Oxford University Press
Digital Learning
Resources

# Discovering Human Sexuality

FIFTH EDITION

Simon LeVay
Janice Baldwin
John Baldwin

Carefully scratch off the silver coating to see your personal redemption code.

**OXFORD**
UNIVERSITY PRESS

## Directions for accessing your

# Oxford Insight Study Guide and Additional Digital Course Materials

***Discovering Human Sexuality 5e*** comes with a wealth of powerful tools to help you succeed in your course.

**Follow these steps to access your resources:**

Visit oup.com/he/levay5e

Select the edition you are using, then select student resources for that edition

Follow the on-screen instructions, entering your personal redemption code when prompted

For assistance with code redemption or registration, please contact customer support at **learninglinkdirect.support@oup.com**. or 855-281-8749.

# Discovering Human Sexuality

## FIFTH EDITION

# Discovering Human Sexuality

## FIFTH EDITION

**Simon LeVay**
*West Hollywood, California*

**Janice Baldwin**
*University of California
Santa Barbara*

**John Baldwin**
*University of California
Santa Barbara*

**SINAUER ASSOCIATES**

NEW YORK    OXFORD
OXFORD UNIVERSITY PRESS

**On the Cover**

Senior couple © Ashley Armstrong/
Design Pics/Corbis; All others © Sinauer
Associates/Oxford University Press

*Discovering Human Sexuality*, Fifth Edition
Oxford University Press is a department of the University of Oxford. It furthers the University's objective of excellence in research, scholarship, and education by publishing worldwide. Oxford is a registered trade mark of Oxford University Press in the UK and certain other countries.

Published in the United States of America by Oxford University Press

198 Madison Avenue, New York, NY 10016, United States of America

© 2021, 2019, 2015, 2012, 2009 Oxford University Press
Sinauer Associates is an imprint of Oxford University Press.

For titles covered by Section 112 of the US Higher Education Opportunity Act, please visit www.oup.com/us/he for the latest information about pricing and alternate formats.

Address editorial correspondence to:

Sinauer Associates
23 Plumtree Road
Sunderland, MA 01375 U.S.A.

Address orders, sales, license, permissions, and translation inquiries to:

Oxford University Press U.S.A.
2001 Evans Road
Cary, NC 27513 U.S.A.
Orders: 1-800-445-9714

Library of Congress Cataloging-in-Publication Data

Names: LeVay, Simon, author. | Baldwin, Janice I., author. | Baldwin, John D., 1941- author.

Title: Discovering human sexuality / Simon LeVay, West Hollywood, California, Janice Baldwin, University of California, Santa Barbara, John Baldwin, University of California, Santa Barbara.

Description: Fifth Edition. | New York : Sinauer Associates : Oxford University Press, 2021. | Revised edition of the authors' Discovering human sexuality, [2019] | Includes bibliographical references and index. | Summary: "An evidence-based, accessible introduction to the study of sexuality and the diverse ways in which it brings joys and challenges to our lives. Now in its fifth edition, Discovering Human Sexuality has established itself as a popular and widely praised text that respects diversity both in the sexual world and among the students who read it. The backgrounds of the authors— in biology, sociology, teaching, and writing—have made possible a text that is multidisciplinary, authoritative, sex-positive, and a delight to read. The scope of Discovering Human Sexuality ranges from homosexuality in ancient Greece to the recent Harvey Weinstein sexual harassment scandal while covering a stunningly diverse array of topics. Questions considered include: How does the menstrual cycle work? What's "splitting the bamboo"? Can premature ejaculation be treated? If a man has undetectable levels of HIV, can he have sex without condoms? Which sex offenders will repeat their crimes? Is there a gay gene? What's wrong with polygamy? Is emergency contraception abortion? This book gives factual answers to important questions and provides material for informed debate for issues without a single solution"-- Provided by publisher.

Identifiers: LCCN 2020028914 (print) | LCCN 2020028915 (ebook) | ISBN 9780197522578 (paperback) | ISBN 9780197522608 | ISBN 9780197522585 (epub)

Subjects: LCSH: Sex (Psychology) | Sex (Biology) | Sex--Social aspects. | Sexual disorders.

Classification: LCC BF692 .L47 2021 (print) | LCC BF692 (ebook) | DDC 306.7--dc23

LC record available at https://lccn.loc.gov/2020028914

LC ebook record available at https://lccn.loc.gov/2020028915

9 8 7 6 5 4 3 2 1
Printed in the United States of America

# About the Authors

**Simon LeVay, PhD** is a British born neuroscientist turned science writer and teacher. He has served on the faculty of Harvard Medical School and the Salk Institute for Biological Studies, and has taught at Harvard, the University of California, and Stanford University. He is the author or coauthor of twelve books, including *Gay, Straight, and the Reason Why: The Science of Sexual Orientation*, Second Edition (OUP, 2017).

**Janice Baldwin, PhD** and **John Baldwin, PhD** are sociologists at the University of California, Santa Barbara. They have been collaborators and writers on many papers and projects in the area of sex, sexuality, and sex education. The Baldwins co-teach a dynamic undergraduate Human Sexuality course at UCSB that has been regularly voted the Best Course there, and they have been named Best Professors multiple times. They also co-created—with their upper division students—a sex information website: SexInfoOnline.

# Brief Contents

# Contents

# 3  Men's Bodies   61

# 4  Sex Development and Diversity   91

# 5 Attraction, Arousal, and Response   127

# 6 Sexual Behavior 157

# 7 Sexual Relationships 193

# 8 Fertility, Pregnancy, and Childbirth 229

# 9   Contraception and Abortion   269

# 10 Sexuality across the Lifespan: From Birth to Adolescence 315

# 11 Sexuality across the Lifespan: Adulthood   349

# 12 Sexual Orientation   379

# 13 Atypical Sexuality 415

# 14   Sexual Disorders   451

# 15 Sexually Transmitted Infections    483

# 16 Sexual Assault, Harassment, and Partner Violence    519

# 17  Sex Work  555

# Sex and Evolution   589

# Preface

*This past year was tough, making the switch to LeVay et al., but I'm glad I did it. Discovering Human Sexuality is unique in both approach and content. The authors have a point of view, but still provide balanced coverage of controversial issues. The boxes are wonderful. One of the things I like about it is the inclusion of historical and cross-cultural detail in the boxes. It's a very readable and beautiful book. The illustrations and diagrams are excellent—the best of any text I have ever used.*

Josephine Caldwell-Ryan
Southern Methodist University

*Discovering Human Sexuality*, Fifth Edition, is the continuation of a textbook that originated in 2003 with the publication of *Human Sexuality* by Simon LeVay and Sharon Valente. Since then, the book has gone through several changes of authorship, format, and title. One consistency, however, has been the identity of the lead author. Another has been the book's high academic and pedagogical standards, which have earned it a prominent place in the market and broad praise from reviewers and users, including the kind words cited above.

The Second Edition of *Human Sexuality* appeared in 2006 with the same two authors. For the 2009 edition, however, Janice Baldwin replaced Sharon Valente. Also, we decided to produce two distinct versions of the book. One of them—*Human Sexuality*, Third Edition—continued the approach pioneered in the earlier editions. The other, which we titled *Discovering Human Sexuality*, was a somewhat shorter and more accessible version that demanded less prior knowledge on the part of the students, especially in the area of biology. John Baldwin joined LeVay and Janice Baldwin as third author of this version.

For the 2015 edition we decided to merge the two versions into one, which we titled *Discovering Human Sexuality*, Third Edition. It was a difficult decision to make because both versions had been successful in the marketplace and each served a somewhat different need. However, the workload involved in producing two different textbooks at the same time was excessive. In addition, we realized that we could incorporate the best features of *Human Sexuality* into *Discovering Human Sexuality* by judicious changes to the text and by the addition of two appendices containing more advanced "optional" material.

Thus the present, Fifth Edition of *Discovering Human Sexuality* is in fact the seventh edition overall. We are very gratified that the text has remained so popular with instructors, some of whom have been with us since 2003.

## Features of *Discovering Human Sexuality,* Fifth Edition

Important features of *Discovering Human Sexuality* distinguish our book from competing texts:

EVIDENCE-BASED APPROACH   We believe that human sexuality is an academic subject like any other, meaning that it should be grounded in reason. Throughout the book, we have sought to present statements that are supported by data, ideas that are tested or testable, and recommendations that are based on research. There are many unanswered questions in sexuality, of course—questions about how abnormal modes of sexual expression (paraphilic disorders) develop, for example, and how best to treat them. In dealing with these controversies, an evidence-based approach demands a nondogmatic style and a willingness to admit that not everything is known. We hope that some students will feel challenged to enter the field of sex research themselves in order to help fill those gaps in our understanding.

Some human sexuality texts contain a great deal of advice to students, especially in the area of relationships. Much of this advice has no objective basis and seems designed more to transmit the authors' values than to foster an authentic learning experience. In *Discovering Human Sexuality*, we keep the total quantity of advice down and try to ensure that the advice we do give has been "field-tested."

Literature citations are, of course, an important element of an evidence-based book. We have been surprised by how cavalierly some competing books deal with this issue—quite commonly, citations in the text are not matched by any corresponding entries in the bibliography. In *Discovering Human Sexuality* we have made every effort to ensure that references are fully documented. Another common practice that we consider unacademic is referring to original research studies by citing magazine or newspaper articles that mention them, rather than the journal articles in which the research was presented. Our policy has been to cite original sources wherever possible, and to use magazine and newspaper references for the kinds of topics they excel at, such as news stories, cultural trends, and the like.

EMPHASIS ON DIVERSITY   Today's college students come from a wide range of backgrounds, and in their adult lives they will have to deal with people very different from themselves. Our text presents this diversity in a detailed and nonjudgmental fashion. For example, with regard to sexual orientation, we go far beyond "gay," "bisexual," and "straight":

We talk about the ever-changing history of the butch-femme dichotomy in lesbian culture, women whose self-identity is too fluid for one-word labels, gay men who are "bears" or "bear cubs" or into the leather scene, what it's like to be gay and Asian-American or Native American, how the gay experience differs for different generations of Americans and for gay people around the world, and so on. Similarly, we take pains to discuss racial, ethnic, and religious diversity, as they affect sexuality, and of course diversity in the actual modes of sexual behavior—including some of the more unusual forms of sexual expression such as "adult babies" and men whose partners are (literally) dolls.

PRESENTATION STYLE   Simon LeVay, Janice Baldwin, and John Baldwin are all experienced authors of college textbooks. In creating *Discovering Human Sexuality*, we have pooled our writing skills to ensure that the text is fully accessible, engaging, and relevant to students of diverse backgrounds. The result of these combined efforts is, we believe, the most readable and student-friendly human sexuality text on the market.

ART PROGRAM   Another way that we have striven to maintain both comprehensibility and interest is through the illustrations. One might think that it would be a simple matter to illustrate a book on human sexuality, but in reality it is a significant challenge. Illustrating some of the concepts discussed in this book, especially in its more biologically oriented sections, requires a great deal of thought and design skill. Sinauer Associates, our long-time publisher now operating as an imprint of Oxford University Press, is an industry leader in the use of art as a pedagogical medium. Thanks to our publisher's efforts, many complex topics, such as the regulation of the menstrual cycle, have been given a visual representation that gracefully parallels and clarifies the accompanying text. Nearly every two-page spread in the book offers one or more illustrations—photographs, drawings, diagrams, graphs, or charts—relevant to the text on that spread. Besides their informative value, illustrations offer important visual relief. Some of our competitors' texts contain sequences of up to ten pages without a single illustration—a definite challenge to the average student's attention span.

BOXES   The 77 boxes are an important feature of the book. They attempt to broaden the reader's horizons with a more in-depth look at specific questions than is possible within the main text: Is there more than one kind of female ejaculation? What's it like to be a rubber fetishist? Why do some Amazonian peoples believe that a child can have several fathers? What have been the consequences of the Harvey Weinstein scandal? In tackling these and many other questions, the boxes provide breaks from the steady flow of the text and allow students to consider specific issues in a more relaxed and informal way.

Other aids to learning and revision include key terms (indicated by boldfaced type and defined in a running glossary), FAQs (frequently asked questions), discussion questions, chapter summaries, web resources, and recommended reading materials.

*Discovering Human Sexuality* on Oxford Learning Link (oup.com/he/levay5e) is an invaluable learning aid which parallels the text with a thorough set of animations, activities, web links, quizzes, and other resources. Learning Link activities are referenced in blue type in the printed text. In addition, a complete set of instructor supplements is available to qualified adopters of the text or e-book. See the section on Digital Resources for details on the full range of material that accompanies *Discovering Human Sexuality*. An alternative to the printed text, the *Discovering Human Sexuality* enhanced e-book combines our high quality text content with multimedia and self-assessment activities to accompany each learning objective, and delivers a more engaging and interactive learning experience. The enhanced e-book version of *Discovering Human Sexuality* is available via RedShelf, VitalSource, and other leading higher education e-book vendors.

## The Fifth Edition

Although we have kept the overall structure of the textbook unchanged from the previous edition, we have taken the opportunity of the new edition to make some significant changes and additions:

- We have added discussions of many topics that were not covered, or only briefly covered, in earlier editions. One example is the controversy over changes to Title IX regulations made by the Trump administration—changes that will impact college students who have experienced sexual violence as well as students accused of perpetrating such violence. Another is the COVID-19 pandemic, which has had many consequences in the sexual sphere.

- We have added new boxes on a wide range of topics, including "Intersex and Sports" (Box 4.2), "Are Today's Children Being Sexualized?" (Box 10.3), "Child Sex Robots" (Box 13.5), "Sex Work in the Time of Plague" (Box 17.1) (a look at the impact of COVID-19 on sex work), and "The World According to Pornhub" (Box 17.5).

- We have of course taken the opportunity to update the book with the latest research, surveys, statistics, laws, medical advances, contraceptive techniques, and cultural happenings.

# Acknowledgments

Producing a modern college textbook such as this one requires the combined efforts of a much larger group of professionals than the three of us who are privileged to have our names on the front cover. The production team has created a textbook of outstanding visual quality and educational value.

Those with whom we have had the most enduring contacts are executive editor Jessica Fiorillo, senior psychology editor Jane Potter, production editor Alison Hornbeck, and photo researcher Mark Siddall, but many others labored behind the scenes to ensure the book's high quality. The complete team is listed in the credits; each member played an indispensable role.

During the writing and production of this textbook the COVID-19 pandemic has caused enormous suffering and the disruption of almost every aspect of American life. The production team members have had to adjust to working in their home environment, and like everyone they have had to cope with anxiety, stress, and perhaps personal loss. Yet production has gone forward in the same efficient, timely, and good-humored fashion as with all previous editions. For this we are enormously grateful.

# Reviewers

We acknowledge with gratitude the extensive and constructive comments made by the people who reviewed chapters of *Discovering Human Sexuality* for the new edition. These reviewers are listed below. Helpful comments have also come from the Baldwins' students at the University of California, Santa Barbara.

Kelly J. Ace, *Delaware County Community College, Wilmington*
Philip Batten, *Wake Forest University*
Jennifer Butler, *Case Western Reserve University*
Voon Chin Phua, *Gettysburg College*
Jen Danilowski, *Valencia College*
Terry Dennison, *University of Oklahoma*
John Edlund, *Rochester Institute of Technology*
Raymond Hames, *University of Nebraska*
Lisa Hoopis, *Rhode Island College*
Chris Jones, *College of the Desert*
Kellie McCants-Price, *Anne Arundel Community College*
Jason McCoy, *Cape Fear Community College*
Erin Moore, *Old Dominion University*
Barbara Oswald, *Cleveland State University*
Dr. Syed Raziuddin, *Daley College*
Pamela Regan, *California State University, LA*
Edie Sample, *Metropolitan Community College*

Christina Scott, *Whittier College*
Maren Scull, *University of Colorado Denver*
Sandra Sgoutas-Emch, *University of San Diego*
Justine Shuey, *Montclair State University*
Susan Sprecher, *Illinois State University*
Ebo Tei, *University of Arkansas at Pine Bluff*
Carrie Watson, *Arizona State University*
Sarah E. Wright, *University of South Carolina*

# Credits

Executive Acquisitions Editor, Jessica Fiorillo
Senior Production Editor, Alison Hornbeck
Production Manager, Joan Gemme
Production Specialist/Cover Designer, Meg Britton Clark
Book Designer, Annette Rapier
Digital Resource Development Editor, Karissa Venne
Photo Researcher, Mark Siddall
Permissions Supervisor, Michele Beckta
Marketing Manager, Joan Lewis-Milne
Editorial Assistant, Morgan Delahunt
Marketing Assistant, Corinne Cramer
Copy Editor, Wendy Walker
Indexer, Grant Hackett

Special thanks to the Oxford University Press sales force, which has ensured that this title reaches all the right people and worked tirelessly to support its use.

## Optimize Student Learning with the Oxford Insight Study Guide

All new print and digital copies of *Discovering Human Sexuality* include access to the Oxford Insight Study Guide, a data-driven, personalized digital learning tool that reinforces key concepts from the text and encourages effective reading and study habits. Developed with a learning-science-based design, Oxford Insight Study Guide engages students in an active and highly dynamic review of chapter content, empowering them to critically assess their own understanding of course material. Real-time, actionable data generated by student activity in the tool helps instructors ensure that each student is best supported along their unique learning path. Learn more at **oxfordinsight.oup.com**.

# Digital Resources

to accompany *Discovering Human Sexuality*, Fifth Edition

## Oxford Learning Link   (oup.com/he/levay5e)

## For the Student

The *Discovering Human Sexuality*, Fifth Edition Oxford Learning Link includes a variety of study and review aids—all available at no additional cost to students purchasing the enhanced e-book or a new print copy. The site includes the following:

- *Enhanced e-book* includes the full text with integrated Self-Assessments, Animations, and Activities.
- *Chapter Outlines* provide an overview of each chapter.
- *Chapter Summaries* give the student a thorough review of each chapter's content.
- *Activities* (for selected chapters) include dynamic illustrations, matching activities, and labeling exercises that help the student learn and understand complex concepts and anatomical (and other) terms.
- *Animations* (for selected chapters) illustrate complex processes.
- *Flashcards* help the student master the hundreds of new terms introduced in the textbook.
- *Web Links* provide a set of online sites and resources relevant to each chapter.

## Learning Cloud

Learning Cloud delivers a wealth of automatically-graded quizzes and study resources for *Discovering Human Sexuality*, along with an interactive e-book, all in an intuitive, web-based learning environment.

## Optimize Student Learning with the Oxford Insight Study Guide

All new print and digital copies of *Discovering Human Sexuality* include access to the Oxford Insight Study Guide, a data-driven, personalized digital learning tool that reinforces key concepts from the text and encourages effective reading and study habits. Developed with a learning-science-based design, Oxford Insight Study Guide engages students in an active and highly dynamic review of chapter content, empowering them to critically assess their own understanding of course material. Real-time, actionable data generated by student activity in the tool helps instructors ensure that each student is best supported along their unique learning path. **Learn more at oxfordinsight.oup.com.**

## For the Instructor

Oxford Learning Link provides instructors using *Discovering Human Sexuality* with a wealth of resources for use in course planning, lecture development, and assessment. Contents include:

- *Textbook Figures & Tables*: All of the figures and tables from the textbook, formatted for optimal legibility when projected. Complex images are provided in both a whole and split version.
- *PowerPoint Resources*: Two ready-to-use presentations are provided for each chapter:
  - A lecture presentation that includes text covering the entire chapter, with selected figures.
  - A figure presentation that includes all of the figures and tables from the chapter, with titles on each slide, and complete captions in the Notes field.

- *Instructor's Manual*: The Instructor's Manual provides instructors with a variety of resources to aid in planning their course and developing their lectures. For each chapter, the manual includes a chapter overview, a chapter outline, the complete chapter summary, class discussion questions, teaching resources, and suggested readings.

- *Media Guide*: The Media Guide includes extensive lists of suggested video segments (and full-length titles) that are ideal for use as lecture starters or other in-class activities. Video suggestions (with links and sources) are provided for topics across all chapters, and suggested discussion questions are included.

- *Test Bank*: The Test Bank consists of a broad range of questions covering all the key facts and concepts in each chapter. Each chapter includes multiple-choice and essay questions. All questions are keyed to Bloom's Taxonomy, aligned to learning objectives, and referenced to specific textbook sections. Available in multiple formats, including MS Word, TestGen, and Common Cartridge (for import into learning management system).

## Learning Cloud

Learning Cloud by Oxford University Press delivers a wealth of study resources and automatically-graded quizzes for *Discovering Human Sexuality* in an intuitive, web-based learning environment. A built in color coded gradebook allows instructors to track student progress. Learning Cloud includes:

- *Enhanced e-book*: A complete e-book is integrated into Learning Cloud and includes in-text links to Activities and Animations, and in-line Self-Assessment questions per section.

- *All Student Resources*: Activities, Animations, Outlines, Summaries, Learning Objectives, Web Links, and Flashcards.

- *Online Quizzes*: Multiple choice and fill-in-the-blank.

## Oxford Learning Link Direct

Oxford Learning Link Direct brings all of the high quality digital teaching and learning tools for *Discovering Human Sexuality* right to your local learning management system. Instructors and their LMS administrators simply download the Oxford Learning Link Direct cartridge from Oxford Learning Link, and with the turn of a digital key, incorporate engaging content from Oxford directly into their LMS for assigning and grading.

To learn more about any of these resources, or to get access, please contact your local OUP representative.

# Value Options

## Enhanced e-book

(ISBN 978-0-19752-258-5)
*Discovering Human Sexuality*, Fifth Edition is available as an e-book, in several different formats, including RedShelf, VitalSource, and Chegg. All major mobile devices are supported.

- *Self-Assessments* at the end of each Key Concept test students on that section's Learning Objectives and provide them with immediate feedback, facilitating participation and increasing retention of the content.

- Links to Activities and Animations are also included.

## Looseleaf Textbook

(ISBN 978-0-19752-260-8)
*Discovering Human Sexuality* is also available in a three-hole punched, looseleaf format. Students can take just the sections they need to class and can easily integrate instructor material with the text.

# Activities and Animations

The following activities and animations are found in the enhanced e-book
and on Oxford Learning Link at **oup.com/he/levay5e**.

| | | | | |
|---|---|---|---|---|
| **Activity 2.1** | The Vulva | | **Animation 2.1** | The Pap Test |
| **Activity 2.2** | Internal Anatomy of the Vulva | | **Animation 2.2** | Ovarian and Uterine Cycles |
| **Activity 2.3** | The Female Reproductive Tract: Frontal View | | **Animation 2.3** | The Reproductive Years |
| **Activity 2.4** | The Female Reproductive Tract: Midline View | | **Animation 3.1** | The Mechanism of Erection |
| **Activity 2.5** | Main Processes of the Menstrual Cycle | | **Animation 4.1** | Development of the Male and Female Reproductive Tracts |
| **Activity 2.6** | Internal Structure of the Lactating Breast | | **Animation 8.1** | How a Home Pregnancy Test Works |
| **Activity 3.1** | The Male External Genitalia | | **Animation 8.2** | Standard In Vitro Fertilization |
| **Activity 3.2** | Internal Structure of the Erect Penis and the Urethra | | **Animation 9.1** | Vasectomy |
| **Activity 3.3** | The Scrotum and Its Contents | | **Animation 9.2** | Tubal Sterilization |
| **Activity 3.4** | Internal Structure of the Testicle and Epididymis | | **Animation A.1** | Mitosis |
| **Activity 3.5** | The Male Reproductive Tract | | **Animation A.2** | Meiosis |
| **Activity 3.6** | Anatomy of the Prostate | | | |
| **Activity 7.1** | Definitions of Sexual Relationships | | | |
| **Activity 7.2** | Sternberg's Seven Types of Love | | | |
| **Activity 15.1** | Milestones in the Global HIV/AIDS Pandemic | | | |
| **Activity A.1** | Differences and Similarities between Meiosis and Mitosis | | | |

Sexuality is the soul of dance.

# 1

# Sexuality: Pathways to Understanding

Sexuality is a central theme of human existence. At its best, sexuality charges our lives with energy, excitement, and love. It offers a deep sense of connectedness, capable of spanning and healing social divisions. It creates family, the primary unit of society and the cradle of future generations.

At its worst, sexuality brings anguish, violence, and disease.

To begin our exploration of this powerful and mysterious force, we first ask what the terms "sex" and "sexuality" mean and why sexuality is a topic worth studying. We go on to review some of the ways in which human sexuality has changed between the origin of our species and the present day. Our purpose is to make clear that, even though there may be some eternal truths about sexuality, it is not static: It changes slowly as a result of evolutionary forces, and much faster under the influence of culture.

Over the last few decades, research has affected people's sex lives in important ways, usually for the better. In this chapter we describe the variety of methods by which sexuality can be studied and give examples of the impact such research has had.

To treat the topic of human sexuality fairly we must approach it with open minds, with respect for diversity and social justice, and with all the modes of inquiry that have been used to illuminate human nature. Approached in this way, the topic is not just another step in your college career; it is a personal voyage of discovery that will help you enjoy the best that sexuality has to offer—and avoid the worst.

## 1.1 Sexuality Is a Broader Concept than Sex

**LEARNING OBJECTIVES**
After reading this section you should be able to:

1.1.1   Give two different meanings for the word "sex."
1.1.2   Explain the distinction between sex and sexuality.

**sex**   The distinction between female and male, or sexual behavior.

**sexuality**   The feelings, behaviors, and identities associated with sex.

**sexual reproduction**   The production of offspring genetically related to two parents.

**asexual reproduction**   The production of offspring genetically related to only one parent.

The term **sex** has two meanings. First, it means the distinction between female and male—a distinction that, as we'll see in later chapters, is not as clear-cut as you might imagine. Second, it means engaging in sexual behaviors. These behaviors may be very obviously sexual because they involve genital phenomena such as vaginal lubrication, penile or clitoral erection, orgasm, and so on. But they also include activities that do not directly center on the genitals, such as finding sex partners, as well as behaviors such as kissing that may or may not be sexual depending on context. Both meanings of "sex" are central to this book.

The term **sexuality** includes the two meanings of "sex" but also goes beyond them to encompass the entire realm of human experience that is more or less closely connected with sex. It means, for example, our gendered traits—the psychological traits that differ, to a greater or lesser extent, between women and men. It means our sexual and romantic attractions and relationships—who we find attractive or fall in love with and how we establish, maintain, or dissolve sexual partnerships. It means becoming a parent (or preventing that from happening). It also includes the two-way relationship between our personal sexual identities and social structures such as the law, religion, and medicine. We touch on all these aspects of sexuality in this book, but even in 621 pages we cannot do all of them the justice they deserve.

## 1.2 Sexuality Has Changed over Time

**LEARNING OBJECTIVES**
After reading this section you should be able to:

1.2.1   Explain the meaning of sexual selection.
1.2.2   Compare the influence of religion, social classes, and urbanization on sexuality.
1.2.3   Describe how marriage has changed throughout history and recently.
1.2.4   Briefly describe the research or achievements of Freud, Hirschfeld, Stevens, Sanger, Kinsey, and Masters and Johnson.

Most—but not all—women and men experience sexual desire and engage in sexual relationships at some point in their lives. This has likely been true across the course of human history and prehistory, and it is true around the world today. But the ways in which these desires and relationships express themselves have been extraordinarily varied. Here we sketch some of the changes that have occurred over time.

### Sexuality has been influenced by evolution

Nearly all species—both animals and plants—have the capacity for **sexual reproduction**. That is, they can produce offspring by combining the genetic contributions of two different parents, a female and a male. In many species, females are also capable of **asexual reproduction,** that is, without any genetic contribution from a male, but this capacity was lost in the evolution of mammals, including ourselves. The reasons why evolution has favored sexual over asexual reproduction are discussed in Appendix A.

In some species, reproduction is not the only or even the main function of sex. One of our closest primate relatives, the bonobo, enjoys a remarkably exuberant sex life: These animals engage in far more sexual behavior than is necessary for producing offspring, and they have sexual contacts with many different partners. The majority of sexual contacts between bonobos cannot lead to pregnancy, either because the female is not in the fertile phase of her reproductive cycle at the time of the contacts, or because the contacts are between two individuals of the same sex. Thus bonobos have clearly evolved functions for sex that have no direct relevance to reproduction; these functions are thought to include social bonding and the resolution of conflicts (de Waal, 2016).

Something similar is true for ourselves, at least in contemporary societies. The average American women spends 31 years of her life trying *not* to get pregnant, according to a study by the Guttmacher Institute (Guttmacher Institute, 2014). This commonality between bonobos and modern humans suggests that the capacity and desire for non-reproductive sex may have evolved among the common ancestors of bonobos and humans, who lived 7 million years ago.

In fact, according to psychologists Christopher Ryan and Cacilda Jethá, early humans enjoyed a promiscuous lifestyle quite similar to that of present-day bonobos (Ryan & Jethá, 2010). Other scholars, however, have argued for a more restrained sexuality, comparable to that of primates that form pair bonds, such as gibbons. This is the first of numerous scholarly controversies that will be mentioned in this book; there are many important questions concerning human sexuality for which cut-and-dried answers cannot yet be provided. This particular controversy may be difficult to resolve, given that it concerns human behavior in the very distant past.

© Ma Xiaobo Photography China/Corbis

▲ Male primates, such as these golden snub-nosed monkeys, often fight over access to females.

Another phenomenon observed in both humans and other animals is *competition* for sex partners: Males often compete for access to the most fertile females, while females often compete for the attention of high-ranking males. You don't have to be a sex researcher to know that these kinds of competition are prevalent in our own species today. It's likely that competition for partners has characterized sexuality throughout human history and prehistory, and that as with other species this competition has driven the evolution of sex differences in appearance and behavior—a process known as **sexual selection**. Nevertheless, sex differences between men and women are less marked than in some other species, and not all the sex differences that do exist can be attributed to sexual selection: Cultural factors also play an important role, as we'll see in Chapter 4.

Early in the evolution of our species, humans probably lacked understanding of the connection between **coitus** (penile-vaginal intercourse) and reproduction. Even today, there are human cultures where people are unaware of biological facts that seem obvious to us, such as the fact that a child has just one father or that pregnancy and childbirth result from a single act of coitus (**BOX 1.1**).

Over the course of human history the trend toward an increasingly conscious understanding of how sex "works" has influenced human sexuality in directions that seem counterintuitive in evolutionary terms. For example, the knowledge that the release of semen (the male ejaculate) in the vagina is what causes pregnancy led to the introduction of contraceptive practices. These included withdrawal of the penis prior to ejaculation—a form of **contraception** known already in biblical times—and the use of various kinds of barriers placed in the vagina. Similarly, methods intended to interrupt an established pregnancy—by use of certain herbs or poisons, or by black magic—were widely used in pre-modern times, with varying success. As methods for contraception and abortion have improved over the centuries, so has it become increasingly possible to enjoy the pleasures of sex without its natural consequences. This has undoubtedly increased people's—especially women's—willingness to engage in sex both within and outside of established relationships.

**sexual selection** Evolutionary changes driven by competition for mates.

**coitus** Penile-vaginal intercourse.

**contraception** Prevention of pregnancy.

## BOX 1.1
## Meet My Dads

No matter how many men a woman has sex with, any child she bears has only a single biological father—the man whose sperm fertilized the woman's ovum. In most cultures around the world, people accept this reality of single paternity, yet anthropologists have discovered an exception among many of the indigenous tribal societies of lowland South America (Amazonia and nearby areas). Here people believe that a man's semen remains in the woman's body indefinitely after sexual intercourse, so if several different men have sex with her before she delivers a child, then all of them contribute to the making of that child (Beckerman & Valentine, 2002).

This belief is called **partible paternity** ("divisible fatherhood"). By studying language relationships among the societies where partible paternity is found, anthropologist Robert Walker of the University of Missouri and his colleagues have traced it back to the distant past, probably to the time when the lowlands were first settled and the settlers spoke a common language (Walker et al., 2010).

What benefit does the concept of partible paternity confer? Anthropologists such as William Crocker of the Smithsonian Institution have found that the societies that believe in partible paternity engage in distinctive sexual practices (Crocker & Crocker, 2003). They may participate in rituals in which women engage in sex sequentially with multiple men. And unlike in other cultures, where men typically guard their wives from sexual contact with other males, men in these Amazonian tribes may freely offer their wives to male relatives as well as to powerful men who are actual or potential allies.

This Araweté woman of Brazil may believe that two or more men fathered her son.

© Sue Cunningham Photographic/Alamy

Partible paternity, and the practices associated with it, benefit women's efforts to raise children. That's because the multiple "fathers" of a given child may give gifts in exchange for sex, may support or protect the child, or may at least refrain from killing the child. (The killing of infants and children by men has traditionally been a significant cause of mortality in Amazonian cultures.) The men with whom a woman chooses to have sex are often related to each other and often live together, so women are choosing men who are both motivated and able to help support her child (Ellsworth et al., 2014).

What about the men? On the face of it, the notion of partible paternity seems to disadvantage them, because they may end up supporting children who are not biologically theirs. On the other hand, they are "hedging their reproductive bets" by spreading their semen widely. This may be of particular value to high-status men, who gain disproportionate access to other men's wives, thanks to partible paternity. In addition, partible paternity gives men some assurance that their biological children will have male support in the event of their own premature death—something that's all too common in Amazonia.

This still leaves unanswered the question of why partible paternity is common in lowland South America but rare elsewhere. The answer may be related to the importance of kinship and alliances in those societies, combined with a general absence of material wealth. In such circumstances paternity may be used as a unit of wealth that can be traded, as it were, in social networks.

**partible paternity** The belief that two or more men may be fathers of the same child.

## Society has changed sexuality

Human sexuality has been greatly influenced by the development of social structures. When people lived in small, independent groups, sexuality was only lightly regulated. Take the issue of nudity: When Christopher Columbus first encountered the native people of the Caribbean, he was surprised to find that most of them, both men and women, went naked. The same is true for some hunter-gatherer peoples even today. With the emergence of larger communities with centralized authority, nudity was restricted, in part with the aim of reducing sexual arousal, preventing the sight of sexual arousal in others, and eliminating sexual conflicts. Marriage was formalized, and nonmarital sex was discouraged to a greater or lesser degree.

Organized religion played a role in these changes. Although teachings have varied greatly among the major religions (such as Christianity, Hinduism, Judaism, and Islam), they have often fostered procreative **heterosexual** sex within marriage while labeling other forms of sexual expression as sinful. For most of the two millennia since the foundation of Christianity, for example, its teachings forbade all nonmarital sex, **homosexual** sex, masturbation, contraception, abortion, and polygamy. Even marital sex was restricted to coitus in certain positions, and it was forbidden on certain days of the week and during Lent. Priests were commonly barred from marriage or any kind of sexual activity. This changed to some extent after the sixteenth-century Reformation, when Western Christianity splintered into numerous denominations, some of which have become much more liberal in the area of sexual ethics compared with the Catholic Church.

The development of large-scale societies led to stratification of societies into classes, with the rich and powerful at the top and the masses below them. What class you belonged to greatly influenced your sex life. Take India: The *Kama Sutra*, compiled around the second century CE, described innumerable ways for men to obtain sexual pleasure and give sexual pleasure to women (Vatsyayana, 1991) (**FIGURE 1.1**). It also described sex between women and between men. But the *Kama Sutra* was written for and about the idle rich. If the sex lives of low-caste Indians were anything like they are today, they involved hasty, fully clothed couplings with the minimum of pleasure or romance (Nath & Nayar, 1997).

Another way in which class influenced sexuality had to do with **polygamy**. Most human cultures have permitted men to have more than one wife. In early Islam, polygamy was legitimized for an entirely beneficent purpose—to provide for the many women whose husbands died in warfare. In general, though, polygamy has benefited rich and powerful men, because they had sufficient means to engage in the practice. Polygamy reduced the numbers of available women and thus made it harder for poor men to afford even one wife. What's more, polygamy has often been connected with the idea that women are men's property—if a rich man has many cattle, why shouldn't he have many wives? By banning polygamy, the Christian religion attempted to promote a more gender-equitable society.

Across history, large numbers of men have been deprived of a sex life altogether by being **castrated**—that is, by having their testicles removed, and sometimes the penis also. Such men were called **eunuchs**. Castration was carried out as a punishment among criminals or prisoners of war or, if done before puberty, to produce asexual male slaves who could serve certain roles, such as court attendants, harem guards, dancers, or singers (Wilson & Roehrborn, 1999). In general, castration served the interests of non-castrated men, especially powerful men, and it therefore represents another way in which class and sexuality interact.

Thankfully, castration is no longer practiced, except as a medical procedure for the treatment of prostate cancer or as an element of sex-change surgery. And individuals—in Western countries at least—are

**heterosexuality** Sexual attraction to, or behavior with, persons of the opposite sex.

**homosexuality** Sexual attraction to, or behavior with, persons of the same sex.

**polygamy** Marriage to or (mostly in animals) mating with more than one partner.

**castration** Removal of the testicles or testicles and penis.

**eunuch** A man who has been castrated.

▲ **FIGURE 1.1** The *Kama Sutra* describes a wide variety of sexual positions.

permitted much more freedom of sexual expression than was the case a century or so ago, in part on account of the waning influence of organized religion on public policy.

Yet social class still influences sexuality today. News stories over the past few years have exposed the sexual secrets of many rich or powerful people—nearly all of them men. These individuals have obtained, or sought to obtain, multiple sex partners by means of financial, material, or professional inducements; by sexual assault or harassment; or by illegal sexual contacts with underage girls or boys. We've learned that wealth and power not only facilitate such behavior but also confer a sense of sexual entitlement and invulnerability, just as they have throughout history. The less affluent among us, even if we might desire to act in the same fashion, mostly lack the means to do so.

### Urbanization has been a curse and a blessing

An important effect of cultural change has involved sexually transmitted infections. When people lived in small groups and stayed in restricted areas, they tended to reach a biological accommodation with the infectious agents (bacteria and viruses) present in that population, such that their effects were not especially severe. Increases in population density and long-distance travel changed this picture: The organism that causes syphilis, for example, was present in the native populations of the Americas long before the arrival of Columbus and other explorers, but when these men returned to Europe, bringing the organism with them, it unleashed a devastating epidemic (Rothschild et al., 2000). Potentially fatal infections such as with the human immunodeficiency virus (HIV—the virus that causes acquired immune deficiency syndrome [AIDS]) spread primarily in cities, and in the process they made sex itself seem frightening and sinful.

A more beneficial effect of urbanization has been the strengthening and validation of sexual diversity. When you were "the only gay in the village," you were unlikely to find a sex partner or even to have any clear understanding of who you were. City life, on the other hand, facilitated the development of communities where being gay was normal and gay relationships flourished. The concept of "the homosexual" as a distinct kind of person only really took hold in the 19th century, as cities like Berlin, London, and New York attracted thousands of migrants from rural areas and from overseas. By the time of the 1880 census, New York had passed the million mark, and soon thereafter a thriving gay culture established itself (Chauncey, 2019).

The media and the internet have facilitated a kind of "virtual urbanization," which in some ways is even more influential than simply living together in a city. Television has encouraged millions of people to imitate the same role models, in sexuality as in other matters (**BOX 1.2**). The internet has enabled more active participation. Thus, however uncommon your sexual identity or your sexual desires, a few keystrokes will tell you all about them, and a few more will put you in contact with others like yourself, whether in your home town or across the globe. As a result, the concept of "normality" has expanded greatly, such that few sexual "kinks" are still stigmatized as shameful or named as mental disorders.

### Marriage has been transformed

Yet another important change has been the radical decline in birth rates that has taken place in most countries, starting in the late 18th century. By 2010 the number of children born to the average American woman had fallen from 7 or 8 to about 2 (**FIGURE 1.2**), and by 2018 it was 1.7 (National Vital Statistics Reports, 2019a). Today, there are plenty of people who choose to have no children at all—something that used to be quite unusual, except for those in religious orders. This steady decline in birth rates over the last two centuries was not accompanied by any equivalent decline in people's interest in sex. Thus the idea has gained currency that sex has a legitimate emotional or recreational function, quite distinct from the desire for children.

**double standard** The idea that acceptable behavior is different for men than for women.

The institution of marriage has changed over time. In many traditional societies marriage signified the transfer of ownership of a woman from her father to her husband; marriages were negotiated and often involved large bridal payments. A woman was expected to be a virgin when she married, but a man could be forgiven or even admired for sexual activity before or outside of marriage (This was an example of the **double standard**, by which males and females were, and still may be, held to different moral codes.) Within marriage, the husband's and wife's roles were quite distinct: The husband was the breadwinner, the wife the homemaker and child rearer, perhaps with the help of servants.

Before the 20th century, marriage was for life: Divorce was quite uncommon and was only permitted in cases of proven adultery. Divorce laws were greatly liberalized over the course of the 20th century, and now nearly half of all U.S. marriages

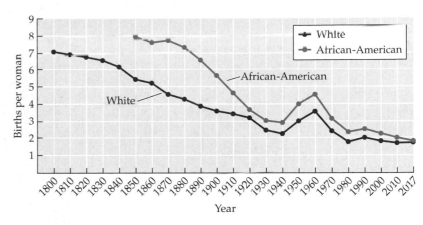

▲ **FIGURE 1.2  Declining birth rates**  This graph shows the average number of children born to American women between 1800 and 2015. The data for white and African-American women are plotted separately. Historical data for other minorities are not available—current fertility rates are highest for Hispanic women at 2.0 children per woman. (After M. Haines. 2008. In *EH.Net Encyclopedia*, Robert Whaples [Ed.]. http://eh.net/encyclopedia/fertility-and-mortality-in-the-united-states/ and J. A. Martin et al. 2017. *Births: Final data for 2015. National Vital Statistics Report* 66(1). US DHHS, CDC, National Center for Health Statistics: Hyattsville, MD.)

# BOX 1.2
# The Media: TV or Not TV?

A classic study conducted in the 1970s took advantage of a unique opportunity to examine the effects of the media—specifically, television—on the psychological development of girls and boys. Up until 1973 the residents of a certain small town in British Columbia were unable to receive television broadcasts, on account of the mountainous terrain, but in that year the Canadian Broadcasting Corporation agreed to install a transmitter in the community. A group of faculty and students at the University of British Columbia, led by social psychologist Tannis MacBeth Williams, decided to study the effects of the new medium on the residents of the town, to which they gave the fictitious name "Notel" (T. M. Williams, 1986).

The researchers interviewed and tested children in Notel before broadcasts started, and again 2 years later. They did the same in two "control" towns—towns that were similar to Notel in most respects but that had received television broadcasts for many years previously. The part of the study that concerns us had to do with children's ideas about appropriate sex roles. Before the broadcasts began, Notel's children had attitudes that were significantly more flexible than those of children in the two comparable towns that already had television. By 2 years after the beginning of television transmissions, the attitudes of Notel's girls and boys had become much more distinct from each other, and comparable to those of children in the other towns. The girls had particularly marked changes in their attitudes toward peer relationships, while the boys showed

marked changes concerning future occupations—both in the direction of what is traditionally expected of girls and boys. All in all, the Notel study demonstrated a powerful effect of television in promoting stereotypical sex roles. Of course, it's possible that television promotes more flexible attitudes today than it did in the 1970s, but some more recent studies suggest that television and other media have been slow to move beyond traditional stereotypes (Collins, 2011).

For good measure, television also made Notel's children less creative, poorer readers, more aggressive, and dumber—at least, they scored slightly lower on IQ tests.

▶ **FIGURE 1.3** **Reinventing marriage** This 2013 wedding of an interracial, same-sex couple would have been doubly shocking a generation or two ago—and still is to some Americans.

© iStock.com/MilamPhotos

**cohabitation** A live-in sexual relationship between individuals who are not married to each other.

end in divorce rather than death. What's more, it's now widely accepted that women are sexually active before marriage and that couples may **cohabit** (live together) before marriage or without marrying at all. And the birth of children outside of marriage, once a shocking secret, is now more or less routine: Four out of 10 U.S. births are now to unmarried women, who may be single or cohabiting with a man or with a woman. This change is part of a worldwide trend (Griffin, 2018).

Up until the mid-20th century the great majority of Americans considered interracial marriage to be morally wrong. According to opinion polls, only 4% of Americans approved of black–white marriages in 1958, as compared with 87% in 2013 (Gallup, 2013), and such marriages were illegal in 24 states. Attitudes changed gradually after World War II: In 1967 the U.S. Supreme Court established a constitutional right to marry across racial lines, and by 2015 17% of all Americans were marrying partners of a different race or ethnicity (Pew Research Center, 2017c). In 2015 the Supreme Court recognized a similar right for same-sex couples, but gay couples who marry today are joining an institution that has lost a great deal of its former significance (**FIGURE 1.3**).

## Sex researchers followed diverse paths

Research into some aspects of sex, such as reproductive anatomy, goes back centuries, but sexual behavior and sexual relationships were not studied in any systematic way until the late 19th century. The early sex researchers faced a great deal of misunderstanding and prejudice, and their most valuable achievement was to bring sex out of the shadows, more than anything useful they found out about it. Here are brief sketches of some individuals whose work has had a significant impact on how people think about sex and sexuality.

**Sigmund Freud (1856–1939)** was an Austrian neurologist and the founder of psychoanalysis. This school of thought placed the origin of sexual problems in the operations of the unconscious mind, especially during infancy or childhood. Because psychoanalytic treatment required consultations between patient and analyst that might go on for years, Freud created a means by which sexologists could earn a living. His theoretical approach contrasted with that of the German physician and gay rights pioneer Magnus Hirschfeld, who promoted biological ideas about sexuality (**BOX 1.3**).

## BOX 1.3
# Freud and Hirschfeld: Contrasting Theories on Sexual Orientation

About a century ago, two European doctors proposed radically different theories to account for why some people are sexually attracted predominantly to members of the other sex while others are attracted to members of the same sex or to both sexes—a characteristic we now call sexual orientation. In Vienna, Sigmund Freud (**FIGURE A**) developed a theory that was based on the concept of an unconscious mind, whose operations could supposedly be probed by psychoanalytic techniques such as free association, the interpretation of dreams, and slips of the tongue. The unconscious mind, though hidden from view and free from moral restraints, nevertheless resembled the conscious mind in many respects—both were capable of rational thought, planning, memory, and emotion.

In Freud's conception, the unconscious mind was more broadly focused in its sexual desires than was the conscious mind. This was particularly true during early childhood, which he believed included autoerotic and homosexual phases as well as incestuous desires directed toward one or the other parent. Freud thought that the "normal" progression to adult heterosexuality could be derailed in various ways, often involving unconscious emotional processes such as a hostile, too-close, or jealous relationship with a parent or sibling. These phenomena could lead to what Freud called **perversions**, that is, mental states in which adult sexual desires were directed toward atypical targets, such as people of the same sex (homosexuality), inanimate objects (fetishism), and so on. or they could lead to **neuroses**, in which the sexual element was supposedly repressed from consciousness altogether and reemerged in the form of nonsexual traits and disorders, such as obsessive-compulsive behaviors, depression, or "hysteria."

In Berlin, Magnus Hirschfeld (**FIGURE B**) took a quite different view. Hirschfeld proposed the existence of two neural centers in the brain that were responsible for sexual attraction to men and to women, respectively. He suggested that during early fetal life all humans possessed both centers, but later one center grew and dominated, while the other regressed. In men, of course, it was usually the center for attraction to women that persisted, while in women it was the center for attraction to men. Only in a small proportion of fetuses—those who would become homosexual adults—did development take the opposite course. Hirschfeld believed that sex hormones (then understood in only a very rudimentary way) channeled development in one direction or

(A)                    (B)

(A) Sigmund Freud (1856–1939). (B) Magnus Hirschfeld (1868–1935).

another and that people also had a genetic predisposition to same-sex or opposite-sex attraction.

In many ways, the views of Freud and Hirschfeld represented opposite approaches to understanding the mind and sexuality. Freud tried to understand the mind in terms of processes that, though hidden, were inherently *mental*—unconscious thoughts. And he believed interpersonal relationships held the key to sexual orientation and other aspects of adult sexuality. To Freud, getting to your adult sexuality was a long, sometimes chaotic drama in which the unconscious mind took the leading role. Hirschfeld, on the other hand, tried to reduce the mind to relatively simple *nonmental* phenomena such as the growth and activity of nerve cells, hormone secretion, and information encoded in the genes. In Hirschfeld's view, these phenomena controlled sexual development in a manner that was largely independent of family relationships and other aspects of life experience. To Hirschfeld, getting to your adult sexuality was a process that unfolded mechanistically without your active participation—it simply happened to you.

Freud's theories came to dominate most people's ideas about the mind and sexuality through the early and middle part of the 20th century, while Hirschfeld's theories languished in obscurity. Toward the end of the century, however, a noticeable shift of views occurred. To some people, Freud's theories began to seem capricious, poorly substantiated, or inspired by prejudice (against women especially). Meanwhile, scientific advances tended to bolster a biological view of sexuality.

*(Continued)*

**BOX 1.3**
## Contrasting Theories on Sexual Orientation (*continued*)

Studies in animals showed that prenatal hormone levels do indeed influence sexual behavior in adulthood, and family studies supported the idea that genes do have some influence on sexual orientation in humans.

Probably the dominant view at present is that both approaches offer potential insights into human sexuality. There must be some biological underpinnings to our thoughts and behaviors, and exploring these underpinnings is likely to tell us a lot about why people differ from one another sexually. On the other hand, it seems likely that some aspects of

human sexuality need to be studied at the level of thoughts—in other words, by a cognitive approach. Thus, even if neither Freud's nor Hirschfeld's theories turn out to be entirely correct, they may both have contributed useful styles of thinking to the discussion.

**perversion**  An obsolete term for atypical sexual desire or behavior, viewed as a mental disorder.

**neuroses**  Mental disorders such as depression that, in Freudian theory, are strategies for coping with repressed sexual conflicts.

**Nettie Stevens (1861–1912)** was an American biologist who worked at Bryn Mawr College and the Carnegie Institution of Washington. Around 1905 Stevens noticed that male and female animals, including humans, possess different complements of sex chromosomes—a pair of X chromosomes in females and an X and a Y chromosome in males. Everything we now know about how males and females develop flows from that fundamental discovery, as we detail in Chapter 4.

**Margaret Sanger (1879–1966)** was an American social activist who campaigned tirelessly and effectively for women's right to learn about and practice contraception. She worked in an era when the cycle of pregnancy and child care trapped many women in ill health and poverty, yet contraception was highly stigmatized and in some jurisdictions illegal. On one occasion Sanger's activities landed her in prison—whereupon she taught contraceptive techniques to her fellow inmates. She founded an organization that later became Planned Parenthood. Sanger's efforts helped free women from reproductive slavery. Sanger was not herself a sex researcher, but she introduced an effective contraceptive (a diaphragm—see Chapter 9) from Europe, and she promoted research that led eventually to the contraceptive pill.

**Alfred Kinsey (1894–1956)** of Indiana University is the sex researcher best known to the American public. Trained as a zoologist, he and his colleagues undertook large-scale sex surveys in the United States in the middle years of the 20th century. Kinsey published the results of these surveys in two lengthy volumes, *Sexual Behavior in the Human Male* (1948) and *Sexual Behavior in the Human Female* (1953). The "Kinsey Reports" became best sellers, and Kinsey himself became a celebrity whose lectures were attended by thousands (**FIGURE 1.4**). What excited people's interest was the surprisingly high prevalence of stigmatized or illegal sexual behaviors such as sex between men or between women or sexual contacts with animals.

**William Masters (1915–2001)** was an American gynecologist. He and his research assistant (later his wife) **Virginia Johnson (1925–2013)** studied sex in the laboratory (**FIGURE 1.5**). They measured many different genital and physiological phenomena in both women and men as their volunteers engaged in solo or coupled sex. They published their observations in a 1966 book, *Human Sexual*

▲ **FIGURE 1.4** **Let's talk about sex** Sex researcher Alfred Kinsey (far right) lectures at the University of California, Berkeley, in 1949.

*Response*, which became yet another sexual best seller. The best-known feature of the book was its representation of genital responses as a four-stage cycle, as described further in Chapter 5.

With these brief historical and biographical notes we want to highlight the fact that sexuality, and the ways people have thought about sexuality, have changed greatly over time. And where we are today in the United States is very unlikely to be the final word on the topic. Sexuality will change, for all kinds of reasons. Over the course of your lifetime, scientific progress is likely to greatly diminish the risk of sexually transmitted infections or unintentional pregnancy, perhaps to the point that they are no longer significant problems. That might change people's attitudes and behaviors in areas like casual sex or pornography. Social and political developments will greatly impact contentious sexual topics such as abortion, but we cannot predict whether the trend will be toward more permissive or more restrictive attitudes. As for sex robots, you or your children may be able to choose between living, life-like, and better-than-life sex partners—in which case the freedom to make such choices may become a contentious social and political issue.

In a word, it is up to your generation to construct the human sexuality of the future.

▶ **FIGURE 1.5** **Masters and Johnson** studied the physiology of sexual behavior.

## 1.3  Sexuality Can Be Studied with a Wide Variety of Methods

**LEARNING OBJECTIVES**

After reading this section you should be able to:

1.3.1   Name four ways in which biomedical research has helped make our sex lives better and safer.

1.3.2   Explain the distinct meanings of social psychology, cognitive psychology, and evolutionary psychology, and give one example of how a branch of psychology has been used to study sexuality.

1.3.3   Evaluate the pros and cons of surveys and "big data" as methods to learn about people's sexuality.

1.3.4   Name five elements of the Declaration of Sexual Rights.

We could fill a whole book with an account of the methods that are being used to study human sexuality. Here, we pick out some of the key areas and highlight certain research studies that illustrate the methods that are available.

### Biomedical research focuses on the underlying mechanisms of sex

Biomedical research is the approach that has the greatest practical impact on people's sex lives. Here are a few examples of achievements in this field:

- Hormone-based contraception and abortion
- Drug treatments for reproductive cancers
- Drug treatments for erectile disorder, premature ejaculation, and low sex drive in men
- Methods to prevent, cure, or effectively treat sexually transmitted infections
- Technologies to treat infertility in women and men
- Improvements in the safety of pregnancy and childbirth

**sexual orientation**   The direction of an individual's sexual feelings: sexual attraction toward persons of the opposite sex (heterosexual), the same sex (homosexual), or both sexes (bisexual).

The introduction of modern imaging technologies has enabled the direct study in humans of topics that earlier could only be studied in non-human animals. This is particularly true for brain function, which can now be studied with a variety of imaging techniques (**FIGURE 1.6**). In addition, the deciphering of the human genome is enabling all kinds of advances, such as the ability to ascertain the sex of a fetus and to diagnose certain fetal abnormalities on the basis of a simple blood sample drawn from the mother. And as we'll discuss in later chapters, current research is attempting to home in on genes that influence such important traits as a person's **sexual orientation** or their interest in casual sex.

In recent years a great deal of research has been devoted to the development of drugs for women who complain of low interest in sex or difficulty in sexual arousal. In 2015 the U.S. Food and Drug Administration (FDA) approved one such drug, flibanserin (sold as Addyi), and another, bremelanotide (Vyleesi), was approved in 2019. Yet a great deal of controversy has surrounded these drugs. On the one hand, their approval was urged by those

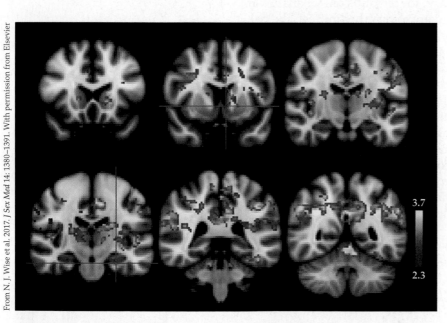

From N. J. Wise et al. 2017. *J Sex Med* 14: 1380–1391. With permission from Elsevier

▲ **FIGURE 1.6   Sex on the brain**   These images show (in red and yellow) the location of brain activity correlated with orgasm in women, obtained with a scanning technique called functional magnetic resonance imaging, or fMRI. The images represent combined data from 10 women. Orgasm-related activity is distributed over a network of regions, some of which are known to be involved in processing of sexual or pleasurable information.

who felt that women's sexual problems had long been ignored by the pharmaceutical industry. On the other hand, detractors pointed out that the drugs are very expensive, their benefits are limited, and they can have significant side effects. It has also been argued that women's sexual problems are rooted in psychological and social issues more than in any physiological dysfunction. We revisit these issues in Chapter 14.

## Psychology includes diverse approaches to sexuality

**Psychology,** the study of mental processes and behavior, has splintered into numerous overlapping subdisciplines, each of which tends to use distinct methods. The branch of psychology most significant to the study of sexuality is **social psychology**—the study of how we think about, influence, and relate to other people. Social psychologists concern themselves with all kinds of sexual matters, such as sexual attraction and relationships, violence between intimate partners, and anti-gay prejudice.

Here's one example of how social psychologists tackle an important question relating to sexuality. Researchers at the University of California, Los Angeles (UCLA), led by Neil Malamuth, have been interested in the question of whether portrayals of sexual violence in the media and pornography make men more accepting of such violence and more willing to commit it, as has been asserted by many **feminists** (Malamuth, 2018). In one study, male college students were randomly assigned to either of two groups. One group watched movies that portrayed sexual violence against women—specifically, movies in which a woman was raped but subsequently fell in love with her rapist. The other students—the **control group**—watched movies that contained no sexual violence. A few days later the students were given a sexual attitudes questionnaire. The results supported the feminist contention: Male students who watched sexually violent movies expressed significantly more accepting attitudes toward sexual violence than the men in the control group. This finding, as well as those of related studies by Malamuth's group and others, suggest that exposure to images of sexual violence really does make some men more likely to commit sexual assaults. This only applies to men with certain predisposing characteristics, however, as we will discuss further in Chapter 16.

**Cognitive psychology** is the study of internal mental processes. As an example, there's a well-known stereotype that gay men are "like women" and lesbians are "like men." How true is this? To find out, cognitive psychologists have conducted many studies comparing a variety of mental traits, skills, and attitudes in gay and straight people. Researchers at the University of Haifa, in Israel, for instance, picked empathy, which is the ability to detect and feel the emotions of other people. This trait is typically better developed in women than in men. Consistent with the stereotype, the researchers found that gay men scored higher on tests of empathy than straight men, whereas lesbians scored lower than straight women (Perry et al., 2013). Still, looking at the entire body of research in this field, gay people show a patchwork of gender-typical and gender-atypical traits, and what's true on average is not necessarily true about individuals. We review this topic further in Chapter 12.

**Evolutionary psychology** seeks to explain how evolution has molded our genetic endowment to favor certain patterns of sexual feelings and behaviors. One idea in evolutionary psychology is that because reproduction is so much more demanding for females than for males, genes have evolved that cause females to be very picky in their choice of sex partners. As a result, other genes have evolved that cause males to engage in competitive and risky sexual displays—displays that are intended to influence females' choices.

It's well established that men are more likely than women to engage in risky behaviors, but it's not clear whether the risks we take in everyday life—such as when we cross a busy street—are actually sexual displays. To help answer this question, an international group of evolutionary psychologists descended on Britain's

---

**psychology** The study of mental processes and behavior.

**social psychology** The study of one's relationships to others.

**feminism** The movement to secure equality for women; the study of social and psychological issues from women's perspectives.

**control group** A group of participants included in a study for comparison purposes.

**cognitive psychology** The study of the information-processing systems of the mind.

**evolutionary psychology** The study of the influence of evolution on mental processes or behavior.

Courtesy of David McIntyre

▲ **FIGURE 1.7** **Looking for love?** Crossing the street in front of traffic can be a form of sexual display, according to research at the University of Liverpool.

Liverpool University (Pawlowski et al., 2008). They stationed themselves near the campus's busiest crosswalk, and over a period of 3 months they observed how 1,000 men and women crossed the street (**FIGURE 1.7**). Specifically, they noted how much risk the students took in crossing (i.e., whether they crossed when vehicles were approaching) and who else was present when each person crossed. As might have been expected, the researchers found that men took more risks than women. The interesting finding, though, was that the presence of women nearby significantly *increased* the likelihood that a man would attempt a risky crossing, whereas the presence of men nearby did not influence his decision one way or another. Women, on the other hand, paid little or no attention to who was present, regardless of their sex, when they decided whether to cross. The researchers concluded that even a mundane act such as crossing a street can be motivated in part by the urge to engage in sexual displays—but only for men in the presence of women. Women do engage in sexual displays—when they flirt, for example—but these displays don't commonly take the form of risk-taking behavior.

## Cultural anthropology focuses on sexual diversity across cultures

**Cultural anthropologists** study ethnic and cultural diversity in sexual attitudes, behavior, and relationships. This kind of research generally involves fieldwork. An example is the research into the concept of partible paternity in Amazonia that is discussed in Box 1.1.

Another example closer to home concerns the Native American tradition of "two-spirit" (i.e., male+female) people—individuals, usually born male, who incorporated both a male and a female identity and who were accorded a special role in their communities. They are described in more detail in Chapter 4. The study of two-spirit people challenges assumptions about **gender** that are prevalent in most Western societies, because they indicate that individuals can embody both female and male gender traits (Sheppard & Mayo, 2013).

## Sociologists focus on the connection between sex and society

**Sociology** is the scientific study of society. Sociologists make a unique contribution to the study of human sexuality by linking the sexual behaviors and attitudes of individuals to larger social structures. Sociologists examine how sexual expression varies with age, race, national origin, religious and political beliefs, place of residence, educational level, and so on. Such studies are often carried out by means of sex surveys.

We already briefly mentioned the surveys conducted by Alfred Kinsey in the mid-20th century. More recent surveys have improved on Kinsey's methodology by using modern random-sampling and data-analysis techniques, and by allowing respondents to enter answers directly into computers, thus avoiding the potential embarrassment of face-to-face questioning.

The most comprehensive of the modern surveys was the 1992 **National Health and Social Life Survey (NHSLS)**, which was initiated in part as a response to the AIDS epidemic (Laumann et al., 1994). A smaller but more contemporary study is the ongoing **National Survey of Sexual Health and Behavior (NSSHB)**, run by researchers at Indiana University (National Survey of Sexual Health and Behavior, 2019). This study

**cultural anthropology** The study of cultural variations across the human race.

**gender** The collection of psychological traits that differ between males and females.

**sociology** The scientific study of society.

**National Health and Social Life Survey (NHSLS)** A national survey of sexual behavior, relationships, and attitudes in the United States, conducted in the early 1990s.

**National Survey of Sexual Health and Behavior (NSSHB)** A national survey of sexual behavior in the United States, based at Indiana University and published in 2010.

has collected survey data at regular intervals since 2009. Here is a sample of the findings from that survey, along with some questions for you to think about:

- When asked about their most recent sexual experience, men nearly always reported that their partners experienced orgasm, but about 1 in 3 women said that they themselves did not do so. What do you think could be the reason for this discrepancy?

- Far more women than men said that they experience physical pain during coitus. Are there ways men could help women enjoy pain-free sex?

- Adults using a condom for sex were just as likely to rate the event positively in terms of arousal, pleasure, and orgasm as when having sex without one. If you or your partner have used condoms, is this finding consistent with your personal experience?

- The percentage of women and men who said that they have had sex with same-sex partners was much higher than the percentage who said they were lesbian, gay, or bisexual. Why might people who say they are heterosexual engage in non-heterosexual sex?

Another valuable source of information is the **General Social Survey (GSS)**, which is run by sociologists at the University of Chicago. The GSS has been asking Americans pretty much the same questions at 1- or 2-year intervals since 1972, which has made it possible to learn how people's attitudes on sexual issues have changed over time.

A British survey—the **National Survey of Sexual Attitudes and Lifestyles (Natsal)**—has been published periodically since 1994; the fourth survey, due to be carried out in 2021, will break new ground by combining a computerized questionnaire with biological data obtained from health records and blood samples (Natsal, 2019).

Random-sample surveys are likely to encompass very few if any individuals who belong to "minorities within minorities," such as Asian-American lesbians or HIV-positive Christian adolescents, yet the combination of such characteristics can strongly affect how individuals are viewed and treated by society as a whole. In fact, every individual is unique in the sense that they stand at the intersection of many demographic and sexual variables; this reality is encapsulated in the expression **intersectionality**. To bring out the individuality of interviewees, **qualitative researchers** may engage them in free-format, in-depth discussions that allow for self-expression

**General Social Survey (GSS)**
A long-running periodic survey of the U.S. population run by the National Opinion Research Center.

**National Survey of Sexual Attitudes and Lifestyles (Natsal)**
A periodic British survey of sexual behavior, relationships, and attitudes.

**intersectionality** Interactions between different aspects of a person's identity, such as race and sexual orientation.

**qualitative research** In-depth but non-numerical study of social phenomena.

◀ Participants in sex surveys give more honest responses when they can do so without the presence of investigators.

**case history** A description of the course of a disorder as it has affected a specific individual.

**big data** The search for patterns and trends in very large data sets.

**script theory** The analysis of sexual and other behaviors as the enactment of socially instilled roles.

**ethnography** The study of a cultural group, often by means of extended individual fieldwork.

**sexology** The scientific study of sex and sexual disorders.

on the part of interviewees and subjective interpretation on the part of researchers. In the medical and psychiatric fields the results of such discussions may be published in the form of sexual **case histories**.

One way in which sex researchers have attempted to avoid the shortcomings of surveys is by mining what is often called **big data**, meaning the enormous quantity of personal information that has been gathered by online search engines, social-media corporations, and the like. For example, American surveys regularly find that there are far fewer gay men in conservative states than in more gay-friendly states, but when Seth Stephens-Davidowitz analyzed millions of searches for pornographic videos on the website Pornhub, he found that roughly the same proportion of men's porn searches in all states were for gay porn (Stephens-Davidowitz, 2017). You've probably already thought of a possible reason for this discrepancy, but if not we discuss the issue in more detail in Chapter 12. Researchers who use this kind of methodology are more likely to call themselves data analysts than sociologists, but they are asking the same basic questions.

Sociologists are also interested in the mechanisms by which social structures (ranging from the family to the mass media) mold individual feelings and behaviors. One influential idea is that society gives us "scripts" and "roles"—ways of presenting ourselves to others as we interact socially. We can select from many different scripts and alter them as creatively as we wish. This idea has been referred to as **script theory** (Wiederman, 2015). The script theory approach helps us understand cause and effect in sexual matters. Researchers at Brigham Young University, for example, found that frequent pornography use by college students is associated with more frequent engagement in casual sex. This association may come about because pornography use strengthens an internal script that validates sexual permissiveness (Braithwaite et al., 2015).

Sociologists may also engage in **ethnographic** fieldwork, immersing themselves in their participants' lives in the same way that cultural anthropologists do. For example, Staci Newmahr, then a graduate student in sociology at the State University of New York (SUNY) at Buffalo, wanted to explore the lives and motivations of people who engaged in BDSM activities (Newmahr, 2011). ("BDSM" means the infliction or receipt of pain, humiliation, and the like as a sexual or recreational outlet.) To do so, Newmahr joined a BDSM club and submitted to treatments that you might consider extreme, or at least well beyond the usual requirements for a Ph.D. We report on some of her findings in Chapter 13.

## Organizations promote sex research

As we have seen, women and men in a variety of academic disciplines and walks of life have made important contributions to our understanding of human sexuality. Increasingly, however, there is a perception that sex research, or **sexology**, is an academic discipline in its own right. This discipline is an unusual one in that it demands expertise in a variety of disciplines, including biology, psychology, anthropology, and sociology.

Numerous organizations at local, international, and global levels now foster sex research. In the United States, the Society for the Scientific Study of Sexuality (SSSS, or "Quad-S") publishes the *Journal of Sex Research* and other periodicals. The American Association of Sexuality Educators,

© Yaacov Dagan/Alamy Stock Photo

▲ Science lab? Sex researcher Staci Newmahr participated in BDSM scenes like this one for her graduate thesis.

Counselors and Therapists (AASECT) and the Society for Sex Therapy and Research (SSTAR) certify educational programs in sex education and therapy. There are also institutes devoted to research or training in issues of sexuality, such as the Kinsey Institute (which is affiliated with Indiana University), and special-purpose organizations such as the Guttmacher Institute (which focuses on family planning issues).

At an international level, two organizations stand out. The International Academy of Sex Research publishes the *Archives of Sexual Behavior*. The World Association for Sexual Health (WAS), which represents sex research and sexual health organizations from 53 countries, has issued a universal Declaration of Sexual Rights (World Association for Sexual Health, 2014). The full declaration is available online; we summarize the main rights as follows:

- The right to freedom from discrimination on the basis of sex, marital status, sexual orientation, or gender identity
- The right to choose one's sexual behaviors, partners, and relationships, with due regard to the rights of others
- The right to freedom from sexual violence, coercion, harassment, exploitation, and trafficking
- The right to privacy in sexual matters
- The right to the highest attainable standard of sexual health
- The right to scientifically accurate sex education and information
- The right to reproductive choices, including access to fertility treatment, contraception, and abortion
- The right to redress and justice for violations of sexual rights
- The right to demonstrate and advocate on matters related to sexuality

In 2019 the WAS supplemented its 2014 declaration with a Declaration on Sexual Pleasure, which urged governments, other organizations, and educators to "promote sexual pleasure in law and policy as a fundamental part of sexual health and well-being" (World Association for Sexual Health, 2019).

## Summary

- Sex means either the distinction between male and female, or sexual behavior. Sexuality means the entire field of human experience that is connected with sex.

- Many species can reproduce without sex, but humans can only reproduce sexually. Sexual selection is a process whereby competition for sex partners has promoted the evolution of anatomical and behavioral differences between males and females. In some species, including ourselves, additional functions for sex have evolved that have no direct connection with reproduction.

- The establishment of large-scale societies and governments led to the regulation of sexuality. In stratified societies the sexualities of people at the top and bottom of the social ladder have come to differ greatly.

- Marriage has undergone many changes, from a contract arranged by men to a more voluntary and egalitarian arrangement that benefits both partners. The banning of polygamy by the early Christian church laid the groundwork for greater equality in marriage. Organized religion has often established moral codes that restrict sexual expression, especially non-reproductive behaviors.

- Urbanization created favorable conditions for the spread of sexually transmitted infections, but it also has aided the recognition and acceptance of sexual minorities. The internet has fostered communication among people with unusual sexual interests.

- The steep reduction in the birth rate in many countries over the last two centuries has allowed women to take a role in marriage that goes beyond unwanted pregnancies and the extra child-rearing responsibilities they impose. Marriage itself has lost some of its significance in Western societies, as nonmarital

*(Continued)*

## Summary *(continued)*

cohabitation and child rearing, and at-will divorce, have become increasingly common and accepted.

- Influential figures in the history of sexuality include psychoanalyst Sigmund Freud, biologist Nettie Stevens, contraception activist Margaret Sanger, sex survey pioneer Alfred Kinsey, and sexual physiologists William Masters and Virginia Johnson.

- Sexuality can be studied with a wide variety of approaches. The biomedical approach has been based primarily on studies in non-human animals, but recent advances, such as brain-scanning technology and the decoding of the human genome, allow for more direct study of sexual processes in humans. Biomedical research has had major impacts on contemporary sexuality.

- The psychological approach falls into several subdisciplines. Social psychology concerns itself with the diverse ways in which sex influences interpersonal relations. Cognitive psychology is focused on the mental processes, such as sexual arousal, that

underlie sexual expression. Evolutionary psychology is devoted to understanding how evolutionary forces have molded our sex lives. Cultural anthropology investigates the influence of ethnic and cultural diversity on sexual expression.

- Sociologists are concerned with the interactions between the sexuality of individuals and larger societal groupings. Sex surveys are an important tool in this approach. An example of a theoretical social science approach is sexual script theory—the notion that, as a result of constant interaction with others, people learn to follow certain sexual scripts and act out certain roles. Sociologists also do fieldwork in the environments where sexual transactions take place.

- Sexology, or sex research, is gradually asserting itself as an independent and multidisciplinary field of study. National and international organizations, conferences, and journals are devoted to the subject. The World Association for Sexual Health has issued a universal Declaration of Sexual Rights.

---

The **Discovering Human Sexuality** digital resources include activities, animations, flashcards, web links, chapter outlines and summaries, and other study tools.

■ ■ ■ ■ ■ ■ ■ ■ ■ ■ ■ ■ ■ ■ ■ ■ ■ ■

Learn more with this chapter's digital tools, including the **Oxford Insight Study Guide**, at **oup.com/he/levay5e**.

## Discussion Questions

1. Do you think that the sexual behavior of non-human animals has anything to teach us about what is acceptable in human sexual behavior?

2. What course of education would you recommend to someone who plans a career in sex research?

3. To what extent do you think that your religious upbringing and beliefs—or the lack of them—affect your current or future sexual and marital choices?

4. After reading the basics of the World Association for Sexual Health's Declaration of Sexual Rights, do you agree with everything in it? Do you think the declaration fails to address any important topics?

## Web Resources

American Association of Sexuality Educators, Counselors and Therapists (AASECT)
  **www.aasect.org**

Archive for Sexology—English-language site at the Humboldt University of Berlin
  **http://tinyurl.com/lmv4ft5**

Guttmacher Institute   **www.guttmacher.org**

International Academy of Sex Research (IASR)   **www.iasr.org**

Kinsey Institute   **www.kinseyinstitute.org**

Sex Information and Education Council of Canada (SIECCAN)   **www.sieccan.org**

Sexuality Information and Education Council of the United States (SIECUS)
  **www.siecus.org**

Society for Sex Therapy and Research (SSTAR)  **www.sstarnet.org**
Society for the Scientific Study of Sexuality (SSSS)  **www.sexscience.org**
World Association for Sexual Health (WAS)  **www.worldsexology.org**

## Recommended Reading

Ellis, H. (1900). *Studies in the psychology of sex*. Davis.

Freud, S. (1905/1975). *Three essays on the theory of sexuality*. Basic Books.

Kinsey, A. C., Pomeroy, W. B. & Martin, C. E. (1948). *Sexual behavior in the human male*. Saunders.

Kinsey, A. C., Pomeroy, W. B., Martin, C. E. & Gebhard, P. H. (1953). *Sexual behavior in the human female*. Saunders.

Krafft-Ebing, R. v. (1886/1999). *Psychopathia sexualis, with special reference to contrary sexual instinct: A clinical-forensic study*. Bloat.

Masters, W. H. & Johnson, V. E. (1966). *Human sexual response*. Little, Brown.

Mead, M. (1928). *Coming of age in Samoa: A psychological study of primitive youth for Western civilization*. Morrow.

(The books listed above are historically important works but don't necessarily represent current thinking.)

Dabhoiwala, F. (2012). *The origins of sex: A history of the first sexual revolution*. Oxford University Press.

Graupner, H. & Tahmindjis, P. (Eds.) (2014). *Sexuality and human rights: A global overview*. Routledge.

Michael, R. T., Gagnon, J. H., Laumann, E. O. & Kolata, G. (1994). *Sex in America: A definitive survey*. Little, Brown.

Wellcome Collection. (2014). *The institute of sexology*. Gestalten. (An illustrated history of sex research).

No two female bodies are the same.

# 2 Women's Bodies

Women and men are different, both in their bodies—the subject of this and the following chapters—and in their minds. Indeed, bodily differences, especially in the external genitals, are commonly used to decide whether a person is male or female. Yet many similarities and parallels exist between the bodies and minds of men and women— they are only variations on a single theme, after all. And there is considerable anatomical diversity within the categories of male and female.

In fact, some babies are born with bodies that are not easy to categorize as either male or female. What's more, some adults are transgender; that is, they identify with the other sex from their anatomical sex at birth. A transgender person may identify as a man but have a typically female body, or vice versa. We discuss these complexities in later chapters. For now, we deal with the great majority of people who are clearly one sex or the other and who identify as such.

The Bible describes how Eve was fashioned from Adam's rib, but in reality neither men nor women are the original sex from which the other was constructed. Rather, women and men coevolved over millions of years from females and males of our ancestral species.

## 2.1 A Woman's Vulva Includes Her Mons, Labia, Vaginal Opening, and Clitoris

### LEARNING OBJECTIVES
After reading this section you should be able to:

2.1.1 Create a schematic drawing of the vulva and label its components.

2.1.2 Describe the parts of the clitoris and its role in sexual activity.

2.1.3 Explain how microorganisms contribute to the health or disorders of the vagina.

**erogenous zone**  A region of the body whose stimulation causes sexual arousal.

**external genitalia**  The sexual structures on the outside of the body.

**vulva**  The female external genitalia.

**mons (or mons veneris)**  The front-most component of the vulva: a mound of fatty tissue covering the pubic bone.

**pubic hair**  Hair that appears on portions of the external genitalia in both sexes at puberty.

The term **erogenous zone** refers to a region of the body where touch or other forms of stimulation cause or increase sexual arousal. The most obvious erogenous zone is the genital area in both women and men, but the buttocks and anus, as well as the breasts and nipples (especially in women), are also very erotically sensitive. In fact, according to one group of psychologists who asked a large number of women and men about their sexual responses, virtually any part of the body surface is erotically sensitive to some degree or in some circumstances (**FIGURE 2.1**). Thus the whole body could be thought of as a single erogenous zone with several "hot spots." In this chapter we describe those hot spots—most especially the genital area—in terms of their anatomy and function in women, as well as women's internal reproductive organs.

Many girls and women have little understanding of their genital anatomy, in part because the female **external genitalia** are not as prominent or accessible as those of men. In addition, girls often learn that it's "not nice" to inquire or talk about these body parts, or even to take a close look at them. Vague phrases such as "down there" may substitute for specific terms. Plenty of adult women—and men—do not know what the word "vagina" means and could not make a reasonable sketch of a woman's genital anatomy. Thus, the "naming of parts" and the description of their layout is the crucial first stage of education in sexuality (**FIGURE 2.2**).

The word **vulva** is a scientific term that refers to a woman's entire external genital area. The appearance of the vulva varies from woman to woman, a fact illustrated clearly in Figure 2.2B.

The **mons** is a pad of fatty tissue covered by skin and **pubic hair**. It lies immediately in front of the pubic bone. The mons is erotically sensitive, and it may serve as a cushion for the woman's pubic area during sexual activity. The hair helps vaporize odors that arise in specialized sweat glands, similar to those in the armpits, and these odors may act as chemical attractants. (The scientific evidence for this is based mainly on animal research that may not be relevant to humans.) The mons with its pubic hair may also be a visual trigger for sexual arousal in a woman's partner, since it is the most easily visible portion of the vulva. In spite of these possible functions for pubic hair, many women remove some or all of it (**BOX 2.1**).

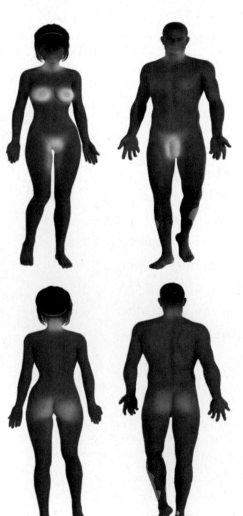

◀ **FIGURE 2.1  The entire body is an erogenous zone.** Finnish researchers asked 528 women and 176 men to mark on a schematic body the regions where they found touch by a partner sexually arousing. These images show the computer-averaged results, with yellow indicating the more sensitive areas and dark brown the less sensitive. Only a few small patches on the man's legs registered as completely insensitive (pink). (From L. Nummenmaa et al. 2016. *Arch Sex Behav* 45: 1207–1216.)

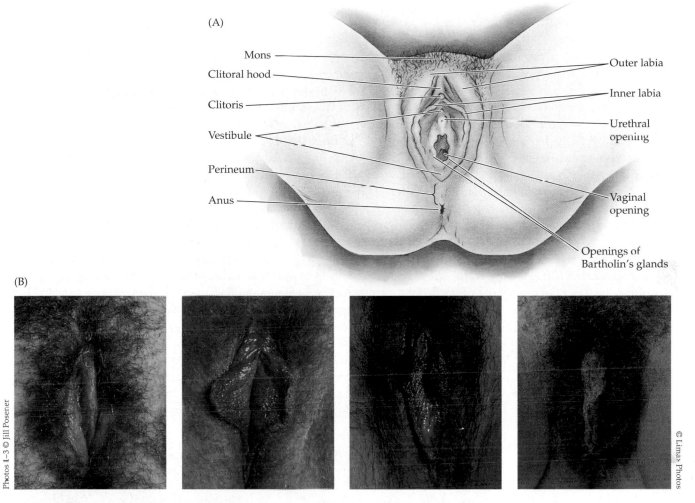

Photos 1–3 © Jill Posener

© Lima› Photos

▲ **FIGURE 2.2    The vulva, or female external genitalia** (A) Vulva with labia drawn apart to show the vestibule, urethral opening, and vaginal opening. The perineum and anus are not part of the vulva. (B) The inner labia are quite variable in shape and color from woman to woman, as these four examples show. (See **Activity 2.1: The Vulva**.)

The **labia** (Latin for "lips") are two pairs of skin folds that extend down from the mons on either side of the vulva. The **outer labia**, or **labia majora**, are padded with fatty tissue and are hairy on the surfaces nearest to the thighs. The skin of the outer labia is often darker than the skin elsewhere, and it is erotically sensitive, especially on the inner, hairless sides of the labia.

The **inner labia**, or **labia minora**, are two thin folds of hairless skin that lie between the two outer labia. (When people use the word "labia" without any qualifier, they usually mean the inner labia.) In some women the inner labia are only visible after parting of the outer labia; in other women they protrude to variable degrees (see Figure 2.2B). The inner labia meet at the back of the vulva, and also at the front, where they form the clitoral hood. The left and right inner labia generally touch each other in the midline when the woman is not aroused, and the area encircled by the labia is called the **vestibule**.

The inner labia are amply supplied with glands, blood vessels, and nerve endings and are very erotically sensitive. During sexual arousal the inner labia swell and darken as they fill with blood, a process called **vasocongestion**. The appearance

**labia**   Two pairs of skin folds that form the sides of the vulva.

**outer labia (or labia majora)**   Fleshy skin folds, partially covered in pubic hair, that extend from the mons.

**inner labia (or labia minora)**   Thin, hairless folds of skin located between the outer labia and immediately flanking the vestibule.

**vestibule**   The potential space between the left and right inner labia.

**vasocongestion**   The swelling of tissue caused by an influx of blood.

## BOX 2.1
## Pubic Hair Removal

Removal of pubic hair—by shaving, waxing, or other methods—is popular among U.S. college students: Most remove at least some of their pubic hair on a regular basis, either for reasons of perceived "hygiene" or in preparation for sex (Gaither et al., 2017). One half of all the female students keep their genital areas entirely hair free, whereas only 1 in 5 men do the same. This sex difference may reflect the preferences of their partners, because 60% of men prefer their partners to be hair free, whereas only 24% of women do so. Hair removal is more common among college-age women and men than among older Americans.

In cross-cultural perspective, pubic hair removal has always been a widespread practice (Craig & Gray, 2018). It features in several origin myths: The Kogi people of Colombia, for example, recounted how men's penises grew from pubic hairs removed and planted in the soil by the female Creator. In Islamic tradition, pubic hair removal was recommended for both women and men by the prophet Muhammad and enforced by Sharia law. Conversely, some cultures, such as that of Japan, have praised abundant pubic hair as highly erotic. In recent years several American and Canadian celebrities have

mentioned that they don't remove their pubic hair, but the reaction hasn't always been positive: When artist Petra Collins posted a photo in which some of her pubic hair was visible above her bikini line, her Instagram account was temporarily shut down (Pai, 2018).

One much-publicized study reported that frequent pubic hair removal—especially complete removal—is associated with a higher incidence of sexually transmitted infections (Osterberg et al., 2017). This may simply be because the people who most often remove their pubic hair are likely to be those who are most sexually active. One infection that is likely to be *reduced* by hair removal is infestation with pubic lice, because lice use the shafts of pubic hair as handholds (see Chapter 15).

A surprising number of women and men manage to injure themselves in the course of pubic grooming. In one national study, 1 in 4 groomers said that they had sustained injuries—most commonly lacerations, followed by burns (Truesdale et al., 2017). Shaving was the method most likely to cause injuries; in men, shaving the scrotum was particularly hazardous. Grooming by another person caused more injuries than self-grooming. Most injuries did not require medical attention.

(A)

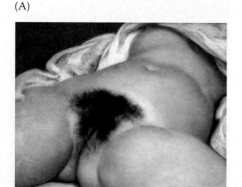

(B)

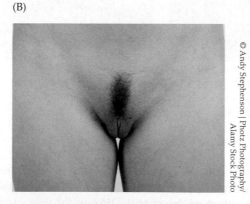

© Andy Stephenson | Photz Photography/ Alamy Stock Photo

(C)

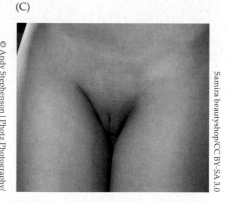

Samira beautyshop/CC BY-SA 3.0

Pubic hair—love it or loathe it? (A) Gustave Courbet's 1866 painting *The Origin of the World* put natural pubic hair front and center. (B) A Brazilian wax removes all pubic hair except a narrow strip. (C) Complete removal of pubic hair.

of the inner labia varies greatly. In some women they are virtually absent and are represented merely by slight ridges on the inner sides of the outer labia. In other women they extend well beyond the outer labia. In some cultures the inner labia are not left in their natural state but are stretched, from childhood onward, with the aim of making the vulva more attractive.

In the contemporary United States, on the other hand, some women and teenage girls request labial reduction or **labiaplasty**—plastic surgery to reduce their inner labia or make them more symmetrical (**FIGURE 2.3**). The American College of Obstetricians and Gynecologists (ACOG) discourages the procedure in adolescents, citing possible harmful complications. The increased desire for labial reduction is probably

**labiaplasty**    Surgical modification of the inner labia.

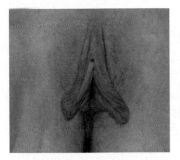 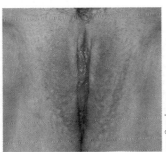

Courtesy of Dr. Robert H. Stubbs. www.psurg.com

▲ **FIGURE 2.3**   A woman's vulva before and after surgical reduction of the inner labia

connected with the increasing popularity of pubic hair removal, which makes the inner labia more visible, as well as with exposure to images of supposedly "ideal" labia in pornographic videos and elsewhere. In reality, the labia of most women who request labial reduction are well within the normal size range, and many are actually at the smaller end of the normal range (Wood, 2018).

In some girls (mostly age 2 to 7) the inner labia stick together, sometimes so completely that it is difficult for the girl to pass urine. These **labial adhesions** often cure themselves over time, but if necessary the labia can be encouraged to separate by regular cleaning or by the application of creams prescribed by a doctor.

The area surrounded by the labia is called the vestibule. Toward the back end of the vestibule are two small glands, called **Bartholin's glands**. The secretions of these glands pass through ducts that open into the vestibule, where they help lubricate the vaginal opening. The Bartholin's glands may only come to a woman's attention if one of them becomes blocked or infected (see Figure 15.23). Farther forward in the vestibule are three important structures: the clitoris, the vaginal opening, and the urethral opening.

### There is more to the clitoris than meets the eye

The **clitoris** is a complex organ, only a portion of which is visible from the outside. This external portion is the clitoral **glans**, a small but highly sensitive knob of tissue positioned at the front of the vestibule. It is about the size of a pearl, and like a pearl, its size can vary. It is covered, or partly covered, by the **clitoral hood**, which is formed by the frontmost portion of the left and right labia minora where they meet in the midline. The glans can be made visible if the hood is gently retracted. The underside of the clitoral glans is attached to the underlying portion of the labia minora by a fold of erotically sensitive tissue known as the **frenulum of the clitoris**. Within the glans is a body called the **corpus spongiosum** ("spongy body"), comprised of **erectile tissue**—a system of vascular spaces that becomes engorged with blood during sexual arousal.

The **shaft of the clitoris**, which is about 1 inch (2 to 3 cm) long, runs upward from the glans, under the hood. Although the shaft cannot be seen directly, it can be felt, and its outline may be visible through the skin of the hood. The tissue within the clitoral shaft consists of two **corpora cavernosa** ("cavernous bodies") that lie side by side. Like the corpus spongiosum, the corpora cavernosa are composed of erectile tissue.

Internally, the two corpora cavernosa of the clitoral shaft diverge from each other, forming the left and right **crura** (singular: crus) of the clitoris. This gives the entire clitoris a wishbone structure (**FIGURE 2.4**). The crura are about 3 inches (7 cm) long; they run backward and downward to either side of the urethra and vagina.

Yet another pair of structures, the **vestibular bulbs**, are closely associated with the clitoris. They are curved masses of erectile tissue that surround the vestibule and underlie the inner labia. Like the crura, the vestibular bulbs are considered to be internal portions of the clitoris.

**labial adhesion**   A condition seen in prepubertal girls in which the left and right inner labia stick together.

**Bartholin's glands**   Two mucus-secreting glands that help lubricate the vaginal opening.

**clitoris**   The erectile organ in females, whose external portion is located at the junction of the inner labia, just in front of the vestibule.

**glans**   The terminal knob of the clitoris or penis.

**clitoral hood**   A loose fold of skin that covers the clitoris.

**frenulum of the clitoris**   An erotically sensitive fold of tissue that connects the labia to the underside of the clitoris.

**corpus spongiosum**   A single midline erectile structure. In both sexes, it fills the glans.

**erectile tissue**   Tissue that stiffens an organ by filling with blood.

**shaft of the clitoris**   The portion of the clitoris next to the glans that can be felt under the clitoral hood.

**corpus cavernosum (pl. corpora cavernosa)**   Either of two elongated erectile structures within the clitoris or penis that also extend backward into the pelvic floor.

**crura (sing. crus)**   The two internal extensions of the corpora cavernosa of the clitoris or penis.

**vestibular bulbs**   Erectile structures beneath the inner labia, on either side of the vestibule.

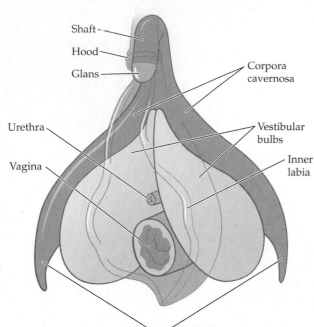

**smegma** A whitish, greasy secretion that can build up under the hood of the clitoris or the foreskin of the penis.

◀ **FIGURE 2.4** **Structure of the clitoris** The inner labia are shown as if transparent. Both the clitoral glans and the vestibular bulbs are composed of corpus spongiosum tissue.

Ointment-like secretions from the underside of the clitoral hood lubricate the motion of the hood over the clitoris, but when these secretions dry and mix with dead cells and bacteria, they form a pasty material called **smegma**, which can collect under the hood. Smegma may be removed, or prevented from accumulating, if the clitoral hood is pulled back and the area is gently washed with soap and warm water.

The clitoris, especially the glans and frenulum, is richly supplied with sensory nerve fibers whose function is to produce sexual arousal. This includes both psychological arousal (the positive excitement that accompanies sexual activity) and physiological arousal (vaginal lubrication and other genital phenomena that facilitate coitus). Thus we can say that the clitoris has both a recreational (pleasure) function and—during a woman's fertile years—a reproductive function (Levin, 2019). Stimulation of the clitoris is the most reliable way for most women to experience orgasm. The clitoris is so sensitive that many women prefer diffuse or indirect stimulation rather than direct touching of the clitoris itself.

During sexual arousal, the clitoris swells and becomes firmer: This is a clitoral erection. The clitoris does not become rigid like the shaft of a man's erect penis, however. That's because the erectile tissue is not surrounded by a layer of tough connective tissue that resists the tissue's expansion. The mechanism of erection is described in more detail in connection with the penis (see Chapter 3), where it has been studied in detail. The process of erection involves not just the shaft and glans, but also the deeper clitoral structures—the crura and vestibular bulbs. Erection of the vestibular bulbs helps to lengthen and stiffen the vagina.

Typically, the glans of the clitoris is visible in the nonaroused state, but it may disappear under the clitoral hood during erection or with increasing sexual arousal, so sexual stimulation of the clitoris may occur through the hood rather than directly on the clitoral glans itself. Still, there's quite a bit of variation from woman to woman in terms of her clitoral anatomy and what kind of clitoral stimulation she finds arousing. The clitoris is more erotically sensitive in the erect than in the flaccid state.

Not all women know that they have a clitoris or understand its function. The clitoris can easily be skipped in sex-education classes, and plenty of women have never had a sex-ed class anyway. If they were discouraged, as girls, from exploring their bodies, and if their partners have no particular interest in their sexual fulfillment, the structure may remain undiscovered.

Genital piercing is a popular form of self-expression in the United States and elsewhere. Some forms of genital piercing, such as the horizontal clitoral hood piercing, are done simply for adornment, but others, such as the vertical piercing, may also enhance sexual stimulation because the ball or jewelry element lies in direct contact with the clitoris (**FIGURE 2.5**). Because of variations in genital anatomy, not all types of piercing are suitable for all women.

As with any piercing, scrupulous hygiene is required during the procedure. About 7% of women experience complications such as infection of the piercing site (Thomas et al., 2015). In some U.S. states, such as New York, it is illegal to perform genital piercing on minors.

Female genital cutting, also known as female circumcision or female genital mutilation, is a traditional but highly controversial practice in some cultures. Cutting or removal of the external parts of the clitoris is a central element in this practice (**BOX 2.2**).

▲ **FIGURE 2.5** **Vertical piercing of the clitoral hood** the most popular genital piercing in women.

## BOX 2.2
## Female Genital Cutting

*I was frozen with fear . . . I peered between my legs and saw the gypsy woman getting ready . . . I expected a big knife, but instead, out of the bag she pulled a tiny cotton sack. She reached inside with her long fingers, and fished out a broken razor blade . . . I saw dried blood on the jagged edge of the blade. She spat on it and wiped it against her dress. While she was scrubbing, my world went dark as my mother tied a scarf around my eyes as a blindfold. The next thing I felt was my flesh, my genitals, being cut away.* (Dirie, 1998)

Like Waris Dirie, author of the foregoing account, more than 200 million women and girls alive today have been subjected to some form of cutting of their external genitals (World Health Organization, 2018b). The various procedures are referred to collectively as **female genital cutting**, female genital mutilation, or (traditionally) female circumcision. The practice is prevalent in 29 countries, most of them in Africa. Eighty percent or more of the women in Djibouti, Egypt, Eritrea, Ethiopia, Gambia, Sierra Leone, Somalia, and Sudan are believed to have been cut. Female genital cutting is also practiced in the Middle East, Indonesia, and elsewhere. It is particularly associated with Islamic cultures, and although female circumcision is not prescribed in the Quran, it is referred to favorably in later Islamic texts and is often perceived to have religious significance.

There are three principal types of female genital cutting. In the least invasive version, known as **sunnah**, the clitoral hood is incised or removed. This procedure is roughly analogous to male circumcision as we know it in the United States. In practice, however, some part of the clitoris itself is often removed during sunnah circumcision.

In the second procedure, known as **clitoridectomy** or excision, the entire clitoral glans and shaft may be removed, along with the hood and sometimes nearby portions of the inner labia. The procedure varies according to local custom.

The third procedure, known as **infibulation**, is the most invasive. It is widely practiced in the Sudan and Somalia. (Waris Dirie is Somali.) The procedure includes clitoridectomy but goes beyond it to include removal of the entire inner labia and the inner parts of the outer labia. The cut or abraded edges of the two outer labia are then stitched together to cover the vestibule. Only a small opening is left for the passage of urine and menstrual blood. When the woman first has coitus, the opening has to be enlarged—by forceful penetration with the penis or other object or by cutting.

Female genital cutting is generally performed by traditional practitioners who lack medical training. It is often done with

Waris Dirie from Somalia has campaigned against female genital cutting.

crude instruments and without anesthesia or attention to sanitary conditions, so there is a risk of potentially fatal complications, including hemorrhage and infection. There has been a recent trend toward the "medicalization" of the procedure—that is, it may be carried out by trained medical personnel. This trend could reduce the rate of complications. The trend is controversial, however, as it may be seen as legitimizing the practice.

The long-term effects of female genital cutting are also controversial. In some cases, especially with infibulation, the procedure can cause serious problems with urination, menstruation, sexual activity, childbirth, and fertility. But some studies have suggested that the harmful effects of the less invasive forms of the practice have been exaggerated (Shell-Duncan & Hernlund, 2000).

Female genital cutting may be done simply because it is a tradition in a given culture. A woman who retains her clitoris may be considered ritually unclean or dangerous to the health of a man who has sex with her. However, there may be a second purpose to the procedure: the reduction of female sexual activity, especially before or outside of marriage. This reduction is achieved either by decreasing the pleasure of sexual acts (especially by removal of the clitoris) or by making them painful or very difficult (as with infibulation). In

*(Continued)*

## BOX 2.2
## Female Genital Cutting (continued)

many cultures in which female genital cutting is practiced, a woman who has not undergone the procedure is not marriageable—which often means that she is condemned to a life of poverty.

Thirty-five U.S. states have laws prohibiting female genital cutting. A federal law doing the same was enacted in 1996, but in 2018 a federal appeals court judge ruled that the law was an unconstitutional invasion of states' rights (Belluck, 2018). Significant numbers of immigrant women have been subjected to genital cutting in their countries of birth, and there are occasional reports of girls being subjected to cutting in the United States (Zopotosky, 2017). Girls may also be cut during "vacations" to their home countries, a practice that also violates U.S. laws. Researchers have estimated that over 500,000 girls are at risk of undergoing genital cutting in the United States (Goldberg et al., 2016), but that estimate is based on an unrealistic assumption, namely that immigrant parents are just as desirous of having their daughters cut as are the populations of their home countries. We prefer to believe that most immigrants respect American values and laws.

The practice of female genital cutting has been strongly condemned by many Americans on several grounds: that it is harmful and dangerous; that it interferes with women's right to self-expression, especially in the sexual domain; that it subjugates women's interests to the purported interests of men; and that it makes irreversible decisions for children before they are able to make those decisions for themselves.

In 2005 the African Union's Protocol on the Rights of Women in Africa was ratified: It requires all 53 member states to prohibit female genital cutting. Since that time reported rates have been falling in most African countries (Odukogbe et al., 2017). It is possible, however, that some of the apparent decline reflects a reluctance to admit to a prohibited practice.

Although campaigning against female genital cutting may seem like an entirely praiseworthy activity, it does potentially conflict with another value, namely respect for cultural diversity and autonomy. While we may use words such as "mutilation" to describe the practice, women in the countries concerned have mostly positive views about it, and many girls

want to have it done as a token of their womanhood and their membership in their culture. "Why should I avoid the exercise when my mother and grandmother went through it?" said one 19-year-old Ugandan woman a year after that country banned the practice (Magga, 2010).

It may be that the greatest progress will come from the work of activist organizations within the cultures concerned. Such organizations now exist in many countries. One possible avenue for change is the institution of "ritual without cutting," in which the traditional rites are preserved but the actual cutting is omitted. The poster shown here was created by a Gambian organization dedicated to ending female genital mutilation and replacing the rite with one that does not involve cutting.

Waris Dirie now runs the Desert Flower Foundation, which campaigns against genital cutting and supports girls and women who have undergone cutting.

**female genital cutting**   Any of several forms of ritual cutting or excision of parts of the female genitalia. Also called female genital mutilation or female circumcision.

**sunnah**   Female genital cutting limited to incision or removal of the clitoral hood.

**clitoridectomy**   Removal of the entire external portion of the clitoris (glans, shaft, and hood).

**infibulation**   The most invasive form of female genital cutting, which involves removal of the clitoris, inner labia, and parts of the outer labia, plus the sewing together of the outer labia over the vestibule.

---

**introitus**   The entrance to the vagina, usually covered early in life by the hymen.

**hymen**   A membrane, usually perforated or incomplete, that covers the opening of the vagina. It may be torn by first coitus or by other means.

### The appearance of the vaginal opening is variable

The vaginal opening, or **introitus**, occupies the rear portion of the vestibule. In newborn girls, the vaginal opening is usually covered by a membranous fold of skin, the **hymen**. The hymen has one or several openings that allow for menstrual flow after a girl begins to menstruate and for the insertion of tampons (**FIGURE 2.6**). In a rare

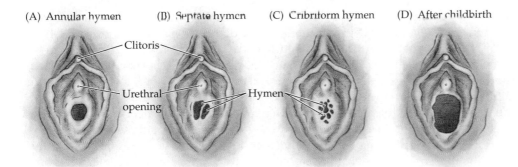

(A) Annular hymen  (B) Septate hymen  (C) Cribriform hymen  (D) After childbirth

Clitoris

Urethral opening  Hymen

▲ **FIGURE 2.6   The hymen is highly variable in structure.** Most commonly it is annular (A); that is, it has a round central opening, which is large enough for passage of the menstrual flow and insertion of a tampon, though it is usually not large enough for coitus. (B) The opening may be crossed by a band of tissue (septate hymen) or (C) by several bands that leave numerous small openings (cribriform hymen). If the openings are very small or are absent entirely (imperforate hymen), the outflow of vaginal secretions and menstrual fluids may be blocked. First intercourse often tears the hymen but leaves it partially intact. (D) Vaginal childbirth removes all but small remnants of the structure. Familiarity with variations in hymen structure is important for professionals who evaluate female sexual assault victims.

condition called **imperforate hymen**, this structure completely closes the vaginal opening. Imperforate hymen is often first diagnosed at puberty because it causes a blockage of menstrual discharge; it is treated surgically to create an opening through which the menstrual discharge can flow.

The hymen may tear or stretch when a woman first has sexual intercourse, which may lead to some pain and bleeding. This phenomenon has led to the traditional notion that the state of a woman's hymen indicates whether or not she has ever engaged in coitus—that is, whether she is a virgin in one meaning of the term (see Chapter 10). One can certainly debate whether a woman's virginity—or lack of it—should be a matter of concern to anyone besides the woman herself. In any case, the state of her hymen is not a reliable indicator of virginity. In some women the hymen undergoes changes at puberty that allow for intercourse without any tearing. Some women may have widened the opening during tampon use or athletic activities, or they may have deliberately stretched the opening with the intention of facilitating first intercourse.

In many Middle Eastern countries it is traditional for a bride's mother or other relative to display the bloodstained sheets from a window after the bride's wedding night, thereby proving to the community that the marriage was consummated and that the bride was indeed a virgin. Of course there may be no stain, for any number of reasons. To guard against this possibility the mother may bring a vial of chicken blood with her.

In some Westernized regions of the Middle East, this ritual has become a lighthearted tradition. In more conservative communities, however, proof of a bride's virginity is still so important that a woman who lacks an intact hymen may undergo an operation to reconstruct one before she marries—even though the state of a woman's hymen is not a reliable indicator of a woman's virginity or nonvirginity (Bentlage & Eich, 2007). Hymen reconstruction is offered by some plastic surgeons in the United States.

The opening of the **urethra** is located between the vaginal opening and the clitoris. Given that the main function of the urethra is to pass urine, you might not consider it a sexual structure, but some women do ejaculate from it during sexual climax (see Chapter 5).

The **perineum** is the erotically sensitive area between the vaginal opening and the anus (or, in males, between the scrotum and the anus). Intestinal bacteria can be spread rather easily from the anus across the perineum to the vagina or urethra,

**imperforate hymen**   A hymen that completely closes the introitus.

**urethra**   The canal that conveys urine from the bladder to the urethral opening.

**perineum**   The region of skin between the anus and the vulva or scrotum.

**pelvic floor muscles** A muscular sling that underlies and supports the pelvic organs.

**pubococcygeus muscles** Muscles of the pelvic floor that runs from the pubic bone to the coccyx (tailbone). In women they form a sling around the vagina.

**reproductive tract** The internal anatomical structures in either sex that form the pathway taken by ova, sperm, or the conceptus.

**vagina** A muscular tube extending 3 to 4 inches (8 to 10 cm) from the vestibule to the uterine cervix.

**coitus** Penetration of the vagina by the penis.

**sexual intercourse** Sexual contact, usually understood to involve coitus.

**birth canal** The canal formed by the uterus, cervix, and vagina, through which the fetus passes during the birth process.

**mucosa** A surface layer of cells that is lubricated by the secretions of mucous glands.

**candidiasis** A fungal infection of the vagina. Also called *thrush* or a *yeast infection*.

which may cause a genital or urinary infection. For this reason, women are advised to wipe themselves in a backward, not a forward, direction after using the toilet.

Important structures underlie the vulva. We have already described the deep extensions of the clitoris. They are associated with various **pelvic floor muscles**, especially the pair of **pubococcygeus muscles**, which are often referred to by the abbreviation "PC muscles" (see **Activity 2.2: Internal Anatomy of the Vulva**). The PC muscles are located to either side of the vagina, and the steady contraction of these muscles stiffens the walls of the vagina during sex, thus increasing sexual sensations for both participants. The PC and other pelvic floor muscles contract even more strongly at orgasm, increasing pleasure, preventing urinary and fecal leakage, and possibly helping to keep semen in the vagina. Exercises to strengthen the PC muscles and other muscles of the pelvic floor (Kegel exercises) have been recommended for the treatment of sexual disorders as well as to prevent the involuntary leakage of urine or feces (incontinence). Kegel exercises are described in Chapter 14.

### The vagina is the outermost portion of the female reproductive tract

As shown in **FIGURE 2.7**, the female **reproductive tract**, when viewed from the front, takes the shape of a letter T. The stem of the T is formed by the vagina, the cervix, and the body of the uterus. The two horizontal arms of the T are formed by the oviducts, also called fallopian tubes, whose ends are adjacent to the two ovaries. The reproductive tract serves the purpose of transport of the female's eggs (ova) and the male's sperm, as well as fertilization, pregnancy, and passage of the fetus during childbirth.

In a woman who is not sexually excited, the **vagina** is a collapsed tube that runs about 3 to 4 inches (8 to 10 cm) upward and backward from the vaginal opening. This length increases with sexual arousal. Penetration of the vagina by the penis constitutes **coitus** or **sexual intercourse**. The vagina plays a role in sperm transport and (along with the cervix) forms the **birth canal** through which a fetus reaches the outside world.

The vaginal wall is highly elastic and consists of three layers: a thin cellular lining, or **mucosa**; an intermediate muscular layer; and an outermost tough, elastic layer. The mucosa can be seen if the inner labia are parted. When a woman is in a nonaroused state, it is pink. The vaginal wall has a series of folds that run around the circumference of the vagina.

The outer third of the vagina, near the vaginal opening, has a structure different from that of the internal portion (see Chapter 4). It is tighter, more muscular, and also more richly innervated than the deeper portion. Thus, most of the sensation during coitus—for both partners—derives from contact between the penis and this outer portion of the vagina.

The vagina is normally inhabited by large numbers of "friendly" bacteria that convert sugars to lactic acid. This bacterial activity usually makes the surface of the vagina mildly acidic (pH 4.0 to 5.0), and this helps to prevent the growth of harmful bacteria. The vagina also normally contains a variety of fungal organisms, especially *Candida albicans*. It sometimes happens that the fungal organisms overgrow, causing inflammation of the vaginal walls, itching, and possibly a thick white discharge. This condition is called **candidiasis**, vaginal thrush, or (in popular language) a "yeast infection," which most women have experienced at least once in their lifetimes (CDC, 2019k). The condition is diagnosed by microscopic examination of the discharge and is treated with antifungal medications. Some of these medications are available without a prescription. It is better to get a medical diagnosis, however, at least for the first episode, because women sometimes use over-the-counter medications for inappropriate conditions, a practice that can lead to the development of drug-resistant infections. Though unpleasant, vaginal candidiasis does not have serious health consequences. Persistent candidiasis can, however, be a sign of an underlying problem with the immune system.

(A) Frontal view

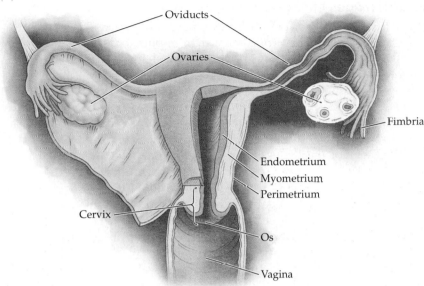

(B) Midline view

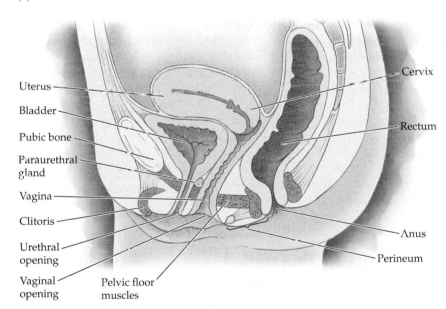

▲ **FIGURE 2.7** **The female reproductive tract** (See Activity 2.3: The Female Reproductive Tract: Frontal View and Activity 2.4: The Female Reproductive Tract: Midline View.)

One of the factors that can predispose women to candidiasis is frequent **douching**—the rinsing of the vagina with a stream of water or other liquid as a "cleansing" or deodorizing procedure. Gynecologists discourage douching, because the vagina is usually a self-cleansing organ. A clear, odorless vaginal discharge is normal and does not require douching or any other treatment. Depending on the time of the menstrual cycle, the normal vaginal discharge may take on a whitish or yellowish appearance. If the discharge develops an unusual appearance or odor, however, this may be a sign of a sexually transmitted infection (STI) or of bacterial vaginosis. These conditions and their treatment are discussed in Chapter 15.

**douche** To rinse the vagina out with a fluid; the fluid so used.

▲ **FIGURE 2.8** **A photocell** can be used to measure female sexual arousal. It is placed against the vaginal wall and tracks the change in color as the tissues become engorged with blood.

**FAQ:** What is "G-spot amplification"?

It's a procedure, such as the injection of collagen into the supposed region of a woman's G-spot, that is claimed to improve its function. The procedure hasn't been shown to be effective or safe, and the American College of Obstetricians and Gynecologists strongly discourages it.

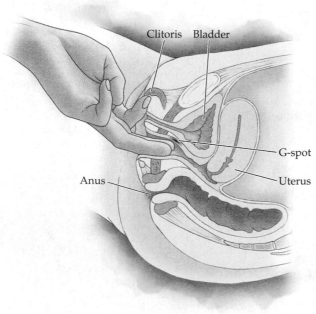

◀ **FIGURE 2.9** **Finding the G-spot** The G-spot is said to be an area of heightened sensitivity on the front wall of the vagina. Many women deny that they have a G-spot, and some sexologists question its existence altogether.

## The vagina undergoes changes during arousal

Like the inner labia, the walls of the vagina swell because of vasocongestion during sexual arousal. As a result, their color changes from pink to purple—the color of venous blood. One way that sex researchers monitor physiological arousal in women is to place a photocell in the vagina to track this color change (**FIGURE 2.8**). Vasocongestion of the vagina and inner labia, combined with the contraction of musculature in the vaginal walls and erection of the vestibular bulbs, cause the vagina to wrap more tightly around the penis during sexual intercourse than would otherwise be the case, which in turn increases sexual stimulation for both partners. For the woman, vasocongestion of the inner labia facilitates motion of the clitoral hood and thus increases stimulation of the clitoris, the structure that is usually most erotically sensitive.

Another response of the vagina to arousal is **lubrication**. This involves a diffuse seepage of watery fluid through all parts of the vaginal mucosa. The fluid is made slippery by the addition of mucus secreted by glands in the cervix. Lubrication serves two functions. First, the lubricant has a near-neutral pH (neither acid nor alkaline), which offers a more sperm-friendly environment than the acidic pH of the nonaroused vagina. Thus, lubrication favors sperm survival and transport. Second, lubrication makes coitus and other stimulation of the vulva easier and more pleasurable for both partners. This natural lubrication can be supplemented with the use of water-based "personal lubricants" if necessary.

## The G-spot is a controversial erogenous zone

Perhaps the most famous and controversial feature of the vagina is the **Gräfenberg spot**, or **G-spot**, named for the German-born sexologist Ernst Gräfenberg, who first described it. Only a minority of women say they have a G-spot, but for those who do, it is an area of heightened sensitivity on the front wall of the vagina, about 1 to 2 inches (3 to 5 cm) from the vaginal entrance (**FIGURE 2.9**). Deep pressure at this location can first trigger the desire to urinate, but continued stimulation is sexually arousing and is said to trigger an orgasm that is different in quality from an orgasm caused by stimulation of the clitoris (Ladas et al., 2004).

What is the structural basis of the G-spot, if it exists? Gräfenberg believed that it was the location where the vagina presses against the urethra. Another proposed candidate is a pair of **paraurethral glands** (also known as Skene's glands), which lie on either side of the urethra close to the vagina (see Figure 2.7B). Their ducts open into the urethra. Yet another candidate is a tangle of nerves and blood vessels that is said to lie at the reported location of the G-spot (Ostrzenski et al., 2014).

The findings of the most detailed recent study, by a group at the University of Melbourne, Australia, were entirely negative: The researchers dissected 13 female cadavers and failed to find any discrete structures at the purported location of the G-spot (Hoag et al., 2017). We believe that this finding is correct. It is still possible, however, that a particular pattern of innervation, not visible on dissection, makes a localized region of the vagina more erotically sensitive than surrounding areas. Alternatively, orgasms attributed to a G-spot may be mediated by underlying structures such as the deep portions of the clitoris.

## 2.2  The Anus Can Also Be a Sex Organ

**LEARNING OBJECTIVES**

After reading this section you should be able to:

2.2.1   Describe the functional difference between the external and internal anal sphincters.

2.2.2   Explain why anal sex often requires use of a lubricant.

Both heterosexual and homosexual couples may engage in penetration or manual or oral stimulation of the **anus**—anal sex (see Chapter 6)—so the anus needs to be described along with the more obviously sexual structures. The anal orifice is located at the back of the perineum (see Figure 2.7.B). It is kept tightly closed most of the time by contraction of the external and internal anal **sphincter** muscles. You can feel these sphincters by inserting your finger a short way into the anus. The external sphincter is under conscious control—you can squeeze down on your finger or release the tension at will. The internal sphincter is not ordinarily under voluntary control; thus, it can cause problems during anal penetration. With experience a person can learn to relax this sphincter too.

Beyond the sphincters lies the **rectum**, the lowermost portion of the gastrointestinal tract. It is usually empty of feces except immediately before a bowel movement. The rectum is a much larger space than the anus, so most of the pleasurable sensation generated during anal sex (for both partners) derives from penetration of the anus itself (which is both relatively tight and richly innervated), rather than from penetration of the rectum. In women, the structure in front of the rectum is the vagina. Stimulation of this and other nearby structures during anal sex may also contribute to sexual arousal.

The anus and rectum are lined by mucosa, but unlike the vaginal walls, this surface does not provide significant amounts of lubrication. Thus, most people who engage in anal sex use some type of lubricant. Other health concerns regarding anal sex are discussed in Chapter 6. Although we are postponing discussion of STIs until Chapter 15, it's worth mentioning now that condoms offer significant protection from STIs during anal sex, just as they do during vaginal sex.

## 2.3  The Uterus Serves a Double Duty

**LEARNING OBJECTIVES**

After reading this section you should be able to:

2.3.1   Create a schematic drawing of the female reproductive tract and label its components.

2.3.2   Describe the purpose of the Pap test and how it is performed.

2.3.3   Explain the differences between uterine polyps, uterine fibroids, and endometriosis.

2.3.4   Evaluate the pros and cons of (a) removing the entire uterus, (b) conserving the cervix, and (c) removing the ovaries along with the uterus (assuming a woman's uterus needs to be removed).

The **uterus** or womb—the inward continuation of the female reproductive tract beyond the vagina—is a hollow organ that lies within the pelvic cavity (the portion of the abdominal cavity that is surrounded by the bones of the pelvis). In a nonpregnant woman the uterus is about the shape and size of a small upside-down pear (see Figure 2.7). The narrow part, the **cervix**, protrudes into the deep end of the vagina. A woman can feel her cervix by inserting one or two fingers deeply into the vagina until she touches something that feels like the tip of her nose. She can see her cervix with the help of a mirror, a flashlight, and a speculum (an instrument that holds open the walls of the vagina) (**BOX 2.3**).

**lubrication**   The natural appearance of slippery secretions in the vagina during sexual arousal, or the use of artificial lubricants to facilitate sexual activity.

**Gräfenberg spot (G-spot)**   A possible area of increased erotic sensitivity on or deep within the front wall of the vagina.

**paraurethral glands**   Glands situated next to the female urethra, thought to be equivalent to the prostate gland in males. Also known as Skene's glands.

**anus**   The opening from which feces are discharged.

**sphincter**   A circular muscle around a tube or orifice whose contraction closes it.

**rectum**   The final, straight portion of the large bowel. It connects to the exterior via the anus.

**uterus**   The womb; a pear-shaped region of the female reproductive tract through which sperm pass and where the conceptus implants and develops.

**cervix**   The lowermost, narrow portion of the uterus that connects with the vagina.

## BOX 2.3
## Genital Self-Examination

If you're a woman and you've never really taken a close look at your genital area, now may be a good time to do so.

Genital self-examination has several potential benefits. If you are reluctant or embarrassed to pay attention to your sexual anatomy, doing so in connection with this course may help you overcome these inhibitions and become more comfortable with your body. Are there aspects of the way your vulva looks that seem to you especially attractive, unattractive, or unusual, and if so, why? Vulvas differ greatly from woman to woman, especially in the distribution of pubic hair, the size and visibility of the clitoris, and the shape and color of the inner labia, but your anatomy is no more or less "normal" than any other woman's. Finally, by becoming familiar with your vulva, you can more easily recognize any changes that may call for medical attention.

To get a good look at your vulva, you should use a hand mirror and possibly a flashlight (see figure). Look while in a variety of postures and from a variety of angles. Be sure you can recognize the parts that are described in the text. Also, explore them with your fingers: What do they feel like to your fingers, and what do your fingers feel like to them? Use your fingers to gently draw back the clitoral hood and to separate the labia, thus getting a view of the vestibule. If you become sexually aroused in the course of examining yourself, notice how the appearance of your vulva changes.

If you are curious to see the inside of your vagina and your cervix, you will need a flashlight and a vaginal speculum. This is a two-armed, "duck-billed" device made of plastic that holds the walls of the vagina apart. (Speculums can be obtained through women's health organizations. They come in three sizes; a small is probably right unless you have reason to think you need a larger one.) First, wash the speculum with soap and water, rinse it with water, and practice opening, locking, and unlocking it. Then lubricate the speculum with a water-based lubricant (or just water). With your knees apart, use the fingers of one hand to separate your labia. With the other hand, hold the

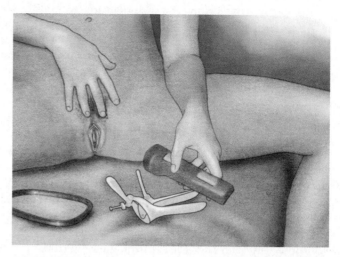

Genital self-examination. The white instrument is a speculum.

speculum, with handle up and the twin arms closed, and slide it gently into your vagina. Any discomfort should be a signal to pause and relax, and if comfortable insertion isn't possible, you should stop. Once the speculum is fully in place, gently open and lock the arms so that you now have both hands free to hold the mirror and flashlight. By shining the flashlight onto the mirror, you should be able to see your cervix, which looks like a rounded knob with a central hole or slit (the os). The appearance of the cervix varies around the menstrual cycle and from woman to woman. Some women may see fluid-filled sacs on the cervix protruding through the os; these are usually harmless. To remove the speculum, first unlock and close the arms, then gently withdraw it. You should carefully wash the speculum with soap and water, rinse it, and put it away in a clean place. Self-examination with a speculum helps a woman get to know her own body, but it isn't a practical way to diagnose medical problems or a substitute for regular professional checkups.

If you're a man and you have a female friend who has already examined her own cervix, it's possible that she would be willing to let you take a look under her guidance.

---

**os** The opening in the cervix that connects the vagina with the cervical canal.

**mucus** A thick or slippery secretion.

**endometrium** The internal lining of the uterus.

**myometrium** The muscular layers of the wall of the uterus.

**perimetrium** The outer covering of the uterus.

A constricted opening—the **os**—connects the vagina to a short canal that runs through the cervix. The cervical canal contains numerous glands that secrete **mucus**, which enters the vagina and may reach the outside of the body as a vaginal discharge. The amount and consistency of this mucus varies around the menstrual cycle (see "The menstrual cycle has three phases," below).

The cervical canal opens into the cavity of the uterus proper. The wall of the uterus has three layers: an inner lining (**endometrium**), a muscular wall (**myometrium**), and a thin, outer covering (**perimetrium**) that separates the uterus from the pelvic cavity, as shown in Figure 2.7A.

The endometrium must switch between two reproductive functions—first, the transport of sperm up the reproductive tract toward the site of fertilization, and then the implantation and nourishment of an embryo. Because these two functions require very different organization, the structure of the endometrium changes over the menstrual cycle. A visible sign of this reorganization is **menstruation**—the shedding of part of the endometrial lining and its discharge, along with some blood, through the cervix and vagina.

The myometrium is composed primarily of muscles that are not under voluntary control. Involuntary contractions of the myometrium during labor play a vital role in delivery of the fetus. Myometrial contractions (often perceived as menstrual cramps) are also thought to aid in the shedding and expulsion of the endometrial lining at menstruation. The perimetrium, which forms the outer lining of the uterus, is continuous with the peritoneal membrane that lines the abdominal cavity and all of the abdominal organs.

Very occasionally a woman may have two uteri located side by side in the pelvis, either of which is capable of sustaining a pregnancy. In 2019 a Bangladeshi woman gave birth to a premature baby from one uterus and, four weeks later, to twins from her other uterus; all three babies survived (O'Kane, 2019).

### Cancer can affect the cervix or the endometrium

Cancer of the cervix (cervical cancer) strikes about 13,000 American women annually and causes about 4,200 deaths. The main factor predisposing women to cervical cancer is infection with human papillomavirus (HPV), a virus that is sexually transmitted. Less important risk factors include chlamydia infection, smoking, and immune system dysfunction.

The death rate from cervical cancer has dropped by more than half since the 1970s. Much of this reduction can be attributed to the use of regular **Pap tests**—named for the pathologist George Papanicolaou (1883–1962), who developed the test. For the Pap test, the clinician holds the vagina open with a speculum and wipes a sample of cells and mucus from the cervix using a brush and a spatula (**FIGURE 2.10**). The sample is spread on a slide and examined under a microscope. If the cells show precancerous changes, the health care provider may proceed to a more detailed examination of the cervix using an operating microscope. This procedure is called **colposcopy**. During the colposcopy, the provider may take biopsies or destroy precancerous lesions by freezing or other methods.

At the same time as the Pap test, a second sample may be taken from the cervix to test for the presence of HPV—specifically, the types of HPV that can cause cervical cancer (see Chapter 15).

If a precancerous lesion escapes detection (most likely because the woman has not had a Pap test for several years, or has never had one), it may progress to true invasive cervical cancer. Symptoms of cervical cancer may include an abnormal, sometimes bloodstained vaginal discharge, pain during intercourse, or bleeding during intercourse. Of course, these symptoms are not specific to cervical cancer, but a woman who experiences them should see a doctor right away to ensure that if cancer is present, it is detected as soon as possible.

In the future, the incidence of cervical cancer may drop significantly as women who were vaccinated

**menstruation**   The breakdown of the endometrium at approximately monthly intervals, with consequent loss of tissue and blood through the vagina.

**Pap test**   The microscopic examination of a sample of cells taken from the cervix or (less commonly) the anus.

**colposcopy**   The examination of the cervix with the aid of an operating microscope.

FAQ: I've had the HPV vaccine. Do I still need Pap tests?

Yes, some cervical cancers are not caused by HPV.

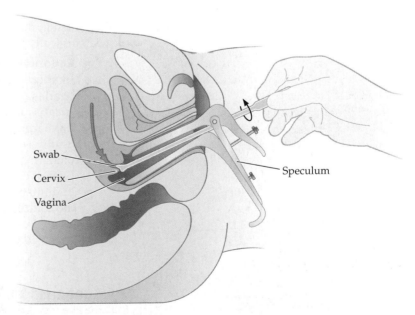

Swab
Cervix
Vagina
Speculum

▲ **FIGURE 2.10**   **The Pap test**  A sample of cells is taken from the cervix. (See **Animation 2.1: The Pap Test**.)

**pelvic examination** A visual and digital examination of the vulva and pelvic organs.

**endometrial cancer** Cancer of the endometrium of the uterus.

**hysterectomy** Surgical removal of the uterus.

**fibroid** A noncancerous tumor arising from muscle cells of the uterus.

**uterine polyp** A tissue growth from the endometrium that bulges into the uterine cavity.

**endometriosis** The growth of endometrial tissue at abnormal locations such as the oviducts.

**prolapse** The slipping out of place of an organ, such as the uterus.

against HPV as teenagers enter their cancer-prone years. HPV and HPV vaccines are discussed in detail in Chapter 15.

ACOG recommends that women age 21 to 29 have a Pap test alone every 3 years. From ages 30 to 65 women should have a Pap test and an HPV test every 5 years. After age 65 women can stop having either test so long as earlier tests have given negative results. There are some exceptions to these recommendations—the complete guidelines are available online (ACOG, 2017a).

A **pelvic examination**, in which a clinician palpates the abdominal organs with a gloved finger inserted into the vagina, may also be performed, but ACOG recommends that this exam be done only if the woman's medical history or symptoms indicate that it is advisable (ACOG, 2018).

**Endometrial cancer** (often called uterine cancer) strikes about 60,000 American women annually and causes about 12,000 deaths. Endometrial cancer is usually treated by removal of the entire organ (**hysterectomy**). Sometimes other pelvic organs, such as the oviducts and ovaries, must also be removed, depending on how advanced the disease is. Chemotherapy, radiation therapy, or a combination of both is commonly added to improve the woman's chances of survival.

## Other uterine conditions include fibroids, endometriosis, abnormal bleeding, and prolapse

Historically, almost any physical or psychological ailment that a woman might suffer from was blamed on the uterus (**BOX 2.4**). These days the list is restricted to a few conditions that involve actual pathological changes in the organ. Besides cancer, these are the major troublemakers:

- **Fibroids** are noncancerous tumors of smooth muscle that grow within or outside the uterus (**FIGURE 2.11**). They are very common: 20% to 25% of women develop them, usually after the age of 30 but before menopause. They are often asymptomatic, but they can cause pain and abnormal bleeding. When fibroids do cause symptoms, they can be removed surgically or destroyed by blockage of the arteries that supply them with blood. If the woman does not want to have children in the future, hysterectomy is an option.

- **Uterine polyps** are tissue growths, usually noncancerous, that grow into the cavity of the uterus from the endometrium. They can cause irregular bleeding, often in menopausal or postmenopausal women. They can be removed surgically by a procedure resembling an early abortion.

  - **Endometriosis** is the growth of endometrial tissue at abnormal locations within the pelvic cavity, such as on the oviducts, the ovaries, or the outside of the uterus. These patches of endometrial tissue are most likely derived from cells in the menstrual discharge that pass backward up the oviducts into the pelvic cavity. The most common symptom of endometriosis is pelvic pain; this pain may be worse before or during the menstrual period, or at the time of ovulation, or it may be ongoing. Endometriosis can cause infertility. There is no simple cure for the condition. Pain medications are helpful, as are oral contraceptives. Sometimes the patches of endometrial tissue can be removed surgically.

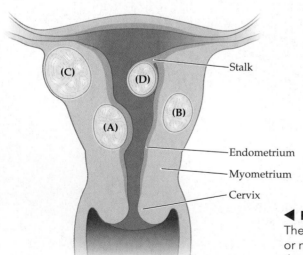

◀ **FIGURE 2.11** **Fibroids are noncancerous tumors of the uterus.** They may be located on the endometrium (A), within the myometrium (B), or near the outer surface of the uterus (C). Sometimes they are attached to the inner or outer surface of the uterus by stalks (D).

## BOX 2.4
## Hysteria

Think "hysteria" and you probably imagine crowds of people running in panic from a nonexistent fire. But the word hysteria derives from the Greek word *hustera*, meaning womb, and it has a long history as a medical term referring to physical and mental problems that were supposedly caused by that organ. These problems included choking, breathlessness, palpitations, faintness, weight gain, weight loss, too much or too little interest in sex, insomnia or excessive sleep, muscle spasms, depression, irrational fears, and a whole lot more. Up until the 19th century, hysteria was the second most common medical diagnosis, after fever.

Why was all this blamed on the womb? The fundamental reason was that all doctors were men. Two thousand years of medical tradition held that the male body was the ideal human form, so female bodies—and in particular women's distinct reproductive organs—were a sign of imperfection, though a necessary imperfection, of course. "The woman is less perfect than the man in respect to the generative parts," wrote the second-century Greek physician Galen. "For the parts were formed inside her when she was still a fetus, but could not emerge and project on the outside, and this, though making the organism that was being formed less perfect, provided no small advantage for the race, for there needs must be a female."

Since the perfect male body had no place for a womb, the belief arose that the womb did not have a fixed abode within a woman's body, but migrated around, causing havoc wherever it went. "It is very much like an independent animal within the body" wrote Galen's contemporary Aretaeus, "for it moves around of its own accord and is quite erratic. Furthermore, it likes fragrant smells and moves toward them, but it dislikes foul odors and moves away from them. When it suddenly

moves upward and remains there for a long time and presses on the intestines, the woman chokes, in the manner of an epileptic, but without any spasms. For the liver, the diaphragm, lungs and heart are suddenly confined in a narrow space. And therefore the woman seems unable to speak or to breathe." Doctors lured errant uteri back into the pelvis by placing pleasant fragrances at the woman's vulva.

During the 19th century medical thinking about hysteria shifted from the uterus to the mind, in part because men were sometimes diagnosed with the same condition (Carter, 1853). Nevertheless, the sexual connection persisted: It was thought that hysteria resulted from sexual frustration, and women diagnosed with hysteria were advised to get married or, if already married, to have marital sex more frequently.

In 1896 Sigmund Freud, the founder of psychoanalysis, proposed that hysteria resulted from childhood molestation. As an example, he described how one patient's nervous cough expressed her unconscious wish to perform oral sex on her father. Perhaps in reaction to such wild ideas, hysteria gradually disappeared as a medical or psychiatric diagnosis during the 20th century.

Woman supposedly suffering from hysteria, a once-popular term encompassing a variety of physical and mental problems in women. This woman was a patient at the Salpêtrière neurological hospital in Paris, around 1870.

---

- Abnormal endometrial bleeding can be caused by some of the conditions we have already discussed, but it can also occur for a variety of other reasons, or for no apparent reason at all. It can be treated with certain oral contraceptives, by surgery, or (if very persistent) by hysterectomy.

- **Prolapse** is a downward sagging of the uterus into the vagina. It is caused by weakening of the ligaments that support the uterus and of the muscles of the pelvic floor. The condition is seen most often in elderly women who have had at least one child, because both aging and childbirth weaken the structures that support the uterus. Uterine prolapse may be treated by a variety of surgical techniques or by insertion of a plastic ring that keeps the uterus in place. Kegel exercises help to prevent uterine prolapse.

## Should hysterectomy be so common?

About half a million hysterectomies are performed in the United States annually, and 1 in 3 women has had a hysterectomy by the age of 60. The associated costs exceed $5 billion annually. Medical research indicates that many hysterectomies are unneeded.

In a premenopausal woman hysterectomy puts an end to menstruation and renders the woman infertile, but the operation does not have hormonal effects unless it is accompanied by removal of the ovaries, which is often done to eliminate the risk of ovarian cancer. Hysterectomy should not interfere with a woman's enjoyment of sex or her ability to engage in coitus or experience orgasm. In some cases the cervix can be left intact, making it even less likely that there will be any impairment of the woman's sexual pleasure. In that case, however, she remains at risk of cervical cancer and will need to continue regular Pap tests. Hysterectomy is often accompanied by removal of the ovaries: This eliminates the risk of ovarian cancer but triggers menopausal symptoms and increases the risk of osteoporosis.

The chances that a woman will undergo a hysterectomy are influenced by seemingly irrelevant factors such as her race and the region of the country where she lives. This suggests that some hysterectomies are unnecessary. Women with noncancerous disorders of the uterus should be aware of the increasing range of options for treatment.

Although it is widely stated that hysterectomy rates have fallen dramatically since the beginning of the century, this may not in fact be the case. The reason for the apparent drop may have to do with a shift in the locations where hysterectomies are performed—from hospitals, where statistics are collected, to outpatient clinics, where they may not be (Cohen et al., 2017).

## The oviducts are the site of fertilization

At the upper end of the uterus, the reproductive tract divides into two symmetrical branches—the **oviducts** (see Figure 2.7A), also called fallopian tubes, uterine tubes, or simply "tubes." They could be thought of as continuations of the uterus, although they are not defined as such. Each oviduct is about 4 inches (10 cm) long and forms a pathway between the uterus and the left or right ovary. Fertilization of an ovum by a sperm takes place in one of the oviducts.

The interior surface of the oviducts is lined with **cilia**, microscopic hairlike structures that wave in a coordinated fashion toward the uterus. Sperm moving from the uterus toward the ovary have to swim against the current set up by the beating cilia, rather like salmon swimming upstream, but this current is too slow to offer a serious impediment to healthy, fast-moving sperm.

The portion of each oviduct near the uterus is relatively narrow, but it widens somewhat nearer the ovary. The oviduct ends in a flared opening with a fringe composed of fingerlike extensions. This fringe is known as a **fimbria**. Each fimbria lies near, but is not actually fused with, the ovary on that side of the body. The function of the fimbria is to catch the ovum after it is released from the ovary. Like the rest of the two oviducts, the left and right fimbrias are lined with cilia that help draw the ovum into the oviduct.

A surprising observation is that, after removal of one oviduct, the remaining oviduct can catch ova released from either ovary (Ross et al., 2013). This suggests that the oviduct secretes some factor capable of attracting ova from a considerable distance.

A continuous pathway extends from the outside of a woman's body, up her reproductive tract, and into the pelvic cavity. The body has many mechanisms to prevent disease-causing organisms from migrating up this pathway: For example, the presence of mucus in the cervix acts like a plug, hindering the passage of microorganisms. In some circumstances, however, sexually transmitted organisms can travel part or all of the way up the pathway, causing inflammation in the reproductive tract or even within the pelvic cavity. This kind of infection is known as **pelvic inflammatory disease** (**PID**).

---

**FAQ:** Does hysterectomy eliminate PMS symptoms?

Not necessarily, because the hormonal cycles continue after hysterectomy, albeit without menstruation.

---

**oviduct**  Either of two bilateral tubes that lead from the uterus toward the ovaries, the usual site of fertilization. Also called a fallopian tube.

**cilia**  Microscopic, hairlike extensions of cells, often capable of coordinated beating motions.

**fimbria**  The fringe at the end of the oviduct, composed of fingerlike extensions.

**pelvic inflammatory disease (PID)**  An infection of the female reproductive tract, often caused by sexually transmitted organisms.

**ovary**  The female gonad, which produces ova and secretes sex hormones.

**gonad**  An organ that produces ova or sperm and secretes sex hormones.

**follicle**  A fluid-filled sac that contains an egg (ovum), with its supporting cells, within the ovary.

**ovum (pl. ova)**  A female gamete, or egg.

## 2.4 The Ovaries Produce Ova and Sex Hormones

### LEARNING OBJECTIVES

After reading this section you should be able to:

2.4.1   Explain the two functions of the ovaries.

2.4.2   Draw and label a mature ovarian follicle.

2.4.3   Name the hormones secreted by the ovaries and describe their functions.

2.4.4   Create a diagram illustrating the hormonal interactions between the hypothalamus, the anterior pituitary gland, and the ovaries.

The **ovaries**—a woman's **gonads**—are paired organs located on either side of the uterus. They are egg-shaped structures measuring about 1 to 1.5 inches (3 cm) long. A woman's ovaries and a man's testicles are about the same size and shape.

Under the microscope, an adult woman's ovary can be seen to contain a large number of **follicles** at various stages of development (**FIGURE 2.12**). Each follicle consists of an **ovum**, or egg cell, surrounded by fluid and supporting cells.

The ovaries have two distinct functions. The first is to release ova in a process called **ovulation**. A newborn female has about a million undeveloped ova in each ovary, but these numbers decline throughout life. By puberty a woman has about 200,000 ova in each ovary. During her reproductive life she typically releases only one mature ovum per menstrual cycle. Thus, only a tiny fraction of a woman's ova are actually ovulated during her lifetime. Much greater numbers of ova die during the process of maturation and are reabsorbed by the body.

The second function of the ovaries is the production and secretion of sex hormones (**TABLE 2.1**). These hormones regulate the monthly menstrual cycle (**BOX 2.5**). The ovarian hormones are mostly **sex steroids**, which are fatty molecules derived from cholesterol. The sex steroids come in three classes: (1) **estrogens**, of which the main representative is **estradiol**; (2) **progestins**, mainly **progesterone**; and (3) **androgens**, mainly **testosterone**.

Both the female gonads (ovaries) and the male gonads (testicles) make all three classes of sex steroids, but in differing amounts. The ovaries secrete relatively large quantities of estrogens and progestins, which are therefore sometimes thought of as "female hormones." The ovaries secrete relatively *small* quantities of androgens,

**ovulation**   Release of an ovum from an ovary.

**sex steroid**   Any of the steroid hormones that are active in sexual and reproductive processes.

**estrogens**   Any of a class of steroids—the most important being estradiol—that promote the development of female secondary sexual characteristics at puberty and that have many other functions in both sexes.

**estradiol**   The principal estrogen, secreted by ovarian follicles.

**progestins**   Any of a class of steroids—the most important being progesterone—that cause the endometrium to proliferate and help maintain pregnancy.

**progesterone**   The steroid hormone secreted by the ovary and the placenta that is necessary for the establishment and maintenance of pregnancy.

**androgens**   Any of a class of steroids—the most important being testosterone—that promote male sexual development and that have a variety of other functions in both sexes.

**testosterone**   The principal androgen, synthesized in the testicles and, in lesser amounts, in the ovaries and adrenal glands.

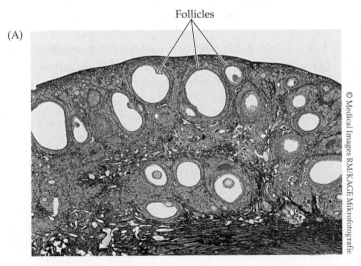

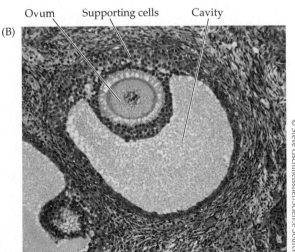

▲ **FIGURE 2.12   Microscopic structure of the ovary** (A) Ovarian follicles. Low-power view of an ovary, showing a number of follicles. (B) Higher-power view of a single follicle, showing the central cavity and the ovum surrounded by supporting cells.

**menarche** The onset of menstruation at puberty. (Pronunciations vary; MEN-ar-kee is most common.)

but these small amounts are supplemented by androgens from another source, the adrenal glands, which lie on top of the kidneys.

Several medical conditions can affect the ovaries. The most significant is ovarian cancer: It strikes about 23,000 American women annually, and about 14,000 women die of the disease. Risk factors for ovarian cancer include older age (the median age at diagnosis is 65), a family history of the disease, possession of cancer-promoting genes, early **menarche** (the onset of menstruation), late menopause, not having children, obesity, and prolonged hormone-replacement therapy. The use of oral contraceptives for more than 5 years *decreases* the risk of ovarian cancer by about 60%.

Early ovarian cancer is usually asymptomatic, and no screening tests have been shown to reduce mortality in average-risk women. Women with a family history of ovarian cancer can be tested for the possession of cancer-causing genes—damaged

**TABLE 2.1  Principal sex hormones and their actions**

| Class/subclass of hormone | Name | Site of production | Main targets | Main hormonal actions |
|---|---|---|---|---|
| **SEX STEROIDS** | | | | |
| **Estrogens** | Estradiol | Gonads | Widespread in body and brain | Feminizes body at puberty; contributes to menstrual cycle; increases density of bone; ends growth of limb bones at puberty; feedback inhibition of gonadotropins; maintains sex drive |
| **Androgens** | Testosterone | Gonads, adrenal cortex | Widespread in body and brain | Masculinizes body and brain during fetal development and at puberty; anabolic effects; maintains sex drive; feedback inhibition of gonadotropins |
| | 5α-Dihydro-testosterone (DHT) | External genitalia, prostate gland, skin (converted from testosterone) | External genitalia, prostate gland, skin | Development and maintenance of male external genitalia and prostate gland; adult male patterns of hair distribution |
| **Progestins** | Progesterone | Ovary (corpus luteum), placenta | Uterus | Contributes to menstrual cycle; maintains pregnancy |
| **PROTEINS/PEPTIDES** | | | | |
| **Releasing hormones** | Gonadotropin-releasing hormone (GnRH) | Hypothalamus | Anterior lobe of pituitary gland | Causes release of gonadotropins |
| **Gonadotropins** | Follicle-stimulating hormone (FSH) | Anterior lobe of pituitary gland | Gonads | Stimulates maturation of ovarian follicles; stimulates spermatogenesis |
| | Luteinizing hormone (LH) | Anterior lobe of pituitary gland | Gonads | Stimulates secretion of gonadal steroids; stimulates ovulation |
| | Human chorionic gonadotropin (hCG) | Conceptus | Ovary | Maintains corpus luteum |
| **Other** | Prolactin | Anterior lobe of pituitary gland | Breast | Prepares breast for lactation |
| | Growth hormone | Anterior lobe of pituitary gland | Widespread in body | Stimulates growth spurt at puberty |
| | Inhibin | Gonads | Anterior lobe of pituitary gland | Feedback inhibition of gonadotropin secretion |
| | Oxytocin | Hypothalamus (transported to posterior pituitary for secretion) | Breast, uterus | Milk letdown; uterine contractions during labor; role in orgasm; other nonreproductive functions |
| | Anti-Müllerian hormone (AMH) | Developing testes | Müllerian ducts | Causes regression of Müllerian ducts during male fetal development |

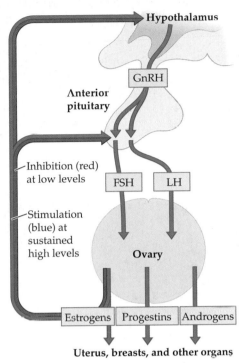
versions of BRCA1 and BRCA2—which are the same genes that cause breast cancer, discussed later in the chapter. Typically, ovarian cancer makes itself known by abdominal swelling, a constant feeling of a need to urinate or defecate, digestive problems, or pain in the pelvis, back, or leg. Treatment typically involves surgery to remove as much of the tumor as possible, as well as chemotherapy. Often the cancer has spread beyond the ovary by the time of diagnosis, so the survival rate is low: Only about 1 in 2 women survives for 5 years.

Another condition affecting the ovaries is the presence of **ovarian cysts** (fluid-filled sacs). These may be discovered when they cause pain, or they may be diagnosed during a pelvic exam. In women of reproductive age, the cysts are usually normal ovarian follicles that have not yet ovulated or that have grown larger than usual. These usually regress without treatment. Nevertheless, cysts can also be a sign of cancer, especially when found in prepubescent girls or in postmenopausal women.

**Polycystic ovary syndrome** (**PCOS**) is a poorly understood condition in which the ovaries secrete high levels of androgens. It is very common: As many as 1 in 5 women worldwide have it (Klein, 2018). The condition may cause irregular menstruation,

**ovarian cysts**   Cysts within the ovary, which can arise from a number of different causes.

**polycystic ovary syndrome (PCOS)**   A condition marked by excessive secretion of androgens by the ovaries.

infertility, and a male-like pattern of facial and body hair. Ovarian cysts are often, but not always, present. PCOS is not curable, but most of the symptoms can be controlled with contraceptive pills or other drugs.

## 2.5 Menstruation Is a Biological Process with Cultural and Practical Aspects

### LEARNING OBJECTIVES

After reading this section you should be able to:

2.5.1  Create a diagram showing the phases of the menstrual cycle and the approximate number of days for each phase.

2.5.2  Create a schematic diagram showing how the circulating levels of progesterone, estradiol, and testosterone vary throughout the cycle.

2.5.3  Discuss examples of contrasting cultural attitudes toward menstruation.

2.5.4  List possible practices and treatments to alleviate PMS.

2.5.5  List the reasons that might cause menstruation to cease in a woman who has previously menstruated normally.

The menstrual cycle has one obvious external sign: menstruation, also known as menses, a menstrual period, or simply a period. This is the vaginal discharge of endometrial tissue and blood that women experience at approximately monthly intervals during their fertile years. It is brought about by a complex internal mechanism that involves the ovaries, the brain, the pituitary gland, and the uterus.

The length of the menstrual cycle varies greatly among women and can also vary from one cycle to the next in the same woman. Most women have cycles lasting between 24 and 32 days, but cycles as short as 20 days or as long as 36 days are not unusual or unhealthy. Cycle length tends to be irregular for several years after the cycles begin at puberty. Health care providers should ask teenage girls about their menstrual cycles, both in order to provide information and reassurance and to identify problems needing medical attention. Cycles are also irregular at the approach of menopause. Menstrual cycles cease during pregnancy and, to a less predictable degree, during the time when a mother is breastfeeding her infant. Certain forms of hormonal contraception also suppress ovulation (see Chapter 9).

A woman's menstrual period lasts somewhere between 2 and 6 days (most commonly 4 to 5 days). The total amount of fluid lost varies greatly from woman to woman and from period to period but is typically about 1 fluid ounce (30 mL). A fully soaked tampon of normal absorbency holds about 5 mL of fluid, so a woman who is using tampons and has a 30-mL flow can expect to use at least six tampons per period. No more than half of a normal menstrual flow consists of blood.

### The menstrual cycle has three phases

Although menstruation, or the **menstrual phase**, is the obvious outward sign of the menstrual cycle, the cycle's most significant internal event is ovulation, which involves the release of an ovum from one or the other ovary about midway between one menstrual period and the next. Some women feel abdominal pain (so-called **mittelschmerz**—German for "middle pain") at the time of ovulation and may even be able to tell from the location of the pain whether the ovum was released from the left or right ovary.

The portion of the menstrual cycle between menstruation and ovulation is called the **preovulatory** or **follicular phase** because it is marked by the maturation of follicles in the ovaries. The portion of the cycle between ovulation and menstruation is called the **postovulatory** or **luteal phase** because it is marked by the presence of a **corpus luteum**—a hormone-secreting structure formed from the single follicle that ruptured at ovulation.

A typical 28-day cycle is divided up roughly as follows: The menstrual phase occupies days 1 through 5, the preovulatory phase occupies days 6 through 14, and

---

**FAQ:** Is it true that women who live together get their periods at the same time?

Some studies do report evidence for "menstrual synchrony," but the weight of the evidence suggests that any such synchronization is purely coincidental.

---

**menstrual phase**  The days of the menstrual cycle on which menstrual bleeding occurs.

**mittelschmertz (German: middle pain)**  Abdominal pain experienced by some women at the time of ovulation.

**preovulatory phase (or follicular phase)**  The phase of the menstrual cycle during which follicles are developing in the ovaries.

**postovulatory phase (or luteal phase)**  The phase of the menstrual cycle between ovulation and the beginning of menstruation.

**corpus luteum**  A secretory structure in the ovary derived from an ovarian follicle after ovulation.

the postovulatory phase occupies days 15 through 28 (**FIGURE 2.13**). Of these three phases, the postovulatory phase is the most constant: It usually lasts 14 days, give or take 2 days. Most of the variation in total cycle length is accounted for by variation in the menstrual and preovulatory phases (see **Animation 2.2: Ovarian and Uterine Cycles**).

Besides her menstrual period, another cyclical change that a woman may notice involves her cervical secretions. For the first few days of the preovulatory phase her cervix may secrete no mucus at all, and her vagina may feel dry. As ovulation approaches, the amount of mucus increases. At first it may be cloudy or sticky, but just before and during ovulation, for about 4 days, the mucus is much more abundant, it is clear in color, and its consistency is thin and stretchy, like raw egg white. This kind of mucus facilitates the movement of sperm into and through the cervical canal. After ovulation the quantity of mucus declines; it becomes thicker in consistency and whitish in color. Observing these changes in cervical mucus can be helpful for women who are trying to become pregnant (Chapter 8) as well as for those trying to avoid pregnancy (Chapter 9).

### The cycle is driven by hormonal changes

During the menstrual phase, much of the inner lining of the uterus—the endometrium—sloughs off, thus beginning the process of preparing the uterus for the development of a fresh endometrium whose properties facilitate the transport of sperm. The sloughing-off process is triggered primarily by a drop in the circulating level of the hormone progesterone. Blood levels of estrogens also drop at this time. These and other processes are represented diagrammatically in **FIGURE 2.14**.

High FSH levels at the start of the preovulatory phase promote the development of about 15 to 20 immature follicles in the ovaries. These follicles secrete estrogens and androgens, so the levels of these sex steroids in the bloodstream gradually rise during the preovulatory phase. The estrogens cause the endometrium in the uterus to thicken. In the latter part of the preovulatory phase, the cervix secretes a type of mucus that permits the passage of sperm, greatly increasing the chances of fertilization. By this time all but one of the 15 to 20 immature follicles in both ovaries have died, and the remaining one (which can be in either the left or right ovary) grows larger.

Toward the end of the preovulatory phase—about 36 hours before ovulation—estrogen levels rise high enough that their feedback influence on the hypothalamus switches from inhibition to stimulation (see Box 2.5), triggering a surge in the secretion of GnRH, LH, and FSH (see Figure 2.14). This surge drives the final development of the one remaining follicle, which expands to a diameter of about 1 inch (25 mm). The follicle creates a bulge on the wall of the ovary. At the moment of ovulation, the bulge breaks, releasing the ovum and its halo of supporting cells. The fimbria of the oviduct on that side actively reaches out and catches the ovum, and the waving of cilia propels it into the oviduct. The moment of ovulation has been captured on video—see Web Resources at the end of this chapter.

If sperm are present in the oviduct, one of them may fertilize the ovum. Otherwise, the ovum simply dies after about 24 hours in the oviduct. The woman's body has no immediate way of "knowing" if fertilization has occurred. Therefore, for about 2 weeks after ovulation, the uterus changes its structure to prepare for a possible

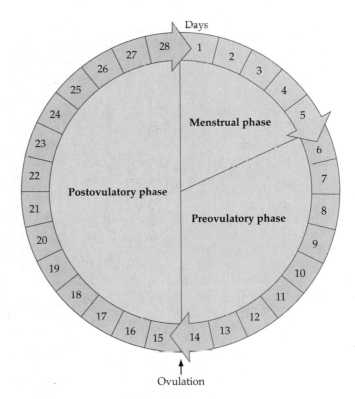

▲ **FIGURE 2.13** **A 28-day menstrual cycle** When cycles are markedly longer or shorter than 28 days, it is because of differences in the lengths of the menstrual and/or preovulatory phases; the postovulatory phase is nearly always close to 14 days long, as shown here (see **Animation 2.2: Ovarian and Uterine Cycles**).

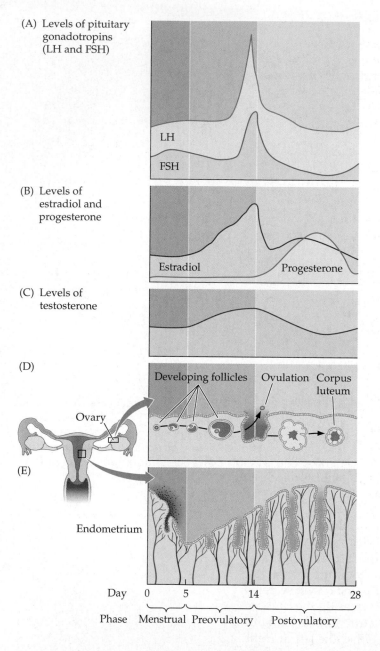

(A) Levels of pituitary gonadotropins (LH and FSH)

LH

FSH

(B) Levels of estradiol and progesterone

Estradiol

Progesterone

(C) Levels of testosterone

(D)

Developing follicles   Ovulation   Corpus luteum

Ovary

(E)

Endometrium

Day    0    5    14    28

Phase    Menstrual   Preovulatory   Postovulatory

◀ **FIGURE 2.14**   **Main processes of the menstrual cycle** (A–C) Changes in the circulating levels of the major hormones involved in the cycle. (D) The development of an ovarian follicle, the release of the ovum at ovulation, and the conversion of the follicle to a corpus luteum. (E) The breakdown of the endometrium during the menstrual phase, followed by its regrowth during the preovulatory and early postovulatory phases. (After A. J. Vander et al. 1985. *Human Physiology: The Mechanisms of Body Function*, 4th Ed. McGraw-Hill: New York.) (See **Animation 2.2: Ovarian and Uterine Cycles** and **Activity 2.5: Main Processes of the Menstrual Cycle**.)

pregnancy, regardless of whether fertilization has occurred or not. This process is guided by the hormones secreted from the remnants of the ruptured follicle, which transforms itself into a secretory structure, the corpus luteum. The predominant hormone secreted by the corpus luteum is progesterone, along with some estrogens. Progesterone stimulates the endometrium to thicken even further and become richly supplied with blood vessels. In this state it is capable of supporting an embryo. Progesterone also causes the cervical mucus to change its properties, such that sperm cannot easily travel through it.

If fertilization does not occur, the corpus luteum eventually begins to degenerate; hence, the hormones it produced in the second half of the menstrual cycle drop to lower levels. As the endometrium loses its hormonal support, it begins to break down. The resulting flow of blood and endometrial tissue marks the beginning of the next menstrual period and a new cycle. (See **Animation 2.3: The Reproductive Years**.)

Like the uterus as a whole, the cervix undergoes changes throughout the menstrual cycle. During the menstrual phase the cervix is easy to feel with a finger because it is firm to the touch and it protrudes downward within the vagina. In the course of the preovulatory phase the cervix becomes softer and rises higher in the vagina, so it may be hard to reach or to distinguish from the vaginal walls. Around the time of ovulation the cervix secretes abundant mucus. Within a day or so after ovulation the cervix returns to its earlier state.

## The menstrual cycle influences women's sexuality

If women's sexual behavior had reproduction as its sole goal, women would engage in coitus only on the day of ovulation and the 5 preceding days because nearly all pregnancies result from coitus on one of those days. In actuality, women are capable of desiring, initiating, and engaging in sex at any time of the menstrual cycle, as well as during pregnancy and after menopause, when fertilization is not possible. That's because, in humans, sex has functions not directly connected with reproduction, such as building interpersonal bonds based on sexual pleasure, and women's sexuality is not strictly regulated by the hormonal fluctuations of the menstrual cycle.

Still, women's sexual feelings are not completely constant around the menstrual cycle. Sexual desire is somewhat greater when estrogen and androgen levels are at their highest, which is to say on the fertile days leading up to and including the day of ovulation, and lower when progesterone levels are high—that is, during the infertile postovulatory days (Jones et al., 2018). These modest swings in sexual desire do not necessarily cause changes in the frequency of partnered sexual behavior, because a woman may respond to a partner's sexual interest when she is not actively seeking sex herself. Still, the swings in desire are a faint echo of the more striking changes in sexual behavior seen in many other female mammals, which forcefully reject all sexual advances on nonfertile days.

### Attitudes toward menstruation vary

Beyond the basic biology, menstruation has important psychological, cultural, and practical aspects. Most women can remember their first menstrual period more clearly than any other. The event, which heralds their passage into womanhood, is celebrated with special rituals in many cultures, such as the Hindu ceremony of Ritusuddhi, in which the young woman wears a sari for the first time.

Yet negative attitudes about menstruation are also common around the world, especially among men. In western Nepal, for example, menstruating women are widely believed to pollute any people or objects they touch, and they are therefore banished to tiny huts outside of the home, where they are exposed to a variety of hazards, including snakebites. This practice, called *chhaupadi* (meaning menstruating woman), has been made illegal, but it continues (ActionAid, 2019). A similar tradition has existed among the indigenous Dogon people of Mali, as well among the Beta Israel (the Jews of northern Ethiopia) before they emigrated to Israel. The !Xoo people of Botswana believe that menstruating women who go outdoors cause a drought or sicken any livestock they come near (Nhlekisana, 2017).

Contemporary American women have very divergent attitudes toward menstruation. In 1999, Brazilian gynecologist Elsimar Coutinho published his book *Is Menstruation Obsolete?* in which he suggested ways that women could abolish the entire phenomenon. Some women saw his message as a godsend, but others saw it as the ultimate sexist assault—the "perfecting" of women's bodies by making them more like men's. The debate has continued and has intensified with the approval by the U.S. Food and Drug Administration (FDA) of contraceptive regimes that reduce the frequency of a woman's periods or eliminate them completely (see Chapter 9).

In one survey, 17% of female university students said that they used these methods to skip or delay their periods (Lakehomer et al., 2013). As far as is known, abolishing menstruation has no harmful effects on the body, as we'll discuss further in Chapter 9.

### Women use pads, tampons, or cups during menstruation

Most American women who menstruate use tampons, sanitary napkins ("pads"), or panty liners in order to absorb their menstrual flow (**FIGURE 2.15**). Tampons—absorbent plugs, about 1.5 inches (3 to 4 cm) long, made of cotton or synthetic fiber—are placed inside the vagina, sometimes with the help of a plastic or cardboard applicator. They have an attached string that hangs outside the body to facilitate removal. Pads and panty liners are worn on the outside of the body—the main difference between them is that panty liners are thinner and usable only for very light

(A)

(B)

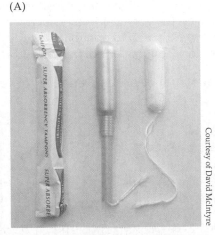
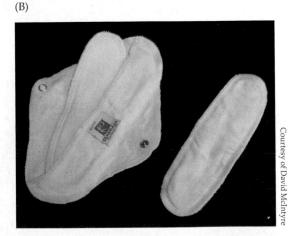

Courtesy of David McIntyre

Courtesy of David McIntyre

▲ **FIGURE 2.15** **Tampons and menstrual pads** (A) Tampons come in varying absorbencies and are available with or without applicators. (B) Most menstrual pads are disposable, but these are washable and made of cotton cloth.

**menstrual toxic shock syndrome**
A rare but life-threatening illness caused by a staphylococcal infection and associated with tampon use.

**menstrual cup** A cup placed within the vagina that collects the menstrual flow.

**menstrual cramps** Sharp pelvic pains that may accompany or precede menstruation.

**dysmenorrhea** Menstrual pain severe enough to interfere with a woman's activities.

**primary dysmenorrhea** Painful menstruation that begins at puberty and has no clear cause.

flow. In the past, most American women used tampons, but recent years have seen a trend toward pads. In less-developed countries pads are far more commonly used than tampons (**BOX 2.6**). Tampon users say that they give more freedom; pad users say that they are more comfortable and safer (Chalabi, 2015).

Use of tampons has been linked to a very rare but dangerous condition known as **menstrual toxic shock syndrome** (Mayo Clinic, 2019j). This condition, caused by a bacterial infection, is marked by high fever, vomiting, diarrhea, rash, and other symptoms, and it is fatal in close to 10% of affected women. Any woman who develops a high fever (102°F, or 38.9°C) while using a tampon should remove the tampon and seek medical attention immediately. To reduce the risk of toxic shock syndrome, a woman who uses tampons is advised to use the least absorbent tampon compatible with satisfactory function and to change tampons every 4 to 8 hours. If a woman takes these precautions, the chances of her developing menstrual toxic shock syndrome are very low.

**Menstrual cups** (**FIGURE 2.16**) are an alternative to pads and tampons. They are worn inside the vagina and block the menstrual flow rather than absorbing it. Menstrual cups have to be emptied and replaced two or three times a day. The three most widely available brands are called the Keeper, the DivaCup, and the Instead Softcup. The Keeper, as its name suggests, is a reusable device—it is made of latex—and it is therefore cheaper over time (and much more environmentally friendly) than tampons or pads. It is placed just a little way into the vagina, so coitus is not possible while wearing it. Another version of the Keeper, called the Moon Cup, is made of silicone. The DivaCup resembles the Moon Cup and is also reusable. The Instead cup, made of soft thermoplastic, is for one-time use only. It is placed deep within the vagina against the cervix, so it permits coitus while it is worn. (It does not function as a contraceptive, however.)

There is no obligation for women to conceal their menstrual flow, and a few women have espoused the idea of "free-bleeding"—that is, simply doing nothing about it (**FIGURE 2.17**). We doubt that the free-bleeding movement will gain many adherents, but media attention to the practice has been a useful reminder that menstruation is a natural and sometimes troublesome part of women's lives.

## Menstrual problems are common but treatable

Many women experience some kinds of health problems associated with their menstrual cycles. These may include painful menstruation, physical or psychological effects in the days before the onset of the menstrual period, and irregular or absent menstrual cycles. For most women menstrual problems are quite minor, but for some they are very disruptive or impair fertility. Luckily, several effective treatments are available for menstrual conditions.

(A)

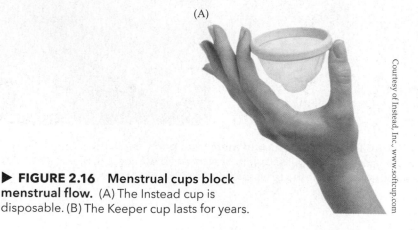

(B)

▶ **FIGURE 2.16 Menstrual cups block menstrual flow.** (A) The Instead cup is disposable. (B) The Keeper cup lasts for years.

Courtesy of Instead, Inc. www.softcup.com

Courtesy of David McIntyre

## BOX 2.6
# Where Tampons Aren't an Option

At 12 to 20 cents apiece, tampons may seem quite inexpensive, but they are beyond the reach of women and girls in many developing countries, especially in Africa. As a result girls may have to remain at home during their periods, causing them to miss many days of schooling in the course of a year. Alternatively, they may absorb or block their menstrual flow with materials that cause pain or predispose to infection, such as crushed newspapers, corn cobs, or even rocks.

The organization Days for Girls addresses this problem by providing reusable menstrual pad kits to schoolgirls in over a hundred countries, including some impoverished communities within the United States (Days for Girls International, 2019). It may surprise you that some Americans cannot afford tampons or pads, but in one survey of poor women in the St. Louis area two out of three women said that they had to go without both on at least one occasion during the prior year (Mundell, 2019).

Each Days for Girls kit is a drawstring bag containing eight washable absorbent liners, two leakproof shields, two pairs of panties, a washcloth, soap, two ziplock bags, and a pictorial instruction sheet. The kits are made by local women or Western volunteers, and they last about 3 years. Distribution of the kits leads to a great improvement in school attendance by girls, and this in turn helps to improve their status in society.

In China, nearly all women use menstrual pads. That's on account of the high cost of tampons; in addition, many Chinese

Ugandan girls with their menstrual pad kits.

Courtesy of Days for Girls International

women believe that tampons prevent harmful substances from leaving the body, or that they rupture the hymen and thus destroy the evidence of a woman's virginity (Yang, 2016). (Tampon insertion may rupture the hymen or enlarge the hole in it, depending on the hymen's structure in that particular woman, the size of the tampons, and how she inserts them.)

Compounding the financial problems are formal and informal taboos in many cultures that make menstruation shameful and difficult to discuss. Because of these taboos girls receive little or no instruction about menstruation or how to cope with it. The stylish bags in which schoolgirls carry their Days for Girls kits do their part to bring menstruation out of the shadows.

## Menstrual pain may or may not reflect underlying pelvic disease

The sloughing off and discharging of endometrial tissue during menstruation is aided by contractions of the muscular layer of the uterus (the myometrium) in a manner somewhat similar to the process of childbirth. These muscle contractions are the cause of the **menstrual cramps** experienced by some women during or shortly before their periods. There can also be persistent, aching pain within the pelvis or in the lower back. The pain may be accompanied by nausea or headaches. Menstrual pain is called **dysmenorrhea** when it is severe enough to limit a woman's activities. Dysmenorrhea is very common, and a family history of the disorder greatly increases a woman's chances of experiencing it (Ju et al., 2014).

There are two kinds of dysmenorrhea:

- **Primary dysmenorrhea** is disabling menstrual pain that is not associated with any diagnosable pelvic condition. It begins at menarche and is especially common among young women who have not had

© Kiran Gandhi

▶ **FIGURE 2.17    Free-bleeding** Musician and women's activist Kiran Gandhi ran the 2015 London Marathon while menstruating, but without a tampon. She wrote: "I ran with blood dripping down my legs for sisters who don't have access to tampons and sisters who, despite cramping and pain, hide it away and pretend like it doesn't exist" (Gandhi, 2015).

**secondary dysmenorrhea** Painful menstruation that begins during adult life, usually as a consequence of a pelvic disorder.

**premenstrual syndrome (PMS)** A collection of physical and/or psychological symptoms that may start a few days before the menstrual period begins and continue into the period.

**premenstrual dysphoric disorder** PMS-associated mood changes that are severe enough to interfere with relationships.

children. Primary dysmenorrhea can be alleviated with heat (e.g., warm showers, or heating pads on the lower abdomen), calcium supplements, plentiful fluid intake, or nonsteroidal anti-inflammatory drugs such as ibuprofen. Exercise and a high-fiber diet are also thought to be helpful. Another strategy is the use of oral contraceptives: The menstrual period experienced during the "off days" of an oral contraceptive regime is often lighter and less painful than a natural menstrual period. And as mentioned earlier, certain types of hormonal contraception make a woman's periods less frequent or abolish them altogether. Thus, hormonal contraceptives are an option for the treatment of dysmenorrhea even in women who do not need them for contraceptive purposes.

- **Secondary dysmenorrhea** is menstrual pain caused by a pelvic disorder. In an affected woman, it usually begins not at menarche but at some point during her reproductive life. Among the possible causes are endometriosis, pelvic inflammatory disease, uterine fibroids, and ovarian cysts. Intrauterine devices (IUDs; see Chapter 9) and even tampons can sometimes cause menstrual pain. Secondary dysmenorrhea may respond to the same treatments listed above for primary dysmenorrhea. If possible, however, the underlying condition should be corrected. Menstrual pain associated with IUD use tends to diminish over time.

The main points to know about disabling menstrual pain are that it should be medically investigated to rule out underlying conditions and that effective treatment options are available.

## Premenstrual syndrome has physical and psychological aspects

It is common for women to experience some form of physical discomfort or negative mood change in the 1 or 2 weeks *before* their periods. If the problems go away soon after the onset of menstruation but recur over several menstrual cycles and are severe enough to interfere with daily living, the condition is called **premenstrual syndrome** (**PMS**). If the psychological symptoms are severe enough to interfere with relationships—including difficult-to-control anger, for example—they may be diagnosed as a psychiatric condition, **premenstrual dysphoric disorder**, which affects no more than 5% of women (Office on Women's Health, 2018a).

Six core symptoms are most useful in defining PMS and distinguishing it from other problems:

- Anxiety/tension
- Mood swings
- Aches
- Altered appetite or food cravings
- Cramps
- Decreased interest in activities

Other symptoms that may occur include breast tenderness, diarrhea or constipation, and "bloating" (the sense of being overloaded with fluid).

The prevalence of PMS is hard to estimate, because the severity of the condition varies so greatly, but at least 90% of women experience at least one of the symptoms listed above (Office on Women's Health, 2018b).

Treatments for PMS include lifestyle changes such as regular exercise, quitting smoking, reducing intake of alcohol, getting sufficient sleep, and managing stress. Selective serotonin reuptake inhibitors (Prozac-type drugs) and calcium supplements often alleviate the condition (Maharaj &

© The Dynamic Duo Studio

▲ Premenstrual syndrome is often portrayed as something worse than it is.

Trevino, 2015). Several studies have reported that PMS symptoms are alleviated by combination-type oral contraceptives (see Chapter 9) when taken on a continuous basis (Yonkers & Simoni, 2018).

PMS is rarely the monster that it is portrayed to be in popular literature. The great majority of women experience few or mild PMS symptoms, and for those who do experience severe symptoms, effective treatments are available. PMS doesn't disqualify the women who experience it from any field of human activity—and dismissing any woman's bad mood or unfriendly behavior with "She's PMS-ing" is ignorant and sexist.

## Menstruation stops during pregnancy—and for other reasons

Most women will notice at some point or another that their menstrual periods have stopped (**amenorrhea**) or have become irregular. The most common reasons for amenorrhea are entirely natural and normal ones: The woman is pregnant, is breastfeeding her baby, or has reached menopause. Irregular periods are also common for some time after the onset of menstruation and during the climacteric—the months or years preceding menopause. But several other factors can interfere with menstruation:

- *Some hormonal contraceptives.* It may take months for menstruation to return after the contraceptive is discontinued.
- *Drugs.* Common culprits include steroids, antidepressants, and some cancer drugs.
- *Stress.* This can delay or prevent ovulation, thus causing irregular periods. If ovulation does occur, stress will not prevent the ensuing menstrual period.
- *Loss of weight for any reason.* This includes anorexia nervosa, severe dieting, and extreme athletic exercise. A woman is at risk of amenorrhea if her body fat drops below 15% to 17% of total weight.
- *Medical conditions.* These include thyroid dysfunction and pituitary tumors.

A girl also may not begin menstruating at puberty (**primary amenorrhea**). This may be due to one of the factors listed above. Alternatively, puberty itself may be delayed for a variety of reasons, or the girl may have a disorder of sex development (see Chapter 4) that makes menstruation impossible.

Unless it is caused by a congenital anomaly, amenorrhea can nearly always be corrected by lifestyle changes or treatment of the underlying condition. Amenorrhea is not harmful in itself—scientists have not identified any health benefit of menstrual bleeding—but the underlying condition may be harmful, and failure to menstruate may cause psychological distress. In addition, a woman is usually unable to become pregnant during the time she is not experiencing menstrual periods. That is not a sure thing, however; a woman who is breastfeeding, for example, may become pregnant before her menstrual periods return, because her first ovulation will not have been preceded by a period.

The reverse condition, excessively heavy menstrual bleeding, affects about 10% of all women. Causes are numerous, the most common being hormonal imbalance and fibroids. Treatment is with drugs such as ibuprofen or hormonal contraceptives, or surgical treatment of the fibroids. Repeated heavy bleeding predisposes a woman to iron-deficiency anemia, so iron supplements are usually recommended.

## Sex steroids affect more than the reproductive tract

Although the main function of sex hormones in women is to regulate the functional state of the uterus and other parts of the reproductive tract during the menstrual cycle, they do have other significant effects:

- Estrogens are responsible for most of the anatomical changes that occur in a girl's body at puberty. Androgens, however, are responsible for the development of armpit and pubic hair.

**mammary glands** The breasts in their functional role as milk-producing glands.

**secondary sexual characteristics** Anatomical characteristics, such as breasts and facial hair, that generally differ between the sexes but are not used to define an individual's sex.

**lobe** A subdivision of a gland or other organ.

**alveolus (pl. alveoli)** A microscopic cavity, such as one of those in the breast where milk is produced.

**areola** The circular patch of darker skin that surrounds the nipple.

- Estrogens maintain bone density, protecting a woman from osteoporosis. They also protect against blood clotting, including the clots that cause heart attacks.

- Progesterone acts on neural centers that control body temperature. Thus, a woman's body temperature rises at least 0.4°F (0.22°C) after ovulation, when progesterone levels rise.

- Progesterone also influences mood: It is an anxiety-reducing agent. Thus, the fall in progesterone levels toward the end of the postovulatory phase of the menstrual cycle can cause or contribute to an increase in anxiety and irritability at that time.

- Both estrogens and androgens act on many regions of the brain to influence women's sexual feelings and behaviors.

## 2.6 The Breasts Have Both Erotic and Reproductive Significance

### LEARNING OBJECTIVES
After reading this section you should be able to:

2.6.1 Create a sketch of the internal structure of the breast.

2.6.2 List at least six risk factors for breast cancer.

2.6.3 List the American Cancer Society's recommendations regarding mammograms.

The breasts, or **mammary glands**, are considered **secondary sexual characteristics**, meaning that they are not components of the genitals but do differ between the sexes. Although both men and women have nipples and some men have a small amount of breast tissue, breasts of significant size are generally a feature unique to women's anatomy. Occasionally, women or men may have extra nipples or even extra breasts, usually located somewhere along the line between the armpit and the groin (**FIGURE 2.18**).

The breast tissue lies between the skin and the muscles of the chest wall; some breast tissue extends up toward the armpits. Each breast consists of about 15 to 20 **lobes** that are separated from one another by fibrous and fatty tissue (**FIGURE 2.19**). The functional units of the breast are microscopic sacs called **alveoli**: Each alveolus is lined by glandular cells that secrete milk into its central cavity. Milk leaving the alveolus travels down the ducts that connect at the nipple. When the baby suckles at the nipple, the stimulation causes milk letdown.

Each nipple is situated at the tip of the breast in the center of a circular patch of darker skin known as an **areola**. Small bumps on the areolar skin around the nipple mark the openings of small glands whose secretions play a role in attracting a newborn infant to the nipple, as described in Chapter 8. The nipples are capable of erection in response to sexual arousal, tactile stimulation, or cold. Many women have sparse hair around the areola.

As with all secondary sexual characteristics, breasts vary considerably among individuals (**FIGURE 2.20**), and there may also be a size difference between the left and right breasts. Variation in breast size is due largely to differences in the amount of fatty tissue in the breast; women with small breasts have adequate glandular tissue to breastfeed an infant.

Breasts are of great erotic significance to many people. For women, tactile or oral stimulation of the breasts (especially the nipples) in the appropriate circumstances is sexually arousing. In contemporary Western culture the appearance or feel of the breasts is an important erotic stimulus to women's sex partners. In some non-Western cultures, on the other hand, men are said to pay little attention to women's breasts beyond recognizing them as an indicator of reproductive maturity. In such cultures women are not obliged to cover their breasts in public.

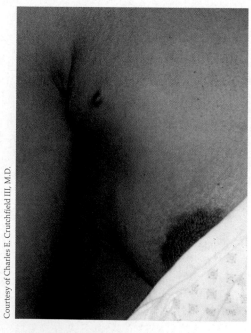

Courtesy of Charles E. Crutchfield III, M.D.

▲ **FIGURE 2.18  An extra nipple,** with some underlying breast tissue, located near the armpit.

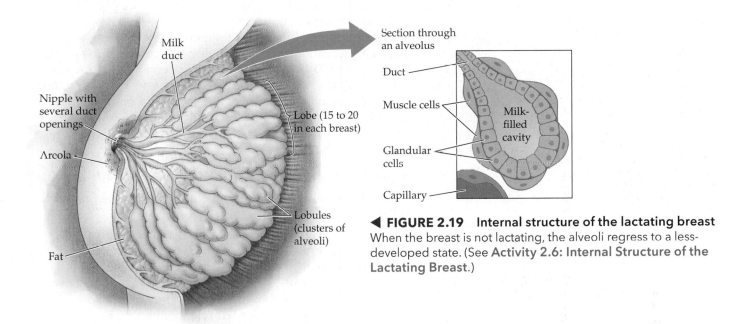

◀ **FIGURE 2.19**  **Internal structure of the lactating breast**
When the breast is not lactating, the alveoli regress to a less-developed state. (See **Activity 2.6: Internal Structure of the Lactating Breast.**)

Girls and young women often fear that their breasts are unattractive—sometimes as a consequence of negative comments they may receive during their middle or high school years. This concern is nearly always unwarranted, because a woman's breasts, as judged by prospective partners, are much more attractive than the woman's own judgments (see Chapter 5). Cosmetic surgery is always an option—about half a million American women had surgery to augment, reduce, equalize, or lift their breasts in 2018 (American Society of Plastic Surgeons, 2019)—but learning to positively value one's natural breasts may be a simpler and more desirable outcome.

## Breast cancer mortality can be reduced

About 265,000 women and 2,000 men are diagnosed with invasive breast cancer in the United States each year, and about 42,000 women and 400 men die of the disease (BreastCancer.org, 2019b). Based on current incidence rates, about 1 in 8 American and Canadian women will be diagnosed with (but not necessarily die of) breast cancer in her lifetime. Women may fear breast cancer not just because of the risk of death, but also because one treatment for the disease—**mastectomy** (surgical removal of the affected breast)—may damage a woman's self-image and affect her sex life.

**mastectomy**  Surgical removal of a breast.

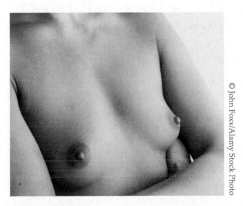
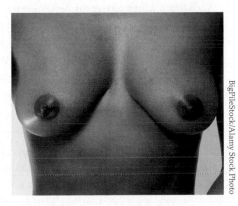
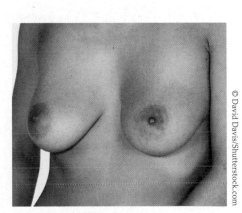

▲ **FIGURE 2.20**  **Breasts vary greatly in appearance.**  There may also be some difference in size between a woman's left and right breast.

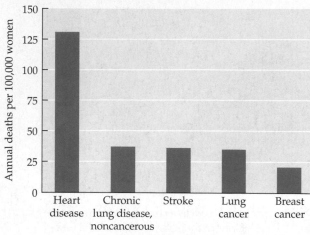

▲ **FIGURE 2.21** **Breast cancer is not the leading cause of death among U.S. women.** The graph shows the most common causes of death among women in the United States and the corresponding death rates. (After National Center for Health Statistics. 2016. *Health, United States, 2015: With Special Feature on Racial and Ethnic Health Disparities.* US DHHS, CDC, National Center for Health Statistics: Hyattsville, MD.)

We don't wish to downplay the seriousness of breast cancer, but it is worth pointing out that, contrary to many women's belief, breast cancer is far from being the leading cause of death for women (**FIGURE 2.21**). Heart disease kills far more women than do all cancers combined. In fact, breast cancer is not even the leading cause of *cancer* deaths among women: Lung cancer kills more women in the United States than does breast cancer. Still, breast cancer is a leading cause of death among middle-aged women.

## Many factors affect the risk of breast cancer

A number of known factors can increase or decrease the chances that a woman will develop breast cancer:

- *Genes.* A woman who has one first-degree relative (mother, sister, or daughter) with breast cancer faces twice the risk of getting the disease as a woman who does not. Women who inherit mutations in genes known as *BRCA1, BRCA2,* or the more recently identified *PALB2* have an increased risk of developing breast cancer (Macedo et al., 2019).

- *Age.* Breast cancer is primarily a disease of older women: About 85% of newly diagnosed cases are in women over 50.

- *Reproductive history.* A modestly increased risk of developing breast cancer is associated with early menarche (before age 12), late menopause (after age 55), having no children, or having a first child after age 30.

- *Alcohol.* Women who consume two to five alcoholic drinks per day have about a 1.5-fold increase in risk of developing breast cancer compared with women who consume fewer than two drinks per day.

- *Obesity.* Women who are obese—especially those whose body fat is concentrated at the waist—face an increased risk of developing breast cancer.

- *Breast size.* Women who wear a C-cup bra have a fourfold greater likelihood of developing breast cancer as compared with women who wear an A-cup (Williams, 2013).

- *Breast density.* Women whose breasts appear dense on mammograms—that is, they consist largely of breast tissue with little fat—are at increased risk of cancer.

- *Radiation.* High doses of X-rays—such as are caused by repeated CT scans involving the chest—increase the risk of breast cancer.

- *Exercise.* Women who exercise several hours a week reduce their risk of developing breast cancer (Fournier et al., 2014).

- *Hormones.* The use of oral contraceptives by young women (age 20 to 34) is associated with a slightly increased risk of breast cancer. (Bear in mind, though, that breast cancer is very uncommon in this age bracket, whether or not oral contraceptives are used.)

Some studies have suggested that low-dose aspirin has a protective effect against breast cancer, but the only long-term randomized trial published to date found no such effect (Cook et al., 2013).

## Regular mammograms are recommended

For many years women were urged to regularly examine their own breasts for lumps. According to the results of two large prospective studies, however, women who are taught breast self-examination (BSE) undergo twice as many breast biopsies as other women but are just as likely to die of breast cancer (Kosters & Goetzsche, 2008). This is probably because the lumps discovered by self-examination, if cancerous, are often too far advanced to be curable. For this reason the relevant professional organizations no longer recommend that women without special risk factors perform BSE, but women who wish to do so can find instructions online (BreastCancer.org, 2019a). Women who notice changes in their breasts should see a clinician right away.

**Mammography** is a breast cancer screening technique that uses low-dose X-rays to image the soft tissues of the breast (**FIGURE 2.22**). Professional organizations have issued varying guidelines; the American Cancer Society (ACS) recommends that women of average risk have annual mammograms starting at age 45, switching to once every two years after age 55 (American Cancer Society, 2019a).

Women who have mammograms according to the recommended schedule do not need breast examinations by a clinician, according to the ACS.

## Treatment depends on the diagnostic findings and the woman's choice

If definitive tests show that the lump is cancerous, the woman and her doctors must decide on the best course of treatment, based on the diagnostic findings, the woman's age and other circumstances, and the woman's own wishes. Early-stage cancers are often treated by "lumpectomy" (removal of the cancerous lump plus some surrounding healthy tissue) plus radiation therapy. More extensive surgery may be advised if the cancer is more advanced. Drugs for treatment of breast cancer include estrogen blockers, such as tamoxifen, and immunotherapeutic drugs such as trastuzumab (Herceptin). Selection of the appropriate drugs is guided by the study of gene expression in the individual woman's tumor.

If a woman's breast must be removed or partially resected, she has several options. She can accept her body's new appearance. She can use an external **prosthesis** to

© 2017 Stefan Rousseau/Associated Press

▲ Actress Angelina Jolie elected to have a double mastectomy on account of her high risk of breast cancer.

**mammography**    Radiographic inspection of the breasts.

**prosthesis**    An artificial replacement for a body part.

(A)

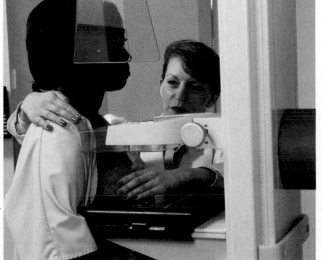

© Keith Brofsky/White/Photolibrary

(B)

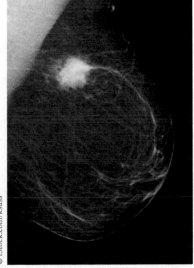

© iStock.com/ksass

◀ **FIGURE 2.22 Mammography** (A) A low-dose X-ray image is taken while the breast is compressed between two plates. (B) This breast lump, visualized as a white patch on the mammogram, is a "ductal carcinoma in situ," the earliest detectable stage and the easiest form of breast cancer to cure.

**breast implant** A tissue substitute that is inserted to augment or replace a natural breast.

conceal the changes in her breast. Or she can have reconstructive surgery, which can be done either at the time of the mastectomy or at a later date (American Cancer Society, 2019b). One type of surgery involves the insertion of a **breast implant** filled with silicone gel or sterilized saline (salt water). This procedure does not affect the chances that the cancer will recur. There can be complications, including pain, leakage of the implant, or arthritis, as well as a gradual deformation of the implant that affects the breast's feel and appearance. Rarely, breast implants have caused the development of a secondary cancer.

Breast cancer and its treatment can affect a woman's sexuality in a number of ways, especially if she has a mastectomy. But in one survey of 800 women with breast cancer, most of whom had surgical treatment, the great majority spoke positively about their lives, including their sex lives (Peltason, 2008).

## Summary

- A woman's vulva (external genitalia) consists of the mons, clitoris, outer and inner labia (labia majora and minora), and vaginal opening.

- A woman's clitoris is a complex erectile organ, only a portion of which (the glans) is visible externally. Stimulation of the clitoris is a major source of sexual arousal in women.

- The outer labia are two fat-padded folds of skin that form the sides of the vulva. The inner labia are two thinner, erotically sensitive folds of skin that enclose the vestibule—they fuse together at the front to form the hood of the clitoris. The vestibule is the space that encloses the entrance to the vagina and the opening of the urethra.

- The female reproductive tract includes the vagina, cervix, uterus, and oviducts. At birth, the infant's vagina is partially covered by a membrane (the hymen), which may be torn at first intercourse or earlier. The inner surface of the vagina is mildly acidic. Frequent douching can disturb the microbial balance, leading to a fungal infection and other problems. The walls of the vagina are more muscular and more sensitive in the outer portion than in the deeper portion. The G-spot is said to be a site of heightened erotic sensitivity on the front wall of the vagina, but its existence is debated.

- The portion of the uterus that connects with the vagina is the cervix, which can be seen by inspection with a vaginal speculum or felt by inserting a finger into the back of the vagina. The main cause of cervical cancer is human papillomavirus (HPV), which is a sexually transmitted infection. Early detection of cancer by means of regular Pap tests has greatly reduced mortality from the disease.

- The uterus serves as a pathway for sperm transport and also for implantation and development of the embryo. Medical conditions affecting the body of the uterus include fibroids, endometrial cancer, abnormal bleeding, uterine prolapse, and endometriosis. Hysterectomies (surgical removal of the uterus) may be done more frequently than necessary.

- The oviducts bring an ovum and sperm together for fertilization, and they transport the resulting conceptus to the uterus. The ovaries are the female gonads; they produce ova and sex hormones. Ovulation is the release of an ovum from an ovary. The ovum enters the oviduct, where if sperm are present, it may be fertilized.

- Steroid sex hormones fall into three classes—estrogens, androgens, and progestins—and are secreted by the gonads (ovaries and testes). Protein and peptide sex hormones include two gonadotropins—luteinizing hormone (LH) and follicle-stimulating hormone (FSH)—that are secreted by the pituitary gland, as well as gonadotropin-releasing hormone (GnRH), which is secreted by the hypothalamus.

- Menstruation—the sloughing off of the uterine lining (endometrium)—is the outward manifestation of the menstrual cycle. A complete cycle usually lasts between 24 and 32 days.

- The menstrual cycle has three phases: the menstrual phase, the preovulatory phase, and the postovulatory phase. The cycle is regulated by hormonal interactions between the hypothalamus, the pituitary gland, and the ovaries.

- Women may use tampons, pads, or menstrual cups to absorb or block the menstrual flow. Some women experience pain during menstruation, or symptoms such as bloating and irritability during the days before menstruation, but many women do not think of their menstrual period as burdensome.

- Women may experience painful periods (dysmenorrhea), a variety of physical and psychological symptoms prior to menstruation (premenstrual syndrome), absence of menstrual periods (amenorrhea), or excessively heavy menstrual bleeding. There are many causes for these conditions, but effective treatments are usually available.

- Besides regulating the menstrual cycle, sex hormones have other functions: They are responsible for the anatomical changes in a girl's body at puberty, they maintain bone density, and they affect brain organization and function—thus influencing a woman's sexual feelings and behaviors in a fashion that varies with the phase of her menstrual cycle.

- A woman's secondary sexual characteristics include her breasts, which combine a sexual function (being a potential source of sexual arousal to her and her partner) with a reproductive function (lactation).

- Breast cancer is the second most common cancer affecting women; risk factors include a family history of the disease, age, childlessness, alcohol use, and obesity. It can be detected early by regular mammographic screening. Most breast lumps are not cancerous. Early-stage cancers can be treated without removal of the entire breast. Some breast cancer treatments, especially chemotherapy and mastectomy, may challenge a woman's sexual self-image or sexual function, but most women who undergo breast cancer treatments are positive about their lives and sex lives.

## Discussion Questions

1. Do you think that genital cutting (circumcision) of girls, in countries where it is a traditional practice, should be permitted or banned? What role do you think the United States should take in this matter?

2. Historically, the clitoris has been largely ignored, and even today it may be neglected in sex-education classes. What do you think is the reason for this?

3. Women may change the appearance of their vulva by hair removal, labial surgery, piercing, tattooing, and so on. What is your opinion of these practices?

4. Make a list of anything you have heard about menstruation. Identify the myths and falsehoods. Compare and contrast these misconceptions with the material in the text and, if you choose, with your own experience or observations.

5. If you currently menstruate, how would you respond to this question: "Would you stop menstruating if you could?" If you don't menstruate, what's your opinion on the matter?

6. Does sexual intercourse during menstruation strike you as appealing or not? Why?

7. What was your reaction to reading about all the gynecological disorders described in this chapter? If you're a woman, did you feel hypochondriacal ("I probably have several of them right now"), bored ("I knew everything about them already"), or empowered ("I've learned things that will help me avoid or deal with them")? If you're a man, did you find it interesting and useful to learn about women's bodies and their disorders, or not? Your instructor and the authors of this book welcome feedback from students.

## Web Resources

American Cancer Society (ACS)  **www.cancer.org**

AnatomyZone. Introduction to female reproductive anatomy  **tinyurl.com/m7x2sbp**

Boston University School of Medicine. Female genital anatomy
**tinyurl.com/km2mofm**

Dr. Susan Love Research Foundation (breast cancer site)  **tinyurl.com/kdc2ehh**

The **Discovering Human Sexuality** digital resources include activities, animations, flashcards, web links, chapter outlines and summaries, and other study tools.

Learn more with this chapter's digital tools, including the **Oxford Insight Study Guide**, at **oup.com/he/levay5e**.

Endometriosis Association   **tinyurl.com/dgj9xq**

Gray, H. *Anatomy of the human body*. The female genital organs   **tinyurl.com/n7c9es2**

Human ovulation captured on video   **tinyurl.com/k86mepw**

Miller, L. NoPeriod.com (site devoted to menstrual suppression)
  **www.noperiod.com**

Museum of Menstruation   **www.mum.org**

National Breast Cancer Coalition   **tinyurl.com/pof66th**

National Cancer Institute   **www.cancer.gov**

National Cervical Cancer Coalition   **www.nccc-online.org**

National Uterine Fibroids Association   **www.nuff.org**

National Women's Health Network   **www.nwhn.org**

Office on Women's Health, U.S. DHHS   **tinyurl.com/mva6uq2**

Ovarian Cancer Research Fund Alliance   **www.ovariancancer.org**

Tostan (Senegal-based organization opposed to female circumcision)
  **www.tostan.org**

University of Delaware. Female reproductive system (histology site)
  **tinyurl.com/mc3mpfs**

## Recommended Reading

Abusharaf, R. M. (Ed.). (2007). *Female circumcision: Multicultural perspectives*. University of Pennsylvania Press.

American Cancer Society. (2005). *A breast cancer journey: Your personal guidebook* (2nd ed.). American Cancer Society.

Angier, N. (2014). *Woman: An intimate geography* (rev. ed.). Virago.

Boston Women's Health Book Collective. (2011). *Our bodies, ourselves: A new edition for a new era* (rev. ed.). Touchstone.

Dodsworth, L. (2019). *Womanhood: The bare reality*. Pinter and Martin.

Ensler, E. (2007). *The vagina monologues*. Villard.

Herbenick, D. & Schick, V. (2011). *Read my lips: A complete guide to the vagina and vulva*. Rowman & Littlefield.

Johnson, M. A. (2013). *Essential reproduction* (7th ed.). Blackwell.

Komisaruk, B. R., Beyer-Flores, C. & Whipple, B. (2006). *The science of orgasm*. Johns Hopkins University Press.

Lightfoot-Klein, H. (2007). *Children's genitals under the knife: Social imperatives, secrecy, and shame*. BookSurge.

Love, S. M. & Lindsey, K. (2015). *Dr. Susan Love's breast book* (6th ed.). Da Capo Lifelong Books.

Nelson, R. J. (2011). *An introduction to behavioral endocrinology* (4th ed.). Sinauer.

Northrup, C. (2010). *Women's bodies, women's wisdom: Creating physical and emotional health and healing* (rev. ed.). Bantam.

Peltason, R. (2008). *I am not my breast cancer: Women talk openly about love and sex, hair loss and weight gain, mothers and daughters, and being a woman with breast cancer*. William Morrow.

Stein, E. & Kim, S. (2009). *Flow: The cultural story of menstruation*. St. Martin's Griffin.

The male body idealized as performance.

# 3

# Men's Bodies

Biologically speaking, men's only reproductive function is to make
and deliver sperm. Everything else—ovulation, fertilization, pregnancy,
childbirth, and lactation—is the responsibility of women. Accordingly,
the reproductive anatomy of men is much simpler than that of women.
What's more, many of men's sex organs are visible on the outside of their
bodies, so they are relatively familiar in appearance. For that very reason,
however, they can also be the cause of considerable anxiety: Many men
are concerned—often needlessly—about whether their genitals look or
perform "right." One of the purposes of this chapter is to normalize the
diversity in the structure and function of men's genitals.

Perhaps because of the social emphasis on male sexuality as
performance, there has been more research into the function of male
genitals than female genitals, particularly with regard to erection. We
therefore take the opportunity in this chapter to discuss the behind-the-
scenes biological control systems that orchestrate male genital
functions, while bearing in mind there are likely to be close parallels
between these systems in women and men.

## 3.1 The Male External Genitalia Are the Penis and Scrotum

### LEARNING OBJECTIVES

After reading this section you should be able to:

3.1.1 Draw and label a diagram of a man's internal and external genital organs.

3.1.2 Evaluate the arguments for and against circumcision of newborn boys.

3.1.3 Explain the differences between balanitis, phimosis, and paraphimosis.

The penis and the scrotum are the parts of the male reproductive system that can be seen from the outside (**FIGURE 3.1**). The testicles, or "balls," are indirectly visible as the twin bulges that give the scrotum its shape, but they are considered part of the internal male reproductive system.

Although men don't usually have the prominent pubic fat pad (the mons) seen in women, they do have a similar distribution of pubic hair. The hair may extend upward toward the navel or merge with the general body hair. Sparse hair usually covers the scrotum.

### The penis combines erotic, reproductive, and urinary functions

Developmentally, the **penis** is equivalent to the clitoris. In a functional sense, however, the penis corresponds to the clitoris, urethra, and vagina all rolled into one, because it is involved in sexual arousal, excretion of urine, and the delivery of sperm. It's no wonder men focus so much attention on the penis and are so gravely concerned when it fails to perform as expected.

The penis in its natural (i.e., uncircumcised) condition has three visible portions: a shaft, a head (or glans), and a foreskin, all of which are hairless. The **foreskin**, or **prepuce**, is a loose, tubular fold of skin that partially or completely covers the glans. In some males—during childhood especially—the foreskin extends well beyond the tip of the glans, where it contracts to form a short canal through which urine passes after it exits the urethra.

Male **circumcision** is the surgical removal of the foreskin, or part of it, exposing all or part of the glans. It may be performed at any age, but most circumcisions in the United States are done soon after birth. With babies, the 5- to 10-minute procedure is facilitated by the use of a clamp or other device. The clinician typically uses a nerve block or another form of local anesthesia to provide pain relief. When circumcision is performed in adulthood, stitches are necessary, and the man needs to refrain from sex, including masturbation, for about 4 to 6 weeks. A nonsurgical device known as PrePex has been approved for adolescent and adult circumcision by the World Health Organization (PR Newswire, 2016) (**FIGURE 3.2**). In Africa, where adult circumcision is encouraged as a means to reduce transmission of HIV (see Chapter 15), the low price and ease of use of PrePex have led to its widespread adoption (Daily Nation, 2016).

In the United States nearly four out of five male adults have been circumcised; most of them were circumcised neonatally prior to discharge from the hospital (CDC, 2018a). Circumcision is most common among whites, less common among African-Americans, and least common among Hispanics and Asian-Americans. Over the last several decades the circumcision rate for newborns has gradually decreased, largely on account of the increasing Hispanic population in the western states (**FIGURE 3.3**). Circumcision rates are lower in Canada than in the United States, and much lower in Europe (Morris, 2016).

Male circumcision is an ancient practice that is religiously prescribed for Muslims and Jews. It has also been practiced as a nonreligious tradition in many cultures.

**penis** The erectile, erotically sensitive genital organ in males.

**foreskin (or prepuce)** The loose skin that partially or completely covers the glans in males who have not been circumcised.

**circumcision** The removal of the male foreskin. In females, a traditional term for "genital cutting."

(A)

(B)

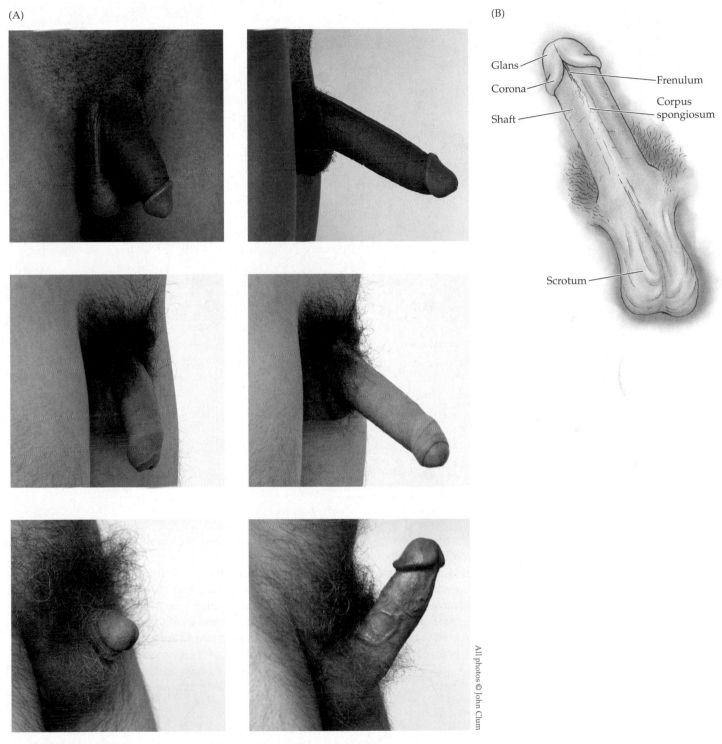

All photos © John Clum

▲ **FIGURE 3.1**  **The male external genitalia**  (A) Three penises in the flaccid state (left) and erect state (right). The middle example is an uncircumcised penis; the other two are circumcised. (B) Drawing of an erect circumcised penis seen from below, showing the glans, corona, and frenulum—the most erotically sensitive portions of the penis. (See **Activity 3.1: The Male External Genitalia**.)

▶ **FIGURE 3.2 Circumcision with the PrePex device** The black elastic ring cuts off blood supply to the foreskin, which dies and is cut off after a few days. The black ring is then removed.

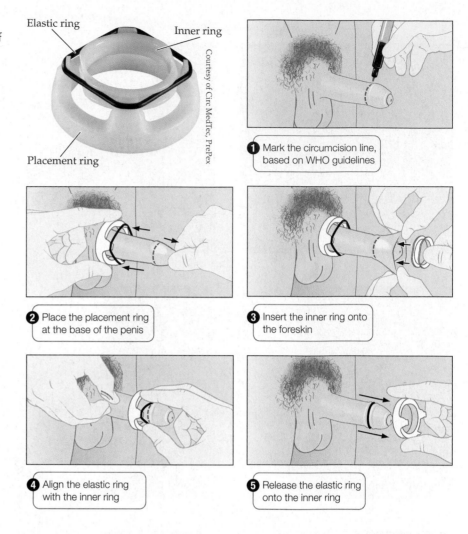

Elastic ring

Inner ring

Placement ring

Courtesy of Circ MedTec, PrePex

**1** Mark the circumcision line, based on WHO guidelines

**2** Place the placement ring at the base of the penis

**3** Insert the inner ring onto the foreskin

**4** Align the elastic ring with the inner ring

**5** Release the elastic ring onto the inner ring

There is some controversy over whether circumcision of male infants should be recommended or discouraged (**BOX 3.1**).

The shaft of the penis contains three erectile structures (**FIGURE 3.4**): two **corpora cavernosa**, which lie side by side and account for the bulk of the penis's erectile capacity, and a single **corpus spongiosum**, which runs along the middle of the undersurface of the penis. The corpus spongiosum extends from the shaft into the **glans**, where it balloons out and fills the entire volume of the glans. Both the corpora cavernosa and the corpus spongiosum extend backward into the body under the pubic bone, forming the root of the penis, which is about 2 inches (5 cm) long.

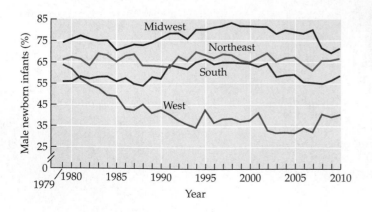

◀ **FIGURE 3.3 Reported infant circumcision rates in the United States** fell between 1980 and 2010, mostly on account of a large drop in the western states. The true rates are probably somewhat higher on account of under-reporting. Data on more recent regional trends are not available. (After M. Owings et al. 2013. *Trends in Circumcision for Male Newborns in U.S. Hospitals: 1979–2010.* National Center for Health Statistics. https://www.cdc.gov/nchs/data/hestat/circumcision_2013/circumcision_2013.htm. Data from National Hospital Discharge Survey.)

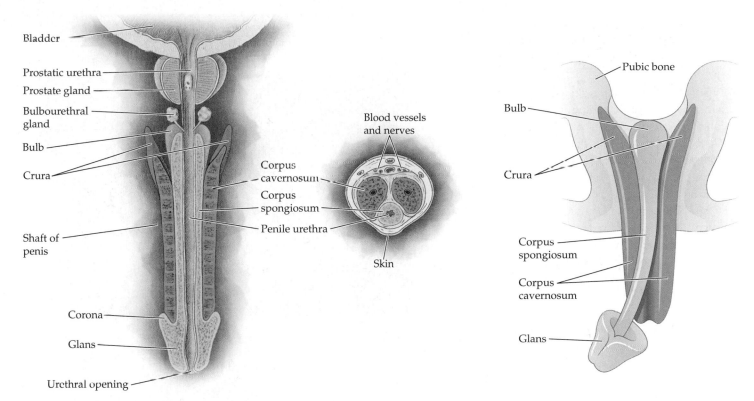

▲ **FIGURE 3.4**   **Internal structure of the erect penis and the urethra**   Note that the corpus spongiosum surrounds the penile urethra and expands at the tip of the penis to form the glans. Because it lacks a tough capsule, the corpus spongiosum is less rigid than the corpora cavernosa when the penis is erect. (After C. M. Dienhart. 1967. *Basic Human Anatomy and Physiology*. Saunders: Philadelphia, PA.) (See **Activity 3.2: Internal Structure of the Erect Penis and the Urethra**.)

At the inner end of the root of the penis, the corpus spongiosum expands into a rounded mass of erectile tissue known as the **penile bulb**. The two corpora cavernosa diverge, forming two **crura** similar to those of a woman's clitoris. As in women, there are several muscles in the pelvic floor that play an important role in the sexual response. These pelvic floor muscles assist with erection of the penis, ejaculation, and orgasm.

The urethra discharges urine from the bladder and discharges semen from internal reproductive glands (see "3.3 The Testicles Produce Sperm and Sex Hormones," later in this chapter). Within the penis, the urethra runs close to the underside, entirely contained within the corpus spongiosum, and emerges at or near the tip of the glans as a slit-like opening.

The shaft of the penis contains other structures, most notably nerves and blood vessels that play an important role in sexual arousal and erection. The skin of the penis is hairless and only loosely attached to the underlying tissue.

The glans has a rim, or **corona**, that encircles the penis. On the undersurface of the penis, the corona comes closer to the tip of the glans than on its upper surface. In this area lies a loose strip of skin named the **frenulum** that runs between the glans and the shaft (see Figure 3.1B). In an uncircumcised man the frenulum attaches to the inside of the foreskin. Although stimulation anywhere on the penis can be sexually arousing, the corona and the frenulum are usually the most erotically sensitive regions.

**corpus cavernosum (pl. corpora cavernosa)**   Either of two elongated erectile structures that are within the penis or clitoris and extend backward into the pelvic floor.

**corpus spongiosum**   A single midline erectile structure that fills the glans; in males it extends backward along the underside of the penis, surrounding the urethra.

**glans**   The terminal knob of the penis or clitoris.

**penile bulb**   An expansion of the corpus spongiosum at the root of the penis.

**crus (pl. crura)**   Internal extensions of the corpora cavernosa of the clitoris or penis.

**corona**   The rim of the glans of the penis.

**frenulum**   A strip of loose skin on the underside of the penis, running between the glans and the shaft.

## BOX 3.1
# Male Circumcision

Circumcision offers some significant benefits but also carries slight risks. One important benefit is reduction by about 90% in the incidence of urinary tract infections in infancy, which can sometimes lead to kidney damage. In adulthood, circumcision confers partial protection from infection with several sexually transmitted viruses and bacteria, including those that cause AIDS, herpes, syphilis, cervical cancer, and anal cancer. (In the case of cervical and anal cancer, the benefit is to the man's sex partners.) In the decade since 2007, when the World Health Organization recommended circumcision for prevention of HIV infection in Africa, nearly 15 million adult men chose to be circumcised, thus averting an estimated half-million infections (World Health Organization, 2017).

Besides its medical benefits, circumcision facilitates hygiene. In uncircumcised men, a substance called **smegma** can build up under the foreskin and over time develop a characteristic odor—something that a man's sex partner may find unpleasant, especially when performing oral sex. This problem can easily be avoided, however, if a man washes under his foreskin whenever he takes a bath or shower.

The risks of circumcision include hemorrhage, infection, and—extremely rarely—damage to the penis. No deaths from conventional circumcision have been reported in the United States in recent times. An Orthodox Jewish circumcision ritual that involves mouth-to-penis contact ("oral suction") has resulted in several cases of herpes infection—two of them fatal—in newborn infants in New York (Campanile, 2017).

Some opponents of circumcision have suggested that the operation reduces the sensitivity of the penis, but physiological testing indicates that this is not the case (Bossio et al., 2016). In fact, one large random-sample study found that circumcision is associated with a slightly *lower* incidence of sexual dysfunctions, especially erectile dysfunction (Laumann et al., 1997). African men who chose to be circumcised expressed a high degree of satisfaction with the results of the

Egyptian circumcision, ca. 2300 BCE. The hieroglyphs on the left read "Hold him so that he doesn't fall" and "It is for your benefit." This is a modern painting based on a stone relief.

procedure (Rosario et al., 2013). The men's wives were twice as likely to say they enjoyed sex as compared with the wives of uncircumcised men (Shacham et al., 2013).

The American Academy of Pediatrics (2015), the American College of Obstetricians and Gynecologists (2017b), and the U.S. Centers for Disease Control and Prevention all believe that the health benefits of newborn male circumcision outweigh the risks. They also agree, however, that it should be the parents' informed choice. The Canadian Paediatric Society (2015), which used to oppose routine circumcision, now takes a neutral stance.

There do exist methods for a circumcised man to recreate a foreskin. These include gradual stretching of the skin of the penile shaft over the glans—a process that takes many months—or the surgical grafting of skin from the scrotum. The results don't closely resemble a natural foreskin, however, and the surgical method frequently leads to complications.

**smegma**　A whitish, greasy secretion that can build up under the foreskin of the penis or the clitoral hood.

---

**FAQ:** Big feet, big penis—true?

No. British urologists measured these body parts in 104 men and found no correlation (Shah & Christopher, 2002).

The size of the penis—in both the flaccid and erect states—varies considerably. In a sample of 1,800 American men who measured their own erect penises, the median length was 14 cm (5.5 inches), and 9 out of 10 men had penis lengths between 10 and 19 cm (4 to 7.5 inches). (**FIGURE 3.5**).

A nonpornographic website illustrates some of this diversity and shows the process of erection (see Web Resources at the end of this chapter). Some men are concerned about the size or shape of their penis, but these dimensions rarely have any significant effect on sexual performance or pleasure (**BOX 3.2**).

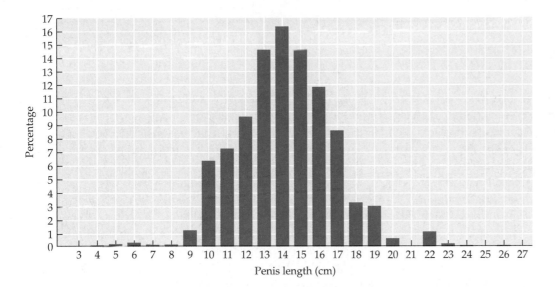

◀ **FIGURE 3.5**  Penis length
This bar graph shows the length of 1,800 American penises, measured by their owners in 1-cm increments from the underside base to the tip, using measurement tools supplied by researchers. Because the researchers offered the men custom-sized condoms based on the provided measurements, it is likely that the measurements were accurate. (After D. Herbenick et al. 2014. *J Sex Med* 11: 93–101.)

Men have been piercing their penises for tens of thousands of years: The practice is depicted in Paleolithic (Old Stone Age) art (Angulo et al., 2011). Men considering a penis piercing should carefully review the potential problems, which can include scarring, damage to erectile tissue, nerve damage, interference with urination, and serious infections such as hepatitis and HIV (WebMD, 2019). Selection of an experienced practitioner who uses scrupulous sanitary techniques is paramount.

## Some disorders affect penile function

Considering the demands that may be placed on it, the penis is a remarkably sturdy organ. Aside from erectile disorder (see Chapter 14) and sexually transmitted infections (see Chapter 15), the penis is subject to only a few medical problems that occur with any frequency:

- **Balanitis** is inflammation of the glans, caused by infection and/or poor hygiene. It is quite common in uncircumcised men. Treatment involves regular cleansing and antibiotics as appropriate.

- **Phimosis** is the inability to retract the foreskin far enough to expose the glans. This is the normal condition in male babies, and it persists in many boys into the teen years. There is no need to treat it unless the flow of urine is affected. Phimosis may also develop as a new condition in adults, especially in association with balanitis, in which case surgical treatment may be required.

- **Paraphimosis** is the entrapment of a retracted foreskin behind the corona of the glans. It can occur as a result of efforts to retract a phimotic foreskin. Paraphimosis is an emergency condition because it can lead to tissue death of the glans. It can usually be reversed without circumcision, but later circumcision is recommended to prevent recurrence.

- **Peyronie's disease** is an unnatural curvature of the erect penis caused by the formation of plaques—dense patches of connective tissue—in the corpora cavernosa. (Many men have some natural curvature of the penis.) Peyronie's disease can cause pain or even prevent penetrative sex. Surgical treatments are available, and the U.S. Food and Drug Administration has approved use of Xiaflex, an enzyme that breaks down connective tissue, for treatment of the condition.

**balanitis**   Inflammation of the glans of the penis.

**phimosis**   A tightening of the foreskin that prevents its retraction from the glans.

**paraphimosis**   Entrapment of the retracted foreskin behind the corona.

**Peyronie's disease**   Pathological curvature of the penis.

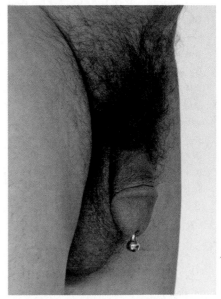

© John Clum

▲ A "Prince Albert" piercing enters the glans through or near the frenulum and exits via the urethra. Urinating standing up can be a challenge with this piercing.

Much rarer than any of these conditions is penile cancer. This condition strikes about 1,200 men in the United States per year and causes about 300 deaths. Infection

## BOX 3.2
# How Big Should a Penis Be?

What do guys think of me in the locker room? How do I stack up against the porn stars I've seen? Am I big enough to satisfy my sex partners—female or male? Am I normal?

"I," of course, is my penis. Most male youths and young men probably ask themselves questions like these at one time or another, fearing that their penises just don't cut it sizewise. Yet not every penis can be below average. Concern about the size of one's penis often represents the "embodiment" of general anxieties about sexual performance and sexual relationships. In addition, though, it often results from ignorance. Penises—especially erect ones—are rarely seen, and those that are seen may belong to male porn stars, for whom having an above-average endowment is more or less a job requirement. This can easily lead to the mistaken belief that one's own penis is inadequate.

In a large internet survey, researchers at California State University, Los Angeles, and at the University of California, Los Angeles (UCLA), found that only 55% of heterosexual men were satisfied with the size of their penis, but 84% of straight women were satisfied with the size of their partner's penis, and only 14% wished it were larger (Lever et al., 2006). Thus, unless a lot of men with small penises are lacking partners altogether, many heterosexual men may be suffering needless anxiety.

There does exist a small industry devoted to the surgical augmentation of the penis. The penis may be lengthened by cutting its suspensory ligament (see figure), followed by many weeks of traction (hanging weights from the penis) or other means to prevent reattachment of the ligament. This procedure extends the apparent length of the penis by 0.5 to 1.0 inch (1 to 2 cm). The procedure only lengthens the flaccid penis, however; the erect penis length is not affected. In obese men, if the penis has become buried in abdominal fat, getting rid of that fat through dieting, liposuction, or a "tummy tuck" will make it more visible (Muneer et al., 2014).

The girth of the penis can be increased by injecting various filler materials under the skin of the penis; the initial results of this procedure can be good, but the penis often comes to look lumpy or otherwise abnormal over time.

Numerous self-help methods have been recommended, such as "jelqing" (repeated squeezing of the penis in a motion that goes from the base to the corona), and drugs and supplements that purport to enlarge the penis are widely advertised, but there is no objective evidence that any of these methods work, and some may cause damage to the penis. Self-injection of filler materials is an exceptionally risky practice (Dellis et al., 2018).

The incidence of complications from penile augmentation surgery is very high (Vardi et al., 2008). The surgery is legal, but according to the American Urological Association, neither surgery nor fat injections have been proven safe or efficacious (American Urological Association, 2016). Although some surgeons report high rates of patient satisfaction, most studies find that men who undergo the surgery are, on average, dissatisfied with the outcome and do not experience improved sex lives afterward (Wessells et al., 1996; Klein, 1999; Li et al., 2006). In most men who seek penis enlargement, the penis is not unusually small, and for that reason they are more likely to be helped by reassurance or psychotherapy than by surgery (Wylie & Eardley, 2007).

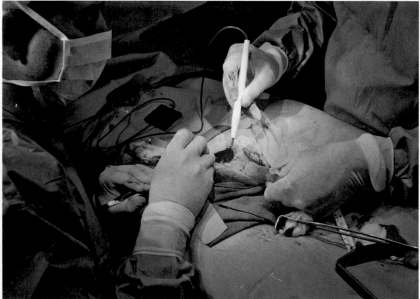

Surgery to lengthen the penis. The operator is pulling on the penis while cutting the suspensory ligament.

Courtesy of Simon LeVay

## BOX 3.3
## Diphallia

"Diphallia" means having two penises. This is the normal condition for snakes and lizards, as well as for some invertebrates, and it also occurs in humans, but very seldom—about once in every 5 million male births. Of the 30 or so individuals known to have been born with diphallia in the United States, the great majority have other congenital malformations, such as a double bladder or a urethra that opens in the wrong place (hypospadias—see Chapter 4) (Tirtayasa et al., 2013). One of the two penises is often small and nonfunctional, and this one may be surgically removed during infancy. It may be that diphallia comes about because of a problem with the molecular signals that define the midline of the body during fetal development.

Extremely rarely, both penises are of equal length and fully functional for urination and sex, without any accompanying malformations. One such instance came to light in 2014, when a man with the username DoubleDickDude went public on Reddit's Ask Me Anything pages (Anonymous, 2014b). Besides having two normally functioning penises, DoubleDickDude is bisexual and has had sex with both men and women, sometimes in three-ways that involve simultaneous oral sex from both partners. Men, he says, are much more enthusiastic about interacting with his penises than women are.

Out of the 9,000+ questions and answers posted on Reddit, here are three:

**How do women react when they find out?**
*"For the most part, girls were nervous and some changed their mind at the last minute. Dudes NEVER change their mind, they always want it even if they're freaked out a little."*

DoubleDickDude's genitals. Neither penis is circumcised.

**Did you ever consider a career in porn?**
*"Yes, but I decided against it . . . The only reason I let photos out is because I thought people might like to know that at least one guy with two normal dicks exists. All the others are pretty scary-looking and I feel for them."*

**What's the best thing about having two penises?**
*"Having two cocks . . . It's great—no complaints."*

A corresponding condition sometimes occurs in women: In this case the woman's vagina has a septum (tissue wall) that divides it into a left and right passageway, each of which leads into a separate uterus. The condition may require surgery, but it is usually compatible with coitus and pregnancy.

---

with certain types of human papillomavirus (HPV—see Chapter 15) is an important factor predisposing men to penile cancer. Detected early, penile cancer can be treated by fairly minor surgical procedures. If the cancer has invaded the deep structures of the penis, however, part or all of the organ may have to be amputated.

In 2016 a 64-year-old Massachusetts man whose penis was amputated on account of cancer received a penis transplant from a deceased donor (Grady, 2016). This novel procedure (pioneered in South Africa) also offers hope to men born with an exceptionally small penis ("micropenis") and to men (such as injured military personnel) who have lost their penis as a result of trauma. In 2018 one such serviceman received a combined penis and scrotum transplant (not including the testicles) at Johns Hopkins School of Medicine. A year later he had partially recovered sensation in his penis and the ability to have an erection (Zaleski, 2019).

Very rarely, boys are born with two penises (**BOX 3.3**). Other congenital disorders are discussed in Chapter 4.

**FAQ:** Is there such a thing as a fracture of the penis?

Yes. Unlike all other great apes, human males lack a bone within the penis that might break, but the term "fracture of the penis" refers to a tear in the capsule of a corpus cavernosum. This can happen when a man's erect penis collides forcefully with his partner's body. There is a cracking noise, severe pain, and a large bruise. The man should go to an emergency room: Surgical repair is usually necessary.

## 3.2 Penile Erection Involves Nerves, Blood, and Chemistry

### LEARNING OBJECTIVES
After reading this section you should be able to:

3.2.1 Identify the regions of the penis that are most erotically sensitive and explain the reason for their high sensitivity.

3.2.2 Describe the mechanism of penile erection, and name the key neurotransmitter involved in this function.

3.2.3 Explain how and why the scrotum regulates the temperature of the testicles.

**genital end-bulbs** Specialized nerve endings found in the genital area that probably detect the tactile stimulation associated with sexual activity.

**autonomic nervous system** The portion of the nervous system that controls smooth muscles and glands without our conscious involvement.

Erection of the penis can occur in response to local stimulation of the genital region, especially of the penis itself. Alternatively, it may occur in response to higher-level inputs, such as erotic thoughts or sensations (sights, odors, and so on) that are processed by the brain.

With regard to local stimulation, the penis (like the clitoris) possesses a unique class of sensory nerve endings termed **genital end-bulbs** (Halata & Munger, 1986) (**FIGURE 3.6**). In these structures, the nerve fibers form tangled knots in the deeper part of the skin. The highest density of genital end-bulbs occurs around the corona of the glans and in the frenulum—the zones generally considered to be the most erotically sensitive regions. It is believed that genital end-bulbs are specialized to respond to the mechanical stimulation that occurs during sexual behavior.

Of course, a man's penis is not his only erogenous zone: A wide zone of genital skin, as well as the anus and prostate gland, are erotically sensitive. So too are men's nipples, though to a varying degree from person to person. In the right circumstances any spot on a man's body can be erotically sensitive, as is also true for women (see Figure 2.1).

Local stimulation of the genital receptors triggers a spinal reflex: That is, nerves carry the information to the spinal cord, which then sends a return signal to the penis that triggers erection. In addition, signals from the spinal cord reach the brain, making the man conscious of the stimulation and increasing his sexual excitement. In the case of a spinal injury that completely separates the spinal cord from the brain, the spinal reflex may continue to function, so stimulation of the penis may still trigger an erection. The nerves that regulate penile erection are part of the **autonomic nervous system** (see Appendix B).

If the stimulation originates in the brain, specific neural pathways transmit the information to the spinal cord and then to the penis. This kind of psychogenic erection cannot occur after an injury that completely severs the spinal cord.

The nerves that innervate the erectile tissue and control the process of erection are not under voluntary control. A man cannot, therefore, develop or lose an erection by a simple act of will.

### Erection is the filling of the penis with blood

Now let's take a look at the erectile tissue itself (**FIGURE 3.7**). We will focus on the two corpora cavernosa of the penis, which have received the most study. The tissue within the corpora cavernosa is like a sponge: It contains numerous collapsible spaces named

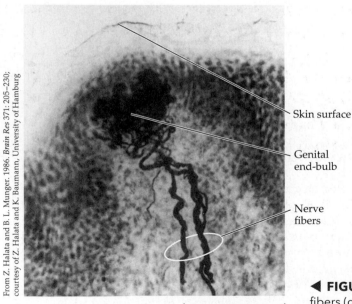

Skin surface

Genital end-bulb

Nerve fibers

30 μm

From Z. Halata and B. L. Munger. 1986. *Brain Res* 371: 205–230; courtesy of Z. Halata and K. Baumann, University of Hamburg

◀ **FIGURE 3.6 Sensory innervation of the penis** A bundle of nerve fibers (circled) approaches the skin surface and forms a dense knot of terminal branches—a genital end-bulb.

**sinusoids**. These spaces are part of the circulatory system; that is, blood enters them from arteries and exits by way of veins. When the penis is in a flaccid state, the arteries are in a constricted state, so little blood can flow into the sinusoids. Erection occurs when neural signals cause the arteries of the penis to open more widely, allowing blood to flow freely into the corpora cavernosa. The resulting expansion of the corpora cavernosa compresses and closes the veins that exit from the erectile tissue, thus preventing blood from leaving the penis. As sexual climax approaches, vasocongestion causes further swelling of the penis, especially the glans, and the pooling of blood within the glans turns it a purplish color.

A neurotransmitter, or neural-signaling molecule, called **nitric oxide** is involved in the triggering of an erection. It is released from the terminals of the nerves that innervate the erectile tissue. As we'll describe in Chapter 14, Viagra and other drugs that help produce erections do so by increasing the sensitivity of the erectile tissue to nitric oxide.

When complete erection occurs, no additional blood can enter the corpora cavernosa. An erection that won't go down—a painful condition called **priapism**—will therefore starve the erectile tissue of oxygen (**FIGURE 3.8**). If an erection persists for more than 4 hours the erectile tissue is at risk of permanent damage and the man should take his penis to an emergency room for treatment.

The ability of the corpora cavernosa to expand is limited by the tough connective tissue capsules that enclose them. This resistance to expansion causes the rigidity of the erect penis. Although both the corpora cavernosa and the corpus spongiosum expand during erection, the corpus spongiosum does not contribute as much to the erect penis's stiffness. The difference in rigidity can be appreciated by feeling an erect penis: The corpus spongiosum, which forms the ridge along the underside of the penis and also occupies the entire glans, is much softer to the touch than the rest of the organ. If the corpus spongiosum were as rigid as the rest of the penis during erection, the urethra would be compressed and ejaculation might be impossible.

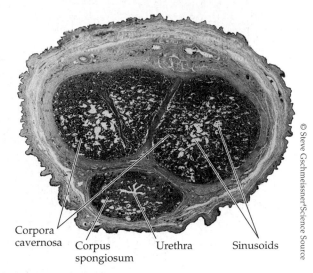

© Steve Gschmeissner/Science Source

▲ **FIGURE 3.7**  **Cross section of the penis** showing the appearance of the erectile tissue within the corpora cavernosa. The small, white collapsible spaces (sinusoids) fill with blood, causing an erection. (See **Animation 3.1: The Mechanism of Erection.**)

**sinusoid**  A vascular space, such as within erectile tissue, capable of expanding when filled with blood.

**nitric oxide**  A dissolved gas that functions as a neurotransmitter in erectile tissue.

**priapism**  A persistent penile erection in the absence of sexual arousal.

## Muscles are also involved in erection

Pelvic floor muscles, including the pubococcygeus muscle, also contribute to erection. If a man's penis is erect but hanging down from the body, a light touch on a sensitive area of the penis, or even on nearby skin, will cause the penis to lift up and project forward or upward. At the same time, the glans of the penis will become more swollen. It is also possible for a man to produce the same reaction voluntarily, without any physical stimulation, by contracting the pelvic floor muscles, which pull on and squeeze the corpora cavernosa and corpus spongiosum in the root of the penis. In spite of the participation of these muscles, we emphasize that the main process of penile erection, described above, is not under voluntary control.

## Erections occur during sleep

Although we usually think of erections as resulting from sexual arousal or behavior, they also occur spontaneously during sleep. They accompany the rapid eye movement (REM) phase of sleep, during which

▶ **FIGURE 3.8**  **Priapism** is named for the Greco-Roman fertility god Priapus, who was always shown with a superhuman erection. This coin was minted by the Roman city of Nicopolis, in what is now Bulgaria. The image of Priapus is an allusion to the city's wealth and power. For mere mortals, an erection that won't go down calls for prompt medical attention.

Classical Numismatic Group, Inc. http://www.cngcoins.com/CC BY-SA 2.5

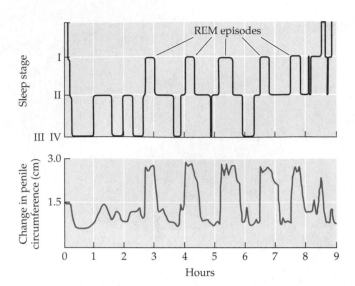

◀ **FIGURE 3.9** Penile erections accompany REM sleep.
The graph shows an entire night's sleep (9 hours) for a healthy young man. The upper trace indicates the stages of sleep as determined by electroencephalography (EEG): Stage I is light sleep, stage II is intermediate-level sleep, and stages III and IV are both deep sleep. The five REM episodes, shown here as being stage I, are actually a distinct kind of sleep characterized by rapid eye movements. The lower trace shows changes in penile circumference (3.0 cm = maximal erection). Note that the erections occur during the REM episodes. (Adapted from sleepsources.org by permission.)

vivid dreams are experienced (**FIGURE 3.9**). The dreams may be erotic in nature and may culminate in **nocturnal orgasms**, or **nocturnal emissions** (also called *wet dreams*), but erections accompany all REM phases, whatever their dream content. Four out of five men report experiencing nocturnal emissions at some time in their lives, most commonly in their teen years (Kinsey et al., 1948). Spontaneous erections may occur during daytime too.

**nocturnal orgasm (or nocturnal emission)** Orgasm or ejaculation during sleep. Also called *wet dream*.

**scrotum** The sac behind the penis that contains the testicles.

**testicle (or testis; pl. testes)** The male gonad: one of the two glands within the scrotum that produce sperm and secrete sex hormones.

The function of nocturnal erections is not certain, but it is suspected that they serve to oxygenate the erectile tissue and to prevent fibrosis (scarring) and loss of elasticity. Nocturnal genital arousal is common in women as well as men, and one study reported that about one in five young women experienced orgasms during sleep (Henton, 1976).

## The scrotum regulates the temperature of the testicles

The **scrotum**, or scrotal sac (**FIGURE 3.10**), is a loose bag of skin that hangs down behind the penis and contains the two **testicles**, or **testes**.* In adult men the scrotum is lightly covered with hair, and it possesses numerous sweat glands that help to regulate the temperature of the scrotal contents. Stimulation of the scrotal skin is sexually arousing in most men, though not to the same degree as stimulation of the most sensitive areas of the penis. Underneath the scrotal skin lies a sheet-like smooth muscle. Contraction of this muscle in response to cold (and also during sexual arousal—especially near orgasm) causes the scrotal skin to wrinkle and appear thicker. This makes the skin a more effective insulator and also brings the testicles closer to the body, warming them.

* Although the terms "testicle" and "testis" denote the same thing, "testicle" is used when referring to the anatomical structure, whereas "testis" is generally used when referring to its function or early development.

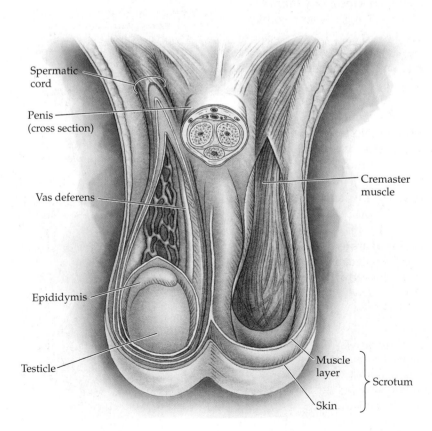

◀ **FIGURE 3.10** The scrotum and its internal structure (See **Activity 3.3: The Scrotum and Its Contents**.)

## 3.3 The Testicles Produce Sperm and Sex Hormones

### LEARNING OBJECTIVES

After reading the section you should be able to:

3.3.1  Identify the structures of the spermatic cord and describe their functions.

3.3.2  Describe the most common disorders that can affect the testicles, including one that is a medical emergency.

3.3.3  Explain the functions of testosterone and estrogens in males.

The testicles, or male gonads, have two functions that are analogous to those of the ovaries (female gonads): They produce **sperm**, or **spermatozoa**, and secrete sex hormones. Men do not become pregnant, and they lack any structures equivalent to the uterus or oviducts. However, men do need to create and store large numbers of sperm, mix them with other secretions, and deliver the resulting **semen** to the urethral opening for ejaculation. These functions require a number of structures, including several specialized glands and assorted pieces of tubing to connect everything together.

The testicles are twin egg-shaped structures that can easily be seen or felt within the scrotal sac. The testicles are not completely symmetrical: One (usually the left) hangs lower, and one (usually the right) is slightly larger. Each testicle weighs about 0.4 to 0.5 ounces (11 to 14 g) and lies within a protective capsule. Above and behind each testicle is an **epididymis**, through which sperm pass after leaving the testicle.

Before considering the structure of the testicle, let's take a look at the **spermatic cord**. This cord is the testicle's lifeline—a bundle of structures that connect the testicle with several crucial organs inside the body. The spermatic cord runs through the **inguinal canal**—a 1.5-inch (4 cm) tunnel through the abdominal wall in the region of the groin. Incidentally, the inguinal canals are weak points in the abdominal wall and are frequent sites of hernias, in which parts of the intestines bulge through the abdominal musculature.

A layer of muscle tissue known as the **cremaster muscle** wraps the spermatic cord and forms a sling around the testicle. The cremaster contracts automatically in response to cold, pulling the testicle toward the body, and thus helps to regulate the temperature of the testicle.

Within the spermatic cord runs the **vas deferens**, the tube that carries mature sperm away from the epididymis. In addition, the spermatic cord contains arteries, veins, and nerves that supply the testicle. The arteries and veins run close to each other, an arrangement that facilitates the transfer of heat from the arterial to the venous circulation. This helps keep the temperature of the testicle below the temperature of the remainder of the body.

With all these temperature-regulating elements, it should be no surprise to learn that the testicles require a specific temperature range for the production of sperm, which is several degrees below core body temperature. Warming the testicles to core body temperature for prolonged periods decreases a man's sperm count and reduces fertility. The sperm count recovers after the testicles return to their preferred temperature range. Increased temperature does not affect the other function of the testicles—hormone production—to any significant extent.

The internal structure of the testicle (**FIGURE 3.11**) is dominated by the **seminiferous tubules**, a set of about a thousand fine, highly convoluted tubes. The seminiferous tubules are the site of sperm production, or **spermatogenesis**. The spaces between the tubules are occupied by **interstitial cells**, which secrete sex hormones—mainly testosterone (see below).

Each sperm cell, whose structure is described in the following section, is the product of a 64-day process of cell division and maturation that begins within a

**sperm (or spermatozoon; pl. spermatozoa)**  The male gamete, produced in the testicles.

**semen**  The fluid, containing sperm and a variety of chemical compounds, that is ejaculated from the penis at male sexual climax.

**epididymis**  A structure, attached to each testicle, where sperm mature and are stored before entering the vas deferens.

**spermatic cord**  Either of two bilateral bundles of structures that include the vas deferens, blood vessels, and the cremaster muscle and that pass through the inguinal canal to a testicle.

**inguinal canal**  A short canal passing through the abdominal wall in the region of the groin in males, through which the spermatic cord passes.

**cremaster muscle**  A sheet-like muscle that wraps around the spermatic cord and the testicle.

**vas deferens (pl. vasa deferentia)**  Either of the two bilateral ducts that convey sperm from the epididymis to the ejaculatory ducts.

**seminiferous tubules**  Convoluted microscopic tubes within the testicle that are the sites of sperm production.

**spermatogenesis**  The production of sperm.

**interstitial cells**  Cells located between the seminiferous tubules in the testicle that secrete hormones.

(A)

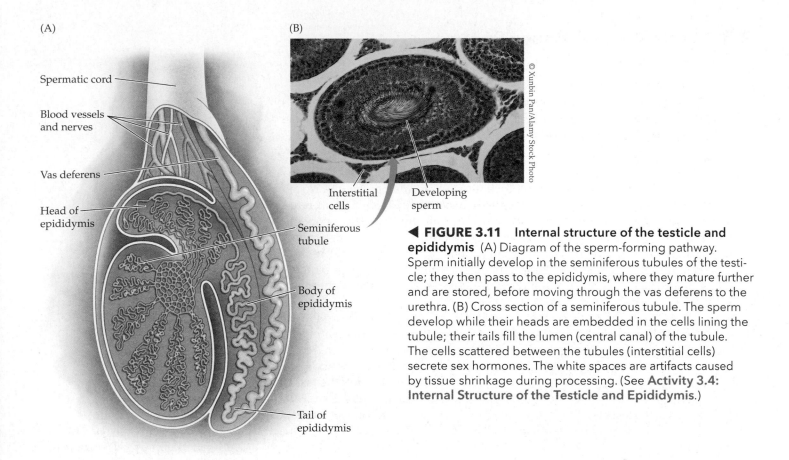

Spermatic cord

Blood vessels and nerves

Vas deferens

Head of epididymis

Seminiferous tubule

Body of epididymis

Tail of epididymis

(B)

© Xunbin Pan/Alamy Stock Photo

Interstitial cells

Developing sperm

◀ **FIGURE 3.11** **Internal structure of the testicle and epididymis** (A) Diagram of the sperm-forming pathway. Sperm initially develop in the seminiferous tubules of the testicle; they then pass to the epididymis, where they mature further and are stored, before moving through the vas deferens to the urethra. (B) Cross section of a seminiferous tubule. The sperm develop while their heads are embedded in the cells lining the tubule; their tails fill the lumen (central canal) of the tubule. The cells scattered between the tubules (interstitial cells) secrete sex hormones. The white spaces are artifacts caused by tissue shrinkage during processing. (See **Activity 3.4: Internal Structure of the Testicle and Epididymis.**)

**FAQ:** I've never seen an elephant's testicles—do they have them?

Yes, male elephants do, but they are internal. An elephant's body temperature is lower than a human's, especially during the night, and it is not high enough to impair spermatogenesis.

seminiferous tubule. Of course, huge numbers of sperm develop simultaneously. The average man produces about 150 million sperm per day—day after day for several decades. Yet these numbers have been declining in recent times, for a variety of reasons (**BOX 3.4**).

After leaving the seminiferous tubules, the immature sperm travel to the epididymis. The epididymis has the shape of the letter C and is attached to the top and back surface of the testicle. It contains a single extremely convoluted tubule. Sperm spend about a week traversing this tubule, during which time they become about a hundredfold more concentrated. They also mature functionally, gaining the capacity for forward motion. Still, this swimming motion is sluggish and undirected, and it does not contribute to the sperm's transport along the reproductive tract. Rather, this transport is a bulk motion caused by contractions of the walls of the tract.

## Cancer and other disorders can affect the testicles

About 8,700 cases of testicular cancer are diagnosed in the United States annually, but less than 400 men die of the disease (American Cancer Society, 2018). In other words, it is usually a curable condition. It most commonly strikes men in their 20s or 30s. Risk factors include a history of undescended testicles, other developmental abnormalities of the testicles, and Klinefelter syndrome (see Chapter 4).

Testicular cancer is usually diagnosed when the individual or his health care provider notices a lump or an increase in size in one testicle. There may also be a sudden accumulation of fluid in the scrotum, pain in the testicle, or an ache or heaviness in the lower abdomen, groin, or scrotum. A provisional diagnosis is made by means of an ultrasound scan; the definitive diagnosis is made by removing the entire affected testicle through an incision in the groin and examining it microscopically.

## BOX 3.4
## Declining Sperm Counts

In 1992 a Danish research group published some disturbing news about male fertility (Carlsen et al., 1992). According to their meta-analysis of about 60 prior studies that employed standardized sperm-counting techniques (**FIGURE A**), average sperm counts in several Western countries dropped by nearly half between 1940 and 1990—from 113 million to 66 million sperm per milliliter of semen. This drop was accompanied by a drop in ejaculate volume from 3.4 mL to 2.75 mL (from 0.11 to 0.09 U.S. fluid ounces) and by an increase in the prevalence of certain male reproductive disorders, such as undescended testicles (cryptorchidism) and testicular cancer.

Although there have been critics of the Danish study, more recent studies have generally confirmed the reality of the decline, and they have found that it has continued up until the present, including among American men (Chang et al., 2018) (**FIGURE B**). Current estimates are in the range of 40 to 50 million sperm per milliliter, which is already in a "gray area" within which male fertility may be affected (see Chapter 8). What's more, among the sperm that remain, there are more "duds" than "studs": One very large study conducted in China found that, in semen samples collected in the period 2011–2015, an average of 89% of the sperm were misshapen (see Figure 8.3) and 53% did not move normally. Both these values, as well as total sperm counts, were dramatically worse than were found 10 years earlier (Huang et al., 2017).

Why is this decline happening? One trivial explanation—more frequent ejaculation—has been ruled out by studies that control for the length of abstinence prior to specimen donation. The increased popularity of tight-fitting pants or underwear, which keep the testes too warm, may be a contributing factor (Redford, 2015), as may an increasingly sedentary lifestyle (Gaskins et al., 2014).

Most attention, however, has been focused on the possibility that the decline is caused by environmental pollutants, especially by endocrine disruptors—agricultural pesticides and other industrial chemicals that mimic or antagonize sex hormones (Sifakis et al., 2017). Effects of this kind have been well established in animal studies; epidemiological and laboratory research suggests that they occur in men too (Buck Louis et al., 2014; Sumner et al., 2019).

Other factors may also play a role. Mothers who are obese or who smoke or drink during pregnancy, or who bottle-feed rather than breastfeed their babies, may have sons with smaller testicles in childhood and/or reduced sperm counts in adulthood (Sharpe, 2012). And finally, the increasing popularity of in vitro fertilization (IVF) is a factor, though only a minor

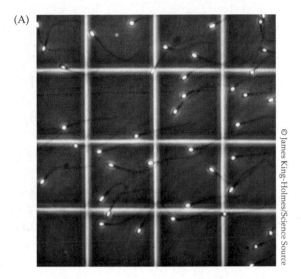

(A)

© James King-Holmes/Science Source

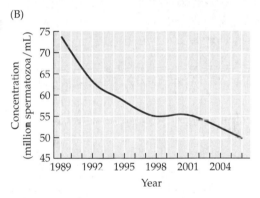

(B)

Sperm are counted in a precisely calibrated chamber (A). Estimated sperm counts for a 35-year-old man in France from 1989 to 2006 (B). (B after M. Rolland et al. 2013. *Hum Reprod* 28: 462-470.)

one so far: Males conceived by a common IVF technique known as intracytoplasmic sperm injection (ICSI) (see Chapter 8) tend to have very low sperm counts in adulthood—less than 20 million sperm per milliliter—probably because they inherit the same problems with sperm development that caused their fathers to be infertile (Belva et al., 2016).

Low sperm counts are becoming more problematic as women are, on average, beginning families at a later age. A sperm count that is perfectly adequate to fertilize a 25-year-old woman may be much less so for a woman of 40. All in all, it is likely that declining sperm counts will accelerate the decline in birth rates in many countries—a decline that up until now has been caused largely by social factors.

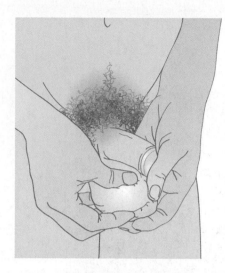

▲ **FIGURE 3.12** Testicular self-examination

**orchitis** Inflammation of a testicle.

**epididymitis** Inflammation of the epididymis.

**varicocele** Enlargement of the veins that drain the testicle.

**hydrocele** A collection of fluid around a testicle.

**testicular torsion** Twisting of a testicle that cuts off its blood supply.

**testosterone** The principal androgen, synthesized in the testes and, in lesser amounts, in the ovaries and adrenal glands.

**FAQ:** I'm a young guy, but I'm not that interested in sex. Is my testosterone level low?

There are many possible reasons for a low sex drive, including psychological or social factors, asexuality (see Chapter 5), or hormonal problems. A testosterone test can be done, and if your testosterone levels are low, the reason can be investigated. In the unlikely event that you need a supplement, your doctor can prescribe testosterone skin patches.

By itself, the removal of one testicle is not debilitating: The remaining testicle can compensate, and the missing testicle can be replaced with a prosthesis, if the man wishes. Unfortunately, further treatments—lymph node dissection, radiation, or chemotherapy—may be necessary, and these have the potential to interfere with erectile function and sperm production. Men with testicular cancer who may want to father children in the future have the option of depositing semen samples in a sperm bank before treatment.

The following noncancerous conditions can affect the testicles or nearby structures:

- **Orchitis** is an inflammation and swelling of a testicle, caused by infection with a variety of organisms, some of which may be sexually transmitted.

- **Epididymitis** is an inflammation of the epididymis, caused by trauma or by infection with *E. coli* or any of a number of sexually transmitted organisms.

- A **varicocele** is an enlargement of the veins that drain the testicles, causing the spermatic cord to feel lumpy. It can be surgically corrected.

- A **hydrocele** is a collection of fluid in the membrane-lined space surrounding one testicle. It can be drained or surgically corrected.

- **Testicular torsion** is a twisting of a testicle and its spermatic cord, which cuts off the testicle's blood supply. Torsion causes sudden and severe pain; it must be treated within a few hours or the affected testicle may die from the lack of blood.

Regular testicular self-examination is recommended for men at increased risk of testicular cancer (**FIGURE 3.12**). There are no objective data about its value for men at average risk, but the exam is simple enough. To do the exam, choose a warm location, such as the shower, so that the scrotal sac is relaxed. Roll each testicle in turn between thumb and fingers. The surface of the testicle is usually fairly smooth, and the epididymis can be felt as a soft, elongated structure behind and above each testicle. One testicle is normally slightly larger than the other, but it is a matter of concern if one testicle has enlarged since the last time you examined it. Also feel for any lumps, rounded or irregular masses, changes in the consistency of a testicle, or tender areas. None of these signs are definitive indicators of cancer, but they merit medical attention.

## The testicles secrete sex hormones

Like women's ovaries, men's testicles manufacture and secrete three kinds of sex steroids: androgens, chiefly **testosterone**; estrogens, chiefly estradiol; and progestins, chiefly progesterone. These hormones are synthesized by the interstitial cells (see Figure 3.11).

Although all three classes of hormones are present in both sexes, their actual levels in the blood differ considerably. In men, testosterone levels are roughly 10 times *higher* than they are in women, while the concentrations of estradiol and progesterone are roughly 10 times *lower*. (These are approximations because hormone levels in women vary greatly throughout the menstrual cycle.) Circulating testosterone has a half-life of less than an hour. In men, the level of testosterone in the blood is variable: It peaks every 2 to 4 hours, and it is also higher during the night and morning than during the afternoon or evening (**FIGURE 3.13**). These fluctuations do not cause corresponding fluctuations in a man's sex drive or sexual performance, so far as is known, but they make it difficult to assess a man's testosterone status on the basis of a single blood draw.

The main functions of these sex hormones in men are as follows:

ANDROGENS  Before birth, testosterone drives development of the fetus—especially the fetal genitalia—in the male direction. Testosterone is also responsible for most of the changes associated with male puberty and for maintenance of these characteristics thereafter. Testosterone acts on the brain in fetal and adult life, promoting the establishment and expression of male-typical gendered traits. It is the chief hormone responsible for the maintenance of the sex drive in men. Testosterone does not regulate sexuality on a minute-to-minute or hour-to-hour basis. Rather, it influences some fairly durable features of brain organization.

Testosterone is an anabolic hormone—it promotes the buildup of tissue, especially muscle, and it increases the oxygen-carrying capacity of the blood. The anabolic effects of testosterone and related androgens are the reason that athletes of both sexes may use them to promote tissue growth, including muscle development. Such use in competitive sports is generally banned, and it carries significant health risks (**BOX 3.5**).

To exert some of its effects, testosterone has to be converted to the more potent androgen **5α-dihydrotestosterone** (**DHT**) in the target tissues. This is true for genital tissues and the skin, but not the brain. Drugs that block this conversion are used to treat enlargement of the prostate as well as male pattern baldness. Androgens such as testosterone and DHT strongly influence the distribution of head, body, and pubic hair in both sexes.

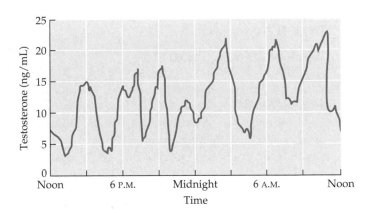

▲ **FIGURE 3.13**   **Testosterone cycles in a man**
Testosterone levels in the blood peak every 2 to 4 hours, and mean levels are higher from midnight to noon than from noon to midnight. (After M. H. Johnson and B. J. Everitt. 2000. *Essential Reproduction*, 5th ed. Blackwell: Hoboken, NJ.)

ESTROGENS   As in women, estrogens help maintain bone density in men, and they also terminate the growth of the limb bones after puberty. (Men who are genetically insensitive to estrogens continue to grow after the end of puberty, reaching 7 feet [2.1 m] or more in height.) In addition, estrogens are required for male fertility: They promote the maturation and concentration of sperm in the epididymis.

PROGESTERONE   The only clearly established function for progesterone in men is as a metabolic precursor for androgens and estrogens. When given as drugs, however, progesterone and synthetic progestins lower men's sex drive, suggesting that progesterone may have a hormonal effect on the brain that counteracts the effect of androgens.

As you can see, it is an oversimplification to think of androgens as "male" hormones and estrogens and progestins as "female" hormones. All three classes of hormones have functions in both sexes.

**5α-dihydrotestosterone (DHT)**
An androgen derived from testosterone that plays an important role in the development of the male external genitalia.

## The brain and pituitary gland regulate hormone levels

As with women's ovaries, men's testicles are linked with the hypothalamus and pituitary gland by a hormonal control loop (**FIGURE 3.14**). The same hormonal messengers—gonadotropin-releasing hormone (GnRH), follicle-stimulating hormone (FSH), and luteinizing hormone (LH)—play similar roles in the two sexes. GnRH, secreted by the hypothalamus, stimulates the secretion of FSH and LH by the pituitary gland. FSH stimulates spermatogenesis in the testicles, and LH stimulates the synthesis and secretion of sex hormones. The androgens in turn exert a negative feedback effect, damping the secretion of the hormones from the hypothalamus and pituitary.

Men's bodies do not experience any monthly hormonal cycle equivalent to that in women.

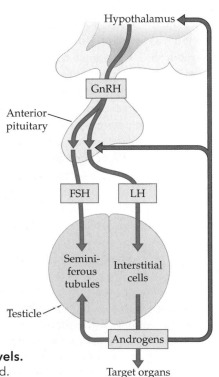

▶ **FIGURE 3.14**   **A feedback loop controls male hormone levels.**
Stimulatory influences are shown in blue, inhibitory influences in red.

## BOX 3.5
# Steroids and Sports

Athletes have abused steroids for decades. Androgens such as testosterone have anabolic effects: They increase muscle bulk and strength—an obvious benefit in many sports. Most professional sports organizations prohibit their use, enforce the prohibition by urine or blood testing, and impose lengthy bans on offenders.

Steroid-abusing athletes or their trainers have devised numerous methods to avoid detection. Some athletes have employed sleight of hand to deliver "clean" urine, rather than their own, into collection flasks. Some have catheterized themselves and filled their bladders with clean urine before being tested. Some have lied about their locations during training, thus making themselves unavailable for testing prior to competition. In 2016 Russian authorities were found to have broken into storage facilities and switched their athletes' sample flasks with flasks of clean urine. As a result Russian track-and-field athletes were banned from competing as a national team at the 2016 Olympic Games, and it is expected that a similar ban will be in force at the 2021 Olympics (Panja, 2019).

Testosterone is naturally present in the body, of course, so some athletes who have taken exogenous testosterone had the hope that its levels in urine or blood would test within or near the normal range. American cyclist Floyd Landis tried this in the 2006 Tour de France, and he won the event, but the ratio of testosterone to other steroids in his blood turned out to be abnormal. In addition, the isotopic composition of his testosterone showed that it was synthesized from plant precursors and was therefore a pharmaceutical. Landis was stripped of his medal. He later admitted to abusing steroids, and he implicated other cyclists, including seven-time Tour de France winner Lance Armstrong, who was also stripped of his medals.

Another tactic has been to use **designer steroids**, which are synthetic steroids that are not naturally present in the body but nevertheless have strong anabolic effects (Rahnema et al., 2015). Designer steroids are used for the specific purpose of avoiding detection in drug tests. Some of these compounds, such as one named tetrahydrogestrinone, or THG, were unknown to science before they were used by athletes. Once a test for THG was developed, numerous athletes who had used the drug were identified, including four members of the Oakland Raiders football team.

Although all anabolic steroids are illegal to possess or use without a prescription in the United States, a designer steroid may not be on the list of drugs banned by sports authorities until its existence is recognized—after which another designer steroid may take its place. For that reason many experts believe that entire classes of drugs—such as all

According to U.S. prosecutors, illegal use of a designer steroid altered the head and body of the female Olympic cyclist Tammy Thomas.

drugs that activate the androgen receptor—should be banned, rather than specific compounds.

Obviously, the abuse of androgens by athletes harms their clean competitors by putting them at a disadvantage. But it also harms the abusers themselves because androgens can have serious and potentially fatal ill effects (Mayo Clinic, 2019g). In men they can cause the development of breasts (gynecomastia), baldness, testicular atrophy and fibrosis, infertility, enlarged prostate, liver damage, and cardiovascular disease, as well as mental effects including pathological aggressiveness, lowered or heightened sex drive, and depression. In women, besides some of these same effects, they also cause the appearance of facial and body hair, a deeper voice, changes in facial structure (see figure), an enlarged clitoris, and irregular or absent periods. In pregnant women they may harm the fetus.

In recent years professional athletes have probably reduced their use of anabolic steroids, on account of improved testing methods, more severe sanctions, and the development of alternatives. At the same time, the use of steroids by non-professional athletes and bodybuilders, who are less likely to be tested, may have become more prevalent (Otterson, 2017).

**designer steroids**  Synthetic steroids intended to evade detection in drug tests.

Because the brain is involved in the regulation of testicular function, life experiences can affect a man's testosterone levels. Entering into a steady romantic relationship or marriage, for example, lowers a man's testosterone levels, and separation raises them again. Becoming a father also lowers testosterone levels (Grebe et al., 2019).

## 3.4 Several Glands Contribute Secretions to Semen

### LEARNING OBJECTIVES

After reading this section you should be able to:

3.4.1　Explain the pathway taken by sperm from their birthplace to ejaculation.

3.4.2　Describe the three conditions that can affect the prostate.

3.4.3　Label a drawing of a sperm and explain its functions.

3.4.4　Describe the mechanism of ejaculation.

3.4.5　Identify the glands involved in the production of semen.

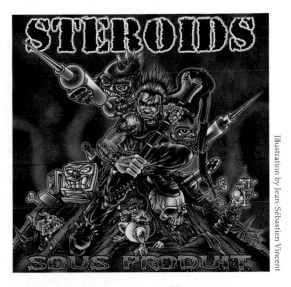

▲ Album cover by a French punk-hardcore band illustrates the popular image of sex steroids.

The sperm pass from the epididymis into the vas deferens on that side, which then passes up through the spermatic cord into the abdomen, past the bladder, and down toward the prostate gland (**FIGURE 3.15**). Each vas deferens is not only a transport route but also a storage reservoir for mature sperm, which have been concentrated by the epididymis into a paste-like mass. Further progress of the sperm occurs not by their own motility, but by muscular contractions of the walls of the vas deferens. These contractions occur just before ejaculation.

The **seminal vesicles** are a pair of glands that lie behind the bladder. Their name is misleading: They are not storage areas for semen, but rather glands that add their secretions to the semen. The duct of each seminal vesicle joins the vas deferens on that side, and the combined duct is thereafter named the **ejaculatory duct**. The left and right ejaculatory ducts join the urethra as it passes through the prostate gland. From that junction on, the function of the urethra is to pass urine or semen as needed.

**seminal vesicles**　Two glands situated to either side of the prostate; their secretions are components of semen.

**ejaculatory duct**　Either of the two bilateral ducts formed by the junction of the vas deferens and the duct of the seminal vesicle. The ejaculatory ducts empty into the urethra within the prostate.

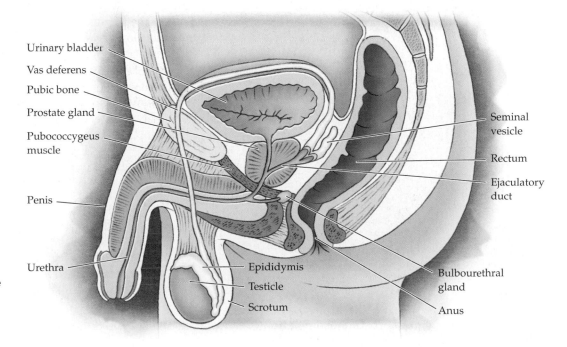

▶ **FIGURE 3.15　The male reproductive tract** Note how the prostate gland surrounds the urethra as it exits the bladder. Enlargement of the prostate can interfere with urination. (See **Activity 3.5: The Male Reproductive Tract**.)

Urinary bladder
Vas deferens
Pubic bone
Prostate gland
Pubococcygeus muscle
Penis
Urethra
Epididymis
Testicle
Scrotum
Seminal vesicle
Rectum
Ejaculatory duct
Bulbourethral gland
Anus

**prostate gland** A single gland located at the base of the bladder and surrounding the urethra; its secretions are a component of semen.

**prostate cancer** Cancer of the prostate gland.

**prostate-specific antigen (PSA)** An enzyme secreted by the prostate gland; its presence at high levels in the blood is suggestive of, but not diagnostic of, prostate cancer.

**radical prostatectomy** Surgical removal of the entire prostate gland and local lymph nodes.

**prostatitis** Inflammation of the prostate gland, either acute or chronic.

**chronic pelvic pain syndrome** An alternative, more inclusive term for "chronic prostatitis."

The **prostate gland** (often referred to simply as "the prostate") lies in the midline immediately below the bladder. It completely surrounds the urethra as it exits the bladder. The normal prostate is slightly larger than a walnut. The secretion of the prostate is a cloudy, alkaline fluid; at ejaculation, this fluid is pumped into the urethra by the contraction of muscle fibers within the gland. (See **Activity 3.6: Anatomy of the Prostate.**)

A health care provider can check the condition of the prostate gland by inserting a gloved finger into the anus and feeling the gland through the front surface of the rectum (**FIGURE 3.16**). In this way, the provider can assess whether the prostate gland is tender or enlarged or contains lumps. If you wish to examine your own or your partner's prostate gland, instructions are available online (Guth, n.d.), but self-examination requires some dexterity and is not a substitute for a professional exam.

The most serious disorder that can affect the prostate gland is **prostate cancer**. This is the most common nonskin cancer among American men: About 1 man in 9 will be diagnosed with the disease in his lifetime, and 1 in 41 of all men will die of the condition. Still, a diagnosis of prostate cancer is very far from being a death sentence: In fact, a man who is given this diagnosis has very nearly the same likelihood of being alive 5 years later as a similarly aged man without the condition (American Cancer Society, 2019d). Risk factors for prostate cancer include advanced age, a family history of the disease, African American race, and obesity.

The early symptoms of prostate cancer may include problems with urination, blood in the urine or semen, or pain in the lower back or hips. Abnormally high or increasing blood levels of a prostate-derived enzyme, **prostate-specific antigen** (**PSA**), are suggestive of prostate cancer, but other prostate conditions such as the two mentioned below can also raise PSA levels, as can diagnostic procedures and even bicycle riding* (Mejak et al., 2013). Routine PSA screening is controversial because of its potential to lead to unnecessary biopsies and surgery.

Definitive diagnosis is made by biopsy, which can also determine whether the cancer is aggressive or slow-growing. If the cancer is aggressive, treatment commonly involves **radical prostatectomy**, which means surgical removal of the entire gland, the seminal vesicles, and nearby lymph nodes. Unfortunately this procedure has serious sexual side effects: It puts a permanent end to ejaculation, and it also usually causes erectile disorder; this is because the nerves that supply the erectile tissue run along the sides of the prostate gland and are likely to be damaged during the operation. If the cancer is slow-growing, especially in an old man, the patient may choose "watchful waiting" rather than surgery, because the cancer may not cause him any problems before he dies of some other condition.

Much more common than prostate cancer are two other conditions that can affect the gland:

- **Prostatitis**—inflammation of the prostate gland—is a disorder that affects men of all ages. It may be acute or chronic. Acute prostatitis may occur as a complication of a urinary tract infection. The symptoms are pain during ejaculation and urination, ongoing pain in the pelvic region or lower back, and a fever. The condition usually responds to antibiotics. Chronic prostatitis, or **chronic pelvic pain syndrome**, is a puzzling and difficult-to-treat condition whose symptoms resemble those of acute prostatitis but are not caused by an

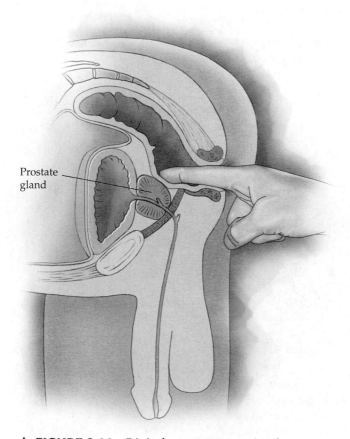

Prostate gland

▲ **FIGURE 3.16** Digital prostate examination

*There is no evidence that bicycle riding harms the prostate.

infection. As indicated by its name, chronic prostatitis can last for months or years (Polackwich & Shoskes, 2016).

- **Benign prostatic hyperplasia** (**BPH**), or "enlarged prostate," is an all-too-common disorder of older men. Besides age, African American race and obesity are risk factors for BPH, but smoking and lack of exercise are not (Kristal et al., 2007). The prostate gland continues to grow slowly throughout adult life, and its growth may eventually constrict the urethra where it passes through the gland. More than half of all men in their 60s and beyond experience chronic urinary problems—weak urine flow, urgency and frequency of urination, and leakage—as a result of BPH. It may be alleviated with drugs, but surgery is sometimes needed. BPH is not a risk factor for prostate cancer.

The last glands that need to be mentioned are the **bulbourethral glands** (or **Cowper's glands**). These two pea-sized glands lie below the prostate gland, and their secretion—a clear, alkaline, mucous fluid—is expelled into the urethra. In many men, secretion from the bulbourethral glands begins early during sexual arousal and can be seen as a drop or two of slippery liquid that appears at the urethral opening sometime between erection and ejaculation; hence its colloquial name, "pre-cum." It's possible that the bulbourethral secretion helps lubricate the passage of the ejaculate through the urethra. During coitus, the alkaline bulbourethral and prostatic secretions may help neutralize the acidic environments within the man's urethra and the woman's vagina, thus increasing the viability of the sperm.

Bulbourethral secretions do not contain sperm. Nevertheless, they can become mixed with sperm remaining in the urethra from a previous ejaculation. This happens chiefly when a man has sex for a second time without urinating between times. In those circumstances, remnants of the first ejaculate that have remained behind in the urethra get mixed in with the bulbourethral secretions from the second episode. In this case the man might unwittingly impregnate his partner during this second episode, even if he doesn't ejaculate or if he delays putting on a condom until just before ejaculating. "Pre-cum" can also contain disease organisms and can therefore be responsible for the spread of sexually transmitted infections.

## What is semen?

Semen, or seminal fluid ("cum" in colloquial English), is the cloudy, off-white fluid that is ejaculated from the male urethra at sexual climax.

The volume of a single ejaculate usually ranges between 2 and 5 mL (5 mL is approximately 1 teaspoonful), but volumes up to 13 mL have been measured (Cooke et al., 1995). The most important component of semen is, of course, the sperm (**FIGURE 3.17**). Each milliliter of semen contains 50 to 150 million sperm, and a normal ejaculate contains between 100 and 700 million sperm.

Each sperm (or spermatozoon) has a tadpole-like structure. The head contains the cell's nucleus with its all-important DNA packed into a dense inert mass. This DNA differs from one sperm to the next, because each sperm carries a different combination of genes from the man's father and mother, and each carries a single sex chromosome, either an X or a Y.

The sperm's tail, or **flagellum**, propels the sperm forward. When we look a little more closely, two other structures become apparent. Capping the nucleus is an **acrosome**,

**benign prostatic hyperplasia** Noncancerous enlargement of the prostate gland.

**bulbourethral glands (or Cowper's glands)** Two small glands near the root of the penis whose secretions ("pre-cum") may appear at the urethral opening during sexual arousal prior to ejaculation.

**flagellum** A whiplike cellular structure, such as the tail of a sperm.

**acrosome** A structure capping the head of a sperm that contains enzymes necessary for fertilization.

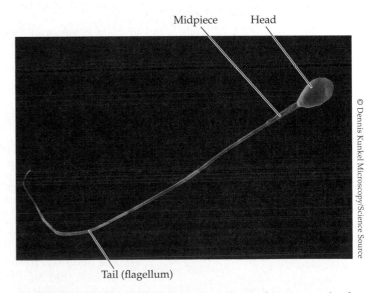

Midpiece    Head

Tail (flagellum)

© Dennis Kunkel Microscopy/Science Source

▲ **FIGURE 3.17** **Human sperm** Colorized micrograph of a single sperm, showing the head, midpiece, and tail or flagellum. The entire sperm is about 50 micrometers long. The acrosome, which caps the sperm head, is not visible as a distinct feature in this micrograph.

▶ **FIGURE 3.18 Glandular contributions to semen** Sperm make up less than 1% of the volume of semen; the rest comes from various glands.

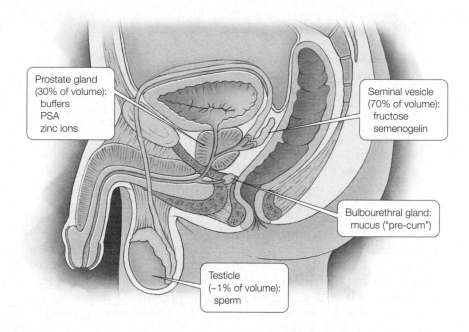

Prostate gland (30% of volume): buffers PSA zinc ions

Seminal vesicle (70% of volume): fructose semenogelin

Bulbourethral gland: mucus ("pre-cum")

Testicle (~1% of volume): sperm

**midpiece** The portion of the tail of a sperm closest to the head, containing mitochondria.

**seminal emission** The loading of the constituents of semen into the posterior portion of the urethra immediately before ejaculation.

which contains a complex suite of receptors and enzymes that are necessary for fertilization of an ovum. The part of the tail nearest the head is slightly thicker than the remainder of the tail and is called the **midpiece**. This section contains mitochondria tightly wound around the tail in a spiral manner. These mitochondria supply chemical energy for propulsion of the sperm.

In spite of the importance of the sperm, they occupy an insignificant proportion (about 1%) of the volume of the semen (**FIGURE 3.18**). The remainder is a mixture of the secretions of the seminal vesicles (about 70% of the total volume) and the prostate gland (about 30%), plus small contributions from the epididymis and the bulbourethral glands. Among the noncellular components of semen are proteins, enzymes, antioxidants, water, and salts, plus the following:

- The sugar fructose is an energy source for the sperm.
- Buffers keep the pH of the semen slightly alkaline (between about 7.2 and 7.8). These buffers protect the sperm from the acidic environment encountered if they are deposited in the vagina.
- A protein called semenogelin is responsible for important changes in semen that occur after ejaculation (**BOX 3.6**).
- The enzyme PSA interacts with semenogelin.
- Zinc ions ($Zn^{2+}$) also interact with semenogelin.
- In men infected with a disease-causing virus such as hepatitis B virus or human immunodeficiency virus (HIV) (see Chapter 15), these viruses may be present at high concentrations in semen.

## Ejaculation requires coordination of muscles and glands

Ejaculation is the forceful ejection of semen from the urethral opening. It is a complex process that requires precise coordination of glands and muscles. Luckily, the spinal cord takes care of most of the details.

Immediately prior to ejaculation, the various components of the semen are expelled from their reservoirs—the left and right vas deferens, the prostate gland, and the seminal vesicles—into the urethra (**FIGURE 3.19A**). This process is called **seminal emission**; it lasts 2 to 3 seconds and can be felt as a pulsing or flowing

## BOX 3.6
## The Secret Life of Semen

You might think that semen is just a bunch of sperm swimming around looking for a cervix. But a great deal more is going on in semen than meets the eye. In fact, it's a hive of physiological and enzymatic activity.

As mentioned in the chapter text, semen consists of contributions from three main sources: the seminal vesicles, which provide the protein semenogelin and the sugar fructose; the prostate gland, which provides zinc ions ($Zn^{2+}$) and the enzyme PSA; and the left and right vas deferens, which convey sperm from the testes. These components are loaded separately into the urethra, but they mix at ejaculation. The mixing may be incomplete, however, in which case the ejaculated semen will show distinct whitish (sperm-rich) streaks and clearer streaks.

When the three components mix, the semenogelin immediately binds to the sperm and immobilizes them. Then the zinc ions cross-link the semenogelin molecules, turning the semen from a fluid into a gel. This process is called coagulation. One biological function of coagulation during coitus is probably to prevent semen from running out of the vagina. In addition, during the coagulation phase, the semenogelin initiates a crucial step in the maturation of the sperm. This step, called capacitation, permits the sperm to move more vigorously and to home in on an ovum.

After coagulation, a slower process begins in which the PSA enzyme starts breaking up the semenogelin, causing the semen to gradually develop a more watery consistency. This process frees up the sperm so that—if they find themselves in a woman's vagina rather than inside a condom or somewhere else entirely—they can begin their migration up her reproductive tract.

The existence of this complex process makes clear why the three components of semen must be produced in different glands: If all three were produced in the prostate gland, for example, the semen would coagulate prematurely. Actually, a small amount of coagulation does occur before ejaculation in some men. These men may notice small globules of tapioca-like gel in their ejaculate, but the globules are harmless and do not impair fertility.

If a man ejaculates into water—for example, during a shower or bath—he may notice that his semen becomes very thick and sticky. That's probably because the PSA in the ejaculate diffuses away or is inactivated, allowing the process of coagulation to proceed further than it normally does.

In some species, such as many rodents, coagulation is a more extreme phenomenon than in humans: Semen ejaculated into the female's vagina forms a solid plug, which serves to prevent other males from copulating with that female.

Because of the role of zinc ions in semen coagulation, zinc deficiency can cause male infertility. Conversely, the cellular receptors that sense the presence of zinc offer a potential target for the development of a male contraceptive.

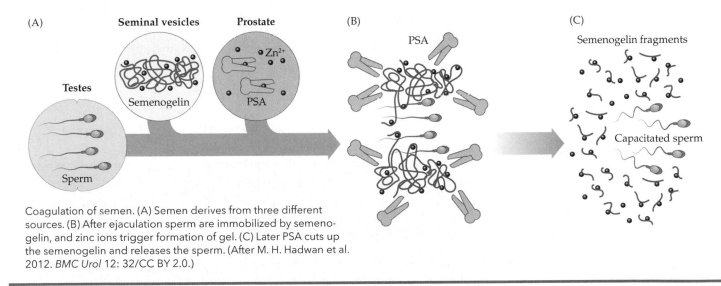

Coagulation of semen. (A) Semen derives from three different sources. (B) After ejaculation sperm are immobilized by semenogelin, and zinc ions trigger formation of gel. (C) Later PSA cuts up the semenogelin and releases the sperm. (After M. H. Hadwan et al. 2012. *BMC Urol* 12: 32/CC BY 2.0.)

sensation at the root of the penis. Once emission begins, the man has the sense that ejaculation is inevitable, although some men are able to halt the process even at this late stage. In that case, the semen simply flows out of the urethral opening, rather than being forcefully ejaculated.

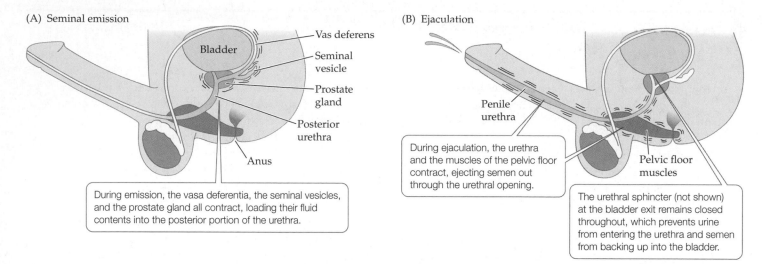

(A) Seminal emission

Vas deferens

Bladder

Seminal vesicle

Prostate gland

Posterior urethra

Anus

During emission, the vasa deferentia, the seminal vesicles, and the prostate gland all contract, loading their fluid contents into the posterior portion of the urethra.

(B) Ejaculation

Penile urethra

During ejaculation, the urethra and the muscles of the pelvic floor contract, ejecting semen out through the urethral opening.

Pelvic floor muscles

The urethral sphincter (not shown) at the bladder exit remains closed throughout, which prevents urine from entering the urethra and semen from backing up into the bladder.

▲ **FIGURE 3.19** Seminal emission and ejaculation

Ejaculation itself (**FIGURE 3.19B**) is caused by a series of rhythmic contractions of the muscular walls of the urethra and the pelvic floor muscles. These contractions, which occur at a rate of about one every 0.8 seconds, can be seen in electrical recordings from the muscles involved (**FIGURE 3.20**). The muscles forcefully squeeze the semen-filled urethra, especially in the region between the prostate gland and the root of the penis. The entire sequence lasts about 10 to 15 seconds.

The urethral sphincter at the outflow of the bladder is usually closed, and it constricts even more tightly at ejaculation in order to prevent the pressurized semen from flowing backward into the bladder. Thus, with nowhere else to go, the semen is expelled from the urethral opening in a series of spurts of decreasing force. If the man ejaculates into free space, the semen may be propelled some distance from the body, but this projectile ability is quite variable from person to person and declines with age. If he ejaculates within a woman's vagina, the semen may be propelled against the cervix, but not into the cervical canal.

"Orgasm" refers to all the events at sexual climax, including the physiological processes just described as well as the intense pleasurable feelings that accompany them. We will discuss orgasm in both sexes in Chapter 5, where we present a comprehensive picture of the sexual response cycle.

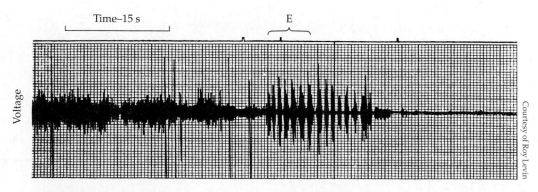

Time—15 s

E

Voltage

Courtesy of Roy Levin

▲ **FIGURE 3.20** **Muscle contractions recorded during male orgasm** This recording was obtained from an electrode placed in a man's pelvic floor muscle. The man was masturbating to orgasm. Seven spurts of ejaculation (E) occurred in synchrony with the first seven contractions of the muscle.

# 3.5 Nudity Is Culturally Regulated

### LEARNING OBJECTIVES

After reading this section you should be able to:

3.5.1 Discuss what social purpose prohibitions on nudity may have served in human history.

3.5.2 Explain the likely consequences for a person walking naked across your campus.

In this and the previous chapter we have discussed men and women's bodies, including their genitals, almost as if they were open for public display. In reality they are not, for the most part. Women's and men's genitals are often referred to as "private parts," highlighting the fact that cultural factors prohibit or limit their exposure.

In societies in which women wear clothing of any kind, they are required to cover the vulva while in public. Even in societies in which women traditionally went without clothing, as among the Kwoma people of New Guinea, men were required to look aside when approached by a woman (Ford & Beach, 1951). Men are usually required to cover their genitals, too, but there are exceptions.

The sight of a woman's vulva is sexually arousing to heterosexual men, as has been shown by controlled experiments conducted in strip clubs (Linz et al., 2000).* Thus, social prohibitions against female nudity have the effect of reducing men's arousal, especially in public. Prohibitions against male nudity may have a similar effect on heterosexual women, even if they are not as "visual" as men when it comes to sexual arousal (see Chapter 5). It therefore seems likely that the prohibition of public nudity reduces sexual arousal, sexual assault, and disputes over potential sex partners—thus facilitating general social cooperation.

Social rules about exposure of the body are indicators of general attitudes toward sexuality. In ancient Greece, male athletes competed without clothing,** and the nude or near-nude body was celebrated in art and sculpture (**FIGURE 3.21A**). In early Christian art, however, clothing served to desexualize the body—or indeed, to de-emphasize the body as a whole—as part of an emphasis on humanity's spiritual nature (**FIGURE 3.21B**).

The 19th century was another period when Europeans went to extraordinary lengths to conceal the body. When bathing at the beach, for example, people wore garments so all-covering as to hamper their ability to swim. These practices were part of a general belief that sexual arousal was dangerous to health, morals, and social order.

In the contemporary United States, attitudes toward nudity are divided. On the one hand, traditional social norms still rule. The "wardrobe malfunction" that exposed Janet Jackson's right breast for half a second at the 2004 Super Bowl triggered over half a million complaints. Nonpornographic websites—even sites that display a lot of skin, like

(A)

(B)

▲ **FIGURE 3.21  Religious attitudes toward the body** (A) Classical Greek sculpture celebrated the beauty of nude or near-nude individuals, including gods, as shown here in this statue of Poseidon, god of the sea. (B) In early Christian times, religious figures (except for Jesus on the cross) were shrouded in all-concealing clothing, as in this eighth-century Byzantine mosaic from Ravenna, Italy.

---

*In the study, researchers from the University of California, Santa Barbara, arranged for exotic dancers to expose themselves, fully naked or with genitals covered, to customers. In questionnaires filled out immediately after the show, the customers exposed to the fully naked dancers reported greater erotic arousal. The study was done in response to a Supreme Court ruling that stated that banning nude dancing did not violate the dancers' First Amendment right to free expression because the "messages" received by the customers were the same whether the dancers were clothed or naked.

** Exposure of the glans of the penis was considered offensive, so athletes often tied off their foreskins to prevent this from happening.

**sexting** Sending sexually explicit text or images via cellphone.

theCHIVE.com—stop short of showing women's nipples or vulvas. Streakers are arrested. And even a man showing up shirtless at a college lecture would probably be met with negative reactions, if only from the professor. State nudity laws vary, but even in states such as California that don't ban public nudity as such, exposing the genitals becomes a misdemeanor if anyone is offended by it.

On the other hand, a more permissive culture has developed in semiprivate settings, especially among young people. The sending of sexually explicit "selfies" by cell phone—**sexting**—is a fairly common practice among high school students (Patchin & Hinduja, 2019), though one that can have legal ramifications (see Chapter 17). Pornography—increasingly viewed by couples or groups—has desensitized many people to naked bodies. Nudity is common in certain environments such as private pools and hot tubs, as well as at "clothing optional" hotels, cruises, and beaches. Women may breastfeed their babies in public—a practice protected by state and federal laws and even encouraged by Pope Francis (Davies, 2014). And alcohol may facilitate the shedding of clothes in some social situations.

Nowhere is the collision between these two cultures more evident than in San Francisco. That city has seen more than its share of nudity over the years, starting with the hippie years of the 1970s. Nude or near-nude people have been common sights in parades, runs, and street fairs, as well as in public spaces in general. In part this may reflect the fact that 60% of Californians claim not to be offended by public nudity (Naturist Education Foundation, 2009). Nevertheless, public opposition to nudity was strong enough that in 2012 San Francisco enacted an ordinance banning nudity in most public spaces, except during permitted parades (Wollan, 2012). (The ordinance did not apply to women's breasts.) The ban triggered nude demonstrations and protest marches. Naked bicycle rides have become a familiar form of nudist activism, not only in San Francisco but in many other cities in the United States and overseas (**FIGURE 3.22**).

If a state or local law prohibits women, but not men, from appearing topless in public, is that unconstitutional discrimination against women? Not according to the Supreme Court of New Hampshire, which upheld a Laconia city ordinance banning topless sunbathing by women only (Associated Press, 2019). In 2020 the U.S. Supreme Court declined to hear an appeal of the case, so for the moment at least it is permissible to apply different legal criteria regarding nudity in women and men (Hurley, 2020).

▶ **FIGURE 3.22 Nude activists** These are participants in a World Naked Bike Ride event in London's Hyde Park.

© Simon Greenwood/Getty Images

# Summary

- The male external genitalia comprise the penis and the scrotum. A man's penis contains three erectile structures and encloses the urethra. Its erotic sensitivity is highest on the glans and frenulum. The foreskin, which covers the glans, is removed in circumcision. Circumcision offers some health advantages, but the prevalence of this operation in the United States is decreasing.

- Health problems affecting the penis include inflammation of the glans (balanitis), inability to retract the foreskin (phimosis), entrapment of the foreskin behind the glans (paraphimosis), pathological curvature of the penis (Peyronie's disease), and penile cancer.

- Penile erection, like clitoral erection, involves vasocongestion. The vascular spaces (sinusoids) fill with blood, under the control of the autonomic nervous system. The neurotransmitter nitric oxide plays a key role in this process.

- The scrotum contains the testicles and has muscular and vascular mechanisms for maintaining them below the internal body temperature.

- A man's internal reproductive structures include six paired structures—the left and right testicle, epididymis, vas deferens, seminal vesicle, ejaculatory duct, and bulbourethral gland—as well as two unpaired midline structures, the prostate gland and urethra.

- The testicles contain seminiferous tubules, in which sperm are produced. Between the seminiferous tubules lie interstitial cells, which secrete sex steroids, including testosterone. The most important health problem affecting the testicles is testicular cancer. This can affect young men, but it is one of the most curable cancers.

- The epididymis is the location where sperm mature and become more concentrated. The vas deferens stores sperm and transports them to the urethra. Sperm constitute only about 1% of the volume of the ejaculate.

- The prostate gland and seminal vesicles add the noncellular portion of semen, which consists of proteins, enzymes, antioxidants, water, salts, fructose, and buffers. The bulbourethral glands produce a slippery secretion ("pre-cum") that may be discharged from the urethra in small amounts before ejaculation.

- The prostate gland can be affected by inflammation (prostatitis), age-related enlargement (benign prostatic hyperplasia), and prostate cancer. It is possible to screen for prostate cancer by regular digital rectal examination and by a blood test (PSA test). The treatments for prostate cancer often have a serious impact on a man's sex life.

- Sexual functions are regulated by the nervous and endocrine systems. Erection of the penis and the clitoris involves a spinal reflex that begins with stimulation of nerve endings in the genital skin. Inputs from the brain powerfully modulate these reflexes. Erection involves the filling with blood of spongy tissue—the corpora cavernosa and corpus spongiosum. The neurotransmitter nitric oxide promotes erection.

- Seminal emission is the loading of the various glandular components of semen into the urethra. It is followed quickly by ejaculation, in which muscular contractions squeeze the urethra and eject the semen in a sequence of pulses from the urethra. Orgasm is the subjective pleasurable experience that usually accompanies ejaculation, along with the physiological events that underlie it.

- In men, testosterone levels and sperm production are regulated by a negative feedback hormonal loop. This involves GnRH secreted by the hypothalamus, the gonadotropins LH and FSH secreted by the pituitary, and testosterone secreted by the testes.

- Testosterone supports the normal structure and function of male genital tissues, has a broad anabolic (tissue-building) effect, guides development in a male direction, and stimulates sexual feelings and behavior. Estrogens are required for sperm development, termination of bone growth after puberty, and maintenance of bone density.

- Most societies prohibit public exposure of the genitals, apparently to regulate sexual arousal and minimize sexual conflicts. Contemporary American attitudes toward nudity vary greatly.

## Discussion Questions

1. How would you advise a couple who asked your opinion regarding whether they should have their son circumcised?

2. Do you consider female and male circumcision ethically equivalent?

3. If a man who is concerned about his small penis wants to have it enlarged surgically, would you consider that a good idea or not, and why?

The **Discovering Human Sexuality** digital resources include activities, animations, flashcards, web links, chapter outlines and summaries, and other study tools.

Learn more with this chapter's digital tools, including the **Oxford Insight Study Guide**, at **oup.com/he/levay5e**.

4. Some have suggested that the problem of illicit steroid use by athletes could be solved by legalizing such use. Do you think that this could be done safely and fairly?

5. Do you think that women and men should be equally entitled to appear topless in public?

## Web Resources

Anatomy Zone: Introduction to male reproductive anatomy **tinyurl.com/lpzruor**

Erection Photos **tinyurl.com/lqjx3of**

Guttmacher Institute: In their own right: Addressing the sexual and reproductive health needs of men worldwide **tinyurl.com/mcfbnur**

Morris, B. J. "Male Circumcision Guide for Doctors, Parents, Adults & Teens: Circumcision: An evidence-based appraisal" **www.circinfo.net**

National Cancer Institute (site with extensive sections on prostate and testicular cancer) **www.cancer.gov**

National Organization of Circumcision Information Resource Centers (NOCIRC) (an anti-circumcision advocacy group) **www.nocirc.org**

Naturist Society **www.naturistsociety.com**

Office on Women's Health. Men's health (There is no federal Office on Men's Health!) **tinyurl.com/km2usaf**

Prostate Cancer Foundation **www.pcf.org**

Prostatitis Foundation **www.prostatitis.org**

Sharpe, L. & Royal, C. Why does semen get stickier in the shower? (a funny and informative Claymation video) **https://tinyurl.com/h5e5o8c**

University of Delaware. Male reproductive system (histology site) **tinyurl.com/lg6594f**

## Recommended Reading

Dodsworth, L. (2017). *Manhood: The bare reality*. Pinter & Martin. (A collection of photos of men's genitals and what the men have to say about them.)

Ellsworth, P. (2014). *100 questions and answers about prostate cancer* (4th ed.). Jones & Bartlett.

Komisaruk, B. R., Beyer-Flores, C. & Whipple, B. (2006). *The science of orgasm*. Johns Hopkins University Press.

McCarthy, B. W. & Metz, M. E. (2007). *Men's sexual heath: Fitness for satisfying sex*. Routledge.

Scardino, P. & Kelman, J. (2010). *Dr. Peter Scardino's prostate book* (2nd ed.). Avery.

Spitz, A. (2018). *The penis book: A doctor's complete guide to the penis*. Rodale.

Heterosexual couple? No—a single model photographed in both female and male gender roles.

# 4

# Sex Development and Diversity

In this chapter we discuss how men and women come to differ from each other. First we describe the origins of the physical sex differences that have been the topics of previous chapters. A cascade of genetic and hormonal factors, operating during both prenatal and postnatal life, guides this process of differentiation. There are also psychological sex differences—in cognition, personality, and sexuality. These differences are also influenced by biological factors, but they are only one part of the story, because social factors also play a role.

A simple male/female dichotomy encompasses most people, but by no means all. In terms of physical differences, there are intersex individuals—those whose anatomical sex is to some degree intermediate or ambiguous. Intersexuality results from unusual genetic or hormonal conditions during development. In terms of mental traits, there are transgender and non-binary individuals—those whose internal sense of their own sex is partially or fully discordant with their anatomical sex at birth. The developmental pathways that lead to a transgender identity are not well understood, but here too biological factors are thought to play some role.

Both intersex and transgender people face many challenges in life, ranging from personal medical issues to broader questions about their position and role in society. Studying and listening to these individuals not only helps us understand their specific circumstances, but also teaches us something about the limitations of terms like "male" and "female," "masculine" and "feminine."

# 4.1 Genes and Hormones Guide Sex Development

## LEARNING OBJECTIVES

After reading this section you should be able to:

4.1.1 Name the sex chromosomes possessed by females and males and explain how this sex difference arises.

4.1.2 Name the precursors of the female and male reproductive tracts, describe what happens to them in both sexes, and identify the hormones that control these events.

4.1.3 Identify homologous structures in the external genitals of females and males, and the common embryonic structures from which they develop.

4.1.4 Describe or sketch how sex hormone levels change from conception to old age in females and males.

**chromosome**  One of the 46 rod-like structures in human cell nuclei that carry a person's DNA.

**homologous**  Corresponding—e.g. carrying the same genes.

**sex chromosome**  Either chromosome (X or Y) of a pair that differs between the sexes.

**X chromosome**  A sex chromosome that is present in two copies in females and one copy in males.

**Y chromosome**  A sex chromosome that is only present in males.

**SRY**  A gene located on the Y chromosome (*Sex-determining Region* of the *Y* chromosome) that causes the embryo to develop as a male.

**Chromosomes** are enormously long but tightly packed sequences of DNA, the molecular carrier of our genetic inheritance. Almost every human cell possesses 46 chromosomes packed into its nucleus, and these come in 23 pairs (**FIGURE 4.1**). The two members of each pair are **homologous**, meaning that they possess copies of the same genes. One chromosome of each pair is inherited from the individual's mother, and one from the father. Under the microscope the two members of each pair are indistinguishable, but each pair of chromosomes has a different appearance from the other pairs.

One of the 23 pairs, now known as the **sex chromosomes**, is an exception to this rule. As already mentioned in Chapter 1, American geneticist Nettie Stevens discovered that male and female animals, including humans, have different complements of sex chromosomes. Females possess a homologous pair of large chromosomes, now known as **X chromosomes**, whereas males carry only one X chromosome, along with a much smaller **Y chromosome**.

One of the sex chromosomes is inherited from the individual's mother, via her ovum; this is always an X. The other is inherited from the person's father, via his sperm. This can be either an X or a Y, because a man's semen contains an approximately equal mixture of X- and Y-bearing sperm. Thus, with rare exceptions, it is the father's genetic contribution to the embryo that determines its sex.

A sex-determining gene called **SRY**, located on the Y chromosome, is the initial switch whose presence (in XY embryos) directs sexual development along a male pathway, and

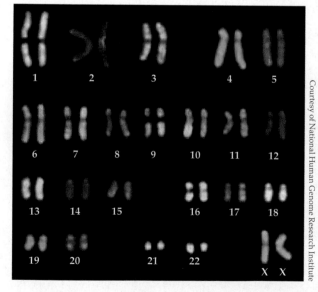
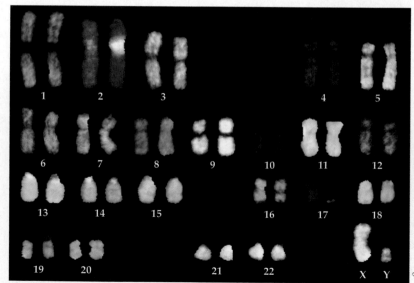

Courtesy of National Human Genome Research Institute

© Phanie/VOISIN/Medical Images

▲ **FIGURE 4.1**  **Human chromosomes** in a woman (left) and a man (right). Women have two X chromosomes, men have one X and one Y. The other 22 pairs of chromosomes are the same. Here, the individual chromosomes have been labeled with a variety of fluorescent chemical probes, each of which binds to the DNA of a single chromosome to identify it. The differences in appearance of the chromosomes in the woman and man are not meaningful: They result from different processing.

whose absence (in XX embryos) allows development to follow a female pathway. Many more genes, linked together in complex networks, are required for the formation of the gonads—the ovaries in females or the testes in males—and for sexual differentiation of the genitals and reproductive tracts (Witchel, 2018). Female development also requires the activity of genes that suppress male development. Thus it may be misleading to describe female development as the "default pathway," as if it somehow happens without active guidance. Because of the complexity of these sex-determining networks, the end result is not always a clear-cut male or a clear-cut female baby, as we will see later.

## Female and male reproductive tracts develop from different precursors

For the first several weeks of development there is no visible difference between female and male embryos. At about 6 weeks after conception, early in the development of the gonads, two pairs of ducts run from the gonads to the outside of the embryonic body at the future site of the external genitalia (**FIGURE 4.2A**). One pair,

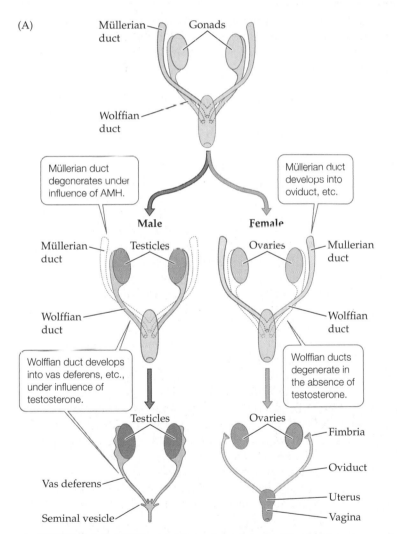

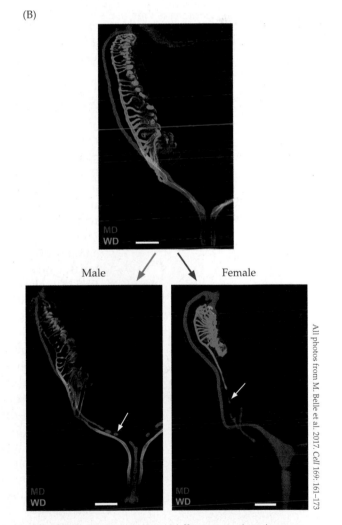

All photos from M. Belle et al. 2017. *Cell* 169: 161–173

▲ **FIGURE 4.2** **Male and female reproductive tracts** develop from different precursor structures (A), the Wolffian and Müllerian ducts. (The male and female gonads [testes and ovaries] have a common origin and do not belong to either duct system.) (See **Animation 4.1: Development of the Male and Female Reproductive Tracts**.) These micrographs of developing reproductive tracts in human embryos (B) are labeled with fluorescent probes. The sexually undifferentiated embryo at 9.5 weeks gestation (top) shows the presence of both Wolffian (blue) and Müllerian (pink) ducts. The male embryo at 10 weeks (bottom left) shows the Müllerian duct beginning to break up (arrow). The female embryo at 13 weeks (bottom right) shows the Wolffian duct beginning to break up (arrow). The white scale bars are 0.4 mm.

**Müllerian duct**  Either of two bilateral ducts in the embryo that give rise to the female reproductive tract.

**Wolffian duct**  Either of two bilateral ducts in the embryo that give rise to the male reproductive tract.

**anti-Müllerian hormone (AMH)**  A hormone secreted by the testes that prevents the development of the female reproductive tract.

**cloaca**  The common exit of the gastrointestinal and urogenital systems; in humans it is present only in embryonic life.

**urethral folds**  Folds of ectodermal tissue in the embryo that give rise to the inner labia (in females) or the shaft of the penis (in males).

**genital swellings**  Regions of the genitalia in the embryo that give rise to the outer labia (in females) or the scrotum (in males).

**genital tubercle**  A midline swelling in front of the cloaca, which gives rise to the glans of the clitoris (in females) or penis (in males).

**anal fold**  The posterior portion of the urethral fold, which gives rise to the anus.

**urogenital sinus**  The common opening of the urinary and genital systems in the embryo.

**hypospadias**  An abnormal location of the male urethral opening on the underside of the penis or elsewhere.

the **Müllerian ducts**, are the precursors of the female reproductive tract. The other pair, the **Wolffian ducts**, are the precursors of the male reproductive tract.

Notice that embryos of *both* sexes begin with a pair of *both* kinds of ducts. Female development involves eliminating the Wolffian ducts and promoting the development of the Müllerian ducts, while male development involves eliminating the Müllerian ducts and promoting the development of the Wolffian ducts. The breakup of the unwanted ducts in each sex is shown in **FIGURE 4.2B**.

Male embryos eliminate the Müllerian ducts by means of **anti-Müllerian hormone (AMH)**. This hormone, secreted by the developing testes, diffuses to the nearby Müllerian ducts and causes them to degenerate. Beginning at about 8 weeks after conception, the testes secrete testosterone. This hormone diffuses down the Wolffian ducts, triggering each one to develop into an epididymis, vas deferens, and seminal vesicle. Testosterone also promotes development of the prostate gland, although this gland is not derived from the Wolffian ducts.

In female embryos, the absence of testosterone causes the Wolffian ducts to degenerate. The absence of AMH allows the Müllerian ducts to persist and to develop into the oviducts, uterus, and deeper part of the vagina. These processes take place at a time when the developing structures are still tiny—note that the scale bars in Figure 4.2B are only 0.4 mm long—so it is a relatively easy matter for hormonal signals to spread from the testes to the ducts.

## Female and male external genitalia develop from the same precursors

Whereas the reproductive tracts of females and males develop from different precursors, the external genitalia of both females and males develop from the *same* early tissues. As shown in **FIGURE 4.3**, at about 4 weeks postconception the embryo's anogenital region consists of a slit known as the **cloaca**. The cloaca is closed by a membrane. It is flanked by two **urethral folds**, and to the side of each urethral fold is a raised region named the **genital swelling**. At the front end of the cloaca is a small midline protuberance called the **genital tubercle**. By 2 weeks later, the urethral folds have fused with each other near their posterior (rear) end. The portion behind the fusion point, called the **anal fold**, eventually becomes the anus. The region of the fusion itself becomes the perineum. Even in adults, the line of fusion is visible as a midline ridge or scar, which you can see on your own perineum with the help of a hand mirror or a phone camera. It is about twice as long in males as in females.

During the fetal period, the region in front of the fusion point, which includes the opening of the **urogenital sinus**, gives rise to the external genital structures in both sexes. As with the internal reproductive tracts, the female external genitalia develop by default—that is, in the absence of hormonal or other external signals. The genital swellings develop into the outer labia. The urethral folds develop into the inner labia, the outer one-third or so of the vagina, and the crura (deep erectile structures) of the clitoris (see Chapter 2). The genital tubercle develops into the glans of the clitoris. Remnants of the cloacal membrane persist as the hymen.

The vagina, therefore, develops from two different sets of tissues. The outer portion of the vagina, which develops from the urethral folds, is more muscular and more richly innervated than the inner portion, which develops from the Müllerian ducts.

In male fetuses, the presence of circulating testosterone, secreted by the testes, is required for the normal development of the genitalia. The urethral folds fuse at the midline, forming the shaft of the penis and enclosing the urethra. If this midline fusion is incomplete, a condition called **hypospadias** results, in which the urethra opens on the underside of the penis or behind the penis (Mayo Clinic, 2017a). The genital

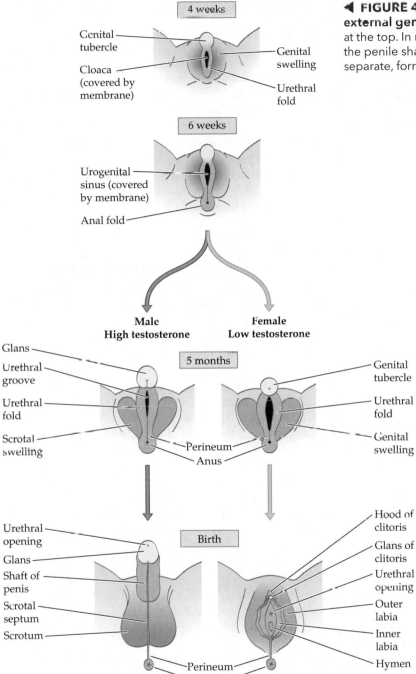

**4 weeks**

Genital tubercle
Cloaca (covered by membrane)
Genital swelling
Urethral fold

**6 weeks**

Urogenital sinus (covered by membrane)
Anal fold

**Male**
**High testosterone**

**Female**
**Low testosterone**

Glans
Urethral groove
Urethral fold
Scrotal swelling
**5 months**
Perineum
Anus
Genital tubercle
Urethral fold
Genital swelling

Urethral opening
Glans
Shaft of penis
Scrotal septum
Scrotum
**Birth**
Perineum
Anus
Hood of clitoris
Glans of clitoris
Urethral opening
Outer labia
Inner labia
Hymen

◀ **FIGURE 4.3  Development of the male and female external genitalia** from common precursor structures, shown at the top. In males, the urethral folds fuse at the midline to form the penile shaft and enclose the urethra. In females, they remain separate, forming the inner labia.

swellings also fuse at the midline, forming the scrotum. The genital tubercle expands to form the glans of the penis. The prostate gland develops—as the homologous paraurethral glands in females probably do—from tissue beneath the urethral folds.

Thus, the same embryonic structures that become the outer labia in females become the scrotum in males. The structures that become the inner labia in females become the shaft of the penis in males. The structure that becomes the glans of the clitoris becomes the glans of the penis in males. These male and female structures are considered homologous because they arise from the same precursors in the two sexes.

(A)

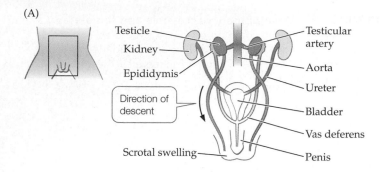

(B)

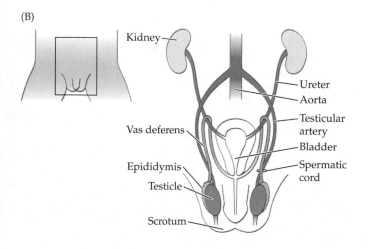

◀ **FIGURE 4.4** **Descent of the testicles** (A) Before descent, at 10 weeks, a fibrous cord (shown here in blue) attaches each testicle to the region of the scrotal swelling. (B) As the fetal body grows, this attachment pulls each testicle down and into the scrotum. Note how the vas deferens (green) and the testicular artery (pink) are pulled after the testicle and how the vas deferens comes to loop over the ureter (the tube, shown here in orange, that carries urine from the kidney to the bladder).

Why isn't female development driven by secretion of estrogens from fetal ovaries in the same way that male development is activated by testosterone from fetal tissues? The answer is probably that fetuses of *both* sexes are exposed to estrogens coming from the mother's body. Thus, if estrogens were the driver for female-typical development, male fetuses too would follow that pathway, at least to some degree.

## The gonads descend during development

In fetuses of both sexes, the gonads (ovaries and testes) begin their development in an area near the kidneys and later move downward. By about 10 weeks postconception they are positioned near the top of the pelvis. In females, the ovaries remain in this position for the remainder of fetal life, but after birth they gradually descend in the pelvis and end up on either side of the uterus.

In males the testes, which may now be called testicles, move even greater distances (**FIGURE 4.4**). At 6 to 7 months postconception they descend into the pelvis, and shortly before birth they move down into the scrotum. As each testicle enters the scrotum, it draws various structures with it, including the vas deferens, blood vessels, and nerves—which make up the spermatic cord. The connection between the pelvic cavity and the testicles is usually sealed off after the testicles descend.

In about 2% of full-term newborn boys, one or both testicles have not yet arrived in the scrotum. In many of these boys, the tardy testicles will arrive within a few weeks after birth, but if they are still no-shows when a boy reaches 3 months of age, the condition is considered a disorder and is termed **cryptorchidism** or simply undescended testicles (Mayo Clinic, 2017b). Usually, the missing testicles have been held up somewhere along the path of their fetal descent—most commonly in the groin. Cryptorchidism is associated with lowered fertility and a doubling in the risk of testicular cancer after puberty (Schneuer et al., 2018). Undescended testicles can usually be moved into the scrotum by a surgical procedure. This is best done before 18 months of age, because if it is delayed, the risk of cancer or infertility increases further.

## Sex hormone levels change over the lifespan

Most prenatal sex development occurs during weeks 8 through 24 of fetal life, when testosterone levels are much higher in male than in female fetuses (**FIGURE 4.5**). A second surge in testosterone production (to adult levels) occurs in males for the first 6 months of postnatal life: This postnatal surge is sometimes called the "mini-puberty." Further maturation of the genitals, including lengthening of the penis, takes place during this time. After that, testosterone levels fall and remain low until **puberty**, the transition to sexual maturity, when they rise to about the same level as during the postnatal "mini-puberty." Testosterone levels then decline gradually over a man's adult lifespan.

In females, both estrogen and testosterone levels are low from conception until puberty, after which the ovaries secrete both estrogen and testosterone, and the levels of the two hormones, as well as progesterone, rise and fall periodically with the

**FAQ:** My baby's testicles did descend, but they're not there anymore. What happened?

The testicles of male infants and toddlers may spend quite a bit of time pulled upward and out of sight by the cremaster muscle. That's not a matter of concern so long as they did complete their original descent.

**cryptorchidism** Failure of one or both testicles to descend into the scrotum by 3 months of postnatal age.

**puberty** The transition to sexual maturity.

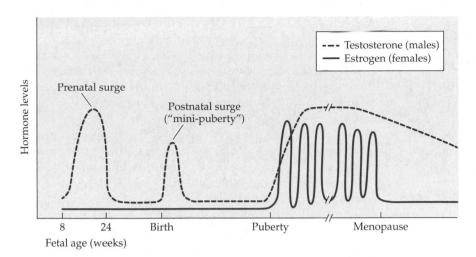

◀ **FIGURE 4.5** **Hormones over the lifespan** This is a highly schematic representation of the levels of testosterone in males and estrogen in females from conception through old age, ignoring pregnancy. Progesterone levels are not shown.

woman's menstrual periods, as was already described in Chapter 2, and they fall again to low levels at menopause. The hormonal events associated with pregnancy, in which progesterone plays a key role, are described in Chapter 8.

Because of the great impact of puberty on psychosexual development, we postpone most of our discussion of this crucial transition to Chapter 10.

At the onset of puberty the testicles and the ovaries begin secreting sex hormones at levels sufficient to initiate reproductive maturity, and the bodies and brains of girls and boys begin to transform into those of women and men.

## The brain also differentiates sexually

Although women's and men's brains are very similar, early hormonal influences do produce some differences in brain organization. After adjustment for sex differences in overall brain volume, at least 10 brain regions are larger, on average, in women than in men, and at least 14 regions are larger in men than in women (Ritchie et al., 2018). The cerebral cortex is a mosaic of regions that are larger in one sex or the other (**FIGURE 4.6**). Considering any one of these regions individually, there is a great deal of overlap in size between women and men, but by measuring a number of these

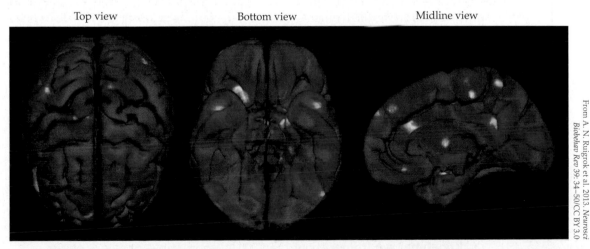

▲ **FIGURE 4.6** **Sex differences in the cerebral cortex** Regions that are larger in women are shown in red; those that are larger in men are shown in blue. Note that the sex differences are not the same in the left and right hemispheres. These images are based on a meta-analysis of numerous quantitative brain-imaging studies.

**disorders of sex development**
Medical conditions producing anomalous sexual differentiation or intersexuality.

**Klinefelter syndrome** A collection of traits caused by the possession of one or more extra X chromosomes in a male (XXY or XXXY).

**Turner syndrome** A collection of traits caused by the possession of one X and no Y chromosome.

**XYY syndrome** A collection of traits caused by the possession, in a male, of an extra Y chromosome.

**triple-X syndrome** A collection of traits caused by the possession, in a female, of three X chromosomes rather than two.

regions it is possible to identify the sex of an individual brain with 93% accuracy (Chekroud et al., 2016; Anderson et al., 2019). Some subcortical regions that play a specific role in sexual behavior, such as a region within the hypothalamus, show even more pronounced differences between the sexes, as will be described in Chapter 12.

There are also sex differences in connections within the brain (Ritchie et al., 2018) as well as in the metabolism of neurotransmitters such as serotonin and dopamine (Barth et al., 2015). Such differences offer a potential explanation for differences in the prevalence of certain mental disorders in the two sexes, such as the greater prevalence of mood disorders (anxiety, depression) among women and the greater prevalence of autism spectrum disorder and alcoholism in men (Li & Graham, 2017).

The difference in circulating androgen levels in the two sexes (higher levels in males than in females) is the main driver of the early sexual differentiation in the brain, as it is in the rest of the body. The brain also "knows" its own intrinsic sex, however, in the sense that the nucleus of each brain cell carries the sex chromosomes corresponding to that individual's sex—XX or XY in most cases. These two influences can be disentangled in experimental animals such as mice. It has been shown, for example, that mice with chromosomally male brains make a greater effort to obtain rewards, such as food, than do those with chromosomally female brains, even in the absence of any hormonal sex differences (Arnold et al., 2016).

## 4.2 Sex Development Is Not Always Binary

### LEARNING OBJECTIVES
After reading this section you should be able to:

4.2.1 Give two examples of disorders of sex development that are caused by atypical complements of sex chromosomes, and name the chromosomal patterns that cause them.

4.2.2 Explain how a chromosomally male fetus develops if it carries a mutation that makes it insensitive to androgens.

4.2.3 Explain the possible anatomical and psychological effects of congenital adrenal hyperplasia.

4.2.4 Explain the sexual development of a chromosomally male individual that lacks the enzyme 5-alpha-reductase.

Given the complexity of the genetic and hormonal cascade that guides sex development, it is perhaps surprising how regularly it leads to one of two binary end points—a healthy, fertile woman or man. Yet deviations from typical female or male development do sometimes occur. Some of these are harmless variations that should be considered examples of sexual diversity—they are differences rather than disorders. Others, however, impair fertility or other aspects of physical health, or are even life-threatening if untreated, and are therefore called **disorders of sex development** (Witchel, 2018). Some examples of these disorders are discussed below.

### Unusual sets of chromosomes affect growth and fertility

The standard sets of sex chromosomes are XX (female) and XY (male), but other combinations are possible. These can arise during cell divisions in the production of ova or sperm, or during the first cell division after fertilization. Embryos with atypical numbers of sex chromosomes are very common, but the great majority die early in development. Among those that survive, the following are the most common variations (Skuse et al., 2018):

- **Klinefelter syndrome**. About 1 in 1,000 live-born babies possesses one or more extra X chromosomes (XXY or XXXY). These individuals are male because they possess a Y chromosome with its SRY gene, which masculinizes their bodies. Some XXY and XXXY males are indistinguishable from XY

**FAQ:** Will a man with Klinefelter syndrome pass it on to his children?

No. He will need medical assistance to become a father, but any children he does have are very unlikely to have Klinefelter syndrome.

males, and these men may not learn that they have an unusual complement of sex chromosomes unless they try, unsuccessfully, to father a child. Others, however, experience a characteristic collection of medical conditions. As children they may have slow motor development and delayed speech. Puberty may be delayed or absent. Men with Klinefelter syndrome commonly have low testosterone levels, small testicles, sparse body and facial hair, and some breast development. They are also generally taller than average (**FIGURE 4.7**). Most XXY and XXXY males have a low sperm count, and they are usually infertile. Regarding their sexual orientation, it is often stated that men with Klinefelter syndrome are no more likely to be gay or bisexual than men in the general population. The limited available evidence, however, suggests that this assumption may be incorrect. In one study, 10.1% of men with Klinefelter syndrome identified as gay or bisexual, as compared to 1.5% of men in a control group—a highly significant difference (Skakkebaek, 2018). Nevertheless the great majority of men with Klinefelter syndrome, including the teenager in the figure, identify as heterosexual.

- **Turner syndrome**. About 1 in 2,500 live-born children has one X chromosome and no Y chromosome (XO). They are girls, since they lack the Y chromosome and its SRY gene. These girls tend to be short, with a characteristic broad chest and neck. They lack functional ovaries, and without medical assistance they do not enter puberty and are infertile. Some may have cognitive deficits, but they are not intellectually disabled (Hong & Reiss, 2014): Women with Turner syndrome have excelled in a variety of careers (**FIGURE 4.8**). Many women with Turner syndrome are actually "mosaics," meaning that their bodies are composed of both XO and XX cells; these women have a milder form of the syndrome (Hook & Warburton, 2014).

- **XYY syndrome**. About 1 in 1,000 babies possesses one X chromosome and two Y chromosomes. They are male, but they may have atypical genital anatomy and low fertility. The cerebral cortex develops in an atypical fashion, intelligence tends to be low, and autism-related symptoms are common (Bryant et al., 2012; Lepage et al., 2014).

- **Triple-X syndrome**. About 1 in 1,000 newborns possesses three X chromosomes (XXX). These babies are girls. They commonly have atypical facial features (wide-set eyes and dental problems) and they may have learning disabilities, but not all XXX girls are affected.

Infertility or impaired fertility are issues that affect the great majority of people with unusual sets of sex chromosomes. Some of them can become parents with the help of assisted reproductive technologies (see Chapter 8).

## The gonads or genitals may be sexually ambiguous

Some disorders of sex development cause the gonads or the genitals to end up in a state that is intermediate between male and female forms or has some features of

▲ **FIGURE 4.7  Klinefelter syndrome** 13-year-old Luke is tall for his age but otherwise physically unremarkable. An interview with him is viewable online at tinyurl.com/u455ybu. People with Klinefelter syndrome vary greatly in physical appearance.

▶ **FIGURE 4.8  Turner syndrome** Dr. Catherine Ward-Melver is a geneticist at Akron Children's Hospital, in Ohio, and past president of the Turner Syndrome Society. Her short stature (4 feet 8 inches, or 1.42 m) is a feature of Turner syndrome.

**intersex** Having a biologically ambiguous or intermediate sex.

**ovotesticular disorder** The possession of both testicular and ovarian tissue in the same individual.

**androgen insensitivity syndrome (AIS)** The congenital absence of a functional androgen receptor, making the body unable to respond to androgens.

**congenital adrenal hyperplasia (CAH)** A congenital defect of hormonal metabolism in the adrenal gland, causing the gland to secrete excessive levels of androgens.

**5-alpha-reductase deficiency** A lack of the enzyme that converts testosterone to 5-alpha-dihydrotestosterone.

both. Persons affected by such conditions may be referred to as (or describe themselves as) **intersex**. Here are some examples:

- **Ovotesticular disorder.** In this rare condition, the affected person possesses both ovarian and testicular tissue—either on different sides of the body or in gonads that contain mixtures of the two tissues. The cause is not usually known, but chromosomal anomalies may be responsible. The appearance of the external genitalia varies, but most persons with this condition look like women and identify as such. They are usually infertile, and they are at increased risk of urinary problems and gonadal (testicular or ovarian) cancer.

- **Androgen insensitivity syndrome (AIS).** This is a genetic condition in XY individuals in which androgen receptors are completely or partially nonfunctional. People with complete AIS lack the reproductive tract of either sex and are therefore infertile: The male tract fails to develop because the Wolffian ducts are insensitive to testosterone, and the female tract fails to develop because the testes still secrete anti-Müllerian hormone. The external genitalia look typically female at birth. The outer part of the vagina does develop, but it is short and blind ending; it can be lengthened by the use of dilators or by surgery in order to permit coitus, if that is desired. The testicles remain inside the body, and they are usually removed surgically at some point on account of a heightened risk of cancer. Persons with complete AIS look like and identify as females, and their condition often remains unrecognized until puberty, when they fail to menstruate. The external changes associated with female puberty can be induced by administration of sex hormones. Individuals with partial AIS have a more variable anatomy, appearance, and sense of which sex they are (see "Gender identity does not always match anatomical sex," below). Some men with a very mild version of AIS may be able to father children.

- **Congenital adrenal hyperplasia (CAH).** This condition is caused by a mutation in one of the genes involved in steroid metabolism. As a result the adrenal glands secrete insufficient levels of the steroids that control salt and water balance, and severe forms of the disorder are fatal if untreated. The adrenals also secrete unusually high levels of androgens. In XX fetuses, which otherwise would develop into typical girls, the high levels of androgens cause a partial masculinization of the genitals: The clitoris is often enlarged, for example, and the labia may be partially fused in the midline (**FIGURE 4.9**). These changes can be prevented by noninvasive prenatal testing and treatment (Kazmi et al., 2017). Most children with CAH are raised as girls, but some children with very marked masculinization are raised as boys.

- **5-alpha-reductase deficiency.** 5-alpha-reductase is the enzyme, present in target tissues such as the genitals, that converts testosterone to the more potent androgen 5α-dihydrotestosterone (DHT) (see Chapter 3). DHT is required for typical male development of the external genitals, but not of the brain. The rare XY babies who lack a functional 5-alpha-reductase enzyme, and who therefore produce no DHT, possess functional testes,

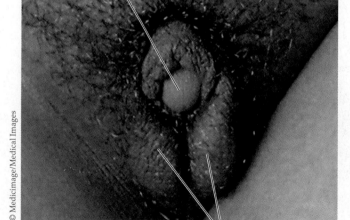

Enlarged clitoris

Fused labia

© Medicimage/Medical Images

▲ **FIGURE 4.9 Partial masculinization of genitalia** in a girl with congenital adrenal hyperplasia. Note that the fused labia resemble scrotal sacs, but they do not contain testicles.

but their external genitalia look female, and they are commonly raised as girls. When they reach puberty, however, the massive increase in testosterone levels is sufficient to at least partially masculinize their genitals and other target tissues, even without the presence of DHT. As a result, these children come to look more like males, both in their genitals and in their general appearance, and from then on they are usually treated as men. Perhaps on account of their brains' exposure to testosterone prenatally, most of these youths willingly embrace their new gender role (Mendonca et al., 2016).

The existence of these various conditions makes clear that a person's sex, or their intersex status, can be defined by several different criteria, which are not necessarily all in agreement with each other:

- **Chromosomal sex** means the possession of XX, XY, or some other complement of sex chromosomes.
- **Gonadal sex** means the possession of ovaries, testes, or a combination of the two.
- **Anatomical sex** usually refers to the possession of the external genitalia typical of females or males, or not clearly one or the other. (Gonadal sex is anatomical too, of course, but this is not so apparent without diagnostic procedures.)
- **Natal sex** means anatomical sex at birth.
- **Assigned sex** means the sex assigned to newborns by doctors or parents. This nearly always corresponds to natal sex, but babies with ambiguous genitals may be assigned to one sex or the other by poorly defined or arbitrary criteria.

For many children with ambiguous genitalia, the cause is not known. Whatever the cause, however, treatment of these children raises a host of difficult ethical questions. Should the child be assigned to one sex or the other, and if so, should the child's genitals be surgically altered in order to bring them into greater conformity with the assigned sex? What should the child be told, and as which sex should the child be raised?

Partly in response to activism by people with intersex conditions, there has been a movement away from early surgery, unless it is medically essential. The idea is to postpone irreversible decisions until affected children are able to make known their own wishes and play an informed role in the decision-making process (Lee et al., 2016). The secrecy and denial that often surround these cases are harmful to children's psychological development and self-acceptance, according to the testimony of intersex people (**BOX 4.1**). In 2017 a well-known supermodel, Hanne Gaby Odiele, came out as intersex (she has AIS) and appealed for an end to unnecessary surgery on intersex children (Wang, 2017).

Children and adults who have unusual sets of sex chromosomes, or who were born with genitals that are not clearly male or female, commonly run into difficulties in their social life. Sometimes these difficulties are truly problematic (**BOX 4.2**). More commonly, though, they could be alleviated or avoided if society didn't feel the need to shoehorn everyone into male or female categories, or if less emphasis were placed on a person's sex as a matter of social or legal significance.

Many people with intersex conditions have posted video blogs about themselves, which can easily be found on YouTube and elsewhere. We recommend that you view some of these blogs to get a better idea of the challenges—and sometimes the blessings—of living with a difference or disorder of sex development.

**chromosomal sex** An individual's sex based on their sex chromosomes.

**gonadal sex** An individual's sex based on their possession of testes or ovaries.

**anatomical sex** An individual's sex based on the appearance of their external genitalia.

**natal sex** A person's anatomical sex at birth.

**assigned sex** An individual's sex as categorized by doctors or others.

## BOX 4.1
# My Life with Androgen Insensitivity Syndrome

Katie Baratz Dalke graduated from the Perelman School of Medicine at the University of Pennsylvania in 2011; she is now a psychiatrist practicing in Philadelphia. She is active in the intersex support and advocacy communities, including with Inter/Act Legal, which supports the civil rights of children born with variations of sexual anatomy, and the AIS-DSD Support Group. She has published work in the area of sex development. She and her spouse recently welcomed a child with the help of a gestational surrogate. Baratz Dalke wrote the following essay for a previous edition of this textbook:

Courtesy of Samuel Dalke

Katie Baratz Dalke

*By all accounts, I was a perfectly healthy and normal baby girl, thriving under the love and attention of my family and constantly seeking opportunities to sing, dance, and try on my mother's dresses and jewelry—the more sparkles, the better!*

*My family's world changed forever when I was 6. That year, I collapsed in the shower with a painful lump in my groin. Convinced I had a hernia, my parents, both doctors, took me to the hospital. But when surgeons operated, they found a testicle that had started descending. Tests soon showed that instead of the typical XX chromosomes found in girls, I had the XY chromosomal complement of boys.*

*The doctor told my stunned parents that I had complete androgen insensitivity syndrome. He assured them that I would grow up normally, fall in love, and have a family through adoption, but they shouldn't tell me that I had XY chromosomes and testicles.*

*My parents did decide to tell me, but gradually. As a young girl, they showed me an anatomy book and told me that the uterus was the nest inside a woman where the baby grew. I didn't have one, but I could adopt a baby that would grow in my heart and be part of my family. I learned about periods and knew I wouldn't get them. Although I was sad that I wouldn't be able to become pregnant and felt different from my girlfriends, I thought that was it—until I turned 16.*

*That year, my sister came home from school with a biology project. Everyone in her class was assigned a condition to research, and she randomly drew AIS. "Mom and Dad, it sounds a lot like Katie," she said at dinner*

*one night. "And there's a woman with Mom's name on the support group website." My parents looked at each other. They'd wanted to wait until I was 18, but there was no going back now. They told me and my brother and sister everything. My dad finished up by saying, "You're still our girl."*

*I was devastated and angry, feeling betrayed by my parents and my own body. Looking back, I know those emotions came from a fear of what was wrong with me, plus the eternal conflict of adolescence: someone else deciding what's best for you.*

*High school was grim. I went through puberty very late, and was taller and thinner than most of the boys all the way through senior year. I had horrible insomnia and tons of anxiety that sometimes veered into depression. I felt as if all of my girl friends were living a life I couldn't access, one marked by the common experiences of periods, dating, and an effortless transition to womanhood. I, on the other hand, had to take estrogen pills to develop a womanly figure, and I had to use a vaginal dilator for 30 minutes a day so that I could comfortably have sex.*

*College was better. In my senior year, I met Sam, a runner and English major with a romantic streak. We started talking, and before I knew it, he was courting me with chocolate-covered strawberries and Marilyn Monroe movies. Shortly after we began dating, I knew that it was time to tell him about my AIS. He listened patiently and assured me that nothing about my genes or gonads changed the way he felt about me.*

*Four years later, we were married on an unseasonably warm New Year's Eve, surrounded by our friends, family, and yes, lots of sparkles. We are beginning our lives together and planning to adopt our children, although I still feel pangs of sadness when I think about how much I'd like to be able to have children biologically.*

*I'm also really involved in the AIS community. It feels incredible to help others with the pain I went through—it was only after finding the AIS Support Group, the summer before college, that I realized AIS could be part of my life without dominating it, and that the loneliness I'd felt abated.*

## BOX 4.2
## Intersex and Sports

In 2018 the International Association of Athletics Federations (IAAF) issued new rules concerning sports participation by women with raised testosterone levels that are caused by an intersex condition. The rules stated that such women must lower their testosterone levels by the use of drugs for at least 6 months prior to competition, if they wish to participate in events where high testosterone levels are known to confer an advantage. The only exception is for women with androgen insensitivity syndrome.

Caster Semenya, an internationally dominant South African runner who identifies and competes as a woman, has XY chromosomes and testosterone levels well above the typical female range. She was therefore banned from competing in the middle-distance track events in which she excels. The ban was upheld on appeal (Court of Arbitration for Sport, 2019).

Decisions of this kind are highly controversial. On the one hand, they traumatize women who did nothing wrong and who often had no idea of their unusual biological status. On the other hand, other athletes whose testosterone levels are within the typical female range may believe that they have no chance of winning against women such as Semenya, any more than they would against a man, or against a woman who raises her testosterone levels artificially by doping. What is your opinion on this question?

Semenya has refused hormone treatment, and she may train for distances other than those from which she has been excluded. "A determined spirit is unstoppable," she tweeted in 2019, and she has received widespread support, including from such sports stars as the former world number one tennis player, Billie Jean King. The IAAF has not softened its stance, for the moment at least, stating that "there are some contexts, sport being one of them, where biology has to trump gender identity" (Mather & Longman, 2019).

Caster Semenya

# 4.3 There Are Sex Differences in Many Mental Traits

### LEARNING OBJECTIVES
After reading this section you should be able to:

4.3.1 Give examples of gender differences in areas other than sexuality.
4.3.2 Give examples of gender differences in the area of sexuality.

There are no measurable mental traits that distinguish unambiguously between men and women, nor, at the other extreme, are there likely to be many that are quantitatively identical in the two sexes. When we talk about psychological sex differences we are talking about matters of degree and not absolute differences.

Still, some sex differences are marked enough to raise important questions about their origin and their impacts on our lives. We first describe some of these differences, without regard to causation. We then go on to discuss theories about how the differences arise.

**gender identity** A person's subjective sense of being male, female, or not exclusively one or the other.

**transgender (or trans)** Having a gender identity that is not fully congruent with one's birth sex.

**sexual orientation** Sexual attraction toward persons of the other sex (heterosexual), the same sex (homosexual), both sexes (bisexual), or neither sex (asexual).

**cognitive** Related to the aspects of the mind that process knowledge or information.

**personality** The collection of mental and behavioral traits, especially those related to emotions and attitudes, that characterizes an individual.

## Gender identity does not always match anatomical sex

In its simplest conception, a person's **gender identity** is their response to the question "Do you feel as if you are a woman or a man?" The great majority of people give the answer that we would expect based on their natal sex, but a few individuals give a different answer: natal women who say they feel like men and natal men who say they feel like women. Such individuals are **transgender**. There are others for whom neither "female" nor "male" satisfactorily describes how they think about themselves.

The existence of transgender individuals, discussed in greater detail later in the chapter, makes us realize that there must be something more to gender identity than simply reporting on one's genitals. At the risk of oversimplifying a complex topic, we can say that sex is the *objective* male/female/other, whereas gender identity is the *subjective* male/female/other, and the two are not always in agreement.

## Women and men differ in a variety of cognitive and personality traits

Some sex differences are seen in aspects of mental life having to do with perception, motor performance, reasoning, judgments, knowledge, and memory—collectively referred to as **cognitive** traits. All cognitive sex differences relate to *averages*; they do not predict the performance of any individual. That said, females (both women and girls) outperform males in reading, writing, and other verbal skills (Reilly et al., 2019) and in fine finger movements, as well as in the ability to recall facts and events (declarative memory) (Ullman, 2016). On the other hand, males outperform females in some visuospatial skills, such as navigation (wayfinding) (Nowak et al., 2015) and mental rotation (**FIGURE 4.10**), as well as in mathematics (Reilly et al., 2015; Flore et al., 2019). The differences just listed are moderate to large in size,* but they are smaller than obvious physical differences between the sexes, such as the difference in average height. Many other cognitive differences show smaller, sometimes trivial differences between the sexes.

Other sex differences have to do with feelings, attitudes, goals, interests, values, and behaviors (including sexual behavior)—traits that loosely cluster under the term **personality**. In large-scale studies, males score higher on assertiveness and physical aggressiveness, risk-proneness, dutifulness (rule-following), emotional stability, and openness to abstract ideas, whereas females score higher on warmth, sensitivity, compassion, anxiety, and openness to change and aesthetics (Kaiser et al., 2019).

Another personality difference has to do with interests, and this is one of the strongest sex differences, statistically speaking: Women's interests are more people-related and empathetic, whereas men's interests are more thing-related. This difference affects the occupational preferences of women and men (Su et al., 2009; Su & Rounds, 2015). Still, it is difficult to disentangle such internal influences from the effects of social expectations and discrimination, which certainly exist.

### There are many differences in sexuality

More directly relevant to the overall subject of this book are sex differences related to sexuality. Here we summarize the most important of these differences, which are discussed in detail in later chapters. All of these differences have been documented in research studies, but all of them describe averages and are not necessarily true when applied to individuals.

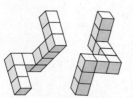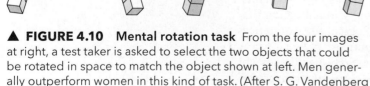

▲ **FIGURE 4.10 Mental rotation task** From the four images at right, a test taker is asked to select the two objects that could be rotated in space to match the object shown at left. Men generally outperform women in this kind of task. (After S. G. Vandenberg and A. R. Kuse. 1978. *Percept Mot Skills* 47: 599–604.)

*For statistics buffs, they show effect sizes (*d*) of about 0.4–1.0.

- Men have a stronger *sex drive* than women—they think more often about sex, have more frequent and more intense sexual fantasies, masturbate more, want more frequent sex, are more likely to initiate sex, make more sacrifices for sex, are more willing to pay for sex, are more interested in casual sex, and are more likely to engage in sexual coercion (see Chapters 5, 7, 10, 16, and 17).

- The criteria for sexual attractiveness differ between the sexes. Women are more influenced than men by the earning capacity of potential partners, whereas men are more influenced than women by their partners' physical appearance and young age (see Chapter 5).

- Women and men both experience *jealousy*, but they tend to experience different *kinds* of jealousy. Women are more likely than men to experience emotional jealousy— that is, to fear that their male partner may commit himself emotionally to a different woman. Men, in contrast, are more likely than women to experience sexual jealousy—to fear that their female partner is being physically unfaithful to them (see Chapter 7).

▲ Wanton violence, such as soccer hooliganism, is largely a male pastime.

- There are differences in the *sexual orientations* of men and women. For example, women are less likely than men to be exclusively homosexual (lesbian or gay) but more likely than men to be bisexual (see Chapter 12).

- Men are much more likely than women to be interested in *unusual forms of sexual expression* ("kinks"), and to experience the pathological forms of sexuality known as *paraphilic disorders* (see Chapter 11).

- The *sexual response cycles* of women and men differ (see Chapter 5). Men are aroused and reach orgasm faster than women. Many women but few men experience multiple orgasms within one cycle of sexual arousal.

- Women's *reproductive capacity* ceases rather abruptly at menopause, whereas men's reproductive capacity declines gradually over the entire adult lifespan (see Chapter 11).

- Reproduction is more of a "gamble" for men than for women: Some men have large numbers of children and other men have none, whereas women are more likely to have some moderate number of children. This variability in reproductive success encourages *sexual risk taking* by men (see below and Appendix A).

- Sexual behavior has more direct potential *consequences* for women—in terms of pregnancy and motherhood—than it does for men, and sexually transmitted infections have a much higher likelihood of impairing fertility in women than in men (see Chapter 15).

Stated in this brief fashion, some of the statements listed above may strike you as more akin to **stereotypes** (opinions about classes of people that are based on overgeneralization or prejudice) than to well-documented facts. As generalizations about average differences between women and men they are valid, but there are also

**stereotypes**   Common opinions about classes of people that are false or overgeneralized.

many important exceptions and nuances that we cannot touch on here. We urge you to withhold judgment until we have had the opportunity to discuss all these topics in greater detail. We should also emphasize that documenting the existence of sex differences says nothing about the morality of women's or men's sexual behavior, nor whether differences that exist today are permanent or changeable.

With regard to all these sex differences in brain organization, cognition, personality, and sexuality, there is still controversy about their reality, magnitude, and meaning. Psychologist Janet Hyde and others believe that most sex differences, if they exist at all, are small, and that they overlap so much as to be irrelevant in any practical context (Fine, 2010; Hyde, 2016). Others say that these critics ignore some large and well-replicated sex differences, and that overlapping traits become far more distinct when measured collectively (multivariate analysis) (Chekroud et al., 2016; Del Guidice, 2019; Kaiser et al., 2019).

## Many sex differences arise early in life

Boys and girls show quite marked differences in behavior from a young age. Even before birth, male fetuses are more active than females, and this difference in activity level increases during childhood (Campbell & Eaton, 1999). Sex differences in toy preferences are detectable as early as 3 months of age and are well established by 1 year (Servin et al., 1999). Boys prefer toy vehicles, toy weapons, balls, and construction toys, while girls prefer dolls and toy kitchen implements. This is a very sizeable difference, but it has decreased somewhat in recent years on account of increasingly diverse preferences by girls (Todd et al., 2018) (**FIGURE 4.11**).

Boys engage in more competitive, strenuous, rough-and-tumble play and aggression than girls do, and girls engage in more conversation and socializing than boys do (Maccoby, 1998; Holmes, 2012). By 4 years of age most boys prefer to play with

▲ **FIGURE 4.11**  **Toy preference test** A child is placed within a circle of toys, and his or her play behavior is videotaped. Later, observers measure the amount of time the child spends playing with toys generally preferred by girls and those generally preferred by boys. Figure 4.12 shows examples of data from this kind of study.

Courtesy of Galen HawkOwl

boys, and most girls with girls. Girls' and boys' play is governed by different moral rules: Girls appeal to social conventions ("The teacher will be angry if we don't play nicely"), while boys appeal to justice-based principles such as ownership ("Hands off the car, it's mine!") (Tulviste & Koor, 2005).

## 4.4 Biological Factors Contribute to Sex Differences

### LEARNING OBJECTIVES
After reading this section you should be able to:

**4.4.1** Give an example of how evolution has promoted gender differences.

**4.4.2** Give an example of how sex hormones during development influence gender differences.

So far, we have attempted to describe sex differences without drawing any conclusions about how these differences arise. We now turn to the topic of causes. Researchers have taken a wide variety of approaches to this topic and have viewed sex differences through the lenses of several different disciplines. We begin by discussing the biological approach.

### Evolutionary forces act differently on females and males

The field of evolutionary psychology investigates how gender characteristics have been molded by a long period of human and prehuman evolution. During this period, the struggle to survive and reproduce has favored the spread of genes that predispose their owners to certain sex-specific traits and behavior patterns. Here are three examples of how evolutionary psychology attempts to explain aspects of women's and men's sexual strategies (Buss & Schmitt, 2019).

INTEREST IN CASUAL SEX  Men's greater interest in casual sex can be explained in terms of evolutionary processes. The cost of fathering a child—when stripped to its biological essentials—is minimal. Women, however, have to invest so much time and resources into pregnancy and child care that they are very limited in the total number of offspring they are able to have. Therefore, it's argued, genes evolved that promote men's interest in casual sex and women's choosiness about who they mate with.

JEALOUSY  Women have always been certain of the identity of their biological children. A man, however, could never be certain which children were his—at least until the invention of DNA testing. According to David Buss of the University of Texas at Austin, this difference between the sexes, persisting over countless generations, led to the spread of genes promoting the different styles of jealousy in women and men described above. Men's sexual jealousy served to reduce the likelihood of rearing children that were not theirs; women's emotional jealousy served to reduce the likelihood that their male partners would abandon them and leave them without resources to rear their children (Buss, 2013).

COGNITIVE  Evolutionary psychologists believe that cognitive differences between the sexes have arisen because of a long-standing division of labor between women and men. Because of their greater physical strength, it is argued, men have always taken a leading role in hunting, warfare, and exploration; women, because of their biologically mandated role in pregnancy and breastfeeding, have taken a leading role in activities near the homesite. Over many generations, such a division of labor might well have favored the spread of genes for different cognitive skills in the two sexes, such as the greater navigating skills of men and the greater hand and finger dexterity of women.

If these ideas are correct, we would expect to find similar evolved sex differences across cultures and across historical periods. This seems to be largely the case. Regarding sexual attractiveness, for example, a research group at the University of Glasgow surveyed the criteria for attractiveness as stated by women and men living in numerous countries. They found that women are more influenced than men by their partner's earning capacity in all countries: This was equally true in countries where women are still economically dependent on men, as well as in egalitarian countries, where women are no more dependent on their partners than men are (Zhang et al., 2019).

In addition, one might expect that nonhuman species (especially those closely related to us) would exhibit some of the same evolved differences that humans do, even without the benefit of human culture. Experiments and field observations show that they often do, for example in the area of play behavior (**BOX 4.3**). And the greater social engagement of girls than boys is echoed in the behavior of female and male monkeys as young as 2 to 3 weeks of age (Simpson et al., 2016).

## Experiments demonstrate a role for sex hormones

Earlier in this chapter we mentioned the structural and functional differences between the brains of women and men. These differences result, at least in part, from differences in circulating levels of sex hormones during fetal life, at puberty, and during adult life. So, do hormones contribute to the psychological differences between the sexes?

Experiments in animals certainly suggest so. Biologists have altered the hormonal environments of fetal rats and monkeys—by adding testosterone to a female fetus, for example, or by blocking the action of a male fetus's own testosterone. In postnatal life the treated females behave in many ways like males, and vice versa.

Although it would obviously be unethical to conduct such experiments in humans, biologists can take advantage of "experiments of nature" in which a similar situation has occurred spontaneously. One example is the condition of congenital adrenal hyperplasia. As mentioned earlier in this chapter, girls with CAH are exposed to high levels of testosterone-like hormones (androgens) that are secreted by their adrenal glands during part of their fetal life. Psychologists have found that some, but not all, of the behavioral traits of these girls are shifted in the masculine direction. The girls with CAH engage in more rough-and-tumble play than other girls, for example, and they prefer "boys' toys" to "girls' toys" (**FIGURE 4.12**). The differences persist into adult life, affecting such things as spatial skills, hobby interests, and career choices (Berenbaum & Beltz, 2016), as well as sexual orientation (see Chapter 12). These observations indicate that the high androgen levels experienced by female fetuses with CAH influence sex-differentiated characteristics throughout their lives.

But do these results say anything about individuals who don't have CAH or other medical conditions? To address this question, researchers have estimated testosterone levels in healthy fetuses—by measuring levels of the hormone in the amniotic fluid or in their mothers' blood (Hines, 2006; Knickmeyer & Baron-Cohen, 2006; Hines et al., 2015). The children born of those pregnancies were studied at various ages after birth. It turned out that fetal testosterone levels predicted a variety of gender characteristics in these children, even within a single sex. The lower a girl's testosterone levels prenatally, for example, the more strongly she would prefer "girls' toys" over "boys' toys" when she was 3 years old.

Another way that biologists have approached this question is by looking for anatomical markers that are thought to be influenced by prenatal testosterone exposure. One marker that has attracted a great deal of attention is the ratio of the length of the index finger (second digit, or

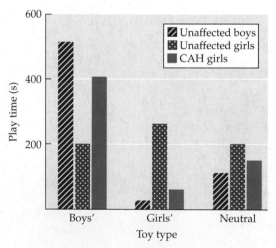

▲ **FIGURE 4.12  Hormones and play**
Exposure to androgens during fetal life influences choice of toys during childhood. Girls with congenital adrenal hyperplasia (CAH), as well as unaffected girls and boys, were observed while playing with toys. The toys available included those generally preferred by boys (e.g., trucks) and those generally preferred by girls (e.g., dolls), as well as gender-neutral toys. The toy preferences of the girls with CAH were more like those of boys than like those of unaffected girls. (After S. A. Berenbaum and E. Snyder. 1995. *Dev Psychol* 31: 31–42.)

# BOX 4.3
# Gendered Play in Primates

If girls' and boys' toy preferences are influenced by internal biological factors, rather than resulting solely from parental encouragement, then we might expect to see similar preferences among our primate relatives. To test this idea, developmental psychologists Gerianne Alexander (of Texas A & M University) and Melissa Hines presented male and female vervet monkeys with the same kinds of toys that they had previously used to test children's toy preferences (Alexander & Hines, 2002). The monkeys' preferences were uncannily similar to those of humans: Male monkeys played more with model cars and balls, for example, and female monkeys played more with dolls (**FIGURES A** and **B**). Similar results have been obtained more recently with rhesus monkeys (Hassett et al., 2008).

Since the monkeys had not seen the test items previously, they could hardly have learned to prefer some toys over others. Probably, some internal process of brain differentiation influences toy preferences in both human and nonhuman primates. It's not that there's an innate representation of the concept of "car" or of any other toys in the brain, of course. Rather, children and monkeys choose toys that facilitate the behaviors they like to engage in, such as active movement in the case of males.

What about primates in the wild, where toy cars and dolls are not available? Primatologists Sonja Kahlenberg and Richard Wrangham observed the behavior of juvenile chimpanzees in Kibale National Park in Uganda (Kahlenberg &

(A)  (B)

From G. M. Alexander and M. Hines 2002. *Evol Hum Behav* 23: 467–479

Monkeys show human-like toy preferences. (A) A female vervet monkey plays with a doll. (B) A male monkey plays with a toy car.

Wrangham, 2010). They found that juvenile females often carried sticks around and appeared to care for the sticks as girls care for dolls, holding them close to their bodies, cradling them, or taking them into their nests to sleep. These juvenile females could not have learned this behavior by imitating their mothers, because the mothers never carried sticks. Juvenile males carried sticks much less often than females, and when they did do so, they used them as weapons or for some other purpose. Because of the similarity of this sex difference in chimpanzees and humans, the researchers suggested that it existed in the common ancestors of the two species, which lived about 6 million years ago.

---

2D) to the length of the ring finger (fourth digit, or 4D)—the so-called 2D:4D ratio (Manning et al., 2014) (**FIGURE 4.13**). Men typically have a lower 2D:4D ratio than women—a shorter index finger relative to the ring finger—and several lines of evidence suggest that this difference is caused in part by the higher testosterone levels that males typically experience during fetal life (Berenbaum et al., 2009; Breedlove, 2010). Researchers have found that the 2D:4D ratio correlates significantly (but not very strongly) with many sex-differentiated characteristics, such as aggressiveness, even within one sex (Hoskins & Ellis, 2014; Turanovic et al., 2017). The 2D:4D ratio also differs between heterosexual and lesbian women, as will be discussed further in Chapter 12.

These kinds of findings suggest a relationship—presumably a causal one—between the brain's exposure to androgens before birth and a variety of sexually differentiated characteristics in childhood and adult life. None of the biological findings mean that prenatal hormones *determine* these characteristics, however. They suggest an *influence*—an influence that may be quite strong for some characteristics and quite weak, or totally absent, for others. Thus, there is plenty of room for other factors to play a role. These may include nonhormonal biological processes, such as aspects of brain development

▲ **FIGURE 4.13  Finger length ratio and gender** The 2D:4D ratio is the length of the index finger divided by the length of the ring finger. The ratio is typically lower in men than women, but it also varies with gender characteristics within each sex.

that are controlled directly by the intrinsic sex of brain cells (Ngun et al., 2011; Bramble et al., 2017), as well as a variety of social and learning factors that we will discuss next.

## 4.5 Life Experiences Mold Gender Roles

### LEARNING OBJECTIVES

After reading this section you should be able to:

4.5.1   Give an example of how socialization promotes gender differences.
4.5.2   Discuss the evidence that imitation is important in the development of gender differences.
4.5.3   Explain how "sexual scripts" influence gender differences.

Newborn girls and boys enter a world that imposes different expectations on girls and boys from the very beginning (**FIGURE 4.14**). Psychologists have discerned a variety of ways in which interactions among individuals, their families, and society help create and strengthen **gender roles**—that is, sets of social behaviors that are perceived as appropriate for males or females. Nevertheless, not all children or adults assume gender roles that are in keeping with conventional ideas. The fact that some individuals flout these expectations suggests that there is more to gender roles than social pressure alone—as can be seen in gender non-binary people.

### Girls and boys are socialized differently

The earliest social influences on a child come from the family. Parents may influence girls' and boys' psychological development by the way they dress them; by the way they decorate their rooms; by the toys they provide (Wong et al., 2013); by the way they attend to, reward, or punish their children's behavior; and by the activities that they initiate with them. Some parents encourage conventional gender roles, while others take a more lenient stance. Even if they do not set out to influence a child's development in this way, parents and siblings may do so simply by virtue of acting as role models.

**gender role**   Social behavior thought to be characteristic of one sex or the other, or some blend of the two.

OBSERVING SOCIALIZATION   Here's just one example of a study in which the influence of family members (older siblings, in this case) on children's sexually

© arek_malang/Shutterstock.com

▲ **FIGURE 4.14   Babies enter a gendered world**  These children have been dressed in the pink and blue outfits that our culture deems appropriate for infant girls and boys, respectively.

**FAQ:** Can I raise my child "gender free"?

You can limit your child's exposure to traditional gender expectations. A few parents have kept their children's sex secret from the world—a strategy that takes considerable effort and doesn't have obvious benefits (Ostroff, 2016).

differentiated behavior was demonstrated and measured (Rust et al., 2000). A British group of psychologists examined the behaviors and interests of over 5,000 3-year-old children; the researchers reduced the data for each child to a single measure of masculinity/femininity. Some of the children had older siblings. Those who had older siblings of the same sex were more sex-typical in their behavior than were children who had no siblings (singletons) (**FIGURE 4.15**). Conversely, children who had older siblings of the other sex were *less* sex-typical than the singletons. These data indicate that the presence of same- or opposite-sex siblings does influence a child's characteristics to an appreciable degree. The influence was modest in size, however, as can be seen in the figure: A child's own sex was a much stronger predictor of her or his behavior than was the sex of the older siblings. Girls with older brothers, for example, were far more feminine than any boys, even boys with older sisters.

Parents are presumably in a stronger position than siblings to influence children's characteristics. This influence is illustrated in a study by researchers at Johns Hopkins University (Pappas et al., 2008). They reported on 40 individuals who, as a result of a variety of intersex conditions, were born with ambiguous genitalia. Although the genitalia of all the children had roughly the same anatomical appearance, those individuals whose parents raised them as boys became increasingly masculine through adolescence and adulthood, whereas those who were raised as girls became increasingly feminine.

Gender socialization also occurs within peer groups, especially with regard to communication styles. From their experiences of talking with same- and opposite-sex playmates, children learn that girls' speech tends to be affiliative (i.e., it serves to establish and maintain connections) whereas boys' speech is more likely to be assertive (i.e., its purpose is to influence the listener). Learning this difference in communication style encourages children to join groups where their style of communication is understood and expected, which is to say children of their own sex (Xiao et al., 2019).

▲ Hadza boy practicing archery, Tanzania.

(A)

(B)

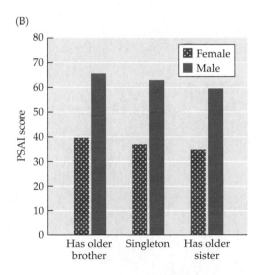

▲ **FIGURE 4.15** **Influence of siblings on gender** (A) Older siblings act as gender role models. (B) The Pre-School Activities Inventory (PSAI) score is a measure of gender-typical activities and interests in which male typical traits score higher and female-typical traits score lower. This figure shows the PSAI score for 5,542 British 3-year-olds, broken down according to whether they are singletons or have older brothers or sisters. The children's gender traits are slightly shifted in the direction of the sex of the older sibling. (After J. Rust et al. 2000. *J Exp Child Psychol* 77: 292–303.)

REWARDS AND PUNISHMENTS   Studies such as the ones just described indicate that social interactions exert an influence but don't pinpoint the exact mechanisms. One possible influence is the way family members use rewards, withdrawal of rewards, or punishments with any given child. Under these circumstances children learn from trial and error, often discovering how their behaviors lead to rewards or avoid punishments. In one study focusing on these learning processes, University of Oregon psychologist Beverly Fagot and her colleagues studied interactions between parents and their 18-month-old infants and then followed the infants for about a year afterward. They found that the infants whose parents reacted to their behavior in the traditional fashion (rewarding or approving of sex-typical behavior and punishing or disapproving of sex-atypical behavior) exhibited more traditionally sex-typical behavior (Fagot et al., 1992). Studies of this kind support the notion that the development of sex-typical traits is influenced by rewards and punishments.

IMITATION   Sex-typical behavior is also influenced by a child's observing and imitating the behavior of parents, older siblings, or other role models, and not just by reward and punishment (Bussey & Bandura, 1984; Grace et al., 2008). In one study, Walter Mischel tracked the eye movements of children while they were watching films featuring male and female characters. In accordance with the theory of observational learning, the children attended more to the same-sex characters in the films than they did to the characters of the other sex. Such behavior could easily lead children to become better acquainted with, and imitate, the behaviors typical of their own sex. And the tendency of children to play with other children of their own sex, mentioned earlier, offers another way in which they can observe and learn sex-typical behavior, this time from their peers (Paechter & Clark, 2007).

The media, particularly television and movies, offer much for children to imitate (**FIGURE 4.16**). We already mentioned the "Notel" study in Chapter 1 (Box 1.2), in which children exposed to television for the first time adopted more stereotypical ideas about male and female gender roles. In more recent studies, a group led by Sarah Coyne of Brigham Young University assessed the exposure of preschool-age girls and boys to Disney Princess and superhero media and toys and then quantified the children's gender-role characteristics one year later (Coyne et al., 2016, 2017). High exposure to princesses predicted an increase in stereotypically female ideas and behaviors, such as playing "house," in both girls and boys. Conversely, high exposure to superheroes predicted an increase in stereotypically male ideas and behaviors, such as fighting—again, in both sexes.

LANGUAGE   The language we speak is another cultural influence on psychological development, but one that we're barely aware of. Children acquire a knowledge of their own sex by 2 to 3 years of age, but this age varies according to the language environment that children are exposed to. Children in Hebrew-speaking households, for example, know their own sex about a year earlier than children in Finnish-speaking households. That's because Hebrew grammar emphasizes sex: Even the Hebrew word for "you" differs according to whether one is addressing a male or a female. Finnish grammar, on the other hand, doesn't specify sex at all. English falls in between, and correspondingly, children in

▲ Mayan mother teaches daughter to weave, Guatemala.

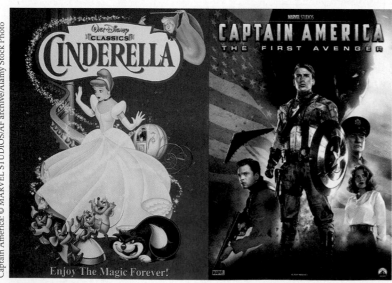

▲ **FIGURE 4.16**   **The media influence gender** Disney Princess and Captain America movies may promote the development of stereotypical gender roles.

English-speaking households learn their sex at an intermediate age (Guiora et al., 1982; Boroditsky, 2011).

There have been efforts in several countries to introduce nongendered pronouns. In Sweden, the newly coined pronoun *hen* has gained some traction as a nongendered alternative to *hon* (she) or *han* (he). Comparable coinages in English, such as *zhe* for he or she, have not been widely accepted, but the nongendered plural *they* has seen increasing usage as a replacement for the gendered singular forms, and we sometimes make use of the singular *they* in this textbook.

LEARNING FROM ADVICE    Language also facilitates the learning of gender roles by means of verbally communicated rules (Baldwin & Baldwin, 2001). When a boy gets hurt and begins to cry, his older brother or father may state the rule "Big boys don't cry." The message is very clear, though the boy may need several months of additional learning before he can control his tears in a broad range of situations. Many girls learn that they are allowed to cry, and they may even get extra attention (a social reward) when they cry. Thus, social advice helps children learn that crying is much more acceptable for females than males. Swearing provides an opposite example: In many households, teenage girls are told more firmly than teenage boys that they should not swear. Gender role advice is communicated not just by family members but also from many other social sources.

Advice-based learning is often backed up by the promise of rewards or the threat of punishments—or reinforced by the social aura of respected role models. The key feature of this form of learning, however, is that advice allows for the acquisition of general concepts that children can apply to a broad range of circumstances, including those that they have not previously encountered. In that way, advice contributes to the creation of durable attitudes and opinions about how girls and boys should behave—viewpoints that may be passed down from generation to generation.

The weight of evidence supports the belief that socialization powerfully influences gender development. But, as with the biological approach, socialization can't explain everything. For example, children who will later become gay or transgender adults often violate some or most gender norms in rather dramatic ways, yet there is no evidence that these children are encouraged or trained to rebel against gender norms. And some children who are born as one sex but reared as the other may reject this kind of social reassignment, as if they somehow know which sex they ought to be (Diamond & Sigmundson, 1997; Reiner, 2004). It therefore seems unlikely that a complete account of gender development can be made in terms of either socialization or biology, and in fact few if any present-day workers in the field would make such a claim.

## Cognitive developmental models emphasize thought processes

Cognitive psychologists believe that studying development requires getting inside children's minds. Children actively seek to interpret the social world in which they live, and in the process they gradually develop a sense of themselves as girls or boys (Martin & Ruble, 2010).

One example of a cognitive developmental model is the **sexual script** theory already mentioned in Chapter 1 (Wiederman, 2015). As the word "script" suggests, this theory asserts that sexual behavior is a form of role-playing, influenced by scripts that we have learned. People are especially reliant on sexual scripts when interacting with prospective partners that they don't know very well. As we'll describe in more detail in Chapter 7, first encounters between heterosexual men and women have traditionally been organized according to scripts governing such matters as what it means to invite someone out for a drink, who pays, and how the man and woman negotiate any sexual interactions.

Scripts can change over time under the influence of culture. Early in the 20th century, for example, oral–genital contact was a form of sex that men largely received

**sexual script**    A socially negotiated role that guides sexual behavior.

from prostitutes and in transient relationships. Now, however, it has become a common and acceptable sexual practice between young adults who are hooking up or dating, and both males and females give oral sex to their partners (Reece et al., 2010b; Wright, 2011). Thus, men and women today follow different scripts about oral sex than their grandparents did.

Scripts influence not only sexual dealings among people, but also the psychosexual development of individuals. Postpubertal boys masturbate a great deal more than do girls, whereas girls' early sexual experiences tend to be with partners. As a consequence, script theory suggests, the meaning of sex for males becomes embedded in the notion of the male's own sexual pleasure, whereas for females it becomes embedded in the notion of relationships.

Sexual scripts are relevant to important social issues such as sexual coercion and pornography. In one longitudinal study of high school students, for example, male students who endorsed a script in which men were expected to take sexual risks were more likely to engage in aggressive sexual behavior (Krahe et al., 2007). Another study found a significant correlation between respondents' pornography use and their engagement in aggressive or degrading behaviors with their sex partners, as if they were enacting scripts learned from pornography (Bridges et al., 2016). (The effects of pornography on users' sexual behavior are controversial and are discussed in more detail in Chapter 17.)

## 4.6 Transgender People Challenge Society's Deepest Divide

**LEARNING OBJECTIVES**
After reading this section you should be able to:

4.6.1   Compare the life experiences of transgender people in Western and non-Western societies.

4.6.2   Compare the life histories of a typical autogynephilic and non-autogynephilic ("classical") trans woman.

4.6.3   Evaluate different strategies for responding to a child who insists they belong to the other sex from their natal sex.

4.6.4   Evaluate the controversy about "rapid-onset gender dysphoria."

4.6.5   Explain some of the stresses and risks to which trans people are exposed.

The term **transgender**, often shortened to **trans**, is used in a broad way to encompass all individuals whose gender identity does not fully correspond with their natal sex. About 0.5% to 0.6% of Americans identify as transgender; the percentages are slightly higher among younger than older age groups and among nonwhite than white Americans (Crissman et al., 2017; Flores et al., 2017). The opposite of transgender is **cisgender**, which refers to the majority of women and men who identify fully with their natal sex. Most transgender people differ from intersex people in that they were born with standard-issue male or female bodies.

In the United States, the focus was for many years on those transgender individuals who sought to change their bodies ("transition") into bodies of the other anatomical sex by medical means, and this has lent a medical or psychiatric flavor to being transgender. Individuals who desire a medical transition are commonly known as transsexual, and they are covered in a later section. We first take a look at the wider population of transgender people, many of whom have no interest in medical treatments.

### Transgender men and women have existed in many cultures

In many non-Western cultures, transgender people have been given special names and accorded special status—often, a spiritual or sacred one. Throughout Polynesia, for example, there existed a class of transgender individuals known as **mahus**. These were natal males who dressed in female (or a mixture of female and male) attire, engaged in women's activities, and had sex with conventional men. *Mahus* were attached to the

**transgender (or trans)**   Having a gender identity that is not fully congruent with one's natal sex.

**cisgender**   Having a conventional gender—masculine if anatomically male, feminine if anatomically female. "Cis" is the opposite of "trans."

**mahu**   A natal male who took a female gender role in Polynesian society and performed ritual dances.

village headman's household and performed sacred dances. In northern India and Pakistan there is an ongoing tradition of **hijras**. These are natal males who cut off their genitals and work as religious dancers or as prostitutes serving men. Thailand has an especially large and visible community of transgender women, who are known as **kathoey** (**FIGURE 4.17**). *Kathoey* are well accepted in the entertainment field and in some jobs typically held by women, but they face discrimination in "male" occupations.

In several native cultures of North America, rituals conducted at or before puberty gave boys the option to choose between the status of conventional males and that of **two-spirit** (male + female) **persons**. Among the Tohono O'odham of the Sonoran Desert, for example, a boy who preferred female pursuits was tested by being placed within a brushwood enclosure, along with a man's bow and arrows and a woman's basket. The enclosure was then set on fire. If, in escaping the flames, the boy took with him the bow and arrows, he became a conventional man, but if he took the basket, he became a two-spirit person. Two-spirit people wore special clothes fashioned from a mixture of male and female attire, practiced mostly female occupations, and engaged in sexual relationships with conventional men. They were often shamans (healers who derived their curative powers from their knowledge of the spirit world), chanters, dancers, or mediators. The two-spirit tradition was studied by anthropologist Walter Williams, then at the University of Southern California, and he described it in a 1986 book, *The Spirit and the Flesh* (W. L. Williams, 1986). The book helped reignite the two-spirit tradition among transgender Native Americans as well as among nonheterosexual Americans generally.*

Transgender men have also been described in many societies. According to legend, anatomically female warriors known as Amazons battled the Greeks during the Trojan War (**FIGURE 4.18**). Since then, the word "amazon" has been used in reference to fierce or powerful females. In the 16th century an explorer described anatomical females among the Tupinamba Indians of northeastern Brazil who adopted a male warrior role (de Magalhaes, 1576/1922); this led to the naming of Brazil's great waterway as the River of the Amazons, or simply the Amazon.

## Many transgender people are "beyond the binary"

Transgender persons who don't seek to transition medically to the other sex may nevertheless identify fully with that sex. They may not transition medically because they don't need to do so in order to express their identity, because they are not satisfied with the likely results, or because they cannot afford the treatments.

Alternatively, they may reject a simple male/female dichotomy. In the latter case they may refer to themselves with such terms as **non-binary**, gender-fluid, genderqueer, or agender, and the conception of transgender identity to which they subscribe is often called the "beyond-the-binary" model (Bettcher, 2014). Some think only of people like themselves as beyond the binary, while others believe that the whole notion of binary gender is an outdated social construction. "My brain is not gendered," said one 18-year-old transgender

▲ **FIGURE 4.17** *Kathoey* Members of the Thai *kathoey* (transgender) band Venus Flytrap.

**hijra** A member of a traditional class of transexual women in northern India and Pakistan.

**kathoey** Trans women in Thailand.

**two-spirit person** In Native American cultures, a person with the spirit of both a man and a woman; a transgender person. Also called *berdache*.

**non-binary** Not conforming to either a conventional masculine or feminine gender identity.

▲ **FIGURE 4.18** **Female warrior** An Amazon prepares to strike a cowering Greek soldier. (Her spear is missing.) This sculpture is from the 350 BCE tomb of Mausolus at Halicarnassus (Bodrum, Turkey).

*More recently Walter Williams was convicted of sex crimes against minors.

**transexual (or transsexual)**
A person who identifies with the other sex and who seeks to transition to the other sex by medical means.

**gender dysphoria** The unhappiness caused by discordance between a person's anatomical sex and gender identity.

**transvestism** Wearing clothes of the other sex for purposes of sexual arousal.

**autogynephilia** A form of male-to-female transsexuality characterized by a man's sexual arousal at the thought of being or becoming a woman.

man. "There's this crazy gender binary that's built into all of life, that there are just two genders that are acceptable. I don't want to have to fit into that" (Quart, 2008).

Thus, if someone tells you that they are transgender, there are several possible meanings to that statement that further acquaintance may clarify. Regardless, it is appropriate to refer to such a person by the nouns and pronouns that they themselves prefer, and it is perfectly acceptable to ask what those terms are.

## Transexual individuals are of more than one kind

Imagine yourself waking up one morning in a body of the other sex. Very likely you would be shocked and would move heaven and earth to get back into your "right" body. That is the kind of discomfort or anguish **transexual** people have to deal with, unless and until they undergo a medical and social transition to the other sex. The unhappiness caused by discordance between a person's natal sex and their gender identity is called **gender dysphoria**. This is a diagnostic category in the American Psychiatric Association's *Diagnostic and Statistical Manual of Mental Disorders (DSM-5)*, but it could also be viewed as a mentally healthy reaction to the difficult situation in which transexual individuals find themselves.

Most transexual men have a characteristic life history. From early childhood they may say they are boys or insist that they want to become boys, and they try to express their masculine identity in their clothing, hairstyles, friendships, activities, and career plans. This often puts them on a collision course with the expectations of family, peers, and the world at large. As they enter puberty, they resent the developing signs of womanhood and may seek to hide them by, for example, binding their breasts. In adulthood they seem quite masculine in many respects, and they are usually sexually attracted to women, but they do not identify as homosexual or lesbian. Rather, they identify as heterosexual men. The well-known expression "man trapped in a woman's body" describes them fairly aptly. They generally seek to transition as early as possible.

Transexual women, on the other hand, fall into two contrasting types with different life histories. The first type, who we may call "classical" transexual women, are pretty much the converse of the transexual men just described. As children they say that they are girls or insist that they want to become girls, and they try to dress as girls and to play with girls. They dislike the man's body that puberty gives them, and they often try to dress and act in such a way as to allow others to accept them as women. Typically feminine mannerisms, gait, and conversational style come naturally to them. They are usually sexually attracted to men, but they identify as heterosexual women, not as gay men. They could be thought of as "women trapped in men's bodies." Transexual women of this type often seek to transition medically and socially in their teen years or young adulthood—as soon as they are legally allowed to do so or as soon as they can raise the money to pay for the necessary treatment.

The second kind of trans women, however, are much less well known to the general public. As children, they do not claim to be girls, and they are only mildly gender-nonconformist, or not at all. When they grow up, they are usually sexually attracted to women, so they are heterosexual with respect to their natal sex, but their interest in women takes an unusual course. In particular, they are erotically aroused by wearing women's clothes—a trait known as heterosexual **transvestism**. Eventually, this kind of ideation may progress to the point that they are aroused by the idea not merely of being in women's *clothes*, but of being in a woman's *body* and possessing female genitals. In other words, their desire to become a woman is fueled by the sex drive and by the desire to incorporate the object of their attractions into themselves, rather than by having a female gender identity. Feminine mannerisms, gait, and conversational style do not necessarily come naturally to these transexual women, and so they may take lessons on how to act like a woman. They tend to seek medical transition later in life, often after they have been heterosexually married and fathered children.

A Canadian sexologist, Ray Blanchard, gave this second developmental pathway the name **autogynephilia**, meaning "being attracted to oneself as a woman" (Blanchard,

**► FIGURE 4.19** **Jonas and Nicole Maines** are monozygotic ("identical") twins. Both were born male, but Nicole transitioned to female as a teenager.

2005). Some sex researchers believe that most male-to-female transexuals who are sexually attracted to women are autogynephilic (Bailey, 2003; Lawrence, 2017).

The cause or causes of transexuality are not well understood. Because, as discussed earlier, sexually differentiated traits are influenced by biological factors such as prenatal hormones, many researchers suspect that such factors also lie behind transexuality. Consistent with this idea, there have been reports of differences in genes (Hare et al., 2009), brain structure (Garcia-Falgueras & Swaab, 2008; Rametti et al., 2011a, 2011b), and finger length ratios (Schneider et al., 2006) between trans- and cisgender individuals of the same natal sex. Twin studies also suggest that genes influence transexuality (Segal, 2000; Diamond, 2013), although not all monozygotic twins (who possess the same genes) have the same gender identity (**FIGURE 4.19**). But the comparative rarity and diversity of transexual individuals, the fact that some of them have had extensive medical treatments, and the autogynephilic/non-autogynephilic distinction all complicate the search for a biological explanation for transexuality.

## Changing sex is a multistage process

No form of psychiatric treatment can bring a transexual person's gender identity into concordance with his or her natal sex. In fact, any attempt to do so would be experienced as a violation of personhood. Therefore, doctors and therapists have followed a different strategy—helping transexual people to achieve their dream of changing their anatomical sex and assuming a gender role that fully corresponds with their gender identity (**FIGURE 4.20**).

Contrary to what many people believe, **transitioning** is not a single event that takes place on a particular day under a surgeon's knife. It is an extended process that has both medical and social aspects, and there are several different ways in which the process may go forward. Four major elements are as follows, according to the World Professional Association for Transgender Health (WPATH, 2017):

- *Assessment, education, and psychotherapy.* Professionals with expertise in the area of transgender health will ask about the clients' life histories, discuss their goals, and educate them about the process and the limitations and risks of transitioning.

**transitioning**   Changing one's physical sex and social gender.

**▲ FIGURE 4.20** **Bruce Jenner** transitioned to Caitlyn Jenner between 2015 and 2017.

▶ **FIGURE 4.21 Effects of cross-sex hormones on female and male bodies** These hormones do not change stature or skeletal structure. Estrogen does not eliminate facial hair or reverse male-pattern baldness in natal males.

**FAQ:** How much does sex change surgery cost?

Anything from $10,000 to $150,000 and higher—the latter being for procedures that include construction of a functional penis or complex facial surgeries. Going overseas (e.g., to Thailand) for surgery is a less expensive alternative, but there could be extra expenses if the person has to return there for treatment of complications.

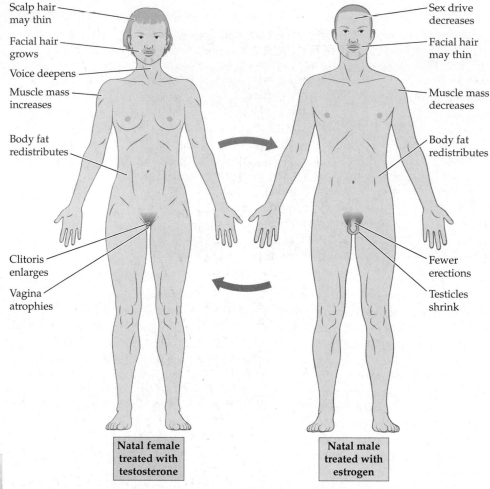

Scalp hair may thin
Facial hair grows
Voice deepens
Muscle mass increases
Body fat redistributes
Clitoris enlarges
Vagina atrophies

**Natal female treated with testosterone**

Sex drive decreases
Facial hair may thin
Muscle mass decreases
Body fat redistributes
Fewer erections
Testicles shrink

**Natal male treated with estrogen**

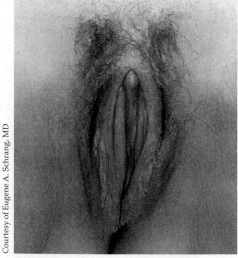

Courtesy of Eugene A. Schrang, MD

▲ **FIGURE 4.22 The vulva after sex-reassignment surgery** The clitoris is constructed from the top surface of the penis with its nerve supply intact and may therefore be capable of triggering orgasm. The clitoris and adjacent labial tissue are covered with mucosa derived from the penile urethra, giving them a pink color. The remainder of the penile skin, including the glans, is inverted to form the vagina. Often, additional skin must be grafted from other areas to make the vagina deep enough for coitus.

- *Hormonal treatment.* For individuals transitioning from natal male to female, some form of estrogen is prescribed. An androgen-blocking drug is often added. Individuals transitioning from natal female to male are given testosterone or a related androgen, and progesterone may be added to stop menstruation. The hormones cause a variety of anatomical and physiological changes, as indicated in **FIGURE 4.21**, but stature and skeletal structure are not affected. Testosterone does not eliminate female breasts. Estrogen thins but does not eliminate the male beard, and it does not reverse male-pattern baldness. The hormonally induced changes may take months to show themselves.

- *Experience in the desired gender role.* WPATH recommends that transitioning clients spend at least a year living in the community in the gender role corresponding to their desired sex, while being monitored and counseled by an experienced therapist. In reality this often does not happen, in part because many trans individuals have difficulty passing as the other sex without medical intervention.

- **Sex-reassignment surgery**, *also called gender confirmation surgery.* For natal males, the key procedures are removal of the penis and testicles; construction of a vagina, labia, and clitoris (**FIGURE 4.22**); and augmentation of the breasts. The vagina may be constructed from the inverted skin of the penis or a graft of intestinal tissue. Other procedures that may be performed include surgery on the vocal cords (to raise the pitch of the voice), liposuction to the waist, reduction of the Adam's apple, and various procedures to feminize the appearance of the face.

- For natal females, surgery can include removal of the breasts, ovaries, oviducts, uterus, and vagina. In addition, a scrotum and penis may be constructed (**FIGURE 4.23**). Construction of a penis that looks natural, contains a functioning urethra, and is capable of erection (with the aid of a pump-and-reservoir system or some kind of stiffening device; see Chapter 14) is a very costly multistage process; the results are far from ideal and complications are common (Hadj-Moussa et al., 2019). For these reasons most transsexual men forgo genital reconstructive surgery. In some clients, the clitoris can be enlarged by hormonal treatment and surgery. This procedure is called **metoidioplasty** (Djinovic, 2018) (**FIGURE 4.24**). The resulting small penis is not generally usable for coitus, but it may be capable of erection and orgasm.

People who have transitioned from one sex to the other have to make many practical decisions (e.g., whether to be open about the sex change or to conceal their past), and they face all kinds of personal and social challenges. They may strive to pass as the other sex, either because passing offers confirmation of their identity, or because it avoids their being labeled as a "pretender" or being subject to abuse (Bettcher, 2014). Alternatively, they may not mind being recognized as transsexual, and their transsexuality may be a meaningful aspect of their social identity.

Establishing sexual and affectional relationships is often difficult. Many organizations provide personal, legal, and political support for transsexual and transgender people (see Web Resources at the end of this chapter), and professional help is available in such matters as voice training. Audio clips illustrating the changes in voice quality that can be achieved with training are available online (Saint Louis, 2017).

Not all transsexual people who wish to change sex do so via the officially recommended route just described. Some educate themselves about transitioning through the internet or peer networks, obtain hormones through irregular channels, and go straight to a private surgeon—perhaps in a foreign country such as Thailand, where costs are lower. Of course, such self-guided treatment carries significant risks.

The outcomes of medically assisted transitions are uncertain, because long-term follow-up and data collection have generally been poor, especially in the United States. A recent study reported on outcomes in Sweden, where centralized medical records are available for the entire population (Branstrom & Pachankis, 2019). In that study, hormonal treatment by itself conferred no benefit in terms of reduced need for mental health care; sex change surgery did confer a benefit, but the magnitude and significance of that benefit has been disputed (Regnerus, 2019).

What medical treatments can accomplish for transsexual people is far short of what they probably wish for, namely a complete transformation of their body into a normal, healthy body of the other sex. Improvements in treatment to bring that desired goal closer would likely lead to better mental health outcomes than those currently reported.

**▲ FIGURE 4.23 Trans man after transition**
This man has had his breasts and ovaries removed. His penis was constructed using tissue grafted from his thigh, and he has testicular implants. The penis has erotic sensitivity but is not capable of erection. Testosterone treatments have masculinized several aspects of his appearance including facial hair and muscle development

© John M. Clum

**sex-reassignment surgery (or gender confirmation surgery)** Surgery to change a person's genitals or other anatomical structures to those of the sex with which the person identifies.

**metoidioplasty** Surgical construction of a small penis from a clitoris.

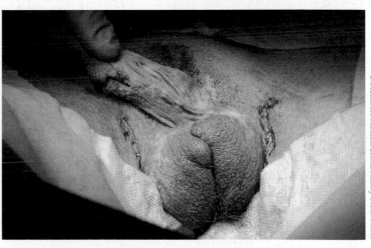

**▶ FIGURE 4.24 Transformation of the clitoris into a small penis** by hormone treatment and surgery (metoidioplasty). This procedure is simpler, less invasive, and less expensive than the construction of a large penis usable for penetrative sex (phalloplasty). This trans man also had a scrotum constructed from labial skin, with saline-filled implants to simulate testicles.

© Media for Medical SARL/Alamy Stock Photo

▲ These four women, members of Pique Resilience Project, experienced the onset of intense gender dysphoria during adolescence, identified as trans men, but later desisted or detransitioned.

**rapid-onset gender dysphoria**
The sudden onset of gender dysphoria in a person who previously had a gender identity congruent with their natal sex.

**transphobia**  Hatred of transgender people.

▲ **FIGURE 4.25**  Trans philosophy professor Talia Mae Bettcher of Cal State LA is also a grassroots activist for the trans community in Los Angeles.

## Early treatment of gender-dysphoric children is controversial

Regarding gender-dysphoric children who want to transition, some centers are now initiating treatment at puberty. Often these children are treated with drugs, such as leuprolide (Lupron), that block the onset of puberty; this prevents the appearance of difficult-to-reverse secondary sexual characteristics such as beards, and it gives the children time to make a more mature decision about whether to transition. According to guidelines issued by the Endocrine Society, it is appropriate to initiate treatment with puberty blockers in the earliest stage of puberty (but not before), and to begin more definitive hormonal and surgical procedures at age 16 (Hembree et al., 2017). This could mean that the child is on puberty blockers for as long as 4 years, and such prolonged treatment can have ill effects, such as a loss of bone density.

In this connection it should be noted that the majority of highly gender-nonconformist children—those who say they are, or want to become, members of the other sex—abandon those ideas at some point, usually around the time of puberty (Green, 1987; Drummond et al., 2008; Wallien & Cohen-Kettenis, 2008). They may well become gay or lesbian adults, but most become satisfied with their natal sex and no longer desire to transition. It has not so far proved possible to distinguish these "desisters" from the minority of gender-nonconformist children who "persist" and become transexual adults. There is therefore some question as to whether treating gender-dysphoric children with puberty blockers does more harm than good (Giovanardi, 2017).

In recent years a new concept or diagnostic category called **rapid-onset gender dysphoria** has been proposed: It has been applied to individuals who are not gender dysphoric during their childhood but who become so during adolescence. This concept, and the controversy surrounding it, is discussed in **BOX 4.4**.

## Trans people struggle for awareness and acceptance

Transgender adults have had a difficult struggle to gain recognition as a group distinct from lesbians and gay men. Of course, the introduction of sex-reassignment surgery in the 1960s, with all the attendant publicity, did educate the public about the phenomenon of transexuality, but it also prompted most people to accept the medical model of transexuality, which, according to some gender theorists, was an attempt to erase trans people by hiding them in their newly assigned sex (Bettcher, 2014).

One factor that has hampered the advancement of trans people is that they are relatively few in number. Thus, their political activism has generally taken place under the umbrella of the much larger gay rights movement. In fact, transgender persons participated in the "Stonewall Rebellion"—the 1969 riot in New York that was a key event in the modern gay rights movement (see Chapter 12).

Still, like bisexual people, trans people have fought to clarify their separate identity. In gay rights and gay pride marches and parades, trans people form their own contingents, and these events now usually carry names such as "March for Lesbian, Gay, Bisexual, and Transgender Equality." Transgender role models are beginning to appear, such as Victoria Kolakowski of California, who was elected as the nation's first transgender trial judge in 2010 (Sheridan, 2010). In academe, transgender professors, such as philosophy professor Talia Mae Bettcher of California State University Los Angeles, have offered role models for trans students (**FIGURE 4.25**).

Legal protections for transgender people lag behind those for gays and lesbians, even though the transgender population is at greater risk of violence and discrimination, which are manifestations of **transphobia**. Only 20 states and Washington, D.C., have hate crime laws that cover transgender identity, and some states have attempted to roll back legal protections that were enacted earlier.

## BOX 4.4
# Rapid-Onset Gender Dysphoria

In 2018 Lisa Littman, a physician and social scientist at Brown University, published a research study in the online journal *PLoS One*. The study concerned a previously little-known mental-health condition that she named **rapid onset gender dysphoria** (**ROGD**) (Littman, 2018). At some point during adolescence, Littman reported, the affected individuals—mostly natal females—expressed a strong dissatisfaction with their natal sex and, often, a wish to transition to the other sex. What distinguished these individuals from other transgender teens was that they lacked any childhood history of gender dysphoria. The numbers of such children have increased dramatically in recent years (Wadman, 2019).

Littman's study was a survey, not of the affected adolescents themselves, but of their parents. These parents typically reported that, prior to the onset of gender dysphoria, their daughters had suffered from another mental health disorder or had some form of neurodevelopmental disability. The girls were strongly involved with social media—specifically, with sites that promoted unqualified acceptance of a young person's stated transgender identity. In addition, they often belonged to friendship circles within which multiple girls expressed gender dysphoria.

Littman suggested that ROGD results from a form of social contagion in which vulnerable girls are persuaded that non-specific negative feelings associated with adolescence mean that they are transgender. Here's how one parent put it: "I believe my child experienced what many kids experience on the cusp of puberty—uncomfortableness! But there was an online world at the ready to tell her that those very normal feelings meant she's in the wrong body."

Littman's paper was highly controversial, because it landed in the middle of a professional debate about how to treat gender-dysphoric children. According to the "watchful waiting" model, providers should support the child and help them explore their feelings about their gender, but not move actively toward transition until the child is mature enough to make an independent decision (Steensma et al., 2013). In some cases watchful waiting includes the use of puberty blockers, as described in the main text. Proponents of watchful waiting point out that significant numbers of gender dysphoric children lose their dysphoria around the time of puberty and embrace a gender consistent with their natal sex. If providers facilitate the transition of such children, they may suffer harms that are difficult to reverse.

In contrast, other providers espouse a "gender-affirmative model of care" (GAMC). These providers believe that "[t]he basic therapeutic tenet of the gender affirmative model is quite simple: When it comes to knowing a child's gender, it is not for us to tell, but for the children to say…[O]nce information is gathered to assess a child's gender status, action is taken to allow that child to exercise that gender" (Ehrensaft, 2017; Gender Dysphoria Affirmative Working Group, 2020). GAMC providers believe that social influences are not responsible for the children's gender dysphoria, but that the negative reactions to dysphoric children are the cause of the psychological problems the children often experience.

Littman's findings and conclusions cast doubt on the GAMC model, but only as it relates to the ROGD subgroup of gender dysphoric children. Her study was heavily criticized by GAMC proponents. For example, Arjee Restar, then a graduate student at Littman's own institution, listed what she considered methodological shortcomings in Littman's study, including her reliance on the parents' statements rather than those of the children themselves (Restar, 2020). Littman countered that she used methods that are standard in the field (Littman, 2020). Littman has also been accused of transphobia.

Some support for Littman's conclusions has come from affected individuals themselves; these include adolescents who have desisted in their attempts to transition, or who transitioned medically or surgically but then came to rethink their decisions and requested help in detransitioning—that is, in changing back to their natal sex and gender. Some desisters and detransitioners, such as those shown in the photograph on the opposite page, formed action groups and posted videos about themselves online (Pique Resilience Project, 2019). These videos received numerous positive comments from other affected teens. Here's one of many similar responses to the just-referenced video:

> I've identified as FTM [female-to-male transgender] for about a year and seven months now. I'm 16 and I realize it's not what I truly identify now and that it's just dysmorphia [dissatisfaction with body appearance] combined with feeling apprehensive towards femininity. I've already come out to my parents and grandparents and uncles and aunts and entirely socially and have no idea how to retract it all. I'm terrified and embarrassed.

The debate has become acrimonious and personal. It's easy to lose hold of the fact that the proponents of both models sincerely wish the best for their clients or patients. And no one in either school of thought doubts the reality of gender dysphoria or transgender identity in general—the discussion only relates to the ROGD children. Many individuals who transition feel reborn into their true selves, and by transitioning they may rescue themselves from lives of anguish or self-harm.

(A)

(B)

Both photos © Associated Press

▲ **FIGURE 4.26** **Transphobic violence** 17-year-old Gwen Araujo of Newark, California (A), was beaten to death by four men who realized that she was anatomically male after two of them had sex with her. All four of the men, three of whom are shown in (B), were convicted of murder or manslaughter and sentenced to prison terms ranging from six years to life (Fraley, 2016).

In 2019 at least 26 transgender individuals—most of them women of color—were murdered in the United States (Human Rights Campaign, 2020), and much larger numbers were assaulted on account of their status as transgender (**FIGURE 4.26**). The murder of a trans teenager, Gwen Araujo, in California in 2002 received enormous publicity and helped trigger the founding of the National Center for Transgender Equality, which advocates for rights and protections for the transgender community.

Transgender people have faced considerable challenges regarding their legal status. Some states require evidence that a person's original gonads have been removed in order for the sex on their birth certificate to be changed. This is not the case for many transgender individuals, even for those who identify fully with the other sex. There are many different documents and forms of identification that indicate a person's sex, and the various agencies that issue them may not all have the same rules and requirements.

If a transgender person does not identify with either sex, procedures may be even more difficult. In 2016 a 53-year-old natal male named James Shupe from Portland, Oregon, was granted legal certification as having a non-binary gender—a first in the United States (Woodstock, 2017). He was assisted in this by Lambda Legal, a pro-LGBT legal support organization. Shupe had cross-sex hormone treatments and changed his first name to Jamie, but two years later he reverted to a male identity, saying that he had been in the grip of mental illness when he initially transitioned (Shupe, 2019). Another Portlander, a 27-year-old natal male then named Patrick Abbatiello, obtained legal recognition as genderless in 2017 and took the single legal name Patch (O'Hara, 2017). As far as is known, Patch has not had medical treatments and remains happy with their agender status.

Some states permit babies with ambiguous genitals to be issued with birth certificates in which sex is designated as "other," "intersex," or "non-binary," and some intersex adults have successfully requested changes to their birth certificates to include such designations. Several states are now willing to mark anyone's driver's license as "X" (sex unspecified) as an alternative to M or F, if so requested. No state has gone so far as to omit the M/F box completely, however.

In 2009 the federal Hate Crimes Prevention Act authorized federal prosecution of hate crimes based on gender identity, wherever they may occur. The first person to be convicted of murder under this statute was Joshua Vallum, a member of a Mississippi street gang. In 2015 he beat his ex-girlfriend Mercedes Williamson to death with a hammer after his friends discovered that she was trans. In 2017 Vallum received a 49-year prison sentence (Stack, 2017).

Growing up trans or non-binary can be a very stressful experience. Victimization, depression, substance abuse, and self-harm are common, especially when there is a lack of family support (Newcomb, 2019). Even so, recent years have seen a great increase in public interest in, and support for, trans people, and there is reason to expect that their lives will become far more rewarding in the future—both to themselves and to the communities with whom they share their lives.

## Summary

- Sex is usually determined by the sex chromosomes: The XX pattern leads to female development, and the XY pattern leads to male development. The key player in male development is the gene SRY, on the Y chromosome, which induces the embryo's genital ridges to become testes. In the absence of SRY, other genes induce the genital ridges to become ovaries.

- The male and female internal reproductive tracts develop from different precursors—the Wolffian and Müllerian ducts. In XY embryos, the testes secrete anti-Müllerian hormone (AMH), which causes the Müllerian ducts to regress, as well as androgens, which cause the Wolffian ducts to develop further and produce the male internal anatomy. In XY embryos lacking functional androgen receptors (a condition called androgen insensitivity syndrome), neither the male nor the female reproductive tract develops. In XX embryos, the lack of AMH allows the Müllerian ducts to develop further, and the lack of androgens allows the Wolffian ducts to regress, producing the female internal anatomy.

- The external genitalia of females and males develop from common precursors. The urethral folds give rise to the inner labia in females and to the shaft of the penis in males. The genital swellings give rise to the outer labia in females and the scrotum in males. The genital tubercle forms the glans of the clitoris in females and the glans of the penis in males. Male-typical development of the external genitalia requires the presence of testosterone and its conversion to 5α-dihydrotestosterone (DHT). In female fetuses exposed to high levels of androgens (as in congenital adrenal hyperplasia), the external genitalia are partially masculinized.

- Male and female brains differ in structure, chemistry, and function. Some sexual differentiation of the brain occurs prenatally—high levels of androgens drive male-typical brain development, and low levels permit female-typical development. At puberty and thereafter, estrogens become important in establishing and maintaining female-typical body structure and function and also influence the brain.

- Examples of atypical sex development include chromosomal anomalies such as Klinefelter syndrome (XXY or XXXY) and Turner syndrome (XO), as well as genetic conditions that affect sex hormone production (e.g., congenital adrenal hyperplasia) or the body's sensitivity to sex hormones (e.g., androgen insensitivity syndrome). The proper treatment of children with ambiguous genitalia is a subject of controversy.

- Many psychological characteristics differ to a greater or lesser extent between females and males. Gender identity is a person's core sense of being a female, a male, or some combination of the two. Gender roles are the sets of behaviors that represent a person as male, female, or non-binary.

- On average, women outperform men in fine movements, verbal fluency, and some aspects of memory. Men outperform women in some cognitive traits, such as visuospatial skills. Personality differences include greater aggressiveness in men.

- In the area of sexuality, men and women differ in the strength of sex drive, interest in casual sex, interest in visual sexual stimuli, styles of jealousy, sexual orientation, interest in unusual forms of sexual expression, likelihood of engaging in coercive sex, sexual risk taking, willingness to pay for sex, frequency of masturbation, sexual response cycles, and the duration of reproductive capacity over the lifespan. Most psychological sex differences show considerable overlap between the sexes, and their significance is debated.

- Many psychological sex differences arise early in life. Boys are typically more active and aggressive; girls are more interested in socializing. Boys and girls tend to prefer different toys, and both prefer to associate with children of their own sex. Sex-specific interaction

*(Continued)*

## Summary (continued)

styles develop within these same-sex groups. Differences in other cognitive traits emerge gradually during childhood.

- Biological factors help create sex differences. These include genes that have evolved to help men and women improve their reproductive success. A role for sex hormones, especially during prenatal life, is illustrated by experiments on animals, by observation of humans affected by endocrinological disorders, and by the study of anatomical markers (such as finger length ratios) that are correlated with gender traits.

- Socialization influences sex differences. This can happen through the innumerable rewards and punishments that children receive from parents and others. Imitation also has an important influence on gender roles.

- Several cognitive developmental models stress the importance of children's thought processes in the development of gender identity. In sexual script theory, the learning of gender roles involves the social negotiation of roles, such as those to be played by the man and woman in heterosexual relationships.

- Transgender people are those whose gender identity does not fully correspond to their natal sex. Transexuals are transgender people who seek to change their anatomical sex: They may transition from male to female (transexual women) or from female to male (transexual men). The change may involve hormone treatment and sex-reassignment (gender confirmation) surgery, or just hormone treatment. All transexual women and some transexual men have a childhood history of strong gender nonconformity. They dislike

the bodily changes induced by puberty and may attempt to conceal them. They are usually homosexual in the sense that they are sexually attracted to persons of the same natal sex as themselves. They usually do not identify as gay, however, but rather as heterosexual individuals of the sex with which they identify. Some transexual women are sexually attracted to women: Some or most of these individuals have a different developmental history, in which their desire to change sex develops out of a wish to incorporate the sex characteristics of their preferred sexual partners (women) into their own bodies (autogynephilia).

- Transitioning is a multistage process. It includes assessment and psychotherapy, living for some period in the identity of the other sex, hormonal treatments, and, often, sex-reassignment surgery. Genitals can be transformed into those of the other sex, but the procedure is expensive and, particularly in the case of female-to-male reassignment, can yield inadequate results. Not all people who transition undergo genital surgery. Many transexual women and men are satisfied with the results of sex reassignment and are able to surmount the social and sexual challenges of post-transition life.

- Many transgender people do not seek sex reassignment, for a variety of reasons. They may not fully identify with either sex. Some believe that sex reassignment would be unnecessary if society could be persuaded to abandon its obsession with the binary nature of gender. All transgender people face the possibility of discrimination and victimization, and many states fail to offer them specific protections.

---

The **Discovering Human Sexuality** digital resources include activities, animations, flashcards, web links, chapter outlines and summaries, and other study tools.

∙ ∙ ∙ ∙ ∙ ∙ ∙ ∙ ∙ ∙ ∙ ∙ ∙ ∙ ∙ ∙ ∙ ∙

Learn more with this chapter's digital tools, including the **Oxford Insight Study Guide**, at **oup.com/he/levay5e**.

## Discussion Questions

1. Imagine that you have just become the proud parent of a newborn baby, but the nurse-midwife or pediatrician tells you that it's not clear whether your baby is a girl or a boy. Do you think this child would be stigmatized and disadvantaged? How? Consider what you would do and why.

2. If you or your partner was pregnant and learned that your baby will be born with Turner or Klinefelter syndrome, what would you decide to do about it, and why? What would be the likely impacts of such a syndrome on your child's life?

3. Do you think that this chapter presents a balanced account of psychological differences between the sexes, and of research into the origins of these differences? If not, why not? Did anything you read surprise you or cause you to reconsider your beliefs in this area?

4. How would you react if your young daughter insisted she was a boy and asked to go to school in boys' clothes? Would you mention the possibility that she might eventually be helped to change anatomical sex? Would you stress the likelihood that she would eventually accept a female identity?

## Web Resources

Accord Alliance (group concerned with the health care of people with differences and disorders of sex development)  **www.accordalliance.org**

Androgen Insensitivity Syndrome Support Group  **www.aissg.org**

CARES Foundation (congenital adrenal hyperplasia education and support)  **www.caresfoundation.org**

Gender Inn (bibliographic source for books, articles, and websites concerning gender)  **www.genderinn.org**

GLAAD. Transgender Resources  **tinyurl.com/jwsjj55**

InterACT (advocates for intersex youth)  **www.interactadvocates.org**

Klinefelter Syndrome Information and Support  **www.klinefeltersyndrome.org**

National Center for Transgender Equality  **www.transequality.org**

National Public Radio: Two families grapple with sons' gender identity (radio program that describes two opposing therapeutic strategies for helping gender-dysphoric children)  **tinyurl.com/lxvdc5a**

Turner Syndrome Society of the United States  **www.turnersyndrome.org**

World Professional Association for Transgender Health  **www.wpath.org**

## Recommended Reading

Baron-Cohen, S. (2012). *The essential difference: Men, women, and the extreme male brain.* Penguin.

Beltz, A. M., Blakemore, J. E. O. & Berenbaum, S. A. (2013). *Sex differences in brain and behavioral development.* In: Rubenstein, J. & Rakic, P. (Eds.), Neural circuit development and function in the brain (Vol. 3 of Comprehensive Developmental Neuroscience). Academic.

Bertelloni, S. & Hiort, O. (Eds.). (2010). *New concepts for disorders of sex development.* Karger.

Bornstein, K. & Bergman, S. B. (2010). *Gender outlaws: The next generation.* Seal.

Buss, D. M. (2016). *The evolution of desire: Strategies for mating* (rev. ed.). Basic Books.

Colapinto, J. (2000). *As nature made him: The boy who was raised as a girl.* HarperCollins.

Drescher, J. & Byne, W. (Eds.). (2012). *Treating transgender children and adolescents: An interdisciplinary discussion.* Routledge.

Erickson-Schroth, L. (2014). *Trans bodies, trans selves: A resource for the transgender community.* Oxford University Press.

Mayor, A. (2014). *The Amazons: Lives and legends of warrior women across the ancient world.* Princeton.

Miller, D. I. & Halpern, D. F. (2014). The new science of cognitive sex differences. *Trends in Cognitive Sciences,* 18, 37–45.

Pfaff, D. (2010). *Man and woman: An inside story.* Oxford University Press.

Wade, L. & Ferree, M. M. (2019). *Gender: Ideas, interactions, institutions* (2nd ed.). W.W. Norton.

Sexual attraction, arousal, and response form a natural sequence.

# 5

# Attraction, Arousal, and Response

In sex, one thing leads to another. To be more specific, a predictable sequence of mental and bodily processes characterizes sexual interactions. In this chapter we present these stages as follows: sexual attraction to a potential sex partner, psychological sexual arousal, and the physiological changes in the genitals—the sexual response cycle—that precede and accompany sexual behavior. This sequence is not universal. Sometimes people engage in sex without prior attraction or arousal, for example, and only become aroused as a consequence of their behavior. But the three sequential stages provide a useful storyline or framework for discussing the key processes underlying sexuality.

To describe the basic structure of this sexual sequence, we must postpone consideration of many issues that relate to it in important ways: how we negotiate sexual interactions, how we enter into sexual relationships, what specific forms of sexual contact we engage in, and how the aging process influences our sexual psychology and performance. What is left, however, is the central core of sex: wanting it, and getting it.

## 5.1 Sexual Attraction: It Takes Two

**LEARNING OBJECTIVES**

After reading this section you should be able to:

5.1.1 Explain how masculinity–femininity, symmetry, and averageness influence the attractiveness of faces.

5.1.2 Evaluate the evidence that cultural and situational factors influence men's preferences among women of varying body mass indexes.

5.1.3 Give an example of choice blindness in judgments of attractiveness.

5.1.4 Describe the circumstances in which familiarity increases or decreases attraction, and explain the Westermarck effect.

5.1.5 Discuss the potential benefits and problems associated with being asexual.

Sexual attraction is an erotically charged orientation toward a specific other person. The attraction may be calm and controlled ("He's a really charming guy"), or it may be madly impetuous ("If I don't have sex with her in the next 5 minutes, there is no God"). It may be felt at first meeting, or it may build over time. The attraction may be mutual, or it may be one-way. It may be accompanied by feelings of love and commitment, or not.

Sexual attraction is different from simple *liking*. In fact, we may be sexually attracted to people we dislike or to people we don't know well enough to like or dislike. Sexual attraction is also different from the judgment that a person is attractive. A heterosexual woman might judge that another woman is attractive, for example, but not be sexually attracted to her. Sexual attraction is also different from mate choice: We may choose to cohabit with someone, marry someone, or even have sex with someone for entirely nonsexual reasons. And sexual attraction is different, at least in part, from romantic love.

Because sexual attraction involves two people, we may approach it in two ways. First, we may ask, "What causes a person to be attractive?" Second, we may ask, "What causes a person to experience attraction?" Both questions are important, but we begin with the former. We are asking, essentially, "What is beauty?"

### Beauty is not entirely in the eye of the beholder

If we define beauty as the attributes that combine to make a person sexually attractive, then beauty can include many things, ranging from physical traits such as appearance, voice quality, and odor to nonphysical attributes such as personality, behavior, and social circumstances. These nonphysical attributes are decisive in the long run, but our looks are usually the first cues to attractiveness that are available to others. We therefore consider physical appearance before other aspects of beauty (**FIGURE 5.1**).

The saying "Beauty lies in the eye of the beholder" suggests that everything is subjective or idiosyncratic—that no objective characteristics make a person more or less attractive to others. In fact, however, psychologists have found a considerable degree of consensus on the topic of beauty. They have identified certain characteristics that influence the perceived attractiveness of faces and other physical features, no matter who is doing the judging.

MASCULINITY–FEMININITY   There are differences between the structures of women's and men's faces: Women typically have fuller lips and larger eyes* than men, for example, while men have wider jaws and noses and larger chins. These sex differences are small during childhood but increase greatly at puberty under the influence of sex hormones. They are therefore indicators of reproductive maturity and fertility, so we would logically expect them to influence judgments of attractiveness.

**FAQ:** I think that mixed-race people are especially attractive. Any science on that?

Yes. Both computer-morphing and real-life studies have found that mixed-race faces are, on average, rated more attractive than faces of the individual races from which they are descended.

---

*This refers not to the entire eyeball but to the portion of the eye that is visible between the eyelids.

◀ **FIGURE 5.1** Human faces offer astonishing diversity, and no two people would place them in the same order of attractiveness. Yet there do seem to be some universals that affect people's judgment.

Top: © iStock.com/real444; © Fotoluminate LLC/Shutterstock.com; © Fotos593/Shutterstock.com; © iStock.com/monkeybusinessimages. Middle: © iStock.com/Anita_Bonita; © iStock.com/Lopolo/Shutterstock.com; © Paul Banton/Shutterstock; © iStock.com/ajr_images. Bottom: © iStock.com/drbimages; © iStock.com/DMEPhotography; © mimagephotography; © Sveta Yaroshuk/Shutterstock.com

That is in fact the case, at least with regard to women: Women's faces are judged to be most attractive when they are situated at the extreme feminine end of a masculinity–femininity spectrum (Little et al., 2011; Van Dongen, 2014) (**FIGURE 5.2**). This is true regardless of whether the viewer is male or female and regardless of whether the images are derived from the faces of European, African, or Asian women. It's no wonder, then, that women who want to look attractive use cosmetics in ways that increase their apparent femininity and exaggerate their differences from male faces.

From V. S. Johnston et al., 2001. *Evol Hum Behav* 22: 251–257

▲ **FIGURE 5.2** **The face that changes sex** Seven frames from a movie of a face that gradually morphs from hypermasculine (left) through androgynous (center) to hyperfeminine (right).

(A)                (B)

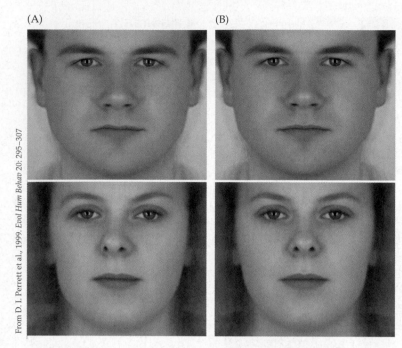

▲ **FIGURE 5.3** **Symmetry increases attractiveness.**
(A) Naturally asymmetrical male and female faces. (B) The same faces manipulated to make them symmetrical. Most viewers rate the symmetrical faces as more attractive, even though they are not generally aware that symmetry is being adjusted.

With men's faces, it's more complicated. Extremely masculine faces, such as the leftmost image in Figure 5.2, may be very attractive, but they may also be judged as cold or unkind, which reduces their attractiveness (Perrett et al., 1998). Thus, studies in which viewers are asked to adjust the masculinity–femininity of a computer-generated male face have yielded inconsistent results (Perrett, 2010; Van Dongen, 2014), and the overall relevance of this dimension of male attractiveness is probably not great.

SYMMETRY Animals look for symmetry in their mates. So do humans, both in industrialized countries and in hunter-gatherer societies (Little et al., 2007). The more symmetrical a person's face, the more attractive, sexy, and healthy that person seems to others (Fink et al., 2006; Perrett, 2010) (**FIGURE 5.3**). Symmetry raises the attractiveness of the remainder of the body, too. This preference for symmetrical features is not present in young children but develops between 5 and 9 years of age (Vingilis-Jaremko & Maurer, 2013).

Evolutionary psychologists have proposed a reason to explain why symmetrical features are more attractive than asymmetrical ones (Little et al., 2011). Because a single genetic program guides the development of the left and right sides of the body, asymmetrical features may develop if the person's genetic makeup is less robust or if the genetic program is derailed in some way, such as by an infection. Some studies do report that people with asymmetrical features are more likely to experience a variety of disorders, but others have failed to observe such an association, especially with regard to the slight asymmetries that are commonly present in the general population (Pound et al., 2014). Thus, it is plausible, but not proven, that evolution has given us the ability to detect asymmetries on account of a connection to ill health.

Curiously, when people are shown half of a face—either left or right side—they rate it as more attractive than when presented with the entire face of the same person (Sadr & Krowicki, 2019). What matters, then, is not the presence of symmetry but the absence of asymmetry.

AVERAGENESS Composite faces generated by averaging a considerable number of individual faces are rated as more attractive than any of the individuals that contributed to the composite (Foo et al., 2017) (**FIGURE 5.4**). This may seem improbable, because the phrase "average looking" is hardly a compliment. However, the attractiveness of such composites derives in large part from the fact that they emphasize features common to many faces and are therefore very familiar. Indeed, if you look at the composite face in Figure 5.4 for long enough, the individual faces that contributed to the composite may begin to look more and more unusual. Computer-averaged faces also tend to be very symmetrical. Individual faces that happen to resemble such composites, such as that of President John F. Kennedy, are judged to be especially attractive. They are also difficult to caricature in cartoons, because they have few "unaverage" features to emphasize.

## Evolution and culture influence the attractiveness of bodies

Throughout most of human history and prehistory the abilities to fight and to hunt have been of primary survival and reproductive value to men. In a study led by

**FAQ:** Do women find men's body hair attractive?

Generally not, but chest hair is a turn-on for some women (Dixson & Rantala, 2016).

▶ **FIGURE 5.4** **Attractiveness of computer-averaged faces** The composite face (A) is rated more attractive than any of the 16 individual faces (B) from which it was derived.

(A)

(B)

Aaron Sell of Griffith University in Australia, raters (mostly women) viewed upper-body photographs of men whose strength had been measured but not revealed to the raters (Sell et al., 2017). The participants consistently rated the men's attractiveness according to their measured strength, using broad shoulders and a V-shaped torso as their main cues. Thus evolutionary pressures exerted over millennia appear to shape women's judgments of male attractiveness today, even though men's physical strength has lost most of its adaptive value in our contemporary world.

**Body mass index** (**BMI**) is another physical characteristic that influences judgments of attractiveness, but here both evolution and culture seem to play a role. BMI is a person's weight in kilograms divided by the square of the person's height in meters. (BMI calculators, many using pounds and feet, can be found online.) The "healthy" BMI range has been defined as 18.5 to 25, but the median BMI in the contemporary United States is near the top of this range (about 24.5 for women in their 20s), so by this standard nearly half of U.S. women in this age range are overweight (BMI of 25 to 30) or obese (BMI greater than 30). A high BMI is generally caused by a high percentage of body fat.

In a number of studies, male and female raters have been asked to judge the attractiveness of women varying in BMI. (They have been shown photos of bodies only, without the faces.) In the United States and other Western countries these raters have preferred women with BMIs around 18 to 22—that is, well below average and near the low end of the healthy range. From these findings, one might be tempted to conclude that slimness is universally preferred. Yet during certain periods in Western history, such as the 17th century, a high BMI was considered much more attractive than it is now. Cross-cultural studies have also demonstrated quite diverse preferences. And people's preferences can change over time—even from minute to minute, depending on circumstances (**BOX 5.1**).

Media trendsetters can strongly influence what is considered attractive. An example: Data analyst Seth Stephens-Davidowitz analyzed porn searches that mentioned "big butts" (Stephens-Davidowitz, 2017). After about 2010 the number of these searches, and of searches for methods to increase butt size, increased dramatically. "Big ass" is now a more popular Pornhub search term than "big tits" (Buzzfeed, 2019). Stephens-Davidowitz attributed this change to one person—social media superstar Kim Kardashian, whose ample posterior has been a topic of intense public interest (**FIGURE 5.5**). Butt augmentation procedures—usually involving the transplant of fatty tissue from other areas of the body—increased by an estimated 250% during the five years after 2010 (Healthline, 2019).

From the general appearance of a person's face and body, we can assess their age, which is an important criterion for attractiveness in women, at least according to men. When judging women solely by physical appearance, straight men find

**body mass index (BMI)** A person's weight in kilograms divided by the square of their height in meters.

▲ **FIGURE 5.5** **Bubble butt diva** Kim Kardashian.

## BOX 5.1
# Culture and Body Weight

In African societies, especially those exposed to food shortages, large women tend to be admired more than they are in contemporary Western cultures, where life for many people is an all-you-can-eat buffet (**FIGURE A**). A British and South African group of researchers asked what would happen to people's preferences if they moved from one culture to the other (Tovee et al., 2006). They first assessed the preferences of white men and women in the United Kingdom and of rural Zulu men and women in South Africa. The white Britons found women with a body mass index (BMI) of around 20—that is, on the thin side of average—to be most attractive, and attractiveness fell off steadily both below and above that value (**FIGURE B**). The Zulus in South Africa gave high ratings to women with BMIs of 20 and above, with no suggestion of a falloff in attractiveness up to a BMI of at least 40. Only on the lower side of 20 was there a rapid drop in attractiveness.

The researchers then investigated a third group of individuals, namely South African Zulus who had migrated to Britain within the previous 18 months. As shown in Figure B, these recent transplants quickly changed their preferences, exhibiting much the same lack of interest in heavier women as is typical of white Britons. In other words, this study suggested that BMI preferences, at least over the upper part of the range, are strongly influenced by the cultures or circumstances in which people find themselves. The low attractiveness ratings for very *underweight* women could be hardwired, however. This would make sense in evolutionary terms, because severely underweight women are unlikely to be fertile.

If preferences of this kind can change over months, can they change over minutes? In two studies, researchers waylaid male students entering and leaving a college dining hall, and they tested the students' preferences for women of varying BMIs (Nelson & Morrison, 2005; Swami & Tovee, 2006). Indeed, the hungry men who were entering the hall preferred heavier women than did the full-bellied men who were leaving it.

These findings don't mean that hungry men view women as edible. Rather, they exemplify a general pattern in which men in a state of deprivation (hungry or poor) are attracted to women who can demonstrate (through body size, maturity, or other cues) that they have access to resources (Pettijohn et al., 2009).

Over the last few decades many cultures that embraced obesity have come to stigmatize it. In part this has to do with increased food security, but television and Hollywood movies may also have spread a culture of thinness. In a study carried out in rural Nicaragua, for example, a group led by Tracey Thornborrow of the University of Lincoln in the United Kingdom tested the preferences of men living in villages that did or did not have television service (Thornborrow et al.,

(A) By Western standards of beauty these South African Zulu women may be considered too heavy, but Zulu men find overweight and average-weight women equally attractive. (B) Body mass index and beauty. This figure plots the BMI and beauty of 50 women (each symbol within a category represents one woman) as rated by three mixed-sex groups of raters: white Britons (circles), Zulus in South Africa (squares), and Zulus within 18 months of migrating to Britain (triangles). After migrating to Britain, the Zulus' preferences shifted toward the typical Western pattern: Their attraction to women with high BMIs decreased. The vertical arrow shows the median BMI for U.S. women in their 20s. (After M. J. Tovee et al., 2006. *Evol Hum Behav* 27: 443–456.)

2018). In the villages with TV, men preferred women with slimmer bodies than did men in the no-TV villages.

Given the apparent low valuation of obesity in Western culture, you might imagine that women with a high BMI would have difficulty finding sex partners. In reality that isn't the case, according to researchers at Chapman University (Frederick & Jenkins, 2015). They found that average-weight and overweight women reported about the same number of sex partners. Underweight women, on the other hand, did report significantly fewer partners.

women most attractive in their late teen years and decreasingly so thereafter (Buss, 2011). This makes sense in evolutionary terms, because young women are at their most fertile and have the most years ahead to nurture children. Straight women's judgments of men's physical attractiveness do not vary nearly so much with the men's age, but young women generally prefer men who are somewhat older than themselves. The age preferences of gay people are similar to those of their heterosexual peers (Silverthorne & Quinsey, 2000).

A striking real-world illustration of the sex difference in age preference comes from an analysis of messaging behavior on the OkCupid dating website (Rudder, 2010). In their early 20s, men typically message women who are about 2 years younger than themselves, whereas women in that age group tend to message men who are about 2 years older than themselves. In the older age ranges the 2-year age difference increases for men (they seek women who are more than 2 years younger than themselves), whereas it decreases and eventually disappears for women—they message men who are about the same age as themselves. An exception to this generalization is the MILF/cougar phenomenon: a small contingent of younger men who are drawn to older women, and vice versa. (MILF stands for "mothers I'd like to fuck.")

The cosmetic enhancements that people use to increase their own attractiveness often involve the exaggeration of sexually differentiated traits. Breast augmentation is a well-known example in Western society, but breast reduction is also a common procedure—it is done either for cosmetic reasons or to relieve back or neck pain (**FIGURE 5.6**).

It's worth stressing that the process of judging visual attractiveness is a largely *unconscious* process. When people are asked to choose the more attractive of two women's faces, for example, and then asked why they found that face more attractive, they will give detailed, persuasive reasons for their choice, as if they had carefully thought the matter through before choosing. But if they are deceived into thinking that the face they *rejected* was the one they chose, they usually fail to notice the deception and give equally detailed and persuasive reasons why *that* face was the more attractive one (Johansson et al., 2014) (**FIGURE 5.7**). This phenomenon has been called **choice blindness**. It's as if consciousness simply provides a plausible explanation for choices that are made at a deeper level of the mind.

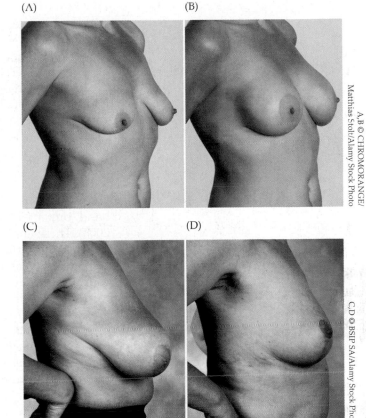

▲ **FIGURE 5.6   Improving on nature**  Before and after breast augmentation (A and B) and breast reduction (C and D).

**choice blindness**   Unawareness of the actual reasons for a preference, along with the unconscious invention of fictive reasons.

▲ **FIGURE 5.7   Choice blindness**  (A) The person is asked to decide which of two faces is more attractive—the left one in this example. (B) By sleight of hand he is made to think he picked the other face. (C) He will then give a detailed explanation for why that face is more attractive.

### Attractiveness involves senses besides vision

Although we tend to rely on our eyes in assessing the physical attractiveness of potential partners, especially in the first moments of meeting them, other senses also play a role. If that were not true, blind people could not experience sexual attraction, but they do. Here's how one blind person expressed it on an online bulletin board: "If anything I think being blind has made me kinkier and more intense as you touch a lot more. Being blind, I would have to say sex is better and deeper, feeling your way around a body you get to know everywhere."

Besides touch, hearing and smell may also be important. Men's voices generally have deeper pitch than those of women, reflecting the sexual differentiation of the larynx at puberty. Women find men with deep voices more attractive than those with higher-pitched voices, and in hunter-gatherer societies fertile women bestow their favors more readily on deep-voiced men (Apicella et al., 2007). Men, on the other hand, prefer women's voices that are higher-pitched than average (Feinberg et al., 2008). These are further examples of sexually differentiated traits being particularly important criteria for physical attractiveness.

Body odor can have a strong influence on a person's attractiveness. In one study conducted by Swiss and German researchers, men sniffed pads that had been used to collect armpit secretions from women on the peak fertility days of their menstrual cycles (the late follicular phase) (Lobmaier et al., 2018). The men were in remarkable agreement about how attractive each odor was. What's more, attractiveness was correlated with the women's sex hormone levels: high attractiveness was correlated with high estrogen and low progesterone levels. In other words, hormonal patterns indicative of high fertility could be recognized by men through their effects on body odor.

Some researchers, however, have gone further, claiming that volatile chemicals released into the air from women's or men's bodies trigger or modify sexual arousal in persons exposed to them, even when those persons are not conscious of having smelled anything. Such substances, which are derived from sex hormones, have been referred to as **human sex pheromones**. Research in this area is very incomplete, however, and the findings are conflicting. If human sex pheromones do exist, their influence is limited: They may help identify the sex of a person with whom one is interacting, mildly increase or decrease attraction, or modify a person's mood (Zhou et al., 2014; Ferdenzi et al., 2016). Yet even these effects failed to show up in carefully controlled trials of two leading sex pheromone candidates (Hare et al., 2017). What we can be sure of is that human sex pheromones, if they exist, don't elicit the automatic mating behaviors that are triggered by sex pheromones in insects and some vertebrates.

To summarize the research on physical attractiveness, we can say that there are some respects in which beauty is not in the eye of the beholder but, rather, reflects objective, universal attributes of men and women. The attributes that make for attractiveness give indications of a person's health, strength, fertility, or genetic fitness. In addition, however, circumstances such as food availability and hunger, and cultural phenomena such as television and social media, help shape what we consider sexually attractive.

One last point: Physical attractiveness confers many advantages in life—economic, relational, and so on (Hamermesh, 2011), but also some disadvantages. Controlled experiments simulating a business environment have shown that very attractive women, but not very attractive men, are judged (both by women and men) as less truthful, and more deserving of termination, than their average-looking peers (Sheppard & Johnson, 2019). The reason for this negative effect of physical attractiveness, according to the authors of the just-cited study, is that seeing beautiful women induces a sense of sexual insecurity in both women and men.

**human sex pheromones** Volatile substances released from men's and women's bodies that are thought to influence sexual feelings in others.

### Behavior and personality influence sexual attractiveness

All this talk of physical beauty can have a downside, because it can provoke anxiety among people who think that their faces or bodies fall short of the standards necessary to attract a desirable partner. Yet this kind of anxiety is seldom justified. For one thing, people tend to underestimate their own physical attractiveness. For another, they can improve their attractiveness by means of all the technologies—from cosmetics to plastic surgery—that human ingenuity has devised. And most important, they can influence their attractiveness through their behavior.

In fact, we may speak of a behavioral or psychological beauty that can be independent of physical beauty. Behavior and personality tend to influence attractiveness more slowly than appearance does, because they are not so immediately apparent. But even in a still photograph, behavior matters: Smiling faces are judged to be more attractive than those with neutral expressions, at least when the faces are looking directly at the observer (Jones et al., 2006).

Another simple behavior affecting attractiveness is gait (manner of walking or running). Because they have wider hips, women rotate and tilt their hips more than men when walking, and they also take shorter strides. Wearing high heels forces women to exaggerate or "hyperfeminize" these behavioral traits. Psychologists at the University of Portsmouth, in England, created "point-light displays" of women walking—that is, computer screen displays that showed only the positions of LED lights attached to the women's joints. The displays created from women walking in high heels were judged by both women and men to be much more attractive than those from the same women in flat shoes (Morris et al., 2013).

Presumably, sexual attractiveness influences the desirability of partners for casual encounters or dating relationships more than it does for longer-term, live-in relationships such as marriage, because long-term relationships involve so much more than sex. To get some insight into the spectrum of traits that influence sexual attractiveness, therefore, we do best to look at studies that have questioned men and women about the traits they would value in a casual or short-term sex partner. Most such studies report that physical appearance is the most important criterion used by both men and women in forming initial judgments of attractiveness (Hatfield et al., 2012), but many personality traits are also highly rated, including trustworthiness, warmth, and a sense of humor (Regan et al., 2000). These are traits that are likely to be important in any relationship. In *Maxim* magazine's (unscientific) 2013 sex survey, for example, over half the women respondents cited "He's funny" as the most important quality in a boyfriend (*Maxim*, 2013). It may be that, even when people are "hooking up," they are still unconsciously evaluating the person they are hooking up with as a potential long-term partner (Sprecher & Regan, 2002). In any event, general "likability" traits seem to intensify sexual attraction.

In one study, men and women were asked to list desirable characteristics in romantic partners and then were invited to a speed-dating event. The dates they chose were not those whose characteristics matched their previously stated preferences (Eastwick & Finkel, 2008). For example, a woman who rated high earnings as the most important criterion for selecting a romantic partner actually chose the lowest earner of the men she talked with at the event. Thus, people might not have a clear idea of what they are looking for in a sex partner until they actually meet someone who appeals to them—another example of the limited role of conscious processes in sexual attraction.

It has been reported over and over again that men are more interested than women in the physical attractiveness of their prospective sex partners,

▲ At speed-dating events, people's choices may not be based on conscious criteria.

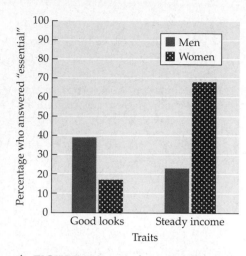

▲ **FIGURE 5.8  Bucks versus beauty**
This figure shows the percentage of heterosexual men and women (age 26–35) who consider good looks or a steady income "essential" in a long-term partner. (After M. R. Fales et al., 2016. *Pers Individ Differ* 88: 78–87.)

**Coolidge effect**   The revival of sexual arousal caused by the presence of a novel partner.

**habituation**   A psychological or physiological process that reduces a person's response to a stimulus or drug after repeated or prolonged exposure.

**Westermarck effect**   The lack of sexual attraction between individuals, such as siblings, who lived together during their childhood.

whereas women are more interested than men in their partners' education, intelligence, social status, or wealth (**FIGURE 5.8**). Regarding education, for example, a group of Belgian economists analyzed 3,600 profile reviews on Tinder, a mostly heterosexual dating app, and found that women strongly preferred highly educated partners, whereas education didn't influence men's preferences one way or the other (Neyt et al., 2019). (We speculate that men would pay more attention to education on a matchmaking site like eharmony, where a partner's long-term compatibility is relevant.)

## Familiarity may increase or decrease attraction

We have discussed evidence that there is some consensus in the way that attractiveness is judged: Certain individuals are judged to be very attractive by most people, and other individuals are judged to be less so. If that were the whole story, the most attractive people would use their looks and personalities to pair off with other very attractive people, and the rest of us would have to make do with less attractive mates. There would be a sorting out of the population into desirable couples, less desirable couples, and downright undesirable couples.

But that's not how it works out, because consensus judgments give way to more person-specific judgments as people become more familiar with each other. Psychologists Paul Eastwick and Lucy Hunt documented this process in a variety of ways (Eastwick & Hunt, 2014). In one study, they asked heterosexual students, at the beginning of the semester, to rate the opposite-sex students in the class on such variables as attractiveness, warmth, and potential for success. At this time, when the students had known each other only briefly, there was a considerable measure of agreement about the relative desirability of different students. Eastwick and Hunt repeated the survey at the end of the semester, by which time the students had had the opportunity to get to know each other much better. By this time, the consensus had largely broken down: There was very little correlation between the ratings made by different students. In fact, similar findings emerged from a variety of experiments: The more people know each other, the more person-specific judgments supplant consensus judgments—with regard not just to physical attractiveness but to a broad spectrum of personality traits. To the extent that intimate relationships develop between people who already know each other, people are not competing for the "hottest" partners so much as they are searching for their own individual soul mates.

Thus, how attractive we find people is strongly influenced by our prior experience, but this influence can work in either direction, making people more attractive or less attractive. In general, mere exposure to any stimulus—whether it be the music of a particular composer or a particular kind of food—makes us like that stimulus better when we encounter it again, even if we don't remember having experienced it before. The same is true of faces: The mere fact of having seen a face before makes us judge it as more attractive than if we were seeing it for the first time. That is true for women viewing faces of either sex, as well as for men viewing men's faces, but when men view a woman's face a second time, they find that face *less* attractive—an observation that presumably reflects men's greater interest in sexual novelty (Little et al., 2014).

In this connection, it's well known from animal experiments that males who have just mated will mate again more promptly if presented with a novel female. This is called the **Coolidge effect**.* There has never been a full-scale test of the Coolidge effect in humans, but here's something close: Researchers at the University of North Dakota

---

*According to legend, President Calvin Coolidge and his wife were once touring a farm. Soon after their arrival they were taken off on separate tours. When Mrs. Coolidge passed the chicken pens, she paused to ask the man in charge if the rooster copulated more than once each day. "Dozens of times," was the response. "Please tell that to the president," Mrs. Coolidge requested. When the president passed the pens and was told about the roosters, he asked, "Same hen each time?" "Oh no, a different hen each time." "Please tell that to Mrs. Coolidge," said the president.

(Plaud et al., 1997) recruited male psychology students for a study that involved listening to erotic tapes narrated by a female student. (As if further incentive were needed, the students received $20 and research credit.) The students' sexual arousal—monitored by a strain gauge placed around the penis (**FIGURE 5.9**)—declined if the same tapes were repeated, but their arousal remained high if new tapes were played. This negative effect of familiarity, known as **habituation**, lasted for several weeks at least. Unfortunately, we're not aware of a comparable study of female students.

Familiarity during childhood has particularly long-lasting negative effects on attraction. Being close to another child (such as a sibling) during early childhood makes it unlikely that one will find that person sexually attractive in adult life (De Smet et al., 2014). This phenomenon is known as the **Westermarck effect**, named for the Finnish anthropologist who first described it. The Westermarck effect is an evolved mechanism that reduces the likelihood of matings between siblings, which are genetically disadvantageous (Lieberman & Billingsley, 2016). Siblings who do not live together as children, however, do not experience the Westermarck effect and may experience strong sexual attraction to each other as adults; this phenomenon is sometimes referred to as genetic sexual attraction.

Although we don't discuss falling in love until Chapter 7, we should mention the obvious, which is that falling in love vastly increases the physical and behavioral attractiveness of the beloved. Physical flaws and distracting tics may suddenly seem like special features that make the person delightfully unique—for as long as love lasts, at least. In this situation, beauty may truly lie in the eye of the beholder.

## Women's perceived attractiveness varies around the menstrual cycle

For women who are naturally cycling (i.e., not using hormonal contraception), their sexual attractiveness to men varies around the cycle: They are most attractive during the "fertile window" leading up to ovulation, when estrogen levels are high, and less attractive after ovulation, when progesterone levels are high (Puts et al., 2013). The increased attractiveness during the fertile window is due to subtle changes in facial appearance, voice quality, and body odor (Haselton & Gildersleeve, 2016). Female lap dancers in strip clubs receive much higher tips near the time of ovulation than at any other time in the cycle (Miller et al., 2007) (**FIGURE 5.10**). Women also pay more attention to grooming, makeup, and clothing during their fertile window (Haselton et al.,

▲ **FIGURE 5.9 A penile strain gauge** The loop of rubber tubing contains mercury, whose electrical resistance increases as the loop is stretched by the erection of the penis.

**FAQ:** How come I'm sexually aroused when I don't want to be?

Sexual arousal is not under conscious control, and it's common and harmless for arousal to occur in circumstances that seem inappropriate. Rarely, arousal may be so persistent as to constitute a disorder (see Chapter 14).

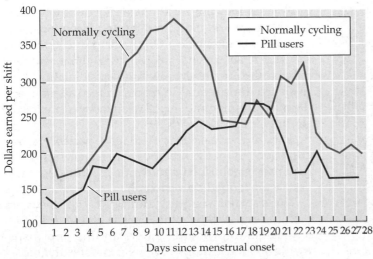

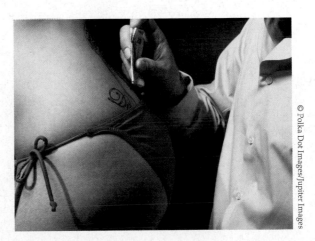

▲ **FIGURE 5.10 Lap dancers' earnings around the menstrual cycle** In normally cycling women, there is a broad peak in earnings between about 9 and 14 days after the onset of menstruation. This peak corresponds approximately to the fertile window leading up to ovulation. In women taking contraceptive pills, which often prevent ovulation, this peak is lower and occurs at a different time. (After G. Miller et al., 2007. *Evol Hum Behav* 28: 375–381.)

2007). However, compared with the females of many other mammalian species, who may be totally unattractive and unreceptive to males outside of their fertile windows, the changes around women's menstrual cycles are relatively subtle.

## Asexual women and men do not experience sexual attraction

All this talk of sexual attraction probably resonates with experiences you have had in your own life. But what do you make of these comments?

*I've never in my life had a dream or a sexual fantasy about being with another woman. So I can pretty much say that I have no lesbian sort of tendencies whatsoever. But I've never had a dream or a sexual fantasy about being with a man either—that I can ever, ever remember.*

*I didn't find the act something I enjoyed. I guess I thought, "What's the big whoop? Why are they so interested in this thing?" I don't get anything out of it. (Prause & Graham, 2007)*

For reasons unknown, some people experience no (or very little) sexual attraction over their entire lifetime. These **asexual** men and women may still experience romantic attraction in the sense of desiring psychological intimacy with a specific partner, but they do not desire to express that intimacy in physical sex. Estimates of prevalence vary, but something like 1% of American adults are asexual (Poston & Baumle, 2010; Bogaert, 2012).

Asexuality is different from a conscious decision not to engage in sexual relationships (sexual abstinence). Nor does it stem from a morbid fear of sex, from repressed homosexuality, or from problems in sexual performance such as erectile disorder. In fact, self-identified asexual men masturbate at about the same frequency as other men (Yule et al., 2017). This suggests that the difference between asexual and sexual men lies not in the pleasure that genital stimulation and orgasm can provide, but in the interpersonal aspect of sexual desire. There are some indications that asexuality may have a biological basis (Yule et al., 2014). There is some overlap between asexuality and mild forms of autism, but many asexual individuals are not autistic to any degree (Yule & Brotto, 2017).

Self-identified asexual men and women say that their lack of sexual attraction has both positive and negative effects on their lives (Prause & Graham, 2007). On the plus side, they have more free time and are spared the complications of negotiating sexual relationships, sexually transmitted infections, and unwanted pregnancies. On the negative side, they may worry about what is wrong with them, and they may have difficulty maintaining close relationships while rebuffing sexual advances. In fact, asexual people often do enter into sexual relationships, not for the sex but for the relationship.

Some individuals do not usually experience sexual attraction but may do so toward persons with whom they have established a romantic relationship. Such people are termed **demisexual**.

The Asexual Visibility and Education Network (AVEN—see Web Resources at the end of this chapter) works to promote understanding and dispel myths about asexuality. AVEN promotes the recognition of asexuality as a legitimate sexual orientation (**FIGURE 5.11**).

**asexual** Describes a person who does not experience sexual attraction.

**demisexual** Describes a person who experiences sexual attraction only in the context of a strong emotional bond.

© Lucy/Shutterstock.com

▲ **FIGURE 5.11** **Asexual pride** Asexual women and men believe that asexuality is an alternative sexual orientation comparable to being lesbian, gay, etc. Hence the acronym "LGBTA" is sometimes used.

This mention of "sexual orientation" reminds us that a person's sexual orientation, defined as the predisposition to experience sexual attraction to one sex or the other, or to both or neither, is the most dramatic example of an internal trait influencing sexual attraction. Because of its personal and social significance, however, we dedicate an entire chapter to it (see Chapter 12).

# 5.2 Sexual Arousal Has Multiple Roots

**LEARNING OBJECTIVES**

After reading this section you should be able to:

5.2.1 Explain why people might experience sexual fantasies that don't correspond to their desired sexual activities in real life.

5.2.2 Describe how sex hormones and conditioning can influence sexual arousal.

Sexual arousal is an acute psychological state of excitement marked by sexual feelings, attractions, or desires. It is a motivational state, meaning that it provides the drive for sexual behavior. In addition, sexual arousal is a physiological state marked by changes in the genitalia such as erection of the penis or lubrication of the vagina. Psychological and physiological arousal usually go together, but not always.

Sexual arousal may be triggered by external events, such as seeing a sexually attractive person, witnessing someone's sexually suggestive behavior such as undressing, or viewing sexual activity in real life or in pornographic videos. Alternatively, arousal may result from physical stimulation of the genitals or other parts of the body. Just thinking about sex may trigger arousal, and sometimes sexual arousal happens without any obvious cause.

## Fantasy is a common mode of sexual arousal

Sexual **fantasy**—imagined sexual experiences during waking hours—is a route by which internal mental processes promote sexual arousal. The great majority of men and women engage in sexual fantasy, and people who place a positive value on fantasy are more sexually assertive—in terms of asking for sex, requesting contraceptive use, and refusing unwanted sex—than those who feel bad about such fanta-

**fantasy** An imagined experience, sexual or otherwise.

sies (Santos-Iglesias et al., 2013). Men engage in sexual fantasies more than women, but women increase the frequency of their sexual fantasies near the time of ovulation (Dawson et al., 2012). Fantasies may occur during regular activities, or they may accompany masturbation or partnered sex.

As for the content of sexual fantasies, common themes involve the kinds of behaviors people actually engage in or would like to engage in. But "forbidden" themes are also popular: In one computer-aided analysis of nearly a quarter-million sexual fantasies posted on an online site, fantasies involving incest were extremely prevalent (Seehuus et al., 2019). (Incest-related porn searches are also common—see Chapter 17.)

Even more surprising is the fact that about half of all women experience erotic fantasies of being physically coerced into sex, which they would do anything to avoid in real life (Bivona & Critelli, 2009). (Again, this theme is common in women's porn searches.). Here is one woman's account of a rape fantasy:

▲ In your fantasies you can have sexual experiences that might be unobtainable in real life. This is *The Dream of the Fisherman's Wife* by the 19th-century Japanese artist Hokusai.

*This friend of mine comes over and immediately shoves me against the wall, pinning my hands over my head and kisses me passionately. I tell him to stop, that it's wrong and we can't do this. He says he doesn't care; he cannot wait another minute. His motivation is satisfying his own sexual hunger. While my hands are still pinned over my head he uses his other hand to tear off my clothes, not caring if they rip. We're both naked and he kisses me all over my body. I am begging him to stop, telling him it's wrong and that we can get caught any minute. He picks me up and screws me against the wall. At first it hurts but it feels so good that I can't help but enjoy it. When we're done he leaves because he knows my boyfriend is going to be over soon. I am torn between the pleasure and knowing that it's morally wrong. (Bivona & Critelli, 2009)*

There are several possible explanations for the prevalence of rape fantasies (Ziegler & Conley, 2016). Among them are the following:

- By fantasizing that they have no choice in the matter, women avoid feeling guilty about the fantasy.
- Rape fantasies are really fantasies of sexual power: The woman is so irresistible that men cast aside their inhibitions against sexual violence.
- Rape fantasies are simply part of a general openness to a variety of sexual experiences.

According to a study by Jenny Bivona and colleagues at the University of North Texas, women who experience rape fantasies are relatively high in self-esteem, have more frequent sexual fantasies and a wider variety of fantasies, and have generally more positive attitudes toward sex than women who do not have rape fantasies (Bivona et al., 2012). Their findings suggest that rape fantasies are part of a general openness to experience, more than they are fantasies of power or strategies to avoid guilt (**FIGURE 5.12**).

▶ **FIGURE 5.12 Swept away** This is *The Rape* [meaning seizure] *of the Daughters of Leucippus* (1618) by Peter Paul Rubens. The women are being forcibly abducted, but in women's fantasies it may be the men who are "swept away"—by the women's beauty.

It hardly needs saying, but knowing that a woman has rape fantasies in no way entitles a man (or woman) to force sex on her. The only context in which coercive sex might be acted out is in the context of a BDSM scene, in which the interaction is agreed on in advance and either partner is able to terminate the scene at will (see Chapter 13).

Contrary to what one might expect, many women and men who identify as heterosexual have occasionally experienced homosexual fantasies (Joyal et al., 2014). Again, this may be part of a general openness to experience rather than a sign that these individuals are really bisexual or gay.

Another counterintuitive finding is that most asexual women and men do experience sexual fantasies, especially in the context of masturbation (Yule et al., 2017). Their fantasies are less frequent than those of other individuals, however, and they are less likely to feature any sexual interaction with others. They may, for example, feature sexual activity between fictional characters, or even activity that is not overtly sexual at all.

Although sexual fantasies are only in the mind, they influence behavior. In an Israeli study, participants were instructed to fantasize about sex with their regular partner or with another person (Birnbaum et al., 2018). Participants who fantasized about their partner were more motivated to have sex with their partner and also to engage in nonsexual behaviors benefiting the relationship, whereas fantasizing about sex with someone else seemed neither to promote nor inhibit sex with the partner. Thus guided sexual fantasy could play a role in sex and relationship therapy (see Chapter 14).

## Gonadal steroid hormones influence sexual arousability

Testosterone, the principal gonadal steroid hormone in men, does not by itself cause sexual arousal, no matter how high its concentration in the blood. It does, however, have an important long-term influence on our sexual *arousability*—that is, our capacity to experience sexual arousal in response to a variety of stimuli (Corona et al., 2016). The clearest connection between testosterone levels and sexual arousability is found in boys at around the time of puberty. Boys experience a great increase in sexual feelings and behaviors at the time of the puberty-associated rise in testosterone levels. Even more direct evidence comes from the study of boys with delayed puberty: Treating such boys with testosterone causes them to think more about sex and engage in more sexual behavior, whereas treatment with an inactive placebo has no such effect (Finkelstein et al., 1998).

Testosterone levels also influence sexual arousability in adult men. **Hypogonadal** men—those who experience a profound reduction in testosterone levels for any reason—suffer a gradual decline in sexual desire and activity, and this decline can be reversed by testosterone replacement therapy (see Chapter 14). Most young and middle-aged men have levels of testosterone that are well above the "ceiling" for its effect on arousability, however. In other words, variation in the testosterone levels among these healthy men does not account for variation in their sexual feelings and behavior—or it does so to only a small degree. Testosterone is one of many substances used as **aphrodisiacs** (**BOX 5.2**), but it's doubtful that extra testosterone enhances sexual desire or performance in healthy men.

Sexual arousability in women is more complex because at least two groups of gonadal steroid hormones are involved—androgens (including testosterone) and estrogens—and their levels vary around the menstrual cycle, as described in Chapter 2. It appears that both estrogens and androgens contribute to sexual arousability, but there is some debate about their relative importance (Cappelletti & Wallen, 2016; Davis et al., 2016). In part, the effects of estrogens are indirect: They maintain the capacity of the vagina to lubricate during sexual arousal, and low estrogen levels may lead to vaginal dryness and hence to painful intercourse, which in turn may cause a decline of interest in sex.

**hypogonadal** Producing insufficient levels of sex hormones.

**aphrodisiac** A substance believed to improve sexual performance, enhance sexual pleasure, or stimulate desire or love.

**FAQ:** I've lost interest in sex since I started using Propecia for my thinning hair—is there a connection?

Propecia blocks conversion of testosterone to the more powerful androgen dihydrotestosterone. It does reduce sexual desire and impair performance in some users, and these side effects may arise or persist after stopping the drug (Guo et al., 2016). Talk with your doctor about this.

## BOX 5.2
# Aphrodisiacs and Drugs

Aphrodisiacs—named for the Greek goddess of love, Aphrodite—are substances intended to improve one's own sexual desire, sexual performance, or sexual pleasure or to cause someone else to respond to one's advances or to fall in love. In the last case, they may be called "love potions."

Traditionally, the belief that certain substances are aphrodisiacs has been based on magical thinking, especially the "law of similarity," which holds that "like produces like" (Frazer, 1922). Thus, aphrodisiacs have been derived from things that resemble penises (e.g., rhinoceros horns) or vulvas (e.g., oysters; **FIGURE A**) or from the sex organs or secondary sexual structures of animals, such as bull's testicles, the bacula (penis bones) of seals (**FIGURE B**), and deer velvet (the skin covering the growing antlers of male deer). It's not likely that any of these substances work, unless simply by the power of suggestion.

Eastern medical practitioners have long claimed that ginseng root is useful in the treatment of sexual disorders. Controlled scientific studies have had mixed results: Ginseng root performed no better than an inactive placebo in the treatment of sexual dysfunctions in women (Chung et al., 2015), but an extract of ginseng berry (which has a different chemical makeup from the root) did modestly improve erectile function in men with erectile disorder (Choi et al., 2013). Botanicals such as ginseng are poorly regulated and are not necessarily safe simply because they are natural products. Especially in non-Western countries, herbal aphrodisiacs are often adulterated with Viagra or similar drugs (Agrawal & Mishra, 2016).

Another class of substances that is sometimes used as aphrodisiacs is that of recreational drugs. Here the issue is not so much whether they work—they often do—but their safety. The following are some examples:

- Amyl nitrite ("poppers") and related drugs such as butyl nitrite, which are administered by inhalation, produce a brief rush, during which time sexual feelings are enhanced and the pleasurable sensations of orgasm are intensified. It is dangerous to use these drugs in combination with Viagra or related drugs, since a life-threatening drop in blood pressure can result. Even used alone, they can have serious harmful effects in people with cardiovascular or breathing problems.
- Marijuana has different effects in different people. In some it induces relaxation that makes sex more enjoyable. In others it increases anxiety. In chronic users it may cause difficulty in experiencing orgasm (Johnson et al., 2004).
- Methamphetamine ("meth") is said to intensify the pleasure of sexual experiences. It is a highly addictive drug, however. With repeated use, it damages the

(A)

(B)

(A) Oysters' reputation as aphrodisiacs probably results from their slight resemblance to vulvas. (B) The penis bone (baculum) of a ringed seal. The collection of animal materials for their supposed aphrodisiac properties threatens the survival of some species.

brain's dopamine system. It may eventually make orgasm unattainable even with the help of the drug.
- Cocaine—which increases the levels of dopamine at synapses—can enhance sexual sensations in moderate doses, but in high doses or with chronic use it can cause erectile difficulties as well as the inability to achieve orgasm.
- MDMA (Ecstasy) is a serotonin-related drug that can increase sexual arousal. With repeated use it can damage the brain's serotonin system. It can cause psychological problems such as depression and anxiety that persist after drug use ceases.
- Heroin and other opiates, when injected intravenously, produce a rush that users often describe as resembling orgasm, but these dangerous drugs lower the sex drive and impair sexual performance.
- Alcohol is a central nervous system depressant that can facilitate sexual expression by removing inhibitions. Frequent use can lead to premature ejaculation in young men (Akre et al., 2014). In large amounts it can impair sexual performance.

A safety issue that applies to the use of all recreational drugs in a sexual context is that they may impair judgment, thus promoting unsafe sex, sexual victimization (whether the drug is taken by the perpetrator or the victim), or sexual encounters that are later regretted. In addition, use of illegal drugs can have legal consequences.

## Conditioning may influence arousal

**Classical**, or **Pavlovian**, **conditioning** is the name given to a form of associative learning first studied by the Russian physiologist Ivan Pavlov in the early 20th century. Pavlov observed that dogs salivate automatically when they smell food (which is an "unconditioned stimulus"—that is, one that naturally triggers a response). Pavlov presented a sound, such as the clicking of a metronome, just before a dog was given food. Over time, the dog began to salivate to the sound alone—which had become a "conditioned stimulus" due to its repeated association with food.

Classical conditioning influences sexual arousal, although the effects are not generally very strong or durable (H. Hoffmann, 2017). A research group based in the Netherlands conducted experiments with women that were somewhat analogous to Pavlov's experiments (Both et al., 2008; Brom et al., 2014). In this case the unconditioned stimulus was genital stimulation with a vibrator, which typically elicits sexual arousal. In conjunction with the vibratory stimulus, the women were shown a test photo of a heterosexual couple engaging in sex. (The photo was presented subliminally—that is, it was shown too briefly for the women to be conscious of it.) As a control, a different photo of heterosexual sex was shown while the vibrator was turned off. Later the test photo, unaccompanied by the vibrator, elicited more genital blood flow than did the control photo, suggesting that the association of the test photo with genital stimulation turned the test photo into a conditioned stimulus.

In this study the conditioned stimulus (the photo of heterosexual sex that accompanied the genital stimulation) was in itself potentially arousing sexually; the effect of the conditioning was simply to make it more so. By extension, it's conceivable that the same process could explain how a person becomes sexually aroused by an object—such as a shoe—that originally was not sexually arousing at all. What it might take would be for the person to repeatedly use or fantasize about the object while masturbating or having sex. We will discuss this issue when we cover unusual forms of sexual expression, such as fetishism, in Chapter 13.

There are also reports that sexual arousal to a stimulus can be *reduced* rather than increased by conditioning, at least for a short period of time (Both et al., 2017). In this so-called **aversive classical conditioning**, the unconditioned stimulus is something unpleasant, such as an electric shock; when paired with a conditioned stimulus such as an erotic image it may temporarily reduce sexual arousal to that image. Aversive conditioning has a bad reputation because, historically, it was used in largely futile attempts to abolish forms of sexual expression then considered undesirable or pathological, such as homosexuality (see Chapter 12). More recently, aversive conditioning has been used in attempts to abolish sexual attraction to children in pedophiles, but there is no long-term effect of the treatment (Harvard Mental Health Letter, 2010). Besides the lack of effect, there are serious ethical questions regarding the use of what is essentially a punitive treatment regime for psychological problems.

**classical (or Pavlovian) conditioning**
A form of behavioral learning in which a novel stimulus is tied to a preexisting reflex.

**aversive classical conditioning**
A form of classical conditioning in which the unconditioned stimulus is painful.

**sexual response cycle**
The sequence of physiological processes that accompany sexual behavior.

## 5.3 Sexual Arousal Follows a Response Cycle

### LEARNING OBJECTIVES
After reading this section you should be able to:

5.3.1 Name the phases of the sexual response cycle as proposed by Masters and Johnson.

5.3.2 Describe what happens during orgasm in women and men.

5.3.3 Explain the origins of the two kinds of "female ejaculation."

5.3.4 Discuss the variety of response cycles that may be seen in women and men.

5.3.5 Describe the possible roles of oxytocin and prolactin in the sexual response cycle.

In Chapters 2 and 3 we described some of the genital phenomena that accompany sexual arousal in women and men. We now attempt to tie these phenomena together into a coherent sequence or process—the **sexual response cycle**. This cycle goes forward in a fairly similar way regardless of how arousal occurs (e.g., through partnered sex or by solitary masturbation).

The best-known description of the overall response cycle is the one developed by Masters and Johnson (introduced in Chapter 1), in which they divided the process into four phases: excitement, plateau, orgasm, and resolution.

### In the excitement phase, genital responses begin

The **excitement phase** is just what it sounds like: the period during which the physiological signs of sexual arousal begin. In women it is marked by swelling and opening up of the inner labia, vaginal lubrication, a deepening in the color of the inner labia and the vaginal walls due to **vasocongestion**, erection of the clitoris and nipples, swelling of the breasts, and an increase in heart rate and blood pressure (**FIGURE 5.13**). The uterus elevates within the pelvis; this is known as the tenting effect.

In men the excitement phase is marked mainly by erection of the penis (**FIGURE 5.14**). In healthy and highly aroused young men the process of erection takes less than a minute—perhaps as little as 10 seconds. Usually the corpora cavernosa become erect first, followed more slowly by the corpus spongiosum. In older men, men who have health problems affecting erection, or men who are not highly aroused, the process of penile erection may take many minutes.

**excitement phase** The beginning phase of the sexual response cycle.

**vasocongestion** Tissue swelling caused by increased filling of local blood vessels.

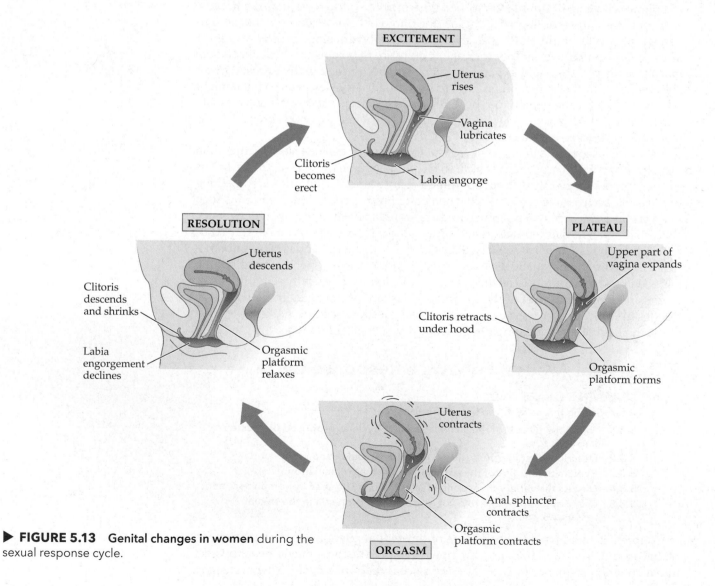

▶ **FIGURE 5.13** **Genital changes in women** during the sexual response cycle.

Also during the excitement phase, contraction of the cremaster muscle begins to elevate the testicles. The skin of the scrotum becomes firmer and more wrinkled because of contraction of the underlying muscle layer. The nipples may also become erect.

Of course, the various components of the excitement phase don't always occur together or to the same degree. The duration of the excitement phase also varies, from less than a minute to an hour or more.

## In the plateau phase, arousal is maintained

The **plateau phase** is a state of high arousal that may be maintained for some time, from several minutes to several hours (in the case of extended lovemaking). Among men, there is considerable variability in how long a man is able (or wishes) to remain in the plateau phase before reaching orgasm. In women, physiological events that occur during the plateau phase include the thickening and tightening of the outer third of the vagina and the surrounding muscles of the pelvic floor. This causes the outer part of the vaginal canal to narrow, so (if coitus is occurring) it grips the penis more tightly. This tense outer region of the vagina and surrounding tissues is called the **orgasmic platform**. The inner part of the vagina, in contrast, tends to balloon out and lengthen, so it does not grip the penis at all tightly during coitus.

During the plateau phase, the glans of the clitoris usually disappears under its hood. The breasts may swell further, and the areolae may become engorged and

**plateau phase**   The phase of the sexual response cycle during which arousal is maintained at a high level.

**orgasmic platform**   The outer portion of the vagina and surrounding tissues, which thickens and tenses during sexual arousal.

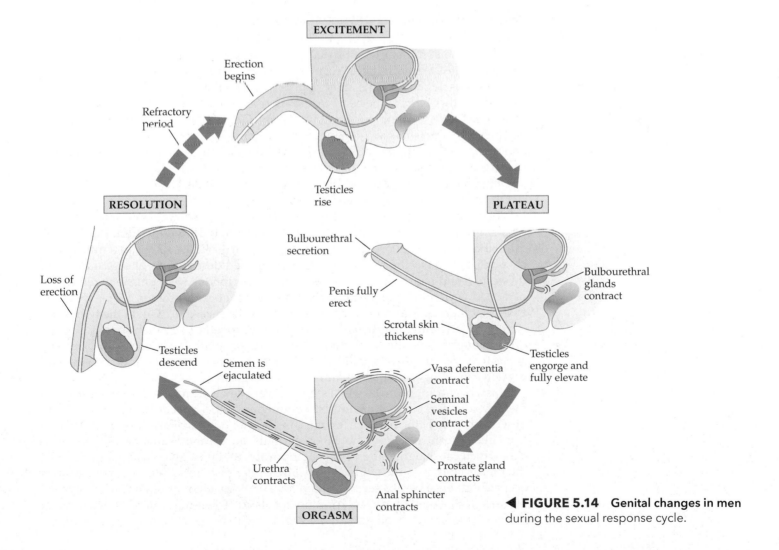

**◀ FIGURE 5.14   Genital changes in men** during the sexual response cycle.

**myotonia**   A general increase in muscle tension.

**orgasm**   The intense, pleasurable sensations at sexual climax, along with the physiological processes that accompany them.

swollen, making the nipples appear less prominent than before. In some women, the breasts or other parts of the body may take on a flushed appearance. Heart rate and blood pressure increase further, accompanied by a general increase in **myotonia**, or muscle tension, throughout the body.

In men, secretions from the bulbourethral glands ("pre-cum") may appear at the urethral opening during the plateau phase. The erection of the penis becomes stronger and is less readily lost. The testicles elevate farther. According to Masters and Johnson, the testicles also swell by a variable amount (Masters & Johnson, 1966), although we are not aware of more recent studies confirming this. Heart rate and respiration rate increase, accompanied by a general increase in muscle tension.

The term "plateau," which means a flat region, suggests a steady state in which not much is changing, physiologically speaking. This may be misleading, however. Sometimes a person passes rapidly from excitement through plateau to orgasm. (This may be because the person deliberately tries to reach orgasm quickly or because he or she has difficulty in delaying orgasm.) In such cases the plateau phase may be a brief period of rapidly increasing arousal that is difficult to distinguish from the excitement phase. If the plateau phase is maintained for an extended time, however, there are likely to be periodic increases and decreases in arousal, depending on the stimulation the person is experiencing, distraction, fatigue, and other factors. Thus, the plateau phase is more of a general concept than a definable episode within each and every sexual experience.

## Orgasm is the climax of sexual arousal

**Orgasm** is the subjective experience of intense pleasure and release at sexual climax, as well as the accompanying physiological processes. As previously discussed in Chapter 3, it is very similar in women and men. Orgasm is usually felt as a brief series of muscle contractions in the genital area, but the sensation often radiates out to involve other parts of the body. Respiration rate, heart rate, and blood pressure all reach peak levels during orgasm. Muscle contractions may occur anywhere in the body. In men orgasm is accompanied by two genital events described in Chapter 3: emission, in which the various components that make up semen are released into the urethra, and ejaculation, in which the semen is forcefully expelled from the urethral opening. Some women also ejaculate during orgasm (**BOX 5.3**).

Orgasm may be experienced as a brief period of altered consciousness or as a loss of control. The person experiencing orgasm may groan or shout involuntarily. Orgasm is usually felt as a release of sexual tension, followed by calm. What about the actual sensation of orgasm in women and men—is it the same? In a much-cited study conducted in the 1970s, researchers collected descriptions of orgasm written by women and men. Experts who read these descriptions were unable to tell which had been written by women and which by men (Vance & Wagner, 1976). This suggests that there is little if any difference in the experience of orgasm in the two sexes.

In men, ejaculation and orgasm usually occur together, so much so that they are often thought to be the same thing. However, ejaculation can occur without any subjective orgasm—that is, without the intense feeling of pleasure and release—and orgasm can occur without ejaculation (a "dry orgasm").

Masters and Johnson, as well as more recent sex researchers, have investigated the physiological basis of the muscle contractions experienced during orgasm. (We described some of the research, on men, in Chapter 3.) In women, the spasms derive from intense contractions of the pubococcygeus muscle and nearby pelvic floor muscles, which cause tightening of the outer portion of the vagina. The anal sphincters, the uterus, and even the oviducts may also undergo contractions. The contractions occur about once per 0.8 second, and a total of about eight or ten occur in a typical orgasm. This would give a total duration of about 10 seconds, but researchers using a different method (blood flow in the vaginal wall) came up with a longer estimate

## BOX 5.3
## Female Ejaculation

You might think that ejaculation would be a purely male experience, but some women say that they experience a discharge of some type of fluid from the urethra at sexual climax. There are two kinds of discharge: In one kind, a small amount (a few drops to a teaspoonful or so) of a milky or pearly fluid is discharged, usually without great force. In another kind, a larger quantity of clear fluid is discharged, sometimes with sufficient force to project the fluid away from the woman's body ("squirting"). Videos illustrating squirting can readily be found online.

The low-volume, milky discharge appears to be a secretion from the paraurethral glands. As described in Chapter 2, these small glands, which are probably equivalent to the much larger prostate gland in men, lie just in front of the front wall of the vagina, in close proximity to the urethra, but are highly variable in size and position (Wimpissinger et al., 2009). Some researchers believe that they are the anatomical basis for the G-spot. The ducts of these glands open into the urethra about 1 inch (2 cm) back from the urethral opening. Consistent with this interpretation, the low-volume discharge contains an enzyme characteristic of secretions from the male prostate gland (Belzer et al., 1984). The functional role of this kind of discharge in women, if any, is unknown. Because the male ejaculate consists in part of prostatic secretions, the paraurethral ejaculation in women is a partial parallel to male ejaculation—minus the sperm, of course.

The high-volume, clear discharge has been much more controversial, with some sexologists doubting the reality of the phenomenon or interpreting it as urine. To solve the riddle, sexologist Gary Schubach recruited volunteers who stated that they experienced large-volume discharges (Schubach, 2001). Schubach observed that these women did indeed expel large volumes—3 ounces (100 mL) or more—of watery fluid from the urethra at orgasm.

To investigate the origin of this fluid, Schubach passed a fine rubber tube (catheter) through the urethra of some of the women, past the ducts of the paraurethral glands and into the bladder (see figure). The women then masturbated or were stimulated by their partners to orgasm. The idea was that if the

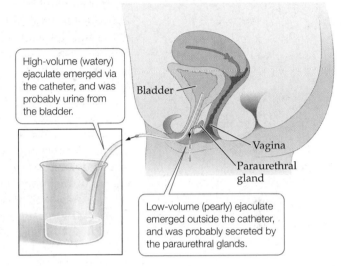

High-volume (watery) ejaculate emerged via the catheter, and was probably urine from the bladder.

Bladder

Vagina

Paraurethral gland

Low-volume (pearly) ejaculate emerged outside the catheter, and was probably secreted by the paraurethral glands.

Gary Schubach's experiment to determine the origin of fluids ejaculated by women. A catheter was inserted through the urethra into the bladder, and the women masturbated or were stimulated to orgasm.

fluid was urine, it should exit the urethra via the inside of the catheter, but if it was a secretion from the paraurethral glands or other nearby glands, it should exit the urethra outside the catheter. In all cases, the high-volume fluid expelled at orgasm exited via the inside of the catheter. Schubach's conclusion: High-volume female ejaculation involves the expulsion of urine from the bladder. This conclusion was reinforced by the findings of a more recent study conducted in France (Salama et al., 2015). These researchers imaged the pelvis of women before and after they experienced a high-volume ejaculation: The bladder contained urine before the ejaculation but was empty immediately afterward.

Some of the women in Schubach's study also released the low-volume, opalescent discharge. This fluid emerged outside the catheter, consistent with an origin in the paraurethral glands.

Both types of discharge may legitimately be referred to as "female ejaculation," but only the low-volume, milky discharge has anything in common with male ejaculation.

(20 seconds), which corresponds more closely to the average duration of orgasm as indicated by women in a laboratory setting (26 seconds) (Levin & Wagner, 1985).

There has long been debate about whether women experience different kinds of orgasms depending on what parts of their genitals are stimulated. According to Masters and Johnson, the key physiological signs of orgasm in women—rhythmic contractions of the muscles around the outer part of the vagina—are the same no matter how orgasm is triggered and are probably the result of direct or indirect stimulation of the clitoris (Masters & Johnson, 1966). Masters and Johnson placed relatively little emphasis on erotic sensitivity within the vagina itself.

A different view has been put forward by Barry Komisaruk and Beverly Whipple (of Rutgers University) and several colleagues (Ladas et al., 2004; Komisaruk et al., 2006). According to studies by this group, stimulation of the clitoris and stimulation of the anterior wall of the vagina (a region thought to include the G-spot—see Figure 2.9) give rise to two different orgasmic sensations. Clitoral orgasms, they say, involve sensations more or less restricted to the area of the clitoris itself, whereas vaginal orgasms are described as involving the entire body. Yet a third kind of sensation is said to be elicited by direct stimulation of the cervix. The differences arise, according to these authors, because these three regions are connected to the brain via different neural pathways.

The idea that clitoral and vaginal stimulation lead to different kinds of orgasm has received some support from an ultrasound study. A French-Italian research group placed ultrasound probes in three women's vaginas and then asked the women to masturbate to orgasm by stimulation either of the clitoris or the vagina (Buisson & Jannini, 2013). Orgasms induced by clitoral stimulation were accompanied by increases in blood flow within the external portion of the clitoris only, whereas orgasms induced by vaginal stimulation were accompanied by movement and blood-flow increases throughout the deep portions of the clitoris and neighboring tissues.

Another research group found that women reported different kinds of orgasms but said that the location stimulated (clitoris versus vagina) is not as relevant as psychological factors and relationship quality (King et al., 2011; King & Belsky, 2012). All in all, there is a need for more research to clarify the nature and basis of different orgasmic experiences in women.

Although orgasms are usually triggered by genital stimulation, the site of stimulation or the site where the orgasm is experienced may sometimes be located far from the genital area (**BOX 5.4**). Some women and an occasional man say that they can reach orgasm from nipple stimulation alone (Anonymous, 2014a).

People generally describe their orgasms in very positive terms, but there can also be "bad" orgasms. Orgasms can be downright painful, as in men with acute prostatitis, or they can be accompanied or followed by severe headaches, or even by panic attacks (Reinert & Simon, 2017). Orgasms can be experienced in a negative way because they occur during coerced or pressured sex, or when a person feels obliged to have an orgasm—either to fulfill a partner's expectations or to bring a sexual encounter to a conclusion (Chadwick et al., 2019). Seeing orgasm as the "climax" of sex may not only load the orgasm with anxiety; it may also make everything else seem less than climactic, thus minimizing the rewards of non-orgasmic sex. And finally there are those notorious faked orgasms, which we discuss in Chapter 14.

## Brain imaging suggests where orgasm may be experienced

The subjective experience of orgasm must result from some kind of activity in the brain, but where in the brain does that activity occur? To study this question in men, a Dutch group (Holstege et al., 2003) used a functional brain-imaging technique (PET scanning). The researchers took scans in two conditions: when the participant was being manually stimulated by his female partner but was not experiencing orgasm, and in the same situation when he was experiencing orgasm (**FIGURE 5.15**). One scan was then digitally subtracted from the other to show the pattern of activity that was specifically associated with orgasm. The researchers found that the most active region was a zone in the midline of the brain including part of the thalamus and nearby structures. Interestingly, this same region has been shown to be active during a heroin rush. It contains many neurons that use dopamine as a neurotransmitter; dopamine is believed to be involved in brain processes that have to do with pleasure and reward. Activity in the cerebral cortex—seat of our intellectual lives—decreases

## BOX 5.4
## Foot Orgasms

Two clinical case histories illustrate that orgasms may be stimulated or experienced far from the genitals, especially when there has been neurological damage. In the first case, psychologist V. S. Ramachandran, of the University of California, San Diego, interviewed a man whose foot had been amputated some time previously (Ramachandran & Blakeslee, 1999). "I actually experience my orgasm in my [missing] foot," he told Ramachandran, "and therefore it's much bigger than it used to be, because it's no longer confined to my genitals."

Ramachandran noted that the area of the brain's cerebral cortex that maps the foot lies next to the area that maps the genitals. It's known that when a part of the body is missing, the region of the cerebral cortex that maps the missing body part may be commandeered by neighboring cortical areas. Thus it seems that genital inputs to the cerebral cortex invaded the empty representation of this man's amputated foot, leading to misinterpretation of the location of his orgasms.

In the second case, a woman who had sustained neurological damage during an intensive-care emergency later

Feet may be especially sexy because they are located next to the genitals in the brain's map of the body.

complained that stimulation of her left foot (in nonsexual contexts) triggered unwanted orgasmic sensations (Waldinger et al., 2013). In the clinic, electrical stimulation applied to her foot triggered an instant orgasmic sensation that spread from her foot to her genital area. Conversely, electrical stimulation of the left side of her vagina triggered an orgasmic sensation that spread to her left foot. The researchers speculated that the original neurological damage was followed by regeneration of sensory nerves to the wrong body regions. The unwanted orgasmic sensations were eliminated by surgical destruction of sensory nerves that innervate both a portion of the left foot and the left side of the genital area.

Feet can be highly erogenous zones even in healthy people, and erotic fixations (fetishisms) that focus on body parts involve the feet much more commonly than any other regions (see Chapter 13). It may be that the ready sexualization of the feet has something to do with the neighboring representation of feet and genitals in the cerebral cortex.

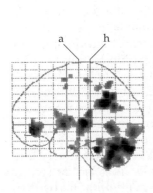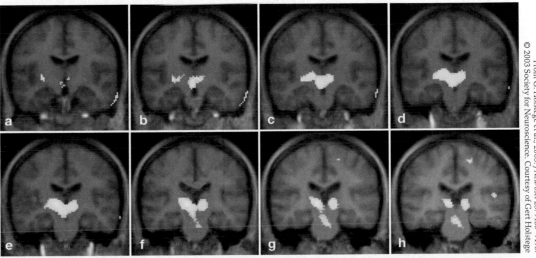

▲ **FIGURE 5.15    Brain activity during orgasm in a man, as revealed in a PET scan**  The most active areas (yellow) involve subcortical structures such as the thalamus. Brain activity during sexual arousal before orgasm has been subtracted from the image.

**nucleus accumbens** A nucleus within the basal ganglia that is part of the brain's reward system.

**resolution phase** The phase of the sexual response cycle during which physiological arousal subsides.

greatly during orgasm. This may reflect a switching off of cognitive or behavioral processes that would otherwise inhibit orgasm. These decreases in cerebral activity during orgasm are not shown in Figure 5.16.

More recently, the Dutch group extended their observations to women: Again, there was activation of dopamine-related systems and a general drop in activity in the cerebral cortex (Georgiadis et al., 2006). The Rutgers University group has also observed activation of dopamine-related systems during orgasm in women. In particular, they saw heightened activity in the **nucleus accumbens**. Portions of the nucleus accumbens appear to serve as a final common pathway for reward and pleasure: The evidence for this is that, given the opportunity, animals will electrically stimulate their own nucleus accumbens in preference to any real-world reward such as food or sex. Thus, the activation of this region during orgasm may help explain why the experience of orgasm is usually experienced as intensely pleasurable.

There is much more going on in the brain during sexual attraction, arousal, and behavior than the events mediating orgasm, of course. We present a more comprehensive overview of the brain's role in sexuality in Appendix B.

### In the resolution phase, arousal subsides

The **resolution phase** is the period during which the physiological signs of arousal reverse themselves. In women, clitoral erection, vasocongestion, and lubrication subside; the vaginal and pelvic floor muscles relax; and the breasts lose their swollen appearance. In men, the penis loses its erection, and the testicles descend within the scrotum. In both sexes, heart rate and blood pressure return to normal levels. Psychological arousal usually subsides too, and there is often a sense of relaxed contentment. Full resolution typically takes about 15 minutes, but resolution is slower if an orgasm has not occurred.

### The phases may be linked in different ways

Although the excitement, plateau, orgasm, and resolution phases are the building blocks of the sexual response cycle, individual cycles may be assembled in a variety of ways (**FIGURE 5.16**). In one type of cycle (shown in green in the figure), the person passes sequentially through the four phases in the sequence just described—excitement, plateau, orgasm, and resolution. This might be called the "standard version" of the response cycle.

A second type of cycle (shown in red in the figure) skips the orgasm phase: The person passes from excitement to the plateau phase and then directly to the resolution phase. Some people may think of this as a sign of something wrong or missing. They might say that the person "failed to achieve" orgasm. Still, the fact is that it is a common type of cycle. Women may describe it as a fully satisfying sexual experience—in fact some women never experience orgasm but nevertheless express satisfaction with their sex lives. Alternatively, they may feel frustrated, especially if the lack of orgasm results from the cessation of stimulation by their partners after their own orgasms.

Men are less likely than women to be satisfied with a sexual experience that doesn't include orgasm—only 34% of men, compared with 50% of women, believe that sex without orgasm can be satisfying, according to a large British survey (Wellings

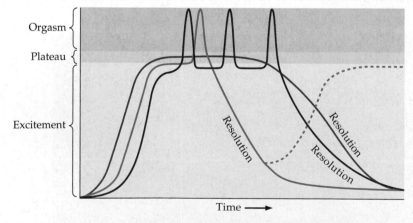

▲ **FIGURE 5.16** **Patterns of sexual response** In the pattern shown in green, a single orgasm is experienced before loss of arousal (resolution), but a new cycle of arousal (dashed line) may begin after resolution. In the pattern shown in purple, the person passes through excitement to the plateau phase and then experiences more than one orgasm, returning to the plateau phase between orgasms. In the pattern shown in orange, the person experiences the plateau phase but no orgasm.

et al., 1994). Besides the loss of the pleasure and release associated with orgasm, men sometimes experience testicular pain ("blue balls"), which is likely due to vasocongestion and anoxia (Chalett & Nerenberg, 2000). Men sometimes plead "blue balls" as a way to pressure their partner into continuing a sexual encounter. That's hardly a compelling argument, because in that situation the condition—if real—could easily be relieved by masturbation. A comparable condition has been described in women, and it has been informally named "blue vulva" or "pink ovaries."

A third type of cycle involves **multiple orgasms** (the purple line in Figure 5.16). A multiple orgasm means a sequence of at least two orgasms, between which the person descends only to the plateau phase of genital arousal (Amberson & Hoon, 1985). It does not refer to having an orgasm, losing one's arousal completely, and then quickly entering another arousal cycle that culminates in a second orgasm.

Multiple orgasms are far more common in women than in men. One survey of college-educated U.S. nurses found that about 43% of them usually experienced multiple orgasms (Darling et al., 1991). No doubt many more women could experience multiple orgasms if they wanted to or if they had the cooperation of their partners. However, women are not necessarily more satisfied with multiple orgasms than with a single orgasm, as many men would imagine. Reports of large numbers of multiple orgasms—up to 50 or so—are based on women who are masturbating with vibrators, rather than engaging in coitus.

Masters and Johnson reported that women can sometimes experience a sequence of orgasms that follow almost directly one after the other with no descent into the plateau phase between them. The orgasms may be considered to form one single, unusually prolonged orgasm. These **serial orgasms** can last from 20 seconds to a minute or so.

A few men—less than one in ten—also experience multiple orgasms (Wibowo & Wassersug, 2016). Sometimes only one orgasm in the series—usually the last—is accompanied by ejaculation, while the previous ones are "dry." Some sexologists believe that all men can learn to have multiple orgasms. For those who wish to try, instructions are available online (Silverberg, 2008). The key, it is said, is learning to separate orgasm from ejaculation by stopping stimulation just short of ejaculation.

A small number of men, however, are naturally capable of experiencing multiple orgasms with ejaculation on each occasion. One such man was observed in the lab while he experienced six orgasms over the course of 36 minutes, without any loss of erection between orgasms. Each of the six events was accompanied by ejaculation, intense psychological arousal, and all the other manifestations of orgasm (Whipple et al., 1998). Videos showing male multiple ejaculatory orgasms can readily be found online. In some cases the men maintain their erection between orgasms with the help of a cock-ring.

## Men experience a refractory period

In spite of the unusual case just described, most men experience a period of time after orgasm during which further sexual stimulation does not lead to renewed erection or a second orgasm. According to Masters and Johnson, this **refractory period** lasts between 30 and 90 minutes. The length of the period varies greatly with age, however, being negligible in some boys around the age of puberty but extending over a day or more in some older men. While the early part of the refractory period may be absolute—that is, the man cannot be physiologically aroused by any means—it may be followed by a relative refractory period during which the man can be aroused by stronger-than-usual stimuli, such as a novel sex partner. This is probably related to the Coolidge effect, described earlier.

## Pituitary hormones influence the sexual response cycle

Two hormones that are secreted by the pituitary gland, oxytocin and prolactin, play roles in the sexual response cycle. The levels of oxytocin in the blood increase during the excitement and plateau phases and then surge dramatically before and during

**multiple orgasms** Two or more orgasms, between which the person descends only to the plateau level of arousal.

**serial orgasms** Two or more orgasms with no more than a few seconds between them.

**refractory period** In males, a period of reduced or absent sexual arousability after orgasm.

orgasm. Adding extra oxytocin (by nasal spray) increases the intensity of orgasm, whereas blocking the secretion of oxytocin decreases it (Murphy et al., 1990; Behnia et al., 2014). Oxytocin probably works both in the periphery (by strengthening the contraction of smooth muscles associated with orgasm) and in the brain (by increasing the pleasurable sensations associated with orgasm).

Prolactin has rather the opposite effect: Artificially *reducing* prolactin levels increases sexual arousal, whereas *increasing* these levels decreases arousal (Kruger et al., 2003). Prolactin is secreted in large amounts at the time of orgasm, and levels of the hormone remain high for at least an hour afterward. Thus, prolactin probably plays a role both in the rapid reduction of arousal during the resolution phase and in the sexual unresponsiveness that characterizes the refractory period. In support of this conclusion, one group of researchers studied a man who was capable of multiple ejaculatory orgasms. They found that he was quite unusual in endocrinological terms, in that no prolactin surge was observed at orgasm (Haake et al., 2002). Thus biological differences in prolactin secretion may explain why some men experience multiple orgasms and others not, and why the length of the refractory period varies from man to man. It is not known whether differences in prolactin secretion are the reason why some women are multi-orgasmic and others not.

The neurotransmitter dopamine also has a sexual function (Kruger et al., 2005). During sexual arousal and orgasm this substance is released in parts of the brain that mediate motivation and reward. Drugs that raise dopamine levels (such as those used in the treatment of Parkinson's disease) may increase sexual responsiveness, whereas dopamine blockers tend to blunt the rewarding properties of sexual activity.

## The Masters and Johnson cycle may be incomplete

Masters and Johnson's four-stage model of the sexual response is primarily a description of physiological processes—effects that one can observe or measure during sexual behavior, such as erection or changes in blood pressure. Since Masters and Johnson's time, researchers have made efforts to place the physiological response cycle into a larger psychological context.

One point is this: Masters and Johnson represented sexual responses in a linear fashion. They described the process as having a beginning (excitement) and an end (resolution), as sketched in Figure 5.16. But sex is not a one-off event in people's lives, of course, so representing sexual responses as a cycle, as shown in Figures 5.13 and 5.14, makes more sense. But this raises the question "What is the connection between the resolution of one sexual event and the next episode of excitement?" According to Beverly Whipple and Karen Brash-McGreer, sexual interactions are followed by a period of reflection, in which the quality of the sexual experience, and the relationship in which it may be embedded, are consciously or unconsciously evaluated (Whipple & Brash-McGreer, 1997). The outcome of this evaluation strongly influences whether and when a person experiences another episode of excitement, and it also affects the emotional quality of any following sexual interactions (Yeung & Pauls, 2016).

Another issue is this: Do the physiological markers of sexual arousal—erection, vasocongestion, lubrication, and so forth—correspond to *psychological* arousal, meaning the person's sense of being sexually excited? There appears to be a difference between men and women in this respect. A man's psychological arousal is usually closely tied to his genital arousal—his mind and his penis are one, so to speak. Women, however, do *not* always feel sexually excited when their genitals are showing every sign of arousal (Suschinsky et al., 2009). It may be that a woman's genital arousal is less obvious to her than is penile erection to a man, or women may be socialized to ignore the messages from their genitals. But the reason for this potential disconnect between physiological and psychological arousal in women remains mysterious and deserves further study. For one thing, it may affect whether drugs that increase genital arousal offer any psychological benefit for women with sexual disorders.

Finally, where does sexual *desire* fit into the overall response cycle? According to Helen Singer Kaplan, sexual desire is the psychological state that precedes and leads to physiological arousal (Kaplan, 1979). This makes intuitive sense: We want to engage in sex, so we do things that cause our genitals to become aroused. But here again, there may be a difference between men and women. For men, Kaplan's model is widely accepted. In the case of women, however, several researchers have moved away from Kaplan's model. Psychiatrist Rosemary Basson proposed that many women, especially those in established relationships, are not motivated to engage in sexual behavior by what we would usually think of as sexual *desire*—"horniness," "sex hunger," "the urge to merge," or whatever you want to call it (Basson, 2000; Basson, 2001). Rather, they have an *interest* in sex that flows from a wish for intimacy with the partner or from an expectation of benefits that may flow from a sexual interaction. This interest is responsive, cognitive, or even intellectual in quality, rather than being the expression of a biological drive. Once physical interactions begin, however, and the physiological processes of sexual arousal are triggered, genital sensations provide a feedback stimulus that reinforces sexual interest and gives it more of the quality of true sexual desire, so a self-reinforcing cycle is set up. Again, this model has implications for the treatment of sexual disorders in women (see Chapter 14).

In fact, a survey by Cindy Meston and David Buss identified no fewer than 237 distinct reasons why people have sex, many of them having nothing to do with sexual attraction, desire, or arousal (Meston & Buss, 2007). These included such reasons as "I wanted the person to feel good about himself/herself," "I wanted to get closer to God," and "I wanted to get back at my partner for cheating on me." Evidently the motivations for engaging in sex can be complex and diverse and can't be encompassed by any single model.

## Summary

- Sexual attraction is a response to another person that is influenced by objective attributes of that person, as well as by both durable and varying characteristics of the person experiencing the attraction.

- The "masculinity" and "femininity" of faces is an important part of their attractiveness. In women, most people find very feminine faces the most attractive. Women's judgments of the attractiveness of male faces vary around the menstrual cycle.

- Another attribute that increases a person's attractiveness is facial and bodily symmetry. One reason we may find symmetry attractive is because it indicates that a person had a healthy physical development.

- One important factor influencing the attractiveness of bodies is the body mass index (BMI). For cultural reasons, lower BMIs are preferred in Western cultures than in some non-Western cultures.

- Youthful appearance—another cue to fertility—is an important trigger for men's attraction to women, but less so for women's attraction to men.

- Attractiveness is strongly enhanced by general "likability" traits such as trustworthiness, warmth, and a sense of humor. When people are given the opportunity to select partners from a large group, however, they don't generally choose the partners who correspond most closely to their stated preferences. This suggests that some aspects of attraction operate below the level of conscious thought.

- Other factors modulating sexual attraction include familiarity and, in women, the phase of the menstrual cycle.

- Some individuals are asexual: They never experience sexual attraction, but they often value close relationships and may engage in sex in order to satisfy their partners.

- Sexual arousal may be triggered internally or by external factors. Internal processes include erotic dreams and sexual fantasies. Fantasies are a healthy part of most people's sex lives.

- Testosterone plays an important role in conferring the capacity for sexual arousal in males, especially at puberty. Testosterone does not play a minute-by-minute role in sexual arousal, however. Both

*(Continued)*

## Summary *(continued)*

testosterone and estrogens may contribute to sexual arousability in women.

- Classical conditioning may increase the sexual arousal that individuals learn to associate with people, body parts, and other things that have been linked with sexual behavior in the past.

- The sexual response cycle has four phases: excitement, plateau, orgasm, and resolution.

- The subjective experience of orgasm is similar in women and men. Many women but few men experience multiple orgasms in a single cycle. Sometimes a response cycle does not include orgasm. A cycle without orgasm may be sexually satisfying, or it may leave the person dissatisfied and in discomfort from vasocongestion that is slow to resolve.

- After orgasm, men but not women experience a refractory period during which they cannot enter a new cycle. The length of the refractory period increases with age but can be shortened by situational factors such as exposure to a novel partner.

---

The **Discovering Human Sexuality** digital resources include activities, animations, flashcards, web links, chapter outlines and summaries, and other study tools.

■ ■ ■ ■ ■ ■ ■ ■ ■ ■ ■ ■ ■ ■ ■ ■ ■ ■

Learn more with this chapter's digital tools, including the **Oxford Insight Study Guide**, at **oup.com/he/levay5e**.

## Discussion Questions

1. Cultural influences shape sexual arousal and attractiveness. Identify the culture of your ancestors, and identify the attributes that your culture finds sexually attractive. For example, are thin women or those with "curves" more attractive?

2. Consider your reactions as you walk around campus or other areas and see people holding hands, kissing, lying on the grass in a passionate embrace, or almost having intercourse. What are your reactions to seeing such behavior? How does your reaction differ depending on whether it is an opposite-sex or same-sex couple? Do you think we should have rules or limits on the extent of public displays of affection or arousal?

3. Should sexual partners discuss what is arousing for each person? What are the costs and benefits of this type of communication? What are your attitudes toward talking with an intimate partner about what is arousing and what is not? Imagine for a moment that your partner had a fascination with your feet and wanted to kiss and touch them. How would your attitudes encourage or discourage this discussion?

4. As a class, make a list of words or phrases (e.g., common expressions, slang, words in other languages) that are used for (1) a woman who has sex with numerous partners, (2) a woman who doesn't engage in partnered sex at all, (3) a man who has sex with numerous partners, and (4) a man who doesn't engage in partnered sex at all. After the list is complete, discuss the attitudes and values it illustrates about men's and women's sexuality. Do you think that a double standard exists?

## Web Resources

Asexual Visibility and Education Network (AVEN)  **www.asexuality.org**

Beautycheck (study of attractiveness, using digitally manipulated faces)  **tinyurl.com/rd92**

Face Research (interactive site at the University of Glasgow)  **www.faceresearch.org**

## Recommended Reading

Bogaert, A. F. (2012). *Understanding asexuality*. Rowman & Littlefield.

Buss, D. (1994). *The evolution of desire: Strategies of human mating*. Basic Books.

Komisaruk, B. R., Beyer-Flores, C. & Whipple, B. (2006). *The science of orgasm*. Johns Hopkins University Press.

Maines, R. P. (1999). *The technology of orgasm: "Hysteria," the vibrator, and women's sexual satisfaction*. Johns Hopkins University Press.

Meston, C. M. & Buss, D. M. (2009). *Why women have sex: The psychology of sex in women's own voices*. Times Books.

Perrett, D. (2010). *In your face: The new science of human attraction*. Palgrave Macmillan.

Portner, M. (2009). The orgasmic mind. *Scientific American Mind, 20*, 26–31.

Rutter, C. (2014). *Dataclysm: Who we are when we think no one's looking*. Crown. (Insights from social media about sexuality and many other topics.)

Swami, V. & Furnham, A. (2007). *The psychology of physical attraction*. Routledge.

Thornhill, R. & Gangestad, S. W. (2004). The evolution of human attractiveness and attraction. In: Moya, A. & Font, E. (Eds.), *Evolution: From molecules to ecosystems*. Oxford University Press.

Erotic sculpture on one of the Khajuraho temples in the Indian state of Madhya Pradesh.

# 6 Sexual Behavior

Which human activities do you consider sexual? Which of these, if any, do you engage in or find enjoyable? Which do you consider morally acceptable, and which strike you as repugnant? Probably no two people would give precisely the same answers to these questions. In this chapter, we survey common forms of sexual behavior, with a central emphasis on sexual practices in the contemporary United States and other Westernized countries. We will defer a discussion of atypical sexual practices to Chapter 13.

Everyone has to make important decisions about their sex life. Questions arise, such as "Do I want to have sex at all, and if so, under what circumstances and in what kind of a relationship? Do I want to have children, and if not, how should I prevent pregnancy? How can I best reduce the likelihood of acquiring or transmitting diseases in the course of sexual encounters?" We will discuss these important topics in later chapters. For the moment, we deal with sexual behavior itself.

## 6.1 People Derive Pleasure from Diverse Sexual Behaviors

### LEARNING OBJECTIVES
After reading this section you should be able to:

6.1.1 Identify and describe more common and less common sexual behaviors.

6.1.2 Describe an experiment that compares the happiness conferred by engaging in sex with that of other activities.

Sexual behaviors can be very diverse, but certain behaviors are the mainstay of sex for most Americans. The National Survey of Sexual Health and Behavior (NSSHB) asked nearly 6,000 Americans whether they had engaged in masturbation, oral sex, coitus (penile-vaginal sex), or anal sex within the previous 12 months (Herbenick et al., 2010b). **FIGURE 6.1** shows the findings for women and men age 25 to 29—the age range in which partnered sexual activity is most frequent. (For college-age women and men the frequency of partnered sex is lower, as described later.) Masturbation, oral sex, and coitus are all very common activities—large majorities of men and women engage in them. Anal sex is less common but far from rare. Most partnered sex is heterosexual— the low figures for homosexual behaviors reflect, very roughly, the percentage of the population that is gay, lesbian, or bisexual. Regardless of the kind of sex and whether it is homosexual or heterosexual, sex with a partner usually makes people happy during the sex act itself and also boosts their ongoing level of happiness (**BOX 6.1**). What's more, partnered sex helps establish, enrich, and maintain durable relationships.

## 6.2 Masturbation Is a Very Common Form of Sexual Expression

### LEARNING OBJECTIVES
After reading this section you should be able to:

6.2.1 Evaluate the reasons for negative and positive attitudes toward masturbation.

6.2.2 Explain how demographic factors influence the prevalence of masturbation.

6.2.3 Describe women's and men's common techniques for masturbation.

**masturbation** Sexual self-stimulation. Sometimes also used to refer to manual stimulation of another person's genitalia.

We have already discussed one way in which people can arouse themselves sexually: through sexual fantasy (see Chapter 5). Because it doesn't involve *doing* anything in the external world, fantasy is not classified as a behavior. But people also have the capacity to arouse themselves sexually through physical stimulation of their own bodies, an activity referred to by the term **masturbation**—or by any of its 1,158 slang equivalents (Urban Thesaurus, 2019). **Self-pleasuring** is another term that is a little more user-friendly than masturbation. It also has the virtue of spelling out something about masturbation that's often ignored—that people do it because they find it enjoyable.

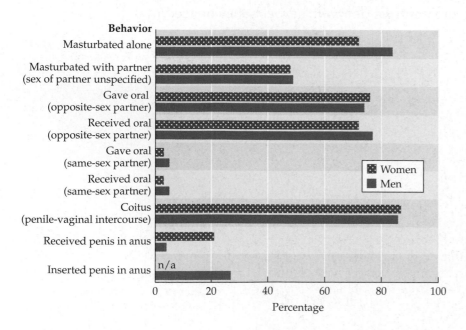

◀ **FIGURE 6.1** Overview of sexual behavior The bar graph shows the percentages of U.S. women and men, age 25 to 29, who said they had engaged in the specified behavior at least once in the previous 12 months. (Data from D. Herbenick et al. 2010. *J Sex Med* 7: 255–265.)

## BOX 6.1
## Sex and Happiness

We concluded the previous chapter by mentioning that people engage in sex for a wide variety of reasons. Nevertheless, pleasure—whether the physical pleasure of sex itself or the emotional pleasure of sexual intimacy—is likely to be the main sexual motivator for most people. To see how pleasurable sex generally is, let's look at two studies that used different approaches to the question.

In a study by Matthew Killingsworth and Daniel Gilbert of Harvard University (Killingsworth & Gilbert, 2010), over 2,000 men and women agreed to be called at random times by an automated iPhone app that asked them what they were doing at the time and how happy they were (see figure). Although the participants spent only a tiny fraction of their time "making love," they were far happier while doing so than at any other time—in spite of the aggravation of being interrupted by an automated phone call! The participants were also least likely to be distracted—to be thinking about something other than the matter at hand—while they were making love. The researchers have established that letting your mind wander from what you are doing is associated with a decrease in happiness, so this focus on sexual activities probably contributes to the pleasure of sex.

The happiness associated with sex lasts well after sex is over. A team led by psychologist Todd Kashdan of George Mason University had 150 college students keep daily diaries in which they recorded their sexual activity over the previous 24 hours as well as their current level of happiness (Kashdan et al., 2018). The students reported an increased level of happiness, as well as an increased sense that their lives were meaningful, that lasted into the following day, but not much longer than that. Conversely, a high level of happiness on a

People are happiest making love   This graph shows the happiness (on a subjective 0-to-100 scale) of 2,250 people contacted at random times during their waking hours by an automated iPhone app. The amount of time spent on each activity is indicated by the size of the circle. (After M. A. Killingsworth & D. T. Gilbert. 2010. *Science* 330: 932.)

given day was not associated with a greater likelihood of sex on the following day. Thus the direction of causation was from from sex to happiness, and not the reverse.

---

The term *masturbation* can mean different things to different people. In an online survey conducted by psychologists at the University of Missouri, almost everyone agreed that touching one's own genitals for sexual pleasure was masturbation, but some respondents said that it wasn't masturbation if a non-manual method such as grinding on a pillow was used, if another person was present, or if the behavior didn't lead to orgasm (Kirschbaum & Peterson, 2018).

Conversely, some respondents said that manually stimulating someone else's genitals *was* masturbation. Commonly, though, the term refers to **autoerotic** (self-arousing) behavior, whether by use of the hand or by other means such as vibrators or pillows, and we use it in that sense here. We include such behavior even in the presence of a sex partner or when performed in a group, so the term "solo sex" doesn't encompass all forms of masturbation. An example of group masturbation is the "circle jerk," which usually involves a group of teenage boys standing in a circle and masturbating, sometimes with the aim of seeing who can ejaculate first.

**autoerotic** Providing sexual stimulation to oneself or being aroused sexually by oneself.

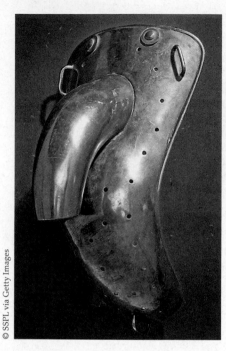

© SSPL via Getty Images

▲ **FIGURE 6.2 Emission Impossible** This is a late-19th-century device intended to prevent male masturbation. The metal shield would have been attached to the body with a lockable harness.

## Negative attitudes toward masturbation are still prevalent

Masturbation is a normal, common, and healthy sexual behavior. It's not always perceived that way, however. In Victorian times (the 19th century), masturbation was considered disgusting, sinful, and unhealthy and was referred to with morally loaded terms such as "self-pollution." According to many authorities of the time, the practice led to "masturbatory insanity" or to "degeneracy," a condition of physical, mental, and moral decay that affected not just the masturbator, but also any offspring that they might have.

Nineteenth-century health manuals recommended a variety of methods for discouraging masturbation, and one could even purchase mechanical devices that prevented the practice (**FIGURE 6.2**). These devices were mostly used on children and patients in mental hospitals who masturbated compulsively and openly. Similar devices are still for sale, but they are now used as bondage toys more than as aids to abstinence.

Few people are campaigning against the evils of masturbation in the United States today, but children may absorb negative attitudes about it from their parents, peers, or religious teachers. The Catholic church still holds that masturbation is a grave sin that can land you in Hell if you die unrepentant (Catholic Education Resource Center, 2004), although there are some Catholic theologians who take a more lenient view (Religious Tolerance, 2011).

In addition, some therapists believe that frequent masturbation, especially while watching pornography, can make it difficult for men to have erections and enjoy satisfying sex with real-life partners. There is also a grass-roots "NoFap" movement whose members aim to desist from masturbation and porn for a period of time in order to "reboot" their sex drives. (The Reddit NoFap community has nearly half a million members, of whom about 5% are women.)* We evaluate these controversial ideas in Chapter 17.

Thus, several factors may combine to make people feel bad about masturbation. In the National Health and Social Life Survey (NHSLS) mentioned in Chapter 1, about half of all the respondents who stated that they masturbated also stated that they felt guilty after they did so. The youngest age group interviewed (18 to 24 years) reported the highest levels of guilt; it is very possible that those under 18 are even more likely to feel guilty about masturbating.

School-based sex education could play an important role in overcoming guilt and other negative attitudes toward masturbation. Some states, such as California, do encourage teachers to discuss the topic in a positive way, but they may have difficulty getting past their own embarrassment and that of their students. In many schools around the nation masturbation is covered in a very perfunctory way, or it isn't mentioned at all. In 1994, when Surgeon General Joycelyn Elders suggested that masturbation should be taught in schools, President Bill Clinton fired her.

Even in Canada, which is generally well ahead of the United States when it comes to sex education, masturbation isn't always on the agenda. In 2015, for example, the province of Ontario introduced a new sex-ed curriculum according to which teachers should inform 11-year-olds that "masturbation is something that many people do and find pleasurable," but three years later Ontario's new Conservative premier canceled the entire curriculum, citing parents' protests (BBC News, 2018). (There is more on sex education in Chapter 10.)

Aside from the pleasure it brings, masturbation may contribute to good health: Frequent ejaculation, whether by solo or partnered sex, is associated with an approximately 20% reduction in the risk of prostate cancer (Rider et al., 2016). The reason for this association is not known, however.

---

*In contrast, there are also online communities of "autosexual" men, such as those at bateworld.com, who prefer masturbation to partnered sex and have no desire to give it up.

## Several demographic factors influence masturbation

Although most people masturbate at least occasionally, the likelihood that people masturbate varies with several demographic factors, according to U.S. data from the NHSLS and NSSHB surveys:

- Men masturbate more than women.

- People over 50 (women especially) masturbate less than those in younger age groups.

- African-Americans masturbate less than other ethnicities.

- The more educated a person, the more likely it is that they masturbate (**FIGURE 6.3**).

- Women (but not men) who have a religious affiliation—especially as fundamentalist Protestant—masturbate less than women who have no religious affiliation.

- People who lack a regular sex partner masturbate slightly more than people who have a partner (**FIGURE 6.4**).

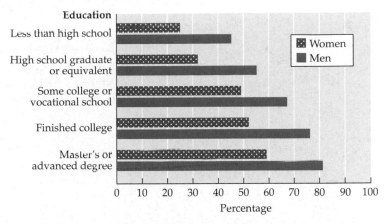

▲ **FIGURE 6.3** **Educational level and masturbation**
This bar graph shows the percentages of U.S. women and men who reported having masturbated at least once in the previous 12 months, broken down by educational level. (Data from NHSLS as reported in E. Laumann et al. 1994. *The social organization of sexuality: Sexual practices in the United States.* University of Chicago Press: Chicago.)

All these data need to be viewed with some caution: It's possible that the differences in the reported prevalence of masturbation reflect, to some degree, differences in the respondents' willingness to admit to engaging in a stigmatized behavior.

Men experience orgasm during masturbation more frequently than women do. In the NHSLS study, 82% of the men but only 61% of the women stated that they always or usually had an orgasm when masturbating. This sex difference is not unique to masturbation: Women are less likely than men to have an orgasm during sex with a partner, too. In fact, the average woman is more likely to experience orgasm when masturbating than when engaged in sex with a partner (Hite, 2003).

Asked *why* they masturbated, the men and women in the NHSLS survey gave similar answers: They did it to relieve sexual tension, for the physical pleasure, and/or because a partner was not available. Some women masturbate to relieve menstrual pain (Ellison, 2000) or migraine headaches (Evans & Couch, 2001; Akkus, 2011).

The survey data lend only limited support to the widespread notion that lack of a sex partner is the major reason for masturbation. People (men especially) who lack partners do masturbate more than those who are partnered, but the difference is not great. More relevant is people's physical or emotional satisfaction with any relationship they may be in. Dissatisfaction with a current relationship is a strong predictor of frequent masturbation (Das, 2007; Regnerus et al., 2017).

## Women use more diverse techniques of masturbation than men

Most of what is known about how people masturbate comes from the work of Masters and Johnson, who observed several hundred men and women masturbating as part of their overall studies of sexual behavior (Masters & Johnson, 1966). Women use quite diverse methods of masturbation (**FIGURE 6.5**). One common technique involves manually stimulating the area of the clitoris with a circular or to-and-fro motion of the fingers. Alternatively, pulling on the inner labia causes the clitoral hood to move back and forth on the clitoral glans, thus stimulating the clitoris

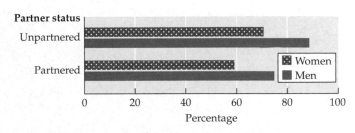

▲ **FIGURE 6.4** **Partner status and masturbation**
This bar graph shows the percentages of women and men age 25 to 29 who reported having masturbated at least once in the previous 90 days, broken down into those who have regular sex partners and those who do not. (Data from D. Herbenick et al. 2010. *J Sex Med* 7(S5): 277-290 and M. Reece et al. 2010. *J Sex Med* 7(S5): 291-304.)

▲ **FIGURE 6.5** Female masturbation

indirectly. (For many women, the clitoral glans is too sensitive for direct stimulation.) Another way of stimulating the clitoris is for a woman to cross her legs and squeeze them together rhythmically. Yet another technique is to rub or press the genital area against some object, such as a bed or pillow. Women sometimes use vibrators, either directly on the genitalia or attached to the back of the hand to give the fingers an extra vibratory motion.

Many men imagine that women masturbate by thrusting their fingers or an object deeply into the vagina, thus simulating coitus. Some women do this, but it is quite a bit less common than clitoral stimulation. Some women say that they can give themselves a different kind of orgasm by stimulation of the region of the vagina thought to include the G-spot.

While manually stimulating the genitals, many women stimulate the nipples or breasts with their free hand. In fact, some women can bring themselves to orgasm by breast stimulation alone. A small number of women can experience orgasm by fantasy alone, without any kind of physical stimulation of the body. One such woman is pop singer Lady Gaga, according to her own statements (Brennan, 2010). These mentally induced orgasms are physiologically identical to those produced by physical stimulation (Whipple et al., 1992).

Men's techniques of masturbation tend to be less varied than women's (**FIGURE 6.6**). The usual method is to grasp the shaft of the erect penis with one hand and move the hand rhythmically up and down, thus stimulating the most sensitive areas of the penis: the glans, corona, and frenulum. Some men like to use a lubricant, such as saliva, oil, soapsuds, or a commercial sexual lubricant—whatever feels good and does not irritate the penis. Because their foreskin glides freely over the glans, men who are uncircumcised have less need for a lubricant.

Alternative methods of masturbation include grinding against an object such as a pillow or the edge of a bed. Some men like to stimulate the nipples or anus with

▲ **FIGURE 6.6** Male masturbation

their free hand or a vibrator while masturbating with the other, but few can reach orgasm without direct stimulation of the penis.

Most men take about 2 to 3 minutes from the beginning of masturbation to reach the point of orgasm, compared with about 4 minutes for women, though these data are old and need to be replicated (Kinsey et al., 1948, 1953). Some men and women like to draw out the experience over a period of many minutes, perhaps approaching orgasm several times and then easing off before finally climaxing; others like to reach orgasm as quickly as possible.

## Gay people masturbate more than heterosexuals

Intuitively, one might imagine that gay men and lesbians would enjoy masturbation more than heterosexual men and women and might masturbate more frequently. Gay people's own bodies, after all, are of the sex that they find sexually attractive, so autoerotic behavior might be more arousing for them than for straight people. According to the NHSLS data, gays and lesbians (or people with recent homosexual experience) do masturbate far more frequently than do heterosexual men and women (**FIGURE 6.7**), and the same finding was reported in a British survey (Gerressu et al., 2008). Gay people also start masturbating about a year earlier than their heterosexual peers (Tenga, 2019).

The difference in masturbation rates was further confirmed in a survey of male German college students: Gay students not only masturbated more frequently (regardless of whether they were partnered or not), but also derived greater pleasure from masturbation (Schmidt, 2000). Furthermore, gay male students were far more likely than straight male students to masturbate in front of a mirror—48% of gay students had done so in the previous 12 months, versus only 18% of straight students (G. Schmidt, personal communication). Comparable data for women are not available.

These findings suggest that gay people's relatively greater interest in masturbation may result from a greater erotic response to their own bodies. (Other explanations are possible, such as that the high rates of masturbation result from a generally stronger sex drive in gay people.) This is not meant to imply that gay people are, in general, erotically focused on themselves. Both lesbians and gay men are as "other directed" in their sex lives as heterosexual men and women (see Chapter 12).

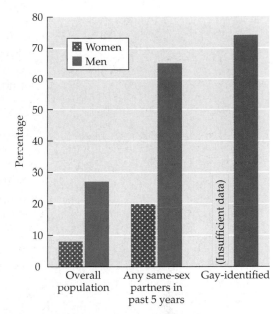

▲ **FIGURE 6.7** **Masturbation and sexual orientation** Homosexual behavior or identity is associated with a high frequency of masturbation. These histograms show the percentages of women and men who masturbate at least once per week. (Data from NHSLS as reported in E. Laumann et al. 1994. *The social organization of sexuality: Sexual practices in the United States.* University of Chicago Press: Chicago.)

## 6.3 The Kiss Represents True Love— Sometimes

### LEARNING OBJECTIVES

After reading this section you should be able to:

6.3.1 Discuss whether sexual kissing is a universal practice, and if not, what kinds of societies don't practice it.

6.3.2 Describe how male and female college students tend to view the purpose of kissing differently.

The kiss has a reputation as the most romantic of sexual behaviors. In art, poetry, music, and film the kiss signifies one thing and one thing only: a passionate love that transcends life itself.

In real life, of course, kisses come in many different degrees and flavors, from the no-contact air-kiss and the perfunctory cheek peck to the wildest oral adventures that tongue, lips, and teeth are capable of. A kiss

▶ **Wet kiss** *Cosmopolitan* magazine reviewed 25 years' worth of MTV Movie Awards "Best Kisses" and assigned all-time number-one ranking to this lip-lock between Ryan Gosling and Rachel McAdams in the 2004 romantic drama *The Notebook*. (*Cosmopolitan*, 2017)

may mean nothing, it may be a way of saying that "real sex" is on the way, or it may solemnify the union of two souls "till death do us part."

Surprisingly, kissing is not as universal a custom as many Westerners might imagine. A team led by anthropologist William Jankowiak of the University of Nevada found evidence of lip-to-lip romantic/sexual kissing in only 45% of the 168 cultures for which information was available, and such kissing was particularly uncommon in unstratified societies—that is, in groups such as hunter-gatherers and simple horticulturalists that lack social classes (Jankowiak et al., 2015).

Members of those non-kissing cultures often express disgust when they see Westerners kissing—a natural enough response, perhaps, when one considers the possibility for the transfer of infectious agents. According to a DNA-based study that employed special marker organisms, a 10-second deep (open-mouth) kiss results in the transfer in each direction of 80 million bacteria (Kort et al., 2014). The vast majority of bacteria and viruses transferred by kissing are harmless, however, and most likely they are already present in the recipient's mouth. The likelihood of acquiring a sexually transmitted infection (STI) through kissing is fairly limited, as discussed further in Chapter 15. You are much more likely to acquire a common cold through kissing than an STI.

Men and women view the purpose of kissing differently. Men (more specifically, male college students) see kissing primarily as a stepping-stone to "real" sex; women, on the other hand, use it to evaluate a person's suitability as a mate or to assess the status of an established relationship (Hughes et al., 2007; Wlodarski & Dunbar, 2014).

Mouth-to-mouth kissing between two straight men used to be a rarity, because doing so would have stigmatized the men as gay. Now that anti-gay attitudes are fading, however, it is becoming increasingly common. About 1 in 10 straight-identified male American college students say that they kiss other straight men on the mouth—as an expression of affection rather than sexual intimacy (Anderson et al., 2019). Similarly, mouth-to-mouth kissing between straight women has become fairly commonplace.

Of course, mouths can roam farther than a partner's mouth. In the heat of passion, almost every body part may be licked, sucked, chewed on, or bitten. Breasts are a perennial favorite. Oral-genital contacts are discussed below. Even the sucking of toes ("shrimping") can be highly arousing to both partners, because, as we stressed in Chapter 2, the entire body is an "erogenous zone."

**FAQ:** Didn't I read somewhere that Japanese teens were licking each other's eyeballs as a sexual turn-on?

You did, but it was Fake News.

**necking**  Kissing or caressing of the head and neck.

**petting**  Sexually touching the partner's body (often taken to exclude the breasts or genitalia).

**heavy petting**  Sexually touching the partner's genitalia or breasts.

**fondling**  Any kind of sexual touching of the partner's body.

**outercourse**  Sexual activities other than coitus, promoted as a means for preventing unwanted pregnancy and reducing the risk of STI transmission.

## 6.4  Sexual Touching Takes Many Forms

**LEARNING OBJECTIVE**
After reading this section you should be able to:

6.4.1   **Describe the various kinds of sexual touching, and what roles they may play in sexual behaviors.**

Simple touching of another person's body can be a powerfully intimate and sexual act. "Necking," "petting," and "heavy petting" are old-fashioned terms used to describe some of this behavior: **Necking** means kissing and touching confined to the head and neck; **petting** means touching skin below the neck—usually excluding the breasts, unless through clothing; **heavy petting** includes touching the breasts or genitals. **Fondling** is a broader term that can indicate any of these behaviors. **Outercourse** is another term used to describe noncoital or nonpenetrative sexual contact, especially when it is practiced as a way to avoid pregnancy or STIs.

General body-to-body contact accompanied by rubbing or thrusting motions of the pelvis that stimulate the clitoris or penis is a common part of sexual activity for many people. When two women engage in this behavior, rubbing their vulvas against each

▲ **FIGURE 6.8**   Tribadism

other's bodies with pelvic thrusting motions, it is called **tribadism** (**FIGURE 6.8**). Another way for two women to bring their vulvas together is by "scissoring"—that is, by spreading their legs and engaging each other like two open pairs of scissors.

People may engage in these behaviors as **foreplay** (behavior designed to increase pleasure and arousal prior to some "main event," such as coitus) or as **afterplay**. But quite commonly, nonpenetrative contacts *are* the main event. Although our culture often depicts coitus as the one essential element of "real" sex, plenty of people derive equal or greater satisfaction from other forms of lovemaking. They may engage in noncoital sex for the sake of variety, to avoid pregnancy and STIs, because coitus is painful or the man has erectile disorder (see Chapter 14), or for the simple pleasure of it. Same-sex couples can't engage in coitus, obviously, but that doesn't limit their sexual satisfaction.

**tribadism**   Sexual behavior between two women who lie front to front and stimulate each other's vulvas with thrusting motions.

**foreplay**   Sexual behavior engaged in during the early part of a sexual encounter, with the aim of increasing sexual arousal.

**afterplay**   Sexual behavior engaged in after coitus or orgasm, or at the end of a sexual encounter.

**fellatio**   Sexual contact between the mouth of one person and the penis of another.

## 6.5   Oral Sex Is Increasingly Popular

### LEARNING OBJECTIVE
After reading this section you should be able to:

6.5.1   Define fellatio, cunnilingus, and anilingus, and explain how they are practiced.

Oral sex has become an increasingly prevalent activity among younger people over the last few decades, both in the United States and elsewhere. Among U.S. college undergraduates, 67% say they have engaged in some kind of oral sex, and 41% have done so in the last 30 days, according to the 2018 National College Health Assessment (ACHA-NCHA) (American College Health Association, 2018).

Oral-genital contacts are of three main kinds: mouth–penis contact (fellatio, also known as a "blow job," "going down on," or "giving head"), mouth–vulva contact (cunnilingus, "eating," or "going down on"), and mouth–anus contact (anilingus or analingus, also known as "rimming").

### Fellatio is oral stimulation of the penis

**Fellatio**, like most sex, is a pretty simple matter (**FIGURE 6.9A**). One person (the "insertee") takes the insertor's penis into her or his mouth and, usually, runs the lips rhythmically up and down the shaft of the penis, keeping them fairly tight to provide optimal stimulation. The insertee may also use the tongue to stimulate the most sensitive portions of the penis: the corona and frenulum.

**FAQ:**   My girlfriend hates the taste of my ejaculate—can I do anything to improve it?

Doctors say "no"; porn stars say "yes"— become a vegetarian, but avoid garlic and asparagus. Experiment and see what works for you and your partner.

▲ **FIGURE 6.9** **Oral sex** (A) Fellatio is sexual contact between a man's penis and his partner's mouth. The partner can be either a woman or another man. (B) Cunnilingus is sexual contact between a woman's vulva and her partner's mouth. The partner can be a man or another woman.

The "insertor" often wants his penis to go deeper and deeper into his partner's mouth as he becomes increasingly aroused, but this may cause gagging, depending on the length of the man's penis and his partner's experience. As with every aspect of two-person sex, good communication is key. The focus on gagging in many porn videos suggests that gagging itself can be eroticized, but this is more likely to be true for the insertor than the insertee.

Fellatio can be continued to the point that the insertor ejaculates. Here again, however, communication is important. Some people don't like the experience of receiving the ejaculate in the mouth or have concerns about disease transmission. As to swallowing the ejaculate, the perennial question is "How many calories does it contain?" The answer: an insignificant amount—less than 5 calories.

In heterosexual contexts, men typically enjoy fellatio more than women do (**FIGURE 6.10**). Thus, it seems that women engage in fellatio to give their male partners pleasure more than as a directly pleasurable experience for themselves. The NHSLS study also found cultural differences; for example, more-educated people tended to enjoy it more than less-educated people.

Persons with drug allergies should not have unprotected oral sex with a partner who is taking that drug. In one much-publicized incident, a woman who was allergic to penicillin performed oral sex on a man who was taking amoxicillin, a penicillin-like antibiotic, and she swallowed the ejaculate. She went into anaphylactic shock but survived (Gomez Caballero et al., 2019).

Not a great deal is known about fellatio in non-Western cultures. One well-studied exception is the Sambia, a small tribal community in New Guinea (Herdt, 2005). Until recently, ritualized fellatio was practiced between older and younger Sambia youths, who were confined in all-male longhouses. This practice was believed to confer the

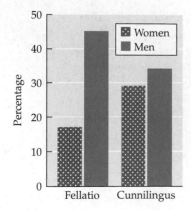

◀ **FIGURE 6.10** **Popularity of oral sex** The graph shows the percentages of women and men who find fellatio and cunnilingus "very appealing." (Data from NHSLS as reported in E. Laumann et al. 1994. *The social organization of sexuality: Sexual practices in the United States*. University of Chicago Press: Chicago.)

physical and spiritual attributes of manhood on the younger boys (the insertees). Besides its ritual significance, this activity provided a sexual outlet for the older youths, who had no access to women. Since the 1990s the longhouse tradition has been abandoned (Herdt, 2019).

## Cunnilingus is oral stimulation of the vulva

In **cunnilingus** (**FIGURE 6.9B**), a woman's partner explores her vulva with tongue and lips. The tongue provides very effective sexual stimulation for many women because it is soft, wet, warm, and highly mobile. Thus, it is much easier to stimulate the clitoris and inner labia in an uninhibited way with the tongue than with, say, the fingers, which may provide too-harsh stimulation to the most sensitive areas, such as the glans of the clitoris. For some women, cunnilingus is the only way by which they regularly achieve orgasm (Hite, 2003).

Considering that men enjoy fellatio more than women, you might expect that women would enjoy cunnilingus more than men. In the NHSLS study, however, slightly more men than women said that they found cunnilingus "very appealing" (see Figure 6.10). It may be that some women's unease with cunnilingus is based on a sense that their genitals are not very attractive and that their partners are only doing it to please them. But in reality men (and women) who perform cunnilingus do mostly find it enjoyable and sexually arousing. Oftentimes women become more comfortable in their own skins as they get older and are therefore more able to enjoy their partners' attention to their erogenous zones. When performing cunnilingus, many men prefer the woman's vulva to be hairless, and that is a large part of the reason why so many young women shave or wax their vulvas.

If a couple arrange themselves in a mutual head-to-genital position, they can perform oral sex on each other simultaneously (**FIGURE 6.11**). This practice is often called "69" or "*soixante-neuf*" (French for "69"). While sixty-nining can be very exciting, it has two possible drawbacks. The first is that each partner may be distracted from enjoying what is going on at one location by the need to attend to the other location. Also, when fellatio is performed in the 69 position, the tongue of the insertee is located on the upper, less sensitive surface of the penis and cannot easily reach the area of the frenulum.

There is little information about the prevalence of **anilingus** (mouth–anus contact). This practice can be very arousing because the skin around the anus is erotically sensitive. Sometimes anilingus is performed as a prelude to anal penetration. Many people avoid anilingus, however, because of negative associations with defecation.

**FAQ:** I've heard that blowing into a woman's vagina is dangerous. Is it?

Blowing into a pregnant woman's vagina as if trying to inflate a balloon may indeed cause an air embolism (blockage of arteries with air) that can be fatal. Whether this can happen in a nonpregnant woman is unclear—we suggest you avoid vigorous blowing.

**cunnilingus**  Sexual contact between the tongue or mouth of one person and the vulva of another.

**anilingus**  Sexual contact between the tongue or mouth of one person and the anus of another.

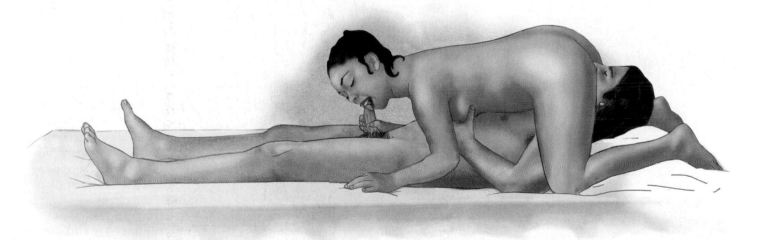

▲ **FIGURE 6.11  Mutual oral sex may be called "69" or "*soixante-neuf*."** Though shown here between a man and a woman, any sex combination can perform this activity.

This concern is to some extent justified by the risk of transmitting disease agents, such as the virus that causes hepatitis A, which is transmitted primarily by the fecal-oral route (see Chapter 15).

Oral-genital contacts are common among nonhuman animals. Among bats, for example, such contacts precede and facilitate copulation (Tan et al., 2009; Maruthupandian & Marimuthu, 2013). Many animals (including a few male humans) are able to orally stimulate their own genitals. Certain male ground squirrels fellate themselves to ejaculation after copulating with females; this behavior may reduce the risk of acquiring STIs (Waterman, 2010).

## 6.6 Most Male-Female Sex Includes Coitus

**LEARNING OBJECTIVES**

After reading this section you should be able to:

6.6.1 Define coitus and describe several different positions couples adopt for it.

6.6.2 Evaluate the pros and cons of the different positions and why they may appeal to different couples.

**coitus** Penetration of the vagina by the penis.

Penetration of the vagina by the penis is called **coitus** (**FIGURE 6.12**), or "fucking" in blunt English. The phrases "sexual intercourse" and "vaginal sex" are usually taken to mean coitus, but they are less well-defined terms that could include other activities. "Coitus" sounds awkward in regular conversation—it's the term preferred by socially inept Sheldon Cooper in the CBS series *The Big Bang Theory*—but the activity itself is central to many people's sex lives. Ninety-five percent of sexual encounters between opposite-sex adults include coitus, according to the NHSLS study, and it is usually the final behavior in an encounter. Sixty-four percent of U.S. college undergraduates have engaged in coitus at least once in their lives, and 45% have done so within the last 30 days, according to the ACHA-NCHA. These figures are very similar to those for oral sex quoted above, which is unsurprising, as the two activities often occur together.

In the late 1990s, two amateur acrobats contributed to science by having sex inside an MRI scanner, thus revealing the inner workings of coitus for the first time (**BOX 6.2**).

### Coitus can be performed in many different positions

Perhaps the most striking thing about human coitus, compared with the same behavior in non-human animals, is the wide variety of positions that a couple may adopt to perform it. Among animals, only our closest primate relatives exhibit any significant degree of variety in this regard: Bonobos, for example, engage in both front-to-front and rear-entry coitus. But humans can and do attempt an almost unlimited number of different positions.

If couples explore the various coital positions, they will discover that each provides a somewhat different physical and emotional experience, and certain ones are preferable in some particular situations. Some positions, for example, allow the man to make thrusting motions of his pelvis but restrict the woman's mobility. Some allow the reverse, while others allow both partners some degree of freedom. Thus, there may be positions that are appropriate when one or the other partner is in an active, take-control mood or, conversely, desires to play a passive role. In some positions, the hands of one or both partners are free to explore and stimulate the other's body; in others, the arms and hands may be occupied in supporting the weight of the body. Some positions require strenuous exertion and cannot be maintained for long periods of time, while others are more relaxed and may be suitable for couples who want to engage in prolonged, leisurely sex, or for obese or

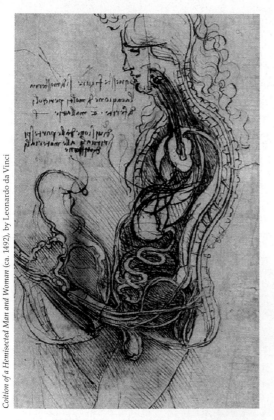

*Coition of a Hemisected Man and Woman (ca. 1492), by Leonardo da Vinci*

▲ **FIGURE 6.12 Coitus as envisaged by Leonardo da Vinci (ca. 1492)** The copulating couple (with the woman only partially shown on the left) are represented as if they had been sliced down the middle.

## BOX 6.2
## Progress in Coitus Research

In Figure 6.12 we show Leonardo da Vinci's anatomical draw-ing of a couple engaged in coitus. Of course, Leonardo didn't really cut people in half in the way that he depicted it—he just imagined it—and as a result, the anatomical details are highly suspect. Leonardo showed the man's penis sticking straight out from his body like a flagstaff. He also had some odd ideas about internal anatomy. If you look back to the drawing, you'll see that there's a tube running from the woman's uterus to her breast, which has no basis in reality. The scientific value of Leonardo's study, however, lay not so much in its veracity, or lack thereof, as in its implied message: that sex was a suitable subject for study.

Half a millennium later, gynecologist Willibrord Schultz and his colleagues at the University of Groningen hospital, in the Netherlands, decided to check on Leonardo's concep-tion of coitus by means of magnetic resonance imaging (MRI) (Schultz et al., 1999). It wasn't easy. First, there was the ques-tion of space. If you have ever been inside an MRI machine, you'll know that it's a tight fit: The tube you lie in is only 20 inches (51 cm) in diameter. Imagine having someone else in there with you, and then going through the contortions required even for missionary-position sex. The researchers had to select smallish volunteers, and in fact, the first couple that succeeded in achieving penetration in the MRI machine was a pair of amateur acrobats.

The researchers had an even more serious problem, however: The male volunteers' penises did not stand up well to the study's high-stress conditions. It took nearly a minute to acquire a single MRI image at that time, and the men just couldn't keep their penises stationary and erect inside the women's vaginas for that long. (Ongoing stimulation is usually required for men to maintain erection.)

Five years after the start of the study, however, two unexpect-ed breakthroughs occurred. The researchers obtained a new MRI machine that could generate an image in a mere 12 sec-onds, and sildenafil (Viagra) came onto the market (see Chapter 14). By swallowing a pill an hour before entering the machine, the men were able to maintain an erection as long as necessary. At last the researchers obtained sharp images of a man's fully erect penis deep within a woman's vagina (see figures).

In these images, the penis is not straight, as depicted by Leonardo, but bent upward, with the hinge point near the abdomen. Thus, the entire penis (including the root of the penis within the man's body) has the shape of a boomerang.

In the images, the sensitive lower surface of the penis presses against the back wall of the woman's vagina, an

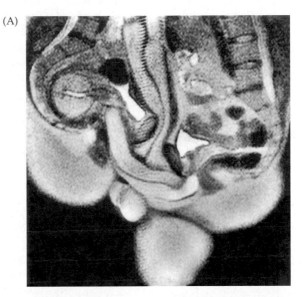

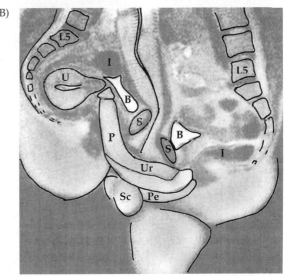

(A) MRI image of a woman (left) and man (right) engaged in coitus. (B) Explanatory drawing. (P = penis; Ur = urethra; Pe = perineum; U = uterus; B = bladder; I = intestine; L5 = fifth lumbar vertebra; Sc = scrotum; S = pubic symphysis) (From W. W. Schultz et al. 1999. *BMJ* 319: 1596.)

arrangement that may be highly stimulating to the man. Yet the penis makes little contact with the front wall of the vagina, which is the location of the controversial G-spot. (The partic-ular women who participated in the study said they did not have G-spots.) These findings support the notion that posi-tions other than the missionary position would provide better stimulation to the female partner, especially if she desires stimulation of the G-spot.

frail people. Yet others may be suitable if the woman is advanced in pregnancy. Some positions allow for eye contact between the man and the woman; this may be crucial for a head-over-heels-in-love couple, but less so for other couples. Some positions provide more erotic stimulation to the man, and others provide more stimulation to the woman; such considerations may be relevant if the couple is trying to reach orgasm simultaneously. Some positions provide the woman with more clitoral stimulation, and some stimulate the area of the G-spot, which may affect the quality of the woman's orgasm or whether she experiences one at all. In short, there seems to be every reason for couples to experiment and to communicate, not just for variety's sake, but in order to suit their sexual activities to their needs.

### The man-above position is a traditional favorite

In spite of the advantages of experimentation, Americans tend to stick to one tried-and-true position for coitus, in which the woman lies on her back with her legs parted and the man places himself above her, supporting his upper body with his hands or elbows (**FIGURE 6.13**). This man-above position is also referred to derisively as the "missionary position," a phrase apparently invented by Alfred Kinsey (Priest, 2001). At the time of his surveys in the 1940s, Kinsey estimated that 75% of Americans had never tried any other position for coitus.

With coitus in the man-above position, one partner guides the man's penis into the woman's vagina. If the woman does this, it may give her a sense of control that otherwise is lacking in the man-above position. Because the man is above, he has to do most of the "work" of coitus (i.e., the pelvic thrusting); the woman's freedom of movement is restricted by the man's body, especially if he is much larger than she is. This position has the advantage of allowing eye contact during sex but the disadvantage that the man's hands are not free to roam over the woman's body.

Simple variations on the man-above position include the woman's achieving more hip flexion by curling her legs around the man's back or even draping them over his shoulders. Such positions allow the man's penis to extend more deeply into the vagina than when the woman's legs are straight or only slightly bent at the knees.

The man-above position generally provides good erotic stimulation for the man—sometimes too good, if he tends to ejaculate more rapidly than he or his partner would like. For the woman, it is more variable. Some women are well stimulated by coitus in this position; for others, there is insufficient stimulation, especially of the G-spot, since the penis is directed toward the rear wall of the vagina.

**FAQ:** Recently, I've noticed some minor bleeding from my vagina after sex—is that something to worry about?

Postcoital bleeding can have many causes, including yeast infections, sexually transmitted infections, fibroids, uterine polyps (growths from the endometrium), and precancerous changes in the cervix. It is definitely a reason to see your doctor.

▲ **FIGURE 6.13** **The man-above position for coitus** is also called the missionary position.

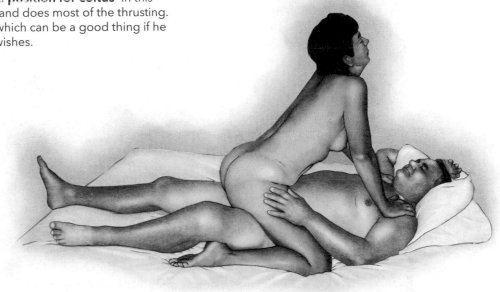

▶ **FIGURE 6.14  The woman-above position for coitus** In this position, the woman is more in control and does most of the thrusting. The man may receive less stimulation, which can be a good thing if he tends to reach orgasm earlier than he wishes.

## The women's movement and porn have encouraged alternative positions

Since Kinsey's time, the sexual revolution and the women's movement have spurred Americans to try positions other than the man-above position. The connection between the women's movement and changes in coital position was well illustrated in 1975, when students at Smith College marked their school's centennial with T-shirts celebrating "A Century of Women on Top."

Online pornography has been another spur to creativity: In one survey of people in the United States and the United Kingdom, 54% of men said that they learned about new sex positions from watching porn (Zava, 2019). For women, their partners were their most-cited source of information—but that information likely originated in porn.

One alternative is the woman-above position (**FIGURE 6.14**). In this position the man lies on his back, and the woman either lies on top of him in a face to face arrangement (which allows full body contact) or sits upright. The woman-above position gives the woman greater control, since she generates much of the thrusting motion. In general, the woman-above position may give the man somewhat less erotic stimulation than the man-above position, and the woman may receive somewhat more stimulation. (This may be helpful if the man tends to reach orgasm more rapidly than the woman does, which is common.) Furthermore, especially when the woman adopts a sitting position, it is relatively easy for her or the man to manually caress her breasts or her clitoris, thus increasing her erotic stimulation further.

In a variation of the woman-above position, the woman sits upright but faces away from the man. This "reverse cowgirl" position allows for deep penetration, but it doesn't allow for eye contact. In fact, all the woman has to look at are the man's feet. Perhaps for that reason, it is not popular: Only about 1 in 25 respondents chose it as their favorite in the Zava survey mentioned above.

Another alternative is the side-by-side position (**FIGURE 6.15**), in which the woman and the man face each other, but each lies with one side directly on the bed. Coitus in this position tends to be relatively relaxed, since neither partner's thrusting is aided by gravity, and penetration tends to be shallow. This may be desirable if the intention is to prolong the sexual encounter or if health concerns restrict one or both partners' ability to expend energy. One problem with side-by-side coitus, however, is that limbs tend to get trapped under bodies and may go numb in the middle of the action. In addition, the penis may become dislodged from the vagina, and reinsertion can be awkward in the side-by-side position. An arm around the waist of the woman can decrease the likelihood of the penis slipping out of the vagina.

▶ **FIGURE 6.15** **The side-by-side position for coitus**
Because both partners are lying directly on a flat surface, it is a less
tiring position and thus can be sustained for longer periods of time.

In rear-entry coitus (**FIGURE 6.16**), the man faces the woman's back. There are several ways of accomplishing rear-entry coitus: The couple may lie side by side with the woman turned away from the man; or the woman may lie prone or adopt a crouching position, or she may stand and lean over some object. Because the penis enters the vagina from the rear, it comes into strongest contact with the vagina's front wall (for potential G-spot stimulation), and penetration tends to be fairly shallow. There are rear-entry positions that give deep penetration, however, such as when the woman is crouching on her knees, with her chest down.

As indicated by its slang name, "doggy style," rear-entry coitus is a reminder of our kinship with the animal world. It has a number of potential advantages and disadvantages. The man may find contact with the woman's back and buttocks arousing, and the fact that the woman's front is free makes it easy for either partner to stimulate her breasts and clitoris during coitus. Rear-entry coitus in the side-by-side ("spooning") position may be the most comfortable position for a woman in the later stages of pregnancy, but nonpregnant people can enjoy this position too. In rear-entry coitus, the angle of penetration of the vagina is ideal for women who like stimulation of the G-spot, but there is no direct stimulation of the clitoris. Another possible disadvantage is that eye contact is limited. Regardless, "doggy style" was the favorite sex position cited by respondents in the Zava survey, beating the missionary position into second place.

◀ **FIGURE 6.16** **Rear-entry coitus** This position leaves the woman's breasts and clitoris free for manual stimulation by either partner.

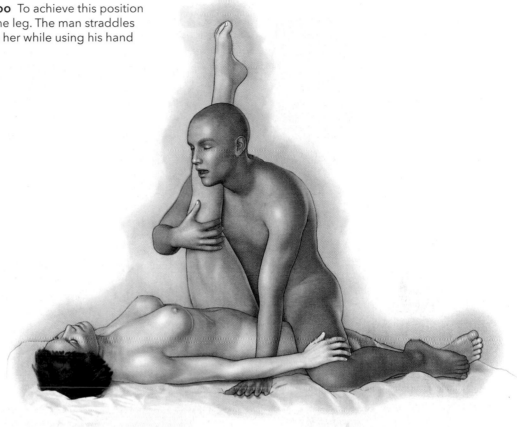

▶ **FIGURE 6.17**  **Splitting the bamboo**  To achieve this position the woman lies on her back and raises one leg. The man straddles the thigh of the other leg and penetrates her while using his hand to raise her free leg even higher.

Some positions allow for very close contact between the man's and the woman's genital areas. An example is the position called "splitting the bamboo" (**FIGURE 6.17**). This position allows for very deep penetration. As is true for many sexual positions, this one requires a certain degree of flexibility. The man should go slowly to avoid the possibility of injury.

In some cultures, heterosexual couples favor coital positions that are uncommon in the United States. In some Pacific Islands cultures, for example, a position called *haku noho* is popular: The man squats in front of the woman, and she places her legs across his thighs, whereupon he pulls her up toward himself and they embrace in a front-to-front fashion (Dixson, 2009).

There are plenty of other coital positions as well as variations on the ones already described. One adventurous couple took up a challenge from *Cosmopolitan* magazine to work their way through all 77 positions described in the 2009 edition of *The Cosmo Kama Sutra* in 77 days. They succeeded with a day to spare, while blogging an amusing and instructive commentary (Anonymous, 2014c).

## 6.7 Anal Sex May Be a Part of Either Heterosexual or Male Homosexual Behavior

### LEARNING OBJECTIVES

After reading this section you should be able to:

6.7.1   Define anal sex and describe the positions that may be used to practice it.

6.7.2   Evaluate the potential problems with anal sex and how to overcome them.

By **anal sex** (**FIGURE 6.18**) we mean penetration of the anus by the penis ("butt fucking"). Anal sex should be distinguished from rear-entry coitus, in which the penis penetrates the vagina from behind. Until 2003, anal sex was illegal in some states.

Although anal sex is often thought of in connection with sex between men, it is not rare in heterosexual sex: In the NSSHB study, about 13% of adult women had engaged in receptive heterosexual anal sex within the past year, whereas only 3.6% of men had engaged in receptive homosexual anal sex. Given that gay men constituted only about 4% of the sample, however, these data do suggest that gay male couples are far more likely to engage in anal sex than are straight couples, which makes sense, as gay male couples have fewer orifices to choose from.

**FAQ:** What is "queefing"?

Queefing, or varting, is the noisy expulsion of air from the vagina—similar to farting, but without the fire hazard.

**anal sex**   Penetration of the anus by the penis, or any sexual behavior involving the anus.

**FAQ:** My track coach tells me that "women weaken legs." Is that true?

Research has found no negative effects of sexual activity on athletic performance by either men or women. During the 2016 Rio Olympic Games, 450,000 condoms were distributed, which works out to 42 per athlete. Twenty-seven world records were set—in sports.

▲ **FIGURE 6.18** **Anal penetration** may be performed by a man on a woman or on another man (as shown here).

Heterosexual couples may engage in anal sex in order to avoid pregnancy, to avoid "having sex" in the narrow sense of the phrase, because the greater tightness of the anus (compared with the vagina) may be stimulating to the man, because anal stimulation is arousing to the woman, or simply for the sake of variety.

The mechanics of anal sex deserve some discussion. The anus is normally kept closed by the sustained contraction of two **sphincter** muscles, the external and internal sphincters (see Chapter 2), and the internal sphincter may go into an even stronger contraction as the penis begins to make entry. Anxiety on the part of the insertee may also promote contractions of the sphincter. For anal penetration to take place without causing discomfort to the insertee, it is usually necessary for the insertor to start very slowly, or to hold a finger or the tip of the penis against the orifice for 15 to 30 seconds or until the sphincter relaxes. People who have some experience with receptive anal sex learn how to relax the sphincter during penetration and tend to enjoy the experience more than first-timers.

Because the anus has no natural lubrication, it is usually necessary to employ a lubricant during anal sex. This lubricant should be water- or silicone-based if, as we recommend, a condom is used. (If a condom is not used, the insertor should urinate soon after withdrawal in order to clear any fecal particles from his urethra.) It has been reported that lubricants containing the spermicide nonoxynol-9 damage the rectal tissue (Phillips et al., 2004), so neither these lubricants nor condoms coated with them should be used for anal sex.

There are anal lubricants containing a numbing agent (benzocaine). While these lubricants may make penetration less painful, they may also increase the risk of trauma by reducing the receptive partner's awareness of potential injury. In addition, erotic stimulation will be lessened for the receptive partner, and the insertive partner's penis may also be numbed if he is not using a condom.

As it passes through the anal orifice, the penis enters the **rectum**, the lowermost portion of the intestinal tract. Repeated thrusting is likely to bring the insertor to orgasm by direct stimulation of the penis. The insertee is stimulated by friction against the anal skin and possibly by the massage of deep structures (especially the prostate gland, if the insertee is male). Only a minority of insertees can be brought to orgasm by anal sex alone, but they may reach orgasm if anal penetration is accompanied by genital stimulation.

To reduce the chances that feces may make an unwelcome appearance during the proceedings, the receptive partner can rinse out their anus and rectum beforehand—a practice called anal douching. Detailed instructions are available online (San Francisco AIDS Foundation, 2017).

There are three general positions that couples can adopt for anal sex. In one, the insertor approaches the insertee from the rear; the insertee may be standing or lying prone but is usually most comfortable with hips flexed. This can be accomplished by lying on one side with knees up, by leaning over an object such as a bed, or by adopting a crouching posture. In a second position, the insertee lies on her or his back, with legs raised and perhaps draped over the shoulders of the insertor, who approaches from the

**sphincter** A circular muscle around a tube or orifice whose contraction closes it.

**rectum** The final, straight portion of the large bowel. It connects to the exterior via the anus.

front. In a third approach, the insertor lies on his back and the insertee sits atop him, facing forward or backward. In this case, the insertee must do most of the thrusting.

The anus can also be penetrated with objects other than the penis, such as a dildo, a finger, or even the entire hand and forearm ("fisting"). Some objects may go into the rectum more easily than they come out, however, triggering an embarrassing trip to the emergency room and, conceivably, surgery to remove the foreign body (Clarke et al., 2005). The medical literature records the extraction of all kinds of objects from the rectum—usually of men—including plastic and glass bottles, cucumbers, carrots and other root vegetables, cigar tubes, and even a baseball. The insertion of any large, hard, or sharp object into the rectum (or for that matter into the vagina) risks causing a dangerous perforation of the wall of the organ, but nonforcible penetration by the penis does not harm the anus or rectum, even when practiced repeatedly over many years (Chun et al., 1997). Regarding fisting, this practice does not usually cause harm, but there are reports of anal or perineal lacerations as well as bowel perforations, which are life-threatening emergencies that have resulted in several deaths (Cappelletti et al., 2016). (Fisting involving the vagina can also cause severe injuries.) Other health concerns related to anal sex are mentioned in Chapter 15.

## 6.8 Men and Women May Have Different Preferences for Sexual Encounters

### LEARNING OBJECTIVE
After reading this section you should be able to:

6.8.1   Describe how heterosexual men and women, and gay men and lesbians, may differ in their preferences for the duration of foreplay and the entire sexual encounter.

People vary considerably in their preferred scenarios for a sexual encounter. Coitus is the preferred culmination of a sexual encounter for most heterosexual people. Some like to precede coitus with extended foreplay, while others like to engage in coitus as soon as both the man and woman are physiologically aroused (i.e., erect and lubricating, respectively).

It is widely believed that women are more interested in extended foreplay than are men, who tend to be more focused on coitus. A Canadian survey of couples in long-term heterosexual relationships casts some doubt on this assumption, however (Miller & Byers, 2004). Both the women and the men in the study believed that women prefer longer foreplay, but their own preferences didn't bear this out: The "ideal duration" of foreplay stated by the women and the men was nearly the same (an average of 18.9 and 18.1 minutes, respectively). Interestingly, the couples' *actual* duration of foreplay (about 11 to 13 minutes) fell well short of this ideal.

Men usually lose their erection soon after ejaculating, and often their psychological arousal with it. Thus, a man who wishes his female partner to feel sexually fulfilled by an encounter may want to delay his own orgasm until his partner is satisfied, whether that satisfaction means orgasm, more than one orgasm, or a certain length or intensity of nonorgasmic sex. A man can delay his ejaculation by any of a number of methods, such as thrusting slowly or using sexual positions that stimulate him less strongly. He can also use techniques taught by therapists specifically to treat **premature ejaculation** (see Chapter 14). Another possibility is not to resist the tendency to ejaculate early but to learn to value and enjoy sexual interactions *after* ejaculation (afterplay), including activities, such as oral or manual sex, that can bring his partner to orgasm even though he himself no longer has an erection.

That women often prefer sex on a more relaxed schedule than men is made obvious when two women get together. According to an unscientific survey by *The Advocate*, a gay and lesbian magazine, 96% of lesbians spend more than 15 minutes on a

---

**FAQ:** Can sex trigger a heart attack?

Yes, but the risk is low and primarily affects people with preexisting heart conditions who don't get regular exercise (Dahabreh & Paulus, 2011).

**premature ejaculation**   Ejaculation before the man wishes, often immediately on commencement of coitus. Also called rapid ejaculation.

lovemaking session, and 39% spend more than an hour (Lever, 1995). Besides taking longer than a typical heterosexual encounter, sexual encounters between women are marked by a greater variety of behaviors and by an emphasis on general body contact in addition to specific genital contacts (Hite, 2003).

While on the topic of same-sex encounters, it's worth pointing out that same-sex couples have one advantage over opposite-sex couples: They are interacting with partners whose basic anatomy, physiology, and psychology are quite familiar to them even before their first sexual experience. Furthermore, people's upbringing often allows them to communicate more effectively on sexual topics with people of their own sex than with people of the other sex. Thus, gay and lesbian couples may find it easier to express their sexual desires and needs. This very familiarity may also create problems, however, by lessening the sense of mystery and tension that energizes heterosexual relationships (LeVay, 2006).

## 6.9 Sex Toys Are Used to Enhance Sexual Pleasure

### LEARNING OBJECTIVES

After reading this section you should be able to:

**6.9.1** Explain what vibrators are and how they may be used in solo and partnered sex.

**6.9.2** Describe the variety of dildos and precautions that should be taken with their use.

**6.9.3** Evaluate the factors that may make for "great sex" beyond the mechanics of sexual practices.

Innumerable natural and artificial objects have been recruited for sexual use at one time or another. Some are widely used, while others serve minority sexual interests or fetishisms or are designed to alleviate sexual disorders.

**Vibrators**, sometimes referred to as "personal massagers," are electrical (usually battery-powered) devices (**FIGURE 6.19**). Their function is exactly what their name implies: to provide vibratory stimulation. These devices vibrate at much higher frequencies than those experienced during "natural" sex. Typically, a vibrator consists of a handle and a vibrating head, whose shape may be designed to stimulate a specific target: clitoris, vagina, the entire vulva, penis, or anus.

Vibrators are very popular among women, because many women need prolonged, continuous clitoral stimulation to reach orgasm, and a vibrator is an effective way to provide it. About half of all women age 18 to 60 have used them, according to a survey by the Center for Sexual Health Promotion at Indiana University (Herbenick et al., 2009). Usage is highest among non-heterosexual women: About 70% of lesbians and 80% of bisexual women have used them, according to the Indiana University survey. Although older women are less likely than younger women to have used vibrators, they are catching up as a more sex-aware generation enters their 50s or 60s: In a more recent but less scientific survey, 2 out of 3 women over 60 said that they had used a vibrator (Depree, 2016).

Vibrators are most often thought of as an aid to women when masturbating alone, and indeed, they are commonly used for that purpose, but women may also use a vibrator during sex with a partner. A woman engaged in coitus or oral sex, for example, may simultaneously stimulate her clitoris with a vibrator. If her partner is a man, he may be unfamiliar with vibrators, or he may believe that a woman who uses one is

**vibrator** An electrically powered vibrating device used to provide sexual stimulation.

Courtesy of Oh My Sensuality, www.ohmysensuality.com

▲ **FIGURE 6.19** **Vibrators** are electrically powered sexual stimulators. The "rabbit vibrator" (center rear) is designed to stimulate a woman's vagina and clitoris simultaneously.

telling him that he is an inadequate lover. (In reality, many women are not brought to orgasm by vaginal penetration alone, no matter who is doing the penetrating.) Most women who use vibrators are comfortable using them in partnered sex, and those who do so have a generally high level of sexual function (Herbenick et al., 2010a).

Men may also use vibrators. About 40% of heterosexual men have used them, usually in the context of sex with a woman (Reece et al., 2010a). There are also vibrators specifically designed for stimulation of the penis—these may have a vibrating sleeve or ring. Alternatively, a vibrator may be used to stimulate the scrotum, perineum, or anus while the penis is stimulated by masturbation or partnered sex.

Many vibrators are now "smart" and can be controlled remotely—they are a useful adjunct to Skype sex and other long-distance booty calls—but they come with certain risks. In 2017 the makers of one smart vibrator, the We-Vibe, paid $3.75 million in settlement of a class action lawsuit brought by users. The lawsuit alleged that the company had secretly tracked how and when people were using their vibrators (Domonoske, 2017).

**Dildos** are sex toys designed for penetration of the vagina or anus (**FIGURE 6.20**). They are not electrically powered; in fact, they predate the discovery of electricity by thousands of years. They may be realistic imitations of a penis (sometimes complete with scrotum), but they also come in a wide variety of other shapes and sizes, some designed to stimulate the clitoris at the same time the shaft of the dildo penetrates the vagina. With another kind of dildo the back end takes the form of a suction cup: The dildo can be parked on a vertical or horizontal surface, so that users can penetrate themselves with the dildo while keeping both hands free for other uses. There are also double-ended dildoes that allow two people to use the same dildo simultaneously.

Yet another kind of dildo is made to fit into a strap that a woman can wear around her hips or around one thigh (**FIGURE 6.21**). Strap-on dildos are mainly designed for sex between women. These devices also have a long history: Women of the Azande people of eastern Sudan traditionally used a banana, manioc, or sweet potato tied around the waist to engage in vaginal penetration with female partners (Ford & Beach, 1951). Heterosexual couples can also employ strap-on dildos: A man who is temporarily or permanently unable to achieve an erection may use one instead of his own penis, or a woman can use one to anally penetrate a man (Queen, 1998).

Dildos designed specifically for anal penetration are called **butt plugs**. The back end of a butt plug is flared to prevent it from getting lost in the rectum. Some butt plugs are shaped or curved in such a way as to facilitate stimulation of the prostate gland—these may be rebranded as **prostate massagers**. They may provide extra erotic stimulation or more intense orgasms, but claims that they provide health benefits for the prostate are dubious.

Finally, there's the **fucksaw** (**FIGURE 6.22**). This is a dildo that can be connected via a special adapter to a reciprocating saw from which the cutting blade has been removed. It produces a pulsing forward-and-back motion that is said to be especially effective for stimulating the region of the G-spot. It needs to be used cautiously to produce pleasure rather than pain or injury. The fucksaw achieved national notoriety in 2011: A Northwestern University psychology professor invited students in his human sexuality class to attend an extracurricular

▲ **FIGURE 6.20**    **Dildos** are designed for penetration of the vagina or anus.

*Courtesy of Oh My Sensuality, www.ohmysensuality.com*

**dildo**    A sex toy, often shaped like a penis, used to penetrate the vagina or anus.

**butt plug**    A dildo designed for anal penetration.

**prostate massager**    A butt plug shaped to stimulate the prostate gland.

**fucksaw**    A sex toy consisting of a dildo attached to a reciprocating saw.

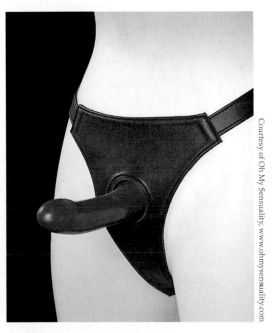

▲ **FIGURE 6.21**    **A strap-on dildo**

*Courtesy of Oh My Sensuality, www.ohmysensuality.com*

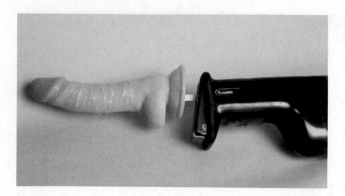

▲ **FIGURE 6.22** A **fucksaw** has three components: a hollowed-out dildo, an adapter, and an electric reciprocating saw.

event in which a woman demonstrated the device in action. The end result was the permanent cancellation of the class.

Dildos are made from a range of materials, but silicone rubber is generally preferred for its flexibility, smooth surface, and ease of cleaning. Dildos usually have to be used with a lubricant. They need to be used gently and with respect for anatomy—that is, they should be moved in the natural direction of the vagina or rectum. It is also best to use small sizes, at least to begin with. (Some health issues connected with the use of sex toys are discussed in Chapter 15.)

There are plenty of sex toys besides vibrators and dildos:

- *Anal beads*. A set of silicone or plastic beads on a string can be inserted into the anus and then pulled out slowly, often at the same time as orgasm (**FIGURE 6.23**). The passage of the beads through the anus can be highly arousing. They are used by both men and women and in both solo and partnered sex.

- *Cock rings*. These are rings made of rigid or elastic materials that are placed around the base of the penis (or the penis and scrotum). They enhance erections, or extend them after ejaculation, by restricting the outflow of blood from the penis. They are especially useful for men with erectile disorder. Cock rings should be worn only for the duration of the sexual activity; prolonged use can damage the erectile tissues of the penis.

- *Masturbatory sleeves*. Basically the inverse of dildos and similarly unpowered, these are for use by men (**FIGURE 6.24**). Some have orifices that are designed to resemble the vulva, the mouth, or the anus, and they all have an inner sleeve with a flesh-like feel.

▲ **FIGURE 6.23** Anal beads The beads shown here are made of a single piece of silicone, making them easier to keep clean than beads on a cord.

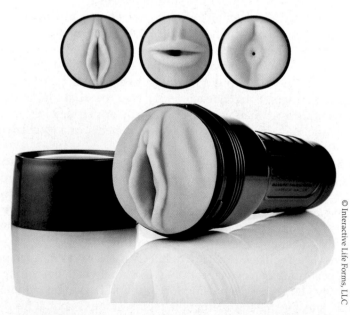

▲ **FIGURE 6.24** **Masturbatory sleeves** have openings for the user to insert his penis. These Fleshlight sleeves are intended to resemble the vulva, mouth, or anus.

- *Erotic dolls.* These are popular with some men. They may be simple blow-up dolls, or they may be very realistic, custom-made dolls that weigh as much as a real person and possess internal skeletons and joints that allow for lifelike positioning. A standard female doll of this kind costs about $6,000, but the price quickly escalates with options such as alternative faces, clothes, or a removable penis to turn her into a "shemale." At a much higher price point are robotic female dolls that can smile, frown, blink, and hold a simple conversation (**FIGURE 6.25**). One of these dolls, named Emma, has "smart moaning technology—she moans louder as touch intensifies," and she even gives weather updates.

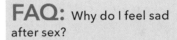

**sex play** A variety of playful activities that add pleasure to sexual interactions.

For most people, sex toys are used in **sex play**—a catchall phrase for activities that add spice and variety to sex. Besides sex toys, sex play can include such things as ice, oil, food, feathers, pillow fights, erotic biting, bondage and other role-playing fantasies, massage, fully clothed sex, striptease, sex with masks or blindfolds, mirrors, or sex in unusual locations. Sex play can incorporate penetrative sex or be a prelude or alternative to it. All that's required is a belief that sex should be fun, as well as an active imagination—and even the latter isn't strictly necessary, given the number of books that offer advice in this area (see Recommended Reading at the end of this chapter).

All sex toys are capable of transmitting infections, so any toy that is to be used by more than one person should be scrupulously cleaned after use. Even after cleaning, STI-causing agents such as human papillomavirus can sometimes be detected on the surfaces of sex toys (Anderson et al., 2014), so it's not a good idea to share sex toys among multiple users.

It's worth stressing that sex is about much more than the mechanical issues that we've been discussing in the previous pages. For a discussion of what really makes for "great sex," see **BOX 6.3**.

**FAQ:** Why do I feel sad after sex?

If you're a woman, you're not alone—1 in 10 women has experienced the post-sex blues within the last month, according to one survey (Bird et al., 2011). The reason isn't known, unfortunately.

▲ **FIGURE 6.25** **Sex with robots** Harmony is a first-generation "intelligent" sex doll that can smile and frown and hold a conversation while enjoying sex with you. Sadly she is still quadriplegic.

© Eduardo Contreras/ZUMA Press Inc/Alamy Stock Photo

## BOX 6.3
## What Is "Great Sex"?

Popular books and magazines tend to stress performance, technique, and novelty as the main elements of sexual satisfaction. But Peggy Kleinplatz, a sex therapist and professor at the University of Ottawa, wanted to find out what really made for "great sex" (Kleinplatz et al., 2009). So she and her colleagues recruited a diverse group of 64 volunteers: sex therapists, members of sexual minorities, and older people, all of whom claimed to have experienced "great sex" or were currently experiencing it. (Curiously, they did not recruit any young, straight, nonprofessional individuals.) On the basis of extended interviews the researchers identified eight major components of "great sex" that were mentioned by most participants:

1. *Being present and focused.* "The difference is when I can really just let go and completely focus and be in the moment and not have that, you know, running commentary going through my head about anything else."
2. *Connection.* "A melding, blurring of identity boundaries so that one feels like you were literally feeling with the other and the distinction between what the other person feels and what you feel seems almost irrelevant."
3. *Intimacy.* "Being loved and wanted, accepted and cherished." "Trust that this partner, whom you trust, will take care of you just as you are taking care of him."
4. *Communication—verbal and nonverbal.* "Being able to listen, to recognize, what, when, even if you're not told, that one kind of touch elicits a certain response in your partner and another does not."
5. *Authenticity, transparency.* "Getting to the point where I am completely stripped bare emotionally, physically, you know, spiritually."
6. *Transcendence, bliss.* "An experience of floating in the universe of light and stars and music and sublime peace."
7. *Exploration, risk taking.* "Where can we take each other? Where can we go?" "An opportunity for creativity." "If you're not having fun, it's not great."

*Great sex is about more than technique.*

8. *Vulnerability.* "It's saying I'm going to jump off this cliff where I'm going to, you know, be naked and be vulnerable and give myself to somebody else and take them in and I hope I feel good after I do that."

Some participants also mentioned the importance of intense physical sensations, such as those of orgasm, or of intense attraction to the other person. ("Oh, my god! If I go another minute without my hands on you, I'll die.")

Based on their analysis of the interviews, the researchers concluded that performance and technique were of secondary importance to most people who experienced "great sex." Indeed, some had great sex in spite of significant sexual disorders. Rather, what mattered was something much more personal. "Being comfortable in one's own skin is the foundation for being authentically present and involved in the moment," Kleinplatz writes. "It is also a prerequisite for revealing oneself and taking a leap of faith with a lover."

## 6.10  Sex May Be in Groups

### LEARNING OBJECTIVE
After reading this section you should be able to:

**6.10.1  Describe different kinds of group sex.**

Most of what we have described so far involves interactions between just two people, but in reality there's no limit to the number of persons who can participate in a single sexual encounter. Group sex may involve three or more people who are in a stable polyamorous relationship (see Chapter 11), or it may be a casual coming together of strangers (a three-way, four-way, etc.) in a swingers' club, bathhouse, or outdoor "cruising" area.

The practical details of group-sex encounters vary widely. Among the possibilities are the following:

- Three people have sex together in various combinations (a three-way or threesome).
- Multiple couples engage in paired sex in a common space (same-room sex).
- Multiple individuals take turns to have sex with one target individual (a "gang bang").
- Multiple individuals engage in more or less random couplings in a common space (an orgy).

The participants in group sex may be all of the same sex (usually gay men) or both sexes. If the latter, the individual contacts may be all heterosexual or a mix of opposite-sex and same-sex contacts. Sometimes there are participants who don't have any physical contact with others but whose arousal comes from watching the proceedings. (In that sense, viewing pornorgraphic videos could be thought of as a form of group sex.)

Although group sex is sometimes viewed as sordid or sinful, it has often been portrayed in art, including religious art (**FIGURE 6.26**). It is also commonly observed among nonhuman animals. Bonobos, for example, are especially fond of group encounters. Some snakes form "mating balls" in which dozens of males attempt to penetrate a single female, but only a few succeed. Threesomes in which one male penetrates a female while being penetrated by a second male have been observed in many mammalian species; whether such couplings are simple mistakes or have some adaptive significance is not known.

© Graham Prentice/Alamy Stock Photo

▲ **FIGURE 6.26** **Orgy in stone** This and many other erotic sculptures decorate the 1,000-year-old Khajuraho temples in the Indian state of Madhya Pradesh.

## 6.11 Sexual Behavior and Attitudes Vary across Cultures

**LEARNING OBJECTIVES**

After reading this section you should be able to:

6.11.1 Describe sexual beliefs and practices in several non-Western societies.

6.11.2 Evaluate the pros and cons of non-Western beliefs and practices as compared with those prevalent in contemporary America.

American culture is in a state of transition with regard to the discussion of sexual practices. On the one hand, one can visit online websites, see video clips, or purchase books that cover not only mainstream sex, but any number of minority interests, from fisting to sex with animals. On the other hand, sex education in schools is still a very controversial topic, reflecting a conflict between traditional negative attitudes toward sex and an increasing desire for openness and realism, especially in the areas of contraception, disease prevention, masturbation, and homosexuality.

### The *Kama Sutra* is the classic work on how to make love

Because attitudes in the United States have been changing so rapidly over the past few decades, open discussion of sexual behavior seems like a modern American phenomenon. In reality, however, some other societies have been more open in the way they deal with sexuality than we are. Nothing illustrates this better than the *Kama Sutra* of Vatsyayana, which was written in India no later than the 5th century.

*Kama Sutra* means "love guide." In Hindu teaching, *kama* ("love") is one of the four goals of life. Unlike the selfless love that is celebrated in Judeo-Christian tradition, however, *kama* includes a hefty dose of erotic pleasure, and this is a central topic of Vatsyayana's book.

Indicative of Vatsyayana's approach, he begins the chapter on sexual intercourse with a discussion of genital size. Unlike current textbooks such as this one, which tend to downplay the significance of size variations, Vatsyayana considers it a major problem if a man's and a woman's genitals are mismatched—particularly if the man is a "hare" (i.e., has a small penis) and the woman is a "female elephant" (i.e., has a large, deep vagina).

In such a case, Vatsyayana recommends penis enlargement, which is to be accomplished by repeated application of the bristles of certain tree-living insects, followed by rubbing the penis with oil for 10 nights and sleeping with the penis hanging down through a hole in the bed. ("He should take away all the pain from the swelling by using cool concoctions.") If this does not provide the woman with satisfaction, the man can use metal or ivory sleeves studded with "pleasure bumps" on the outside. They fit over the penis in a modular fashion, increasing its girth and length as much as desired. (Similar devices, made of plastic or silicone rubber, can be bought in sex toy shops today—they are called cock sleeves.) In an extreme case, says Vatsyayana, the man should forget about his penis altogether and simply tie the tubular stalk of a bottle gourd around his waist with string—another variation on the strap-on dildo.

The *Kama Sutra* is best known for its detailed description of coital positions, which include all the ones we have discussed plus more exotic ones that "require practice." There are also several chapters on foreplay, with detailed instructions for embracing, kissing, touching, slapping, scratching with the nails, and biting. Every kind of foreplay escalates by precise gradations, to slowly increase the degree of passion. Thus, if a man gives a woman a "line of points" (a mark caused by a nip by several teeth), she should respond with a "broken cloud" (a circular arrangement of marks caused by biting down on a large chunk of skin). He, in turn, may respond with the "biting of the boar," and so on.

Vatsyayana covers fellatio in considerable detail and cunnilingus briefly, but he barely mentions anal sex. (According to Indian tradition, the Muslims introduced anal sex in the 11th century.) Vatsyayana describes sex between women, but he sees it as a choice of last resort (e.g., among the women of the king's harem when no man can be smuggled in). Sex between men is chiefly a matter of eunuchs (castrated men) performing fellatio on other men in connection with bodily services such as massage. There is no notion of homosexuality as a stable orientation, but other sources show that both male and female homosexuality were known in ancient India (Vanita, 2001).

Vatsyayana is far more mindful of women's interests than are other ancient texts on sexuality, such as the Roman poet Ovid's *Art of Love* (written in the year 2 CE), which is basically a guide to seduction. Many of Vatsyayana's observations on how men and women interact seem right on target today. But his understanding of women's bodies is rudimentary: He seems not to know of the clitoris, for example.

Whether the open and positive attitude toward sex seen in the *Kama Sutra* was generally typical of Vatsyayana's time is difficult to know. For one thing, the book was written for and about the wealthy classes. The sex lives of the great majority of Indian people in the 5th century are lost to history, but they are unlikely to have been as rich and varied as described in the *Kama Sutra*. Today, the sex lives of poor Indians leave a lot to be desired. This is how two Indian sexologists summarized their survey of Dalit (lowest-caste) women living in cities:

> *Most of these women portrayed their experience with sexual intercourse as a furtive act in a cramped and crowded room, lasting barely a few minutes and with a marked absence of physical or emotional caressing. It was a duty, an experience to be submitted to, often from a fear of beating. None of the women removed their clothes during intercourse since it is considered shameful to do so.* (Nath & Nayar, 1997)

India is, of course, not the only country where women's sexual interests may be subordinated to those of men. In sub-Saharan Africa, many men's preference for "dry sex" reduces women's sexual pleasure and threatens their health (**BOX 6.4**).

There are plenty of books with titles like *The Gay Kama Sutra* or *The Lesbian Kama Sutra*. Whatever their merits, these books have nothing to do with the *Kama Sutra* of Vatsyayana.

## Taoists recommended the avoidance of ejaculation

The followers of the ancient Chinese tradition of Tao ("the Way") believed that the loss of bodily fluids, especially men's semen, drained life energy and hastened death—an idea encapsulated in the saying "If the fuel is exhausted, the flame expires" (Wile, 1992). Taoist men were therefore encouraged to terminate coitus before ejaculation and to allow their sexual excitement to dissipate without loss of semen. Alternatively, a man could experience orgasm, but he should prevent ejaculation by pressing deeply on his perineum, which caused the semen to ascend to the brain and invigorate it. (This is not what actually happens, in case you were wondering: The semen is forced backward into the bladder and is voided when the man next urinates.)

In traditional Taoist teachings women were viewed primarily as donors of life energy to men, who could absorb it through their penises. Because a woman's life

---

## BOX 6.4
## Dry Sex

If the slogan "moisturize, moisturize" was coined by beauty care specialists, it is echoed by sex therapists. Women who don't produce enough natural lubrication are advised to use liberal amounts of off-the-shelf personal lubricant—the wetter, the better.

That advice wouldn't play well in southern Africa, where dry sex is preferred—by men at least. Women often place drying substances in their vaginas before sex: These substances include crushed stone, tobacco, herbs, soil soaked in baboon urine, or the ground-up bark of certain trees. The substances cause the genital tissues to become swollen, hot, and dry, and this provides a tighter, more abrasive sensation that many southern African men prefer. (Most men in this region are uncircumcised, which gives them more loose penile skin to accommodate the unlubricated sliding motion.) Prostitutes who practice dry sex can charge much more than they would get otherwise (Elmes et al., 2014).

For the woman, however, dry sex can be quite painful, and it can cause small tears in the vaginal mucosa, which increase the likelihood of her becoming infected with HIV and other STIs. What's more, the lack of lubrication makes it difficult to use condoms. Yet most women in southern Africa—not just prostitutes, but married women too—engage in the practice. The reason they do so is to please their partners. If a woman doesn't do it, the man may accuse her of promiscuity, which (he will say) causes the vagina to become loose and wet. He may also seek sex elsewhere or even abandon his partner.

This African prostitute can charge more if she practices dry sex.

Thus, the custom of dry sex reflects women's lack of power and the denial of their right to sexual pleasure, somewhat analogous to the case of female circumcision. Fortunately, the custom of dry sex is gradually going out of favor among the urban populations of southern Africa.

Don't confuse "dry sex," as used here, with its meaning in U.S. slang, which usually refers to a man and woman rubbing their genitals against their partners' bodies to the point of orgasm, but without coitus.

▲ **FIGURE 6.27** **An Aka mother and her children** According to Aka beliefs, the birth of a child results from multiple acts of coitus.

**seminal nurture** The belief that fetuses require repeated infusions of semen to grow.

energy weakened as she grew older, men were encouraged to have sex with very young virgins, even before their first menstruation. Needless to say, contemporary Taoist teachings do not include such practices.

### The Aka emphasize the importance of frequent sex

As an example of a contemporary non-Western culture, we'll take a look at sex among the Aka, a hunter-gatherer people who live in the rain forest of the Congo Basin (**FIGURE 6.27**). Aka culture is remarkably egalitarian: They have no dominant leaders, and men and women share their responsibilities, including hunting and child care.

Anthropologists Barry and Bonnie Hewlett, of Washington State University, have spent many years studying the Aka and have interviewed numerous men and women (in their native language) concerning their sex lives (Hewlett & Hewlett, 2010). One of their most striking findings concerns the frequency of sex. Married Aka couples have sex on about three nights every week, and on each of these nights they engage in coitus an average of three times, resting or sleeping between episodes. Men experience orgasm on every occasion, while women do so at least once on every night when they engage in coitus.

While this frequency of sex might not be unusual for American newlyweds, the Aka continue to have sex at roughly the same frequency throughout their fertile years. "I am now doing it five times a night to search for a child," one Aka man told the Hewletts. "If I do not do it five times my wife will not be happy because she wants children quickly." To facilitate this level of performance, Aka men use a sexual stimulant that they obtain by chewing the bark of a certain tree. (This stimulant may be yohimbine, a drug that is sometimes used in the United States for treatment of erectile disorder.)

The Aka men and women told the Hewletts that sex was "hard work"—work that was motivated by the need to produce numerous children in a culture where infant and child mortality is high. Although frequent sex does (within limits) increase the likelihood of pregnancy, the Aka also subscribe to a belief that makes it particularly important to have sex as often as possible. They believe that fetuses require repeated infusions of a man's semen in order to grow, an idea called **seminal nurture**. There is some kinship between seminal nurture and partible paternity, discussed in Chapter 1 (see Box 1.1): Central to both ideas is the belief that several or many coital acts—not just one—contribute to the making of a baby.

Consistent with their emphasis on the reproductive function of sex, none of the Hewletts' male or female interviewees had engaged in masturbation or homosexual behavior, nor had they even heard of these practices. The Hewletts cite the difficulties faced by an anthropologist who tried to obtain semen samples from another rain forest people: "It was very difficult to explain to men how to self-stimulate . . . Despite explicit and lengthy instructions three of four semen samples came to him mixed with vaginal secretions." Although further research might identify some Aka individuals who do practice these behaviors, the Hewletts' observations challenge the notion that nonreproductive sexual behaviors are a human universal.

## 6.12 Many Disabled People Have Active Sex Lives

**LEARNING OBJECTIVES**
After reading this section you should be able to:

6.12.1 Evaluate the ethical conflicts that may arise regarding sexual expression by intellectually disabled people.

6.12.2 Describe the effects on sexual expression of injuries at different levels of the spinal cord, and explain why they occur.

6.12.3 Explain what kinds of advice you could give to people whose sexual behavior is impaired by arthritis.

So far in this chapter, we have discussed sexual behavior as if everyone who wanted to engage in it was fully able-bodied and healthy. That's not the case, of course: Many people have disabilities or illnesses that present challenges to sexual expression. Here we briefly focus on three kinds of disabilities—one that raises questions of choice and competency (intellectual disability) and two that may directly affect sexual behavior (spinal cord injuries and arthritis).

Probably the main thing to understand about disabilities is that they do not generally interfere with sexual desire or they do so only indirectly, in the sense that disabled people may internalize other people's stereotypes of them. Even severely disabled men and women are likely to experience sexual attraction, to fall in love, to desire intimacy, and to make great efforts to consummate those feelings. In one large-scale national study of women with and without disabilities, the disabled women were only moderately less sexually active than the nondisabled women (Nosek et al., 2001) (**FIGURE 6.28**). The differences that did exist were primarily a consequence of the fact that the women with disabilities were less likely to be in a marriage or cohabitation.

There are individuals—sometimes called **devotees**—who are sexually aroused by disabilities or disabled people (Limoncin et al., 2014). For example, they may have a fetishistic interest in limb amputations (see Chapter 13). Disabled people do not generally think of their disability as a central element of their identity, however, so a sexualized focus on the disability may be experienced as dehumanizing. In other cases, though, the devotee may be attracted to the disabled person on account of his or her positive personality traits, such as fortitude, in which case a mutually rewarding relationship may be established. Most partners of disabled persons are not devotees, of course, but are attracted to a particular individual who happens to have a disability.

## Many intellectually disabled people are competent to make sexual choices

In modern societies, people with mild or moderate intellectual disabilities often participate in community life and may live in independent or semi-independent settings. There has been an increasing acknowledgment that most intellectually disabled people have sexual feelings—only some profoundly disabled people seem to lack them. Like anyone else, intellectually disabled people may belong to sexual minorities—they may be gay or lesbian, for example—though this is a possibility that is often ignored by caregivers and others (Noonan & Taylor Gomez, 2010).

Intellectually disabled people have the same constitutional right as other people (under the right to privacy) to make informed choices about sexual activity, to the extent that they are capable of doing so. They also have a right to protection from sexual exploitation, however. In general, it is illegal, as well as reprehensible, for anyone to have sexual contact with an intellectually disabled person if that person lacks the mental capacity to give informed consent. Mental capacity means knowledge about sex, the intelligence to understand the risks and benefits of sexual activity (including an awareness of the social and moral nature of sexual relations), and the ability to make a decision free of coercion (Lyden, 2007).

Luckily, many intellectually disabled people are well within the bounds of competence and chiefly need education in such matters as potential sexual behaviors, appropriate partners, privacy, sexual exploitation, STIs, pregnancy prevention, and the like (Lumley & Scotti, 2001). The Arc, a national organization of and for the intellectually disabled, asserts the right of these people not only to engage in sexual relationships, but also to marry and have children and, if they do have children, to receive assistance in raising them.

People with age-related dementia present a particular ethical dilemma, especially if they are married or in another relationship that predates the onset of their

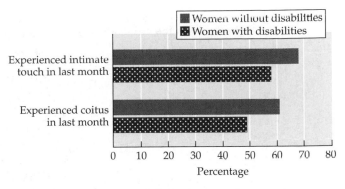

▲ **FIGURE 6.28** **Disabilities have only a moderate effect** on women's sexual activity. (Data from M. A. Nosek et al. 2001. *Sex Disability* 19: 5–40.)

**devotee** Colloquial term for a person whose sexual interests are focused on disabilities.

**quadriplegia** Paralysis affecting almost the entire body below the neck.

**paraplegia** Paralysis affecting the lower half of the body.

disability. A poignant example came up in 2014: A 78-year-old Iowa man, Henry Rayhons, was arrested and charged with felony sexual abuse of his wife, also 78, who had severe Alzheimer's disease and was in a nursing home. The allegation was that he had sex with her after having been told by doctors that she no longer had the competence to consent. Rayhons's sperm were identified on the bedsheets, but he denied that they had done more than hold hands and kiss, and a jury acquitted him (Kaplan, 2015). You may well have sympathy for this man, particularly as his wife died shortly before his arrest. Bear in mind, though, that consent is legally and ethically required for sex within marriage just as it is between unmarried people.

## Spinal cord injuries present a major challenge to sexual expression

Each year there are about 10,000 spinal cord injuries in the United States that result in significant and permanent neurological deficits. The majority of those affected are young or middle-aged men (**FIGURE 6.29**). Most of these injuries result from motor vehicle accidents, violence, sports accidents, or falls. A complete injury at the cervical (neck) level results in almost total loss of movement and sensation below the neck (**quadriplegia**), while injuries at lower levels usually affect the legs and the lower portion of the trunk, including the genitals (**paraplegia**).

One option adopted by many men and women with spinal cord injuries is to make increased use of parts of the body whose movement and sensation are unimpaired. In quadriplegics that may mean primarily the mouth, while for paraplegics it may include the hands and breasts. Many people with spinal cord injuries report that the erotic sensitivity of their unaffected body regions increases over time, so much so that the person may experience orgasm, or highly pleasant sensations comparable to orgasm, from sexual use of those regions. In some cases the sensations may be experienced as if they were coming from the genitalia ("phantom orgasm").

A man with a spinal cord injury may or may not be able to have an erection. If the injury is to the lowest portion of the spinal cord, the man is unlikely to be able to have an erection under any circumstances, because the neural mechanisms that activate erection are located there. If the injury is high in the spinal cord, he probably will be able to have erections in response to sensory stimulation of the genitalia, because the entire reflex loop from the genitalia to the spinal cord and back is intact. In fact, the loss of inhibitory influences from the brain may cause reflex erections to be stronger and more frequent than usual (Elliott, 2009). If the spinal injury is complete, however, the man will not feel any sensations from his penis, erect or not. Nor will he have erections in response to erotic sights or fantasies ("psychogenic erections"), because the long pathways between the brain and the lower spinal cord have been interrupted.

Ejaculation may be possible for men with lower-level injuries, especially if there is not a complete transection of the spinal cord, but a complete upper-level injury generally makes ejaculation impossible because it cuts off signals from the brain centers that are involved in triggering this process. (The brain's involvement in ejaculation is discussed in Appendix B.) Even if ejaculation is possible, it is not likely to be accompanied by the normal subjective sensations of orgasm.

Men with spinal cord injuries who wish to engage in coitus are usually capable of doing so. If the man is paraplegic, he can take the man-above position. He may have to push his flaccid penis into the

▲ **FIGURE 6.29** **Paraplegia typically strikes young men.** Sexual expression is still possible but requires adaptability. (The man in this stock photo is a non-disabled model.)

© iStock.com/JackF

woman's vagina by hand (the "stuffing" technique); the woman can help this process by actively contracting the muscles surrounding the walls of her vagina. The man's penis may then become erect as a result of reflex action as the woman performs thrusting motions. If the man is quadriplegic, the woman does best to kneel astride him and place his penis in her vagina; again, the penis may become erect in response to this stimulation. An additional complication is urinary incontinence. If a urinary catheter is in place, it can be kept in place with the aid of a condom or tape; this, then, will necessitate the use of a lubricant.

Women with spinal cord injuries have deficits roughly comparable to men's: Besides the loss of movement and sensation (depending on the level and severity of the injury), women may lose vaginal lubrication (necessitating use of a lubricant). With lower-level injuries, engorgement of the vulvar tissues may be lost as well. Coitus is possible in several positions, however, including the man-above position or side by side with either front or rear entry.

In one laboratory-based study (Sipski et al., 2001), not quite half of the women with spinal cord injuries were able to reach orgasm, compared with 100% of uninjured women. Ability to reach orgasm was lowest with complete injuries affecting the lowest region of the spinal cord. Among women who did reach orgasm, the time required to do so was longer than among the uninjured women, but the orgasms themselves were similar in quality.

The usual explanation for how women with spinal cord injuries can experience orgasm is that the cord has not been completely severed. Some women with *complete* transection of the cord still report experiencing orgasm in some circumstances, however, especially in response to deep stimulation of the vagina or cervix. It is thought that this is made possible by sensory signals carried in the vagus nerve (one of the cranial nerves), which has sensory branches that innervate the abdomen and pelvis, bypassing the spinal cord altogether (Komisaruk et al., 2004).

If you are an able-bodied and sexually active young person, you may be wondering whether sexual interactions are really worth it for men and women with spinal cord injuries or their partners. The answer, however, is often a resounding "yes"—whether in terms of physical pleasure, intimacy between partners, or the psychological reward of accomplishing such a basic human activity in the face of a major challenge.

## Arthritis is the number-one disability affecting sex

Some disabilities interfere with sexual expression by limiting movement. In this connection, people generally think first of spinal cord injuries, but numerically, the leading villain is arthritis. This collection of conditions (chiefly osteoarthritis, rheumatoid arthritis, and systemic lupus erythematosus) affects an estimated 22% of American adults; women and the elderly are disproportionately affected.

If arthritis affects the large joints, such as the hips, it may interfere with the postures or body movements (such as pelvic thrusting) involved in partnered sex. If it involves the small joints of the hands, it may interfere with masturbation, sensual touching, and tasks requiring dexterity, such as putting on a condom or inserting a diaphragm.

A certain degree of planning can make lovemaking a much more positive experience for people with arthritis. Sex can be timed for a part of the day when the person's arthritis is least bothersome, or medications can be timed to be maximally effective during sex. It may be helpful to precede sexual intercourse with a warm shower, gentle massage, or use of a vibrator to assist arousal.

What about positions for coitus? If the woman has arthritis that affects her hips (one of the most common conditions), the man-above (missionary) position may not be suitable. It may help to modify the man-above position so that the woman keeps her thighs together and the man places his legs on the outside of hers. Alternatively, the rear-entry position is often suitable, either with both man and woman lying on their sides or with both man and woman standing and the woman leaning over and supporting herself on something. If the man's knees or hips are affected, the woman-above position may be the best. If coitus is too painful on a particular occasion, oral or manual stimulation, or use of a vibrator, may be a fine alternative. Each couple can experiment to find what works for them.

## Summary

- Historically, attitudes toward masturbation or auto-erotic behavior have been quite negative. These attitudes derive from moral teachings, from the notion that masturbation is unhealthy, and from a sense that people who masturbate are those who can't find a sex partner. Even today, many people feel guilty about masturbating.

- Masturbation is a common sexual behavior. Factors associated with higher rates of masturbation include a younger age and a higher educational level. Factors associated with lower rates of masturbation include having a regular sex partner, being more religious, and being African-American. Gay people masturbate more than heterosexuals and derive more enjoyment from it. Masturbation does not seem to be simply a substitute for sex with partners.

- Men tend to use a single technique for masturbation—direct manual stroking of the penis—whereas women use a greater variety of techniques, such as manual stimulation of the clitoris, labia, or vagina or rubbing of the vulva against objects. Men experience orgasm during masturbation more frequently than do women.

- Kissing is an important form of sexual expression in the United States, where it often has strong romantic significance, but it is not practiced in all human cultures.

- Sexual touching includes a variety of behaviors short of penetrative sex. It may be a prelude to penetrative sexual interaction (foreplay), or it may form the entire sexual encounter, especially among adolescents.

- Oral sex means contact between the mouth and the penis (fellatio), the vulva (cunnilingus), or the anus (anilingus). Oral sex has become increasingly popular among younger people in the United States and Britain, where 80% to 90% of young people have engaged in it. Like many noncoital sexual behaviors, it is more common among well-educated people.

- About half of U.S. men, but fewer women, find fellatio very appealing. Men and women enjoy cunnilingus about equally; approximately a third of the U.S.

population find it very appealing. Oral sex may be performed mutually in a head-to-genital arrangement; this position is called 69, or *soixante-neuf*.

- Most adult heterosexual couples engage in coitus as the culmination of a sexual encounter. The most popular and traditional position for coitus in the United States is the man-above position ("missionary position"), which requires the man to do most of the pelvic thrusting. The rise of feminism in the 1970s encouraged the exploration of other positions, such as the woman-above position and rear-entry coitus. Each position may have particular advantages and disadvantages for certain couples or in certain situations.

- Anal sex (penetration of the anus by the penis) is practiced in both male–male and female–male encounters. Anal sex can be performed in a variety of positions and does not damage the anus or rectum when performed in a nonforcible manner.

- Some couples like to make coitus almost the entirety of a sexual encounter, while others include much foreplay and afterplay, or even dispense with coitus altogether. Women generally take longer to reach orgasm than do men, so men might have to learn to postpone orgasm in heterosexual encounters when the man and woman wish to experience orgasm at close to the same time.

- Vibrators are electrically powered devices that deliver erotically arousing vibratory stimulation. Men or women may use them, but they are particularly associated with use for masturbation by women and to help women reach orgasm in partnered sex. Dildos are unpowered, sometimes penis-shaped objects used for vaginal or anal penetration, in either partnered or solo sex. Other sex toys include anal beads, cock rings, masturbatory sleeves, and erotic dolls.

- Group sex can take many forms, involving interactions within polyamorous relationships as well as between strangers. Group contacts can be orgies, "same-room sex," and other combinations.

## Summary *(continued)*

- Different cultures vary greatly in the openness with which they discuss sexual behavior. One classic how-to manual on sexual behavior is the *Kama Sutra* (from India, 5th century or earlier). This book demonstrates that explicit discussion of sex is not the sole prerogative of modern Western society. Contemporary India, however, has attitudes toward sex that are less positive than those described in the *Kama Sutra*.

- Among the Aka, an African hunter-gatherer people, couples have sex at high frequencies throughout their fertile years. This practice is connected with the belief that multiple acts of coitus are required to nurture a fetus.

- Most intellectually disabled people experience the same sexual feelings and desires as everyone else. They have a right to make informed choices about sexual behavior if they are capable of doing so. Facilitating the exercise of this right must be balanced against the need to protect intellectually disabled people from

sexual exploitation. With appropriate education, many intellectually disabled people can enjoy active sex lives, and some become parents and raise children.

- Spinal cord injuries can cause a near-complete loss of movement and sensation in the body below the neck (quadriplegia) or in the lower half of the body (paraplegia). Although conscious sensations from the genitalia are often lost, reflex penile erection and vaginal lubrication and engorgement may be preserved, depending on the level of the injury and whether the spinal cord has been completely severed. Most people with spinal cord injuries can engage in coitus if they desire it.

- Some disabilities interfere with sexual behavior by limiting movement or making movement painful. Arthritis is the leading culprit in this respect, with 15% of the U.S. population affected. Nevertheless, people with arthritis can usually engage in pleasurable and rewarding sex if they prepare in advance and choose positions for sex that put the least stress on affected joints.

## Discussion Questions

1. Why do you think a higher educational level is associated with a greater prevalence of masturbation (see Figure 6.3)? How could researchers determine the actual reason? Do you think that teaching about masturbation would help reduce unwanted pregnancies and sexually transmitted infections?

2. Do you think that people in general should not engage in some of the sexual behaviors described in this chapter? Is your view based on your moral beliefs, practical (e.g., health) considerations, or some other reason?

3. Consider your attitudes and beliefs about whether the government should regulate the kinds of sex acts that American adults engage in. Are there any sex acts that should be prohibited? Imagine that you are testifying before a Senate committee, and argue what should or should not be permitted or prohibited. How might the Supreme Court rule on the decision you make?

4. Do you think that it's possible to have "great sex" with a complete stranger? How do your views on this jibe with Peggy Kleinplatz's eight components of "great sex" described in Box 6.3?

## Web Resources

Dr.Ruth.com (Dr. Ruth Westheimer's sex advice)   **www.drruth.com**

The Lover's Guide   **www.loversguide.com**

O.school ("your judgment-free resource for everything sexuality and dating")
   **www.o.school**

The **Discovering Human Sexuality** digital resources include activities, animations, flashcards, web links, chapter outlines and summaries, and other study tools.

Learn more with this chapter's digital tools, including the **Oxford Insight Study Guide**, at **oup.com/he/levay5e**.

## Recommended Reading

Clark, T., Gerstle. C. A., Ihigami, A. & Yano, A. (Eds.). (2013). *Shunga: Sex and pleasure in Japanese art*. Hotei.

Comfort, A. (2009). *The joy of sex: The timeless guide to lovemaking* (rev. ed.). Crown.

Cosmopolitan. (2007). *Cosmo's steamy sex games: All sorts of naughty ways to have fun with your lover*. Hearst.

Dale, L. (Ed.). (2003). *The complete illustrated Kama Sutra*. Inner Traditions.

Frank, K. (2013). *Plays well in groups: A journey through the world of group sex*. Rowman & Littlefield.

Joannides, P. (2017). *Guide to getting it on: Unzipped* (9th ed.). Goofy Foot. (A far more extensive how-to guide than we have been able to present here, copiously illustrated by Daerick Gröss.)

Katz, S. (2014). *Lesbian sex positions: 100 passionate positions from intimate and sensual to wild and naughty*. Amorata.

Lacroix, N. (2014). *Kama Sutra: A modern guide to the ancient art of sex*. Skyhouse.

Lieberman, H. (2017). *Buzz: A stimulating history of the sex toy*. Pegasus.

McRuer, R. & Mollow, A. (Eds.) (2012). *Sex and disability*. Duke University Press.

Schwartz, P. & Lever, J. (2012). *Getaway guide to the great sex weekend*. Worldwide Romance.

Silverstein, C. & Picano, F. (2003). *The joy of gay sex* (3rd ed.). William Morrow. (Gay male sex only.)

Stengers, J. & Van Neck, A. (2001). *Masturbation: The history of a great terror* (K. A. Hoffmann, Trans.). Palgrave.

Vatsyayana. (n.d./1991). *The Kama Sutra of Vatsyayana* (R. F. Burton, Trans.). Arkana.

Consummate love includes passion, intimacy, and commitment.

# 7 Sexual Relationships

In previous chapters we discussed sexual attraction, sexual arousal, and sexual behavior. Now we step back and take a look at the interpersonal frameworks within which partnered sex may occur—in other words, sexual relationships.

Of course, we have to interpret the word "relationship" broadly if we are to encompass the full expression of human sexuality. In common discourse, a "one-night stand"—or an even briefer sexual encounter between strangers—may not constitute a relationship, but for our purposes it does. So does a partnership that lasts a lifetime. So do sexual encounters that involve coercion or payment, although we defer discussion of these two topics to Chapters 16 and 17. What interests us here is the dynamic that brings people together as potential sex partners and keeps them together for minutes, days, or decades.

## 7.1 Sexual Relationships Are Motivated by Many Factors

What propels people into sexual relationships? According to the contemporary Western ideal, there are two leading factors: physical attraction and romantic love. Certainly, these powerful forces inspire many sexual encounters and lasting relationships. But they may be mingled with, or entirely replaced by, a wide variety of other motives. These include the desire for status, security, or profit; the desire to conform or to follow moral beliefs—or, conversely, to rebel; the desire to arouse jealousy; and finally, of course, the desire to have children. Most sexual relationships are probably fueled by some combination of these forces. (See **Activity 7.1: Definitions of Sexual Relationships.**)

Sexual relationships involve more than just two people: They are played out in a larger social, economic, and moral context. Let's begin with the last of these and consider how moral attitudes influence sexuality.

## 7.2 Demographic Factors Affect Sexual Attitudes

### LEARNING OBJECTIVES
After reading this section you should be able to:

7.2.1 **Describe the demographic factors associated with permissive or restrictive attitudes on sexual topics in the United States.**

7.2.2 **Describe how Americans' attitudes on sexual matters have changed over the last 50 years.**

Surveys such as the General Social Survey (GSS—a project of the National Opinion Research Center at the University of Chicago) have found that basic demographic facts about a person, such as sex, age, educational level, region of residence, race/ethnicity, and religion, predict that individual's attitudes on sexual issues (**FIGURE 7.1**). Being male, being young, having a high level of education, living in the Northeast or on the West Coast, and having no religion are all factors associated with relatively permissive attitudes on topics such as premarital, casual, and gay sex. These demographic groups tend to believe that it is morally acceptable to have sex even when it is not in the context of a committed relationship. Being female, old, or less educated, as well as living in the South and being religiously observant, are factors associated with relatively conservative ideas on sex, including the belief that sex is only morally acceptable within a marriage or other committed relationship.

Although survey data imply that people's demographic characteristics can predict, to a considerable extent, their sexual attitudes, we don't mean to downplay the individual aspects of moral reasoning. All kinds of life experiences—an unwanted pregnancy, having a daughter or son come out as gay, and so on—may cause people to reconsider their attitudes on sexual issues.

There have also been long-term changes in societal opinions on sexual matters. For example, you may find it hard to believe that it was ever illegal in the United States for interracial couples to marry or even date, but some states had **antimiscegenation statutes** as recently as the 1960s (**BOX 7.1**). These statutes were based in a broad disapproval of black–white relationships among white Americans. Traces of such disapproval still exist today, even at the level of college students, but now black students—especially those at historically black universities—are more opposed to black–white relationships than are students of other races (Field et al., 2013). Their opposition may be grounded in a desire to save African-American culture from complete assimilation.

**antimiscegenation statutes**
State laws that prohibited marriage (and sometimes cohabitation or sex) between persons of different races.

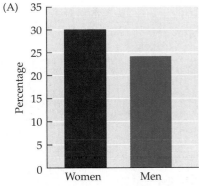

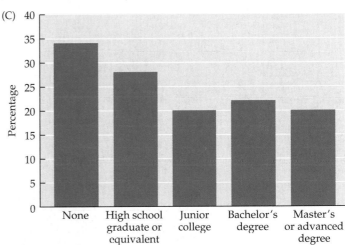

◀ **FIGURE 7.1** **Is premarital sex wrong?** These five figures show the percentage of respondents who believe that premarital sex is "always wrong" or "almost always wrong," based on their sex (A), age (B), education level (C), geographic region (D), and religion (E). (Data from T. Smith et al. *General Social Surveys, 1972–2018*. Sponsored by National Science Foundation. NORC at the University of Chicago. Data accessed from the GSS Data Explorer at gssdataexplorer.norc.org.)

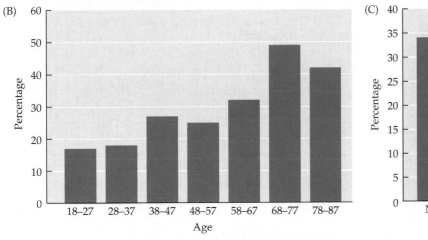

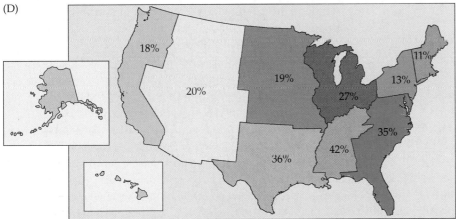

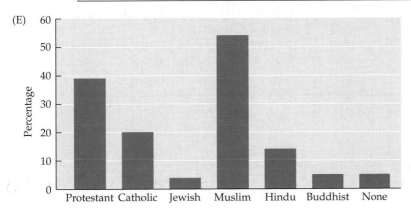

## BOX 7.1
# Who May Marry?

Early in the morning of July 11, 1958, Richard Loving and his wife Mildred were asleep at their home in Central Point, Virginia, when three policemen burst into their bedroom. "Who is this woman you're sleeping with?" they demanded of Richard. Mildred replied, "I'm his wife," and Richard pointed to the marriage certificate hanging on their bedroom wall. "That's no good here," responded the sheriff, and he arrested both of them.

The Lovings (see figure) were an interracial couple (Richard was white; Mildred was African-American). They had married out of state and returned to Virginia to live. They were convicted of violating Virginia's 1924 Racial Integrity Act, which made marriage between a white person and a nonwhite person a felony.

In his sentencing opinion, the judge in the *Loving* case wrote as follows: "Almighty God created the races white, black, yellow, malay, and red, and he placed them on separate continents. The fact that he separated the races shows he did not intend for the races to mix." Although this makes the statute appear to be based on (misguided) moral grounds, historians and jurists believe that it was motivated by white supremacist thinking, because it did not ban marriage between nonwhite persons of different races.

The Lovings were sentenced to a year in prison, but the sentence was suspended provided that they left the state and did not return for 25 years. They moved to Washington, DC, where they appealed the case. In its 1967 *Loving v. Virginia* decision, the U.S. Supreme Court struck down the Virginia statute and affirmed the right to marry across racial lines. The justices based their ruling on the due process and equal protection clauses of the Constitution. These have been interpreted to grant a fundamental right to marry that cannot be denied to certain couples on account of a mere perception of immorality. Some state supreme courts (beginning with California, in a 1948 case titled *Perez v. Sharp*) had reached the same conclusion before the *Loving* decision.

Between 1967 and 2015 the number of interracial couples rose from 3% to 17% of American newlyweds but with great variations across the country, ranging from 3% in Jackson,

Mildred and Richard Loving

Mississippi, to 42% in Honolulu, Hawaii (Pew Research Center, 2017c). Among the many beneficiaries of *Loving* are the current U.S. Supreme Court justice Clarence Thomas and his wife, an interracial couple who live in the same state where Mildred and Richard Loving were convicted 60 years ago.

Although the constitutional battle over interracial marriage has been resolved, the legal principles that were debated then were brought back into focus more recently by the debate over same-sex marriage. In 2008, when the California Supreme Court heard arguments on the gay marriage issue, proponents of such marriage successfully argued that the court's 1948 *Perez* ruling set a precedent that was equally applicable to same-sex couples. And in 2013, when the U.S. Supreme Court struck down the Defense of Marriage Act (which banned federal recognition of same-sex marriage), it cited the *Loving* case in support of its decision. (Same-sex marriage is covered in Chapter 12.) Richard Loving died in 1975, Mildred in 2008. In her last public statement before her death, Mildred Loving spoke out in favor of gay couples' right to marry (Martin, 2008).

A 2016 feature film, *Loving*, directed by Jeff Nichols, told the story of Richard and Mildred Loving. Ruth Negga was nominated for an Oscar for her portrayal of Mildred Loving.

Since the early 1970s the GSS has asked Americans a standard set of questions on a variety of topics related to sexuality (**FIGURE 7.2**). The survey has reported a decline in the percentage of the population who consider sex before marriage "always wrong" and a corresponding rise in the percentage who consider it "not wrong at all." When interviewees have been asked specifically about sex between 14- to 16-year-olds, however—a question that was first asked in 1986—opinions have been far more negative and have not changed significantly over the period during which the question has been asked.

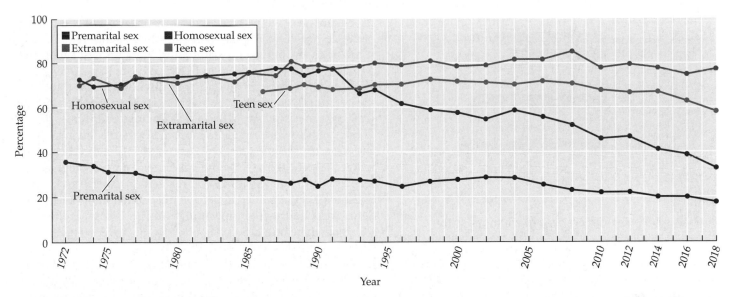

▲ **FIGURE 7.2    Changing attitudes** This graph shows changes in the percentage of the U.S. population who considered premarital sex, extramarital sex, gay sex, and teen sex "always wrong," from 1972 through 2018. The question about teen sex (which was first asked in 1986) specified 14- to 16-year-olds. (Data from T. Smith et al. *General Social Surveys, 1972–2018.* Sponsored by National Science Foundation. NORC at the University of Chicago. Data accessed from the GSS Data Explorer at gssdataexplorer.norc.org.)

With regard to extramarital sex, public opinion has actually become slightly more negative over the years. Between 1973 and 2018, the percentage of people who believed that extramarital sex is "always wrong" increased from 70% to 77%.

With regard to gay sex, opinion has changed in a more complicated way. During the 1980s, when public concern about AIDS was at its height and the disease was largely blamed on gay men, disapproval of gay sex increased to the point that nearly 80% of Americans thought it is "always wrong." Since the early 1990s, however, there has been a very marked liberalizing trend. By 2018 only 33% of Americans believed that gay sex is always wrong. This change has been too rapid to be accounted for by a cohort effect (the replacement of one generation with another, more liberal one); rather, large numbers of individuals must have changed their minds.

In spite of the diversity of attitudes toward the morality of sex, it's worth emphasizing a belief that represents a common moral ground for many people—the idea that it's not the sex act itself, but its context, that has moral significance. In particular, sexual behavior that may endanger established relationships is very broadly disapproved of. This is true not only for marriages but also for nonmarital cohabitations and even—to a lesser extent—for *non*-cohabiting sexual relationships: Most interviewees say that people should not engage in sex outside existing relationships. Evidently, most people place a high moral value on lasting sexual relationships, even when they are not formalized by marriage, and see sexual monogamy as an important factor in preserving them.

## 7.3  Casual Sex Has More Appeal to Men than to Women

### LEARNING OBJECTIVES
After reading this section you should be able to:

7.3.1    Outline the course of a typical campus hookup.

7.3.2    Explain why many college students don't engage in hookups.

7.3.3    Explain why casual sex may be more prevalent and acceptable among gay than straight people.

Proposed activities

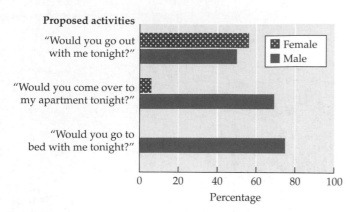

Legend: Female (dotted), Male (solid)

- "Would you go out with me tonight?"
- "Would you come over to my apartment tonight?"
- "Would you go to bed with me tonight?"

0    20    40    60    80    100
Percentage

▲ **FIGURE 7.3** **Sex differences in willingness to engage in casual sex** The figure shows the percentage of female and male college students who agreed to three activities proposed by an attractive but unfamiliar student of the other sex. (Data from R. D. Clark & E. Hatfield. 1989. *J Psych Hum Sex* 2: 39–55.)

**casual sex** Sexual encounters that do not take place within a lasting sexual relationship.

**sociosexuality** Interest or engagement in sex without commitment.

**hooking up** Uncommitted sex with an acquaintance.

▲ Hookups often arise out of social gatherings.

By **casual sex**, we mean sexual encounters that the participants do not view as part of a committed sexual relationship. It includes sex between people who have known each other only very briefly, as well as sex between those who have known each other for some time but do not intend the encounter to be the beginning of a longer sexual relationship. The willingness to engage in casual sex is known as **sociosexuality**.

Surveys show that men are more likely than women to desire and seek casual sex (England & Bearak, 2014). Real-life tests have found the same thing. In a now-classic study, psychologists Russell Clark and Elaine Hatfield performed a "real-life test" of this question. They recruited attractive male and female college students and had them approach unwitting students of the other sex somewhere on a U.S. college campus (Clark & Hatfield, 1989; Clark & Hatfield, 2003) (**FIGURE 7.3**). They were told to say "I have been noticing you around campus and I find you to be very attractive." Then they asked one of three questions: "Would you go out with me tonight?" "Would you come over to my apartment tonight?" or "Would you go to bed with me tonight?"

The male and female "targets" of these requests were about equally willing to go out with the confederate—about half assented to this request. When the request was phrased in ways that referred more explicitly to the desire for casual sex, however, women's responses rapidly fell off—in fact, not a single woman agreed to go to bed with the male confederate, and the women often lent emphasis to the rejection with comments such as "What's wrong with you, creep, leave me alone!" Men's responses, however, became more positive as the proposal became more explicit: 69% of the men agreed to go to the female confederate's apartment, and 75% agreed to go to bed with her, sometimes adding a comment such as "Why do we have to wait until tonight?" In other words, reducing a casual date to its sexual essentials robbed the date of all its appeal to women but actually *enhanced* its appeal to men! More recent experiments of the same kind have largely replicated Clark and Hatfield's findings (British Broadcasting Corporation, 2002; Voracek et al., 2005).

## Hooking up—the new norm?

Although women may be as averse to sex with total strangers as they ever were, some young heterosexual women are becoming more open to engaging in casual, uncommitted sex with acquaintances—sometimes including people they have met that same evening, and sometimes involving other women rather than men (**BOX 7.2**). This practice is often called **hooking up**. Hookups may involve anything from kissing to coitus, are typically unplanned, and arise when young people hang out, party together, and the like. Hookups are more common on college campuses than they were a decade or two ago (Monto & Carey, 2014).

To be clear: Most college students are not having sex with large numbers of partners, and the majority of students who are having sex are doing so within romantic relationships that are monogamous for as long as the relationships last, according to a study at a Canadian university (Netting & Reynolds, 2018). When the American College Health Association asked about 75,000 undergraduate students how many partners they had oral, vaginal, or anal sex with in the previous 12 months, the median answer was just 1. Fully one-third of the students had not had penetrative sex with

## BOX 7.2
# Straight Women, Gay Sex

Pop singer Katy Perry rose to fame in 2008 with the song "I Kissed a Girl," whose lyrics included the following lines: "I kissed a girl just to try it. I hope my boyfriend don't mind it. It felt so wrong. It felt so right. Don't mean I'm in love tonight." With these words Perry put her seal of approval on a form of behavior that has been rapidly gaining in popularity and acceptance: sexual intimacy between young women who are not lesbians. The practitioners may describe themselves as **heteroflexible**, "gayish," or (in the case of college students) "4-year queer" or "BUG" ("bisexual until graduation"). In the 1990s only about 1 in 20 young women said that they had had sex with another woman, but by 2014 about 1 in 8 had done so (Twenge et al., 2016).

There is a long tradition of romantic, physically intimate friendships between teenage girls or young women who later become pillars of heterosexual society (Faderman, 1981; Vicinus, 1989). What distinguishes the current trend is that the behavior is overt rather than hidden and that much of it is quite casual. In fact, part of the purpose of these "lesbian" interactions may be a heterosexual one—to arouse the interest of males. "It's very common to see girls making out at parties," a male Rutgers student told the *Star-Ledger* of New Jersey. "I think it's an attention-getting thing; they only do it in front of guys." A 22-year-old woman said, "The waitresses where I work are doing it right in front of the cooks. They're doing it for attention" (O'Crowley, 2004).

Other young women engage in sexual interactions with women for reasons that have nothing to do with attracting men or with establishing a lesbian identity. It may be a matter of experimentation, the desire to give physical expression to a close friendship, the pressure to follow a trend, or a preference for the safety and mutual understanding of a same-sex relationship. Here's one student's (abbreviated) account:

*I had small crushes on women before, but nothing beyond the realm of my imagination had happened—until I met Amy. Our attraction was, at first, that of two best friends destined to keep in touch for life. But by the end of one listless summer an undeniable sexual heat had developed between us. One night, we got drunk on cheap swill and did the deed. Embarrassed, we giggled*

Katy Perry is straight but she "kissed a girl"—Miley Cyrus, in fact.

*over our small feat for weeks. It was the first and last time we'd make love. But, hot damn, it was amazing!*

*I had other encounters with women, but none quite matched the heady rush that followed the first. I quickly became disenchanted with the notion of, well, going down. How could men manage this for minutes on end? And the soft, sweet feminine touch was no match for the firm, male thrust. There was no getting around it: I was straight.* (Anonymous, 1999)

The prevalence of heteroflexible behavior by women is consistent with other lines of evidence suggesting that sexual orientation is more fluid in women than in men. We discuss this issue in Chapter 12.

Meanwhile, Katy Perry has expanded a bit on her "I kissed a girl" confession. "Truth be told, I did more than that," she said in 2017, on the occasion of receiving an award from the LGBT organization Human Rights Campaign (Fecteau, 2017).

**heteroflexible**  Mostly straight but having some interest in same-sex contacts or relationships.

anyone (American College Health Association, 2016). Still, enough students engage in casual sex, or attempt to do so, to make for a "campus hookup culture"—a culture that affects even those students who don't participate in it.

Sociologist Lisa Wade of Occidental College has studied this culture on several college campuses by having students keep "sex diaries" over the course of several months or years (Wade, 2017). Here's how students described the scenario of a typical hookup: After several "pregame" drinks to loosen up, a group of friends descends on a party, which may be held at a frat house or even on the street if the climate permits. It's extremely crowded, noisy, and dark, and liquor flows freely. The main activity besides drinking is "grinding"; this means dancing in such a way that there is rhythmic contact between a man's (clothed) crotch and a woman's rear. If both the man and woman are sufficiently excited, and both are sufficiently "shitfaced" from drinking, they may go to a room or a private area to have more intimate sex—the hookup itself, which doesn't always include coitus. One way or another, the man reaches his climax; the woman may or may not do so, because the central goal of a hookup is the man's orgasm. Then the couple splits without saying much to each other.

In the campus hookup culture, sex should be "emotionless." The particular emotion to avoid is anything resembling romantic intimacy. Here's how one man described a hookup gone wrong: "She was weird and said some things that you just don't say during a hookup. She wanted to talk about how we felt about each other. Then halfway through she changed her mind about hooking up. It was too late" (Paul & Hayes, 2002). (If he continued in spite of her expressed refusal he was committing a serious crime—see Chapter 16.)

A man and woman who hook up may not have much contact with each other after the event, but during the following day they report to their friends what went down, especially regarding the hotness of their hookup partners. Looks are the major criterion, of course, but other attributes, such as being a collegiate athlete, can make up for average looks—for the men at least. Being chosen by a hot man who could have chosen any number of other women—that's something a woman is going to boast about, even if the sex itself wasn't stellar (Wade, 2017).

## The hookup culture—some like it, some loathe it

Because women, as mentioned above, are typically less interested in (or even averse to) casual sex than men, one group of researchers asked first-year college women what benefits they had experienced from their most recent hookups (Shepardson et al., 2016). The most common response was that they didn't get any benefit from the hookup, but there were also plenty of positive answers, ranging from having fun to starting a dating relationship (**FIGURE 7.4**). One response typified the attitude of many women: "I had sex and received oral sex. I think everyone needs to have a healthy sex life and have sex often. I think as long as you take precautions, sex is good for you."

For some students, though, the hookup culture has significant negatives. About one-third of students choose never to engage in hookups—because they want to remain virgins, because they don't like the idea of emotionless sex, or because they are already in relationships. But even if only a minority of students are actually having frequent casual sex, the idea of a hookup culture dominates campus social life, so students who don't participate often feel like "internal exiles"—especially during their first year, when many students live on campus.

There are also students who would like to hook up but are rejected or excluded. This may be because they are not judged personally attractive enough. Students who commute to school have little opportunity to participate. Lesbian, gay, and transgender students may have their own cliques, but they are not welcome as participants in the hookup culture. Lisa Wade notes an irony here: In their classes, students happily learn to reject the "gender binary" and to celebrate "queerness," but after dark the traditional heterosexual ethic takes over.

© Monkey Business Images/Shutterstock.com

▲ Alcohol fuels many hookups.

▶ **FIGURE 7.4   What women get out of hookups**
First-year female students who had experienced at least one hookup were asked about the benefits they gained from their most recent hookup. The bar graph shows the percentage of different kinds of responses, with examples. (After R. L. Shepardson et al. 2016. *Int J Sex Health* 28: 216–220.)

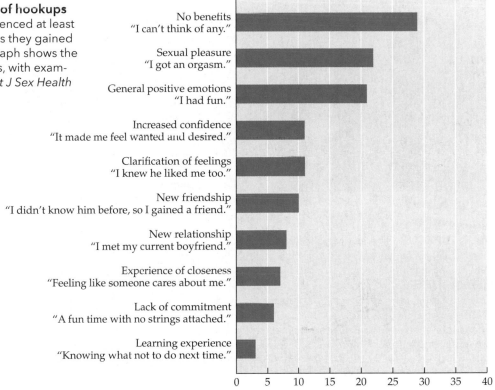

Finally, sexual coercion, sexually transmitted infections, and pregnancy are all possible outcomes for students who hook up. These risks are not a reason to demonize uncommitted sex, but they are real nonetheless, and alcohol is a large part of what makes them so. We don't discuss these issues here, because they are the focus of other chapters. Still, regarding sexual coercion, it's worth making two points: Most hookups are not coerced, but the hookup culture is one in which sexual predators can operate with relative impunity.

Here's a comment from a woman describing a bad hookup experience: "I tried to talk with him about slowing down and that was seen as abnormal by the guy. I felt dirty, sad, and mad. He didn't respect my requests. He used me for his own physical pleasure. I was mad at myself and lied to my friends and said that we didn't have sex" (Paul & Hayes, 2002).

There are many possible factors that have helped create the hookup culture. One that is not widely appreciated has to do with sex ratios. As we discussed in Chapter 1, a person's willingness to engage in sex is a resource whose value varies with scarcity. A generation and more ago, women were in the minority on campus, and they were therefore able to set rules that restricted sex to emotionally committed relationships. Now men are in the minority on many campuses, and they can find various women to approach if the first one turns them down. If a woman wants to be in the party scene, she may feel that she cannot afford to be too prudish. Is this the reason for an increase in the kind of uncommitted sex that men typically favor?

To answer this question, Mark Regnerus and Jeremy Uecker mined data from the College Women's Survey, which covered colleges with widely varying proportions of women and men (Regnerus & Uecker, 2011). On campuses where women were in a small minority, these women were quite likely to still be virgins, even if they had boyfriends. It was as if they could say to their partners, "I'd rather not have sex yet, and if you don't like that, there are plenty of other guys I can choose from." As the proportion of women on campus increased, however, the likelihood that they were virgins decreased steeply, as if the boyfriends could now say, "Give me sex, or some other woman will" (**FIGURE 7.5**). Thus, the general shortage of men on today's campuses does seem to make it easier for men to demand and receive sex.

Our account of the campus hookup culture may resonate with your own experiences. Alternatively, it may strike you as a libelous parody of life at your college. Both reactions are valid, because colleges range over a broad spectrum—from out-and-out party schools to temples of nerdiness. But few colleges make serious efforts to disable the central engine of the hookup culture, which is underage drinking, and colleges that try to do so have limited success (Scott-Sheldon et al., 2016).

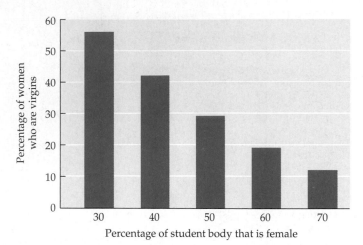

▲ **FIGURE 7.5**   **The sex ratio influences sexual behavior**
The bar graph shows how the likelihood that a college woman is still a virgin varies according to the percentage of female students at her campus. These data are for women with current boyfriends. (Data, in part, from the College Women's Survey [N. Glenn and E. Marquardt. 2001. *Hooking Up, Hanging Out, and Hoping for Mr. Right: College Women on Dating and Mating Today.* Institute for American Values: New York.], as cited in M. Regnerus & J. Uecker. 2011. *Premarital Sex in America: How Young Americans Meet, Mate, and Think about Marrying.* Oxford University Press: Oxford.)

It's easy to dismiss the campus hookup culture as the creation of boorish frat boys, but the culture couldn't exist without the enthusiastic participation of women. Also, the very same men who disrespect women they hook up with are likely, when the time and opportunity finally arrive, to enter into relationships of a quite different flavor—stable relationships in which both men and women are genuinely concerned about their partners' sexual and emotional fulfillment. In fact, according to a study led by social psychologist Neslihan James-Kangal of the University of Cincinnati, young men and women who are involved in the hookup culture already look forward to stable relationships as a long-term goal (James-Kangal et al., 2018).

What about high school graduates who don't go to college? You might think that they would be less sexually active—first, because they are not exposed to the campus hookup culture, and second, because this population has an excess of males, so by the economic argument laid out above, there should be less pressure on women to have sex. The reality, however, is quite the opposite, according to a longitudinal study carried out by a group of social scientists at the University of Washington (Bailey et al., 2008). By 6 months after leaving high school, the participants who didn't go to college were getting much more sex, including more casual sex, than the college students (**FIGURE 7.6**). And whereas 24% of college students in another study said that they were still virgins, only 10% of 18- to 23-year-olds who were not in college said the same thing (Regnerus & Uecker, 2011). It may be that young people who don't go to college have more time for sex, as well as fewer reasons to postpone it. Also, young people who are not in a college environment still have access to a universe of potential sex partners through dating apps.

## Casual sex is more accepted in the gay male community

Casual sex has long been more prevalent among gay men—especially among gay men without steady partners—than in the heterosexual population. In the National Health and Social Life Survey (NHSLS) study, men who identified as homosexual or bisexual reported an average of 3.1 sex partners in the previous 12 months, compared with 1.8 partners for heterosexual men. A more recent large-scale survey of college students found an even greater difference: Gay male students reported more than twice the number of partners as straight male students, and male students who identified as bisexual also had high numbers of partners (Oswalt & Wyatt, 2013). (Not all these sexual encounters were casual ones, presumably.) Interestingly, the highest number of partners (7.6 in the previous 12 months) was reported by men who said that they were "unsure" what their sexual orientation was; apparently these men were making a serious effort to find out.

Explanations for the greater prevalence of casual sex among gay men may include the following:

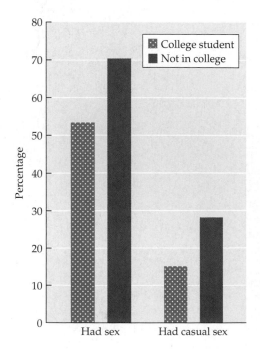

◄ **FIGURE 7.6**   **College students get less sex**  This bar graph shows the percentage of college students and those not in college who reported that they "had sex" and "had casual sex" within the last month. All individuals were surveyed 6 months after leaving high schools in the Seattle area, so the college students were freshmen. (After J. A. Bailey et al. 2008. *J Adolesc Health* 42: 573–579.)

- Gay men are not restrained by women's reluctance to engage in casual sex.

- Pregnancy is not an issue.

- Gay men, who may already be stigmatized by society for their sexual orientation, are less likely to pay attention to public opinion on the topic of casual sex.

**cruising**  Looking for casual sex partners in public spaces.

In addition to gay bars, which are an important feature of gay male life in most U.S. cities, other institutions offer the opportunity for sexual encounters on an even more casual or totally anonymous basis. These include encounters at bathhouses, gyms, outdoor **cruising** areas, and sex parties (Solomon et al., 2011), as well as encounters facilitated by geosocial apps such as Grindr or Scruff (Goedel & Duncan, 2016).

Although engaging in casual sex carries little stigma in gay male communities, not all gay men approve of the practice or engage in it. Some limit their sexual activity because of the risk of acquiring HIV (human immunodeficiency virus—the virus that causes AIDS) or other sexually transmitted infections. Some believe that casual sex gives the gay community a bad name. And, most important, many gay men are involved in monogamous relationships and have no desire to engage in casual sex— or they feel that doing so would endanger their relationship.

There do exist a few bars and other locations where women can meet for casual sex. Skirt Club, for example, is a members-only underground community that organizes gatherings in several cities (Tunell, 2018). Although the gatherings are focused on sex between women, most of the women who participate identify as straight or bisexual, and many have husbands or steady boyfriends. There are also "W4W" sections on hookup websites such as BestCasualSex.com.

Still, very little research has been done on casual sex between women. The National Survey of Sexual Attitudes and Lifestyles identified 175 women who had had at least one sexual encounter with another woman. Of these women, only one had had more than ten female partners in her lifetime. Although the nature of the encounters was not investigated, the low numbers suggest that casual sex between women is uncommon. Even if their numbers are low, however, there clearly is a lively minority of lesbians who thrive on open relationships, polyamory, and casual sex (Munson & Stelbourn, 2013).

## Casual sex can mean more than a hookup

Hookups are generally one-night stands—two people have sex, and that's it. Sometimes two people may have sex repeatedly, however, without committing each other to a durable sexual relationship. These kinds of relationships are of several different types, best known by their colloquial monikers (Wentland & Reissing, 2014):

- A "booty call" is a sexual encounter arranged on short notice, often late at night, between two people who know each other and have sex occasionally. As with hookups, alcohol is often involved.

- "Fuck buddies" are two people who know each other but don't socialize except for regular uncommitted sex. Alcohol is not usually involved.

- "Friends with benefits" are two friends who often socialize non-sexually but who also have sex on a regular basis. Alcohol is not usually involved.

Although these uncommitted relationships are often thought to be about sex only, a Canadian survey of young people in such relationships found that many of the participants mentioned intimacy as an important aspect of the relationship (Rodrigue et al., 2018). In other words, uncommitted relationships are not necessarily loveless.

## Negotiating sex involves flirting

Getting from a regular social encounter to a sexual one involves a set of reciprocal communications known as flirting. A standard set of flirting signals has been

▲ Grindr, Scruff, and similar apps make it easy to find gay sex in your vicinity.

▲ **FIGURE 7.7  Flirting king penguins** Most animal species, including humans, have their own specific courtship behaviors.

**prosociality**  A positive interest in and concern for others.

observed in many different cultures (Eibl-Eibesfeldt, 2007). A woman who is interested in a man smiles, arches her brows, looks down and to the side, and then puts her hands near her mouth and laughs. When both persons are attracted to each other, they move closer, make slight touching movements, nod in agreement, and gaze into each other's eyes. These findings suggested that nature has equipped us with a standard set of flirting behaviors, just as she has with other species (**FIGURE 7.7**).

Flirting allows for mutual evaluation, and for possible rejection, before things get too intimate for either participant to back out gracefully. It also helps avoid more direct behaviors that may be experienced as sexual harassment—so long as both partners remain alert to negative signals.

Heterosexual women and men perceive and respond to flirtation signals somewhat differently. Consistent with what we know about women's and men's sexual strategies, women respond best to signals of emotional commitment, exclusivity, and caring, whereas men respond best to signals of sexual availability (Wade & Feldman, 2016). Thus men do best to express interest in the woman or to offer her gifts or services, whereas women do best to move close to the man, touch him, or rub against him.

When people flirt to establish relationships—what we may call romantic flirting—rather than just for fun or for casual sex, they do well if they communicate their sincerity, positivity, and interest and concern for the other person—traits that are summarized in the term **prosociality**. A sincere, natural smile—as opposed to an "I should smile now" smile—does wonders in this respect (**FIGURE 7.8**). In fact, LeeAnne Harker and Dacher Keltner of the University of California, Berkeley, showed that women who smiled naturally in their high school yearbook photos got married earlier than women who smiled in a more self-conscious way, and their marriages were more satisfying even decades later (Harker & Keltner, 2001). By definition a sincere smile cannot be faked, of course, but it is possible to develop one's own prosociality—by consciously deciding to take more positive interest in others—and the smile will follow.

Romantic flirting works best in a romantic environment. That could be the traditional candlelit dinner, but more effective is the great outdoors—specifically, scenes of natural beauty. Being in or viewing beautiful natural scenery evokes strong prosocial emotions such as liking, trust, empathy, and kindness, which form the basis for romance. This is not just a misty-eyed notion—it has been documented in many experimental studies (Zhang et al., 2014).

The dating apps, such as Tinder, Bumble, and Grindr, have to some extent short-circuited the flirting process. If both partners have "swiped right," it's already clear that the two have some sexual interest in each other. When they meet, they could in principle proceed directly to physical sex. However, increasing numbers of dating app users are looking for love rather than sex, in which case the first meeting may not involve sex at all (Sumter et al., 2017).

 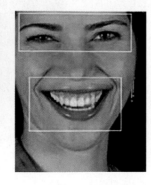

◄ **FIGURE 7.8  Forced and natural smiles** A forced or voluntary smile (left) engages primarily the mouth, whereas a natural smile (right) also engages the eyes. Natural smiles are more effective at communicating openness and positive feelings toward others.

# 7.4 Non-Cohabiting Relationships Are Often Short-Lived

## LEARNING OBJECTIVES

After reading this section you should be able to:

**7.4.1** Describe the roles of social and interpersonal scripts over the course of a non-cohabiting relationship.

**7.4.2** Explain how having sex early in a non-cohabitating relationship and delaying sex until later are associated with different outcomes of the relationship.

One step up the relationship hierarchy from casual sex are sexual relationships between people who are not married or living together but who nevertheless feel some commitment to each other and are physically intimate on multiple occasions. These have traditionally been called "dating" relationships. This term is still in use, but it doesn't necessarily mean that the couples go on traditional "dates." Other possible terms include "partners," "boyfriends" or "girlfriends," "seeing each other," "going steady," and "Facebook official," but we'll use the term **non-cohabiting relationship** because whether two people live together usually says a lot about how committed the relationship is.

Because of all the attention that has been paid to the hookup culture, it's easy to get the impression that non-cohabiting relationships are disappearing, but that's not the case. Certainly there are young people who purposefully select hookups over steady relationships, as mentioned earlier, but there are also many women and men, of all ages, who want a relationship with some degree of commitment but don't want to (or can't) move in together. **FIGURE 7.9** gives some sense of the numbers: By age 20 about 40% of Facebook users describe themselves as "in a relationship," and by age 24 their numbers match those who describe themselves as "single." (The data in the figure do not distinguish between cohabiting and non-cohabiting relationships, but for people in their early 20s most of these relationships are likely to be non-cohabitating.)

For many young people, leaving college marks a transition from casual sex to more organized and lasting relationships. That's because unplanned sexual contacts don't

**non-cohabiting relationship**
An ongoing sexual relationship between two people who do not live together.

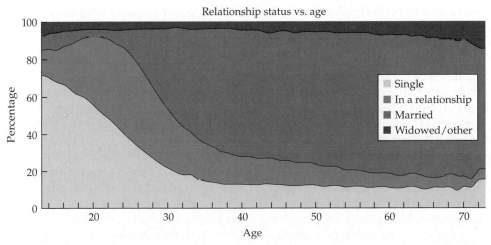

▲ **FIGURE 7.9    Relationship status of U.S. Facebook users as a function of age** Where categories correspond, the self-described Facebook data track U.S. Census data quite closely, but there are some distortions: The percentage of young teens who are married is probably lower than shown here, and the percentage of those over 70 who are widowed is probably higher than shown here. (After S. Wolfram. 2013. *Data Science of the Facebook World*. Stephen Wolfram/Writings. wolfram.com)

**interpersonal scripts** Patterns of behavior that develop between couples.

**serial monogamy** Engagement in a series of monogamous relationships.

happen nearly so readily when a person has left the group-oriented college environment and is now working and living in an apartment. Hence the need for "dating"—but many college graduates find the concept of dating strange and even scary.

To help her students prepare for postcollege life, Boston College philosophy professor Kerry Cronin has them practice real-life dates, in accordance with her instructions (Cicchese, 2014; Wade, 2017):

1. The student must ask for the date face to face, not by text.
2. The student must pay.
3. The would-be date must be a person of real romantic interest to the student.
4. The activity must allow for conversation, not just watching a movie.
5. No alcohol, kissing, or sex.
6. The date must be over by 10 p.m.

For Cronin's students, the most unnerving part is the initial ask, which carries the risk of explicit rejection. As one student commented, "It's easy to hook up with someone you've just met in a dark room after having a few drinks. But asking someone out on a date in broad daylight, and when you actually have to know their name, can be really scary." Yet this student completed his assignment successfully and, at the end of the evening, asked his companion for another date.

If the two people don't know each other well, their first date will have a somewhat formal flavor, because it will be guided by the rules that govern dates in general. As a relationship progresses, however, these kinds of social scripts give way to rules and expectations that are generated by the couple themselves. Such **interpersonal scripts** have an especially strong influence on the couple's sexual interactions—when (if ever) they should begin, what form they should take, where they should take place, and so on.

Sometimes a non-cohabiting relationship leads to cohabitation or marriage. Sometimes it is a brief romance that breaks up when the pair realize that they are incompatible, find better partners, or get separated by external circumstances such as professional relocation. On the other hand, it can also be a durable relationship between two people who for some reason don't want to or are unable to live together. Although we think of non-cohabiting relationships as being the hallmark of young adulthood, plenty of older people—unmarried, divorced, or widowed—also engage in them. In one national study, 14% of Americans over the age of 57 said that they were in such a relationship (Brown & Shinohara, 2013). As people get older, they may become more set in their ways, so even if two people are highly committed to each other, cohabitation may be too disruptive of their daily habits.

Do relationships that begin with hookups, or with sex very early in the relationship, fare worse than more traditional relationships in which sex is postponed until the couple know each other better? Sociologist Anthony Paik of the University of Massachusetts Amherst surveyed 642 individuals in relationships, half of which started off with sex while in the other half sex was delayed until later in the relationship (Paik, 2010). The delayers were indeed more satisfied with their relationships, on average, compared with those who had sex early on. Paik interpreted this finding as a selection effect, however, rather than a result of the early sex itself. In other words, people who began with sex were those who were less interested in a stable relationship in the first place. For someone seeking a committed relationship, Paik concludes, waiting helps weed out potential partners who are mostly focused on instant sexual gratification.

Some men and women who are in non-cohabiting relationships engage in sex outside the relationship (extra-pair sex), but more commonly these relationships are expected to be sexually exclusive, even though the two people do not live together. A person who engages in a series of sexually exclusive relationships with different people over a period of time is said to be practicing **serial monogamy**—a very common lifestyle, especially among adolescents and young adults.

## Long-distance relationships can be very successful

Young people tend to relocate frequently—in order to attend college or to take up a new job, for example. Such moves may lead to the breakup of existing relationships. Still, a surprisingly large number of couples maintain their relationship even when they are too far away for frequent face-to-face contact. The majority of college students already have some experience with such relationships (Stafford, 2011), and even married people not uncommonly live far away from each other.

You might think that, without frequent physical contact, these relationships would quickly wither and die, but in fact they often flourish. Couples in long-distance relationships report levels of satisfaction, relationship stability, and trust that are equal to or greater than those experienced by couples living in the same area. They tend to idealize each other, and their communications, though no more frequent than those of nearby couples, are more intimate in quality and involve more self-disclosure (Jiang & Hancock, 2013). In other words, it may be worth thinking twice before breaking up with someone just because they are going to be on the other side of the country.

## Same-sex relationships follow their own scripts

Same-sex non-cohabiting relationships have not been the subject of a great deal of study, but it's worth raising a few points. First, in many environments (such as high school, college, or work) there is a presumption of heterosexuality. Thus, for a same-sex relationship to get going, there has to be an initial recognition or mutual disclosure that the two people are open to such a relationship. This disclosure, once achieved, may promote a more rapid development of the relationship than would be typical for an opposite-sex couple. Conversely, some same-sex couples may have difficulty achieving intimacy because of inculcated negative feelings about homosexuality (internalized homophobia: see Chapter 12).

For women especially, sexual exploration and the development of a homosexual or bisexual identity may occur in the context of a preexisting and intense same-sex friendship (Peplau et al., 1999). In such cases, the two people may essentially be in love before the question of sexual attraction and sexual behavior comes into play at all. Sexual relationships arising in this situation have a very different meaning than do those between most heterosexual or male–male couples, in which the two people are typically not very emotionally intimate on their first date but may be very conscious of sexual attraction and the possibility of sexual behavior.

The cultural scripts that regulate heterosexual relationships—especially those related to gender roles—may be less relevant in the gay and lesbian communities. Still, certain expectations apply, such as the idea that a person who provides resources is accruing a degree of sexual entitlement. Within some gay subcultures, such as the gay leather or BDSM communities (see Chapter 13), an explicit negotiation of the kind of sexual role-playing that the two participants will engage in is likely (Townsend, 2007).

## Non-cohabiting relationships may evolve rapidly

Non-cohabiting relationships are often very dynamic—they are processes, rather than states of being. The process may be one of growing self-disclosure and love, leading to cohabitation or marriage (Sprecher & Hendrick, 2004). Alternatively, there may be a gradual realization by one or both partners that "this was not meant to be," with a resulting breakup.

Often this dynamic process is viewed as taking place entirely within the relationship—in other words, as an exploration of mutual attraction and compatibility. But it may be affected by a larger sexual marketplace in which both persons consciously or unconsciously assess whether they have struck an equitable deal, given their own sense of self-worth and the range of other individuals in the marketplace (Hatfield & Rapson, 2011). If either partner believes that they can do better, that partner will feel less commitment to the relationship, and the chances of a breakup increase.

Aerial view: © trekandshoot/Shutterstock.com; Woman: © TheVisualsYouNeed/Shutterstock.com; Man: © Damir Khabirov/Shutterstock.com

▲ Absence makes the heart grow fonder. During the 2020 COVID-19 lockdown, cross-town relationships became long-distance, but didn't necessarily suffer for it.

**passionate love** The overwhelming feeling of attraction typical of the early stage of a loving relationship.

**companionate love** Love characterized by intimacy and trust.

You might think that when a dating couple break up, there'd be no more sex, but in fact "sex with an ex" is common, especially among younger people. That's because the breakup marks the end of commitment but not necessarily the end of sexual desire (Birnbaum, 2018). Common wisdom says that pursuing sex with an ex simply prolongs the heartache of the breakup, especially for a person who perceives that they were "dumped" by their partner. But in fact, according to a study led by Stephanie Spielmann of Wayne State University, neither pursuing sex with an ex nor actually having sex with an ex hinders recovery from the trauma of a breakup (Spielmann et al., 2019). A person pining for their ex is more likely than a person who has "moved on" to pursue sex with their ex, of course, but whether they do or not seems to have little effect on the process of recovery. What's more, a breakup is not necessarily forever: Nearly half of all breakups among young people are followed by reconciliation and continuation of the relationship (Halpern-Meekin et al., 2013). Thus urging a person who has been dumped to "get over it" and avoid their ex may be counterproductive.

We will postpone our discussion of more-lasting sexual relationships (cohabitations and marriages) to Chapter 11, where we will also discuss sexual relationships that involve more than two people (polyamory and polygamy). Instead, we now turn our attention to the emotional underpinnings of sexual relationships.

## 7.5 Love Cements Many Sexual Relationships

### LEARNING OBJECTIVES
After reading this section you should be able to:

7.5.1 Describe the elements of Sternberg's love triangle, and how they combine in different ways.

7.5.2 Explain how research on voles may be relevant to human sexual relationships.

Love, in some form or another, is the glue that holds couples in long-term sexual relationships. In contemporary hunter-gatherer societies, love is associated with increased reproductive success, because it motivates men to supply provisions to their female partners—women whose own food-gathering ability is limited by the need to care for young children (Wood & Marlowe, 2013; Sorokowski et al., 2017). This has probably been true throughout human evolution.

### There are different kinds of love

Within the context of sexual relationships, two different kinds of love are apparent. **Passionate love**—also called limerence—means "falling in love" or "being head over heels in love." It is an overwhelming desire for oneness with the beloved person. Passionate love can be a source of joy (if reciprocated) or despair (if not). **Companionate love**, a cooler emotion than passionate love, is a sense of attachment, intimacy, trust, and commitment.

Here's how one teenager explained the difference (Montgomery & Sorell, 1998):

*Being in love with someone and loving someone are two different things; when you're in love with someone, you think they're just wonderful and everything they do is perfect and they have no faults. When you love someone you know about their faults and you realize that they may not be exactly as you want them to be, but you love them in spite of it.*

The capacity for passionate love seems to exist in most or all human cultures (Jankowiak & Fischer, 1992; Hatfield & Rapson, 2005). In one interview with an anthropologist, a woman of the hunter-gatherer !Kung people of the Kalahari Desert of southern Africa drew a distinction between a husband and a lover. A relationship with a husband is "rich, warm and secure," she said, while that with a lover is "passionate and exciting, although often fleeting and undependable." She added that

▲ Pre-Colombian lovers. Ceramic sculpture from the Olmec culture, Mexico.

© Werner Forman/Corbis

"when two people come together their hearts are on fire and their passion is very great. After a while, the fire cools and that's how it stays" (Shostak, 2000).

Passionate love, as this quotation indicates, is often strong early in a relationship. Companionate love may also exist early in a relationship, but it typically increases over a year or so as the couple get to know each other better. If a couple date for some period and then marry, companionate love tends to peak around the time of marriage.

With the passage of time both types of love decline in intensity, according to studies by Elaine Hatfield and her colleagues (Hatfield et al., 2008), and by sociologist Susan Sprecher of Illinois State University (Sprecher, 1999). Even among couples who stay together for decades, both kinds of love gradually weaken, according to Hatfield. That is a statement about averages, of course—some couples may still experience both kinds of love over many years. There may be strategies for extending and strengthening love within a relationship, as we will discuss later.

According to psychologist Robert Sternberg of Cornell University, companionate love is actually a combination of two elements—an emotional element, which he calls **intimacy**, and a cognitive element, which he calls **commitment**. Thus, in Sternberg's model, love consists of three elements in total—passion, intimacy, and commitment—which can be represented as the three vertices of a triangle (Sternberg, 1986; Sternberg, 1997) (**FIGURE 7.10**).

A real-life individual who loves another person is unlikely to experience all three elements to the same degree, so there are seven possible kinds of love based on an individual's love triangle (**FIGURE 7.11**). The person might experience just one of the three elements, or they might experience two elements with little or none of the third, or they might experience all three elements. Sternberg names the single-element kinds of love as follows:

- *Liking* is intimacy without passion or commitment.
- *Infatuation* is passion without intimacy or commitment.
- *Empty love* is commitment without passion or intimacy.

The two-item combinations are as follows:

- *Romantic love* is the combination of passionate and intimate love, without much commitment. Sternberg mentions the love of Romeo and Juliet as an example. (But if you know the play, you might question whether they were low in commitment.)
- *Fatuous love* is the combination of passion and commitment, without much intimacy. According to Sternberg, it is seen in whirlwind romances in which two lovers rush off to get married and set up a home together without ever getting to know each other very well.
- *Companionate love* is the combination of intimacy and commitment without much passion. Perhaps passion has faded, or perhaps the person is in an arranged marriage and passion will build up over time.

Sternberg gives the name *consummate love* to the kind of love that is high in all three elements—passion, intimacy, and commitment.

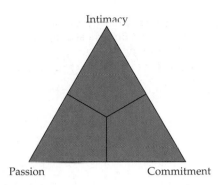

▲ **FIGURE 7.10  Sternberg's love triangle** Robert Sternberg proposed that love consists of three elements—passion, intimacy, and commitment—that can be represented as a triangle.

**intimacy**  The sense of connectedness in an established relationship.

**commitment**  The cognitive component of love: the decision to maintain a relationship.

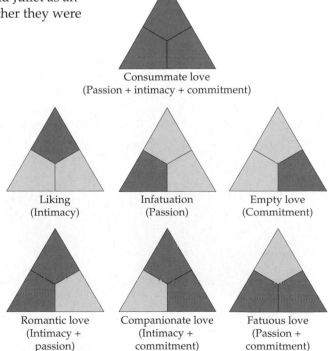

▶ **FIGURE 7.11  Sternberg's seven types of love** are made up of different proportions of passion, intimacy, and commitment. In the figure, intimacy is at the top vertex of each triangle, passion is at the left, and commitment is at the right, as is also shown in Figure 7.10. (See **Activity 7.2: Sternberg's Seven Types of Love**.)

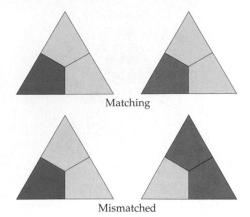

Matching

Mismatched

◀ **FIGURE 7.12 Couples may have matching or mismatched love triangles.** Each member of the upper couple has a triangle approximating Sternberg's "infatuation." In the lower couple, one member's triangle corresponds to "infatuation" and the other member's to "companionate love." According to Sternberg, the upper couple is more likely to be satisfied with their relationship because there is more overlap between their triangles.

These various kinds of love triangles represent love as experienced by an individual. The most satisfying relationships, Sternberg believes, are those in which the two individuals have matching triangles (**FIGURE 7.12**). When two persons' triangles are mismatched, as when one partner is high on commitment but low on passion while the other partner is the reverse, both partners are likely to be dissatisfied.

To get a better idea of how these kinds of love show themselves in actual relationships, we encourage you to evaluate relationships you know about in terms of Sternberg's love triangle. These could be love relationships you have been in yourself, those of your relatives or friends, or relationships in history, literature, or the movies.

### Liking and reciprocal attraction precede falling in love

What actually causes Agustín to fall in love with Bianca, or vice versa? In surveys that ask Agustín what led up to his falling in love with Bianca, Agustín typically mentions that he already liked Bianca, that he perceived that Bianca liked him, that he found Bianca's personality and appearance attractive, that he and Bianca had a lot of similarities, and so on (Pines, 2005).

Still, people may not be conscious of, or able to articulate, the actual factors that caused them to fall in love. (Recall the speed-dating experiments mentioned in Chapter 5, in which people chose partners who didn't resemble their verbally expressed ideals.) One factor rarely mentioned in surveys is the act of having sex, but coitus and orgasm can cause people to fall in love with their sex partners, or at least facilitate it. This may be due to the neurochemical events associated with orgasm, including the activation of dopamine, oxytocin, and vasopressin systems (Young & Wang, 2004).

Is it possible to fall in love at first sight? About half of the U.S. population thinks it is; in fact, 44% of men and 36% of women say that it has happened to them (Gallup Organization, 2001). Since there is no objective test for being in love, it is hard to confirm or refute their claims. But the fact that so many people say they have experienced love at first sight highlights the fact that familiarity is not a necessary ingredient for romantic love.

**FAQ:** I've fallen in love with two different people—can that be?

Most experts say "no." Perhaps one of your "loves" is more of a close attachment than a passionate love.

### Researchers are probing the biological basis of love

Some research has aimed at finding a biological basis for love. One interesting line of animal research focuses on prairie voles (Bosch & Young, 2018) (**FIGURE 7.13**). These small rodents are among the minority of mammals that form life-long pair-bonds, which are established when they first mate. The peptide hormone oxytocin, which is secreted from the pituitary gland during mating, plays a central role in this process. Administering oxytocin to prairie voles causes pair-bond formation even without mating; conversely, blocking the action of oxytocin prevents pair-bonding even when mating does occur. Other species of voles that do not normally form pair-bonds can be induced to do so by transferring some oxytocin-related genes from prairie voles. Thus the critical

Courtesy of Todd H. Ahern, Ph.D., Emory University

▲ **FIGURE 7.13 Prairie home companions** After mating, prairie voles share parental duties and remain together for life. The hormone oxytocin plays a key role in the establishment and maintenance of these relationships.

(A)  (B)  (C)

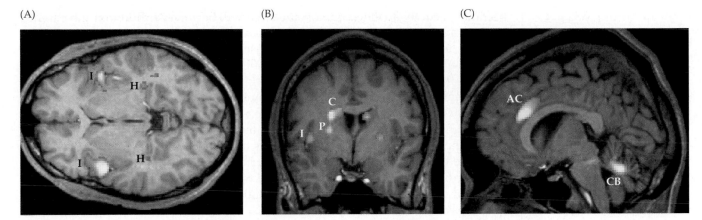

▲ **FIGURE 7.14**  **The brain in love**  These functional brain scans show (in orange and yellow) the brain regions that are more active while a person is viewing a photograph of his or her beloved than while viewing photos of a non-romantic friend. (A) A horizontal slice, showing activity in an infolded region of the cerebral cortex named the insula (I), most strongly in the left hemisphere (bottom), and in the hippocampus (H). (B) A frontal slice, showing activity in the insula and also in the left caudate (C) and putamen (P), structures that are heavily innervated by the dopamine system. (C) Near-midline slice, showing activity in the anterior cingulate cortex (AC) and cerebellum (CB). (After A. Bartels & S. Zeki. 2000. *Neuroreport* 11: 3829–3834.)

importance of oxytocin to pair-bonding in prairie voles has been well established, but whether it plays a similar role in human pair-bonding is not yet known. Other substances believed to be involved in pair-bonding are the peptide vasopressin, which is also a hormone secreted by the pituitary gland, and the neurotransmitter dopamine.

Another way researchers have probed the biology of love is by using functional brain imaging. Two research groups, one at Rutgers University and the other at University College London, scanned the brains of individuals who were intensely in love while they viewed photographs of their beloved (Bartels & Zeki, 2000; Fisher et al., 2006). The results of the two studies were not entirely in agreement, but both showed heavy involvement of brain regions that are rich in receptors for dopamine and oxytocin (**FIGURE 7.14**). The British group went on to show that the brain activity patterns evoked by photographs of one's beloved are similar in everyone regardless of their sex or sexual orientation (Zeki & Romaya, 2010). In fact, a similar activity pattern was seen in mothers who were shown photographs of their baby (but not when shown someone else's baby) (Bartels & Zeki, 2004). Intense love, it seems, is a universal emotional state, regardless of who it is that a person loves.

## 7.6  Life Experiences Mold Our Sexual Relationships

**LEARNING OBJECTIVES**

After reading this section you should be able to:

7.6.1  Explain how attachment styles in childhood may predict relationship styles in adulthood.

7.6.2  Define homogamy and discuss its significance for sexual relationships.

Our relationships are often shaped by life experiences that are not under our control. Here we briefly consider two such factors: our early relationships with our parents, and the social groups in which we live.

### Relationship styles are influenced by childhood attachments

According to research based on **attachment theory**, parenting styles profoundly affect the child's developing personality (Fraley, 2010; Zeifman, 2019). If parents—the mother, especially—respond sensitively to the young child's needs, the child

**attachment theory**  The idea that relationship styles are influenced by the quality of the early parent–child bond.

**homogamy** The tendency of sexually partnered couples, or married couples, to resemble each other in a variety of respects.

becomes securely attached; that is, the child will become confident in the parent's love, will respond positively to the parent, and will seek contact with her or him but will not be unduly disturbed by brief separations. If the parent is rejecting or emotionally distant, the child may avoid intimate interactions with the parent. If the parent is inconsistent or unresponsive, the child may become anxious or ambivalent, often becoming extremely upset when separated from the parent. In avoidant as well as anxious-ambivalent parent–child relationships, the child ends up with insecure attachments, which are much less fulfilling than the secure attachment we described first. Although usually described in terms of these three categories, actual individual attachment styles usually comprise some mixture of the three attachment types.

According to attachment theory, people who were securely attached as children have a basic self-confidence and trust that allows them to enter into intimate relationships with relative ease during adolescence and adulthood. People who were avoidant as children may be uncomfortable with adult intimacy, and their partners may feel they are distant or unresponsive. This can lead to sexual difficulties in the relationship, because both physical and emotional closeness and responsiveness are necessary for long-term sexual satisfaction (Peloquin et al., 2014). People who were anxious or ambivalent as children may have an unrealistic fear of being deserted, and this may cause them to seek an emotional "merger" that actually has the opposite effect—driving the partner away.

To some extent, this relationship between childhood and adult attachment styles has been verified in retrospective and longitudinal studies (Hazan & Shaver, 1987; Simpson et al., 2007). Nevertheless, the relationship is not especially strong—people's attachment styles can change over the course of their lives (Fraley, 2010). This may be because people continuously (but unconsciously) update their attachment styles depending on the types of relationships they experience. Thus attachment theory does not condemn anyone to lifelong failure in love. Rather, it provides insights that can help individuals surmount problems derived from childhood attachment difficulties.

## Couples in relationships resemble each other

One striking fact about couples is how similar the two individuals commonly are to each other. Couples resemble each other far more than would be expected by chance in personal characteristics such as age, height, facial appearance, body mass index, and race, as well as in social dimensions such as religion, educational level, and socioeconomic status. The tendency of sexually partnered couples to resemble each other is called **homogamy**. (Some scholars reserve this term for married couples.)

To some degree, homogamy results from the fact that people tend to find partners within their own social groups; college students are likely to meet other college students, for example. This observation shows that sexual relationships are embedded in larger social structures, but it doesn't say whether homogamy has any *effect* on relationships, either for good or for bad.

There is some evidence, however, that homogamy does contribute to the success and stability of heterosexual relationships. Longitudinal studies have found that couples who resemble each other in a variety of respects are more likely to stay together, and express greater satisfaction with their relationships as time goes by, than couples who are less alike. The most robust correlation seems to be with age: Couples in which the man is much older or younger than the woman face at least twice the risk of breakup, compared with couples that are close in age (Kippen et al., 2013).

Similarity between partners may strengthen relationships because companionate love promotes exactly what one would expect: a companionship. Like friends, partners who are similar

▲ Couples may resemble each other physically and in other ways.

to each other tend to have shared interests and attitudes. Thus, they communicate approval to each other, bolster each other's self-esteem, and help stabilize each other's personalities. In addition, a couple's two birth families are more likely to interact socially and to actively support the couple's relationship if the two partners are similar to each other—in race and religion, for example. Homogamy seems to be especially important early in relationships; dissimilar couples who do manage to stay together for the long term often thrive on their differences, perhaps because they complement each other in useful ways or because their differences maintain an "edge" to the relationship that counteracts boredom.

Homogamy has profound effects on society as a whole, some that may be beneficial and others less so. It helps preserve distinct cultures within American society across the generations, but it also helps maintain or even increase social divisions, and it restricts social mobility and economic opportunity for the disadvantaged (Ford, 2019).

## 7.7 Communication Is a Key Factor in the Success of Relationships

### LEARNING OBJECTIVES

After reading this section you should be able to:

7.7.1   Evaluate the potential benefits and limitations of "active listening."

7.7.2   Explain how disagreements and conflicts can be resolved in ways that strengthen relationships.

7.7.3   Describe the effects on sexual satisfaction of a belief in "sexual destiny" versus "sexual growth."

Many therapists name communication problems as the number-one reason for dissatisfaction in marriages and other long-term relationships. Couples who communicate poorly early on are likely to be dissatisfied with their marriages later. And couples who communicate via aggression are likely to be separated or divorced a few years later.

### Communication may be inhibited by upbringing or by the gender barrier

Communication is a skill that affects many aspects of a relationship. We focus here first on communication in the area of sexuality itself—which is, after all, the topic of this book. In later sections we take a look at more general aspects of communication between intimate partners.

Many couples are reluctant to communicate at all about sexual issues. This reluctance results in part from a tradition of silence about sexual matters that is instilled in young children. Parents tend not to discuss sexual function or genital anatomy with their children, nor do they typically disclose much about their own sex lives or sexual problems. Children quickly learn that sex is a taboo subject. The result is a sense of shame that may profoundly inhibit communication in adulthood.

In heterosexual relationships, the gender barrier may compound communication problems. Boys and young men tend to talk about sexual matters among themselves, as do girls and young women, but they tend to do it in quite different ways, leading almost to separate languages. Young men, for example, may be perfectly comfortable using words such as "dick" and "pussy" among themselves, but the same words may seem vulgar when used with female partners. So men are obliged to use words such as "penis" and "vagina," which may put them in an uncomfortable, almost clinical mindset. When this language difficulty is combined with limited knowledge about the other sex's anatomy and physiology, communication may be severely inhibited. Similarly, girls and young women may discuss sexual and relationship issues at great length among themselves, but they may be quite unprepared to bring up these same issues with men. Additionally, cultural factors inhibit communication in certain groups. Asian-Americans, for example—especially Asian-American women—may find it a very foreign concept to discuss sex or relationship problems, whether with family, partners, or health care providers (Ayuda, 2011; Zhao et al., 2016).

## Marriage and relationship education teaches communication skills

Marriage and relationship education (MRE) programs, developed by several groups, including Howard Markman of the University of Denver, aim to teach basic communication skills that are often as relevant to work and general social life as they are to sexual relationships. At the core of all communication, for example, is one person saying something and the other person listening and responding. In premarital counseling programs, couples may first practice this interaction in a formalized manner. The couple may be seated facing and looking directly at each other, perhaps touching each other. One partner ("Pat") holds a speaker's token such as a floor tile (representing "the floor") and makes a statement such as "Kim, I find myself feeling hurt when you just breeze in and start chatting with the kids as if I'm not there." Pat then yields the "floor" to Kim, who replies by paraphrasing what Pat has just said, such as "You mean, I seem to just take you for granted?" The floor tile changes hands again, and Pat clarifies the initial statement: "Not all the time, just when the kids are around." Another tile change, and Kim gives a response representing a proposed resolution: "You may be right, Pat—sorry! I can understand how you must feel. However much I love the kids, you're the number-one person in my life, and I want to make sure you know it." And so on.

Contrived though such "active-listening" exercises may seem, they teach two important points: the right of one partner to make a clear statement of a potential problem without interruption, and the obligation of the other to provide some feedback—to acknowledge understanding the statement and to process it in a way that will bring the interaction to a satisfactory close. In other words, "uh-huh" might not be a fruitful response to each and every one of your partner's utterances. It's not expected that couples will continue to pass floor tiles to and fro for the rest of their lives, but the hope is that the notion of ordered, reciprocal communication will persist.

Active-listening exercises do run the risk of turning sexual relationships into therapy sessions. Partners are not therapists—outsiders with professional skills—but players *within* the drama. Thus, it doesn't necessarily help to say how much you understand your partner's point of view unless that understanding is accompanied by action and resolution.

Let's make up an illustrative example. You buy a giant flat-screen TV, but your partner is distressed about the unplanned hit to your budget, and they get angry with you. It wouldn't help much for you to say, "I hear what you're saying. I can understand that you're angry that I spent so much money without consulting you." That hasn't put your finances back in order. What actions would show genuine empathy? Returning the TV? Being frugal until you've made up the cost of the TV? Consulting with your partner before every significant purchase in the future? Any or all of these practical responses would stand a better chance of resolving the conflict than apologizing or "understanding."

The long-term value of MRE programs is uncertain. In one longitudinal study by Markman's group, couples were randomly assigned to participate or not participate in an MRE program. For a year or two after the MRE sessions, the participating couples did show evidence of better communication and relationship satisfaction than the controls, but at a 5-year follow-up the differences had become small or nonsignificant (Markman et al., 1993).

## How couples deal with conflict affects the stability of their relationships

Conflicts are inevitable in all but the briefest relationships, but how conflicts are handled is a good indicator of the likelihood that a relationship will last. John Gottman and his colleagues at the University of Washington have carried out numerous longitudinal studies of conflict styles in marriage (Gottman et al., 1998; Gottman &

Levenson, 2000; Gottman & Notarius, 2000; Gottman & Schwartz Gottman, 2017). Typically, the researchers videotape interactions between partners early in their relationship and analyze and quantify the conversations, facial gestures, and body movements—since words alone do not capture the breadth of signals people exchange. Then the researchers follow the relationship for a period of years, evaluating the outcomes.

One of the key findings is that the expression of anger is not necessarily a bad thing. Disagreement and anger cause unhappiness at the time they are expressed, but they open up topics for communication—which may not happen much among couples who use conflict management styles such as withdrawal, defensiveness, criticism, or contempt.

That doesn't mean that couples should just lay into each other with anger—far from it. The University of Washington researchers have found that when conflicts do occur in stable marriages, communications between the partners feature at least five times as many positive interactions as negative ones. Thus, couples who freely express anger during conflict have to balance it out with a high ratio of positive statements and actions if they are to prevent their relationships from dropping below the 5 to 1 ratio. People who get into prolonged fights have to spend hours of "repair work" with positive talk and actions to prevent the anger from harming their relationships. Even more important is attending to the ways that conversations *begin*: People who initiate interactions with "positive start-ups" ("I love how cheerful you are. It brings joy to my life, and our friends notice it too.") are less likely to have later marital breakups than those who use "negative start-ups," meaning starting directly with some kind of complaint or criticism.

Gottman's group claimed to predict, with 92.7% accuracy, whether a couple would divorce or not in the following 4 years, simply on the strength of their positive interactions during repair conversations (Gottman & Levenson, 1999). This claim may be misleading, however, as it is based mainly on the large numbers of couples predicted to stay together who did stay together. In many of Gottman's studies the majority of the couples who were predicted to divorce did not in fact do so. Gottman's statistical methods have been criticized on several counts (Heyman & Smith Slep, 2001; Abraham, 2010). One rigorously designed longitudinal study concluded that there is little causal connection between communication style and marital satisfaction, and that any connection that does exist works in the opposite direction from that suggested by Gottman—that is, poor communication was more likely to be a *consequence* of marital dissatisfaction than a *cause* of it (Lavner et al., 2016).

In troubled marriages and other relationships, a common problem emerges when one partner makes some demand for change in the relationship and the other responds by stonewalling—that is, remaining verbally silent and showing little facial or gestural expression, even though there may be some internal turmoil. It's most often the man who stonewalls, because of gender differences in emotional expressiveness. This pattern of demand and withdrawal precludes the possibility of resolution. Making a couple aware of the demand–withdrawal problem—along with alternative strategies for conflict resolution and positive repair conversations—can help them improve their communication skills.

Therapy based on insights of this kind is known as **behavioral couples therapy (BCT)** (Gottman & Schwartz Gottman, 2017). According to its practitioners, this form of therapy is quite successful in helping rescue troubled relationships, no matter what problems couples have. The BCT therapist introduces the couple to simple behavioral exercises, such as practicing the activity called Catch Your Partner Doing Something

Conflict doesn't harm a relationship...

...if it's followed by plenty of repair work.

**behavioral couples therapy (BCT)**
Therapy focused on improving styles of communication between partners in relationships.

Right, which helps increase the ratio of positivity to negativity in a relationship. The therapist also brings social-learning and cognitive principles to bear on the problems faced by the couple.

Gottman has published research on the importance of trust in intimate relationships (Gottman, 2011). He stresses that trust is based on *behavior* more than on thoughts or words alone. Do each partner's *actions* show "I am here for you" and "You can count on me"? These are behaviors demonstrating that each partner is thinking about *both* of them. If both individuals can do this, it can increase the chances of creating a lasting relationship. These trust-inspiring actions are especially important when times get tough: If each partner's actions show genuine concern for the other, even when problems arise, both of them will come to realize that they have a truly trusting relationship.

Trust does not emerge instantly between two people, which can make it hard for individuals in new relationships to be certain whether they are on the road to developing real mutual trust. But the more often the behavior of each partner demonstrates a sincere concern for the other, the sooner the pair will develop a strong emotional bond, which is the basis of intimate trust—and a loving sexual connection.

Although writers such as Gottman often frame their discussion in terms of heterosexual marriage, the principles they put forward are applicable to any relationship that a couple values and wishes to sustain. In fact, even the less durable relationships that are common in the college years are opportunities for exploring and learning skills for building good relationships. Thus Gottman's "seven principles for making marriage work" are worth studying by anyone who would like to enjoy a lasting and rewarding sexual relationship (**BOX 7.3**).

All couples experience some problems in relationships. Repairing them is crucial. Couples are most likely to survive for the long haul if they can fix the things that go wrong. The sooner and more effectively two people can show that they sincerely want to repair any problems that occur, the more likely they are to nurture their trust and love.

### In sexual relationships, sex matters

Satisfaction with sexual relationships depends in considerable measure on satisfaction with the sex itself, because sex helps establish and maintain intimacy and attachment (Birnbaum & Reis, 2019). In a very large online survey led by David Frederick of Chapman University, respondents who had been in a relationship for at least 3 years were asked about their satisfaction with the sexual aspects of their relationship, both at the start of the relationship and currently (Frederick et al., 2017). The great majority (about 83%) said that they had been satisfied initially, but only about half said that they were still satisfied at the time of the survey; the others were either neutral or dissatisfied. What distinguished those who were still satisfied from the others? They had sex more often, received more oral sex, had more orgasms, engaged in a wider variety of sex acts, paid more attention to creating a sexy mood (e.g., engaged in sexy talk, said "I love you," or created a sexy environment), and talked more with each other about their sex life.

In another study, a Canadian group asked people about their beliefs regarding sexual satisfaction (Maxwell et al., 2017). Some respondents believed in "sexual destiny"—that is, the important thing was to find your sexual soul mate, and good sex would follow. Others believed in "sexual growth"—that is, sexual satisfaction was a matter of effort and hard work, such as learning through trial and error what both partners wanted and how to satisfy them. Those who believed in sexual growth were more satisfied with both the sexual and nonsexual aspects of their relationships than those who believed in destiny. When couples had disagreements or unhappiness concerning sex, the "destiny" people tended to think, "We're not right together," whereas the "growth" people thought, "We can solve this."

Thus couples who invest some energy and creativity into their sex lives maintain their sexual satisfaction over the long term, which in turn helps maintain their overall satisfaction with their relationships.

## BOX 7.3
## Lasting Relationships: Gottman's Seven Principles

John and Julie Gottman (see figure) have studied couples' relationship styles by monitoring their interactions in a laboratory setting. They have then followed these couples over a period of years to see which relationship styles foster and predict lasting satisfaction. They have also examined the long-term effects of various kinds of relationship advice and training. The Gottmans have distilled what they have learned into seven principles (Gottman & Gottman, 2011):

1. *Enhance your love map.* This means developing and updating a detailed mental representation of your partner's history, habits, desires, and fears, including things that you may not have direct knowledge of, such as interaction styles at work. This love map enhances empathy, because you can use it to guess what the problem is, even if your partner does not spell it out for you.

2. *Nurture fondness and admiration.* The fact that you have chosen someone as a partner means that you have seen good and valuable qualities in that person. Even when things get rough, keep this sense of admiration in mind, and express it to your partner.

3. *Turn toward each other.* When your partner seeks attention or support, give it. Turning away from such "bids" causes disconnection and resentment; turning toward the partner fosters connection and passion.

4. *Let your partner influence you.* Treat your partner with honor and respect, and be ready to share decision making and reach compromises. Most women already do this, say the Gottmans, but men often need to make a conscious effort to reciprocate.

5. *Solve your solvable problems.* When there is a difficulty between you that needs resolution, tackle it in a positive way. Start the conversation gently. Make "I" statements.

John and Julie Gottman

Make and accept repair attempts. If either of you becomes aggravated or feels overwhelmed, take a break to cool off. Think about how you can reach a compromise.

6. *Overcome gridlock.* If your conflict goes on and seems to defy resolution, think about whether there is something below the surface—whether one or both of you have unexpressed desires or dreams. Respect each other's dreams, and try to find a way to make both dreams into reality.

7. *Create shared meaning.* Although you are different people, nurture the values you have in common. Develop your own "microculture" that explains and validates your relationship, and make sure it is flexible enough to accommodate change.

Reading the Gottmans' books can help you turn these simple ideas into detailed realities.

# 7.8 Love, Jealousy, and Infidelity Are Intertwined

### LEARNING OBJECTIVES

After reading this section you should be able to:

7.8.1 **Explain the differences in how women and men may experience jealousy in sexual relationships.**

7.8.2 **Evaluate the possible negative and positive effects of jealousy on relationships.**

**Jealousy** is the unpleasant feeling caused by suspicions of—or the discovery of—the infidelity of one's partner.* Infidelity, in this context, could mean anything from an actual sexual contact or relationship with a third party to a mere indication of interest in someone else—as evidenced by looking at, flirting with, or spending time with

**jealousy**   Fear that one's partner may be sexually or emotionally unfaithful.

---

*Jealousy is different from envy—the distress caused by another person's possession of something that one lacks.

▲ Jealousy can help maintain relationships that are threatened by third parties.

**sexual jealousy** Fear that one's partner is engaging in sexual contacts with another person.

**emotional jealousy** Fear that one's partner is becoming emotionally committed to another person.

**FAQ:** My boyfriend is constantly accusing me of seeing someone else behind his back, even though I'm not. What should I do?

Delusional jealousy is a serious disorder that can lead to violence or stalking. Your boyfriend needs to be assessed and perhaps treated by a mental health professional. If he refuses, you should consider whether it's worth staying in the relationship.

that person. At any one time, about 1 in 10 college students is experiencing jealousy, according to an Italian study (Marazziti et al., 2003).

Jealousy can be an acute sensation—the instant stab of jealousy that we may feel when our beloved shows attention to a potential rival. This feeling probably involves a physiological stress response. Alternatively, it can be a gnawing, suspicious frame of mind that takes over a jealous person and colors interactions with his or her partner.

We can break down jealousy into two kinds. The first, **sexual jealousy**, is a fear that one's partner is engaging or seeking to engage in sex with another person. The second, **emotional jealousy**, is a fear that one's partner is committing to another person and might therefore abandon the relationship. Men and women can experience both kinds of jealousy, but men typically experience sexual jealousy more strongly than women, and women typically experience emotional jealousy more strongly than men. This sex difference exists across many or all cultures (Buss, 2011). Regardless of their sex, individuals who have experienced a partner's infidelity in an earlier relationship are liable to experience more intense jealousy in a current relationship (Zandbergen & Brown, 2015).

Have you ever checked out a romantic partner's activities on social media? That's known as "interpersonal electronic surveillance" or, colloquially, "creeping." Most young people have engaged in it at one time or another, the most common motivation being jealousy (Stern & Willis, 2007). "Facebook jealousy" in particular has been the subject of considerable research. The more time romantically involved people spend on Facebook, the more likely they are to experience jealousy, especially of the emotional kind (Muise et al., 2009). Facebook makes it easy—perhaps too easy—for users to monitor the activities of their partners: who they are friending, who they are close to in photos, or how they describe their relationship status. Ambiguous information in these postings then incites further vigilance, and this feedback loop can sometimes lead all the way to cyberstalking (see Chapter 16). People with anxious attachment styles are particularly prone to this kind of escalation (Marshall et al., 2013).

### Jealousy can have a positive function

Evolutionary psychologists see the capacity for jealousy as a hardwired adaptation to certain inescapable facts about reproduction. First, female mammals make a much greater biological contribution to reproduction than do males, but in some species, such as ours, this imbalance may be countered by the extra resources (e.g., food and protection) that males contribute. Second, females can be certain that any offspring they bear are their own; males, however, cannot be certain that they fathered their mates' offspring. Thus, during human evolution, the major reproductive risk for a woman was that a man would take up with another mate, leaving her with insufficient resources to rear her children alone. The major reproductive risk for a man, however, was that he would unwittingly devote a great deal of time and effort to helping rear children who were actually fathered by another man. According to David Buss of the University of Texas, these differences in risks explain why men and women tend to experience different kinds of jealousy—greater sexual jealousy in men and greater emotional jealousy in women (Buss, 2018).

This evolutionary interpretation gains further support from studies that focus on same-sex cheating (Confer & Cloud, 2011). Men are far less disturbed by the idea that their female partner is having sex with another woman than by the idea that she is cheating with a man—presumably because same-sex infidelity cannot lead to the birth of children that he might mistakenly rear as his own. Conversely, women are, if anything, even *more* disturbed by the idea of their male partner cheating with another man than with a woman—perhaps because the implication of homosexuality is seen as carrying an even greater risk of permanent abandonment.

Jealousy often arises when people in relationships receive sexual advances from outsiders. These "mate-poaching" efforts seem to be universal across human cultures (Schmitt, 2004). In addition, people in relationships may themselves be tempted to cheat on their partners, because love—the main glue that holds relationships together—is not always strong enough by itself to preserve monogamy. That's where jealousy attempts to take over the job. And that's where jealousy can have a positive value for the person who experiences it, painful though it is. Jealousy is part of the mechanism that detects and gives salience to cheating by a partner and then motivates action to prevent or end it.

Because our capacity for jealousy has evolved, it is "built in"; thus, it is not always a rational process. A husband doesn't say to himself, "Oh, my wife's on the pill, so I'm not worried if she sleeps around." Evolution knows nothing about pills; it simply provides everyone with an emotional mechanism that has been effective in the past for protecting people's reproductive interests.

Jealousy is neither a good thing nor a bad thing, but rather a psychological response that can have both positive and negative consequences. The negative consequences can be truly horrendous: About 13% of all homicides are spousal murders, most of them triggered by jealousy. Battered women who seek refuge in shelters are commonly there because of spousal jealousy. And many more relationships are poisoned by less extreme expressions of the same emotion.

Several therapists have described useful techniques for distinguishing healthy jealousy, which can help strengthen and maintain loving relationships, from jealousy that is merely destructive, as well as techniques for overcoming the latter kind (Dryden, 1999; Leahy & Tirch, 2008). Self-destructive jealousy, aggressive jealousy, and jealousy that is based on persistent false beliefs about the partner, called **delusional jealousy**, obviously merit therapeutic intervention. Still, one way to deal with jealousy is to act on it, specifically by making oneself more physically attractive to one's partner or by going out of one's way to demonstrate love and commitment. "Men who are successful at keeping their partners often step up their displays of love when threatened with a possible partner defection," writes Buss. "Men who fail in these displays tend to be losers in love" (Buss, 2000).

## 7.9 Unrequited Love Is Painful for Both Parties

### LEARNING OBJECTIVE

After reading this section you should be able to:

7.9.1 **Explain why rejection of a suitor may be a negative experience both for the suitor and the rejector.**

**Unrequited love** is love that is not reciprocated. It may take several forms, according to a study by Robert Bringle and colleagues at Appalachian State University (Bringle et al., 2013):

- A **crush** on someone who is distant and unobtainable, such as a rock star
- A secret crush on a friend or acquaintance
- The actual pursuit of a love object who does not reciprocate
- The longing for a past lover

These ill-starred relationships are common: In Bringle's survey of high school students and young adults, episodes of unrequited love were four times more common than episodes of reciprocated love.

**delusional jealousy** Persistent false belief that one's partner is involved with another person.

**unrequited love** Love that is not reciprocated.

**crush** A short-lived, intense, unreciprocated love, often experienced during adolescence.

© Asian Art & Archaeology Inc./Corbis

▲ This late-19th-century Japanese woodblock print, *Reflected Moonlight*, depicts Lady Ariko, a poet of the medieval Heian court, with her lute, preparing to drown herself because of her unrequited love for a lord. Lady Ariko's poem, which appears at the top right of the print, expresses the anguish of the rejected lover: "How hopeless it is / It would be better for me to sink beneath the waves / Perhaps there I could see my man from Moon Capital."

**suitor** A person who is seeking to establish a romantic relationship with another.

**obsessive relational intrusion** Obsessive pursuit of a person by a rejected lover.

**stalking** Obsessive pursuit of a previous, current, or desired sex partner in such a way as to put that person in a state of fear.

For the **suitor**, rejection hurts, of course. How literally this is true was illustrated in a brain-imaging study (Kross et al., 2011): The brain regions that became active when recently rejected lovers thought about their rejection were the same regions that became active when a painfully hot stimulus was applied to their arms. Persons who have relatively low self-esteem to begin with may be the ones who are most traumatized by a rejection, whereas persons with high self-esteem may bounce back quickly (Waller & MacDonald, 2010).

The rejected suitor often feels "abandonment anger" without actually falling out of love. The blend of anger and continuing love may seem like a contradiction, but it is a common experience (Ellis & Malamuth, 2000). "You can be terribly angry at a rejecting sweetheart but still very much in love," Helen Fisher has written. "In fact, the opposite of love is not hate but indifference" (Fisher, 2006).

The suitor does at least have a "script" to follow. The role of the unrequited lover is familiar to everyone; it is celebrated in one popular song after another. It is a dramatic role with its prescribed times for grief, anger, acceptance, and moving on.

Unrequited love can be thought of as part of the matching process by which people find long-term mates, and in that sense it can have a positive value. In fact, most people can handle a few experiences with unrequited love and emerge unscathed, perhaps stronger for the experience. For a minority, however, especially those with controlling or manipulative personalities or poor communication skills, it may be difficult to take "no" for a final answer, and a single-minded pursuit of the desired person may ensue (Sinclair & Frieze, 2001). This pattern, termed **obsessive relational intrusion**, is one in which the suitor cannot stop obsessing over the desired relationship, perhaps spending hours each day locked in thoughts and feelings about the unreciprocated love. In rare cases this may eventually lead to the criminal behavior known as **stalking** (see Chapter 16).

### The rejector may experience guilt

The person who is the target of unrequited love may not even be aware of the situation—in the case of a secret crush, for example. But a person who is aware of being the object of someone's love and doesn't love in return (a "rejector") is likely to feel guilty. According to research by psychologist Roy Baumeister and colleagues at Florida State University, these guilty feelings may take several forms: guilt at having led the suitor on, even if unintentionally or to a small degree; guilt at not returning the suitor's affection—a violation of the social norm of reciprocity; and guilt at inflicting humiliation on the suitor by telling that person that his or her love is not returned (Baumeister & Dhavale, 2001).

Furthermore, the rejector's role is largely "unscripted": There are few social models for how a rejector is supposed to behave or feel. Thus, the rejector may end up failing to communicate the rejection clearly to the suitor, perhaps representing it as a matter of unfortunate circumstances that might conceivably be overcome in the future ("I'm really too busy to be thinking about relationships right now").

By analyzing numerous accounts of unrequited love told from the perspectives of both suitors and rejectors, Baumeister's group found systematic biases in the way the episodes were recalled (**FIGURE 7.15**). Suitors were much more likely than rejectors to recall that the rejector initially reciprocated the suitor's advances and that the rejector led the suitor on. Rejectors, however, were more likely than suitors to recall that the rejector gave the suitor an explicit rejection and that

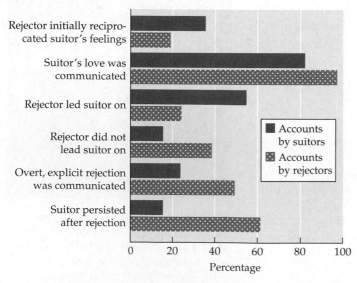

**▲ FIGURE 7.15  Unhappy memories** When college students were asked to recall their experiences of unrequited love—both experiences in which they were rejected and experiences in which they did the rejecting—the two kinds of narratives differed markedly. The figure shows the percentage of "suitor" and "rejector" narratives that included the six listed assertions. (Data from R. F. Baumeister et al. 1993. *J Pers Soc Psychol* 64: 377–394.)

the suitor persisted unreasonably in spite of the rejection. The researchers interpreted these biases as representing efforts by suitors to rebuild their self-esteem and by rejectors to justify themselves and reduce their feelings of guilt.

**extra-pair relationship** A sexual relationship in which at least one of the partners is already married to or partnered with someone else.

## 7.10 Extra-Pair Relationships Have Many Styles and Motivations

**LEARNING OBJECTIVES**

After reading this section you should be able to:

7.10.1 Evaluate the possible motives for engaging or not engaging in extra-pair relationships.

7.10.2 Explain the evolutionary psychological perspective on extra-pair relationships.

As we've just discussed, the capacity for jealousy exists because people who are in coupled relationships, whether dating, cohabiting, or married, may also engage in sexual relationships outside their ongoing partnership. We now turn our attention to the forms and motivations of such **extra-pair relationships**. ("Extramarital relationships" is a better-known phrase, but it is inappropriate here because we are not focusing exclusively on married couples.)

About the only thing that all extra-pair relationships have in common is that, as mentioned earlier, they tend to incur societal disapproval. Either monogamy or serial monogamy is considered the ideal, and anything else is stigmatized, though to varying degrees depending on circumstances. Even fantasies about having sex with a person outside the partnership are widely considered a form of infidelity, in spite of the fact that most men and about half of all women experience them (Yarab et al., 1998).

If we discount fantasies, we are still left with a broad range of behaviors that fall into the category of extra-pair relationships. These behaviors include casual flirting, fondling, genital contact and coitus, and falling in love. Extra-pair relationships may be single encounters, brief "flings," or longer "affairs," or a succession of such relationships may occur with a variety of different partners. They may take place with or without the knowledge or acquiescence of the person's regular partner. They may take place in real life or on the internet (**BOX 7.4**).

### Personal and evolutionary factors influence infidelity

Why do some women and men in our society engage in extra-pair relationships while others do not? Many factors come into play here. Many people refrain from engaging in extra-pair relationships because of moral beliefs, concern for their partners' feelings, or fear of the consequences. Conversely, lack of physical satisfaction, communication, or love in the primary relationship, or prolonged absence of the primary partner, can drive some people into affairs. So can the sense that one is not getting what one deserves in the primary relationship because one's partner is perceived as less attractive or desirable than oneself. So can the sheer excitement of having a new partner or of falling in love all over again. People may also cultivate secondary relationships to provoke a jealous response on the part of the primary partner, to "get even" with the primary partner if that partner is already having an affair with someone else, or to precipitate an end to the primary relationship. Finally, gay people who are heterosexually married may find their only sexual satisfaction in secondary relationships.

People who are in the early stages of a relationship may also cultivate a relationship with a "back burner" partner. This strategy could be either a form of insurance in case the main relationship doesn't work out or simply a means to increase sexual enjoyment or attention. According to a survey of college undergraduates by Jayson Dibble of Hope College and Michelle Drouin of Indiana University–Purdue University Fort Wayne, many students (men especially) cultivate back burners, keeping in touch with them by text, social media, and the like (Dibble & Drouin, 2014).

**FAQ:** My boyfriend and I have great sex, but he also hooks up occasionally with a man—is he gay?

He's more likely to be bisexual or "heteroflexible," but he may come out as gay later. Either way, you need to decide whether you're cool with it, because his behavior isn't likely to change.

## BOX 7.4
## We Just Clicked

When John Goydan of Bridgewater, New Jersey, filed for divorce from his wife Diane and sought custody of their two young children, his legal papers contained dozens of emails, some of them sexually explicit, that Diane had exchanged with a man who called himself "The Weasel." Diane and The Weasel never met, but to John their online romance amounted to adultery. Similarly, "Nadja" considered that her attorney husband "Steve" had cheated on her when their children found erotic correspondence between him and a woman named "Galaxy Queen" on the family computer—even though Steve and Galaxy Queen had confined their romance to the internet (Associated Press, 1996).

What drives people to commit internet infidelity? For the most part, the causes are the same as those that have driven people to cheat on their partners since time immemorial. But the internet offers special incentives—what has been called the "triple-A engine" of accessibility, affordability, and anonymity (Cooper, 2002). Anonymity, in this context, includes selective disclosure and deception—in other words, a level of control over how the other person perceives you that would never be achievable in the real world. And of course it means safety—no hard-to-explain hickeys, no mysterious phone hang-ups, and no sexually transmitted infections. A secure password covers everything.

Diane's and Steve's escapades took place in the 1990s, when text emails were about the only option for cyberlovers. Now the profusion of webcams, videotelephony services, and web-enabled sex toys allow for the exchange of everything but pheromones. In one study, 8% of partnered respondents said that they had engaged in cybersex with people other than their partners (Fricker & Moore, 2008).

Partnered individuals who engage in cybersex with third parties may deny that this constitutes "cheating" ("How can you call it cheating—I've never met her/him—it's not real!"). But people who discover that their partners are engaging in cybersex—whether by being directly told about it, by finding evidence of it on a computer, or by walking in on a cybersex session—do usually consider it cheating (Cravens & Whiting, 2015; Ferron et al., 2017). In fact, even viewing pornography without the involvement of any third party is often considered cheating too. Most of the survey respondents said that their partners' online activities had caused them stress and led them to think of themselves as trauma victims and that it led to a worsening or termination of the relationship. "Now I feel unattractive, ugly, wondering what's wrong with me," wrote one respondent. "I can't sleep or concentrate. I'm missing out on life's happiness, worried, scared all the time."

No doubt there are some people who are able to see their partners' cybersex as "not real" and simply let it go or turn a blind eye to it. Others may be happy to join in on the online activities. But for the majority, cheating online is the same thing as cheating in the real world, and it is seen as betrayal and a breach of trust (Vossler, 2016).

---

Surprisingly, students who said that they were in committed relationships were just as likely to have back burners as those who were not, suggesting that "commitment" at the college level isn't expected to be forever.

Besides the potential threat posed by back burners, people in long-lasting relationships are exposed to another danger, especially as their passionate love weakens over time. This is the possibility of finding new love—but with a different person. It's the stuff of soap operas, but it's often the stuff of real life, too: A man or woman may be deeply attached to his or her regular partner but may also be head over heels in love with someone else.

Personality influences the likelihood of infidelity. In one study a team led by Emma Altgelt, then a graduate student in psychology at Florida State University, assessed the personalities of recently married women and men and then followed them for 3 years, asking them individually whether they or their spouses had engaged in extramarital sexual relationships (Altgelt et al., 2018). The personality factor predictive of infidelity by women was extraversion—the combination of assertiveness and gregariousness. No personality factors were predictive of infidelity by men. However, the personalities of the respondents' *spouses* were indeed predictive of infidelity by either men or women. Individuals whose spouses scored high on neuroticism (emotional instability and anxiety) or extraversion were more likely to be unfaithful than those whose spouses scored low on those factors. This is not to suggest that it's the spouse's fault if a married person cheats. Rather, infidelity needs to be understood in terms of the dynamic between the spouses rather than simply the personality of the one who is unfaithful.

Infidelity has evolutionary roots. This is suggested by the fact that promiscuity is common among non-human animals, including many species that form pair-bonds (that is, **socially monogamous** species). Male animals probably engage in extra-pair sex because it is a relatively inexpensive way to have more offspring, whereas females are more likely to do so to acquire the resources provided by the extra-pair males or to give their offspring better genes than those provided by their regular mates. Evolutionary psychologists argue that similar forces influence human behavior. Steve Gangestad and Randy Thornhill, for example, believe that when women have sex outside of their marriages or regular partnerships, they are unconsciously shopping for better genes (Gangestad & Thornhill, 1997).

If evolutionary forces have contributed to men's and women's tendency to engage in extra-pair sex, one might expect genes to influence who strays and who does not. That is in fact the case. According to a large-scale twin study led by evolutionary psychologist Brendan Zietsch of the University of Queensland, Australia, the heritability of infidelity in men is 62%—which means that 62% of the variability in men's infidelity is accounted for by the genes they inherit (Zietsch et al., 2015). In women the corresponding figure is 40%. In women, but not men, one of the genes that influences infidelity has been tentatively identified by Zietsch's group: It is the gene that encodes the receptor for the pituitary hormone vasopressin. We mentioned vasopressin earlier as a hormone that helps regulate pair-bonding in voles, so this function of the hormone may be conserved widely among mammals.

In addition to these apparent evolutionary forces, we should bear in mind the obvious social factors that influence women and men in different ways when it comes to extra-pair relationships. A man's infidelities tend to be viewed more leniently than those of a woman, and a man often has greater ability to devote time and resources to an outside relationship than a woman does, especially if the woman is pregnant or already has children.

### Extra-pair relationships are uncommon

Americans don't cheat on their spouses or regular partners very often (**FIGURE 7.16**). In the NHSLS study, conducted in 1992, most of the interviewees reported that they had been completely monogamous over the entire duration of a marriage or cohabitation, whereas many of these same people had multiple partners *before* and *after* those long-term relationships. In the GSS data for 2010, only 20% of ever-married men and 14% of women said that they had sex with a person other than their spouse while they were married. And of children born to married women, only about one in a hundred is fathered by someone other than the husband, according to DNA studies (Larmuseau et al., 2017).

It's possible, of course, that survey respondents are less than honest about their extramarital relationships. One study found that married women were much more likely to admit to a recent extramarital relationship when entering their responses into a computer than when they were questioned in a face-to-face

**social monogamy** The formation of pair-bonds or marriages that may or may not be sexually exclusive.

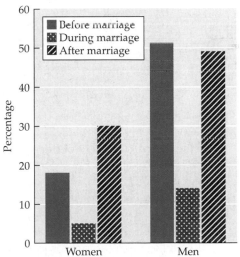

▲ **FIGURE 7.16 Marriage is an interlude of monogamy,** according to NHSLS data. The graph shows the percentage of women and men born between 1943 and 1952 who said they had more than one new sex partner before, during, or after their first marriage. (Data from NHSLS as reported in E. Laumann et al. 1994. *The social organization of sexuality: Sexual practices in the United States.* University of Chicago Press: Chicago.)

interview, as was done in the NHSLS study (Whisman & Snyder, 2007). Even among the women who entered data into the computer, however, only 6% said that they had engaged in a recent extramarital relationship.

The low prevalence of extra-pair sex may surprise some readers, for several reasons. As we've discussed, plenty of factors cause marital problems and increase people's motivation to look for other partners. Viagra and improved health care would seem to make infidelity an increasingly available option for older people. And role models for infidelity are in the news every day. So what stops people from straying? Most likely, it is the fact that 4 out of 5 Americans believe that doing so is morally wrong (see Figure 7.2) and the fact that they value the stability of their long-term relationships more highly than the immediate rewards of infidelity.

Couples therapists often have to deal with issues of infidelity (Hertlein & Weeks, 2007). These therapists are very familiar with the pain, confusion, and anger that infidelity can cause. Therapeutic goals include apology, forgiveness, improvement of communication, and the setting of new ground rules. If the couple cannot recommit to each other, a therapist may guide them to an amicable separation.

## Summary

- People enter into sexual relationships for a variety of reasons: sexual attraction and love; the desire for status, security, or profit; the desire to conform or to rebel; and the desire to have children.

- People tend to judge the morality of sexual behavior by its context, being more approving of sex in committed relationships than of casual or extramarital sex. Beliefs about the morality of sex are tied to beliefs about its purpose. Americans can be grouped into several clusters with characteristic attitudes on sexual matters; to a considerable degree, a particular person's beliefs can be predicted by demographic characteristics such as age, sex, religion, and educational level. Americans have become far more accepting of sex between unmarried individuals and homosexual sex over the past several decades, but disapproval of extramarital and teen sex remains high.

- Casual sex is more appealing to men than to women. In the college environment, "hooking up" (uncommitted sex between acquaintances) is an increasingly common practice. But the prevalence of casual sex in the college environment is lower than most students believe. Alcohol is an important factor in facilitating hookups. Some participants in hookups—women more than men—later regret them and possibly experience mental health consequences, but many others enjoy hookups and have no regrets. Casual sex is more accepted and more prevalent in the gay male community than among heterosexuals or lesbians.

- Flirting behaviors of both sexes are quite stereotyped across cultures, but flirting styles vary with personality. Largely unconscious signals, such as prolonged eye contact, communicate a person's desire to escalate an encounter or, conversely, to terminate it.

- Committed but non-cohabiting relationships (traditionally called dating relationships) tend to be fluid and short-lived, leading either to a live-in relationship or to separation. Those relationships that include sex very early tend to be shorter than those in which sex is postponed, but this is probably a selection effect, not an effect of the sex itself.

- Romantic love exists in most or all cultures. Mutual liking, physical attraction, and other factors promote falling in love. Romantic love appears to be mediated by specific hormones and neurotransmitters and by activity patterns within regions of the brain that process pleasurable sensations.

- Sternberg's theory of love proposes that love consists of three elements—passion, intimacy, and commitment—whose relative contributions may be represented by a triangle. The shape of a person's "love triangle" changes over the course of a relationship. Partners are most likely to be satisfied with their relationship when their triangles match.

- Unrequited love is painful to both suitors and rejectors: to suitors because it denies them their love object and diminishes their self-esteem, and to rejectors because it causes them guilt.

- According to attachment theory, young children's relationships with their parents establish patterns that are repeated in romantic relationships during adulthood.

- Partners in relationships tend to resemble each other in a variety of respects. This homogamy contributes to satisfaction in relationships.

- A couple's communication style predicts their satisfaction with their relationship and its durability. Couples may have difficulty communicating about sexual matters for a variety of reasons, such as a culture of sexual shame. Some premarital counseling programs teach communication skills.

- The ways couples deal with conflict are strongly predictive of how long the relationships will last. Optimal strategies involve not avoiding anger, but rather solving the problems that cause anger and developing numerous positive interactions. Couples do best when hostile interactions are followed with positive "repair" conversations. Couples therapy may focus on altering behavior or on unearthing hidden emotional problems.

- Jealousy, though a painful experience, has a positive function in protecting relationships against infidelity and in testing the strength of love bonds. Sex differences in jealousy—sexual jealousy in men and emotional jealousy in women—may reflect the different reproductive interests that men and women have had over the course of human evolution. Some forms of jealousy are damaging and merit treatment, but well-grounded jealousy can spur constructive efforts to improve the relationship, if those involved have learned to respond effectively to problematic situations.

- Many circumstantial factors influence whether people in long-term partnerships engage in sexual relationships outside those partnerships. National surveys suggest that most married Americans are in fact monogamous for most or the entirety of their marriage.

## Discussion Questions

1. Compare and contrast your beliefs about what is right or wrong in the sexual domain with your peers' and your parents' beliefs (e.g., consider extramarital sex, premarital sex, casual sex, promiscuity, age of consent, homosexual behavior, contraception, abortion, and divorce). Discuss how your attitudes have or have not changed over time.

2. If you have had an experience with a relationship breakup, describe your reactions to that breakup, how it felt, and what you learned. If you have not had a breakup or don't wish to discuss it, imagine the circumstances that would distress you enough to lead to a breakup.

3. Discuss what is important to you about communication and conflict negotiation in a relationship. Are you reluctant to discuss sexual issues? Why? Consider your ability to communicate in light of those factors discussed in the text that hinder communication.

4. Discuss your experiences with jealousy, and compare them with those of your peers.

5. What basis do you think is most effective for selecting a marriage partner— arranged marriage, falling in love, or something else? Why?

## Web Resources

American College Health Association   **www.acha.org**

Beliefnet. Relationships (interfaith site with considerable discussion of sexual and relationship issues)   **tinyurl.com/yav7qy4w**

Go Ask Alice! Relationships (from Columbia University's Health Services)   **tinyurl.com/y7tqax7x**

Gottman Institute   **www.gottman.com**

Loving from a Distance (support group for people in long-distance relationships)   **tinyurl.com/lw2jjek**

> The **Discovering Human Sexuality** digital resources include activities, animations, flashcards, web links, chapter outlines and summaries, and other study tools.
>
> Learn more with this chapter's digital tools, including the **Oxford Insight Study Guide**, at **oup.com/he/levay5e**.

Perel, E. TED Talks: The secret to desire in a long-term relationship **tinyurl.com/b7flgz3**

SexInfoOnline. Love & relationships (from the University of California, Santa Barbara) **tinyurl.com/y8lnjnb6**

## Recommended Reading

Buss, D. M. (2000). *The dangerous passion: Why jealousy is as necessary as love and sex*. Free Press.

Chapman, G. (2017). *The five love languages: Singles edition*. Northfield Publishing.

Davenport, B. (2015). *201 relationship questions: The couple's guide to building trust and emotional intimacy*. Bold Living Press.

Fisher, H. (2016). *Anatomy of love: A natural history of mating, marriage, and why we stray* (rev. ed.). Norton.

Gottman, J., Schwartz Gottman, J., Abrams, D. & Carlton Abrams, R. (2016). *The man's guide to women: Scientifically proven secrets from the "Love Lab" about what women really want*. Rodale.

Gottman, J. M. & Silver, N. (2015). *The seven principles for making marriage work: A practical guide from the country's foremost relationship expert*. Harmony Books.

Hojatt, M. & Cramer, D. (2013). *Positive psychology of love*. Oxford University Press.

Markman, H. J., Stanley, S. M. & Blumberg, S. L. (2010). *Fighting for your marriage* (3rd ed.). Jossey-Bass.

Northrup, C., Schwartz, P. & Witte, J. (2013). *The normal bar: The surprising secrets of happy couples and what they reveal about creating a new normal in your relationship*. Harmony.

Orenstein, P. (2016). *Girls and sex: Navigating the complicated new landscape*. Harper.

Pileggi Pawelski, P. & Pawelski, J.O. (2018). *Happy together: Using the science of positive psychology to build love that lasts*. TarcherPerigee.

Quilliam, S. (2017). *How to choose a partner*. Picador.

Wade, L. (2017). *American hookup: The new culture of sex on campus*. Norton.

Weigel, M. (2016). *Labor of love: The invention of dating*. Farrar, Straus and Giroux.

Young, L. & Alexander, B. (2012). *The chemistry between us: Love, sex, and the science of attraction*. Current.

Pregnancy is an opportunity for sex education.

# 8

# Fertility, Pregnancy, and Childbirth

In earlier chapters we described the production and release of gametes (sperm and ova), the site where they meet (one of the woman's oviducts), and the process by which the resulting embryo differentiates as male or female. We now take a broader look at pregnancy and childbirth from the perspectives of both the conceptus and its parents. In this chapter we assume that couples want to become parents—and parents of healthy children. We will see how a couple can optimize their chances of achieving this goal and how medical science has improved their odds of doing so. In Chapter 9 we will take the opposite tack, looking at strategies to prevent pregnancy and childbirth.

## 8.1 Pregnancy and Childbirth Raise Major Health Concerns

**LEARNING OBJECTIVE**

After reading this section you should be able to:

**8.1.1** Describe current trends in birth statistics in the United States.

In the past, pregnancy and childbirth were events to which women looked forward with a mixture of joy and terror. Joy, because producing and rearing children defined much of a woman's existence. And terror, not just because of the pain of childbirth, but because of the grave risk that pregnancy would end in the death of mother, baby, or both.

Before the advent of modern medicine, no amount of wealth or power could avert the tragic risks of reproduction. Remember England's King Henry VIII (1491–1547) and his six wives? Yes, he had a couple of them beheaded, but two of the remaining four—Jane Seymour and Catherine Parr—died in or soon after childbirth. Of these six women's 11 children, most died in infancy, and only 3 reached adulthood. Memorials to the millions of women who have died in childbirth are everywhere, from India's fabled Taj Mahal to a humble stone in the pioneers' graveyard at Coloma, California, that records the death of 32-year-old Hannah Seater and her newborn son in 1852.

Today the prospects for pregnant women and their fetuses are far brighter than in the past (CDC, 2019g). If we exclude pregnancies that are terminated by induced abortion, 80% of all established pregnancies in the United States culminate in the delivery of a live child. Once a child is born, it has a better than 99% chance of surviving through infancy. And only about 17 per 100,000 pregnancies now lead to the death of the mother. Still, even this figure is worse than the maternal death rates for Canada and many other countries, and the statistics on infant and maternal mortality are worse for some U.S. minorities than they are for the general population. Of all the maternal deaths that occur in the United States, three out of five are preventable, according to the CDC.

Of course, parents want not just a live-born child, but also one who is in the best possible shape to face the rigors of life "on the outside." To achieve this goal, it helps for prospective parents to learn as much as possible about pregnancy, childbirth, and the factors that promote or compromise the health of the mother and her fetus.

Some key facts concerning U.S. birthrates are listed in **BOX 8.1**.

## 8.2 The Fertilization of an Ovum Is Followed by Implantation

**LEARNING OBJECTIVES**

After reading this section you should be able to:

**8.2.1** Describe how and where fertilization and implantation take place.

**8.2.2** Explain the role of human chorionic gonadotropin (hCG) in the establishment of pregnancy.

After semen is ejaculated into a woman's vagina, some spermatozoa rapidly enter the cervix. Those that do not are inactivated within less than an hour by the acidic environment of the vagina. Poor-quality sperm tend to be left behind, so the sperm that reach the cervix are the healthier, more motile ones.

Although spermatozoa are motile, transport from the cervix to the oviducts is mostly passive—it is brought about by peristaltic movements of the cervix, uterus, and oviducts (Brannigan & Lipshultz, 2017). In fact, either sperm or inanimate particles placed in the vagina can reach an oviduct within 5 minutes, which is much too fast for sperm to get there by their own efforts. This passive transport is directed primarily toward whichever oviduct is on the side of the ovary that is ovulating during the current menstrual cycle.

**FAQ:** Can a man get pregnant?

Disregarding Arnold Schwarzenegger in *Junior* (1994), the only men who can become pregnant are transgender men who have not had genital surgery and who stop testosterone treatment.

## BOX 8.1
## Birth Facts

In the United States, birthrates are declining. In 2018, the general fertility rate—the overall birthrate in that year—reached an all-time low of 59 births per 1,000 women age 15 to 44. The statistically average woman now has 1.7 children over her lifetime, well below the level required to keep the population level stable in the absence of immigration (about 2.1 children), and far below historical levels (see figure). Here are some more specific numbers:

- The birthrate for teenagers (age 15 to 19) is falling especially rapidly. In 2018 it reached an all-time low of 17.4 births per 1,000 females, representing a 7% decline from the previous year and a 74% drop from 1960.
- The birthrates for women over 30 and over 40 are increasing at a rate of about 1% per year. Social factors and improved fertility treatments are probably responsible.
- Today 40% of all births are to unmarried mothers.
- The percentage of all births that are twin births is holding steady at about 3%, but the numbers of triplets and higher multiples is declining rapidly and is now down by nearly one-half from the peak rate reached in 1998. This drop is probably due to changes to IVF procedures (implantation of fewer embryos).
- One in three babies are delivered by cesarean section.
- Less than 1% of all babies are born at home.

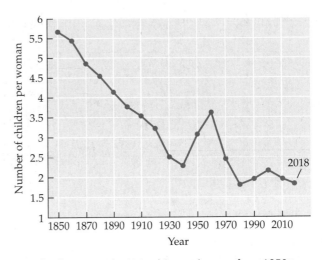

Total fertility rate in the United States, by year from 1850 to 2018. This rate is the average number of children born to a theoretical woman who spends her entire life in the stated year. The 1950–1960 peak results from the post–World War II baby boom; it reflects a shift in the timing of births due to the war, not an increase in the fertility of real women.

*Source*: Data from various sources including J. A. Martin et al. 2019. *National Vital Statistics Reports* 68(13): 1–46. National Center for Health Statistics (NCHS): Hyattsville, MD; J. A. Martin et al. 2010. *National Vital Statistics Reports* 59(1): 1–71. NCHS: Hyattsville, MD; National Center for Health Statistics. *Vital statistics of the United States: 2003, Volume I, Natality*. NCHS: Hyattsville, MD.

---

Sperm that reach the distant end of the oviduct—the end adjacent to the ovary—are fully capable of fertilizing an ovum, but they die within a short time if they fail to do so. Yet we know that sperm can live for up to 6 days in a woman's body, because a woman can become pregnant if she ovulates as much as 6 days after coitus. The explanation for this apparent paradox is that the bulk of the sperm are held back in a "reservoir" at the near end of the oviduct, where they remain in a quiescent state. They are released from the reservoir gradually over a period of a few days; this mechanism allows for fertilization even if coitus and ovulation are not optimally timed (Rodriguez-Martinez, 2007).

Ovulation is the discharge of an ovum from an ovary into the open (internal) end of an oviduct. The ovum is a single very large cell—a female gamete—surrounded by a protective coating called the **zona pellucida**. Once it enters the oviduct, the ovum begins to release a specific chemical attractant, which draws spermatozoa toward the ovum. When a sperm reaches the ovum, its acrosome (see Figure 3.17) breaks down, releasing enzymes that digest the zona pellucida, and allowing the sperm to enter the ovum's cytoplasm. This event is **fertilization**, and it takes place near the open end of the oviduct, far away from the uterus. The single cell produced by fusion of ovum and sperm is called a **zygote**. Once fertilization occurs, no further sperm can enter the ovum.

**zona pellucida** The protective membrane surrounding an ovum and early embryo.

**fertilization** The entry of a spermatozoon into an ovum.

**zygote** A cell produced by fusion of male and female gametes—a fertilized ovum.

**FAQ:** Does conception mean the same thing as fertilization?

In this textbook, yes. Some people use it to mean implantation.

**▲ FIGURE 8.1**   **A human embryo hatching from its zona pellucida** This is a colorized scanning electron micrograph.

**embryo**   In humans, the developing individual up until about 8 weeks of pregnancy.

**implantation**   The attachment of the embryo to the endometrium.

**human chorionic gonadotropin (hCG)**   A hormone secreted by the placenta that maintains the corpus luteum and thus keeps progesterone levels high enough to sustain pregnancy.

About 24 hours after fertilization the zygote divides into two cells, and from then on the new organism is usually called an **embryo**.* The embryo begins migrating down the oviduct toward the uterus, a journey of a few days. Meanwhile, the lining of the uterus is being put into readiness to receive it. This process is initiated by progesterone secreted by the ovary (specifically, by the corpus luteum) during the postovulatory phase of the woman's menstrual cycle.

During its journey the embryo continues to undergo cell divisions, so by the time it reaches the uterus, it consists of a few hundred cells, still confined within the original zona pellucida. Having reached the uterus, the embryo hatches from the zona pellucida (**FIGURE 8.1**) and burrows into the uterine lining—the endometrium. This step is called **implantation**.

Once implanted, the embryo begins to secrete a hormone known as **human chorionic gonadotropin** (**hCG**). This hormone acts on the ovaries to prevent the next menstruation from occurring, and a missed menstrual period is the usual way that a woman learns that she is pregnant.

Many embryos fail to implant, or they only implant briefly and are then lost. In such cases the embryo simply disintegrates and its remains are washed out of the woman's body during her next menstrual period. The woman has no way of knowing that an embryo has existed. Thus, doctors say that pregnancy is "established" only after successful implantation, not at fertilization. In fact, it is thought that only a minority of all zygotes develop to the point of an established pregnancy. Many that do not do so are abnormal in some way, such as possessing an atypical number of chromosomes.

## 8.3   Pregnancy Is Confirmed by Hormonal Tests

### LEARNING OBJECTIVE

After reading this section you should be able to:

8.3.1   **Explain how it is determined whether a woman is pregnant.**

The absence of a menstrual period at the expected time is not a totally reliable indicator of pregnancy. Many women have irregular periods anyway, and even a woman whose menstrual cycle is normally very regular can experience a missed or delayed period due to illness, stress, or some other reason. Conversely, some "spotting" (light bleeding) can occur even when a woman is pregnant. Other symptoms may help to confirm the pregnancy, including breast tenderness, fatigue, and nausea (the beginning of the "morning sickness" that can plague some women during the first 3 months of pregnancy).

Pregnancy tests are designed to test for the presence of hCG in the mother's blood or urine. The most sensitive (and expensive) laboratory tests can detect hCG in the mother's blood almost immediately after implantation—several days *before* a woman would notice a missed period. To get a laboratory test, a woman must see a health care provider.

Another option is to purchase a home pregnancy test kit (**FIGURE 8.2**). These products are convenient and inexpensive—about 20 million are sold in the United States every year. Various brands are available, ranging in price from about $8 to $20. They show the result by the presence or absence of a

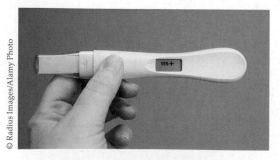

**▲ FIGURE 8.2**   **Home pregnancy test** The user holds one end of the test stick in her urine stream for a few seconds (or dips it into a collected urine sample). This is a digital test. (See **Animation 8.1: How a Home Pregnancy Test Works**.)

---

*Strictly speaking, it is a *conceptus*: It does not become an embryo until 2 weeks after conception, when the nonembryonic tissues, such as the fetal membranes and placenta, have separated from the cells that will give rise to the fetus.

colored line on the test strip, a plus or minus sign, or by the words "pregnant" or "not pregnant" displayed on a screen.

Unfortunately, home pregnancy tests are not nearly as reliable as laboratory tests. In independent studies, many tests have not shown the level of sensitivity claimed by the manufacturers (Cole, 2012; Johnson et al., 2015). Experts recommend waiting to perform a test until 1 week after the date of a missed period, regardless of what it says on the test kit's packaging (Mayo Clinic, 2019c). A negative result obtained before that time should be followed up with a second test a few days later. It is a good idea to perform the test early in the morning, when the urine is concentrated.

Definitive clinical evidence of pregnancy can be obtained at 5 to 6 weeks by means of an **ultrasound scan**. This can determine whether one or more embryos are present, and 2 to 3 weeks later it can detect the fetal heartbeat.

**FAQ:** Will a home pregnancy test detect an ectopic pregnancy?

Not necessarily, because the urinary levels of hCG may be lower than with a uterine pregnancy.

## 8.4 Infertility Can Result from a Problem in the Woman or in the Man

### LEARNING OBJECTIVES
After reading this section you should be able to:

8.4.1 Describe the possible causes of male infertility.

8.4.2 Explain the procedures for in vitro fertilization.

8.4.3 Evaluate the possible causes of female infertility and how these may be overcome.

8.4.4 Explain what causes Down syndrome, its symptoms, and its relationship to maternal age.

For a healthy young couple who are having sex several times a week without any form of contraception, there is about a 20% chance of pregnancy per month. This translates into a 93% chance within the first year. **Infertility** is the term used to describe failure to achieve pregnancy after that period of time. This doesn't mean that there is no further chance of pregnancy, but rather that an investigation to find out why pregnancy has not occurred is warranted.

Infertility is surprisingly common—it affects about 15% of couples worldwide (Agarwal et al., 2015). Fertility problems can be caused by a disorder on the man's side or the woman's side. In about one-third of cases, there are problems on both sides, or the cause can't be identified.

**ultrasound scan** An imaging procedure that depends on the reflection of ultrasonic waves from density boundaries within the body. Also called ultrasonographic scan.

**infertility** Inability (of a man, woman, or couple) to achieve pregnancy.

**subfertility** Difficulty in establishing a pregnancy; arbitrarily defined as the absence of pregnancy after a couple has had frequent unprotected sex for 12 months.

### A variety of factors can reduce sperm counts

A common cause for difficulty in getting pregnant is that the man is producing insufficient or poor-quality sperm. Sperm-related problems are the cause of about 25% of all couples' difficulties in achieving pregnancy. The usual rule of thumb is that a man is likely to be **subfertile** (i.e., have difficulty becoming a father) if he has fewer than 20 million sperm per milliliter of semen, or if the fraction of his sperm that move normally is less than 50%. Sperm abnormalities (**FIGURE 8.3**) can also impair fertility.

There are many potential causes for low sperm counts:

- Undescended testicles, sex chromosome anomalies, infections that cause blockage of the reproductive tract, and intensive chemotherapy can all cause irreversible reduction or failure of spermatogenesis.

- Heating of the testes, as can occur with too-tight clothing, causes a lowered sperm count that is usually reversible.

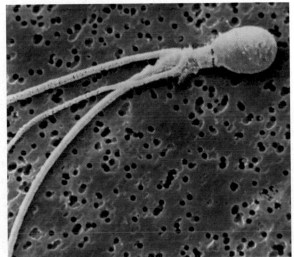

▲ **FIGURE 8.3** Abnormal (multi-tailed) sperm

© Scimat/Science Source

- Men who don't exercise have low sperm counts, but so do men who follow intense training regimens. The sweet spot is in the range of mild to moderate exercise (Hayden et al., 2018).
- Smoking—including marijuana smoking—lowers sperm counts.
- Environmental toxins such as pesticides can lower sperm counts, and they are suspected of having contributed to a general reduction in sperm counts in the United States and other countries over the last several decades, as was discussed in Box 3.4. Men who consume a great deal of fruit and vegetables should try to keep pesticide intake low—by choosing organic produce, for example.
- Normal aging is associated with a gradual decrease in the volume of a man's ejaculate, as well as an increase in the numbers of sperm that are misshapen, move poorly, or contain damaged DNA.
- Finally, genetic factors can impair sperm function in some men (**BOX 8.2**).

## BOX 8.2
# The Scent of an Ovum

We mentioned earlier that spermatozoa are drawn toward the ovum by a chemical attractant. This attractant is thought to be **bourgeonal** or a related molecule. Bourgeonal is a fragrant oil that has an attractive scent similar to that of lily-of-the-valley flowers, and it is a common ingredient in women's perfumes. Unlike the case with almost any other odor, men are more sensitive to bourgeonal than women are, but even among men there's considerable variability in how readily they can detect it. That's because of slight person-to-person variations in the DNA sequence of the gene that codes for the bourgeonal receptor.

This receptor is present not just in the nose, but also on the surface of spermatozoa. This fact motivated two research groups to ask whether problems with the bourgeonal receptor might contribute to male infertility (Ottaviano et al., 2013; Sinding et al., 2013). And sure enough, both groups found that men who were infertile for unknown reasons—that is, the numbers, appearance, and motility of their sperm were all normal—could not smell bourgeonal as well as men of normal fertility. One of the groups went further: They found that the infertile men's sperm were less strongly attracted to a source of bourgeonal than were those of other men, and that they tended to carry certain specific variants of the bourgeonal receptor gene—variants that presumably made the receptor less sensitive. Because this kind of male infertility is caused by the sperm's inability to home in on the ovum, it can be alleviated by in vitro fertilization, in which this step is bypassed.

Lilies-of-the-valley are the traditional flowers carried by brides at their weddings (see figure). Is that because their

Catherine Middleton carried lilies-of-the-valley to her 2011 wedding with Britain's Prince William.

scent is irresistible to their grooms? Perhaps the scene at the altar is a pre-enactment of what may take place, a few hours later, in the woman's oviduct?

**bourgeonal** A floral-scented compound that may be an attractant for spermatozoa.

In cases of problems with sperm quality, a couple can take various steps to achieve pregnancy. If sperm numbers are too low, semen can be collected over a period of time and frozen. Then the entire collected amount can be placed in the woman's vagina or directly into her uterus at a time coinciding with ovulation. This procedure is called **artificial insemination**. If the sperm come from the woman's partner, the technique is usually called artificial insemination by husband, or AIH (although the man could actually be the woman's unmarried partner). Men with normal sperm counts may also store their own sperm for future AIH use.

## Sperm can be donated

Sometimes the male partner is completely infertile, or the couple does not want to use his sperm—as, for example, when he carries a gene for a serious disorder. In such cases, a woman can use **artificial insemination by donor** (**AID**). In this procedure, sperm from a third party are placed in the woman's vagina or uterus.

**Sperm banks** provide suitable semen at a cost of $200 per vial and up. Sperm donors are usually college students who are paid a small fee—typically $50 to $100—to donate semen (by masturbation). Donors can be either totally anonymous or "open-ID," meaning that a child resulting from the donation may contact the donor once he or she has reached the age of 18. There are also private individuals who will donate semen without charge: They can be contacted via the internet, either directly or through a website such as KnownDonorRegistry.com.

A potential problem with sperm donation is that two children fathered by the same donor with different women may unwittingly commit incest when they become adults and therefore produce offspring with an increased risk of inherited disorders (Mroz, 2011). For that reason many American sperm banks set limits on the number of women who can receive sperm from a single donor.

Women who use sperm donors on account of fertility problems are outnumbered by women who do so for other reasons, such as that they are single or are partnered with another woman.

DNA testing has uncovered a disturbing number of cases in which fertility doctors have used their own sperm for AID without the knowledge or consent of their patients. This practice has been criminalized in several states (Mroz, 2019).

## In vitro fertilization can circumvent many sperm problems

Some sperm quality problems may require the use of **in vitro fertilization** (**IVF**). "In vitro" means "in glass," but it's actually in a plastic petri dish. In the standard IVF procedure (**FIGURE 8.4**), the woman is given hormones to promote the development of a group of follicles on a precisely timed schedule. When the follicles are nearly ready to ovulate, a needle is passed into each follicle under ultrasound control, and the ovum is removed by suction. As many as two dozen ova can be harvested in a single procedure. The collected ova are placed in a petri dish, and the man's sperm are then added.

If the man's sperm are not capable of performing even this simplified fertilization task, further variations on IVF are available. The most popular is **intracytoplasmic sperm injection** (**ICSI**), in which a single sperm is injected directly into the ovum by means of a very fine pipette. In fact, even a man who produces no mature sperm at all may be able to father a child: Precursor cells can be used instead. These are harvested by needle aspiration of one of the man's testicles.

Regardless of the exact IVF procedure used, the artificially fertilized ova are usually kept in tissue culture for several days, during which time they divide several times (**FIGURE 8.5**). It is possible at this stage to remove a cell from each embryo without harming it, which allows the chromosomal or genetic makeup of the removed cell to be studied. This **preimplantation genetic screening** (**PGS**) is useful if one of the parents carries a

**artificial insemination** An assisted reproduction technique that involves the placement of semen in the vagina or uterus with the aid of a syringe or small tube.

**artificial insemination by donor (AID)** Artificial insemination using sperm from a man who is not the woman's partner.

**sperm bank** A facility that collects, stores, and provides semen for artificial insemination.

**in vitro fertilization (IVF)** Any of a variety of assisted reproduction techniques in which fertilization takes place outside the body.

**intracytoplasmic sperm injection (ICSI)** Fertilization of an ovum by injection of a single sperm into it.

**preimplantation genetic screening (PGS)** Testing of in vitro fertilization embryos for genetic defects prior to implantation.

(A)

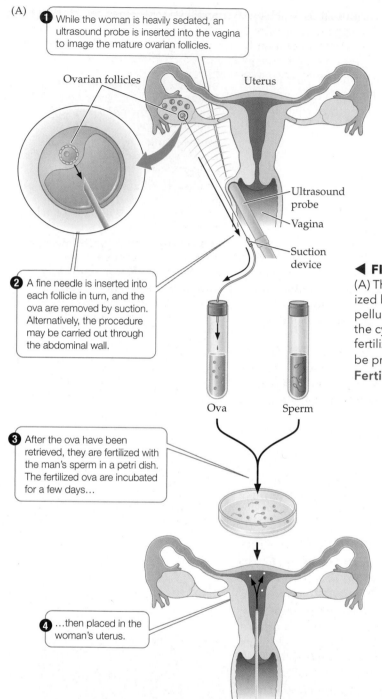

**①** While the woman is heavily sedated, an ultrasound probe is inserted into the vagina to image the mature ovarian follicles.

Ovarian follicles

Uterus

Ultrasound probe

Vagina

Suction device

**②** A fine needle is inserted into each follicle in turn, and the ova are removed by suction. Alternatively, the procedure may be carried out through the abdominal wall.

Ova

Sperm

**③** After the ova have been retrieved, they are fertilized with the man's sperm in a petri dish. The fertilized ova are incubated for a few days…

**④** …then placed in the woman's uterus.

(B)

© david gregs/Alamy Stock Photo

◀ **FIGURE 8.4** **Standard in vitro fertilization**
(A) The steps in the procedure. (B) An ovum being fertilized by sperm in vitro. Many sperm attach to the zona pellucida—the coat around the ovum—but only one enters the cytoplasm of the ovum and fertilizes it. In a natural fertilization within a woman's oviduct, fewer sperm would be present. (See **Animation 8.2: Standard In Vitro Fertilization**.)

disease-causing gene and the couple wants to ensure that their child does not inherit it (Harper & Sengupta, 2012). PGS technology, which is rapidly advancing, presents significant ethical issues (Hens et al., 2013). For example, it allows for would-be parents to choose the sex of their child, even when there is no medical reason to make such a choice (**BOX 8.3**).

A small number of embryos are then placed in the woman's uterus simultaneously—enough to give a reasonable chance that at least one of them will implant and become a fetus. If several implant, the woman is offered the opportunity to have the number reduced by selective abortion (often called "fetal reduction"), but this practice can present risks to the remaining fetuses, and it may also cause psychological problems for some women.

Most of the high-number multiple births that have attracted headlines over the past few years involve mothers who have undergone IVF or other assisted reproduction procedures (see below) and have declined abortion. High-number multiple pregnancies are associated with all kinds of serious risks to the fetuses and the mother. According to professional guidelines, healthy young women should receive either one or two embryos on their first IVF attempt (American Society for Reproductive Medicine, 2013).

A more common problem, however, is not multiple but zero pregnancies: In 2017, only 27% of all IVF attempts in the United States led to a live birth (Society for Assisted Reproductive Technology, 2019). Couples may have to repeat the procedure several times, with no guarantee of ultimate success. The prospects are particularly poor for women over age 40 who use their own ova. Still, over 70,000

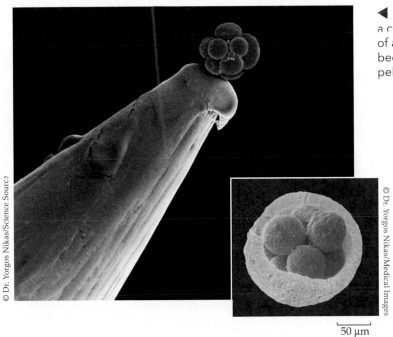

◀ **FIGURE 8.5** **A human embryo** (more accurately called a conceptus), perched on the tip of a pin. The embryo consists of about 10 cells and is 3–4 days old. The zona pellucida has been removed. The inset shows an embryo with the zona pellucida still partially intact.

© Dr. Yorgos Nikas/Science Source

© Dr. Yorgos Nikas/Medical Images

50 μm

babies are born in the United States every year by IVF and related methods, collectively known as **assisted reproductive technologies** (**ART**). These represent nearly 2% of all U.S. births.

IVF is expensive: A single basic treatment cycle, including drugs, costs about $15,000, but clinics often talk women into paying for add-ons of dubious value (Wilkinson et al., 2019). Given that repeated cycles may be necessary, the total bill often exceeds $50,000.

There do remain questions about the safety of ART. ART pregnancies are high-risk pregnancies, and children conceived through ART face a greater likelihood of health problems than those conceived naturally (Esteves et al., 2018). This has partly to do with the health issues in the parents that caused the infertility in the first place. For example, men conceived by ICSI have low sperm counts, probably because they have inherited this problem from their fathers (Belva et al., 2016). ART also introduces its own risks, however, especially because of the higher incidence of multiple births and low birth weight (CDC, 2019a). ART doesn't yet imitate nature closely enough.

### Abnormalities of the female reproductive tract may reduce fertility

The second most common group of conditions affecting fertility are abnormalities of the woman's reproductive tract. Such conditions are responsible for about 20% of infertility cases. The most common site of abnormalities is the oviducts. They can become scarred, obstructed, or denuded of cilia as a consequence of **pelvic inflammatory disease** (**PID**)—a general term for infections of the uterus or oviducts, usually caused by sexually transmitted organisms, such as chlamydia or gonorrhea (see Chapter 15). In such cases it is possible to bypass the oviducts by performing IVF and placing the resulting embryos directly into the uterus. Uterine fibroids and endometriosis can also reduce fertility, which can sometimes be restored by surgery.

### Failure to ovulate can be dealt with by drugs or by egg donation

Another 20% or so of infertility cases are caused by problems with ovulation. We mentioned the failure to begin menstrual cycles at puberty—primary amenorrhea—in

**assisted reproductive technology (ART)** In vitro fertilization and related technologies.

**pelvic inflammatory disease (PID)** An infection of the female reproductive tract, often caused by sexually transmitted organisms.

## BOX 8.3
## Choosing Children's Sex

As they plan for pregnancy, some couples would prefer their children to be of a particular sex, either male or female. At times their preference has a specific medical reason. In particular, if the child is at risk of inheriting a genetic disorder that crops up predominantly in one sex, the couple may want a child of the other sex. This usually means a girl, because most sex-linked disorders affect boys. More commonly, couples want a child of a particular sex for some social reason. For example, they may have one or more children of one sex and now want to "balance" the family with a child of the other sex.

In many cultures boys are commonly preferred over girls. Boys are wanted because they will help with farmwork, because they will bring money into the family, or because their children will carry on the family name. Girls are less desired in some cultures because marrying them off requires hefty bridal payments or because they may be lost to their birth family after marriage and therefore will not support the parents in their old age.

In the past, there has been much "folk wisdom" about how to have a child of a particular sex, but only one technique has actually worked: killing or abandoning newborn children of the unwanted sex. Female infanticide still persists to some extent in India and China. However, the introduction of obstetric ultrasound has provided a simple and inexpensive means to visualize a fetus's genitals and hence to determine its sex, and this can be done as early as 12 to 14 weeks of pregnancy. As a consequence, the practice of aborting female fetuses has become prevalent in some countries, especially India and China, and the sex ratio of newborn children has become skewed toward males. In China, for example, about 113 boys are born for every 100 girls (Zhou, 2016). In both China and India sex-selective abortion is now illegal, and in India it is even illegal to inform a woman about the sex of her fetus. Still, the practice continues (see figure). Strangely, the tiny European country of Liechtenstein has the world's most skewed sex ratio at birth, with 126 boys born for every 100 girls in 2018, according to the CIA's World Factbook (Central Intelligence Agency, 2019).

Considerable efforts have been devoted to the development of methods for selecting a child's sex before pregnancy

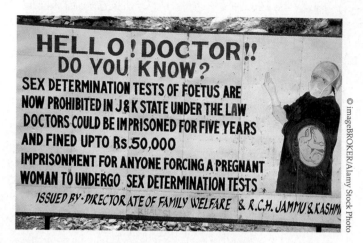

In spite of signs such as this, many pregnant Indian women are able to find out whether they are carrying a female or male fetus.

is established. Because X chromosomes are larger than Y chromosomes, X-bearing sperm contain slightly more total DNA than Y-bearing sperm. A technique called flow cytometry can sense this difference and thus sort out the two kinds of sperm, but not with 100% accuracy. The most reliable method is preimplantation genetic screening. Several embryos are produced by in vitro fertilization, a single cell is removed from each embryo for sex determination, and only embryos of the preferred sex are implanted in the woman's uterus. Although this is mostly done to avoid sex-linked diseases, some fertility clinics also offer the service for the purpose of "family balancing." In the future it may not even be necessary to remove an embryonic cell, because sufficient embryonic DNA to determine an embryo's sex may be obtained from the fluid in which it is cultured (Shamonki et al., 2016).

As with so many issues in the area of reproductive technology, the possibility of selecting children's sex triggers strong reactions. Some say that the practice is morally offensive or will have bad social consequences, such as a skewed sex ratio. Others say that it is a good idea because children will be more like what their parents want and therefore more loved. Some say the practice should be banned; others believe it should be left up to the mother, or to both parents, to decide. What's your opinion?

Chapter 2. A postpubertal (but premenopausal) woman may also stop cycling or cycle irregularly. These conditions can be caused by weight loss, intense athletic training, stress, certain drugs, a pituitary tumor, or reduced ovarian function. Sometimes, failure to ovulate can occur in a woman who is experiencing normal menstrual periods. Most ovulatory problems can be reversed by lifestyle changes, drug treatment, or psychotherapy (if the cause is an eating disorder, for example).

If the woman's own ova cannot be used, she can obtain them from donors. Obtaining ova from female donors is more complex and expensive than sperm donation, however, because the donor must undergo hormone treatment followed by surgical aspiration of the ova from the ovaries, as described earlier for IVF (see Figure 8.4). The donors—who are often college students—are typically paid a few thousand dollars. For both sperm and ova donations, there is a market for donors who are perceived to have desirable traits, and higher fees may be paid in such cases, especially for ova.

## Surrogate mothers bear children for others

If the woman cannot sustain a pregnancy at all—say, because she was born without a uterus, or her uterus is malformed or has been removed, or because her general medical condition makes pregnancy inadvisable—an option is to use a **surrogate mother**. Gay male couples who wish to have children may also make use of this option, as may single men, whether gay or straight.

In traditional surrogacy the surrogate agrees to be artificially (or naturally) inseminated by the male would-be parent, or her ova are fertilized by IVF using his sperm; she then carries the resulting fetus or fetuses to term. Thus the surrogate is the genetic mother of the fetus. In **gestational surrogacy** an embryo is created by IVF, using gametes from both would-be parents or from donors, and it is placed in the uterus of the surrogate. Thus the gestational surrogate is not genetically related to the fetus at all—her fetus could be of a different race, for example.

The motivation of a woman to act as a gestational surrogate can be either altruistic or commercial, or some combination of the two. In altruistic surrogacy the woman is not recompensed beyond her medical and living expenses. Often an altruistic surrogate is a relative of the would-be mother, such as her sister. Even unrelated women can be motivated by altruism, however. "Being a surrogate is like giving an organ transplant to someone, only before you die," one woman told a *Newsweek* magazine reporter, "and you actually get to see their joy" (Ali & Kelley, 2008).

In commercial surrogacy the surrogate's motivation is to make money. Some American women act as commercial surrogates—the wives of servicemen who are overseas for long periods sometimes earn money in this fashion. The legal status of surrogacy varies greatly from state to state; most surrogacies are arranged in states such as California where surrogacy contracts are fully recognized. In some other states, such as Michigan, surrogacy contracts are illegal and unenforceable. Wikipedia maintains a page that lists the current legal status of surrogacy and surrogacy contracts on a state-by-state basis.

Alternatively, the surrogate may live in a foreign country—usually a much poorer country than the one where the would-be parents live. Many countries have banned commercial surrogacy, however. India, once a major center for "surrogacy tourism," banned international surrogacy in 2015. In fact there is a move to ban all commercial surrogacy in that country.

A new option may be on the horizon for women without a uterus, which is to receive a uterus transplant. This procedure was pioneered in Sweden; the first baby born in the United States after a living-donor transplant was delivered at Baylor University Medical Center in 2017, and the first after a deceased-donor transplant was born in 2019 at the Cleveland Clinic. The procedure is still considered experimental.

## Adoption is limited by the supply of healthy infants

Adoption is a low-tech but often very successful way for infertile couples to have children. In the United States, about 60,000 children are adopted through public agencies annually; additional children are adopted privately (Children's Bureau, 2018).

Many more people want to adopt than actually get an adopted child. That's because there has been a major decline in the availability of children for adoption over the last 100 years; the main reason for this has been the greater willingness of unmarried mothers to keep their babies, but legalized abortion and better access to

**surrogate mother** A woman who carries a pregnancy on behalf of another woman or couple.

**gestational surrogacy** A surrogate pregnancy in which the ovum is provided by some other woman than the surrogate mother.

**▲ FIGURE 8.6 Age and infertility**
The graph shows the percentage of women, grouped by age at marriage, who remain childless after a first marriage in spite of continued efforts to produce a child. Note that the likelihood of infertility rises rapidly in the mid-30s. (After M. H. Johnson and B. J. Everitt. 2000. *Essential Reproduction*, 5th Ed. Blackwell: Hoboken, NJ.)

**Down syndrome** A collection of birth defects caused by the presence of an extra copy of chromosome 21.

contraception may also have played a role. Children who are less preferred for a variety of reasons—they are older, they belong to racial/ethnic minorities, they have disabilities, or they belong to sibships that want to be adopted together—are more readily available.

Adopting from overseas is an alternative, though usually an arduous and expensive one. The numbers of overseas adoptions dropped from 23,000 to 4,000 between 2004 and 2018 (U.S. Department of State, 2019). The reasons for the dramatic fall-off in international adoptions include improving economic conditions in the source countries, as well as legal restrictions placed by those countries' governments and by the 2008 Hague Convention.

## Fertility declines with age

A major factor affecting fertility is age—of both the woman and the man. You might imagine that couples stay completely fertile until the woman's menopause, whereupon fertility drops to zero. In reality, fertility drops off steadily beginning in young adulthood, as shown in **FIGURE 8.6**. Already by their mid-30s, about one in four couples is infertile. This decline in fertility has several causes, including more frequent failures to ovulate, decreasing sperm counts and sperm quality, and an increased likelihood of spontaneous abortion early in pregnancy. Age-related infertility is an increasingly important issue because American women have been postponing motherhood: The mean age at which women have their first child rose from 24.9 to 26.8 between 2000 and 2017 and is higher in some groups, such as Asian-Americans (National Vital Statistics Reports, 2017). One strategy to cope with this problem is for the woman to have her eggs frozen early in adulthood for use at a later time. Some companies are starting to pay for this procedure for their employees.

Children who are born to older parents, especially older mothers, also stand a greater risk of having chromosomal abnormalities. One of these causes **Down syndrome**, named for the English physician, John Langdon Down, who first described it in 1862. The chromosomal basis of the disorder was discovered almost a century later by a French research group: Individuals with Down syndrome have an extra copy of chromosome 21 (i.e., three copies instead of two). The extra chromosome results from an error in the meiotic cell divisions that take place during the maturation of gametes prior to fertilization (see Appendix A).

Down syndrome usually includes mild or moderate intellectual disability and a characteristic facial appearance (**FIGURE 8.7**). It affects 1 in 2,000 births at a maternal age of 20, 1 in 900 at age 30, 1 in 100 at age 40, and 1 in 10 at age 49 (National Down Syndrome

**▶ FIGURE 8.7 Down syndrome** (A) A teen with Down syndrome; the syndrome is marked by a characteristic facial appearance and sometimes by other physical anomalies. (B) Chromosome set of a person with Down syndrome, showing the three copies (circled) of chromosome 21.

Society, 2019). Because the great majority of babies are born to younger women, however, four out of five children with Down syndrome are born to women *under* 35. For that reason, current guidelines call for screening for Down syndrome to be offered to all pregnant women, regardless of their age.

Increasing paternal age does not affect the risk of Down syndrome (Thompson, 2019), but it does increase the likelihood that the child will suffer from physical malformations, as well as mental conditions such as autism spectrum disorders and schizophrenia (Mazur & Lipshultz, 2018). This results in part from the accumulation of damaged DNA in the stem cells that maintain a man's sperm supply. In fact, because these cells have to go through so many more rounds of cell division than the equivalent cells in females, fathers are the source of about 80% of all the new mutations that are passed on to the next generation (Jonsson et al., 2017).

In one study, the sons of older fathers were more likely to be "geeks" than those of younger men, where "geekiness" was defined as the combination of social aloofness, mildly restrictive or repetitive behavior, and high intelligence (Janecka et al., 2017). Although geekiness shares some characteristics with mild forms of autism spectrum disorder, it may be an advantageous personality trait in today's knowledge-based economy.

A postmenopausal woman can become pregnant with the aid of reproductive technology: Donated ova can be fertilized in vitro (usually with her husband's sperm), and the embryos can be placed in her uterus. The pregnancy must be supported with hormone treatments. Two Indian women became mothers by this procedure when they were reportedly 70 years old.

© Barcroft Media/Getty Images

▲ Daljinder Kaur, reported to be age 70, and her 79-year-old husband, with their newborn son Arman in 2016.

## 8.5 Many Embryos Do Not Survive

### LEARNING OBJECTIVES
After reading this section you should be able to:

8.5.1 Explain why Rh incompatibility can affect a woman's later pregnancies but not her first one.

8.5.2 Describe the possible causes of ectopic pregnancy and how it is treated.

Nature has not completely mastered the intricate task of creating a normal embryo. Some large fraction—perhaps more than 50%—of all human embryos are genetically abnormal and have little or no chance of giving rise to a viable child. Most of these abnormalities cause defects at the very earliest stages of development. If the ovum is fertilized by two sperm rather than one, for example, the resulting embryo will have three sets of chromosomes rather than the normal two. In some cases, environmental factors such as alcohol consumption, general anesthesia, or X-ray exposure at around the time of ovulation may trigger chromosomal abnormalities.

The great majority of abnormal embryos are lost at some point in their development. Many fail to implant, and the mothers are never aware of their existence. Others implant briefly, causing a transient release of hCG and a slight prolongation of the postovulatory phase, but then die, so menstruation ensues. Of pregnancies that proceed far enough to be detected clinically, about 20% are subsequently lost by spontaneous abortion, usually during the first 3 months. At least half of those have chromosomal abnormalities. In fetuses that make it to term, only 1 in 200 has a chromosomal abnormality.

### Rh factor incompatibility can threaten second pregnancies

One major cause of fetal loss is blood group incompatibility, especially when the fetus possesses the blood group antigen known as **Rh factor**\* and the mother does not

**FAQ:** I have a birth defect. Will I pass it on to my children?

Children of mothers with birth defects have an increased risk of being born with the same defect, especially for cleft palate/lip and limb defects (Skjaerven et al., 1999). Still, 96% of the children of mothers with birth defects are free of all defects. The effects of paternal defects have not been well studied but are likely to be similar.

**Rh factor**   An antigen on the surface of red blood cells that, when present in a fetus but not in its mother, may trigger an immune response by the mother.

---

\*Rh is short for rhesus, a species of monkey that was originally thought to carry this antigen.

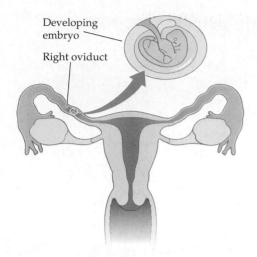

Developing embryo

Right oviduct

▲ **FIGURE 8.8** Ectopic pregnancy can occur in the oviduct (as shown here), on the ovary or cervix, or elsewhere.

**placenta** The vascular organ, formed during pregnancy, that allows for the supply of oxygen and nutrients to the fetus and the removal of waste products.

**ectopic pregnancy** Implantation and resulting pregnancy at any site other than the uterus.

(National Institutes of Health, n.d.). Rh factor is a molecular label on the surface of red blood cells. In cases of Rh incompatibility the fetus will have inherited the factor from its father. The combination of Rh-negative mother and Rh-positive father is common—it is the case for about 10% of all couples in the United States—but only a minority of their pregnancies are marked by problems. These problems arise when the mother develops antibodies against Rh and those antibodies cross the **placenta** and attack the fetus. This does not happen routinely, because the fetus is immunologically isolated from the mother. Nevertheless, the mother may develop anti-Rh antibodies at childbirth if the fetus bleeds into the maternal circulation during delivery. These antibodies develop too late to affect that child, but they may attack a subsequent fetus, destroying its red blood cells and rendering it severely anemic. Such an attack can kill the fetus or newborn child, or it can leave the child intellectually disabled.

Luckily, the initial immune response to a mother's first Rh-positive fetus can be blocked by the administration of an antibody that binds to Rh and hides it from the mother's immune system. If severe anemia does occur in a subsequent pregnancy, the fetus or the newborn child may have to receive a blood transfusion.

### Ectopic pregnancy can endanger the mother's life

Another serious condition that causes fetal loss is **ectopic pregnancy**, which is implantation of the fetus at a location other than the uterus (American College of Obstetricians and Gynecologists [ACOG], 2019a) (**FIGURE 8.8**). This happens in about 1% to 2% of all pregnancies. The most common site of ectopic pregnancy is one of the oviducts (in which case it is called a "tubal pregnancy"), but other possible sites include the cervix, the ovary, and elsewhere within the abdominal cavity.

Ectopic pregnancies can be caused by congenital malformations of the oviducts or uterus, by damage to the oviducts resulting from PID or appendicitis, or by treatment with certain sex steroids and contraceptives that interfere with the normal movement of the embryo into the uterus. About half of all ectopic pregnancies occur without any known predisposing factors, however. The rate of ectopic pregnancy is increasing, and the main culprit is the increasing prevalence of PID due to chlamydia infections (see Chapter 15). Another factor is the increasing number of births to older women, who are more likely to experience ectopic pregnancies (San Lazaro Campillo et al., 2018).

Ectopic pregnancy commonly leads to early spontaneous abortion. Alternatively, as the embryo grows, it may cause internal hemorrhage or rupture of an oviduct, both of which are emergencies that threaten the mother's life. Recognition of the condition is hampered by the fact that the woman may not know she is pregnant—the symptoms can appear within 3 weeks of the beginning of pregnancy. Therefore, if a woman of childbearing age has engaged in coitus recently and experiences unexplained abdominal or shoulder pain, pain on defecation or urination, abnormal vaginal bleeding, or signs of shock, she should see a doctor without delay.

An ectopic embryo cannot survive. If it does not abort spontaneously it may be caused to do so with a drug, methotrexate. Otherwise, the entire oviduct on that side may have to be removed surgically—doing so does not impair the woman's ability to become pregnant so long as the other oviduct is in good condition.

## 8.6 Pregnancy Is Conventionally Divided into Three Trimesters

### LEARNING OBJECTIVES
After reading this section you should be able to:

8.6.1   Explain how a woman's due date is calculated.

8.6.2   Explain what lengths of pregnancy are considered "full-term" and "early term."

Let's return to the happier topic of normal pregnancy. First of all, how long does a normal pregnancy last? Logically, we would time pregnancy from fertilization, or perhaps from implantation, but neither of these events can be used for timing because they don't usually make themselves known to the mother. The only relevant date that the mother is likely to remember is the onset of her last menstrual period, which occurs about 2 weeks before fertilization. Thus, pregnancy is conventionally timed from that date, and a fetus is said to have a **gestational age** based on the number of weeks that have elapsed since the onset of the woman's last menstrual period—even though the embryo didn't actually exist for the first 2 weeks of that time.*

Traditionally, a woman's "due date" is calculated as 280 days, or 40 weeks, from the onset of her last menstrual period. This is the so-called **Naegele's rule,** named for the 19th-century German obstetrician who introduced it. Of course, few births occur exactly on the due date: A "term" pregnancy—one considered to be of normal duration—is taken to mean any pregnancy lasting at least 260 days (37 weeks) and no more than 294 days (42 weeks).

Even within the range of term pregnancies, the best outcomes are associated with deliveries at 39 or 40 weeks, and such deliveries are called "full term." Many women believe mistakenly that 37 weeks is an optimal, full-term pregnancy, and nearly 4% of mothers choose to have an induced early-term delivery (at 37 or 38 weeks) for no medical reason, even though such deliveries are associated with an increased risk of harm to the baby (Fleischman et al., 2010; Kozhimannil et al., 2014). Unless there is a medical reason, mothers and their doctors should allow pregnancies to continue until at least 39 weeks.

In the context of prenatal care, pregnancy is usually divided into three **trimesters,** each 3 months long. These time periods do not correspond to any particular biologically significant milestones but are simply convenient ways to refer to early, middle, and late pregnancy. The growth and appearance of the fetus over the first half of pregnancy is shown in **FIGURE 8.9**.

**gestational age**   A fetus's age timed from the onset of the mother's last menstrual period.

**Naegele's rule**   A traditional rule for the calculation of a pregnant woman's due date: 9 calendar months plus 1 week after the onset of the last menstrual period.

**trimester**   One of three 3-month divisions of pregnancy.

**FAQ:** I'm pregnant, but I'm still having my periods. What's up?

If you're pregnant, the bleeding is not your normal menstrual period. Minor bleeding commonly occurs around the time of implantation. If you're bleeding at later times, consult your doctor promptly; it could be something harmless, but it could also signal a serious problem such as an ectopic pregnancy or a miscarriage.

---

*Some sources use "gestational age" to mean age timed from the date of fertilization. The usage we adopt is the one recommended by the American Academy of Pediatrics.

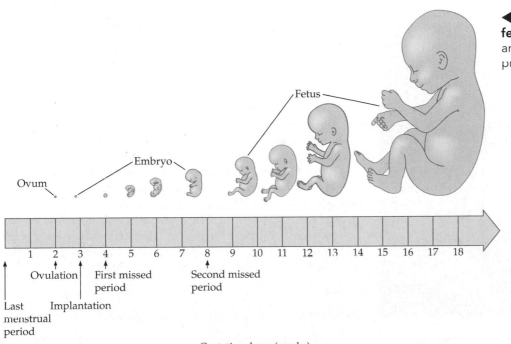

◀ **FIGURE 8.9   Embryonic and fetal growth** and changes in appearance through the 18th week of pregnancy.

Fetus

Embryo

Ovum

1  2  3  4  5  6  7  8  9  10  11  12  13  14  15  16  17  18

Ovulation

First missed period

Second missed period

Last menstrual period

Implantation

Gestational age (weeks)

## 8.7 The First Trimester Is a Period of Major Changes

### LEARNING OBJECTIVES

After reading this section you should be able to:

8.7.1 Describe the elements of prenatal care.
8.7.2 Analyze the substances and activities that may impact fetal development.

The first trimester is in many ways the most significant period of pregnancy. During this time the embryo implants in the uterine wall and sets up a system of hormonal and metabolic communication with the mother. The implanted embryo secretes hCG, which prevents the corpus luteum from regressing and therefore keeps progesterone levels high. Later, the embryo and placenta themselves secrete estrogens and progesterone. These hormones enter the mother's circulation, eventually rising to levels not experienced at any other time of her life. Their main role is to sustain the endometrium, but they also prepare the uterine musculature for childbirth and the breasts for lactation.

During the first 8 weeks of gestational age (which is 6 weeks after fertilization), the embryo develops from a tiny, featureless disk of cells into a miniature human being with all its organ systems present. It is then referred to as a fetus. By the end of the first trimester the fetus is about 4 inches (10 cm) in its longest dimension (crown–rump length) and weighs about 2 ounces (50 g). The external genitalia have differentiated as male or female, and most of the fetus's organ systems are functioning at some primitive level.

The first trimester is an important period for the mother as well. She typically learns that she is pregnant, a piece of news that may bring delight or anxiety. She may have to decide, perhaps in discussions with her partner, whether to continue the pregnancy. Assuming that she goes ahead with it, she is likely to experience some of the early symptoms of pregnancy, especially breast tenderness and morning sickness. Breast tenderness is a sign that the breasts are preparing for nursing (breastfeeding) the infant, even though it will be months before they can actually function. Morning sickness affects about half of all pregnant women, but it varies in degree, from mild nausea upon awakening to persistent and even life-threatening vomiting. Eating bland foods tends to alleviate the condition, which usually disappears by the end of the first trimester. Other symptoms experienced by many women during the first trimester include frequent urination, tiredness, sleeping difficulties, backaches, mood swings, and, sometimes, depression.

**prenatal care** Medical care and counseling provided to pregnant women.

### Prenatal care provides health screening, education, and support

Numerous studies have shown that almost every aspect of pregnancy benefits from **prenatal care**. It decreases the likelihood of maternal, fetal, or neonatal death; fetal prematurity; and low birth weight. Unfortunately, prenatal care is not as widely utilized in the United States as it is in European countries. Within the United States, the percentages of women who receive prenatal care during the first trimester vary greatly with race and ethnicity (**FIGURE 8.10**), and are higher in some states (e.g., Vermont) than others (e.g., Texas).

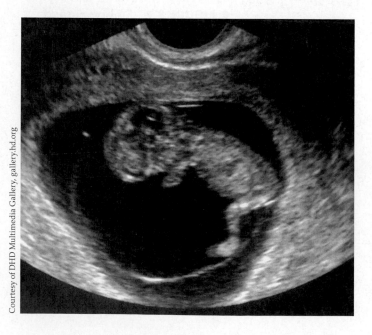

Courtesy of DHD Multimedia Gallery, gallery.hd.org

◀ Ultrasound image of a fetus after 10 weeks.

The reasons that some American women receive inadequate care have to do with psychosocial factors, such as ambivalence about the pregnancy or not believing that prenatal care will be helpful, more than a lack of access to such care (Johnson et al., 2007; Sunil et al., 2010). Some immigrants, especially Latinas, avoid agencies that might provide prenatal care out of fear that they or someone in their family might be deported (Rhodes et al., 2015).

Ideally, prenatal care begins at least 3 months *before* a woman becomes pregnant. This **preconception care** involves several steps a woman should take (CDC, 2018b):

- She should talk to her health care provider about preconception health care and discuss the medications and supplements she is taking.

- She should take 400 micrograms of folic acid daily to reduce the risk of birth defects.

- If she drinks alcohol, smokes, or uses street drugs, she should stop.

- Any medical conditions (e.g., diabetes or obesity) should be under control, and vaccinations, especially for **rubella**, should be up to date.

- An HIV test should be done.

- She should reach and maintain a healthy weight.

- She should avoid exposure to toxic or infectious substances at work and at home.

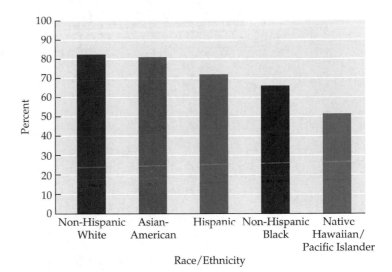

▲ **FIGURE 8.10** **Race and prenatal care** This bar graph shows the percentages of women in various race/ethnicity groups who receive first-trimester prenatal care. Data are for 2016. (After M. J. K. Osterman and J. A. Martin. 2018. *National Vital Statistics Reports* 67(3): 1–13. National Center for Health Statistics: Hyattsville, MD.)

It's important to take care of these issues before pregnancy, not only because they may take time to deal with, but also because some of them are relevant to the very earliest weeks of development, when a woman may not know that she is pregnant at all. Therefore, if there is a chance that she will become pregnant, she should act as if she *is* pregnant.

The first health care visit after conception typically takes place soon after the first missed period. At this point the health care provider takes a history and does a general examination, a Pap smear, a cervical culture (to test for gonorrhea and other conditions), a rubella test (if not done previously), and a test for blood type and Rh factor. A clinical pregnancy test may be done, even if the woman has already done a home pregnancy test. The provider advises the woman on nutrition and related matters, answers her questions, and helps her make informed decisions about how to manage her pregnancy and childbirth.

On one or more occasions during the first trimester, the provider conducts a pelvic exam. Many providers also perform an ultrasound exam at some point during the first trimester, especially if there is some indication of a problem. This exam permits determination of fetal age, the number of fetuses, and the presence of any abnormality such as an ectopic pregnancy. It is not usually possible to discern the fetus's sex by ultrasound during the first trimester.

## Adequate nutrition is vital to a successful pregnancy

An expectant mother needs an extra 250 to 300 calories per day in addition to what she needs to support herself. At term (just before childbirth), a woman typically weighs 20 to 35 pounds (9 to 15 kg) above her prepregnancy weight; this includes the weight of the fetus, placenta, and amniotic fluid, as well as her own increased

**preconception care** Medical care and counseling provided to women before they become pregnant.

**rubella** German measles, a viral infection that can cause developmental defects in fetuses whose mothers contract the disease during pregnancy.

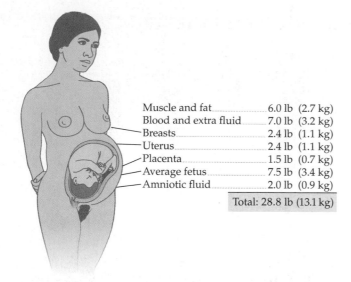

Muscle and fat..............6.0 lb  (2.7 kg)
Blood and extra fluid.....7.0 lb  (3.2 kg)
Breasts.........................2.4 lb  (1.1 kg)
Uterus..........................2.4 lb  (1.1 kg)
Placenta.......................1.5 lb  (0.7 kg)
Average fetus................7.5 lb  (3.4 kg)
Amniotic fluid...............2.0 lb  (0.9 kg)

Total: 28.8 lb  (13.1 kg)

▲ **FIGURE 8.11    Where do those extra pounds go?**
The distribution of extra weight for a woman who gains 28.8 pounds (13.1 kg) during pregnancy. (Data from Mayo Clinic. 2014. *Pregnancy weight gain: What's healthy?* https://tinyurl.com/y7ostwcj.)

**fetal alcohol syndrome**    A collection of physical and behavioral symptoms in a child who was exposed to high levels of alcohol as a fetus.

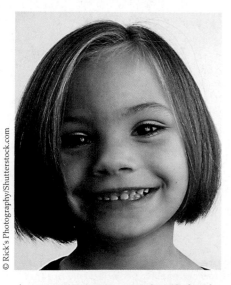

© Rick's Photography/Shutterstock.com

▲ **FIGURE 8.12    A girl with fetal alcohol syndrome** Typical facial features include short eye slits (palpebral fissures), a flat midface, a short nose, an indistinct groove (philtrum) between nose and lip, a thin upper lip, and a small chin.

**TABLE 8.1    Weight gain recommendations according to prepregnancy weight**

| Prepregnancy weight | BMI | Recommended weight gain at term, in pounds (kg) |
|---|---|---|
| Underweight | <18.5 | 28–40 (13–18) |
| Normal weight | 18.6–24.9 | 25–35 (11–16) |
| Overweight | 25.0–29.9 | 15–25 (7–11) |
| Obese | >30.0 | 11–20 (5–9) |

*Source*: Source: Institute of Medicine and National Research Council of the National Academies. 2009. *Weight Gain During Pregnancy: Reexamining the Guidelines*, K. M. Rasmussen and A. L. Yaktine (Eds.), p.3. National Academies Press: Washington, D.C. www.nap.edu.

fat deposits, enlarged breasts, and increased volume of blood and tissue fluids (**FIGURE 8.11** and **TABLE 8.1**). If a woman is already eating healthily, she doesn't need to make significant changes in her diet, but she should be sure that she's taking in adequate amounts of folic acid, calcium, and iron.

Women who begin pregnancy with a normal weight are most likely to give birth to healthy children. Underweight women risk producing underweight children, who are more likely to experience a variety of medical problems. Women who are overweight or obese face an increased risk of certain serious disorders during pregnancy, including diabetes and hypertension. These women are advised to gain less weight during pregnancy than women of normal weight.

There are specific structural changes in women's brains during pregnancy, and these changes last long beyond childbirth (Hoekzema et al., 2017). The changes involve a loss of cortical volume in certain areas devoted to social cognition. You might think that a loss of volume would mean a loss of function, but in reality it is a positive maturational step—one that is also seen during normal puberty in both sexes. The volume loss probably results from the trimming away of irrelevant connections, leaving the cortex better able to carry out specific tasks—in this case those connected with motherhood.

## Tobacco, alcohol, drugs, and radiation can harm the fetus

A pregnant woman needs to avoid a number of agents that can harm the fetus (**TABLE 8.2**). Alcohol and tobacco head this list. Alcohol consumption increases the likelihood of spontaneous abortion, infant mortality, and birth defects, and it is associated with a specific cluster of symptoms known as **fetal alcohol syndrome**. Children with this syndrome (**FIGURE 8.12**) are small and have a characteristic facial appearance, and they may have birth defects. They also exhibit cognitive and behavioral problems that persist into adulthood (Freunscht & Feldmann, 2011). Binge drinking is particularly dangerous. Whether light drinking—one or two drinks per week—harms the fetus is uncertain; for that reason all experts recommend that women who are or might be pregnant abstain from alcohol completely. The severity and nature of the effects of alcohol vary greatly, which has led to the introduction of an umbrella term, fetal alcohol spectrum disorders, analogous to autism spectrum disorders (CDC, 2019b). Caffeine can also be harmful: Each one-cup increment in daily coffee consumption raises the risk of miscarriage by about 7% (Chen et al., 2016).

Smoking is one of the most harmful practices a pregnant woman can engage in (CDC, 2019j). It is associated with an increased likelihood of spontaneous abortion,

**TABLE 8.2**  Examples of substances, infections, and physical agents that can harm the developing fetus

| Agent | Possible consequences |
| --- | --- |
| **DRUGS** | |
| Alcohol | Fetal alcohol syndrome |
| Tobacco | Spontaneous abortion; premature birth; low birth weight; addiction of newborn; sudden infant death |
| Isotretinoin (Accutane) | Heart, brain malformations; intellectual disability |
| Thalidomide | Limb defects; deafness; blindness |
| Vitamins A and D (in excessive amounts) | Fetal malformations |
| Androgens, estrogens | Abnormalities of external genitalia and reproductive tract, especially in females |
| Acetaminophen (Tylenol) | Possible modestly increased risk of ADHD-like behaviors[a] |
| Street drugs (heroin, methamphetamine, cocaine) | Spontaneous abortion; low birth weight; respiratory depression of newborn; addiction of newborn |
| Marijuana | Heart and brain defects |
| **INFECTIONS** (see also Chapter 15) | |
| Rubella | Damage to ears, eyes, heart |
| Genital herpes | Spontaneous abortion; premature birth; birth defects; possibly autism spectrum disorder[b] |
| HIV | AIDS in infancy/childhood |
| Chlamydia | Premature birth; neonatal eye infection |
| **PHYSICAL AGENTS** | |
| X-rays, nuclear radiation | Increased risk of childhood cancer |
| Cosmic radiation (from high-altitude flight, for air crew or very frequent flyers) | Possible increased risk of childhood cancer |
| High body temperature (over 100.4°F, or 38°C) in early pregnancy (from fever, excessive exercise, saunas, hot tubs) | A variety of birth defects |

[a] *Source*: Z. Liew et al. 2014. *JAMA Pediatrics* 168: 313–320.

[b] *Source*: M. Mahic et al. 2017. *mSphere* 2: e00016–17.

premature birth, low birth weight, congenital malformations, and sudden infant death syndrome. Localities that enact bans on smoking in workplaces and public spaces experience a significant drop in the incidence of preterm births (Been et al., 2014).

Many drugs—including prescription, over-the-counter, and street drugs—can harm the fetus. A particularly dangerous drug is isotretinoin (Accutane and its generic equivalents), which is used for the treatment of severe acne. Isotretinoin causes fetal malformations. Because teenage girls have high rates of both acne and unintended pregnancy, the possibility of disaster is real, despite educational programs and stringent prescribing requirements.

Addictive drugs such as cocaine, heroin, and methamphetamine slow fetal development, raise the risk of miscarriage and premature birth, and cause the baby to be born in an addicted state. A pregnant woman, or one who may become pregnant, should also discuss with her doctor all prescription drugs she is taking; often, drugs that are harmful to the fetus or whose safety has not been established can be replaced with safer ones.

**FAQ:** I've heard there's a device I can put in my vagina that plays music to my unborn baby—it's supposed to help her learn to speak earlier. True?

We say let fetuses be fetuses.

Cannabis (marijuana) use has increased dramatically since its legalization in some states. There is an increasing trend toward viewing cannabis as harmless, and while this may possibly be true for adults, it is not true for fetuses. One public-health study found that, after legalization in Colorado, the rate of birth defects in that state rose in parallel with cannabis consumption (Reece & Hulse, 2019). In lab animals cannabis causes defects similar to those seen in fetal alcohol syndrome, and the combination of alcohol and cannabis is especially toxic, because both drugs attack the same molecular targets in the body (Fish et al., 2019).

Vitamin A, though essential for normal fetal development, can cause malformations in excessive doses. Of particular concern is "preformed vitamin A," which is present in liver and eggs and is often added to breakfast cereals, nonfat milk, and other foodstuffs (check the ingredients list for "retinyl palmitate," "vitamin A palmitate," or similar compounds). Pregnant women should limit their intake of these substances to no more than 100% of the recommended daily allowance.

Fish is a nutritious food for both mother and fetus, but it is wise to avoid species that may contain significant amounts of mercury. These are mostly large predator species such as tuna, king mackerel, and swordfish. Information on the mercury content of various kinds of fish and shellfish is available online (U.S. Food and Drug Administration, 2017).

Another agent that can harm the fetus is radiation. X-rays, especially CT scans, should be avoided during pregnancy if possible, although the medical benefits of the X-ray may outweigh the risks in some cases.

## 8.8 The Second Trimester Is the Easiest

### LEARNING OBJECTIVES

After reading this section you should be able to:

8.8.1   Describe the tests that can be used to diagnose fetal abnormalities.

8.8.2   Evaluate the possible benefits and risks of sex and exercise during pregnancy.

The second trimester begins at 13 weeks of gestational age. Most women experience the second trimester as a period of calm and well-being. Morning sickness and most of the other unpleasant symptoms of early pregnancy usually disappear, and this may allow for an increased interest in, and enjoyment of, sex. One symptom that may cause problems during the second trimester is a need for frequent urination, caused by pressure on the bladder from the enlarging uterus. Signs of pregnancy become obvious: The abdomen swells, stretch marks may begin to appear, and the breasts may release small amounts of colostrum, the special kind of milk that nourishes newborn infants.

Around the middle of the second trimester the mother will begin to feel the fetus's movements. This event, known as **quickening**, has always had great psychological significance—it is a major step in the mother's bonding with her child. In early Christian doctrine, quickening was thought to be the time the soul entered into the fetus, so abortion before quickening was not necessarily a sin. The beginning of fetal movement does not mean that the fetus is now a conscious being, however: The cerebral cortex, which is probably the main locus of consciousness, is still at an extremely rudimentary stage of development at the time of quickening.

### Tests can detect fetal abnormalities

At prenatal care visits during the second trimester, the health care provider monitors the fetus's growth and well-being. In addition, tests may be done to check for congenital disorders. These tests may include ultrasound scans, amniocentesis, and chorionic villus sampling.

An ultrasound scan done at the beginning of the second trimester or slightly earlier can reveal evidence suggestive of congenital abnormalities, including Down

**quickening**   The onset of movements by the fetus that can be felt by the mother.

syndrome. When the ultrasound is combined with biochemical tests, about 90% of fetuses with Down syndrome can be identified.

If there are reasons to be concerned about fetal abnormalities, such as advanced maternal age or a history of abnormalities in previous pregnancies, more-invasive tests may be recommended. In **amniocentesis** (**FIGURE 8.13A**), the doctor first determines the precise position of the uterus and the fetus with an ultrasound scan and then passes a thin needle through the front wall of the abdomen into the amniotic sac in which the fetus is floating, avoiding the fetus itself. A sample of the amniotic fluid, containing some free-floating cells derived from the fetus or its membranes, is withdrawn. The information gained through amniocentesis allows for the identification of chromosomal and genetic abnormalities as well as **spina bifida** (incomplete development of the spine and spinal cord). Amniocentesis is usually done at about 15 to 18 weeks of pregnancy, but it is sometimes done as early as 11 weeks.

An alternative to amniocentesis is **chorionic villus sampling** (**CVS**) (**FIGURE 8.13B**). In this procedure, a catheter is passed through the cervix, and a sample of tissue is taken from the placenta. (Chorionic villi are the highly branched tissue projections from the placenta that serve to increase the area of contact with the mother's blood.) The procedure may also be done with a needle inserted through the abdominal wall. CVS is usually done at 10 to 12 weeks of pregnancy. Although it has the advantage of producing results earlier than amniocentesis, CVS identifies only chromosomal and genetic abnormalities, and not spina bifida. Both amniocentesis and CVS can trigger a miscarriage, but the risk is very low (Akolekar et al., 2015).

In the great majority of cases, the outcome of these tests is reassurance that the baby is probably healthy. Unfortunately, a few women do receive the devastating news that the fetus has a serious genetic abnormality. In some cases it may be possible to prevent harm to the fetus by medical treatment during pregnancy, but if not, most women choose to abort the fetus. (Women who are opposed to abortion under any circumstances tend not to seek prenatal testing in the first place.) The earlier diagnosis offered by CVS (compared with amniocentesis) usually makes the decision to have an abortion psychologically easier and medically safer.

**amniocentesis** The sampling of the amniotic fluid for purposes of prenatal diagnosis.

**spina bifida** A congenital malformation caused by incomplete closure of the neural tube.

**chorionic villus sampling (CVS)** The sampling of tissue from the placenta for purposes of prenatal diagnosis.

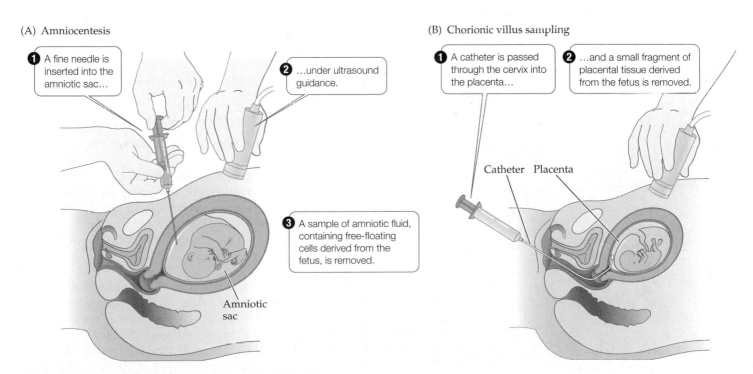

(A) Amniocentesis

① A fine needle is inserted into the amniotic sac…

② …under ultrasound guidance.

③ A sample of amniotic fluid, containing free-floating cells derived from the fetus, is removed.

Amniotic sac

(B) Chorionic villus sampling

① A catheter is passed through the cervix into the placenta…

② …and a small fragment of placental tissue derived from the fetus is removed.

Catheter   Placenta

▲ **FIGURE 8.13**   **Screening for congenital disorders**

**cell-free fetal DNA analysis**
The diagnosis of fetal disorders by sequencing fetal DNA that leaks into the maternal circulation.

**placenta previa** An abnormally low position of the placenta, such that it partially or completely covers the internal opening of the cervix.

**incompetent cervix** A weakening and partial opening of the cervix caused by a previous traumatic delivery, surgery, or other factors.

In 2011, a Hong Kong–based research group showed that it is possible to isolate and sequence the tiny amounts of fetal DNA that leak into the mother's circulation. This **cell-free fetal DNA analysis** allows for the diagnosis of Down syndrome and other chromosomal abnormalities from a simple blood draw, and it can identify the sex of the fetus and whether it is Rh positive or negative (Mayo Clinic, 2019i). The test can be done as early as 10 weeks, but it may take another 2 weeks to get the results. The introduction of the fetal DNA test has led to fewer amniocenteses and CVS procedures being performed than in the past. Positive results may have to be confirmed with one of the more invasive procedures, however, and the test does not detect all fetal abnormalities.

## Sex during pregnancy is healthy

One topic that couples often think about as the mother grows larger is sex: Is it a good idea in the latter half of pregnancy? Can it harm the fetus? The answer is that in a normal pregnancy, the fetus is well protected from almost anything the couple might do during sex, and coitus does not cause miscarriage or bring on labor, even when practiced close to the due date (Sayle et al., 2001; Jones et al., 2011). The only sex practice known to be dangerous during pregnancy is blowing air into the vagina, which can cause a fatal air embolism (blockage of blood vessels by air bubbles). Anal sex is also discouraged on account of the risk of transferring fecal bacteria to the vagina.

About the only other way that sex can harm the fetus is if the mother acquires a sexually transmitted infection (STI) from her partner. Such diseases can be transmitted to the fetus during pregnancy or as the fetus passes through the birth canal. Organisms that cause only mild or moderate problems for adults can be catastrophic for fetuses or newborns. Thus, pregnant women who are sexually active should be extra vigilant concerning the possibility of acquiring an STI, and they should abstain from vaginal sex if either partner has an active herpes outbreak. Condoms are recommended for coitus.

The foregoing applies to *normal* pregnancies. The following medical conditions may make coitus unwise, especially toward the end of pregnancy:

- Threatened miscarriage or premature birth
- Unexplained vaginal bleeding
- Leakage of amniotic fluid
- **Placenta previa**, a condition in which the placenta covers the cervix
- **Incompetent cervix**, in which the cervix opens too early

The woman's health care provider can advise her about whether or when she should refrain from coitus.

Sex during pregnancy may require some modifications to a couple's usual practices (Nagrath & Singh, 2012). As the woman's belly swells, the man-above position for coitus becomes awkward, but there are strategies to make it more practical. For example, placing a couple of pillows under the woman's buttocks will cause her belly to tilt away from the man. Or he can kneel between her legs, again with her buttocks raised on pillows.

The woman-above position is also suitable, especially if the woman sits straight up (facing either forward or backward) to allow more space for her belly. Rear-entry coitus becomes the most practical approach as pregnancy goes on: This may be done doggy style, standing, side by side, or sitting (**FIGURE 8.14**). Some women, especially those with G-spots, find rear-entry coitus very stimulating; for others, simultaneous stimulation of the clitoris

▲ **FIGURE 8.14** **Sex during the later stages of pregnancy** may be facilitated by a willingness to try new positions or sexual activities other than coitus.

by hand or with a vibrator is useful. Side-by-side rear-entry coitus is perhaps the least stressful position during late pregnancy, but it also tends to be the least stimulating because movement is limited.

Of course, coitus is not the only option: Straight people could take their cue from lesbian couples, who enjoy a wide variety of noncoital positions (see Chapter 6). And if a pregnant woman just doesn't feel up to engaging in more athletic interactions, plain kissing and cuddling can be rewarding and reassuring to both partners.

## Moderate exercise during pregnancy is beneficial

Another issue that concerns some women is exercise. Traditionally, pregnant women were thought of as fragile creatures who needed to be spared any kind of exertion. It's now clear that, for most pregnant women, exercise has a positive value in maintaining health and well-being. It is especially useful in counteracting backache, constipation, mood swings, and sleeplessness. Paula Radcliffe, who set a world record in the marathon, delivered a healthy daughter after training up until the day before she went into labor (Kolata, 2007).

▲ Moderate exercise is beneficial to mother and fetus.

© Tetra Images, LLC/Alamy Stock Photo

The American College of Obstetricians and Gynecologists is a bit more cautious (ACOG, 2019b): ACOG recommends that pregnant women engage in moderate, low-impact forms of exercise such as brisk walking—exercises during which "you can talk but you can't sing." A pregnant woman does best to avoid exercises that involve lying on the back or that raise body temperature significantly, and she should not exercise while she has a fever. A pregnant woman should talk to her medical provider about exercise, because there are certain uncommon medical conditions in which exercise may harm the mother or her fetus.

## 8.9 The Third Trimester Is a Time of Preparation

### LEARNING OBJECTIVES
After reading this section you should be able to:

8.9.1 Evaluate the pros and cons of different locations for childbirth.
8.9.2 Compare the aims of different kinds of childbirth classes.

The third trimester begins at 27 weeks of gestational age. At this time, the fetus already weighs about 2 pounds (900 g) and has a decent chance of surviving if born prematurely, although its survival would entail weeks of intensive neonatal care and a six-figure hospital bill. During the third trimester, the fetus increases rapidly in weight; at the time of fastest growth, which is around 33 weeks, the fetus is gaining about 2 ounces (50 g) every day. By the time of birth it has reached a weight of about 7.1 pounds (3.2 kg).

During the third trimester, the fetus performs many of the behaviors that it will need to survive outside its mother, including breathing motions. Its brain is functioning, at least in a primitive way. For example, at 10 weeks before birth the brain can respond to speech sounds and will change its response if, for example, a male speaker is replaced by a female speaker: This is known from the recording of brain activity in babies born 10 weeks prematurely (Mahmoudzadeh et al., 2017).

The mother's uterus undergoes occasional, irregularly spaced contractions. These **Braxton Hicks contractions** (or "false labor") are normal and do not endanger the fetus. Only if the contractions come at regular intervals and become gradually more frequent, stronger, and longer lasting need a woman be concerned that true labor is beginning.

**Braxton Hicks contractions** Irregular uterine contractions that occur during the third trimester of pregnancy. Also called false labor.

Women's experience of the third trimester varies greatly. Some women sail through it serenely, while others are overwhelmed by physical problems (backache, urinary frequency, fatigue, or sleeplessness) or by anxiety about childbirth and motherhood. Couples may find themselves bonding more closely than at any previous time in their relationship, or there may be increasing tension. Depression is not uncommon at this time, particularly among women who do not have partners.

## A hospital is the best location for childbirth if complications are foreseen

On a more positive note, the third trimester is a time of preparation for birth. By this time, the mother will probably have decided where to have her baby. If it is her first baby, she and her partner should be taking classes in preparation for the birth.

Concerning where to have the baby, there are three choices: at home, in a hospital, or (in some areas) in a stand-alone facility known as a **birthing center**. Over 98% of all births in the United States take place in hospitals (Caughey & Cheyney, 2019). The great advantage of a hospital is the immediate availability of obstetricians (physicians who specialize in childbirth) and equipment. The disadvantage is that a hospital can be a relatively impersonal and sometimes intimidating environment, and the mother may feel that less attention is paid to her wishes for the birth process than if she were in her own home.

A birthing center (if one is available) offers a compromise between hospital and home. Most birthing centers are staffed by midwives rather than by physicians. These midwives (especially certified nurse-midwives) are highly trained and experienced in their field. Birthing centers are not as well equipped as hospitals, however, and centers that are staffed only by midwives will not be able to provide certain forms of anesthesia, such as epidurals (see below). It will be necessary to move the mother to a hospital if serious complications arise. For that reason, a birthing center that is part of a hospital complex is preferable to one that is some distance away.

Home is, of course, the most "home-like" setting for giving birth. In principle home birth is cheaper than other options, but it may end up being more expensive for the consumer because many insurance plans don't fully cover home birth. The risk of perinatal death is as high for planned home births as for hospital births, or higher, even though most planned home births are low-risk ones (Snowden et al., 2015). Both ACOG and the American Academy of Pediatrics recommend against home birth.

The most important consideration influencing the choice of location should be the estimated likelihood of complications. The health care provider will advise the mother to have her child in a hospital if labor begins prematurely, if the fetus is not optimally positioned for birth, if there is more than one fetus, if the mother's pelvis is unusually narrow, or if there exist any other medical conditions that increase the risk of complications.

## Childbirth classes prepare parents for birth

Many different kinds of childbirth classes are available to parents. Nearly all provide general education about pregnancy, childbirth, and infant care and encourage

**birthing center**   A facility specializing in childbirth care.

© MBI/Alamy Stock Photo

▲ Childbirth classes help expectant mothers and their partners prepare for the physical and psychological demands of labor.

breastfeeding. Some of the classes incorporate the ideas of the French pioneer in "prepared childbirth," Fernand Lamaze. Reacting against the use of general anesthetics during labor, which was widespread in the 1950s and 1960s, Lamaze asserted that women could experience a pain-free childbirth without anesthetics. The **Lamaze method** has undergone considerable revision in recent years, however (Lamaze International, 2019). It now incorporates the concept that pain plays an important role in labor, helping the mother to act in ways that protect the baby and herself. Women are taught techniques of "active relaxation" that help them to stay focused and to participate fully in the birth process, rather than simply averting their minds from it.

Lamaze teachers do not oppose anesthesia during labor if it seems necessary, and a fair proportion of women who take Lamaze classes do receive some kind of anesthesia. Another type of childbirth preparation, the **Bradley method**, stresses natural childbirth and places a lot of weight on the role of the woman's partner as birth coach (American Academy of Husband-Coached Childbirth, 2019). Although developed by a physician, it is more anti-medical in flavor than the Lamaze method, and women who take classes based on the Bradley method are less likely to accept anesthesia or other medical interventions during labor than are women who take Lamaze classes.

Most hospital-based childbirth classes do not closely follow either the Lamaze or the Bradley model but are based on the experience of the people teaching them. They tend to be eclectic, practically oriented, and responsive to the parents' needs, rather than being based on some overarching theory of childbirth management.

One form of childbirth that has gained some popularity in recent years is water birth. The mother (often with her partner and midwife) sits in a pool or tub of warm water during delivery, and the baby is born underwater. (The baby does not take its first breath until it is brought above the water's surface.) There are no demonstrated benefits of water birth to the baby, however, and some babies born in this fashion have contracted serious lung infections (CDC, 2017h). For this and other reasons ACOG recommends against the practice of water birth (ACOG, 2016).

During the final few weeks of pregnancy, it is useful for women to practice **perineal massage.** This involves manual stretching of the perineum, the region of skin between the vulva and the anus. Perineal massage has been shown to reduce the likelihood of perineal tears (or the necessity for episiotomy—see below) during labor, especially for women expecting their first child (Cochrane Collaboration, 2009). Instructions on how to perform perineal massage are available online (American College of Nurse-Midwives, 2005).

## The fetus also makes preparations for birth

While the parents are preparing themselves for childbirth, so is the fetus. Although the fetus's growth rate slows dramatically after 33 weeks, its organ systems undergo rapid maturation. Much of this preparation for birth is orchestrated by increasing amounts of corticosteroids secreted by the fetus's adrenal glands during the third trimester. Among their effects are important changes in the lungs: These include the production of **pulmonary surfactant**, a detergent-like substance that facilitates opening of the respiratory spaces within the lungs during the child's first drawn breath. Corticosteroids also instruct the fetus's liver to manufacture **glycogen** that will be used to supply the brain's critical glucose needs before, during, and just after birth. Rising corticosteroid levels before birth also affect blood production, switching the hemoglobin in red blood cells to a different form that is better suited to an air-breathing lifestyle. Corticosteroids may be administered to women who are at risk of preterm delivery, for the purpose of accelerating the fetus's preparation for birth.

**Lamaze method** A method of childbirth instruction that focuses on techniques of relaxation and other natural means of pain reduction.

**Bradley method** A method of childbirth instruction that stresses the partner's role as birth coach and that seeks to avoid medical interventions.

**perineal massage** Manual stretching of the perineum in preparation for childbirth.

**pulmonary surfactant** A compound produced in the fetal lung that reduces surface tension and thus facilitates inflation of the lungs with air at birth.

**glycogen** A polymer of glucose used for energy storage.

# 8.10 Labor Has Three Stages

## LEARNING OBJECTIVES
After reading this section you should be able to:
- 8.10.1 Describe the three stages of labor.
- 8.10.2 Evaluate the risks of premature and delayed labor.

**parturition** Delivery of offspring; childbirth.

**labor** The process of childbirth.

**engagement** The sinking of a fetus's head into a lower position in the pelvis in preparation for birth. Also called lightening.

**contraction** In childbirth, a periodic coordinated tightening of the uterine musculature, felt as a cramp.

**softening** The elimination of connective tissue from the cervix, allowing it to thin out and dilate during labor. Also called ripening.

**birth canal** The canal formed by the uterus, cervix, and vagina, through which the fetus passes during the birth process.

**effacement** Thinning of the cervix in preparation for childbirth.

**dilation** In childbirth, the expansion of the cervical canal. Also called dilatation.

**transition** The final phase of dilation of the cervix during labor.

The process of childbirth is referred to scientifically as **parturition**, and more commonly as **labor**. During most of pregnancy, labor is prevented by the inability of the uterine musculature to contract in an organized manner, as well as by the cervix, whose thick wall contains a dense network of connective tissue that resists expansion. Thus, the Braxton Hicks contractions described earlier put some downward pressure on the fetus, but this pressure is easily resisted by the cervix, so the fetus does not move into the birth canal.

Before labor begins, the fetus changes its position in the uterus, as its head sinks deep into the pelvis against the cervix (**FIGURE 8.15**). The mother often notices this event, called **engagement** (or lightening), when a bit of extra space opens up between her breasts and her swollen belly. In first pregnancies, engagement may occur a week or more before birth; in later pregnancies, it occurs shortly before or during labor.

Labor itself takes place in three stages. The first stage consists of the uterine contractions that open the cervix. The second stage is the actual delivery of the baby. The third stage is the period from the delivery of the baby to the delivery of the placenta.

## The first stage of labor is marked by uterine contractions and cervical dilation

Labor may be heralded by the discharge of the mucous plug that seals off the cervix during pregnancy. The plug may be tinged red with blood, and this event is therefore traditionally called the "bloody show." The amniotic sac may also rupture early in labor, or it may be ruptured by a health care provider. The rupture produces a gush or leakage of amniotic fluid from the vagina ("water breaking"). In other cases the sac does not rupture until later in labor.

The first stage of labor can last anywhere from a couple of hours to more than 24 hours. The two main processes that permit childbirth are the strong, coordinated **contractions** of the uterus and the elimination of much of the connective tissue—the **softening** (or ripening) of the cervix (**FIGURE 8.16**).

The effect of the uterine contractions is not yet to move the fetus downward, but to pull the cervix upward so that the vagina and cervix together form a single, continuous **birth canal**. Early in labor, the contractions are fairly mild and spaced 15 to 20 minutes apart. Later, they become more intense and closely spaced—about every 3 minutes.

The softening of the cervix allows **effacement** (thinning out) of the cervix and the gradual **dilation**, or dilatation (opening up), of the cervical canal for passage of the fetal head. When this opening process is complete, the canal measures 4 inches (10 cm) in diameter.

The last part of the first phase of labor, when the cervix dilates from 3 to 4 inches (8 to 10 cm), is sometimes called the **transition**; it is a short period of very intense and frequent contractions. The transition is the part of labor that is most likely to be painful and exhausting, and it is here that the woman can most usefully apply what she has learned in her prenatal classes: relaxing

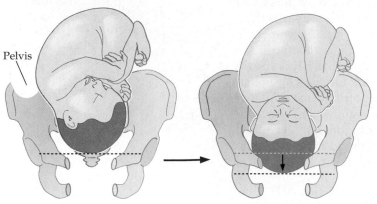

Pelvis

◀ **FIGURE 8.15** **Engagement** is the sinking of the fetus's head deep into the mother's pelvis.

(A) Effacement

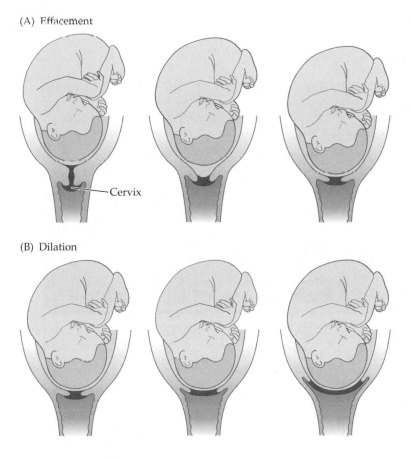

Cervix

(B) Dilation

◀ **FIGURE 8.16   Cervical changes during labor**
(A) Effacement is the thinning of the cervix. (B) Dilation is the opening of the cervix, from fully closed to a width of 4 inches (10 cm).

**FAQ:** I have a tattoo on my lower back—will that stop me from getting an epidural?

Only if the tattoo reads "No epidurals."

rather than resisting the contractions, and directing her attention to forms of natural pain relief that many women find to be useful. These include such seemingly simple activities as walking, pelvic rocking, showering, soaking in a hot tub, sitting on a "birth ball," doing breathing exercises, and using guided imagery.

Some women go through labor with little or no pain (**BOX 8.4**). But for those who *are* experiencing significant pain, several different forms of anesthesia are available. The most widely used is **epidural anesthesia**, which involves the infusion of a morphine-like drug or local anesthetic (or a combination of both) into the back, just outside the membrane that wraps the spinal cord (**FIGURE 8.17**). More than half of all women who give birth in hospitals receive epidural anesthesia (American Pregnancy

**epidural anesthesia**   Anesthesia administered just outside the membrane that surrounds the spinal cord.

(A)                              (B)

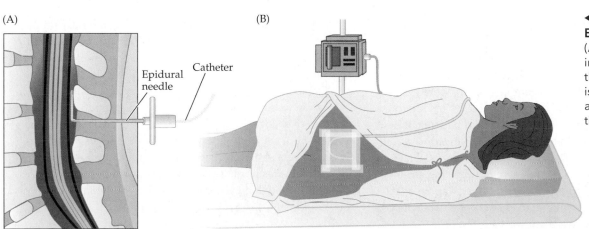

Epidural needle

Catheter

◀ **FIGURE 8.17**
**Epidural anesthesia**
(A) A catheter is guided into the epidural space through a needle, which is then removed. (B) The anesthetic is infused continuously or as needed.

## BOX 8.4
# Pain-Free Childbirth

*This account was provided to us by psychologist Vicki Engelke, who teaches human sexuality at Las Positas College in Livermore, California:*

Women often hear the stories of painful childbirth, which lead us to believe that pain is inevitable. But that wasn't my experience. No two birth stories are the same, but I did learn some things that will help you and your partner look forward to childbirth rather than dread it. Here is what I know:

- *Learn all you can during pregnancy.* Ask other women what they might have done differently, and take the classes offered at the hospital. My doctor recommended the hospital class, which included 1 hour of preparation/talk/circle time with other women and 1 hour of yoga. I got a wealth of information about labor and delivery. The class allowed me to understand the process of childbirth, without judgment, without fear. And talking with other women really helped ease any anxiety that I had.

- *Be your own advocate.* Ask what a typical birth is like with your doctor or at your hospital. My hospital used midwives more than doctors. The only reason I would see a doctor while in labor was if there were problems. I had to ask what they meant by "problems" and why they used midwives. The answers I got helped ease my fears. Be flexible, but if there are some things that are not negotiable, don't negotiate. Case in point: I am more comfortable with my bra on. They told me I'd have to take it off, and when I said no, they were adamant. When I pushed the issue and asked why, they said, "If you need an emergency cesarean, we'll have to cut it off." I said, "Fine, cut it off if you need to, but I want to be comfortable." I kept my bra on through my whole labor.

- *Find what works for you.* I was uncomfortable, so I spent my entire labor on my knees, leaning over the back of the bed. I was in the zone; this allowed me to tune the chaos out that was happening around me. There were people coming and going, staff prodding me, so I just found a position that worked for me. Each time I had a contraction, I moaned! Like the low guttural moan a dog would emit when in danger. Yes, it sounds ridiculous, but it's what worked for me. Of course, it took walking around for a few hours, lying on my side, and rocking on an exercise ball to figure out that those activities, while helpful for a lot of women, were not working for me.

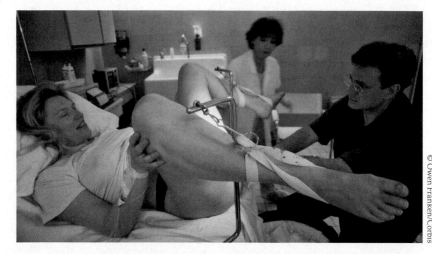

A woman giving birth: It doesn't have to hurt.

© Owen Franken/Corbis

- *Keep in mind that pain is perceptual.* When I tell women my birth story, they don't believe me when I say it was not painful. I had no pain medicine, only Pitocin to help my contractions along. When they ask, "How were you not in pain," it's not an easy answer. To a certain degree, pain is in the mind. What is painful to one woman is more painful to another woman and less painful to yet another woman. How we label pain may have an effect on how we view our own labor and childbirth. The moaning and guttural vibrations that came with the moaning helped ease my contractions. Yes, they were uncomfortable, but I can't say they were painful. As my daughter emerged, the perineum stretched—a lot! But again, the labels I use for pain are different. I felt a strong burning sensation as my perineum tore. For me, this worked—using different words for what I was feeling. My labor was uncomfortable and it included that burning sensation, but it was *not* painful.

- *Honor your journey to motherhood for what it is.* Find the resources that you think will be helpful and get as much information as you can, and above all be flexible! And please, honor each woman's journey; we don't need to judge each other, we are in this together. Lean on each other; let's not one-up one another with our horror stories of childbirth. And if you have a positive story, share it! There are a lot of good stories out there. Is it possible to have a pain-free childbirth without drugs? All I know is that it was possible for me. Fear is what causes pain, so try everything you can to reduce your fear. It certainly couldn't hurt—no pun intended!

Association, 2017). Done properly, this technique provides satisfactory pain relief with minimal impairment of the mother's ability to move and participate in the birth process. Still, no single method is appropriate for all situations or is entirely free of risk. Pregnant women do well to discuss the issue of anesthesia and develop birth plans ahead of time with their health care providers.

Incidentally, it's worth mentioning that our primate relatives have a far easier time with childbirth than women do—for them, the process is quick and seemingly pain-free. Two factors make childbirth so much more challenging for women: First, the large size of the fetal brain, and second, evolutionary changes in the geometry of the pelvis to permit upright gait. Together, these two factors have turned the human birth canal into a perilous obstacle course.

## The second stage is the delivery of the baby

The second stage of labor is the actual passage of the fetus through the birth canal. Although the delivery of the fetus can be accomplished purely by uterine contractions, women usually feel an urge to push, or "bear down." Bearing down—voluntary contraction of the muscles of the abdominal wall and the diaphragm—assists the process by adding to the pressure produced by the uterine contractions; it's very much like straining to pass a constipated bowel movement.

The second stage of labor is quite variable in duration: It may last just a few minutes, or it may take several hours. It is usually lengthier and more stressful for a woman's first delivery than for subsequent deliveries.

In 2010 a German research group succeeded for the first time in imaging the passage of a fetus through the birth canal (**FIGURE 8.18**). What this image vividly illustrates is the large size of the fetus's brain in relation to the space through which it must pass.

Toward the end of the second stage, the baby's head begins to **crown**—that is, appear at the vaginal opening. At this point, if it seems likely that the delivery of the head will tear the vaginal wall, the health care provider may make an incision in the perineum to extend the vaginal opening a short distance backward, toward the anus. This procedure, called an **episiotomy**, is done under local anesthesia.

The thinking behind doing an episiotomy is that, if the vaginal wall is likely to tear anyway, it is better to make a clean incision that can be neatly sewn up afterward. Still, many people feel that episiotomies are done too often, mostly to hurry delivery along, even though speedy delivery does not convey any particular medical benefit.

In the past, episiotomies were performed in the majority of deliveries, but results are just as good if episiotomies are limited to cases with specific risk factors, according to a recent meta-analysis of numerous studies (Jiang et al., 2017). In the United States less than 10% of women now receive episiotomies.

## The newborn child adapts quickly

Once the fetus's head and shoulders have exited the birth canal, the rest of the body follows more easily. The compression of the fetus's chest as it passes through the canal effectively "squeegees" the fluid out of its lungs, thus preparing them for the baby's first breath. With the passage of the entire body through the canal, the second stage of labor is complete. Occasionally the baby is born "in a caul"—that is, partially or completely wrapped in fetal membranes.*

---

*Historically, cauls were thought to be talismans conferring protection against drowning; they could be sold to sailors for considerable sums.

**crowning** The appearance of the fetal scalp at the vaginal opening.

**episiotomy** A cut extending the opening of the vagina backward into the perineum, performed by an obstetrician with the intention of facilitating childbirth or reducing the risk of a perineal tear.

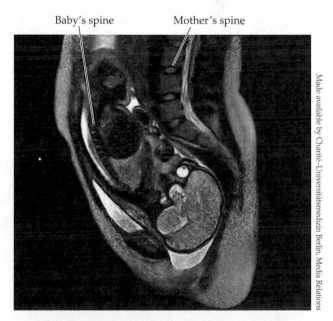

Baby's spine    Mother's spine

Made available by Charité–Universitätsmedizin Berlin, Media Relations

▲ **FIGURE 8.18**  **A fetus passing through the birth canal,** as seen in an MRI image. Note the large size of the fetal brain (outlined in red) in relation to the canal through which it must pass. A research team at Berlin's Charité Hospital developed a special open-field MRI machine to allow women to give birth inside it while receiving all normal medical support.

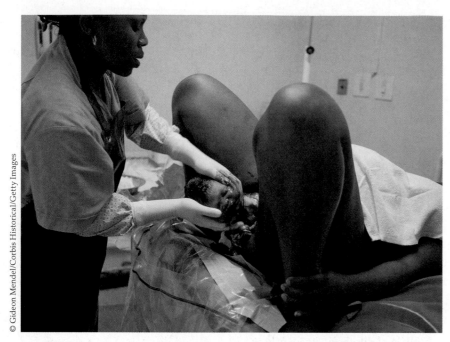

▲ The hard part is over. Once the baby's head and shoulders are free, the rest of its body emerges easily.

At this point, the newborn is still attached to the placenta by the umbilical cord, so the infant is still getting oxygen from the mother's lungs. Very shortly after birth, however, the baby takes its first breath, probably in response to cold and tactile stimulation. Then, in a beautifully orchestrated feat of physiology, the infant's circulatory system reorganizes itself: The fetal system, which largely bypasses the lungs, is replaced by the circulatory pattern seen after birth, in which the lungs receive all the blood from the right side of the heart.

The cessation of pulsation in the umbilical blood vessels can be readily seen. At this point, the cord is clamped and cut (sometimes by the mother's partner), and the baby is finally a free-living individual. The mother is often given the chance to hold and perhaps breastfeed her baby, at least for a short while. Increasing numbers of hospitals are keeping the baby in the mother's room rather than moving it to a nursery.

### The third stage is the expulsion of the placenta

**afterbirth** The placenta, whose delivery constitutes the final stage of labor.

**cesarean section (C-section)** The delivery of a baby through an incision in the abdominal wall and the uterus.

**premature birth (or preterm birth)** Birth that occurs more than 3 weeks before a woman's due date.

The third stage of labor consists of further uterine contractions that separate the placenta from the uterine wall and expel it (along with the other fetal membranes) through the birth canal. This usually takes about 30 minutes, but it can range from a few minutes to an hour or more. The expelled placenta is called the **afterbirth**.

The fetal blood in the afterbirth and the umbilical cord can be donated to a public cord blood bank; it contains stem cells that are of potential use in the treatment of leukemia and related diseases. Storing the blood in a private bank for the baby's own future use is a growing trend, but it doesn't make a whole lot of sense, given the low chance that the baby will ever need it. As for the placenta itself, some mothers who give birth at home eat their placentas, either directly or in the form of dehydrated capsules. This practice is common in some non-human animals, but it is not a typical human behavior in any culture. It has no proven benefits and has the potential for causing a serious infection in the baby or the mother (Elwood et al., 2019).

The process of labor can be shortened, or eliminated entirely, by delivering the baby through **cesarean section** (**C-section**), but the popularity of this practice raises serious concerns (**BOX 8.5**).

### Premature or delayed birth is hazardous

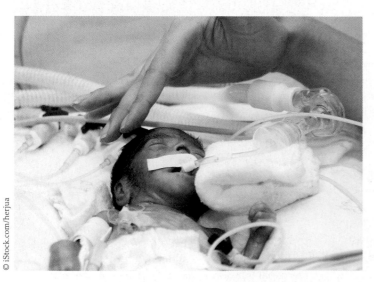

▲ Premature infants have a good chance of surviving, but they require intensive care and may end up with some kind of disability.

Labor is considered premature if it occurs more than 3 weeks before the mother's due date. In most cases of premature labor the cause is not known, but predisposing factors include multiple fetuses, teen pregnancy, the mother's use of tobacco or drugs, malnutrition, and a variety of illnesses during pregnancy.

Premature labor can sometimes be halted with the use of drugs; if not, it leads to **premature birth,** or **preterm birth**. This happens in about 10% of all pregnancies in the United

## BOX 8.5
## Cesarean Section

A cesarean section, or C-section, involves the delivery of a baby through a surgical incision in the front of the mother's abdomen and uterus (**FIGURE A**). The procedure is so named because Julius Caesar was supposedly born by this method (**FIGURE B**). We know that he wasn't, however, because his mother was alive during his childhood; no mothers survived a C-section before the Renaissance period.

In the United States today, one in three hospital births is by C-section. This is a very large increase from a generation ago. The Canadian rate is somewhat lower, at about 26%.

Cesarean sections are done when vaginal delivery is deemed inadvisable for a variety of medical reasons: if the mother's pelvis is too narrow for the size of the fetus, when labor does not progress after a prolonged period and the mother or fetus is becoming exhausted, or when certain complications occur during labor. A C-section may also be performed if the fetus's position is unfavorable for birth—that is, it is in some orientation other than head down and cannot be manipulated into the head-down position—or if the placenta is blocking the baby's passage into the birth canal. Another medical indication for a C-section may be to avoid exposing the baby to an infection present in the birth canal, such as herpes. For unknown reasons, a woman in whom labor is induced with drugs—an increasingly common practice—is twice as likely to end up having a C-section as a woman who is allowed to go into labor on her own schedule (Zhang et al., 2010).

Still, some C-sections are performed electively—that is, without any medical reason. The mother may request the procedure because she fears a painful childbirth, she believes that a vaginal delivery will impair her sex life afterward, or even because she doesn't want to attend childbirth classes. Some doctors also favor C-sections for nonmedical reasons: These procedures are much less likely than vaginal deliveries to lead to malpractice suits, and preplanned C-sections are easier to fit into a doctor's schedule than unpredictable natural births.

Emergency C-section may well save the life of mother or child, but any C-section is major surgery and should not be done without good reason. A review of 79 studies, including randomized trials, indicated that elective C-section presents significantly more risks to mother and child than natural childbirth (Belizan et al., 2007).

The World Health Organization believes that governments should try to keep national C-section rates no higher than 5% to 10% of all births.

(A)

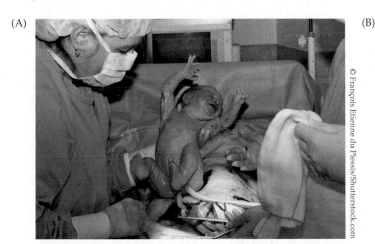

© François Etienne du Plessis/Shutterstock.com

(B)

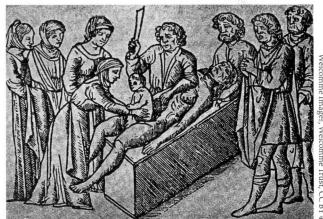

Wellcomme Images; Wellcomme Trust, CC BY 4.0

(A) A baby being delivered by cesarean section. (B) This didn't happen: The supposed birth of Julius Caesar by C-section, as imagined in a medieval woodcut.

States. The earliest time at which a preemie has a reasonable chance of viability (with intensive care) is about 24 weeks of gestational age, making the baby 16 weeks premature. At 23 weeks of gestation about 25% of preemies survive; at 22 weeks survival is rare (Manktelow et al., 2013).

Premature birth is dangerous to the baby's health. About 75% of all neonatal deaths (aside from those associated with congenital defects) strike the 10% of babies who are born prematurely. Most babies born before 28 weeks experience complications affecting

**delayed labor**   Labor that occurs more than 3 weeks after a woman's due date.

**induced labor**   Labor induced artificially by drugs.

**postpartum period**   The period after birth.

**lochia**   A bloody vaginal discharge that may continue for a few weeks after childbirth.

**postpartum depression**
Depression in a mother during the postpartum phase.

the eyes, brain, lungs, or intestines (Kluger, 2014). Preterm babies, especially those who are small for their gestational age or who are born very prematurely, have a higher likelihood of dying during childhood or experiencing long-lasting physical and behavioral disabilities, compared with babies delivered at term (López Bernal & TambyRaja, 2000; Swamy et al., 2008). Effects last into adulthood: In their 30s, people who weighed less than 1 kg (2.2 pounds) at birth are less likely to be married or have children than their peers, and their earnings are significantly lower (Saigal et al., 2016).

Labor that occurs more than 3 weeks past term is considered **delayed labor**: About 10% of babies are born at least this late. Like premature labor, delayed labor has risks. The fetus may grow too large to pass through the birth canal, and in a minority of cases the placenta may cease to adequately nourish the fetus, so it is born too small for its gestational age. Post-term babies are about three times more likely to die neonatally than are babies born at term. To avoid these ill effects, drugs such as oxytocin and prostaglandins may be used to **induce labor**. This practice itself carries some risk, but it does at least allow for the date of delivery to be planned ahead of time.

All these statements about premature and post-term babies are about risks, of course, not certainties. Many of these babies thrive both in childhood and adulthood. Still, the findings make clear how desirable it is for a baby to be born within 3 weeks of the mother's due date.

## 8.11  The Period after Birth Places Many Demands on Parents

**LEARNING OBJECTIVES**
After reading this section you should be able to:

8.11.1   Describe the possible causes of postpartum depression.
8.11.2   Evaluate the changes to relationships that may result from parenthood.

The weeks after birth are called the **postpartum period**. Although there can be medical problems for the mother during this period, including serious ones such as infections acquired during the birth process, its main feature is physical recovery from the stresses of pregnancy and childbirth. A vaginal discharge continues for a few days after parturition and is then replaced by small volumes of a dark, bloody discharge known as **lochia**; this ceases after a few weeks, but spotty bleeding may continue for 6 to 8 weeks. The uterus gradually shrinks back to its original dimensions, episiotomy or C-section incisions heal, and the mother's levels of estrogens and progesterone, which dropped precipitously at delivery, eventually return to more normal levels.

Psychologically, the postpartum period is a highly variable experience. On the plus side, the mother has the relief of putting pregnancy behind her and the joy of a new baby. Over the first few days after childbirth, these positive feelings tend to dominate. After that, however, the mother faces a great deal of stress. She finds herself back home and devoting a great deal of time and effort to looking after her infant, yet she still needs quite a bit of "mothering" herself. In this situation, the degree of support she receives from her partner or others makes an enormous difference to her psychological well-being.

### Postpartum depression may be accompanied by disordered thinking

Many women experience variable moods after childbirth, including periods of sadness and crying ("baby blues"). In about 1 in 10 women this sadness is sufficiently intense and sustained to be diagnosed as **postpartum depression** (Stewart & Vigod, 2019). This susceptibility to depression peaks in the period between 10 and 20 days after the birth, but it can linger for several months. Postpartum depression often impairs the mother's ability to care for her baby.

In a small minority of women, postpartum depression is accompanied by a serious disruption of thinking: This is called **postpartum depressive psychosis,** or simply **postpartum psychosis**. On rare occasions, this disorder can lead to infanticide or suicide. In a 2001 case Andrea Yates, a Houston woman with a prior history of postpartum depressive psychosis, drowned her 6-month-old daughter as well as her four older children. After two trials Yates was found not guilty by reason of insanity; she is now confined in a state mental hospital.

The factor most predictive of postpartum depression is a prior history of depression or other mood disorders, especially during pregnancy. Psychosocial factors, such as the lack of a partner or stressful economic circumstances, often play a role. In China, where boys are strongly preferred over girls, women who give birth to girls are nearly three times more likely to experience postpartum depression than those who give birth to boys (Xie et al., 2007).

Biological factors have not been identified with certainty, but the hormonal and metabolic changes at parturition, especially the severe drop in estrogen levels, are good candidates. Nevertheless, postpartum depression is quite commonly a continuation of depression experienced during pregnancy, when estrogen levels are high. The U.S. Preventive Services Task Force urges that all women be screened for depression both during pregnancy and after giving birth (United States Preventive Services Taskforce, 2016).

As with depression in general, SSRI-type antidepressants, such as sertraline (Zoloft), have been shown in well-controlled trials to alleviate the symptoms of postpartum depression; these drugs do not pose a risk to breastfeeding infants. A new drug, brexanolone (marketed as Zulresso) was approved specifically for treatment of postpartum depression in 2019, but its high cost will likely limit its use, as will the requirement that it be administered as a 60-hour intravenous infusion. Aside from drugs, counseling and peer support are helpful, as are strategies to help the mother get the sleep she needs.

## Childbirth and parenthood affect sexuality

The postpartum period is one of low or absent sexual activity, especially coitus, for most women. There are plenty of reasons for this: They are exhausted from the travails of pregnancy and childbirth, they are preoccupied with maternal responsibilities, and the vulva takes time to recover from the stresses of parturition, especially if there has been an episiotomy or a spontaneous tear that had to be sewn up. In addition, low postpartum estrogen levels tend to decrease vaginal lubrication, making coitus uncomfortable. Obstetricians often recommend that women wait about 6 weeks before resuming coitus, and most women do wait about that long or a little longer (McDonald & Brown, 2013). But after an uncomplicated delivery with no tearing or episiotomy, a woman can safely resume coitus at 3 weeks, if comfort allows. Contraception is necessary even that soon after childbirth.

Some women may be concerned that pregnancy and parturition have reduced their attractiveness (perhaps on account of weight gain or stretch marks) or their ability to enjoy coitus and satisfy their partners (perhaps because of stretching of the vagina). These fears are ill founded. Weight gain can be reversed, and it may not reduce attractiveness even if it isn't. Stretch marks fade. The vagina tightens. (This process can be aided by Kegel exercises; see Chapter 14.)

Although nearly all couples resume sex within a few months after childbirth, the transition to parenthood can have profound and often negative effects on their relationship and their sexuality. These effects have been studied most carefully for married couples. For the average couple, marital conflicts increase about ninefold after the birth of the first child, the perceived quality of the marriage drops precipitously,

© WENN Ltd/Alamy Stock Photo

▲ Pop superstar Adele experienced depression after the birth of her son Angelo in 2012. "You don't want to be with your child; you're worried you might hurt your child; you're worried you weren't doing a good job," she said 4 years later. "I felt like I'd made the worst decision of my life." (Robinson, 2016)

**postpartum depressive psychosis (or postpartum psychosis)**
Postpartum depression accompanied by seriously disordered thinking.

**FAQ:** I'm just getting back into sex after having my baby, but milk leaks out when I orgasm.

That's normal: The oxytocin surge at orgasm is triggering milk letdown. Try some strategically placed towels, or nurse your baby just before sex.

husband and wife adopt more stereotypical gender roles, the husband withdraws into work, and the frequency of marital conversations and sex goes into a steep decline (Gottman & Notarius, 2000). Of course, not every couple is the "average" couple: Some marriages and cohabitations blossom—especially those in which the baby was truly wanted by both partners (Council on Contemporary Families, 2009).

## 8.12 Breastfeeding Is the Preferred Method of Nourishing the Infant

### LEARNING OBJECTIVES
After reading this section you should be able to:

8.12.1 Explain the differences between colostrum and mature milk.

8.12.2 Evaluate the benefits of and possible problems with breastfeeding.

Breastfeeding—the trait that links humans with all other mammals—represents many things: a complex physiological process, a wellspring of intimacy between mother and child, and a source of physical and psychological health for both. In addition, it is a focus of controversy—between those who promote the virtues of breastfeeding and those who see it as something that technology and the demands of modern society have rendered obsolete or excessively burdensome.

### Lactation is orchestrated by hormones

**lactation** The production of milk in the mammary glands.

**prolactin** A protein hormone, secreted by the anterior lobe of the pituitary gland, that promotes breast development, among other effects.

**milk letdown reflex** The letdown of milk in response to nipple stimulation, mediated by oxytocin.

As described earlier, the breasts are ready to **lactate** (produce milk) by about the fourth month of pregnancy. The main hormone that promotes lactation—**prolactin**—is secreted in ever greater amounts as pregnancy proceeds. Once estrogen and progesterone levels drop, as they do at childbirth, prolactin triggers copious lactation, so the milk glands in the breasts become distended with milk.

While prolactin promotes lactation, oxytocin is responsible for the release of milk from the breast tissue into the milk ducts and nipples. The baby's sucking on the nipples triggers oxytocin release and the **milk letdown reflex**. Interestingly, this reflex is readily "conditioned": After a mother has nursed for some time, simply the sound of her baby crying or the mother's actions in preparing to nurse may trigger the milk letdown reflex. Suckling also promotes the continued secretion of prolactin after birth. Thus, if the mother does not breastfeed her infant, prolactin secretion declines, and the breasts gradually cease to produce milk.

In addition to hormones, a pheromone is involved in breastfeeding (Schaal et al., 2019). The tiny areolar glands that surround the nipples secrete a volatile substance whose identity is not known. If a cotton swab is wiped on these glands and then held near the nose of a newborn baby, it will trigger suckling behavior, even if the baby is asleep and no breast is nearby. The nipple pheromone is probably responsible for the "breast crawl"—the phenomenon whereby a newborn baby placed on its mother's abdomen will crawl unaided toward a breast and latch onto the nipple (Mother and Child Health and Education Trust, 2016). A video showing this behavior is available online (*Daily Mirror*, 2016). Excessive cleaning of the nipple prior to nursing may remove the nipple pheromone and make it difficult for the baby to "latch on."

### The content of breast milk changes over time

For the first few days after birth, the material secreted by the breasts is not mature milk, but a thick, yellowish special milk

▲ Breastfeeding cements the bond between mother and infant.

called **colostrum**. This material is lower in fat and sugar than mature milk but richer in proteins, especially antibodies. These protect the infant against a wide variety of infectious organisms and other antigens to which the mother has been exposed at some point in her life. Because colostrum is low in calories and is produced in limited amounts, a breastfeeding baby may lose up to 10% of its birth weight while waiting for the mature milk to come in. This is completely normal.

Over the first 2 weeks after birth, the breast secretions gradually become mature milk (**TABLE 8.3**) and increase greatly in volume. By 3 weeks after birth, a breastfed baby is drinking a little over 2 pints (1 L) of milk per day, which provides about 700 calories of energy. Most of that energy comes from the fat content of the milk. Of the proteins in milk, some are digested to provide amino acids for protein synthesis, while others resist digestion and serve as enzymes, antibodies, growth factors, and the like (Lönnerdal, 2003).

| **TABLE 8.3** | **Main constituents of mature human milk** |
|---|---|
| Water | Approximately 90% |
| Sugar (lactose) | Approximately 7% |
| Fat | 3%–6% |
| Proteins | 0.8%–0.9% |
| Amino acids | Includes all essential amino acids |
| Vitamins | Includes A, B1, B2, B12, C, D, E, K |
| Energy content | Approximately 19 calories per fluid ounce (650 calories per liter) |

## Infant formula is an alternative to breast milk

Over most of human history, mothers had little choice but to breastfeed their babies. Unmodified cow's milk is not a satisfactory substitute for human milk, at least for young infants. If women could not breastfeed or did not wish to do so, they would sometimes have their babies breastfed by other women who had milk to spare—perhaps because they had lost their own babies. Such women were called **wet nurses**. In the 20th century, the industrial production of **infant formula** began, and breastfeeding largely gave way to bottle-feeding in Western countries. Most formula is based on cow's milk that has been modified to make it more digestible; soy-based formula is recommended only for infants who cannot digest cow's milk.

In the 1950s only about one in five American women breastfed their infants, but beginning in the 1970s the numbers began to rise. This shift was propelled by medical research, which demonstrated that breastfeeding has specific health benefits, and by the women's movement, which rejected the image of breastfeeding as demeaning. Breastfeeding became a cause, spearheaded by La Leche League International. Currently, about 83% of American mothers breastfeed their babies initially, but that figure drops to 58% at 6 months and 36% at 1 year (CDC, 2018c).

**colostrum** The milk produced during the first few days after birth; it is relatively low in fat but rich in immunoglobulins.

**wet nurse** A woman who breastfeeds someone else's infant.

**infant formula** Manufactured breast milk substitute.

## Breastfeeding has many advantages and some drawbacks

Breastfeeding, compared with bottle-feeding, has many advantages (Office on Women's Health, 2018c):

- *Health benefits for the baby.* Breastfed babies are less likely to develop infectious illnesses such as pneumonia, botulism, bronchitis, bacterial meningitis, staphylococcal infections, influenza, ear infections, rubella, and diarrhea, and they are also less prone to asthma. These benefits are experienced mainly during the period of breastfeeding; the long-term physical health of breastfed and bottle-fed infants is about the same. But there do seem to be long-lasting cognitive benefits: In one randomized trial, prolonged, exclusive breastfeeding was associated with a higher IQ and better academic performance at the age of 6.
- *Health benefits for the mother.* By stimulating the release of oxytocin, breastfeeding helps shrink the uterus to its

▲ In many non-Western cultures, the contraceptive effect of prolonged breastfeeding plays an important role in the spacing of a woman's children.

**mastitis** Inflammation of the breast.

prepregnancy size and reduces postpartum bleeding. It also helps the mother shed the excess weight she gained during pregnancy. (Breastfeeding is nature's own liposuction.) It may also reduce her risk of ovarian cancer and early (premenopausal) breast cancer.

- *Psychological benefits to the mother and infant.* Breastfeeding helps establish a close bond between mother and child. Breastfeeding is usually pleasurable and relaxing for the mother.

- *Convenience and less expense.* Breastfeeding is much less expensive than formula-feeding, even considering the extra food the mother must consume to support it. Breastfeeding is more convenient than formula-feeding in the sense that no preparations are required: The breast milk is always there, perfectly prepared, at the right temperature, and sterile. Breastfeeding is also far better for the environment than formula-feeding.

- *Contraceptive effect.* In some non-Western cultures women nurse their children for several years after birth, and intensive nursing is associated with a reduction in fertility. Most American women do not nurse so intensively, however, and they stand a good chance of becoming pregnant even if they continue to nurse.

Breastfeeding also has several potential disadvantages:

- *Health problems for the mother.* Women who breastfeed sometimes develop inflamed nipples, which make nursing painful, or their breasts become uncomfortably engorged with milk. About 20% of women develop **mastitis** (inflammation or infection of the breast), often as a consequence of cracked nipples or a blocked milk duct. These conditions can be easily treated, however.

- *Health problems for the baby.* The infant can acquire some infections, including HIV and hepatitis, from the mother via her milk. Many drugs (including contraceptives) can pass from the mother to the child via milk and may harm the child. A mother who is taking medication and plans to breastfeed should discuss all drugs with her physician.

- *Inconvenience.* Although breast milk comes already prepared and warmed, the process of feeding it to the baby takes considerable time—several hours each day. It can be a real challenge for women to balance breastfeeding with workplace demands. One option is for the mother to remove milk with a breast pump and refrigerate it so that a caretaker—or perhaps the mother's partner—can rewarm it later and feed it to the baby by bottle.

Numerous organizations would like to see more women breastfeed their babies. Still, if a woman cannot do so for one reason or another, she should not feel that she has failed her child. Formula-fed infants can thrive as well as breastfed ones.

If a mother does breastfeed her infant, when should she stop? The American Academy of Pediatrics has recommended that babies be exclusively breastfed for 6 months, with continued partial breastfeeding for 1 year or more (American Academy of Pediatrics, 2012). There is no harm in breastfeeding throughout or even beyond the toddler years.

# Summary

- The onset of pregnancy is marked by a missed menstrual period and other symptoms. It can be confirmed by urine or blood tests that detect the human chorionic gonadotropin hormone (hCG) secreted by the implanted embryo.

- Infertility or subfertility can be caused by problems in the man or in the woman. If this condition results from low sperm count or sperm quality, in vitro fertilization (IVF) may still make pregnancy possible. An alternative is artificial insemination with donated sperm.

- Abnormalities of the female reproductive tract, resulting from sexually transmitted infections or other causes, can reduce fertility. The oviducts are the most common site of such problems. These abnormalities can sometimes be corrected surgically. Alternatively, embryos produced by IVF can be placed directly into the uterus.

- Problems with ovulation can often be treated with drugs. An alternative is the use of donated eggs.

- If a woman cannot sustain pregnancy at all, surrogate motherhood and adoption are possible options.

- Fertility declines steadily with age in both sexes. Age also raises the likelihood of fetal abnormalities such as Down syndrome.

- Many embryos do not survive. Many of those that fail to implant or that die early in pregnancy are abnormal. Other conditions, such as Rh factor incompatibility or ectopic pregnancy, can cause fetal loss or harm the fetus or the mother.

- Pregnancy lasts about 9 months and is conventionally divided into three trimesters. The first trimester may be marked by symptoms such as morning sickness. It is a critical period of fetal development during which the main body plan is laid out and organ systems develop. This process can be impaired by maternal infection or poor nutrition or by use of alcohol, tobacco, or a variety of drugs. Prenatal care offers important benefits, but many women do not receive such care in early pregnancy.

- The second trimester is usually easiest for the mother. The fetus can be screened for congenital abnormalities, and its sex can be determined at this time. Moderate exercise benefits the mother. The frequency of sexual activity tends to decline during pregnancy, but for most women there is no health reason for abstaining from coitus.

- In the third trimester both the parents and the fetus make preparations for birth. Childbirth classes teach strategies to facilitate delivery and to minimize pain.

- Labor has three stages. In the first stage, uterine contractions and cervical softening prepare the birth canal for the passage of the fetus. In the second stage, the fetus passes through the canal and is "delivered." Rapid physiological changes adapt the infant to an air-breathing existence. In the third stage, the placenta (afterbirth) and fetal membranes are expelled.

- Difficult births may necessitate surgical widening of the vaginal opening (episiotomy) or delivery via an abdominal incision (cesarean section). In the United States, episiotomy is performed much less often than in the past, but one in three women deliver by C-section. Various forms of anesthesia are available if labor is excessively painful. Methods of pain relief that do not rely on medications are also available.

- Premature and delayed labor are associated with increased risks of harm to the fetus.

- The postpartum period, after birth, is a time of recovery for the mother but is marked by depression with disordered thinking in a few women.

- The birth of a child, especially a first one, can bring great happiness, but it also causes major stresses. Marital satisfaction tends to decline after the transition to parenthood, and the frequency of sexual activity decreases.

- Hormones prepare the mother's breasts for lactation and mediate the release of milk during breastfeeding. The content of milk changes during the weeks after childbirth. Breastfeeding has significant advantages over formula-feeding, but formula-fed infants can thrive too.

## Discussion Questions

1. Imagine that for some reason you or your partner were not able to become pregnant by sexual intercourse. Discuss your preference for some alternative method of becoming parents. Discuss what the pros and cons of each solution would be for you.

2. Would you feel OK about paying a woman in a third-world country to go through pregnancy on your behalf?

3. Do you think that IVF clinics should help postmenopausal women who want to become pregnant, regardless of their age?

4. Imagine that you or your partner were pregnant and learned that the fetus had a genetic defect such as the one that causes Down syndrome. Discuss the costs and benefits of the options available to you (e.g., abortion, delivering the child and putting it up for adoption, or keeping and raising the child) and the rationale behind each one.

5. Do you think that the capability to select a child's sex prenatally is a good thing or a bad thing, and why? Do you think the practice should be permitted, discouraged, restricted, or banned?

6. Do you think it is right or sensible for a 70-year-old woman to have a baby? What about in a country like India, where many women consider it a disgrace to die childless? What about a man who becomes a father at that age?

7. Imagine that you are, or your partner is, happily pregnant and expecting a normal delivery. Would you elect to deliver the child at home, in a hospital, or in a birthing center? Would you prefer a medical doctor or a certified nurse-midwife to deliver your baby? Why?

8. Your baby is born and is healthy. Discuss the pros and cons of breastfeeding versus bottle-feeding. Which would you select? How long do you think breastfeeding should continue? Give your reasons.

9. What reasons can you list for having no children, or just one child?

## Web Resources

American Congress (also the College) of Obstetricians and Gynecologists
  **www.acog.org**

American Society for Reproductive Medicine   **www.asrm.org**

La Leche League International (organization that promotes breastfeeding)
  **www.llli.org**

National Down Syndrome Society   **www.ndss.org**

Society for Assisted Reproductive Technology   **www.sart.org**

## Recommended Reading

Cunningham, F., Leveno, K., Bloom, S., et al. (Eds.). (2014). *Williams obstetrics* (24th ed.). McGraw-Hill.

Gilbert, R. M. (2006). *The eight concepts of Bowen theory: A new way of thinking about the individual and the group*. Leading Systems.

Haimowitz, R. & Sinha, V. (2010). *Made in India*. Chicken and Egg Pictures. (Feature documentary about commercial surrogacy.)

King, T. L., Brucker, M. C., Osborne, K. & Jevitt, C.M. (2019). *Varney's midwifery* (6th ed.). Jones & Bartlett.

La Leche League International. (2010). *The womanly art of breastfeeding* (8th ed.). Ballantine.

Marsh, M. & Ronner, W. (2019). *The pursuit of parenthood: Reproductive technology to uterus transplants*. Johns Hopkins University Press.

Mayo Clinic. (2011). *Guide to a healthy pregnancy*. Good Books.

Twine, F. W. (2015). *Outsourcing the womb: Race, class, and gestational surrogacy in a global market* (2nd ed.). Routledge.

Weschler, T. (2006). *Taking charge of your fertility* (10th ed.). HarperCollins.

Condom assembly line. Globally, about 8 billion condoms are produced per year.

# 9 Contraception and Abortion

The previous chapter treated pregnancy as a natural consequence of vaginal intercourse. Most men and women, however, experience substantial periods of life during which they want to engage in sexual relationships but do not want to produce children. In fact, the typical American woman is capable of becoming pregnant for 34 years of her life but spends 31 of those years trying to avoid pregnancy. Human ingenuity has come up with a wide variety of methods for preventing pregnancies and—if necessary—ending them. These methods, often referred to collectively as family planning, are the topic of this chapter.

# 9.1 Birth Control Has a Long History

**LEARNING OBJECTIVES**

After reading this section you should be able to:

9.1.1 Describe the various outcomes of unintended pregnancy in the United States.

9.1.2 Evaluate the factors that should be considered in choosing a method of contraception.

**infanticide** The intentional killing of a newborn or very young child.

In the ancient world, the problem of unwanted pregnancies was often dealt with after the children's birth, by neglecting, abandoning, or directly killing them—a practice now known as the crime of **infanticide**. (The skeletons of numerous newborn babies have been found under the ruins of Roman-era brothels in England and Israel.) Abortion was also widely practiced, usually by consuming certain abortion-inducing herbs. Ergot—a fungus that infects rye—was used to induce abortion until quite recent times, even though it is almost as dangerous for the mother as it is for her fetus.

Various forms of contraception were used, though probably with limited success. These methods involved placing some substance, such as olive oil or a vinegar-soaked sponge, in the vagina before sex or douching with wine or vinegar afterward. The withdrawal method of contraception has been known for millennia and is mentioned in the biblical story of Onan, who "spilled his semen on the ground" to avoid impregnating his deceased brother's wife.

Male condoms—sheaths placed over the penis—also have a long history. The 18th-century Italian adventurer and ladies' man Giacomo Casanova made frequent reference to them in his memoirs, and this helped popularize them (Casanova, 1789/2015). Most early condoms were made from animal intestines, and they were so expensive that they had to be used repeatedly. Thus they had to be tested by inflating them with air before each use (**FIGURE 9.1**). Mass-produced vulcanized-rubber condoms (hence "rubbers") became available at the end of the 19th century, followed by latex condoms in the 1930s.

Diaphragms—barriers that cover the cervix—were originally natural objects, such as squeezed half-lemons. (The lemon half acted as a barrier; the lemon's acidity had some spermicidal action.) A reasonably effective artificial diaphragm was invented in the 1880s. Diaphragms were the main form of contraception used by women until the 1960s. In the 1920s Ernst Gräfenberg (of G-spot fame) developed an effective intrauterine device (IUD).

Scientific discoveries about the endocrinological basis of the menstrual cycle led to the introduction of oral contraceptives ("the pill") for women in the 1960s. Oral contraceptives, which consist of drugs related to sex hormones, were so effective that they almost eliminated the fear of unwanted pregnancy for many women and thus helped spur the "sexual revolution" of that time, although many other factors were at work. Most recent developments in contraceptive technology employ sex steroids or related compounds.

## Feminists led the campaign to legalize contraception

The history of contraception in the United States is not merely a story of technological advances, however, but also one of profound social conflict.

© Interfoto/Alamy Stock Photo

▲ **FIGURE 9.1** **Safety check** Nineteenth-century users tested condoms by blowing into them before use.

At least until the end of the 19th century, contraception was viewed by many as morally offensive because it subverted what was thought to be the natural or divinely intended function of sex: procreation. Indeed, that is still the official position of the Roman Catholic Church today, except that "fertility awareness" methods are permitted (see section 9.6). Early proponents of contraception were harassed, fined, or jailed.

Margaret Sanger (1879–1966) and other early feminists led the struggle to legalize contraception in the 20th century (**BOX 9.1**). The birth control movement did not achieve definitive success until the 1960s and 1970s, when two decisions of the U.S. Supreme Court (*Griswold v. Connecticut*, 1965, and *Eisenstadt v. Baird*, 1972) overthrew laws that banned the use or distribution of contraceptives. These rulings were based on a constitutional right of privacy and in fact helped establish that right.

Following these decisions, federal and state governments began supporting family planning initiatives—for example, through the Medicaid program. The AIDS epidemic, which began around 1980, boosted the social approval of one form of contraception—condoms—because it offered protection against the transmission of HIV. But contraception remains controversial in some quarters even today, especially with regard to its use

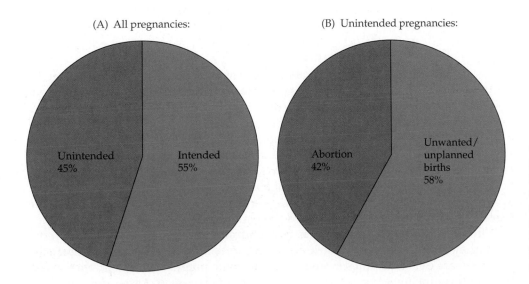

▲ Ideally, couples who engage in sex and who don't want children will cooperate to ensure that pregnancy doesn't occur, but a self-reliant method, or one that is evident in use, may allay concerns about a partner's reliability.

by teens. Much of this debate centers on whether schools should provide information about contraception and access to contraceptives. Because of this controversy, the U.S. government has been much less active in the field of contraception services, education, and research than have governments in many other industrialized countries. Thus, much of the burden of education and service provision has fallen on nongovernmental organizations such as Planned Parenthood.

## Contraception has not yet solved the problem of unintended pregnancy

Every pregnancy should be a wanted pregnancy and a source of joy to the pregnant woman and her partner. The reality can be very different, however (Guttmacher Institute, 2019c) (**FIGURE 9.2**). Forty-five percent of all pregnancies in the United States are unintended, meaning that the woman did not want to become pregnant at all or she did not want to become pregnant at that particular time. Forty-two percent

(A) All pregnancies:

Unintended 45%

Intended 55%

(B) Unintended pregnancies:

Abortion 42%

Unwanted/ unplanned births 58%

◀ **FIGURE 9.2 Unintended pregnancy in the United States** (A) Percentages of all pregnancies that are intended or unintended. (B) Percentages of unintended pregnancies that are terminated by abortion or that lead to unwanted or unplanned births. (Data from L. B. Finer and M. R. Zolna. 2016. *N Engl J Med* 374: 843–852.)

## BOX 9.1
## Margaret Sanger and the Birth Control Movement

Margaret Higgins Sanger was born in Corning, New York, in 1879. Her mother, Anne Higgins, died at age 50 after bearing 11 children, and Sanger attributed her early death to the burden of too-frequent pregnancies. Sanger trained as a nurse and in 1902 married an architect. The couple had three children and then moved to New York City. Working as a visiting nurse on the Lower East Side, Sanger came to realize that unrestricted births were putting a crushing economic and health burden on working-class women. Their all-too-frequent response to this burden—illegal or self-induced abortion—was killing many of them. In 1914 Sanger began publishing a radical feminist monthly called *The Woman Rebel*, which included appeals for the right to practice birth control. Sanger was indicted under the Comstock Law, which forbade the dissemination of information about contraception. She jumped bail and spent a year in Europe. While there, she visited a birth control clinic in the Netherlands, where women were being fitted with a new type of diaphragm, and she later imported this diaphragm into the United States.

Sanger returned to the United States in 1915 to face the charges against her, hoping to make her trial into a showcase for the birth control cause. The charges were dropped, however, because of widespread public sympathy for Sanger—especially because her only daughter had died that same year. She therefore went on a national lecture tour to promote birth control and was arrested in several cities.

In October 1916 Sanger opened the country's first birth control clinic, the Brownsville Clinic in Brooklyn, New York. The police closed it down after just 9 days of operation. Sanger was arrested and, because she refused to pay a fine, spent 30 days in prison. While in prison she taught contraceptive methods to other inmates.

Margaret Sanger (1879–1966).

The Brownsville affair drew widespread sympathy and financial support to her cause. Although she lost the appeal of her conviction, the appellate court did rule that physicians could provide contraceptive information for medical reasons. This ruling allowed Sanger's group to open a doctor-staffed birth control clinic, and others followed. In 1917 Sanger began publication of a monthly, the *Birth Control Review*, and in 1921 she founded the American Birth Control League, forerunner of Planned Parenthood Federation.

Sanger died in 1966, a year after the U.S. Supreme Court, in *Griswold v. Connecticut*, declared that married couples had a constitutional right to use birth control.

of these unintended pregnancies, or about 1 in 5 of all pregnancies, are terminated by abortion; the remainder lead to unwanted or unplanned births. Unintended pregnancies entail costs to state and federal governments of over $20 billion per year to cover medical care and welfare payments.

Among American women who are sexually active and fertile but don't want to become pregnant, about two-thirds make consistent use of some contraceptive technique, and these women are very unlikely to become pregnant. The other one-third, however, don't use contraceptives at all or use them inconsistently, and these women account for 95% of all unintended pregnancies. In other words, contraception works—but only if people use it, and do so consistently.

Who are the women who become pregnant without wanting to? Overwhelmingly, they are poor. Women whose family incomes are below the U.S. federal poverty level are over five times more likely to become pregnant unintentionally than those whose incomes are at least double the poverty level. Other demographic factors associated with unintended pregnancy are being unmarried, being young, and having relatively little education. The good news is that the unintended pregnancy rate is declining in all American demographic groups. Just in the 3 years from 2008 to 2011 the rate of unintended pregnancies among all women age 15 to 45 fell by 18%, and among those age 15 to 17 the rate fell by an astonishing 44%. Data for more recent years are not available, but a continuing decline in abortion rates (which we will discuss later) suggests that there has been a corresponding decline in the rate of unintended pregnancies.

The facts in the above paragraphs come from the website of the Guttmacher Institute. This is a nonprofit organization devoted to research, education, and policy development in reproductive health, with an emphasis on contraception and abortion. The Guttmacher Institute's website and those of Planned Parenthood, the Centers for Disease Control and Prevention, and the Mayo Clinic (see Web Resources at the end of this chapter) are generally the most reliable sources of information regarding the topics covered in this chapter, and they may be more up to date than what you read in this edition of our textbook, whose text was finalized in 2020.

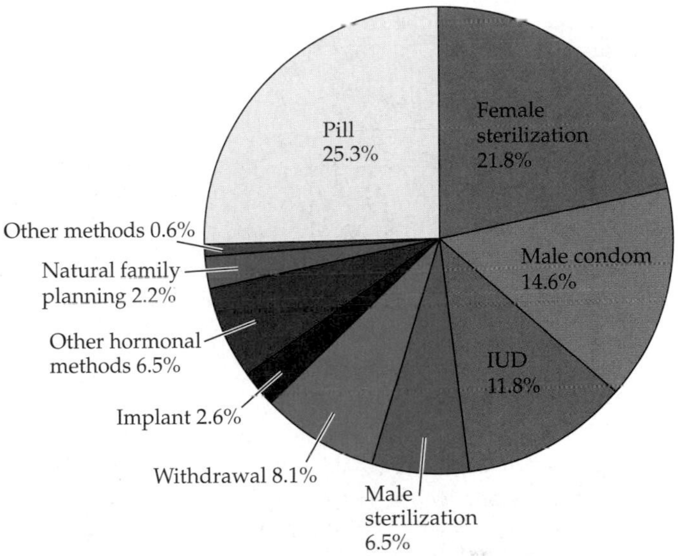

### Different users have different contraceptive needs

A wide variety of contraceptive methods are available, each of which has certain features that make it more or less attractive for individual users (**FIGURE 9.3**). The data in the figure are for all women age 15 to 44 who use contraception. Sterilization is uncommon among young users, of course: Among women age 20 to 24, only 3% depend on female or male sterilization, whereas among women age 40 to 44 the majority do so.

Here are the main issues that people who are choosing a contraceptive technique should consider.

- *How reliable is the method?* With some methods, such as oral contraceptives, less than 1% of users will become pregnant in a single year, provided they practice the method properly. This percentage is called the **perfect-use failure rate** of the method. All humans are fallible, however; a woman might forget to take the pills for a day or two, for example, or a man's fingernail might tear a condom while he is putting it on. Thus, the **typical-use failure rates** of contraceptive methods tend to be higher—about 7% for pills. Only a few methods have typical-use failure rates below 1%; these are methods that you can basically forget about once you have taken the initial steps. We summarize information about the reliability of the most common methods of contraception in **FIGURE 9.4**.

- *How safe is it for me?* We describe general risks associated with the various methods listed in this chapter. Individual users may have risk factors that make specific methods inadvisable for them.

- *Do I need the method to be reversible?* For most young people the answer is "yes," but for older adults who are certain they don't want more children, irreversible contraception (sterilization) may be preferable.

- *Do I need STI protection?* The protection against sexually transmitted infections offered by condoms is an important added advantage of this method, especially for women and men who are not in long-term monogamous relationships. Of course, condoms can be added to methods that don't offer STI protection, such as pills.

**▲ FIGURE 9.3  Usage of contraceptive methods** The pie chart shows the percentage of all contraceptive users in the United States who use each method. "Other methods" include diaphragm, sponge, spermicide, and others. (Data from M. L. Kavanaugh and J. Jerman. 2018. *Contraception* 97:14–21.)

**perfect-use failure rate**
The percentage of women using a contraceptive technique correctly who will become pregnant in the course of a year.

**typical-use failure rate**
The percentage of women using a contraceptive technique with a typical degree of care who will become pregnant in the course of a year.

▶ **FIGURE 9.4** **Failure rates for contraceptive methods** The failure rate is the typical percentage of women using this method who will become pregnant during the first 12 months of use. The two percentages under each method show the failure rates with perfect use (left) and with typical use (right). None of these percentages are precise. Notes: (1) The failure rate for the sponge is higher for women who have previously given birth than for women who have not (see text). (2) Failure rates vary among different IUDs (see text). (3) Failures with sterilization, especially male sterilization, are mostly the result of resuming unprotected sex too early. Failures at later times are rare (see text). (After J. Trussell et al. 2018. In *Contraceptive Technology*, 21st ed., R. A. Hatcher et al., eds., pp. 95–120. Ayer Company Publishers, Inc.: New York, with data from J. Trussell. 2011. *Contraception* 83: 397–404.)

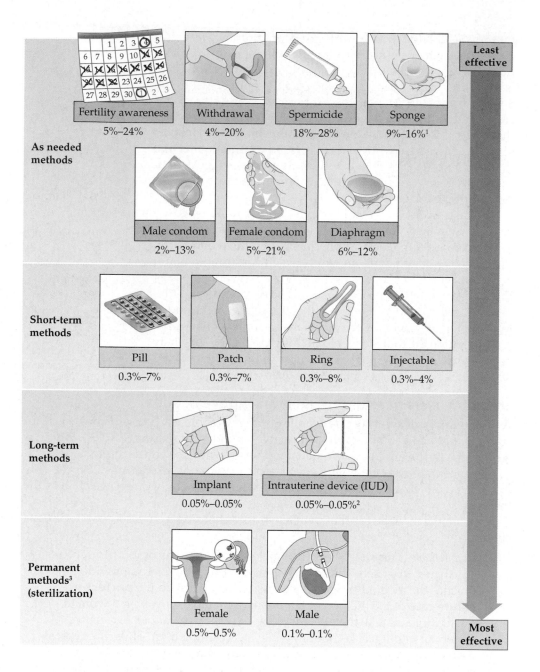

- *How easy is the method for me to use?* Some methods, such as condoms, require some time and attention before or during every sexual encounter. Some methods require taking pills on a rather precise schedule. Some require regular visits to a health care provider. How burdensome these requirements are depends on your individual circumstances and personality.

- *How much will it cost?* Some methods require substantial upfront expenditure, some require continual purchases over time, and some are free, or nearly so.

- *Will I be in control?* For some users, it may be important to be in charge of the contraception method, rather than leaving the responsibility to partners who might not be reliable.

Don't be discouraged by the high typical-use failure rates shown in Figure 9.4. "Failure" is defined in a very broad way that includes, for example, women who say they use a certain method but in fact never do so. You can do better than that!

# 9.2 Physical Methods Block Sperm Transport

**LEARNING OBJECTIVES**

After reading this section you should be able to:

9.2.1 Describe the different kinds of male condoms and how they should be used.

9.2.2 Evaluate the pros and cons of male and female condoms, diaphragms, and spermicides.

We begin with reversible physical methods, some of which have a long history of safe and successful use.

## Male condoms are reliable when properly used

The **male condom** (**FIGURE 9.5**) is a disposable sheath that is placed over the penis before coitus. It works simply by preventing semen from entering the vagina; thus, it is described as a **barrier method** of contraception. Some condoms come precoated with the spermicide nonoxynol-9, which kills sperm chemically. The amount of spermicide on coated condoms is probably not enough to be effective in the event that the condom breaks, however, and the presence of the spermicide shortens the shelf life of the condom and increases its cost. In addition, as discussed later in this chapter, the frequent use of spermicides can cause health problems for the woman. For all these reasons, spermicide-coated condoms are not recommended. When used properly (**FIGURE 9.6**), condoms are an effective contraceptive.

Most condoms are made of latex. Others are made of synthetic materials such as polyisoprene, polyurethane, or nitrile (synthetic latex), or they are derived from animal tissue ("lambskin" condoms). Latex condoms are the cheapest: They cost less than $1 apiece when bought in multipacks, and they can be picked up for free at many colleges and at hundreds of other locations nationwide (Condomfinder, 2019).

Latex condoms should be used in conjunction with water-based or silicone lubricants only. Oils, fats, lotions, Vaseline, and any lubricants containing those substances will weaken the latex and will likely cause the condom to break.

Some men and women are allergic to latex. Another potential disadvantage of condoms—whether latex or synthetic—is that they lessen the sensitivity of the penis. This might be helpful for men who tend to ejaculate earlier than they wish, but some men have difficulty maintaining an erection when using a condom; this can be true for both vaginal and anal sex (Graham et al., 2006; Li et al., 2020).

Polyisoprene condoms are stretchy like latex and therefore fit snugly. Some people find that they provide a better sensation than latex condoms, and they smell better. They are suitable for people (men or their partners) who are sensitive to latex.

Polyurethane condoms are much less stretchy than latex condoms. Thus, if the right size is chosen, it will fit well without the tight feeling of a latex condom, but if it is too large, it may easily slip off. Both polyisoprene and polyurethane condoms are effective contraceptives. They can be used with water-, silicone-, or oil-based lubricants. Many such condoms come already lubricated with a silicone-based lubricant.

Latex and synthetic condoms are impermeable to disease agents, including HIV. For that reason they are often used in combination with other contraceptive methods, such as pills, that don't offer STI protection, as well as for sexual activities such as anal sex where pregnancy is not an issue. In real-world usage,

**male condom**   A sheath placed over the penis as a contraceptive and/or to prevent disease transmission.

**barrier method**   Any contraceptive technique in which a physical barrier, such as a condom or diaphragm, prevents sperm from reaching the ovum.

**FAQ:** I'm sensitive to nonoxynol-9. Are there alternatives?

You may be able to find spermicides containing octoxynol-9. In Canada and Europe, spermicides containing benzalkonium chloride are available.

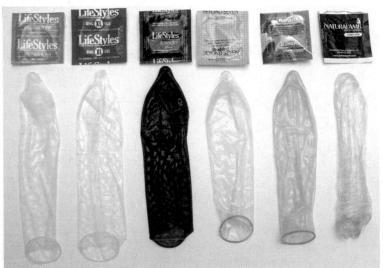

David McIntyre

▲ **FIGURE 9.5**   **Male condoms** come in a variety of types, sizes, and even flavors.

**1** Open condom pack. Use a new condom for each act of intercourse if any risk of pregnancy or STI exists.

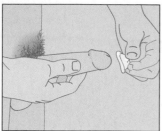

**2** Before any genital contact, place the condom on the tip of the erect penis with the rolled side out.

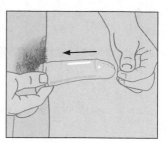

**3** Unroll the condom all the way to the base of the penis.

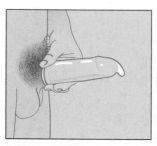

**4** Immediately after ejaculation, hold the rim of the condom and withdraw the penis while it is still erect.

**5** Throw away the used condom safely (in the trash, not the toilet).

**6** With latex condoms, use only water-based or silicone lubricants.

▲ **FIGURE 9.6 How to use a condom** These are the instructions recommended by an expert committee of the World Health Organization. If the condom doesn't have a pouch at the tip to contain the ejaculate, some sources suggest making one by pinching the tip while unrolling the condom. (After L. Warner and M. J. Steiner. 2018. In *Contraceptive Technology*, 21st ed., R. A. Hatcher et al., eds., pp. 431–450. Ayer Company Publishers, Inc.: New York.)

## FAQ: Are latex condoms OK for vegans?

Most latex condoms employ the milk protein casein in the manufacturing process. Look for "casein-free," or use synthetic condoms.

however, the anti-STI protection offered by condoms is less than perfect, on account of various forms of misuse. Among these, the most common are the application of inappropriate lubricants and the failure to use a condom throughout the entire sexual episode (Smith et al., 2015).

Natural-tissue "lambskin" condoms are made from sheep intestines. They feel more natural in use than other condoms, but they are more expensive, and they may have a disagreeable odor. More importantly, they are *ineffective* in preventing the transmission of HIV and other viral STIs. That's because they have pores large enough to permit the passage of viruses. Thus, they should be used only if STIs are not a concern.

Condoms come in quite a variety of sizes, styles, colors, and even flavors. A standard-size condom, which measures about 7 inches (180 mm) long by 2 inches (51 mm) across when flat, will fit most men, but there are smaller ("snugger fit") and larger ("large," "magnum," "magnum XL") condoms available, as well as a condom called myONE Perfect Fit that is customized to any of 60 sizes. (The company's website explains how to order the correct size.) There are also condoms whose width is greater near the tip, condoms with various kinds of ribbed or bumpy surfaces (to increase sensation), condoms with a skin desensitizer (to delay the man's orgasm), and condoms that glow in the dark (possibly useful for men who can't find their penises).

If condoms are going to be a part of your life for the foreseeable future, it may be worth ordering one of the sampler kits that are available on the internet. These kits contain many different types of condoms from a variety of different manufacturers. (Testing them all could add spice to your relationship and provide material for an interesting term paper.) Just be wary of natural-tissue or novelty condoms that may not provide adequate contraception or disease protection.

Condoms do sometimes break or slip off. Usually this is because of some kind of misuse, such as the use of old or inappropriately sized condoms, insufficient lubrication, or the use of oil-based lubricants with latex condoms. Very infrequently, even properly used condoms break. According to one study of broken condoms returned to their manufacturer, most of these failures involve "blunt puncture," in which repeated thrusting by the head of the penis stretches the condom until it breaks (White et al., 2008). Strategies to prevent breakage include inspection of the condom before and during sex, use of plenty of water-soluble lubricant, changing condoms during prolonged coitus, or using thicker condoms.

Among college students who engage in vaginal sex and use some form of contraception, about two-thirds say they use condoms—often in combination with another contraceptive method such as the contraceptive pill (American College Health Association, 2018). This figure should be viewed with caution, however: Total U.S. condom usage as calculated from survey data vastly exceeds actual condom sales, meaning that many people exaggerate their condom usage (Stephens-Davidowitz, 2017).

## BOX 9.2
## Male Contraceptives of the Future?

Imagine never having to use a condom again. Many research groups are trying to make that dream a reality—by developing alternative, more acceptable forms of male contraception. Here's a sampler of the technologies that are being explored (Thirumalai & Page, 2019):

- *Intra-vas devices (IVDs).* These are plugs that are placed inside the vasa deferentia, blocking the flow of sperm (see figure). Alternatively, the vas deferens can be blocked with an injected gel (Parsemus Foundation, 2019). To restore fertility, a second injection flushes out the gel.

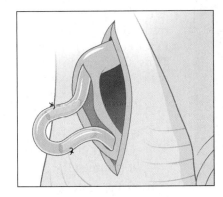

Intra-vas plugs block sperm transport along the vasa deferentia. This procedure, which is still in development, can be more easily reversed than a vasectomy.

- *Androgens.* Testosterone and other androgens exert a feedback inhibition on the production of the gonadotropic hormones, which in turn causes a reduction in sperm counts (see Figure 3.14). To be effective without causing unwanted side effects the androgen must be supplemented with a progestin, or a single drug with both actions may be used. Another drug under development is 7α-methyl 19-nortestosterone, known as MENT, which can be delivered as a subdermal depot (like Nexplanon in women). The advantage of this drug is that it cannot be converted to DHT (see Chapter 3), and it therefore doesn't cause unwanted peripheral effects such as an enlarged prostate (Population Council, 2019).

- *"Dry orgasm" pills.* Several drugs have been developed that disrupt the action of smooth muscle within the vas deferens or the urethra. These drugs can prevent sperm from being mixed into the semen or can cause the semen to be ejaculated retrogradely into the bladder.

- *Immunology.* Some men are infertile because they possess antibodies directed against their own sperm. It is possible to trick the immune systems of healthy men into developing antibodies against sperm or other elements of the male reproductive system.

- *Retinoic acid blockers.* Retinoic acid, a metabolite of vitamin A, is required for spermatogenesis. Drugs that prevent the attachment of retinoic acid to its receptors in the testicles have been shown to block sperm production in a reversible fashion in laboratory animals.

- *Sperm immobilizer.* A start-up company named Eppin Pharma is working on a drug that acts like semenogelin (see Box 3.6), but unlike semenogelin, it resists breakdown by PSA, so the sperm remain immobilized and cannot migrate up the female reproductive tract.

It's uncertain whether any of these methods will make it through clinical trials into general use. The Male Contraceptive Initiative website provides up-to-date information about the field (Male Contraceptive Initiative, 2019).

Advantages of the male condom:

- It is cheap and readily accessible.
- It is reliable when properly used.
- It offers significant but incomplete protection against STIs.
- It lacks the possible side effects of hormone-based contraceptives.
- Its use is fully and immediately reversible.

Disadvantages of the male condom:

- Putting on a condom can interrupt lovemaking.
- The man must withdraw promptly after ejaculating.
- Condoms reduce the pleasure of sex for many users.
- Some men have difficulty maintaining an erection while using a condom.
- Reliability is less than ideal in typical use, mostly due to failure to use condoms consistently.

Because condoms have drawbacks, there is considerable research into other potential methods of male contraception (**BOX 9.2**).

▲ **FIGURE 9.7** **The female condom** is made of nitrile (synthetic latex). It is an effective contraceptive, but it is less popular in the United States than in some other countries.

**female condom** A nitrile rubber pouch inserted into the vagina as a contraceptive and/or to prevent disease transmission.

**diaphragm** A barrier placed over the cervix as a contraceptive.

## Female condoms are relatively intrusive

The **female condom** is made of nitrile rubber. It resembles a large male condom, but it is stiffened by rings at each end (**FIGURE 9.7**). The ring at the closed end lies loose inside the condom; it fits around the cervix rather like a diaphragm (see below). The ring at the open end is attached to the condom; it is large because it is intended to stay outside the body. Thus, the condom covers the entirety of the vagina and adjacent parts of the vulva. The condom comes with lubricant on the inside, and additional lubricant for the outside is supplied with the condom.

Advantages of the female condom:

- The female condom is the only contraceptive controlled by the woman that probably offers substantial protection from STIs, including HIV.
- It can be inserted ahead of time, thus avoiding any interruption of lovemaking.
- It does not require the man to maintain an erection during use, and it does not constrict the man's penis.
- Its use is easily and immediately reversible.
- It can be used for anal sex if the inner ring is removed.

Disadvantages of the female condom:

- The method feels awkward initially, though it becomes easier with practice.
- The female condom tends to be less appealing to men than to women; part of the reason for this is that some men consider the protruding free end unaesthetic.
- There is the possibility that the man will accidentally insert his penis into the vagina outside of the condom.
- Sometimes the entire condom may be drawn into the vagina during coitus. To prevent this, it may be necessary to hold the outer ring of the condom.
- Male and female condoms should not be used simultaneously, because the friction between them may pull one of them out of place.

The female condom has not gained wide acceptance in the United States, but some couples may find that it works well for them. Larger numbers of female condoms are distributed in developing countries, where there is a greater need for women to control their own contraception.

## Diaphragms and cervical caps are inconvenient but have few side effects

The **diaphragm** (**FIGURE 9.8**) used to be a very popular form of contraception prior to the development of oral contraceptives, but it is now used by fewer than 1 in 100 American women. It is a dome-shaped piece of silicone or latex that is stiffened by a spring-like strip around its perimeter. It fits against the walls of the vagina, covering the cervix. It works by preventing sperm from entering the cervix. However, sperm can migrate around the edges of the diaphragm, and it must therefore be used in conjunction with a spermicidal cream or jelly, which is placed inside the dome of the diaphragm and around the rim. Latex diaphragms, like latex condoms, are damaged by oil-based lubricants.

▲ **FIGURE 9.8** **Diaphragms have lost popularity** in the United States but are still widely used elsewhere.

The diaphragm should be left in place for at least 6 hours after sex, but no more than 24 hours in total. For repeated sex while the diaphragm is still in place, more spermicide should be placed in the vagina without dislodging the diaphragm.

Advantages of the diaphragm:

- It is somewhat less intrusive than condoms because it can be inserted ahead of time and does not usually affect sensation during sex.
- Long-term use of the diaphragm is associated with a lowered risk of cervical cancer, probably because the diaphragm offers some protection against infection of the cervix with human papillomavirus, the virus that causes cervical cancer.

Disadvantages of the diaphragm:

- It is inconvenient, because of both the necessity for professional fitting and the need for insertion, removal, and cleaning.
- It can occasionally get dislodged during coitus.
- The diaphragm's failure rate is significantly greater than that of hormone-based methods and slightly greater than that of condoms. The failure rate is even higher for women who have previously given birth.
- It provides much less disease protection than condoms.
- The spermicide may cause irritation, which may increase the risk of STI transmission.
- Some women find that they develop urinary tract infections with diaphragm use.

Variations on the diaphragm include the **cervical cap**, a smaller device that holds onto the cervix like a suction cup. The **FemCap** is the only cervical cap available in the United States; it has a raised brim that lies against the wall of the vagina, as well as a strap for easier removal.

In general, diaphragms and cervical caps may be acceptable options for women who need to be in charge of their own contraception but cannot or do not want to use hormone-based methods.

## Spermicides are not very reliable when used alone

Some women use **spermicides** as their sole method of contraception. Spermicides are chemicals, usually nonoxynol-9, that destroy sperm with a detergent-like action that disrupts their cell membranes. Spermicides come in the form of contraceptive foams, jellies, creams, suppositories ("inserts"), or dissolvable films (**FIGURE 9.9**). They are placed deep in the vagina no more than 2 hours ahead of time (and preferably much closer to the time of coitus). Suppositories and some other spermicides need time to dissolve, so they should be inserted at least 10 minutes before coitus. (Carefully follow the instructions that come with the product.) All spermicides must be left in place for at least 6 hours afterward in order to complete the killing of sperm; therefore, the woman should not rinse out her vagina during this time. (Nor does she need to do so after that time has elapsed.) If a woman has coitus again during this 6-hour period, she must insert more spermicide before each act.

One spermicide contraceptive, the Today sponge, sits against the cervix like a diaphragm and thus creates a partial physical barrier in addition to releasing spermicide. It is said to be effective for multiple acts of intercourse over 24 hours.

Advantages of spermicides:

- They are readily available without a prescription.
- They are inexpensive.
- They have few side effects, except in the case of allergic reactions and irritation, which is mostly associated with frequent use.

**cervical cap** A small rubber or plastic cap that adheres by suction to the cervix, used as a contraceptive.

**FemCap** A type of cervical cap that has a raised brim.

**spermicide** A chemical that kills sperm, available as a contraceptive in a variety of forms, such as foams, creams, and suppositories.

(A)

David McIntyre

(B)

© Garo/Phanie/Science Source

▲ **FIGURE 9.9** **Spermicides come in a variety of forms.** Vaginal contraceptive foam and Encare inserts (A) and contraceptive sponges (B) contain the spermicide nonoxynol-9.

Disadvantages of spermicides:

- Spermicides can hardly be recommended as the sole means of contraception, because their failure rate is quite high—about 25% for the foams and possibly higher for the suppositories. They are better suited for use in combination with barrier methods. The Today sponge may be a little better, with a reported 16% failure rate in typical use.

- Spermicides, used alone, offer no significant protection against several STIs, including gonorrhea, chlamydia, and HIV. In fact, frequent use of spermicides (more than twice a day) can cause genital irritation or lesions, thus increasing the likelihood of acquiring or transmitting HIV and other infections.

## 9.3 Hormone-Based Methods Are Easy to Use

### LEARNING OBJECTIVES

After reading this section you should be able to:

9.3.1 Explain how combination and progestin-only pills work, and their pros and cons.

9.3.2 Define menstrual suppression and explain how it is achieved.

Several different hormone-based contraceptive methods are available. They differ in the kinds and amounts of hormones they contain, as well as in their form of delivery. Because oral contraceptives (pills) are so popular—they are the choice of about one in four women who use any kind of contraception—and because they come in a number of significantly different formulations, we will devote most of our attention to them.

Contraceptive pills (**FIGURE 9.10**) contain either a combination of two hormones—an estrogen and a progestin—or just one hormone, a progestin. Both hormones are synthetic. Synthetic steroids are used because they are broken down in the body much more slowly than the natural hormones, so the pills need be taken only once a day. Among U.S. undergraduate college women who engage in coitus, nearly 60% say that they use contraceptive pills (American College Health Association, 2016).

## Combination pills offer health benefits

The most commonly used type of contraceptive pill is the **constant-dose** (or "monophasic") **combination pill**. Such pills, of which there are many different brands as well as generic versions, usually contain between 20 and 50 micrograms (μg) of estrogen (in a synthetic form known as ethinyl estradiol) and between 0.1 and 1.0 milligrams (mg) of a progestin. (Part of the reason for the varying progestin doses is that progestins vary in potency: 0.1 mg of one may be the equivalent of 1.0 mg of another.) Typically, a woman takes one pill a day for 21 days, followed by no pills or by inactive "dummy" pills for 7 days. Some formulations that contain very low doses of hormones shorten the drug-free interval to 4 or even 2 days.

Another kind of combination pill is the **triphasic** (or "multiphasic") **combination pill** (examples are Ortho-Novum 7/7/7 and Tri-Norinyl). In these pills, the amounts and ratios of estrogen and progestin vary around the cycle, in order to minimize the total doses of hormones and decrease side effects. As with most constant-dose pills, triphasic regimens involve a 7-day drug-free interval. Triphasic pills are more expensive than constant-dose pills, but they have not been shown to be more effective or safer.

One site of action of combination pills is the brain—specifically, the hypothalamic-pituitary control system, whose function is altered in ways that prevent ovulation. The other site is the cervix: The hormones in combination pills cause the cervix to secrete thick mucus that prevents sperm from entering the uterus.

Combination pills also promote development of the endometrium, as would happen naturally during the postovulatory phase of the menstrual cycle. During the drug-free portion of the cycle, therefore, the endometrium breaks down and bleeding occurs. This bleeding simulates a natural menstrual period, although the menstrual flow may be less than a woman normally experiences.

Ovarian follicles develop during the drug-free interval, just as they do during the early days of a normal menstrual cycle. A woman is just as well protected from pregnancy during the drug-free days as during the rest of the cycle, because the further development of these follicles is suppressed as soon as the next cycle of pills begins. If a woman forgets to begin the next cycle of pills, however, the developing follicles can proceed to ovulation within a couple of days or so, potentially leading to pregnancy. Thus, if she is in doubt about the number of drug-free days that have elapsed, a woman does better to restart the cycle of pill taking, beginning too early rather than too late.

Many physicians prefer to prescribe pills containing as little estrogen as possible (i.e., 20 μg or thereabouts) because it is primarily the estrogen in combination pills that is responsible for the health risks associated with these products (see disadvantages below). Low-estrogen combination pills are as effective in preventing pregnancy as are higher-estrogen products. They do not always regulate the woman's menstrual cycle as effectively, however, and this can be a reason why some women discontinue low-estrogen combination pills.

Advantages of combination pills:

- With perfect use, combination pills are extremely reliable: Less than 1% of women who use these pills correctly will become pregnant per year. Unfortunately, it is easy to forget a pill or two. Thus, the typical-use failure rate is about 7%—significantly better than that for condoms or behavioral methods (see below), but significantly worse than the rate for sterilization or the intrauterine device (IUD). Remember, though, that a woman doesn't

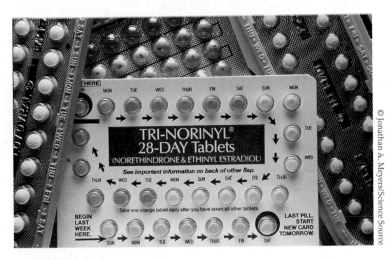

▲ **FIGURE 9.10** **A variety of combination-type contraceptive pills** in 28-day dispensers. Note the orange dummy pills, seen at the bottom of the photograph, for the 7 no-drug days.

© Jonathan A. Meyers/Science Source

**constant-dose combination pill**
An oral contraceptive regimen in which all pills (except any dummy pills) contain the same drug dosage.

**triphasic combination pill**
An oral contraceptive regimen that varies the doses of estrogens and progestins around the menstrual cycle.

**FAQ:** Is it safe to take St. John's wort while on the contraceptive pill?

No. St. John's wort, an unregulated medicinal herb used to treat depression, accelerates the breakdown of the pill's ingredients in the body and may therefore raise the likelihood of pregnancy.

have to be "typical": She can come close to "perfection" by planning her pill-taking schedule carefully, by using a reminder app, or by adding condoms to the mix.

- They are convenient and neither interfere with the spontaneity of sex nor diminish the sensations of coitus.

- They are easily reversible. Fertility should return to normal levels by 3 months after stopping the combination pill. (If the woman doesn't wish to become pregnant, she should use an alternative contraceptive technique immediately after stopping the pills.)

- They have very significant health benefits quite aside from the avoidance of pregnancy (which is a health benefit in itself). Use of combination pills for 10 years is associated with an 80% reduction in the risk of both ovarian and endometrial cancers, and this reduced risk persists for at least 20 years after stopping pill usage. Many women experience lighter menstrual flows and diminished or absent menstrual cramps, premenstrual symptoms,* and midcycle pain when on the pills. Pill usage also reduces the prevalence or severity of iron-deficiency anemia, endometriosis, ovarian cysts, acne, hirsutism (excessive facial and body hair), and noncancerous conditions of the breast. The health benefits of contraceptive pills can be so great, for many women, that some experts recommend their use even by women who don't need contraception.

Disadvantages of combination pills:

- They offer no protection against STIs, including HIV. (However, condoms can be added for disease protection.)

- The woman needs to remember to take the pills regularly each day.

- The method is not evident to the woman's partner unless he is present every day when she takes a pill. Thus, he has no objective assurance that the woman is employing effective contraception.

- The combination pill can have side effects. Frequently reported side effects include nausea, breast pain, increased breast size, irregular bleeding, abdominal pain, back pain, decreased vaginal lubrication, weight gain, blotchy discoloration of the skin, emotional lability (e.g., crying for little reason), and decreased or increased interest in sex. Nevertheless, controlled trials have found no increase in these problems in women using combination pills as compared with nonusers (Grimes & Schulz, 2011). Regarding weight gain, a large longitudinal study conducted in Sweden found that women using the combination pill did gain weight over time, but no faster than women who did not use the pills (Lindh et al., 2011).

- Among the less common but more serious side effects are hypertension (increased blood pressure) and disorders of blood clotting, which can cause heart attacks, strokes, and other ill effects. Although these

**FAQ:** I threw up—did I lose the pill I took?

Episodes of vomiting or diarrhea may interfere with absorption of the pill. Abstain from coitus or use alternative protection until you've taken active pills for 7 days after you've returned to normal digestive health. With progestin-only pills, abstain or use alternative protection for 48 hours, while continuing to take pills as usual.

© Eo naya/Shutterstock.com

▲ As a 37-year-old smoker, this woman faces a heightened risk of experiencing serious side effects if she uses combination-type contraceptive pills.

---

*One combination pill, Yaz, is specifically approved by the U.S. Food and Drug Administration (FDA) for treatment of premenstrual symptoms, especially psychological ones. Yaz was tested against a placebo, however, and not against other combination pills, so it may not in fact be superior to other pills when used for this purpose. Yaz is more likely to cause blood clots than other contraceptive pills (Larivee et al., 2017).

complications are rare, they can be fatal. The risk for women over 35 who smoke is particularly high, and such women are usually advised not to use combination pills.

- There has been a great deal of public concern about whether hormonal contraceptives increase the risk of breast cancer. Earlier studies reported that they did not. According to a large study conducted in Denmark, however, they do increase the risk of developing breast cancer before age 50 by about 20 percent (Morch et al., 2017). This is not a large increase in absolute terms: It represents about 1 extra case per 8,000 users per year. Whether the increased risk persists into the older age range in which most breast cancers occur was not addressed in the Danish study. Moreover, some experts have suggested that the study was flawed by a failure to consider various confounding factors such as alcohol use (Kaunitz et al., 2018). In other words, the important question of whether hormonal contraceptives increase the risk of breast cancer has still not received a definitive answer, but if they do so it is by a small amount. This potential risk should be weighed against the pill's known benefits, including the very sizeable reduction in the risk of two other gynecological cancers, as mentioned above.

- Among women who use oral contraceptives for more than 2 years, the risk of glaucoma—a serious eye disorder characterized by increased intraocular pressure—is about twice the risk for nonusers (Y. E. Wang et al., 2016). Women who are or have been on the pills for extended periods should have periodic eye exams.

- Oral contraceptives may raise the risk of depression. In most women this effect is small if it exists at all, but in adolescents age 15 to 19 there does appear to be a moderately increased risk (Skovlund et al., 2016).

It's important for a user of combination pills to know what to do if she inadvertently misses taking a pill. If she has delayed taking a pill by less than 12 hours, she should simply take the missed pill immediately and then take the next pill at the normal time (even if that means taking two pills on one day). If she has delayed by more than 12 hours, she should do the same thing; in addition, however, she should use other protection or abstain from coitus until she has taken an active pill every day for 7 consecutive days. Furthermore, if she has had unprotected coitus during the week leading up to the day she realizes she's missed a dose, she should use emergency contraception (see Section 9.7).

### Continuous use of combination pills eliminates menstrual periods

The standard combination-pill regimen calls for a 7-day drug-free interval every month, which allows for withdrawal bleeding akin to a menstrual period. The only known function of a menstrual period, however, is to prepare the woman's uterus to receive and transport sperm. If pregnancy is not desired, menstrual periods offer no known health benefit and in fact present health concerns such as menstrual pain, premenstrual symptoms, and iron-deficiency anemia in some women. For that reason, some contraceptive pills have been designed to reduce the frequency of menstrual periods or eliminate them entirely:

- Several brands of combination pills—the best-known is **Seasonale**—are designed to be taken continuously for 12 weeks, followed by a 7-day drug-free interval, and so on. Thus, the user experiences 4 menstrual periods per year instead of 13.
- Slightly different versions, **Seasonique** (**FIGURE 9.11**) and **Camrese**, contain the same drug combination except that the pills taken during the 7-day

**FAQ:** I'm overweight—will contraceptive pills work for me?

Yes—excess weight has little if any effect on the pill's efficacy (Trussell et al., 2009).

**Seasonale**   An extended-use contraceptive pill.

**Seasonique**   An extended-use contraceptive pill.

**Camrese**   An extended-use contraceptive pill.

▲ **FIGURE 9.11** **Seasonique contraceptive pills** come in a 3-month pack. The seven yellow pills contain a low dose of estrogen only, allowing for a menstrual period during that week.

---

**FAQ:** If I suppress my periods, won't some bad stuff back up in my body?

No—the biological function of menstruation is not to get rid of "bad stuff" but to change the structure of the endometrium into a form more suitable for sperm transport.

---

**Amethyst** A contraceptive pill designed to completely abolish a woman's periods.

**Quartette** An extended-use contraceptive pill.

**progestin-only pill** An oral contraceptive that contains progestin but no estrogen. Also called the mini-pill.

---

interval contain a low dose of estrogen rather than being completely inert; this regime is helpful for women who experience heavy bleeding during the drug-free interval.

- Yet another combination pill, **Amethyst** (also available under other brand names or as a generic), contains the same drug combination as Seasonale or Seasonique, but at lower doses. Amethyst is packaged for continuous year-round use with no drug-free intervals at all, so the user can kiss her periods goodbye.

Although extended-use contraceptives do suppress menstrual periods, irregular spotting or breakthrough bleeding is common, especially in the early months of use, and can sometimes be quite severe. One extended-use pill, **Quartette**, is similar to Seasonique, but it decreases the likelihood of breakthrough bleeding by increasing the estrogen dosage over the course of the 12 period-free weeks.

It is also possible to get the same menstrual suppression effect with regular, much less expensive combination pills, simply by skipping the drug-free days and taking an active pill every day. Because of the many options for menstrual suppression, a woman does best to select the regime that is best for herself, in consultation with her doctor.

In some countries menstrual suppression has become so popular that tampon sales have declined considerably. In the United Kingdom they dropped by a quarter just between 2012 and 2016 (Morley, 2017).

## Progestin-only pills have fewer side effects

The **progestin-only pill** contains a very low dose of a progestin and no estrogen. For example, several brands contain just 0.35 mg of the progestin norethindrone. Compare that with the 1.0 mg of norethindrone, plus an estrogen, in some popular combination pills. How can a pill that contains so much less of an active ingredient have a reliable contraceptive effect? And if it does, why don't the combination pills go out of business? The answer is that the progestin-only pill works differently from the combination pill, requires greater care in use, and has some unique side effects.

The progestin-only pill does not reliably shut down ovulation, although it does do so in some women. It works mainly through its effect on the cervical mucus, making it thick and hostile to sperm transport. It may also make the endometrium resistant to implantation. These actions do not require such high levels of progestin as those needed to prevent ovulation, and they do not require the presence of estrogens.

The effects of each progestin-only pill last a very short time—barely 24 hours. Therefore, a woman who uses this method of contraception must be very careful not to miss taking the pills at the proper time. (If she does miss a dose by more than 3 hours, she should abstain from coitus or use alternative protection for 48 hours, while continuing to take her pills at the normal times. If she has had unprotected sex during the time she missed one or more pills, she should use emergency contraception—see Section 9.7.) There is no 7-day drug holiday every month, as with the combination pill: The progestin-only pill must be taken every single day for as long as this method is used.

With perfect use, the progestin-only pill is just as reliable as the combination pill. There is a widespread assumption that it is less reliable in typical use because of the requirement for accurately timed dosing, but this has not been documented in clinical trials.

Many of the advantages and disadvantages of progestin-only pills are similar to those of combination pills. For example, both pills are associated with the same increased risk of breast cancer (Morch et al., 2017). Here we list the differences between the two pills.

Advantages of progestin-only pills over combination pills:

- Progestin-only pills lack the estrogenic side effects of combination pills. They may be an alternative for women who experience serious side effects with the combination pill.
- Mothers who are breastfeeding their infants can use progestin-only pills, beginning 6 weeks after birth.

Disadvantages of progestin-only pills over combination pills:

- Unlike the combination pill, the progestin-only pill tends to disrupt women's menstrual cycles. In fact, irregular bleeding and spotting are reasons some women discontinue this form of contraception. This effect is highly variable from woman to woman, however, and does not have major health consequences so long as total blood loss is not increased. Plenty of women continue to have regular menstrual cycles while using progestin-only pills—presumably, these are women in whom the pills do not suppress ovulation.
- Progestin-only pills double the risk of depression in adolescents (Skovlund et al., 2016). This applies also to non-oral progestin-only methods (see below).
- Because progestin-only pills block the implantation of fertilized ova, women who believe that a fertilized ovum has the same moral status as a fetus or newborn baby may have qualms about using them. Progestin-only pills do not interfere with an established pregnancy, however.

Given the wide variety of contraceptive pills available—with more coming on the market all the time—a woman who is considering this form of contraception should consult with a knowledgeable professional who can recommend a pill suited to her needs and who can suggest appropriate changes if side effects crop up. Because a woman may take birth control pills for years, it is important that she keep herself well informed to ensure that she is taking the one best suited to her.

## 9.4 Hormones Can Be Administered by Non-Oral Routes

### LEARNING OBJECTIVES

After reading this section you should be able to:

9.4.1 Evaluate the pros and cons of the various non-oral hormonal contraceptive methods.

9.4.2 Explain what the major disadvantage of IUDs is, and how it may be overcome.

We now shift our attention to hormone-based contraceptives that are administered by some route other than by mouth. The methods we consider depend entirely on the slow release of hormones from some kind of "depot"—a reservoir that is inside or outside of the woman's body. The general advantage of non-oral over oral contraceptives is that they don't require taking a pill every day. Most women on contraceptive pills forget to take one from time to time, and this fact makes non-oral hormonal contraceptives more reliable in typical use.

A general disadvantage of the non-oral methods is that they have been in use for a much shorter time than pills, so their reliability and possible long-term effects (whether beneficial or harmful) have not been as thoroughly researched. It's reassuring that the hormones used are generally similar to those in contraceptive pills, but non-oral administration does introduce some functional differences. For example, the rate of drug delivery is usually more constant than with a once-a-day pill, and the drug does not pass through the liver before reaching the rest of the body, as happens with pills. These differences could affect the cumulative drug load experienced by hormone-sensitive tissues.

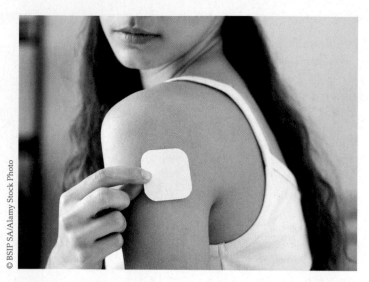

© BSIP SA/Alamy Stock Photo

▲ **FIGURE 9.12** **The Xulane patch** releases an estrogen–progestin combination that is absorbed through the skin.

**Xulane** A contraceptive patch.
**NuvaRing** A contraceptive ring placed in the vagina.

## Transdermal patches last a week

Transdermal patches look like large, square Band-Aids, but they contain a hormonal contraceptive that diffuses slowly into the body through the skin. The only transdermal contraceptive patch currently available in the United States is named **Xulane** (**FIGURE 9.12**). In Canada a similar patch is named Evra.

Xulane contains an estrogen and a progestin, so it's equivalent to a combination-type oral contraceptive. The woman has many choices as to where to place the patch, but she should not place it on a breast, and she should select a new location each time (to reduce the likelihood of skin reactions).

Each patch is left on for 1 week. The woman uses three in a row and then goes for a week without a patch, resulting in a 4-week cycle, just as with the combination pill. She will probably have (or begin) a period during the patch-free week. She should apply a new patch after the 1-week gap, even if her period hasn't yet stopped.

Generally, the advantages and disadvantages of Xulane are similar to those of combination-type contraceptive pills, but there are a few differences:

Advantages of Xulane (compared with combination pills):

- It requires fewer actions on the part of the user, and compliance is better.
- It is more evident in use and thus offers more assurance to the woman's partner that effective contraception is being used.

Disadvantages of Xulane (compared with combination pills):

- There may be local skin reactions, which, if severe, could necessitate discontinuance.
- The patch may become loose or fall off, though this is uncommon.
- As with the combination pill, Xulane is not advised for women over 35 who smoke.
- For women who weigh more than about 200 pounds (90 kg), the patch might not deliver enough hormones for reliable contraception. (This may be a particular concern when using the Canadian Evra patch, which contains 20% less estrogen than the U.S. version.)
- A woman using the patch experiences a higher total drug load than a woman who uses an equivalent combination pill, and the risk of serious side effects, such as blood clots, may be higher with the patch. The FDA has deemed this a serious enough issue to warrant a "black box warning," a safety warning with extra emphasis.

## Vaginal rings last 3 weeks

Contraceptive hormones can be absorbed by the vagina, and the **NuvaRing** takes advantage of this phenomenon (**FIGURE 9.13**). It is a flexible ring, about 2.1 inches (54 mm) in diameter, and it is placed deep within the vagina. (Its exact placement doesn't matter.) Like the combination pill and the Xulane patch, it releases a combination of an estrogen and a progestin. The ring is kept in place for 3 weeks and then removed. There is a week's break to allow for a menstrual period, and then a new ring is inserted.

As with the Xulane patch, the hormones released by the NuvaRing spread through the whole body. Thus, the side effects of the NuvaRing are probably similar to those of combination pills. These effects include an increased risk of blood clots, especially for women over 35 who smoke.

Advantages of the NuvaRing (compared with Xulane):

- The woman has to take fewer actions per month (two versus four), which may improve compliance.
- There are no skin reactions.
- Estrogen exposure is lower.
- The ring is not visible.

Disadvantages of the NuvaRing (compared with Xulane):

- The ring may occasionally slip out. (If it does, it should be washed in cool water and replaced.)
- It can cause vaginal irritation or a discharge.
- Some women or their partners report feeling the NuvaRing during coitus. However, the ring can be taken out beforehand; if so, it should be replaced within 3 hours.
- The NuvaRing must be protected from heat prior to use.

▲ **FIGURE 9.13** **The NuvaRing** is a flexible hormone-releasing ring that is placed in the vagina.

A new vaginal ring called **Annovera** was approved by the FDA in 2018. As with the NuvaRing, the ring is placed in the vagina for 3 weeks, followed by a 1-week break, but the same ring can be reused for 13 cycles (i.e., 1 full year).

## Depo-Provera lasts 3 months

The contraceptive **Depo-Provera** is administered by intramuscular injection or (in a different formulation called **Depo-SubQ Provera**) by subcutaneous injection. Depo-Provera is a slow-release (depot) form of a progestin, medroxyprogesterone acetate (**FIGURE 9.14**). A single Depo-Provera injection provides contraception for 3 months. The subcutaneous formulation can be self-injected.

Depo-Provera is usually administered within a few days of the onset of menstruation to ensure that the woman is not pregnant. Repeat injections should not be delayed for more than 2 weeks beyond the 3-month approved period, or pregnancy may occur.

Initially, a woman who uses Depo-Provera may experience irregular bleeding. After a year of use, however, at least 50% of women experience complete cessation of menstruation. Some women consider this a worrisome side effect, while others consider it a convenience.

Advantages of Depo-Provera:

- With a typical-use failure rate of 3%, Depo-Provera is more reliable than contraceptive pills. Failures are almost always caused by neglecting to get injections on time—something that a conscientious woman should be able to avoid.
- It doesn't require the user to do anything aside from getting the injections. Teenagers can easily conceal their use of Depo-Provera from their parents, if that is necessary.
- The eventual cessation of menstrual periods may appeal to women with menstrual problems.

Disadvantages of Depo-Provera:

- Depo-Provera offers no protection against STIs.
- Irregular, sometimes prolonged bleeding is a common problem, especially in the early months of use. Approximately 20% to 25% of women discontinue Depo-Provera during the

**Annovera** A vaginal contraceptive ring that lasts for a year.

**Depo-Provera** An injectable form of medroxyprogesterone acetate, used as a contraceptive in women or to decrease the sex drive in male sex offenders.

**Depo-SubQ Provera** A form of Depo-Provera designed for subcutaneous injection.

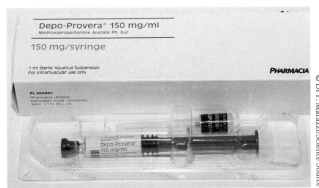

▲ **FIGURE 9.14** **Depo-Provera** is an injectable progestin that provides 3 months of contraceptive protection.

**contraceptive implant** A device implanted in the body that slowly releases a hormonal contraceptive.

**Nexplanon** An implanted hormonal contraceptive.

**intrauterine device (IUD)** A device placed in the uterus as a contraceptive. Also called intrauterine contraceptive (IUC).

first year for this reason. Less common side effects can include decreased sex drive, depression, liver damage, acne, and hair loss.

- Some women experience weight gain while on Depo-Provera: Adolescents and young women who are already overweight are particularly likely to do so (Burke, 2011).

- Once injected, Depo-Provera cannot be removed, so if side effects occur, it may take 3 months for them to go away.

- Although Depo-Provera is a fully reversible contraceptive, it may take as long as a year for a woman to return to full fertility after discontinuing the injections.

- Some women experience a loss of bone density while on Depo-Provera, which could increase their chances of experiencing bone fractures later in life—a serious health issue for postmenopausal women. Because of this risk, the FDA issued a black box warning that advises against the use of Depo-Provera for more than 2 years unless other birth control methods are inadequate (FDA, 2016). Women who are taking Depo-Provera should be sure they get adequate calcium in their diet, or they should take calcium supplements.

## Implants are extremely reliable

**Contraceptive implants** are small rods containing contraceptive hormones that are implanted under the skin. They are as reliable as sterilization but are fully reversible. The only implant currently available in the United States is **Nexplanon** (**FIGURE 9.15**). This is a flexible, matchstick-sized rod that releases a progestin. A health care provider inserts the rod under the skin of the woman's upper arm—the procedure takes about 1 minute. The implant provides protection against pregnancy for at least 3 years.

Advantages of Nexplanon (compared with Xulane or NuvaRing):

- It requires no action on the part of the user beyond the insertion and removal by a health care provider.

- Because the user does not have to do anything, it is probably more reliable. In typical use, it may be the most reliable of any hormonal contraceptive technique.

Disadvantages of Nexplanon (compared with Xulane or NuvaRing):

- Initial expenses are higher—$400 to $800 for the exam, the Nexplanon, and the insertion—but these may be covered by insurance. Removal costs about $100. Because it lasts so long, the cost of Nexplanon per month of use is quite low.

- Because it contains a progestin only, irregular bleeding is common. Up to 30% of women have the implant removed by 2 years after implantation, often because of bleeding.

- The reliability of Nexplanon in women weighing over 220 pounds (100 kg) is uncertain.

## IUDs require little attention

**Intrauterine devices** (**IUDs**) are plastic objects, usually in the shape of a T, that are placed in the uterus. An IUD must be inserted by a trained health care professional. It is passed through the cervix while folded up inside an insertion tube; once it is in the uterus, the insertion tube is removed, and the IUD unfolds (**FIGURE 9.16**). A plastic thread, attached to the bottom of the T, is left trailing through the cervix. Every month after her period, the woman or her partner must feel inside the vagina to be sure that the thread is in place and that no part of the IUD itself has moved down into the vagina. The thread also helps in

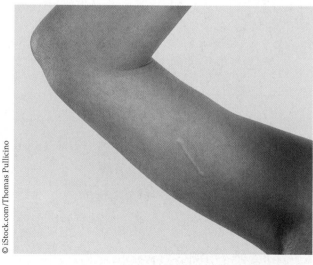

▲ **FIGURE 9.15** **The Nexplanon contraceptive implant** is barely visible under the skin of this woman's upper arm. In some women, it is not visible at all.

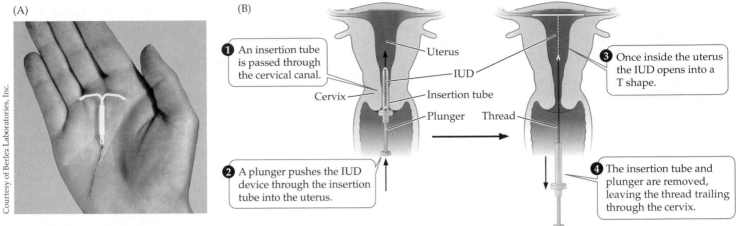

▲ **FIGURE 9.16** **IUD insertion** (A) The Mirena IUD. (B) Insertion of the Paragard IUD. The Mirena is inserted in a similar way.

the removal of the IUD, which is also done by a professional. (Women should never attempt to remove their own IUDs.)

Currently, five models of IUDs are available in the United States: four models that release the progestin levonorgestrel (**Mirena**, **Skyla**, Kyleena, and Liletta) and one model that releases copper (**Paragard**). The contraceptive action begins immediately with the Paragard; with the others, the woman should use other protection for the first week after insertion. IUDs remain effective for a period of years that varies between models (**TABLE 9.1**).

Advantages of the IUD:

- All five IUDs are highly effective; in fact, they are nearly as effective as female sterilization.

- Once inserted, IUDs are convenient and nonintrusive, requiring only the monthly thread check.

- With the progestin-releasing IUDs, menstrual cramping and bleeding may be reduced and sometimes abolished altogether.

- Fertility returns very soon after removal of the device.

- IUDs offer significant protection against endometrial cancer. In fact, already existing early-stage endometrial cancer, as well as precancerous changes, can in many cases be cured by insertion of the Mirena IUD (Pal et al., 2018).

Disadvantages of the IUD:

- The one-time costs are fairly high—$500 to $1,000—but they are usually covered by health insurance. There are no subsequent costs, unless condoms are added for disease prevention.

- Some cramping and irregular bleeding may occur, but these symptoms usually go away after a short period of use. With the Paragard, menstrual flows may increase and remain high as long as the device is in place.

- The progestin-releasing IUDs can have side effects such as nausea, headache,

**Mirena** A hormone-releasing IUD that is effective for 5 years.

**Skyla** A hormone-releasing IUD that is effective for 3 years.

**Paragard** A copper-containing IUD.

**TABLE 9.1** Characteristics of IUDs

| Model | Lasts for | Total amount of hormone in IUD | Failure rate | Effects on menstrual bleeding |
|---|---|---|---|---|
| Mirena | 6 years | 52 mg | 0.2% | Decrease after several months |
| Liletta | 3 years | 52 mg | 0.2% | Decrease after several months |
| Kyleena | 5 years | 19.5 mg | 0.2% | Variable |
| Skyla | 3 years | 13.5 mg | 0.2% | Variable |
| Paragard | 12 years | 0 mg | 0.8% | May increase |

and breast tenderness. Most users experience no side effects or side effects that are too mild to motivate users to have the IUDs removed (Hardeman & Weiss, 2014).

- The progestin-releasing IUDs carry the same increased risk of breast cancer as contraceptive pills (Morch et al., 2017).

- IUDs offer no protection against STIs. This is their main disadvantage, but it can be readily overcome by combining with condoms.

- IUDs do not prevent ectopic pregnancies as effectively as they prevent normal (intrauterine) pregnancies, probably because the site of implantation is farther away from the IUD. Therefore, in the very unlikely event that an IUD user becomes pregnant, the risk of the pregnancy being ectopic is increased (Sivalingam et al., 2011).

- Very occasionally an IUD may prove difficult to remove.

An estimated 85 million women use IUDs worldwide, and the great majority are very satisfied with them.

## 9.5 The Availability of Hormonal Contraceptives May Be Limited

### LEARNING OBJECTIVE
After reading this section you should be able to:

**9.5.1** Explain possible difficulties with obtaining hormonal contraceptives, especially for teenagers.

The 2010 U.S. Affordable Care Act ("Obamacare") included provisions intended to make contraception more affordable and accessible. Specifically, it extended medical insurance to more people and mandated that insurers cover contraceptive drugs and devices without co-pays or deductibles. In 2017 the Trump administration introduced an exception to this mandate for insurers and employers who object to providing this coverage on religious grounds. The mandate is the subject of ongoing litigation.

Even with coverage, obtaining hormonal contraceptives such as pills and patches involves inconvenience and possible expense on account of the necessity to obtain a doctor's prescription, and teens who are dependent on their parents' coverage may not want their use of contraceptives to become known. Ten states and Washington, D.C. allow pharmacists to prescribe most hormonal contraceptives at the point of sale, but it is often difficult to locate pharmacies that provide this service, because the pharmacists must undergo special training. An online tool helps with locating a participating pharmacy, but it is good to call ahead to make sure that a qualified individual will be on duty (Birth Control Pharmacies, 2019).

Many birth control professionals recommend that hormonal contraceptives be recategorized as over-the-counter drugs so that they can be purchased without a doctor's or pharmacist's prescription, by both adults and adolescents (Upadhya et al., 2017). This could raise costs for consumers with medical insurance, however, as over-the-counter drugs are not usually covered by insurance.

Many college students can obtain contraceptive pills through their college's student health services, but they may want to compare prices with those offered by big-box pharmacies such as Target or Walmart. Another option is the service offered by online pharmacies, including the pharmacy run by Planned Parenthood. The woman completes an online questionnaire and the pills are mailed to her, or the prescription can be sent electronically to a convenient brick-and-mortar pharmacy. These services do a good job of screening for contraindications (e.g., a history of blood clots) (Jain et al., 2019). Prices vary greatly, so it's worth checking several sites; the average cost is about $300 for a year's supply, including the initial visit.

# 9.6 Behavioral Methods Can Be Demanding

**LEARNING OBJECTIVES**

After reading this section you should be able to:

9.6.1 Explain how fertility awareness methods work.

9.6.2 Evaluate the reasons why withdrawal and outercourse are only moderately effective methods.

For couples who do not want to use "artificial" contraception of any kind for moral or other reasons, there are contraceptive options that depend simply on the manner or timing of sexual encounters. Although these options are considered by some to be more "natural" than other forms of contraception, and although they are inexpensive and free of the side effects of other methods, they make such demands on their users that their reliability in typical use is well below that of the best artificial methods.

## In fertility awareness methods, couples avoid coitus during the fertile window

Nearly all pregnancies result from coitus during the fertile window, which is the 6-day period leading up to and including the day of ovulation. Therefore, a woman who avoids coitus during the fertile window will greatly decrease the likelihood of pregnancy (Jennings & Arevalo, 2011). **Fertility awareness methods** of contraception, sometimes called "rhythm methods" or "periodic abstinence methods," depend on knowing the time of the fertile window (**FIGURE 9.17**). Because this time cannot be known precisely, the woman has to be abstinent for more than 6 days, but the required length of abstinence varies from method to method and from woman to woman.

The **standard days method** is the simplest fertility awareness method: It is usable by women who have regular menstrual cycles lasting between 26 and 32 days. (About three out of four women meet this criterion.) Counting the first day of menstruation as day 1, the woman simply abstains from coitus on days 8 to 19 or uses condoms on those days.

Some women use CycleBeads™, a set of color-coded beads developed at Georgetown University (**FIGURE 9.18**) to help them keep track of the days on which they may and may not have unprotected sex. The woman pushes a rubber ring from bead to bead each day, and the color of the current bead tells her whether coitus is safe or not. Several websites and smartphone apps claim to help women track their menstrual cycles and fertile days, but these resources are liable to give inaccurate results, and according to a 2019 report some of these apps pass on potentially embarrassing personal information to Facebook (BuzzFeed News, 2019).

Some idea of the limitations of the standard days method comes from a prospective study of 221 healthy women who identified the dates of their ovulations precisely using hormonal tests on their urine (Wilcox et al., 2000). From

**fertility awareness methods**
Contraceptive techniques that rely on avoiding coitus during the woman's fertile window. Also called rhythm methods or periodic abstinence methods.

**standard days method**
A simplified fertility awareness calendar method of contraception usable by women with regular cycles.

**FAQ:** Can I get pregnant during my period?

The chances are low but increase somewhat toward the end of the period, especially if you have long periods or short or irregular cycles. Also, women sometimes experience light bleeding ("spotting") at midcycle. If you mistake this for your menstrual period and have unprotected sex, you could very easily become pregnant.

▶ **FIGURE 9.17  Timing methods make different demands on women,** depending on the regularity of their cycles. (A) A woman who cycles quite regularly needs to abstain from unprotected sex for only about 9 days per month. (B) A woman who cycles irregularly may have to abstain for 16 days or more because of greater uncertainty as to when ovulation will occur.

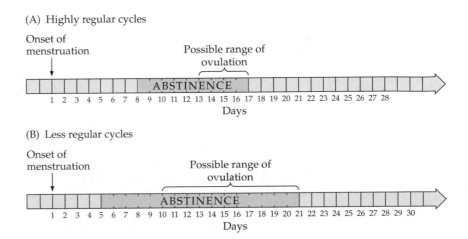

(A) Highly regular cycles

Onset of menstruation

Possible range of ovulation

ABSTINENCE

1 2 3 4 5 6 7 8 9 10 11 12 13 14 15 16 17 18 19 20 21 22 23 24 25 26 27 28
Days

(B) Less regular cycles

Onset of menstruation

Possible range of ovulation

ABSTINENCE

1 2 3 4 5 6 7 8 9 10 11 12 13 14 15 16 17 18 19 20 21 22 23 24 25 26 27 28 29 30
Days

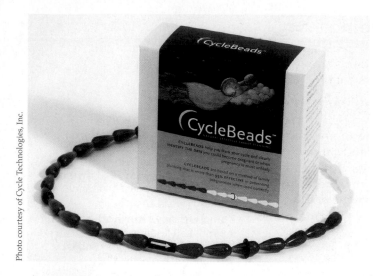

Photo courtesy of Cycle Technologies, Inc.

▲ **FIGURE 9.18** CycleBeads™ may help women apply the standard days method of contraception.

these data the researchers calculated that the women stood a minimum 10% chance of being within their fertile window for no less than 15 days of each cycle (days 6 to 21). In other words, the average woman using this method has to avoid unprotected coitus on about half of all days.

With the **calendar rhythm method**, the woman first keeps track of the length of her menstrual cycles over 6 to 12 cycles and notes the length of the shortest and longest cycles. She subtracts 18 from the number of days in her shortest cycle to identify the first no-sex day in her cycle, and she subtracts 11 from the number of days in her longest cycle to identify the last no-sex day in her cycle. So, for example, if her shortest cycle is 24 days and her longest cycle is 34 days, then she must abstain from unprotected sex from day 6 (24 minus 18) to day 23 (34 minus 11) of her cycle. This method is usable by women with cycles that are too irregular for the standard days method, but it rules out a large number of days. For these reasons it is not widely used or recommended.

Using the **cervical mucus method**, the woman monitors changes in her cervical mucus around the menstrual cycle. In the simplest version of the method, called the TwoDay method, the woman does not concern herself with what the mucus is like but simply notes each day whether she has *any* secretions. She asks herself two questions: "Do I have any secretions today?" and "Did I have any secretions yesterday?" If the answer to *both* questions is "no," the chances of becoming pregnant are low. If the answer to *either* question is "yes," the chances of becoming pregnant are high. The TwoDay method has been validated in large-scale studies; used correctly, fewer than 4 out of 100 women will become pregnant per year (Arevalo et al., 2004), but typical-use failure rates are higher. Other methods, which involve checking the consistency of the mucus, are also available (Planned Parenthood, 2019). These methods may allow for a few more safe days per cycle.

The **sympto-thermal method** combines awareness of cervical secretions with the monitoring of body temperature: The woman measures her basal body temperature every day with a digital thermometer before getting up. She stops having unprotected sex on the first day of cervical secretions. Her temperature drops slightly on the day of ovulation and then rises abruptly by at least 0.4°F (0.22°C) on the day after ovulation. Women can resume unprotected sex 2 days (or, to be extra safe, 3 days) after the rise in temperature.* For both the cervical mucus and the sympto-thermal methods, the woman needs to have at least one detailed consultation with a family planning provider; otherwise she is likely to make mistakes while she is familiarizing herself with the techniques.

Advantages of fertility awareness methods:

- They are inexpensive or free.
- They are usable by people who consider other forms of contraception unacceptable.
- They avoid the side effects and health risks of other forms of contraception.
- They are completely and immediately reversible.

**calendar rhythm method**    A fertility awareness method of contraception that takes account of variability in the length of a woman's menstrual cycles.

**cervical mucus method**    A fertility awareness method of contraception that depends on observing changes in the cervical mucus.

**sympto-thermal method**    A fertility awareness method of contraception that depends on the measurement of basal body temperature and the testing of cervical mucus.

---

*An ovum survives for no more than 24 hours after ovulation. The 2- to 3-day wait is necessary because of uncertainty in the temperature determination and also because of the slight chance that a second ovulation might occur up to 24 hours after the first.

Disadvantages of fertility awareness methods:

- They are considerably less reliable than some other methods (see Figure 9.4). This is a particular problem because users of these methods are often opposed to the use of abortion as a backup measure in the event pregnancy occurs. However, a couple who use a fertility awareness method to have children less frequently rather than to avoid pregnancy altogether might find the method perfectly adequate.

- They require a great deal of abstinence from coitus. Of course, the couple could use an alternative form of contraception, such as condoms, during the fertile period.

- The more accurate fertility awareness methods (i.e., cervical mucus and sympto-thermal methods) are quite demanding of time and attention.

- With the calendar rhythm method, a woman needs to keep track of her cycles for at least 6 months before even beginning to use the method.

- There is no protection from STIs, including HIV, if condoms are not used.

## The withdrawal method is simple but challenging

In the **withdrawal method** of contraception (also called "coitus interruptus"), the man removes his penis from the woman's vagina before he ejaculates. Being so simple, the method is very popular, especially among young people: In one survey, nearly one in three women age 15 to 24 said they used it. Unfortunately 21% of the women who used withdrawal experienced an unintended pregnancy, as compared with 13% of their peers who used some other method of contraception (Dude et al., 2013). Some studies have come up with even higher failure rates—up to 27% per year of use (Kowal, 2011).

One reason for failure of the method is that some sperm may be present in the pre-ejaculatory fluid, or "pre-cum." Normally, this fluid contains no sperm, but it could contain some if the man ejaculated earlier, did not urinate afterward, and is now having sex for a second time. These sperm can be cleared out by urinating and wiping off the tip of the penis before the second episode.

If this were the only way in which the method could fail, it would probably be one of the most reliable forms of contraception. A more common reason for failure, however, is that the man doesn't pull out soon enough or far enough. He simply gets carried away, or he doesn't get sufficient warning of the impending ejaculation. In the process of withdrawal he may spill semen on the labia, from where some hardy sperm may make it all the way into the woman's reproductive tract.

Advantages of the withdrawal method:

- It requires no advance preparation.
- It is free and always available.
- It enables the man to take responsibility for contraception.
- It can be combined with condom use for extra protection.
- There are no medical side effects or health risks.

Disadvantages of the withdrawal method:

- Reliability is only moderate. It is not recommended for men who ejaculate prematurely or have difficulty telling when they are going to ejaculate, or for teenagers.
- It provides little or no disease protection.

**withdrawal method** A method of contraception in which the man withdraws his penis from the vagina prior to ejaculation.

© View Stock/Alamy Stock Photo

▲ Noncoital sex is an excellent form of contraception for responsible couples who communicate well.

**outercourse** Sexual activities other than coitus, promoted as a means for preventing unwanted pregnancy and reducing the risk of STI transmission.

Although we are not enthusiastic about the withdrawal method, given the availability of better contraceptive options, the method has been of great importance in global terms. It has played a key role in the "demographic transition"—the dramatic decline in family size that accompanies modernization. Thanks to the withdrawal method, countries such as Turkey have undergone the demographic transition without the widespread adoption of medical contraceptive techniques (Ciftcioglu & Erci, 2009).

## Noncoital sex can be used as a means of avoiding pregnancy

Knowing that only penile-vaginal intercourse can lead to pregnancy, many couples engage in other forms of sexual activity, including everything from kissing and fondling to body-on-body contact, hand stimulation of the genitals, and oral and anal sex. Sometimes these alternative forms of sex are promoted as a way to avoid pregnancy; in that context, they may be referred to as **outercourse**—the opposite of intercourse. (Some people exclude any form of penetrative sex from the definition of "outercourse.")

Advantages of noncoital sex:

- It is completely reliable if adhered to. (Semen must not be deposited near the vaginal opening, however, or transferred to the vagina after ejaculation by manual or body contact.)
- It is free and requires no preparation.
- It has none of the side effects that may be associated with other forms of contraception.
- For teens who have not yet engaged in coitus, it may be valued as a way to preserve "vaginal virginity."
- There is some STI protection, depending on what kinds of noncoital activities are engaged in. (Anal sex is at least as risky as coitus, and more so in the case of HIV.)

Disadvantages of noncoital sex:

- It misses out on what many heterosexual men and women consider the most pleasurable and intimate kind of sex.
- Some people may find it difficult to refrain from coitus once noncoital sex is under way, and if coitus does happen, contraception may not be available.

The main keys to successful outercourse are to decide what kinds of sex you will and will not engage in, discuss this with your partner *before* any sexual behavior begins, and have condoms ready in case plans change.

## Combining long-acting methods and condoms makes sense

As we mentioned earlier, there is no single best contraceptive method for everyone, and a consultation with a birth control professional is the best way to settle on a method that's the best for you and your partner or partners. Nevertheless, for many college-age women, the long-acting reversible methods make a great deal of sense, combining as they do a very high effectiveness with unparalleled ease of use—you just get it and forget it. The Mirena and Liletta IUDs are particularly worth considering because of their tendency to lessen menstrual symptoms. Condoms should also be used for STI protection, unless both partners are certain that STIs are not an issue.

Most contraceptive methods affect the environment in various ways, and this may also be a factor influencing your choice of a method (**BOX 9.3**).

---

## BOX 9.3
## Contraceptives and the Environment

Young people who care about the environment may want to know how it will be affected by their contraceptive practices. One often-expressed concern is that the hormones in contraceptive pills will end up in waterways and affect wildlife or pollute our drinking water. This is a legitimate concern: Synthetic hormones such as ethinyl estradiol—the estrogen in most combination pills—do leave a woman's body in urine and end up at wastewater treatment plants. Some or all of the hormones pass through the plants unchanged and are discharged into rivers and lakes. Here they can disrupt the sexual development of fish and other aquatic animals (see the figure), and this can happen even at concentrations so low that they are difficult to detect. The estrogenic load imposed by contraceptives is very small, however, in comparison with the much larger amounts of estrogenic compounds that are present in these waters naturally or that result from the discharge of industrial pollutants (Laurenson et al., 2014). Thus if everyone stopped using birth control pills, there would be little beneficial effect, unless all other sources of these pollutants were eliminated.

Contraceptive hormones have sometimes been detected in drinking water, though at miniscule levels that are unlikely to be of any concern. Domestic water filters typically fail to remove them. You could avoid them by drinking bottled water, but you would be liable to get a higher (but still tiny) load of estrogenic chemicals from the plastic bottles the water is sold in.

The Catholic Church has been one of the loudest voices warning of the contraceptive pill's environmental effects. In a 2009 statement the Vatican's newspaper spoke of the the pill's "devastating ecological effects" and claimed that it is contributing to the rise in male infertility (*Catholic News-Herald*, 2009). This view is somewhat suspect because the Vatican opposes contraception for other reasons.

With condoms the main issue is biodegradability. Plastic condoms are not degradable. Latex and lambskin condoms are made of biodegradable materials, but the manufacturing process makes them more resistant to breakdown. Lambskin

Two genetically male frogs copulating; the lower frog was turned into a female by exposure to an estrogenic pollutant. Their union produced healthy but all-male offspring.

From Hayes et al., 2010

is the most degradable, but even with these you can't really toss your used condoms into the bushes. And in landfills nothing breaks down, on account of the dryness of the landfill interior, so garbologists—scientists who drill down into landfills to see what's there—find condoms in decades-old strata.

Developing the rubber plantations where latex is harvested has been an incentive to deforestation, although the amount of latex devoted to condoms is not great.

One of the least-polluting contraceptive devices is the copper-releasing Paragard IUD, because copper is not harmful and in fact is an essential trace element. However, any contraceptive method that suppresses or lessens menstrual flows is a boon to the environment—not because the flows themselves are polluting, but because of all the tampons, pads, insertors, and wrappings that don't have to be manufactured, transported, or disposed of.

Fertility experts at the Population Council have pointed out the connection between inadequate contraception and climate change (Bongaarts & Sitruk-Ware, 2019). Globally, an estimated 44% of all pregnancies are unintended, mainly on account of poor access to contraceptive education and services. Because population growth is a major driver of climate change, increased availibility of contraception and improved contraceptive technology could, over the long term, lead to substantial reductions in the emission of greenhouse gases.

## 9.7 There Are Contraceptive Options after Unprotected Coitus

**LEARNING OBJECTIVES**

After reading this section you should be able to:

9.7.1 Explain how the two kinds of emergency contraceptive pills are used.

9.7.2 Evaluate the use of an IUD for emergency contraception as compared with pills.


**FAQ:** Can I use my regular contraceptive pills for emergency contraception?

We don't recommend it. Plan B and generics are readily available without a prescription. There is an online procedure to get ella, which is shipped overnight.

**emergency contraception** Use of high-dose contraceptives to prevent pregnancy after unprotected sex.

**Plan B One-Step** A progestin used for emergency contraception.

**Next Choice One-Dose** A progestin used for emergency contraception.

**ella** A form of emergency contraception that is effective for 5 days after sex.

You got carried away. He said he was going to pull out. She said she was on the pill. The condom broke. The diaphragm slipped. Who cares how it happened? It's 11:00 PM, and your whole life—as a parent—is passing before your eyes. What next?

A woman's first impulse is to rinse out the contents of her vagina—preferably with something that will kill sperm. Coca-Cola is said to be the traditional favorite of teens.* Some women use water, a commercial douche, or spermicidal foam.

None of these methods is recommended as a regular form of postcoital contraception. Even the spermicidal foam, which is probably the best of the options just mentioned, is a highly unreliable way to prevent pregnancy when applied after coitus, because some sperm are likely to have gotten beyond the reach of the spermicide before it is ever placed in the vagina. For that reason, it would be best for a woman in this situation to assume that sperm have made it into her cervix. She now has two effective options to prevent pregnancy: taking pills, or having an IUD inserted.

The pill method is called **emergency contraception**. Two kinds of pills are available for this use. The first kind contains 1.5 mg of the progestin levonorgestrel.** Brand names are **Plan B One-Step** (**FIGURE 9.19**) and **Next Choice One Dose**, and there are several generics. The main way by which levonorgestrel works is by preventing ovulation. It reduces the likelihood of pregnancy by 60% to 90% when taken up to 3 days after sex, and there is a weaker effect for 2 days after that. These pills can be bought by anyone, and they are usually found with other family planning products at drugstores. They do not cause the loss of an already established pregnancy.

The other type of pill (brand name **ella**) contains a progesterone-blocking drug called ulipristal. It remains fully effective for up to 5 days after sex. Again, the main action of ella is to block ovulation. A prescription for ella is required, whatever the woman's age, and it is considerably more expensive than the levonorgestrel pills—about $60 including an online prescription.

The efficacy of all these emergency contraceptive pills is thought to be lower in overweight or obese women. The levonorgestrel pills appear to lose their efficacy at a body mass index (BMI) of about 26, while ella retains some efficacy up to a BMI of about 35*** (Office of Population Research, 2014). Heavier women should not try to compensate by taking higher doses unless this is recommended by new guidelines.

Given that Plan B One-Step and the other versions of levonorgestrel can be bought by anyone without a prescription, it may make sense for sexually active women to buy a dose ahead of need. That way it can be taken quickly after unprotected sex, when it is most likely to be effective. Generic versions can be bought online for about $20.

---

*The 2008 Ig Nobel Prize—an award honoring comical science—was bestowed on two groups who studied whether Coca-Cola is an effective spermicide. One group found that it is; the other found that it isn't. One thing's for sure: It leaves a sticky mess.

**Note that this is a far higher dose of levonorgestrel than the *microgram* amounts that are contained in some regular contraceptive pills.

***For a 5-foot 5-inch (1.63 m) woman, a BMI of 26 corresponds to a weight of 152 pounds (69 kg), and a BMI of 35 corresponds to a weight of 204 pounds (92.5 kg).

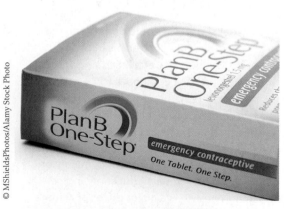

▲ **FIGURE 9.19** **Plan B One-Step** is a progestin, levonorgestrel, specifically packaged for use as an emergency contraceptive.

© MShieldsPhotos/Alamy Stock Photo

A completely different strategy to prevent implantation is to have an IUD inserted. The Paragard IUD is used for this purpose. Of course, this is a much more expensive and inconvenient option than taking pills. However, it is nearly 100% reliable—only 10 failures have ever been reported. The IUD can be inserted up to 5 days after coitus, or even later so long as it is not more than 5 days after ovulation. (With a 10-day wait, it may work by inducing an early abortion.) Furthermore, the IUD can be left in place, in which case it will provide very reliable contraception for up to 12 years, depending on the type of IUD. Alternatively, it can be removed as soon as the woman has had her next menstrual period. The Paragard IUD is not affected by a woman's body weight, so it is a good option for heavier women.

## 9.8 Sterilization Is Highly Reliable

**LEARNING OBJECTIVES**

After reading this section you should be able to:

9.8.1   Evaluate who might consider sterilization as a contraceptive option.

9.8.2   Explain why a man should not engage in unprotected sex immediately after a vasectomy.

9.8.3   Compare the pros and cons of female versus male sterilization.

**Sterilization** is a surgical procedure that puts an end to fertility. Various procedures have this effect. Here we focus on surgical procedures that are used to terminate fertility *electively* in otherwise healthy men and women: vasectomy in men and tubal sterilization in women. Both methods work by preventing sperm from reaching an ovum.

Sterilization is a serious issue for any individual or couple. Although, as we'll see below, sterilization procedures can be successfully reversed in some cases, there is no guarantee of success, so people who choose sterilization should be clear in their minds that they want to end their fertility permanently. People select sterilization under a number of circumstances:

- They simply don't want children and are certain they will never change their minds. (However, doctors may be reluctant to sterilize healthy young men or women who don't have children.)

- They have had enough children and are confident that they will want no more, even if they remarry or their children die.

- A medical condition makes pregnancy a serious health hazard.

- They have a significant likelihood of passing on a serious congenital disorder.

The majority of people who choose sterilization are married couples with children. Among heterosexual couples in the United States who use contraception, about 27% rely on female sterilization, and 9% rely on male sterilization (Bartz & Greenberg, 2008). The greater popularity of female than male sterilization is perhaps surprising, given that sterilization is a much simpler and less expensive procedure in men. Part of the reason is that insurance plans are more likely to cover sterilization for women than for men.

The increasing availability and popularity of long-acting reversible contraceptive methods has led to a recent decline in sterilization rates. For women, contraception is only required up until menopause, of course, so depending on the woman's age long-acting reversible methods may easily bridge the at-risk years.

### Vasectomy is a brief outpatient procedure

**Vasectomy** is a very simple and safe procedure that is usually done under local anesthesia (**FIGURE 9.20**). The physician locates the vas deferens inside the scrotal

**FAQ:** I don't have sex very often. Could I just rely on emergency contraception?

It is not recommended. Emergency contraceptive pills are considerably less reliable than other methods of hormonal contraception and can be more expensive.

**sterilization**   A surgical procedure to eliminate fertility in either sex.

**vasectomy**   A male sterilization technique that involves cutting or tying off the vas deferens from each testicle.

▶ **FIGURE 9.20** **Vasectomy** is a relatively simple procedure that can be performed under local anesthesia. (See **Animation 9.1: Vasectomy.**)

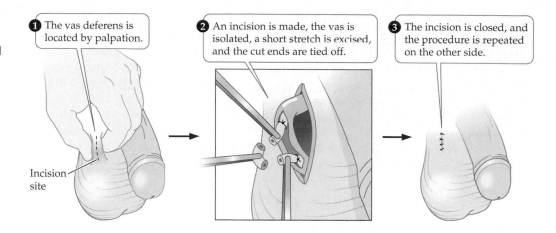

**1** The vas deferens is located by palpation.

Incision site

**2** An incision is made, the vas is isolated, a short stretch is excised, and the cut ends are tied off.

**3** The incision is closed, and the procedure is repeated on the other side.

sac, makes a small incision, and cuts out a short segment of it. The free ends are tied, cauterized, or sealed with clips to prevent them from rejoining. The incision is then closed with a couple of stitches, and the procedure is repeated on the other side. In an alternative "no scalpel" procedure, the scrotal skin is pierced with sharp-tipped forceps. Because the incision is so small, it needs no stitches and heals faster. (See Web Resources at the end of this chapter for a full-length video of the procedure.) With either method the man can go home directly after the procedure.

The man should refrain from strenuous exercise for a couple of days after surgery. He can usually resume sexual activity in about a week. He is not yet sterile, however, because sperm remain in the portion of each vas deferens above the cut, so he must continue to use another contraceptive method such as condoms. It takes about 15 to 20 ejaculations, over a period of about 3 months, to get rid of these sperm. The man's semen should be checked microscopically for absence of sperm before he engages in unprotected coitus.

Complications of the procedure can include bleeding, infection, and—in about 18% of cases—the appearance of lumps formed by leaked sperm. These usually clear up by themselves, but they can be treated surgically if necessary.

Vasectomy is extremely reliable; early failure can result if the man resumes unprotected sex too soon. Late failure, which is very rare, can result from spontaneous reconnection of a vas deferens or other unusual causes.

About the only way that vasectomy can harm a man's sex life is if he feels psychologically damaged by the procedure. For most men, it's quite the opposite: They and their partners are able to enjoy sex more because they no longer have to worry about contraception or pregnancy. The procedure has no effect on sexual desire, the ability to perform, testosterone levels, or secondary sexual characteristics. Because sperm form such a small component of semen, there is no noticeable reduction in the volume of the ejaculate.

Of course, there are men who for one reason or another end up wanting the procedure reversed. In an operation called **vasovasostomy**, the surgeon, using an operating microscope, locates the two cut ends of each vas and sews them together. The procedure is expensive, however, and has no more than about a 50% chance of success. Quite aside from the difficulty of getting a functional reconnection, the man may have formed antibodies against his own sperm, which interfere with sperm production.

Some men deposit a sperm sample in a sperm bank prior to the vasectomy procedure, with the hope that they can become fathers via artificial insemination in case they change their minds. There is no assurance that this will be possible, however, as there will be only a limited amount available.

**vasovasostomy** Surgery to reverse a vasectomy.

Advantages of vasectomy:

- It is almost 100% reliable.
- Once accomplished, it is totally convenient and free.
- Vasectomy is cheaper, simpler, and safer than female sterilization

Disadvantages of vasectomy:

- Vasectomy is not reliably reversible. Attempts at reversal are very expensive.
- The upfront expenses are considerable if they are not covered by insurance.
- There is no STI protection.

## Tubal sterilization is more invasive and expensive

**Tubal sterilization** (female sterilization) is quite analogous to male sterilization: In a process called **tubal ligation** the oviducts are tied and cut, cauterized, or closed off with clips or other devices (**FIGURE 9.21**). The result is that ova and sperm cannot meet. Tubal sterilization is a more invasive procedure than vasectomy, however, since it involves entering the abdominal cavity. Many sterilizations are done after childbirth or after an abortion, while the woman is in a surgical setting. (She has to give consent for the procedure.)

There are two main procedures for tubal sterilization, called laparoscopy and mini-laparotomy. These procedures differ not so much in what is done to the oviducts, but in the surgical approach. In a **laparoscopy**, no extended incision is made in the abdominal wall. Instead, a viewing instrument (laparoscope) is inserted through one tiny incision, and an instrument to clamp or cut the oviducts is inserted through another. Sometimes the two instruments are combined into one, and only a single incision is made. The laparoscopic procedure is less stressful than mini-laparotomy, requires no stitches afterward, and can be done under either local or general anesthesia. Often, the woman can go home the same day.

In a **mini-laparotomy** or "mini-lap," a small scalpel incision about 1 inch (2.5 cm) long is made somewhere between the navel and the mons pubis. The oviducts are located and pulled to the incision, where they are tied and cut, or closed with clips, and then allowed to slip back into their normal position. The incision is then sewn up. Recovery takes a few days.

Tubal sterilization, like any internal surgery, can occasionally cause hemorrhage or infection. General anesthesia, if used, also carries some risk. These or other complications occur in 1% to 4% of cases, but they can usually be dealt with effectively. In the United States there are one to four deaths for every 100,000 tubal sterilizations. In general, one can say that tubal sterilization is a very safe procedure, but not quite as safe as vasectomy. In some cases, tubal sterilization can be

**tubal sterilization**   Any procedure that prevents sperm transport in the oviducts.

**tubal ligation**   A procedure in which the oviducts are blocked by tying them off.

**laparoscopy**   Abdominal surgery, such as tubal sterilization, performed through a small incision with the aid of a laparoscope (a fiber-optic viewing instrument).

**mini-laparotomy**   Abdominal surgery, such as tubal sterilization, performed through a short incision.

▶ **FIGURE 9.21**  Tubal sterilization (A) Laparoscopic procedure for tubal ligation. (B) A portion of the oviduct may be excised and the ends tied off, as shown here, or the oviduct may be closed off by cauterization or the application of clips. (See **Animation 9.2: Tubal Sterilization.**)

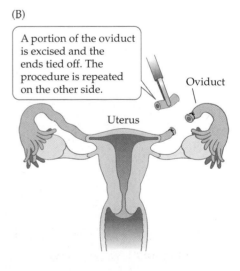

(A) Surgical instruments and a laparoscope are inserted through separate small incisions in the abdominal wall.

Laparoscope
Operating channel
Forceps
Oviduct
Uterus

(B) A portion of the oviduct is excised and the ends tied off. The procedure is repeated on the other side.

Oviduct
Uterus

**Essure** A method of tubal steriliza-tion that blocks the oviducts by use of metal coils.

reversed by microsurgical techniques, but the operation is very expensive, and success is quite unpredictable.

Like vasectomy, tubal sterilization has no effect on other aspects of sexual functioning. Menstrual cycles usually continue as before, and a woman's interest in sex and her physiological reactions during sex are undiminished. She may enjoy sex more because she is no longer concerned about pregnancy.

The advantages and disadvantages of tubal sterilization are very similar to those of vasectomy, but there are a few important differences between the two.

Advantages of tubal sterilization (compared with vasectomy):

- The woman is sterile regardless of who she has sex with.
- The loss of fertility is immediate.
- Tubal sterilization is associated with a 20% decrease in a woman's risk of ovarian cancer, perhaps because tying off the oviducts prevents the passage of carcinogenic substances through the oviducts to the ovaries (Gaitskell et al., 2016).

Disadvantages of tubal sterilization (compared with vasectomy):

- Tubal sterilization is more invasive and therefore slightly riskier.
- It is more expensive.
- Recovery is longer (but shorter than with most other surgeries).

Another method of tubal sterilization called **Essure** was available up until 2018. It involved insertion of metal coils into each oviduct. The manufacturer of Essure discontinued the product in 2018 on account of poor sales and the occurrence of complications in some women. Women who have already had Essure coils inserted do not need to have them removed unless they experience problems, which is unlikely.

## 9.9 Disabled Persons Have Special Contraceptive Needs

### LEARNING OBJECTIVE

After reading this section you should be able to:

9.9.1 Explain why some disabled persons have special contraceptive needs, and how these can be met.

Many men and women with physical and mental disabilities are sexually active, but they may face special challenges related to contraception, and they tend to use less effective contraceptive methods than their nondisabled peers (Wu et al., 2017). People with a movement disorder, arthritis, multiple sclerosis, or a spinal cord injury may not be able to put on a condom, insert a diaphragm, or check an IUD. Oral contraceptives are not advisable for women with reduced mobility, because they may raise the risk of blood clots. IUDs are not advisable if the woman does not have normal sensation in the pelvic area. If the disabled person has a nondisabled partner, that partner may be able to help with the tasks, or the partner may be willing to take on responsibility for contraception themselves.

Contraception is a particularly important issue for intellectually disabled female adolescents and young women, who face a heightened risk of sexual abuse and who may not be able to comply with the usual contraceptive regimens. Careful counseling, repeated over time and tailored to the particular young woman's needs, is often required. Progestin hormone injection methods may be particularly useful for these women; the reduction in menstrual periods associated with these contraceptives may be an advantage in itself. Still, the ethical requirement for informed consent applies to intellectually disabled persons just as it does to other people.

Disabled people are more likely to use sterilization and less likely to use long-acting reversible methods than nondisabled people. While there could be good reasons for this difference, there have been suggestions that it results from external pressure—from family members, contraception providers, or institutions—rather from any preference expressed by the disabled persons themselves (Wu et al., 2019). If so, disabled persons and those who interact with them should be aware of the 2008 U.N. Convention on the Rights of Persons with Disabilities, which promotes "full and effective participation in society on an equal basis with others," including in issues related to reproductive health (United Nations, 2008).

## 9.10 Lack of Access to Contraception Is a Global Problem

**LEARNING OBJECTIVE**

After reading this section you should be able to:

9.10.1 Evaluate the barriers to the availability of contraception globally and in the United States.

An estimated 214 million women in developing countries want to avoid pregnancy but are not using a modern contraceptive method (World Health Organization, 2018a) (**FIGURE 9.22**). Although these women may use traditional methods, such as withdrawal, many end up needing abortions, which are often unsafe, or they give birth to unplanned or unwanted children.

One reason is the prevalence of organized opposition to contraception, especially from the Roman Catholic Church. The Philippines, for example, is a country where explosive population growth is stymieing attempts to eliminate poverty, but the Catholic Church (to which most Filipinos belong) has long prevented the government

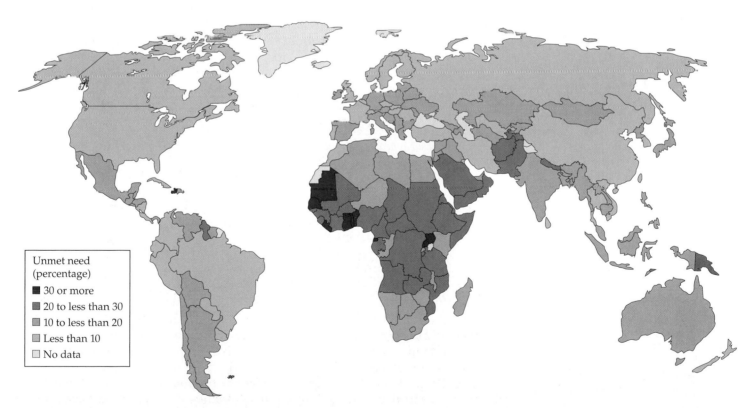

Unmet need (percentage)
- 30 or more
- 20 to less than 30
- 10 to less than 20
- Less than 10
- No data

▲ **FIGURE 9.22 Where contraception is lacking** The map shows the percentage of married or cohabiting women age 15 to 49 who have an unmet need for family planning. (From Trends in Contraceptive Use Worldwide 2015 [ST/ESA/SER.A.349], by United Nations, Department of Economic and Social Affairs, Population Division © 2015 United Nations. Reprinted with the permission of the United Nations.)

from initiating any contraception programs. Finally, in 2012, President Benigno Aquino signed into law the Responsible Parenthood and Reproductive Health Act, which allowed for government assistance with contraception and also mandated sex-education classes in state schools. Members of the Roman Catholic Church challenged the law, and in 2015 the country's Supreme Court blocked its most important provisions. In 2017, however, President Rodrigo Duterte ordered expanded access to contraception, saying, "Three's enough" (National Public Radio, 2017).

Another reason for the lack of access to contraception is poverty and limited education. Efforts by the United Nations, individual governments, and nongovernmental organizations have gradually improved the situation, but even now 13% of women globally have unmet contraceptive needs (United Nations, 2019). Further improvement will depend on economic advancement in developing countries, not only because people who are better off are more able to afford contraception but also because they are more motivated to restrict family size. In addition, as countries advance economically, women typically acquire more influence over their reproduction.

Looking at Figure 9.22, you might conclude that the United States has overcome any barriers that might interfere with access to contraception, but that's not the case. According to the American College of Obstetricians and Gynecologists, several factors limit access for some women (ACOG, 2017):

- *Knowledge deficits.* An emphasis on abstinence-only sex education in some states has left girls and young women ignorant of contraceptive options and susceptible to misperceptions, such as that contraceptive pills work by causing early abortion.

- *Restrictive legal climate.* Twenty states limit minors' access to contraceptive services in some fashion. Parental notification or permission may be required, for example, which is a serious problem for some teens.

- *Cost and insurance coverage.* Because the United States lacks universal health care, some women cannot afford contraceptive services. Recent political developments have raised the prospect that contraceptive services may no longer be provided cost-free to all insured women or those on Medicaid.

- *Religion-based barriers.* Ten of the largest health care systems in the United States are affiliated with the Catholic Church, and these systems often restrict access to contraceptive services.

- *Unnecessary medical procedures.* Many doctors insist on performing pelvic examinations or other unnecessary procedures and tests before initiating hormonal contraception.

## 9.11 Several Safe Abortion Procedures Are Available

**LEARNING OBJECTIVES**
After reading this section you should be able to:
9.11.1 Describe how abortions are performed at different stages of pregnancy.
9.11.2 Evaluate the pros and cons of surgical versus medical abortion.

**induced abortion** An abortion performed intentionally by medical or surgical means.

**therapeutic abortion** An abortion performed to safeguard a woman's life or health.

**elective abortion** An abortion performed in circumstances when the woman's health is not at risk.

An **induced abortion** is the intentional termination of a pregnancy. In this chapter we use the term "abortion" to refer exclusively to induced abortions rather than spontaneous abortions (miscarriages) (**BOX 9.4**).

An abortion induced in order to safeguard the mother's health is termed a **therapeutic abortion**. An abortion induced because the woman chooses not to carry the fetus to term is referred to as an **elective abortion**. An elective abortion may be performed because the pregnancy is not wanted (e.g., contraception failed or was not used, or the pregnancy resulted from rape) or because the fetus

## BOX 9.4
## Abortion in the United States: Key Statistics

- Eighteen percent of all established pregnancies in the United States (aside from those that end in miscarriage) are terminated by abortion. An estimated 862,000 abortions were performed in 2017. The rate has been dropping steadily over the last 30 years. Based on current rates, about one in four American women will have an abortion by the age of 45.

- Most abortions are done for social, not medical, reasons (see table).

- Young, single women are the major recipients of abortion. Twelve percent of all abortions are performed on minors.

- About half of all women who have abortions say that they were using some kind of contraceptive technique (though probably not perfectly) when they became pregnant.

- Minority women are disproportionately represented among women who have abortions.

- Two-thirds of all abortions are performed at 8 weeks or earlier.

- Fewer than 5 in 10,000 legal first-trimester abortions result in a complication requiring hospitalization. Legal abortion performed by 8 weeks of pregnancy has a 1 in 1,000,000 chance of causing the mother's death. Abortion performed at or after 21 weeks has a 1 in 11,000 chance of causing the mother's death.

**Most Important Reason Given for Abortion**

| Reason given | Percentage of women |
|---|---|
| Not ready for a(nother) child; timing is wrong | 25 |
| Can't afford a baby now | 23 |
| Have completed my childbearing; have other people depending on me; children are grown | 19 |
| Don't want to be a single mother; am having relationship problems | 8 |
| Don't feel mature enough to raise a(nother) child; feel too young | 7 |
| Would interfere with education or career plans | 4 |
| Physical problem with my health | 4 |
| Possible problems affecting the health of the fetus | 3 |
| Was a victim of rape | <0.5 |
| Husband or partner wants me to have an abortion | <0.5 |
| Parents want me to have an abortion | <0.5 |
| Don't want people to know I had sex or got pregnant | <0.5 |
| Other | 6 |
| Total | 100 |

Source: After L. B. Finer et al. 2005. *Perspect Sexual Reprod Health* 37: 110–118.

is known or suspected to have some defect or disease. In some countries, but not in the United States, abortions are commonly performed because the child is of the nonpreferred sex—usually female. India and China are most frequently mentioned in this regard.

The moral status of abortion and the degree to which governments should restrict or regulate the practice are highly contentious issues in contemporary society. In this section, we first describe the technology of abortion and then discuss the social conflicts that surround it.

Abortion can be performed by physically removing the fetus and its membranes from the uterus, in which case it is referred to as a **surgical abortion**. Alternatively, drugs can be administered that cause the death and expulsion of the fetus in a **medical abortion,** which resembles a miscarriage.

### Vacuum aspiration is the standard first-trimester surgical method

Surgical abortions are carried out in different ways depending on the age of the embryo or fetus. During the first trimester, most surgical abortions are performed

**surgical abortion**   An abortion induced by a surgical procedure.

**medical abortion**   An abortion induced with drugs. Also called medication abortion.

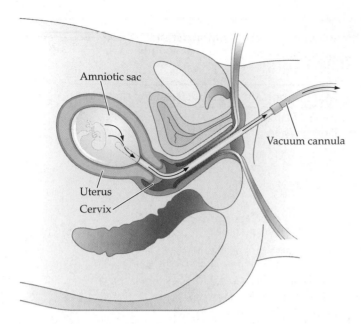

▲ **FIGURE 9.23** **Vacuum aspiration** is the abortion procedure most commonly used in the first trimester.

by **vacuum aspiration** (**FIGURE 9.23**). This procedure—which accounts for the majority of all abortions in the United States—is done on an outpatient basis with local anesthesia or sedation.

The health care provider first dilates the cervix by passing a series of metal rods of increasing diameter through the cervical canal. Once the cervix has been dilated, the provider passes a cannula (tube) into the uterus. The other end of the cannula is connected to a pump that applies suction. (With very early abortions, suction may be applied by hand, using a syringe.) The suction breaks up the embryo or fetus and its membranes and removes them from the uterus. This process takes less than 5 minutes. The extracted tissue is examined to ensure that the abortion is complete. The provider may insert a curette (a metal loop) to clean the walls of the uterus of any remaining tissue.

The woman remains in the clinic or doctor's office for an hour or so before going home. She may experience some bleeding and cramping over the following week or two. The woman should refrain from coitus for 2 weeks to allow the cervix to close fully. Complications are rare but can include heavy bleeding, infection, or perforation of the uterus.

### Dilation and evacuation is used early in the second trimester

Vacuum aspiration abortions can be performed up to about 14 weeks of pregnancy, but the majority of second-trimester abortions are performed using a different procedure, called **dilation and evacuation** (**D&E**). Most D&Es are done in the period from 13 to 16 weeks, but they are sometimes done up to 20 weeks or even later.

D&Es are usually performed under general anesthesia in a hospital but may be performed with sedation in an outpatient setting. The procedure is fairly similar to vacuum aspiration, but the cervix has to be dilated more widely. Therefore, a 2-day procedure is commonly employed. On the first day, a sterilized stick made from the seaweed *Laminaria* is inserted into the cervical canal. The stick absorbs fluid and expands, gently opening the cervix. On the following day, a suction cannula is used to remove fluid and some tissue, and then the remainder is removed with forceps or other instruments. Finally, the lining of the uterus is cleaned with a curette.

The D&E is a very safe procedure, but it has a somewhat greater likelihood of complications, such as excessive bleeding, than vacuum aspiration abortion.

### Induced labor and hysterotomy are performed late in the second trimester

Late in the second trimester, the D&E procedure becomes more risky, and alternative surgical techniques may be used. In one method, the provider simply induces premature labor. This may be accomplished by **saline-induced abortion**—that is, by injecting a salt solution into the amniotic sac. Alternatively, and more commonly, labor is induced by administration of a prostaglandin. The drug is either injected into the amniotic sac or administered by means of a vaginal suppository. Contractions usually begin within an hour or so, and the fetus is expelled within 48 hours.

If the woman's health is such that labor seems risky, the fetus may be removed by means of a **hysterotomy**, a surgical incision in the abdomen and the uterus. Neither induced labor nor hysterotomy is performed very frequently—each of them accounts for less than 1% of all abortions in the United States, and some states impose legal restrictions on these procedures.

**vacuum aspiration** An abortion procedure in which the conceptus is destroyed and removed by suction.

**dilation and evacuation (D&E)** A procedure involving the opening of the cervix and the scraping out of the contents of the uterus with a curette (a metal loop). D&E may be done as an abortion procedure or for other purposes.

**saline-induced abortion** An abortion induced by use of a strong salt solution.

**hysterotomy** An abortion performed via a surgical incision in the abdominal wall and the uterus.

## Medical abortions are two-step procedures

Medical abortions (also called medication abortions) can be performed anytime up to 7 to 9 weeks after the start of the last menstrual period. Medical abortions accounted for 39% of all nonhospital abortions in the United States in 2017, and 60% of all abortions performed up to 10 weeks (Guttmacher Institute, 2019a).

The drug most commonly used is **mifepristone**. Mifepristone blocks progestin receptors—the cellular molecules that recognize and respond to progesterone and similar hormones. Recall that progesterone, secreted by the corpus luteum and later by the placenta, is required to keep the uterus in a state capable of sustaining pregnancy (**FIGURE 9.24**). In the presence of mifepristone, the progestin receptors do not "see" progesterone, so it is as if progesterone is absent. The endometrium begins to break down and ceases to support the fetus, which consequently detaches from the endometrium and dies.

In about 5% of women the remains of the fetus and its membranes are expelled by spontaneous uterine contractions. In most cases, however, it is necessary to give a second drug, the prostaglandin **misoprostol**, to induce contractions. The misoprostol is usually taken 2 or more days after the mifepristone. Bleeding begins within 24 hours of taking misoprostol, and the entire abortion process takes no more than a few days. A follow-up visit to the clinic is usually necessary to ensure that the abortion is complete, but an FDA-approved research program known as TelAbortion allows for the entire abortion procedure to be conducted without in-person clinic visits (TelAbortion, 2020).

Medical abortions work in about 96% of cases. If the procedure should fail, the woman must have a surgical abortion because the fetus is likely to have been seriously damaged.

Advantages of medical abortion (compared with surgical abortion):

- It requires no invasive surgical procedure.
- It can be performed earlier than surgical abortion—as soon as pregnancy is confirmed.
- The abortion may seem more like a natural miscarriage.

Disadvantages of medical abortion (compared with surgical abortion):

- Medical abortions take longer and require more active participation on the part of the pregnant woman. A surgical abortion is over within minutes, whereas a medical abortion typically takes a few days and requires a total of two or three visits to the provider.
- Medical abortions are liable to cause more cramping and bleeding.
- Medical abortions cannot be performed after 7 to 9 weeks from the beginning of the last menstrual period.

**mifepristone**   An anti-progesterone drug used to induce abortion. Also known as RU-486.

**misoprostol**   A prostaglandin used in medical abortions.

① In normal pregnancy, the endometrium is sustained by progesterone.

Progesterone   Uterus

Endometrium

② Mifepristone blocks the action of progesterone, leading to breakdown of the endometrium and death of the embryo.

Progesterone

Mifepristone

③ Misoprostol, given a few days later, causes myometrial contractions and expulsion of the fetal remains.

Misoprostol

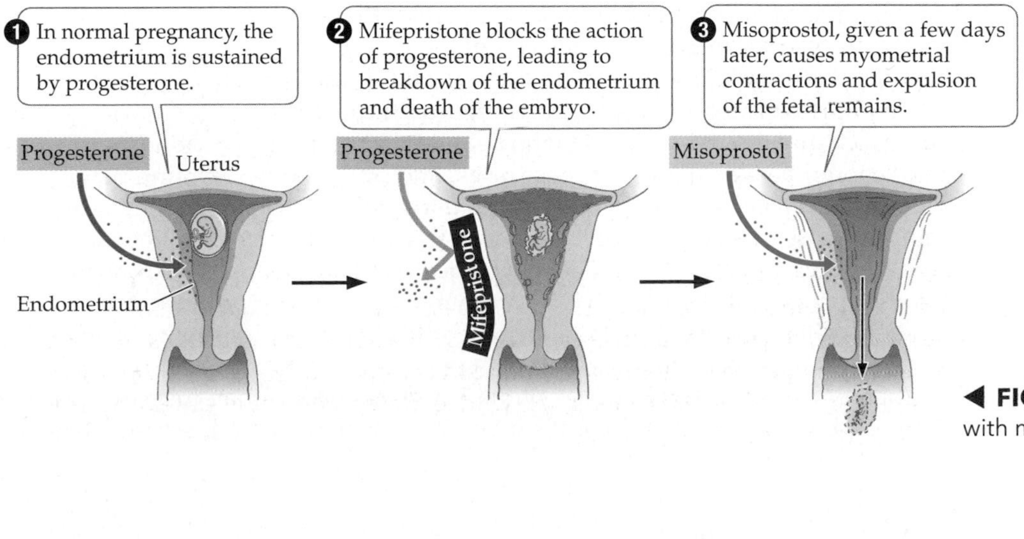

◀ **FIGURE 9.24**   Medical abortion with mifepristone and misoprostol.

- For anyone who is trying to conceal the abortion, having the abortion at home may be a disadvantage.

- Another disadvantage of having the abortion at home is the possibility of seeing the fetal remains, which may disturb some women.

## Abortions do not cause long-lasting ill effects

An uncomplicated surgical or medical abortion does not affect a woman's subsequent fertility. Some studies suggest an increase in the risk of premature birth, and in rare instances a surgical abortion can damage the uterine wall, making it difficult for the woman to become pregnant in the future (Mayo Clinic, 2019a).

Immediately after an abortion, a woman may feel sadness, stress, relief, or some other emotion. There has been a controversy over the question of whether abortion causes any harmful long-term psychological effects. Some people have claimed that women who have had an abortion suffer from a "post-abortion stress syndrome" marked by regret, guilt, anger, insomnia, depression, anxiety, emotional withdrawal, drug dependence, and intrusive thoughts about the "missing child" (Rue, 1997; Coleman et al., 2009). This syndrome is supposed to resemble the post-traumatic stress disorder experienced by some military veterans.

Yet based on the best evidence, the post-abortion syndrome does not exist. Women who have had an abortion are more likely to experience psychological problems than other women, but this is because women with psychological problems are more likely than other women to have abortions in the first place (Steinberg & Finer, 2011). And teenagers—supposedly the group most vulnerable to the post-abortion syndrome—suffer no psychological ill effects from having abortions (Warren et al., 2010). According to a study of nearly 1,000 women who requested abortions at U.S. clinics, those who received abortions were no more likely to experience stress symptoms than those whose requests were denied (on account of the fetus's advanced age) (Biggs et al., 2016).

## 9.12 Americans Are Divided on Abortion, but Most Favor Restricted Availability

### LEARNING OBJECTIVES
After reading this section you should be able to:

9.12.1 Explain why "pro-choice" and "pro-life" may not be the polar opposites that these terms suggest.

9.12.2 Describe some of the restrictions on abortion that have been enacted recently by some states.

9.12.3 Suggest reasons why the abortion rate is declining.

In its landmark 1973 decision in *Roe v. Wade*, the U.S. Supreme Court ruled that states could not enact outright bans on abortions performed before the age of fetal viability, which was taken to mean before the end of the second trimester of pregnancy. Since that time, Americans have remained divided on the issue of abortion.

The abortion debate is often portrayed as if there are simply two opposing camps: **pro-life**, meaning people who believe that elective abortion is wrong and that it should be illegal in all or most cases, and **pro-choice**, meaning people who believe that women should be allowed to make all or most abortion decisions for themselves. By these criteria 61% of Americans are pro-choice and 38% are pro-life (Pew Research Center, 2017e). There have been no great changes in these numbers in recent years, but the issue has become more politically polarized: Increasing numbers of Democrats support abortion rights, whereas increasing numbers of Republicans oppose them.

When polls give interviewees a wider range of choices than just pro-choice or pro-life, it becomes apparent that the interviewees' views are not strictly polarized.

**pro-life** Opposed to abortion; believing that abortion should be illegal under most or all circumstances.

**pro-choice** Believing that abortion should be legal under some or all circumstances.

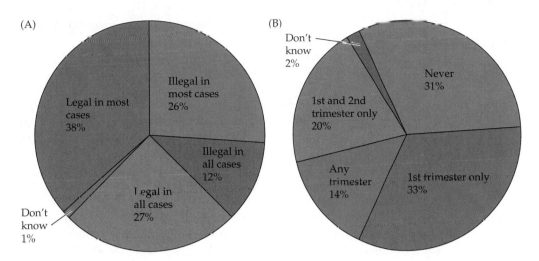

(A)

Illegal in most cases
26%

Legal in most cases
38%

Illegal in all cases
12%

Legal in all cases
27%

Don't know
1%

(B)

Don't know
2%

Never
31%

1st and 2nd trimester only
20%

1st trimester only
33%

Any trimester
14%

▲ **FIGURE 9.25** **Americans' views on abortion are not as simple as "pro-life versus pro-choice."** (A) Only minorities of Americans have extreme opinions in response to the question "Under what circumstances should abortion be legal?" (B) Abortion is considered more acceptable when it is done early: The graph shows the percentage of Americans who believe abortion should be permitted during different time intervals within pregnancy. (A after Pew Research Center. 2019. *Public opinion on abortion*; data from PRC's online American Trends Panel. Pew Research Center: Washington, D.C. B data for 2018 after Gallup. n.d., "Abortion A-Z". Accessed May 2020 via https://tinyurl.com/y5zx4nfo.)

Relatively few people favor either complete legality or a complete ban (**FIGURE 9.25A**). One of the issues that most strongly influences people's opinions is the timing of abortion: Many people believe that abortion should be permissible in the first trimester, but far fewer believe that it should be permissible in the second or third trimester (**FIGURE 9.25B**). In this respect, Americans tend toward a more conservative position than was spelled out in *Roe v. Wade*, which made abortion legal in both the first and second trimesters.

Furthermore, while 60% of Americans think that the *Roe v. Wade* decision was a good thing, this does not mean that they agree with the core of the decision, which was that a woman has a right to an early abortion for any reason: Only 44% of Americans shared that perspective in 2016 (National Opinion Research Center, 2016). Americans generally are in favor of the notion that a woman should be able to have an abortion if her life is at risk, if the fetus is likely to have a congenital disorder, or if the pregnancy resulted from rape. In contrast, they are *not* in favor of the idea that a woman should be allowed to have an abortion for a reason of mere convenience—such as the fact that having the baby would interfere with her career. Seventy percent of Americans believe that abortion under these circumstances should be illegal, contrary to the *Roe v. Wade* ruling.

How do views on abortion vary with major demographic variables? Women and men do not differ significantly in their representation in the pro-choice and pro-life camps (Pew Research Center, 2017c). The main variables that do correlate with abortion views are religious beliefs, political affiliation, educational level, and age. People with strong religious beliefs or who are Republicans are more likely to have restrictive views on abortion, while Democrats, people who are more highly educated, and younger people are more likely to have permissive views.

While the Roman Catholic Church holds to its doctrine that elective abortion is a grave sin, a hint of a more nuanced view was given in the church's Year of Mercy—2015. For that year, it was announced, priests

© Associated Press

▲ The abortion debate is often portrayed as a conflict between extreme pro-life and pro-choice activists, but many Americans hold intermediate positions.

would be authorized to forgive the sin of abortion, something that up until then only bishops were able to do. Pope Francis later made this dispensation permanent.

## The availability of abortion is decreasing

Under pressure from anti-abortion activists, policies regarding abortion have become more negative in many states. In 2019, the Guttmacher Institute rated 22 states as "hostile" or "very hostile" to abortion rights, as compared to only 4 such states in 2010 (Guttmacher Institute, 2019b). Only one state (California) was rated "very supportive" of abortion rights (**FIGURE 9.26**).

Anti-abortion activists hope that the *Roe v. Wade* decision will eventually be reversed, and they have been heartened by a rightward shift in the ideological makeup of the U.S. Supreme Court during the Trump administration. Short of that goal, however, activists have sought to restrict the right to abortion or to limit women's access to abortion services. The Guttmacher Institute has state-by-state information on these restrictions (Guttmacher Institute, 2020). Here are some examples:

- Many states have enacted mandatory 24-hour or 72-hour waiting periods and mandatory counseling about abortion. The counseling often provides misleading, disputed, or incorrect information. In Arkansas, for example, women must be told that medical abortions can be safely "reversed" after they receive the first of the two drugs—by means of high doses of progesterone—even though this has not been scientifically verified.

- Some states require parental consent for a minor to have an abortion. (If consent can't be obtained, the minor can generally seek permission from a judge.)

- Some states have enacted measures that make it difficult for abortion clinics to function. For example, a 2013 Texas law required doctors performing

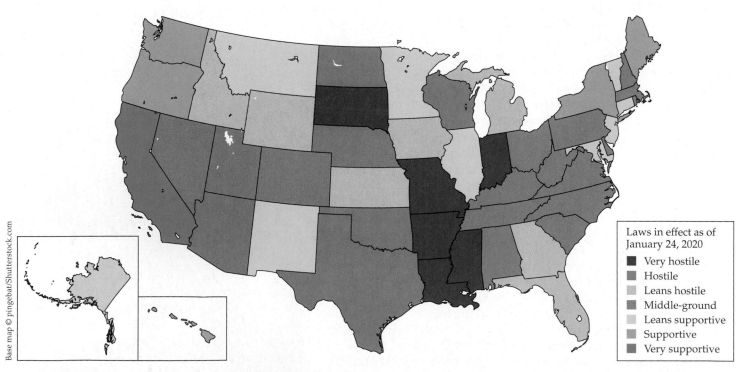

Base map © pingebat/Shutterstock.com

Laws in effect as of January 24, 2020

- Very hostile
- Hostile
- Leans hostile
- Middle-ground
- Leans supportive
- Supportive
- Very supportive

▲ **FIGURE 9.26** **Policies on abortion vary by state and by region** The West Coast is supportive of abortion rights, the Northeast is supportive or neutral, and the South is hostile; other regions are a patchwork of support or hostility. The criteria used to establish these ratings are available online. (After E. Nash. 2020. *State Abortion Policy Landscape: From Hostile to Supportive.* Guttmacher Institute: New York. © 2020 Guttmacher Institute. gu.tt/HostileSupportiveStates.)

abortions to have admitting privileges at a nearby hospital; this restriction resulted in the closure of 35 of the state's 42 abortion clinics. The law was later overturned by the U.S. Supreme Court (Liptak, 2016).

- Many states limit the use of public funds to pay for abortion services in most circumstances.

- Fetal homicide laws have been expanded or reinterpreted by some states to include self-induced abortions (**BOX 9.5**).

- Some states have passed laws that are clearly unconstitutional under *Roe v. Wade*—laws that ban elective abortions outright or lower the fetal age threshold to ages long before the age of viability. These laws cannot be enforced, but their proponents hope that the ensuing litigation will provide the Supreme Court with the opportunity to overthrow *Roe v. Wade*. Yet a

---

## BOX 9.5
## Feticide

Most states have fetal homicide or "feticide" laws, although the details vary from state to state. The laws were originally aimed at providers of illegal abortions, but they later came to be used against people (usually the male partners of pregnant women) who caused the death of a fetus in the course of an assault or murder. In 2018, for example, an Indiana teen, Aaron Trejo, was charged with murder and feticide because he killed his girlfriend when she was 6 months pregnant. In 2019, Trejo pleaded guilty to both charges, and in the following year he received a 65-year prison sentence (Beacham, 2020).

More controversially, feticide laws have been modified or reinterpreted so that they can be directed against pregnant women themselves, if they cause the deaths of their fetusus by some means other than legal abortion. In 2013, for example, a 33-year-old Indiana woman, Purvi Patel, showed up at a hospital emergency room complaining of bleeding from her vagina. She said that she had delivered a fetus that she believed to be dead and that she disposed of it in a dumpster, where the fetus was eventually found. According to court papers, investigators found text messages on her mobile phone referring to drugs that she allegedly took to cause an abortion. In August 2014 Patel was charged with feticide. She was found guilty and sentenced to 20 years' imprisonment, but the conviction was overturned by the Indiana Court of Appeals; the court ruled that the state's feticide law was not intended to be used to prosecute women for their own abortions (Associated Press, 2016c). Another Indiana woman, Bei Bei Shuai (see figure), was charged with feticide after her fetus died when she tried to commit suicide by swallowing rat poison. Immense public pressure led to a deal in which she pleaded guilty to a lesser charge and was released (Penner, 2013).

The broader purpose of feticide laws has been to establish the principle that fetuses are persons with rights distinct from

Bei Bei Shuai was charged with feticide because her fetus died as a consequence of a suicide attempt.

those of their mothers. Although these laws are not usually applicable in the context of legal abortions, they create a paradoxical situation in which an embryo or fetus of a certain age may have full rights of personhood (in the case of an assault on a pregnant woman, for example) but no rights at all in the case of a legal abortion. Thus feticide laws tend to foster the belief that legal abortion may also be a violation of the fetus's rights. This may have been the intention of legislators who created these laws and prosecutors who make use of them.

© Matt Stroshane/Stringer/Getty Images

▲ **FIGURE 9.27 Anti-abortion extremism** In 1994 Paul Hill shot and killed an abortion provider and a clinic security guard. Hill was sentenced to death and was executed in 2003. These pro-life activists were expressing their support for Hill at the time of his execution.

strong majority of Americans (60%) want *Roe v. Wade* to remain in force, compared with only 33% who want to see it overthrown (Gallup, 2019a).

- Some anti-abortion activists have put abortion providers in a state of fear by threatening or harassing them, and some extremists within the movement have actually murdered abortion providers (**FIGURE 9.27**).

Another strategy used by anti-abortion activists has involved the establishment of deceptive "crisis pregnancy centers." These facilities advertise in a fashion suggesting that they provide abortion services, but once a woman arrives at the center, she is exposed to misinformation and shaming, which is intended to change her mind about having an abortion. These centers may be located in the same building or even on the same floor as real abortion clinics, and they may use deceptive names such as "PP Inc."

The result of these combined activities has been to greatly reduce the availability of legal abortion in the United States. Six states—Kentucky, Mississippi, Missouri, North Dakota, South Dakota, and West Virginia—now have only one abortion clinic. Many women live 100 miles or more from the nearest provider, and if there is a mandatory waiting period, they will have to make that trip twice—a severe burden for working women or single mothers. Those clinics that are still operating in hostile states are often kept under siege by demonstrators who hope to put them out of business by dissuading pregnant women from entering.

The abortion rate in the United States is steadily declining in all age groups and is now less than half of what it was in the early 1980s (Guttmacher Institute, 2019a). The drop may in part be due to the restrictions and pressures described above. A more significant factor, however, has been the decline in the number of unintended pregnancies, and this decline has resulted largely from improved contraception practices, especially the adoption of long-acting reversible contraceptives (Lindberg et al., 2018). This is a development that all sides of the abortion debate can be happy with.

## Summary

- Although various forms of contraception have been known since ancient times, moral repugnance, restrictive laws, and lack of knowledge prevented effective contraception in the United States until the 20th century. Margaret Sanger led the struggle to legalize contraception, to educate the public about contraceptive methods, and to introduce improved methods. Contraception was not fully legalized in the United States until 1972. Even today, about 3 million unintended pregnancies occur in the United States every year, on account of nonuse or failure of contraceptive methods.

- All currently available contraceptive methods have advantages and disadvantages. Different people have different contraceptive needs in terms of reversibility, reliability, cost, and so on, so no one method is best for all users.

- Male condoms (sheaths that cover the penis) require careful use to prevent failure and are somewhat intrusive, but they are cheap and readily accessible and

offer significant protection against STIs. They are the only contraception method controlled by the male that is reversible (aside from withdrawal). Female condoms offer similar benefits but are far less popular than male condoms.

- Diaphragms and cervical caps are other barrier methods of contraception. They are used in conjunction with spermicides to prevent the entry of sperm into the cervix. They are less intrusive than condoms, but they provide less pregnancy and disease protection and are fairly inconvenient to use. Spermicides used by themselves are not very reliable, and overuse of spermicides can cause vaginal irritation and raise the risk of STI transmission.

- Contraceptive pills contain either a combination of estrogen and progestin or progestin only. They work by blocking ovulation and by rendering the uterus hostile to sperm transport. They are fairly convenient once prescribed, nonintrusive, and very reliable if taken regularly. They offer no STI protection. Estrogen-containing pills may have a number of side effects as well as some long-term health risks and benefits. Progestin-only pills often cause irregular bleeding.

- Some contraceptive pills may be taken in an extended fashion that reduces the frequency of menstrual periods or eliminates them entirely.

- Hormone-based contraceptives may also be administered by non-oral routes, including injections (Depo-Provera), contraceptive patches (Xulane), vaginal rings (NuvaRing), or implants placed under the skin (Nexplanon). These non-oral methods have the advantage of greater reliability than pills in typical use.

- Intrauterine devices (IUDs) render the uterus hostile to sperm transport. They are very reliable and convenient once inserted. They offer no STI protection, but this can be provided by adding condoms.

- In fertility awareness methods, couples avoid having sex near the time of ovulation, which they can determine by a variety of techniques, including simple calendar calculations, body temperature measurements, or examination of cervical mucus.

- In the withdrawal method, the man withdraws his penis prior to ejaculation. Globally, this method has made a major contribution to population control, but many couples find it difficult to practice, especially if the man tends to ejaculate early or without warning.

- Noncoital sex (outercourse) is a reliable form of contraception if adhered to strictly.

- Emergency contraception involves taking a high dose of oral contraceptives within a few days after unprotected sex or failure of a barrier contraceptive. These drugs prevent ovulation. Another postcoital contraceptive technique is the insertion of an IUD.

- Sterilization is the cutting and/or tying off of the vasa deferentia (in men) or the oviducts (in women). Either procedure prevents sperm and ovum from meeting and is almost completely reliable in preventing pregnancy. The majority of sterilizations are done in women, but the procedure is simpler, safer, and less expensive in men. Although intended to be permanent, sterilization can be reversed in some cases. Sterilization is generally chosen by couples who have all the children they desire.

- Globally, poverty, religious proscriptions, and other factors severely limit access to contraception.

- In the United States, about 1 million abortions are performed every year. Most abortions are done in the first trimester of pregnancy by the vacuum aspiration method, in which the cervix is dilated and the contents of the uterus are removed by suction under local anesthesia. A slightly more complex procedure, dilation and evacuation (D&E), is used early in the second trimester.

- Early abortions may also be induced with drugs. Medical abortion is a two-step procedure involving the administration of a drug that terminates the pregnancy (mifepristone), followed about 2 days later by a second drug (misoprostol) that induces contractions and the expulsion of the fetal remains.

- Women who choose abortion do not experience negative psychological consequences.

- The moral and legal status of abortion is contentious. The extreme anti-abortion (pro-life) position is that abortion is always wrong and should be illegal, except perhaps when done to save the mother's life. The extreme opposing (pro-choice) view is that a woman should have the right to choose abortion under any circumstances. Most Americans describe themselves as pro-life or pro-choice but actually hold to an intermediate position, believing that abortion should be permitted under certain limited conditions, such as early in pregnancy or when the fetus has a congenital defect.

- The U.S. Supreme Court's 1973 decision in *Roe v. Wade* established a woman's constitutional right to have an abortion for any reason before the age of fetal viability. In recent years, however, pro-life activists have used a variety of strategies to restrict the availability of abortion.

## Discussion Questions

1. Your sister or best friend asks you to help her decide which contraceptive method is best for her. She says she could not take pills, use a diaphragm, or use the rhythm method because she is too forgetful. She does not want to have to contemplate an abortion, because it is against her values. Recommend two forms of contraception that would be suitable, and describe the pros and cons of each method. Compare their actions and side effects. Compare their reliability.

2. A teenager tells you that she has no risk of getting pregnant because she can tell when her boyfriend is about to ejaculate by the look on his face, and she makes him pull out. How could you help her understand the risks of this method? What alternative methods would you suggest? Describe how they work and their advantages and disadvantages.

3. What are your own views about abortion? What do the laws say about abortion in your state, and what changes, if any, would you like to make in them?

4. What improvements in contraceptive technology would you most like to see?

## Web Resources

Bedsider. Birth control methods **www.bedsider.org/methods**

California Vasectomy and Reversal Center (includes vasectomy video) **www.californiavasectomyreversal.com/vasectomy.html**

Centers for Disease Control and Prevention: Contraception **http://tinyurl.com/ycp494eb**

Guttmacher Institute **www.guttmacher.org**

Ipas (an organization dedicated to the global availability of contraception and safe abortion) **ipas.org**

Male Contraception Initiative **www.malecontraceptive.org/**

Marie Stopes UK **www.mariestopes.org.uk**

NARAL Pro-Choice America **www.naral.org**

National Abortion Federation **www.prochoice.org**

National Right to Life Committee **www.nrlc.org**

Planned Parenthood Federation of America **www.plannedparenthood.org**

Science Daily. Birth control news **http://tinyurl.com/y6u9ufmf**

## Recommended Reading

Chesler, E. (1992). *Woman of valor: Margaret Sanger and the birth control movement in America*. Simon & Schuster.

George, R. P. & Tollefsen, C. (2008). *Embryo: A defense of human life*. Doubleday. (Makes the case that an embryo is a full human being entitled to legal protection.)

Hatcher, R. A., Trussell, J., Nelson, A. L., et al. (2018). *Contraceptive technology* (21st ed.). Managing Contraception LLC. (This massive and frequently updated work is the principal reference volume in the field of contraception.)

Hatcher, R.A., Zieman, M., Lathrop, E., et al. (2020). *Managing contraception 2019-2020 for your pocket* (15th ed.) Managing Contraception LLC.

Sanger, M. (1938/2004). *The autobiography of Margaret Sanger*. Dover.

Solinger, R. (2005). *Pregnancy and power: A short history of reproductive politics in America*. NYU Press.

Wicklund, S. (2007). *This common secret: My journey as an abortion doctor*. Public Affairs.

In many Latino cultures a girl's transition to sexual maturity is marked by a *quinceañera* celebration.

# 10

# Sexuality across the Lifespan: From Birth to Adolescence

No two lives are alike, yet sexuality does unfold in a somewhat predictable manner across the lifespan. In fact, a person's age is one of the best predictors of that person's sexual behavior and relationships. Early sex researchers tended to focus on a narrow age range within the total lifespan—from adolescence to midlife—when sexuality has its greatest social relevance. Yet sexuality is a work that is already in progress at birth and remains so throughout life. This chapter focuses on the dynamic changes in sexuality during childhood and adolescence. Chapter 11 focuses on the variations in sexuality during adulthood.

## 10.1 Some Forms of Childhood Sexual Expression Are Common

**LEARNING OBJECTIVES**

After reading this section you should be able to:

10.1.1 Compare the sexual knowledge of U.S. and European children.
10.1.2 Describe common solitary and partnered sexual activities in children.

Studying childhood sexuality is difficult. Adults have very limited memories of their childhood and no recollection at all of their infancy. Infants cannot be interviewed about their sex lives. Older children can be interviewed, but their understanding may be limited, and interviewer suggestions might too easily influence their replies. In addition, parents and society in general may be reluctant to permit questioning of children on sexual matters. Direct observation of children's sexual behavior may be difficult if the behavior is infrequent, and ethical and legal considerations also limit the use of this approach. Thus, observational studies have generally involved asking intermediaries, such as parents or teachers, about sexual behavior they happened to have witnessed among children under their care, rather than direct observation of such behavior by researchers. Because of these problems, the total number of studies of childhood sexuality has been very limited.

### In contemporary Western culture, children are insulated from sex

Before the 19th century, families generally slept together, so young children sometimes observed and learned about adult sexual behavior. Also, because farming was the most common occupation, children saw animals mating, becoming pregnant, and giving birth. Climate permitting, young children frequently went naked, so it was easy for them to explore and learn about their own anatomy and that of their siblings and friends.

During the 19th century, however, a belief developed that children needed to be kept in a state of sexual innocence. Despite the changes since then, especially in terms of formalized sex education, children today often experience a conspiracy of silence on sexual matters. Many parents, for example, do not permit their children to see them naked or to witness their sexual encounters, in part because some therapists have suggested that these experiences are harmful to children and may even represent a form of sexual abuse. Research on this topic has led to reassuring findings, however. In one 18-year longitudinal study—the UCLA Family Lifestyles Project— young children who saw their parents naked or engaging in sex were no more likely to experience psychological problems in later childhood or adolescence than children who did not (Okami et al., 1998). In fact, there was a tendency for them to have *fewer* problems—a finding that is in line with another, retrospective study (Lewis & Janda, 1988) (**FIGURE 10.1**).

Children, especially younger ones, express a lot of curiosity about "where babies come from" and other sexual matters. Some parents are very forthcoming, using these questions as an opportunity to teach their children the basic facts of sexuality in an age-appropriate fashion (**BOX 10.1**). But other parents are evasive: They may give fairy-tale explanations, tell their children that they are too young to know such things, or express disapproval of the questions. Thus, many children remain remarkably uninformed about sexual matters. In one survey conducted around 1980, researchers found that North American children lagged far behind children in other Western countries in terms of their sexual knowledge (Goldman & Goldman, 1982). Nine-year-olds, for example,

▲ Do young children have a sex life? What do you think?

© iStock.com/Paz Ruiz Luque

## BOX 10.1
## Talking with Children about Sex

**Talk early and often**    Toddlers should learn the names for their genitals along with other body parts ("These are your toes, and this is your penis"—or "vulva" or "vagina"). Progress from there in an age-appropriate manner through high school. Each stage facilitates later stages: It's a lot easier to talk about a man putting his penis into a woman's vagina if you and the child have already become comfortable with talking about those body parts.

**Use teachable moments**    Rather than postpone everything to a "big talk about sex"—which may never happen—take advantage of opportunities that arise, such as when the child is undressing, sees a sibling or parent's genitals or nude art (see figure), witnesses sexual intimacy on television or in real life, or sees animals mating or giving birth. Take advantage of a subsequent pregnancy and childbirth, or the puberty of a sibling, to talk about these processes. Above all, respond simply and accurately to the child's questions. If children ask about the meaning of a word they hear from peers, respond candidly and in a relaxed, nonjudgmental manner. The question "Where do babies come from?" needs to be answered several times over, in increasing detail, beginning with something like "Babies grow in a special place inside the mother" and later explaining about eggs and sperm and how they come together. Respond to things the child has heard or witnessed at school or from friends: If the child announces that "Andy has two mommies," for example, that would be a good opportunity to talk about gay relationships and alternative parenting styles.

**Balance negatives with positives**    If you see your child masturbating, for example, then (depending on your own beliefs on the topic) you may want to say something like "That feels good, doesn't it? It's fine to do that, but it's best to do it in your bedroom. People like to do that when they're by themselves." When talking about sexual behavior, talk in an age-appropriate way about the physical and emotional pleasure of sexual contact and intimate relationships—including the specific body parts, such as the clitoris, that are involved—as well as the responsibilities and risks that sexual intimacy involves.

**Anticipate events**    That's especially important for the bodily and psychological changes that accompany puberty. A mother can teach her daughter (or her son, for that matter) about menstruation either in words or with aids such as pictures or her own unused and used tampons. Puberty comes earlier than parents expect, and by the time schools get around to the subject, half the class may have pubic hair. There are dozens of books suitable for kids—check out booksellers' websites under the search term "puberty."

There are many opportunities to teach one's child about sex and reproduction.

**Acknowledge diversity**    Help your child or teen understand that there is no single "normal" size or shape for genitals or breasts; no single "normal" time for the growth spurt, menarche, a sexual relationship, falling in love, or marriage; and no single "normal" sexual orientation.

**Communicate your values**    Let your child know your views on when sex is acceptable—whether it should be restricted to marriage or to emotionally committed relationships, or whether it has a place outside of those relationships. If you believe that your teen is ready for some forms of sexual contact, but not for others, say so. Ask for your child's views on these questions, and if you disagree, present the reasons for your point of view rather than simply laying down the law. Explain the core values, such as respect for others, or your religious beliefs that underlie your opinion.

**Give practical advice**    Bear in mind that most teens become sexually active well before leaving home. Adults can help teens avoid the serious pitfalls of adolescent sexuality without encouraging them to engage in sex. Explain the specific steps they can take to reduce the likelihood of pregnancy and STIs. Remember that, depending on your school's sex-education policy, there may be little or no instruction in contraceptive methods, especially in such practical matters as where to obtain contraceptives. It's unlikely that you'll be able to answer all the spoken or unspoken questions your teen will have about sex, so tell them about teen-oriented sex-education websites such as For Teens (www.plannedparenthood.org/teens) and Sex, Etc. (www.sexetc.org).

◀ **FIGURE 10.1** **Nudity** allows children to familiarize themselves with anatomical sex differences.

were mostly unable to give accurate answers to simple questions such as "How can anyone know whether a newborn baby is a boy or a girl?"

Nothing much has changed in this regard since the 1980s. In a 2012 study, Sandra Caron and Carie Ahlgrim of the University of Maine asked 6-year-old girls and boys from the United States and three European countries to make drawings in answer to the question "How are babies made?" and also to explain their drawings verbally (Caron & Ahlgrim, 2012) (**FIGURE 10.2**). Although the total number of children was small, the poor performance of U.S. and British children was striking.

## Some children engage in solitary sexual activity

Sexual behavior may begin before birth. Using ultrasonography, researchers have seen male fetuses developing penile erections and touching their penises in an apparently purposeful way (Meizner, 1987). A female fetus was observed touching her vulva repeatedly over a period of 20 minutes, a behavior that culminated in generalized body contractions resembling an orgasm (Giorgi & Siccardi, 1996).

Newborn babies sometimes exhibit penile erections or vaginal lubrication (Martinson, 1976; Masters et al., 1982). These responses are not necessarily brought about

(A)

"I think they are made by a mom and a dad, but I am not sure how; maybe during a special time when they are alone." (Boy, United States)

(B)

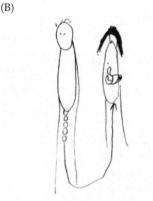

"The drops of the man come together with the egg of the mother. The baby grows and becomes bigger and then when it is big enough it comes out of the mother." (Boy, The Netherlands)

(C)

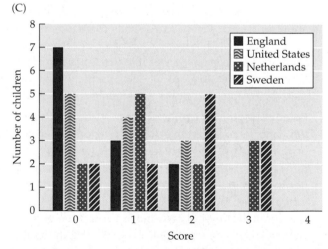

▲ **FIGURE 10.2** **How are babies made?** (A) Drawing made in response to this question by an American 6-year-old boy with his verbal explanation. (B) Drawing and explanation by a 6-year-old Dutch boy. (C) Scores of 6-year-olds from four countries (12 children from each country) on the Children's Sexual Awareness Scale, which required an accurate knowledge of the contributions of male and female to making a baby, its prenatal growth, and the birth process. Possible scores ranged from 0 (no answer) to 4; no child scored 4. (From S. L. Caron and C. J. Ahlgrim. 2012. *Am J Sex Ed* 7: 16–36.)

© Owen Franken/Corbis

by what we would normally consider *sexual* stimuli, however. Rather, it seems that erections in young boys are part of a generalized arousal response. Less is known about these responses in girls at that age.

Infants and young children of both sexes commonly touch their genitals. The great majority of mothers in European countries report having witnessed such behavior, whereas only about half of American mothers say that they have seen genital touching (Friedrich et al., 2000; Larsson et al., 2000). This cross-national difference could be real, but it could also reflect a greater openness of European mothers to the concept of childhood sexuality.

By 15 to 19 months of age some girls and boys rhythmically stimulate their genitals by hand or by rubbing their genitals against an object (Galenson,

▲ Very young children's tactile exploration may lead to autoerotic behavior.

1990). Roughly one in five parents has witnessed such masturbatory behavior in their child before the age of 6: Again, the numbers are higher in some European countries than in the United States (Friedrich et al., 1998; Larsson & Svedin, 2002b). In a survey of daycare professionals in Finland, 70% of respondents said they had a child in their group who masturbated openly (Cacciatore et al., 2020). Parents may misinterpret their young children's masturbatory and orgasmic behaviors as a sign of epilepsy or some other neurological disorder, and doctors may need to reassure such parents that this kind of masturbatory behavior is normal and healthy (Yang et al., 2005; Ajlouni et al., 2010).

According to Alfred Kinsey, this masturbatory behavior sometimes climaxes in what looks like an orgasm, even in children just a few months old (Kinsey et al., 1948; Kinsey et al., 1953). There has been very little research in this area since Kinsey's time, but one Chinese study reported on a girl who masturbated to orgasm from about 5 months of age until at least 8 years of age (B. Zhu et al., 2011). What was clear from this longitudinal case history was that the rather ambiguous behaviors seen in infancy developed gradually into a more explicit and purposeful masturbatory style. When she was old enough to be questioned about the behavior, the girl said that she did it for the pleasure it generated.

According to studies that are based on parents' reports, the prevalence of masturbation declines markedly during childhood (Friedrich et al., 1998). In retrospective studies, on the other hand, adolescents recall very little sexual activity in early childhood but a marked increase in sexual interest and behavior as puberty approaches. Among those who recall having masturbated before puberty, for example, the mean age of first masturbation is 8 to 10 years of age (Larsson & Svedin, 2002a).

These conflicting data illustrate the difficulty of conducting research on childhood sexuality. We may guess, however, that the decrease in sexual behavior with age that is reported by parents is only apparent: It could result from the fact that children learn to conceal sexual behavior. The failure of adolescents or adults to recall masturbation in early childhood could reflect the general impermanence of memory at that age.

According to the American Academy of Pediatrics, sexual behaviors by young children can fall anywhere on a spectrum from those that are normal, common, and harmless to others that are highly problematic and merit bringing to the attention of child protective services—because in some cases they may indicate that the child was sexually abused (American Academy of Pediatrics, 2019).

## Sex with others can occur during childhood

Besides solitary sexual activity, children's sexual behavior may involve others (**TABLE 10.1**). It is common for young children to show their genitals to adults or to other children and to attempt to view the genitals of others. Such activities begin in the second year of life, and about half of all parents have witnessed it by the time a child

**TABLE 10.1** Percentages of children engaging in sexual behaviors

| | Ages 2–5* | | Ages 6–10** | |
| --- | --- | --- | --- | --- |
| | GIRLS | BOYS | GIRLS | BOYS |
| Tries to look at people when they are nude | 26.9 | 26.8 | | |
| Touches genitals at home | 43.8 | 60.2 | | |
| Masturbates with hand | 15.8 | 16.7 | 8.5 | 18.1 |
| Kisses other children | 7.1 | 7.9 | 44.0 | 34.0 |
| Shows genitals to other children | 6.4 | 9.3 | 22.5 | 28.3 |
| Touches other child's genitals | 8.8 | 4.6 | 19.0 | 16.5 |
| Shows genitals to adults | 13.8 | 15.4 | | |
| Inserts objects into other child's vagina or anus | | | 4.2 | 10.2 |
| Puts penis in other child's mouth | | | – | 4.7 |
| Vaginal intercourse | | | 0.7 | 3.9 |
| Anal intercourse | | | 0 | 3.2 |

*Data for U.S. children age 2–5, based on reports of parents or caregivers. No data for blank cells.
*Source*: W. Friedrich et al. 1998. *Pediatrics* 101: E9.

**Data for Swedish children age 6–10, based on recollections of young adults. No data for blank cells.
*Source*: I. Larsson. 2002. *Arch Sex Behav* 31: 263–273.

reaches the age of 5 or 6. Not only parents but also preschool staff report seeing this kind of behavior (Davies et al., 2000; Larsson & Svedin, 2002b).

In addition, there may be sexual or quasi-sexual contacts between children. (We say "quasi-sexual" because these behaviors may not have what adults would consider a sexual motivation.) Children often hug and kiss each other. They may also attempt to touch each other's genitals. Sometimes these behaviors are incorporated into games such as "show," "doctor," "house," and the like. In a study carried out at UCLA about half the mothers reported that their children had engaged in this type of behavior before the age of 6 (Okami et al., 1997).

Only very small numbers of children engage in more adultlike sexual behavior, such as coitus (or pretended coitus), oral or anal sex, or insertion of a finger or an object into the vagina or anus. At first glance, this might seem surprising, given that coitus-related behaviors (presenting and mounting) are almost universal among the young of nonhuman primates. Bear in mind, however, that children (at least in contemporary American culture) have little opportunity to observe adults engaged in sexual behavior beyond kissing and hugging. Because imitation may play a large role in the learning of interpersonal sexual behavior in childhood, one would not expect to see many children attempting coitus or other forms of penetrative sex.

While most sexual behaviors between young children are voluntary, some are not. In one study, 13% of adolescents recalled childhood experiences of being coerced into a sexual contact by another child—the method of coercion being trickery, bribes, threats, or physical force. Eight percent recalled being the perpetrator in such coercive acts (Larsson & Svedin, 2002a).

For the most part, solitary and interpersonal sexual behaviors by children seem to be harmless. Even involuntary sexual experiences, if trivial in nature, may not be serious enough to warrant any kind of concern (**FIGURE 10.3**). Children who engage in sexual play with other children are just as likely to be well adjusted in the teenage years as children

▲ **FIGURE 10.3 Involuntary but harmless**
This boy may not have consented to being kissed, but he's unlikely to be traumatized by it.

Courtesy of Devadarshan Gurumayum

◀ **FIGURE 10.4**  **Lepcha girls** require coitus in order to develop into women, according to traditional beliefs of the Lepcha people of Sikkim, India.

who do not, according to one longitudinal study carried out at UCLA (Okami et al., 1997). When adolescents or young adults are asked to describe how childhood sexual experiences made them feel, most reply with positive descriptors such as "curious," "excited," or "happy," and most say that these experiences were "normal." But a minority report that the experiences made them feel "shamed," "guilty," or "embarrassed." Girls experience more negative feelings than boys, children who are coerced experience more negative feelings than those who participate willingly, and Americans experience more negative feelings than Europeans (Larsson & Svedin, 2002a; Reynolds et al., 2003).

## Cultures vary in their attitudes toward childhood sexuality

Children in many non-Western societies have traditionally engaged in sexual behaviors, but societies have varied in whether they encouraged, tolerated, or suppressed them (Frayser, 1994). It was noted on the Polynesian island of Mangaia, for example, that children traditionally have had the opportunity to observe the sexual behaviors of adults and have been freely permitted to engage in sex play and masturbation (Marshall, 1971). Similarly, the Chewa people of Malawi have encouraged their children to play at being husband and wife in little huts situated away from the village. The Lepcha people of northern India have believed that coitus is necessary for girls to mature into women (**FIGURE 10.4**), and several tribes in New Guinea have believed that ingestion of semen (by male-on-male fellatio) is necessary for boys to develop into men (Herdt, 2005).

More commonly, however, adults exert some degree of restraint on children's sexual expression. There are usually mild restraints on heterosexual play or masturbation during early childhood, but they may become stronger during later childhood, when girls and boys tend to be more strictly segregated. These restraints are stronger in societies in which sexual restraint is expected of adults; thus, children are essentially being prompted to learn the sexual attitudes they are expected to show in adulthood.

Anthropological studies, as well as observations in nonhuman primates, suggest that children learn how to perform sexually by observing adults' behaviors and by rehearsing those behaviors with other juveniles (Josephs, 2015) (**FIGURE 10.5**). In contemporary Western societies there may be little opportunity for such direct observation, so children's sexual learning may depend on sex education, the media, or pornography.

**FAQ:** I'm having a hard time teaching my 5-year-old to pee standing up. He's not circumcised, and pee goes everywhere.

Just slightly retracting his foreskin may help him achieve a better stream, but don't force it. If that doesn't help, he may have to continue sitting down for a few years. Plenty of adult men prefer urinating that way.

▲ **FIGURE 10.5**  **Front-row seat** Infant bonobos can't help learning about adult sex.

## 10.2 Some Children Have Sexual Contacts with Adults

**LEARNING OBJECTIVES**

After reading this section you should be able to:

10.2.1 Explain who are the most likely persons to sexually molest girls and boys.

10.2.2 Describe the factors influencing how harmful various kinds of adult–child sex may be.

If only the occasional child had sexual contact with an adult, this topic might be better dealt with in the context of atypical sexuality (see Chapter 13) or sexual assault (see Chapter 16). But in fact these childhood experiences are fairly common. In a large national survey of adults, about 1 in 10 interviewees said that they had experienced at least one sexual contact with an adult during their childhood; of these, 75% were female and 25% were male (Perez-Fuentes et al., 2013). Similar figures have been reported worldwide (Barth et al., 2013). Larger numbers of children have noncontact experiences, such as witnessing a man expose his genitals to them.

We therefore consider it appropriate to discuss adult–child sex in this chapter. We look at the issue only from the point of view of the child, however, focusing particularly on the harm that such contacts may do. The adults who have sexual contact with children are discussed in Chapter 13.

### Most adult–child contacts involve older children and are single encounters

According to the National Health and Social Life Survey (NHSLS), most children who have sexual experiences with adults or adolescents have only one such experience—or if they have multiple experiences, they are all with the same person. For girls, that person is most often an adult male and less often an adolescent male. For boys, it is most commonly an adolescent female, less often an adolescent male, and even less often an adult male. The data also show that 80% to 90% of adult–child contacts involve the adult touching the genitals of the child. Oral contacts and vaginal or anal penetration are much less common.

How old are children when they have sexual contact with adults or adolescents? The most likely age for a child of either sex to have sexual contact with a male is 7 to 10 years, but about one-third of such contacts occur in the under-7 age bracket. The most likely age for a boy to have contact with a female is 11 to 13 years. The females involved are usually adolescents who are a few years older than the boys.

In most cases, the child knows the adult, who is often a relative or family friend (**TABLE 10.2**). Girls are more likely to be molested by relatives, boys by family friends. Less than 10% of contacts are with strangers. As the table shows, girls as a group are equally likely to have contacts with fathers and stepfathers, but these figures are misleading, because many more girls live with their fathers than with stepfathers. Thus a girl who lives with her stepfather is at considerably greater risk of being molested by him than is a girl who lives with her biological father. Children who grow up in unhappy families are more than twice as likely to experience sexual abuse as those who experience a happy family life (Finkelhor et al., 1990).

**TABLE 10.2** Percentage of adult–child sexual contacts identified by relationship and child's sex

| Relationship of adult to child | Child's sex | |
|---|---|---|
| | GIRL | BOY |
| Father | 7 | 1 |
| Stepfather | 7 | 1 |
| Older brother | 9 | 4 |
| Other relative | 29 | 13 |
| Teacher | 3 | 4 |
| Family friend | 29 | 40 |
| Mother's boyfriend | 2 | 1 |
| Older friend of child | 1 | 4 |
| Other person known to child | 19 | 17 |
| Stranger | 7 | 4 |

*Source*: Data from NHSLS as reported in E. Laumann et al. 1994. *The social organization of sexuality: Sexual practices in the United States.* University of Chicago Press: Chicago.

*Note*: The percentages add up to more than 100 because some children had contacts with more than one adult.

### Some kinds of adult–child sex are more harmful than others

The effects of adult–child sex on children are controversial. In the minds of most members of the public, politicians, and jurists—as well as some therapists—such contacts are always extremely harmful to the child. As a result, adults convicted of child molestation are punished more severely than almost any other criminals. Sentences of 60 or more years of imprisonment may be imposed for serious offenses, especially if those convicted have prior records.

According to numerous studies, children who have had sexual contacts with adults do indeed experience more harmful consequences than do comparison groups of children who have not had such contacts. The harmful effects of these contacts are also more severe than the effects of nonsexual maltreatment (Lewis et al., 2016). These effects include both short-term effects (e.g., fearfulness, depression, inhibition of emotions, hostility, and antisocial behavior) and long-term effects (e.g., mood disorders, phobias, panic disorder, antisocial personality, suicidality, substance abuse, poor academic performance, premature sexual activity, sexual promiscuity, exposure to sexually transmitted infections [STIs], and sexual victimization of others) (Chen et al., 2010; Maniglio, 2013). In general, externalizing (i.e., behavioral) problems are more common in boys and internalizing problems (i.e., mood disturbances and suicidality) are more common in girls. Personal accounts confirm the traumatic effects that sexual abuse of children can have (Lopez, 2013).

A somewhat different picture emerges, however, when the details of the adult–child contacts are taken into account. The children who are most likely to experience adverse effects are, not surprisingly, those who were physically coerced into a sexual contact (Molnar et al., 2001; Stander et al., 2016). Sexual contacts that are repeated over a long period of time, that are with a family member or caregiver, or that involve a very large age difference may also be more likely to cause harm than isolated or nonincestuous contacts or those with a small age difference between the child and the older person. Contacts that involve sexual penetration are more harmful than those that do not (Najman et al., 2005). Girls are also more likely to experience harm than boys.

Because most adult–child contacts are single events and don't involve physical coercion or penetrative sex, it's possible that most contacts cause little or no harm. According to meta-analyses and original studies by psychologist Bruce Rind of Temple University and his colleagues, most children who experience sexual contacts with adults suffer no long-term adverse consequences, or only mild ones (Rind et al., 1998; Rind, 2001).

The Rind studies provoked a great deal of controversy: Some researchers have reached different conclusions (Najman et al., 2005; Najman et al., 2007), while others have confirmed Rind's findings (Ulrich et al., 2005/6). In a 2018 study that used data from the NHSLS, Rind reported that men who, when they were postpubertal minors, had sexual contact with adult men were just as healthy, happy, and successful in their careers as men who did not have such contacts (Rind, 2018). These data did not relate to more vulnerable populations: girls, or boys molested before puberty.

The issue of adult–child sex and its consequences is greatly complicated by problems of recall. Ideally, children would give reliable testimony about sexual contacts they had recently experienced, and adults would have accurate memories of childhood sexual experiences. Unfortunately, neither is necessarily the case. Children can be induced to believe and report events that didn't happen, and adults can be induced to "recover" supposedly repressed memories of childhood sexual abuse, even when such memories are demonstrably false (**BOX 10.2**).

## Strategies to prevent adult–child sex are quite effective

Even if many children are left unscathed by sexual contact with adults, the fact remains that some children are indeed traumatized. These children are at risk of developing **post-traumatic stress disorder** (**PTSD**), just as adult rape victims are (see Chapter 16). One aspect of this disorder is **dissociation**—the tendency to "stand outside" the traumatic experience and to fail to experience the normal emotional responses to it. Another common trait shown by sexually abused children is

**post-traumatic stress disorder (PTSD)** A cluster of physical and psychological symptoms that can affect persons who have experienced severe trauma.

**dissociation** The distancing of oneself from the emotions evoked by some traumatic experience or memory.

## BOX 10.2
## Sex and Suggestibility

How would you like to serve 21 years in prison for crimes you didn't commit—crimes so monstrous as to challenge anyone's credulity? This is what happened to Fran and Dan Keller, a Texas couple who were wrongly convicted of child molestation in 1992, spent 21 years in prison, and were not finally exonerated until 2017 (see figure).

The Kellers ran a day care center near Austin. In 1991 the mother of a 3-year-old girl who attended the center went to the police, saying that her daughter had been treated by a therapist for behavioral problems and that the child told the therapist that she had been sexually abused by the Kellers. Under intense questioning and pressure, the child—and later several other children—described scenes of ritual sexual abuse. The Kellers, they said, had put blood in their Kool-Aid, sacrificed and buried babies, cut off the arm of a gorilla, enacted satanic scenes in graveyards, dismembered a passerby with a chainsaw, and taken the children to Mexico to be sexually abused by military officials—among many other lurid crimes.

The Keller trial happened during a national "sex panic," when many innocent people were accused of ritual sexual abuse of young children. In 1992, for example, a Missouri woman who was in therapy with a church counselor "remembered" that she was repeatedly raped by her father—a minister—between the ages of 7 and 14, that she became pregnant as a result, and that she was forced to perform an abortion on herself with a coat hanger. When her story was publicized, her father had to resign his post as a minister. Before he could be tried, however, a medical examination revealed that the daughter had never been pregnant and, in fact, was still a virgin. The therapist paid $1 million in settlement of the case.

Dan and Fran Keller after their release from prison.

Numerous studies document that memories can be inculcated. The leading figure in this field of research is Elizabeth Loftus (now at UC Irvine), who testified in many sexual abuse cases (Loftus & Davis, 2006). In her best-known experiment, Loftus instilled her subjects with false memories of having been lost in shopping malls as children, along with various things that happened to those children while lost. Others have instilled "childhood memories" of hospitalization for an ear infection, of the sprinklers going off in a store, of an accident at a wedding reception, and the like. Nothing distinguishes these false memories from real ones—except that they are false.

The state of Texas paid the Kellers $3.4 million in reparations for their wrongful conviction and imprisonment. What the state cannot do is give the Kellers their lives back.

---

self-blame. Therapy may be focused on helping the child to experience the missing emotions and to realize that the adult perpetrator was the sole guilty party.

Many schools have programs intended to teach young children how to avoid sexual encounters with adults by learning to distinguish between "good touch" (e.g., patting and hugging) and "bad touch" (e.g., genital fondling). One simple instruction that children often receive is never to allow anyone to touch them on parts of their body that are covered by a bathing suit. Programs of this kind have been quite effective in reducing the incidence of sexual abuse (Davis & Gidycz, 2000; Finkelhor et al., 2014).

There has been some concern that these programs might inculcate sex-phobic attitudes. A study of college-age women, however, concluded that women who participated in these prevention programs during their childhood were as well adjusted sexually as other women, and were much less likely to have experienced adult–child sexual contact subsequent to the instruction (Gibson & Leitenberg, 2000).

Whatever the reason, child sexual abuse is much less common than it was in the past (Jud et al., 2016). Substantiated cases of such abuse dropped by 60% between 1992 and 2010 (Goode, 2012), and there has been a similar decline in online sexual solicitation of children (Mitchell et al., 2013).

# 10.3 Preadolescence May Be Marked by an Increase in Sexual Interest

**LEARNING OBJECTIVE**

After reading this section you should be able to:

**10.3.1 Describe the process of gender segregation during preadolescence and how it may affect non-heterosexual children.**

The period between about 8 years and 12 to 13 years of age is often called **preadolescence**, or more informally the "tween years." During this period the biological processes of puberty begin. Preadolescence may be marked by some degree of increased sexual feelings and behaviors, but this varies greatly from one individual to another.

In the United States, where many young children receive little or no sex education, the early preadolescent years (say, around age 8 or 9) are the time when most children learn about coitus and other "facts of life." Much information is spread through peer networks, so comical misunderstandings are the rule. For example, children may fail to understand the difference between the anus and the vaginal opening or may think that babies grow in the mother's stomach and emerge via the navel.

Concern has been expressed in recent years that children, especially preadolescent children, are being prematurely "sexualized" by television, social media, pornography, and other manifestations of mass culture. We assess this issue in **BOX 10.3**.

## Preadolescent children segregate by sex

Preadolescent children spend much of their free time in all-male or all-female groups. Obviously, this pattern of socialization minimizes their opportunities for heterosexual interactions. Nevertheless, some older preadolescents do engage in sexual behavior with the other sex. According to the CDC's Youth Risk Behavior Survey, 6% of children under the age of 13 have engaged in sexual intercourse (CDC, 2014).

The fact that preadolescent children socialize primarily with peers of the same sex facilitates same-sex sexual behavior. Boys may engage in paired or group masturbation, for example. It's possible that preadolescents who later become gay adults enjoy such behavior more than those who become straight adults, but the behavior is certainly not indicative of a child's sexual orientation, either at the time of the behavior or later in life.

## Strict gender norms may traumatize children who become gay or transgender adults

Actually, preadolescent children who will become gay, lesbian, or transgender adults tend to distinguish themselves not so much by their sexual behavior, but by gender nonconformity in a variety of nonsexual traits (see Chapter 12). A boy who will become a gay man may be less interested in contact sports than other boys, for example, while a girl who will become a lesbian may be *more* interested in such sports than other girls. Such gender nonconformity may be apparent in earlier childhood, and it may worry parents or teachers, but young children themselves are usually blind to it, so gender-nonconformist children are not seriously disadvantaged within their peer groups.

During the preadolescent years, however, gender norms become much stricter, both within peer groups and with respect to the expectations of adults. The problems are more severe for gender-nonconformist boys than for girls because some degree of masculinity in a girl may actually be an advantage: A degree of athleticism, aggressiveness, or competitiveness, for example, may help her gain a leadership position in her peer group. Boys who are unmasculine or who are overtly feminine, however, may find themselves excluded from both their male and female peer groups and may have to content themselves with the company of other "misfits" at

**preadolescence** The age range including the beginning of puberty, from approximately age 8 to 12 or 13 years.

## BOX 10.3
## Are Today's Children Being Sexualized?

In the British dating show *Naked Attraction*, a clothed contestant inspects the fully naked bodies of six strangers, starting with their feet (see figure). After close inspection of their buttocks, genitals, and breasts, the contestant gradually whittles the six down to two, and then takes his or her own clothes off to make the final choice. Once fully familiarized with each other's bodies, but ignorant of anything else, the two go off on a date, and they later report back on what transpired.

Unlike British TV, American network television does not permit full nudity, but there's still plenty of nudity that's been blurred out, as well as reality shows in which sex transpires just off camera, or *Bachelor*-type shows where the aim is to outcompete your rivals for the attention of some latter-day Adonis. What effect, if any, does this "pornified" television, as well as pornography itself and all the other sex-related material in the media, have on children who may see it, whether by choice or accident?

According to a widely expressed point of view, children who view this kind of material risk being "prematurely sexualized"—taught, in other words, to think, feel, and act in sexual terms that are well beyond what children might naturally experience. It is usually girls who are the subject of concern: They are taught, according to a task force of the American Psychological Association, to present themselves as sex objects and to believe that they could and should become sexually active. In the process, girls become dissatisfied with their bodies, lose self-esteem, and fall prey to anxiety, depression, and other disorders (American Psychological Association, 2007). To the extent that there is any concern about boys, it is that they are taught to judge girls by their looks alone, and to seek casual sex before they or their sought-after partners have the emotional maturity to do so responsibly and safely.

There is little doubt that some process of this kind does go on, and it may begin at a very young age—as for example with young girls who are entered by their parents in beauty pageants. Nevertheless, there are also reasons to doubt that the sexualization phenomenon is as pernicious as it is often portrayed. For one thing, children are not "blank slates" who remain sexually innocent unless and until the wicked world comes calling. Rather, boys and girls come preloaded with certain sexual tendencies. In this, they are no different from the young of other primates, who spontaneously rehearse male- and female-typical sexual behaviors long before puberty. Sexual innocence is "something that adults wish upon children, not a natural feature of childhood itself," according

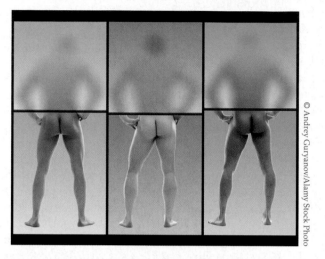

Booty contest. This is how hopefuls line up on Britain's *Naked Attraction* to be selected for a date.

© Andrey Guryanov/Alamy Stock Photo

to the British educational psychologists Debbie Epstein and Richard Johnson (Epstein & Johnson, 1998). And according to Allison Moore and Paul Reynolds of Edge Hill University in the United Kingdom, "[T]o define the sexualization of childhood as inherently negative and to conflate this with the sexual expression and desires of children and young people is deeply problematic" (Moore & Reynolds, 2018).

What's more, children themselves are rarely asked about their views on the matter. When they are, they often show that they understand the difference between the make-believe world of the media and the reality of their own lives. Moore and Reynolds quote one 13-year-old girl as follows: "When you see girls on TV like in music videos, and basically everywhere, they're all sexualized. Basically everywhere, you don't see a girl on TV that isn't sexualized. Guys aren't encouraged to see a girl's personality. In the media it's all about how they look, and getting to that girl for stuff." This girl at least was not a victim of sexualization so much as a critic of it.

If *Naked Attraction* does promote sexual objectification, it at least does so in a gender-equitable way: Women on the show choose men, women choose women, men choose men, men choose women, and any of them can be cis- or transgender. Gender roles, as traditionally defined, are nowhere in evidence.

Looking back on your own "tween" years, what effect, if any, did seeing sex in the media have on your own psychological development? Do you think children are being "prematurely sexualized," and if so, what would you like to see done about it?

the fringes of childhood society. Furthermore, epithets such as "faggot" and "dyke" are used with increasing frequency in the preadolescent years, and hearing these epithets may begin the internalization of homophobic attitudes by the children who hear them. Of course, the degree to which children who will become gay adults experience these problems before adolescence varies greatly, depending on how gender-nonconformist they are as well as on their parents' attitudes, the schools they attend, and so on.

Children who will become transgender adults are likely to be at least as gender-nonconformist as those who become gay adults, and often more so. We already discussed the social difficulties experienced by many of these children in Chapter 4. It's the responsibility of parents and schools to establish an environment in which the bullying of gender-nonconformist children is not permitted. These children can offer a positive learning experience in the area of tolerance, acceptance, and respect for diversity.

## 10.4 Puberty Is a Period of Rapid Maturation

### LEARNING OBJECTIVES
After reading this section you should be able to:

10.4.1 Describe the sequence of bodily changes that occur during puberty in girls and boys.

10.4.2 Explain how the timing of puberty contributes to the greater average height of men than women.

10.4.3 Name two proposed reasons why children are entering puberty earlier than in the past.

**Puberty** is the transition to reproductive maturity. It is marked by biological changes that affect the entire body: These include anatomical and physiological maturation of the external and internal genitalia, the development of secondary sexual characteristics such as breasts in girls, a growth spurt, and changes in the brain that affect behavior, especially in the area of sexuality. We will first describe all these changes, and then we will go on to discuss their timing and the mechanisms that bring them about.

**puberty** The biological transition that confers the capacity to be a parent.

### Puberty is marked by visible and invisible changes

In girls, the most noticeable change in the external genitalia is the appearance of pubic hair (**FIGURE 10.6**), but in addition, the outer and inner labia become more prominent, the vagina deepens, and the vaginal wall thickens. Underarm hair appears a little later than pubic hair.

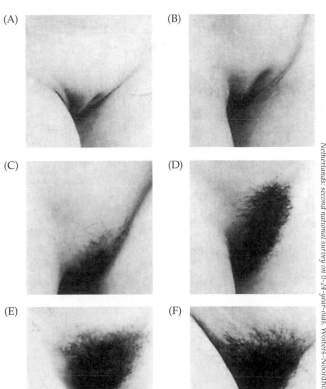

▶ **FIGURE 10.6  Typical development of pubic hair in girls at puberty** (A) Prepubescent state: No hair is visible. (B) Sparse, long, downy hair grows along the labia. This stage occurs at about 8.8 years in blacks and 10.5 years in whites, but with considerable variability. (C) Coarser, curly hair grows along the labia. (D) Hair covers the labia. (E) Hair spreads over the mons but not to the adult extent or density. (F) Hair forms an adultlike "inverted triangle" and extends to the inner surface of the thighs; this final pattern varies considerably among women, and many women trim or remove their pubic hair. Note: We use these old, much-published black-and-white images because contemporary ethical standards make taking photographs of minors' genitals problematic.

All photos from J. C. Van Wieringen et al., transl. from Dutch by Marja Jokel, 1971. *Growth diagrams 1965 Netherlands: second national survey on 0–24-year-olds*. Wolters-Noordhoff: Groningen

(A)

(B)

(C)

(D)

(E)

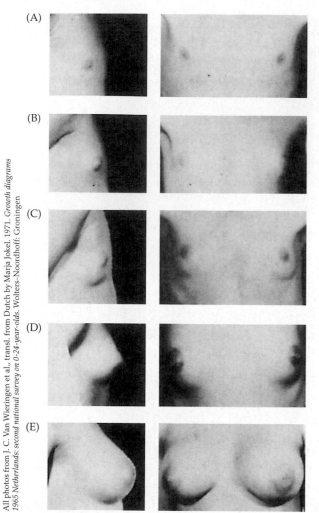

All photos from J. C. Van Wieringen et al., transl. from Dutch by Marja Jokel. 1971. *Growth diagrams 1965 Netherlands: second national survey on 0–24-year-olds.* Wolters-Noordhoff: Groningen

◀ **FIGURE 10.7** Typical development of breasts in girls at puberty, seen in side and frontal views (A) Prepubescent appearance. (B) Breast bud stage: The nipple, areola, and nearby breast tissue form a small mound at about 8.9 years (for black girls) or 10 years (for white girls). (C) Further enlargement of the areola and breast occurs. (D) The nipple and areola project out from the breast. (E) Adultlike stage: The areola is now flush with the breast; only the nipple projects forward.

Inside a girl's body, puberty is marked by a spurt of growth in the ovaries, uterus, and oviducts. The oviducts, which before puberty have a somewhat contorted course, become straighter. The cervix begins to produce the characteristic secretions of adult life. In the ovaries, some follicles begin to mature.

Female breasts are important secondary sexual characteristics that develop at puberty. Breast development goes through several stages (**FIGURE 10.7**). The breasts first emerge as small mounds—the **breast buds**—centered on the nipples. As breast development continues, both the nipple and the surrounding areola come to project forward from the breast, and the areola enlarges. With the completion of breast development, the areola lies flush with the breast once more, and only the nipple projects.

The onset of menstruation is called **menarche** (pronunciations vary; MEN-ark-ee is the most common). The first menstrual period is often quite slight—perhaps just a single episode of spotting rather than a several-day flow. Even so, menarche is a highly memorable event in most women's lives (**BOX 10.4**).

After menarche, menstruation may be irregular for a year or two. Furthermore, the initial menstrual cycles tend not to be accompanied by ovulation. For this reason, an adolescent may not be capable of becoming pregnant for up to 2 years after menarche. However, there is much variation in this respect.

For boys, an early sign of puberty is the enlargement of the testicles and scrotum (**FIGURE 10.8**). The penis grows in length and then in girth, and pubic hair appears. The larynx (voice box) grows and the vocal folds thicken, leading to a deepening of the voice.

Many boys experience growth of the glandular tissue of the breasts, called **gynecomastia**, during the latter part of puberty (**FIGURE 10.9**). Breast development is driven by estrogen, and in some boys a great deal of estrogen is produced by enzymatic conversion from testosterone (Swerdloff & Ng, 2019). The enlarged breasts generally disappear within about 3 years, but while they are present, they may cause intense embarrassment; psychological support is important. Medical or surgical treatments are available for boys who are highly distressed about the condition.

First ejaculation may occur with masturbation or during sleep (nocturnal emission). Initially, the semen may lack mature sperm; in fact, a male can be infertile for a year or two after his first ejaculation. It's a good idea for parents to mention nocturnal emissions when they are discussing puberty with their sons, because otherwise boys may be surprised and frightened by the experience: Some imagine that it is a medical abnormality or a punishment for masturbation, for example.

The extent of facial and body hair is highly variable among individuals as well as between ethnic groups. One puberty-associated trait that afflicts many teens, especially boys, is acne. The key feature of acne is the blockage of oil-producing glands associated with hair follicles—most commonly on the face, neck, or back. The blockage is caused by an excess production of oil and shedding of skin cells within the glands. The blocked glands become a breeding ground for a common skin bacterium, *Propionibacterium acnes*. The blocked gland is called a whitehead if

**breast bud**   The first stage of breast development at puberty.

**menarche**   The onset of menstruation at puberty.

**gynecomastia**   The development of breasts in males.

**epiphyseal plates**   The growth zones in limb bones, which cease to function after puberty.

▶ **FIGURE 10.8** **Typical development of male external genitalia at puberty** (A) Prepubescent appearance. (B) Enlargement of the scrotum and testicles. This stage usually occurs at between 11 and 13 years. (C) Increase in the length of the penis and further enlargement of the scrotum. (D) Increase in the size of the penis, especially the glans, and appearance of pubic hair. (E) Adultlike appearance.

(A) (B)
(C) (D)

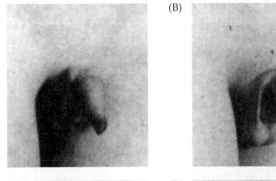
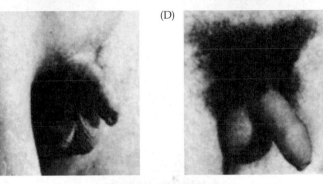
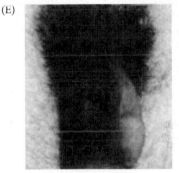

(E)

it is below the skin, a blackhead if it reaches the surface, and a pimple or pustule if it becomes inflamed. Severe acne can lead to permanent scarring. The condition can be treated with topical (local) medications containing benzoyl peroxide, salicylic acid, or sulfur. Severe cases may be treated with the oral drug isotretinoin (Accutane), but this drug can have serious side effects, including fetal defects if taken by pregnant women.

One of the most visible processes of puberty is the growth spurt, which takes place over a period of about 5 years. During this time girls gain about 10 inches (25 cm) in height, and boys gain about 11 inches. The spurt in height ends when the **epiphyseal plates**—the cartilaginous growth zones near the ends of the limb bones—cease functioning and turn into bone.

The spurt in height is not the only growth change during puberty. There are changes in skeletal structure, with girls developing wider hips and boys developing wider shoulders. Body composition also changes: By adulthood, men have 50% more bone and muscle mass than women, and women have twice as much body fat as men. Of course, these are statements about averages—there are plenty of muscular women and pudgy men. Variations in body composition among individuals of both sexes are influenced by many factors, such as genetics, diet, and levels of physical exercise.

During puberty, the brains of boys and girls diverge from each other, both in structure and in function (see Figure 4.5). These changes are long-lasting—that is, they are not easily reversed by changes in the amounts or kinds of sex hormones to which the brain may be exposed during adult life (Schulz & Sisk, 2016; Sisk, 2017). In rodents, the representation of the genitals in the cerebral cortex doubles in size at puberty, and the neurons within this area undergo maturational changes, which are accelerated by sexual experience (Lenschow et al., 2016; Sigl-Glöckner et al., 2019). Whether this also true in humans is not yet known.

Paralleling these brain changes are dramatic psychological developments. Some of these processes—such as an increase in sensation-seeking and risk-taking behaviors—are fairly similar in girls and boys, although boys typically show more risk-taking behavior. Both girls and boys experience an increase in sexual interest, attraction, and behavior (whether autoerotic or partnered), but most girls develop attraction to males whereas most boys develop attraction to females, while a minority of girls and boys develop same-sex or bisexual attractions, or no sexual attractions at all (asexuality). (We discuss how sexual orientation develops in Chapter 12.)

Similarly, both boys and girls become more susceptible to mental disorders as they go through puberty, but the kinds of disorders that strike girls and boys tend to differ: Girls (and adult women) are more liable to anxiety, depression, and eating disorders,

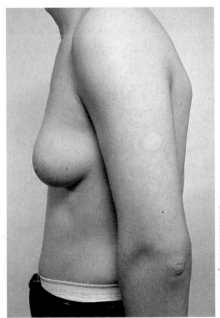

▶ **FIGURE 10.9** **Gynecomastia** is breast development in a boy or man.

## BOX 10.4
## My First Period

Most women recall the circumstances surrounding their first menstrual period. The event is experienced in very different ways by different girls, depending on the culture in which they grow up and how their parents or schools have prepared them for it (see figure). Here are some first-person accounts. The first two are from the website ExperienceProject.com, where girls or women can contribute their recollections. The last two are from a similar site that is no longer online:

*I was 11 and my sister was 8. She and I were changing our clothes for bed and she just said, "Look—does that mean you're gonna have a baby?" I looked down and saw a big red spot. My mom was working a night shift so I called her, crying. For some reason, I couldn't stop crying. I was so sad. Now, I am happy to see the red spot some months!*

*I got my first period during the summer between 6th and 7th grade. My friends and I always talked about periods and we were all excited to get them. I was raised where getting your period was a joyous thing. I was at home with my BFF in my bedroom, and I went to the bathroom. I sat down and saw the blood. I jumped up and started screaming until my friend came in, and we jumped for joy. She ran and got my mom and she talked to us about it, and the three of us had a Girls Night Out. It was the best day of my life. The funny thing was that my BFF got her period the next day.*

*I come from India and girls' first periods were celebrated in a very grand fashion. In India, particularly southern India, a girl's first menstruation is a matter of great joy to the community. Initially for the first three days she is not allowed to touch anything in the household nor participate in any household chores. After the three days all the*

Courtesy of Kathy Pickus, Dot Girl Products

The Dot Girl's First Period Kit was designed and marketed by two sisters who were unprepared for their own menarches. The kit includes five menstrual pads with disposal bags, two hand wipes, a reusable heating pad, and an answer book/diary.

*women of the community are invited to a grand function exclusively for women. Everyone gives her gifts, usually jewelry. From then on she always puts the red spot on her forehead, which signifies womanhood.*

*I was a few hours late to school, arriving in the middle of music class. All I wanted to do was crawl to my seat and quietly die. I was so sure everyone must know. The guy I had a crush on sat near me in that class. As I reached my seat, he called over to me. God! The last thing I wanted was for him to know! I figured he was going to ask why I'd been late, and what could I say? I'd lie, of course, but I was sure it would show in my face. But he didn't ask that. Instead he said, "Hey, why do you look especially nice today?"*

whereas boys (and adult men) are more liable to conduct disorders such as antisocial behavior and drug abuse. It is as if the strong emotions that are awakened during puberty are more likely to be internalized in girls, and more likely to be externalized (expressed in behavior) in boys (Eaton et al., 2012).

### Puberty occurs earlier in girls than boys

The timing of puberty is quite variable from individual to individual, so during the early teen years children of the same age may have reached very different stages of development (**FIGURE 10.10**). Nevertheless, the various processes of puberty occur in a fairly predictable sequence. For girls, the earliest events of puberty are the appearance of pubic hair and the breast bud stage of breast development, which occur at a median age* of about 9 years of age in black girls and about 10 years of age in white,

---

*The median age is the age at which half the individuals have reached that stage of development and half have not.

Hispanic, and Asian girls (Biro et al., 2013). Girls' growth spurt begins about 1 year after the beginning of breast development. Menarche occurs at about 12.5 years (CDC, 2017c). Final height is reached at about 16 years of age.

In boys, the penis and testicles begin to enlarge at the age of about 10 years, pubic hair appears at about 11, the growth spurt begins at about 12, first ejaculation occurs at about 13, and the voice reaches adult pitch at about 15. The growth spurt ends at about 17, but some additional slow growth may occur for 2 to 3 years after that. As with girls, some of these stages occur 6 months to a year earlier in black boys (Herman-Giddens et al., 2012).

Because the early stages of puberty occur earlier in girls than in boys, boys experience a longer prepubertal childhood than girls. One striking result is the difference in the adult height of men and women. Boys have about 2 more years of childhood growth before the growth spurt begins, which gives them an extra 3 inches

▲ **FIGURE 10.10** **The timing of the growth spurt varies.** These girls are all 12 years old.

(7.5 cm) of height. Add the extra inch (2.5 cm) gained over girls during the growth spurt itself, and adult men end up 4 inches (10 cm) taller than women, on average.

Over the past century a number of Western countries have experienced a trend toward the earlier onset of puberty in both girls and boys. In the United States, children are entering puberty 1 to 2 years earlier than they did in the 1970s, and a similar phenomenon has been observed in many other countries (Herman-Giddens et al., 2012; Biro et al., 2013; Eckert-Lind et al., 2020). Changes in diet—specifically, the introduction of plentiful, calorie-dense food that allows children to grow faster and put on more fat—are probably the main reason (Parent et al., 2016). Part of the evidence for this is that girls with a high body mass index (BMI) enter puberty earlier than other girls, and the average BMI of prepubertal girls has been rising steadily for many years. Another factor may be the increasing presence of **endocrine disruptors**—industrial pollutants that mimic the action of sex hormones—in food or in the environment (Fisher & Eugster, 2014).

**endocrine disruptors** Substances that interfere with development by mimicking sex hormones.

Although puberty is beginning earlier, the later stages of puberty, such as the termination of limb bone growth, are happening at the same age or even at a later age than previously (Parent et al., 2016). Thus the overall duration of puberty is longer than it was a century or so ago.

## 10.5 Puberty Is Orchestrated by Hormones

### LEARNING OBJECTIVES
After reading this section you should be able to:

10.5.1 Analyze the roles of androgens and estrogens in puberty in girls and boys.

10.5.2 Delineate the cascade of signals that initiate puberty.

10.5.3 Explain the physical and psychological problems that may be caused by precocious puberty.

So far, we have simply described the major phenomena associated with puberty. But what triggers and orchestrates these phenomena? Let's start by looking at the

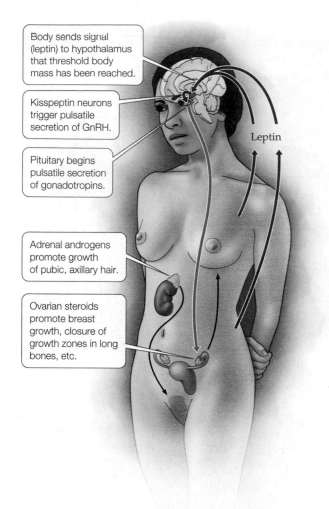

Body sends signal (leptin) to hypothalamus that threshold body mass has been reached.

Kisspeptin neurons trigger pulsatile secretion of GnRH.

Pituitary begins pulsatile secretion of gonadotropins.

Adrenal androgens promote growth of pubic, axillary hair.

Ovarian steroids promote breast growth, closure of growth zones in long bones, etc.

Leptin

▲ **FIGURE 10.11    Hormonal control of puberty**
This figure shows the chain of events that drive puberty in girls. The regulation of puberty in boys is similar, except that the principal gonadal steroids are androgens, especially testosterone. Signals from body fat may be less important in boys.

proximate (immediate) causes, then track back to the earlier events that get puberty under way (**FIGURE 10.11**).

The proximate causes of most of the phenomena of puberty are hormones—in particular, *androgens* and *estrogens*, along with growth hormone. Although estrogen effects predominate in girls and androgen effects predominate in boys, both androgens and estrogens are needed in both sexes for normal completion of puberty.

The levels of testosterone and other androgens rise steadily in both sexes during puberty, but they reach much higher final levels in men than in women. Androgens are responsible for muscle development, change of voice, and spermatogenesis (in combination with the gonadotropin follicle-stimulating hormone [FSH]), as well as the appearance of pubic and underarm hair in both sexes. In males, androgens are also responsible for the pubertal development of the external genitalia, prostate, seminal vesicles, sebaceous glands, and facial and body hair (and for male-pattern baldness), but full development of these characteristics requires the conversion of testosterone to the more potent androgen 5α-dihydrotestosterone (DHT) in the target tissues (see Chapter 3).

The very high levels of testosterone reached during puberty in boys drive their brain development in a male-typical direction and therefore promote male-typical gender characteristics. Boys who were unmasculine or positively feminine in childhood often become more conventionally masculine during puberty; in fact, boys who say they want to be girls quite commonly change their minds at puberty.

Estrogens (in combination with growth hormone and progesterone) promote development of the breasts. By their actions on the hypothalamus, estrogens and progesterone trigger menarche and are required for the maintenance of menstrual cycles thereafter. These hormones also have more general effects on the brain, affecting mood, memory, and other characteristics. Whether estrogens have a direct effect on women's sexual feelings and behaviors is uncertain, but they may do so indirectly by their effects on the genitals (such as increased vaginal lubrication) that make sex more pleasurable. Surprisingly perhaps, testosterone also promotes sexual desire in women (Davis & Davison, 2012).

In males, estrogens are required for the normal functioning of the epididymis in concentrating sperm and are therefore necessary for male fertility. In both sexes, estrogens are responsible for an increase in bone density at puberty, as well as for the closure of the epiphyseal plates at the end of the pubertal growth spurt. Thus, individuals who cannot manufacture estrogens, or who lack estrogen receptors, keep on growing after the end of puberty and may become exceptionally tall (Sharpe, 1997).

What drives the increase in circulating sex steroids during puberty? The initial rise in androgen levels, which triggers the appearance of pubic and underarm hair in both sexes, is due to an increase in androgen secretion by the adrenal glands. The main increase in sex steroids during puberty, however, is due to an increase in secretion by the gonads. This gonadal secretion is driven by an increase in the release of the gonadotropins luteinizing hormone (LH) and follicle-stimulating hormone (FSH).

Gonadotropin secretion is triggered, in turn, by an increase in the secretion of gonadotropin-releasing hormone (GnRH) by the hypothalamus. This increase is a key event during puberty. The rest of the body seems to be primed from early childhood to heed the call of GnRH; only the lack of GnRH prevents puberty from taking place at 2 or 3 years of age. Thus, we would like to know why GnRH secretion increases when it does, rather than earlier or later.

## The body signals its readiness for puberty to the brain

Why then does GnRH secretion increase when it does, rather than earlier or later? It appears that the increase is triggered when the body has reached a certain critical weight, weight-to-height ratio, or body fat ratio (the proportion of body weight that is fat). The timing of puberty correlates better with body weight than with chronological age. In girls, the pubertal growth spurt begins at an average weight of 66 pounds (30 kg). In boys, puberty is triggered at a higher body weight than in girls: about 121 pounds (55 kg).

Menarche occurs at an average weight of 103 pounds (47 kg). Thus girls who are overweight for their age experience menarche earlier than thin girls, and very thin girls may not experience menarche at all (**primary amenorrhea**). Furthermore, if women lose most of their body fat after puberty—as can happen during famines, as a consequence of eating disorders such as anorexia nervosa, or even as a result of extreme athletic activity—their menstrual cycles may cease (**secondary amenorrhea**).

How might the brain know when the body has reached a certain weight or composition? One key player is **leptin**, a peptide hormone that is secreted by fat cells (Sanchez-Garrido & Tena-Sempere, 2013; Zhang & Gong, 2018). In general, leptin levels in the blood provide an indication of how much fat the body has accumulated. It makes sense for a puberty-inducing signal to come from fat cells, especially in girls, because a girl should not become reproductively mature until she has accumulated the energy stores necessary to sustain pregnancy. Supporting the idea that leptin helps trigger puberty is the finding that girls with a mutation in the gene for the leptin receptor do not enter puberty (Clement et al., 1998).

The role of leptin in male puberty is still unclear. Overweight boys, like overweight girls, enter puberty earlier than normal-weight boys, but boys who are heavy enough to be defined as obese enter puberty *later* than other boys (Lee et al., 2016). This may be because estrogen, secreted by body fat, counteracts the action of leptin in triggering male puberty.

Leptin does not directly activate the GnRH-secreting cells of the hypothalamus. Rather, leptin, along with other chemical and neural signals, stimulates a group of hypothalamic neurons that manufacture and secrete a signaling molecule named **kisspeptin** (Cortes et al., 2015). Kisspeptin in turn stimulates the GnRH neurons to secrete GnRH, and the rare individuals who lack the receptor for kisspeptin—like those who lack the receptor for leptin—fail to enter puberty.

In summary, puberty is the end result of a long chain of chemical signals:

$$\text{Body fat} \rightarrow \text{leptin} \rightarrow \text{kisspeptin} \rightarrow \text{GnRH} \rightarrow \text{gonadotropins} \rightarrow$$
$$\text{gonadal sex steroids} \rightarrow \text{target tissues.}$$

Why so complicated? Probably because it allows for metabolic and environmental factors to modulate the process, including feedback signals from the target tissues and the gonads. One example: The hormone melatonin, which is secreted by the pineal gland and helps regulate the sleep–wake cycle, interacts with kisspeptin. There is concern that long-term use of melatonin by children or adolescents may delay or otherwise interfere with the processes of puberty (Boafo et al., 2019). Melatonin is not approved by the U.S. Food and Drug Administration for use in children.

## Puberty may come too early or too late

Disorders affecting the timing of puberty are fairly common (Howard et al., 2019). Puberty may begin too early (**precocious puberty**), too late (**delayed puberty**), or not at all. Untreated, these conditions can cause a great deal of distress to the affected individuals and their families.

Puberty has generally been diagnosed as precocious if it begins before age 8 in girls or 9 in boys (Leger & Carel, 2016). Because puberty in the general population has been starting earlier than it used to, especially for girls, there is some question

**primary amenorrhea** The failure to begin menstruating at puberty.

**secondary amenorrhea** The cessation of menstruation at some time after menarche.

**leptin** A hormone secreted by fat cells that acts on the hypothalamus.

**kisspeptin** A signaling molecule in the hypothalamus that promotes the onset of puberty.

**precocious puberty** Puberty that begins earlier than normal.

**delayed puberty** Puberty that begins later than normal.

▲ Because of his precocious puberty, Patrick Burleigh towered over his childhood peers.

about whether these criterion ages should be revised downward. After all, about 10% of white and Asian-American girls, 15% of Hispanic girls, and 23% of black girls have some breast development by age 7 (Biro et al., 2010). The great majority of children who enter puberty between 7 and 8 (girls) or between 8 and 9 (boys) do not need treatment (Kaplowitz & Bloch, 2016).

Precocious puberty can cause a child to end up shorter than normal because some years of prepubertal growth will have been lost. In addition, early sexual maturity may cause psychological and social problems for the child, especially for girls (Mrug et al., 2014). These girls tend to have low self-esteem on account of the physical differences between them and their peers. They may become targets for sexual advances that they cannot easily repel, and they themselves may develop sexual feelings that they don't know how to cope with.

The earlier children enter puberty, the earlier they are likely to become sexually active. Problems such as early pregnancy, STIs, smoking, alcohol and substance abuse, disruptive behavior, delinquency, and suicidality are all more common among children who enter puberty early than among those who do so at an average time, although it is not clear whether these outcomes are direct consequences of early puberty.

Most cases of precocious puberty are described as "idiopathic," meaning that they have no obvious cause, but increasing numbers of children with precocious puberty have been found to carry mutations in one of the genes that regulate the function of the pituitary gland, and other children may have a congenital malformation of the gland. In girls, puberty may be triggered by disorders of the ovaries that cause premature secretion of estrogen.

One man who experienced precocious puberty starting at age 2, on account of a gene running in his family, described the turmoil it created:

> [T]he shame—and the shaming—became a constant in my life. Much of it came from my preoccupation with sex. I began experiencing sexual impulses at such an early age I don't remember a time before needing to find an outlet for them. "I'll show you mine if you show me yours" became an obsession. What was an innocent game of discovery for other 4-year-olds became, by virtue of my sexually capable body, decidedly less innocent for me. I had one friend in particular; I'll call her Abigail . . . She and I were inseparable. Our favorite variation of "I'll show you mine if you show me yours" took place in the bathroom. The game was simple: I would try to pee through Abigail's legs while she peed on the toilet. This was impossible because I inevitably had an enormous erection. I was 5. I didn't understand my drive for sex. I simply felt it and felt compelled to act on it, but I wasn't old enough to act in any identifiably sexual way. I didn't even know what sex was. (Burleigh, 2019)

Precocious puberty is often treated with a drug that blocks the secretion of the pituitary hormones LH and FSH (see Chapters 2 and 3). One such drug is leuprolide (Lupron).* A similar drug, named histrelin, is being increasingly used because it can be administered as a one-time implant that works for 2 years but can be removed at any time. Either drug is continued until the child reaches an age or height more appropriate for puberty. (In Chapter 4 we discussed the use of leuprolide to delay puberty in children who wish to change their anatomical sex.)

Puberty is considered delayed if the early signs of puberty do not appear by age 13 in girls, or by age 14 in boys (Lee & Houk, 2016). Delayed puberty is much more

---

*Leuprolide is a GnRH-like peptide and it therefore binds to GnRH receptors on the gonadotropin-secreting cells of the pituitary. These cells are activated only by *pulsatile* GnRH stimulation, however; when leuprolide is *continuously* present, the cells become desensitized and cease to secrete gonadotropins.

common in boys than in girls. Again, a specific cause cannot usually be identified, but many or most cases are thought to be inherited. Undernourishment or chronic illness may also play a role. Puberty does eventually begin in most cases, so patience is often the best treatment. It is sometimes possible to jump-start the process with a short course of testosterone (for boys) or estrogens (for girls). Because a delay in puberty allows for more years of childhood growth, persons with delayed puberty are often taller and longer of limb than those who went through puberty at a typical age.

Boys castrated before puberty never go through puberty without medical treatment. Historically, some boy singers were castrated to produce adult males with high-pitched and strangely beautiful voices. Thankfully this is no longer done, but one of the last of these *castrati*, a member of the choir of the Vatican's Sistine Chapel, made a recording in 1902 that is available online (YouTube, 2019).

## 10.6  Adolescence Is a Time of Sexual Exploration

### LEARNING OBJECTIVES
After reading this section you should be able to:

10.6.1  Analyze the biological and social factors influencing the age of partnered sexual activity.

10.6.2  Explain how pluralistic ignorance can affect a teenager's sexual beliefs and behaviors.

10.6.3  Evaluate the effectiveness of abstinence-only and comprehensive sex education programs.

10.6.4  Describe the psychological meanings that virginity loss may have for different people.

The term **adolescence** is used to mean roughly the teen years (13 to 18, or 13 to 20). The beginning of adolescence may correspond to the biological events of puberty, such as menarche or first ejaculation. The end of adolescence, however, when it morphs into "emerging adulthood," is not a well-defined event (Tanner & Arnett, 2016). In fact, the concept of adolescence could be considered a social construction, designed to accommodate the ever-widening gap between the age of reproductive maturity and the age at which society grants men and women full adult freedoms and responsibilities. In many preindustrial societies adolescence was not recognized as a distinct phase of life: At puberty, children transitioned directly to adult rights and responsibilities (LeTendre, 2020).

**adolescence**  The period of psychosexual and social maturation that accompanies and follows puberty.

The beginning of adolescence is usually marked by a great increase in a boy's or girl's sexual feelings and often by an increase in sexual behavior as well. This sexual awakening may in part be a response to the obvious bodily changes that accompany puberty. In addition, however, the rising blood levels of sex hormones, especially testosterone, seem to directly activate the brain circuitry that produces sexual feelings and urges in both girls and boys. An adolescent's testosterone level is quite a strong predictor of when she or he will begin to engage in partnered sex (Pringle et al., 2017), but social factors are also important (see below). American teens typically have their first experience of partnered genital sex (not necessarily coitus) at the age of 16 (Vrangalova & Savin-Williams, 2011).

### Many cultures have puberty rites
Puberty, and the consequent increase in sexual feelings and expression, is an important event in a young

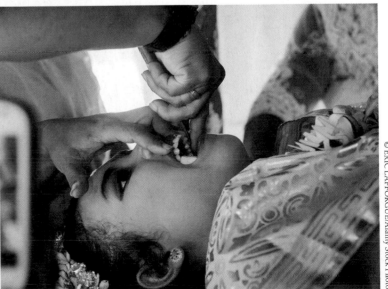

▲ On the Indonesian island of Bali, traditional puberty rites include the filing down of the incisor teeth, which is said to inhibit evil traits such as lust.

**bar mitzvah**  Jewish coming-of-age ceremony for boys.

**bat mitzvah**  Jewish coming-of-age ceremony for girls.

**quinceañera**  Hispanic coming-of-age ceremony for girls.

person's life and has been marked by special coming-of-age ceremonies in many cultures (Levesque, 2011). In girls, puberty includes a dramatic event—menarche—and girls' puberty rites are usually centered on this event. One example is the Western Apaches' Sunrise Ceremony. This 4-day ceremony is a reenactment of the Apache origin story, in which Changing Woman had sexual intercourse with the sun, thus bringing forth the Apache hero, Slayer of Monsters. The ceremony, which involves dancing, running to the compass points, and much else, emphasizes the four life goals of physical strength, a good disposition, prosperity, and a healthy old age. (Videos of the ceremony can be found online.)

For boys, puberty rites may be simple or complex. On the Chuuk Islands in the western Pacific, a boy whose pubic hair and facial hair become noticeable simply puts on an adult loincloth and goes to live in the men's quarters. Among the Keraki of New Guinea, however, puberty rites take up to a year. The boys undergoing initiation are gathered in a clearing, where they are shown a sacred musical instrument, the bullroarer, and struck a blow on the back with a heavy banana stalk. There follows a parade and a feast. The boys are confined for nearly a year in a special longhouse. At the end of this period the boys return home and take on the role of adults. Body modifications, including circumcision, skin scarring, and tattooing, are common features of male puberty rites around the world (see Chapter 3).

In the contemporary United States, puberty rituals may be associated with certain religions and ethnic groups. An example is the Jewish combination of religious instruction and family celebration called **bar mitzvah** for boys and **bat mitzvah** for girls. Hispanics have the **quinceañera**, a celebration for girls who reach the age of 15 and (traditionally, at least) have maintained their virginity. It incorporates a Catholic Mass as well as a traditional *vals* (waltz) danced by the girl and her male escort, along with 14 *damas* and *chambelanes* ("bridesmaids" and their escorts).

## There are social influences on teen sexual behavior

Although the physiological processes of puberty play a key role in kick-starting adolescents' sex drive, social influences on teen sexuality also play an important part, especially with regard to sexual behavior with partners. Thus, the overall proportion of the U.S. population who say they first had sex before they were 15 is about 16% (Finer & Philbin, 2013), but it differs greatly among different groups. The percentage is higher among less educated, less religious, and less affluent people (Halpern et al., 2000b; CDC, 2007) (**FIGURE 10.12**).

To some extent these causes act directly on individuals. For example, individuals from more affluent backgrounds may postpone sexual initiation because they are preoccupied with school and other career-related activities, or because they are more alert to the potential negative consequences of early sexual activity such as unplanned pregnancy and STIs. But there is also an effect of community norms, because the sexual behavior of individual adolescents is strongly influenced by their perception of peer expectations (Santelli et al., 2004). Thus, adolescents are likely to initiate sexual activity early if their community has a low average income, few college graduates, a high crime rate, or high

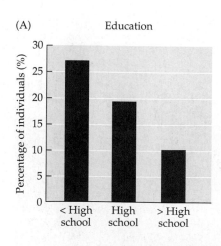

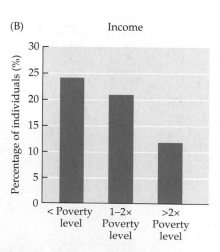

▲ **FIGURE 10.12  Social influences on early sex**  The graphs show the percentages of individuals who engaged in vaginal, oral, or anal sex before the age of 15, broken down by (A) education and (B) economic status. (Data from C. D. Fryar et al. 2007. *Advance Data from Vital and Health Statistics* 384: 1–15. National Center for Health Statistics: Hyattsville, MD.)

unemployment. It is likely that such communities offer adolescents few challenging goals and therefore give them little motivation to work hard and avoid risky sexual activities that could keep them from attaining their dreams.

Another factor associated with the early initiation of sexual activity is having a significantly older boyfriend or girlfriend (Halpern et al., 2007). This is hardly surprising, given that older partners are likely to be more sexually experienced and eager to initiate their younger partners.

Television may promote early entry into sex by portraying sexual relationships and activities among young people, often in a highly glamorized and unrealistic fashion, as we discussed in Box 10.3. But not all TV shows glamorize sex, of course. MTV's *Teen Mom* reality series, for example, highlights the tough situations faced by working-class teen mothers, so it may encourage teens to delay sex or use contraception more effectively. On the other hand, it may actually promote teen pregnancy simply by virtue of the attention paid to the girls or young women on the show—they're on television, after all. What do you think?

Some cultural forces attempt to dissuade teens from engaging in sexual behavior. In faith-based **virginity pledge programs** (or purity pledge programs), such as True Love Waits and Silver Ring Thing, teens make a commitment to abstain from sex until (heterosexual) marriage. The programs may portray marital sex as something precious, but they also instill a fearful attitude toward sex in the teen years (Manning, 2015).

A large controlled prospective study found that pledge taking had no effect on sexual activity. In fact, most of the pledge takers later denied ever having taken a pledge—probably because they didn't want to admit that they had already broken it (Rosenbaum, 2009). One famous pledge taker and breaker—singer-songwriter Nick Jonas—explained his fall from grace this way: "I came from an incredibly religious home. . . . But as you do, you grow up, you live life. It was about me being a man and being OK with my choices" (Bossip, 2016).

School-based sex-education programs that only promote abstinence also have a poor track record (Santelli et al., 2017). In one study mandated by the U.S. Congress, students were randomly assigned to attend or not attend **abstinence-only programs** and then were followed up for several years. Attending a program had no effect on any measure of the teens' subsequent sexual behavior (Trenholm et al., 2007). States that legally mandate abstinence-only sex education have the highest rates of teen pregnancy and HIV infection (Elliot et al., 2017). According to professionals concerned with the health of adolescents, abstinence-only sex education is not only ineffective, it is also unethical, because it denies adolescents information about sexuality to which they are entitled as a human right (Society for Adolescent Health and Medicine, 2017). Yet currently, 19 states mandate the promotion of abstinence only until marriage. And same-sex marriage may not qualify, because five of those states mandate that students be provided with only negative information about homosexuality (Guttmacher Institute, 2019).

**Comprehensive sex-education programs**, which discuss the risks of sex as well as the means (such as contraception) to mitigate those risks, have had better results: Teens who are exposed to such programs do not engage in more or earlier sex but are more likely when they do engage in sex to do so in a responsible and safe fashion (Carter, 2012). Under President Obama there was a major shift of federal sex-education funds from abstinence-only to comprehensive programs, but President Trump's 2017 budget proposal steered sex-ed funds back toward abstinence-only programs (Quartz, 2017). Only 18 states and the District of Columbia require school sex-ed programs to include a description of contraceptive methods (Guttmacher Institute, 2017b).

Although the content of school sex-ed programs varies considerably from state to state, and from country to country, teens themselves have a fairly consistent set of views on the topic (**BOX 10.5**).

▲ Pop idol Nick Jonas wore his purity pledge ring around his neck, but he didn't keep the pledge.

**virginity pledge programs**
Programs in which teens take formal pledges not to have sex before marriage.

**abstinence-only programs**  Sex-ed programs that teach abstinence and omit mention of safer-sex practices, homosexuality, etc.

**comprehensive sex-education programs**  Sex-ed programs that discuss abstinence as well as safer-sex practices, sexual and gender diversity, etc.

## BOX 10.5
## Sex-ed—What Teens Say

Sixty-nine studies, carried out in countries as diverse as Iran, Sweden, and the United States, have asked teens for their reactions to their sex-education classes. Sociologist Pandora Pound and her colleagues at the University of Bristol, England, reviewed these studies (Pound et al., 2016). In spite of major differences between countries in the content of the classes, she found that the teens' reactions were remarkably uniform (see figure). The following themes cropped up repeatedly:

**The subject matter is embarrassing to both teachers and students**  *We had Miss Plum, she was a PE teacher but she cried. So we just felt sorry for her. Like it was so horrible.*

*Yeah, some people are too scared to say things, so they cover that up by being noisy and disrupt the class.*

**Teachers deal with this by being too "scientific"**  *They never really talked about sex. Like the sperm goes up the fallopian tube, hits the egg . . . we don't care about that.*

*Everything we got in our class had a really clinical feel, it's just like information but it's not related to yourself.*

**Teachers deal with this by moralizing**  *All they ever do is talk about the dangers of sex and that, and nothing about the pleasure.*

**Teachers avoid a lot of important topics**  *You just were taught about sexual intercourse causing pregnancy, but you were never taught about masturbation; you were never taught about oral sex—all the other types of sexual practices.*

*They don't really go into the whole relationships thing partly because . . . they don't want us to have relationships.*

*They don't mention anything about same-sex relationships or homophobia.*

Students may ignore sex education that's not relevant to their lives.

*They didn't really talk about how sex will affect you as a person and how it affects your emotions.*

**Students from ethnic minorities, and much younger children, value sex-ed classes more**  *You get some good information in these classes. All my mother would tell me, she would tell me like myths, hypothetical things, things that old ladies from generation to generation will tell her.*

**Peer educators and outside experts do a better job than regular teachers**  *They treated us with respect, they treated us like fellow students.*

*She was not ashamed of it, we saw that she thought it was fun to talk about it, that she really thought it was fun, her job.*

### Social media have risks and benefits

In recent years a great deal of attention has been paid to the effects of social networking tools on teen sexuality. Through these media teens engage in "impression management," meaning that they seek to maximize their desirability to potential romantic partners. On Facebook, for example, teens (like adults) are able to control how they appear to others in ways that are not possible in face-to-face interactions, such as by the choice, manipulation, and frequent changes of their profile photographs, and by selective or untruthful accounts of their activities and relationships (Stephens-Davidowitz, 2017).

Thus, in following their peers on social media, teens can very easily come to believe that they themselves are relatively unattractive, uncomfortable, or unsuccessful in their love lives or that their own sexual morality differs markedly from that of their peers. Such a pattern of distorted beliefs—known as **pluralistic ignorance**—can overwhelm their own behavioral norms and cause them to make themselves more available sexually, or more willing to engage in risky sexual practices, than they would otherwise.

**pluralistic ignorance**  A mistaken belief that one's values, opinions, or behaviors differ from those of one's peers.

Most research on this topic has been done on college students (Holman & Sillars, 2012; Barriger & Velez-Blasini, 2013), but the phenomenon is likely to be even more pervasive among younger teens because they have less well-established personal norms and are less able to critically evaluate their peers' postings and texts.

Another issue with social media has to do with privacy. Many young people do not understand how difficult it is to restrict the dissemination of information about themselves via social media. Gay or lesbian youths, for example, may unintentionally out themselves to their parents or others, or they may be outed by third parties such as gay organizations that the individual joins (Fowler, 2012). Similarly, teens may "sext" nude or sexually suggestive photographs of themselves to intimate partners, only to find that these photographs have become much more widely available.

Moreover, it is a federal and state felony to post, send, or receive "lascivious images of the genitals or pubic area" of a person under 18, even if that person is one-self. ("Lascivious" means "intended to arouse sexual desire," so it would not include, for example, the photos of pubertal development that accompany this chapter.) Only a small percentage of teens send or receive these kinds of images (Crimes Against Children Research Center, 2014), and of those who do, an even smaller percentage run into trouble with the law. Still, penalties for these activities can include severe sentences. In 2017, for example, a 19-year-old Virginia man was sentenced to lifelong registration as a "violent sex offender" because, just after he turned 18, he received five pictures of an underwear-clad 13-year-old girl with whom he had been conducting an online romance—a girl he never met in person (Skenazy, 2017).

In spite of these negatives, social media can also have positive value, for example in the dissemination of information relating to sexual health. Moreover, social media and the internet as a whole can be of great significance to teens who are members of sexual minorities or who have uncommon sexual interests, especially in countries where they face legal or social oppression.

## Males masturbate more than females

One of the most common sexual behaviors among adolescents is masturbation. But adolescents often feel guilty about masturbating, believe that the practice is harmful, and taunt others about masturbation as schoolyard insults. Thus, adolescents are often reluctant to admit that they masturbate, making the topic difficult to research. In one longitudinal study, for example, only about one-third of 13-year-old boys said that they masturbated, but when these same individuals were reinterviewed in adulthood, more than twice as many said that they had masturbated at that age (Halpern et al., 2000a).

Many studies show that the frequency of masturbation increases during early and mid-teen years and that boys masturbate more frequently than girls. But girls have been catching up: In the mid-20th century only 39% of young women said that they had ever masturbated during childhood or adolescence; by the early 21st century, 84% reported having done so (Bancroft et al., 2003). Although substantial numbers of both boys and girls begin masturbating before puberty, the onset of masturbation is much more closely synchronized with the onset of puberty in boys than it is in girls (**FIGURE 10.13**). This suggests a more powerful hormonal influence on masturbation in boys.

## The sexual activity of American teens increased and then decreased

Cultural changes over the last half-century or so have had a strong influence on adolescent sexuality in the United States. In the period immediately after World War II, most adolescents' goals were focused on completing schooling, working, marrying, and starting a family. Adolescents dated in the late 1940s, and this behavior was important for their social standing and the development of gender-appropriate roles, but dating at that time generally involved sexual behavior short of coitus. Engaging in coitus and risking pregnancy endangered the social status of unmarried young adult females. The status of males was not endangered in the same way—exemplifying the

▶ **FIGURE 10.13** **Masturbation and puberty** Female and male college students were asked about the age at which they first masturbated and their age at puberty, defined as menarche (girls) or first ejaculation (boys). The graphs (plotted in number of years before and after puberty) show that the onset of masturbation is not closely tied to puberty in girls (A), but it is in boys (B). (After J. Bancroft et al. 2003. In *Sexual development in childhood*, J. Bancroft [Ed.], pp. 156–185. Indiana University Press: Bloomington, IN.)

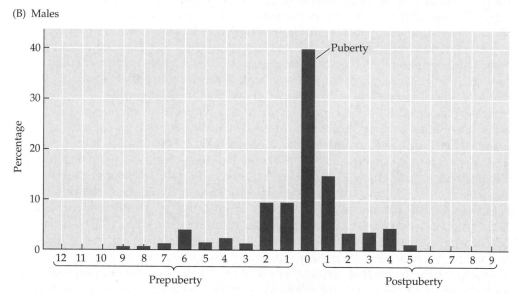

(A) Females

(B) Males

sexual "double standard"—but males generally found it difficult to persuade females to have intercourse with them, and some turned to prostitutes.

Many social changes since the 1940s and 1950s caused teenage sexual activity to increase, especially among girls (**FIGURE 10.14**). One was the introduction of oral contraceptives in the 1960s. Another was the legalization of abortion in the United States in 1973. Yet another was the introduction of effective treatments for some STIs. These factors reduced the risks of coitus for women, including adolescents. Another factor was feminism, which encouraged women to attend college, enter the workforce, and postpone marriage. All these changes together made it easier for young women to begin having sex without fears of pregnancy or disease.

Even so, "losing one's virginity" is still a significant event in many teens' or young adults' lives. According to repeated surveys of students at Illinois State University, males report more pleasure than females during their first sexual intercourse, and females report more feelings of guilt. Over the last two decades, however, women's guilty feelings during first intercourse have lessened, and their sense of pleasure has increased (Sprecher, 2014).

All in all, these changes led to a considerable increase in the numbers of sexually experienced adolescents as compared with their numbers 50 or 60 years ago. This increase came to an end around 1990, however: Between 1991 and 2015 the proportion of high school students who had ever had sexual intercourse dropped significantly—from 54% to 41%—and this drop was particularly marked among

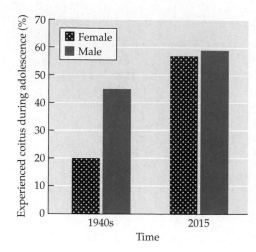

◀ **FIGURE 10.14** **Coitus has become more common among teens.** The graph shows the percentages of females and of males who experienced coitus during adolescence (by age 18 or 19) in the 1940s and in 2015. The 1940s data refer to coitus by age 19; the 2015 data refer to coitus by grade 12. (1940s data from A. C. Kinsey et al. 1948. *Sexual Behavior in the Human Male*. Saunders: Philadelphia, PA; A. C. Kinsey et al. 1953. *Sexual Behavior in the Human Female*. Saunders: Philadelphia, PA; 2015 data from L. Kann et al. 2016. *MMWR Surveill Summ* 65(6): 1–174.)

the younger students (9th and 10th grades) (CDC, 2016b). What's more, even those teens who engage in coitus don't do so very often: In 2010, only 27% of 17-year-old males said they have done so even once within the previous 90 days (Herbenick et al., 2010b), and more recently one in four 20-year-olds said they had never experienced coitus (Guttmacher Institute, 2017a). The reason for this drop in sexual activity by teens is not clear, but it parallels the drop in sexual activity among adults, as mentioned in Chapter 6.

There are differences in teen sexual activity related to race/ethnicity (**FIGURE 10.15**). Black teens are the most likely to have experienced coitus, and Asian-American teens are the least likely. The black/white difference is particularly marked at early ages: Thus, 18% of black teens have already experienced coitus by age 13, compared with only 4% of white teens (Lindberg et al., 2019). (These figures are based on the recollections of high school students, which may have been distorted by cultural expectations.) Black teens, on the other hand, are less likely than white teens to have engaged in oral sex, especially cunnilingus. In this, they reflect the attitudes of their elders, because oral sex is much less popular among blacks generally than it is among whites (Laumann & Michael, 2000). Hispanics are more like whites in this respect.

Asian-Americans and Pacific Islanders (AAPIs) are a small but very diverse group who often get overlooked in surveys. Far fewer AAPI high school students have ever engaged in coitus than have students of other origins. This could be read as consistent with the stereotype of Asian-Americans as the "model minority." When AAPI teens do finally engage in coitus, however, they are just as likely as other teens to do so without protection or while under the influence of alcohol or drugs (Grunbaum et al., 2000), so their "modelness" doesn't necessarily carry over into the details of their sexual activities. Part of the reason for this may be a traditional reluctance of Asian-Americans to discuss sexual matters within their families or with health care providers: Many Asian-American females have never discussed sexual matters with their parents (Meneses et al., 2006). The more acculturated to mainstream U.S. society they are—speaking English at home, for example—the more the sexual behavior of Asian-American youths comes to resemble that of other U.S. teens (Tong, 2013).

Perhaps even more striking than the racial differences are differences related to academic achievement (CDC, 2015b). As shown in **FIGURE 10.16**, high school students who earn mostly D's and F's are more than twice as likely to have experienced coitus as those who earn mostly A's. Of course the low-achieving students are unlikely to go to college; thus the difference between the sexual activity of college students and their noncollege peers, illustrated in Figure 7.6, has its roots in the high school years.

Oral sex is common among U.S. teens; among those age 15 to 19, 51% of males and 46% of females have engaged in oral sex with an opposite-sex partner (CDC, 2017c). In part, oral sex may be popular because it is a way to have sex without loss of "vaginal virginity" and without risking pregnancy. About half of all young Americans have oral sex on some occasion prior to their first experience of vaginal intercourse. Nevertheless, engaging in oral sex doesn't seem to be a long-term strategy for avoiding coitus, because the great majority of teens who have engaged in oral sex have engaged in vaginal sex too, according to the National Survey of Family Growth (NSFG) data. This suggests that, for most teens, oral sex is something they add to their sexual repertoire because of the pleasure it brings, not as a substitute for coitus. Anal sex is much less common than oral sex—only about 1 in 10 adolescents has engaged in it—and again, it is practiced mainly by teens who have already begun to experience vaginal intercourse.

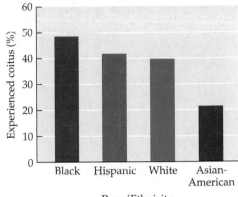

▲ **FIGURE 10.15 Ethnicity and sexual initiation** This bar graph shows the percentages of U.S. 15- to 19-year-olds who have ever experienced coitus, according to their race/ethnicity. (Data from L. Kann et al. 2016. *MMWR Surveill Summ* 65(6): 1–174. Data for Asian-Americans from H. C. Hahm et al. 2006. *Perspect Sexual Reprod Health* 38: 28–36.)

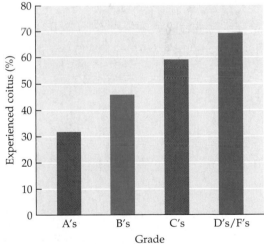

▲ **FIGURE 10.16 Academic achievement and sexual initiation** This bar graph shows the percentages of U.S. high school students who have ever experienced coitus, according to the grades they most frequently earn. The data have been controlled for race and sex, meaning that those factors do not account for the differences seen here. (After Centers for Disease Control and Prevention. 2015. *Sexual risk behaviors and academic achievement.* [tinyurl.com/y7dhru4t]; data from D. K. Eaton et al. 2010. *MMWR Surveill Summ* 59(5): 1–142.)

Teenagers can easily violate age-of-consent laws when they engage in sexual activities, especially if one partner is older than the other. A remarkable example concerned a Georgia youth, Genarlow Wilson, who had oral sex with a willing 15-year-old girl when he was 17. In 2005 Wilson was convicted of aggravated child molestation and sentenced to 10 years of imprisonment. After he had been behind bars for 2 years, the Supreme Court of Georgia ordered him released; he later attended and graduated from Morehouse College. He helped found a nonprofit that works to support black youth in the Atlanta area (Sturdivant, 2019).

### The meaning of "virginity loss" varies

"Losing one's virginity" usually refers to a person's first experience of penile-vaginal intercourse (coitus). According to a qualitative study by Laura Carpenter of Vanderbilt University, however, many young people think of it more as a mental event than a mechanical one (Carpenter, 2005). So, for example, being raped might not constitute a loss of virginity. Also, those who only have sex with same-sex partners never experience coitus, so for them other behaviors, such as oral or anal sex, or any sex leading to orgasm, may count as loss of virginity, or they may not think of it as an event worth defining. More importantly, the emotional meaning of losing one's virginity varies from person to person. According to Carpenter, there are four common viewpoints:

- *Virginity loss is a gift*. It is something valuable that one gives to a partner in a loving relationship. For people who see it this way, virginity is not really "lost," because it becomes part of the extended self that includes the intimate partner.
- *Virginity loss is the erasure of a stigma*. Virginity is a sign of "irredeemable dorkiness," so losing virginity is an end in itself, and it doesn't have to happen in the context of a loving relationship.
- *Virginity loss is part of a process*. This point of view interprets virginity loss as one stepping-stone out of many on the path to male or female adulthood. Gay people are especially likely to take this point of view, because they experience virginity loss as part of the process of coming out.
- *Virginity loss is a sacrament*. Some young people see abstinence as a form of worship and losing one's virginity as a mutual gift to God. These people typically avoid almost all forms of sexual intimacy before marriage.

However virginity loss is viewed ahead of time, the actual event doesn't always live up to expectations. Here's how one young man interviewed by Carpenter described his experience:

*I was so nervous, it was my first time, and I didn't want to look foolish. I tried to do what I saw the people do in the porno movies, move my body in a certain way, and do it really fast. She was saying to me, "There's another person here, you know." I ejaculated very quickly. I was, like, just interested in getting myself off and didn't even think about her. I felt like I had really fucked this thing up.*

## 10.7 Teen Sexuality Is Central to Identity Development

### LEARNING OBJECTIVES

After reading this section you should be able to:

10.7.1 Give possible reasons why teen casual sex and teen pregnancy have been on the decline.

10.7.2 Evaluate the potential positive and negative aspects of teen pregnancy and parenthood.

Although public attention focuses mainly on the possible negative consequences of teens' sexual behavior, and on ways to prevent it, we shouldn't ignore the positive role that sexuality plays in the process of growing up. Adolescence involves the development of a sense of self and a social identity independent from one's parents. Answering questions about one's sexuality figures centrally in this process. Teens must answer many such questions: "What am I looking for in sexual relationships? What is my sexual orientation? How attractive am I? Who might I attract as a sexual partner, and what are the best ways for entering into a partnership? How does my sexuality relate to other aspects of my identity, such as my career goals, my ethnic origins, or my religion?"

The development of a sense of self is vital to practical sexual concerns. For example, adolescents of both sexes need to be able to refuse unwanted sex, including sex without a condom. In one study of black teenage girls in Birmingham, Alabama, girls with a high evaluation of themselves—including a positive ethnic identity, high self-esteem, and a positive body image—communicated better with their partners concerning condom use and were more likely to refuse unprotected sex than were other girls (Salazar et al., 2004).

Developing a sense of self is not a purely intellectual process—it is not achieved simply by reason or introspection. Rather, it requires social exploration and learning. This exploration takes place chiefly in the milieu in which sexual interactions are likely to arise—namely, in one's peer group. This is not to say that parent–teen interactions are unimportant, however. In the Birmingham study, for example, girls who spoke frequently with their parents about sexual matters were nearly twice as likely to refuse unwanted sex as those who did not (Sionean et al., 2002).

Given all that you may have heard about the harmful consequences of early sexual behavior, it may be surprising to learn that, in a study of seniors in a rural New York high school, those students who became sexually active earlier than average, or who had a higher-than-average number of sex partners, did not report any lesser well-being than those students who became sexually active at an average age or who had not yet become sexually active. In fact, the girls who became sexually active early reported higher levels of well-being than their peers (Vrangalova & Savin-Williams, 2011). If they can avoid STIs and pregnancy, teens may derive a positive benefit from sex and sexual relationships.

**serial monogamy**  Involvement in a series of monogamous relationships.

## Teen relationships are often short-lived

For some adolescents, sexual exploration involves **serial monogamy**, in which the youth has a series of exclusive dating relationships with girlfriends or boyfriends, or with both (see Chapter 7). Within such serial relationships adolescents can discover what gives them pleasure and how to interact intimately with another person. Typically, the sexual content of these relationships progresses during the adolescent years from kissing and fondling to non-coital orgasmic contacts, and possibly to coitus.

According to some social commentators and newspaper investigations, however, the "hookup culture" has come to the American high school, largely replacing traditional non-cohabiting relationships. As one 17-year-old girl told the *New York Times*, "The couple thing is overrated—it gets too clingy" (Denizet-Lewis, 2004). Another sign of the decline in adolescent dating relationships is that

▲ Teen sexual relationships often have a playful quality.

teens increasingly attend proms and similar events without specific "dates": They may attend solo or in groups of friends (College Confidential, 2014).

Yet the statistics collected by the CDC offer little support for the notion that casual sex has been on the increase at the high school level. According to their national Youth Risk Behavior Survey, the percentage of high school students who have had four or more sex partners in their lifetime has been *falling* steadily from year to year—from 18.7% in 1991 to 9.7% in 2017 (CDC, 2018f). This suggests that if a hookup culture does exist in the adolescent years, it involves only a small minority of young people.

With the loosening of traditional attitudes over the last few decades has come an increasing interest among adolescents in issues of gender and sexual orientation. Most teens, regardless of their sexual orientation or gender identity, are likely to know something about sexual minorities and the cultures that they have established, and many have openly gay, bisexual, or transgender teens in their peer groups. As a result, they are aware of a greater range of sex and relationship options than were their predecessors. The once-rigid categories of "straight" and "gay" have morphed, for some teens, into "mostly straight" and "mostly gay." We will explore this topic further in Chapter 12.

In spite of these positive changes, life is still stressful for some lesbian, gay, and bisexual (LGB) adolescents. These youths are much more likely than their straight peers to experience bullying, miss school out of safety concerns, feel sad or hopeless, and contemplate or attempt suicide, according to a nationwide survey by the CDC (CDC, 2016a). Regarding suicide attempts, for example, 29% of LGB youths in grades 9 to 12 said that they had attempted suicide, as compared with 6% of straight students. Transgender and non-binary youth experience even higher rates of suicidality: In a 2018 study, 51% of female-to-male teens and 42% of male-to-female teens reported having made at least one suicide attempt (Toomey et al., 2018). (Not all teens who attempt suicide actually intend to die; nevertheless, a history of a prior suicide attempt is the strongest predictor of a subsequent completed suicide.)

### Teen pregnancy is declining but is still too common

Teenage pregnancy is not an inherently bad thing, of course. Evolution has equipped girls with the capacity to have children soon after puberty, and until modern times most did so. In many developing countries females are still expected to marry in their mid-teens and bear children shortly thereafter. What's more, there are some advantages to becoming a mother early. These include a lesser likelihood of fertility problems, a decreased risk of breast cancer later in life, and the ability to look after and enjoy one's children while still in the full vigor of young adulthood. Some U.S. teenagers are able to successfully incorporate pregnancy and motherhood into their lives—with help from their partners, their parents, or social services, as personal accounts testify (Noffsinger, 2014). Those who have difficulty may eventually recover from the disadvantages of early, unassisted motherhood. In fact, the very experience of being a mother helps some previously aimless teenagers focus on their life goals and strive for success (SmithBattle, 2007).

In spite of these positive points, the outcome of pregnancy is not a happy one for many American teenagers (Power to Decide, 2019). The majority of teen pregnancies (about four out of five) are

**FAQ:** If a teen gets pregnant, does the father have any legal say over whether she has an abortion or not?

No, but his wishes and his commitment to parenthood (or lack of it) often influence her decision.

▲ This teenage mother and her child are likely to face economic hardship.

© Zoonar GmbH/Alamy Stock Photo

unintended, and one-third of all teen pregnancies end in abortion. When unintended pregnancies continue to term, the children born of them are less likely to be breast-fed and more likely to have health problems than other children. If the pregnancy is intended, it may be for less than satisfactory reasons, such as a desire for the self-esteem or social status that is imagined to go with motherhood. Frequently the father is out of the picture before the child's birth or soon thereafter—often his name does not even appear on the birth certificate. When the father can be identified, he is often significantly older than the mother. Although most teen fathers do want to be good parents, circumstances often make that role difficult. If the mother and father marry, the likelihood of marital breakdown and divorce is high. Pregnancy and motherhood impair teenagers' opportunities for education and employment—many drop out of school—so children of teenage mothers typically grow up in poverty and are more likely than other children to drop out of school themselves.

Perhaps because of increasing awareness of these negatives, the teen birth rate has declined quite dramatically in the United States: In 2018—the most recent year for which data are available—it was at a record low of 17.4 births per 1,000 females age 15 to 19 (Pew Research Center, 2019c) (**FIGURE 10.17**). This is less than one-third the peak rate in 1991. The decline has been caused by a decrease in the pregnancy rate, not by an increase in abortions, which have actually fallen. The decline in the pregnancy rate is due mostly to improved contraceptive use (Lindberg et al., 2016). In spite of the decline, teen birth rates are twice as high among Hispanic and black Americans as among white Americans, and the overall rates are higher in the United States than in many other developed countries, including Canada.

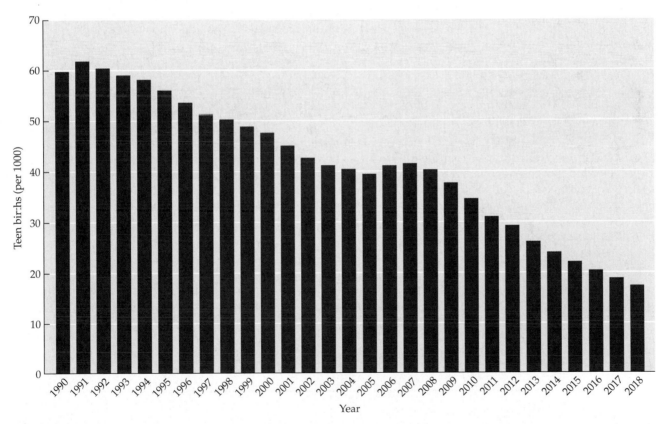

▲ **FIGURE 10.17** **Declining teen births** The figure shows the number of births per 1,000 U.S. females age 15 to 19, from 1990 to 2018. (Data from USHHS Office of Adolescent Health. 2016. *Trends in Teen Pregnancy and Childbearing: Teen births*. [tinyurl.com/kbmplbh] and J. A. Martin et al. 2019. *National Vital Statistics Reports* 68(13): 1–46. National Center for Health Statistics: Hyattsville, MD. )

# Summary

- Basic physiological responses of sexual arousal are seen in infants and young children. They are often triggered by a wide range of stimuli, such as strong emotions of any kind. Masturbation is common in young children, and other sexual behaviors, such as the display of genitals or the inspection of other children's genitals, are also quite prevalent. These behaviors may be incorporated into sexual games such as "doctor." Young children rarely engage in adultlike sexual behavior, however.

- Some non-Western societies tolerate or encourage childhood sexual behavior, while others attempt to restrain it. In the contemporary United States, children are often prevented from engaging in or learning about sexuality.

- Some children, usually older ones, have sexual contacts with adults. These contacts are usually one-time events rather than ongoing relationships. Most adults who have sexual contacts with children are relatives or acquaintances of the child, rather than strangers. Coercive or repeated adult–child sexual contacts can cause long-lasting psychological trauma. Noncoercive, single-event contacts may cause little or no harm.

- In preadolescence, children tend to socialize in same-sex groups and to impose strict gender codes, expecting gender conformity. This practice can be traumatic for gender-nonconformist children. Although segregation by sex limits opportunities for heterosexual encounters, a few children do engage in coitus before the age of 13.

- Puberty is the transition to reproductive maturity. It is marked by development of the genitalia, the appearance of secondary sexual characteristics, a growth spurt, the onset of menstruation in girls and ejaculation in boys, and changes in the brain that lead to sexual behavior and psychological sex differences.

- The onset of puberty is triggered by a complex chain of events: the attainment of a criterion body size or body fat ratio; the communication of this information to the hypothalamus by the hormone leptin; the activity of kisspeptin neurons; the secretion of GnRH; the secretion of LH and FSH by the pituitary; the secretion of sex steroids by the gonads; and the effect of sex steroids on the body and brain.

- Puberty begins at a median age of about 10 (9 years in black children). Children are entering puberty at younger ages than was the case in the past; a likely cause is the faster growth and increasing obesity of contemporary children. Puberty is generally considered precocious (early) if it begins before age 8 in girls or 9 in boys, but some experts believe that the criterion age for girls should be lowered to 7. Puberty is considered delayed if it does not begin by age 13 or 14 in girls or by age 14 in boys.

- Many cultures mark puberty by special celebrations or rites. Examples practiced in the United States are the Jewish bar/bat mitzvah and the Hispanic *quinceañera*.

- Adolescence is usually defined as the teen years. In early adolescence, rising sex hormone levels trigger an increasing interest in sex. Most adolescent males masturbate frequently, but females do so less often.

- Adolescent heterosexual behavior gradually progresses from kissing and fondling to coitus, oral sex, and, sometimes, anal sex. Some characteristics of teen sexual behavior reflect personal and demographic factors such as education and ethnicity. The availability of reliable contraception and modern views of women's roles in society have modified teen sexual behavior over the last several decades. Social media have also affected teens' sexuality, in both negative and positive ways.

- Virginity pledge programs and abstinence-only sex education have little or no effect on teens' sexual behavior. Comprehensive sex education, which includes practical information for those teens who will be sexually active, leads to safer sexual practices and does not increase teens' sexual activity.

- Teen pregnancy rates have declined over the last two decades, mostly on account of improved use of contraceptives, but it is still higher in the United States than in Canada or other developed countries. It is also higher among Hispanic and black teens than among white or Asian-American teens. About one in three teen pregnancies are terminated by abortion. Teenage mothers and their children face numerous problems, but some thrive.

## Discussion Questions

1. What are your attitudes and values about what is normal sexuality during child-hood? If you were a parent and found your child engaging in sexual exploration with the child next door, how would you respond?

2. Assuming you had some sex-ed classes in middle or high school, did your own experiences resemble, or differ from, those of the students quoted in Box 10.5? Would you be comfortable teaching such a class yourself?

3. Do you recall whether you experienced puberty at the same time as your peers, or earlier or later than most? How did the timing of your puberty affect you, or how were your early- or late-developing peers affected?

4. In high school, were you able to discuss sexual and relationship issues freely with your parents? How might you hope to do a better job if and when you become a parent?

The **Discovering Human Sexuality** digital resources include activities, animations, flashcards, web links, chapter outlines and summaries, and other study tools.

Learn more with this chapter's digital tools, including the **Oxford Insight Study Guide**, at **oup.com/he/levay5e**.

## Web Resources

Center for Sexual Health Promotion, National Survey of Sexual Health and Behavior (2010) (includes much information about teen sexuality **www.nationalsexstudy.indiana.edu**

Gay Teen Resources   **www.gayteenresources.org**

National Campaign to Prevent Teen and Unplanned Pregnancy **www.thenationalcampaign.org**

Planned Parenthood. For teens   **www.plannedparenthood.org/teens**

Sex, Etc. (website for teens by teens)   **www.sexetc.org**

SexInfo (from the UC Santa Barbara sociology department) **www.soc.ucsb.edu/sexinfo**

Silver Ring Thing (virginity pledge program)   **www.silverringthing.com**

Wikipedia: Ages of consent in North America (This article appears to be accurate and up to date, but Wikipedia articles can change unpredictably or become outdated.)   **tinyurl.com/7xneeae**

## Recommended Reading

Bancroft, J. (Ed.). (2003). *Sexual development in childhood*. Indiana University Press.

Carpenter, L. M. (2005). *Virginity lost: An intimate portrait of first sexual experiences*. New York University Press.

Kumanov, P. & Agarwal, A. (Eds.). (2016). *Puberty: Physiology and abnormalities*. Springer.

Levine, J. (2002). *Harmful to minors: The perils of protecting children from sex*. University of Minnesota Press.

Saleh, F. M., Grudzinskas, A. J., Jr. & Judge, A. M. (Eds.). (2014). *Adolescent sexual behavior in the digital age: Considerations for clinicians, legal professionals and educators*. Oxford University Press.

Sales, M. J. (2016). *American girls: Social media and the secret lives of teenagers*. Knopf.

Steinberg, L. (2019). *Adolescence* (12th ed.). McGraw-Hill.

Sexuality is a lifelong voyage of discovery.

# 11 Sexuality across the Lifespan: Adulthood

Adulthood is not a fixed state of being but a story with many episodes. Among them, for most men and women, is finding a true love, then living together as a couple. Yet cohabitation and marriage are changing. For some, wedding vows represent a necessary commitment to sexual loyalty and parenting. For others, marriage is something temporary or unnecessary. Yet regardless of the setting, successful intimate relationships require as much care and nurturing as any children that may be born of them.

Over the course of adult life, a person's sexuality faces many challenges. These include the task of establishing and maintaining durable relationships and perhaps additional challenges, such as parenthood, separation, menopause, physical decline, and bereavement. As people face these issues, their sexual lives change, but not necessarily for the worse. Sexuality, like life in general, always seems to offer opportunities for growth.

## 11.1 In Young Adulthood, Conflicting Demands Influence Sexual Expression

**LEARNING OBJECTIVES**

After reading this section you should be able to:

11.1.1 Describe general trends in the frequency of sexual activity in the United States.

11.1.2 Assess the accuracy of the belief that cohabitation harms subsequent marriage.

In Chapter 7 we discussed the kinds of sexual relationships that adults may engage in. We now attempt to describe how those relationships structure individual life courses. We begin with collective data—data that describe "generic" Americans, with their off-white skin color, predominantly heterosexual orientation, and 1.72 children.

### Most young men and women have only a few sex partners

In 2018, the median age at first marriage in the United States was 29.8 years for men and 27.8 years for women, up from a post–World War II minimum of 22.5 and 20.1 in 1956, when they were the lowest in U.S. history (U.S. Census Bureau, 2019). Assuming an age of 13 for puberty, men can therefore expect a period of about 17 years between puberty and marriage, and women can expect a period of about 15 years. These figures conceal a great deal of diversity, however. In fact, based on current trends, it is likely that about one in four of today's young people will never marry in their entire lives. For that reason we do not use the term "premarital" in this book, except when referring to people who are known to have subsequently married.

Most unmarried young adults are sexual, of course. By many measures, young adulthood includes men's and women's peak sexual years. It includes the years of most frequent sexual behavior (including masturbation), greatest fertility, and greatest physical attractiveness (for females as perceived by males, at least—see Chapter 5). Typically, young people spend a portion of this period without a steady sexual relationship, a portion in one or more non-cohabiting ("dating") relationships, and a portion in one or more cohabitations.

Given all one reads and hears about sex among young adults, the actual statistics are perhaps surprising. Between the ages of 20 and 24, only 30% of men and 25% of women report having had more than one opposite-sex sex partner in the previous 12 months, according to data from the National Survey of Family Growth (NSFG) for 2011 (CDC, 2011b) (**FIGURE 11.1**). In a more recent NSFG survey, respondents age 15 to 44 were asked whether they had had five or more opposite-sex partners in the previous 12 months: Only 4.0% of males and only 1.7% of females said yes (CDC, 2017e). Some young adults have sexual contact with same-sex partners, of course: In the NSFG survey, 5.6% of young men and 15.8% of young women reported at least one same-sex partner within the previous year.

Even by their late 20s about 3% of the population have had no partnered sexual experiences (defined as oral-genital, vaginal, or anal sex) in their lifetimes (Haydon et al., 2014). Some of these "adult virgins" may have been unable to find sex partners on account of social ineptness or severe disability, but many will have chosen not to have sex because of a lack of sexual attraction to anyone (asexuality—see Chapter 5), for religious reasons, or because they are focused on other life goals. Adult virgins perceive themselves as stigmatized on account of their lack of sexual experience; this perception seems to be correct, because both

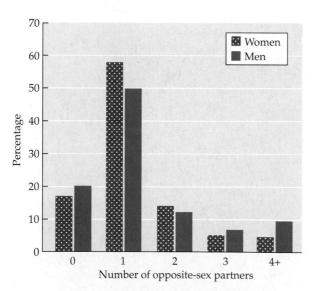

▲ **FIGURE 11.1 Heterosexual activity by young adults** This bar graph shows the percentages of women and men age 20 to 24 who reported the stated number of opposite-sex partners within the previous year. (Data from R. Stepler. 2017. *Number of US adults cohabiting with a partner continues to rise, especially among those 50 and older.* Pew Research Center: Washington, D.C.; US Census Bureau Table AD-3; and, Pew Research Center analysis of 2007 and 2016 Current Population Survey, Annual Social and Economic Supplements [IPUMS].)

sexually experienced adults and adult virgins themselves view adult virgins as less desirable sexual or romantic partners (Gesselman et al., 2017).

There has been an across-the-board decline in the frequency of sex in recent years: The average American has sex about nine times per year less often than in the late 1990s (Twenge et al., 2017). While all groups, including Millennials, are trending in the same direction, the drop has been most marked among those who are college educated, married, or in their 50s.

Many other affluent countries besides the United States are experiencing a similar trend. The statistics for the U.K. are similar to those for the U.S. (Wellings et al., 2019). In Japan, the so-called "herbivore men"—adult men who have little interest in sex or marriage—have taken part of the blame for a profound drop in the total fertility rate, to just 1.4 children per woman, since the 1980s (World Bank, 2019).

▲ Young adults typically spend several years dating and relating before they move in with a partner.

### Dating relationships are short-lived

We already discussed dating relationships—steady sexual relationships between people who are not living together—in Chapter 7. Such relationships are of course very common in young adulthood. Nevertheless, they are typically short-lived. In one study of newly established dating couples, only 23% remained in that relationship a year later (Sassler et al., 2016), 27% had progressed to a cohabitation, and the remaining 50% had already broken up.

In the view of some experts, a factor leading to the breakup of dating relationships is that the participants have an excessively romantic or idealistic view of sexual relationships; in other words, they may believe that establishing a relationship involves locating one's sole true love and that being in love is enough for a relationship to succeed. Based on this belief, some experts have designed programs intended to "de-romanticize" young people's ideas about relationships (Kerpelman et al., 2009). Nevertheless, a Canadian group recently found the opposite, namely that romantic beliefs actually benefit young adults' commitment and satisfaction in dating relationships (Vannier & O'Sullivan, 2017). Perhaps they do so because they lead to generous interpretations of the partner's actions and motives and thus to increased trust.

**cohabitation** A live-in sexual relationship between two persons who are not married to each other.

### Cohabitation is an increasingly prevalent lifestyle

Most men and women hope to enter into a durable, live-in sexual relationship—a cohabitation or marriage—eventually. Often, a desire for children comes into play here, but even people who don't currently want children commonly want to be part of a long-term, loving relationship.

**Cohabitation** is the word we use to describe the relationship of a couple—opposite-sex or same-sex—who live together in a sexual relationship without being legally married. Cohabitation has become an increasingly common form of relationship over the past few decades, both in the United States and in other Western countries. In 2016 there were about 9 million cohabiting couples in the United States, up from 7 million in 2007 (Pew Research Center, 2017d) (**FIGURE 11.2**). Among couples who marry before their mid-30s, 7 out of 10 have lived together for some period of time before marrying (Kuperberg, 2019).

Although so many people now make their first live-in relationship a cohabitation, only a small fraction of the U.S. population (about 10% of

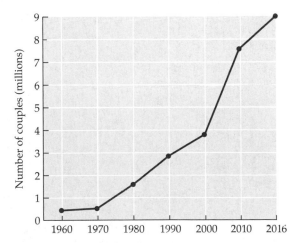

▲ **FIGURE 11.2  Cohabitations are on the rise** This graph shows the numbers of unmarried, cohabiting couples in the United States (uncorrected for population growth). (Data from A. Chandra et al. 2011. *Natl Health Stat Report* 36: 1–36. National Center for Health Statistics: Hyattsville, MD based on data from *CDC/NCHS, National Survey of Family Growth*, 2002 and 2006–2008.)

▲ Brad Pitt and Angelina Jolie cohabited for 9 years and had several children before marrying in 2014—and splitting up 2 years later.

young adults and 7% of all adults) is cohabiting at any given time (Pew Research Center, 2017d). That's because cohabitations typically last only a short time. After 3 years, only about one-third of cohabiting couples are still cohabiting; the others have married or split up.

Cohabitation is considerably more common in Canada than in the United States. Cohabiting couples ("common-law couples" in Canadian terminology) constitute 21% of all Canadian couples, and 40% of all couples in the province of Quebec (Statistics Canada, 2017).

## Cohabitation has diverse meanings

Many cohabiting couples appreciate the informality of their relationship. They may feel less burdened by social expectations and less constrained by traditional roles than if they were married. It may be easier to preserve financial independence, if that is desired, and terminating a cohabitation is much simpler than terminating a marriage. Couples of this kind may not face any impediment to getting married; they just don't place any particular value on marriage as an institution. This is a very common perspective in Canada and the United Kingdom, but less so in the United States.

Still, there is a trend, both in the United States and other Western countries, toward treating cohabitations more like marriages from a legal perspective, especially if the cohabitation has lasted a long time. Thus cohabiting couples should be aware that a separation, if it happens, might not be the clean financial break that they had imagined. If the couple has generated significant assets during their cohabitation, one partner may be legally compelled to make payments ("palimony") to the other after their separation, as if they had been married. This can apply to both opposite-sex and same-sex couples.

On the downside, cohabiting couples are often denied many rights provided automatically to married couples. Therefore, cohabitation can bring bureaucratic hassles, especially if there are children. People who cohabit have to draw up wills, durable powers of attorney, revocable trusts, or other documents if they want their wishes to be respected in case of incapacity or death. There are plenty of horror stories about people who have had their cohabitational partners die, only to be evicted from their shared home by their partners' relatives.

For some couples, cohabitation is a "trial marriage," whose explicit or unstated purpose is to test their compatibility before marrying and having children. Some cohabitations are between old people—widowed or divorced—who see no particular need to marry, because they will not have children, or who prefer not to marry, in order not to disturb pension or inheritance arrangements.

For many couples, cohabitation is not perceived as an alternative to marriage but as an alternative to *dating*. In other words, the decision to cohabit may be driven more by economic considerations or convenience than by a deep sense of commitment. During the 2020 COVID-19 pandemic, some dating couples were motivated to cohabit because restrictions on movement limited their opportunities to meet otherwise (Keane, 2020).

Given that non-cohabiting relationships tend to be short-lived, we wouldn't necessarily expect couples who cohabit as an alternative to dating to stay in such a cohabitation for long periods of time. And indeed, "serial cohabitation" is an increasingly prevalent lifestyle (Kroeger & Smock, 2014).

About 20% of women become pregnant during their first cohabitation, and about 40% of cohabiting couples already have children (of one or both partners) living with them (National Marriage Project, 2010; CDC, 2013a). Children born to cohabiting couples—like any children born to unmarried women—used to be termed

**illegitimate**, and they were stigmatized with pejorative terms like "bastard." Such negative attitudes have largely evaporated in Western societies, except among the most conservative groups. There may still be legal concerns, however: If a cohabiting woman has a baby, the parental rights and obligations of the woman's partner are less well defined than if the couple were married.

For a variety of reasons, couples who are cohabiting feel less committed to each other and are more exposed to jealousy and other stresses than married couples (Pollard & Mullan Harris, 2013). This has the effect that domestic violence is more common between cohabiting couples than between married couples. In the extreme case, a cohabiting woman is nine times more likely than a married woman to be killed by her partner (Shackelford & Mouzos, 2005).

In general, though, cohabitation and marriage confer about the same degree of mental well-being: People in either type of relationship are significantly happier than people who are not living with any partner (Perelli-Harris & Styrc, 2018). And cohabitational relationships are significantly more durable than dating relationships. Even by 3 years after moving in together, only 27% of couples have broken up: 32% are still cohabiting and 40% have married (CDC, 2017c). Not surprisingly, couples who are engaged—that is, they have declared their intention to marry—experience greater well-being than other cohabiting couples because engagement signifies optimism about the future trajectory of the relationship (Willoughby & Belt, 2016).

### Cohabitation does not harm a subsequent marriage

Some tradition-minded people still believe that sex outside of marriage is immoral and that it is therefore wrong for a couple to live together before they get married. In fact, cohabitation used to be called "living in sin." Aside from the purely moral argument, conservatives may say that living together before marrying increases the likelihood that a married couple will be unhappy and will eventually divorce. To support this assertion, they may cite studies that supposedly demonstrate this so-called cohabitation effect (Pennsylvania Catholic Conference, 2009).

For couples who married recently (since the mid-1990s), however, there is little difference in divorce rates between cohabitors and "direct marriers" (Manning & Cohen, 2012). That is because as the proportion of couples who cohabit has increased, preexisting differences between them and the direct marriers have lessened. And further, what little "cohabitation effect" remains is the result of an age discrepancy: Couples who cohabit before marriage are necessarily younger when they cohabit than when they marry, and live-in relationships established by younger couples are less stable than those established by couples in their mid-20s or later (Kuperberg, 2014).

If relationships are timed from when couples first move in together, regardless of whether they are in a marriage or a premarital cohabitation, the "cohabitation effect" disappears. Thus, for those who want their live-in relationships to last a long time, the message isn't "Don't cohabit before you marry," but rather "Don't cohabit *or* marry while you're still in your teens or early 20s."

Today's young adults (Millennials and Gen Zers) have much more permissive attitudes toward cohabitation than their elders: Only 12% of them think that cohabitation is a bad thing for society, as compared with 41% of Americans born before 1945 (Pew Research Center, 2019a).

## 11.2 Marriage Takes Diverse Forms

### LEARNING OBJECTIVES

After reading this section you should be able to:

11.2.1 Identify the societal functions of marriage.

11.2.2 Describe the variety of marriages or marriage-like relationships that are not monogamous.

**illegitimate**  When applied to children, an obsolete term meaning born to unmarried parents.

**FAQ:** When I marry, will whatever I have now become his too?

No—in most states your preexisting assets remain your sole property, so long as you keep them separate from shared assets.

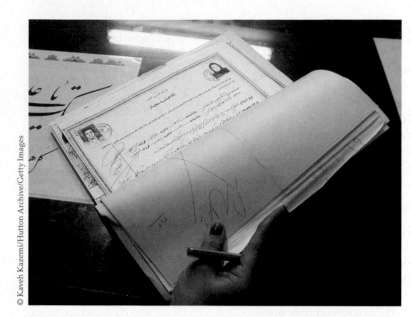

**▲ FIGURE 11.3 Temporary marriage certificates in an Iranian registry office** The X that has bled through to the back of the green certificate indicates that the allotted time span for that marriage has expired.

**mut'a** In Shia Islam, a contract to marry for a fixed period of time.

Most, if not all, human cultures have formalized heterosexual unions in some way, but the manner in which this has been done has varied greatly. In ancient Israel, one way for a couple to wed was simply to let it be known that they had had intercourse. In India, a wedding is an elaborate ceremony that takes up the best part of a week and involves lengthy rituals and enormous expense, particularly on the part of the bride's parents. In the United States, getting married can mean anything from a quick visit to a government office to a multimillion-dollar union of dynasties. According to The Knot—the leading online wedding-services marketplace—the average U.S. wedding in 2019, including the engagement ring, cost $33,900 (The Knot, 2020).We suspect that this is an overestimate, however—one that was arrived at by ignoring the large number of simple registry-office weddings.

Marriage is not always intended to be permanent. The Shiite branch of Islam, for example, has a temporary marriage known in Arabic as **mut'a** (**FIGURE 11.3**). The partners specify the terms of this marriage, including its duration, in advance. *Mut'a* may last for as little as 30 minutes if the man and woman want to have just a one-time sexual encounter, or it might last for a year if, for example, a man is living away from home for that period of time and wants a temporary wife for the duration. It is a real marriage in the sense that any offspring of the relationship are legitimate. There is a sexist element to *mut'a*, however, because it is open to married or unmarried men, but only to unmarried women. In some parts of the Islamic world, short-term *mut'a* has become a cover for prostitution, including child prostitution. This practice has been facilitated and commercialized by some Shia clerics in Iraq, according to a 2019 investigation by *The Guardian* (London) (Al-Maghafi, 2019).

## The formalization of sexual unions has social and personal functions

Formalizing sexual unions by marriage has a variety of purposes:

- In some cultures, women are still viewed as men's property; in such cultures, marriage is a contract marking the transfer of a woman from her father to her husband.

- Marriage may bring the couple's extended families together; this was an important function of marriage in traditional societies, in which marriages were often used to end vendettas or to create social alliances.

- To the extent that childbearing is limited to married couples, marriage gives society the power to regulate who may have children (by banning incestuous marriages, for example).

- Marriage creates an environment favorable for child rearing, by identifying two people as responsible for children's rearing and support.

- By publicly identifying two people as a couple, marriage is widely seen as obliging others to respect the sexual exclusivity of their relationship, thus reducing social friction and making paternity more certain.

- By making it difficult for a man and woman to separate, marriage is intended to stabilize their union and ensure that they stay together long enough to rear any children that they may have.

**FAQ:** Should we get genetic testing before we get married?

It's only recommended if one or both of you are at increased risk based on your family history or if one or both of you are of Ashkenazi Jewish descent. Genes for several inherited disorders are unusually prevalent in this population (UCSF Health, 2019).

© Kaveh Kazemi/Hutton Archive/Getty Images

## Many societies have permitted polygamy

Nearly all Americans think of a marriage as involving just two people—monogamy—and the law reinforces this attitude: Anyone who marries someone while still married to someone else is committing the crime of **bigamy**. Thus, you might be tempted to think that monogamy is the only legally or culturally recognized form of sexual relationship around the world, but that is not the case. Anthropological studies indicate that **polygamy**—having more than one spouse at the same time—is, or has been, commonplace.

Polygamy involving one man with more than one wife is known as **polygyny** ("many women"); polygamy involving one woman with more than one husband is known as **polyandry** ("many men"). Because polygyny is much more common than polyandry, the term "polygamy" is often used to mean polygyny.

Out of 853 preindustrial societies analyzed in one survey, 84% permitted polygyny, and in most of these cultures polygynous unions were legally recognized (Fisher, 1989). Today, most Islamic countries permit polygyny, as does India, though only for its Muslim citizens. The exact arrangements in polygynous societies vary. Often, the initial mate has some kind of official status as "principal wife." In some societies polygynous relationships are permitted but not legally formalized. In such cases, the later mates may be **concubines** whose attachment to the household is impermanent and whose children have no inheritance rights.

In early Islam a sizable fraction of the male population died in battle; thus one function of polygyny was to provide for war widows and their children. In some parts of the Islamic world this is still a relevant factor. "Our men fight wars and die; women stay alive," said the founder of a Palestinian matchmaking website. "This is why my project supports polygamy" (Al Waheidi, 2017).

Most societies have roughly equal numbers of men and women, however, and so not every man in such a society can have multiple wives. In fact, most men in polygynous societies have just one wife at best; it is the wealthy and powerful men who have many. The extreme cases were the **harems** associated with Oriental rulers. According to Jewish legend, King Solomon had a harem of a thousand wives, each of whom prepared a banquet every evening in the faint hope that he would dine with her. Harems were traditionally watched over by **eunuchs** (castrated men).

Polygyny is connected to the idea that women are men's property: If a rich man has many cattle, why shouldn't he have many wives? Thus, the Christian prohibition of polygyny, which distinguishes it from many other religions, such as Islam, can be viewed as an attempt to ensure some equity in marriage. Still, shades of polygyny persist in Western culture: Some wealthy men support mistresses, and a polygynous culture persists among some fundamentalist Mormons (**BOX 11.1**). In addition, it has been estimated that 50,000 to 100,000 American Muslims are in polygynous marriages; typically the man marries one woman legally and the others in religious ceremonies that are not legally recognized (Hagerty, 2008).

Polyandrous societies are less common than polygynous societies. In some, resources are so limited that a man cannot maintain a wife and children on his own. That has been true for poor, high-altitude communities in Tibet and other parts of the Himalayas (Samal et al., 1997). In these

**bigamy**   In law, the crime of marrying someone while being already married to another spouse.

**polygamy**   Marriage to more than one spouse at a time.

**polygyny**   The marriage or mating of one male with more than one female.

**polyandry**   The marriage or mating of one female with more than one male.

**concubine**   A woman who cohabits with a man but is not his wife, usually in a polygamous culture.

**harem**   The quarters for wives and children in a polygamous Muslim household.

**eunuch**   A man who has been castrated.

© China Photos/Getty Images

▲ Tibetan polyandrous family. Cai Zhuo with her two husbands, who are brothers, and their son.

## BOX 11.1
# Mormon Polygamy

Joseph Smith (1805–1844), the founder of the Mormon faith, secretly married between 30 and 40 women, some of them already married and some as young as 14. His nephew Joseph F. Smith, who became the sixth president of the church, married 6 women and fathered 43 children (see figure). Many early Mormons believed that polygamy was a necessary path to the highest salvation.

The practice of polygamy drew the Mormons into conflict with the U.S. government, which passed anti-polygamy laws and refused to grant Utah its statehood. In 1890 the church disavowed polygamy, and when Utah finally became a state in 1896, its constitution banned the practice.

In spite of the official end of Mormon polygamy (also called "plural marriage"), "Mormon fundamentalists" continue the practice in isolated areas. As many as 30,000 polygamists may be living in Utah and nearby states today. The church has excommunicated them and opposes their identification as Mormons.

The Mormon polygamists have mostly kept a low profile, but in the late 1990s one of them, Tom Green, went on national television with his five wives. Green was charged with bigamy and, later, with child rape (Green's first wife gave birth when she was only 13 years old). He was convicted and served 6 years in prison. Another polygamist leader, Warren Jeffs, controlled a community of several hundred people, many of whom moved to the YFZ ("Yearning for Zion") ranch near Eldorado, Texas. In 2011 he was convicted of aggravated sexual assault against children and sentenced to life imprisonment (Associated Press, 2011). Seven other men at the ranch had already been convicted on related charges.

The legal campaign against polygamists runs counter to the recent trend toward greater respect for individual freedom in sexual arrangements. For that reason, the ACLU of Utah has opposed the bigamy statute that has been used to prosecute some Mormon polygamists. In 2013 a federal district court ruled that plural marriage cannot be criminalized if none of the participants are legally married (Bailey, 2013).

Early Mormon leader Joseph F. Smith (1838–1918) with some of his wives and children.

On the other hand, children in polygamous families are more liable to experience a variety of mental health problems, educational difficulties, and social problems, as compared with children in monogamous families (Al-Sharfi et al., 2016). Law enforcement and child welfare officials allege that incest, physical and sexual abuse of children, poverty, welfare and tax fraud, and criminal nonsupport of children are rife in Mormon polygamous communities (Eckholm, 2007). Some feminists have argued that Mormon polygamy is a form of trafficking in women (Kwek, 2016).

In addition, polygamy in these communities creates a situation where there are too many young men for the numbers of available women. To solve this problem, many teenage boys have been banished from their communities for seemingly minor violations of church teachings, such as listening to music or talking to girls (Eckholm, 2007). These "lost boys" are ill prepared for life in mainstream America.

In 2020 Utah decriminalized bigamy, reducing it from a felony to an infraction comparable to a parking ticket (Vejar, 2020). The motivation for the change was to allow polygamists who are victims of crimes to come forward without fear of being prosecuted themselves. It was necessary to keep a minimal penalty in order to conform with the state's constitution.

communities, a woman may be married to two or more brothers. This arrangement prevents the subdivision of scarce arable land, and it also ensures that any children are genetically related to all husbands. Polyandry may also arise as a response to a shortage of women, according to a study by anthropologists Kathrine Starkweather and Raymond Hames (Starkweather & Hames, 2012). Those authors identified over 50 societies where polyandry is permitted, so these kinds of marriages are not as rare as commonly believed.

The United Nations has condemned polygamy, placing it alongside child marriage and other women-harming practices that "have no place in any society" (UN News, 2018). While a solid majority of Americans has long been opposed to polygamy, the numbers who believe that the practice is morally acceptable increased from 7% in 2003 to 18% in 2019 (Gallup, 2019a). This increase parallels a general liberalization of attitudes on sexual topics, such as same-sex marriage.

## Polyamory includes a variety of non-monogamous relationships

Somewhat related to polygamy is **polyamory** (Anapol, 2010). This is a catchall term for people who openly and intentionally participate in non-monogamous ("poly") relationships. A related term is "open relationship," meaning a relationship in which the partners don't object to the other person being sexually active with third parties. Poly relationships do not generally violate bigamy laws unless the participants attempt to legally formalize their relationships.

Some polyamorists are **swingers**, or "mate swappers." Swingers are usually couples (married or otherwise) who engage in casual sex with like-minded others, often at sex clubs. Whether they visit these clubs as couples or separately, the main point is that both partners are aware of and happy with what they are doing. Swingers often see their lifestyle as a way of avoiding the desire or necessity for secret extramarital affairs. According to one survey, swingers say that their marriages are happy and that swinging contributes to marital stability (Bergstrand & Blevins Williams, 2000). On the negative side, studies conducted in the Netherlands have found that a substantial proportion of people seeking treatment for sexually transmitted infections are swingers and that the use of multiple recreational drugs is very common in this population (Dukers-Muijrers et al., 2010; Evers et al., 2019). There are dating apps, such as Feeld, that cater to swingers and the polyamorous community generally.

Some polyamorists form stable, sexually linked groups of three or more people who usually live together as a family. This phenomenon is called **group marriage**, or **polyfidelity**. Such arrangements have surprisingly deep roots in America. From 1848 to 1881, one group of about 250 people flourished as the Oneida Community in upstate New York. Every man in the community was considered to be married to every woman, and exclusive sexual relationships were forbidden. Excessive pregnancies were prevented by "male continence," which meant that men were expected not to ejaculate during coitus.

Many of the hippie communes of the 1960s and 1970s practiced polyfidelity in one form or another. A notable example was the Kerista Commune located in San Francisco's Haight-Ashbury district. The commune had about 30 members, divided into four clusters of about 8 individuals each. Within each cluster, sleeping partners changed every night, the schedule being arranged by computer. Most of the men underwent vasectomy before joining the group.

While polyamory no longer has the visibility it enjoyed in the 1960s, it is still quite widespread. According to an analysis of data from the National Survey of Sexual Health and Behavior, out of all Americans who are in sexual relationships, 4% say that their relationships are consensually non-monogamous (Levine et al., 2018). (Another 8% say they are in *non*-consensual non-monogamous relationships—i.e., they or their partners are "cheating"—but that is not what we are discussing here.) People who identify as gay/lesbian or bisexual are far more likely to be in poly or open relationships than those who identify as straight.

Within group marriages, a variety of sexual relationships can exist (**FIGURE 11.4**). Usually, members are expected not to have sex with outsiders, and this lessens the risk of sexually transmitted

**polyamory** The formation of non-transient sexual relationships in groups of three or more.

**swingers** Couples who agree to engage in casual sexual contacts with others.

**group marriage (or polyfidelity)** Three or more people living together in a marriage-like relationship.

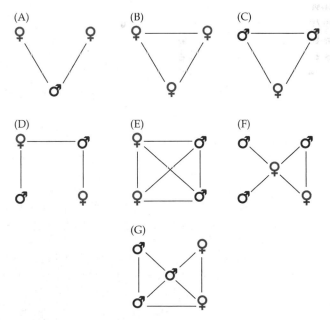

▲ **FIGURE 11.4 Polyamory** Polyamorists are small groups of people linked by sexual bonds. "Poly" relationships are highly diverse. They may consist of three (A–C), four (D, E), five (F, G), or more persons. All the members of a group may have sexual interactions with one another (B, C, F), or they may have sex only in certain combinations (A, D, F, G). The sexual interactions may be all heterosexual (A, D), all homosexual (B), or both heterosexual and homosexual (C, E, F, G).

▲ Companionate marriage had its origins in ancient Rome. This couple is portrayed in a wall painting from the city of Pompeii (79 CE).

infections as compared with swinger groups. Relationships within a group marriage may not all be equivalent: There may be "primary," "secondary," and "tertiary" relationships involving different degrees of commitment. Bisexuality is common in the "poly" community, especially among the women, but it is not universal.

Polyamorists adopt a wide variety of rules or ethical codes to regulate their sexual relations. Although polyamory presents an interesting alternative to standard monogamous relationships, its appeal is limited by the problem of jealousy, which often tears sex-sharing groups apart. Successful polyamorists say that they intentionally cultivate an emotion that is the very opposite of jealousy, namely a pleasure in the knowledge that their partners are enjoying sexual relations with others. This emotion has been called **compersion**. In general, men are more able to feel compersion with regard to their female partner's *emotional* involvement with others, whereas women are more able to feel compersion with regard to their male partner's *physical* involvement with others (Mogilski et al., 2019). This difference is consistent with the sex differences in jealousy that we discussed in Chapter 7.

A group of social psychologists at the University of Michigan reviewed all the evidence relating to the advantages and disadvantages of monogamy as compared with other arrangements such as polyamory (Conley et al., 2013). They found no evidence to support the common belief that monogamy is superior to other kinds of sexual or marital arrangements.

## 11.3 The Institution of Marriage Is Evolving

### LEARNING OBJECTIVES
After reading this section you should be able to:

11.3.1 Describe historical and current changes in the nature and meaning of marriage.

11.3.2 Identify demographic factors associated with the likelihood of being married.

To understand the place of cohabitation and marriage in people's lives today, it's important to recall that the Western institution of marriage has changed greatly over the centuries. In ancient Greece, marriage was not companionate—a wife was not expected to be a social partner to her husband but was chiefly there to have children (who were then looked after largely by slaves). **Companionate marriage** had its origins in Roman culture, and it got a boost from the banning of polygamy by the early Christian church. It did not reach its heyday, however, until the 19th and early 20th centuries, when the improved education of women led to their being seen as more desirable companions for men.

Before industrialization and the shift of the population to cities, a married couple typically formed the core of a large extended family that dwelled together under one roof. Although some Americans, especially Hispanics, still maintain that pattern to some degree, the average household size in the United States now numbers fewer than three people; most married couples live alone or accompanied only by their children, and the number of children has fallen dramatically. In 1800, the average American woman had eight live-born children over her lifetime; now she has just under two.

In the 19th century the average age at first marriage was fairly high, especially for men, who couldn't marry until they had the means to support a family (**FIGURE 11.5**). During the 20th century people married progressively younger, reaching a minimum of the early twenties in the post–World War II years. Since then the age at first marriage has increased steadily and is showing no signs of leveling off.

**compersion** Pleasure at one's partner's sexual involvement with others.

**companionate marriage** A form of marriage in which the husband and wife are expected to be emotionally intimate and to engage in social activities together.

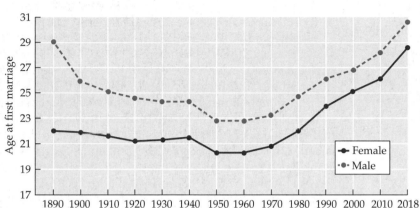

▲ **FIGURE 11.5   Age at first marriage** reached a minimum in the post–World War II era and has since climbed back to near (male) or beyond (female) Victorian levels. (After U.S. Census Bureau. 2017. *Historical marital status tables*. Data from *Decennial Censuses, 1890 to 1940, Current Population Survey, Annual Social and Economic Supplements, 1947 to 2018*. U.S. Census Bureau: Washington)

## Companionate marriage makes the availability of divorce a necessity

The institution of companionate marriage suffers from several problems. Most notably, companionate marriage demands intimacy and affection, yet not all couples are capable of sustaining these feelings over a lifetime, so companionate marriage has driven demand for access to no-fault divorce.* Indeed, the divorce rate has skyrocketed since Victorian times (see "A Variety of Factors Bring Relationships to an End" later in this chapter). Yet the availability of divorce makes marriage a less serious commitment in the first place. Essentially, it converts marriage from a permanent status to a contractual relationship.

A sign of the increasingly contractual nature of marriage is the appearance of custom-designed legal agreements. These include **prenuptial agreements**, which are used primarily to specify the distribution of wealth in the eventuality of divorce, and **postnuptial agreements**, which are similar agreements made after marriage. In addition, three states (Louisiana, Arkansas, and Arizona) have an institution called **covenant marriage**. This is an optional form of marriage that does not allow for no-fault divorce. In 2005 Governor Mike Huckabee of Arkansas and his wife Janet converted their 30-year marriage to a covenant marriage. In spite of their example, no more than about 1% of couples in those three states choose the covenant option.

A companionate marriage implies some kind of equivalence between the two spouses, and in most cases that means between husband and wife. Indeed, past generations would be amazed at the similarity of the roles of men and women in present-day marriages—especially in terms of the distribution of breadwinning, household, and decision-making responsibilities. That's not to say that women earn as much as men (they don't [(Payscale.com, 2019)]) or that men do an equal share of housework or child care (they don't [(Pew Research Center, 2017a)]). Still, the fact that these activities are shared at all is a major break from the past. This increasing equivalence of women and men has been brought about not only by the education of women and their entry into the labor market, but also by the decline in the number of children produced by women during marriage. This lack of or small number of children minimizes the biologically distinct roles of men and women.

In the case of same-sex marriages, traditionalists often express the opposite concern, especially when the couple has children. It may be asserted that one gender is

**prenuptial agreement**   A contract signed before marriage, spelling out the disposition of wealth in the event of divorce.

**postnuptial agreement**   A financial agreement between spouses.

**covenant marriage**   A form of marriage that requires a stronger vow of commitment than a regular marriage and that makes divorce harder to obtain.

*In all U.S. states a married person may obtain a no-fault divorce without his or her partner's consent. Some feminists have criticized this system as harmful to women.

"missing," along with the parenting style and role-modeling that are imagined to be the province of that gender (Family Research Council, 2019). Research does not support this concern, as we discuss further in Chapter 12.

Whether individuals are in opposite-sex or same-sex marriages, the contemporary world thinks of them as all-purpose companions. They are expected to be romantic partners, friends, economic collaborators, fellow workers in the home, and colleagues in parenting. And they are expected to sustain all these relationships with far less support from relatives or neighbors than was customary a generation or two ago.

It is no small challenge, but for many it works: Surveys have consistently found that married people are happier than the unmarried (Rothman, 2016). Being married is better than being rich: In a 2008 poll, more married people in the lowest income bracket said they were "very happy" (56%) than did unmarried people in the highest income bracket (50%) (Gallup & Newport, 2008). The greatest happiness, however, was reported by those who were both married *and* wealthy (67%).

## Marriage is becoming a minority status

So is marriage on the way out? It's certainly on the decline. Currently, 50% of Americans over age 18 are married; that's down from 72% in 1960. Just between 2001 and 2017 the marriage rate (marriages per 1,000 people per year) fell by 16% (CDC, 2018d).

Of course, these general statistics conceal major demographic variations in marriage rates. The rate has declined most steeply among younger and less-educated people. There are also very marked differences between different racial/ethnic groups: Asian women are the most likely to be married, and black women the least likely (**FIGURE 11.6**). The majority of black children live in households where their fathers are not present (U.S. Census Bureau, 2010). The absence of fathers can be traced to low employment and wages for black men, increasing employment for black women, and a history of welfare policies that favor single mothers. Among black families living in the suburbs, however, living arrangements are much more like those of other middle-class Americans. Furthermore, black single-mother families are often strengthened by the presence of other relatives

(A)

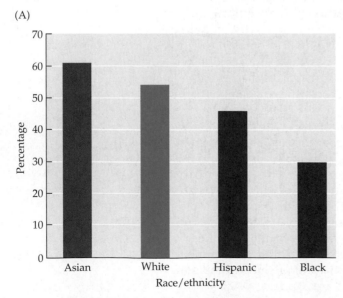

(B)

▲ **FIGURE 11.6** **Race and marriage** (A) This bar graph shows the percentage of Americans age 18 and older who are married, by race/ethnicity (Pew Research Center, 2017b). (B) Black women are much more likely to be single mothers than are women of other racial or ethnic groups. (After K. Parker and R. Stepler. 2017. *As U.S. marriage rate hovers at 50%, education gap in marital status widens.* Pew Research Center: Washington, D.C. https://tinyurl.com/yy9w7t3k.)

in the household or by strong kinship links outside of it (Taylor, 2010).

Income is a very important factor influencing marriage in the United States. For men, the likelihood of being married rises steeply with increasing personal income (U.S. Census Bureau, 2017) (**FIGURE 11.7**). For women there is little indication of such a relationship, probably because women with little or no personal income are more likely to be married to well-off men than the reverse.

## Relationship options have diversified

A generation or two ago, couples had two starkly different options: to live together in a legally unrecognized (and sometimes illegal) cohabitation, or to marry. Today, the dividing line between cohabitation and marriage has blurred. Cohabitation has become more like marriage: It has lost much of its stigma, and it has gained some of the legal and financial benefits that were formerly restricted to married couples. And marriage has become more

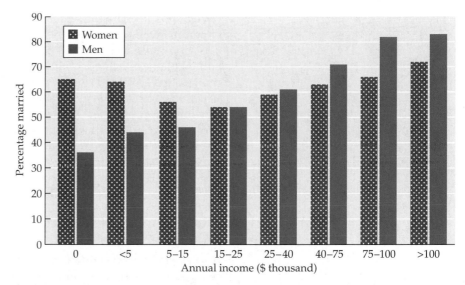

▲ **FIGURE 11.7** **Marriage and income** The bar graph shows the percentages of men and women, age 40 to 44, who are married and living with their spouses, broken down by personal (not joint) income. (Data from U.S. Census Bureau. 2017. *America's families and living arrangements: 2016*. U.S. Census Bureau: Washington. http://tinyurl.com/yc8gjcq2.)

like cohabitation: Separation and divorce are less stigmatized, couples can file their taxes separately, and same-sex couples—who previously could only cohabit—can now marry.

In addition, a kaleidoscope of intermediate arrangements has come into being under the designations **domestic partnership** and **civil union**. Domestic partnerships offer some of the rights of marriage; civil unions offer most or all of these rights except for the name "marriage." The original impetus to formalize such arrangements came from the gay community, and after same-sex marriage became legal, many jurisdictions terminated the civil union option. Domestic partnerships are still widely available, however, and offer advantages to some couples, regardless of their sexual orientation.

**domestic partnership**   A legal arrangement that confers some or most of the rights and obligations of marriage.

**civil union**   A legal arrangement that confers most or all of the rights and obligations of marriage except the name.

## 11.4 Most Long-Term Couples Are Satisfied with Their Sex Lives

### LEARNING OBJECTIVES
After reading this section you should be able to:

11.4.1   Identify reasons why the frequency of marital sex declines over time.

11.4.2   Analyze possible strategies to maintain sexual satisfaction in marriage.

This and the following sections deal mainly with heterosexual married couples because those are the people on whom most researchers have focused their attention. It's likely, however, that much of what we have to say is relevant to long-term relationships in general, including same-sex relationships.

Married (and cohabiting) couples generally seem happier with their sex lives than the frequency of their sexual activities would suggest. According to National Health and Social Life Survey (NHSLS) data, married women are less likely than dating women to have sex more than twice a week. They are also less adventurous sexually and less likely to experience orgasm. Nevertheless, women's physical satisfaction with sex is much greater in long-term relationships than in short-term relationships, and their emotional satisfaction is higher in marriage than in any other type of relationship. The same is true for men, except that men have a high likelihood of experiencing orgasm regardless of the kind of relationship they are in.

Why would this be? There could be at least two different reasons. These results could be an artifact reflecting different demographic characteristics among the various groups studied. Alternatively, it could be that marriage somehow confers satisfaction—especially emotional satisfaction—on the sexual aspects of relationships. The NHSLS researchers carried out a statistical analysis to resolve this question and came up with the following answer (Waite & Joyner, 2001). For men, demographics are key—when men are matched for other characteristics, they are about equally likely to be satisfied by sex within marital or nonmarital relationships. Women, however, do derive extra emotional satisfaction from sex within a married relationship simply by virtue of that relationship being a marriage.

## The frequency of sex declines over the course of long-term relationships

Sexual interactions between married partners decline with increasing duration of marriage and also with age. According to the 2010 National Survey of Sexual Health and Behavior (NSSHB) (Reece et al., 2010), the proportion of married men and women having sex (coitus) at least once per month decreases from over three in four in early adulthood to about one in four after age 70 (**FIGURE 11.8**).

Several factors probably contribute to this decline in sexual activity. First, there is a loss of sexual interest associated with **habituation**; that is, increasing familiarity between the partners is associated with the dimming of passionate love. Second, there is a long-lasting decline in sexual interest and frequency of coitus following the birth of children. Finally, a decline in sexual behavior is associated with the process of aging itself, which is accompanied by declining health and fitness and falling levels of sex hormones. As you can see from Figure 11.8, a rapid decrease in sexual activity begins around age 50, which is about the age of women's menopause (see below).

Another issue has to do with housework. The average heterosexually married man today does far more housework than his father or grandfather did, even if he still doesn't take a 50% share. It's widely believed that this makes for a happier and therefore sexier marriage. But the truth turns out to be different, according to a U.S.-Spanish collaboration (Kornrich et al., 2012). This group analyzed data from the U.S. National Survey of Families and Households. The more egalitarian the marriage (in terms of the husband sharing household chores, for example), the *lower* was the frequency of marital sex, according to their analysis. "It's the first time in history we are trying this experiment of a sexuality that's rooted in equality and that lasts for decades," sex therapist Esther Perel told the *New York Times*. "It's a tall order for one person to be your partner in Management Inc., your best friend and passionate lover. There's a certain part of you that with this partner will not be fulfilled. You deal with that loss. It's a paradox to be lived with, not solved" (Gottlieb, 2014).

On a more positive note, sociologists Pepper Schwartz and Janet Lever have conducted numerous studies and surveys of what factors keep sex alive in long-term relationships. In their *Getaway Guide to the Great Sex Weekend* they distill what they've learned into three pieces of advice: First, maintain good sexual communication, which includes building anticipation of sexual encounters; second, be willing to try new things (new locations,

**habituation** A psychological or physiological process that reduces a person's response to a stimulus or drug after repeated or prolonged exposure.

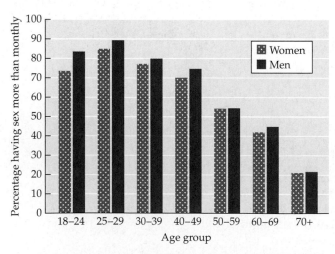

▲ **FIGURE 11.8** **Marital sex becomes less frequent with increasing age.** This bar graph shows the percentage of married women and men having sex more than once per month, for different age ranges. (Data from D. Herbenick et al. 2010. *J Sex Med* 7(S5): 277–290 and M. Reece et al. 2010. *J Sex Med* 7(S5): 291–304.)

new sex toys, new positions) to ward off sexual boredom; and third, take the time to set the right mood for romance.

## Marital satisfaction declines during middle age

Marital satisfaction also falls off over time, although to a highly variable degree (Musick & Bumpass, 2006); some couples remain very satisfied with their marriage over a long lifetime. Two life events are particularly likely to trigger a drop in satisfaction. One is the birth of the first child: Childbirth is associated with a significant drop in women's sexual desire, and this drop in desire leads to a drop in marital satisfaction (McNulty et al., 2019). Childbirth also reduces the amount of "quality time" in the relationship, as well as a perception by both husbands and wives (but particularly by wives) that each is having to shoulder an unfair share of family responsibilities (Lawrence et al., 2008). The other significant life event is the entry of the oldest child into adolescence (Cui & Donnellan, 2009): The father and mother often have differences over how to cope with the stresses associated with having an adolescent child.

It has often been said that women are less satisfied with their marriages than men, but a recent meta-analysis found that not to be the case, at least for the general population (Jackson et al., 2014). Wives in marital therapy are indeed less satisfied than husbands, according to the meta-analysis, but this may simply be because unhappy wives bring their spouses into therapy, whereas unhappy husbands don't.

A variety of factors influence how satisfied a couple remains with their marriage as the years roll by, some of which have been discussed in earlier chapters. As mentioned in Chapter 5, for example, physical attractiveness of the wife (but not of the husband) at the start of the marriage predicts more lasting satisfaction—on the part of both partners—with the marriage at later times (Meltzer et al., 2014).

Also, people's personalities, as measured by the "Big Five" factors of extraversion, agreeableness, conscientiousness, neuroticism, and openness, tend to change over the course of their married lives, especially during the first few years of marriage (Lavner et al., 2018). Some of these changes may benefit marital satisfaction: Men become more conscientious, and women become less neurotic (e.g., less liable to feel stressed-out or worried). On the other hand, some changes are likely to harm marital satisfaction: Both men and women become less agreeable (e.g., less likely to be interested in other people's problems), men become less extraverted (e.g., less likely to initiate conversations), and women become less open (e.g., less imaginative or interested in abstract ideas). The extent to which these personality changes happen varies from couple to couple, but they may in some cases lead to a sense that "he/she is not the person I married."

Marital satisfaction matters not just for people's happiness but also for their physical health—especially for men. Thus men who display a lot of anger in marital conflicts tend, over many years, to develop the symptoms of cardiovascular disease. Men who "stonewall," on the other hand, tend to develop symptoms of musculoskeletal disease (Haase et al., 2016). How could **psychosomatic effects** like this come about? Probably because anger is accompanied by an increase in blood pressure and other cardiovascular phenomena that, over time, injure the heart and blood vessels, whereas stonewalling is accompanied by muscle tension, which over time harms muscles and joints, leading to arthritis and other disorders. Regardless of how these health effects come about, the end result is dramatic: Men and women who describe their marriages as "happy" or "pretty happy" live significantly longer than those whose marriages are "not too happy" (Whisman et al., 2018).

There is of course a great deal of variation among both men and women in how their marital satisfaction changes as the years pass. Interestingly, research suggests that people already have some idea at the time they marry—although only unconsciously—how successful their marriage is going to be (**BOX 11.2**).

**FAQ:** When we have our marriage license, are we legally married?

Requirements vary, but usually the license must be signed by the couple and the officiant of a civil or religious marriage ceremony, and then filed for the issuance of a marriage certificate, before the state will recognize your marriage.

**psychosomatic effects** Effects of the mind on the body.

## BOX 11.2
## You Know the Future of Your Marriage

When newlywed men or women are asked about their future satisfaction with their marriage and then followed over a period of years, their answers have virtually no predictive value: People don't seem to have any clue about how their marriages are going to work out (Lavner et al., 2013). But social psychologist James McNulty (of Florida State University, Tallahassee) and several colleagues suspected that there might be more to it than that. They devised an experiment to probe beneath the surface of newlyweds' minds (McNulty et al., 2013).

First, the researchers assessed the conscious feelings of the experiment participants toward their spouses by means of a simple questionnaire. Then they sidestepped the participants' conscious minds by using an **implicit association test**. In the test, participants were very briefly exposed to photos of their spouses or various control faces. Immediately thereafter they had to decide as quickly as possible whether a certain emotionally loaded word (e.g., "love" or "sickness") was "good" or "bad." The more positive feelings the participants had toward their spouses, the more they were biased toward a "good" response, so it took them less time to associate "love" with "good" than to associate "sickness" with "bad"—and vice versa if they had negative feelings. Thus, by calculating the ratio of the "good" to the "bad" response times, the researchers could get an estimate of the participants' "automatic" feelings about their spouses.

After the test the participants were followed for 4 years, and every 6 months they were asked how satisfied they were with their marriages. In agreement with previous studies, the

Young couples want to know the future—but perhaps they know already.

participants' consciously expressed feelings bore no relationship to their later satisfaction (or lack of it) with their marriages. But the "automatic" feelings revealed by the implicit association test did bear a relationship: The more positive these feelings, the less likely the participants were to experience any decline in marital satisfaction over the follow-up period. Thus it appears that newlyweds do have an implicit knowledge of how their marriage is going to work out, even if they are not conscious of it or are unable or unwilling to express it. It's possible that this kind of approach could be useful in marriage counseling.

**implicit association test** A psychological test designed to reveal unconscious or unexpressed feelings.

## 11.5 A Variety of Factors Bring Relationships to an End

### LEARNING OBJECTIVE
After reading this section you should be able to:

**11.5.1 Identify factors associated with marital breakups and marital stability.**

Till death do us part? Not really. In 2018 there were 46 divorces, and an unknown number of permanent separations, for every 100 marriages (U.S. Census Bureau, 2020). Thus only about half of all marriages go the full distance.

The divorce rate—the percentage of married persons who divorce per year—rose steadily from the 1960s until 2000. Since 2000 the divorce rate has fallen by about 20%. This improvement is somewhat illusory, however. It results in large part from the fact that couples who are especially prone to divorce, namely economically disadvantaged young people, are now less able to marry in the first place.

Married couples usually break up because they are unhappy in their marriages, but there are many possible causes for that unhappiness (Härkönen, 2015). In fact, the famous opening sentence of Leo Tolstoy's novel *Anna Karenina* sums it up: "All happy families are alike; each unhappy family is unhappy in its own way."

## Several demographic factors increase the likelihood of a breakup

In the preceding section (and in Chapter 7), we discussed some of the family circumstances and psychological factors that seem to promote or prevent the breakup of marriages and other long-term relationships. In a broader, demographic sense, the likelihood of marital disruption is linked to three major factors: age at marriage, ethnicity, and educational level.

Marriage during the teen years increases the risk of disruption. If the woman is under 18 at the time of marriage, the chances of breakup within 10 years are double what they are for women over 25 (one in two versus one in four). The reasons for the vulnerability of teen marriages probably include the immaturity of the partners, the economic stresses of early marriage, and the fact that some teen marriages are "shotgun" (forced by pregnancy).

Race/ethnicity has a significant effect on marital stability. Asian Americans have the most stable marriages, followed by Hispanics, whites, and then blacks (**FIGURE 11.9**) (CDC, 2012).

On the positive side, a college education does wonders for marital stability (CDC, 2012) (**FIGURE 11.10**): If you graduate from college, your first marriage will have a 75% chance of lasting at least 15 years. Throw in a few other favorable demographics (**TABLE 11.1**), and your marriage will be almost divorce-proof.

Similarity between partners increases marital stability, at least in the early years of marriage, according to NHSLS data. Thus, married couples who have different religions are more likely to break up than are couples who share the same religion. Interracial couples are more likely to break up than same-race couples (Bratter & King, 2008). Large age differences also increase the chances of a breakup.

## There are more personal reasons for breakups

When individual divorced people are asked about why their marriages ended, they refer not to demographic variables, but rather to specific problems in their own marriages (de Graaf & Kalmijn, 2006). These problems include psychological incompatibility, behavioral problems (including drinking and drug use), and abuse.

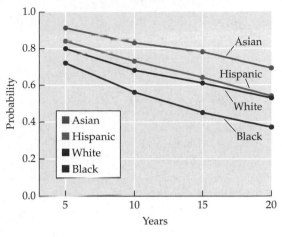

▲ **FIGURE 11.9  Ethnicity influences the durability of marriage.** This figure shows the probability that couples of each race/ethnicity will still be together at 5, 10, 15, and 20 years after they marry. Marriage duration is longest for Asian Americans and shortest for blacks. (After C. E. Copen et al. 2012. *National Vital Statistics Reports* 49: 1–22. National Center for Health Statistics: Hyattsville, MD.)

### TABLE 11.1  Your divorce calculator

| Factors | Percent decrease in risk of divorce |
|---|---|
| Earning over $50,000 annually (vs. under $25,000) | 30 |
| Having graduated from college (vs. not completed high school) | 25 |
| Having a baby 7 months or more after marriage (vs. before marriage) | 24 |
| Marrying at over 25 years of age (vs. at under age 18) | 24 |
| Coming from an intact family of origin (vs. having divorced parents) | 14 |
| Having a religious affiliation (vs. having none) | 14 |

*Source*: W. B. Wilcox. 2010. *The State of Our Unions 2010*. National Marriage Project and Institute for American Values: Charlottesville, VA; based on data from M. D. Bramlett and W. D. Mosher. 2002. *Vital Health Stat* 23(22): 1–94.

*Note*: Overall, almost half of U.S. marriages end in divorce, but each of these factors reduces the chances of divorce by the stated percentage. Each figure represents the contribution of the stated factor in isolation from other factors—for example, the effect of graduating from college does not include the effect of the higher income that college graduates typically enjoy.

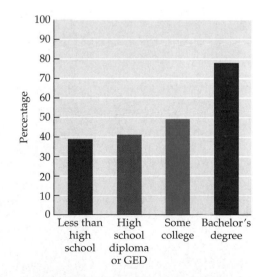

▲ **FIGURE 11.10  Education makes for stable marriages.** This bar graph shows the percentages of women of different educational levels whose first marriages last at least 20 years. (After C. E. Copen et al. 2012. *National Vital Statistics Reports* 49: 1–22. National Center for Health Statistics: Hyattsville, MD.)

Infidelity, as you might imagine, is one of the strongest predictors of imminent breakup. Husbands cheat about three times more often than wives, but the disruptive effect is the same regardless of the sex of the cheater (DeMaris, 2013).

In non-Western societies, infertility is often seen as an adequate justification for divorce (Inhorn, 1996). As discussed in Chapter 8, a couple's infertility is about equally likely to result from problems in the man as in the woman, but tradition- ally it is the woman who takes the blame. In Pakistan, for example, a woman who does not have a live birth within a few years of marriage—or who does not produce a son—may experience verbal and physical abuse at the hands of her husband or in-laws, and she may eventually be sent back to her parents' home (Sami & Ali, 2006).

In contemporary Western societies couples rarely cite infertility as the reason for a breakup, but it can play a role nonetheless. A Danish group studied women who were married or cohabiting and who attended a clinic for a fertility problem; those women who did not subsequently give birth to a child were three times more likely to divorce or separate than the women who succeeded in giving birth (Kjaer et al., 2014).

## 11.6  Marital Disruption Can Have Negative and Positive Consequences

### LEARNING OBJECTIVES
After reading this section you should be able to:

**11.6.1**  Analyze the potential harms and benefits associated with divorce.
**11.6.2**  Identify the effects of remarriage on income, sexual activity, and children's well-being.

In the immediate aftermath of a divorce, negative emotions such as anger, guilt, sad- ness, or fear for the future often predominate. Yet divorce is a mixed bag in terms of its effects on the ex-spouses and any children they may have.

### Divorced men and women can suffer psychological, physical, and economic damage

When marriages end, there are all kinds of negative consequences that go far beyond the bitter feelings of the breakup itself (Amato, 2010). Divorced people have higher rates of psychological and physical ill health (including higher mortality) than do married people. They are less happy, less sexually active, more socially isolated, and more prone to substance abuse. Divorced women—who often retain physical custody of children— generally experience a severe drop in per capita household income. (Divorced men, on the other hand, may see a rise in per capita household income.) The children of divorced parents experience a heightened risk of depression, behavior problems, low academic performance, substance abuse, criminality, and early sexual activity. Couples who separate without divorcing may experience similar problems: This is particularly relevant to separated black couples, who tend to remain in that state without divorcing for much longer than do white or Hispanic couples (Raley et al., 2015).

Of course, not all these ill effects can be blamed on divorce or separation per se: They may well be the ongoing conse- quences of the kind of marriage that preceded the breakup. People who divorce are generally unhappy in their marriages, and if divorce were not possible, they might become even less happy and might eventually experience impairments in their mental and physical health at least as severe as those that affect divorced men and women. What is really desirable is to

▲ Statistically, this interracial couple stands a much higher chance of breaking up than do couples of the same ethnicity. Interracial couples may lack the social supports that help sus- tain marriage. Even so, there are plenty of interracial couples who enjoy long, happy marriages.

© KeyStock/Shutterstock.com

increase people's marital satisfaction to the point that they won't want to split up in the first place. We discussed some strategies to accomplish this earlier in this chapter and in Chapter 7.

## Divorce may be the start of a new life

To some extent, the concept of divorce as an unmitigated evil has arisen from a religious conservative tradition that uses terminology such as "failed marriages" and "broken homes," that refers to the children of divorced parents as "victims," and that sees rising divorce rates as a symptom of society's "moral decay." In reality, marital disruption can also have positive consequences. In fact, if it didn't, it would be hard to explain why divorce and separation are so popular.

The benefits of divorce include escape from an unhappy, possibly abusive, relationship and the potential for forming a better one. Divorce is always a challenge, but for some people, women especially, it can be the key that unlocks previously untapped sources of talent, energy, and resolve. For gay or bisexual men and women who are in opposite-sex marriages, divorce may be an opportunity to "come out of the closet" and develop more-fulfilling same-sex relationships.

For all these reasons, divorce is sometimes seen as a cause for celebration: an occasion to be marked with a party and perhaps gifts to make up for whatever the ex took with them. To satisfy this need, the crowdfunding site Plumfund allows users to set up divorce funds or divorce gift registries. You can buy divorce cups on Amazon, but they express very different sentiments for women ("Congrats on your divorce—We hated him") and for men ("King of whatever is left").

## Many divorced people remarry

It's common for divorced or widowed men and women to marry again; in fact, about 4 in 10 U.S. marriages involve at least one partner who has been married previously (Pew Research Center, 2014). But the remarriage rate, like the marriage rate, has fallen dramatically in recent years. The drop has been particularly marked for the younger age groups: In 1960, 72% of young (under age 35) divorcees had remarried, but by 2013 this figure had dropped to 42%.

Remarriage brings economic and other benefits. The median incomes of remarried Americans are the same as those of Americans who remain in their first marriage, and they earn about $5,000 more than those who stay divorced. Remarriage is also associated, not surprisingly, with an increase in sexual activity—clear evidence that the general decline in sexual behavior during marriage is not solely a biological effect of aging.

Unfortunately, children of divorce tend to remain disadvantaged when their mothers remarry: The adverse effects that strike children of divorced parents (see above) also affect stepchildren. Still, the differences between the well-being of stepchildren and children whose parents are still married are not great: Most stepchildren fare quite well in such areas as behavior and academic performance (Ganong & Coleman, 2016).

Second and later marriages are somewhat less durable than first marriages. For example, a woman 25 years old or older has a one in four chance of breaking up within 10 years when she marries for the first time, but if she has been married previously, she has a one in three chance of breaking up within the same period. In other words, experience gained from the first marriage doesn't seem to stabilize later marriages. Bear in mind, though, that it's a special subset of people who remarry—namely, those who have already divorced at least once. These people may have personality traits or economic

**FAQ:** How can we stop fighting?

Get more sleep. Shortened sleep triggers marital hostility and also harms the body (Wilson et al., 2017).

© Denise Truscello/WireImage/Getty Images

▲ Divorce, Vegas style. Former Miss USA Shanna Moakler celebrated her 2006 split from drummer Travis Barker with a party at the Bellagio Hotel, complete with divorce cake.

**climacteric** The transition to infertility at the end of a woman's reproductive life, lasting for several years and culminating in menopause.

**perimenopause** The phase prior to menopause that is marked by irregular menstrual cycles.

**menopause** The final cessation of menstruation at the end of a woman's reproductive years.

### FAQ: Can divorced Catholics remarry in the church?

Strictly speaking, no—because the Catholic Church doesn't recognize divorce. But they can have their former marriages annulled (declared to have never existed) for a variety of reasons, and then marry in the church.

circumstances that reduce marital stability, or they may see less moral or practical value in lasting marriages.

### Does marriage have a future?

Marriage is not just a romantic goal: It is also a major engine of wealth creation, because a married couple is so much more efficient economically than the same two people living independently. Thus, as marriage becomes increasingly restricted to the wealthier and better-educated sectors of American society, a social and economic problem is created. The institution of marriage has come to reinforce the divide between America's haves and have-nots and to facilitate its persistence across the generations (Kearney & Levine, 2017).

If the decline in marriage were simply a matter of cohabiting couples neglecting to visit the marriage registrar's office, as is widely the case in Europe, there would be no harm to anyone except the wedding industry. But in reality, marriage is declining in significant part because it has become an unattainable dream for many poorer Americans. Changes in the labor market—in particular, the less-rewarding employment prospects for people with a high school education or less—greatly limit many young people's ability to marry. Thus, strengthening education and employment opportunities may be an important step toward restoring a central place for marriages—and marriage-equivalent cohabitations—in American society.

The great majority of college students do desire and expect to get married and have children one day. But unlike their parents or grandparents, they also stress the importance of giving themselves time to enjoy life, travel, and take advantage of sexual freedom before the more dutiful burdens of marriage overtake them. To some, marriage is so remote in their minds that they associate it with the end of life. "I don't want to die alone," said one student when asked why he planned to marry. Some students, though, take a more positive view. One 20-year-old woman said: "[Being 30 and married is] when your life is really gonna kick into gear" (Regnerus & Uecker, 2011).

## 11.7 Menopause Marks Women's Transition to Infertility

### LEARNING OBJECTIVES

After reading this chapter you should be able to:

11.7.1 Explain the "grandmother hypothesis" for menopause.
11.7.2 Describe the possible negative and positive effects of menopause.
11.7.3 Assess the benefits and risks of menopausal or postmenopausal hormone therapy.

Midlife has major effects on the sex lives of both men and women. The effects are more dramatic in women, so we discuss those first.

When women reach their early or mid-40s, they may find that their menstrual periods become less regular. This change marks the onset of a gradual transition to infertility—a phase called the **climacteric**, or "change of life." The first portion of the climacteric, when a woman misses some menstrual periods but has not stopped menstruating completely, is called **perimenopause**. **Menopause** is the final cessation of menstrual cycles. Because of the irregularity that commonly precedes menopause, a woman can't *know* that her last period was in fact her last until some time afterward. Conventionally, menopause is said to be "confirmed" after 12 months without a period—in the absence of health factors that might be responsible for the amenorrhea.

Among American, Canadian, and European women, menopause occurs at a median age of 51, but with considerable

© Flashpop/Getty Images

▲ Menopause is an aspect of aging, but it comes at what we now consider midlife.

▲ **FIGURE 11.11** **Life after menopause is adaptive—for killer whales.** A post-reproductive female, at right, leads her adult son and two adult daughters in a search for Chinook salmon in the Pacific Northwest.

variation. Some women reach menopause in their early 40s; others continue to menstruate into their late 50s or even early 60s. Menopause tends to occur earlier—as early as the mid-40s—in South America and Asia, probably on account of disadvantageous socioeconomic conditions (Palacios et al., 2010).

Women's fertility declines well before menopause, but a woman can't be sure that she's incapable of becoming pregnant until menopause is confirmed. Plenty of women in their 40s think that they are unlikely to conceive, let their guard down with regard to contraception, and then are surprised to find themselves pregnant. Particularly at risk are women who use fertility awareness methods of contraception: That's because the cycles of perimenopausal women are too irregular to allow for reliable timing of ovulation.

Although people often focus on the negative aspects of menopause, namely the loss of fertility or the symptoms that may accompany it, evolutionary biologists look at menopause in a different way, asking why women have evolved the capacity for many years of active life *after* cessation of reproduction. They suspect that the reason has to do with the resources, such as food and knowledge, that postmenopausal women have been able to provide to their adult children, thus enabling them to be more prolific and successful parents. This is the so-called grandmother hypothesis of menopause (Cant & Croft, 2019). It is supported by data showing that, in premodern times, women who lived for many years after menopause had more surviving grandchildren than those who did not. Also, females of a few non-human species also experience a significant period of postreproductive life, and this trait may be adaptive (beneficial in an evolutionary sense). For example, female killer whales, which can live for 50 years after giving birth for the last time, use their experience to lead their offspring to food supplies, thus benefiting their offspring's survival and reproductive success (Brent et al., 2015; Nattrass et al., 2019) (**FIGURE 11.11**).

## Menopause may be caused by depletion of ova

A woman's genes influence the age at which she will enter menopause (Stolk et al., 2012). In addition, women who have had fewer pregnancies, who have short cycle lengths, who have had one ovary removed, or who don't use oral contraceptives are all likely to experience menopause earlier than other women. Several lifestyle factors influence age at menopause, sometimes in ways one might not expect: Smoking and being a vegetarian are associated with earlier menopause, whereas engaging in strenuous exercise, having a high body mass index, and drinking alcohol are associated with later menopause (Morris et al., 2012).

It appears that women are born with the capacity for a certain number of ovarian cycles and that the main reason for the transition to infertility may be the depletion of the cells that give rise to ova (Depmann et al., 2015). By the time of menopause, the ovaries contain very few such cells. Surgical removal of the uterus (hysterectomy) in

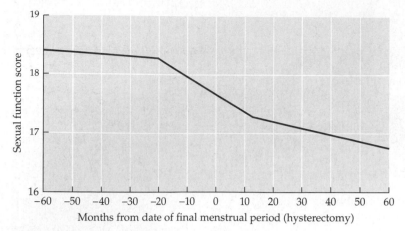

**▲ FIGURE 11.12 Menopause affects sexual function.** This figure charts the mean sexual function scores of 1,396 women over the menopausal transition. Zero on the x-axis indicates the time of the final menstrual period. (After N. E. Avis et al. 2017. *Menopause* 24: 379–390.)

**vasomotor control** The physiological regulation of peripheral blood flow.

**hot flashes (or hot flushes)** Episodes of reddening and warmth of the skin associated with menopause.

**osteoporosis** Reduction in the mineral content of bone, predisposing an individual to fractures.

**menopausal hormone therapy** Use of hormones to treat symptoms occurring during or soon after menopause.

**isoflavones** Estrogen-like compounds of plant origin.

**FAQ:** My mother thinks she may be entering menopause. Should I buy her one of those menopause test kits?

No—those tests will only give a meaningful result at a point when it is already obvious to your mother that she has reached menopause. A copy of the *Menopause Guidebook* (see Recommended Reading at the end of this chapter) would be a more useful gift in the same price range.

a premenopausal woman puts a stop to menstruation but not to the hormonal processes that underlie the menstrual cycle. If the ovaries are removed, however, menopause occurs immediately.

## Women may experience a decline in sexual function at menopause

The most detailed information about the effect of menopause on women's sexuality comes from the Study of Women's Health Across the Nation, which followed over 1,300 women over the menopausal transition (Avis et al., 2017). The research condensed several measures of sexual functioning—including sexual desire, arousal, emotional satisfaction, ability to experience orgasm, and pain—into a single measure of sexual functioning (**FIGURE 11.12**). This function remained stable until about 20 months before the women's final menstrual period, whereupon it began a rapid decline. From about 1 year after the final menstrual period, sexual function continued to decline but at a slower pace. According to the researchers' statistical analysis, the decline in sexual function was not related to vaginal dryness, anxiety, or depression.

Although Figure 11.12 charts the overall trend, it masks a considerable degree of variability. Part of the variability in the study represented racial differences: Japanese American women experienced the greatest decline in sexual function, whereas black women experienced the least decline. Nonbiological factors such as relationship issues, attitudes toward sex and aging, and cultural background also have an impact on sexual function over the time surrounding menopause (Avis et al., 2005; Hayes et al., 2008). Bear in mind that androgens play a significant role in female sexual desire, and although some androgens come from the ovaries, they are also secreted by the adrenal glands. This latter supply continues after menopause and is often sufficient to maintain a high level of sexual interest.

The psychological effects of menopause on sexuality are diverse. For women who believe that the main or only purpose of sex is reproduction, the loss of fertility at menopause may lead to a loss of interest in sex. For the larger number of women, who see an emotional or recreational significance in sex, menopause may actually be welcome because it removes the fear of unwanted pregnancy and makes contraception unnecessary. Such women may get increased pleasure from sex for that reason. (The risk of sexually transmitted infections may still make the use of condoms advisable, of course.)

## Decreased hormone levels affect a woman's physiology

The reduction in circulating ovarian hormones, especially estrogens, has direct effects on the body. These effects can include a reduction in vaginal lubrication in response to sexual arousal, a rise in the pH (decrease in acidity) of vaginal fluids, and sometimes a thinning of the walls of the vagina. In some women these changes may lead to painful coitus and vaginal inflammation. However, many perimenopausal and postmenopausal women do not experience these vaginal symptoms.

Menopause (and perimenopause) may be accompanied by a variety of other symptoms that can influence sexual expression indirectly. The reduction in estrogen levels often leads to instability in **vasomotor control** (the control of blood vessels), so many menopausal women experience **hot flashes** or **hot flushes** (dilation of blood vessels in the skin that may cause reddening, a sensation of warmth, and perspiration, sometimes followed by a cold chill), as well as night sweats, headaches, tiredness, and heart palpitations (bouts of accelerated or irregular heartbeats). Sleep problems are also common. The extent to which these menopausal symptoms occur and how bothersome women find them is highly variable. Symptoms often disappear within a few years after menopause, even without medical treatment, but some women continue to experience symptoms until the age of 60 or beyond (Gartoulla et al., 2018).

Lowered estrogen levels may also have long-term health effects (Levin, 2015). The most significant of these are **osteoporosis** (a loss of bone density), which carries a risk of fractures and vertebral compression (**FIGURE 11.13**), and changes in blood lipid (fat) chemistry, which increase the risk of cardiovascular disease. In addition, there are noticeable effects on the skin (loss of thickness, elasticity, hydration, and fat content).

## Hormone therapy can reduce menopausal symptoms

Menopausal women have the option of taking sex hormones or other drugs to compensate for the loss of their own ovarian hormones and thus to alleviate the symptoms of menopause. This practice is called **menopausal hormone therapy.** The most common regimen is a combination of estrogens and progestins, which may be formulated as a single pill such as Bijuva, which was approved by the U.S. Food and Drug Administration in 2018. The estrogens alleviate symptoms such as hot flushes and vaginal dryness and reduce the incidence of osteoporosis and fractures. Progestins are added to protect the woman from one unwanted side effect of the estrogen treatment, which is an increased risk of endometrial cancer. For women who have had a hysterectomy, this risk is not an issue, so the therapy may consist of estrogens alone. For women in whom vaginal symptoms are the main problem, estrogen can be administered directly to the vagina by means of a ring, tablets, or cream. Hormone therapy not only relieves menopausal symptoms but also improves the general quality of life for women whose menopausal symptoms are severe (Utian & Woods, 2013).

Hormone therapy also has risks, which include an increased likelihood of heart disease, stroke, and dementia. Medical opinions on the balance of risks and benefits have varied over the years. Here's a summary of the current guidelines issued by the North American Menopause Society and endorsed by many other professional organizations: Women who are under 60 or within 10 years of their last menstrual period may benefit from hormone therapy if they experience severe hot flushes or run an elevated risk of bone loss and fractures (North American Menopause Society, 2017). The risks for older women generally outweigh possible benefits, according to the guidelines. Nevertheless, a very large randomized trial whose results were published in 2017 found no increased risk of death among women who took hormone therapy for a median of 6 years, and this was true even for women in their 70s (Manson et al., 2017). The findings of this study offer some reassurance to older women who are considering hormone therapy.

There has been a search for alternative, more "natural," therapies for menopausal symptoms and for long-term postmenopausal use. In particular, there has been interest in **isoflavones**, which are plant-derived molecules with an estrogen-like structure. Unfortunately, carefully controlled studies have found little or no effect of isoflavones in reducing menopausal symptoms, bone loss, or breast cancer (Levis et al., 2011; Chen et al., 2014). Lifestyle choices such as exercise (especially weight-bearing exercise such as walking), keeping a healthy weight, not smoking, and eating a healthful, calcium-rich diet are likely to reduce menopausal symptoms and postmenopausal health risks more effectively than any "natural" pills.

The use of testosterone in the treatment of women's sexual disorders is discussed in Chapter 14.

(A)

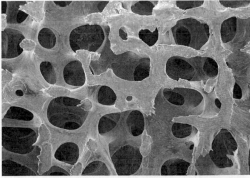

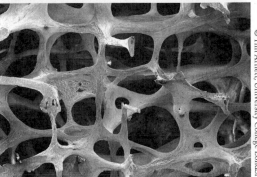

0.2 mm

(B)

▲ **FIGURE 11.13 Osteoporosis** (A) Low estrogen levels after menopause can lead to thinning of the mineral structure of bone. These are scanning electron micrographs showing the microscopic structure of a healthy vertebra (spinal bone) (top) and an osteoporotic vertebra (bottom). The non-mineral tissue has been removed. (B) Osteoporosis can cause collapse of vertebrae, resulting in increasingly stooped posture, but exercise, diet, and drugs can help prevent this process.

## 11.8  Men's Fertility Declines Gradually with Age

**LEARNING OBJECTIVE**

After reading this section you should be able to:

**11.8.1  Assess the controversy regarding testosterone supplementation for older men.**

**andropause**  In men, the gradual decline of fertility with age; a hypothetical male equivalent of menopause.

Men do not experience a sudden or complete cessation of fertility comparable to menopause. Instead, they experience a gradual reduction in fertility and sexual function with aging, evidenced by declining sperm counts and ejaculate volume, an increased likelihood of erectile disorder (see Chapter 14), and decreased sexual desire and frequency of sex. More general changes associated with aging include loss of muscle bulk and bone density, changes in the skin and hair, and possible cognitive changes such as memory impairment.

Some people refer to this collection of changes as the "male menopause," or **andropause**, but these terms are misleading if they are taken to suggest that the changes are sudden or result in a total cessation of reproductive function. Sperm counts decline, but some men in their 80s have fathered children.

Although men don't go through their own menopause, heterosexual men are often affected by the menopause of their female partners. In one interview study, men mentioned being distressed by their partners' irritability, waning sex appeal or sexual engagement, and difficulty in discussing the topic either with their partners or with others (Liao et al., 2015). The topic was perceived as taboo because it was a "woman thing," because it was thought of as a sexual matter, or because it was seen as the beginning of old age. Nevertheless there were also more positive comments. "I keep saying to her, 'This should be the summer of your life. You know you're not going to get pregnant again. I'm not going to need to use condoms so we should have fun.'"

Driven in part by pharmaceutical advertising, middle-aged American men are increasingly coming to believe that their decreased libido, declining athletic ability, or general world-weariness are symptoms of a medical condition, "low T," which can and should be corrected with testosterone supplements (patches or injections). The reality is different: Testosterone levels do not affect sexual functioning in middle-aged or aging men until they fall below a level that is not commonly encountered (O'Connor et al., 2011).

With regard to middle-aged or older men whose testosterone levels do test low, there are conflicting data about the long-term benefits and risks of testosterone supplementation. An obvious concern for men of any age is that testosterone treatment may increase the risk of developing prostate cancer or accelerate the growth of preexisting, undiagnosed cancers, and it might worsen benign enlargement of the prostate, a common condition in older men. Nevertheless, a recent controlled study of men with abnormally low testosterone levels found that testosterone therapy markedly *improved* the symptoms of enlarged prostate, even though it caused a slight enlargement of the gland. The therapy also improved sexual function and did not have any adverse effects (Haider et al., 2018). Bear in mind, though, that findings in hypogonadal men say nothing about testosterone's benefits or risks in men with sexual or other problems whose testosterone levels are within the normal range.*

As one might expect, the frequency and quality of sexual contacts decrease steadily with advancing age and with declining health, for both women and men. Yet psychological factors

▲ The sexuality of this older couple is important to the well-being of their relationship.

© FilippoBacci/Getty Images

*We don't give numbers here because testosterone levels can be measured and expressed in a variety of ways, and the levels considered normal vary with age.

also play an important role. In one prospective study, individuals in their 50s and 60s who had a positive attitude toward aging or who felt younger than their chronological age got more pleasure from sex than other people (Estill et al., 2017).

Sexual activity itself seems to keep people healthy as they age. In a longitudinal study conducted in Wales, middle-aged men who experienced two or more orgasms per week were half as likely to die over the following 10 years as men who had less than one orgasm per month (Davey Smith et al., 1997). Heart disease was the cause of death against which sexual activity offered the most protection. The direction of cause and effect in this study is not entirely clear, but it is part of a growing body of research suggesting that sex is good for older people's health. In another longitudinal study from Britain, both men and women who had low interest in sex at the beginning of the study were the most likely to subsequently develop serious illnesses, including cancer (Jackson et al., 2019).

# 11.9 Old People Face Challenges to Their Sex Lives—Often Successfully

**LEARNING OBJECTIVES**

After reading this section you should be able to:

**11.9.1** Identify the biological, medical, and social challenges to sexual expression by older women and men.

**11.9.2** Describe the variety of attitudes to sex expressed by older people.

One of the most striking findings about sex and aging is the difference in the impact of aging on men and women's sexuality. Young men typically have a stronger sex drive than women by various measures, as we discussed in Chapter 4, but this sex difference increases greatly as people age. In an AARP survey, over half of all women over 70 said that they never had sexual thoughts, fantasies, or erotic dreams, compared with only about 12% of men of the same age (**FIGURE 11.14**). Correspondingly, 80% of men over 70 said that a sexual relationship was important to their quality of life, whereas only 39% of women said the same thing (American Association of Retired Persons, 2010).

In considering these numbers, it's important to bear in mind that heterosexual women face an increasing shortage of potential sex partners as they age. This is because men die younger than women, tend to partner with women who are younger than themselves, and are much more likely than women to be in a same-sex relationship (four times more likely, in the AARP data). Thus, far more older men than older women have regular sex partners (**FIGURE 11.15**). It's likely that more older women would value and think about sex if sex partners were available. Still, even solo sex shows a major sex difference in the AARP data: Nearly three times more men than women masturbated at least once per week.

Among the AARP respondents who did have a sex partner, almost equal percentages of women and men said that they were satisfied with their sex lives (56% and 59%, respectively). Being married, being healthy, experiencing little stress, exercising frequently, and of course having frequent sex were all predictors of sexual satisfaction. About half of partnered men and women in the 70+ group said that their partners were physically attractive, and two-thirds said that their partners "loved them deeply."

## Aging is accompanied by physiological changes in the sexual response

About half of all sexually active older people experience at least one bothersome sexual problem, which we discuss in detail in Chapter 14.

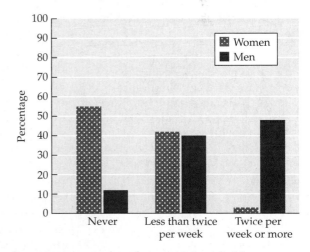

▶ **FIGURE 11.14** **The sex drive in old age** Survey participants over 70 were asked the question "How frequently have you had sexual thoughts, fantasies, or erotic dreams?" The bar graph shows the percentages of women and men who never had such thoughts, had them less than twice a week, or had them more frequently. (Data from L. Fisher et al. 2010. *Sex, Romance, and Relationships: AARP Survey of Midlife and Older Adults.* © 2010 AARP. All rights reserved.)

(A)

(B)

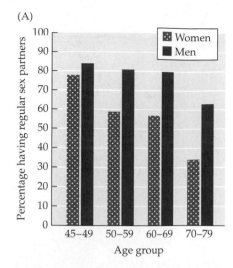

© Darren Modricker/Corbis

▲ **FIGURE 11.15  The partner gap** (A) This bar graph shows the percentages of men and women in different age groups who have a regular sex partner. (B) Because of the imbalance between the sexes, a single older man may be a hot property. (Reprinted from L. Fisher et al. 2010. *Sex, Romance, and Relationships: AARP Survey of Midlife and Older Adults.* © 2010 AARP. All rights reserved.)

Some of these problems are caused by changes in the physiological processes underlying sexuality. For men, these changes include the following:

- The penis becomes erect more slowly in response to either tactile or mental stimulation. The erect penis is less hard. Some degree of erectile dysfunction is reported by about 30% of men in their 60s and the majority of men over 70 (Shamloul & Ghanem, 2013).
- Ejaculatory volume is smaller, and the semen is discharged less forcefully. (It may flow out slowly or even flow backward into the bladder.)
- The erection is lost more rapidly.
- The refractory period (time before another erection and ejaculation are possible) is longer.

Women may experience the following changes:

- The walls of the vagina become thinner, and the entire vagina may become shorter and narrower. (This condition can be alleviated with local application of estrogens.)
- Vaginal lubrication decreases. Nearly half of women over age 65 report vaginal dryness (Mayo Clinic, 2017c).
- There are fewer contractions during orgasm.
- There is a more rapid decrease in arousal after orgasm.

### Medical conditions, drugs, and social factors can impair the sexuality of older people

Medical conditions that become more common with advancing age can also impair sexual performance. These conditions include arthritis, heart disease, osteoporosis, incontinence, diabetes, chronic obstructive pulmonary disease (emphysema and chronic bronchitis), and obesity. Surgeries such as prostatectomy, mastectomy, and hysterectomy can affect sexual performance, either directly, or indirectly by causing pain or embarrassment.

Older people take more prescription drugs than younger people, and many of these drugs can interfere with sexual performance. Examples include antihypertension drugs, diuretics, tranquilizers and antidepressants, cancer chemotherapy, ulcer medicines, and anticoagulants. (Individual drugs vary, as do patients' responses to them; alternative drugs can often be prescribed that do not impair sexual desire or performance.)

Psychological and social factors can impair sexual expression in older people, especially in women. In one study of over 4,000 postmenopausal women, lack of a partner (usually through widowhood) was the most-cited reason for a lack of sexual activity; followed by the partner's medical problems or sexual dysfunction; their own health problems, menopause-related symptoms, or low sex drive; and relationship difficulties (Harder et al., 2019). The difference between the sex drives of aging women and aging men was highlighted in a University of Michigan survey of people between the ages of 65 and 80: Fifty percent of the men but only 12% of women said that they were "extremely interested" or "very interested" in sex (National Poll on Healthy Aging, 2019).

For older couples who have difficulty with coitus (because of physiological changes in one or both partners), it might make good sense to practice oral sex instead. However, people in the oldest age groups came of age at a time when oral sex was relatively uncommon and was practiced mainly by the better-educated levels of society. This age cohort did not necessarily join the rush to oral sex in the 1960s; in fact, nearly half of them have never had a single experience of fellatio or cunnilingus, according to NHSLS data, and many of them probably consider these behaviors immoral or unappealing.

## Old age may be a time for romance

Old people are just young people, later. They display the same spectrum of sexual attitudes and experience the same diversity of sexual feelings and relationships. The comments of individual women and men show that sex in old age can be frequent or nonexistent, a pain or a joy, just as it can be for the young (**BOX 11.3**). Yet there is something about romance that is characteristic of old age—something that was well expressed by author and runner Eve Pell, who at the age of 70 married a fellow athlete, 80-year-old Sam Hirabayashi. In a *New York Times* piece titled "The Race Grows Sweeter Near Its Final Lap," she wrote as follows (Pell, 2013): "Old love is different. In our 70s and 80s, we had been through enough of life's ups and downs to know who we were, and we had learned to compromise. We knew something about death because we had seen loved ones die. The finish line was drawing closer. Why not have one last blossoming of the heart? . . . Young love, even for old people, can be surprisingly bountiful."

---

## BOX 11.3
## Seniors on Sex

In 2014 Gloria Steinem, a leader in the 1970s women's liberation movement, reached her 80th birthday. She marked the occasion by speaking positively about her dwindling libido, saying, "The brain cells that used to be obsessed [with sex] are now free for all kinds of great things" (Collins, 2014). Britain's *Guardian* newspaper asked its readers for their reactions, and several hundred British and American women obliged (Spencer, 2014). Their remarks give some idea of the diverse ways in which aging affects women's sex lives. Here are some samples:

*My lack of sex drive has been enormously liberating. I look back with some regret at the years I wasted on men. I've recently, at age 60, completed a BSc in Computer Science and I now work as a software engineer.*

*For me, diminished libido is yet another manifestation that my time has passed. Outliving my vitality has not made me feel happy, free, or wise.*

*I had zero sex drive until my gyno prescribed testosterone cream. It made a huge difference. I recently fell in love with a man who is 73 and I'm having the best sex of my life and am multi-orgasmic for the first time. Hooray senior love.*

*Far from dwindling, my sex drive has surged since menopause. Sex toys are my best friends.*

This comment comes from a different source (Kleinplatz et al., 2009):

*It's just the huge warmth of being with somebody that you've been in bed with for 40-plus years and still feeling that immense rush of joy, that–you know–what a gift!*

And here are some comments from men, culled from a variety of online sources:

*I started taking a daily drug for erections and it makes me feel like 20 again.*

*I had a laser treatment for BPH [enlarged prostate]. Since then I have been unable to sustain an erection, nor am I able to ejaculate.*

*My appetite for sex is about normal. The problem is that my wife no longer feels that way. All the fun and excitement has gone from our sex life.*

*There's a great beauty in the freedom from necessity. Sex becomes more a matter of choice and is more interesting and intriguing for each partner.*

*I am experiencing the best sex ever. I can attribute it to the mutual love that I have with my partner. We have sex almost daily.*

If your grandparents are available and agreeable, why not get their perspectives on sex in old age? They may be happy to know that at least one person has an interest in their sex lives.

# Summary

- Young adults typically spend a few years "hooking up" and/or dating before they enter their first live-in relationships, but the average number of sex partners during this period is quite low. Sexual desires have to compete with other interests, such as the pursuit of education or career advancement.

- For many adults, the first live-in relationship is a nonmarital cohabitation. Cohabitation may serve simply as a convenient alternative to dating, or it may represent a committed relationship without the legal trappings of marriage. Cohabitation does not harm a subsequent marriage.

- Marriage has had many different functions and forms. Many past and present human societies have allowed polygamy. In the United States, polyamory, Mormon polygamy, and same-sex marriage exemplify non-standard marital arrangements.

- Western society is moving from a traditional, one-size-fits-all institution of marriage to a greater variety of live-in sexual relationships. Because women have fewer pregnancies than in the past and are more likely to be in the labor market, distinct gender roles in marriage have diminished. People are marrying later and divorcing more readily; marriage may soon become a minority status for American adults. Nevertheless, most people desire to be in some kind of monogamous, long-term relationship.

- Married men and women tend to have less sex than those who are dating or cohabiting, and they are less adventurous sexually, but their physical and emotional satisfaction with their sex lives is high. For women, simply being married makes sex more satisfying. However, marital satisfaction tends to decline over time.

- One in three marriages breaks up within 10 years. The likelihood of breakup is increased by a number of factors, such as early (teen) marriage, dissimilarity between husband and wife, and low educational level. A college education is associated with marital stability.

- Divorced people experience a variety of physical and psychological ill effects, but many divorced men and women remarry.

- Menopause—the final cessation of menstrual cycles—is the culmination of a gradual transition to infertility in women. The hormonal changes of menopause can impair the physiological processes of sexual arousal and may be accompanied by a decline in sexual interest and activity.

- Hormone therapy can alleviate menopausal symptoms. Postmenopausal women over 60 are discouraged from using hormone therapy, because of cardiac and other risks.

- Men experience a gradual decline in fertility, physiological arousal, and sexual interest, rather than a rapid transition to infertility. A few men father children in old age.

- Many people continue to experience sexual desire into old age. The physical expression of this desire may be compromised by declining physiological responsiveness (for example, erectile disorder or loss of vaginal lubrication), by a variety of medical conditions and drugs, or by the lack of a partner. Nevertheless, many older women and men continue to engage in sexual behavior, including masturbation, coitus, and noncoital contacts.

---

The **Discovering Human Sexuality** digital resources include activities, animations, flashcards, web links, chapter outlines and summaries, and other study tools.

∎ ∎ ∎ ∎ ∎ ∎ ∎ ∎ ∎ ∎ ∎ ∎ ∎ ∎ ∎ ∎ ∎ ∎

Learn more with this chapter's digital tools, including the **Oxford Insight Study Guide**, at **oup.com/he/levay5e**.

## Discussion Questions

1. Describe your ideal marriage partner or cohabiting partner and his or her characteristics (e.g., appearance, personality, and occupation). What circumstances or conflicts (if any) do you think would lead you to consider a separation or divorce (e.g., infidelity, refusal to have children, disease, or cross-dressing)?

2. Why do you think the divorce rate for college graduates is so much lower than it is for people without college degrees?

3. Identify the myths and what you "have heard" about menopause. Contrast these descriptions with the facts. What behaviors are characteristic of menopause? Do men have a "change of life"?

4. Describe the advice you would give to your mother or an older female friend who asks you to explain the pros and cons of menopausal hormone therapy. Do you think the fact that menopause is a natural part of the aging process should discourage women from attempting to counteract its effects with hormone treatment?

5. Think about your grandparents or people who are older than 60. What are your beliefs and thoughts about sex among older people? What do you think are the barriers to enjoying a happy sex life after 60?

## Web Resources

DivorceNet  **www.divorcenet.com**

North American Menopause Society  **www.menopause.org**

Parents Without Partners  **www.parentswithoutpartners.org**

Study of Women's Health Across the Nation  **www.swanstudy.org**

Unmarried Equality  **www.unmarried.org**

## Recommended Reading

Bogle, K. A. (2008). *Hooking up: Sex, dating, and relationships on campus.* NYU Press.

Cherlin, A. J. (2010). *The marriage-go-round: The state of marriage and the family in America today.* Vintage.

Easton, D. & Hardy, J. W. (2009). *The ethical slut: A practical guide to polyamory, open relationships and other adventures* (2nd ed.). Celestial Arts.

Finkel, E. J. (2017). *The all-or-nothing marriage: How the best marriages work.* Dutton.

Gottman, J., Schwartz Gottman, J., Abrams, D., & Carlton Abrams, R. (2018). *Eight dates: Essential conversations for a lifetime of love.* Workman Publishing.

Jenkins, C. (2017). *What love is: And what it could be.* Basic Books.

Levine, S. B. (2013). *How we love now: Women talk about intimacy after 50.* Plume.

Michaels, M. A. & Johnson, P. (2015). *Designer relationships: A guide to happy monogamy, positive polyamory, and optimistic open relationships.* Cleis Press.

North American Menopause Society. (2015). *Menopause guidebook* (8th ed.). (Can be ordered at www.menopause.org.)

Northrup, C., Schwartz, P. & Witte, J. (2014). *The normal bar: The surprising secrets of happy couples and what they reveal about creating a new normal in your relationship.* Harmony.

Sex, love, marriage, and child rearing are all options for same-sex couples.

# 12 Sexual Orientation

The direction of our sexual attractions—to the other sex, to our own sex, or to both sexes—has a profound influence on our personal and public lives and on how we are viewed and treated by others. In this chapter we first ask what sexual orientation is and how it develops. We then turn to the social aspects of sexual orientation. Here we largely neglect heterosexuality because that topic is a leading theme of most other chapters of this book. Instead, we focus on gay people—lesbians and gay men. What is causing their rapid emergence from a history of discrimination and exclusion? How do their life courses differ from those of heterosexual men and women, beginning in childhood? What subcultures exist within the larger gay community? What causes some people to fear or dislike lesbians and gay men, and how can these negative attitudes be changed?

Finally, we take a look at what might be the least understood sexual orientation: bisexuality. Bisexual men and women are the subject of considerable scientific and social controversy. Does bisexuality even exist—or are we all bisexual? And by being attracted to both women and men, do bisexual people enjoy the best of all possible worlds— or the worst?

# 12.1 There Is a Spectrum of Sexual Orientations

### LEARNING OBJECTIVE

After reading this section you should be able to:

**12.1.1** Describe the differences between the distributions of male and female sexual orientations.

**sexual orientation** The direction of a person's sexual feelings: sexual attraction toward persons of the other sex (heterosexual), the same sex (homosexual), or both sexes (bisexual).

**heterosexuality** Sexual attraction only (or predominantly) to persons of the other sex.

**homosexuality** Sexual attraction only (or predominantly) to persons of one's own sex.

**bisexuality** Sexual attraction to persons of both sexes.

**straight** Colloquial term meaning "heterosexual."

**gay** Colloquial but now-standard term meaning "homosexual," applicable to men or women.

**bi** Colloquial term meaning "bisexual."

**lesbian** Homosexual, applicable to women only.

**Kinsey scale** A 7-point scale of sexual orientation devised by Alfred Kinsey.

**Sexual orientation** is the dimension of personality that describes the balance of our sexual attraction to the two sexes. At either end of this continuum are **heterosexuality** (attraction only to persons of the other sex) and **homosexuality** (attraction only to persons of one's own sex). Between these two endpoints lie degrees of **bisexuality**—sexual attraction to both sexes. The colloquial terms **straight** and **gay** have come to replace the more clinical-sounding words "heterosexual" and "homosexual" in most contexts, and bisexual people may simply call themselves **bi**. The term "gay," as we and many others use it, can apply to either homosexual men or homosexual women. An alternative term that applies only to homosexual women is **lesbian**. This term comes from the Greek island of Lesbos, home of the ancient poetess Sappho, who wrote passionate love poems to other women.

In his pioneering studies, Alfred Kinsey developed a 7-point scale of sexual orientation that ranged from group 0 (exclusively attracted to the other sex) to group 6 (exclusively attracted to the same sex), with the intervening groups defining various degrees of bisexuality. Although well known to the public, the **Kinsey scale** is less widely used by researchers today than it was in the past, chiefly because it suggests finer gradations of sexual orientation than are usually supported by scientific studies. Instead, modern researchers often use a 5-point scale (**FIGURE 12.1**).

In terms of numbers, the distribution of sexual orientations is strongly biased toward the heterosexual end of the continuum. In most random-sample surveys, at least 80% to 90% of American men and women say that they are attracted sexually only to persons of the other sex, and another several percent say that they are attracted "mostly" to the other sex. At the other end of the spectrum, only about 1% of men and women say that they are attracted exclusively to persons of the same sex as themselves. If we include in the definition of gay people those who say they are attracted "mostly" to the same sex, their numbers sometimes rise to about 2% to 3% of the population (CDC, 2017d).

These surveys likely underestimate the numbers of gay and bisexual people, because some respondents may be reluctant to admit to same-sex attraction. By analyzing internet usage, data scientist Seth Stephens-Davidowitz estimated that the true percentage of gay Americans is about 5% (Stephens-Davidowitz, 2017). Curiously, Americans consistently estimate the size of the gay community to be about 24% of the population, which is far beyond any plausible value (Gallup, 2019b). It may

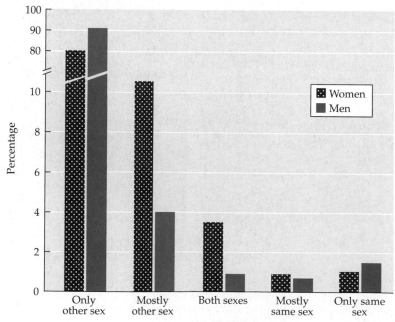

◀ **FIGURE 12.1 Distribution of sexual orientations** This bar graph shows the direction of sexual attraction for U.S. men and women age 18 to 44, based on data from the National Survey of Family Growth. Note the break in the y-axis and the change of scaling to allow for clearer representation of the non-heterosexual groups. (Data from CDC. 2017. *Key statistics from the National Survey of Family Growth - S Listing.* Centers for Disease Control and Prevention, National Center for Health Statistics: Washington, D.C.)

be that this inflated estimate is a consequence of the media attention that has been paid to gay people in recent years.

More men than women are exclusively homosexual, whereas more women than men are about equally attracted to both sexes. This is true regardless of whether people are asked about their attractions or how they identify themselves. Furthermore, when sexual orientation is assessed by measuring the genital arousal (penile erection or vaginal vasocongestion) of study participants while they are viewing erotic images or videos of females or males, the sex difference in sexual orientation is even more pronounced: The great majority of men are aroused much more strongly by one sex than the other, whereas many or most women show arousal to both sexes (Chivers, 2017).

In an online survey that encompassed men and women in 28 countries, roughly the same percentages of respondents in every country (3 to 10 percent) stated that they were predominantly attracted to people of their own sex (Rahman et al., 2020). The percentages were not correlated with social factors such as the stage of economic development or the degree of gender equality in each country.

There are many other aspects of sexual attraction that might logically be included within the term "sexual orientation," such as the preferred age or race of one's sex partners. Traditionally, however, the term refers only to the balance of same-sex versus other-sex attraction, and that is how we use the term here. Other aspects of sexual attraction are dealt with elsewhere in this book.

Lesbian, gay, and bisexual people are often linked with transgender people under the umbrella term "LGBT" or with an even wider range of identities such as LGBTQQIAP—sometimes shortened to LGBT*—which stands for lesbian, gay, bisexual, trans, queer, questioning, intersex, asexual, and pansexual. Trans people certainly have some overlap and shared concerns with people who are gay, lesbian, or bisexual, as we discuss in this chapter and elsewhere in the textbook. But gender identity is distinct from sexual orientation: Knowing that someone is transgender does not tell us whether they are sexually attracted to males or females or to both sexes. That is why we cover gender identity and transgender people in Chapter 4 rather than here.

**gender-variant**   Atypical in gender characteristics.

## 12.2 Sexual Orientation Is Not an Isolated Trait

### LEARNING OBJECTIVE

After reading this section you should be able to:

12.2.1   **Explain how the relationship between childhood gender characteristics and adult sexual orientation has been verified.**

Lesbians and gay men have often been thought of as having many characteristics of the other sex. Words such as "effeminate" or "queeny" have been applied to gay men, and "mannish" or "butch" to lesbians, usually with derogatory implications. These are stereotypes—false or overgeneralized beliefs about classes of people.

Some gay people themselves, however, have promoted the idea that they are **gender-variant** (**FIGURE 12.2**). Others have rejected this notion, asserting that they differ from straight people only in "who we love."

You probably know at least one or two gay people. If you are gay yourself, you may have scores of gay friends and acquaintances. Either way, you can hardly have failed to notice that lesbians and gay men are a very mixed bunch. Some are entirely conventional in

© Fox Photos/Stringer/Getty Images

▲ **FIGURE 12.2   Novelist Radclyffe Hall (1880–1943)** (standing, with her partner Una Troubridge) portrayed lesbians, including herself, as resembling men.

their gender characteristics, some are a trifle nonconformist, and some are flagrant gender rebels. Straight people are not always so "straight acting," either. But are there gender-related differences between gay and straight people considered as entire groups?

Psychologists have studied this issue by examining gender-related traits in large numbers of gay and straight people. They find that gay people—*on average*—do differ, in a number of gender-related traits, from straight people of the same sex (LeVay, 2017). In fact, these differences are apparent well before people become aware of the direction of their own sexual attractions. During childhood, boys who later become gay men tend to be less focused on typical boys' toys and boys' activities, to be judged by others as unmasculine or girlish, and to have less stereotypically male career plans. For girls who later become lesbians, the opposite is true: Such girls tend to prefer boys' toys and activities, to be judged by others as unfeminine or boyish, and to have male-typical career plans.

These conclusions are based on prospective studies of gender-conformist and gender-nonconformist children (Xu et al., 2019) (**BOX 12.1**) and on the recollections of gay and straight adults. In one particularly convincing study, raters watched childhood video clips provided by gay and straight adults (without knowing which was which); they rated the "pre-gay"* children as far more gender-nonconformist than the "pre-straight" children (Rieger et al., 2008). It is not possible to predict with certainty the future sexual orientation of even extremely gender-nonconformist children, but many or most of them—feminine boys especially—do become gay adults.

This relationship between childhood gender nonconformity and adult homosexuality has been reported in both Western and non-Western cultures. For example, a group based at Lethbridge University in Canada found a strong relationship of this kind among the Istmo-Zapotec–speaking people, a pre-Columbian culture in the Mexican state of Oaxaca (Gomez Jimenez et al., 2020).

In adulthood, gay and bisexual men describe themselves as less masculine—*on average*—than do straight men, and lesbians and bisexual women describe themselves as less feminine, on average, than do straight women. Gays and lesbians are also shifted toward the other sex in their choice of occupations and recreational interests (Lippa, 2020). All these differences hold up across several different regions of the world, including non-Western cultures (Lippa, 2008; Ueno et al., 2013; Semenyna & Vasey, 2016).

Gay men are—*on average*—gender-atypical in some of the sex-differentiated cognitive traits that we discussed in Chapter 4 (LeVay, 2017; Xu et al., 2017). They are less aggressive than straight men; perform less well on some tasks at which men typically excel, such as targeting accuracy and mental rotation; and perform better on some tasks at which females typically excel, such as verbal fluency, object-location memory, and face recognition. Lesbians on average also score in a gender-atypical fashion in some tests—doing better than heterosexual women in mental rotation and worse in object-location memory, for example.

To some extent, it is possible to identify a person's sexual orientation on the basis of unconscious behaviors such as body motions and voice quality (Rule, 2017). This ability is referred to colloquially as **gaydar**. The cues that gaydar relies on are gender-atypical behaviors, for the most part.

In short, there is a partial correlation between sexual orientation and other aspects of gender, and any theory of sexual orientation needs to explain the existence of this correlation. Gays and lesbians are certainly not transgender, but

**gaydar**  The ability to recognize gay people on the basis of unconscious behaviors, voice quality, gait, and so on.

---

*We use the term "pre-gay" in reference to children who later become gay adults, regardless of their childhood identity or characteristics.

they are distinctly atypical, on average, in some gender-related traits. These differences between gay and straight people are generally more consistent for men than for women.

---

## BOX 12.1
## Boys Will Be Girls

There has long been "folk wisdom" to the effect that feminine boys have a high chance of becoming gay when they grow up. In the late 1960s, psychiatrist Richard Green of UCLA initiated an ambitious prospective study to test the truth of this notion (Green, 1987). He recruited 66 families in which there was a son (age 4 to 10) who was markedly feminine. These were not just slightly unmasculine boys. Here's an excerpt from one interview Green had with a five-year-old boy, "Richard," whose parents brought him to Green because of his persistent cross-dressing, role-playing as a girl, and avoidance of male playmates:

> Green: Have you ever wished you'd been born a girl?
>
> Richard: Yes.
>
> Green: Why did you wish that?
>
> Richard: Girls, they don't have to have a penis.
>
> Green: They don't have to have a penis?
>
> Richard: They can have babies. And—because they— it doesn't tickle when you tickle them here.
>
> Green: It doesn't tickle when you tickle them here? Where your penis is?
>
> Richard: Yeah. 'Cause they don't have a penis. I wish I was a girl.
>
> Green: You wish you were a girl?
>
> Richard: You know what? I might be a girl.

Green also recruited 56 boys as matched controls; these boys were chosen without regard to their gender characteristics. He interviewed the boys and their parents repeatedly during the boys' childhood, adolescence, and (in many cases) young adulthood.

The central finding of the study could hardly be more striking. The control boys became, with one slight exception, totally heterosexual (see figure, which includes data only for the boys who could be followed into adolescence or adulthood). Of the feminine boys, the majority became gay or bisexual. Although many of the feminine boys wished they were girls, most of them actually became fairly conventional gay men who were no more obviously feminine than gay men in general, and only one expressed an interest in sex-reassignment surgery.

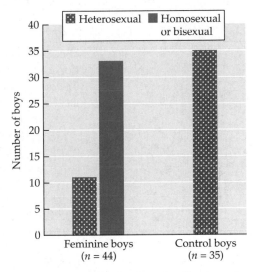

(After R. Green. 1987. *The "Sissy-Boy Syndrome" and the Development of Homosexuality*. Yale University Press: New Haven, CT.)

In spite of the marked difference in outcomes for the two groups, we should make a couple of cautionary points. First, some of the feminine boys were entirely heterosexual at their last interview. In fact, "Richard" was one of these. It's possible that some of these "heterosexual" youths would have come out as gay or bisexual if they had been followed over a longer period. However, childhood characteristics are not entirely predictive of adult orientation, even for these extreme gender-nonconformist children. Second, most gay men do not have a history of such radical gender nonconformity during their childhood; in fact, some recall a very conventionally masculine childhood.

Richard Green's 20-year study is now considered a classic in the field of sexology; its findings have been confirmed in a variety of ways by later research. Green was a heterosexual man, but he dedicated a great deal of his life to understanding and supporting gay and trans people. In the 1970s he was active in the movement to declassify homosexuality as a mental illness. He also had a law degree, which he used to argue for gay and transgender rights in court cases and the political arena. Green died in 2019.

## 12.3 Diverse Theories Attempt to Explain Sexual Orientation

**LEARNING OBJECTIVES**

After reading this section you should be able to:

12.3.1 Compare psychodynamic, social, and biological theories of sexual orientation.

12.3.2 Evaluate the evidence that prenatal sex hormones influence sexual orientation.

12.3.3 Evaluate the evidence that genes influence sexual orientation.

What causes a person to become heterosexual, bisexual, or homosexual? This question has aroused a great deal of interest and controversy over the years. In popular discourse, the question has often been phrased in such forms as "What makes people gay?"—as if heterosexuality didn't require any explanation. In reality, of course, heterosexuality, homosexuality, and bisexuality all need some kind of explanation.

Most theories of sexual orientation could be described as either psychological or biological. Psychological theories attempt to explain the development of a person's sexual orientation in terms of internal mental processes, especially as they are affected by interaction with others, rewards and punishments, and so on. Examples include psychoanalytic and socialization theories. Biological theories, in contrast, attempt to explain sexual orientation in terms of phenomena such as brain circuitry, hormones, genes, and evolution.

### Freud proposed psychodynamic models

Throughout most of the 20th century, the thinking about sexual orientation centered on the psychoanalytic theories of Sigmund Freud. Freud saw heterosexuality as the "normal" culmination of a complex, multistage process of psychosexual development (Freud, 1905/1975). This process, he believed, included a homosexual phase in early childhood that is later forgotten. The "normal" developmental process could be disrupted by abnormal relationships within the family: These could include a mother who was too "close-binding" or "seductive" toward a child, a father who was too distant or hostile, intense sibling rivalry, or penis envy—the trauma supposedly suffered by a girl when she discovered that she lacked a body part possessed by her father or brother. If these phenomena blocked "normal" development, the child might remain stuck in the early homosexual phase. Freud suggested a variety of other mechanisms by which a person might become homosexual. None of them have been substantiated by scientific research.

### Sexual orientation has been attributed to socialization

One potentially very powerful form of socialization consists of sexual interactions. In this vein, it has often been suggested that both male and female homosexuality result from consensual same-sex experiences in boarding schools, from molestation during childhood, from rape during young adulthood, or from other early sexual experiences. Again, though, the evidence does not support such ideas. People who attend single-sex boarding schools do have more same-sex sexual experiences during that time than people who don't attend such schools, but they are no more likely to be gay in adulthood (Wellings et al., 1994). In some studies gay adults are more likely than straight adults to report having experienced sexual abuse during their childhood, but this doesn't mean that the abuse caused the homosexuality. Rather, the direction of causation appears to be the other way around: Gender nonconformity in childhood, which is common in children who become gay (see above), raises the risk that a child will experience sexual abuse (Xu & Zheng, 2017). Regardless of this issue, many or most gay people become aware of same-sex attraction before their first sexual experience of any kind.

Socialization effects could, of course, be much more subtle than those just described and could include important cognitive aspects. For instance, women's sexual feelings are more strongly modulated by considerations of love and intimacy than are those of men, and they may for that reason be more responsive to life events and sexual scripts (see Chapter 1), which might give their sexual orientation greater fluidity than that of men (Diamond et al., 2017).

Many desires and behaviors, including sexual ones, are "contagious," meaning that they spread in friendship networks. This is especially true during adolescence, when young people shift their allegiance from family to peer groups. To see if this was true for same-sex attraction, an international group of psychologists, sociologists, and public health specialists examined data from the U.S. National Longitudinal Study of Adolescent Health (Brakefield et al., 2014). In this study nearly 15,000 adolescents were asked about their sexual feelings, desires, and behaviors, and they were also asked to identify their friends. As expected, the researchers found that many phenomena, such as becoming sexually active and desiring to enter into a romantic relationship, were strongly influenced by a teen's friendship networks, but neither identifying as gay/lesbian nor desiring to enter a same-sex romantic relationship showed any influence of this kind. On the basis of this and other studies, it appears that social factors have little if any influence on sexual orientation, at least during the teen years.

Although the influence of socialization on sexual orientation is ambiguous at best, socialization does strongly influence how gay people think of themselves and how they live their lives: Some learn to feel guilty about their sexuality and have to fight those feelings in adulthood, while others grow up in supportive families and peer groups, with the result that they feel comfortable in their own (gay) skins.

### Biological theories focus on prenatal hormones and genes

The leading biological theory of sexual orientation proposes that sexual orientation, like other aspects of gender, reflects the sexual differentiation of the brain under the influence of prenatal sex hormones. In the simplest version of this theory (**FIGURE 12.3**), everything depends on androgen levels during a sensitive period of prenatal development. Fetuses whose brains are exposed to high levels of androgens during this period (mostly males, but a few females) will be sexually attracted to women (**gynephilic**) in adult life; conversely, fetuses whose brains are exposed to low levels of androgens (mostly females, but some males) will be sexually attracted to men (**androphilic**) in adult life. Alternatively, it might be not the hormone levels themselves but the brain's sensitivity to hormones that differs between "pre-gay" and "pre-straight" fetuses.

The prenatal hormone hypothesis could explain why gay people are, on average, gender-atypical in a variety of traits besides their sexual orientation, as described above. We would just need to suppose that differences in androgen levels during development affect the differentiation not only of brain circuits that are responsible for sexual orientation, but also of brain circuits that mediate some other gendered traits, such as targeting accuracy or verbal fluency.

The prenatal hormone theory has a solid basis in animal research: The preference of animals such as rats for male or female sex partners can be modified by

**gynephilic**   Sexually attracted to women.

**androphilic**   Sexually attracted to men.

---

**FAQ:** Why don't gay people fall in love with themselves?

A developmental mechanism ensures that people don't fall in love with persons they grew up with, such as siblings. Presumably this same effect rules out oneself as a target of romantic love.

---

▶ **FIGURE 12.3   The prenatal hormone theory of sexual orientation**  In its simplest form, this theory proposes that adult sexual orientation depends on the level of androgens to which the brain is exposed during a sensitive period of fetal development. Most males and a few females exceed some threshold of androgen exposure and therefore become attracted to females (gynephilic). Most females and a few males fall below that threshold level and therefore become attracted to males (androphilic). In the figure, the threshold has been arbitrarily set at a value that would produce more homosexual males than females, corresponding to what has been observed in most studies.

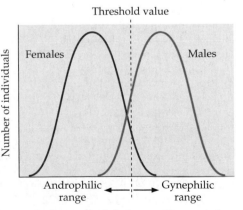

**medial preoptic area** A region of the hypothalamus involved in the regulation of sexual behaviors typically shown by males.

**INAH3** Third interstitial nucleus of the anterior hypothalamus—a neuronal cell group in the hypothalamus that differs in size between men and women and between gay and straight men.

experimental manipulation of their androgen levels during development (Alexander et al., 2011). Of course, it is not ethically possible to do comparable experiments in humans. As we mentioned in Chapter 4, however, the condition of congenital adrenal hyperplasia (CAH), in which human fetuses are exposed to high levels of androgens regardless of their sex, offers an equivalent "experiment of nature." Consistent with the prenatal hormone theory, women with CAH are more likely to experience same-sex attraction and engage in same-sex relationships than are control groups of women such as their unaffected sisters (Meyer-Bahlburg et al., 2008; Gondim et al., 2018). This suggests that the findings of the animal studies are relevant to humans too.

Of course, CAH is a rare medical condition. Do the findings in CAH-affected persons say anything about people who don't have such a condition? To study this question, researchers have looked for biological markers related to sexual orientation in the general population. Neuroscientist Simon LeVay (one of the authors of this textbook) focused on the hypothalamus. We mentioned this brain region in Chapter 2 and Chapter 3 on account of its participation in the regulation of sex hormone levels and the menstrual cycle. From studies in animals, it appears that a region at the front of the hypothalamus known as the **medial preoptic area** is involved in the regulation of sexual behaviors typically shown by males, including the preference for female partners (**FIGURE 12.4**). Within the medial preoptic area is a cell group that is typically larger in males than in females. In humans it has the name **INAH3**. Again, based on animal experiments, it appears that this sex difference results from differences in circulating sex hormone levels during the prenatal period when this region of the brain is developing. LeVay measured the volume of INAH3 in autopsied brains of gay and straight men. He reported that the volume was significantly smaller in the gay men than in the straight men and that the volume in the gay men was not significantly different from the volume found in women (LeVay, 1991). A replication study found a difference of the same kind, though smaller in degree (Byne et al., 2001). A research group at Oregon Health and Science University made similar findings in

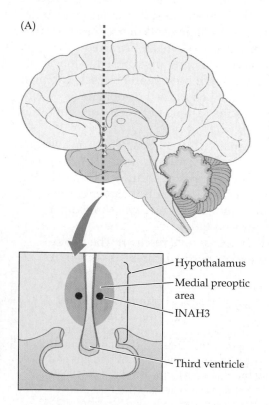

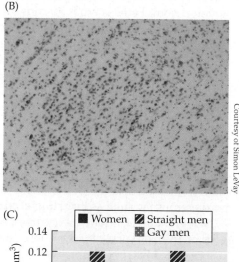

*Courtesy of Simon LeVay*

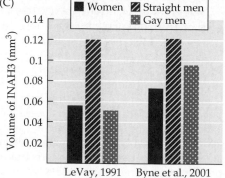

▶ **FIGURE 12.4**

**The hypothalamus and male sexual orientation** (A) A cell group known as INAH3 lies within the medial preoptic area of the hypothalamus, a region concerned with male-typical sexual behavior. (B) Microscopic view of INAH3 in a man; INAH3 is the oval-shaped cluster of darkly stained cells occupying most of the center of the image—it measures about 0.5 mm across. (C) Two autopsy studies found that INAH3 is smaller in women and gay men than in straight men, but they did not agree on the magnitude of the difference. (Data from S. LeVay. 1991. *Science* 253: 1034–1037 and W. Byne et al. 2001. *Horm Behav* 40: 86–92.)

the brains of domestic sheep—a species in which about 8% of males are naturally homosexual (Roselli & Stormshak, 2009). And a Dutch group found that INAH3 in male-to-female transexual individuals is similar in size to INAH3 in heterosexual women and smaller than in heterosexual men (Garcia-Falgueras & Swaab, 2008).

A variety of other biological differences between gay and straight people have been reported (LeVay, 2017). These include differences in the relative size of the left and right cerebral hemispheres, in the function of the inner ear, in eye-blink reflexes, and in anatomical features such as the relative lengths of the fingers and the ratio of arm length to height. Regarding finger length ratios, we mentioned in Chapter 4 that the ratio of the length of the index finger to that of the ring finger, the 2D:4D ratio, is lower in men than in women, but is also correlated with some gendered characteristics within one sex. Biopsychologist Marc Breedlove and colleagues at Michigan State University have reported that the finger length ratios of lesbians are shifted to lower values—that is, toward male-typical ratios—as compared to heterosexual women (Williams et al., 2000; Breedlove, 2019). Because finger length ratios are strongly influenced by sex hormone levels during early development, Breedlove's findings (which have been confirmed by other labs) point to a role for sex hormones in the development of women's sexual orientation. Studies that have compared finger length ratios in gay and straight men have not come up with consistent findings.

There also appear to be some differences between gay and straight people in their facial appearance: People can distinguish between still photos of gay and straight people's faces at above-chance levels (Rule, 2017). Two Stanford computer scientists trained a neural network that could make this distinction much more accurately than humans (Wang & Kosinski, 2018). Based on detailed analysis of the data, it appeared that the neural network based the distinction more on facial structure than on cues that could be controlled by the persons in the photos, such as facial expressions. None of these traits are "diagnostic" of an individual's sexual orientation, but differences emerge when large numbers of gay and straight people are compared. In most of these studies, including the face study just described, the traits under investigation are reported to be sex-atypical (or intermediate between the sexes) in gay men or lesbians, and such findings have been interpreted as further evidence in support of the prenatal hormone theory.

It's possible that a fetus's *genes* affect its sex hormone levels or the sensitivity of its developing brain to these hormones. Family and twin studies indicate that genes do indeed have a significant influence on sexual orientation. Finding one gay person in a family increases the likelihood of finding others, as if genes running in certain families increase the likelihood of family members being gay. Monozygotic, or "identical," twins—who share the same genes—are much more likely to share the same sexual orientation than are nonidentical twins, who do not (**FIGURE 12.5**) (Långström et al., 2010). Genetic factors account for somewhere between one-third and one-half of the total causation of men's sexual orientation, according to these studies. Genes have a weaker but still significant influence on women's sexual orientation.

Using DNA analysis, molecular geneticists have attempted to locate or identify the genes that influence sexual orientation (Hu et al., 1995; Sanders et al., 2015). In the most recent study, a team led by Andrea Ganna of the Massachusetts Institute of Technology and Harvard University examined the genomes of nearly half a million women and men who had been asked whether they had ever had sex with someone of the same sex* (Ganna et al., 2019). Those who said yes were significantly more likely to carry one or

---

*This question about a behavior that may have occurred on only one occasion is not an ideal way to assess a person's sexual orientation. It seems likely, though, that the small numbers of people who answered yes (3% to 4% of the total) consisted in large part of gay or bisexual people, whereas the great majority of the remainder were probably not gay.

▲ **FIGURE 12.5   Gay identical twins**
Joshua and Jacob Miller of the pop duo Nemesis.

more of five genetic variants, which were located on five different chromosomes. Some of these variants appeared to involve genes concerned with the regulation of sex hormones or olfaction. It seems, however, that the genetic influence on sexual orientation is distributed over a considerable number of genes, each of which contributes only a small effect. There does not appear to be a single "gay gene" that acts like a powerful on/off switch to control the preference for same- or other-sex partners. This "polygenic" pattern of inheritance has been seen for many other mental traits. Identifying some of the genes involved in the development of sexual orientation might help us understand in evolutionary terms why homosexuality exists (**BOX 12.2**).

Boys who have older brothers are more likely to grow up gay than boys who don't (Blanchard, 2017). Adoption studies indicate that this birth order effect is not

---

## BOX 12.2
## Why Gay Genes?

The idea that genes cause people to be sexually attracted to their own sex is puzzling. How could such genes survive in the population if they cause their owners to engage in non-reproductive sex? Many gay people are in fact parents (as discussed in a later section), but they do have fewer children, on average, than their heterosexual peers, so this question is a significant one. Gay genes should die out, but they don't, to judge by the apparent persistence of homosexual behavior since ancient times (see figure).

Researchers have put forward a number of ideas to explain this paradox. Most of these ideas relate to gay genes in men, because the genetic influence on sexual orientation is stronger in men than in women.

Most theories involve the supposition that not everyone who possesses a gay gene is actually gay. Let's say, for example, that a man is gay because he has inherited genes causing him to be sexually attracted to males. This man's female relatives, such as his sisters, have a good chance of inheriting the same genes, because of their genetic relatedness to him. But in these female relatives these genes might also increase their attraction to males, making them "hyperheterosexual," as it were, and causing them to engage in more heterosexual sex and have more children. In this way the man's gay genes could be transmitted to the next generation, albeit not via the gay man's own offspring. This theory has some empirical support, because the female relatives of gay men do in fact have significantly more children than other women, according to several studies (Camperio Ciani et al., 2015).

Another idea is that gay males increase their sisters' reproductive success by their behavior: Not being parents themselves, they might be able to devote resources to their sisters, enabling them to have more children and helping those children survive and reproduce in their turn. Here again, then, the man's gay genes are perpetuated via his female

© dbimages/Alamy Stock Photo

Khnumhotep and Niankhkhnum were confidants of a pharaoh who ruled Egypt about 4500 years ago. Because of the intimacy evident in their portraits, and because they were buried in the same tomb, they are thought to have been a same-sex couple—the earliest in history whose names are known today. Both men had wives and children.

relatives, but not because of any direct effect of the genes on those relatives. Evidence concerning this idea is mixed. In Western countries such as the United States and United Kingdom, gay men do not seem to devote more resources to their female relatives than straight men do. Among the native inhabitants of American Samoa, on the other hand, *fa'afafine* (biological males who assume a "third-gender" role and who are sexually attracted to conventional men—see Chapter 4) do provide substantial support to the children of their female relatives, according to studies by researchers at the University of Lethbridge in Canada, and this support could help explain why some female relatives of *fa'afafine* have higher-than-usual numbers of children (VanderLaan et al., 2017).

These are only two out of several ideas that have been proposed to explain the persistence of gay genes (LeVay, 2017; Jeffery et al., 2019). If and when specific gay genes are identified and their mode of action is understood, it will become easier to select the most plausible theories.

caused by the social experience of living with an older brother. Rather, it appears to operate through some biological mechanism whose nature is still being investigated (Bogaert et al., 2018).

## 12.4 The Gay Community Has Struggled for Equal Rights

**LEARNING OBJECTIVES**

After reading this section you should be able to:

**12.4.1** Identify significant landmarks in the history of the gay rights movement in the United States.

**12.4.2** Compare the ways gay people are treated in the United States and some other countries.

As with some other minorities, gay people's identity has been powerfully molded by a history of oppression and by the struggle to overcome that oppression (Faderman, 2016). Thus, to understand the gay community today, it is necessary to have some knowledge of its political history, a history that began in Europe rather than in the United States.

### The gay rights movement began in Germany

The world's first gay rights organization, the Scientific-Humanitarian Committee, was founded in Berlin in 1897. The main figure behind this group was Magnus Hirschfeld (see Box 1.3), a gay Jewish doctor and sexologist who developed a biological theory of sexual orientation and gender. For 30 years Hirschfeld led the struggle to have the German sodomy statutes overthrown, but his efforts were ultimately unsuccessful. During the Nazi period several thousand German gay men, and a much smaller number of lesbians, were sent to concentration camps, where most of them died.

The first enduring American gay rights organization, the Mattachine Society, was founded in Los Angeles in 1950, and the first lesbian organization was founded in San Francisco five years later. These organizations functioned largely as support groups for gays and lesbians, who were generally reviled at that time. In the mid-1960s, more politically active gay organizations sprang up on the East Coast and began a series of actions, such as picketing the White House to protest the firing of gay federal employees (**FIGURE 12.6**).

Early on the morning of June 28, 1969, a riot erupted outside the Stonewall Inn, a bar in New York's Greenwich Village that catered to gay men, transvestites, and trans women. The rioters were protesting against a police raid—something that gay bars endured frequently in those days. Street demonstrations continued for several nights. These demonstrations were followed by the formation of more-confrontational gay rights organizations. The Stonewall Riots are often viewed as the starting point of the modern gay rights movement.

It may be difficult for you to imagine what life was like for gay people at the time of the Stonewall Riots. Homosexuality was officially listed by the American Psychiatric Association as a mental disorder. Sex between men or between women was illegal in most states, and most Americans thought that gay sex was morally wrong. Gay people had no legal protection from discrimination and were often dismissed from public or private employment on the basis of their sexual orientation. Not a single openly gay person had ever been elected to public office, and there were few if any gay role models

▲ **FIGURE 12.6** **Early gay activists** picket the White House in 1965.

**come out of the closet (or come out)** Reveal a previously concealed identity, such as being gay.

in most occupations. Yet many gay people thrived "under the radar," and new gay organizations, such as the Metropolitan Community Church (founded in 1968), gave gays and lesbians opportunities to socialize beyond the bar scene.

The 1970s were a period of rapid change. The first gay rights marches took place in 1970. In 1971, the National Organization for Women (NOW) officially acknowledged the role of lesbians in that organization. In 1973, homosexuality was deleted from the *Diagnostic and Statistical Manual of Mental Disorders* (*DSM*), the American Psychiatric Association's handbook. In 1974, the first openly gay person won elected office (Massachusetts State Representative Elaine Noble), and others followed (**BOX 12.3**).

During the 1970s, urban gay districts such as San Francisco's Castro Street drew thousands of young gay men from around the country and became the centers of their sexual, social, and political lives. Homosexuality became a topic of considerable public interest, and while many people continued to despise gays and lesbians, others became sympathetic. By 1977, about 40 cities had enacted some kind of anti-discrimination ordinance.

The AIDS epidemic began around 1980, and by the end of the decade the disease had taken the lives of more than 65,000 Americans, the majority of whom were gay or bisexual men (CDC, 1989). The initial public and political response to AIDS was to ignore it or dismiss it as a "gay disease" (Shilts, 1987). In reaction, countless

## BOX 12.3
## Gay Martyrs

Harvey Milk was a city supervisor of San Francisco. In 1977 Milk was the first openly gay man to be elected to city government in the United States (**FIGURE A**). During his short tenure as supervisor (1977–1978), Milk helped lead the successful campaign to reject California Proposition 6, which would have forced the state to fire openly gay teachers. He was also instrumental in passing San Francisco's first gay rights ordinance.

On November 27, 1978, shortly after Proposition 6 was rejected, Milk and San Francisco Mayor George Moscone were shot dead in their city hall offices by Dan White, an anti-gay city supervisor. White was convicted of the double murder, but he received an extraordinarily light sentence—fewer than eight years in prison. After his release he committed suicide. Milk's life has been commemorated in a biography (Shilts, 1982), plays, music, and the 2008 feature film *Milk* starring Sean Penn.

David Kato was a Ugandan gay rights activist and the co-founder of Sexual Minorities Uganda (**FIGURE B**). At the age of 38 he came out as gay—he may have been the first person in Uganda to do so. In October 2010 a Ugandan tabloid newspaper published photographs of Kato and other gay Ugandans under the banner "Kill Them." Three months later Kato was beaten to death by a man wielding a hammer. The assailant was convicted of the murder and was sentenced to 30 years' imprisonment. His motives have not been clarified. "David showed tremendous courage in speaking out against hate," stated then President Barack Obama. "He was a powerful advocate for fairness and freedom" (White House, 2011).

(A)  (B)

(A) Harvey Milk (1930–1978) (right, with Mayor George Moscone). (B) David Kato (ca. 1964–2011), seen in the documentary *Call Me Kuchu*.

© Roger Ressmeyer/Corbis

© From *Call Me Kuchu*, 2012, Wright Film Company.
© AF archive/Alamy Stock Photo

thousands of gay men were motivated to involve themselves in AIDS activism and gay activism. Lesbians, who during the 1970s had been involved in feminist causes more than in specifically lesbian or gay ones, joined forces with gay men and founded co-gender organizations. Gays and lesbians **came out of the closet** in droves. Americans came to *know* gay people—not just the distant, famous ones, but also family members, neighbors, and coworkers. The percentage of Americans who said that they personally knew someone who was gay rose from 30% in 1983 to 87% in 2016 (Rubin, 2000; Pew Research Center, 2016). It seems likely that this increased familiarity with gay people has been an important factor in changing public attitudes toward them.

All in all, pro-gay attitudes have dramatically increased over the last 30 years, as revealed by opinion polls that asked the same questions in the 1990s and again more recently (**FIGURE 12.7**). There have also been important judicial and legislative decisions affecting gay people:

- In 2002, the U.S. Supreme Court ruled that state laws banning gay sex were unconstitutional.

- In 2003, the Massachusetts Supreme Court paved the way for gay marriage in that state.

- In 2011, the U.S. Armed Forces accepted openly gay and lesbian recruits into their ranks for the first time.

- In 2015, the U.S. Supreme Court ruled that state laws banning same-sex marriage were unconstitutional.

- By 2017, 22 states had enacted laws banning discrimination against gay people, and in states without such laws 87 cities had passed comparable ordinances.

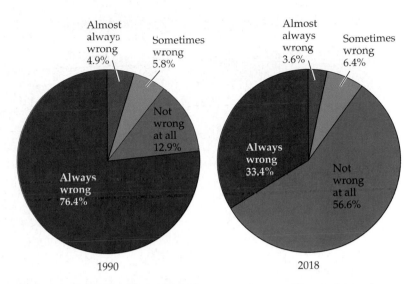

▲ **FIGURE 12.7** **Changing views on gay sex** These charts show responses of Americans in 1990 and 2018 to the question "What about sexual relations between two adults of the same sex—Is that always wrong, almost always wrong, sometimes wrong, or not wrong at all?" "Don't knows" have been excluded. (Data from T. Smith et al. *General Social Surveys*, 1972–2018. Sponsored by National Science Foundation. NORC at the University of Chicago. Data accessed from the GSS Data Explorer at gssdataexplorer.norc.org.)

## Gay rights are a global issue

Here are two shortened but otherwise unedited letters sent to AVERT, an international organization combating AIDS (AVERT, 2014):

*Hi my name is B am 19. I live in Addis Ababa, Ethiopia . . . i am gay i knew that i'm gay befor 8 years when i was in grade 5. I'm ashamed of it and even it is unthinkable to expose that I am gay. I'm always think that i am sinner and God will never give me mercy. Sometimes i think to sucide my self. I'm now university student all my dorm mates talk about girls but even i don't have an idea about girls. . . . My gay friends in z campus are dissmissed becaus of they are gay. I can't learn every time i am alone think about my sexual orientation. As ethiopian orthodox church is dominant homosexuality is so punishable abtu 26 yrs in prison that is why am afraid. What can i do?*

*Hi my name is Jane and I'm an ordinary South African girl. I've recently admitted to myself that I'm a lesbian but it wasn't easy doing so. . . . I feel as though I've made more friends since I've come out and I'm really coming out of my shell at an alarming rate. . . . It helps that I've got a few friends who are also bisexual/lesbian. I've also learnt that love just happens and you start to have a great life once you begin to remain true to yourself.*

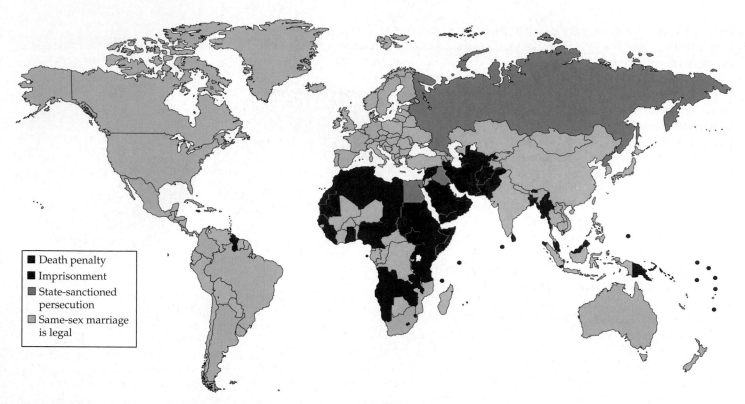

▲ **FIGURE 12.8** **Your gay vacation planner** This map shows countries that permit same-sex marriage (green) and those with statutes punishing gay sex with the death penalty (black) or imprisonment (brown). Countries with state-sponsored persecution of gay people but no statutory penalties are shown in orange. (After L. R. Mendos. 2019. *State-Sponsored Homophobia 2019: Global Legislation Overview Update*. ILGA World: Geneva.; updated to May 2020.)

As these letters suggest, the status of lesbians and gay men varies greatly around the world (**FIGURE 12.8**). Some countries, especially in Western Europe, have a tradition of social tolerance that has allowed their gay citizens to sidestep some of the inequities that their American counterparts have experienced. In France, for example, sex between men has been legal since 1791, whereas it was a crime in some U.S. states as recently as 2002. Also, the religious right—typically a source of opposition to gay rights—is a much less significant political force in most European countries than it is in the United States. In many European countries anti-gay discrimination and gay bashing are less common than in the United States, and gay culture flourishes. Canada has also been relatively accepting of gay people, as exemplified by the fact that same-sex marriage became legal nationwide 10 years before that happened south of the border.

South America is a mixed bag in terms of how gay people are seen and treated. Argentina may be the most progressive: Gay sex has been legal there since the 19th century, and gay marriage since 2010. Three other countries allow gay marriage (Brazil, Colombia, and Uruguay). But hate crimes, police harassment, and discrimination against LGBT people are very common throughout the continent. Brazil in particular has a tragic record of homophobic and transphobic violence: In 2018, 420 LGBT Brazilians were murdered, according to the gay rights organization Grupo Gay de Bahia (Hermanson, 2019).

More than 2.5 billion people live in countries where gay sex is illegal and gay people lack legal protections. These include most countries in Africa (except South Africa) and the Middle East (except Israel), and some countries in South and Southeast Asia. Homosexual acts are punishable by the death penalty in 10 Muslim-majority countries, of which 8 actually implement the penalty (ILGA, 2019). Police harassment of gay people is common in many countries, including countries where gay sex is ostensibly legal.

LGBT Americans are not immune to harassment, discrimination, and violence in countries where the local gay population is subject to these abuses. In Egypt, for example, police have used dating apps to entrap gay foreigners. Advice for LGBT travelers is available online (Fergussen & Fergussen, 2019).

Islamic traditions are partially responsible for negative attitudes toward homosexuality: Muhammad is believed to have authorized the death penalty for sex between men. Nevertheless, Westerners have also facilitated the spread of anti-gay attitudes. In many countries, such as India, sodomy statutes were originally imposed by European colonialists. More recently, evangelical Christians from the United States have stirred up anti-gay sentiment in sub-Saharan Africa, especially in Uganda (Blake, 2014).

In 2011 the United Nations Human Rights Council passed a resolution expressing "grave concern at acts of violence and discrimination, in all regions of the world, committed against individuals because of their sexual orientation and gender identity" (Associated Press, 2011). Of the 47 nations represented on the council, 19 voted against the resolution: These included Russia, Pakistan, Saudi Arabia, Jordan, Nigeria, and Uganda. Two years later, Russia enacted a law banning "propaganda of non-traditional sexual relations," which potentially criminalized any public manifestation of gay identity or culture. The passage of the law was followed by arrests of gay activists and by a surge in anti-gay violence. The Russian Republic of Chechnya has seen especially brutal repression of gay people (United Nations, 2017). Canada, but not so far the United States, has welcomed gay Chechen refugees (Harms, 2019).

The clampdown on gay people throughout much of the world is in part a reaction against an increasing openness and activism by gays and lesbians themselves. What do you foresee as the ultimate outcomes of these conflicts?

In this section we have made the assumption that homosexuality is the same the world over. That is quite likely true at the basic level of people's sexual attractions to males and females, but sexual orientation has not been conceptualized in the same way in all regions of the world or in all periods of history. In particular, more attention has often been paid to gender characteristics than to the direction of sexual attraction: Gender-variant individuals have been recognized and named widely around the world, as we discussed in Chapter 4, but homosexual individuals, if they've been recognized at all, have usually been assigned to the gender-variant "types" mentioned in the box, like *fa'afafine* or *mahu*. Recently, though, the Western concepts of gay, lesbian, and bisexual as categories defined by sexual attraction have largely replaced the traditional concepts in many parts of the world.

## 12.5  Growing Up Gay Presents Challenges

### LEARNING OBJECTIVES
After reading this section you should be able to:

**12.5.1  Identify factors that may traumatize or support the lives of gay children.**

**12.5.2  Describe the typical stages of coming out as gay.**

It's possible that at some future time, people's sexual orientation will be of as little significance as, say, their handedness. For now, however, many gay people grow up in a hostile environment, and the experience of this hostility may strongly color their worldviews as adults.

We mentioned above that many gays and lesbians are somewhat gender-nonconformist as children. Of course, there's a lot of variation among individuals. Some pre-gay children act like miniature transexuals and cannot be cajoled or forced by any means to behave like conventional children of their own sex. Others fit easily into the conventional mold. The majority are probably somewhere in the middle—not quite conventional boys and girls but not outrageously unconventional either.

Pre-gay children's positions on this gender continuum strongly affect their growing-up process. Markedly gender-nonconformist children "out" themselves before they even enter kindergarten. Parents may already suspect—with good reason—that a child is likely to become gay, and they may do everything in their power to prevent it. A "sissy" boy may quickly become the least favorite child in the family—especially in the eyes of his father. For tomboyish girls, it's less predictable—some such girls thrive.

Initially, a gay child's experiences in school may be unremarkable, but trouble often crops up in the preadolescent years (age 8 through 13). Children form same-sex social networks at this age and rigorously enforce gender norms, so a child who is gender-nonconformist may be excluded from friendship groups and even verbally abused. This can happen even before the child becomes aware of same-sex attraction—in fact, some of these children don't become gay at all. But it's all the same to their peers. Terms of abuse such as "faggot" and "dyke" are used commonly in preadolescent and adolescent school society, and teachers do not always make serious efforts to stop this abuse.

It's not possible to provide a single image of what it's like to grow up gay. For some youths, it can be an unrelenting torment. Some are rejected by their parents or run away from home, perhaps becoming prostitutes in the nearest big city. It has been estimated that about 40% of homeless youth in the United States identify as lesbian, gay, bisexual, or transgender (Williams Institute, 2012). Gay youths are three times more likely to attempt suicide than their heterosexual peers (Marshal et al., 2011); it is gay youths exposed to childhood abuse, parental rejection, or peer victimization who account for this high rate of suicidality (Flynn et al., 2016). One tragic example: A 9-year-old Denver boy, Jamel Myles, came out as gay to his classmates, only to be greeted with abuse and demands that he kill himself. After four days of this, he did so (Moye, 2018).

For increasing numbers of today's adolescents, however, growing up gay can be relatively painless or, indeed, a very positive experience—one in which their identity as gay may take a back seat to a richer kaleidoscope of sexual and social engagement (Savin-Williams, 2016). Even some preteens are getting in on the act: In stark contrast to the fate of James Myles, one gay-identified fifth-grader, Ella Briggs of East Hampton, Connecticut, received the enthusiastic support of her peers when she was elected Kid Governor of the state.

Circumstances that have improved the lives of many gay youths include the existence of role models, the frequent discussion of gay issues on youth-oriented television shows and online sites, the presence of support organizations such as Gay-Straight Alliances in some schools (**FIGURE 12.9**), the efforts of some teachers to confront anti-gay attitudes and bullying, and the greater willingness of some parents to accept and love their gay or gender-nonconformist children. Given the continuing trend toward acceptance and respect for gay people, we may predict that growing up gay will be a more widely positive experience for the next generation of gay youth in America.

## Coming out is a lifelong process

Although there are some analogies between gay people and ethnic minorities, there is one major difference: Ethnic minority children are usually brought up by parents of that same minority, whereas most pre-gay children are brought up by straight parents. Thus, whether or not gay people are "born gay" in a *biological* sense, they are usually "born straight" in a *social* sense: They are born into a predominantly straight culture, and everyone (including probably

▲ **FIGURE 12.9**   A high school Gay-Straight Alliance group with their faculty advisor.

© Jeffrey Isaac Greenberg 8/Alamy Stock Photo

themselves) expects them to become heterosexual adults. Coming out of the closet, though it may involve a dramatic moment or two, is really a lifelong voyage away from the social expectation of heterosexuality and toward a fully integrated and healthy gay identity (Rosario et al., 2011). That individual voyage repeats, to some extent, the social and political history of gay people as a whole.

The process of coming out has several elements. The first is coming out to oneself; that is, realizing and consciously accepting that one is gay. Although it is only the first step in the process of coming out, it is the hardest step for many gay people, especially those who grow up in a social setting that strongly disapproves of gays and lesbians or whose religion labels homosexual behavior as immoral. Some gay people live in denial for many years, perhaps even for their entire lives.

The second element in most gay people's life stories is coming out to others (Ryan et al., 2015). Unlike the tragic example mentioned in the previous section, coming out to others is usually a gradual process: A gay adolescent may come out first to another gay youth, a best friend, a sibling, or a counselor. Parents tend to find out late; gay adolescents fear parental rejection, sometimes with good reason. However, many parents whose initial reaction is negative go through a rapid change of heart after their child comes out, and they may even take an activist role and join a pro-gay organization such as PFLAG (formerly Parents, Families and Friends of Lesbians and Gays), which has over 400 chapters in the United States.

The third element of coming out is joining a gay or lesbian community. For some gay men, that means moving to a big city that has a well-developed gay community. An example is West Hollywood, California, an independent city within Los Angeles whose population is about one-third gay men. Lesbians tend to be more scattered, but some smaller cities, such as Northampton, Massachusetts, have become centers of lesbian life. In locations such as West Hollywood and Northampton, gay people can find communities that offer sex partners, acceptance, and a wide range of gay or lesbian cultural institutions.

Moving to a "gay mecca" has lost quite a bit of the significance it once had for young gay people, however. That's because many young lesbians and gay men can now find other gay people, be openly gay, and experience some degree of organized gay life in the communities in which they grew up. In addition, the internet, with its endless opportunities for gay networking, chat, and cybersex, has delivered the gay community to gay youth in their own homes. Meanwhile, cities known for their gay nightlife, such as West Hollywood, are being invaded by gay-friendly straight people. Even San Francisco's Castro District, the most famous of all gay meccas, faces an identity crisis as straight people move in and gay bars close or take on a more generic identity (Kane, 2014).

One problem with moving to a gay mecca is that it may also represent a flight from other aspects of a gay person's cultural identity. In becoming openly gay and moving to a gay-friendly community, many young gay people isolate themselves from their ethnic roots, their religion, and their extended families. Thus, an important fourth element of coming out for many gay people is integrating the gay side of their identity with other aspects of who they are. This may involve returning to their roots or participating in organizations that straddle the boundary that they have crossed—for example, gay Catholic groups, gay Asian groups, or gay Deaf groups.

Sometimes the person who seems the least gay has the hardest time coming out. That was certainly true for former Patriots and Chiefs offensive tackle Ryan O'Callaghan (6 feet 7 inches, 330 pounds), who came out to the world in 2017 at the age of 34. He had no difficulty hiding his sexuality while he was an NFL player, though at the cost of inward torture, and he always planned to commit suicide once his playing career was over. It took months of intense therapy, and a sympathetic general manager, to change that outcome (Zeigler, 2017).

## Lesbians and gay men are well represented in certain occupations

Lesbians and gay men are found in all walks of life. Yet, as we mentioned above, gay people are more likely to violate gender norms in their occupational preferences than are heterosexual men and women (Ueno et al., 2013). What about the actual occupations of gay Americans? One research group investigated this question through data mining of the U.S. Census Bureau's American Community Survey (Tilcsik et al., 2015) (**TABLE 12.1**). The jobs in which gays and lesbians were highly overrepresented (compared with their same-sex straight peers) were characterized by three factors: (1) They were jobs dominated by persons of the other sex (e.g., gay men working as flight attendants, lesbians as mechanics), (2) they were jobs requiring a high level of social perceptiveness (e.g., psychologist), and (3) they were jobs allowing people to perform their work without a great deal of reliance on others (e.g., technical writer, home appliance installer). The occupation with the highest proportion of both lesbians and gay men was psychologist. In viewing the table, bear in mind that there are also plenty of gay people in occupations where they are not overrepresented.

One reason for mentioning these apparent occupational preferences is to highlight the fact that gay people are not simply people who get together to have sex, nor are they simply a community united in resistance to oppression. They also, to a degree, share common interests and a common sensibility. If and when gay people are fully accepted by mainstream society, it is not likely that they will be completely assimilated and disappear from view as a distinct group, as has happened to left-handers, for example. More probably, homosexuality will retain a special salience, and gay people will be valued for their unique gifts.

**TABLE 12.1** Gay occupations

**Female-majority occupations**

| HIGHEST PROPORTION OF LESBIANS AMONG FEMALE WORKERS | HIGHEST PROPORTION OF GAY MEN AMONG MALE WORKERS |
| --- | --- |
| 1. Psychologists (S, T) | 1. Flight attendants (S) |
| 2. Probation officers/correctional treatment specialists (S, T) | 2. Hairdressers, hair stylists, cosmetologists |
| 3. Training and development specialists and managers (S) | 3. Nurse practitioners (S, T) |
| 4. Sociologists (S, T) | 4. Transportation attendants, except flight attendants (S) |
| 5. Social and community service members (S, T) | 5. Travel agents (S, T) |

**Male-majority occupations**

| HIGHEST PROPORTION OF LESBIANS AMONG FEMALE WORKERS | HIGHEST PROPORTION OF GAY MEN AMONG MALE WORKERS |
| --- | --- |
| 1. Bus and truck mechanics and diesel engine specialists | 1. Actors (S, T) |
| 2. Elevator installers/repairers (T) | 2. News analysts, reporters, and correspondents (S, T) |
| 3. Heating, A/C, and refrigeration mechanics/installers (T) | 3. Artists and related workers (S, T) |
| 4. Home appliance repairers (T) | 4. Agents/managers of artists, performers, athletes (S, T) |
| 5. Security and fire alarm systems installers (T) | 5. Producers and directors (S, T) |

*Source*: Data from A. Tilcsik et al. 2015. *Adm Sci Q* 60: 446–481.

*Note*: Listed here are the female-majority and male-majority occupations with the highest proportion of lesbians among female workers and those with the highest proportion of gay men among male workers. "Gay" and "lesbian" individuals were identified in U.S. Census data as men or women in a same-sex marriage or cohabitation; thus they include an unknown fraction of bisexual individuals, and they omit gays and lesbians who are not in a live-in relationship. S indicates a job requiring above-average social perceptiveness; T indicates a job with above-average task-independence.

## 12.6 Gay People Who Belong to Minorities Have Special Concerns

**LEARNING OBJECTIVE**

After reading this section you should be able to:

**12.6.1** Identify some gay men and women who belong to racial/ethnic minorities.

As far as is known, roughly similar proportions of different racial or ethnic groups in the United States are gay or lesbian. Nevertheless, the experience of being gay can be different for members of minorities. For one thing, there were until recently few or no role models for gay people within their own minority communities.

That situation is now changing, as increasing numbers of minority public figures have come out as gay or bisexual (**FIGURE 12.10**). Here are a few examples: singer/songwriter Willow Smith, professional football player Ryan Russell, and television news anchor Don Lemon (African American); singer Ricky Martin, U.S. District Judge Nitza Quiñones Alejandro, and singer Vicci Martinez (Hispanic); and model Jenny Shimizu, actor George Takei, and gay rights activist Urvashi Vaid (Asian American).

Nevertheless, many minority gay people have to deal with cultural traditions that make heterosexual marriage into a near-sacred obligation (for oldest sons in many Asian American cultures, for example) or that place taboos on the discussion of sexual topics in general, especially for women. Thus, acknowledging their own gay identity might, for some minority gay people, come at a cost of distancing themselves from their communities or their cultural roots.

Besides facing anti-gay attitudes within their own communities, gay minorities often have to deal with rejection by white gay people. On gay dating apps like Grindr, statements like "Not into Black or Asian" or "Keep it white or Latin" are commonplace.

Members of sexual minorities who are nonwhite may develop their own cultural institutions. A striking historical example is that of the "voguing balls"—elaborate contests in dance, drag, and "realness" that sprang up among gay and transgender African Americans and Hispanics in the 1980s. The lifestyle surrounding these balls

▲ **FIGURE 12.10**  Judge Nitza Quiñones Alejandro and football player **Michael Sam** are role models for minority lesbian and gay youth.

▶ **FIGURE 12.11** The documentary film
*Paris Is Burning* brought voguing to the
attention of a wider audience.

constituted a parallel universe that was largely unknown to most Americans until it
was made the topic of a notable documentary film, *Paris Is Burning* (1991) (**FIGURE
12.11**). Although largely wiped out by the AIDS epidemic, the voguing culture has
more recently made a comeback, and it has influenced mainstream entertainers such
as Lady Gaga and RuPaul (Clark, 2015).

When thinking about "minorities within minorities," the numbers of people
located at these intersections can be very limited. There are only an estimated 750
gay male little people in the United States, for example. They don't have to find each
other to find romance, of course, but average-sized gay men sometimes seek out little
men more out of curiosity or fetishistic interest than out of genuine attraction to them
as individuals (Juzwiak, 2015).

## 12.7 Gay Sex Has Its Own Style

### LEARNING OBJECTIVE

After reading this section you should be able to:

**12.7.1** Describe differences between the sexual practices of straight
and gay women and men.

With the exception of coitus, most sexual behaviors that male–female couples engage
in are also practiced by same-sex couples. It's worth pointing out some differences,
however. Most obviously, no one has gay sex in order to procreate, so physical pleasure and emotional intimacy are the principal reasons for engaging in sex.

Among the sexual behaviors practiced by female couples are kissing, fondling,
oral or manual breast stimulation, body-to-body rubbing involving the vulva (tribadism), "scissoring," cunnilingus, rimming (anilingus), manual stimulation of the
clitoris, penetration of the vagina or anus with a finger or sex toy, and sex play
involving elements of bondage/dominance/sadomasochism (BDSM play; see Chapter 13). Women in relationships with women are, on average, more likely to experience orgasm and find those orgasms more satisfying than women in relationships
with men (Blair et al., 2018). This may be because women understand better than
men what turns women on.

Among behaviors practiced by male couples are kissing, fondling, nipple stimulation, body-to-body rubbing, penis-to-penis rubbing ("frot"), fellatio, anal penetration with the penis or fingers or sex toys, intercrural (between-the-thighs) intercourse, and BDSM play. Many of these behaviors can be either unidirectional or reciprocal (for example, reciprocal fellatio, or "69").

Same-sex couples take their time over sex (Masters & Johnson, 1979). Lesbians may spend a great deal of time on breast and nipple stimulation, for example, before focusing on the genitals and may extend the entire sexual interaction for well over an hour. Gay men often bring each other close to orgasm and then back off, thus prolonging sexual pleasure and causing a more intense orgasm when it finally arrives.

Although nearly all lesbians and many gay men confine their sexual activity to paired encounters in the privacy of their own bedrooms, some gay men have sex in other places, including secluded outdoor spots whose locations become known through word of mouth or dedicated "cruising" websites. The gay slang term "cruising," by the way, means looking for casual sex partners in public spaces. This activity has become much more efficient in recent years, thanks to gay hookup apps that inform the user about other available men in the vicinity, along with their photos and interests.

**Bathhouses** are another location for sex between men. Gay bathhouses are facilities in which large numbers of men cruise for partners in cubicles, steam rooms, or dimly lit open spaces. As with outdoor cruising areas, sex may be in pairs or in groups. Early in the AIDS epidemic, bathhouses were closed down in many cities, but some still operate or have reopened, usually under city regulations that attempt to enforce safer sex practices.

There may be reasons for outdoor and bathhouse sex that are purely practical: Home may be too far away, or the participants may want to hide their sexual orientation or sexual activities from people they live with (parents, wives, or steady boyfriends). In addition, however, men may seek out these locations for the thrill of the hunt, the risk of public exposure, or the chance to have sex with a number of strangers in a short time.

Although gay male culture includes and is fairly accepting of outdoor sex, bathhouses, and group sex, it's worth reemphasizing that large numbers of gay men do not engage in these practices, preferring to live in monogamous relationships that, aside from their same-sex aspect, are indistinguishable from the relationships of most heterosexual Americans.

**bathhouse** A facility, usually in the form of a private club, used for casual sex between men.

## 12.8 There is Diversity among Gay People

### LEARNING OBJECTIVES
After reading this section you should be able to:

12.8.1 Explain what the terms butch, femme, top, and bottom mean in reference to gay people.

12.8.2 Evaluate the options for gay people who want to become parents.

We have already mentioned several differences that may exist within the population of gay and lesbian Americans. We now look at how diversity shows itself in the kinds of relationships that gay people establish.

### Some same-sex couples differ in gender characteristics

"One of my moms is kind of like my dad, and my other mom is the girly mom," explained Noah, the 10-year-old son of a lesbian couple, Roxanne and Kelly Prejean (Bagby, 2008). Noah was echoing, on the basis of his own experience, a concept that has enjoyed varying degrees of acceptance within the gay community over the years—the idea that gay people can be divided into subtypes on the basis of gender characteristics and that gay couples should consist of one gender-conformist and one gender-variant partner.

**butch** Masculine-acting, often used to describe certain lesbians.

**femme** Feminine-acting, often used to describe certain lesbians or bisexual women.

**bear** In gay slang, a burly gay man with plenty of body hair.

**FAQ:** I'm a woman who's had several boyfriends, but they all turned out to be gay. Is something wrong with me?

Women who associate predominantly with gay men may do so because they appreciate the gay male sensibility, because they feel safe in such relationships, or because they want intimacy without sex. There's nothing wrong with you, but if you want a lasting sexual relationship, you need to look elsewhere.

A generation or two ago, this concept ruled many lesbian communities in the United States (Kennedy & Davis, 1983). The two kinds of lesbians were called **butch** and **femme**: The butch lesbians looked, dressed, and acted like men and took a dominant role in sex, while the femme lesbians were like heterosexual women and took a submissive role in sex. A lesbian couple would consist of a butch–femme pair. Similarly, gay men were thought to be of two kinds, sometimes referred to as "tops" and "bottoms": Tops were defined by a preference for the insertive role in anal intercourse and were relatively masculine and dominant generally, while bottoms preferred the receptive role and were more feminine. With this thinking, lesbian and gay male relationships were "regularized": Although they were same-sex relationships, they mimicked heterosexual relationships in the sense that they were formed by the union of partners, one more masculine and one more feminine.

Since those years there has been a relaxation and splintering of gender norms among both lesbians and gay men. Today's gay and lesbian communities are characterized by a kaleidoscopic variety of "types" and a generally more playful attitude toward gender. Lesbians who identify as butch ("dykes"*) and those who identify as femme still exist, but their behaviors and relationships are no longer regulated by strict cultural codes. No one would be surprised to see two butch or two femme lesbians forming a couple, for example—something that would have been unusual in the 1950s.

As for tops and bottoms among gay men, these descriptors are still current, but many gay men define themselves as "versatile," meaning that they enjoy both insertive and receptive sex roles (Moskowitz et al., 2008; Moskowitz & Hart, 2011), and plenty of gay couples are not composed of top-and-bottom pairs.

### Gay people aren't all of a kind

Even if same-sex partners don't differ from each other in gender characteristics, they often differ in other ways. In both the United States and Europe, live-in gay and lesbian couples—gay couples especially—are much more likely than straight couples to differ from each other in such demographic characteristics as age and educational level (Schwartz & Graf, 2009; Verbakel & Kalmijn, 2014).

There are other subtypes among gay people that form the basis of sexual subcultures. Among gay men there exists an extensive BDSM culture, which overlaps with the "leather community." BDSM practitioners are not necessarily gay, of course, but they are a far more visible and accepted subculture within the gay community than in the heterosexual world. Leather bars are common in gay communities. San Francisco has a (mostly gay) Leather Pride Week, which culminates in the BDSM-focused Folsom Street Fair, where you can get spanked for free. Some lesbians are also involved in leather or BDSM practices. Most gay people think of leather and other BDSM practices as a normal but minority sexual interest. We take a closer look at BDSM in Chapter 13.

Another gay subculture is that of **bears** (Moskowitz et al., 2013; Edmonds, 2015). A stereotypical bear is an overweight or obese man with plenty of body hair (**FIGURE 12.12**). It's not really appearance or body type that defines a bear, however, so much as an attitude:

▲ **FIGURE 12.12** **Bears** form a well-known subculture within the gay male community. These men are participants in United Bears Barcelona, a Spanish bear festival.

*Originally a term of abuse directed at lesbians in general, the term "dyke" has been reclaimed by some butch or politically radical lesbians to identify themselves.

specifically, a rejection of the necessity to conform to the "pretty boy" or "muscle boy" images so popular elsewhere in the gay world, combined with a warm, nonjudgmental personality. Bears generally pair up with other bears fairly like themselves, but older bears may also pair up with younger "bear cubs." In the past bears have often been stigmatized by other gay men on account of their appearance, but they have recently become much more visible and accepted: A gay pride parade would no longer be complete without at least one truckload of bears. There are numerous social organizations for bears in most parts of the United States, and they can meet up through their own social networking app, Growlr.

Lesbians don't have such prominent sexual subcultures as gay men, although, as just mentioned, some lesbians are into BDSM practices. Lesbians do have innumerable *social* subcultures, ranging from literary salons to softball leagues to women's music festivals. The music festivals are Woodstock-like events, but they combine music with art, crafts, discussion groups, and many other activities.

Beyond these social diversities, the lesbian/straight and gay/straight dichotomies are themselves under siege, especially among women. While many non-heterosexual women remain out-and-out lesbians, others move fluidly between relationships with both men and women (Diamond, 2008). Some of these women, especially those who describe themselves as femme, may identify as bisexual rather than lesbian (Rosario et al., 2009). But others—both women and men—reject these kinds of classifications altogether, preferring to define their sexual desires in terms of the specific people they are attracted to, rather than by overall classes of partners (**BOX 12.4**). Thus, they challenge the centrality of sexual orientation as we currently define it.

## BOX 12.4
## Beyond Gay and Straight

Straight, gay, bi—or none of the above? Harris Wofford defied categorization.

In 1948, at the age of 22, Wofford married Clare Lindgren, with whom he had three children. The couple remained happily married for 48 years, until Clare's death in 1996. Wofford had a distinguished career in public service, including a stint as president of Bryn Mawr College and another as a U.S. senator for Pennsylvania.

Five years after Clare's death, Wofford met 25-year-old Matthew Charlton on a Fort Lauderdale beach. The two men felt an immediate attraction, in spite of the 50-year age difference. After living together as a couple for 15 years, Wofford and Charlton married in 2016. Wofford died in 2019 at the age of 92.

It's not that uncommon for men to embark on a same-sex relationship after a long period of heterosexual marriage. For the most part, though, such men say that they knew they were gay all along and that they married a woman for reasons that didn't involve sexual attraction.

Such a history didn't fit Wofford, according to an op-ed piece that he wrote for the *New York Times* shortly before his and Charlton's 2016 wedding. "Too often," he wrote, "our society seeks to label people by pinning them on the wall—straight, gay or in between. I don't categorize myself based

Harris Wofford (1926–2019).

on the gender of those I love. I had a half-century of marriage with a wonderful woman, and now am lucky for a second time to have found happiness."
*Source:* Wofford, 2016.

The term "queer" also has some relevance when talking about diversity. Originally an abusive slang term aimed at homosexuals, "queer" was reclaimed by gay people in the late 20th century. Over time, especially in the 1980s and 1990s, it developed a somewhat different meaning from "gay": It was used as a self-identifier by those non-heterosexual people who took pride in nonconformity, rejected strict categories, and considered themselves cultural or political revolutionaries. More recently the meaning of queer has expanded to include almost any kind of nonconformity—not always in the sexual or gender domain. The opposite of queer is "heteronormative," which refers to the body of ideas and values that are assumed to characterize conventionally heterosexual people, or that supposedly give them a moral superiority.

## Some gay people are parents

Because sex between two men or two women is nonprocreative, you might think of lesbians and gay men as being without children. That's not always the case, however. About 22% of cohabiting female couples, and 11% of male couples, have their own children living with them; other same-sex couples may have children who have already left home, and single lesbians and gay men may also be parents. An estimated 6 million Americans have at least one parent who is gay, lesbian, bisexual, or transgender (Gates, 2013; U.S. Census Bureau, 2013).

Where do these children come from? Most come from opposite-sex relationships, such as marriages—many lesbians and gay men have been in such relationships before coming out as gay, or are still in them. Increasing numbers of lesbians and gay men, however, are producing and rearing children as gay couples or, less commonly, as single gay people (**FIGURE 12.13**).

Gay people who wish to become parents can avail themselves of most of the reproductive options described in Chapter 8 (Mamo, 2007). Lesbians can simply have sex with a man or use artificial insemination, perhaps utilizing sperm from one of their partner's male relatives or a friend. Gay men can employ a surrogate mother, who may be artificially inseminated or made pregnant through in vitro fertilization. They can also adopt a child. Either way, becoming parents is an expensive proposition for most gay male couples.

The ultimate wish of gay would-be parents is probably for both partners to be the true genetic parents of their children. Some gay male couples mix their sperm prior to artificial insemination. This practice randomizes and conceals the identity of the genetic father, but it does not produce a genetically blended embryo, of course, since only one sperm fertilizes the ovum. Experiments in laboratory animals have demonstrated that it is possible to create offspring from two female or two male parents (Deng et al., 2011; Li et al., 2016); it's unclear whether this technology will ever be applicable to human same-sex parenting.

The legal status of gay parenting, co-parenting, and adoption is evolving rapidly. Same-sex couples are legally entitled to adopt in all states, but some states require them to be married. If one person is the legal parent (biological or adopted) of a child, some states allow that person's same-sex partner to petition for second-parent adoption. State-by-state information is available online (Lifelong Adoptions, 2019). The American Academy of Pediatrics and the American Psychological Association have put themselves on record as supporting gay adoptions. Adopting from abroad can

© Associated Press

▲ **FIGURE 12.13** **Married with children** Canadians Jeff Hall and Emil Florea with their two pairs of twins, who were produced with the help of surrogate mothers.

be difficult for married gay couples because most of the source countries forbid adoption by gay people, and the fact that someone is gay becomes all too apparent if that person is in a same-sex marriage.

There have been dozens of studies of children brought up by gay (mostly lesbian) parents. Based on a review of these studies, the American Psychological Association, the American Psychiatric Association, and several other professional groups jointly declared that "there is no scientific basis for concluding that gay and lesbian parents are any less fit or capable than heterosexual parents, or that their children are any less psychologically healthy and well adjusted" (Gilfoyle, 2010). More recent studies continue to refute the notion that having gay parents jeopardizes a child's health or welfare (Bos et al., 2016; Farr, 2016).

## 12.9 Changing One's Sexual Orientation Is Difficult or Impossible

**LEARNING OBJECTIVE**
After reading this section you should be able to:

**12.9.1** Describe the legal status of treatments to change people's sexual orientation in the United States.

During the 1950s and 1960s many gay men (and a few lesbians) tried to become straight by psychoanalysis or other forms of psychotherapy. The market for this kind of treatment has dwindled in recent years, but there is still enough demand to keep a small number of therapists in business. There are also groups that offer to help individuals get rid of homosexual feelings by religious counseling.

In 2009 an expert panel of the American Psychological Association concluded there is no convincing evidence for success of any conversion treatments and that some evidence indicates that these treatments may be harmful to the persons who undergo them (American Psychological Association, 2011). The harmful effects include depression and thoughts of suicide. More recent studies have supported the panel's conclusions (Dehlin et al., 2015). By 2019, 18 states and numerous cities had enacted laws or ordinances banning the application of conversion treatments to minors (Movement Advancement Project, 2019).

What is difficult or impossible to change is the direction of one's sexual *attractions*—a person's sexual orientation, as we define it. People can certainly choose to change their sexual *behavior*, and some gay people do decide to enter heterosexual relationships for moral or practical reasons. In doing so, however, they risk inflicting long-lasting distress on themselves and their partners.

## 12.10 Homophobia Has Multiple Roots

**LEARNING OBJECTIVES**
After reading this section you should be able to:

**12.10.1** Evaluate the various possible causes of homophobia.

**12.10.2** Describe the status of hate-crime laws with respect to gay people in the United States.

Antagonistic feelings and behaviors directed toward gay people are common. They range all the way from the simple belief that homosexual behavior is wrong—a belief held by one in three Americans in 2019—to the killing of lesbians and gay men by a few hate-filled **gay bashers**. The most horrific example in recent times was the Pulse nightclub shooting in Orlando, Florida, in June 2016, in which 49 people, most of them LGBT Latinos, were murdered by an Islamist terrorist. (This hardly needs saying, but the vast majority of American Muslims reject anti-gay violence, and there are

**gay bashing** Hate crimes against gay people. Sometimes includes verbal abuse as well as physical violence.

**homophobia** Prejudice against homosexuality or gay people.

**heterosexism** The cultural establishment of heterosexuality as the normal and preferred form of sexual expression.

numerous organizations that represent or support gay Muslims in the United States and overseas [Muslims for Progressive Values, 2017]).

The word **homophobia** literally means *"fear* of homosexuality," but it has come to be used for the entire spectrum of anti-gay attitudes and behaviors, and that is how we use it here. A variety of different factors probably contribute to homophobia, so it may be difficult to unravel the causes of a particular person's anti-gay attitude or to figure out what sparked a particular hate crime.

Related to homophobia is **heterosexism**: This is a social norm by which all people are expected to be heterosexual, or the idea that heterosexuality is intrinsically superior to other forms of sexual expression. Homophobia is a personal attitude; heterosexism is the institutionalized prejudice that allows homophobia to flourish and that denies gay people equal rights.

## Cultural indoctrination transmits homophobia across generations

Some children and adults learn to dislike homosexuality and gay people by receiving anti-gay messages from parents, teachers, peers, religious authorities, political figures, and so on. The messages can be quite vocal and explicit: The Roman Catholic Church, for example, labels homosexuality a moral disorder, calls gay sex sinful, and has actively opposed gay marriage and other gay rights initiatives in the United States and worldwide.

Many American evangelicals express similar views: In 2017 a group of leading evangelicals issued a "Nashville Statement," which included the following: "We affirm that it is sinful to approve of homosexual immorality or transgenderism and that such approval constitutes an essential departure from Christian faithfulness and witness" (Coalition for Biblical Sexuality, 2017). In the same year one well-known radio pastor, Kevin Swanson, claimed that Hurricane Harvey was a punishment dealt on Houston by God because the city had elected a "very, very aggressively pro-homosexual mayor" (Wanshel, 2017).*

Regular participation in organized worship is the strongest demographic predictor that a person will disapprove of gay sex (**FIGURE 12.14**). Nevertheless, plenty of religious denominations or congregations are gay affirmative, and many religiously observant individuals support gay rights or are openly gay themselves.

Another factor that correlates strongly with people's attitudes toward gay people is their beliefs about the cause of homosexuality. Persons who think that being gay is a choice that people make are far more likely to espouse anti-gay attitudes than those who think of homosexuality as a trait that people are born with (**BOX 12.5**). Why people's thinking of homosexuality as a choice should predict their anti-gay attitudes is somewhat perplexing, but the correlation has held up in many studies and opinion polls (Collier et al., 2014; Overby, 2014). Perhaps disliking people for an inborn trait feels too close to racism. As for gay people themselves, the great majority deny that they chose to be gay (Herek et al., 2010), but some (more lesbians than gay men) do experience their orientation as a choice.

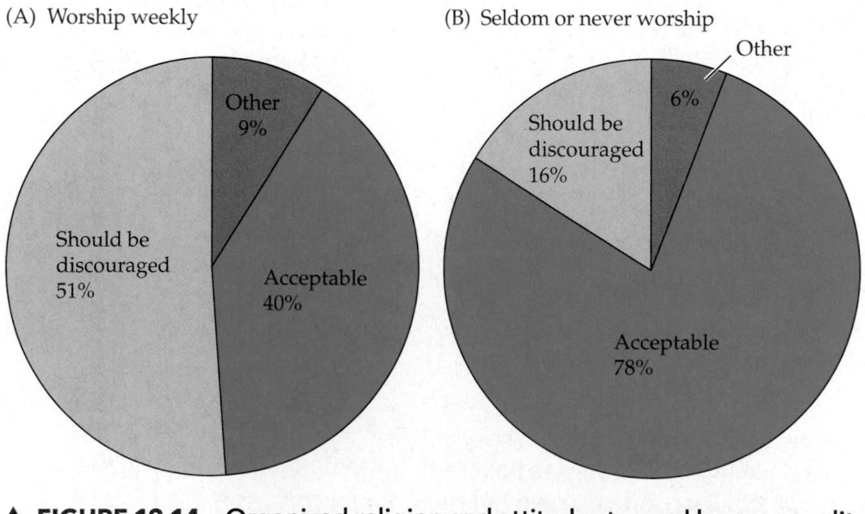

**(A) Worship weekly**

Other 9%

Should be discouraged 51%

Acceptable 40%

**(B) Seldom or never worship**

Other 6%

Should be discouraged 16%

Acceptable 78%

▲ **FIGURE 12.14** **Organized religion and attitudes toward homosexuality** These charts show the percentages of Americans who believe that gay sex is morally acceptable or should be discouraged among (A) those who worship weekly and (B) those who seldom or never worship. (After Pew Research Center. 2014. *U.S. Religious Landscape Study 2014: Views about homosexuality*. PRC: Washington, D.C.)

* There is a long history of blaming natural disasters on homosexuality. The sixth-century Roman emperor Justinian, for example, made male–male sex illegal on the grounds that "crimes of this description cause famines, earthquakes, and pestilence" (Crompton, 2003)

## BOX 12.5
## Born That Way? And Does It Matter?

Considering that our sexual orientation is such a key part of who we are, trying to understand how sexual orientation develops seems like a worthwhile enterprise just for its own sake. But people's beliefs about sexual orientation are closely tied up with their attitudes toward gay people, so this area of research may also have social or even political repercussions.

Many surveys have asked Americans about the origins of sexual orientation, usually by means of simplified questions like "Are gay people born that way, or is it something they learn or choose?" Until recently most surveys have come up with roughly equal numbers of respondents who answer one way or the other.

Some of these surveys have gone on to ask questions like "Would you be OK if your child was taught by a gay teacher?" or "Do you support same-sex marriage?" Very consistently since these polls began, people who believe gays are "born that way" or that homosexuality has a biological basis have expressed far more gay-friendly attitudes than those who believe that homosexuality is learned or chosen. In one study, belief in a biological basis for homosexuality was associated with a 40-point increase in the percentage of people who consider homosexuality morally acceptable (Haider-Markel & Joslyn, 2008).

Is there a causal connection here? Four psychologists at the University of Valencia in Spain set out to find the answer (Frias-Navarro et al., 2015). One hundred ninety students filled out a questionnaire that assessed their beliefs about the causation of homosexuality. Then half the students, selected at random, read biological materials (including a summary of Simon LeVay's hypothalamus study, mentioned in the text) that pointed toward a born-that-way causation. The other half read materials pointing toward the idea that homosexuality is something environmental or learned. The students then took the beliefs assessment a second time. Not surprisingly, students who read the biological materials shifted their opinions toward the born-that-way position, and those who read the other materials shifted toward the learned position.

Next, the psychologists had all the students complete a questionnaire that assessed their agreement or disagreement with a long list of statements like "If a child is adopted by a same-sex couple, he/she will surely have psychological problems in the future" and "I have nothing against people with a homosexual orientation, but I don't think it's appropriate to call the union between same-sex couples 'marriage.'" Those

Most gay people believe they were born gay.

students who had read the biological materials gave significantly more gay-friendly responses—they were more likely to support gay marriage and gay parenting, for example—than those who had read the materials suggesting that homosexuality is learned.

The conditions of this study were somewhat artificial—in particular, it's not known whether the changes in the students' attitudes persisted after completion of the study. Still, there are indications of a similar effect in real life—for some people, at least. In 1991, for example, the editorial-page editor of the *Arizona Republic* newspaper, William Cheshire, reversed his previously anti-gay views and wrote columns in support of pro-gay legislation. This, he wrote, was the result of reading research papers that indicated a biological basis for homosexuality. "I was persuaded that it was not something voluntary," he said in an interview, ". . . and then one's whole theological and moral perspective shifts, and then you begin to view the problem entirely differently, and that's what happened to me" (Taylor, 1992).

In an ideal world, the causation of homosexuality wouldn't matter: People would evaluate gays and lesbians as individuals or by assessing the benefits or harms that homosexuality confers on society. That's a future worth working toward, but in the meantime causation is a big part of the mix. And according to national polls, the percentage of Americans who think that homosexuality is "something one is born with" rose from 13% in 1977 to 42% in 2015 (Pew Research Center, 2015). This trend was roughly paralleled by increasingly positive views on gay rights issues.

**femiphobia** Prejudice against femininity, especially of males.

## Gay people are seen as rule breakers

One motivation for anti-gay prejudice is the sense that gay people break rules—not just society's rules, but what seems to some heterosexual people to be the natural order of things. Gay people break these rules by engaging in gay sex, but, in addition, they may do so by being recognizably gender-nonconformist (Wellman & McCoy, 2014). In fact, the earliest experience of anti-gay prejudice that many pre-gay children experience is really a prejudice against gender transgression. Sometimes this attitude is called **femiphobia** because it is directed most strongly against males who act like females, rather than vice versa. Even some gay men are femiphobic, devaluing other gay men who seem at all feminine, or feeling bad about themselves on account of their perceived femininity (Sanchez & Vilain, 2012).

People who view lesbians and gay men as transgressors tend to be those who themselves live by very strict rules (Young-Bruehl, 1996). Extending this same line of thought, is it possible that people who hate or actually attack lesbians and gay men are fighting homosexual urges within themselves? The thinking behind this idea is that their anti-gay attitude is part of a defense mechanism that helps these people control, hide from, or mask their own transgressive feelings.

Some studies have come up with experimental evidence in support of this hypothesis. Henry Adams and his colleagues at the University of Georgia tested the genital responses of self-described "heterosexual" men, of whom some had homophobic attitudes and did not (Adams et al., 1996). All the men were genitally aroused by erotic videos of females, but many of the homophobic men were also aroused, though less strongly, by the male videos (**FIGURE 12.15**). In a more recent study that used viewing time as a measure of sexual orientation, many of the homophobic men spent more time looking at male images than did any of the nonhomophobic men (Cheval et al., 2016). The findings of both studies suggest that strongly homophobic attitudes are associated with homosexual feelings that the person denies or is not aware of. In both studies some homophobic men were not at all aroused by the male images, however, so there are likely to be other factors that can trigger the development of anti-gay feelings.

From time to time, politicians, preachers, and others who promote an anti-gay agenda are caught in situations that raise questions about their own sexuality. One example involved Bishop Eddie Long, pastor of a Georgia megachurch and "one of the most virulently homophobic black leaders" (Southern Poverty Law Center, 2007). In 2010 Long faced four lawsuits from young men who claimed that he used his pastoral office to coerce them into sexual relations. Long promised to fight the

▶ **FIGURE 12.15  Do homophobic men have homosexual urges?** These graphs show the penile responses of homophobic and nonhomophobic men, all of whom identified themselves as heterosexual, to videotapes containing heterosexual or homosexual images. Both groups responded to the heterosexual videos, but only the homophobic men responded to the homosexual videos. (After H. E. Adams et al. 1996. *J Abnorm Psych* 105: 440–445.)

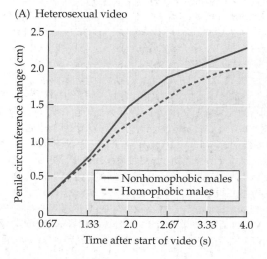

(A) Heterosexual video

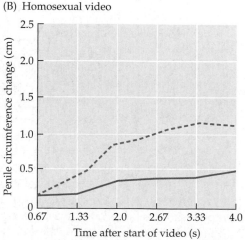

(B) Homosexual video

accusations but eventually settled the lawsuits on undisclosed terms. He never admitted to being gay, but in 2017 he said in a sermon, "I had a moment [when] I wanted to kill myself and was ready" (Boone, 2017). He died later that year. Anti-gay feelings directed against oneself are referred to as **internalized homophobia**.

## Overcoming homophobia is a communal enterprise

Considerable research has been done on methods to overcome anti-gay attitudes. Because these attitudes have such diverse roots, it is unlikely that any one strategy will be successful by itself.

To some extent, a reduction of homophobia can be engineered through legislation and other public policy measures—by the passage of nondiscrimination and hate-crime statutes, for example. Thirty-three states and the District of Columbia now have hate-crime statutes that include sexual orientation, and 22 of these also include gender identity as a protected category (Human Rights Campaign, 2019) (**FIGURE 12.16**). The U.S. federal hate-crime law was expanded to include sexual orientation and gender identity in 2009.

Nevertheless, social science research suggests that people's attitudes toward gays and lesbians, as in other matters, are most readily influenced by interactions with relatives, friends, coworkers, and other people with whom they have personal contact. Recent history supports the same view; for example, as mentioned earlier in the chapter, there has been a large increase over the last two decades in the number of Americans who know a gay person, and there has been a dramatic easing of anti-gay attitudes over the same period.

This trend has greatly benefited the current generation of gay youth, of course, but it has benefited non-gay youth too—boys and young men especially. Less intimidated by the fear of being labeled gay, they are able to express same-sex intimacy in ways that were off-limits earlier. Researchers have noted increased physical and emotional intimacy among straight youths and a greater willingness to include gay peers among their intimate friends (McCormack & Anderson, 2014). There has also been a trend toward young people describing themselves as "mostly heterosexual," meaning that they might not be averse to some sexual exploration with a same-sex friend (Savin-Williams & Vrangalova, 2013).

**internalized homophobia**
Anti-gay feelings that some gay people absorb from the larger society.

**FAQ:** In Egypt I saw lots of men holding hands in public. Does that mean that Egyptians are cool with homosexuality?

Not at all. In some countries homosexuality is such an alien concept that traditional displays of intimacy between men—which can include hand-holding, kissing, and feeding each other—don't trigger any suspicion that they are in a sexual relationship.

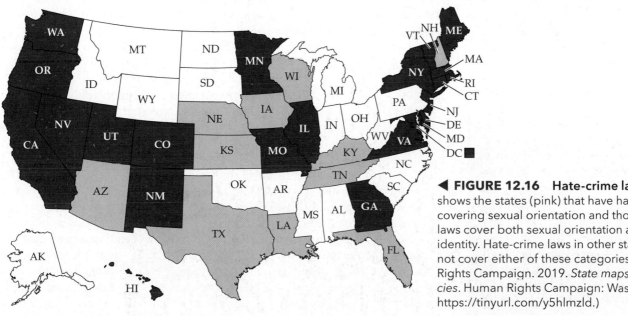

◀ **FIGURE 12.16   Hate-crime laws** This map shows the states (pink) that have hate-crime laws covering sexual orientation and those (red) whose laws cover both sexual orientation and gender identity. Hate-crime laws in other states (white) do not cover either of these categories. (After Human Rights Campaign. 2019. *State maps of laws & policies*. Human Rights Campaign: Washington, D.C. https://tinyurl.com/y5hlmzld.)

## 12.11 Bisexual People Are Caught between Two Worlds

**LEARNING OBJECTIVES**

After reading this section you should be able to:

12.11.1 Explain differences between the sexes with regard to bisexuality.
12.11.2 Explain how the causes of biphobia and homophobia may differ.

"Labels put people in boxes, and those boxes are shaped like coffins." That was how Chirlane McCrae, former lesbian activist and now wife of New York's Mayor Bill de Blasio, explained her sexual orientation to *Essence* magazine (Villarosa, 2013). McCrae is one of many people who reject the simple heterosexual/homosexual dichotomy. On the other hand, within the gay male community one sometimes hears the mantra "Straight, gay, or lying"—the idea that claiming to be attracted to both sexes is a form of self-delusion or a convenient fiction (Carey, 2005). What's the truth of the matter?

### The prevalence of bisexuality depends on definitions

Population-based surveys suggest that bisexuality—when defined as *any* degree of sexual attraction to both men and women—is more prevalent than exclusive homosexuality in both sexes (see Figure 12.1). But the majority of bisexual people defined in this manner are far more attracted to the other sex than to the same sex, and they may be described as "mostly heterosexual" rather than "bisexual" (Savin-Williams, 2017). If bisexuality is defined as a *roughly equal* attraction to the two sexes, it is much less common, especially in men. In the 2018 General Social Survey, 5.6% of women but only 0.6% of men identified as bisexual.

In fact, some sex researchers have questioned whether male bisexuality exists at all, at least when sexual orientation is assessed by measuring the genital responses to erotic videos. Most men who identify as bisexual respond far more strongly to videos featuring men than to those featuring women, meaning that they are in fact homosexual by physiological criteria (Freund, 1974; Rieger et al., 2005). But men who fulfill strict criteria for bisexuality—who don't just call themselves bisexual but also have a history of sexual and romantic relationships with partners of both sexes—do show genital arousal to both women and men (Rosenthal et al., 2011). Thus there is no real question about the existence of truly bisexual men, even if such men are not very common. This conclusion, long maintained by bisexual men themselves, is now broadly agreed on by sex researchers (Jabbour et al., 2020).

Within the gay male community there has been a tradition of skepticism about male bisexuality. This is because the term "bisexual" has often been used by young men who are on the path to an adult gay identity (Lever, 1994; Rosario et al., 2006). They may have used the "bisexual" label because of uncertainty about their true feelings or as a convenient crutch on their way out of the closet. This conclusion is also supported by the results of data mining by the dating site OkCupid. Among 18-year-old males on the site who identified as "bisexual," only about 1 in 5 sent messages to both men and women; most of the others sent all their messages to men (OKtrends, 2010). In another study, gay men who had identified as bisexual in the past were asked whether they had actually been bisexual during that earlier period. The great majority said no; most of these said they had identified as bisexual because they thought others would accept them more readily as bisexual than as homosexual (Semon et al., 2017). Again, this is not to deny the existence of bisexual men but to emphasize that any study of male "bisexuality" needs to carefully distinguish between those men who are sexually attracted to both sexes and those who are not.

The situation with female bisexuality is almost the opposite of the one just described for men. That is to say, when women's genital responses to erotic

▲ Bisexual comedian Margaret Cho.

videos are tested, most women respond to both male and female videos, regardless of whether they identify as straight or bisexual. Only some lesbian-identified women respond selectively to female videos (Dawson & Chivers, 2014). These findings, which are consistent with a body of other evidence, do not disprove the existence of exclusive heterosexuality in women. Rather, they show that, in women, there is not always a straightforward connection between patterns of physiological arousal and those of verbally stated sexual attraction. Most men can figure out their sexual orientation by monitoring their genitals; few women can do so.

The percentage of American women who identify as bisexual has increased markedly in recent years—from 1.8% in 2008 to 5.6% in 2018, according to the General Social Survey. Most of that increase was driven by young women: in the 18-to-24 age group, the percentages rose from 2.7% to 7.5% over the same time period. We doubt that there has been an actual increase of this magnitude in young women's bisexual attractions: Rather, it seems likely that young women are becoming aware of, or feel socially encouraged to acknowledge, feelings that went unrecorded in earlier years. There was no equivalent increase in bisexual identification by men, or of lesbian/gay identification by either sex, over the same period.

Psychologist Lisa Diamond followed about 80 young non-heterosexual women over a period of 10 years (Diamond, 2008; Diamond, 2016). At the onset of her study, all the women described themselves as "lesbian," "bisexual," or "unlabeled." Over the course of the study many of the women changed their self-descriptions, but there was no overall trend in one direction or another. Rather, the women adopted identities that matched their current relationship patterns. Diamond's work suggested not only that women's sexual orientation is more fluid than men's, but also that there is little distinction between different kinds of non-heterosexual women, such as lesbian and bisexual, when women's lives are viewed over a longer term. For some women, these labels are not as important as the specific individuals to whom they are attracted. Thus Chirlane McCrae, when asked about her attraction to Bill de Blasio, said, "I didn't think: 'Oh, now I'm attracted to men.' I was attracted to Bill."

Another complicating issue is that many self-identified bisexual people are not attracted to men and to women in the same way. For example, a bisexual man may be more emotionally attracted to women but more physically drawn to men. Alternatively, the strength of a person's attraction to one or the other sex might change over the lifespan. Unidimensional measures of sexual orientation do little justice to these complexities.

Other personality traits that are not directly associated with sexual orientation influence where a man or woman stands on the sexual orientation spectrum. One example is novelty seeking (or its close relative, sensation seeking). This trait is heritable, and it is linked to possession of a particular variant of a dopamine receptor gene. Men who possess this genetic variant are far more likely than other men to have sex with both men and women (Hamer, 2002). Matthew Stief and colleagues at Cornell University found that bisexual individuals score higher than other people in sexual sensation seeking (e.g., "I like to have new and exciting sexual experiences"), sexual curiosity ("If I were invited to an orgy, I would accept"), and sexual arousability ("When a sexually attractive stranger accidentally touches me, I easily become aroused") (Stief et al., 2014). Another study found that among men who identify as bisexual, only those who showed genital arousal to both sexes scored high in sexual curiosity (Rieger et al., 2013). In other words, it's as if there's a developmental process that drives people's main attractions to males or to females, as well as one or more other personality factors, partly biological in nature, that broaden their sexual horizons, causing them to have sexual interest in persons of their nonpreferred sex.

You might think that when bisexually identified men or women enter committed sexual relationships, they would do so in roughly equal numbers with same-sex and other-sex partners. But that's not the case: If one partner in a committed relationship identifies as bisexual, the other partner is nearly always of the other sex, according to

▲ Bisexual punk rocker Billie Joe Armstrong.

**pansexuality** Sexual attraction to persons of any sex or gender. Also called omnisexuality.

**biphobia** Prejudice against bisexuals.

**bisexual erasure** Ignoring or denying the existence of bisexual people.

a large random-sample survey (Herek et al., 2010). That may be because the pool of potential heterosexual partners is so much larger, or because it's simpler and more socially acceptable to be in a heterosexual relationship.

The term **pansexuality** (or omnisexuality) overlaps considerably with bisexuality, but it is a broader term, referring to sexual or romantic attraction to persons of any sex or gender identity, including persons with nonstandard identities (Rice, 2015). People who identify as pansexual often think of themselves as "gender-blind," meaning that a person's sex or gender is simply not a factor influencing their attractiveness. Many people who identify as bisexual, on the other hand, use different criteria for the attractiveness of men and women or relate sexually to men and women in different ways.

## Bisexual people face prejudice

Being bisexual has certain advantages: "It doubles your chance of a date on Saturday night," as Woody Allen is reputed to have said. But bisexual men and women are exposed to prejudice and discrimination (**biphobia**). This is particularly true for bisexual men, who are perceived more negatively than any other minority sexual orientation (Helms & Waters, 2016). In one study, bisexual men were evaluated as being more confused, untrustworthy, and open to new experiences, and less monogamous and less able to maintain a long-term relationship, as compared with either straight or gay men (Zivony & Lobel, 2014). Another stereotype about bisexual men is that they are especially likely to spread HIV and other sexually transmitted infections.

By calling these beliefs stereotypes, we don't mean that they are necessarily flat-out wrong: We've just mentioned evidence that bisexual people may be relatively open to new sexual experiences, and some young people who identify as bisexual may be, if not "confused," at least in a state of uncertainty about their sexual orientation. But these beliefs are stereotypes when applied indiscriminately against the entire population of bisexual people with the aim of denigrating them.

Anti-bisexual stereotypes are harmful at a personal level, of course, but also at a political level. Here's one example: In opposing legal protection for bisexual people, then U.S. Senator Don Nickles said, "Bisexual by definition means promiscuous, having relations with both men and women" (Religious Tolerance.org, 2012). Nickles's comment reflects a general tendency for conservatives to define words like "heterosexual," "homosexual," and "bisexual" in terms of sexual behavior rather than sexual attraction.

Another manifestation of prejudice against bisexual people is when other people deny that they exist or simply ignore them. These attitudes have been called **bisexual erasure**, a phenomenon that has caused bisexual people to be largely invisible. Not only straight people but also gays and lesbians may participate in bisexual erasure, if they assume that everyone who identifies as bisexual is simply a gay person who is halfway out of the closet or someone who just wants attention (Alarie & Gaudet, 2013; Eisner, 2013).

These negative views about bisexual people are changing, however, especially among the young and well educated. We mentioned earlier that increasing numbers of young people are describing themselves as "mostly heterosexual." Such people are especially likely to reject negative stereotypes about bisexual people because they have recognized at least a trace of bisexuality in themselves. Another factor promoting acceptance of bisexual people is the emergence of self-identified bisexual role models in some walks of life. Examples include actresses Drew Barrymore and Angelina Jolie, feminist leader Patricia Ireland, choreographer Paul Taylor, fashion designer Calvin Klein, and businessman/politician Michael Huffington. Still, bisexual role models (especially male ones) are in short supply outside of the arts and the entertainment industry.

Bisexual Americans have lagged behind gays and lesbians in developing a community identity. A Bisexual Center was founded in San Francisco in 1976, and various regional bisexual organizations sprang up. Bisexuals formed their own contingents in gay rights marches beginning in the late 1980s, and the 1993 March on Washington for Lesbian, Gay and Bi Equal Rights and Liberation was the first national event to include "bi" in its name. BiNet, a national-level bisexual organization, was formed in 1990. The American Institute of Bisexuality, founded in 1998, publishes an academic journal, the *Journal of Bisexuality*. Several important books by or about bisexuals have appeared since the early 1990s (see Recommended Reading at the end of this chapter).

Bisexuals debate whether they should ally closely with lesbians and gay men, forge an independent social identity, or act as some kind of bridge between heterosexual and homosexual people. The bisexual community is very much a work in progress.

### Lesbian, gay, straight, bi, other—more alike than different

This chapter has necessarily emphasized what distinguishes people of different sexual orientations, whether in their biological development, their cognitive and personality traits, their communities, or their life experiences. It's important to know something about these differences, both because they offer a window into an important aspect of human nature and because they help us relate to people whose sexual orientations differ from our own.

Still, we wrap up the chapter by emphasizing that nearly all of us experience sexual and romantic attraction in similar ways, regardless of our sexual orientation. Nearly everyone has had or will have the experience of falling in love for the first time, for example, and it feels the same, regardless of who one falls in love with. Here's how an African American rap artist, Frank Ocean, described the experience in a Tumblr post (Ocean, 2012):

> *4 summers ago, I met somebody. I was 19 years old. He was too. We spent that summer, and the summer after, together. Everyday almost, And on the days we were together, time would glide. Most of the day I'd see him, and his smile. I'd hear his conversation and his silence. Until it was time to sleep. Sleep I would often share with him. By the time I realized I was in love, it was malignant. It was hopeless. There was no escaping, no negotiating with the feeling. No choice. It was my first love, it changed my life.*

## Summary

- Sexual orientation defines how a person's disposition to experience sexual attraction varies with the sex of potential partners. It can be represented on a 5- or 7-point scale from heterosexual (attracted to people of the other sex only), through varying degrees of bisexuality, to homosexual (attracted to people of one's own sex only). A small percentage (2% to 3%) of the population is homosexual. Exclusively homosexual men are more common than exclusively homosexual women. The percentage that is bisexual depends greatly on the definition used but is always higher in women than in men.

- Lesbians and gay men, although very diverse, tend to be sex-atypical in their self-described masculinity or femininity, in cognitive and personality traits, and in occupational interests. This gender nonconformity is evident in children who later become gay adults.

- A variety of theories have been put forward to explain how sexual orientation develops. According to Freudian psychoanalytic theory, heterosexuality emerges from a complex sequence of stages of psychosexual development; the disruption of several of these stages may lead to homosexuality. According to socialization theories, a child's ultimate sexual orientation is molded by innumerable rewards and punishments given by parents and others.

- According to biological theories, sexual orientation is affected by factors such as prenatal hormone levels, which are thought to influence the organization of brain systems responsible for sexual attraction. Genes also influence sexual orientation, especially

*(Continued)*

## Summary *(continued)*

in men, but the specific genes involved have not yet been identified.

- The modern gay rights movement began in 19th-century Germany and spread to the United States after World War II. A key event was the Stonewall Rebellion, riots in New York City in 1969 that led to the politicization of the gay community. The AIDS epidemic, which began around 1980, devastated gay male communities. It was also the spur to more effective political action and to greater openness on the part of gay people.

- The rapid advances made by lesbians and gay men have made them the focus of a cultural conflict between conservative and progressive forces in American society. The same conflict is playing itself out worldwide; in some countries, gay people have gained greater acceptance than in the United States, while in others gay sex is still a crime.

- Pre-gay children who are markedly gender-nonconformist typically experience taunting, abuse, or efforts to normalize them. For gay people, psychological development is a process of "coming out." This process involves several stages: self-realization and self-acceptance, disclosure to others, joining the gay community, and integrating one's homosexuality with other aspects of one's cultural identity.

- Gay sex and gay relationships are quite similar to their heterosexual counterparts. Gay men tend to be more sexually adventurous and to have more partners than lesbians or heterosexual people, but monogamous gay relationships are also common.

- There is diversity within the gay and lesbian communities. Some lesbians identify as "butch" (more masculine) and some others as "femme" (more feminine). Some gay men have preferred sex roles as "tops" or "bottoms," but many are "versatile." Within the gay male community there is a leather/BDSM subculture as well as a "bear" community that rejects the prevalent gay standards of male beauty.

- Many lesbians and some gay men are parents, either from earlier heterosexual relationships or as a result of a variety of reproductive strategies that are open to gay couples. The children of gay parents generally thrive: They may experience some taunting in school, but they are as well adjusted as the children of straight parents.

- Anti-gay attitudes and behaviors (homophobia) have multiple roots. These roots include cultural indoctrination, an image of homosexuality as a transgression of social rules, and a defense mechanism against real or feared personal homosexual tendencies. Overcoming homophobia depends primarily on personal interactions in everyday life.

- Bisexual men and women have the advantage of a wider potential range of sexual experience, but they also face social stigma ("biphobia"). They may be mischaracterized as closeted gay people, as oversexed, as spreaders of AIDS, or as inconstant partners. Bisexuals have attempted to forge a social and political identity that is at least partially separate from that of gay people.

---

The **Discovering Human Sexuality** digital resources include activities, animations, flashcards, web links, chapter outlines and summaries, and other study tools.

. . . . . . . . . . . . . . . . . . .

Learn more with this chapter's digital tools, including the **Oxford Insight Study Guide**, at **oup.com/he/levay5e**.

## Discussion Questions

1. How do your views on homosexuality compare with those of your grandparents, your parents, and your college peers?

2. Your friend tells you, "A person can tell if someone is gay without even asking them." Do you agree or disagree with this statement? If you agree, what clues you in to a person's sexual orientation?

3. You are a board member of a local school district. This school district proposes to start a program in which openly gay faculty would provide support, information, and role models for students. Would you support or discourage this program? Give a rationale for your answer. What would the effect of the program be on the students?

4. Imagine that you have always been attracted emotionally and sexually to your own sex and that your family has rather traditional religious and conservative views. Would you tell your family about your attraction? If you were to disclose your sexual orientation to your family, how would you do it? What do you think their response would be?

5. Researchers find more evidence of bisexuality and sexual fluidity among women than among men. Do you think this says something profound about men's and women's sexuality, or does it have more to do with how boys and girls are acculturated to think about sexual attraction and sexual relationships?

6. The text lists three characteristics of occupations in which gays and lesbians are overrepresented. How do you think gay people acquire the personalities that allow them to be successful in those occupations?

## Web Resources

American Civil Liberties Union (ACLU). LGBT Project page
   **www.aclu.org/lgbt-rights**

American Institute of Bisexuality   **www.bisexual.org**

Asian Pacific Islander Queer Women and Transgender Coalition   **www.apiqwtc.org**

BiNet USA   **www.binetusa.org**

Bisexual Resource Center   **www.biresource.net**

Center for Positive Sexuality   **www.positivesexuality.org**

Gay, Lesbian and Straight Education Network (GLSEN)   **www.glsen.org**

WGBH Educational Foundation. Homophobia questionnaire   **tinyurl.com/jmgq**

Human Rights Campaign (political and educational organization for the gay, lesbian, bisexual, and transgender communities)   **www.hrc.org**

Lambda Legal (the main gay and lesbian legal organization)
   **www.lambdalegal.org**

National Center for Lesbian Rights (NCLR)   **www.nclrights.org**

National LGBTQ Task Force (serves the same communities as the Human Rights Campaign, but with an emphasis on grassroots activism)
   **www.thetaskforce.org**

PFLAG (formerly Parents, Families and Friends of Lesbians and Gays)
   **www.pflag.org**

## Recommended Reading

Diamond, L. M. (2008). *Sexual fluidity: Understanding women's love and desire.* Harvard University Press.

Faderman, L. (2015). *The gay revolution: The story of the struggle.* Simon & Schuster.

Garber, M. (2000). *Bisexuality and the eroticism of everyday life.* Routledge.

Herek, G. M. (Ed.). (1998). *Stigma and sexual orientation: Understanding prejudice against lesbians, gay men, and bisexuals.* Sage.

LeVay, S. (2017). *Gay, straight, and the reason why: The science of sexual orientation* (2nd ed.). Oxford University Press.

Ochs, R. & Williams, H.S. (Eds.). (2014). *Recognize: The voices of bisexual men.* Bisexual Resource Center.

Owens-Reid, D. & Russo, K. (2014). *This is a book for parents of gay kids: A question and answer guide to everyday life.* Chronicle.

Rust, P. C. R. (Ed.). (2000). *Bisexuality in the United States: A social science reader.* Columbia University Press.

Savin-Williams, R. C. (2001). *Mom, Dad, I'm gay: How families negotiate coming out.* American Psychological Association.

Schwartz, E. F. (2016). *Before I do: A legal guide to marriage, gay and otherwise.* New Press.

Stein, M. (Ed.). (2019). *The Stonewall riots: A documentary history.* NYU Press.

For some, sexuality is inextricably tied to fetish objects or to behaviors outside the sexual norm.

# 13 Atypical Sexuality

Most of us, at one time or another, have experienced an unusual sexual fantasy or have tried out some "kinky" sexual practice. Such thoughts and behaviors may add spice to our sex lives and help maintain our interest in sexual relationships. But have you ever been sexually aroused by a horse? Have you ever masturbated while holding an item of lingerie? Have you ever enjoyed having your sex partner inflict pain on you during sex? Such unusual desires take a central place in the sex lives of some people—most of whom are men. These desires become problematic only if they cause distress to the people who experience them or if they are acted out in behaviors that harm others or run afoul of the law. In this chapter we describe a variety of atypical sexual desires and behaviors, discuss theories about what causes them, and present treatment options if treatment is called for.

## 13.1 Sexual Variety Is the Spice of Life

*The blows fell rapidly and powerfully on my back and arms. Each one cut into my flesh and burned there, but the pains enraptured me. They came from her whom I adored, and for whom I was ready at any hour to lay down my life.*

*She stopped. "I am beginning to enjoy it," she said, "but enough for today. I am beginning to feel a demonic curiosity to see how far your strength goes. I take a cruel joy in seeing you tremble and writhe beneath my whip, and in hearing your groans and wails; I want to go on whipping without pity until you beg for mercy, until you lose your senses. You have awakened dangerous elements in my being. But now get up."*

*I seized her hand to press it to my lips.*

*"What impudence." She shoved me away with her foot. "Out of my sight, slave!"*

—*Venus in Furs* (Sacher-Masoch, 1870/2000)

**kink** Colloquial term for an unusual sexual desire or behavior; a paraphilia.

**sadism** Sexual arousal by the infliction of pain, bondage, or humiliation on others, or by witnessing the recipient's suffering.

**masochism** Sexual arousal from being subjected to pain, bondage, or humiliation.

**sadomasochism (S/M)** The infliction and acceptance of pain or humiliation as a means of sexual arousal.

**bondage** The use of physical restraint for purposes of sexual arousal.

Does this passage strike you as an example of healthy sexuality? Or was one or both of the participants mentally deranged? Richard von Krafft-Ebing, the 19th-century encyclopedist of sexual "aberrations," was so impressed by Leopold von Sacher-Masoch's autobiographical account that he borrowed the author's name to create the term "masochism," which he saw as a psychiatric disorder.

Today, however, most sex researchers believe that only a small province within the realm of atypical sexuality needs to be cordoned off as "disordered" (**FIGURE 13.1**). We cover that province later in this chapter. For now, we discuss variant sexual interests and practices—or **kinks** in common parlance—as, at worst, harmless oddities and, at best, creative strategies to enrich sexual experiences and to strengthen relationships. Someone who has these interests may be called a kink-identified person or, more colloquially, a kinkster.

One feature that most unusual forms of sexuality have in common is that far more men than women experience and enact them. For that reason, we often use male pronouns to describe individuals in this chapter.

## 13.2 Sadomasochism Involves the Infliction or Receipt of Pain or Degradation

**LEARNING OBJECTIVES**

After reading this section you should be able to:

13.2.1 Define sadism, masochism, and BDSM.
13.2.2 Explain how consent is established in BDSM practices.

In regular discourse, the word **sadist** may be applied to any cruel person, and the word **masochist** to anyone who is a "glutton for punishment." When these terms are used by sexologists, however, they refer to people who are sexually aroused by physical pain or psychological humiliation. Sadists are sexually aroused by inflicting such pain or humiliation on others (or by witnessing the recipient's suffering); masochists are sexually aroused by experiencing pain or submitting to humiliation themselves.

The term "sadism," like "masochism," was coined by Krafft-Ebing from the name of a real person—in this case the Marquis de Sade (1740–1814) (**FIGURE 13.2**). The two terms are often combined into the single word **sadomasochism (S/M)** because they may coexist in the same person or involve reciprocal interactions between a sadist and a masochist.

Sadomasochism, narrowly defined, involves the infliction, or enjoyment, of physical pain—by such practices as spanking, paddling, whipping, piercing, cutting,

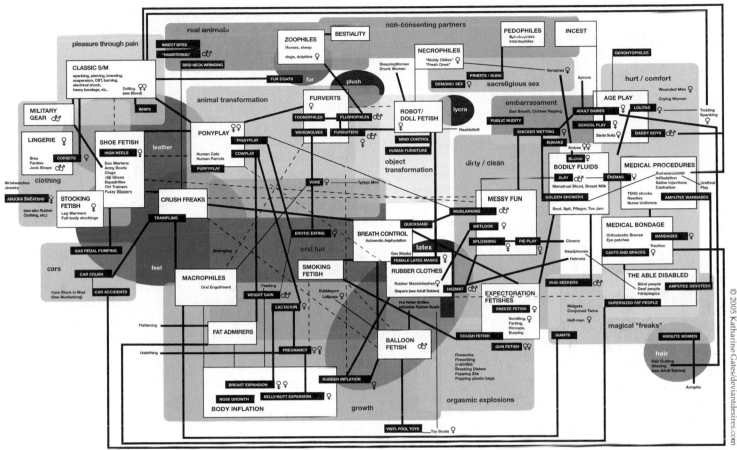

▲ **FIGURE 13.1   A map of "deviant" sexuality** by Katharine Gates (see Recommended Reading at the end of this chapter), showing the clustering of traits into conceptual categories, with their links. Only small regions of this map cover forms of sexual expression that are definitely abnormal or illegal (especially the blue section labeled "non-consenting partners"), but other regions may be considered pathological if they cause distress to the people who experience them. This diagram should be viewed as one writer's attempt to organize the diversity of atypical sexual expression, rather than as a definitive or consensus-based analysis.

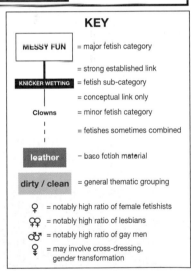

branding, nipple clamping, or "cock-and-ball torture." This last item includes many different methods for inflicting pain on a man's genitals, some of which risk injury.

Alternatively (or in addition), the emphasis may be on psychological torture. This may include placing someone in a humiliating position by means of **bondage** (restraints), verbal abuse, or **dominance** (enslavement). The person may be forced to engage in some degrading activity, such as licking his tormentor's boots, verbally acknowledging his enslavement, being led around on all fours like a dog, or being urinated or defecated on. **Submission** is the key element—it may be experienced as erotic by both the dominant and the submissive partner. Accoutrements like military uniforms or a dungeon-like decor can intensify the psychological pressure on the submissive partner.

**BDSM** is the term generally used for the entire collection of sexual behaviors involving the infliction of, or submission to, pain, humiliation, restraint, and the like. What the letters BDSM originally stood for is lost to history, but bondage, dominance, discipline, submission, sadism, and masochism are commonly mentioned. A Google search under the keyword "BDSM" in 2020 elicited 354 million hits, so BDSM

**dominance**   The use of humiliation or subservience for purposes of sexual arousal.

**submission**   Taking the subservient role in BDSM activity.

**BDSM**   An all-inclusive term for forms of sexual expression that involve inflicting and receiving physical pain, restraint, or humiliation.

◀ **FIGURE 13.2** **Donatien Alphonse François de Sade, better known as the Marquis de Sade,** described his own sadistic interests in *The 120 Days of Sodom,* a book that he wrote while imprisoned in the Bastille.

is obviously a topic of widespread interest. Any attempt to label BDSM as "sick" or "disordered" would risk pathologizing a significant fraction of the population. BDSM practitioners do not experience higher rates of mental health or relationship problems than other people (Brown et al., 2019).

As with other forms of variant sexual expression, BDSM may be practiced with all degrees of intensity. Most couples probably engage in some slapping, wrestling, or biting from time to time as a way of heightening their sexual arousal. For many people, BDSM represents a fashion statement or a cultural identity, perhaps validated by an occasional visit to a BDSM sex club (**BOX 13.1**). Other people may spend a great deal of time pursuing BDSM interests: They may seek out partners at sex clubs or via the internet, or they may create BDSM "dungeons" in their own homes.

Some individuals are so focused on the infliction or receipt of pain or humiliation that the usual physiological manifestations of sex, such as erection, ejaculation, and orgasm, play little or no role. At some BDSM parties, especially those that are semipublic, penetrative sex and even genital exposure may be banned.

Within the BDSM community, individuals who subject others to pain or humiliation are referred to as "tops" or "doms" (dominants) while those who prefer to be on the receiving end are "bottoms" or "subs" (submissives). It seems that subs are quite a bit more common than doms, and appreciable numbers of subs are female. In fact, a survey of the general Canadian population found that more women than men (28% versus 19%) answered yes to the question "Have you ever been sexually aroused while suffering, being dominated, or being humiliated?" (Joyal & Carpentier, 2017).

Good female doms are in short supply and are much sought after in heterosexual BDSM communities. For gay men, of course, that's not a problem; in fact there exists a flourishing gay male BDSM subculture. Because female doms are hard to find, some heterosexual male masochists pay for the services of a **dominatrix**—a woman who inflicts pain or humiliation in a BDSM setting. There is a small but flourishing lesbian BDSM community (**FIGURE 13.3**), as well as communities in which gay and straight men and women mingle freely.

**dominatrix** A woman who acts the role of the dominant partner in a BDSM setting.

The phrase "safe, sane, and consensual" is a popular summary of the ethical principles that should guide BDSM practices. Of these, consent is perhaps the most important, but it is sometimes difficult to verify, because compulsion or a master–slave relationship is often a part of the sexual activity (or "scene") itself. "Stop, stop!" may mean "More, more!" Establishing consent is an ongoing process. Before the scene, perhaps as a part of flirtation or foreplay, the partners negotiate what will transpire and set limits for behavior. (For example, they may agree that no blood is to be drawn or that condoms are to be used for any sexual penetration.) During the scene, there may be brief interruptions to check that the sub is still OK with what is going on. In addition, the participants often have prearranged "safe words" or nonverbal signals that cue the dom to desist. After the BDSM scene, the partners usually share a period of cuddling, intimacy, or more conventional sex, during which they may review what has transpired, thus learning for future occasions what is exciting and what should be avoided.

▲ **FIGURE 13.3** **Two female BDSM enthusiasts** prepare for a Mardi Gras celebration in Sydney, Australia.

## BOX 13.1
## In the Dungeon

Staci Newmahr, a sociologist at SUNY Buffalo, undertook an ethnographic study of the heterosexual BDSM scene at a club in a northeastern U.S. city (Newmahr, 2011). That meant getting personally involved; she submitted to flogging by a BDSM practitioner:

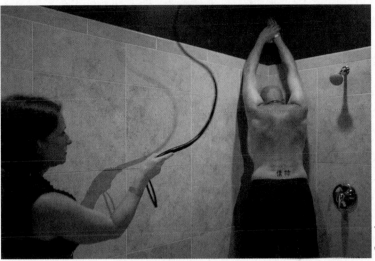

© David McNew/Getty Images

> He began with two-handed flogging, which I had never seen him do, and he was quick and light and agile. I really wouldn't have thought that he'd be so dexterous with them. After a few minutes—maybe ten or fifteen, but I'm not the best one to ask—he checked in with me. I said I was fine. I was still facing the cross [an X-shaped frame to which she was tied by her hands and feet].

> The next thing I felt was an enormous thud across my back. I turned to look at him. He had taken all nine of his floggers in his hands, and hit me with them in one blow. Trey is over six feet tall and nearly 200 pounds. The floggers alone must have weighed thirty pounds.

> At some point, about midway through the scene, he switched to a singletail. Each time the whip landed, it burned me—a tiny precise sharp hotness that lasted just a half-second short of unbearable. He threw it fast, slicing my skin with one blow after the other, diagonal down the left shoulder, then the right, then the left—then a shot across the middle of my back. It fucking hurt.

> We played for three hours. When our scene ended the dungeon was closing and many of the onlookers had gone to their rooms. The ones that remained approached us to compliment us.

Newmahr found that many or most members of the BDSM club took an "essentialist" view of themselves, thinking of their interest in BDSM as something they were born with. As one practitioner told her:

> The interest [in SM] was literally the first thing that I can remember about most of the world. It's why I say it's so deeply ingrained in who I am. It's more today than a sexual orientation, than a gender identity—it's SM. It's really where I identify with; it's that strong.

The members of the club also had an essentialist perspective on the particular role they took in BDSM activities. "My name is Jane," a person might say, "I've been a member for 2 years, and I'm a submissive." People's roles could change, but that was viewed as something like coming out of the closet, more than as a real change of identity. People might be labeled as "a top who can't admit it" or "a submissive and doesn't know it yet." Nevertheless, it's clear that actual BDSM practices rely heavily on socially constructed "scripts" that are derived from literature (e.g., de Sade), modern media, and person-to-person communication.

Although many members of the club viewed BDSM as sexual in nature, overt sexual activity was not a significant part of the club scene that Newmahr investigated. In many gay BDSM clubs, on the other hand, sexual activity may be part of the public scene or something that goes on in more private areas of the club.

These kinds of communications are of particular importance in male–male BDSM scenes, which tend to involve more intense interactions than what typically takes place in male–female or female–female scenes. BDSM scenes that challenge the bottom's tolerance or that approach the boundaries of safety or consent are known as "edge play." Serious injuries and even deaths do sometimes occur during BDSM activities; it's not a good idea to plunge into edge play without first gaining experience from the milder BDSM scenes and learning from skilled practitioners.

Zak Krevitt © 2016

▲ **FIGURE 13.4** **Puppy play** is a BDSM variant that is popular with some gay and bisexual men.

**fetish** Sexual fixation on an inanimate object, material, or part of the body.

**partialism** A fetishistic attraction to a specific part of the body.

An interesting offshoot of BDSM is puppy play (or pup play) (**FIGURE 13.4**). Puppy play scenes usually involve two gay or bisexual men, one of whom dresses and acts like a dog, and the other as his handler. Although the two men are clearly in a dominant/submissive relationship, often involving anal sex with the puppy as the recipient, there is little or no infliction of pain; instead, the relationship can be quite friendly. Sometimes a handler controls two or more puppies. Important to a puppy is the sense that he is losing his regular self in his new role. One puppy described it like this:

*And then finally pulling on this tight leather hood that I've got that literally has a dog's face, muzzle, that kind of thing so normally when I pull the hood on for myself that is very much that's the point where I kind of allow myself to shed the ability to talk and with the ability to talk it kind of allows me then to almost Zen like enter a much more preverbal state; I stop talking so I stop thinking in words and it becomes a much more emotional primal headspace that I allow myself to then fall into.* (Langdridge & Lawson, 2019)

On the surface, BDSM activities involve entirely negative feelings such as pain, fear, and anger. Dedicated BDSM practitioners, however, assert the very opposite: that the relationship of power, trust, and dependency that exists between top and bottom represents a condition of heightened intimacy and that a participant in a BDSM scene may enter an altered state of consciousness that amounts to a spiritual experience.

## 13.3 Most Fetishes Are Related to the Body

**LEARNING OBJECTIVE**
After reading this section you should be able to:

13.3.1 Explain the differences between partialism, media fetishism, object fetishism, and urolagnia.

Most of us find that certain items of clothing or certain perfumes are especially effective in enhancing a partner's sexual attractiveness—and whole industries depend on that fact. For many of us, particular body parts—for example, breasts, penises, buttocks, legs, or feet—carry a special erotic charge. When any such sexual attraction comes to play a central role in a person's sexual life, it is known as a **fetish**.

The most common fetishes are associated with the human body (**FIGURE 13.5**). If the focus is on specific body parts, it is called **partialism**. Alternatively, the arousing stimulus may be something worn on the body, such as women's lingerie or jewelry, or a general feature of the body, such as obesity (eroticized by "fat admirers" or "chubby chasers").

As shown in the figure, a remarkably high proportion of fetishes are directed toward feet and shoes. Why this should be so is something of a mystery. Sigmund Freud proposed that feet are taken as a symbolic representation of the penis. It may also be relevant that feet are often hidden from view, inside shoes or stockings, perhaps giving them a special allure. (Hands, which are much more visible and are frequently touched, are rarely the focus of fetishes.) The frequent eroticization of feet might also have to do with the close proximity of the feet and the genitals in the brain's map of the body, as discussed in Box 5.4. Other common

© Mark Peterson/Corbis

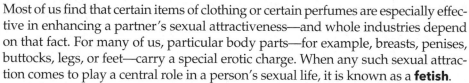

◀ Fetishism is erotic fixation on inanimate objects or, as here, on certain body parts.

body fetishes are for body fluids (e.g., urine), hair, and body modifications (e.g., piercings).

In **media fetishism**, fetishistic desire is directed toward *materials*—such as leather, rubber, silk, or fur—that are arousing regardless of the specific object into which they are fashioned. Usually, however, the material is most arousing when it is worn on the body as an item of clothing. Sacher-Masoch was a fur fetishist as well as a masochist.

Besides normal body parts, a few men have fetishistic attractions to abnormal body parts such as congenital malformations or amputation stumps, while some other men are sexually aroused by the thought of having malformations or amputations themselves, and they may actually seek to have an amputation to satisfy their desire (Brugger et al., 2016). Within the world of amputation fetishism, these two kinds of men are referred to as "devotees" and "wannabes," respectively. (There may also be men who seek to have an amputation for nonsexual reasons.)

Fetishism involving inanimate objects not associated with bodies—called **object fetishism** or **objectophilia** or **objectum sexuality**—is much less common, but it does occur. Most of what we know about object fetishism comes from a website created by and for objectophiles (Objectum Sexuality Internationale, 2013). Sometimes the love object is a well-known landmark: An American woman, for example, fell in love with the Eiffel Tower, "married" it, and changed her name to La Tour Eiffel (Cassar, 2016), and another American woman fell in love with a roller coaster (**FIGURE 13.6**). The majority of objectophiles have physical sexual contact with their love objects or (if the objects are very large or far away) with scale models of them. According to the website, objectophilia is not a fetish, because the loved objects have sentient spirits that reciprocate the objectophiles' love. Even though this may be an objectophile's sincere belief, it is not factually correct and therefore is not relevant to the question of whether objectophilia is a fetish. One respect in which object fetishism does differ from most other fetishes, however, is that many objectophiles are women. Also according to the website, some objectophiles have Asperger's syndrome, which was reclassified by the American Psychiatric Association's 5th edition of *Diagnostic and Statistical Manual of Mental Disorders (DSM-5)* as an autism spectrum disorder. It is marked by difficulty in establishing social relationships with human beings. This might facilitate the displacement of a person's sexual and romantic attractions from people to inanimate objects.

That fetishistic interests are common is made obvious by a visit to any sex shop or sex toy website, both of which offer a wide variety of fetish-related objects. Fetish-related videos make up 25% or more of the output of some large adult video companies. Some smaller companies, such as Kink Video and RedBoard Video of San Francisco, specialize entirely in fetish videos. The term "fetish" is used broadly in the sex industry, however, and may include bondage/dominance and almost any other sexual behavior aside from "vanilla sex" (conventional intercourse). In fact, this broader use of the term has spread into general

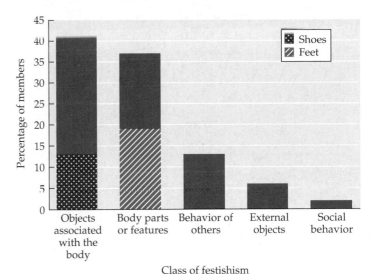

▲ **FIGURE 13.5**  **Prevalence of different classes of fetishes** based on membership in Yahoo groups devoted to single fetishes. The total number of group members was 136,040, and the bar graph breaks these down according to five classes of fetishes. Note that body parts or objects associated with the body constitute by far the most prevalent kinds of fetishes. Within those two categories, note the high prevalence of foot and shoe fetishes. (Data from C. Scorolli et al. 2007. *Int J Impot Res* 19: 432–437.)

**media fetishism**  Sexual attraction to materials such as rubber or silk. Also called material fetishism.

**object fetishism (or objectophilia or objectum sexuality)**  Sexual arousal by objects that are not associated with bodies.

▲ **FIGURE 13.6**  **Object fetishist** Amy Wolfe, a church organist from Pennsylvania, fell in love with a roller coaster, rode it over 3,000 times, and stated her intention to marry it, even though she also had relationships with spaceship models and a banister railing.

use; for example, a person who is sexually aroused by crushing animals or by being crushed is generally known as a "crush fetishist," even though the arousal is to a BDSM-like behavior rather than to a physical object (**BOX 13.2**).

How does a person express fetishistic sexuality? A foot fetishist may incorporate foot worship into sexual foreplay with his partner. He may spend a lot of time watching foot fetish videos or visiting foot fetish websites. He may belong to groups of people who share the same interest. A lingerie fetishist may spend a lot of time purchasing (or

## BOX 13.2
## Crush Fetishes

On a June afternoon in 1999 two Okeechobee, Florida men came across a Honda Passport SUV with its engine running and a man's legs sticking out from under its left rear tire. The victim, Bryan Loudermilk, was alive, and so the men backed the SUV off of him, but he died later that day.

This wasn't a run-of-the-mill wheel-change mishap. Loudermilk had laid himself down in a shallow trench with a board and pillow over his belly, and someone—whose identity was never discovered—drove the SUV onto the board and left it there. It later emerged that Loudermilk had done this many times before without serious injury. This time, though, the SUV's pressure was too great, or he was left for so long in that position that parts of his body died of anoxia.

Loudermilk was a crush fetishist—a person, usually a man, who is sexually aroused by crushing animals or inanimate objects, by watching someone else doing this, or by being crushed himself. Loudermilk was also a foot fetishist, and he drew pictures of himself as a tiny person being stomped on by a giant woman dressed as a goddess and wearing open-toed sandals (Reischel, 2006).

Although there are ways to act out a crush fetish legally and safely—by watching one's girlfriend stomp on insects, for example—these fetishes may escalate into activities that are cruel, illegal, or deadly. A more recent example involved 54-year-old Brent Justice of Houston, Texas. In 2016 he was sentenced to 50 years' imprisonment—later reduced to 20 years—for filming his nearly naked girlfriend mutilating and killing puppies, kittens, and other animals, and for distributing the resulting videos on the internet. His girlfriend received a 10-year sentence (Boroff, 2016).

In response to public concern about crush videos, Congress enacted the Animal Crush Video Prohibition Act in 2010. Nevertheless, it is usually difficult to identify and prosecute the producers of these videos, because the identity of the actors is often concealed and the videos are difficult to find. Sleuthing by People for the Ethical Treatment of Animals (PETA) led to the arrest of Brent Justice and several other perpetrators.

Although crush fetishes often involve the torturing and killing of animals, the motivation behind them seems more con-

Being stomped on by powerful women can be a sexual thrill for male crush fetishists.

© Catalin Petolea/Alamy Stock Photo

nected to masochism than sadism, because the fetishist usually identifies with the crushed animal, not the person doing the crushing. Some crush videos show women stepping on tiny model cars or houses; this makes the women seem gigantic and all-controlling and thus heightens the fetishist's arousal.

As with most unusual forms of sexuality, the reason why some men develop crush festishes isn't known. The fetish often appears early in life. Loudermilk wrote in a letter, "I used to catch lizards and frogs and put a little super glue on their bellies and stick them to the floor next to my teacher's desk so that I would be able to see her step on the victim." Another man recounted how he became sexually aroused at the age of 10 by seeing Liz Taylor grind her stiletto heel into Richard Burton's foot in the film *BUtterfield 8* (Reischel, 2006). Whether these early experiences triggered the development of fetishes, or whether they were simply the first manifestations of a preexisting trait, is unclear.

stealing) items of women's underwear and viewing and touching them during solitary masturbation, or he may ask his partner to wear specific items that he finds arousing. He may even wear these items himself (see the section on cross-dressing below).

At what point does someone with fetishistic interests deserve to be called a fetishist? There is no universal agreement about this: Some authorities reserve the term "fetishist" for a person whose interest clearly crosses the line to a mental disorder (see the section on paraphilic disorders below), but others hold that someone who is strongly invested in fetishism, even if not diagnosable as having a mental disorder, can be called a fetishist. We take the second view—*we use the term "fetishist" without any implication that the person has a disorder.*

Some men have a fetishistic interest in urination. A famous example was Havelock Ellis (1859–1939), a prominent English sex researcher, who described his own inability to experience sexual arousal except by watching women urinate. This kind of fetishism is called **urophilia.** Thus defined, urophilia is very uncommon, but there are plenty of men who are aroused to a varying degree by urinating on their partners or being urinated on by them, without being dependent on urination for sexual arousal. "Water sports" and "golden showers" are colloquial phrases referring to sexual activities involving urination.

The internet has had a major impact on the lives of fetishists, as it has for all people with minority sexual interests (**BOX 13.3**). It has facilitated communication among fetishists, thus bolstering self-acceptance and satisfaction and reducing the likelihood that fetishists will feel the need to seek psychological help. It has also promoted awareness about fetishism in the general population. Thus, the internet has played a key role in "normalizing" fetishism and other uncommon forms of sexual expression.

**urophilia**  Sexual fixation on urination.

## BOX 13.3
## Rubber Fetishism and the Internet

The following is an interview by one of the authors with "Ataraxia," a 59-year-old Pittsburgh man who is a rubber fetishist (or "rubberist") and founder of the International Association of Rubberists and its website, Rubberist.net:

**Is rubber fetishism a mental illness?**
*That's what I thought for the first half of my life. I got out of the Navy because of it. And on the way out their psychiatrists told me, "There's not a whole lot we can do to cure this, so why don't you learn to enjoy it?" That's where I came up with "Ataraxia," which means "peace of mind."*

**What kinds of problems do fetishists have?**
*One problem is spousal: With many of them, their wives are either not into it at all, or they barely tolerate it. And then there's the social aspect, where people think that we're kinky and therefore dangerous. We're not: We don't hurt anybody.*

**What's the purpose of Rubberist.net?**
*The aim is to help others go through that process I went through. Before the internet, fetishists might think they were the only one in the world.*

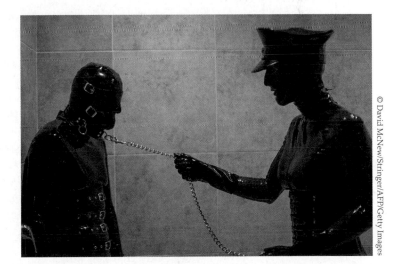

Rubber fetishists.

**What can they find on the site?**
*Personal stories, as well as practical information, like how to make rubber clothing or where to get it. News, culture, surveys. And a way to meet other rubberists. They can*

*(Continued)*

© David McNew/Stringer/AFP/Getty Images

*post on a bulletin board or jump into a conversation. About 1000 rubberists visit the site every day.*

**What kinds of people visit the site?**
*Ninety percent or more are male. There's some confusion because some are transgendered. True female rubberists are rare. As for sexual orientation, my site tends to be heterosexually oriented, but it includes a lot of material that is not specifically straight or gay. There are plenty of gay rubber sites. Life is easier for gay fetishists—they can find partners without too much trouble.*

**What are the options for straight ones?**
*They can grin and bear it, or they can reach some sort of compromise, as I did with my wife. Some of the younger women are more open to it.*

**Is there a connection between rubber and BDSM, like there is between leather and BDSM?**
*Yes, a large proportion of rubberists are into that—mostly the bondage side of it.*

**What's the psychology of rubber fetishism?**
*Mostly it's the sense of encasement. The term is "total enclosure," which means covering every inch of your body with rubber—making two or three layers if you can. It's a combination of the sense of tightness and being shielded from the rest of the world. I think it's a "return to the womb" kind of thing—the warm, moist, enclosing environment, it seems like a womb. It seems to be a phenomenon of the industrialized world. About a third of our members are from England.*

## 13.4 People Cross-Dress for a Variety of Reasons

**LEARNING OBJECTIVES**
After reading this section you should be able to:

13.4.1 Evaluate the different possible motivations for cross-dressing.
13.4.2 Explain the sequence of sexual interests that can progress to autogynephilia.

Some people repeatedly or continuously wear the clothes of the other sex. Both men and women may **cross-dress**, and they do so with a wide variety of motives.

There may be entirely nonsexual reasons for cross-dressing. Women have often cross-dressed in order to pass as men and thus obtain male employment or other privileges of masculinity. Several hundred women disguised themselves as men in order to participate as soldiers in the American Civil War (**FIGURE 13.7**). Nowadays, male attire may be more practical for many activities. In fact, as women have gained increasing parity with men, traditionally masculine attire, such as blue jeans and T-shirts, have become unisex.

Alternatively, men or women may dress as the other sex for entertainment purposes or to mock stereotypical gender expectations or fashion norms. This is called doing **drag**. In this case their clothing, makeup, and hairstyle are likely to be an over-the-top caricature, not a real attempt to replicate the typical dress of the other sex. Many, but not all, drag artists are gay men, in which case they are often called "drag queens." Female performers who dress in male attire may be called "drag kings."

For transgender people, wearing the clothes of the gender with which they identify is a natural expression of their gender identity. Trans people do not typically wear these clothes for purposes of erotic arousal or as a parody. They are only "cross" dressing with respect to their natal (birth) sex, not their gender identity or (if they have physically transitioned) their current sex. Trans people who reject the gender binary may dress in a manner that expresses this attitude—perhaps in some combination of male-typical and female-typical attire or in attire that is not conventionally congruent with their physical appearance (e.g., a skirt with a beard).

**cross-dressing** Wearing the clothing of the other sex, for any of a variety of reasons.

**drag** The wearing of exaggeratedly feminine clothing by a man, or male clothing by a woman, often for entertainment purposes.

## Transvestism is a sexual drive to cross-dress

Yet another class of cross-dressers comprises heterosexual individuals (nearly all men) who wear clothes appropriate to the other sex because they find the practice itself sexually arousing. This is therefore a form of fetishism, and its technical name is transvestic fetishism, or simply **transvestism**. (Again, the use of the term "fetishism" here is not intended to brand this form of sexual expression as a mental disorder.) Transvestic fetishism is not especially rare: One random-sample study of the general population of Sweden found that 2.8% of men and 0.4% of women had engaged in at least one episode of transvestic fetishism (Långstrom & Zucker, 2005).

Many heterosexual transvestites keep their cross-dressing secret, for fear of public ridicule or rejection by their partners. Others venture out in public while cross-dressed, and they may be sexually excited by doing so. Many heterosexual transvestites are married; some conceal their cross-dressing from their wives, but others tell their wives or it is discovered by accident. Wives are commonly disturbed by cross-dressing behavior and may worry that their husbands are gay. Some wives come to accept their husbands' cross-dressing, however, and couples may even incorporate it into their sexual activities.

It seems that there is a continuum of traits in which heterosexual men's sexual desires move from their usual target—women—to *representations* of women that can be progressively stripped away, co-opted, and internalized (Blanchard, 1993; Bailey, 2003). The first stage in this continuum is regular fetishism, in which a woman's identity is represented by an object, such as a piece of feminine attire that is separable from the woman and can be completely owned and controlled by the man. In the second stage (transvestic fetishism), the clothing that represents the woman is put on, rather than simply viewed or handled. Later, the man may be sexually aroused by fantasies in which he imagines *being* an alluring woman, including the possession of breasts and female genitalia. This phenomenon is called **autogynephilia** (see Chapter 4). Finally, the man may seek sexual satisfaction in actually transitioning to the female sex (see Chapter 4). Most fetishists do not progress through this series of traits, of course, but autogynephiles often have regular fetishism and transvestic fetishism in their prior history.

Certainly, not all heterosexual cross-dressers go this route. For others, cross-dressing may lose some of its erotic significance over time and become a matter of gender expression more than sexual expression. Such men may join the Society for the Second Self (more commonly known as Tri-Ess), a support organization that organizes events at which heterosexual cross-dressers can socialize in a safe and accepting atmosphere. Support of this kind is important because heterosexual cross-dressers may encounter a lot of misunderstanding or ridicule.

## Some men are aroused by trans women

While on the subject of gender variance, it's worth mentioning that some men have a specific sexual attraction to transgender or transexual women—most commonly to those who look feminine and have breasts but still have male genitals ("she-males" in popular speech) (Blanchard, 1993). Such men may be referred to as **trans-attracted**, or more colloquially as transfans. A term in common use—"tranny chaser"—is considered derogatory by many trans people. There is also a technical term for this form of sexual

▲ **FIGURE 13.7** **Cross-dressing soldier** Frances Clalin (left), a mother of three children, disguised herself as Union cavalryman Jack Williams (right) and participated in numerous Civil War battles alongside her husband.

Left: Minnesota Historical Society; Right: Library of Congress

**transvestism** Wearing clothes of the other sex for purposes of sexual arousal. The term is sometimes applied to cross-dressing for any reason.

**autogynephilia** A form of male-to-female transexuality characterized by a man's sexual arousal at the thought of being or becoming a woman.

**trans-attracted** Sexually attracted to transgender persons.

▶ Drag king (left) and drag queen (right).

© PYMCA/Getty Images

© Zoonar GmbH/Alamy Stock Photo

expression—"gynandromorphophilia," meaning sexual attraction to persons with elements of both female and male anatomy—but it has far too many syllables to deserve widespread use. We prefer "trans-attraction." The numbers of trans-attracted men are not small, to judge by the large number of "she-male" websites that cater to their interests, as well as the many streetwalking prostitutes who are recognizably transgender (see Chapter 17). Most are heterosexual, not gay, but many heterosexual transfans are autogynephilic (Rosenthal et al., 2017). Thus a transfan's attraction to she-males could be driven by a desire to be in the body of a woman while still able to perform sexually as a male. Still, the phenomenon of trans-attraction remains something of a puzzle.

## 13.5 There Are Many Uncommon Kinks

### LEARNING OBJECTIVES
After reading this section you should be able to:

13.5.1 Describe the sexual interests of adult babies and furries.
13.5.2 Explain the possible motivation for cuckolding.

There is an almost endless list of sexual fetishes and kinks that we don't have space to discuss here. Some of them have been graced with Greek-sounding names such as coprophilia (sexual arousal by feces or defecation) and formicophilia (sexual arousal by being crawled on by ants). For those interested in learning more, a good starting point would be Figure 13.1 and the book *Deviant Desires* from which it is taken (Gates, 2017). Here we pick three examples that, while uncommon, involve enough practitioners to allow for the development of communities devoted to them.

### Adult babies reenact infancy

**infantilism** Sexual satisfaction from acting as an infant.

**adult baby** An adult who obtains sexual satisfaction from acting as if he is a baby or toddler.

Some men derive sexual satisfaction from acting as if they were infants or toddlers. A technical term for this behavior is **infantilism**, but most men in this group don't consider it an illness or seek professional help, and they simply call themselves **adult babies** (Zamboni, 2019). Not all adult babies perceive their activities as being sexually motivated.

Adult babies may wear diapers or toddler clothes, sit in baby chairs, drink from baby bottles, sleep in cribs, and talk and act in a baby-like fashion. Sometimes there are BDSM elements: The man may play a role in which returning to babyhood is a punishment to which he is forced to submit. Adult babies are not interested in sexual contacts with actual babies.

If a man's sexual interest is largely focused on the wearing of diapers, he may call himself a "diaper lover." Diaper lovers may masturbate while wearing diapers, or they may act in more authentically baby-like fashion by wetting or soiling the diapers. Some diaper lovers wear diapers under their regular clothes during daily activities, like adults with incontinence.

As with so many other minority sexual interests, adult babies have been normalized by the internet. In the past they may have thought they were the only people in the world to have an erotic interest in babyhood, but now they are served by many websites and internet-based groups. On some websites, for example, adult babies can hire "babysitters" who will play that role for an hourly fee, doing such things as pampering, feeding, or disciplining the adult baby, or changing his diapers.

### Furries wear animal costumes

Men and women who socialize in animal costumes are known as **furries**. They come to public attention on account of their conventions: It is natural to ask what's going on when half the guests at a hotel are dressed as bears, cats, dogs, or roosters. Furry "animals" are anthropomorphic; that is, they take on the visual appearance of animals but can talk, stand on their hind legs, and exhibit human personalities, like the animal characters in Disney cartoons.

Some observers have claimed that there's nothing sexual about being a furry, and that is doubtless true for some participants (Herzog, 2017). But in a detailed survey of 334 male furries, 96% of the respondents acknowledged at least some sexual motivation, and 47% said that sex was their main reason for being a furry (Hsu & Bailey, 2019). Many of the men said that they were sexually aroused both by other furries and by the idea of being a furry themselves, and many were in romantic relationships with other male furries. Furries often feel like outsiders, either because they are not heterosexual, or because they have traits such as autism spectrum disorder or tics that can make regular social life difficult or embarrassing. Socializing as a furry bypasses these issues: It confers an automatic lovability—at least in the eyes of other furries (Soh & Cantor, 2015). What most clearly distinguishes furries from the puppy play practitioners described earlier is that there are no BDSM connotations and no "human" handlers. In furryland, everyone is a furry.

### Some men are turned on by their partner's infidelity

In traditional usage, a cuckold was a man whose wife had a secret lover. That meaning still exists today, but there is also a kink called **cuckolding** in which a man is sexually aroused by watching his partner have sex with someone else—usually another man. That other man may be referred to as a "bull." Here's how one man described witnessing his wife having sex with a younger man:

> *Sometimes I am with my wife during these sessions, holding her hand or kissing her, but mostly I just watch. Occasionally, I even stay outside the room, drinking or chatting with others. The first few times, I had mixed emotions, but now I find it extremely exciting. . . . Our relationship is better for these events; we are closer than before, and I love seeing her receive such pleasure.* (Anonymous, 2019)

The desired bull is often a stereotypically hypermasculine man, such as a black man with a large penis, apparently because that triggers an eroticized sense of inferiority in the male partner (Ley, 2009). The woman may increase his humiliation by, for example, mocking his supposedly too-small penis or requiring that he suck the other man's ejaculate out of her vagina—a practice known colloquially as

**furry**   A person who socializes in animal costumes.

**cuckolding**   Being sexually aroused by watching one's partner have sex with another person.

"creampie eating." Evidently cuckolding incorporates elements of swinging, voyeurism, and masochism. Cuckolding relationships are also quite common among gay men, and there is a genre of gay pornography devoted to the practice (Lehmiller et al., 2018).

## 13.6 Paraphilic Disorders Cause Distress or Harm Others

**LEARNING OBJECTIVES**

After reading this section you should be able to:

13.6.1 Explain how *DSM-5* distinguishes between a paraphilia and a paraphilic disorder.

13.6.2 Describe the characteristics and sexual history that many people with paraphilic disorders have in common.

13.6.3 Define exhibitionism, voyeurism, and frotteurism.

So far in this chapter, we have discussed feelings and behaviors that, though uncommon, are generally agreed to lie within the realm of healthy or, at worst, harmless sexual expression. We now turn to sexual desires or behaviors that are problematic enough to be considered disorders.

At this point we need to introduce the terms "paraphilia" and "paraphilic disorder." Until recently, the term "paraphilia" meant any unusual and persistent sexual desire that caused distress to the person experiencing it or that led to behavior that harmed others or involved them without their consent. In other words, a paraphilia was by definition a psychiatric disorder. However, *DSM-5*, issued in 2013, altered the definition of **paraphilia** to mean "any intense and persistent sexual interest other than sexual interest in genital stimulation or preparatory fondling with phenotypically normal, physically mature, consenting human partners." A great example of committee-speak! The phrase "phenotypically normal" presumably means not being intersex or transgender, having missing limbs, or being anything other than a garden-variety woman or man. So a paraphilia, according to *DSM-5*, now means basically any uncommon sexual desire or behavior that plays a central role in a person's sex life (but it doesn't include homosexuality or bisexuality). On the other hand, **paraphilic disorders** are defined as the subset of paraphilias that justify clinical intervention because they cause distress or impairment to the individual or because they may lead to behaviors that entail the risk of harming others.

What the editors of *DSM-5* tried to achieve by this change was to make a clear distinction between uncommon sexual desires or behaviors in general (paraphilias) and those desires and behaviors that are problematic (paraphilic disorders). Thus the "kinks" that we've described up to this point are paraphilias by the *DSM-5* definition. We did not use the term "paraphilia" earlier in this chapter, however, because in spite of the change in the *DSM*'s definition, the word inevitably retains a medicolegal flavor, as has been noted by critics (First, 2014). Telling your "furry" friend that they have a paraphilia won't endear you to them. Thus, we don't wish to perpetuate a tradition of turning innocuous forms of sexual expression into mental illnesses or crimes merely because they are rare or seem strange to the average person.

Let's discuss a specific example. We have already described sadism as an unusual form of sexual desire that can be expressed in mutually fulfilling behavior involving consensual partners. According to the *DSM-5*, however, a paraphilic disorder called **sexual sadism disorder** can be diagnosed if both of the following conditions are met:

1. Over a period of at least 6 months, [the person experiences] recurrent and intense sexual arousal from the physical or psychological suffering of another person, as manifested by fantasies, urges, or behaviors.

**paraphilia** A persistent, intense sexual desire or behavior that is uncommon or unusual.

**paraphilic disorder** A paraphilia that causes distress or harms others.

**sexual sadism disorder** Sexual arousal by the suffering of others, viewed as a paraphilic disorder.

2. The person has clinically significant distress or impairment in important areas of functioning, or has sought sexual stimulation from behaviors involving the physical or psychological suffering of two or more nonconsenting persons on separate occasions.

Note that the two alternatives presented within the second condition—distress to the sadist or harm to others—highlight two distinct roles for psychiatrists and other professional therapists: (1) caring for their patients and (2) protecting the general public. Sometimes, as when a child molester confides in a psychiatrist about crimes he has committed or plans to commit, the psychiatrist may be put in a difficult ethical position, in that the principle of doctor–patient confidentiality may conflict with legally mandated reporting requirements. U.S. courts have ruled that health care professionals must inform law enforcement if the public is at risk.

*DSM-5* lists nine categories of paraphilic disorders: (1) sexual masochism disorder, (2) sexual sadism disorder, (3) transvestic disorder, (4) fetishistic disorder, (5) exhibitionistic disorder, (6) voyeuristic disorder, (7) frotteuristic disorder, (8) pedophilic disorder, and (9) the catch-all category "paraphilic disorders not otherwise specified."

The first four categories in this list cover forms of sexual expression that we discussed earlier, in the context of normal sexual expression. All that we need say about them here, then, is that they are diagnosable as paraphilic disorders if (and only if) they cause significant distress to the person who experiences them or risk harming other people who are exposed to them. We will focus our attention on the other four specific paraphilic disorders, as well as some that fall into the "not otherwise specified" category. The paraphilic disorders that come to medical or legal attention most often are those that involve victims (**FIGURE 13.8**).

We can make some generalizations about paraphilic disorders:

- They are often extensions or exaggerations of common sexual desires and behaviors.

- Far more men than women develop them.

- Paraphilic disorders begin at an early age—usually around the time of puberty or early adolescence—and tend to become more pronounced over time.

- People who start out with one kind of paraphilic disorder may eventually exhibit multiple forms; by the time they come to professional attention, 54% report experiencing more than one disorder, and 18% report four or more (Abel & Osborn, 2000).

- Certain personality traits are common among people with paraphilic disorders: These include a lack of social skills (especially in dealing with women), a sense of inadequacy, depression, and sometimes a sense of rage against women.

- People with paraphilic disorders commonly have cognitive distortions, believing, for example, that their behaviors are sexually exciting or beneficial to the people they target.

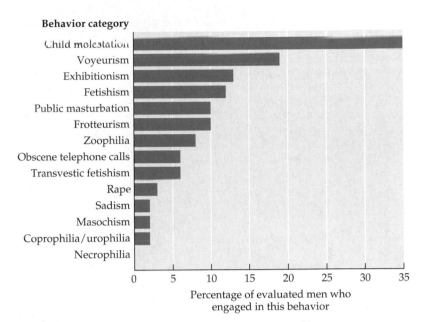

▲ **FIGURE 13.8** **The prevalence of paraphilias** among men being evaluated clinically for suspected inappropriate sexual interests. Of course, these behaviors are biased toward those that bring men to medical or legal attention, namely, those that involve victims. "Coprophilia/urophilia" refers to sexual fixation on defecation or urination. No men in this sample had necrophilic interests. (Data from G. G. Abel and C. A. Osborn. 2000. In *New Oxford Textbook of Psychiatry*, M. G. Gelder et al. [eds.]. Oxford University Press: Oxford.)

**exhibitionism**   Sexual arousal by exposure of the genitals to strangers.

**indecent exposure**   The crime of exposing the genitals or female breasts in public—exact legal definitions vary.

**telephone scatalogia**   Sexual arousal from making obscene telephone calls.

## Exhibitionists expose themselves to nonconsenting persons

The paraphilic disorder called exhibitionistic disorder, or simply **exhibitionism**, applies to people who are sexually aroused by the act or fantasy of exposing their genitals to unsuspecting strangers. Typically, an exhibitionist (or "flasher") will station himself in some location where women are present but that offers little danger of his being identified or arrested. As a woman approaches, the man will step into her line of sight and open his coat to expose his genitals. Alternatively, he may remove a book or newspaper that conceals them. During this action, the man may fantasize having a sexual interaction with the woman. He may masturbate and ejaculate while doing so; alternatively, he may flee and masturbate later, using his recollection of the event as an arousing stimulus. In legal terms, this behavior is the crime of **indecent exposure**, which commonly leads to mandatory registration as a sex offender. The internet has enabled remote forms of exhibitionism such as the sending of unsolicited "dick pics" (Hayes & Dragiewicz, 2018). Several states have made this a crime or are in the process of doing so.

Exhibitionism is defined *behaviorally*—by what people do—rather than as a sexual preference. Exhibitionists are no more excited by exposing themselves than by other forms of sexual expression, to judge from studies that measure genital arousal (Marshall & Fernandez, 2003). Rather, exhibitionists often exhibit high rates of many different kinds of sexual behaviors—a trait called hypersexuality (see below) (Murphy & Page, 2008).

An exhibitionist often misinterprets his victim's reactions—whether of surprise, shock, fear, or amusement—as a reciprocation of his sexual interest. Because of this cognitive distortion on the exhibitionist's part, the woman's emotional reactions tend to reward him and promote a continuation of his behavior. Women who encounter an exhibitionist do best to stay calm and simply walk away, although there is the option of attempting to have the man arrested if circumstances permit.

Exhibitionism is very common: In one survey of college students, over 40% of women and 12% of men said that they had witnessed at least one episode (Clark et al., 2014). Most of the victims had strong emotional reactions to the event: They felt violated, angry, or scared. Less than 1 in 10 of the victims reported the event to the police.

Genital exposure for nonsexual reasons, such as public urination, skinny-dipping, or "streaking," may trigger prosecution for lewd conduct, but is not usually considered indecent exposure. These forms of sexual exposure are not likely to result in registration as a sex offender, although the laws of some states do allow for such a penalty.

## Obscene telephone calling is related to exhibitionism

There is an auditory version of exhibitionism in which the perpetrator derives sexual arousal from making sexually suggestive remarks to a nonconsenting person. This is usually done by telephone, so it is called obscene telephone calling or **telephone scatalogia**. This term does not cover prank phone calls that may have sexual content but are not made for purposes of sexual arousal. Nor does it cover phone sex between willing partners.

The perpetrator (almost always a man) calls a known or unknown victim (usually a woman) and makes sexual suggestions or utters obscenities. Sometimes the caller boasts about his sex organs. Sometimes he makes threats in an attempt to coerce the recipient into a sexual act or a lewd conversation, or he may pose as a sex researcher in order to ask intimate questions as if they form part of a survey. In the latter case he may try to pass as a female.

Improved technology for tracing calls, and the widespread removal of public pay phones, has made obscene telephone calling riskier for the perpetrator than in the past, and the number of such calls may be on the decline. But some women are still

**FAQ:** I've been getting obscene phone calls—what should I do?

Note the exact time and date of the call(s), the name or number from which it originates (if it shows), a description of the voice (e.g. sex, age, accent) and the words spoken, and file a police report with this information. (This may require a visit to a police station.) Also file a complaint with your cell phone service provider—they may place a "trap" on the phone. Obscene text messages should be saved and reported in a similar way.

plagued by them. Women who staff suicide hotlines and other 24-hour services are particularly likely to be victimized.

## Voyeurs are aroused by watching others

Voyeuristic disorder, or simply **voyeurism**, means obtaining sexual arousal from watching unsuspecting people (usually women) while they are undressing, naked, engaged in sexual behavior, or urinating or defecating (Lavin, 2008). Typically, voyeurs ("peepers") carry out their activities in a discreet fashion, such as by peering through a bedroom window from a dark location. Thus, even though they may masturbate while watching, they are usually safe from arrest and may never come to the attention of the women who are being observed. Some voyeurs may use mirrors or camera phones to peer under women's clothing or look through peepholes into dressing rooms or toilets. A gynecologist at Johns Hopkins Health System photographed the genitals of as many as 8,000 women and girls who were his patients, using a secret pen camera; after his activities came to light, he committed suicide, and the hospital agreed to pay $190 million in settlement of the case (CNN, 2014).

Voyeurism is probably even more common than exhibitionism. It could be considered an extension of normal male sexuality, which includes a strong visual component (**FIGURE 13.9**). Many adolescent or adult males might take advantage of an opportunity to watch women who are undressed or engaged in sexual activity, especially if they can do so "guilt free" because the woman's bedroom is in plain sight from their own window or from the street. About half of all adolescent males report having engaged in such behaviors (McConaghy, 2005). The popularity of pornographic videos and webcam models (see Chapter 17) reflects a similarly widespread voyeuristic interest; the main moral difference is that voyeurism is practiced without the watched person's consent.

In many U.S. states voyeuristic acts remain legal so long as no trespassing, photography, or video recording is involved. The distribution of photographs or videos obtained surreptitiously for sexual purposes is illegal everywhere.

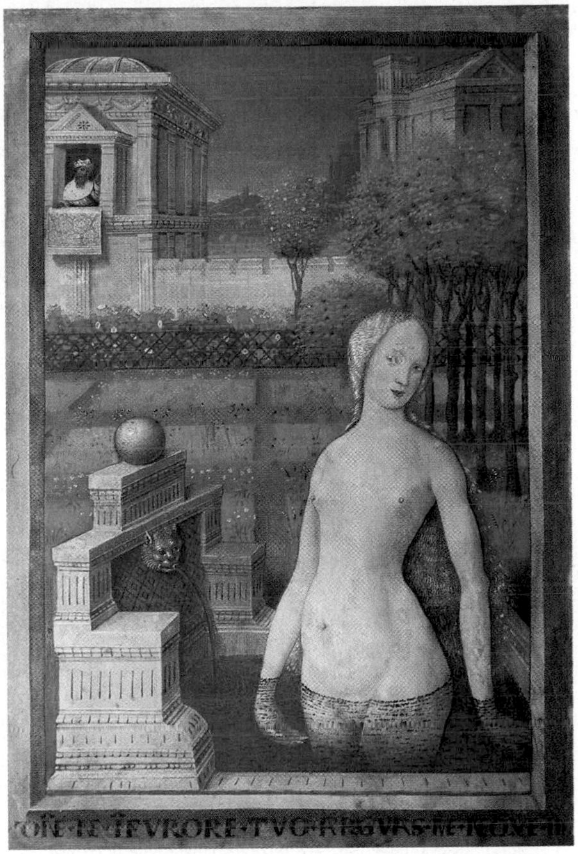

*From The Hours of Louis XII*

▲ **FIGURE 13.9   Biblical voyeurism**  King David spying on Bathsheba, from Jean Bourdichon's Book of Hours (ca. 1500).

## Frotteurism involves surreptitious physical contact

Frotteuristic disorder, or **frotteurism**, means obtaining sexual arousal from physical contact with others—usually women—in public places without their consent and often without their knowledge (Lussier & Piché, 2008) (**BOX 13.4**). A frotteur ("groper") seeks out women in places that are sufficiently crowded that physical contact goes unnoticed—subway cars, elevators, crowded bars, dances, concerts, sporting events, and the like. He rubs his erect penis, hand, leg, or an object such as a newspaper against the woman's thighs, buttocks, vulva, or breasts. Because he may ejaculate under his clothes during the encounter, the frotteur may wear a plastic bag or condom around his penis to prevent any visible staining of his clothes. If he is arrested, evidence of such precautions may be used to prove his criminal intent. Other frotteurs may expose themselves and ejaculate directly onto their victim's clothing, however.

In the survey of college students mentioned in the section on exhibitionism above (Clark et al., 2014), 24% of women and 7% of men reported having been victims of frotteurism. These figures were closely matched by a national survey (Stop Street Harassment, 2014). The true percentages are likely to be higher because people in a crowded environment are not always aware that they are being touched by a frotteur. Besides the victims' immediate emotional responses to the event, more than one-third reported suffering long-term psychological consequences, and many changed their

**voyeurism**  Sexual arousal from watching persons while they are undressing, naked, or engaged in sex.

**frotteurism**  Sexual arousal from touching or rubbing the genitals against strangers without their consent or without their knowledge, as in a crowded public place.

## BOX 13.4
## Frotteurism: First-Person Accounts

The following two accounts describe groping incidents on subway trains, with contrasting outcomes:

*He stands on the platform, still holding me with his gaze as the doors close and I finally yell out loud, "That man just groped me." I frantically look to others around me—for help, for comfort, for acknowledgment—but I get nothing but averted eyes and a small shrug from a woman who clearly does not want me to involve her. It was awful—I was ashamed that I could barely find my voice to confront my offender. I was embarrassed when the people who witnessed it couldn't find their voice at all. I'd never felt so violated and alone as I did riding those next few stops.* (Nyugen, 2015)

*A man on the train . . . tried to rub himself against me. . . . My instinct made me turn around, and I saw this person exposed in front of me, wearing a condom. There are really no proper words to describe the anger and sense of violation that one feels when something like that happens to you. I confronted him, announcing to the subway car at the top of my lungs what he had been doing to me. I also enlisted other passengers to help me detain him . . . all of us taking pictures on our cell phones. "That's it!" I screamed. "You're getting fucking arrested." Upon exiting the train the perpetrator was immediately arrested by transit police. He was later convicted and is now a registered sex offender for life. And he was deported, too.* (Briggs, 2014)

And this is part of a statement by a man who has been convicted of groping over 20 times:

*Something's compelling me to do it, has been compelling me to do it, and it's never been addressed. The "why" I do anything and any of the things, is because I am totally just twisted. . . . If I walk out of this with treatment, I don't care how much time I do. If I walk out of here and I can get treatment because I want that more than any-*

To counter frotteurism, the Tokyo subway bans all men from certain cars during rush hour.

*thing in the world. I want this to end. They know I'm sick. They know something's wrong with me. They know I'm not a violent person. They know that I'm sorry I was ever born to do the things I do.* (McEntyre, 2017)

From time to time transit police conduct stings to catch offenders. The associated publicity may deter offenders for a while, but after repeated sting operations New York's subway system is still seeing close to 1,000 reported offenses per year (Conley, 2017). Subway groping is a particular problem in Tokyo, Japan, where the behavior has long been an accepted part of the culture: There's a genre of Japanese pornography devoted to it. Subway trains in Tokyo now have certain cars that are reserved for women (see figure). In addition, activist groups have held repeated demonstrations in subway stations to bring attention to the problem (DW News, 2019). Reducing overcrowding by increasing subway service would be an effective countermeasure, but that seems to be an unattainable goal in Tokyo, New York, or anywhere else.

behavior—for example, by monitoring their proximity to others in public spaces. Only about 5% of the victims reported the event to the police.

Again, frotteurism could be viewed as an extension of conventional sexuality; many heterosexual men would like to "cop a feel" of an attractive female stranger with whom they find themselves in close proximity, and some actually indulge this wish. Still, a great deal of the "groping" that is done in public places represents the persistent activity of dedicated frotteurs, rather than the occasional acts of otherwise conventional men. In the New York City subway, one-third of all groping arrestees have at least two prior convictions for the same offense (Daily News, 2019). Given that most groping goes undetected or unpunished, it's likely that these men have devoted much of their free time to the practice.

With all three of these behaviors—exhibitionism, voyeurism, and frotteurism—it is the lack of consent that makes them into disorders (and crimes). There is of course nothing wrong with self-exposure, watching a naked person, or touching him or her sexually, if it is done in a private and consensual situation.

## 13.7  Some Adults Are Sexually Attracted to Children

### LEARNING OBJECTIVES
After reading this section you should be able to:

13.7.1  Explain the different meanings of pedophilia and child molestation.

13.7.2  Analyze possible reasons why many Catholic priests sexually molest boys.

13.7.3  Explain the aims of B4U-ACT and Virtuous Pedophiles.

Few topics in the area of human sexuality arouse such strong feelings, or are the focus of so many news stories, as that of sexual contact between adults and children. In Chapter 10 we discussed this issue from the point of view of the children who experience such contacts, and we described the harm that many such children suffer. Here we revisit the issue from the point of view of the adults: people (usually men) who are sexually attracted to children or youths below the legal age of consent or who actually engage in sexual contact with them.

### Pedophilia and child molestation are not synonymous

The terms "pedophilia" and "child molestation" denote different but overlapping concepts (**FIGURE 13.10**). A **pedophile** is a person—nearly always a man—who has a persistent sexual attraction to prepubescent children, generally defined as children under the age of 11. To meet the definition of pedophilia, a person's sexual attraction to children must be greater than, or equal to, his attraction to adults. In other words, a person who does experience some sexual attraction to prepubescent children, but less than he does to adolescents or adults, is not to be regarded as a pedophile.

Pedophilia is a paraphilia, according to *DSM-5*, but it is only a **pedophilic disorder** if the person is distressed by his sexual attraction to prepubescent children or if he is at risk of expressing his attraction in actual sexual contacts. Thus it is possible to be a pedophile without having a mental disorder, according to *DSM-5*. Some experts disagree with this idea, but the lead editor of this section of *DSM-5*, Ray Blanchard, has defended it with a rhetorical question: "If you take an individual who has a very strong erotic attraction for children, but who has never acted on it, who never would act on it, who agrees that society's prohibition of adult child sexual interactions should be in place, do you want to say this individual has a mental disorder?" (Stuart, 2013). What's your opinion?

Pedophiles generally become aware of their sexual attraction to children in early adolescence—most commonly at the age of 12 to 14 (**FIGURE 13.11**). This is about the same time that nonpedophilic males become aware of their sexual attraction to females or to males. Thereafter, pedophilic attraction remains unchanged over the lifespan.

Some pedophiles actually molest children, but some do not. They may refrain from doing so because they believe it is wrong, are afraid of the consequences, or can obtain sufficient sexual gratification from older partners, from fantasies, or from viewing child pornography. (The last of these is a crime—see Chapter 17.)

**pedophile**  A person whose sexual feelings are directed mainly toward prepubescent children.

**pedophilic disorder**  Pedophilia that causes distress or that is expressed in sexual contacts with children.

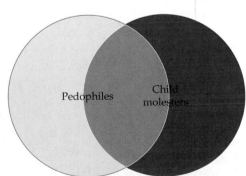

▲ **FIGURE 13.10  Pedophiles and child molesters** are distinct but partially overlapping populations. The degree of overlap between these two populations is uncertain.

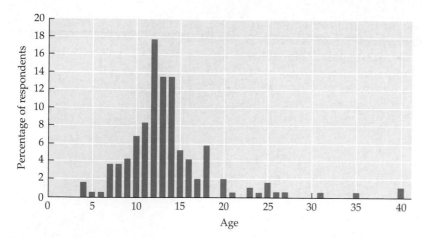

**▲ FIGURE 13.11** **Age at onset of attraction to children** This bar graph shows the responses of 192 adults (190 males, 2 females) attracted to minors when they were asked the question "How old were you when you first had a preferential attraction to boys or girls younger than yourself?" (After B4U-ACT. 2011. *Youth, Suicidality, and Seeking Care*. B4U-ACT, Inc.: Westminster, MD. Retrieved from http://tinyurl.com/y737z3bm.)

**hebephile** An adult whose sexual attraction is directed mainly toward pubescent children.

**autopedophilia** Sexual arousal by the fantasy of being a child.

**erotic target identity inversion** Sexual arousal by the fantasy of being the kind of person to whom one is sexually attracted.

**child molester** An adult who has had sexual contact with a prepubescent child.

Some adults are primarily attracted to children who are going through puberty—pubescent children—roughly in the 11- to 14-year-old range. These adults, termed **hebephiles**, do not fit the definition of pedophiles given above. Hebephilia is not a diagnostic category in *DSM-5*, although some of the *DSM* editors believed that it should be.

For pedophiles and hebephiles, their attraction to children is not just sexual but also romantic in nature. Most report that they have fallen in love with a child at least once in their lives (Martijn et al., 2020).

Most pedophiles have a preference for children of a particular sex. Heterosexual pedophiles predominate; they outnumber homosexual pedophiles in a ratio of about 2:1 or 3:1 (Blanchard et al., 2000). Because gay men are sometimes accused of being pedophiles, it's worth emphasizing the obvious: Homosexual pedophiles are not the same thing as regular gay men, any more than heterosexual pedophiles are the same thing as regular straight men.

Kevin Hsu and Michael Bailey of Northwestern University conducted a survey of 475 men who were sexually attracted to children (Hsu & Bailey, 2017). Nearly half of the men stated that they were sexually aroused, not only by children, but also by the fantasy of being children themselves, as if they had incorporated the objects of their sexual attraction into themselves. By analogy with autogynephilia, as described earlier (see Section 13.4), the researchers named this phenomenon **autopedophilia**. Bailey has suggested that the pop star Michael Jackson, who died in 2009, was autopedophilic, based on his known attraction to boys and his adoption of a childish appearance and voice, as well as his stated identification with Peter Pan, the fictional boy who refused to grow up (Bailey, 2009). Autogynephilia and autopedophilia are examples of a more general phenomenon whereby external objects of sexual attraction may be incorporated into oneself; this phenomenon has been called **erotic target identity inversion** (Freund & Blanchard, 1993; Brown et al., 2020).

Pedophilia is an exaggeration of a sexual interest that exists fairly widely in the male population. You may be reluctant to believe that many "normal" men are sexually aroused by children, but this has been demonstrated in laboratory studies. Arousal is generally greatest in response to older children, and to girls in heterosexual men and to boys in homosexual men (Freund et al., 1989). Quite a few of these adults are only prevented from acting on their attraction to children by fear of punishment: In an online survey conducted by researchers at the University of Colorado, 6% of men, as well as 2% of women, said there was some likelihood that they would have sexual contact with a child if they were guaranteed that they would not be caught (Wurtele et al., 2013).

## "Child molestation" is a behavioral and legal term

A **child molester** (or sexual offender against children) is any adult who has sexual contact with a child. In the context of child molestation the legal definition of "child" varies between jurisdictions, but in U.S. federal law it includes anyone under the age of 18.

Some child molesters are pedophiles or hebephiles; others molest children for a variety of other reasons, such as the lack of available older partners, the desire to hurt a child's parent (perhaps an ex-girlfriend of the perpetrator), alcohol or drug intoxication, or neurological damage. The majority of child molestation convictions are for nonpenetrative acts, such as touching a child's genitals or buttocks.

Some child molesters have sexual interactions with their own children or step-children; these are called **intrafamilial child molesters** or incest offenders. Others, **extrafamilial child molesters**, have interactions with children outside their immediate families. There are differences between these two types of molesters. Extrafamilial molesters are more likely to engage in penetrative sex with their victims, to injure their victims, to molest boys, to repeat their offenses, and to be exclusive pedophiles (as assessed by penile plethysmography), compared with men who molest their own children (Rice & Harris, 2002; Blanchard et al., 2006).

Female child molesters are uncommon, but they do exist. Cases in which female teachers enter into sexual relationships with male teenage students grab the head-lines from time to time. In one much-publicized case, a 34-year-old Seattle teacher, Mary Kay Letourneau, who was married and the mother of four children, began an affair with a 13-year-old student, Vili Fualaau, and had two daughters by him. After Letourneau served a seven-year prison sentence for child rape, she and Fualaau reunited, and in May 2005 they married. The Fualaaus earned a reported $750,000 from the sale of their wedding video to the television show *Entertainment Tonight*. They remained married for 12 years but split up in 2017, 21 years after their initial affair (Carlson & Helling, 2017).

Vili Fualaau denied that he was a "victim," and that viewpoint is common. When eBaum's World Forum posted photographs of female teachers accused of sexu-ally abusing their underage male students, typical male readers' comments included "Lucky kids," "I'd be the last to press charges," and "Where can I find some of these 'pedophiles'?" (Hayes & Carpenter, 2010). Still, we don't condone sex with underage boys any more than we do with underage girls; if the teens are too young to give consent, then adults who have sex with them are committing a serious offense no matter which sex the minors may be.

## Priests and others may molest children under their care

Over the last 25 years, an unfolding scandal has involved revelations about Roman Catholic priests, both in the United States and elsewhere, who sexu-ally molested children under their pastoral care. Church authorities relo-cated many of the offending priests rather than suspending them or report-ing them to the police—whereupon some of them reoffended in their new locations. By 2019, over 5,000 U.S. priests were reported to have abused as many as 10,000 minors, of whom about 80% were boys. (Many of the reported offenses occurred decades ago.) In just one state, Pennsylvania, a grand jury report identified over 1,000 children abused by priests (Goldstein & Otterman, 2018).

While most offenders have been parish priests, some higher officials have been involved. In 2019, for example, Pope Francis "defrocked" (removed from the clergy) Cardinal Theodore McCarrick, Archbishop of Washington, D.C., on account of sexual misconduct with minors and young adults over a period of many years (Dias & Horowitz, 2019). Legal actions arising from priestly abuse have led to settlements totaling over $3 billion; these settlements have forced 21 U.S. dioceses and religious orders to file for Chapter 11 bankruptcy* (BishopAccountability, 2019).

The fact that Catholic priests are not permitted to marry could be one factor contributing to the high prevalence of abuse. That is, it may make the seminary

---

*Chapter 11 bankruptcy means that the organization is protected from creditors while it undergoes a court-supervised financial reorganization.

**intrafamilial child molester**
A person who has had sexual contact with his own children or stepchildren. Also called incest offender.

**extrafamilial child molester**
A person who has had sexual contact with children outside his immediate family.

© Associated Press

▲ Catholic priest John Geoghan was known to the archbishop of Boston as a frequent molester of children, but he was shuffled from parish to parish over a period of 30 years, during which time he continued his offenses. In 2002 he was sentenced to a nine-year prison term; in the following year he was murdered by a fellow inmate.

**minor-attracted person (MAP)**
Someone whose predominant sexual attractions are to children or youths under the legal age of consent.

and the priesthood a desirable option for men who want to avoid marriage because they are not attracted to adult women, or it may make the men more likely to abuse children by denying them a sexual outlet within marriage.

Of course, Catholic priests are not the only people who may violate their fiduciary responsibilities to children. Many Scout leaders, doctors, teachers, and sports coaches have been convicted of molesting minors. Over 12,000 Boy Scouts have been sexually molested by troop leaders and others, according to the testimony of a researcher hired by the Boy Scouts of America (BSA) (Christensen, 2019). As a result of litigation arising from these cases the BSA filed for Chapter 11 bankruptcy in 2020.

In the field of sports, one much-publicized 2012 case involved Penn State's assistant football coach Jerry Sandusky, who was convicted on 45 counts of sexually abusing boys. Sandusky was sentenced to 30 to 60 years in prison, and other university officials were indicted for covering up Sandusky's crimes. In 2017 seven female former gymnasts accused the doctor for the U.S. Olympic gymnastics team, Larry Nassar of Michigan State University, of sexually assaulting them by fondling and penetration with his fingers, and dozens of other women later made similar accusations. Nassar received a 60-year prison sentence in federal court and another 175 years on state charges.

To sum up, any occupation in which adults have one-on-one contacts with children carries the risk of sexual abuse. Scrupulous background checks are important, but the best means of preventing such abuse is to ensure close supervision of all adult–child contacts.

### Some organizations support "minor-attracted persons"

Men who are sexually attracted to underage youths or children—sometimes called **minor-attracted persons** or **MAPs**—risk arrest and lengthy prison sentences if they attempt to satisfy that attraction with physical contacts. Even if they do not make any such attempts, their lives are likely to be stressful and lonely. In one survey, 45% of these men said that they had seriously contemplated suicide, most commonly in their mid- to late teen years (B4U-ACT, 2017).

B4U-ACT is a Maryland-based nonprofit that supports minor-attracted people (B4U-ACT, 2019). It is run by a mix of minor-attracted people and mental health professionals who take a nonjudgmental view of them. Its purpose is to promote mental health services, public understanding, and mutual support for minor-attracted people and to help them lead fulfilling lives while remaining within the law. Another organization, Virtuous Pedophiles, is a mutual support group for MAPs who do not want to have sexual contacts with children, because they believe that such contacts are wrong (Virtuous Pedophiles, 2017).

One out-of-the-closet member of Virtuous Pedophiles named Todd has given an on-camera interview, viewable on YouTube, in which he gave a detailed account of his life (Hales, 2019). "I would rather die a virgin than harm a child," Todd said. "I want young MAPs to understand that they're not doomed to offend—that's nonsense. I feel that can become a self-fulfilling prophecy. . . . And I want to show that non-offending MAPs exist."

Some pedophiles may make use of child sex dolls. Whether having sex with child dolls encourages or discourages offending against actual children is a question that arouses strong opinions, but it hasn't been answered in evidence-based studies (**BOX 13.5**).

Whatever your views on the morality of sex between adults and minors, it's worth noting that the age of legal consent (the age at which a person is deemed capable of consenting to sexual contact with others) varies significantly from jurisdiction to jurisdiction. In the United States it ranges from 16 to 18, depending on the state. Internationally, the age of legal consent is commonly 14, 15, or 16—Canada raised its age of consent from 14 to 16 in 2008. Thus, there does seem to be room for debate about the age at which youths are capable of giving meaningful consent to sexual activity with adults.

## BOX 13.5
## Child Sex Robots

We opened Chapter 1 with the headline "Child sex robots are coming to America," and we raised the question of whether the introduction of such robots would be harmful or beneficial. So far as we know, child sex robots don't yet exist, but there are adult sex robots (with limited capabilities), as described and illustrated in Chapter 6. There are also life-size child dolls, made by companies in China and Japan. One Japanese company's website states that their dolls are not intended to be used for sexual purposes, but the way the dolls are posed and photographed on the website suggests otherwise. It would certainly be possible to make robotic versions, and such robots would likely find a niche market.

The owner of the Japanese company, Shin Takagi, describes himself as a pedophile who doesn't molest children, and he thinks of his company's mission as helping other pedophiles to resist temptation. "We should accept that there is no way to change someone's fetishes," Takagi told *The Atlantic*. "I am helping people express their desires, legally and ethically. It's not worth living if you have to live with repressed desire" (Morin, 2016).

In 2013 a Canadian man who ordered what was alleged to be a child sex doll from China was charged with possessing child pornography. After a legal process lasting 7 years he was acquitted in a non-jury trial (CBC News, 2020). Child sex dolls have showed up in various places in the United States, and several states are moving to ban them, or have already done so, on the theory that owning or using such a doll would encourage

pedophiles to molest real children. No doubt the robotic versions will also be banned if and when they show up.

Reactions from professionals concerned with child molestation have been mixed. Juliet Grayson, a therapist who was co-founder of the U.K. organization Specialist Treatment Organization for the Prevention of Sexual Offending (StopSO), agrees with Takagi. "I do know of a man who had children dolls—he had two and was very happy to use them rather than touching a child. This wasn't great but better than nothing," Grayson told *The Independent* (Revesz, 2017). The newspaper got a contrasting opinion from Britain's National Society for the Prevention of Cruelty to Children, whose development director said, "There is no evidence to support the idea that the use of so-called child sex dolls helps prevent potential abusers from committing contact offences against real children."

Ethicist Litska Strikwerda of Twente University in the Netherlands has argued that child sex robots can and will be banned under the theory of legal moralism, which holds that laws may be used to prohibit behaviors that are widely considered immoral, even in the absence of logical reasons for the prohibition (Strikwerda, 2017). That would make sex with child robots the moral equivalent of same-sex incest and other behaviors that have been criminalized simply because most people are disgusted by them.

There is a need for experimental studies on the question of whether sex dolls encourage or discourage illegal sexual behaviors.

---

# 13.8 A Variety of Other Paraphilic Disorders Exist

### LEARNING OBJECTIVES
After reading this section you should be able to:

13.8.1 **Evaluate the legal and moral status of sex with nonhuman animals.**

13.8.2 **Explain what aspects of sexual violence might cause a person to be diagnosed as having a paraphilic disorder.**

Besides the paraphilic disorders already discussed, there are many others, some specifically listed in *DSM-5* and others not. The following are some examples.

### Zoophiles are sexually attracted to animals

Sexual contact between humans and nonhuman animals—a behavior traditionally called **bestiality**—is not particularly rare (Earls & Lalumière, 2009). In the Kinsey studies, about 3.6% of women and 8% of men stated that they had had at least one sexual contact with an animal after adolescence. Among men raised on farms, nearly half had had sexual contact with an animal, and about 17% reported a contact leading to orgasm. In such contacts, the man may penetrate the animal vaginally or anally or may induce the animal to fellate him or penetrate him anally.

**bestiality** Sexual contact between a person and an animal.

▲ Bestiality as portrayed in a sculpture at Lakshmana Temple, Khajuraho, India.

**zoophilia**  A persistent preference for sexual contacts with animals.

**necrophilia**  A paraphilia involving sexual arousal from viewing or having contact with dead bodies.

Most human–animal contacts occur during the preadolescent or adolescent years and constitute only a tiny fraction of the person's total sexual activity. In the Córdoba Department of Colombia, for example, the majority of boys in rural areas have sex with female donkeys for several years after puberty, and even fall in love with them, but eventually graduate to female humans (Stoneage, 2012). Such culturally sanctioned practices can hardly be considered a sign of a paraphilic disorder.

A few people—mostly men—do persist in having sexual contacts with animals throughout their lives, however, largely to the exclusion of human sexual contacts. This condition is called **zoophilia**. In one study, two-thirds of zoophiles (or "zoos") stated that they would rather have sex with an animal than with a human (Williams & Weinberg, 2003). In one case study, a man was found (by penile plethysmography) to be sexually aroused more strongly by horses than by any other species, including humans (Earls & Lalumière, 2002). A first-person account (also written by a horse lover) asserted that zoophilia is a matter of romantic intimacy and not merely physical gratification (Matthews, 1994). This is an almost universal theme in writings by zoophiles, some of whom describe themselves as being "married" to particular animals. Some zoophiles think of attraction to animals as their sexual orientation (Miletski, 2017).

In 2005 a 45-year-old aerospace engineer in Washington state died of a perforated colon after being anally penetrated by a stallion. The man had been one of a group of men who visited a farm to have sex with horses. At the time, Washington had no law banning sex with animals, but it passed one in the aftermath of this case. Five years later another Washington man was found to have kept four stallions and seven large-breed male dogs for sexual purposes. The man had been an outspoken proponent of sex with animals and said that his life partner of 10 years was a horse named Capone. He was sentenced to three years of imprisonment, and another man was sentenced to three months in jail for having sex with dogs at the same location (Clarridge, 2010).

Although household pets and farm animals are the main objects of zoophilic desire, some zoophiles have been romantically attracted to, and had sex with, more exotic animals such as dolphins (Saincome, 2013). Speaking of marine life, we showed a 19th-century Japanese painting of sex between a woman and two octopuses in Chapter 5 (p. 139). While that painting probably represented a fantasy, there are plenty of *hentai* videos—Japanese anime porn—that focus on "tentacular sex."

Most U.S. states explicitly criminalize bestiality—as of 2017, only Hawaii, Kentucky, New Mexico, West Virginia, and Wyoming did not (Wisch, 2017). Even in those five states sex with animals may be prosecuted under other laws, such as those related to gross indecency or animal cruelty. In Canada, any sexual contact with animals was criminalized in 2019.

Whether it is truly cruel to animals to have (pain-free) sex with them has been questioned by moral philosophers (Singer, 2001). But quite apart from any moral considerations, having sexual contact with animals does risk acquiring a number of serious infections.

## In necrophilia, nonresistance of the partner may be arousing

**Necrophilia** is a sexual fixation on corpses (Hickey et al., 2016). It is a rare paraphilic disorder, with probably fewer than 200 cases having been reported in the scientific literature. Still, there is enough interest in necrophilia to keep some internet bulletin boards busy. Necrophiles may take positions as mortuary workers or other jobs that give them access to dead bodies.

Most necrophiles are men, but in 1979 one female mortuary worker in Sacramento, California, named Karen Greenlee absconded with the body of a 33-year-old while driving it to a funeral, and she spent 2 days with it before being arrested (Parfrey, 2000). She admitted to having sex with the corpses of numerous young men, and when asked about her motivation, she said, "That body is just lying there, but it has what it takes to make me happy. The cold, the aura of death, the smell of death, the funereal surroundings, it all contributes." (We should emphasize the obvious, which is that the overwhelming majority of mortuary workers are not necrophiles.)

Necrophiles may view or touch a dead body while masturbating or may actually have penetrative sex with it (**FIGURE 13.12**). Apparently, it is the lack of resistance or rejection by the dead person that is the usual motivator for necrophilic behavior (Rosman & Resnick, 1989). In fact, some men are turned on when their (living) sex partners feign unconsciousness, "play dead," or join them in necrophilic fantasies. Such activities may not be entirely harmless, because some men have committed murder to satisfy their necrophilic interests.

"Hatred" by Pietro Pajetta, 1896

▲ **FIGURE 13.12** **This painting by Pietro Pajetta** represents necrophilia as the revenge of a rejected suitor.

Not all states criminalize sex with corpses, and in those that do, the interpretation of the law is often murky, as was highlighted by an unusual case in 2006. A 20-year-old Wisconsin man was smitten with the photograph of a woman who had died in an accident a few days earlier. One night he and two companions drove to the cemetery where she was buried, after stopping off at a Walmart store to buy condoms. They dug down to the woman's concrete vault but could not break into it. Shortly thereafter they were apprehended by the police, and the ringleader—who had often expressed the desire to have sex with a dead body—was charged with attempted third-degree rape.

Wisconsin had a statute banning sex with corpses, but the defendant argued that it only applied to cases where the sex act took place in conjunction with a murder. The trial court, and an appeals court, agreed with him. But the prosecutors appealed the case to the Wisconsin Supreme Court, which ruled that the statute did cover sex with a dead person who had not been murdered. The ringleader eventually received a two-year prison sentence (Associated Press, 2008).

## Sexual violence can be paraphilic

Not all violent forms of sexual expression warrant diagnosis as paraphilic disorders. Consensual S/M scenes are not usually an indication of a paraphilic disorder, nor are most cases of rape (though rape is a crime, of course). If a person has a persistent and distressing fixation on sexual violence, however, or commits acts of nonconsensual sexual violence *because the violence itself is sexually arousing*, the person probably has a paraphilic disorder. This condition is not specifically listed in *DSM-5*. There was a proposal to introduce a "paraphilic coercive disorder" in *DSM-5*, but it was rejected. The reason for the rejection was the fear that ordinary rapists would be placed in this category: This could have led to rapists being detained indefinitely after the expiration of their sentences, by a medicolegal procedure called "civil commitment."

Some of the most notorious serial killers, such as Jack the Ripper, or Jeffrey Dahmer—who killed, dismembered, and ate portions of 17 boys or youths in the Milwaukee area for sexual gratification—clearly had a paraphilic disorder of this kind. (Dahmer was also a necrophile.) Paraphilic sexual killers often have a complex mental disorder, including brain damage, psychosis, and a history of severe childhood abuse (Pincus, 2001). Nevertheless, these crimes are not impulsive. Typically, they are carefully planned and involve hours or days of torture before the victim is finally killed. The perpetrator often records his crimes as videos or in diaries.

**autoerotic asphyxia**
Self-strangulation for purposes of sexual arousal.

One sexual serial killer who generated enormous publicity was Gary Ridgway (the "Green River Killer"). In 2003 Ridgway pleaded guilty to murdering 48 young women and girls—mostly prostitutes—in the Seattle area over a period of 16 years. He killed most of the women by strangling them during sexual encounters. In his confession Ridgway expressed contempt for prostitutes, but this seems to have been merely what permitted him to direct his murderous sexual impulses at them, rather than being the actual motive, which—while obviously pathological—remains obscure. Ridgway escaped the death penalty by agreeing to provide information about his victims and the location of their bodies.

Some masochists inflict pain or suffering on themselves without the aid of a partner. A particularly dangerous form of this behavior is **autoerotic asphyxia**, in which the practitioner partially asphyxiates himself while masturbating. Although this behavior can have the aim of enhancing sexual arousal, it is often connected with BDSM ideation and practices (**BOX 13.6**).

## BOX 13.6
## Autoerotic Asphyxia

"When you find my body hanging . . . with a tight noose around my neck, do not look for a murderer. I have executed myself. I say execute rather than suicide because I didn't really intend to hang unto death." This cryptic note was found next to the strung-up, half-naked body of a young Canadian man. Indeed, the cause of his death was not murder, nor was it suicide. It was autoerotic asphyxia—a sexually charged near-death experience that went a step too far (Blanchard & Hucker, 1991).

People who practice autoerotic asphyxia do so in order to increase the intensity of orgasm by constricting the flow of blood to the brain during masturbation. The practitioners of this behavior—mostly male—may tighten a belt around their necks or suspend themselves by a noose, often using a closet rail, rafter, or tree. Alternatively, they may put their head in a plastic bag. The cerebral cortex is partially knocked out by the resulting lack of oxygen, and its normal inhibitory influence on lower centers of the brain is removed. This probably results in the same kind of heightened, semiconscious orgasm that some people experience with the use of nitrite inhalers, or "poppers."

At least two prominent individuals have died in circumstances suggestive of autoerotic asphyxia. One was Australian rock star Michael Hutchence (lead singer for INXS), who died in 1997. (His death may have been suicide, however.) The other was American actor David Carradine: In 2009 he

© Pictorial Press Ltd./Alamy Stock Photo

Actor David Carradine is thought to have died by autoerotic asphyxia.

was found hanging naked in a Thai hotel room, with a rope around his neck and genitals (McShane, 2009).

For many practitioners, autoerotic asphyxia is about more than experiencing a supernormal orgasm. To judge by the death scenes of victims, it is often linked with a complex of paraphilic elements, including bondage, punishment, and (very commonly) transvestic fetishism (Tattoli et al., 2017). One victim was found dressed in women's clothes and surrounded by documents containing passages such as "the law of the land for any man dressed as a woman and found guilty is that he be hanged." Another was found hanging in front of a computer that had been playing a "snuff video" (a movie depicting a real or staged murder, perhaps in a pornographic context) (Vennemann & Pollak, 2006). A survey of living practitioners of autoerotic asphyxia confirmed the connection with masochism, transvestic fetishism, and other paraphilic behaviors (Hucker, 2011).

Never experiment with autoerotic asphyxia: It carries a dire risk of accidental death if the practitioner passes out before he has time to release whatever is constricting his neck. (Loss of consciousness occurs just 10 or 11 seconds after complete strangulation.) Over 400 deaths have been reported in the forensic literature (Sauvageau & Racette, 2006; Sauvageau & Geberth, 2009), and the true numbers are probably much higher because many cases are misidentified as suicides. Deaths have occurred even when a second person has been present.

## 13.9 Sex Offenders Do Not Necessarily Repeat Their Offenses

### LEARNING OBJECTIVE

After reading this section you should be able to:

**13.9.1** Evaluate the factors that raise or lower the likelihood of recidivism by sex offenders.

Sex offenders, especially offenders against children, are widely perceived as incorrigible monsters who will inevitably repeat their offenses if given the chance. This perception has led to draconian measures against convicted sex offenders: very long prison sentences, denial of parole, detention after the completion of sentences, and compulsory drug treatments (see below). Sex offenders are generally placed on sex offender registries, and there are currently over 700,000 registered sex offenders in the United States (Dillinger, 2019). Some of these offenders committed their offenses as juveniles—some as young as 11 years old. Placing these children on sex offender registries brands them for life and largely excludes the possibility of rehabilitation (Human Rights Watch, 2013).

The names and addresses of all registered sex offenders must be accessible to the public (**FIGURE 13.13**). In some states the police are required to notify the public when a registered sex offender moves into a neighborhood. Registered sex offenders are subject to many burdens that are not imposed on other criminals who have completed their sentences. These include restrictions on where an offender can live—sometimes to the point that there is no place in a given town where an offender can live, except perhaps under a freeway overpass.

Although sex offender registries are very popular with the public, there is little or no evidence that the registries do anything to protect children or prevent **recidivism** (Levenson, 2018). In fact, the recidivism rate for most sex offenders (the probability that they will commit another sex offense) is no more than 7% at five years (Helmus et al., 2012); this is well below the rates for most other offenders. Some sex offenders are at higher risk of reoffending—these include men who have already committed more than one offense, whose previous offenses involved violence, or who have antisocial personality disorder. These high-risk offenders have an approximately 22% recidivism rate at 5 years after release, but if they are offense free at 10 years, there is only a small chance that they will offend again (Hanson et al., 2014). In other words, high-risk sex offenders do not remain high risk forever.

## 13.10 There Are Numerous Theories of Paraphilic Disorders

### LEARNING OBJECTIVES

After reading this section you should be able to:

**13.10.1** Contrast the various theories for the causation of paraphilic disorders.

**13.10.2** Explain what is meant by the "cycle of abuse."

Understanding the causes of uncommon sexual desires and behaviors might lead to effective treatment or prevention of those that are unwanted—that is, paraphilic disorders. Yet theories to explain why people develop these desires are very diverse. This may in part reflect the diversity of sexual desires themselves, ranging as they do

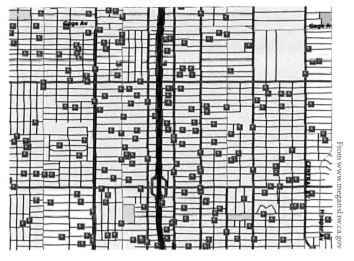

From www.meganslaw.ca.gov

▲ **FIGURE 13.13　Sex offender in your backyard?** In densely populated areas, most people have a registered sex offender living within a block or two. This screenshot from the California sex offender registry website shows (in blue squares) the residences of sex offenders in a fairly typical area of Los Angeles.

**recidivism**　The tendency of convicted offenders to reoffend.

**FAQ:** What crimes result in registration as a sex offender?

Occasionally, people have ended up as registered sex offenders as a result of trivial offenses such as public urination, but the great majority of registered offenders have been convicted of serious crimes such as rape, sexual assault, and sexual offenses against children. Criteria vary from state to state, and the decision is sometimes up to the judge: Take a look at your state's online registry.

▶ **FIGURE 13.14** **Familial pedophilia** This Canadian family tree has nine male pedophiles (red squares), all attracted to prepubescent girls, in four successive generations. Open squares are non-pedophilic men, and circles are women. The pattern suggests the presence of a gene predisposing to pedophilia that is transmitted directly from father to son. (After A. Labelle et al. 2012. ISRN *Psychiatry* 2012: 692813.)

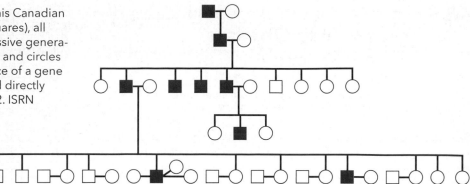

from minority sexual interests such as fetishism—which only become disorders by virtue of any distress they may cause—to highly abnormal desires that may trigger grave sex crimes.

BIOLOGICAL FACTORS   Paraphilic disorders and sex offenses sometimes run in families, suggesting the existence of genes predisposing individuals to them (Labelle et al., 2012; Langstrom et al., 2015) (**FIGURE 13.14**). There are also reports of differences in brain structure and function between pedophiles and nonpedophiles (Poeppl et al., 2014; Fonteille et al., 2019). These findings need to be interpreted cautiously, however, because they might relate to personality traits (such as impulsiveness) that would cause a pedophile to act on his attractions, rather than relating to the attraction itself (Kärgel et al., 2017).

LEARNING PROCESSES   Some kink-identified people, as well as people with paraphilic disorders, recall incidents from their childhood that might be interpreted as triggering the development of these sexual traits by some kind of learning process such as **conditioning** (see Chapter 5). Some researchers have reported that it is possible to "sexualize" nonsexual stimuli by conditioning (**FIGURE 13.15**), which could be interpreted as the experimental creation of a fetishism (Plaud & Martini, 1999). Again, caution is advised, because experiments of this kind have generally yielded weak, inconsistent, or impermanent results. This could of course be because the study participants have been adults, whose sexuality may be less malleable than that of young adolescents.

**conditioning**   The modification of behavior by learning through association and/or reinforcement.

**courtship disorder**   A paraphilia or cluster of paraphilias seen as a disorder of normal courtship behavior.

**hypersexuality**   Excessive sexual desire or behavior.

**obsessive-compulsive disorder (OCD)**   A mental disorder marked by anxiety, repetitive thoughts or urges, and behaviors that temporarily relieve those urges.

**cycle of abuse**   The cycle in which some abused children grow up to perform similar forms of abuse on others. Also called victim–perpetrator cycle.

DISORDERS OF COURTSHIP   The usual process by which a man acquires a sex partner consists of four stages: (1) location and evaluation of a potential sex partner; (2) initial nontactile interactions, such as smiling, displaying attractive features, and talking with the partner; (3) tactile interactions such as embracing and fondling; and (4) genital sex. Each of these stages has a paraphilic counterpart: (1) voyeurism, (2) exhibitionism and obscene telephone calling, (3) frotteurism, and (4) paraphilic rape. In the 1980s Kurt Freund and colleagues suggested that some higher organizing principle that normally ties the elements of male courtship together into a coherent sequence has been lost in people with paraphilic disorders. This could leave the individual elements in a state of psychic disorder that allows them to be expressed inappropriately (Freund & Blanchard, 1986). Freund gave this concept the name **courtship disorder**.

ESCAPE ROUTE   Another idea is that paraphilic disorders are caused by the blockage of normal avenues of sexual expression. A person who can't explore typical sexual relations might turn to alternative, atypical ones. What could cause such

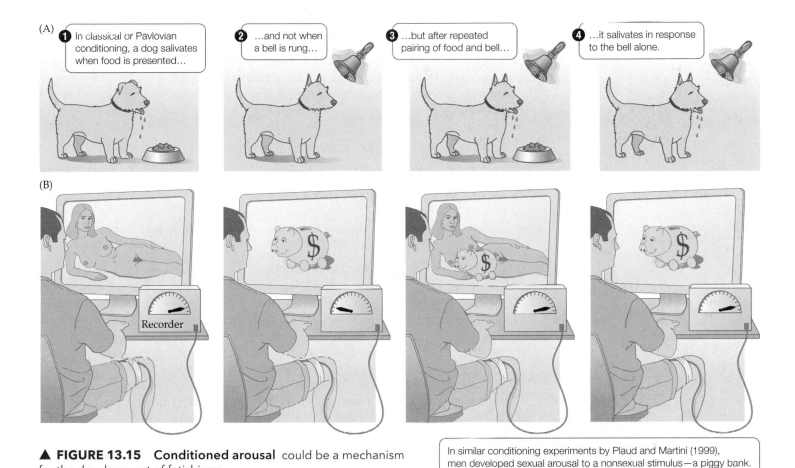

**▲ FIGURE 13.15  Conditioned arousal** could be a mechanism for the development of fetishisms.

In similar conditioning experiments by Plaud and Martini (1999), men developed sexual arousal to a nonsexual stimulus—a piggy bank.

a blockage? As mentioned above, some studies have reported that men with paraphilic disorders are deficient in social skills and relate poorly to women. Such personality traits might hamper adolescents' attempts to establish conventional sexual relationships and might lead them to explore atypical activities that require few or no social skills.

INFLUENCE OF OTHER TRAITS  It is possible that certain personality traits or disorders make the development of paraphilic disorders more likely. These traits could include **hypersexuality** (an excess of sexual desire that shows itself in compulsive masturbation and the devotion of a great deal of time to sexual fantasy, pornography use, and the pursuit of sex partners), as well as **obsessive-compulsive disorder** (**OCD**), attention-deficit/hyperactivity disorder (ADHD), impulsivity, mood disorders, and alcohol and drug dependency (Kafka, 2008; Laws & O'Donohue, 2008).

CYCLE OF ABUSE  Most victims of childhood abuse do not become abusers when they are adults (**FIGURE 13.16**). Nevertheless, abusers are more likely to have a history of childhood victimization than are other men, according to numerous studies (Seto, 2008). This is called the **cycle of abuse**. The correlation is particularly strong between childhood sexual abuse and adult pedophilia (Nunes et al., 2013). It is not known why some abused children become abusers and others do not.

© UPPA/Zuma Press

**▲ FIGURE 13.16  Breaking the cycle** Former U.S. senator Scott Brown of Massachusetts was sexually abused as a child. He had some behavior problems as a teenager but did not become a sexual abuser. His life illustrates the fact that there is no inevitability to the "cycle of abuse."

In summary, researchers have proposed a variety of ideas to explain the development of paraphilic disorders and unusual sexual desires in general. Because no single idea seems adequate, there have been attempts to develop integrative theories that involve interactions among multiple causal factors (Ward & Beech, 2008). However, a comprehensive and persuasive picture of how people come to develop and act on paraphilic desires remains an elusive goal.

## 13.11 Theories of Causation Have Suggested a Variety of Treatments

**LEARNING OBJECTIVES**

After reading this section you should be able to:

**13.11.1** Explain the differences between cognitive therapy and relapse prevention therapy in the treatment of paraphilic disorders.

**13.11.2** Compare the use of selective serotonin reuptake inhibitors (SSRIs), anti-androgen drugs, and castration in the treatment of paraphilic disorders.

Most people with paraphilic disorders do not seek treatment of their own accord. They may be pressured into doing so by spouses, or they may be referred to mental health professionals by the courts. For convicted sex offenders, attending some kind of risk reduction program might be a condition of their sentencing or parole.

The fact that people with paraphilias do not usually initiate their own treatment makes that treatment difficult, both practically and ethically. For example, a person who is incarcerated may be highly motivated to feign a disappearance of his paraphilic interests. A child molester may learn to control his penile responses during laboratory testing, for example, to make it seem that he is no longer aroused by images of children. Some reports of treatment successes probably result from uncritical acceptance of such "cures."

### Conditioning is intended to change sexual desires

If paraphilic disorders result from conditioning or other forms of learning, then it might be possible to treat them by driving the learning process in reverse or by fostering new learning processes that lead to more typical sexual desires or behaviors. Treatments based on these ideas are called **behavior therapy**. One of these techniques is **aversion therapy**. In this approach, aversive (unpleasant) experiences are paired with something that was previously experienced as attractive, in hopes of making it unattractive or even repulsive. If a man is attracted to prepubescent girls, for example, he is shown pictures of girls or told to masturbate to fantasies of girls, but these pleasant experiences are paired with something unpleasant, such as the smell of ammonia or disgusting images.

Another technique, **masturbatory reconditioning**, does not rely on aversive stimuli. A man who is sexually excited by prepubescent girls is instructed to masturbate to fantasies of girls but to switch his fantasies to focus on adult women just as orgasm is approaching—in order that images of adult females will become positively conditioned by association with the pleasant experience of orgasm. The hope is that, after many repetitions of such experiences over weeks or months, the man will gradually lose his paraphilic interests and develop sexual arousal to more acceptable targets. This kind of "positive control" has largely replaced aversion therapy because it is less likely to instill negative feelings such as guilt or anger.

### Cognitive therapy is aimed at preventing repeat offenses

In **cognitive therapy** (which is often combined with the conditioning treatments just described) the aim is to correct the disordered thinking that the man uses to justify or rationalize his behaviors. For example, the man may believe that his behavior is sexually arousing to his victims or benefits them in some way. In that case, therapy

**behavior therapy** Treatment of mental disorders by training of behavior.

**aversion therapy** A form of behavior therapy that attempts to eliminate unwanted desires or behaviors by associating them with some unpleasant experience, such as a noxious smell.

**masturbatory reconditioning** The attempt to change a person's sexual attractions by control of fantasy content during masturbation.

**cognitive therapy** Therapy based on changing a person's beliefs and thought processes.

will be aimed at helping him realize that his behavior is harmful, rather than helpful, and will attempt to awaken some empathy toward his victims. In fact, empathy training is one of the most commonly used techniques in the treatment of sex offenders including pedophiles, because well-developed cognitive empathy is a characteristic of pedophiles who are able to resist the urge to offend (Schuler et al., 2019).

Another approach seeks to remove blockages to normal sexual expression. The therapist will attempt to strengthen the man's social skills, self-esteem, assertiveness, and desire for intimacy. The man may be encouraged to practice interactions with women, including such basic matters as how to behave on a date and how to deal with conflicts and jealousy.

In yet another approach, called **relapse prevention therapy**, the offender is trained in how to identify the situations that may trigger a repeat offense and how to avoid or cope with those situations. This may include mental tricks, such as "thought stopping," that interrupt obsessive ideation—"I've got to stop thinking about young girls and focus more on my wife." Training may also include very practical issues, such as avoiding locations that offer temptations to offend, and committing to jobs or hobbies. These programs also encourage the development of peer relationships that can give the offender a sense of purpose and acceptance. Although aimed primarily at sex offenders, relapse prevention therapy can also be used to treat paraphilias that don't involve criminality or victims but do distress the people who experience them.

These various forms of therapy are often conducted in small groups (**FIGURE 13.17**). Group therapy doesn't just save time and money: Peer interaction is an important therapeutic tool in itself (Levenson & Macgowan, 2004).

## The efficacy of psychological treatments is limited

Although some of these therapeutic strategies have been employed, alone or in combination, for several decades, there is surprisingly little evidence that they work, whether "working" is taken to mean curing paraphilic disorders or merely stopping criminal recidivism. Probably the most thorough study was the Sex Offender Treatment and Evaluation Project (SOTEP), funded by the state of California (Marques et al., 2005). The study began in 1985. Sex offenders were randomly assigned either to be treated with a state-of-the-art intervention program that focused on relapse prevention or to receive no treatment. Individual offenders were treated for many years, both during and after incarceration. Follow-ups continued until 2005. The outcome: Offenders who participated in the program were just as likely to reoffend as were offenders who dropped out of the program or never took it.

More recent studies have found that psychological treatments such as cognitive therapy and relapse prevention do have a modest effect in preventing recidivism; this beneficial effect is greater in adolescents than in adults, as one might expect (Kim et al., 2016). Treatment is also more effective with offenders in the community than with those who are in prison or other institutions, perhaps because offenders in the latter group are more likely to be repeat offenders.

**relapse prevention therapy**
Therapy aimed at training a person to avoid or cope with situations that trigger the undesirable behavior.

▶ **FIGURE 13.17** **Relapse prevention** Social worker Karen Swearingen leads a discussion in an education group for sex offenders at the Circleville Juvenile Correctional Facility in Ohio.

**Good Lives model** A form of therapy for sex offenders that focuses on improving the individual's ability to achieve a broad range of life goals.

**Circles of Support and Accountability (COSA)** A program of community support for released sex offenders.

**selective serotonin reuptake inhibitors (SSRIs)** A class of drugs, including antidepressants such as Prozac and Lexapro, that may depress sexual function.

The search for better treatments continues. One approach focuses on helping the person implement a meaningful plan based on the **Good Lives model** while living in the community (Good Lives Model, 2014). This plan is the collection of skills and knowledge that enable him to attain "primary human goods": life, health, knowledge, excellence in work and play, autonomy, inner peace, friendship, and spirituality. In a related approach, known as **Circles of Support and Accountability (COSA)**, a group of community volunteers pledges to help a sex offender follow principles similar to those of the Good Lives model. One review concluded that COSA offers modest benefits in terms of reduced reoffending (Clarke et al., 2017).

## Drug treatments interact with neurotransmitters or hormones

As an alternative to psychological interventions, or in combination with them, many researchers and clinicians have turned to drug treatments. One class of drugs that has been widely used is that of the **selective serotonin reuptake inhibitors** (**SSRIs**), which are antidepressants such as Prozac. These drugs affect the activity of two neurotransmitters, serotonin and dopamine, in the brain. For reasons not well understood, they tend to lower a person's interest in sex. Although this can be a bothersome side effect when these drugs are given to treat depression, it is helpful in lowering sex drive in men with paraphilic disorders. In addition, these drugs tend to relieve obsessive-compulsive conditions, which, as mentioned above, often contribute to paraphilias. SSRIs are used in the treatment of the less severe paraphilic offenders, such as exhibitionists.

A more radical pharmaceutical approach is to interfere with the production or action of testosterone, the principal hormonal driver of male sexuality (**FIGURE 13.18**). One anti-androgen drug used for this purpose is Depo-Provera. As described in Chapter 9, Depo-Provera is a synthetic injectable progestin that is used as a long-term contraceptive in women. In men Depo-Provera depresses the secretion of GnRH by the hypothalamus, which results in a steep decline in testosterone secretion by the testes (see Chapter 3). The end result is a profound drop in testosterone levels and a concomitant reduction in sexual desires and behaviors. Leuprolide (Lupron), a drug we mentioned in Chapter 10 in connection with the treatment of precocious puberty, produces similar results. Yet another drug, cyproterone acetate, blocks testosterone receptors, thus making the body and brain insensitive to the hormone.

Use of these hormone-blocking drugs to prevent the expression of paraphilic behavior—an approach sometimes referred to as "chemical castration"*—is far from ideal. The drugs do not cure paraphilic disorders in the sense of redirecting sex offenders' sexual desires into more acceptable channels; they simply decrease sexual desire and arousal generally. Still, they are often effective in eliminating criminal sexual behavior over periods of many years. Drug treatments (possibly in combination with psychological methods) are more effective in reducing recidivism than psychological treatments alone (Kim et al., 2016). Some states, such as California and Louisiana, have mandated Depo-Provera treatment for serious or recidivist sex offenders.

## Castration is a treatment of last resort

Surgical castration (removal of the testicles) removes a man's main source of androgens, including testosterone. The surgery is followed by a rapid drop in circulating androgen levels and a slower, somewhat variable decline in sexual desires and behaviors, including physiological responses such as erection and ejaculation (Zverina et al., 1990). Castration may be more effective than other treatments for the prevention of sexual recidivism (Sreenivasan & Weinberger, 2016).

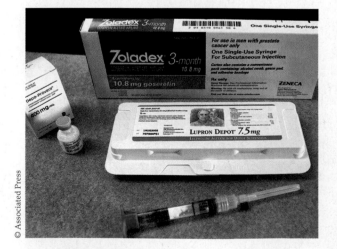

▲ **FIGURE 13.18** **Drugs used to treat sex offenders** include the injectable progestin Depo-Provera and the GnRH blockers Lupron and Zoladex.

*We do not particularly like this term, because unlike surgical castration, drug treatment is reversible.

A very small number of repeat offenders in the United States have opted for castration and have subsequently been released into the community. There is a serious question about whether such a choice is truly voluntary, however, if the price of refusal is lifelong detention. This issue, as well as a sordid history of forced sterilizations in the early 20th-century United States (Dowbiggin, 2003), has made the voluntary castration of sex offenders a distasteful notion to many Americans. Voluntary castration of sex offenders is done in some other countries, including the Czech Republic and Germany, and at least one bioethicist has defended the practice as "useful for reconfiguring a life that has gone badly awry" (McMillan, 2014).

## 13.12  Few "Kinks" Are Disorders

### LEARNING OBJECTIVE

After reading this section you should be able to:

**13.12.1   Explain how medicalizing sexual diversity can create a stigma against unconventional forms of sexual behavior.**

Because the previous few sections have dealt with serious sexual disorders or crimes, we need to reinforce what we said at the beginning of the chapter: Most unconventional or uncommon forms of sexual desire and behavior are neither disorders nor crimes, but simply instances of sexual diversity. Sex researchers and psychiatrists have tended to medicalize this diversity, for example by giving each uncommon form of sexual expression a Greek-sounding name, akin to a medical diagnosis: podophilia (foot fetishism), katoptronophilia (arousal from sexual activity observed in mirrors), klismaphilia (arousal from the administration of enemas), and so on. These terms are sometimes useful for their specificity, but more commonly they create an unjustified aura of scientific understanding, and we have therefore used them sparingly in this chapter. Even the word "paraphilia" serves little real purpose, now that *DSM-5* has redefined it to mean any uncommon form of sexual expression. The colloquial term "kink" is more readily understood and carries no implication of sickness or criminality.

## Summary

- Most variations in sexual desire and behavior are not mental disorders but represent minority interests or a means of adding excitement to sexual relationships.

- Bondage/dominance and sadomasochism (collectively known as BDSM) involve sexual arousal by the infliction or receipt of humiliation, degradation, or physical pain. BDSM practices generally take place in safe, consensual settings.

- Fetishism is sexual arousal by objects, materials, or body parts. Transvestic fetishists are sexually aroused by cross-dressing, but not all cross-dressers are fetishists—others may cross-dress for practical reasons, for entertainment purposes, or as an expression of a transgender identity.

- The boundary between normal and abnormal sexuality is imprecise and subjective and is defined socially as well as medically. According to the American Psychiatric Association, paraphilias are uncommon sexual desires or behaviors, which we have referred to as kinks; those paraphilias that cause significant distress, social dysfunction, or harm to others are called paraphilic disorders. Paraphilic behaviors directed at nonconsenting persons are illegal.

- In general, paraphilias are extensions or exaggerations of normal sexual feelings or behaviors. Far more men than women have paraphilias. It is common for a person to develop multiple paraphilias over time. Persons with paraphilic disorders who commit sex offenses may have psychological problems and deficient social skills, and some have suffered child abuse, but others have ordinary personalities and histories.

- Exhibitionists are sexually aroused by exposing their genitals to others (usually women) in public places. Making obscene phone calls is a variation on exhibitionism. Voyeurs spy on women who are undressed

*(Continued)*

## Summary (continued)

or engaged in sex. Frotteurs make body contact with women in crowds.

- Pedophiles are sexually attracted to prepubescent children more than to adults. Pedophiles and child molesters are overlapping but nonidentical groups. Most pedophiles are attracted to children of one sex more than the other. Hebephiles are aroused by pubescent children. Children are sometimes molested by adults with fiduciary responsibilities toward them, such as Catholic priests, teachers, and Scout leaders. There are organizations that aim to help minor-attracted adults avoid sexual contacts with children.

- Zoophiles are aroused by sexual contact with animals. Necrophiles are aroused by dead bodies. Autoerotic asphyxia is often combined with BDSM elements; it is a highly dangerous practice.

- Although rape is not in itself a paraphilic disorder, the commission of violent sexual acts is considered paraphilic if the perpetrator experiences the violence itself as sexually arousing. Paraphilic sadism has motivated many notorious serial killers.

- Recidivism—the tendency for criminals to repeat their offenses—is lower among sex offenders than among many other kinds of offenders. Certain factors, such as antisocial personality disorder or a history of violence, are associated with an increased likelihood of recidivism.

- A variety of theories attempt to explain paraphilias. Biological theories attribute paraphilias to neurological or genetic disturbances. Behavioral theories see them as the result of distorted learning processes or as the result of a blockage of normal sexual expression. It has also been suggested that paraphilic disorders result from the disintegration of the normal behavioral sequence of courtship (courtship disorder). In some cases—but not all—the experience of abuse during childhood can be the trigger for the abuse of others in later life.

- The various theories of paraphilia have led to diverse forms of treatment. Behavioral approaches, such as aversion therapy, attempt to help people unlearn their paraphilias and acquire more conventional sexual desires. Psychotherapeutic approaches include cognitive therapy, which attempts to correct paraphilic thinking; social skills training programs, which encourage normal communication with women; and relapse prevention programs, which help sex offenders identify and avoid situations in which they are likely to reoffend. There is little evidence that any of these methods are successful in preventing recidivism.

- Biological approaches to treatment include the use of drugs that reduce testosterone levels or block testosterone's effects, as well as selective serotonin reuptake inhibitors. The drugs appear to be quite effective but can have serious side effects. Castration is an effective but rarely used method of preventing recidivism by men who commit repeated, serious sex crimes.

---

The **Discovering Human Sexuality** digital resources include activities, animations, flashcards, web links, chapter outlines and summaries, and other study tools.

· · · · · · · · · · · · · · · · · · · ·

Learn more with this chapter's digital tools, including the **Oxford Insight Study Guide**, at **oup.com/he/levay5e**.

## Discussion Questions

1. Do you think society should place any legal restrictions on the expression of non-coercive sex practices (e.g., those undertaken as a solo activity or with a consenting partner)? Give a rationale for your point of view.

2. People with paraphilias often find it very difficult to give them up. Compare the advantages and disadvantages of various treatments (e.g., psychotherapy, behavior therapy, drug therapy).

3. Strippers may exhibit their genitals. Are they exhibitionists?

4. If you were confronted by an exhibitionist who exposed himself, what would you do? Why?

5. A pedophile who has been arrested for molesting a child argues that he has a sexual compulsion that he cannot resist. Do you think treatment should be legally mandated? Which treatments do you think would be best for him, and why?

6. The Catholic Church has faced an ongoing controversy over reports that priests have had sexual contacts with minors. In several cases the priests received counseling and were moved to other parishes, where they repeated their behavior. Take

a position on what an institution (e.g., religious or educational) should do about reports of child molestation. Should the institution handle the accusation itself, or should it turn the matter over to the police? If the reports of molestation are accurate, how should the perpetrators be treated? What should be done to prevent further incidents?

7. Imagine that you're a therapist who is counseling a couple. The woman has caught the man cross-dressing. What questions would you ask him to find out what's really going on and whether he has a paraphilia? How would you advise the couple?

8. How would you respond if you learned that a sex offender had moved into your neighborhood? How can public safety be balanced against the right of someone who has "served his time" to get on with his life?

## Web Resources

American Professional Society on the Abuse of Children   **www.apsac.org**

Association for the Treatment of Sexual Abusers   **www.atsa.com**

Oh Joy Sex Toy: An unconventional orgy by Salem. (Comic strip about group sex at a furries convention)   **https://tinyurl.com/uvkhlg7**

Tri-Ess (organization for heterosexual cross-dressers)   **www.tri-ess.org**

U.S. Department of Justice. Dru Sjodin National Sex Offender Public Website (NSOPW)   **www.nsopw.gov**

## Recommended Reading

Bering, J. (2013). *Perv: The sexual deviant in all of us*. Scientific American.

De Sade, Marquis. (1966). *The 120 days of Sodom, and other writings* (R. Seaver & A. Wainhouse, Trans.). Grove. (Original work written in 1785 and published in 1904.)

Dekkers, M. (1994). *Dearest pet: On bestiality*. Norton.

Gates, K. (2017). *Deviant desires: A tour of the erotic edge*. powerHouse.

Largier, N. (2007). *In praise of the whip: A cultural history of arousal*. Zone.

Laws, D. R. & O'Donohue, W. T. (Eds.). (2008). *Sexual deviance: Theory, assessment, and treatment* (2nd ed.). Guilford.

Newmahr, S. (2011). *Playing on the edge: Sadomasochism, risk, and intimacy*. Indiana University Press.

Ortmann, D. M. & Sprott, R. (2012). *Sexual outsiders: Understanding BDSM sexualities and communities*. Rowman & Littlefield.

Sacher-Masoch, L. v. (2000). *Venus in furs*. Viking Penguin. (Full text available online at www.gutenberg.org/ebooks/6852.) (Original work published in 1870.)

Seto, M. C. (2013). *Internet sex offenders*. American Psychological Association.

Smith, M. (2014). *The erotic doll: A modern fetish*. Yale University Press.

St. Clair, J. (2015). *Bark!* Nazca Plains Corporation. (About puppy play).

Talese, G. (2016). *The voyeur's motel*. Grove. (A nonfiction account of a man who bought a motel in order to spy on his guests' sexual activities.)

Terry, K. J. (2012). *Sexual offenses and offenders* (2nd ed.). Cengage Learning.

Weiss, M. (2011). *Techniques of pleasure: BDSM and the circuits of sexuality*. Duke University Press.

Sexual problems are common but usually treatable.

# 14 Sexual Disorders

We turn now from uncommon forms of sexual expression to common problems that can interfere with any kind of sexual relationship. A number of mental and physical conditions can impair sexual interest or arousal or make sexual interactions painful or unrewarding. Most of these conditions are reduced functions, such as a lack of interest in sex or a difficulty with erection, lubrication, or orgasm. Some, however, represent overexcitable states, such as premature ejaculation and excessive sexual behavior. Either way, these problems are common. For the most part, they are more readily treatable than the paraphilic disorders discussed in Chapter 13. The major factor impeding their successful treatment is people's reluctance to discuss sexual problems openly with their partners or to seek appropriate professional advice and therapy.

# 14.1 Sexual Disorders Are Common

**LEARNING OBJECTIVE**

After reading this section you should be able to:

14.1.1   Describe how a sex therapist, a sex surrogate, and a urologist may assist a person with a sexual disorder.

**primary disorder**   A disorder that is not preceded by any period of healthy function.

**secondary disorder**   A disorder that follows some period of healthy function.

**situational disorder**   A disorder that appears only in certain circumstances.

**sex therapist**   A person who treats sexual disorders, usually by means of psychotherapy and sexual exercises.

**urologist**   A physician who specializes in disorders of the urinary and genital systems.

**endocrinologist**   A physician who specializes in hormonal disorders.

**sensate focus**   A form of sex therapy that involves graduated touching exercises.

**sex surrogate**   A person who engages in sexual relations with a client as part of a sex therapy program.

Large numbers of women and men have problems with some aspect of sexual function. For example, many young men say they ejaculate too early, and many young women say they experience pain during sex. Yet sexual difficulties can usually be alleviated—by psychological treatment, drug therapy, or some combination of the two (Lipshultz et al., 2016).

Estimates of the actual prevalence of the various sexual disorders vary greatly from study to study and from country to country, probably because of differences in the definitions used and in the populations studied—in their age ranges, for example (McCabe et al., 2016). We will therefore not burden you with detailed statistics about the prevalence of individual disorders. It is generally agreed, however, that men and women tend to experience different kinds of sexual problems. Men's problems most commonly have to do with sexual performance, whereas women's problems most commonly have to do with sexual feelings (**FIGURE 14.1**).

In spite of this generalization, there is a fair amount of overlap and commonality between the problems encountered by the two sexes. Some performance issues, such as difficulty experiencing orgasm, are quite common among women, for example, and some men are troubled by a lack of interest in sex, especially as they age.

Sexual disorders can be primary, secondary, or situational. A **primary disorder** is one in which the person has never experienced healthy function. A **secondary disorder** is one that appears after some period of healthy function. A **situational disorder** is one that appears in some circumstances but not in others.

## A multidisciplinary approach to treatment is preferred

A person who has a sexual disorder may visit a family doctor, a psychotherapist, or some other nonspecialist provider. Sometimes these professionals resolve the problem satisfactorily: For example, a family doctor might write a prescription for a drug that successfully treats a man's erectile disorder, or a therapist might help a person work through relationship difficulties that are interfering with sexual pleasure.

Commonly, though, sexual problems are complex and multifaceted. In this case the person or couple who has the problem may benefit from the combined insights of a group of experts—experts who focus on sexual disorders from different perspectives. One of these experts is likely to be a **sex therapist**, a clinical psychologist or psychotherapist who specializes in sexual problems (**FIGURE 14.2**). In addition, there may be a physician (such as a **urologist** or an **endocrinologist**) and a physiotherapist who can give instruction on Kegel exercises (described later in the chapter) and other methods of improving genital function.

Sex therapy may be provided to individuals or to couples. The details will vary according to the clients' needs, but the therapist will frequently do the following:

- Inquire about the clients' history and relationships—including such matters as any experience of sexual abuse.

- Listen to the clients' account of the specific problems that bring them to the therapist.

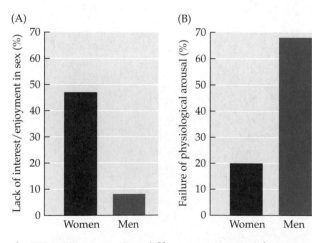

▲ **FIGURE 14.1   Sex differences in sexual dysfunctions** The bar graphs show the percentages of 533 men and 577 women attending a sexual problems clinic who complained of (A) lack of interest/enjoyment in sex and (B) failure of physiological arousal. (Data from P. Warner et al. 1987. *Sex Marital Ther* 2: 115–126. )

- Provide information: Some clients have very little knowledge about sex.
- Advise on relaxation and communication between partners.
- Teach exercises to improve sexual function. A frequently used set of exercises is called **sensate focus**, described in **BOX 14.1**.
- Advise on how to avoid pain and increase pleasure during sex.
- Help clients integrate the sexual and nonsexual aspects of their relationships.

Sex therapists do not engage in sexual interactions with their clients—the recommended exercises are practiced as "homework" rather than in the therapist's office. However, a few clients may be helped by interaction with a **sex surrogate**, also called a partner surrogate. This is a woman or man who has intimate or sexual contacts with clients as part of a treatment program, usually under the guidance of a sex therapist. Although sex surrogates are not officially licensed, many are professionally trained and certified (International Professional Surrogates Association, n.d.).

▲ **FIGURE 14.2** **A sex therapist** may recommend a combination of psychotherapy, sexual exercises, and drugs to alleviate sexual problems. Success is more likely when both partners participate in therapy.

## BOX 14.1
## Sensate Focus

Sensate focus is a set of touching exercises for couples who want to build closer intimacy and overcome sexual difficulties in their relationship (Weiner & Avery-Clark, 2017) (see figure). As the name implies, these exercises involve focusing on the physical sensations of gently touching and being touched, to the exclusion of other thoughts. The couple could be you and your partner—and that might mean two women, two men, or a woman and a man. For any couple, the procedure is the same.

After finding some free time and a quiet place—and turning off your cellphones—you and your partner undress and make yourselves comfortable, perhaps lying face-to-face with partial or full body contact. You may spend the first five minutes or so simply focusing on relaxed breathing. Then with your free hand you (the toucher) gently caress a nonerogenous zone of your partner (the "touchee"), such as the back. You can use your bare fingers or, if it feels good, some kind of massage oil. But we're not talking massage here: The motions should be gentle caresses, barely indenting the skin, if at all, and slow, slow, slow. If in doubt, go slower.

In sensate focus exercises, one partner is pleasured by the other but lets go of any responsibility to reciprocate.

Focus your mind on what your fingertips are feeling as your partner's skin drifts slowly by. At first, probably, you will experience intrusive thoughts—sometimes anxious ones, such as "This is weird" or "Am I going at the right speed?" or "Is my partner enjoying this?" or "Is it time to switch roles yet?" These thoughts, and all the other anxieties that

*(Continued)*

**BOX 14.1**

## Sensate Focus (continued)

may be interfering with your sex life, will gradually recede and disappear as you consciously bring your attention back to the sensations at your fingertips. You are doing this for your own pleasure, not your partner's.

After an agreed-on period of time, such as 10 or 15 minutes, you and your partner exchange roles. When you are the touchee, your role is not to provide a running commentary (no "Ahh, that feels good!" or "A little lower down please"). Instead, you just lie there, muscles relaxed, breathing relaxed, and focus on the movement of your partner's fingers and the pleasurable sensations they afford you. Again, in time this consciously willed focus becomes easier to maintain and causes intrusive or anxious thoughts to fade away. It's just two people individually experiencing the pleasure of the moment, but a pleasure that is generated by a shared activity. You may or may not become genitally aroused—it doesn't matter. If you do become genitally aroused, however, don't switch the agenda to regular sex, because that will invite any problems and anxieties that are interfering with your sex life to come flooding back.

At the end of the session, spend a few minutes discussing what transpired. Tell your partner honestly how you felt, even if it was unpleasurable or created anxiety for you for some or all of the time. Now is the time, if you wish, to tell your partner how his or her touch might be made more pleasurable for you on future occasions.

If you are doing sensate focus exercises under the guidance of a sex therapist, at your next meeting with the therapist you will discuss what transpired. She or he will probably suggest that you repeat the exercise several times until you and your partner are completely comfortable with it. Then, the therapist will suggest that you graduate to another region of the body. The sessions will be organized in a sequence, beginning with nonerogenous zones (perhaps the head and shoulders, with both partners fully dressed) and progressing to naked caressing of the back, the front, and then the genitals, over a period of a few weeks. The genital sessions may start with manual touch. Later sessions may involve oral sex and/or coitus, or perhaps tribadism or anal sex, depending on what the couple would like to engage in.

Sensate focus is a basic exercise whose purpose is to overcome performance anxiety, "spectatoring," and other distractions that impair many couples' ability to focus on the sheer pleasure of sexual interactions. Depending on the particular difficulty that an individual or a couple is experiencing, more specific exercises are available. If you feel that you could benefit from sensate focus or other exercises but don't want to consult a therapist, we suggest you read one of the books that covers these topics in detail (see Recommended Reading at the end of this chapter).

**FAQ:** Can I get sex therapy online?

Some sex therapists do offer information and advice online. This will not be the equivalent of a person-to-person meeting, but it may be useful for people who are too embarrassed, too busy, or too remotely located to visit a therapist's office. Check that the therapist is AASECT certified.

**female sexual arousal disorder** Lack or insufficiency of physiological sexual arousal in women.

**sexual interest/arousal disorder** Lack of interest in sex or insufficient sexual arousal, when it causes distress.

## 14.2 Female Sexual Arousal Disorder Involves Insufficient Genital Response

### LEARNING OBJECTIVE

After reading this section you should be able to:

14.2.1 Describe the symptoms of female sexual arousal disorder and the possible means to alleviate it.

In women, the three early processes of physiological arousal are vaginal lubrication, engorgement of the vaginal walls, and clitoral erection. These processes are often accompanied by psychological arousal—the feeling of sexual excitement. The absence or insufficiency of any of these processes can make coitus unpleasurable or downright painful. **Female sexual arousal disorder** is a term used to refer collectively to these problems (Meston & Stanton, n.d.).

In the fifth edition of *Diagnostic and Statistical Manual of Mental Disorders* (DSM-5), problems with sexual arousal and problems with sexual desire are grouped together under the diagnostic term **sexual interest/arousal disorder**. This makes some sense because a lack of sexual desire and a lack of genital arousal can trigger or exacerbate each other. Nevertheless, the two issues are conceptually and practically distinct, so we deal with them separately here. This section is about arousal problems; problems with sexual desire are covered toward the end of the chapter.

Insufficient lubrication during sex is a common complaint, especially after menopause. In postmenopausal women, the condition may well respond to hormone treatment, although such treatment carries some risks, as discussed in Chapter 11. Estrogens may be administered orally or directly to the vagina in the form of creams, tablets, or slow-release rings. (Application to the vagina does not eliminate the health risks associated with estrogen treatment, because the hormone spreads into the general circulation.) If poor lubrication is the woman's only problem, however, hormone treatment may be "overkill": Over-the-counter water-based lubricants do a good job, are inexpensive, and have few, if any, side effects. The lubricant may be applied to the woman's vagina, to her partner's penis, or to anything else that is inserted into the vagina.

Because PDE5 inhibitors (Viagra-type drugs—see below) have proved so successful in the treatment of erectile disorder in men, as described later in this chapter, it was hoped that they might prove equally useful in women with sexual arousal disorder. Results so far have been disappointing, however. One large U.S. study found no benefit at all from use of Viagra—it merely caused unpleasant side effects such as headaches (Basson et al., 2002). One subgroup of women is helped by Viagra, however: These are women who experience arousal difficulties as a side effect of antidepressant medications (Nurnberg et al., 2008).

Erectile disorder is often thought of as an exclusively male problem, but women can experience a lack of clitoral erection. Clitoral erectile disorder can coexist with absence of vaginal engorgement; both can be caused by diseases that compromise the blood vessels supplying the genitalia (Goldstein & Berman, 1998). A small battery-powered pump called the Eros Clitoral Therapy Device has been approved for treatment of this condition (**FIGURE 14.3**). A soft plastic cup is placed over the clitoris, and a partial vacuum is produced. This increases blood flow into the clitoris and nearby structures. Women who used the device reported moderate benefits in terms of increased sensation, lubrication, and satisfaction with sex, and the benefits lasted for at least four weeks after treatment (Alexander et al., 2018). The device is also useful for women in whom genital arousal is impaired by a neurological disorder such as multiple sclerosis or spinal cord injury (Alexander et al., 2017).

Psychotherapy and sex therapy can play an important role in the treatment of female arousal disorder. We will postpone discussion of these types of therapy until after we have covered other aspects of sexual dysfunction in women.

Some women experience the very opposite of female arousal disorder: They are troubled by frequent, unwanted, or near-continuous physiological arousal, including vasocongestion, tingling, and sensitivity of the genital area. Orgasm does not relieve the condition, or does so only briefly. Because the physiological arousal is completely disconnected from any subjective sexual arousal or desire, it can be extremely distressing.

This condition is called **persistent genital arousal disorder** (**PGAD**) (Goldmeier et al., 2014). Another name, "restless genital syndrome," has also been applied to the condition because it resembles (except for location) the better-known restless legs syndrome, and the two conditions may occur together. It has been suggested that PGAD is caused by entrapment or other damage to the sensory nerves that innervate the genitals (Klifto & Dellon, 2019) . Restless legs syndrome is thought to be a brain disorder, however, so if the two conditions are related, there is probably a brain basis for PGAD also. Sex therapy, electrical stimulation, and a variety of drugs have proved helpful in alleviating the disorder.

▲ **FIGURE 14.3** **The Eros Clitoral Therapy Device** increases blood flow to the clitoris and the surrounding area by producing a partial vacuum.

© 2018 NuGyn, Inc. (www.eros-therapy.com)

**persistent genital arousal disorder (PGAD)** Long-lasting physiological arousal in women, unaccompanied by subjective arousal or pleasure. Also called *restless genital syndrome*.

## 14.3 There Are Many Reasons for Sexual Pain in Women

**LEARNING OBJECTIVES**

After reading this section you should be able to:

14.3.1 Define dyspareunia and describe its possible causes.

14.3.2 Describe vaginismus and how it may be treated.

**dyspareunia** Pain during coitus.

**vulvodynia** Chronic pain in the vulva with no clear cause.

**provoked vestibulodynia** Painful sensitivity of the vestibule to touch or pressure.

Pain during sex is called **dyspareunia** (Mayo Clinic, 2019f). This problem is quite common: About 7.5% of sexually active women experience it, according to a U.K. survey (Mitchell et al., 2017), and it is especially common among young women. Dyspareunia can severely impact women's sex lives and relationships.

The following is a partial list of causes of dyspareunia:

- Allergic reactions to foreign substances, such as latex, spermicides, soap, or (rarely) semen
- Insufficient genital arousal, especially insufficient vaginal lubrication
- Developmental malformations, intersex conditions, or a persistent unbroken hymen
- Scars from vaginal tearing during childbirth or from episiotomy, hysterectomy, sexual assault, or female genital cutting
- Vaginal atrophy (a thinning of the vaginal walls that occurs with aging)
- Acute or chronic infections or inflammation of the vagina, internal reproductive tract, or urinary tract, including several sexually transmitted infections and pelvic inflammatory disease
- **Vulvodynia**—chronic pain in all or part of the vulva without an obvious cause
- **Provoked vestibulodynia**—the commonest form of vulvodynia, in which pain is experienced when some part of the vestibule is even lightly touched
- Endometriosis (see Chapter 2)
- Vaginismus (see next section)

The treatment of dyspareunia depends on the diagnosis. Infections may be treatable with antibiotic, antiviral, or antifungal drugs. If the problem is vaginal dryness, a lubricant can be used, or the woman's natural lubrication may be improved by prolonging foreplay or by clitoral stimulation before coitus. Because natural lubrication sometimes decreases during the course of prolonged arousal, it may be useful to add a lubricant during the course of lovemaking. If the dryness is associated with vaginal atrophy, treatment with estrogens (by mouth or by local administration) is an option. If there is a suspected latex allergy, polyurethane condoms can be substituted. Endometriosis can be treated with drugs or with surgery.

Provoked vestibulodynia can usually be effectively treated with cognitive behavioral therapy, as described in **BOX 14.2**. This form of treatment has been validated in a randomized controlled trial (Bergeron et al., 2016). Other options include massage, local anesthetics, non-SSRI antidepressants, corticosteroids, estrogens, and Botox injections. The majority of these treatments have limited experimental support however (Bergeron et al., 2020). If other treatments fail, surgical removal of the pain-eliciting areas (vestibulectomy) has been shown to be effective for many women.

### Vaginismus may make intercourse impossible

Some women have no obvious vaginal abnormalities, and yet they cannot experience coitus: Penetration of the vagina by the penis, or by any other object, is impossible on account of a combination of intense anxiety, pain, and pelvic muscle tension. Here is one woman's account:

## BOX 14.2
## Dyspareunia: A Case History

This is an abridged account of a case of provoked vestibulo-dynia described by Yitzchak Binik and his colleagues at McGill University Health Centre, reproduced by permission (Binik et al., 2007). It illustrates the application of cognitive behavioral therapy to this condition.

*Heather and Steven, ages 31 and 35, were referred by their gynecologist with a diagnosis of provoked vestibulodynia. The gynecologist had also referred them to a physical therapist, and pelvic floor rehabilitation had already begun when the couple came to see us.*

*Heather and Steven had been married for 5 years and reported a good relationship. Heather was an accountant and Steven was a pharmacist. They planned to have children but wanted to wait until the genital pain problem was resolved. The couple had begun to limit all forms of sexual contact, and both experienced self-doubt, each wondering how they were contributing to the problem.*

*Their family histories were similar; each had one parent who had been depressive and who was absent for long periods of time from the daily routine of family life. The two had always done well in school, excelled in sports, and had had significant past romantic relationships before meeting one another. They currently lead busy and active lives, with many nights taken up by work or sports.*

*The genital pain had begun a few years ago but had been bearable until a year previous, when it had worsened following a particularly stressful time in Heather's career. The problem had affected Heather's sexual desire, which fluctuated but had generally decreased. They both believed that intercourse was an important part of sex and felt inadequate for not engaging in it more often.*

*Initial goals were to explore factors related to Heather's desire fluctuations and to decrease the intensity of her genital pain. Among the first issues worked on was lifting some of the obstacles to having uninterrupted time together and to find ways to connect other than sex. Heather often leaned on Steven for support, and in return Steven tended to overprotect Heather to the point of neglecting his own needs. We also did some cognitive restructuring to separate sex from intercourse and to reduce catastrophizing about pain. Information was provided about vulvar vestibulitis, and sex education focused on broadening their definition of sex and on decreasing the emphasis they placed on intercourse. Both Steven and Heather were very receptive to these interventions and made significant attempts to integrate new knowledge and behaviors between sessions.*

*Heather and Steven were seen for a total of 18 sessions. The couple learned to create high-quality moments for intimacy and sex and felt more connected than at the start of therapy. They developed coping strategies, for example, opening up more to each other about their respective difficulties. In doing so, they learned that they could cope with intermittent episodes of pain.*

*During therapy we learned that both felt unlovable at times and that this drove many of their reactions to each other. Heather improved her management of emotions, and Steven began to concentrate more on his own needs. At the end of therapy, both reported that sexual desire was no longer a major issue and that the pain was negligible.*

*Both Heather and Steven dealt with their difficult childhoods by placing a high value on creating a healthy marriage; in addition, they were obviously committed to doing whatever work was necessary to ensure this outcome. The fact that they had previously enjoyed pain-free sex may have contributed to Heather's recovery from pain and restoration of her sexual desire. The relationship work that was accomplished during the course of therapy helped Steven become less passive both inside and outside of the bedroom. Finally, the increased emotional intimacy of the couple along with the decreased focus on intercourse may have helped the couple to reinject passion into their sex life.*

---

*My husband and I waited until we were married to have sex. To our disappointment, our wedding night was not the magical, lovemaking night we had envisioned. I had told him about my fear of intercourse, and he said we could take it slow. . . . When we did try, I became very tense and afraid and my legs would snap shut, and my arms would push him away. I went to the gynecologist who could not examine me [on account of my fear and pain] and told me "to relax." We have been trying to have intercourse for three years without success and are getting worried because we really want to start a family.* (Perez et al., 2016a)

This form of dyspareunia is known as **vaginismus**. This condition was originally thought to be the result of spasm of the vaginal walls, but experimental studies have failed to detect this spasm (Perez et al., 2016b). The focus has shifted to psychological factors as the cause, namely the crippling anxiety that is always present. Some sexologists believe

**vaginismus**   Inability to experience coitus due to pain, or fear of pain, and tension in the muscles surrounding the outer vagina.

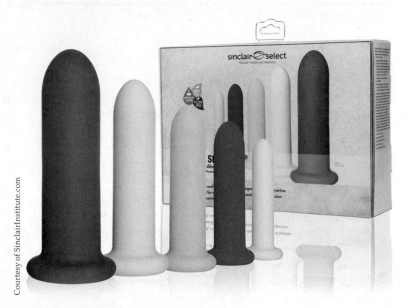

Courtesy of SinclairInstitute.com

▲ **FIGURE 14.4** **Vaginal dilators** of gradually increasing sizes may be used in the treatment of vaginismus.

**vaginal dilator** A plastic cylinder used to enlarge the vagina or to counteract vaginismus.

**anorgasmia** Difficulty experiencing or inability to experience orgasm. In women, also called *female orgasmic disorder.*

that this anxiety results from early traumatic experiences (such as experiencing or witnessing sexual assault) or from the inculcation of very strict or sex-negative attitudes during childhood and adolescence. The anxiety appears to be the primary cause; the pain and the tension in the pelvic floor muscles are consequences.

A mix of psychotherapy and sex therapy is the favored option for treatment of vaginismus. The psychotherapy may be aimed at identifying and overcoming the root cause of the woman's aversion to coitus. The sex therapy may include general exercises such as sensate focus. In fact, the key ingredients of sensate focus—the emphasis on relaxation, focus on the pleasure of gentle touch, and the gradual shift from nonerogenous zones to the vulva—are ideally suited to resolving the anxiety felt by women with this condition.

One sex therapy exercise specific to vaginismus is the use of **vaginal dilators** (**FIGURE 14.4**): Once having mastered the relaxation exercises, the woman (usually with her partner present) inserts the smallest dilator, while continuing to focus on relaxing her pelvic floor muscles. After she becomes comfortable with this dilator, she gradually progresses to a dilator that is the same size as her partner's penis. The great majority of women are able to engage in coitus after a few such sessions, and most report a lessening or disappearance of fear and pain (Ter Kuile et al., 2015). Another option is the use of Botox injections to relax the affected muscles directly (Werner et al., 2014).

Objective evidence for the efficacy of any treatments for vaginismus is limited. While many uncontrolled studies report benefits, a meta-analysis of randomized controlled studies found only a trend toward a benefit that did not reach statistical significance, because many of the women in the control groups experienced improvements comparable to those reported by the treated women. No difference in the efficacy of the various treatment methods was observed (Maseroli et al., 2018).

The *DSM-5* dropped the term vaginismus and folded these symptoms with other forms of dyspareunia into a new entity called genito-pelvic pain/penetration disorder (GPPPD). Quite apart from the cumbersome terminology, however, many sexologists prefer to keep the term vaginismus because it specifies a particular causal factor, namely the anxiety about coitus.

## 14.4 Difficulty in Reaching Orgasm Is Common among Women

**LEARNING OBJECTIVES**
After reading this section you should be able to:

14.4.1 Describe the possible causes of anorgasmia.
14.4.2 Explain how cases of anorgasmia with different causes may require different treatments.
14.4.3 Evaluate the potential downsides of faking orgasms.

"Orgasm is the end goal of sex; therefore, if you haven't reached orgasm during sex you have not fulfilled your goal." This comment is typical of those made by nearly all participants in a study of college-age women's and men's beliefs about sex (Opperman et al., 2014). Thus, even though sex without orgasm can be satisfying, especially in an emotional sense, most young women who rarely reach orgasm during coitus or other forms of sex consider this a problem and would like to solve it—in which case they are said to have **anorgasmia**, or female orgasmic disorder (Cohen & Goldstein, 2016).

In the National Health and Social Life Survey (NHSLS), 71% of women (compared with only 25% of men) said that they did not always experience orgasm during sex with their regular partners. But much fewer numbers of women experience orgasm so infrequently that they are seriously distressed or are motivated to seek some kind of remedy.

## Psychotherapy and directed masturbation may be helpful

If a woman doesn't reach orgasm with her partner, the root of the problem may lie more with the partner than with herself. If her partner is a man, he may suffer from sexual disorders such as erectile dysfunction or premature orgasm (see below), which prevent her from being sufficiently aroused. Treating his disorder may solve the problem. Or her partner may be uninterested in her sexual satisfaction or not know how to satisfy her. The problem could lie in a failure to communicate each other's needs—something that a sex therapist could help them with.

If the root of the problem is in the woman herself, there may be numerous possible causes, including the following:

- There may be a lack of education about female genital anatomy and function.

- Psychological factors such as anxiety, depression, the effects of sexual abuse, embarrassment, or excessive focus on the partner's pleasure may interfere.

- The problem may be a side effect of a variety of drugs, especially antidepressants. (About half of all women taking selective serotonin reuptake inhibitors [SSRIs] report difficulty in experiencing orgasm.)

- Some medical conditions, especially those that cause neurological damage, such as vascular disease or multiple sclerosis, can make it difficult to experience orgasm.

- Pelvic surgery, including hysterectomy, may impair orgasm.

- The biological changes that accompany aging, specifically during or following menopause, make it difficult for some women to experience orgasm.

- Anatomical differences may be problematic. It has been reported that the vulvas of anorgasmic women differ from those of orgasmic women. Specifically, the glans of the clitoris is reported to be smaller, and both the glans and body of the clitoris are located farther from the vagina (Wallen & Lloyd, 2011; Oakley et al., 2014).

- Anorgasmia often occurs as a secondary consequence of other sexual difficulties, especially difficulty with sexual arousal. A woman who is not aroused is not going to have an orgasm.

If a woman is anorgasmic for no obvious reason, the clinician or therapist will suggest different strategies depending on the details of the problem. If the woman can experience orgasm with masturbation but not with partnered sex, it may be possible to suggest modifications of partnered sex that will allow orgasm to occur. First, the therapist will reassure the couple that it is common for a woman not to experience orgasm with vaginal stimulation alone: According to a nationally representative survey led by Debby Herbenick of Indiana University, 9% of women never experience orgasm during coitus, and 37% only do so if clitoral stimulation is added to the vaginal stimulation (**FIGURE 14.5**). Another 36% of women do experience orgasm during coitus alone, but the orgasm is more intense with clitoral stimulation added. Only 18% of women say that vaginal stimulation by itself is adequate for orgasm and that clitoral stimulation doesn't add anything (Herbenick et al., 2018).

Thus, when a woman complains that she doesn't climax during coitus, a therapist will likely encourage the couple to add clitoral stimulation—by hand or mouth, or with a vibrator (Laan et al., 2013) (**FIGURE 14.6**). This stimulation can be provided by either partner and can take place before, during, after, or instead of coitus.

**FAQ:** My partner loves me but he cannot bring me to orgasm during intercourse—what should we do?

More partnered women reach orgasm through oral sex (cunnilingus) than any other means. To reach orgasm during coitus, try the coital alignment technique described below, or add a vibrator to the mix.

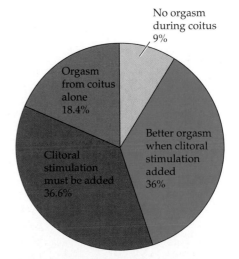

▲ **FIGURE 14.5** **What women want** This pie chart shows the percentages of women who experience orgasm during coitus with and without clitoral stimulation. (After D. Herbenick et al. 2017. *J Sex Marital Ther* 44: 201–212.)

▶ **FIGURE 14.6  Helping a woman experience orgasm during partnered sex**  If a woman has difficulty experiencing orgasm during coitus, it may be helpful to adopt a position, as here, that allows either partner to provide clitoral stimulation by hand or with a vibrator.

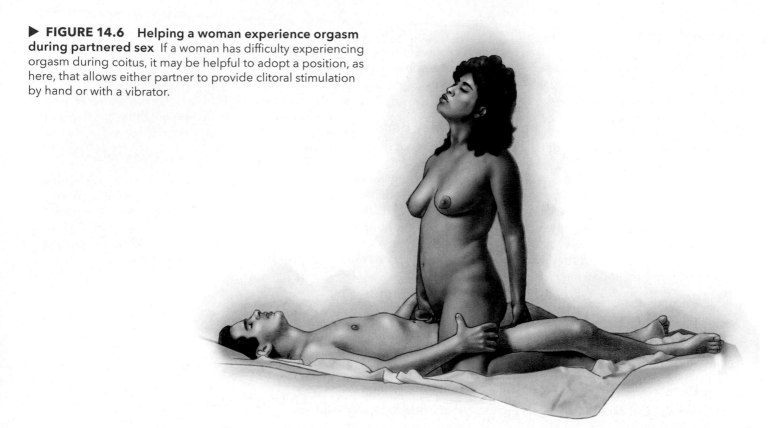

**coital alignment technique (CAT)**
A variation of the man-above position for coitus that increases clitoral stimulation.

One variant on the man-above position, known as the **coital alignment technique** (**CAT**), was specifically developed by sex therapist Edward Eichel and his colleagues with the purpose of helping women experience orgasm during coitus (Eichel et al., 1988; Pierce, 2000). In CAT, the man enters the woman in the man-above position but then slides a few inches forward over her pelvis so that the upper surface of the base of his penis is pressing against her clitoris. (This is the "riding high" position.) Now, during the inward stroke of coitus, the man's penis moves downward rather than upward, and it glides over the woman's pubic bone and clitoris like a bow over violin strings. By adjusting the upward and downward pressure exerted by each partner during the coital cycle, they turn the coital strokes into a series of gentle collisions between penis and clitoris so that the whole coital motion is more of a vibration than a friction. The method is helpful not only because it adds clitoral stimulation but also because the stimulation of the clitoris and the vagina follows a synchronized rhythm.

Encouraging couples to communicate better about their sexual feelings and the sexual activities that are most arousing can be very helpful as well. Men do not automatically know what their female partners find sexually arousing. A man may rush from foreplay to coitus before his partner is sufficiently aroused, in which case coitus may be a turn-off for her, rather than a turn-on. The man may stimulate the woman's nipples or clitoris too strongly—these are tender areas, after all. A postmenopausal woman may take longer to become aroused than she did earlier in her life. All these things can make it difficult for the woman to experience orgasm. In an environment in which the woman feels free to let her partner know whether the things he is doing are working or not, these difficulties can often be resolved.

If the woman does not experience orgasm under any circumstances, a somewhat different strategy is called for. Bear in mind that over half of all women say that they never masturbate, according to NHSLS data. Thus, if they are open to trying masturbation, they may be helped to experience orgasm for the first time. Sex therapy for anorgasmia often includes a program of self-stimulation, in which the woman begins with visual and manual exploration of her naked body and later progresses to genital stimulation. Vibrators are particularly useful in these kinds of exercises. Sometimes this directed masturbation program is accompanied by exercises in the use of fantasy or erotic materials. In addition, the woman may be encouraged to perform **Kegel exercises (BOX 14.3)**, although these are more useful for improving the quality of orgasm than for helping women experience orgasm at all. Sensate focus exercises with a partner are often added.

As might be expected, directed masturbation programs are most successful at helping women reach orgasm during masturbation. The great majority of women are able to do so by the end of a sex therapy program, but fewer are able to transfer this newfound capacity to partnered sex (Heiman, 2007).

**Kegel exercises** Exercises to strengthen pelvic floor muscles, with the aim of improving sexual function or alleviating urinary leakage.

## BOX 14.3
## Kegel Exercises

Kegel exercises strengthen the muscles of the pelvic floor (Mayo Clinic, 2019d). They were developed in the 1950s by Arnold Kegel, a urological surgeon at UCLA, for the purpose of helping women overcome urinary incontinence. The pelvic floor muscles are also involved in sexual functions, however, and women (as well as men) with strong pelvic floor muscles enjoy better sexual function. Thus Kegel exercises have also been promoted as a way to improve sexual function, both in women and in men.

The first step in doing Kegel exercises is to identify the muscles that need to be exercised. The usual recommendation is for the person to begin to urinate and then to voluntarily interrupt the flow of urine. The muscles that accomplish this are the pubococcygeus muscles (see figure) and possibly other muscles of the pelvic floor. Alternatively, you can place a finger in the vagina (or the anus, if you're a man) and squeeze down on the finger. (You should try not to assist this effort by clenching your buttock muscles.) Another possibility, if you're a man, is to raise your erect penis (hands-free) while standing, an action that requires contraction of pelvic floor muscles attached to the root of the penis (see Chapter 3). These muscles participate in erection and ejaculation. At first having an erection is necessary so that you can see that you are contracting the right muscles; once you know how to contract them, you can do the exercise with a flaccid penis.

After learning how to contract your pelvic floor muscles, begin a regular program of exercises. Do these exercises without a finger insertion, unless you need to recheck that you are using the right muscles. The routine for each repetition is squeeze-hold-release. At the beginning it may be difficult to hold a contraction for more than a second or so. But with practice you will be able to hold the contraction for several

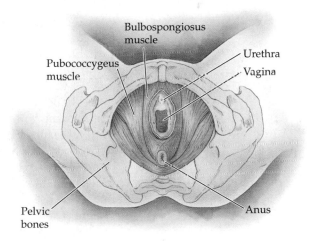

Kegel exercises are designed to strengthen the pelvic floor muscles.

seconds. One recommended routine to aim for is a set of ten three-second contractions, three times a day. In an alternative routine, which requires less attention to timing and counting of reps, you perform 3 contractions, each for the duration of two normal breaths and separated by two normal breaths; this routine is performed four times each day for a total of 12 contractions (Bridgeman & Roberts, 2010). Some guidelines recommend at least 30 10-second contractions per day (Mayo Clinic, 2014). If you'd like your smartphone to share the experience, there are apps to analyze data transmitted wirelessly from an intravaginal sensor.

Most randomized controlled clinical trials of Kegel exercises have focused on whether they reduce urinary or fecal incontinence. (They do.) Some studies have also asked additional questions about sexual function, and the findings are generally positive, according to a review (Ferreira et al., 2015).

© iStock.com/AleksandarNakic

▲ Orgasm—genuine or faked?

Directed masturbation programs work better for women with primary (lifelong) orgasmic disorder than for women who develop the problem after some years of satisfactory orgasmic functioning. In the latter group of women, the problem usually reflects relationship difficulties, other psychological issues, or medical conditions that are not addressed by masturbation training.

## Faked orgasms offer a questionable solution

If a woman (or a man) doesn't experience orgasm during an episode of partnered sex and this causes a problem, a possible solution is to fake one. It may not be possible to replicate the vaginal contractions associated with a genuine female orgasm—let alone the ejaculation associated with a male orgasm. Still, the vocalizations and facial expressions can certainly be faked, though with variable effectiveness depending on the person's acting skills.

Faked orgasms are the stuff of lore and legend. Among adults who have engaged in coitus, 67% of women and 28% of men say they have faked an orgasm at least once (Muehlenhard & Shippee, 2010). In a survey of a nationally representative sample of women, most of those who had faked orgasm said that they did so because they wanted their partner to feel successful, they liked the person and didn't want them to feel bad, or they wanted to bring sex to an end (Herbenick et al., 2019). Another reason some women give for faking orgasm is to heighten their own sexual arousal (Barnett et al., 2019).

Can a man tell if a woman is faking orgasm? In one study, researchers put this question to 326 college undergraduates (Knox et al., 2008). The male students were much more likely than the female students to believe that men could tell. Presumably that's because if a woman successfully fakes an orgasm, she knows that the man was unable to tell, but the man doesn't. Alternatively, he might know that she faked the orgasm but might say nothing in order to avoid embarrassing her, in which case she would overestimate his gullibility.

Women who don't fake orgasms realize that doing so can create problems. Here are some comments on the topic from nonfakers (Opperman et al., 2014): "If I don't orgasm I'm not gonna fake one because that's not gonna help anyone. It just means he would do whatever he thought caused the orgasm again"; "He would realize I was faking and then be upset because of it"; and "It's very dishonest and as sexual activity is part of being in love, it wouldn't benefit the relationship."

## 14.5 Lack of Interest in Sex Is Not Necessarily a Problem

### LEARNING OBJECTIVES

After reading this section you should be able to:

14.5.1 Evaluate the potential benefits, limitations, and risks of drugs used to treat hypoactive sexual desire disorder in women.

14.5.2 Explain how social circumstances can lead to a low interest in sex.

A significant number of women (estimates range from about 3% to 30%, depending on the criteria used) have little or no desire to engage in sexual activities of any kind (McCabe & Goldhammer, 2013). The proportion of women who are uninterested in sex increases with age. Many older women who lack interest in sex are not troubled by their lack of interest and should not be thought of as having a disorder. Thus in one study of women age 65 to 79, 88% of the participants had low sexual desire, but only 15% of them—mostly those who had partners—were troubled about it (Zeleke et al., 2017). Still, that 15% represents a lot of women who would like to regain a desire for sex. When women are troubled enough by a lack of interest in sex to seek professional help, the condition falls into the *DSM-5* diagnostic category sexual interest/ arousal disorder, but it may also be referred to by the more specific name **hypoactive sexual desire disorder (HSDD)** (Goldstein et al., 2017).

Problems with sexual desire often come to therapists' attention in cases of **discrepant sexual desire**, where one partner in a relationship is more interested in sex than the other. Because women are more likely than men to experience a lack of interest in sex, it's not uncommon for heterosexual couples to be mismatched in this respect, with the man wanting sex more than the woman. Here's how one 21-year-old woman described the situation (Meston & Buss, 2009):

> Having been with my previous boyfriend for three years, our sex life declined due to my disinterest. At times his discontent with the situation was so overwhelming and disruptive to the rest of our lives that I would feign interest and have sex with him just to make him happy, in part because I felt I wasn't holding up my end of the relationship sexually.

Situational factors such as child-rearing responsibilities, which usually affect women more than men, tend to exacerbate this gender-based discrepancy in sexual desire.

HSDD is often a result of depression. Unfortunately antidepressant drugs, especially SSRIs, may actually worsen the loss of interest in sex (Lorenz et al., 2016).

It's important to distinguish between HSDD and asexuality—a topic discussed in Chapter 12. Asexuality is a long-lasting—often lifelong—absence of sexual attraction to others. Asexual people may nevertheless masturbate, and they may experience sexual arousal without that arousal being directed toward other people. HSDD, on the other hand, is a global lack of interest in sex, and it usually develops after an earlier period of life in which the person did experience strong sexual feelings.

## Estrogen or androgen treatment may improve sexual desire in women

Women's sexual desire is influenced by two classes of sex steroids, estrogens and androgens, but in normal circumstances estrogens are the dominant factor (Cappelletti & Wallen, 2016). The levels of estrogens drop in women who have very little body fat for any reason, such as demanding athletic regimens, starvation, or eating disorders, as well as after menopause. In these circumstances, sexual desire can decline or disappear. Some women continue to initiate sexual activity long after menopause, however. Their behavior may reflect the importance of a loving relationship and cultural factors in sexual desire, or it may depend on the continuing presence of sex steroids secreted by the adrenal glands.

In premenopausal women who are not menstruating and have low sexual desire, an interest in sex usually reappears when body weight returns to normal and menstruation resumes. In postmenopausal women with low sexual desire, interest in sex may reappear with hormone therapy (i.e., treatment with either an estrogen or an estrogen plus progestin). The positive effect of hormone treatment on sexual desire is probably twofold: Part of it is due to the direct effect of estrogens on the brain, and part is due to improved physiological arousal (vaginal lubrication, engorgement, and clitoral erection), which makes sex more pleasurable and therefore rekindles an interest in it.

Administration of testosterone (via transdermal patches or implants) for the treatment of HSDD is controversial. The U.S. Food and Drug Administration (FDA) has not approved the use of testosterone for this purpose, because of the risk of masculinizing side effects, which can include male-pattern baldness, growth of facial and chest hair, acne, and possibly heart disease (Harvard Women's Health Watch,

**hypoactive sexual desire disorder**
Low or absent interest in sex, when this condition causes distress.

**discrepant sexual desire**
The situation in which one partner in a relationship has much more interest in sex than the other.

▲ Elite female athletes, especially in sports where extreme leanness is an advantage, may experience a drop in sex hormone levels, which puts them at risk of developing sexual disorders, including a lack of interest in sex.

2013). According to a consensus statement issued by an international group of professional societies, however, testosterone is safe and effective for treatment of HSDD in women who are postmenopausal (whether naturally so or as a result of removal of their ovaries), but only so long as the levels of testosterone in a woman's blood are raised no higher than those normally seen in premenopausal women (Davis et al., 2019). For this purpose some countries (but not the United States) have approved a low-dose testosterone patch named Intrinsa. The consensus statement did not support the use of testosterone for the treatment of HSDD in *pre*menopausal women.

In 2015 a drug named flibanserin (trade name Addyi), which acts on the serotonin system in the brain, was approved for treatment of low sexual interest or arousal in premenopausal women. The efficacy of this drug in increasing women's sexual interest is minimal, however, according to a meta-analysis of studies, and it can have worrisome side effects, including daytime somnolence (Jaspers et al., 2016). Another drug, bremelanotide (trade name Vyleesi), was approved for the same purpose in 2019.* This drug must be self-injected at least 45 minutes before expected sexual activity. As with flibanserin, side effects (including elevated blood pressure) are a significant issue, as is the cost (nearly $1,000 for a four-pack).

## Sex therapy may be helpful for low sexual desire in women

Sex therapy is an alternative (or possibly additional) option in the treatment of low sexual desire in women (Goldstein et al., 2017). As with other sexual problems, sex therapists often use a combination of cognitive and behavioral approaches. The cognitive portion may involve challenging negative beliefs and expectations that interfere with sexual desire (such as the idea that low sexual desire is simply "part of who I am") and helping the woman and her partner improve their communication skills. The behavioral portion will likely include sensate focus and other exercises that do not make excessive demands on the woman's interest in becoming sexual. Case reports support the usefulness of the sex therapy approach; large-scale outcome studies have not been done.

Another approach that has proven useful in women troubled by low sexual desire is mindfulness-based therapy: Mindfulness is a form of meditation in which a person focuses nonjudgmentally on his or her own mental state in the present moment (Brotto & Basson, 2014). Mindfulness therapy has also been reported to be helpful in the treatment of some kinds of dyspareunia (Brotto et al., 2019).

## Alternative views on women's response cycles may influence treatment options

In Chapter 5 we described Rosemary Basson's model of women's sexual arousal, in which sexual desire may be generated or amplified once a woman begins to engage in the physical stimulation of sexual behavior (Basson, 2001; Basson, 2007).

---

*Bremelanotide has a curious history. This drug activates receptors in the brain for a hormone named melanocortin, one of whose functions is to stimulate skin pigmentation. Drugs of this type were originally tested as sunless tanning agents, but male volunteers who took them experienced spontaneous penile erections, and this led to successful trials of bremelanotide in the treatment both of male erectile disorder and of low sexual desire in women. Portman, D. J., Edelson, J., Jordan, R., et al. (2014). Bremelanotide for hypoactive sexual desire disorder: Analyses from a Phase 2B dose-ranging study. *Obstetrics and Gynecology, 123 Suppl 1*, 31S.

In other words, a woman may not be conscious of any desire for sex, but she may be willing to engage in sex as an expression of intimacy or to please her partner. Once sexual interactions begin, sexual desire may be awakened in response to her physiological arousal.

Women who have sexual disorders are especially likely to endorse Basson's model (Sand & Fisher, 2007). Here's an example from Basson (2007):

> Caroline, age 55 and 6 years postmenopause, was referred because of low sexual desire— for some 8 to 10 years in her estimation, and for some 20 years according to her husband, George. George recalled how Caroline's sexual interest decreased with each of her three pregnancies, recovering only partially in between, and then plummeted some 8 years ago around menopause. There had been minimal sexual activity since that time. . . . . After hearing that many women have close to zero spontaneous desire but go ahead anyway and engage in sex, having previously ensured their partner's knowledge and skill in giving them sexual pleasure and satisfaction, Caroline totally changed her situation around between the first and second visit. We had suggested the couple might begin to discuss bringing back into their lives some nonintercourse sexual caressing and some "date-like" contexts. However, apparently no discussion occurred—just action. Caroline went ahead and instigated two sexual episodes with her husband, inclusive of intercourse, during the 7 days between the visits. . . . We simply congratulated the couple and were pleased to find that their progress continued when they were seen some 6 months later. This truly appears to be an example of therapy that consisted entirely of giving information.

If desire does follow physiological arousal for some women, then problems with physiological arousal could be an important cause of low sexual desire, and treatments for these problems could help restore missing desire. In addition, recognition of the importance of motivations for sex other than sexual desire itself points to a wider view of sexual disorders and their treatment. Indeed, Basson postulates a "sexual interest disorder" that is much broader than the traditional "hypoactive sexual desire disorder" and that takes account of social and other situational factors.

Not everyone agrees that these issues should be "medicalized" by labeling them as a disorder (Tiefer, 2002). In fact, some physicians have claimed that hypoactive sexual desire disorder is a diagnosis invented by the pharmaceutical industry for the purpose of selling drugs to treat it (Meixel et al., 2015). Still, there is general agreement that relational and social factors do play an important role in women's sexual feelings—probably much more so than for men. Consider the following case history provided by a family physician (Candib, 2002):

> A 32-year-old Salvadoran married woman, a documented immigrant, works 40 hours cleaning houses, looking after her two children and her husband's aging mother, cares for the house, and does all the housework and cooking. She [visits] her family physician with an urgent concern about sex. She reports that for the last few months she has not been interested in having sexual relations, and she worries that her husband will seek sex elsewhere. Family history reveals that her mother died when she was young. She was raised by an older brother in whose home she was a servant. She was never sexually abused but felt neglected and poorly treated by her brother and sister-in-law. She became pregnant on the first episode of intercourse, married promptly, immigrated to the U.S., and never had any further partners. Further inquiry reveals that communication between her and her husband about sex or the relationship is minimal and that he is not affectionate. Nevertheless, she finds him to be a good provider and good father. She has no interest in other partners or in divorce. She reports that although she used to become sexually aroused, she has never had orgasm. She takes oral contraceptives and wonders if they are the cause of her lack of interest. She does not feel depressed, although sometimes she is tired for days on end, but she wonders if her husband could be depressed.

**premature ejaculation** Ejaculation before the man wishes, often immediately on commencement of coitus. Also called *early* or *rapid ejaculation*.

To deal with the issues raised by this kind of account, a group of feminist-oriented psychologists, sex therapists, and social workers put forward a revised conceptualization of women's sexual problems (Working Group for a New View of Women's Sexual Problems, 2001; Wood et al., 2006). This model categorizes sexual problems under four major headings:

- *Sexual problems due to sociocultural, political, or economic factors.* These include lack of information about sex or lack of access to relevant services, culturally imposed anxiety about one's attractiveness or shame about one's sexual orientation, conflicts between one's own cultural norms and those of the dominant culture, and lack of interest in sex due to family and work obligations.

- *Sexual problems relating to the partner and the relationship.* These include sexual inhibition resulting from relationship conflicts or unequal power, different desires, poor communication, or the partner's health or sexual problems.

- *Sexual problems due to psychological factors.* These include sexual aversion due to past trauma, feelings of attachment or rejection, depression, anxiety, or fear of the consequences of sex or of refusing sex.

- *Sexual problems due to medical factors.* These include painful intercourse or lack of physiological arousal caused by physical issues listed earlier in this chapter.

Women in the real world, such as the woman in the case history above, might well have problems in several of these categories. Viewed in this way, women's sexual problems demand an integrative approach to treatment—one that addresses biological, psychological, social, and cultural factors that may impair or facilitate a rewarding sex life (Leiblum, 2007; Weeks et al., 2015; Perelman, 2016a).

## 14.6 Premature Ejaculation Is Men's Number One Sex Problem

**LEARNING OBJECTIVES**
After reading this section you should be able to:

**14.6.1** Explain the stop-start method for treating premature ejaculation.
**14.6.2** Explain the options for medical treatment of premature ejaculation.

Turning now to men's sexual problems, we start with the one that is the most common, at least among young men: **premature ejaculation**. This condition, also called early or rapid ejaculation, is ejaculation that occurs before the man wants it to (Mayo Clinic, 2019h). If the man's intention is to engage in coitus, he might ejaculate before he can place his penis in the woman's vagina, at the moment he does so, or quickly thereafter. Some authorities give a particular cutoff time for a clinical definition of premature ejaculation: One minute after onset of coitus is a widely used criterion (Althof et al., 2014). Still, it's really the distress caused by the problem, more than the precise timing, that is relevant. Premature ejaculation must be a persistent problem, not just an occasional phenomenon, to merit a diagnosis.

Perhaps as a consequence of watching pornography, many young people (both male and female) think that a healthy man should be able to continue coital thrusting without ejaculation for as long as he wishes, and that any man who cannot do so has a sexual disorder. This is not the case, however. Whether they want to or not, most healthy men will ejaculate after a very few minutes of thrusting: two to eight minutes is the typical range, and five minutes is the average (Rowland et al., 2010). Contrary to what one might imagine, men tend to ejaculate more rapidly as they get older (**FIGURE 14.7**)

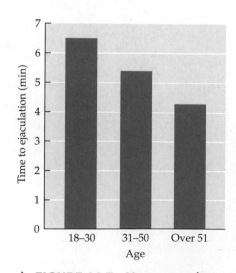

▲ **FIGURE 14.7 Young men last longer.** This bar graph shows the duration of coital thrusting before ejaculation for different age groups of men. (M. D. Waldinger et al. 2005. *J Sex Med* 2: 492–497.)

## There are different kinds of premature ejaculation

Premature ejaculation can be a primary, secondary, or situational disorder. As an example of the last of these, premature ejaculation might occur during partnered sex but not during masturbation.

The following two vignettes (Althof, 2007) illustrate some of this diversity:

*John, a 6-foot-2-inch, well-muscled 30-year-old, sought consultation because he had developed rapid ejaculation with his new partner of 6 weeks. . . . With some embarrassment John revealed that he was intimidated by Kim. She was a beautiful, successful woman, the CEO for a small corporation, and he felt "dominated" by her.*

*Jim, a 58-year-old businessman, . . . described never being able to last more than 15 seconds with any sexual partner. He had read books about premature ejaculation and diligently practiced the exercises, to no avail. This "disability" was a great source of shame for him, and he felt that it had greatly interfered in his relationships prior to marriage and in both of his marriages.*

The traditional view of premature ejaculation, espoused by Masters and Johnson, was that it results from learning. They suggested that a man whose early sexual experiences are conducted in haste and anxiety (perhaps in the back seat of a car or in the parents' family room) might become conditioned to reaching orgasm very quickly (Masters & Johnson, 1970). Psychological theories such as this seem most plausible in cases where premature ejaculation is situational (as with John in the first vignette above).

Another idea, based on animal research as well as pharmaceutical studies in humans, is that lifelong premature ejaculation is caused by a dysfunction in neurotransmitter mechanisms. In particular it has been shown that men who experience lifelong premature ejaculation (such as Jim in the second vignette) often carry a particular variant of a gene associated with dopamine neurotransmission (Santtila et al., 2010; Eltonsi et al., 2017).

A man who is troubled by premature ejaculation is likely to try various kinds of self-devised remedies for his condition, such as distracting himself during sex with irrelevant thoughts. Such remedies rarely work and, even worse, often prevent the man or his partner from having a rewarding sexual experience.

## Sex therapy helps some men

The clinician's first task is to reassure the man that he is not a sexual failure and that premature ejaculation is a common condition that can usually be successfully treated. The mainstays of treatment are sex therapy and drugs, and the combination of these two modalities may offer the greatest benefit (Althof, 2016).

One aspect of sex therapy is simply talking through the history of the man's condition and the factors that may exacerbate it. In the first vignette above, for example, it quickly became clear that interpersonal dynamics lay behind John's premature ejaculation—specifically, the power relationship between John and his partner—and this became the focus of discussion. In other cases, it may be useful to concentrate on cognitive distortions. These distortions can range from discounting the positive ("My partner says she is satisfied because she doesn't want to hurt my feelings") to all-or-nothing thinking ("I am a complete failure because I come quickly") or catastrophizing ("If I fail tonight, my girlfriend will dump me").

Sex therapy exercises are useful in some cases. These often include the same sensate focus exercises already described. In addition, there are exercises specifically designed for premature ejaculation. One example is the **stop-start method**:

- Initially, the man masturbates alone, bringing himself to a medium level of excitement. (He may be taught to think about sexual arousal on a 10-point scale, 10 being orgasm, and to focus on staying in the 5- to 7-point range.)

**stop-start method** A sex therapy technique for the treatment of premature ejaculation that involves alternating between stimulating and not stimulating the penis.

(A)

(B)

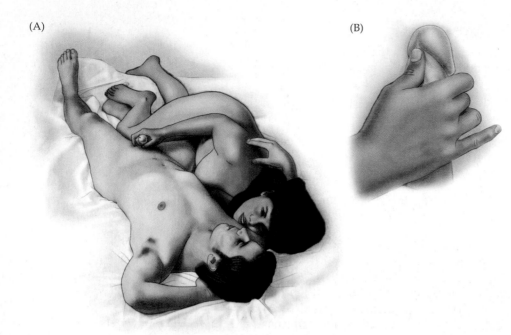

◀ **FIGURE 14.8 Sex therapy exercises for premature ejaculation** Position of a couple for "stop-start" exercises directed at premature ejaculation. (A) The man lies on his back with his legs apart. His partner lies to one side and partly astride him, so that she can manually or orally stimulate his genitals. (B) The "squeeze technique" for premature ejaculation. When the man is close to orgasm, he communicates this fact to his partner with a prearranged signal. (Some couples do this with random timing.) The partner then grasps the man's penis with a thumb on the frenulum and squeezes firmly for a few seconds. This diminishes the man's urge to ejaculate and possibly causes a partial loss of his erection.

He learns to recognize what the 8- and 9-point levels feel like and then stops masturbating to avoid such high levels of arousal. This is repeated a few times, until he is finally allowed to masturbate to orgasm. He does these exercises several times a week for several weeks, with the goal of being able to stimulate his penis for 15 minutes without ejaculating. Some studies have reported beneficial effects of using a vibrator during these exercises, because the strong effect of the vibrator can lead to partial desensitization of the penis to more natural stimuli (Ventus et al., 2019).

- In the next stage, the man and his partner are together, in a position such as that shown in **FIGURE 14.8A**. She (assuming it's a woman) stimulates his penis by hand or orally, but he asks her to stop before he climaxes. Masters and Johnson recommended that the partner firmly pinch or squeeze the man's penis, just below the glans, at the time that stimulation ceases, as a means of reducing his arousal (**FIGURE 14.8B**). Again, the goal is to be able to experience sexual stimulation for 15 minutes without ejaculation.

- The third stage progresses to coitus. The woman simply places the man's penis in her vagina, and the couple lies still for a prolonged period. The idea is that the man gets accustomed to the sensations of coitus without being too excited. Then the woman begins to move slowly, but the man tells her to stop whenever he nears orgasm. The woman can apply the squeeze technique in this situation too, as necessary. She can squeeze the base of his penis when it is still partially inserted in her vagina. After several repetitions, the man is allowed to ejaculate. As the exercises proceed, the man should be able to postpone his ejaculation for a longer and longer time.

Unfortunately, about three in four men who try sex therapy are not successful in overcoming premature ejaculation, or they experience an initial improvement followed by a relapse (Althof, 2007). Specialists recommend various methods to prevent relapses, such as repeating the initial exercises periodically and having regular follow-up visits with the therapist.

## Drug treatment may be effective

The drugs used to treat premature ejaculation are mostly SSRIs—antidepressants such as Prozac, Paxil, and Zoloft. Of the SSRIs that are currently available in the United States, paroxetine (Paxil) is the one most commonly used. In one randomized, double-blind study of men with severe premature ejaculation, a six-week course of paroxetine increased the time between commencement of coitus and ejaculation from about 20 seconds to 2.5 minutes (**FIGURE 14.9**), whereas the placebo had no effect at all. Another SSRI, dapoxetine (Priligy), has also been shown to be effective; this drug has a short lifetime in the body, so it is taken one to three hours before expected sexual activity rather than on a once-a-day basis.

Another class of drugs that have proven effective is that of PDE5 inhibitors. These are Viagra, Cialis, and similar drugs, discussed in greater detail below. PDE5 inhibitors have been shown in controlled trials to work as well as SSRIs and better than sex therapy with the squeeze technique (Martyn-St James et al., 2017). The combination of a PDE5 inhibitor and an SSRI may work even better than an SSRI alone.

Topical anesthetics such as lidocaine can be used to delay ejaculation by numbing the penis. The numbness may be perceived as unpleasant, however. In addition, unless a condom is used, the anesthetic may irritate or numb any region with which the man's penis comes into contact: This could be the partner's vagina, mouth, or anus.

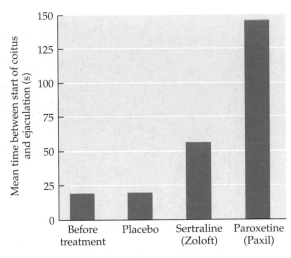

▲ **FIGURE 14.9  Drug treatment for premature ejaculation** Effect of six weeks of treatment with a placebo or one of two SSRIs. (Data from M. D. Waldinger et al. 2001. *J Clin Psychopharmacol* 21: 293–297.)

## 14.7  Delayed Ejaculation Is Not Well Understood

**LEARNING OBJECTIVE**

After reading this section you should be able to:

14.7.1  Compare the treatment options for delayed ejaculation.

**Delayed** (or absent) **ejaculation** is the opposite of premature ejaculation: The man can reach the point of ejaculation and orgasm only with difficulty or not at all (Williams & Johnson, 2016). Sometimes delayed ejaculation is specific to a certain kind of sexual behavior, such as coitus or partnered sex generally; in other cases the man may not be able to reach orgasm under any circumstances. Either way, it is a fairly uncommon problem: Estimates of its prevalence range from less than 3% to about 8% of the male population. As with premature ejaculation, delayed ejaculation can be a lifelong problem, or it may be acquired at some point in adult life.

The cause or causes of delayed ejaculation are not well understood. Some therapists have proposed psychological or behavioral causes (Perelman, 2013). For example, it has been suggested that delayed ejaculation affects men who have become accustomed since adolescence to frequent, lengthy masturbation using a tight grip and vigorous strokes, or who masturbate by rubbing their penis against bedding or rough surfaces (Keesling, 2006). It is equally possible, however, that these men masturbate often and vigorously *because* they have such difficulty experiencing orgasm any other way (Hartmann & Waldinger, 2007). Alternatively, too much viewing of pornography could be the cause, as will be discussed in Chapter 17. It should be possible to correct either of these problems by changing the man's habits. Sometimes stopping masturbation for a few weeks makes it easier for a man to reach orgasm during partnered sex.

Other models suggest that sexual shame, inculcated during upbringing, leads to an inhibition of the orgasmic process or that the root cause is a lack of sexual desire. In either of these cases, more in-depth psychotherapy would be needed to identify and correct the problem. Delayed ejaculation can also follow some traumatic life event, such as a relationship crisis. Or perhaps the man's thought processes during sex are so distracting or negative that they interfere with sexual arousal.

In a minority of cases delayed ejaculation has obvious biological causes, such as neurological damage. It can also result from the use of certain drugs, including antihypertensive drugs, major tranquilizers, and antidepressants. If it is caused by drugs, the condition can usually be treated by switching to a different drug or by adding

**delayed ejaculation** Difficulty achieving or inability to achieve orgasm and/or ejaculation. Also called *male orgasmic disorder*.

a second drug that counteracts this side effect. For example, delayed ejaculation caused by SSRIs is often successfully treated by adding or substituting the non-SSRI antidepressant bupropion (Wellbutrin).

Bupropion is sometimes helpful even when delayed ejaculation is not caused by SSRIs. In general, though, there is no broadly effective drug treatment for the condition (Martin-Tuite & Shindel, 2019). Sometimes the use of a vibrator and lubricant jelly helps (Wincze, 2009). If the man can reach orgasm through masturbation but not with his partner, he may be encouraged to do exercises in which his partner is gradually incorporated into his masturbatory activities. Alternatively, some experts believe that reducing solo masturbation, especially masturbation in conjunction with viewing pornography, makes it easier for a man to reach orgasm with his partner (Sadowski et al., 2016). We revisit this issue in Chapter 17, where we consider the possible harmful effects of pornography.

A few men have no difficulty reaching orgasm but never ejaculate. This is most likely a neurological problem. Even if the condition cannot be corrected, such men can usually become fathers via medically induced ejaculation using vibratory or electrical stimulation or by harvesting sperm directly from the testes.

Delayed ejaculation is often difficult to treat successfully, but occasionally a simple solution presents itself. One sexually naive Orthodox Jewish couple came to a therapist because they couldn't have children. They said that they lay together without moving during intercourse, waiting for the man to ejaculate, but he didn't. The therapist suggested that they try thrusting, whereupon pregnancy quickly followed, and they ended up having eight children (Perelman, 2016b).

## 14.8 Erectile Disorder Has Many Causes and Treatments

**LEARNING OBJECTIVES**

After reading this section you should be able to:

14.8.1 Describe the possible causes of male erectile disorder.

14.8.2 Explain the circumstances in which PDE5 inhibitors are or are not likely to alleviate erectile disorder.

14.8.3 Describe the options for men who have lost the capacity for erection following prostatectomy.

**Erectile disorder (ED)** (also called erectile dysfunction) is a recurrent inability to achieve an adequate penile erection or to maintain it through the course of the desired sexual behavior—if such inability causes distress to the man or difficulty between the man and his partner. The condition may be partial or complete, and it may be a primary, secondary, or situational disorder. Estimates of the prevalence of ED among American men vary from 21% to 58% (Kessler et al., 2019). All studies agree that the prevalence increases as men age: Most men in their 70s and beyond experience some degree of ED. Nevertheless, ED can occur in young men, and when it does, young men are more likely to seek help. Thus about one in four men who seek help for ED are under 40 years of age (Capogrosso et al., 2013).

### Erectile disorder can have physical or psychological causes

A great variety of factors can cause or contribute to ED, ranging from entirely physical factors to entirely psychological ones (Glina et al., 2013). Here are some of the chief villains:

- *Behavioral/lifestyle factors.* These may include smoking (which doubles the risk of erectile disorder), chronic alcohol abuse, obesity, and lack of exercise. Extended bicycle riding has been suggested as a causal factor on

**erectile disorder (ED)** A persistent inability to achieve or maintain an erection sufficient to accomplish a desired sexual behavior, such as coitus, to orgasm. Also called *erectile dysfunction.*

account of potential damage to nerves or blood vessels supplying the penis, but research studies have not demonstrated a connection (Duffy et al., 2016).

- *Medical conditions.* These include diabetes, hypertension, atherosclerosis ("hardening of the arteries"), and prostate surgery.
- *Drugs.* Certain tranquilizers, diuretics, antidepressants, and some recreational drugs can cause ED. The drug finasteride (Propecia or Proscar) is of particular concern: It can cause lasting erectile dysfunction, even at the low dosage used for treatment of male-pattern baldness (Guo et al., 2016).
- *Injuries.* These include spinal cord injury, injury to the nerves and blood vessels that supply the penis, and injury to the penis itself.
- *Psychological factors.* These include performance anxiety, distraction, inadequate stimulation, relationship difficulties, stress, and depression.
- *Developmental issues.* These include childhood trauma, sexual orientation issues, and religious taboos.

▲ Smoking, alcohol use, and obesity all increase the risk of erectile disorder.

Often, erectile disorder results from an interplay of physical and psychological factors, which reinforce each other and need to be disentangled (Goldstein, 2000; Rosen, 2007). For example, a middle-aged man may notice on some occasion that his penis doesn't become erect as fast as he expected. This may be part of the normal physiological aging process, compounded by some circumstance such as tiredness or alcohol use. But the next time he has sex, the memory of that event may cause him to fear that he will embarrass himself, that he will fail to satisfy his partner, or that he will cause his partner to think that he has lost interest in her or him. These anxieties may then make his erectile difficulties worse by distracting him from the pleasure of sex, thus triggering a downward spiral of dysfunction.

## Simple measures may alleviate the problem

Sometimes the cause of ED can be removed rather simply. If the problem is caused by a prescription drug, for example, it may be possible to substitute another drug that does not have the same side effect. Lifestyle changes such as quitting smoking, reducing alcohol consumption or drug use, losing weight (if the person is obese), and beginning an exercise program may alleviate erectile difficulties (Bach & Brannigan, 2016).

If the man can develop an erection but loses it during sex, he may be able to maintain the erection for a longer period simply by placing a constricting elastic band ("cock ring") around the penis after the erection has developed. (The ring should be taken off as soon as it has served its purpose, to avoid damaging the erectile tissue.)

## Psychological treatments may be useful

If a man's erectile difficulties appear to result from psychological or relationship issues, he may seek out a sex therapist. One common objective in sex therapy is to reduce anxiety. This may be accomplished by means of sensate focus exercises, as described in Box 14.1. These exercises are thought to be useful for less severe cases or early stages of erectile disorder. The particular aim will be to help the man enjoy sensual contacts without worrying about whether he has an erection or not.

A more "talky" way of treating erectile disorder is **cognitive restructuring** (Nobre, 2017). Here the aim is to overcome negative beliefs that create anxiety and thus worsen the man's problem. For example, the man may be convinced that a first-class erection and coitus are the be-all and end-all of sex. When the man realizes that he can fully satisfy his partner by means other than coitus, his anxiety may be reduced to the point

**cognitive restructuring**
A technique to overcome psychological problems by talking through the negative beliefs that underlie them.

By prescription only for men with erectile dysfunction (ED), 2.5 mg, 5 mg.

▲ Advertising for Viagra, Levitra, and Cialis links the drugs with relatively young, healthy men.

**FAQ:** I've heard that Viagra makes men want more sex— is that true?

Viagra doesn't have any direct effect on sexual desire, but it may do so indirectly by making a man more confident in his ability to perform.

that his erectile difficulties also decrease. Simply reassuring men that it is normal for the process of erection to take longer as they age can be very helpful.

Even more important may be efforts to resolve relationship problems. These problems may be of various kinds (Rosen, 2007). The man's self-esteem in the relationship may be traumatized by a loss of status, such as may follow loss of a job or development of an illness. His experience of intimacy may be damaged by an extramarital (or extra-pair) relationship or by the birth of a child. His partner's or his own perceived attractiveness may be diminished by aging, obesity, or alcoholism. The impact of these issues on erectile function may be lessened by bringing them out into the open and trying to resolve them in one-on-one psychotherapy, in couples therapy, or even in group therapy. Sex therapy can be combined with drug treatment.

## PDE5 inhibitors have become the leading treatments

The 1998 introduction of the PDE5 inhibitor sildenafil (Viagra, now available as a generic) revolutionized the treatment of ED, allowing many cases to be treated successfully by first-line physicians rather than by specialists or sex therapists.* Besides Viagra itself there are now three other PDE5 inhibitors approved for the treatment of erectile disorder: Levitra (vardenafil), Cialis (tadalafil), and Stendra (avanafil). The efficacy of these drugs in improving the quality of life of men with ED has been well documented in placebo-controlled trials, and the men's partners also experience much more satisfying sex lives as a result (Yafi et al., 2016).

How do PDE5 inhibitors work? As mentioned in Chapter 3, during sexual arousal the neurotransmitter nitric oxide is released from nerve endings within and near the erectile tissue. Blood vessels supplying the erectile tissue respond to nitric oxide by dilating, so blood flow into the erectile tissue increases. PDE5 inhibitors enhance the blood vessels' response to nitric oxide. Thus, in the presence of PDE5 inhibitors, even subnormal activity in the nerves supplying the penis can trigger an adequate erection.

If there is no activity in the nerves, however, PDE5 inhibitors do not cause an erection. What this means is that simply swallowing a Viagra tablet does not produce an erection—there has to be sexual excitation as well. And if the nerves are not functioning—if they have been destroyed in the course of prostate surgery, for example—then none of the PDE5 inhibitors are likely to work, no matter how sexually excited the man may feel.

PDE5 inhibitors must not be taken in conjunction with certain other substances, most especially nitrate- or nitrite-containing drugs (drugs prescribed for heart pain or abused as the inhaled recreational drugs "amyl," "rush," or "poppers"). The reason for this is that combining these drugs can cause a life-threatening drop in blood pressure. It is also dangerous to take any of these drugs *after* use of a PDE5 inhibitor—up to 48 hours after in the case of Cialis (Murphy et al., 2018).

PDE5 inhibitors can cause a variety of undesirable side effects, such as headache, facial flushing, or visual disturbances. Cialis is longer-acting than the other drugs—it works for up to 36 hours, and it is also available in a formulation for daily rather than as-needed use. This appeals to many men because it allows for greater spontaneity in sexual activities. In addition, the daily-use formulation alleviates the symptoms of enlarged prostate, which is common in older men with ED. As a result Cialis has become the market leader among PDE5 inhibitors. Still, the long duration of Cialis's action means that side effects may also be prolonged. If this is a problem,

---

*As with bremelanotide, the therapeutic value of sildenafil was discovered serendipitously during its development for another purpose—in this case, for the treatment of angina, or heart pain.

▶ **FIGURE 14.10** Prostaglandin E₁ produces an erection when injected directly into the corpora cavernosa.

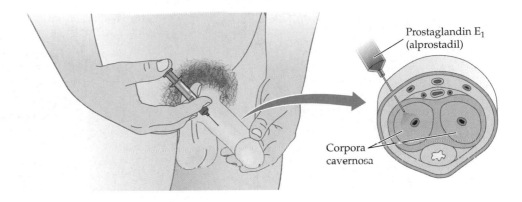

Stendra may be a better choice—it acts within 15 minutes, has a milder side-effect profile than Cialis, and is broken down in the body much more quickly (Wang et al., 2014).

Do these drugs do anything for men who *don't* have ED? One study compared the effects of Viagra and an inactive placebo on sexual performance in healthy men (Mondaini et al., 2003). The drug was no different from the placebo in terms of the quality of the men's erections or orgasms, but the men who took Viagra did experience a shorter refractory period after ejaculation before they could develop an erection again. The pornographic video industry is well aware of this effect: Viagra is frequently used by male actors who need to perform several times in the course of a one-day shoot.

Recreational use of PDE5 inhibitors by young men without ED is fairly common, but we advise against it. In the absence of medical supervision, serious side effects can occur; in addition, recreational users may lose confidence in their ability to perform satisfactorily without the drug (Harte & Meston, 2012).

Some men are not helped by PDE5 inhibitors, even if their ED has a clear biological cause. These include men whose penile nerves have been destroyed by prostate surgery, as mentioned above. However, the drug **prostaglandin E₁** produces a very reliable erection in any circumstances, so long as the erectile tissue itself is still intact. This drug has to be delivered locally to the penis, either by self-injection into the corpora cavernosa (**FIGURE 14.10**) or by means of a soft pellet that is pushed into the urethra.

Testosterone supplementation (via transdermal patches) does not alleviate ED, even in men with diagnosed or suspected low testosterone levels (Huo et al., 2016).

**prostaglandin E₁** A hormone that can be injected into the penis to produce an erection.

**vacuum constriction system** A device for treating erectile disorder that creates a partial vacuum around the penis, thus drawing blood into the erectile tissue.

## Erectile disorder can be treated with devices and implants

Nondrug methods can also help men who experience ED. One such method is a **vacuum constriction system** (**FIGURE 14.11**), versions of which are made by several manufacturers. (A medical-grade device recommended by a doctor is likely to work better

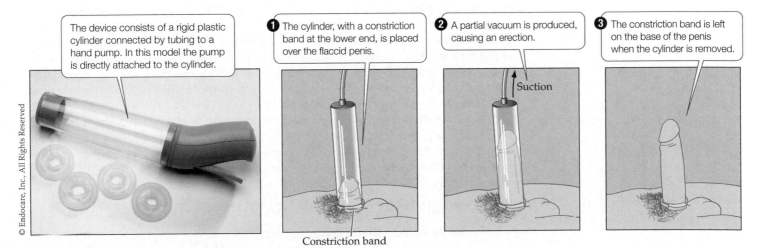

The device consists of a rigid plastic cylinder connected by tubing to a hand pump. In this model the pump is directly attached to the cylinder.

**1** The cylinder, with a constriction band at the lower end, is placed over the flaccid penis.

**2** A partial vacuum is produced, causing an erection.

Suction

**3** The constriction band is left on the base of the penis when the cylinder is removed.

Constriction band

▲ **FIGURE 14.11** **Vacuum constriction systems** produce an erection by drawing blood into the penis.

▶ **FIGURE 14.12** Penile implants

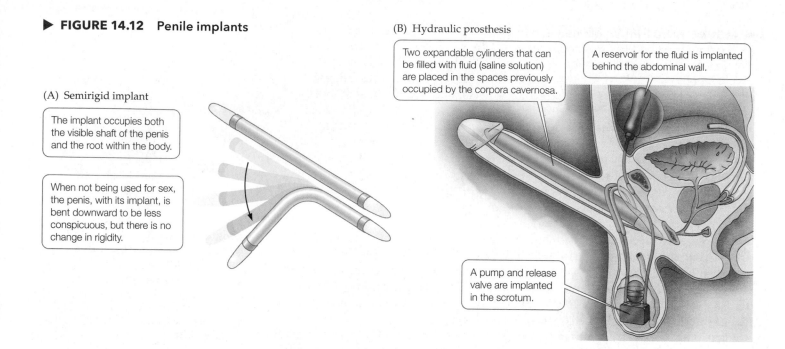

(A) Semirigid implant

The implant occupies both the visible shaft of the penis and the root within the body.

When not being used for sex, the penis, with its implant, is bent downward to be less conspicuous, but there is no change in rigidity.

(B) Hydraulic prosthesis

Two expandable cylinders that can be filled with fluid (saline solution) are placed in the spaces previously occupied by the corpora cavernosa.

A reservoir for the fluid is implanted behind the abdominal wall.

A pump and release valve are implanted in the scrotum.

**penile implant**   An implanted device for treatment of erectile disorder.

and more safely than one bought in a sex store.) The man lubricates his penis, places a clear plastic cylinder over it, and then produces a partial vacuum inside the tube with the aid of a pump powered by hand or by a battery. The vacuum draws blood into the erectile tissue. Once an erection has been attained, the man slips a constriction band off the end of the cylinder onto the base of the penis. The band blocks the veins that drain blood from the penis and thus maintains the erection after the cylinder is removed. The presence of the constriction band may interfere with ejaculation, however.

A more invasive and expensive treatment involves the surgical insertion of a **penile implant** (**FIGURE 14.12**). One kind of implant is a semirigid plastic rod that keeps the penis permanently stiff enough for coitus. It is relatively easy to have inserted surgically, but the permanent erection may be difficult to conceal and therefore embarrassing in some circumstances. Another kind of implant is hydraulic; it is filled from a reservoir that is implanted under the groin muscles. The pump and valves that control the filling and emptying are placed in the scrotum, where they can be accessed manually through the skin. This kind of implant is costlier and more prone to malfunction, and the erect penis is not usually as long as it was originally. On the positive side, the hydraulic implant is more discreet and produces a more natural-seeming erection than the semirigid implant.

With the advent of effective drug treatments for ED, implants have lost most of their popularity, but they are still useful for men whose erectile tissue has been damaged by scarring or other processes. Having an implant does not usually interfere with the capacity for orgasm or ejaculation.

It may eventually be possible to cure ED by the use of stem cells derived from the patient himself. The studies conducted so far, which have involved no more than about 60 men, have yielded inconclusive results, but some of the men reported an improvement in erectile function (Lokeshwar et al., 2020).

## 14.9 Men May Have Little Interest in Sex

### LEARNING OBJECTIVE

After reading this section you should be able to:

14.9.1 Explain the circumstances in which testosterone patches may or may not be expected to increase a man's interest in sex.

As with women, a man who has no interest in sex may not experience this as a problem. Young men who are asexual have little or no desire for partnered sex, and they may be fine with that. Other young men may be too focused on school or career to think about sex. Many older men have little interest in sex on account of declining testosterone levels, and again this may not cause any problems.

On the other hand, a man may feel that his low sexual desire is causing him to miss out on one of life's major pleasures, or he may be having sex with his regular partner but only out of a desire to satisfy her or him—an obligation that is difficult to fulfill over the long term. In such cases, as with women with similar problems, his condition comes under the *DSM-5* heading sexual interest/arousal disorder or the more specific category hypoactive sexual desire disorder (Krakowsky & Grober, 2016).

High-volume endurance exercise can cause men to lose interest in sex, probably because it lowers testosterone levels (Safarinejad et al., 2009; Hackney et al., 2017). A variety of psychological factors can also reduce a man's interest in sex. These may include, for example, a lack of attraction to his spouse or regular partner, bereavement, illness, disability, depression, or inculcated sex-negative attitudes. Or he may have no desire for sex because he knows that he is likely to experience erectile difficulties or premature ejaculation.

If psychological factors are at work, psychotherapy, relationship counseling, or behavioral sex therapy may alleviate the problem. Lack of sexual desire caused by low testosterone can be reversed by testosterone supplementation—usually via transdermal patches (Cunningham et al., 2016). This treatment is unlikely to be of use if testosterone is in the normal range, however, which is the case in the great majority of young men. What's more, testosterone supplementation can have a variety of side effects. The notion that testosterone supplementation or replacement has a broadly beneficial effect on health is incorrect (Emmelot-Vonk et al., 2011; Huo et al., 2016). In fact, testosterone is the main reason why men die earlier than women: In one study based on historical records, castration early in life (which causes lifelong testosterone deficiency) actually *increased* men's life expectancy by 14 to 19 years (Min et al., 2012).

▲ As a means of restoring interest in sex, using testosterone patches has benefits, limitations, and risks.

*Courtesy of David McIntyre*

## 14.10 Sexual Pain Is Uncommon in Men

### LEARNING OBJECTIVE

After reading this section you should be able to:

**14.10.1 Give possible reasons why a man might experience pain during sex.**

Pain during sex is not something that men experience at all frequently, and *DSM-5* does not list pain as a male sexual disorder. Even so, sex can sometimes be painful for men. The pain can result from acute or chronic prostatitis, Peyronie's disease, or phimosis, all of which are described in Chapter 3. In one form of phimosis, movement of the foreskin over the glans is limited by an unusually short frenulum (**FIGURE 14.13**). A man with that condition may be able to avoid pain by using a condom, but a urologist can often resolve the problem with minor surgery or by performing a circumcision. Finally, allergic reactions to latex or soap can cause pain during sex for either men or women.

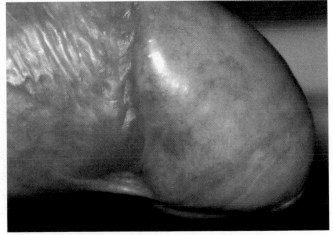

*Lead Holder/CC BY-SA-3.0*

▶ **FIGURE 14.13 A short frenulum** can distort the glans when the penis is erect, and cause pain during sex.

## 14.11 Too Much Interest in Sex Can Cause Problems

**LEARNING OBJECTIVES**

After reading this section you should be able to:

14.11.1 Evaluate the arguments for and against sex addiction as a valid diagnosis.

14.11.2 Explain treatment options for people who complain of an excessive sex drive.

**hypersexuality** Excessive sexual desire or behavior.

**sex addiction** The idea that a person may be addicted to sexual behavior by a mechanism similar to that of substance addiction.

Some people—men, for the most part—spend several hours each day masturbating, viewing pornography, participating in sex-related online chat rooms, using commercial phone sex services, seeking casual sex partners in bars, making unwelcome sexual advances to acquaintances or strangers, using prostitutes, or having anonymous sex with multiple partners in bathhouses or sex clubs. They often feel that they have lost control of their own behavior. In fact, these activities may so take over their lives as to threaten their careers and relationships and expose them and their partners to HIV and other sexually transmitted infections.

How to understand and treat such problems is a subject of controversy (Walton et al., 2017; Kingston, 2018). For one thing, sex researchers and therapists don't want to be seen as "sex-negative," so they may be tempted to deny that there is anything wrong or to say that the problem lies with the person's guilty feelings about the behavior rather than with the behavior itself. And certainly, some people with strongly inculcated negative beliefs about sex may come to a therapist on account of a frequency of masturbation or pornography use that few other people would consider problematic. In such a case, reassurance that their behavior is normal and harmless may be all that is needed.

Another commonly expressed view is that the activities described above should be regarded simply as bad or criminal behavior and that making them into a disorder absolves people of responsibility for their own actions. This view is particularly common when the behavior involves victims, a topic that we cover in Chapter 15.

When excessive sexual behavior, or the urge to engage in such behavior, is viewed as a disorder, it is often called **hypersexuality**. In the view of many experts, this is an appropriate term for the collection of behaviors listed at the top of this section, especially when the person longs to stop the behavior but feels unable to do so. Hypersexuality is not listed as a disorder in *DSM-5*, however.

In some cases hypersexuality has an obvious pathological cause, as for example when it follows brain injury, dementia, epilepsy, or the use of certain drugs, especially drugs that activate dopamine systems in the brain (Moore et al., 2014). In these conditions the abnormal nature of the person's sexual behavior is clear because it represents a radical departure from his or her behavior prior to the onset of the medical condition. It is as if an "internal censor," which normally limits a person's quest for self-gratification, has been damaged or lost. In fact, something like this may be true of hypersexuality in general: It has been reported in brain imaging studies that men with hypersexual behavior have impaired functional connections involved in the regulation of emotion-driven behavior (Schmidt et al., 2017).

From a more psychological perspective, hypersexuality may be viewed as an obsessive-compulsive disorder—a behavior pattern driven by a need to reduce anxiety, like compulsive hand washing—or as an impulse control disorder, which means a pleasure-seeking behavior that persists regardless of harm, such as impulsive gambling or shopping. The developmental mechanisms for such disorders are not well understood; one idea is that traumatic childhood experiences, such as parental abuse, play a role (Kingston et al., 2017). For LGBT people, hypersexual behavior may result from the anxieties induced by social stigma or "minority stress" (Hatzenbuehler & Pachankis, 2016).

Some experts believe that hypersexuality is a form of addiction and therefore use the term **sex addiction**. This concept was popularized by Arizona-based sexual

▲ Actor Colin Farrell is one of many celebrities who have described themselves as addicted to sex.

health counselor Patrick Carnes (Carnes, 2001), and there are plenty of therapists who follow Carnes's model. The term has come into popular use, driven in part by media attention to self-described sex addicts such as actor Colin Farrell (Lynch, 2015).

Certainly the craving for sex can resemble the craving for addictive drugs, especially in terms of its cyclical nature (**FIGURE 14.14**). On the other hand, the concept of sex addiction has been criticized on several grounds: that excessive sexual behavior lacks the classic signs of addiction such as tolerance (the need to have greater doses over time to produce the same "high") or physical withdrawal symptoms (Kafka, 2013); that there are functional brain differences between people who exhibit hypersexuality and people who are addicted to alcohol or drugs (Prause et al., 2015); or that the term "sex addiction" stigmatizes sexual behaviors that actually fall within the range of healthy sexual expression (Ley et al., 2014; AASECT, n.d.).

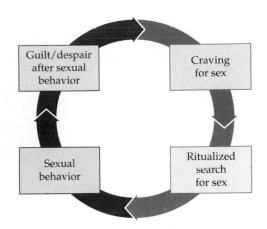

▲ **FIGURE 14.14  Hypersexual behavior** often takes the form of a four-stage cycle. (After P. Carnes. 2001. *Out of the shadows: Understanding sexual addiction*, 3rd edition. Hazelden: Center City, MN.)

### Treatment depends on theoretical models

Traditional talk therapy may be used to explore possible origins for hypersexuality in childhood trauma. Cognitive-behavioral treatments, such as relapse prevention therapy (see Chapter 13), have also proven useful. In addition, drug treatment can be very effective. SSRIs are the drugs most commonly used for this purpose (Leppink & Grant, 2016). Indeed, the effectiveness of these antidepressants in the treatment of many cases of hypersexuality could be taken as supportive evidence that hypersexuality belongs to the family of obsessive-compulsive disorders, because SSRIs are known to be helpful in the treatment of those conditions.

If a person's hypersexual behavior is diagnosed as sex addiction, he or she may be referred to a residential sex addiction facility or encouraged to join an organization like Sexaholics Anonymous, which offers a 12-step program comparable to those developed for alcohol and drug addiction (Carnes & Adams, 2019). The focus will be on getting out of the swamp, not on finding out how the person fell into the swamp in the first place. The goal, as with substance abuse, may be abstinence or sobriety, but that's a tricky concept to apply to sexual behavior, because the sex drive is natural and inborn, whereas the drive to consume alcohol or drugs is acquired. How much sexual behavior is acceptable for people who are diagnosed as being addicted to sex is a disputed issue within the therapeutic community. The American Association of Sexuality Educators, Counselors and Therapists (AASECT) takes a broadly negative view of the sex addiction model; AASECT asserts that the efficacy of addiction-based treatment methods is not supported by evidence (AASECT, n.d.).

If you yourself are troubled by obsessive thinking about sex, or by a sense that you can't stop yourself from engaging in undesired sexual behaviors, the most likely reason is that you're a human being. While counseling, therapy, or medication may be valuable options for some, for most it's sufficient to accept your flaws and focus on other goals. In time you will look back and smile at your college-age anxieties.

## 14.12  LGBT People Have Special Concerns

**LEARNING OBJECTIVE**
After reading this section you should be able to:

**14.12.1**  Describe ways in which sexual problems may affect non-heterosexual and heterosexual people differently.

Men and women who belong to sexual minorities face the same kinds of sexual problems and disorders as do heterosexual men and women and benefit from the same kinds of treatments. Yet in certain ways sexual orientation or gender identity is especially relevant in the context of sexual disorders:

▶ Lesbian couples, perhaps more than other couples, may lose interest in sex over time.

© iStock.com/SolStock

- Some gay people are in heterosexual marriages or relationships. The gay partner may have performance difficulties or avoid sex as a result of a lack of sexual attraction, and this in turn is likely to create problems for the person's partner and for the relationship as a whole. Surprisingly, though, many gay people perform quite well in heterosexual relationships.

- Lesbian, gay, and bisexual people may have a culturally induced sense of shame or self-hatred about their sexual orientation (internalized homophobia or biphobia). "Gay-affirmative" therapy addresses this issue, not merely by rejecting negative stereotypes, but also by building on the strengths of gay people and gay couples (Wang et al., 2016).

- Some gay men have developed an unreasonable fear of sex because of the AIDS epidemic, anxiety about sexual practices in a relationship in which one of the partners is HIV-positive, or feelings of guilt as AIDS "survivors."

- Anal penetration, practiced by some gay men, can present performance difficulties for either the receptive or the insertive partner. Advice on how to deal with these problems is not always easy to come by (see Chapter 6).

- Transgender and transexual people may have special concerns about sexual practices. They may be dissatisfied with their genitals and not wish to use them in sex. If they have undergone genital surgery, they and their partners will have to deal with the functional limitations of their new genitals. In a European survey of trans women and men, many of whom had undergone genital surgery, about one-third of respondents said they had difficulty in experiencing orgasm (Kerckhof et al., 2019). In addition—although this is not a sexual dysfunction in a narrow sense—more than one in four respondents said they had difficulty initiating sexual relationships.

- Although all couples can lose interest in sex with each other over time, this may occur particularly commonly for lesbians. In one survey of lesbians over 50 years old who had female life partners, 57% said that they had sex "a few times a year" or "never" (Averett et al., 2012). Long-time lesbian couples may place more emphasis on their emotional connection than on physical sex, in which case they may not experience the low frequency of sex as a problem. Still, lesbian couples who wish to reinject some passion into their relationship can follow the same recommendations that apply to all established couples: Make time for each other, introduce novelty (dates and trips, new sexual positions or sex toys, sex in new locations), express romantic feelings, and resolve conflicts.

Men and women who belong to sexual minorities may fear that they will not receive understanding treatment from heterosexual physicians and therapists and therefore may not seek help with their sexual problems. The American Psychological Association's Division 44 consists of over 1,500 gay or gay-affirmative members and has published guidelines for psychotherapy with lesbian, gay, and bisexual clients (American Psychological Association, 2017). The Association of Gay and Lesbian Psychiatrists provides referrals (Association of LGBTQ Psychiatrists, 2017). There is also a searchable database of transgender therapists (*Psychology Today*, 2019).

## Summary

- Sexual disorders are clinical problems requiring treatment only if they cause distress. Treatment may involve some combination of drugs, psychotherapy, and sex therapy exercises. Sensate focus exercises are commonly recommended.

- "Female sexual arousal disorder" refers to difficulties with vaginal lubrication or engorgement or with clitoral erection. Insufficient lubrication is common, especially after menopause; it can be dealt with by the use of lubricants. Hormone replacement often restores physiological arousal in postmenopausal women. Sex therapy exercises may be helpful.

- In women, painful coitus (dyspareunia) can result from a wide variety of biological causes, including insufficient lubrication, infections, allergies, developmental malformations, scars, and vaginal atrophy. It can often be treated by correcting the underlying condition.

- In vaginismus, coitus is impossible because of some combination of pelvic muscle tension and pain or fear of pain. It is treated by psychotherapy and sex therapy exercises, including the use of vaginal dilators.

- Many women have problems with orgasm. Some have never experienced it, and some do not experience it during partnered sex or during coitus. A biological cause for orgasmic disorder cannot usually be identified. Sex therapy for anorgasmia may include a program of directed masturbation or sensate focus exercises. A woman may be helped to experience orgasm during partnered sex or coitus by adding effective clitoral stimulation, trying different positions, or extending the duration of the sexual interaction. It may also be helpful to address relationship problems.

- Women are more likely than men to experience a lack of interest in sex. Sex hormone levels strongly influence sexual desire. Women who are distressed by a lack of sexual desire may be helped by treatment with estrogens, androgens, or a combination of the two, but androgen treatment can cause unwanted or harmful side effects. Sex therapy may help people with low desire "let go" of thought patterns that interfere with sexual pleasure, such as a perceived obligation to ensure their partner's satisfaction. Lack of sexual desire has to be evaluated in a broad context, which includes not just medical problems but also psychological, relationship, and socioeconomic issues.

- The causes of premature ejaculation, a very common male sexual disorder, are poorly understood. A man who ejaculates too soon may be helped by sex therapy exercises in which he learns to maintain his arousal at a medium level for extended periods of time. Premature ejaculation can also be treated with selective serotonin reuptake inhibitors (SSRIs).

- Difficulty in reaching ejaculation or orgasm is fairly uncommon in men but may be caused by certain drugs, such as SSRIs. It may be treated by changing or adding drugs or by sensate focus exercises in which the man and his partner progressively explore each other's bodies while avoiding performance demands.

- Many conditions can lead to problems with penile erection; these include smoking, use of alcohol and certain prescription or recreational drugs, diabetes, cardiovascular disease, spinal cord injury, and prostate surgery. Among psychological factors that may impair erectile function, performance anxiety is probably the most important. Treatment of erectile

(*Continued*)

# Summary (continued)

disorder can include alleviation of the underlying disorder, psychotherapy, or the use of a PDE5 inhibitor (Viagra-type drug). The nondrug treatments available include vacuum devices and penile implants.

- Excessive sexual desire or behavior (hypersexuality) in either sex can be caused by neurological damage, various mental illnesses, or certain drugs. Hypersexuality may include frequently repeated and seemingly involuntary involvement in masturbation, partnered sex, pornography use, telephone sex, and the like. Such behaviors may be classed as compulsive disorders, and like other such disorders, they often respond well to SSRIs. The use of the term "sex addiction" to describe these conditions is controversial.

- LGBT people may experience the same sexual difficulties as other people, but there are some concerns specific to sexual or gender minorities. Some gay people are in relationships with opposite-sex partners, which may make it difficult to engage in or enjoy sexual interactions. Internalized homophobia may impair sexual desire, pleasure, or performance. Anal penetration, widely practiced by gay men, can cause pain. Trans people may be unhappy with their genitals, and if they undergo sex-reassignment surgery, their new genitals may not perform as well as desired, especially as regards to orgasm. LGBT-affirmative therapists are skilled in helping non-heterosexual men and women overcome problems of these kinds.

---

The **Discovering Human Sexuality** digital resources include activities, animations, flashcards, web links, chapter outlines and summaries, and other study tools.

▪ ▪ ▪ ▪ ▪ ▪ ▪ ▪ ▪ ▪ ▪ ▪ ▪ ▪ ▪ ▪ ▪

Learn more with this chapter's digital tools, including the **Oxford Insight Study Guide**, at **oup.com/he/levay5e**.

## Discussion Questions

1. "Many people have sexual disorders but are prevented by embarrassment or ignorance from seeking treatment that could help them." "Many people have unrealistic expectations about sex and therefore demand treatments, such as drugs or psychotherapy, when there's really not much wrong with them." Which of these two statements describes contemporary U.S. society more accurately, in your opinion, and why?

2. A married woman friend complains to you that she cannot reach orgasm during intercourse with her husband. If you were a therapist, what questions would you ask her, and what recommendations would you give her?

3. Do you think faking orgasm is acceptable behavior, and if so, under what circumstances?

4. An older male friend complains that he has been unhappy with his sexual performance and unable to sustain an erection over the past two years. How would you advise him about the various treatment options available?

5. Do you think that anxiety about performance, or excessive attention to one's partner's sexual satisfaction, can interfere with one's own sexual pleasure or performance? If so, what steps could be taken to alleviate the problem?

6. Some old people have lost interest in sex but are not bothered by that fact. If they were to take a pill that somehow restored their sex drive, do you think that would improve their lives, or would it simply create extra problems for them?

## Web Resources

American Association of Sexuality Educators Counselors and Therapists (AASECT)  **www.aasect.org**

American Board of Sexology  **www.americanboardofsexology.com**

International Society for Sexual Medicine. Sexual health conditions  **www.issm.info/sexual-health-conditions**

National Vulvodynia Association  **www.nva.org**

Society for Sex Therapy and Research  **www.sstarnet.org**

## Recommended Reading

Brotto, L. A. (2018). *Better sex through mindfulness: How women can cultivate desire.* Greystone Books.

Cass, V. (2007). *The elusive orgasm: A woman's guide to why she can't and how she can orgasm.* Da Capo.

Goldstein, A., Pukall, C. & Goldstein, I. (2011). *When sex hurts: A woman's guide to banishing sexual pain.* Da Capo Lifelong.

Hall, K. S. K. & Graham, C. A. (Eds.). (2012). *The cultural context of sexual pleasure and problems: Psychotherapy with diverse clients.* Routledge.

Ogden, G. (2018). *Expanding the practice of sex therapy* (2nd ed.). Routledge.

Lipshultz, L. I., Pastuszak, A. W., Goldstein, A. T., et al. (2016). *Management of sexual dysfunction in men and women.* Springer.

McCarthy, B. (2015). *Sex made simple: Clinical strategies for sexual issues in therapy.* PESI.

Mintz, L. (2017). *Becoming cliterate: Why orgasm matters—and how to get it.* HarperOne.

Nagoski, E. (2015). *Come as you are: The surprising new science that will transform your sex life.* Simon & Schuster.

Weeks, G. R., Gambescia, N. & Hertlein, K. M. (2016). *A clinician's guide to systemic sex therapy* (2nd ed.). Routledge.

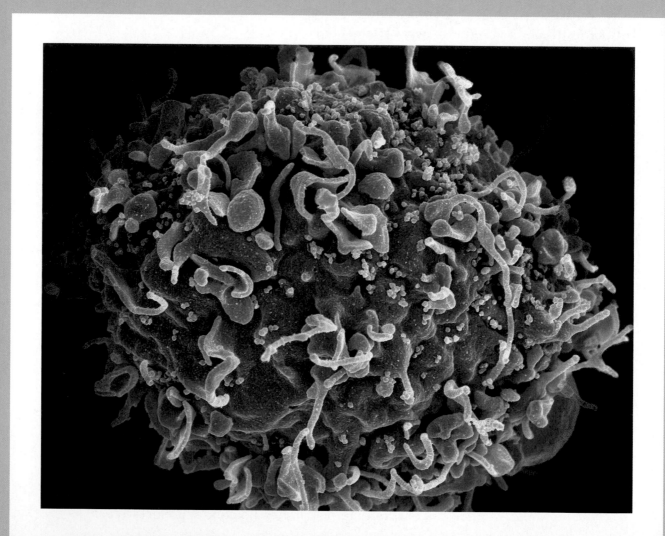

HIV viruses (yellow) attached to a human T cell, in a colorized scanning electron micrograph.

# 15 Sexually Transmitted Infections

The sustained physical intimacy of sexual contact offers an ideal opportunity for many disease-causing agents to spread from one person to another. Some of these organisms are highly specialized for transmission by the sexual route, while others can spread either sexually or by alternative means. The existence of sexually transmitted infections (STIs) has always added an element of risk to sex, and that has strongly influenced people's sexual behaviors and attitudes. The AIDS epidemic, which struck the United States in the late 1970s and continues to cause immense human suffering worldwide, is just the most recent example.

Medical research has brought spectacular advances in our knowledge of the causes of STIs and in many cases has given us the power to prevent or treat them. Yet there are deep social conflicts about how the battle against STIs should be conducted. These conflicts, rooted in moral differences about the nature and purpose of sexuality, have undercut the effectiveness of public health campaigns aimed at eliminating STIs.

Women and men who educate themselves about STIs can greatly reduce their risk of acquiring one. If they do contract one, they are in a better position to participate in effective treatment and can minimize the risk of passing the infection on to others.

## 15.1 Venereal Diseases Were Once Seen as Punishment for Sexual License

**LEARNING OBJECTIVE**

After reading this section you should be able to:

**15.1.1** Describe factors that have caused the prevalence of STIs to increase or decrease over time.

**sexually transmitted infection (STI)** Infection with a disease agent during sexual contact.

**venereal disease** Obsolete term for a sexually transmitted infection.

**syphilis** A sexually transmitted infection caused by a spirochete, *Treponema pallidum*.

A **sexually transmitted infection** (**STI**) means infection with a disease agent through sexual contact. Any contagious disease may be transmitted between sex partners, of course, but the term STI is reserved for those conditions for which sexual contact is the main route, or one of the main routes, by which they spread from person to person.

Until about a generation ago, STIs were called **venereal diseases**, after Venus, the Roman goddess of love. The archetypal venereal disease was **syphilis.** The first European cases of this disease were described in the mid-1490s, a year or two after Christopher Columbus discovered the New World. It is likely that Columbus or his sailors brought the disease from the Americas, where it had been endemic (Harper et al., 2011). For centuries, syphilis was essentially untreatable; it spread inexorably and returned to America with the colonists. By 1918, an estimated 1 in 22 Americans was infected (Amstey, 1994).

During the 19th century, there was very little sympathy for people with syphilis. They were thought to have brought the disease on themselves by engaging in sinful behavior. Except for innocent wives infected by their husbands, people with syphilis were denied admission to hospitals for the poor. The facial disfiguration that commonly accompanied late-stage syphilis was taken as proof that the disease was divine retribution for wrongdoing.

Until the mid-20th century, young men commonly used prostitutes as a sexual outlet prior to marriage—a practice that promoted the spread of syphilis and other STIs. Prostitutes were blamed, but of course the men who visited them played an equal role. Military servicemen in particular used prostitutes in huge numbers: During World War I, over 10,000 U.S. Army personnel had to be discharged from active duty on account of STIs, and nearly 7 million duty days were lost (Korzeniewski, 2012).

In the past, men used primitive condoms to protect themselves from syphilis and other diseases. Many other men refrained from sex altogether for fear of infection. Thus, syphilis and other STIs helped make sex seem like something frightening and evil.

Syphilis still exists in America, but over the last several decades it has become much less common. This has resulted from medical advances, beginning with the discovery of the causative bacterium in 1905 and the introduction of the first effective antibiotic 4 years later. Grassroots activism and public health campaigns have also played an important role, as well as the decline of prostitution as a social institution. Unfortunately, as we'll see, the disease is proving harder to wipe out than was expected just a few years ago.

The history of AIDS has mimicked that of syphilis in many respects: the importation of the causative agent from another continent (in the case of AIDS, Africa), its rapid spread, the initial lack of any effective treatment, the stigmatization of those who were affected, and the gradually increasing success in combating the epidemic, thanks to medical advances, social activism, and public health campaigns. The main difference is that the process has been compressed into a couple of decades rather than half a millennium. At present, AIDS can only be held at bay, whereas syphilis can now be cured.

Courtesy the National Library of Medicine

▲ Anti-VD (venereal disease) posters in the mid-20th century often blamed prostitutes and promiscuous women for the spread of syphilis and gonorrhea.

# 15.2 STIs Are Still a Major Problem in the United States

**LEARNING OBJECTIVE**

After reading this section you should be able to:

**15.2.1 State which demographic groups (age, race, location, sexual orientation) are most and least likely to acquire reportable STIs.**

Here are some basic facts about STIs in the United States (American Sexual Health Association, 2019):

- One in two sexually active persons will contract an STI by age 25.
- Nearly 20 million new infections with STI-causing organisms occur in the United States every year.
- About half of these infections occur in 15- to 24-year-olds.
- Undiagnosed STIs cause about 24,000 women to become infertile every year.
- The United States has the highest incidence rates for curable STIs of any developed country—even higher than many developing countries.
- The incidence of new cases of several STIs—especially chlamydia, gonorrhea, and syphilis—has been rising rapidly in recent years (Scott-Sheldon & Chan, 2019).

Some STIs occur much more commonly than others. Furthermore, because some STIs are readily treatable while others persist for a lifetime, there are enormous differences in the numbers of Americans who are carrying the various STIs at any one time (**TABLE 15.1**).

Some STIs are **reportable diseases**, meaning that medical professionals who encounter cases are required to notify state or federal authorities. The main federally reportable STIs are syphilis, gonorrhea, chlamydia, and HIV/AIDS. In reality, many cases of these diseases go undiagnosed or unreported. The prevalence of STIs that

**reportable disease** A disease whose cases must by law be reported to health authorities.

**TABLE 15.1** Estimated incidence and prevalence of some important STIs in the United States

| STI | Incidence (estimated number of new cases per year) | Prevalence (estimated number of people currently infected) |
|---|---|---|
| Trichomoniasis | 1 million | 3.7 million |
| Syphilis | 35,000 | 117,000 |
| Gonorrhea | 583,000 | 270,000 |
| Chlamydia | 1.8 million | 1.8 million |
| Genital herpes | 776,000 | 24 million[a] |
| Human papillomavirus (HPV) | 14 million | 79 million |
| Hepatitis B[b] | 21,000 | 850,000 |
| HIV[b] | 39,000 | 1.1 million |

*Source*: CDC. 2019. *Sexually Transmitted Diseases Surveillance 2018*; HHS.gov. 2019. *Hepatitis B basic information*; HIV.gov. 2019. *U.S. statistics*. U.S. Department of Health and Human Services: Washington, D.C. and Atlanta, GA; and other sources.

[a]In age range 15–49; total is higher.

[b]Hepatitis B and HIV infections are not all by sexual contact.

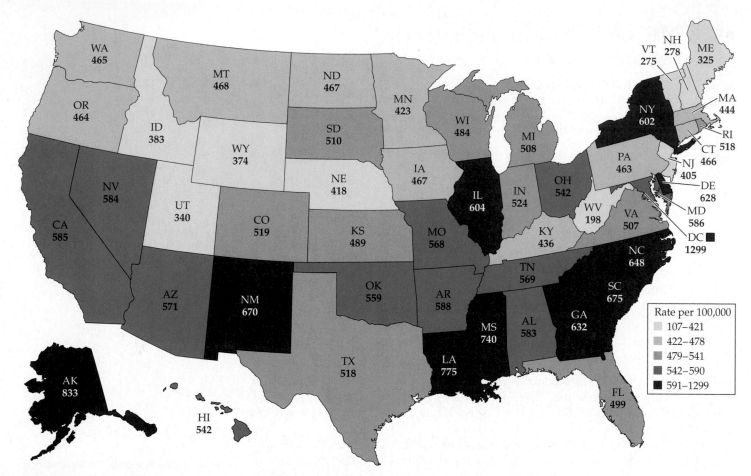

▲ **FIGURE 15.1** **Highest STI rates are in the South and Alaska** This map shows the number of new infections of chlamydia, the most common reportable STI, per 100,000 population, in 2018. Washington, D.C., had a rate higher than any state (1299/100,000). Other STIs had a similar distribution, but syphilis rates were highest in California. (After CDC. 2019. *Sexually Transmitted Diseases Surveillance 2018*. U.S. Department of Health and Human Services: Atlanta.)

are not reportable, such as herpes and human papillomavirus, is usually estimated on the basis of surveys.

The overall statistics cited in Table 15.1 mask important differences in how STIs affect various demographic groups within the United States. Most STIs are more common in the South than elsewhere (**FIGURE 15.1**). They are more common among African Americans and less common among Asian Americans than they are among white Americans. And—with the possible exception of chlamydia—they are more common among gay and bisexual men than among heterosexual men or women of any sexual orientation. Individuals who stand at the intersection of all three of these ill-starred demographics, namely black gay and bisexual men who live in the southern United States, are at far greater risk of acquiring an STI than are other Americans.

We focus here on those STIs that are most commonly encountered in the United States and Canada (**TABLE 15.2**). We describe them in a sequence based on what causes them, beginning with visible organisms and progressing down the size scale to viruses. This also represents a sequence of increasing seriousness: Insects and mites are an annoyance, but viruses can be killers.

What's the difference between "sexually transmitted infection (STI)" and another commonly used phrase, "sexually transmitted disease (STD)"? A sexually transmitted

**TABLE 15.2  Basic STI facts**

| STI (causative agent) | Typical symptoms | Diagnostic tests | Treatment |
|---|---|---|---|
| **INSECTS AND MITES** | | | |
| Pubic lice | Itching at site of infestation | Visual recognition | Topical insecticide |
| Scabies (scabies mite) | Itching, rash | Microscopic examination of skin scrapings | Topical insecticide |
| **PROTOZOA** | | | |
| Trichomoniasis (*Trichomonas vaginalis*) | Foul-smelling vaginal discharge, vaginal itching | Microscopic examination of discharge | Oral metronidazole (Flagyl) |
| **BACTERIA** | | | |
| Syphilis (*Treponema pallidum*) | Primary: chancre at site of infection; Secondary: rash, fever; Latent period: none; Tertiary: widespread organ damage | Primary: microscopic examination of discharge; Secondary: blood test (antibodies to *T. pallidum*) | Penicillin by injection |
| Gonorrhea (*Neisseria gonorrhoeae*) | Thick, cloudy discharge from urethra, vagina, or anus; may be asymptomatic or cause PID | DNA test on discharge or urine | Oral antibiotics |
| Chlamydia (*Chlamydia trachomatis*) | Thin discharge from urethra, vagina, or anus; local pain or irritation; often asymptomatic | DNA test on urine or swabs from penis, cervix, etc. | Oral azithromycin |
| **VIRUSES** | | | |
| Herpes (herpes simplex virus 1, herpes simplex virus 2) | Recurrent outbreaks of blisters or fissures localized to site of infection; may be painful | DNA tests on blood or swabs from sores, or visual recognition | Oral antivirals; not currently curable |
| Genital warts (human papillomavirus type 6 or 11) | Painless genital or anal warts | Visual recognition | Destruction of warts by freezing, podophyllin application, laser treatment, or surgical excision |
| Precancerous changes in cervix or anus (human papillomavirus type 16, 18, or others) | None at early stages | Microscopic examination of sample from cervix or anus (Pap test) | Destruction of abnormal cells by freezing; prophylactic vaccine (Gardasil 9) |
| Hepatitis B | Jaundice, fever; recovery common, but may cause chronic hepatitis and liver failure | Blood test (antibodies to virus) | No specific treatment for acute infection; antivirals available for chronic hepatitis |
| Hepatitis A | Jaundice, nausea, flu-like illness; no progression to chronic hepatitis | Blood test (antibodies to virus) | No specific treatment |
| HIV/AIDS (human immunodeficiency virus) | Acute flu-like illness; after latent period, opportunistic infections, cancers, wasting | Blood test or saliva (antibodies to virus; alternatively, DNA test) | Combination of several oral antiviral drugs; not currently curable |

*Note:* This table lists only the major STIs and their typical symptoms, most commonly used diagnostic tests, and usual forms of treatment.

infection occurs when an agent such as a bacterium enters a person's body during a sexual encounter and establishes itself there. A sexually transmitted disease is the harm to a person's health that may be caused by such an infection. Some people who acquire a sexually transmitted infection experience no health consequences, or they do so only a long time after acquiring the infection: Such people are called **asymptomatic carriers**. The importance of asymptomatic carriers is that they can sometimes infect other people, and they themselves may fall ill at a later time.

**asymptomatic carrier**  Someone who is infected with a disease organism but is not experiencing symptoms.

## 15.3 Lice and Mites Are More of an Annoyance Than a Danger

### LEARNING OBJECTIVES

After reading this section you should be able to:

15.3.1  Describe how pubic lice can be removed from the body and clothing.

15.3.2  Describe the life cycle of scabies mites.

**pubic lice**  Insects (*Phthirus pubis*) that preferentially infest the pubic region.

**scabies**  Infestation with a mite (*Sarcoptes scabiei*) that burrows within the skin.

Two species of lice (head and pubic lice), as well as scabies mites, are specialized for living on or in human skin. Of these, pubic lice and scabies mites are frequently spread by sexual contact and are therefore discussed here. These conditions are usually called "infestations" rather than "infections" or "diseases." They do not usually cause serious harm to the body, but they are very bothersome conditions that, luckily, can be quickly and effectively treated.

### Pubic lice itch, and that's all they do

**Pubic lice** (*Phthirus pubis*) are popularly known as "crabs," but they are insects, not crustaceans (**FIGURE 15.2**). They are small but visible—a large adult louse may measure about 0.04 inches (1 mm) across and is dark or tan colored, while newly hatched lice are considerably smaller and colorless. Pubic lice are flat, so they can lie very close to the skin; this makes them hard to dislodge. In addition, they grasp two nearby hairs with their clawlike legs, anchoring themselves in place. Once anchored, they burrow their mouthparts into the skin between the hairs and gorge themselves on their host's blood. The amount of blood lost is trivial, but the infestation can cause severe itching.

Pubic lice are happiest living among pubic hairs because the spacing between hair shafts in that region is optimal for them. They can also spread to other hairy areas of the skin, however, such as the armpits, eyebrows, and the general body surface of hairy people.

Pubic lice lay eggs ("nits"), which they glue onto hairs near the base. They are visible as tiny bumps on the hairs. It takes about a week for the nits to hatch and begin the cycle anew. Both the lice and their nits may fall off the body and end up on bedding, underwear, or towels. The lice can survive in these locations for 2 days at the most, but the nits can survive for a week. It is therefore possible to acquire a louse infestation either by direct contact with an infested person or by using that person's bedding, clothing, or towels. Most infestations are probably passed on by direct contact, however. Sleeping with someone is the most favorable situation for transmission.

Diagnosing pubic lice is a simple matter of looking for the insects in the region of irritated skin, digging one out, and watching it wave its legs. Pubic lice are probably the one STI that you don't need a medical degree to diagnose.

Pubic lice are treated with insecticidal lotions or shampoos. If over-the-counter medications don't work, it may be necessary to get a prescription for a more effective insecticide, lindane. Because this chemical is potentially toxic if misused, it is important to follow instructions carefully. Pubic lice and nits may also be removed by close shaving of all affected areas. Removing the nits by hand is tedious work requiring sharp eyesight—hence "nitpicking."

### Scabies may be transmitted sexually or nonsexually

**Scabies** is an infestation with *Sarcoptes scabiei*, a parasitic mite that, if it were ten thousand times larger, would be truly scary (**FIGURE 15.3**). The mites are only about 0.5 mm across, however, and they are not usually seen, because they spend most of their

© Oliver Meckes/Science Source

1 mm

▲ **FIGURE 15.2  Scanning electron micrograph of pubic lice**  The claws at the ends of the insects' legs are well shaped to clamp onto oval-shaped hair shafts.

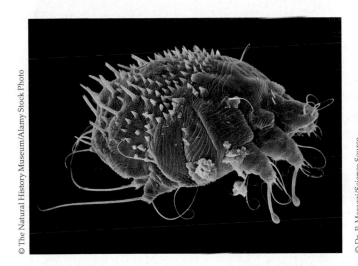 

© The Natural History Museum/Alamy Stock Photo

© Dr. P. Marazzi/Science Source

◀ **FIGURE 15.3**
**A scabies mite** (left) and a severe case of scabies rash (right).

time in tunnels that they dig within the superficial layers of the skin. The tunnels themselves are visible as reddish tracks, spots, or pustules. If the infested person is sensitive to scabies mites, there may also be a generalized rash even in places where no mites are located. Unlike lice, scabies mites do not require hairy skin. In fact, they are commonly found in hairless areas such as the wrists, elbows, knees, penis, breasts, back, or between the fingers.

The female mites live for about 2 months below the skin in their tunnels, laying eggs every few days. The eggs hatch after 3 to 8 days. The young go through a couple of juvenile stages and then return to the skin surface as adults to mate. Impregnated females burrow into the skin again, completing the cycle.

The itching caused by scabies infestations can be severe: Infested people may scratch themselves to the point of causing sores, which can become infected. Scabies spreads from person to person quite easily, so it is common wherever people live in crowded conditions. Sexual contact is just one of many modes of transmission, but a common one for adults.

Scabies is best diagnosed by a physician, who may examine skin scrapings under a microscope. Over-the-counter remedies are unlikely to work, but there are several prescription options, including a topically applied lotion containing permethrin, which is left on for several hours or overnight before being washed off. A repeat treatment 7 to 10 days later may be necessary. As with pubic lice, possibly infested clothes and bedding must be washed and dried on a hot cycle or left unused for two weeks.

## 15.4 Trichomoniasis Is Caused by a Protozoan

### LEARNING OBJECTIVES
After reading this section you should be able to:

15.4.1 Indicate the approximate percentages of trich-infected women and men who have symptoms.

15.4.2 Explain why these percentages are relevant to treatment.

**Trichomoniasis** (or **"trich"**) is an infection of the vagina or the male urethra and prostate gland with *Trichomonas vaginalis*. This organism is not a bacterium, but rather a single-celled protozoan with a bundle of whiplike flagella; it measures about 5 by 10 micrometers and thus is not visible to the naked eye (**FIGURE 15.4A**). In women, trichomoniasis is marked by a foul-smelling, greenish, or frothy discharge from the vagina. There may be vaginal itching and redness, as well as abdominal discomfort or the urge to urinate frequently. Many women, however, are asymptomatic carriers.

**trichomoniasis (or "trich")**
Infection with the protozoan *Trichomonas vaginalis*.

(A)

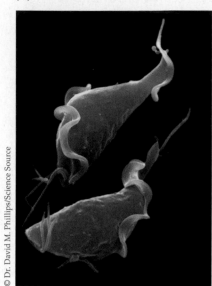

© Dr. David M. Phillips/Science Source

(B)

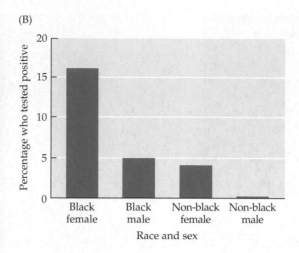

◀ **FIGURE 15.4** **Trichomoniasis**
(A) *Trichomonas vaginalis*. The bundle of whiplike processes carries receptors that specifically recognize and bind to the cells of the vaginal lining. (B) Percentage of young adults (age 15 to 35) in Baltimore who tested positive for trichomoniasis, by sex and race (black or non-black). The majority were asymptomatic. (After S. M. Rogers et al. 2014. *PLOS ONE* 9: e90548. https://doi. org/10.1371/journal.pone.0090548.)

Women who do have symptoms develop them within 6 months of infection, which usually happens through coitus. The trichomoniasis organism survives poorly outside a human host or even on the outside of the body, so nonsexual transmission is thought to be rare. Pregnant women with trichomoniasis are more likely than other women to give birth prematurely, and their babies may be underweight.

In men, trichomoniasis infections are usually asymptomatic. Sometimes they are marked by a slight discharge from the urethra, the urge to urinate frequently, and pain during urination.

In a random-sample study of 2000 young adults living in Baltimore, 7.5% of the entire sample tested positive for trich, but there were major disparities based on sex and race: Women were more likely to test positive than men, and black women and men were more likely to test positive than their nonblack counterparts (Rogers et al., 2014) (**FIGURE 15.4B**). Among the participants who tested positive, 73% of the women and 98% of the men had no symptoms.

Trichomoniasis is diagnosed by microscopic examination of specimens from the vagina or the urethra. A more sensitive diagnostic method is to culture the organism—that is, to grow it in the laboratory; this process takes a few days and is more expensive.

Trichomoniasis can be cured with a single oral dose of metronidazole (Flagyl or its generic equivalents). The infected person's partner(s) should be treated at the same time, whether symptomatic or not; otherwise partners may continue to swap the infection back and forth between them.

## 15.5 Bacterial STIs Can Usually Be Treated with Antibiotics

The main sexually transmitted bacterial infections in the United States are syphilis, gonorrhea, and chlamydia. These cause diseases that can be fatal in themselves (syphilis), impair fertility (gonorrhea and chlamydia), or facilitate HIV infection (all three). Treated promptly, however, they can be readily cured, and complications can be avoided.

## 15.6 Syphilis Is Down but Not Out

### LEARNING OBJECTIVES
After reading this section you should be able to:

15.6.1 Describe the stages of an untreated syphilis infection.
15.6.2 Explain which demographic groups are most at risk of syphilis.

**spirochete** Any of a class of corkscrew-shaped bacteria, including the agent that causes syphilis.

Syphilis is caused by infection with a corkscrew-shaped bacterium, or **spirochete**, with the name *Treponema pallidum* (**FIGURE 15.5**). Syphilis is spread by direct contact, nearly always sexually. (It can also spread from mother to fetus.) If not treated, syphilis can last a lifetime and eventually cause death.

## Untreated syphilis progresses through three stages

A man or woman can acquire syphilis by sexual contact with a person who is in the primary or secondary stage of the disease or in the first year or so of the latent phase (see below). Most commonly, infection comes from a syphilitic sore, or **chancre**\* (**FIGURE 15.6**), which exudes a fluid containing huge numbers of spirochetes. The chancre is often painless. It may be visible on the penis or labia, or it may be hidden inside the vagina, on the cervix, inside the anus or rectum, or even inside the mouth. Thus, it may or may not be possible to tell whether a sex partner has a chancre.

The spirochetes penetrate the skin and multiply at the site of infection. Between 10 and 90 days (usually about 21 days) after infection, a chancre appears at that same site. This condition is known as **primary syphilis**. The chancre

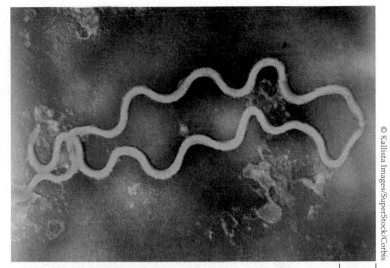

▲ **FIGURE 15.5** *Treponema pallidum,* the bacterium that causes syphilis.

10 μm

begins as a red bump that then breaks down, becoming a sore or ulcer. The chancre has a hard, rubbery rim and a wet or scabbed-over interior. If left untreated, it will heal by itself within 3 to 6 weeks. Because a chancre is a break in the skin, it greatly facilitates the transmission of an even more serious pathogen, HIV.

**Secondary syphilis** may begin while the primary chancre is still visible, or it may be delayed for several weeks. The main sign of secondary syphilis is a painless rash, which classically affects the palms of the hands and the soles of the feet but may also occur elsewhere (**FIGURE 15.7**). The rash takes the form of red or reddish-brown blotches. It is often accompanied by a fever, swollen lymph nodes, sore throat, and muscle pain. If left untreated, these symptoms generally disappear within a few weeks.

In many individuals, the spirochetes are not eliminated at the end of the second stage but continue to multiply in the body, even though the symptoms are gone. After about a year of this **latent phase**, the person is no longer infectious to sex partners. A pregnant woman can pass the organism to her fetus, however. The fetus may be stillborn, die neonatally, or develop severe neurological impairment.

During the latent phase, the spirochetes continue to multiply within the body at a slow rate. They may gradually invade the cardiovascular system, the bones, the liver, and the nervous system without initially causing any symptoms.

Eventually—sometimes decades after infection—syphilis may begin to do serious damage. This phase is called **tertiary syphilis**; it occurs in about 15% of untreated individuals. Large ulcers may appear on the skin or internal organs. The disease may attack the heart, the central nervous system, or the skeleton. Tertiary syphilis is now thankfully rare, but its very rarity, combined with the variety of sites that may be attacked, can make it difficult for today's physicians to diagnose.

## Syphilis has resisted elimination

Syphilis is diagnosed by recognizing the clinical signs and symptoms, by finding spirochetes in the fluid discharge from the primary chancre, or by detecting antibodies to these organisms in the blood. During the first year after infection, a single large injection of a long-acting form of penicillin is curative; at later times a more prolonged course of the drug may

**chancre** A primary sore on the skin or a mucous membrane in a person infected with syphilis. (Pronounced SHANK-er.)

**primary syphilis** The first phase of syphilis, marked by the occurrence of a chancre.

**secondary syphilis** The second phase of syphilis, marked by a rash and fever.

**latent phase** An asymptomatic phase of syphilis or other infectious disease.

**tertiary syphilis** The third phase of syphilis, marked by multiple organ damage.

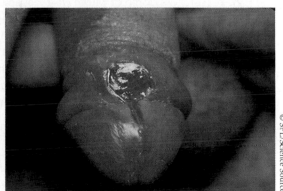

▲ **FIGURE 15.6** **Primary syphilitic sore** (chancre) on the penis.

---

\*Not to be confused with *chancroid*, a different STI that is rare outside of tropical countries.

▲ **FIGURE 15.7 Secondary syphilitic rash** may appear on the hands, as here, on the soles of the feet, or elsewhere on the body.

be required. Having had syphilis in the past does not protect a person from reinfection. Happily, no penicillin-resistant strains of *T. pallidum* have emerged since the first use of this antibiotic to treat syphilis in the 1940s.

The introduction of antibiotic treatment, along with other public health measures, greatly reduced the prevalence of syphilis in the United States from the 1 in 22 rate in 1918, mentioned earlier. In 2000 the rate of new cases was so low (about 2.5 new infections per 100,000 people) that public health officials spoke hopefully of eliminating the disease. By 2016, however, the syphilis rate had rebounded to 10.8 new infections per 100,000 people (CDC, 2019i).

There are three distinct but interconnected syphilis epidemics in the United States. One is a heterosexual epidemic among black men and women in the southern states. This epidemic has persisted for well over a century (**BOX 15.1**). The second is a more recent series of outbreaks among gay and bisexual men in large cities, including Washington, Los Angeles, New York, San Francisco, and Atlanta. A man who has sex with men is over 100 times more likely to be infected with syphilis than a man who has sex with women only, or a woman whatever the sex of her partners (CDC, 2017g). A third syphilis epidemic is brewing among drug users, gang members, and their shared female partners in regions of the country that are badly affected by the current increase in illicit drug use (J. Hoffman, 2017; CDC, 2019f).

## BOX 15.1
## The Tuskegee Syphilis Study

One of the most shameful episodes in the history of American medicine began in 1932, when U.S. Public Health Service researchers initiated a study of the effects of untreated syphilis on several hundred African American men living near Tuskegee, Alabama (see figure). The aim of the project was to follow the natural history of the disease, to study whether there were differences between the disease in black and in white people, and to compare symptoms during life with autopsy findings after death. (The study initially had a treatment element, but this was soon abandoned.)

The researchers, some of whom were based at the Tuskegee Institute (now Tuskegee University, a historically black college), recruited black farmers, renters, and laborers who had latent syphilis. That is, they had progressed beyond the first two stages of the disease but had not yet shown systemic symptoms. Most of the participants thought that they were being treated for their condition, but in reality they only received dubious medications such as "tonics."

The study continued for decades, and 13 research papers described the findings. In 1947, penicillin was recognized as the standard of care for syphilis. In the same year, the Nuremberg Code was promulgated in response to the atrocities committed by doctors in Nazi Germany. The code

Drawing blood from a participant in the Tuskegee study.

declared that informed consent must be a condition for participation in medical experiments. Nevertheless, the Tuskegee experiment continued, and the men being studied were not told that a simple and effective treatment was now available. In fact, the researchers went to considerable

# 15.7   Gonorrhea Can Lead to Infertility

**LEARNING OBJECTIVES**

After reading this section you should be able to:

15.7.1   Describe the symptoms of gonorrhea in women and men.

15.7.2   Explain why gonorrhea is a matter of great concern for women.

15.7.3   Contrast the development of antibiotic resistance in syphilis and gonorrhea.

**Gonorrhea** ("the clap," "the drip") is caused by infection with the bacterium *Neisseria gonorrhoeae*. The symptoms of gonorrhea develop quickly—within 2 to 10 days after infection in most people. In women, the initial site of infection is usually the cervix. Symptoms include a yellow or bloody vaginal discharge, bleeding during coitus, and a burning sensation when urinating. Sometimes—perhaps in the majority of cases—the initial infection is asymptomatic. In men, the usual site of infection is the urethra, and the symptoms are a discharge of pus from the urethra (**FIGURE 15.8**) and pain on urination. Like women, men can be infected with gonorrhea without experiencing symptoms.

Both men and women can be infected rectally through receptive anal sex. The symptoms of rectal infection include a rectal discharge, anal itching, and, sometimes, painful bowel movements with fresh, bright-red blood on the surface of the feces. In women, a vaginal infection can spread to the rectum. Infections of the mouth or pharynx can occur as a result of oral sex, especially fellatio, with an infected person.

**gonorrhea**   A sexually transmitted infection caused by the bacterium *Neisseria gonorrhoeae*.

---

lengths to prevent them from receiving treatment at the hands of other doctors. Thus the moral status of the study changed radically.

The study did not end until 1972, when a CDC researcher who was opposed to the continuation of the study gave an account of it to an Associated Press reporter. The ensuing publicity led to the rapid termination of the project. By that time, however, dozens of the men had died of the disease, and 22 wives, 17 children, and 2 grandchildren had contracted it, probably as a result of the study's nontreatment policy.

In 1974 a lawsuit brought on behalf of the survivors was settled for $10 million. In May 1997, President Clinton, responding to pressure from civil rights activists and the Congressional Black Caucus, formally apologized to the survivors in a White House ceremony. In response, one of the survivors, Herman Shaw, declared that "it is time to put this horrible nightmare behind us as a nation. We must never allow a tragedy like the Tuskegee study to happen again."

Contrary to widespread belief, no one was deliberately infected with syphilis during the Tuskegee study. Nevertheless, that did happen in the late 1940s in Guatemala. According to historian Susan Reverby of Wellesley College, doctors from the U.S. Public Health Service infected Guatemalan

prisoners and mental patients with syphilis without their knowledge or consent (Reverby, 2011). They did this either by exposing them to infected prostitutes (some of whom had syphilitic material placed in their vaginas just before contact with the prisoners) or by inoculating the individuals directly with syphilis-infected tissue. Later these people were treated with penicillin to cure any syphilis infection that took hold. The lead doctor on this project was later involved in the Tuskegee study.

These events exemplify a long tradition of abusive medical research on black Americans, prisoners, orphans, asylum inmates, and other disadvantaged groups. Research practices have changed greatly since the time of the Tuskegee study. It is unthinkable that such a project could be carried out in the United States today. These historical abuses should remind us of the need for continuing vigilance to ensure the protection of research participants, but they should not discourage members of any minority from seeking medical care or participating in research. In fact, the participation of minorities (including gay men and lesbians as well as people of minority racial groups) in research is essential if we are to ensure that medical advances benefit all Americans and harm none.

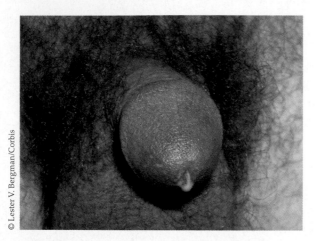

© Lester V. Bergman/Corbis

▲ **FIGURE 15.8 Gonorrheal urethritis in men** is usually marked by painful urination and a discharge of pus from the urethra.

**FAQ:** Should I get tested for gonorrhea? I've never had symptoms.

The CDC recommends that all sexually active women under 25 and all men who have sex with men get tested annually.

**pelvic inflammatory disease (PID)**
An infection of the female reproductive tract, often caused by sexually transmitted organisms.

**epididymitis** Inflammation of the epididymis.

**expedited partner therapy**
Giving antibiotics to an infected person to pass on to his or her sexual contacts.

**chlamydia** A sexually transmitted infection caused by infection with the bacterium *Chlamydia trachomatis*.

Untreated gonorrhea usually resolves in a few months (W. Zhu et al., 2011). Unfortunately, serious complications can occur. In women, a gonorrheal infection can spread into the uterus and oviducts, causing **pelvic inflammatory disease** (**PID**). In some women, PID symptoms are the first symptoms of gonorrhea to be noticed. These symptoms can include abdominal cramps and continuous pain, vaginal bleeding between menstrual periods, vomiting, and fever. PID may cause scarring of the oviducts, resulting in infertility or subfertility and a heightened risk of ectopic pregnancy. In men, the infection can spread to the epididymis (causing pain in the scrotum) or to the prostate gland. **Epididymitis**, like PID, can affect fertility. Other organ systems can be affected in both sexes, and babies can become infected—usually in the eyes—during the birth process. To prevent this, all newborns in the United States are given antibiotic eye drops.

Gonorrhea is usually diagnosed by the detection of the bacterium's DNA in the discharge or in urine. It is also possible to make a diagnosis by culturing the organism from a sample of the discharge.

In 2018 there were about 179 cases of gonorrhea per 100,000 people in the United States (CDC, 2019e). This rate is far below historical levels, but it is an 83% increase from the historic low in 2009. Rates are highest in the southeastern United States.

At one time, gonorrhea was readily treatable with standard antibiotics such as penicillin and tetracycline. Unlike the organism that causes syphilis, however, *N. gonorrhoeae* has shown a remarkable ability to develop drug resistance—five different classes of antibiotics have lost efficacy against some strains of the organism. The CDC now recommends that all cases of this disease be treated with a more advanced antibiotic, ceftriaxone (delivered by injection), in combination with an oral antibiotic, azithromycin, but CDC experts predict that gonorrhea will eventually become resistant to this drug regimen too. Newer antibiotics are in clinical trials (Taylor et al., 2018).

It's important for infected people to notify their partners so that they too may be treated before serious complications develop. Women in particular may have few or no symptoms, at least initially, so they may not seek medical treatment unless they know that their sex partner is infected. In a novel strategy known as **expedited partner therapy**, persons treated for gonorrhea may be given antibiotics to pass on to their sexual contacts without those contacts having to see a doctor themselves (CDC, 2019d). This strategy is far from ideal in medical or public health terms; the fact that the CDC has sanctioned it demonstrates how concerned they are by the recent increase in the prevalence of gonorrhea and other STIs.

Infection with gonorrhea does not trigger a lasting immune response, so a person who has recovered from an infection is not protected from reinfection. Efforts to develop a vaccine against gonorrhea have so far been unsuccessful.

## 15.8 Chlamydia Causes a Common Infection with Serious Complications

**LEARNING OBJECTIVES**
After reading this section you should be able to:

15.8.1 Describe the symptoms of a sexually transmitted chlamydia infection, and its most serious long-term complication if untreated.

15.8.2 Explain the CDC recommendations for routine chlamydia testing and treatment.

**Chlamydia** is the commonest of all reportable infectious diseases—1.8 million cases were reported in the United States in 2018 (CDC, 2019i). Reported cases in the United States rose from 17 to 540 per 100,000 people between 1985 and 2018. This huge long-term increase was due in large part to increased recognition of a condition that

▶ **FIGURE 15.9  Chlamydia**  This colorized electron micrograph shows a cell that has been infected with chlamydia. The cell's nucleus is at upper right. The *Chlamydia trachomatis* organisms live within an intracellular vacuole (the white space), where they are protected from immune attack. The larger (red) *C. trachomatis* organisms are metabolically active: They secrete chemical signals that take control of the host cell's metabolism, and they also divide. The smaller, dark forms are inert but highly infectious *C. trachomatis* organisms that are destined for export.

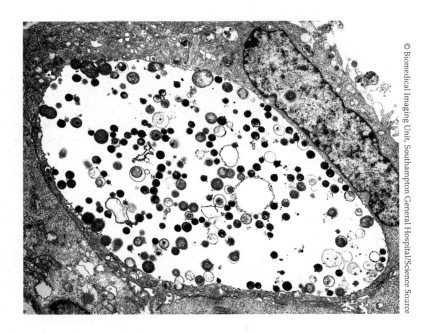

had previously been diagnosed as a nonspecific genital infection. Nevertheless, the actual incidence of chlamydia is now believed to be increasing rapidly, just as is the case for syphilis and gonorrhea.

The causative agent, *Chlamydia trachomatis*, is a bacterium, but an unusual one (**FIGURE 15.9**): Like viruses, it is active inside cells and exists outside of cells only in the form of inert but highly infectious particles. Besides its role in causing an STI, this bacterium is a leading cause of blindness in tropical countries, where it is transmitted by eye-seeking insects.

In the United States and Canada, chlamydia is usually spread by genital contact. Symptoms appear a few days to 3 weeks after infection. In men, the organism infects the urethra, causing a thin discharge (different from the thick discharge of gonorrhea) and burning pain during urination. As with gonorrhea, the organism can migrate farther up the male reproductive tract and cause epididymitis or prostatitis. Chlamydia is suspected of causing some cases of male infertility (Bryan et al., 2019).

In women, the organism infects the cervix (**FIGURE 15.10**) or urethra, causing irritation, a thin vaginal discharge, and painful urination. But 75% of infected women (as well as 50% of infected men) experience no symptoms. In both men and women, chlamydia infections can also occur in the rectum and in the mouth or throat if those parts have been involved in sexual contact with an infected partner.

Like gonorrhea, chlamydia can migrate up the female reproductive tract and cause PID (whether the initial infection was symptomatic or not). Up to 40% of women with untreated chlamydia infections develop PID; 20% of these women with PID will become infertile, and 9% of them will have an ectopic pregnancy. About half of all cases of PID are probably caused by chlamydia infections. In other words, chlamydia is a far more serious STI than one might imagine based on its immediate symptoms—or lack of symptoms.

As with gonorrhea, chlamydia can spread from an infected woman to her infant during childbirth, causing a serious but treatable eye or respiratory infection. Testing (and, if necessary, treatment) of all pregnant women is recommended.

Certain variants of the *C. trachomatis* bacterium can infect the lymphatic system, causing abscesses in the groin or elsewhere. This condition, called **lymphogranuloma venereum**, is a separate disease from the standard chlamydia infection. Although it

**lymphogranuloma venereum**
Infection of the lymphatic system by certain strains of *Chlamydia trachomatis*.

(A)

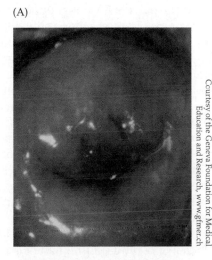

(B)

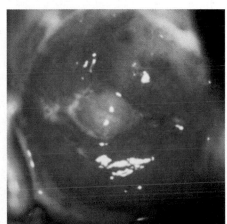

▲ **FIGURE 15.10**  **(A) Normal cervix and (B) cervical inflammation caused by chlamydia,** as seen on visual examination through the vagina. (Not every healthy cervix looks exactly like the one on the left.)

**bacterial vaginosis** A condition in which the normal microorganisms of the vagina are replaced by other species, causing discomfort and a foul-smelling discharge.

has long been considered a tropical disease, it has been diagnosed with increasing frequency in the United States and Europe, especially among men who have sex with men.

Chlamydia is usually diagnosed from cell samples obtained from the penis or cervix. (The cervical sampling procedure is different from the Pap test described in Chapter 2.) Chlamydia can also be diagnosed from urine samples. Chlamydia can be cured with a single dose of an antibiotic, usually azithromycin. Unlike with gonorrhea, drug resistance is uncommon, so far at least. Reinfection from an infected partner can easily occur, so it's important that partners be tested and successfully treated before they resume sexual contact.

Chlamydia is common among young, sexually active men and women across the United States. As many as 1 in 10 of all adolescent girls is infected, and the figures for older adolescents in urban areas may be even higher. By age 30, about half of all sexually active women show evidence of current or prior chlamydia infection.

The CDC recommends that all sexually active women under 25 be tested for chlamydia once per year, as well as older women who have had a new sex partner and all pregnant women. Since the test merely involves giving a urine sample—and taking a single dose of an antibiotic if the test is positive for chlamydia—it is a small price to pay for peace of mind.

## 15.9 The Status of Bacterial Vaginosis as an STI Is Uncertain

### LEARNING OBJECTIVES
After reading this section you should be able to:

15.9.1 Describe the symptoms of bacterial vaginosis.
15.9.2 Explain the reasons why it is important to treat bacterial vaginosis.

**Bacterial vaginosis** is a condition in which the normal vaginal microorganisms—mostly acid-producing bacteria known as lactobacilli—are replaced by a variety of other bacterial species. The vaginal secretions become less acidic (pH rises), the vagina develops a characteristic fishy odor, and there may be itching, pain, and a thin, off-white discharge. Many women who have bacterial vaginosis have no symptoms, however.

Bacterial vaginosis is uncommon in women who have not had sexual intercourse, but it is very common among sexually active women, especially those who have multiple partners. Vaginal douching, which disturbs the bacterial ecosystem within the vagina, increases the likelihood of developing vaginosis, as does the insertion of substances such as oils and petroleum jelly.

While it is clear that engaging in sex increases the likelihood of developing bacterial vaginosis, it is not clear whether sexually transmitted organisms are responsible for the condition. That does seem to be the case for female-to-female sexual contact, however: Lesbians whose partners have bacterial vaginosis are much more likely to have the condition themselves, compared with lesbians whose partners do not have it (Forcey et al., 2015). As to the question of heterosexual transmission, at least one of the organisms that characterize bacterial vaginosis, *Gardnerella vaginalis*, can also infect men; such infections may be asymptomatic, or they may be accompanied by urethritis (see below). Nevertheless, the CDC does not recommend routine treatment of males whose partners have been diagnosed with bacterial vaginosis.

In a minority of women, bacterial vaginosis may lead to serious complications, such as PID and (in pregnant women) premature delivery. Having bacterial vaginosis makes it easier for a woman to acquire STIs such as chlamydia, gonorrhea,

**FAQ:** Will vaginal probiotics cure my bacterial vaginosis?

No.

and HIV. What's more, having bacterial vaginosis greatly increases the risk that an HIV-positive woman will transmit HIV to male sex partners (Cohen et al., 2012).

Bacterial vaginosis can be treated effectively with antibiotics, and it is especially important for pregnant women with the condition to be treated, because it can cause premature birth and low birth weight. Relapses can occur; treating the male partners of affected women does not reduce the likelihood of recurrence.

# 15.10 Urethritis Can Be Caused by a Variety of Organisms

### LEARNING OBJECTIVE

After reading this section you should be able to:

15.10.1 Describe the possible causes and symptoms of sexually transmitted urethritis.

**Urethritis**, an infection or inflammation of the urethra, is very common. It is not necessarily caused by sexually transmitted bacteria, but it often is. We already mentioned gonorrhea as a cause of urethritis in men. Urethritis caused by other organisms, especially when it occurs in men, is referred to as **nongonococcal urethritis** (**NGU**). One such organism is *Gardnerella vaginalis*, mentioned above, but the most common agents are chlamydia, also discussed above, and an organism named **Mycoplasma genitalium**, often referred to by an informal abbreviation, Mgen.

Mgen is a tiny flask-shaped bacterium; it has the smallest genome of any known nonviral organism. It attaches to the outer membranes of cells in the urinary tract and enters the cytoplasm, where it reproduces (**FIGURE 15.11**). As with chlamydia, it can spread to the female reproductive tract and cause PID. Like gonorrhea, Mgen has shown a remarkable ability to develop resistance against most antibiotics.

**urethritis** Inflammation of the urethra, usually caused by an infection.

**nongonococcal urethritis (NGU)** Urethritis not caused by gonorrhea.

**mycoplasma genitalium** A group of very small cellular organisms that may cause urethritis.

(A)

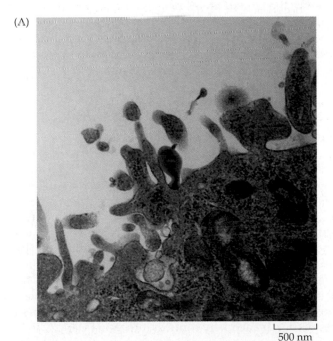

500 nm

(B)

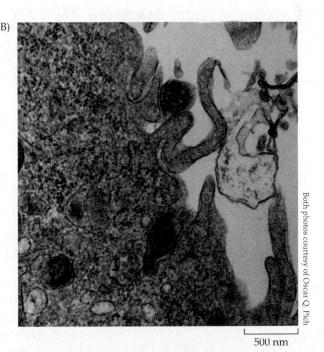

500 nm

Both photos courtesy of Oscar Q. Pich

▲ **FIGURE 15.11** *Mycoplasma genitalium* attaching itself to the outer membrane of a cell (A) and entering the cell's cytoplasm (B). The organism has been colorized for ease of identification.

Urethritis causes pain during urination and, often, a urethral discharge. The infection can spread to the bladder (cystitis) and reproductive tract. If gonorrhea has been ruled out, the doctor may treat the urethritis with antibiotics without attempting to identify the specific organism responsible. As with any STI, partner notification is important.

## 15.11 Viral STIs Can Be Dangerous and Hard to Treat

**Viruses** are extremely small infectious particles (10 to 200 nanometers in diameter). When not inside a host cell, viruses are metabolically inert but infectious. A virus's genome consists of either DNA or RNA and is very limited in size: It may possess as few as 10 genes, compared with about 1000 genes for a bacterium. Once inside a host cell, the viral genes take over the cell's metabolic machinery in order to replicate. This replication may occur right away and be followed by the release of new viral particles. Alternatively, the viral genes may persist in the cell in an inactive form for months or years before coming out of hiding and generating new viral particles.

Many viral diseases are self-limiting because they trigger an effective immune response in the infected person. Some viruses have found ways to protect themselves from their host's immune system, however. Viral infections are not treatable with antibiotics. A variety of effective antiviral drugs exist, but they are rarely curative, and they often have serious side effects.

In the following sections we discuss five viruses or classes of viruses: a pox virus, herpes simplex viruses (HSV), human papillomaviruses (HPV), hepatitis viruses, and the human immunodeficiency virus (HIV). This sequence corresponds approximately to the increasing seriousness of the diseases they cause. Besides the familiar viruses just listed, there is always the possibility that a new viral STI will be imported into the United States or will be recognized for the first time (**BOX 15.2**). The novel coronavirus that has caused the 2020 COVID-19 pandemic is not an STI, but the close contact required for sex can readily transmit the virus, so it has presented an especially great threat to sex workers and their clients (see Chapter 17).

**virus** An extremely small infectious agent. When not inside a host cell, viruses are metabolically inert but infectious.

**molluscum contagiosum** A skin condition marked by small raised growths; it is caused by a pox virus.

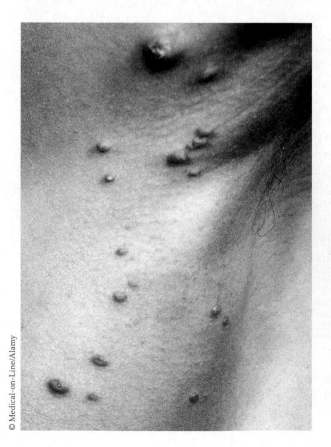

© Medical-on-Line/Alamy

## 15.12 Molluscum Contagiosum Is a Self-Limiting Condition

**LEARNING OBJECTIVE**
After reading this section you should be able to:

15.12.1 Describe the symptoms and treatment of molluscum contagiosum.

**Molluscum contagiosum** is a skin condition caused by a pox virus. It is characterized by small growths that appear as bumps on the skin up to about the size of a pencil eraser (**FIGURE 15.12**). Each bump has a central pit or dimple. The virus is transmitted by direct skin-to-skin contact or by contact with infected clothing or towels. In adults the most common affected site is the genital area, in which case sexual transmission is the likely route of infection (Mayo Clinic, 2019e).The condition does not cause any serious health problems,

◀ **FIGURE 15.12** **Molluscum contagiosum** takes the form of small growths on the skin.

## BOX 15.2
## Zika—The Virus That Came and Went

In late 2014 an epidemic of infections with the Zika virus broke out in Brazil (Ferraris et al., 2019). This RNA virus, which originated in Africa, is transmitted by tropical mosquitoes of the genus *Aedes*. Infection causes a short, flulike illness, but often there are no symptoms. Infection in a pregnant woman, however, can cause catastrophic damage to her fetus's developing brain (see **FIGURE A**).

In 2016 about 5000 cases were diagnosed in the United States. Nearly all of these were in individuals who had traveled to heavily affected areas, such as Brazil, or who lived in the southernmost areas of the United States, where *Aedes* mosquitoes are endemic. Nevertheless, at least 48 individuals contracted the virus from sexual contact with infected persons.

After men have recovered from the illness, the virus persists at high levels in their semen for several months. In women, on the other hand, the virus disappears from genital fluids much more rapidly. Therefore, male-to-female and male-to-male transmission are much more likely than female-to-male or female-to-female transmission.

Luckily, 2017 saw a precipitous decline in the number of reported cases (**FIGURE B**), and the World Health Organization declared the global health emergency over. In the United States only three sexually transmitted cases were reported in 2017, and none in 2018 or 2019 (CDC, 2020). A few cases were diagnosed in travelers returning from affected areas.

Zika, like HIV, teaches us that we must constantly be on the alert for new STIs. The causative agents do not necessarily come from overseas; they may evolve from organisms already present in the community. An example is a type of urethritis caused by the bacterium *Neisseria meningitidis*. It has long been known that this bacterium is responsible for outbreaks of meningitis (inflammation of the coverings of the brain), and that it can be spread by sexual contact. Recently, however, a strain of the bacterium known as ST 11 has emerged as a cause of sexually transmitted genital infections (Jannic et al., 2019). This bacterium can exist asymptomatically in the throat for years, but when a carrier engages in oral sex his or her partner may develop urethritis. Even though the carrier has acquired the throat infection long before, the newly infected person may wrongly accuse the partner of infidelity.

(A) Small head size (microcephaly) in a baby whose brain was damaged by the Zika virus before birth. (B) Course of the Zika epidemic in the United States (all cases, not just those transmitted sexually). (After V. Hall et al. 2018. *Morb Mortal Wkly Rep* 67: 265–269.)

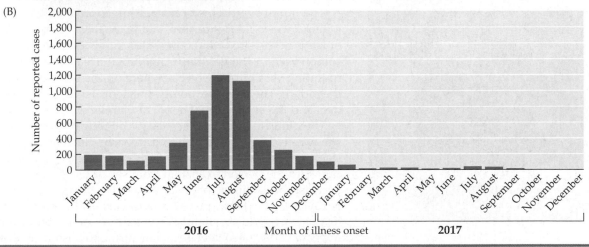

and it usually disappears within a few months of its first appearance, but several treatments are available, the most common being removal of the growths by freezing. Because it is so contagious, people with molluscum should take care to prevent others from coming into contact with the growths.

## 15.13 Genital Herpes Is a Lifelong Infection

**LEARNING OBJECTIVES**

After reading this section you should be able to:

15.13.1 Explain the differences between HSV-1 and HSV-2 in terms of the typical ways they are acquired, the sites of outbreaks, and the long-term likelihood of recurrences.

15.13.2 Describe the course of a typical herpes outbreak.

15.13.3 Evaluate possible means for a person with herpes to avoid infecting others.

The genetic material of herpesviruses is DNA (**FIGURE 15.13**). Two herpesviruses, herpes simplex 1 and 2 (HSV-1 and HSV-2), may be transmitted sexually. The term **herpes** can refer to a condition caused by either of these viruses.*

HSV-1 is the usual cause of **oral herpes**, often in the form of "cold sores" on the lips. Many people acquire HSV-1 nonsexually during childhood—from social kissing, for example. After the initial infection the virus remains in the body in a suppressed state (see the section on recurrent outbreaks below), but in some people cold sores recur from time to time. Regardless of whether they experience recurrences of oral herpes or not, people who were infected with HSV-1 during childhood are usually resistant to genital infection with HSV-1, even if they receive oral sex from a partner infected with HSV-1.

For some reason, childhood infections with HSV-1 have been on the decline for years. While that spares people from oral herpes, it means that they lack immunity to HSV-1 in adulthood. They are therefore susceptible to **genital herpes** if they receive oral sex—either fellatio or cunnilingus—from a partner infected with HSV-1, particularly if that partner has a cold sore at the time. Thus genital herpes caused by HSV-1 has become increasingly prevalent.

HSV-2 infection does not usually happen during childhood. Rather, the virus is acquired in adolescence or adulthood during sexual contact with a partner infected with HSV-2. Most transmissions are from the genital or anal area of one person to the genital or anal area of the other; genital-to-oral and oral-to-genital transmission does occur but is much less common.

The initial symptoms of herpes infection usually appear within 2 weeks after exposure, taking the form of an outbreak of sores at the site of infection. This site is most commonly somewhere in the genital or anorectal area or on the surrounding skin but may be elsewhere on the body or around the mouth. The most frequently affected sites are the penis in men and the labia, clitoral hood, or vaginal walls in women.

The outbreak may be preceded by tingling or itching at the site where the outbreak is about to occur. Such anticipatory signs are useful, especially in later outbreaks, because they can warn the person to abstain from sex or use protection (to decrease the likelihood of giving herpes to a sex partner) and to begin taking medication (see below). Shortly after any anticipatory signs, a reddish, slightly elevated spot or cluster of spots appears. A day or so later, the spots turn into blisters (**FIGURE 15.14**). The blisters then break, leaving sores or ulcers that give rise to a clear discharge. Alternatively, there may be cracks in the skin or mucosa, rather than blisters. The discharge from the

**herpes** An infection caused by herpes simplex virus type 1 or 2 (HSV-1 or HSV-2).

**oral herpes** Herpes infection of the mouth, caused by HSV-1 or (less commonly) HSV-2.

**genital herpes** An infection of the genital area caused by HSV-1 or HSV-2.

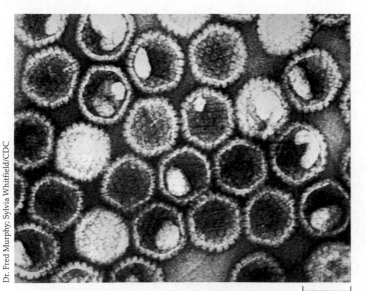

Dr. Fred Murphy; Sylvia Whitfield/CDC

150 nm

▲ **FIGURE 15.13 Particles of herpes simplex virus 2 (HSV-2),** the usual causative agent of genital herpes, are shown in an electron micrograph, using negative contrast. Each viral particle measures about 200 nanometers in diameter. The DNA cores are visible as dense, light-colored clumps within some of the particles.

*The skin condition called shingles is caused by a different herpesvirus that is not sexually transmitted.

(A)

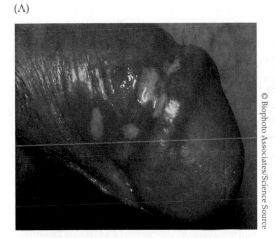

© Biophoto Associates/Science Source

(B)

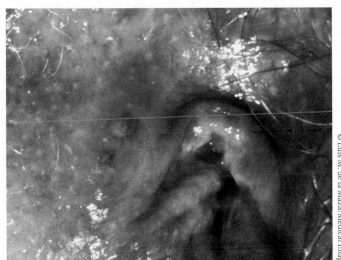

© Luis M. de la Maza/Medical Images

▲ **FIGURE 15.14** **Herpes outbreaks** commonly occur (A) on the shaft of the penis or (B) on the vulva.

blisters or cracks contains immense numbers of viral particles and is highly infectious. After a few more days, the sores crust over, dry up, and gradually heal and disappear.

Herpes outbreaks may be painless or mildly itchy—especially if they occur on a less sensitive patch of skin. In that case, they may not come to the person's attention at all. Alternatively, the outbreaks may be quite painful. If they are in a site that is contacted by urine, the act of urination may be extremely painful.

The initial herpes outbreak may be accompanied by fever and swollen lymph nodes or, rarely, by more serious symptoms. Also, the virus can be spread to other parts of the body, including the eyes, by the person's fingers. This can happen only during the initial outbreak.

### Recurrent outbreaks are the rule

Unless the immune system is compromised, the primary infection is quickly resolved, and the sores disappear within a couple of weeks. However, some viral particles enter the terminals of sensory nerve fibers in the vicinity of the infection site. They are then transported up the nerve fibers to the nerve cell bodies, which are located in ganglia close to the spinal cord. Once the viral particles have reached the cell bodies, they may remain inert for weeks, months, or a lifetime. In this location, they are protected from the host's immune system.

At some point, a new round of viral replication occurs, and the viral particles are carried back down the nerves to the original infection site or nearby, where they cause another outbreak of sores. Because the host's immune system has already been exposed to the virus, the second and later outbreaks are usually less severe than the first, and during these later outbreaks the virus cannot be spread to other parts of the body.

A few people infected with genital herpes caused by HSV-2 may experience only the initial outbreak, but the great majority continue to experience outbreaks indefinitely. Typically, the frequency of outbreaks decreases over time, from a median of six outbreaks in the first year to three outbreaks in the fifth year. When genital herpes is caused by HSV-1, recurrent outbreaks are less frequent and commonly cease altogether after a year.

It is widely believed that most HSV-2 infections are asymptomatic, because the majority of people who have been infected (as documented by the presence of antibodies to HSV-2 in their blood) deny any history of herpes outbreaks. However, many of these "asymptomatic" carriers have outbreaks that they haven't noticed

**FAQ:** I get cold sores—does that mean I'm immune to genital herpes?

Your cold sores are probably caused by HSV-1, in which case you are protected from genital herpes caused by that virus. You are not protected from genital herpes caused by HSV-2, however, although the symptoms may be less severe.

**FAQ:** My herpes seems to come back when I'm stressed out—is there a connection?

There have been conflicting findings on this. A meta-analysis did find a connection between stress and herpes recurrences, but the connection was less strong for genital than for oral herpes (Chida & Mao, 2009).

**FAQ:** My boyfriend has oral herpes—can he give me genital herpes through oral sex when he's not having an outbreak?

There's little research on this. If it's HSV-1, you may already be infected— most college-age Americans are— in which case you're unlikely to experience further harm. If he takes acyclovir or valacyclovir continuously, it will lessen the likelihood of your getting infected, whether it's HSV-1 or HSV-2.

**human papillomavirus (HPV)**
Any of a group of viruses that can be sexually transmitted and that cause genital warts or other lesions; some types predispose infected persons to cancer of the cervix or anus.

because they are painless and in an inconspicuous location (Sabo, 2010). It's not known how many people carry HSV-2 but never have outbreaks. What's important, though, is that many people have HSV-2 but don't know it.

During outbreaks, herpes sufferers can very easily transmit the disease to their sex partners. People with herpes are generally most infectious from the time they experience the first symptoms to the time that all their sores are dry and crusted over. HSV-2 can sometimes be detected on the affected area of skin during times when no outbreak is present, as well as in the genital area of individuals who deny having outbreaks (Tronstein et al., 2011). It's believed that herpes can sometimes be contracted from a partner when no outbreak is present (Mayo Clinic, 2019b). Even so, the chances of infection are much higher during an outbreak, and people with herpes who carefully watch for outbreaks and who abstain from sex during those times are going a long way toward protecting their partners from infection. The guidelines published by the World Health Organization only recommend abstention from sex while symptoms are present (World Health Organization, 2019). Condoms reduce the risk of transmission, as do certain drugs (see below).

A herpes-infected pregnant woman can transmit the infection to her child during the birth process, and the infection can be fatal to the infant or leave it severely disabled. Mother-to-infant transmission can be prevented by delivering the baby via cesarean section.

### Drug treatment can shorten or prevent outbreaks

Genital herpes is sometimes diagnosed simply from the patient's history and from clinical observation of the sores. Herpes is often difficult to recognize, however, and other, more serious diseases can closely mimic herpes. Also, simple inspection cannot distinguish whether herpes was caused by HSV-1 or HSV-2, but the distinction is important because of the difference in the long-term course of the two diseases. For all these reasons, both the CDC and independent experts recommend that the diagnosis be confirmed by laboratory tests either on samples swabbed from the sores or on blood samples.

The mainstays of treatment are acyclovir (Zovirax and generic equivalents) and valacyclovir (Valtrex and generics). Oral tablets are more effective than topical ointments. If a course of oral acyclovir or valacyclovir is begun at the first sign of an outbreak, the outbreak is shortened and may never get to the point of producing a discharge. People who are bothered by frequent or painful outbreaks can take acyclovir or valacyclovir on a continuous basis as a preventive measure. Doing so reduces the frequency of outbreaks or eliminates them entirely, and it also greatly lowers (but doesn't eliminate) the chance that partners will be infected.

An RNA-based vaccine against HSV-2 has proven effective in laboratory animals and entered clinical trials in 2020 (ClinicalTrials.gov, 2020).

## 15.14 Human Papillomaviruses Can Cause Genital Warts—and Cancer

**LEARNING OBJECTIVES**
After reading this section you should be able to:

15.14.1 Explain the possible effects of infection with HPV types that do not cause cancer.

15.14.2 Describe the possible locations of cancers caused by HPV in women and men.

15.14.3 Explain why it is important to be vaccinated against HPV at a young age.

**Human papillomaviruses** (**HPV**) are DNA viruses that fall into about 100 different types, out of which over 40 can infect the urogenital tract or the skin near the genitalia. Transmission is usually by sexual contact. Once inside a host cell, the virus can remain in an inactive form; alternatively, it can spur cell division, leading to the appearance of **genital warts** (**FIGURE 15.15**) or other skin lesions. The types of papillomaviruses that cause common skin warts (such as those on the hands) do not generally infect the genitals.

Genital warts usually appear a few months after infection, but many infected people have no warts or other symptoms. The warts are benign (noncancerous) tumors that are typically located at the vaginal opening, within the vagina, on the cervix, on the penis, at or within the anus, or even in the mouth. They can be single soft pink bumps or more elaborate cauliflower-like growths. They are unsightly and highly infectious, but they are usually painless and do not often cause serious health problems. These raised genital warts are most frequently caused by HPV types 6 and 11, which rarely cause cancer.

More dangerous are HPV types 16 and 18. These are not common causes of raised genital warts. They can cause other kinds of lesions in the genital region, including flat lesions that may be precancerous, but most commonly there are no symptoms. The problem with these HPV types is that, in women, they can eventually promote the development of cervical cancer (**FIGURE 15.16**). In fact, HPV infection is the principal cause of this disease. A key strategy in preventing the progression from HPV infection to cervical cancer is the Pap test.

These same two types of HPVs (16 and 18) can also cause anal cancer; in fact, HPV (in the form of types 16 and 18 and several others) is thought to be responsible for 9 out of 10 cases of this disease. HPV infection of the anus occurs most readily during unprotected receptive anal sex. Anal cancer is not very common: About 5500 women and 2700 men develop the disease in the United States annually, and it causes about 1000 deaths (American Cancer Society, 2019c). Some specialists recommend regular anal Pap tests for at-risk groups, but there is no positive evidence of benefit from such screening. Although anal warts rarely lead to anal cancer, people who have had anal warts are at increased risk of anal cancer, simply because they are more likely than other people to have been infected with the cancer-causing types of the virus.

HPV infection is also an increasingly common cause of cancers of the throat and of the vulva. According to a random-sample survey, nearly 7% of U.S. teens and adults carry HPV in their mouths. These infections were acquired through oral sex and possibly also through deep kissing. Only a small minority of these infections will progress to throat cancer, but HPV now causes more cases of throat cancer than cervical cancer (Kaiser Family Foundation, 2019).

Unlike the situation with HSV, the fact that a pregnant woman has been infected with any type of HPV is unlikely to have any adverse effect on her fetus or newborn child. Very rarely, the infant can develop warts in the mouth or respiratory tract; these are treatable, but they can recur.

An estimated 50% to 75% of sexually active men and women acquire an HPV infection at some point in their lives, and HPV is the most common STI in the United States in terms of the number of new infections per year. In one study that followed a large group of HPV-negative female college students, over 60% had acquired an HPV infection by 5 years later (Baseman & Koutsky, 2005). Most infected people eventually clear the virus from their bodies and become noninfectious to others within a couple of years from the initial infection, but an estimated 79 million Americans are currently infected and potentially infectious to others.

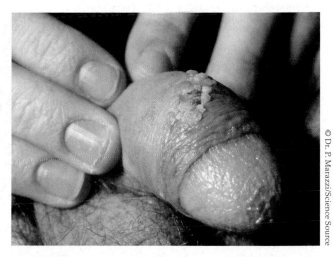

▲ **FIGURE 15.15   Genital warts on the penis**
Genital warts vary greatly in appearance.

© Dr. P. Marazzi/Science Source

**genital warts**  Wartlike growths on or near the genitalia or anus, caused by infection with human papillomavirus.

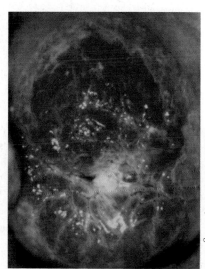

Courtesy of the Geneva Foundation for Medical Education and Research, www.gfmer.ch

▶ **FIGURE 15.16   Cervical cancer** as seen on visual examination through the vagina. Compare with the normal cervix shown in Figure 15.10A. Most cases of cervical cancer are caused by HPV infection.

A clinician can remove genital warts by a variety of means, such as by cutting them off, by freezing them with liquid nitrogen, by laser ablation, or by applying podophyllin or other agents. HPV may not be eliminated from the body by these treatments, however, and the warts sometimes recur.

### An HPV vaccine is available

The HPV vaccine available in the United States is known as Gardasil 9. The "9" refers to the fact that it offers protection against nine types of HPV—the four types mentioned above and five others. Together, these nine types account for most cases of genital warts and about 90% of all cervical cancers. The remaining 10% of cervical cancers are probably not caused by HPV.

The CDC recommends that Gardasil 9 be administered to all children (with a few exceptions) at the age of 11 or 12, although it can be given as early as age 9. For children under 15 the vaccine is given as two doses spaced 6 to 12 months apart; for those 15 or older it is given as three injections spread over 6 months. The CDC's Vaccines for Children program makes Gardasil 9 available at no cost to uninsured minors.

Although males cannot develop cervical cancer, the vaccine offers three benefits to them: protection against most genital warts, likely protection against anal and oral cancers caused by HPV, and protection against becoming an HPV carrier who can infect others.

To be effective against a given HPV type, the vaccine must be administered *before* a person becomes infected by that type. Ideally, therefore, children or adolescents should be vaccinated before they become sexually active. However, vaccination may still be useful for people who have already been infected, as it will protect them against the HPV types to which they haven't been exposed.

An earlier version of Gardasil ("Gardasil 4") protected against only four types of HPV. Individuals who received that vaccine may want to discuss with their doctors whether it's a good idea to get revaccinated.

Gardasil 4 is known to be effective for at least 10 years (Ferris et al., 2017); the same is likely to be true for Gardasil 9, but it has not been in use for long enough to be sure of that. It is known to be effective for at least 6 years (Huh et al., 2017).

The introduction of the HPV vaccine is a major advance in the battle against STIs as well as cancer. Unfortunately, over half of all American children have not received the vaccine or have only received the first dose, and the great majority of children do not receive complete vaccination before the age of 13, when the likelihood of sexual activity increases greatly (Bednarczyk et al., 2019). Some parents are reluctant to have their children vaccinated, out of unfounded fears that the vaccines are harmful or that they will encourage unsafe sexual activity. In some states, such as California, children as young as 12 can consent to receiving the HPV vaccine without their parents' involvement.

Evidence for how effective an HPV vaccination campaign can be comes from Britain, where centralized records are available. Prior to the introduction of Gardasil 4 in 2008, over 15% of sexually active teenage girls were infected with the types of HPV that the vaccine protected against; by 2018 that percentage had dropped to zero. This was true even for unvaccinated girls, because enough girls were vaccinated to knock the virus out of circulation—this phenomenon is called "herd immunity" (Public Health England, 2020).

## 15.15 Hepatitis Viruses Can Be Sexually Transmitted

**LEARNING OBJECTIVES**

After reading this section you should be able to:

15.15.1 Describe how the hepatitis A and hepatitis B viruses may be sexually transmitted.

15.15.2 Explain a simple means to avoid infection with both hepatitis A and hepatitis B.

---

**FAQ:** Does HPV vaccination in childhood make Pap tests unnecessary?

No. The risk of developing cervical cancer is greatly reduced but not eliminated.

---

**FAQ:** Does HPV vaccination work for life?

It's too soon to know, but Gardasil 9 protects for at least 6 years and probably longer (Huh et al., 2017).

Viruses that attack the liver, called **hepatitis viruses**, belong to a number of unrelated types, of which the best known are hepatitis A, B, C, D, and E. The most important of these viruses in terms of sexual transmission is hepatitis B, followed by hepatitis A.

The **hepatitis B** virus can be picked up by coitus or by anal or oral sex with an infected partner, as well as by contact with contaminated blood (by sharing needles, for example). The signs and symptoms of hepatitis B include **jaundice** (yellowing of the skin and mucous membranes—**FIGURE 15.17**), fever, general malaise, and tenderness and swelling of the liver. The majority of people with hepatitis B recover uneventfully and become noninfectious to others, but in about 6% of infected people (and a much higher percentage of young children) the infection progresses to a chronic state, which can lead to scarring (cirrhosis) of the liver, liver cancer, and fatal liver failure. Chronically infected people remain infectious to others. Several drugs are available for treatment of chronic hepatitis B, but they need to be taken for many months and are more likely to suppress symptoms than to actually eliminate the virus from the body.

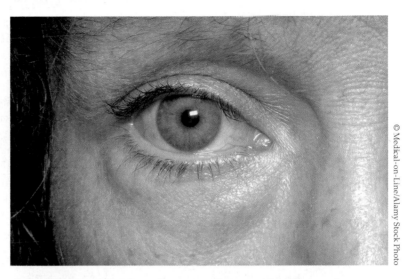

▲ **FIGURE 15.17** **Jaundice** is a yellowing of the skin and mucous membranes, seen most easily in the whites of the eyes. It is usually caused by liver disease, including sexually transmitted hepatitis infections.

Routine vaccination of children against hepatitis B was implemented in the United States in 1991, and the incidence of the disease has dropped by about 90% since then. Nevertheless, about 850,000 Americans are chronically infected.

The **hepatitis A** virus is transmitted by the fecal-oral route; that is, viral particles in the feces of an infected person get into the mouth of another. The virus can be spread nonsexually among people living in crowded or insanitary conditions. Sexual transmission occurs most readily via anal sex. Large outbreaks have occurred in gay male communities in Colorado and New York. The symptoms are similar to those of hepatitis B but are usually milder. The disease does not progress to a chronic state, and no one remains infectious after recovery. There is no specific treatment.

Individual vaccines are available against hepatitis A and against hepatitis B, and there is a combined vaccine against both A and B (Twinrix). The combined vaccine is administered as three injections over 6 months.

The hepatitis C virus is another important cause of chronic liver disease. It is not commonly transmitted via sexual contact, but some cases have been reported among men who have sex with men, especially those who engage in forms of rough sex where there may be exposure to blood.

**hepatitis viruses** Viruses that cause liver disease.

**hepatitis B** Liver disease caused by the hepatitis B virus, a virus that is often transmitted sexually.

**jaundice** Yellowing of the skin and mucous membranes, caused by liver disease.

**hepatitis A** Liver disease caused by the hepatitis A virus. It is sometimes transmitted sexually.

**acquired immune deficiency syndrome (AIDS)** The disease caused by the human immunodeficiency virus (HIV); its onset is defined by the occurrence of any of a number of opportunistic infections, or on the basis of blood tests.

## 15.16 AIDS Is Caused by the Human Immunodeficiency Virus

### LEARNING OBJECTIVES

After reading this section you should be able to:

15.16.1  Rank sex acts in order of decreasing risk of acquiring HIV from an infected partner.

15.16.2  Describe the features of the various stages of HIV/AIDS.

15.16.3  Evaluate the various means to avoid acquiring and transmitting HIV infection.

**Acquired immune deficiency syndrome** (**AIDS**) was first described in 1981. Nearly uniformly fatal if untreated, the disease has spread as a devastating epidemic in the United States and worldwide (**TABLE 15.3**). It is caused by the

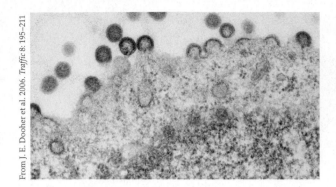

From J. E. Dooher et al. 2006. *Traffic* 8: 195–211

▲ **FIGURE 15.18**  **HIV particles** at various stages of assembly, budding, and release from the outer membrane of a cell. The cell's nucleus is at bottom right. Each viral particle is about 110 nanometers in diameter.

**human immunodeficiency virus**
**(HIV)**  The retrovirus that causes AIDS.

**retrovirus**  An RNA virus whose genome is transcribed into DNA within the host cell.

**human immunodeficiency virus (HIV)** (**FIGURE 15.18**). This is a **retrovirus**, meaning that its genetic material, RNA, is transcribed into DNA once it enters the host cell. "Retro" refers to the fact that transcription runs backward in comparison with the usual DNA-to-RNA direction.

The abbreviation "HIV/AIDS" is used to refer to the entire course of HIV infection, including its nonsymptomatic stages, its early symptomatic stages, and the later more serious symptomatic stages that fulfill the criteria for actual AIDS.

HIV evolved from a very similar virus that infects chimpanzees in west-central Africa. Molecular sleuthing indicates that the initial transmission from chimpanzees to humans occurred in the country of Cameroon, probably in the late 19th century. The first people to be infected may have been involved in the killing and butchering of chimpanzees for "bush meat." The virus spread to Kinshasa, Democratic Republic of the Congo, where around 1920 it evolved into the form of the virus that is the cause of the current epidemic (Faria et al., 2014).

Although the first human cases must have been in Africa, the first outbreak to be recognized as a new disease struck gay men in San Francisco, Los Angeles, and New York in the mid- to late 1970s. (See **Activity 15.1: Milestones in the Global HIV/AIDS Pandemic.**) HIV has since spread by other routes, including heterosexual sex, contaminated needles, blood transfusions, and perinatal transmission from mother to child, but two out of three infections in the United States still result from sex between men (**FIGURE 15.19A**). Young gay and bisexual men and African Americans of both sexes (**FIGURE 15.19B**) are particularly at risk of acquiring and passing on the virus.

The rate of new HIV infections in the United States has remained steady at about 39,000 per year since 2012, but this statistic masks a mixture of both good and bad news. In the large cities that have long been the core of the epidemic, the rate of new infections is falling: In Philadelphia, for example, new diagnoses fell by 14% just between 2017 and 2018, partly on account of a 36% decrease among black gay and bisexual men (City of Philadelphia, 2019). In rural America, on the other hand, the opioid crisis is spurring new outbreaks of HIV infection, as users switch from pills to needles, which are often shared (Thrasher, 2019).

HIV/AIDS has spread around the world, but it has caused the worst humanitarian disaster on the continent where it originated—Africa. Two-thirds of all new HIV infections occur in sub-Saharan Africa. In at least nine sub-Saharan countries, 10% or more of the adult population carry HIV, and AIDS-related deaths have orphaned millions of children and devastated national economies.

There is increasingly hopeful news regarding the global pandemic, however: The rates of both new infections and deaths have fallen by about half since their peaks around the turn of the century (AVERT, 2019). The rise and fall of the epidemic is illustrated by statistics from South Africa: From the beginning of the epidemic to 2004, AIDS caused the average life expectancy at birth to fall by 9 years—from 62 years to 53 years—but since 2004 life expectancy has rebounded to its original level. This recovery happened mainly because of the increasing availability of effective antiviral drugs (Nordling, 2016). The AIDS pandemic is not spiraling out of control as some had feared a decade or so ago.

**TABLE 15.3**  HIV/AIDS statistics for the United States and worldwide (figures are approximations or estimates)

|  | United States (2018) | Global (2018) |
|---|---|---|
| Cumulative AIDS deaths[a] | 690,000 | 35 million |
| AIDS deaths per year[a] | 16,000 | 770,000 |
| Persons currently infected with HIV | 1.1 million | 38 million |
| New HIV infections per year | 39,500 | 1.7 million |

*Source:* After HIV.gov. 2019. *U.S. statistics: Fast Facts and Global statistics: The Global HIV/AIDS Epidemic.* U.S. Department of Health and Human Services: Washington, D.C.
[a]Deaths from any cause of persons diagnosed with AIDS.

## Sexual transmission is chiefly by coitus and anal sex

HIV can be transmitted from person to person by a variety of means, including blood transfusions, accidental needlesticks, and needle sharing by drug abusers. The most common mode of transmission is by sexual contact, however, and that is the topic that concerns us here.

According to an analysis of numerous studies by CDC experts, the risk of acquiring an HIV infection through unprotected sex with an HIV-positive partner varies greatly depending on the kind of sex act performed (**FIGURE 15.20**). The risk is highest for receptive anal sex (a man or woman being anally penetrated by a man's penis). For insertive anal sex and receptive penile-vaginal sex the risk is much lower, and it is even lower for insertive penile-vaginal sex. During coitus, in other words, the virus is transmitted more readily from man to woman than from woman to man. Transmission is very unlikely to occur during any kind of oral sex, but a few cases have been reported.

The risk to the insertor is about 60% lower if he is circumcised than if he is not, at least in the case of vaginal sex (World Health Organization, 2014). Adult circumcision does not impair sexual sensation, performance, or satisfaction, but it does require a several-week abstinence from sexual activity (see Chapter 3).

The reason why receptive anal sex is so much riskier than receptive vaginal sex is not entirely clear. Both the vagina and the rectum are populated by large numbers of immune system cells that are capable of being infected by HIV (McElrath et al., 2013). The difference may be that the lining of the rectum is thinner and more easily abraded than that of the vagina, so that viral particles enter the body more readily.

The use of condoms greatly reduces the likelihood of transmission. With perfect condom use the likelihood of transmission is probably negligible, but an appreciable fraction of people who say they use condoms consistently do acquire HIV (Smith et al., 2015). The transmission risk also varies greatly depending on the stage of the infected partner's disease, on whether they are being successfully treated, and on whether the noninfected partner is taking prophylactic drugs (see below).

The presence of preexisting STIs such as syphilis, gonorrhea, herpes, or chlamydia facilitates transmission in either direction. In fact, any condition that causes ulcers or other damage to the skin or mucosa increases the risk of transmission. Coitus during a woman's menstrual period increases the risk of woman-to-man transmission.

The risk of acquiring HIV by any kind of woman-to-woman sexual contact is low, but instances have been

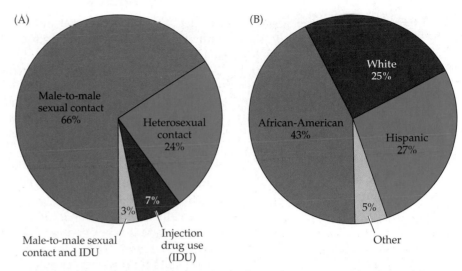

▲ **FIGURE 15.19** **The demographics of HIV diagnoses in the United States** (A) Mode of infection. (B) Racial/ethnic breakdown of infections. (After CDC. 2020. *HIV Surveillance Report, 2018* [Updated]; vol. 31. U.S. Department of Health and Human Services: Atlanta.)

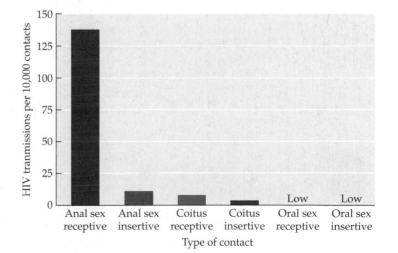

▶ **FIGURE 15.20** **Risky sex** This bar graph shows, for various kinds of sexual contact with an HIV-infected partner, the number of HIV transmissions that are expected to occur per 10,000 contacts. (Data from P. Patel et al. 2014. *AIDS* 28: 1509–1519.)

**CD4 T lymphocyte** A type of lymphocyte that carries the CD4 receptor; one of the major targets of HIV.

**seroconversion** The change from negative to positive on an antibody test, such as occurs a few weeks or months after HIV infection.

**early symptomatic HIV infection** Health problems caused by HIV, especially those that occur before the criteria for an AIDS diagnosis have been met.

**antiretroviral drugs** Drugs effective against retroviruses.

reported. Of course, bisexual and lesbian women can contract HIV infection from sex with men or from injection drug use.

The risk levels shown in Figure 15.20 may seem reassuringly low, but bear in mind that they relate to single acts. A person might engage in a thousand such acts within the space of a few years (with either a single or multiple partners), thus dramatically increasing his or her likelihood of becoming infected. Sex should not be a game of Russian roulette; your aim should be to eliminate the risk of acquiring HIV or—if you are HIV-positive—of passing it on to others.

## HIV infection progresses in a characteristic way

Now let's look in more detail at the course of the disease following HIV infection (AIDSinfo, 2019). During the weeks after the initial infection, the virus multiplies inside cells in the person's blood and lymph nodes. Its main target is the **CD4 T lymphocyte**, a type of white blood cell that is a central player in the body's immunological defenses. During this initial period there are no symptoms, and the infected person's immune system has not yet produced significant levels of antibodies to the virus. Thus, the person is "HIV-negative," meaning that the usual HIV blood test, which detects the presence of antibodies to HIV, gives a negative response. Nevertheless, the virus itself is present at high levels and can be detected by a technique called the polymerase chain reaction. Thus, the person is capable of infecting other people. This is the reason why members of high-risk groups are not allowed to donate blood, even if they test HIV-negative. (Modern screening methods detect HIV in donated blood within 7 to 10 days of infection.)

At some point, usually between 6 weeks and 6 months after infection, the infected person's immune system does mount a response to the virus—antibodies appear in the blood, and the person tests HIV-positive. This change is called **seroconversion**. Seroconversion may be preceded or accompanied by an acute flulike illness marked by fever, nausea, muscle pain, and sometimes a rash; however, some people experience no symptoms at all during this phase. Even those who do may mistake the symptoms for some other illness.

The body's immune response to the HIV greatly reduces the level of virus in the infected person's blood. The symptoms of acute illness subside, and the person now enters a prolonged asymptomatic period, or latent phase, that may last 7 to 10 years or even longer. Sexual contact with an HIV-infected partner is only about one-tenth as likely to result in transmission of the infection during the latent period as it is before seroconversion, according to a study conducted in Africa (Wawer et al., 2005). The latent period is so much longer, however, that there are far more opportunities for infection, especially if the HIV-infected person is unaware that he or she is carrying the virus.

Some signs and symptoms may begin to appear several years before the diagnosis of AIDS. These signs include thrush (a fungal infection of the mouth and throat), shingles (a painful rash caused by reactivation of a latent chicken pox infection), unexplained fever, diarrhea, night sweats, and a generalized swelling of lymph nodes. To distinguish these disorders from full-blown AIDS, these disorders are referred to collectively as **early symptomatic HIV infection**.

HIV-positive people are considered to have AIDS when their CD4 levels drop from the normal 1000 to below 200 cells per microliter or when certain illnesses appear. These include opportunistic infections, such as unusual forms of pneumonia or meningitis, as well as certain cancers, extreme weight loss, or dementia. Without treatment, people diagnosed with AIDS (not just HIV infection) typically survive for less than a year before succumbing to one of the complications of the disease.

## Antiretroviral drugs suppress but don't eliminate HIV

**Antiretroviral drugs** fall into four classes that target specific phases of the virus's replication cycle (**FIGURE 15.21**):

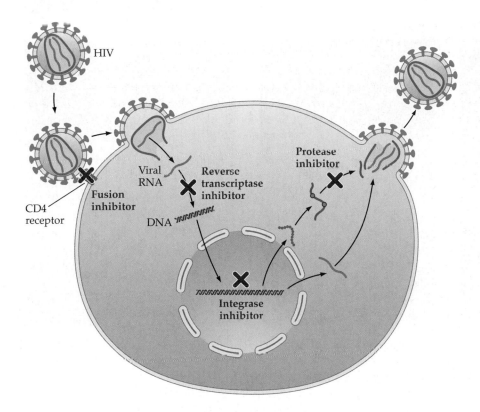

◀ **FIGURE 15.21**   **HIV replication cycle** and the sites of action of antiretroviral drugs.

- Fusion inhibitors, or entry inhibitors, block the attachment of the virus to the host cell or the fusion of the viral and host cell membranes, thus preventing the virus from entering the cell.

- Reverse transcriptase inhibitors block the transcription of viral RNA into DNA.

- Integrase inhibitors block the insertion of this DNA into the host cell's own genome.

- Protease inhibitors block the cutting of newly synthesized viral proteins into the shorter lengths that are required for function.

Typically these drugs are administered in combinations of three or more different drugs, to attack the virus on several fronts and reduce its ability to develop resistance. The multiple drugs may be combined into a single pill.

Antiretroviral therapy has greatly reduced the death rate from AIDS in the United States and other countries (**FIGURE 15.22**). An HIV-positive 20-year-old who is treated effectively now has a life expectancy only a year or two less than that of an HIV-negative person of the same age (Antiretroviral Therapy Cohort Collaboration, 2017). What's more, an HIV-positive person in whom the virus is "undetectable"—defined as having less than 200 copies of the viral DNA per mL—has effectively no risk of passing HIV on to another person. This fact is encapsulated in the slogan "Undetectable = Untransmittable," or "U = U," which has been endorsed by NIH's top HIV/AIDS experts (Eisinger et al., 2019). Still, current antiretroviral therapy has several shortcomings: It does not eradicate the virus from the body, so the drugs must be taken indefinitely; drug resistance can develop; and the drugs may have serious side effects.

Both the U.S. government and the World Health Organization recommend that antiretroviral treatment begin as soon as a person is diagnosed as having HIV. Early treatment improves an HIV-positive person's long-term health, and it also reduces the likelihood that he or she will pass on the virus to others.

**FAQ:**  My HIV viral load is now "undetectable," and my boyfriend takes Truvada every day. Can we have anal sex without a condom?

So long as you are virally suppressed (<200 copies/mL), you won't transmit HIV to your boyfriend, according to the CDC, regardless of whether he takes Truvada or not. Condoms still offer protection against other STIs and assurance in case your viral levels rebound.

(A)

(B)

(C)

▲ **FIGURE 15.22** **Living with HIV** (A) Basketball star and businessman Magic Johnson announced he had HIV in 1991. (B) Figure skater Rudy Galindo announced he was HIV-positive in 2000. (C) Safer-sex advocate Rebekka Armstrong (shown when she was a *Playboy* Playmate) has been HIV-positive since 1994.

**post-exposure prophylaxis (PEP)**
A drug treatment designed to prevent establishment of an infection after exposure to a disease agent such as HIV.

**pre-exposure prophylaxis (PrEP)**
A drug taken before exposure to a disease agent to prevent infection.

FAQ: Can I take Truvada just when I have sex?

In one study, participants took two pills before sex, one pill the next day, and one the day after. No one who complied with this regimen became infected (Molina et al., 2017).

Although antiretroviral therapy cannot eradicate an established HIV infection, it might prevent an infection from taking hold if administered immediately after exposure to the virus. This **post-exposure prophylaxis** (**PEP**) has been used with some apparent success in cases of occupational exposure (needlesticks among medical personnel), sexual assaults by HIV-positive men, and sexual encounters between sero-opposite couples—couples where one partner is infected and the other is not (McCarty et al., 2011). People who believe they have been exposed to HIV should get medical advice immediately. To reduce the risk of mother-to-child transmission, a brief course of antiretroviral therapy can be administered to the mother before delivery, as well as to her newborn baby.

It is also possible to take antiretroviral drugs *before* exposure to HIV, in order to prevent an infection from taking hold. This is called **pre-exposure prophylaxis** (**PrEP**) (CDC, 2017f). A once-daily pill named Truvada (a combination of two antiretroviral drugs) is used for this purpose. Compliance with the Truvada regimen is not always consistent. For that reason, long-acting forms of PrEP—injections, implants, and vaginal rings—are under development (HIV.gov, 2019a). One of these, an integrase named cabotegravir that is packaged into long-lived nanoparticles, needs only to be injected once every 8 weeks. It proved more effective than oral Truvada in a large trial, probably because of better adherence by users (Ryan, 2020). This form of PREP may have been approved by the FDA by the time you read this.

The U.S. Public Health Service has recommended PrEP for all HIV-negative members of high-risk groups, such as anyone who has an HIV-positive partner, and for men who have multiple male partners and don't always use condoms. PrEP is now widely used by HIV-negative white gay men in major cities such as San Francisco and New York, but it is used much less widely by at-risk women and in the South, where new infection rates are high. Only 10% of PrEP users are black, even though 44% of new HIV infections are among African Americans (HIVandHepatitis.com, 2016).

In spite of an enormous research effort over 30 years, no vaccine has so far provided reliable protection from infection with HIV. New candidate vaccines are currently in clinical trials. Regardless of the outcome of these trials, epidemiologists are increasingly optimistic that the AIDS pandemic can be halted without a vaccine.

## 15.17  You Can Reduce Your STI Risks

**LEARNING OBJECTIVE**

After reading this section you should be able to:

**15.17.1  Evaluate different strategies to reduce the risk of acquiring STIs.**

In spite of the many medical advances documented in this chapter, STIs remain a major public health problem. In fact several STIs, including syphilis, gonorrhea, and chlamydia, are actually increasing in prevalence, as we have documented in earlier sections. What's the reason? Decreased use of condoms is probably the main one: Condom sales are falling by about 3% per year (Beras, 2019). Less frequent sex by young people may be part of the reason for the fall in sales, but there are other likely factors: the increasing popularity of contraceptive methods that don't require condoms; the introduction of PrEP, which eliminates the risk of contracting HIV; and the HPV vaccine, which reduces the risk of infection with one of the commonest STI agents. Yet people who abandon condom use for these reasons increase their risk of contracting one of the "big three" STIs listed above.

We now consider the various ways in which you can protect your own health and collectively put a dent in the dismal STI statistics.

### Abstinence prevents STIs

Although it may seem too obvious to be worth saying, people who have no sexual contacts with others cannot acquire or transmit any infection by the sexual route. Complete abstinence from sexual contacts has other potential benefits besides disease prevention. It offers complete protection against unwanted pregnancy. It allows people to concentrate their time and energies on nonsexual relationships as well as on nonsexual goals. "Abstinence" is interpreted in different ways by different people, however. If it is interpreted to allow for sexual contacts other than coitus, it may not offer much protection against STIs (see the section on sexual behaviors below).

### Sexually active people can reduce their risk of STIs

People who do not choose to be abstinent still have options for reducing their risk of acquiring STIs. Two ways they can do this is to reduce the total number of people with whom they have sexual contact and to select partners who are less likely to have STIs:

- A person who has had many previous sex partners is more likely to have an STI than someone who has had few or no partners.
- An injection drug user may have acquired an STI by nonsexual means.
- Someone with whom you can feel comfortable discussing STI issues is likely to be a safer partner than someone who avoids the topic.
- Someone you know well is more likely to tell you if they have an STI than someone you just met.

There are mobile phone apps, such as Healthvana, that make it easy to get tested for STIs and to communicate the results to potential sex partners. If you don't have that information, just looking at your partner's genitals offers some degree of protection: Sores, warts, herpes lesions, and genital discharges are obvious warning signs, if you are willing to just take a look.

If you already have an STI, telling your prospective sex partners about it is not just the right thing to do; it might also save you from serious legal jeopardy (**BOX 15.3**).

## BOX 15.3
## Partner Notification

In late April 2002, state health officials knocked at the dorm room of Nikko Briteramos, a 6-foot-7 basketball star at tiny Huron University in South Dakota. A few weeks previously, Briteramos had been told that he was HIV-positive—the discovery was made when he attempted to donate blood. Now the officials wanted to interview him about his sex partners in order to notify them of their possible exposure to the virus. But Briteramos didn't let the officials into his room. The reason soon became obvious: He was in bed with his girlfriend. That same day, Briteramos was arrested and charged with five counts of intentionally exposing his girlfriend to the AIDS virus through unprotected sex. He received a suspended 5-year prison term, and after violating the terms of his probation, he spent 18 months in prison (Simon, 2002).

Probably few of you would dispute that it is wrong for people who know they are HIV-positive to engage in unprotected sex without telling their partners of their HIV status. Even if a condom is used, you might question the morality of withholding this information. South Dakota is one of 21 states that make such behavior a crime regardless of whether the virus is actually transmitted or not. Nevertheless, California is moving in the other direction: In 2017 it reduced the crime of knowingly exposing someone to HIV from a felony to a misdemeanor, with a maximum penalty of 6 months in jail (CNN, 2017a).

Consider the situation in which people who haven't been tested might still have reason to believe they are infected with HIV or another STI. This issue came before the Supreme Court of California in 2006. A woman sued her ex-husband for damages because he infected her with HIV. He had denied having engaged in any risky sex before or outside of their marriage, but she discovered emails that revealed his "rampant, high-risk secret homosexual lifestyle," according to her lawyers' statements. The court ruled that the case could proceed, and the woman was eventually awarded $12.5 million in damages (BakersfieldNow.com, 2008).

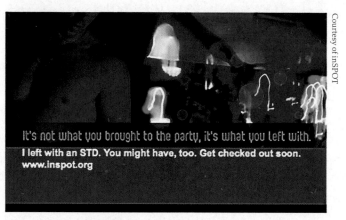

It's not what you brought to the party, it's what you left with.
I left with an STD. You might have, too. Get checked out soon.
www.inspot.org

This is from a friend at **inSPOT** the [STD] Internet Notification Service for Partners Or Tricks.

This inSPOT card is designed for peer-to-peer STI notification.

The majority of states have enacted mandatory partner notification laws. Although the details vary from state to state, these programs often require medical personnel or officials to ask HIV-positive people about their sexual contacts and to inform those partners about their risk of exposure. In most states, however, HIV-positive people are not legally required to provide the names of their sexual contacts. In that sense, even "mandatory" programs are voluntary.

An online application known as inSPOT is designed to facilitate peer-to-peer notification. Persons who have been diagnosed with an STI (not necessarily HIV) can go to the website (www.inspot.org) and select an e-card (see figure). They type in the email addresses of up to six of their sex partners, select an STI (including HIV), add an optional personal message, and send it to their partners under their own name or anonymously. When recipients click on the card, they are linked to a page with information about that STI and a variety of resources such as clinic addresses.

Different individuals may have different likelihoods of acquiring an STI even when their total numbers of sex partners and their sexual behaviors are the same, on account of demographic variations in STI prevalence. For example, we mentioned above that HIV prevalence is much higher among gay and bisexual black men than among other groups. This is not because these men have more partners or use condoms less than gay or bisexual men of other races—in fact they have *fewer* partners and engage in *less* unprotected sex, according to a study by Michael Newcomb and Brian Mustanski of Northwestern University (Newcomb et al., 2014). However, this same study found that the sex partners of gay and bisexual black men are about 11 times more likely to be other black men than is true for members of other racial groups, so each sexual encounter is much more likely to be with an HIV-positive partner. In other words, gay and bisexual black men form an interconnected network within which HIV infection can readily spiral out of control, in spite of relatively cautious sexual behavior by individuals within the network.

## Some sexual behaviors are riskier than others for STI transmission

As we've already discussed in the case of HIV, women and men who are sexually active can greatly influence their likelihood of acquiring or transmitting an STI by their choice of sexual behaviors. Coitus, anal sex, and anilingus (mouth-to-anus contact) are high-risk sexual behaviors, with anal sex being the riskiest with regard to HIV transmission. Anilingus has a low likelihood of transmitting HIV, but it is a risky practice because of the likelihood of transmission of hepatitis A or B (in the anus-to-mouth direction), as well as other STIs.

Oral sex (fellatio or cunnilingus) is a moderate-risk behavior. Although transmission of HIV by oral sex is unlikely, this route readily transmits some other STIs, such as gonorrhea and syphilis. Other sexual behaviors, such as kissing, fondling, hand–genital contact, and general body contact, are low-risk behaviors. They are certainly not free of risk—herpes and syphilis, for example, can both be transmitted by these behaviors—but they are so much safer than the high- and moderate-risk activities described above that they offer a sensible alternative for sexually active people when STI transmission is a concern.

The use of sex toys is risky if the toys are not kept scrupulously clean. Sex toys should not be shared.

Experimental studies have shown that people are willing to engage in much riskier sex when they are sexually aroused than at other times (Skakoon-Sparling et al., 2016). For that reason, people do well to discuss safer-sex practices with their prospective partners before things get too hot.

Having sex while you or your partner is under the influence of alcohol or drugs increases the chances that you will ignore all the information in this chapter.

## Condoms are the mainstay of STI prevention

The condom is the key to STI prevention for sexually active people, especially for those who are not in a long-term relationship. The proper use of condoms has already been described in the context of contraception (see Chapter 9). Two points are worth reemphasizing in the context of STI protection:

1. Natural-tissue condoms ("skins"), although possibly effective as contraceptives, do not provide adequate protection against STIs, because they have pores through which viruses can pass. No disease agents can pass through an unbroken latex or polyurethane condom, and the same is true for female condoms.

2. Anal sex places greater demands on a condom than does vaginal sex, so extra-strength condoms are recommended. This is particularly important when the insertive partner is known to be HIV-positive.

Some people wash and reuse condoms. We (and the CDC) strongly advise against this. Reused condoms are more likely to slip off, break, or develop holes—they are designed for one-time use only.

The condom is—let's face it—a pretty medieval solution to a 21st-century health crisis. We look forward to the day when advances in prophylaxis, vaccines, and non-barrier contraception—combined with better sex education—will consign the condom to history. In the meantime, it's a lifesaver.

> **FAQ:** Is there any way to reduce STI risk during cunnilingus?
>
> For oral stimulation of the vulva or the anus you can buy flat sheets of latex called "dams" or use kitchen plastic wrap. Water-based lube between the dam and skin may improve sensation.

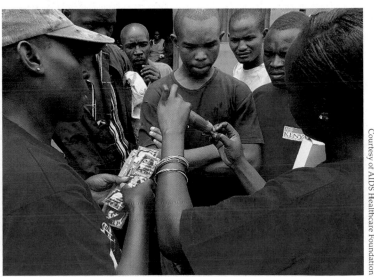

Courtesy of AIDS Healthcare Foundation

▲ Condom education by the AIDS Healthcare Foundation in Nigeria.

## 15.18 Not Everything Is an STI

### LEARNING OBJECTIVE
After reading this section you should be able to:

**15.18.1 Identify several conditions that are often mistaken for STIs.**

By this point, you quite likely have diagnosed several STIs in yourself, including a couple of fatal ones! If so, it's time for a reality check. HIV is uncommon in the college student population and very uncommon among heterosexual students. Hepatitis usually cures itself. Syphilis and gonorrhea can be easily cured with antibiotics. Herpes won't kill you.

Students often mistake other medical conditions, or even perfectly healthy traits, for STIs. **FIGURE 15.23** shows some examples of conditions that are not STIs but might be interpreted as such by people without medical training. Shaving the pubic area may cause a rash that is misinterpreted as herpes. Little bumps around the head of the penis, called "pearly penile papules," are natural and harmless growths, not genital warts caused by HPV. (Some women have similar skin tags on or near the clitoris.) A round swelling on the labia is more likely to be caused by a blocked mucous gland than any kind of STI. Canker sores within the mouth have many possible causes, but they are not the result of infections, sexual or otherwise.

We encourage you to take all reasonable steps to protect your own health and that of your sex partners. By all means, get yourself checked out if you are in doubt about whether you have an STI or would like to be screened for HIV. But don't let fear of AIDS or other STIs so preoccupy you as to leave no room for emotional or physical intimacy.

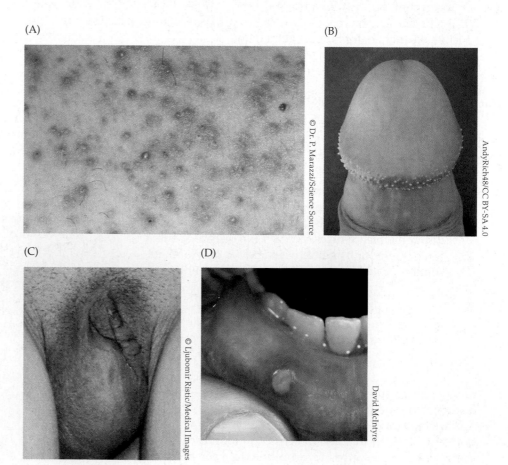

(A) © Dr. P. Marazzi/Science Source
(B) AndyRich48/CC BY-SA 4.0
(C) © Ljubomir Ristic/Medical Images
(D) David McIntyre

▶ **FIGURE 15.23 We're not STIs.** (A) Folliculitis, such as might be caused by shaving pubic hair. (B) "Pearly penile papules" are harmless little bumps that ring the glans of the penis in some men. (C) This cyst on the labia was caused by blockage of the duct of a mucous gland. (D) A canker sore in the mouth may result from accidental biting or other causes.

# Summary

- Nearly 20 million new cases of sexually transmitted infections (STIs) occur annually in the United States. STIs are caused by lice, mites, protozoans, bacteria, and viruses. In spite of medical advances, STIs remain a major public health problem. They also bolster common perceptions of sex as something dangerous or immoral.

- Skin infestations that can be transmitted sexually include pubic lice and scabies. Pubic lice attach themselves to hair shafts, especially in the pubic region. Scabies mites burrow under the surface of the skin. Both infestations can cause severe itching but do not otherwise threaten health. Pubic lice and scabies mites can be eliminated by use of insecticidal lotions or shampoos.

- Trichomoniasis is an infection of the vagina or urethra by a protozoan. In women it causes discomfort, a vaginal discharge, and the urge to urinate frequently. In men, the infection is usually asymptomatic. It is generally eliminated by a single oral dose of Flagyl.

- Syphilis is caused by infection with the bacterium *Treponema pallidum*. The disease has several stages. Primary syphilis is marked by a sore (chancre) at the site of infection. Some weeks later, a rash and fever occur (secondary syphilis). The infection then becomes latent, but it may eventually attack a variety of organ systems (tertiary syphilis) and cause death. The disease is readily curable with penicillin in its early stages.

- Gonorrhea is caused by infection with the bacterium *Neisseria gonorrhoeae*. In men it usually infects the urethra, causing a discharge of pus and painful urination. In women it can infect the cervix, causing a vaginal discharge. The infection in women is commonly asymptomatic, but it can spread to the internal reproductive tract, causing pelvic inflammatory disease (PID) and reduced fertility. Rectal and oral infections can occur in either sex. Gonorrhea can be treated with antibiotics, but antibiotic resistance is an increasing problem.

- Infection with the bacterium *Chlamydia trachomatis* is very common. It can cause a urethral or vaginal discharge and painful urination, but many infected men and women do not have symptoms. Anal and oral infections can occur. Chlamydia is readily treatable with antibiotics. In women, untreated chlamydia infections can lead to PID.

- Bacterial vaginosis is a condition, sometimes transmitted sexually, in which the vaginal lactobacilli are replaced by other organisms. There is a characteristic fishy odor and a thin discharge. It can be treated with antibiotics.

- Molluscum contagiosum is a common skin condition caused by a pox virus. It consists of small skin growths that usually disappear permanently after a few months. Although any kind of interpersonal contact can allow for transmission, molluscum in the genital area is usually the result of sexual transmission.

- Genital herpes is a very common condition caused by infection with the herpes simplex virus type 1 or 2 (HSV-1 or HSV-2). It causes an outbreak of sores at the site of infection, which is usually somewhere in the anogenital region but can also be in the mouth. The initial outbreak heals spontaneously, but it may be followed by further outbreaks at the same location that recur for the remainder of the person's life. Herpes infection is incurable, but outbreaks can be treated or prevented with antiviral drugs. When transmitted from a mother to her baby during the birth process, herpes can be a life-threatening condition.

- Human papillomaviruses (HPV) cause genital warts and other lesions of the genital skin and urogenital tract. Genital warts can be removed by a variety of treatments. Some HPV types (not those that cause bulky, raised genital warts) infect the cervix and are the principal cause of cervical cancer and anal cancer. An HPV vaccine (Gardasil 9) is available; it should be administered to girls and boys before they become sexually active.

- Hepatitis A and B are viral infections of the liver that can be acquired sexually as well as by other routes. Anal sex (especially oral-anal contacts) are the sexual behaviors most likely to transmit hepatitis A. Hepatitis B is transmitted by coitus or oral sex; in a minority of cases it leads to chronic liver disease and liver cancer. No cure exists for either form of hepatitis, but effective vaccines are available.

- Acquired immune deficiency syndrome (AIDS) is caused by infection with the human immunodeficiency virus (HIV). The virus originated in central Africa, but a worldwide pandemic began with outbreaks in gay male communities in the United States in the late 1970s. Transmission now occurs by both

*(Continued)*

## Summary *(continued)*

male–female and male–male sexual contacts (principally by coitus and anal penetration), as well as by exposure to contaminated blood. Female-to-female transmission is uncommon.

- HIV infection is marked by an acute illness followed by a several-year asymptomatic period. Eventually the infection impairs the person's immune system to the point that certain opportunistic infections and cancers may occur. Symptomatic AIDS is a life-threatening condition that cannot be cured, but it may be held in check with a combination of drugs that interfere with various stages of the virus's replication cycle. These drugs are slowing the global AIDS epidemic. There is no HIV vaccine, but high-risk populations can take antiviral drugs (Truvada) as prophylaxis against infection.

- Women and men can reduce their risk of acquiring STIs by a variety of means. Complete sexual abstinence offers complete protection from sexual transmission. Sexually active people can reduce their risk by keeping the number of their sexual partners low (ideally, by forming a mutually monogamous relationship), by discussing STIs and sexual history with prospective partners, by getting tested for STIs, and by engaging in relatively low-risk sexual behaviors as an alternative to coitus or anal sex. Careful and consistent use of condoms is another key to lowering the risk of acquiring and transmitting STIs.

---

The **Discovering Human Sexuality** digital resources include activities, animations, flashcards, web links, chapter outlines and summaries, and other study tools.

▪ ▪ ▪ ▪ ▪ ▪ ▪ ▪ ▪ ▪ ▪ ▪ ▪ ▪ ▪ ▪ ▪ ▪ ▪

Learn more with this chapter's digital tools, including the **Oxford Insight Study Guide**, at **oup.com/he/levay5e**.

## Discussion Questions

1. Can you think of any circumstances in which it would be acceptable for someone who has an STI not to inform his or her sex partner? If others in your class have a different opinion, discuss the reasons for your differing views, and attempt to reach a consensus on the subject.

2. Do you think that there are any circumstances in which a person should be legally punished for transmitting a serious STI to a partner? Or do you think that such action is counterproductive? Should people simply be held responsible for protecting themselves from STIs?

3. Imagine you are embarking on a sexual relationship with your first partner or a new partner. How would you bring up the matter of STIs and what to do about them? Try to imagine the actual conversation you would have and what the difficulties might be.

4. Imagine you are returning to your high school to give a half-hour presentation about STIs. What age students would you choose to speak to? What would be the main goals you'd like to accomplish? Do you think any particular styles of communication would be most effective? Is there any way in which you think you could do a better job than an STI specialist from the local health department?

## Web Resources

American Sexual Health Association   **www.ashasexualhealth.org/stdsstis**

Centers for Disease Control and Prevention. HIV/AIDS   **www.cdc.gov/hiv**

Centers for Disease Control and Prevention. Sexually transmitted diseases (STDs) **www.cdc.gov/std**

It's Your (Sex) Life (MTV's website on STDs and birth control) **www.itsyoursexlife.com**

NMAC (National Minority AIDS Council)   **www.nmac.org**

UNAIDS   **www.unaids.org**

University of California, San Francisco. HIV InSite   **hivinsite.ucsf.edu/InSite**

## Recommended Reading

Grimes, J. (2016). *Seductive delusions: How everyday people catch STIs*. Johns Hopkins University Press.

Holleran, A. (2008). *Chronicle of a plague, revisited: AIDS and its aftermath*. Da Capo.

Jones, K. (ed.). (2016). *Sexually transmitted diseases sourcebook* (6th ed.). Omnigraphics.

Marr, L. (2007). *Sexually transmitted diseases: A physician tells you what you need to know* (2nd ed.). Johns Hopkins University Press.

Reverby, S. (2009). *Examining Tuskegee: The infamous syphilis study and its legacy*. University of North Carolina Press.

Protesters against the appointment of Brett Kavanaugh to the U.S. Supreme Court in 2018. Christine Blasey Ford testified that he attempted to rape her when they were teenagers.

# 16

# Sexual Assault, Harassment, and Partner Violence

This chapter deals with the dark side of sex. Sex is not limited to balanced, happy interactions between loving couples. It can be grossly one-sided, involving sexual desire on one person's part and disinterest, perhaps aversion, on the other's. It can involve physical assault or an ongoing pattern of harassment. And intimate sexual relationships can be marred by cruelty and violence.

We touched on these issues earlier: In Chapter 7 we discussed the difficult feelings resulting from unrequited love, as well as the breakup of relationships. In Chapter 13 we described paraphilic disorders such as exhibitionism that can lead to the victimization of others. Here we take a broader look at sex as a context for physical and psychological injury. We omit one important form of sexual victimization—that of children by adults—because we covered this topic in Chapters 10 and 13.

## 16.1 What Is Sexual Assault?

**LEARNING OBJECTIVES**

After reading this section you should be able to:

16.1.1 Define the terms sexual assault, rape, statutory rape, date rape, and acquaintance rape.

16.1.2 Describe the demographics associated with high or low risk of experiencing a sexual assault.

16.1.3 Evaluate the reasons why victims of sexual assault often don't report the crime to the police.

**sexual assault** Coercive or non-consensual sexual contact; a broader category of behaviors than rape.

**rape** Penetrative sex accomplished by force or the threat of force.

**statutory rape** Penetrative sex when a partner is legally unable to give consent on account of young age, intellectual disability, or unconsciousness.

**date rape** Rape by a social acquaintance or someone the individual is dating.

**acquaintance rape** Rape by a person known to the victim.

**Sexual assault** is a broad term covering any violent or nonconsensual act involving physical contact of a sexual nature. As used here, and in general discourse, it includes rape, which is the most serious kind of sexual assault. As a criminal charge, however, it is often reserved for non-rape acts—that is, acts in which actual sexual penetration did not take place or cannot be proven.

**Rape** or "forcible rape" means penetration of the vagina or anus by the penis or any other body part or object or penetration of the mouth by the penis, when performed by force or the threat of force. Penetration does not have to be complete: Even a slight penetration is sufficient for the act to be considered rape. Forced deep kissing (i.e., penetration of the mouth by the tongue) is not rape, but it would certainly qualify as sexual assault. By these definitions, women are capable of committing rape and men are capable of being raped, but the great majority of rape convictions are for rapes of women by men.

**Statutory rape** means coitus, anal penetration, or oral penetration performed without force but also without the partner's consent; it is usually applied to cases in which the partner cannot legally give consent on account of young age or mental incapacity. When we use the term "rape" without qualification, we are excluding statutory rape.

Another frequently used term is **date rape**: This is not a legal term but an informal way of referring to rape that occurs in the context of a social or romantic interaction between two people. It includes situations in which some form of sexual interaction is already under way, whereupon one person continues to sexual penetration against the will of the other person. **Acquaintance rape** includes date rape but also covers any rape where the perpetrator is a friend or acquaintance of the victim.

For a sexual assault charge to have legal validity, it must usually be shown that the victim made evident to the perpetrator her or his unwillingness to engage in the act that is the subject of the charge. This unwillingness is often expressed by physical resistance, but not necessarily: A verbal refusal is sufficient, because the courts are aware that physical resistance is sometimes impossible or unwise. The fact that the victim consented to one sex act, such as oral sex, is not a defense if the charge relates to another act, such as coitus.

Sexual assault laws do not cover every sexual situation. There exists a gray area in which a person isn't comfortable with having sex but hasn't said either "yes" or "no" and hasn't offered even token resistance to the sexual advances. This is unlikely to be considered criminal sexual assault, but it might be grounds for disciplinary action in a college setting, as we'll discuss later.

It's important to be aware that the laws governing rape and sexual assault vary considerably from state to state, and there are often different degrees of these crimes that incur different penalties. We recommend that you find out how these terms are legally defined in your own state (FindLaw, 2019a; FindLaw, 2019b).

Some forms of unwanted touching—such as might occur in a workplace, for example—may not amount to sexual assault, but if they are repeated over time, they may constitute sexual harassment, a topic discussed later in the chapter.

**FAQ:** Don't women sometimes provoke rape by the way they dress or act?

Women's clothing or actions may increase or lessen their risk of being raped, but nothing they do or fail to do changes the culpability of the rapist.

## Young women are the most frequent victims

Sexual assault statistics are subject to a variety of errors and distortions; the least unreliable numbers are those derived from random-sample surveys of the U.S. population, such as the National Criminal Victimization Survey (NCVS) conducted by the U.S. Department of Justice (Bureau of Justice Statistics, 2019a), and the National Intimate Partner and Sexual Violence Survey (NISVS) conducted by the CDC (CDC, 2018e). According to the NISVS:

- 36% of women and 17% of men say they had experienced a sexual assault during their lifetime.*

- 19% of women and 1.5% of men say they had experienced an attempted or completed rape in their lifetime.

- Among women who were sexually assaulted, 96% of the perpetrators were male; among men, 82% of the perpetrators were female.

- Among women, Asian Americans reported the lowest rate of sexual assault; mixed-race women and Native Americans reported the highest rates.

- Four out of five individuals who sexually assaulted women were known to their victims (**TABLE 16.1**).

**TABLE 16.1** Perpetrators of sexual assault against women

| Relationship of perpetrator to victim | Percent of all women |
|---|---|
| Current or former intimate partner | 45 |
| Family member | 18 |
| Person of authority | 8 |
| Acquaintance | 50 |
| Stranger | 19 |

*Source*: S. G. Smith et al. 2017. *The National Intimate Partner and Sexual Violence Survey (NISVS): 2010-2012 State Report*. National Center for Injury Prevention and Control, Centers for Disease Control and Prevention: Atlanta, GA.

*Note*: The figures are the percentages of women who said they had been sexually assaulted by each kind of perpetrator. The percentages add up to more than 100 because some women reported assaults by more than one kind of perpetrator.

The risk of rape is highest for young women: Among female rape victims 81% were raped (or were raped for the first time) before their 25th birthday, and 43% were raped before their 18th birthday, according to NISVS data. Nevertheless, there is some risk of sexual violence against women of any age, including elderly residents of nursing homes, who may be especially vulnerable on account of physical or mental incapacity (CNN, 2017c).

In the NCVS data, the victimization rate of 2.7 per 1000 in the year 2018 represented a more than twofold increase since 2014, when the reported rate was 1.1 per 1000. It's doubtful that this startling increase was real, however—particularly because it was not matched by any equivalent increase in nonsexual assaults over the same time span. It may be that it was due, at least in part, to Americans' increasing willingness to talk about their experiences of sexual victimization—a willingness encouraged by the #MeToo movement (see below)—rather than to an actual increase in the crime rate. In other words, the lower rate in earlier years is likely to have been an underestimate.

Although the circumstances of sexual assault vary greatly, what is common to most such crimes is their severe effects on the women or men who experience them. These effects are illustrated by first-person accounts of rape (**BOX 16.1**).

## Most sexual assaults are not reported

According to the NCVS, fewer than one in three rapes and sexual assaults are reported to the police. This is considerably lower than the rate for violent crimes in general. Reporting rates are highest when the perpetrators are strangers and lowest when they are current or former spouses or partners. Victims who do not report rapes most frequently give one of the following reasons:

- It was a personal matter.
- They were afraid of reprisals.
- They wanted to protect the perpetrator.
- They believed the police were biased or would do nothing.
- In addition, LGBT victims of sexual assault may be hesitant to report crimes that occur within the community that is their main source of support.

---

*Because "lifetime" meant "up until the interview," the overall lifetime experiences would likely be higher.

## BOX 16.1
## It Happened to Me

Rape is a horrific experience for the victim, regardless of the exact circumstances of the rape or the level of violence involved. Here we present three accounts by rape survivors. The first account, by "Steph," describes the most common form of rape: male-on-female acquaintance rape that includes the involvement of alcohol or drugs (Survive-UK, 2001):

*The girl invited me to a party that her friends were having. So I went there with her. I met the girls having the party, and they seemed very nice. I started talking to a guy who seemed to be a few years older than me. He was very nice and polite. Maybe I should have seen it coming.*

*I had a boyfriend at the time, so I just talked to him with only intentions of friendship. To make this story shorter, I ended up in a room with him. I have no idea how. He ended up touching me and removing quite a bit of my clothing. I struggled and I cried the whole time. He took off his pants as well. Then he tried to go inside of me, which he succeeded at. But to be very blunt, it was only a few thrusts of going in and out. It was all so horrible and hurt so much. I ended up getting out from underneath of him. Not quite sure how. He apologized as I ran out of the room very quickly.*

*Since I was a virgin at the time, I think I lost my virginity to him. However, it might sound silly, but I do not consider that to be very true. I consider it to be the time with my boyfriend now. In my head I have a definition of losing virginity that involves love. What he did to me did not contain any love.*

Male-on-male rape can happen in prison, as well as elsewhere. Here is an account by "Taz" (Just Detention International, 2014):

*Two of the "homies" that I use to be tight with come by my building and ask me to take a walk. I didn't think nothing of it so I went and we landed up at one of their cells. One of the dudes leaves and blocks the door from the outside. The other one starts telling me to give him head and I tell him I don't get down that way. That just because I'm gay doesn't mean I'll have sex with everyone. So he gets mad and punches me in the stomach. I lose my wind and before I can catch my breath I'm laying face down on the bottom bunk with lotion and grease between my ass and I'm being sexually violated. I blackout from the pain and not wanting to feel anything. . . .*

UC Berkeley student Sofie Karasek breaks down as she testifies in 2013 at the California State Legislature about her experience of campus sexual assault. Karasek later cofounded the organization End Rape on Campus.

*Department of Corrections did a mock investigation that lasted about 10 days. Then I went in front of the committee who basically said I was making things up just like all the gays do. We have sex with people then cry rape. I was so mad I wanted to strangle everyone in the room. I had to deal with nightmares and sleepless nights right after the incident. I even tried to commit suicide by overdose.*

The third account is by a woman who was raped by three lesbians (Experience Project, 2014):

*After a while one of them said it was now my turn to pleasure them. I said I didn't want to, & that's when the mood changed! Two of them dragged me onto the floor on my back & held me down while the other sat on my face & ground her pussy hard against my mouth. I struggled but they were too strong & too determined. they each took turns on my face, the others holding me down all the while, then one of them let go of me & moved away. I couldn't see what she was doing, but suddenly I felt my legs being forced apart & raised up. Then she was between my thighs & I felt something being pushed into my vagina—to my horror, she was wearing a "strap on" dildo—quite a big one—and she was fucking me. . . . The more they raped me, the more I struggled. Eventually I passed out, and when I came to sometime later, I was alone on the floor, naked.*

Although this should go without saying, none of the incidents recounted in this chapter represent characteristic sexual behavior by any group, whether male or female, straight or gay.

© Max Whittaker/Prime Collective

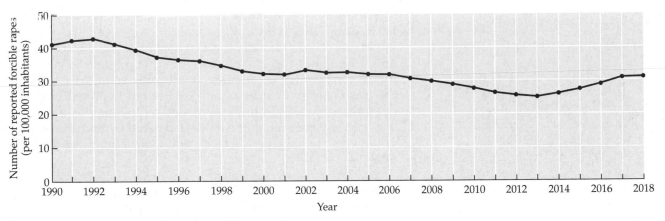

**▲ FIGURE 16.1   U.S. rape rates, 1990 to 2016**
This graph shows the number of reported forcible rapes per 100,000 inhabitants, based on FBI statistics. In 2013 the FBI changed its definition of rape from vaginal penetration only to the expanded definition given in Section 16.1. This had the effect of increasing total numbers by about 30%, but all figures shown here are based on the earlier definition in order to illustrate trends over time. (After Disaster Center. 2019. *United States Crime Rates 1960–2018*. Accessed via http://tinyurl.com/qtj24. Data from Bureau of Justice Statistics. 2005. *Crime in the United States 1960–2004* and Federal Bureau of Investigation. 2019. *Crime in the United States 2018*. U.S. Department of Justice: Washington, D.C.)

Most rape prevention organizations encourage people who have been sexually assaulted to report the crimes. They believe that doing so can help the victims regain a sense of control and can reduce the likelihood that the perpetrators will offend again. Even if they are not prosecuted, the fact that their names are on file with the university or police can facilitate their prosecution for later offenses. Still, the decision to report or not report any sexual assault is a deeply personal one that only victims can make for themselves.

Although police statistics miss many sexual assaults, they are useful for evaluating long-term trends. There has been a slow decline in the incidence of reported rapes since a peak in 1980, followed by a rise since 2014 (**FIGURE 16.1**).

## 16.2  Sexual Assaults in College Are Becoming Less Common

### LEARNING OBJECTIVES
After reading this section you should be able to:

16.2.1  Explain the "cold-to-hot empathy gap" as it relates to college sexual assault.

16.2.2  Evaluate the reasons why fraternity members and athletes are responsible for a disproportionate share of college sexual assaults.

16.2.3  Analyze the political and legal controversy about the application of Title IX to college sexual misconduct.

16.2.4  Explain incapacitated rape and the substances used to perpetrate it.

In the American College Health Association's 2019 survey, 13% of female undergraduate students said they had experienced some form of nonconsensual sexual contact in the course of the previous 12 months, and 3.0% said they had been raped. Male students reported significant but lower rates of sexual victimization (**TABLE 16.2**). Members of racial, sexual, and gender minorities report higher rates of victimization than other students, and "double minorities" are especially at risk: Five out of the nine black trans students surveyed between 2011 and 2013 said that they had been sexually assaulted within the previous 12 months (Coulter et al., 2017).

**TABLE 16.2** Sexual assaults in college

| Type of nonconsensual act | Female (%) | Male (%) |
|---|---|---|
| Sexual touching | 13 | 4 |
| Attempted sexual penetration | 5 | 1 |
| Sexual penetration | 3 | 1 |

*Source*: American College Health Association. 2019. *National College Health Assessment II Reference Group Data Report–Spring 2019*. American College Health Association: Silver Spring, MD.

*Note*: This table shows the percentages of U.S. undergraduate students who said they had experienced nonconsensual sexual acts in the previous 12 months.

Some studies have come up with higher figures. In one study led by Kate Carey of Brown University, for example, 28% of incoming female college students said that they had already experienced an attempted or completed rape, and that number rose to 37% by the start of their sophomore year (Carey et al., 2015). Part of the reason for differences among studies has to do with varying definitions of rape. In the Brown study, for example, a woman was said to have been raped if she had been "overwhelmed with arguments" to have sex—a tactic that would not meet the legal definition of rape.

Disturbing though the statistics are, sexual violence against college students dropped by about half from the mid-1990s to 2016, according to NCVS data (Bureau of Justice Statistics, 2017). And there is nothing about being in college that makes sexual assault especially likely. In fact, in the NCVS surveys, female college students were significantly *less* likely to say they had been sexually assaulted than women of the same age who were not college students.

Some sexual assaults on college students take place off campus and are perpetrated by nonstudents, perhaps by strangers. Nevertheless, most occur on campus—more specifically, after 6 PM in the victim's own residence. Most victims know the perpetrator, who is usually a classmate, friend, ex-boyfriend, current boyfriend, or acquaintance. Thus, many of these crimes could be described as "acquaintance rapes" or "date rapes," although the rapes may occur in the context of hookups rather than traditional dates. About one in five campus rapes involve additional injuries, such as bruises and cuts.

A phenomenon that contributes to date rape in a college setting as much as elsewhere is what has been called the "cold-to-hot empathy gap." This means that as people become sexually aroused, they become more strongly motivated to consummate their desire, and they pay less attention to moral issues such as consideration for the interests of the other person. This effect parallels the effect of sexual arousal on people's willingness to risk acquiring or transmitting sexually transmitted infections (STIs), as described in Chapter 15.

The cold-to-hot empathy gap was strikingly demonstrated in a study by Dan Ariely of Duke University and George Loewenstein of Carnegie Mellon University (Ariely & Loewenstein, 2006). These researchers had male students answer questions about their likely sexual behavior in a range of situations. The questions were asked while the students were in two different states: while they were in a normal unaroused state ("cold"), and while they were highly aroused sexually through masturbation and viewing of erotic images ("hot"). The men expressed a greater interest in a diverse range of sexual options, and a greater willingness to take morally questionable steps to obtain sex, when they were aroused than when they were not (**FIGURE 16.2**). Thus, it appears that people—college men at least—are not aware while "cold" of how much their decision making may change when they are "hot."

▲ An acquaintance rape–prevention workshop at Hobart College, New York.

© Bob Mahoney/Time Life Pictures/Getty Images

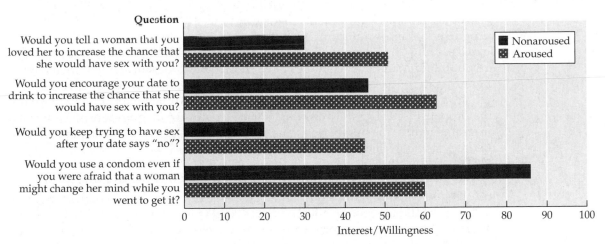

**Question**

Would you tell a woman that you loved her to increase the chance that she would have sex with you?

Would you encourage your date to drink to increase the chance that she would have sex with you?

Would you keep trying to have sex after your date says "no"?

Would you use a condom even if you were afraid that a woman might change her mind while you went to get it?

■ Nonaroused
▨ Aroused

Interest/Willingness
(0  10  20  30  40  50  60  70  80  90  100)

▲ **FIGURE 16.2** **In the heat of the night** This bar graph shows the averaged responses of 35 male (presumably heterosexual) college students to a series of computer-generated questions, while they were unaroused and again while they were highly sexually aroused by masturbation and viewing of erotic images. For each question the participant could place a cursor anywhere from 0 (no) to 100 (yes). These are four examples from a larger set of questions. (Data from D. Ariely and G. Loewenstein. 2006. *J Behav Decis Mak* 19: 87–98.)

## Many college sexual assaults are committed by fraternity members and athletes

Male students who join fraternities are three times more likely to commit sexual assaults than those who do not, according to two studies (Loh et al., 2005; Foubert et al., 2007). Fraternity members were no more likely than non-members to have committed sexual assaults *before* entering college, suggesting that the culture of some fraternities encourages sexual assault in a variety of ways. These may include demands for the display of what is thought to be traditional masculinity, an emphasis on alcohol consumption, and the inculcation of "rape myths." An example of such myths is the belief that a woman's refusal to have sex is actually a ploy intended to encourage more forceful advances. This particular myth came to nationwide attention in 2010, when members of Yale University's Delta Kappa Epsilon fraternity marched to the Women's Center chanting "No means Yes" (and worse) (Korn, 2010). The University imposed a 5-year partial ban on DKE activities—which was largely ineffective, however (Park, 2019).

Members of collegiate sports teams have an unenviable record as perpetrators of sexual violence. In 2017, for example, rape or attempted rape charges were brought against football players at the University of South Dakota, Oregon State University, Ohio State University, the University of Memphis, Cerritos College, and Wheaton College. Many studies have reported that male college athletes are more likely to commit sexual assaults than non-athlete men, but the size of the difference has varied between studies and also with the exact form of coercion that was specified (**TABLE 16.3**). The increased likelihood of committing sexual assault is true both for members of intercollegiate teams and for recreational athletes (Young et al., 2017). The higher rate of coercive behaviors by athletes is due to higher alcohol consumption, socialization to the "jock" culture (i.e., peer group pressure), and selection for aggressive personalities (Sonderland et al., 2014). Another factor may be the sense of entitlement that goes with athletes' celebrity status.

**TABLE 16.3** Sexual coercion by college athletes and non-athletes

| Type of behavior | Athletes (%) | Nonathletes (%) |
|---|---|---|
| I insisted on sex when my partner did not want to (but did not use physical force) | 32.3 | 26.8 |
| I used threats to make my partner have sex | 9.7 | 0 |
| I used force (like hitting, holding down, or using a weapon) to make my partner have sex | 9.7 | 1.1 |

*Source*: B.-R. Young et al. 2017. *Violence Against Women* 23: 795–812.
*Note*: This table shows the percentages of athletes and nonathletes at an NCAA Division I university who said they had engaged in the stated behaviors at least once in their lifetimes.

In spite of the well-documented associations mentioned above, it's important to recognize that most fraternity members and college athletes have not committed sexual assaults and are unlikely to do so in the future. What's more, the associations are not immutable: Several studies have shown that programs to help members of higher-risk groups reject rape myths and feel more empathy toward women can reduce their propensity to commit coercive sexual acts (Foubert et al., 2007). Usually this propensity is assessed by students' answers to survey questions; whether the programs reduce the number of actual assaults is less clear—some experts believe that they do not (Malamuth et al., 2018).

## Colleges must balance the rights of the accuser and the accused

In 2011 the Obama administration issued guidelines that forcefully reminded colleges of their obligation to protect students from sexual violence under Title IX, the federal law that prohibits gender discrimination in schools receiving federal funding (U.S. Department of Education, 2011). Among other things, the guidelines instructed college administrations to use a "preponderance of the evidence" criterion in judging sexual misconduct cases; this is the lowest standard of proof, requiring only that it is more likely than not that the assault occurred. It also allowed colleges to bar the accused from being represented by a lawyer or from cross-examining the accuser.

The new policies were widely challenged. In 2014, for example, 28 Harvard Law School professors demanded that the school's sexual misconduct policy be rescinded, claiming that the new procedures were overwhelmingly stacked against the accused (Bartholet, 2014). In 2016 a federal court ruled that an accused student was denied due process, citing among other things the low standard of proof used in the case (Shatz, 2016).

The Trump administration rescinded the Obama-era rules and proposed new rules regarding sexual misconduct cases, which were finalized in May 2020 (U.S. Department of Education, 2020). These offered greater protections to students accused of sexual misconduct, including the requirement for live hearings at which the complainant can be cross-examined by an advisor or attorney for the accused. In addition, the rules allow (but do not require) schools to raise the standard of proof to the next level, which is "clear and convincing proof," as well as allowing accused students to have legal representation at hearings. The rules potentially benefit the victims of sexual misconduct too, by providing them with other options such as mediation, restorative justice, or dropping the case, none of which were allowed under the earlier rules (Mott, 2018). They also protect complainants from retaliation, even if the outcome of the case is in favor of the accused. Although the new rules now have the force of law rather than simply being guidelines, their legality could be the subject of further litigation, and they could be modified or reversed by future administrations, subject to Congressional approval.

Speaking of litigation, colleges risk being sued if the college's action or inaction facilitated a sexual assault. A student at Utah State University, for example, received a payout of $250,000 on account of a rape by another student; according to her allegation, five other women had reported sexual assaults by the same man to college authorities prior to her rape (United Educators, 2019). If the assaults are by college faculty or staff the payouts are likely to be much larger: In 2019 the University of Southern California reached a $250 million settlement with women who alleged sexual mistreatment by a gynecologist at USC's student health center. In 2018 Michigan State University agreed to pay $500 million to women and girls sexually abused by gymnastics team doctor Larry Nassar. Nassar is currently serving a 175-year prison sentence (Smith, 2019).

College hookups are inherently risky situations in which date rape can readily occur. In fact, it is not always easy to distinguish between a consensual hookup and a rape, because in real-world hookups, "consent" is often expressed not verbally but by a sequence of actions and inactions whose meanings may be difficult to interpret, especially if alcohol is involved. Without wishing to minimize the responsibility of

**FAQ:** I didn't fight back—will people blame me?

People understand that rape victims' main concern is to survive. Rapists can be successfully prosecuted without evidence that the victim fought back, even when no weapon was involved.

(A)

© Loop Images Ltd/Alamy

(B)

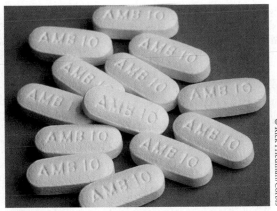

© Rick Friedman/Corbis

◀ Alcohol (A) is a far more widely used date rape drug than Ambien (B) or other chemicals.

rape perpetrators in any circumstances, we emphasize that women (and men) can best protect themselves from date rape by avoiding situations in which sexual interactions can get out of control—which often means situations in which one or both parties have been drinking heavily.

We also urge both women and men to express in words their desire or unwillingness to engage in specific sexual acts, rather than relying on ambiguous body language. Far from spoiling the atmosphere, a quick "Would you like to go down on me?" or "Yes, I'd like to have sex with you—if you use a condom" builds trust and intimacy.

## The number one "date rape drug" is alcohol

In recent years, a lot of attention has been paid to the role of drugs or alcohol in facilitating date rape (Office on Women's Health, 2013). Such rapes are termed **incapacitated rapes**, and they are very common. In the Brown University study mentioned earlier, 83% of the rapes were said to have been incapacitated rapes.

Among the drugs that have been used by rapists to incapacitate their victims are flunitrazepam (Rohypnol, a Valium-type tranquilizer), gamma-hydroxybutyrate (GHB, a central nervous system depressant), the veterinary anesthetic ketamine, and the sleep aid zolpidem (Ambien). The misuse of Ambien came to public attention in 2014 when former New Orleans Saints safety Darren Sharper faced five rape or sexual assault charges in California, Louisiana, and Arizona: Sharper was alleged to have used Ambien to facilitate at least some of these rapes. In 2016 he was sentenced to 20 years in prison (Associated Press, 2016b).

In contrast to the relatively infrequent use of the above-mentioned drugs, alcohol is a very common factor in facilitating sexual assault and rape (Bliss, 2013). In one analysis, nearly 3 million women in the United States had been victims of rapes in which the rapists gave their victims alcohol or other drugs with the intention of facilitating rape. Another 3 million women drank heavily of their own accord, and men took advantage of their self-incapacitated state to rape them (Kilpatrick & Resnick, 2013). The very fact that a woman is drinking is sometimes interpreted as a signal that she wants sex, according to an experimental study of college men and women (Maurer & Robinson, 2008). In reality, however, the more alcohol a woman

**incapacitated rape**  Rape in which the victim was unable to resist on account of intoxication by alcohol or drugs.

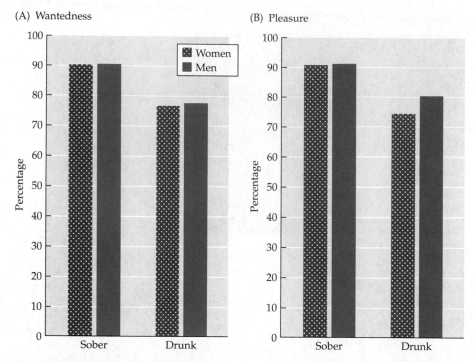

**▲ FIGURE 16.3 Alcohol and sex** (A) Wantedness: These bar graphs show the percentages of male and female college undergraduates who described their most recent sexual encounter as "very much" or "moderately" wanted, where both partners were sober or drunk. (B) Pleasure: These bar graphs show the percentages of students who described their most recent sexual encounter as "extremely," "quite a bit," or "moderately" pleasurable. Encounters where just one partner was drunk (not shown) were rated similarly to those in which both were drunk. The data are based on 7000 replies to a survey of undergraduate students at Indiana University. (After D. Herbenick et al. 2019. *J Am Coll Health* 67: 144–162.)

has consumed, the less a man is entitled to take anything she says or fails to say as conveying her consent to sex.

Of course, alcohol also promotes rape when consumed by the rapist—by reducing his inhibitions. One half of all sexual assaults are committed by perpetrators who are under the influence of alcohol (Abbey & Ortiz, 2008). It's not just that men who happen to be drinking are more likely to rape. Rather, men often drink with the conscious intent of facilitating sexual behaviors that they would not engage in otherwise (Cowley, 2014). All in all, alcohol is certainly the number one "date rape drug," whether consumed by the rapist or the victim. The fact that alcohol is so often involved should not cause us to excuse rapists or blame victims: It is simply a fact that everyone needs to be aware of.

Although alcohol is often involved in sexual assaults, most college students—both men and women— recall their sexual encounters as both wanted and pleasurable even if they were drunk at the time, according to a large survey of students at the University of Indiana (Herbenick et al., 2019) (**FIGURE 16.3**). Thus the fact that one or both partners were drunk doesn't by itself mean that sex was traumatic in any way, according to the subjective assessment of the participants. College policies that equate *all* drunken sex with sexual assault are therefore unrealistic, according to the Indiana researchers. Still, sex while sober is both safer—less risk of STIs, pregnancy, or legal consequences—and more meaningful.

## 16.3 Sexual Assault Can Have Severe Effects on the Victim

### LEARNING OBJECTIVES
After reading this section you should be able to:

16.3.1 Explain the appropriate steps that should be taken in the aftermath of a sexual assault.

16.3.2 Describe the potential long-term psychological harms of sexual assault and steps that may be taken to aid recovery.

Women can take many steps to reduce the likelihood that they will be raped or sexually assaulted (**BOX 16.2**). If a woman does experience such an event, however, many options and services are available to help her, speed her recovery, and reduce the long-lasting psychological harm that rape may cause.

### Services are available for rape victims

The first and foremost step toward recovery is getting medical attention. The best place for this is an emergency room or a specialized forensic clinic, in which the staff

## BOX 16.2
# Reducing the Risk of Sexual Assault

In a just world, neither women nor men would have to think about the risk of sexual assault when going about their daily lives. That is a world that we should aspire to create. In the meantime, though, it is sensible to take precautions to reduce the risks. Adopting this point of view does not reduce rapists' culpability for their crimes, nor does it constitute "victim blaming."

Many rape crisis centers and rape prevention organizations offer the following advice:

### General
- A man who has sexual contact with you against your will is committing a serious crime, no matter what his relationship to you and no matter what the circumstances. By reporting the crime, you can help prevent victimization of someone else
- Prepare yourself for "fight or flight": Take self-defense and fitness classes (see figure).

### Preventing acquaintance rape
- Until you know a man well, meet him in a group environment in which there are other women present, or in a public place.
- Consider paying your own way so that there can be no basis for "quid pro quo" thinking.
- Avoid drugs and excessive alcohol use, and take the man's use of either, or his attempts to persuade you to use them, as a warning sign. Be explicit if you don't want to have intercourse (or any kind of sex). Be assertive.
- If the man commences an assault, protest vehemently, threaten to call the police, and escape from the situation if possible or create a loud disturbance to attract attention to what he is doing.

### Preventing stranger rape
- Make your home secure. If you are a woman living alone, do not make that fact obvious. Do not open the door to strangers.
- Keep your car doors locked whether you are inside or outside of the car. Park where it will be safe for you to return—think about what the environment will be like after dark. Avoid deserted or ill-lit places. Never pick up hitchhikers or hitchhike yourself.
- If you jog, etc., do it with friends or at times and places that other people are doing the same.

Learning to resist sexual assault.

- If you find yourself in a threatening situation, run away. If that's not possible, resist forcefully. Fighting and creating a loud disturbance are more effective than pleading or offering no resistance.
- Carry an alarm device such as an air horn. If you carry any kind of weapon, be sure you know how to use it and how to prevent it from being used against you. Know what the law is: Generally, a person who is in imminent danger of rape may legally inflict whatever injury is necessary to prevent it, but no more than that.

### If you become a victim of a sexual assault
- Whether or not there was a completed rape, call the police or go to an emergency room immediately or call 1-800-656-HOPE, the National Sexual Assault Telephone Hotline.
- Do not shower, wash, douche, urinate, change your clothes, eat, drink, or clean up the location of the assault before you go—you may be destroying evidence. Take a change of clothes with you.
- If the assailant was a stranger, try to remember his appearance and clothes and any details, such as a car license plate number or any part of it.
- If you do not report the assault right after it happens, do so later. Consider contacting a rape crisis center, where you can get expert advice and understanding in a confidential environment.

▲ Rape crisis centers provide education, advocacy, and support to victims.

are trained in the appropriate medical and reporting procedures. A victim can also go to her own doctor, but that option may involve a delay, and the doctor might not have adequate expertise. Many colleges and rape crisis centers will provide a rape advocate—a volunteer who will accompany the victim to the hospital and provide various kinds of practical and emotional support.

Survivors of sexual assault are not legally obliged to cooperate with police inquiries or to press charges. In many communities, a woman can have a full, evidence-collecting examination and still not press charges. Thus, she can keep her options open until she is sure whether or not she wants to pursue the matter legally. (Even if she doesn't press charges, the record of her victimization may be of assistance in the prosecution of the perpetrator if he subsequently assaults another woman.) The desire not to report the crime should not prevent a woman from getting medical attention. Most states—those that receive federal funds under the 2005 Violence Against Women Act—are required to provide medical forensic exams to sexual assault victims without cost, but the billing departments at some hospitals are unaware of that requirement (Kaiser Health News, 2019).

Providers who examine rape victims must assess and treat the physical and psychological injuries that the victims have sustained. Careful assessment is important because there may be injuries of which the victim is unaware—particularly if, as is likely, she is in a state of emotional shock. Providers can assess the likelihood of pregnancy or disease transmission and suggest steps to prevent either eventuality. As described in Chapter 9, emergency contraception can be used within the 5 days after coitus to reduce the likelihood of pregnancy. Prophylaxis against STIs may include antibiotics. If there seems to be a substantial risk of HIV transmission, a short course of antiretroviral medications (post-exposure prophylaxis) might be advised.

Samples collected from the victim's body or clothing can be analyzed for DNA that might identify the perpetrator. Until recently, many of these **rape kits** were never analyzed, mostly on account of the cost. A nationwide backlog of about 250,000 kits had accumulated by around 2015, but starting in 2015 the Manhattan District Attorney's office and the federal government paid for the testing of 100,000 kits, leading to over 1000 arrests and hundreds of convictions. An example: Tracy Rios of Tempe, Arizona, was raped by a person known to her in 2002, but her rape kit remained untested for 15 years, and her case lapsed. "I lost faith in the system: I thought they didn't care," she told PBS. In 2017 her rape kit was finally tested with money from the Manhattan DA's office; this led to her rapist being convicted and given a 7-year prison sentence (PBS, 2019). Although many kits are still waiting to be tested, most jurisdictions are reducing their backlogs or have actually cleared them.

Counseling, both in the immediate aftermath of the rape and in the longer term, plays a vital role in helping "victims" of rape become "survivors." Many schools and colleges, rape crisis centers, and governmental agencies offer such counseling, which may be conducted on either an individual or a group basis.

Several organizations, including Men Can Stop Rape (see Web Resources at the end of this chapter), work to reduce rape by encouraging men to act responsibly toward women and to speak up in the face of attitudes and actions that encourage sexual aggression (**BOX 16.3**).

## Rape can inflict long-lasting harm

The effect of sexual assault is likely to extend far beyond the immediate shock or any physical injury that the victim may sustain. This is particularly true for individuals who have experienced a completed rape. Different people react to the immediate experience in different ways—some with an emotional outpouring, some with tightly controlled feelings—but all are at risk of developing the symptoms of **post-traumatic stress disorder** (**PTSD**). (In the context of sexual assault, this may be called "rape

**rape kit** Samples collected from a rape victim's body or clothing for the purpose of identifying the perpetrator.

**post-traumatic stress disorder (PTSD)** A cluster of persistent physical and psychological symptoms seen in victims of catastrophic events, such as sexual assault or other violence.

## BOX 16.3
## Ways Men Can Prevent Sexual Violence

The following action agenda, compiled by Men Can Stop Rape, is reproduced here by permission.

### Be Bold

- **Define your own manhood.** Consider how common messages such as "don't take no for an answer" play a role in creating unhealthy and unsafe relationships. Choose what kind of man you want to be.

- **Understand from a female's perspective.** Ask a woman you know how often and in what situations she has feared being sexually assaulted. How has this affected her daily life? Does she know someone who has been assaulted? How has it affected her? Listen and learn.

- **Get a guy's perspective.** Ask a friend—how would it feel to be viewed as a potential rapist? How would he react if a woman or girl in his life—his mother, a sister, a girlfriend, or a friend—was sexually assaulted?

- **Take note of pop culture's messages.** Daily, we're surrounded by movies, TV shows, magazines, and video games that sometimes communicate harmful messages about masculinity and relationships. Ask how images in popular culture affect how you view yourself and women.

- **Pledge to be a man of strength.** Don't ever have sex with anyone against their will. Pledge to be a man whose strength is used for respect, and not for hurting others.

- **Support survivors of rape.** Rape will not be taken seriously until everyone knows how common it is. By learning to sensitively support survivors in their lives, men can help

Poster created by Men Can Stop Rape.

both women and other men feel safer to speak out about being raped and let the world know how serious a problem rape is.

### Be Strong

- **Talk it over first.** Create a space to speak honestly about sex: Listen to your partner, state your desires openly, and ask questions if a situation seems unclear.

- **If drunk or high, wait for consent.** If your partner is drunk or high and can't give consent, back off and wait until you both are ready to enthusiastically say yes.

### Take Action

- **Choose your words carefully.** When you put down women, you support the belief that they are less than human. It is easier to ignore a woman's decisions or well-being if she is seen as inferior. Choose respectful language.

- **Stand up.** You will probably never see a rape in progress, but you will hear attitudes and see behaviors that degrade women and promote a culture of violence. When your friend tells a rape joke, let him know it's not funny.

- **Get involved.** Join or donate to an organization working to prevent violence against women. Rape crisis centers, domestic violence agencies, and men's anti-rape groups count on donations for their survival and always need volunteers to share the workload.

---

trauma syndrome.") The symptoms may include feelings of numbness or disconnection, alternating with flashbacks and preoccupation with the assault; irrational self-blame; anxiety, depression, or anger; sleeplessness; inability to concentrate; and physical symptoms such as headaches and digestive disturbances.

In the first 2 weeks after the assault, 94% of women have symptoms of PTSD, and 46% still exhibit symptoms at 3 months after the event. Even several years later, women who have been sexually assaulted are at increased risk of depression, anxiety, and substance dependency. Not surprisingly, women who have been raped often experience sexual problems, including lack of physiological arousal (especially lubrication) and pain on intercourse, as well as more general problems with pelvic function, such as vestibulodynia (pain when touched in the area of the vestibule—see Chapter 14), urinary tract problems, and irritable bowel syndrome (Postma et al., 2013).

Many forms of help can facilitate a rape victim's psychological recovery. Partners, family, and friends can offer practical and emotional support by such steps as the following:

- Offer a place to stay.
- Be willing to listen in a loving and nonjudgmental fashion.
- Accept the victim's account of what happened.
- Emphasize that the rape was not the victim's fault.
- Give the rape survivor time and space to make her own decisions about how to deal with the situation.

Various forms of therapy can be used to prevent or treat the psychological harms caused by sexual assault (Gilmore et al., 2018). Rather than general supportive counseling, cognitive methods show the best results. An example is **prolonged exposure (PE) therapy**. In this approach, the client recalls the traumatic event in a safe and supportive environment, usually in combination with relaxation techniques, such as breathing exercises, to counteract negative emotions. The procedure for recall entails not just remembering the event but describing it aloud to the therapist in as vivid detail as possible, and this is done repeatedly over a series of sessions, as well as in the form of "homework" between sessions. In addition to this imagined re-exposure, the client is encouraged to experience real-life re-exposure—not to the assault, obviously, but to circumstances associated with it that may trigger painful emotions. Best results are obtained if PE therapy is begun within hours of the assault, and some emergency rooms and rape crisis centers have staff trained to provide such treatment. In general, cognitive treatments such as this one benefit about two-thirds of the people who undergo them.

It's useful to bear two points in mind. First, recovery from rape, as from other traumatic events, does not occur overnight, whatever therapeutic measures are undertaken. Second, most people who have experienced rape or sexual assault are eventually able to recover, think of themselves as survivors rather than victims, and get on with their lives.

## Male victims have special concerns

Regarding female-on-male victimization, narrowly defined rape (physically forced coitus) is uncommon, but it does sometimes occur when the man already has an erection and the women forces him to penetrate her, or when the man develops an erection in the course of a sexual assault (CDC, 2011a). The fact that a man develops an erection does not mean that he wants to have sex, but it may cause him to feel an irrational guilt about the event. This is illustrated by the following account of an attempted female-on-male rape (Fogg, 2013):

> When I was at a student party, . . . a very drunk (and physically rather large) woman came on to me, very strongly indeed. I tried to escape with a tactical toilet break. She followed me, forced me up against the basin, pushed her tongue into my mouth and her hand into my jeans. I had to summon up quite a lot of physical strength to escape. This may sound strange, but my understanding of the incident, then and now, was not that I had narrowly escaped being raped by her, but that she had narrowly escaped being raped by me. When her hand grasped my cock it reacted and for a moment I considered letting her have her wish.

More commonly, a woman may engage in coitus or other forms of sexual contact with a man without violence but without his consent—as, for example, when he is incapacitated by alcohol or drugs or is underage.

There are many similarities between men's and women's experiences of sexual victimization, but there are also some differences. Men (or male youths) who have

**prolonged exposure (PE) therapy** A form of extended psychotherapy for victims of rape or abuse in which they are encouraged to recall the traumatic event in a safe environment.

been sexually assaulted by women may experience little support or understanding from their peers, who may treat the matter as a joke. Male victims may believe that rape crisis centers, medical staff, therapists, and the legal system are all geared toward seeing males as perpetrators and thus are not likely to be sympathetic or helpful to male victims. Oftentimes this belief is false, because professionals who deal with sexual assault are familiar with the fact that men can be victimized. Even if false, however, this belief tends to inhibit male victims from obtaining the help they need. In addition, men may feel guilty about being sexually assaulted, because they feel they have violated an ethic of masculinity.

Rapes of males in prisons are something of a special case, not only because they are mostly committed by other males, but because they involve considerations of power as well as sex. Historically, prison authorities have not taken effective steps to prevent prison rape or to punish offenders. This changed somewhat with the passage in 2003 of the Prison Rape Elimination Act, which authorized funds for programs to study the problem and reduce its prevalence. While male-on-male prison rape does occur, it is not as widespread as people often imagine: In one survey, just 1.7% of male inmates of U.S. prisons (as well as 6.9% of female inmates) said that they had been sexually victimized by other inmates within the previous 12 months (Bureau of Justice Statistics, 2013b).

### Sexual, gender, and some racial minorities experience greater risk

Non-heterosexual men and women experience more sexual victimization than those who are straight (Bureau of Justice Statistics, 2016). In the NISVS, bisexual women and men reported the highest rates of sexual victimization; gay men were also victimized more often than heterosexual men (CDC, 2013b) (**FIGURE 16.4**). The difference between reported victimization rates for lesbian and heterosexual women was not significant. A very similar pattern was found in a large survey of college students (Coulter et al., 2017).

In the just-mentioned college survey, transgender people reported higher rates of victimization than cisgender people. Black students reported higher rates than white students, whereas Asian and Hispanic students reported lower rates. Students belonging to more than one minority were at especially high risk: For example, black trans students were exposed to a calculated 58% risk of being sexually victimized within a single year, as compared with a less than 3% risk for Asian-Pacific cisgender men.

Trans women are at greater risk than trans men (Kenagy, 2005). Most trans victims report that homophobia or transphobia was the motivation for the assault. "In my neighborhood, either they want to beat you up or they want a free blow job," said an interviewee in one survey (Bockting, 1998). To make matters worse, transgender people, especially those who belong to racial minorities or are immigrants, do not always receive culturally competent care from rape crisis programs (Seelman, 2015).

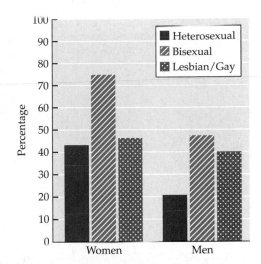

▲ **FIGURE 16.4 Sexual assault and sexual orientation** This bar graph shows the percentages of heterosexual, bisexual, and gay or lesbian adults who reported having experienced sexual violence at least once in their lifetime. "Violence" included noncontact events such as nonconsensual exposure to a person's genitals. (Data from M. L. Walters et al. 2013. *The National Intimate Partner and Sexual Violence Survey (NISVS): 2010 findings on victimization by sexual orientation*. National Center for Injury Prevention and Control, Centers for Disease Control and Prevention: Atlanta, GA.)

## 16.4 Rape Laws Have Become More Protective of Victims

### LEARNING OBJECTIVES

After reading this section you should be able to:

16.4.1 Explain the most important provision of rape shield laws.

16.4.2 State the approximate proportions of sexual assault reports that lead to arrests, of arrests that lead to convictions, and of convictions that incur prison sentences, as well as the percentage of rape allegations that are found to be false.

As recently as the 18th century, women in Western societies were considered the property of men, and rape of women was considered an offense against men—against the woman's father if she was unmarried or against her husband if she was

**rape shield laws**   Laws that protect rape victims—for example, by limiting the introduction of evidence about their prior sexual behavior.

married (Geddes & Lueck, 2000). A woman who was raped lost value, was shamed, and brought shame on her family. Thus, her kinsfolk might reject her, in addition to seeking vengeance on the rapist. These ideas persist in some traditional patriarchal societies. In Pakistan there have even been incidents in which village courts have ordered that a young woman be raped as punishment for an earlier rape of a different woman committed by her brother, the motivation being to bring shame on her brother's entire family (CNN, 2017b).

In India, an estimated 99% of rapes go unreported to the police, because a survivor often expects the police to do nothing or to further traumatize her in a variety of ways (Changoiwala, 2019). Nevertheless, public outcry in the wake of some recent atrocities—gang rapes involving torture and murder—have spurred a movement for justice reform and greater social awareness of the problem.

U.S. law inherited from English common law the concept of a "marital exemption" to rape, meaning that it was not rape for a man to force sex on his wife. The thinking was that the wife had given consent to sex by virtue of her marriage vows and could not retract it. Marital rape did not become a crime in all U.S. states until 1993. Even today, many states allow a man to have sex with his wife in circumstances that would constitute *statutory* rape if it took place between unmarried persons, such as when the wife is unconscious, mentally impaired, or underage. (In some states, youths can marry below the age of consent—usually with parental or court permission.)

As an informal extension of the marital exemption, the legal system used to be quite forgiving of rapes that occurred between cohabiting or socially acquainted couples, rapes of dates or pickups, or rapes of prostitutes. The women in these circumstances were viewed as having voluntarily placed themselves at the man's disposal. Simply demonstrating that the victim was of "unchaste character" was often enough to get the rape charges reduced or to secure an acquittal. Evidence that the victim used contraceptives even though unmarried, that she frequented bars, or that she had a reputation as a promiscuous woman might be introduced for this purpose. In other words, rape laws were used primarily to protect "women of virtue"—women who either were virgins or were married to someone other than the perpetrator.

## Reforms began in the 1970s

The women's movement brought about many significant changes in the ways in which the legal system and the general public view rape. Beginning in the 1970s, **rape shield laws** were introduced. These laws protect rape victims in a number of ways, most notably by preventing the alleged perpetrator from introducing evidence about the victim's prior sexual history. In other words, the defendant can no longer escape from legal penalty by painting the victim as a "slut." In some cases these laws have ruled that courts can prohibit public identification of the victim; such provisions have been struck down by the courts, but in general the media do now respect victims' privacy.

Laws have also been modified to introduce a range of sexual offenses in addition to rape as traditionally defined. These offenses are called "sexual battery," "sexual assault," "forcible or aggravated sodomy," and the like. The definitions of such offenses vary considerably from state to state. The key point is that it is no longer necessary to prove that coitus occurred, which makes it easier to obtain convictions in many cases—although the sentences are often much lighter than for a rape conviction. In addition, it is no longer necessary in many states to prove that the victim physically resisted the rape or assault, nor is it necessary to provide corroborating evidence from third parties.

## What happens to men who rape?

Since the majority of rapes are not reported to law enforcement officials, we can assume that the majority of rapists go unpunished. In 2018, reported rapes in the United States totaled 139,000, and there were 25,000 rape arrests, so even when a rape is reported, the chances that this will lead to an arrest for rape are not high (FBI, 2019) (Some reports lead to arrests on lesser charges.)

About half of all men arrested for rape are convicted (usually of felony rape)—most, after a guilty plea. Over two-thirds of convicted defendants receive a prison sentence; the average term is 14 years. Convicted rapists typically serve about half of their prison terms before release. At any one time, about 165,000 people—86% of them male—are incarcerated in state prisons for rape or sexual assault (Bureau of Justice Statistics, 2019b).

Some rape reports are false, of course. After investigation, about 5% of rape reports are found to be false, and some unknown further percentage are equivocal—it's not clear whether they are false or not (Ferguson & Malouff, 2016). This suggests that false rape allegations are neither common nor especially rare. Documented motives for false rape allegations include revenge, regret at having consented to sex, desire for sympathy or attention, need for an alibi (e.g., for an illicit affair that has been discovered), material gain (e.g., to dispose of a rival for a promotion), and mental illness (O'Neal et al., 2014; De Zutter et al., 2018). When one considers the devastating consequences a rape conviction can have for the accused person, the need for caution in evaluating rape allegations should be clear.

The fact that a woman retracts a rape allegation or refuses to cooperate with an investigation does not necessarily mean that her initial allegation was false. There are several reasons why a woman may retract a true rape allegation; we revisit this issue in the context of intimate partner violence (see Section 16.7).

In a further illustration of the difficulty of fairly adjudicating these cases, it can also happen that a woman who was found to have made an untrue rape allegation—and who was convicted of filing a false police report—is later proven to have been raped in exactly the way that she initially claimed (Armstrong & Miller, 2017). The risk that actual rape victims may be disbelieved and even prosecuted is a factor in why many victims are reluctant to report the crimes in the first place.

## Repeat offending is common

According to a study by the U.S. Department of Justice, about 8% of people who spend time in state prisons for rape or sexual assault are arrested for another rape or sexual assault within 9 years of their release, and 67% are arrested for any offense (Bureau of Justice Statistics, 2019c). These figures are lower than those for non-sexual assault, where the corresponding numbers are 44% for another non-sexual assault and 83% for any offense.

By themselves, this statistic suggests that rape is a sporadic crime that perpetrators are not especially likely to repeat. As with other crimes, however, many convicted rapists have committed more rapes than those for which they were arrested or convicted (Weinrott & Saylor, 1991). This raises the possibility that a significant fraction of all rapes are committed by repeat offenders.

An illustrative case at the college level is that of Elton Yarbrough, a 23-year-old economics major at Texas A&M University who was convicted and sentenced to 18 years in prison for a single offense: raping a female British exchange student while she was intoxicated. At his trial, however, four other women testified that he had raped them under similar circumstances (Diaz, 2010).

To study whether this kind of repeat offending is common, psychologists David Lisak and Paul Miller surveyed 1882 male college students. In total, these students admitted to having committed 483 acts that met the definition of rape or attempted rape, but 91% of these rapes were committed by just 76 men—a median of 3 rapes per man—and these men also committed many other acts of interpersonal violence (Lisak & Miller, 2002). One study reported different findings, namely that most college sexual assaults are one-time offenses (Swartout et al., 2015). Nevertheless, a recent very large multi-campus survey that looked specifically at alcohol-fueled sexual assaults found results similar to those of Lisak and Miller: 87% of such assaults were committed by serial perpetrators, who committed an average of five assaults each (Foubert et al., 2019). These findings suggest that there is a specific rapist "type," in which case identifying and prosecuting the perpetrator of a single sexual assault may avert multiple assaults in the future.

## 16.5  Why Do Men Rape?

**LEARNING OBJECTIVES**

After reading this section you should be able to:

16.5.1  Explain Malamuth's confluence model of sexual aggression.

16.5.2  Evaluate social factors that may encourage or discourage sexual assaults.

Understanding the reasons why some men rape seems like an important first step toward developing effective strategies for preventing rape. This question has been approached from a variety of different perspectives, and there is no consensus on the most important reasons.

### Rape may have evolutionary roots

Forced copulation is quite common among nonhuman animals, including some of our close primate relatives such as orangutans (Huppin et al., 2019). In some species in which forced copulation occurs, it is clearly an evolutionary adaptation; that is, the behavior has evolved because it increases the animals' reproductive success. Whether the human capacity for rape is an evolutionary adaptation has been the subject of much debate. It could have evolved simply as a by-product of selection for adaptive traits such as sexual desire and aggressiveness, which have evolved for reasons that have no direct connection with the reproductive benefits or costs of rape (Thornhill & Palmer, 2000; Dadlez et al., 2009).

Evolutionary theory is less useful to our understanding of why particular individuals commit rape and others do not. However, it has been observed in several species that males turn to rape as a secondary strategy when regular courtship is unsuccessful, which could be relevant to some cases of human rape. We discuss this topic in more detail in Appendix A.

▲ Gang rape? Five male mallard ducks attempt to copulate with one (barely visible) female.

### Some characteristics distinguish rapists from nonrapists

Researchers have focused a great deal of attention on men who commit rape. The hope is that through such study it might be possible to identify personality traits, early experiences, or other factors that predispose these men to commit their crimes.

There are no well-established biological differences between rapists and nonrapists. For example, rapists do not have higher testosterone levels than nonrapists (Wong & Gravel, 2016). There is evidence for the existence of genes that predispose men to commit sexually aggressive crimes (Langstrom et al., 2015), but the actual genes have not been identified.

Some extremely violent rapists have severe personality disorders or are driven by sadistic impulses (see Chapter 13). The majority of rapists, especially those who commit acquaintance or date rape, are fairly unremarkable people, but in a statistical sense, at least, they do differ from nonrapists. For one thing, they tend to be of lower socioeconomic status and to have had less education; this could hamper their ability to acquire voluntary sex partners and thus make rape a more attractive option, in accordance with evolutionary theory (Miller, 2014).

Rapists tend to have worse relationships with their parents, to have more self-centered personalities, and to have less capacity for **empathy**, as compared with nonrapists (Chantry & Craig, 1994; Gannon et al., 2008). These attributes are common in other criminal offenders, so they do not by themselves account for a proclivity to rape.

Neil Malamuth of UCLA and his colleagues have carried out extensive studies of men (both college students and others) to investigate factors associated with an inclination to sexual aggression (Malamuth & Hald, 2017). On the basis of their findings they proposed a "confluence model" to account for why some men commit sexual assaults while most others do not (**FIGURE 16.5**). In the model, sexual aggression manifests itself when two developmental pathways coexist. The "antisocial/impersonal sex" pathway begins with an abusive environment in the childhood home, including violence between the parents or physical or sexual abuse of the child. This then leads to delinquent behavior by the child or youth, followed by early sexual initiation and sexual promiscuity. The "hostile masculinity" pathway begins with a broadly hostile personality that allows for an acceptance of violence against women, which leads to narcissism and a tendency to be sexually aroused by the act of dominating women. When these two pathways converge in the same person, they drive sexually aggressive behavior. Even then, however, another personality factor, namely a well-developed sense of empathy, can block the expression of this behavior.

It has often been claimed that male-on-female rape is motivated by hatred of women or the desire to control them, rather than by sexual desire. The truth seems to be that either factor, or a combination of both, may trigger rape. Here are two statements by rapists about their victims that illustrate contrasting motivations, both from a period when rape was far more prevalent than it is today:

> I couldn't stand [my teacher]. I used to humiliate her. I used to hit her in the ass with paperclips because I hated her, man. (Sussman & Bordwell, 1981)

> She stood there in her nightgown, and you could see right through it—you could see her nipples and breasts, and, you know, they were just waiting for me. (Groth, 1979)

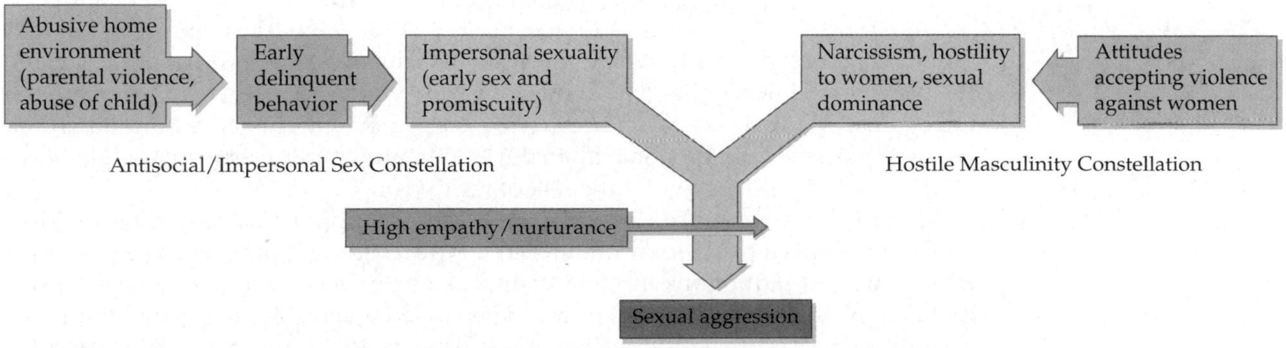

**empathy**  The ability to share or understand other people's feelings.

▲ **FIGURE 16.5  The confluence model of sexual aggression** proposes that for sexual aggression to occur, two developmental pathways must converge in the same individual. Even when they do, a sense of empathy can prevent the manifestation of aggression. (After N. M. Malamuth and G. M. Hald. 2017. In *The Wiley handbook on the theories, assessment, and treatment of sexual offending*. D. P. Boer [Ed.], Wiley: West Sussex, U.K.)

### Social forces influence the likelihood of rape

Social scientists and feminists have generally taken the view that rape is a learned behavior. Here is an expression of this point of view by Diana Russell, professor emeritus of sociology at Mills College in Oakland, California (Russell, 1984):

> *Males are trained from childhood to separate sexual desire from caring, respecting, liking or loving. One of the consequences of this training is that many men regard women as sexual objects, rather than as full human beings. . . . [This view] predisposes men to rape. Even if women were physically stronger than men, it is doubtful that there would be many instances of female rapes of males: Female sexual socialization encourages females to integrate sex, affection, and love, and to be sensitive to what their partners want.*

Here is a specific example that seems to illustrate a "culture of rape" in at least one sector of U.S. society. After the 2000 Puerto Rican Day parade in New York, a mob of men assaulted, stripped, groped, or sexually abused 50 women in Central Park. There was no intervention by police or bystanders. Some bystanders did provide videotapes to the police, but these videotapes were broadcast repeatedly on local TV stations, further traumatizing the victims. To some cultural critics, the media reaction to the event focused inappropriately on "mob psychology" and ignored the culture of sexism that permitted it to occur (Katz & Jhally, 2000).

Current feminist thinking on the topic of rape emphasizes the multiplicity of social factors that may influence the likelihood of sexual violence (Canan & Levand, 2019). These include the social and economic oppression of women; patriarchal values, including the emphasis on aggressive masculinity; class inequalities; and the intersection of sexual-, gender-, and race-based identities such as we mentioned earlier.

In the United States, social forces work not only to encourage rape but also to restrain it. One social institution, the criminal justice system, presents a major deterrence to would-be rapists. In the 2000 Puerto Rican Day case just mentioned, for example, 30 men were charged and 18 were convicted for their roles in the incident and given sentences of up to 5 years of imprisonment (Finkelstein, 2001). In many parts of the world there would have been no prosecutions in connection with an incident of this kind. The power of social controls is illustrated by what happens when they collapse, as may happen during police strikes, war, or civil unrest (**BOX 16.4**).

## 16.6  Intervention Programs Are of Uncertain Value

**LEARNING OBJECTIVE**

After reading this section you should be able to:

**16.6.1  Explain the Safe Dates program for rape prevention and how its effectiveness has been tested.**

One way to prevent sex offenders from reoffending is to keep them in prison, and the very long sentences handed down to some sex offenders—especially sex offenders against children—are designed to do exactly that. On the other hand, it would be more humane (and economical) to develop treatment programs that might allow offenders to be released with little risk of recidivism.

Many efforts have been made to develop and apply such treatments. Most employ cognitive-behavioral therapy in a group setting. Some of these programs have reported reductions in recidivism, but the effects have been small: In one meta-analysis, treatment reduced recidivism by only about 6% compared with non-treated controls (Lösel & Schmucker, 2005). Some more recent studies have reported reductions of as much as 40%, but these tend to be the less well-designed ones; the more rigorous studies that assign participants at random to treatment or control groups have found little or no treatment effect (Marshall & Marshall, 2016). In other words, the efficacy of any treatment program to prevent sex offenders from repeating their offenses remains in doubt.

## BOX 16.4
## Rape and War

Among the horrors of war and "ethnic cleansing," rape has long held a preeminent place. Rape serves to terrorize and humiliate the enemy, to reward victorious troops, and to propagate the victors' genes.

Among the most notorious users of wartime rape were the Mongols, who swept across Asia in the 13th century. After killing most of the men and children in the conquered cities, they systematically raped the women, either immediately or after enslavement. The Mongol leaders—Genghis Khan and his male relatives—always had first choice among the captured women. Thanks to this behavior, at least 16 million contemporary Asian men possess a Y chromosome inherited from Genghis Khan's family, meaning that they are descended from the Khans in an unbroken male line (Zerjal et al., 2003).

Rohingya women were raped as part of a program of ethnic cleansing by the armed forces of Myanmar in 2017.

Wartime rape was banned by the 1949 Geneva Conventions, and the systematic use of rape, as employed by the Mongols, was more recently declared an instrument of genocide (United Nations, 1994). Yet it continues. In 2017, when the armed forces of Myanmar drove the Rohingya ethnic minority out of the country, rape was one of the tools (besides murder and the burning of villages) employed in the campaign. Here is what happened to one Rohingya woman, Rashida Begum, as recounted by a CNN reporter who interviewed her in a refugee camp in Bangladesh (Abdelaziz, 2017):

*"We saw the military digging holes (for mass graves). We were five women with our babies," Rashida said, almost in a whisper. "They grabbed us, dragged us into the house, and shut the door."*

*The soldiers snatched Rashida's baby son from her arms and killed him.*

*"I just screamed, I cried but they wouldn't listen to us. They don't even understand our language," Rashida recalled.*

*The uniformed men showed her no mercy. They slit Rashida's throat and tore off her clothes. She was brutalized and raped alongside the four other women. As Rashida lost consciousness, the men set the house alight and left them for dead.*

*"I thought I was already dead, but when my skin started to burn I woke up," she said.*

*Naked and disoriented, she ran out of the flames and hid in a nearby field, but she wishes she had not survived.*

*"It would be good if I too died because if I died then I wouldn't have to remember all these things. My parents were killed too, lots of people were killed," Rashida said as tears streamed down her face.*

---

Given that sexual violence begins early, some rape prevention programs aim at adolescents who are beginning to date. A team led by Vangie Foshee of the University of North Carolina developed a program aimed at eighth-graders that they named Safe Dates. The program consisted of a 10-session curriculum, a poster competition, and a play. To test the effectiveness of the program, the researchers randomly assigned schools to receive or not receive the program. Students exposed to the program were less likely to either perpetrate or be victims of sexual violence or other forms of abuse, and the beneficial effects lasted at least 4 years (Foshee et al., 2004). The Safe Dates program has been widely adopted, and Foshee's group has developed a family-based version of the program, as well as a program designed specifically for teens who have been exposed to domestic violence (Foshee et al., 2016).

# 16.7 Intimate Partner Violence Is a Crime with Many Names

## LEARNING OBJECTIVES

After reading this section you should be able to:

16.7.1 Identify the risk factors for experiencing intimate partner violence.

16.7.2 Describe the cycle of intimate partner violence.

16.7.3 Describe the kinds of help available to victims of intimate partner violence.

**intimate partner violence**
Violence within a sexual or romantic relationship.

The terms have changed over the years—from "wife beating" to "battering" to "spousal abuse" to "domestic violence" to **intimate partner violence**. The ugly reality remains the same: violent acts committed within what are supposed to be loving sexual relationships.

According to the NISVS, 1 in 5 women and 1 in 12 men in the United States have experienced some kind of contact violence at the hands of an intimate partner over their lifetime (CDC, 2019h). Thankfully, serious intimate partner violence—aggravated assault, robbery, and sexual assault—has become much less common over the last 25 years: The rates for both women and men were more than 3 times higher in the mid-1990s than they are now. Most of the decline happened before 2010 (Bureau of Justice Statistics, 2013a); since then the rates have remained level or have risen slightly.

Of the criminally violent acts committed by intimate partners, the majority are simple assaults, meaning assaults that are carried out without a weapon and that cause no injury or only minor physical injury. About one-third are aggravated assaults, robberies*, or sexual assaults (**FIGURE 16.6**). About 50% of the crimes are reported to the police. Contemporary definitions of intimate partner violence often include psychological abuse, which might not rise to the level of criminality.

Risk factors for experiencing intimate partner violence include being divorced or separated, bisexual, or African American, or having a low income. The association with poverty is particularly marked: Women living in the lowest-income households experience intimate partner violence at seven times the rate of women in affluent households.

Intimate partner violence is a particular problem on college campuses. In one study (Graham et al., 2016), about 1 in 10 students in heterosexual relationships reported having been physically injured by their partners. These injuries were usually minor ones, such as bruises, that would not have qualified the attacks as aggravated assaults. In addition, about 4 in 10 students had suffered some kind of psychological assault (**FIGURE 16.7**). There was little difference between the rates of assault committed by the male and female partners. About the same injury rate was reported by men in same-sex relationships. Women in same-sex relationships, on the other hand, reported considerably higher rates of injury, both physical and

▲ In 2016 Amber Heard accused her then husband Johnny Depp of smashing an iPhone into her face. Depp has denied doing so.

© Andrea Raffin/Alamy Stock Photo

---

*Robberies in legal terms are thefts that involve physical injury or the threat of injury.

psychological There were also very wide regional differences: The injury rates at colleges in Louisiana, for example, were more than double the rate in Utah.

These wide differences show that dating violence is by no means an inevitable concomitant of the college experience; thus, there should be opportunities to reduce its prevalence at the worst-affected institutions. Measures to reduce heavy drinking are leading candidates because intimate partner violence, like rape, is strongly associated with alcohol use on campus. Among male and female students who are heavy drinkers, over half have committed some kind of aggression (including psychological aggression) against an intimate partner in the previous 12 months (Fossos et al., 2007).

More significant than the physical injuries in most cases are the psychological effects of intimate partner violence: PTSD, depression, suicidal thoughts, and suicide attempts (Devries et al., 2013). The specific type of PTSD that occurs in these circumstances may be called "battered-woman syndrome," but it is not only women who experience it (Walker, 2009). The syndrome is often characterized by **learned helplessness**—a depressive condition following multiple experiences in which attempts to escape abuse have not succeeded and are therefore no longer attempted.

Those who physically abuse their intimate partners may also do so online. **Cyber dating abuse** can include abusive texts or cellphone calls, emailed threats, use of social media sites to post or solicit hateful statements about the partner, and the distribution of sexually explicit images of the partner without his or her consent. Obviously it's not possible to physically assault someone online, but in one study of teenagers, 34% of those students who said they had perpetrated cyber dating abuse also admitted to physically assaulting their dating partners, whereas only 2% of non-perpetrators did so (Zweig et al., 2013). And abuse at a distance can be deadly: One Massachusetts teenager was convicted of involuntary manslaughter for sending text messages to her 17-year-old boyfriend that urged him to commit suicide, even though she was not physically present at the scene of his death (Li, 2019).

Young children are present in over one-third of the households where a woman is subjected to intimate partner violence (Bureau of Justice Statistics, 2011). These children very often witness the violence directly, and they are at risk of being assaulted themselves. The violent atmosphere may profoundly affect the children's social development, increasing the likelihood that they, too, will commit intimate partner violence, abuse children, and exhibit other behavioral problems in adolescence and adulthood.

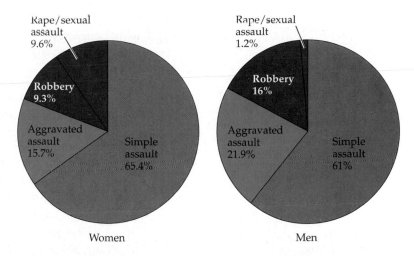

▲ **FIGURE 16.6** Violent crimes against intimate partners
These pie charts show that simple assaults are the most common violent offenses against both female and male intimate partners. Sexual violence against male intimate partners is very uncommon. Although these two pie charts are the same size, bear in mind that the total victimization of female intimate partners is much greater than of male partners. (Data from S. Catalano. 2013. *Intimate Partner Violence: Attributes of Victimization, 1993–2011. Special Report NCJ243300*. Based on *National Crime Victimization Survey, 2002–2011*. U.S. Department of Justice, Bureau of Justice Statistics: Washington, D.C.)

**learned helplessness**   Depression associated with failure to escape intimate partner violence.

**cyber dating abuse**   Abusive online behavior between dating or other sex partners.

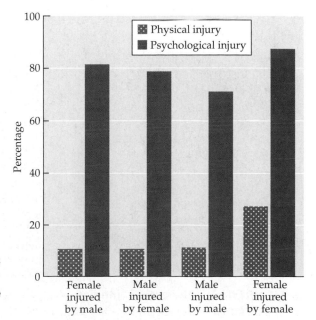

▶ **FIGURE 16.7** **Intimate partner violence in college** This bar graph shows, for U.S. college students who had been in an intimate relationship for at least a month, the percentage who said they had suffered a physical (usually minor) injury or psychological aggression at the hands of their partners. The results are charted separately for heterosexual, male–male, and female–female couples. (After L. M. Graham et al. 2016. *J Interpers Violence* 34: 1583–1610.)

## Intimate partner violence follows an escalating cycle

Domestic violence typically occurs as one phase of a three-phase cycle of violence (National Center for Health Research, 2019) (**FIGURE 16.8**):

1. *The tension-building phase.* In this phase, the longest of the three, the abuser may be increasingly moody, nitpicky, or sullen. He may threaten the victim or commit minor assaults or property damage. The victim may attempt to stop the progression of the cycle by trying to calm him, by avoiding confrontation, or by satisfying his demands—by keeping the children quiet, having food ready on time, and so on. (Although we use "he" and "she" for the abuser and victim respectively here, bear in mind that not all intimate partner violence is perpetrated by males on females.)

2. *The violent phase.* The actual violent behavior constitutes the shortest phase, typically lasting no more than a day. It often occurs during a bout of binge drinking (Wilson et al., 2017). The victim tries to protect herself (and her children if she has them), fights back, kicks the abuser out, or flees. The victim, other family members, or neighbors may call the police, who have usually been to this address several times before.

3. *The reconciliation phase.* In this phase, the perpetrator is apologetic and tries to make amends by declarations of love. He promises to cease the abusive behavior, to stop drinking, or to seek treatment. He showers the victim with gifts and attention. The victim is relieved and happy, forgives the abuser, and returns to him (or allows him back, if he has been kicked out). The victim may retract statements made to the police, with the hope of stopping legal proceedings, or may lie to doctors about the cause of her injuries.

Often, the severity of the violence escalates from cycle to cycle, so it may be more descriptive to refer to an "upward spiral of violence" rather than a cycle. In the worst cases, relationships degenerate into a condition of nonstop violence: In a study of cases in which police were called to scenes of domestic violence, 35% of the victims said that they were assaulted every day (Brookoff et al., 1997).

## Breaking up is hard to do

Sympathetic outsiders who see a victim—usually a woman—sticking with her abusive mate through escalating cycles of violence often ask, "Why on earth does she stay with that awful man?!" Some of the answers to this question are apparent from narratives written by the victims themselves (Weiss, 2004). Information also comes from research studies (Walker, 2009).

Victims of intimate partner violence may stay with their partners because they are socially isolated, are economically dependent, lack self-esteem, or believe that separation and divorce are wrong. They may irrationally believe that the battering is their own fault. In addition, victims may fear that breaking up will bring shame on them and that the perpetrators will pursue and punish them—a fear that is frequently justified. Victims may also fear that their children will suffer in a breakup. Perpetrators may sense and reinforce all these traits; in particular, they often keep the victims socially isolated and punish them for reaching out to any potential sources of help. Nevertheless, many victims do eventually break free from their abusive relationships and are able to start new lives.

In LGBT relationships, abusers may have additional means of preventing their victims from escaping from the relationships (National Domestic Violence Hotline, 2017). They may threaten to "out" their partners to relatives or coworkers; they may say that their partners, on account of their LGBT status, deserve to be punished and will not get any help from others; or they may claim that aggression is "normal" in LGBT relationships.

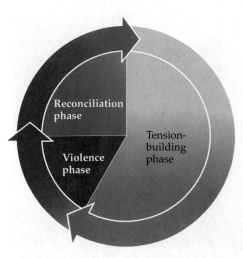

▲ **FIGURE 16.8** **The cycle of intimate partner violence**

## Help is available

Services are available to help those who are experiencing intimate partner violence, whether or not they remain in an abusive relationship:

- Emergency room staff are trained to treat domestic violence injuries and to recognize their cause. When a victim has multiple head and neck injuries at different stages of healing and there is no other predisposing factor, such as a neurological disorder, domestic violence is likely to be the cause.

- Law enforcement officers and lawyers can assist a domestic violence victim who decides to leave an abusive relationship by arresting the abuser or by helping the victim obtain a restraining order. In some states, such as California, prosecutors will continue domestic violence cases even when the victims retract their accusations (the "no-drop policy"). Legal assistance is often available to low-income victims.

- Hotlines, battered women's shelters, women's crisis centers, and city social services can provide practical assistance for women who leave abusive relationships temporarily or permanently.

- Psychotherapists and support groups can help abused women understand the process of victimization and regain the strength and motivation to end it. Interventions such as short courses of cognitive-behavioral therapy are quite effective (Arroyo et al., 2017).

Services for male victims and for victims of same-sex abuse are less well developed than those for women who are abused by men. Still, most public services for abuse victims are gender neutral, and the gay and lesbian organizations in many metropolitan areas have domestic violence services. The Los Angeles LGBT Center, for example, provides survivors' groups, a batterers' treatment program, crisis counseling, shelter referrals, and educational programs (Los Angeles LGBT Center, 2019).

# 16.8 Sexual Harassment Occurs in Many Environments

### LEARNING OBJECTIVES

After reading this section you should be able to:

16.8.1 Explain the differences between quid pro quo and hostile environment workplace sexual harassment.

16.8.2 Evaluate the measures individuals may take to prevent, end, or seek redress for workplace sexual harassment.

**Sexual harassment** is unwelcome sexual behavior in the workplace or in other structured environments. Most sexual harassment is perpetrated by men on women, but men are sometimes sexually harassed, either by women or by men. Women may also be sexually harassed by other women.

Besides being motivated by sexual desire, sexual harassment may also be an expression of a wish by men to control women. This idea is supported by some experimental studies. For example, Jennifer Berdahl of the University of Toronto reasoned that if sexual harassment is motivated by sexual desire, women who meet feminine ideals will be most harassed, but if it is motivated by a desire to control women, then women who *violate* feminine ideals will be most harassed. She found, in both college and work environments, that it was indeed the gender violators who were most harassed— that is, the women who showed stereotypically "masculine" traits such as assertiveness, dominance, and independence (Berdahl, 2007). This supported the idea that an important motivation for sexual harassment is to "keep women in line."

**sexual harassment** Unwanted sexual advances or other intimidating sexual behavior, usually in the workplace.

**quid pro quo harassment**
Unwelcome sexual advances, usually made to a worker in a subordinate position, accompanied by promises or threats.

**hostile environment harassment**
Sexual harassment involving a pattern of conduct that creates an intimidating work environment.

**third-party sexual harassment**
Indirect negative effects of sexual harassment on other employees, or sexual harassment by nonemployees.

Unwelcome sexual behavior can arise in faculty–student relationships at colleges and in relationships between doctors, therapists, lawyers, ministers, and other professionals and their patients or clients. Such behaviors are not always illegal, but they are widely prohibited by college administrations, professional governing bodies, and the like.

## There are two kinds of workplace sexual harassment

Sexual harassment in the workplace takes two different forms. The first involves an explicit or implicit "deal": "If you go out with me, I'll see that you get a merit raise" or "If you don't have sex with me, you can kiss your job goodbye." This kind of sexual harassment is called **quid pro quo** (literally "what for what?") **harassment**. It is generally considered the more reprehensible kind—if the facts are not in dispute, there can be little doubt about its illegal and damaging nature.

Unfortunately the facts often *are* in dispute. As with sexual assault allegations, quid pro quo harassment allegations quite often come down to the credibility of the accuser and the accused. An example came up in 2014 in the form of an unusual "she says, she says" case. A female Yahoo employee accused a female executive of coercing her into sex. Allegedly, after the employee refused further sex, the executive responded by giving her a poor performance review and removing her as project leader. Yahoo sided with the executive, saying that the employee had provided no evidence to support her allegations, and the executive countersued the employee for defamation (Soper, 2014). In 2015 both suits were dismissed after the two sides reached a nonmonetary settlement.

The second kind of sexual harassment, called **hostile environment harassment**, involves a pattern of unwelcome attention, advances, or statements that make life difficult for the victim. The behavior must relate to the victim's sex, but it need not be sexual in nature; for example, if the victim is a woman, it can consist of repeated disparaging comments about women in general. This kind of harassment causes a great deal of suffering, but it is not so easy to characterize and document. For one thing, it depends on the victim's reactions to the perpetrator's actions. Men are less likely to be psychologically injured by sexual advances from women than women are by sexual advances from men. Even among women, some will feel more harmed than others. Also, in many cases, it's not obvious how effectively the victim has communicated to the harasser how unwelcome the behavior is. Thus, it's not always easy to draw the line between acceptable social behavior and sexual harassment.

Employees who are not themselves the object of sexual harassment may suffer harm as a consequence of the harassment of others. For example, if an employer uses the promise of a promotion to obtain sexual favors from one employee, another employee may lose out on that promotion. Alternatively, the knowledge that sexual harassment is rife may degrade the work environment for employees who have not been harassed themselves. Such employees are entitled to file a suit claiming **third-party sexual harassment**.*

Hostile environment harassment cases often involve free speech issues. In a 1994 case, University of New Hampshire professor Donald Silva got himself into trouble during a technical writing class. In attempting to explain the meaning of the word "simile," Silva quoted the words of belly dancer Little Egypt: "Belly dancing is like Jell-O

© Katarzyna Białasiewicz/123RF

▲ What a man may think is acceptable social behavior may be experienced by a woman as sexual harassment.

---

*This term also refers to sexual harassment by outsiders, such as delivery persons or company clients.

on a plate with a vibrator under the plate." Seven women in the class complained of sexual harassment, and Silva was ordered to apologize and undergo counseling. He refused and sued the school, whereupon the school suspended him without pay. Two years later, a federal court ordered Silva reinstated, saying that the school had violated his First Amendment free speech rights (Honan, 1994). The school had to pay Silva substantial damages. In general, sexual harassment means a pattern of behavior, not a one-time incident such as in the Silva case.

In most cases it is the employer rather than the actual harassing person (if they are different) who is charged or sued in sexual harassment cases. And it is the *pattern* of conduct that matters: A man could express an interest in a romantic relationship with a woman—by asking her for a date, for example—without getting himself into trouble, but if he repeatedly asked after she said no, then she would have good cause to file a complaint. It is usually important to be able to document that the employer knew about the ongoing harassment and did nothing to stop it. For that reason a person who files a complaint about harassment increases the likelihood that the employer will be held liable for future harassment—either of the complainant or other victims of the same perpetrator.

Workplace sexual harassment, if not quickly stopped, may escalate to sexual assault, in which case the perpetrator himself or herself faces criminal charges. The intermingling of harassment and assault was a consistent theme in the crimes of Hollywood movie mogul Harvey Weinstein and the many other individuals accused of sexual misbehavior in the wake of the 2017 Weinstein revelations (**BOX 16.5**).

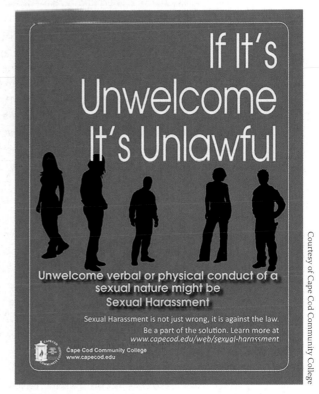

▲ A sexual harassment awareness poster.

## Sexual harassment often begins early

For many children, sexual harassment begins as soon as they enter puberty—if not before. In a survey of middle schoolers led by Dorothy Espelage, then at the University of Illinois at Urbana-Champaign, verbal sexual harassment was commonly reported, but acts involving physical contact were much less frequent (Espelage et al., 2016) (**TABLE 16.4**). In another study Espelage and her colleagues followed over 3000 children through middle school into high school (Basile et al., 2018; Espelage et al., 2018); they found that perpetration of bullying and homophobic name-calling in middle school, as well as a lack of empathy, was predictive of both sexual and nonsexual violence in high school. It seems then that the roots of intimate partner violence lie in childhood, well before children become sexually active.

It is possible that many sexually colored incidents in schools are of no great significance. A school in Lexington, North Carolina, for example, earned national ridicule in 1996 when it suspended a 6-year-old boy for kissing a female classmate (Nossiter, 1996). But sexual harassment in school can be persistent and traumatic, as was made clear by the 4000 letters received by *Seventeen* magazine in response to an article and poll on the subject (Stein, 1999). Here is one typical letter, from a 12-year-old Mexican American student in Michigan:

**TABLE 16.4** Types of sexual harassment experienced in school by students in grades 5 to 8

| Type of harassment | Percent who experienced harassment "often" or "occasionally" |
|---|---|
| Made sexual comments, jokes, gestures, looks | 23.8 |
| Said you were gay or lesbian | 8.3 |
| Touched, grabbed, or pinched you in a sexual way | 8.3 |
| Spread sexual rumors about you | 5.1 |
| Showed you sexual pictures, photographs | 4.9 |
| Forced you to kiss | 2.6 |
| Made you touch private parts | 0.7 |

*Source*: D. L. Espelage et al. 2016. *Child Youth Serv Rev* 71: 174–183.

## BOX 16.5
## The Weinstein Effect

In October 2017 *The New York Times* reported that Harvey Weinstein, then one of Hollywood's most prominent movie executives, had reached legal settlements with at least eight women who had accused him of sexual harassment and unwanted sexual contact (Kantor & Twohey, 2017). These cases were not previously known to the public, because the settlements included nondisclosure clauses.

The allegations against Weinstein reprised similar allegations that had been made earlier against many high-status individuals. In fact, the U.S. Equal Employment Opportunity Commission has a name for the phenomenon—"superstar harassment"—as well as an explanation: "Often . . . superstars are privileged with higher income, better accommodations, and different expectations. That privilege can lead to a self-view that they are above the rules, which can foster mistreatment" (Equal Employment Opportunity Commission, 2016). Superstars are not necessarily well known to the general public, but they are towering figures within their own fields or organizations.

Yet the Weinstein case differed from earlier cases in that it triggered an outpouring of similar allegations so numerous that they constituted a social revolt. First, scores of other women made similar or even more serious allegations against Weinstein. But within a few weeks similar allegations were made against many other men. By 5 months after Weinstein's exposure 71 other men prominent in politics, entertainment, industry, and other fields had been fired or forced to resign after being accused of sexual harassment (Almukhtar et al., 2018). These included U.S. Senator Al Franken, television host Charlie Rose, and actor Kevin Spacey (who was accused of sexually harassing males). Under social media hashtags such as #MeToo, countless women recounted their own experiences, not always at the hands of celebrities.

While the early allegations mostly concerned sexual harassment, some men were accused of more serious crimes. American financier Jeffrey Epstein, who already before the Weinstein revelations had served a prison sentence for procuring a minor for prostitution, was sued by several women for various kinds of sexual abuse, and then in 2019 he was arrested and charged with conspiracy to traffic minors for sex. He died while in detention awaiting trial, apparently by suicide.

Many prominent people had socialized with Epstein, sometimes on his private island in the Caribbean. One of his associates was Prince Andrew, the second son of Britain's Queen Elizabeth, who was accused by a 31-year-old woman of holding her as a sex slave when she was 17. (The age of consent in Britain is 16.) Andrew denied the allegations, but the queen relieved him of his official duties, and many individuals and organizations cut their ties to him.

Actress Ashley Judd, seen here in a 1997 photo, was one of the first women to publicly accuse film producer Harvey Weinstein (right) of sexual harassment.

Not surprisingly, the Weinstein scandal and its global repercussions have inspired diverse and contradictory interpretations. One point of view is that superstar harassment is a consequence of the way that boys are raised. Thus, psychologist Niobe Way of New York University believes that society rewards and places in positions of power males who reject intimacy-based relationships in favor of aggressive sexuality (Blair, 2017).

Some conservatives have pointed to potentially unhealthy aspects of the current social revolt against sexual harassment. For example, scholar Christina Hoff Sommers of the American Enterprise Institute, who is well known as a critic of what she calls "victim feminism," has claimed that the Me Too movement has elements of a sex panic, comparable to the panic about satanic ritual sexual abuse at a day care center that we described in Box 10.2 (Sommers, 2017). Some men have been punished on the basis of questionable evidence of wrongdoing (Yoffe, 2019).

Harvey Weinstein denied engaging in any nonconsensual sex, but he was fired from his company and expelled from the Academy of Motion Pictures. In 2018 he was charged in New York with several sex crimes, including rape. In 2020 he was convicted on two charges and sentenced to 23 years in prison.

*In my case there were 2 or 3 boys touching me, and trust me they were big boys. And I'd tell them to stop but they wouldn't. This went on for about 6 months until finally I was in one of my classes in the back of the room minding my own business when all of them came back and backed me into a corner and started touching me all over. So I went running out of the room and the teacher yelled at me and I had to stay in my seat for the rest of the class.*

A common theme of the letters, as in this one, was the lack of concern shown by teachers and school officials; often the harassed students felt that they were treated as offenders rather than victims.

Schools are beginning to take sexual harassment more seriously, partly as a result of successful legal actions by students who have been harassed. The key case was that of LaShonda Davis, a fifth-grade student in Forsyth, Georgia. A male classmate sexually taunted Davis for months, but the school authorities failed to stop the abuse. With the help of the ACLU, LaShonda's mother sued the school board, and the case went all the way to the U.S. Supreme Court. In 1999 the court ruled in her favor, stating that federally funded schools that are willfully indifferent to student-on-student sexual harassment can be held liable. Since then schools have made greater efforts to prevent harassment and to respond appropriately to harassment allegations.

## Sexual harassment harms its victims

Although adults are better able to resist sexual harassment than are schoolchildren, the harmful effects of harassment in adulthood are still considerable (Willness et al., 2007). The effects on harassed workers include decreased job satisfaction, lower organizational commitment, withdrawing from work (with ensuing financial difficulties), physical and mental ill health, and even symptoms of PTSD. Employers also suffer in terms of lost productivity and the costs of insurance premiums or claim settlements.

While sexual harassment of a college student by a faculty member is clearly wrong, what about consensual relationships? The problem here is that, even if there isn't an actual quid pro quo (e.g., better grades for sex, or worse grades for refusing sex), there will almost always be the appearance of one. Thus most college policies prohibit all sexual relationships between faculty members and those students for whom they have some academic responsibility. Some schools go further. UC Berkeley bans sexual *or romantic* relationships between faculty members and their own students. A few schools, such as the College of William & Mary and the University of Pennsylvania, prohibit sexual or romantic relationships between faculty members and *any* undergraduate students. (It is the faculty member, more than the student, who risks disciplinary action.) Brigham Young University's honor code prohibits sexual activity between all unmarried persons, including between unmarried students, and if the two persons are of the same sex even holding hands can be a violation, according to interviews with BYU students by the *Salt Lake Tribune* (Tanner, 2019).

## Victims of sexual harassment can take steps to end it

Many organizations, such as the AFL-CIO, the National Partnership for Women & Families, and Feminist Majority, have formulated recommendations for dealing with sexual harassment:

- Know your rights. Consult the written policies of your organization, business, or school concerning sexual harassment.
- Tell your harasser that he or she is harassing you. Recount what he or she is doing, explain how it affects you, and demand that it stop. Be sure your tone of voice, facial expression, and body language match the seriousness of your message. Don't accept any excuses the harasser may offer or be sidetracked by diversionary topics. If the harassment is so severe that you

**stalking** Obsessive pursuit of a previous, current, or desired sex partner in a way that puts that person in a state of fear.

**cyberstalking** Stalking via the internet.

**intimate partner stalking** Stalking of a current or former spouse or other intimate partner.

might anticipate a violent response to your complaint, do not confront the harasser directly but go to a supervisor.

- Keep a journal documenting every incident of harassment as it happens, how it affected you, and how you responded. Keep photographs or the originals of any offensive messages or images you receive. Don't erase offensive text messages or emails.

- Tell other people, such as trusted coworkers, about the harassment as it occurs. Ask whether others have experienced sexual harassment from the same person, whether they have witnessed the harassment that you have experienced, and whether they will support you if you take action.

- If the harasser does not stop the offensive behavior or responds with any vindictive action, complain to your supervisor, your supervisor's boss, your union steward, your personnel department, your principal, or your student advisor, or file an official complaint via the channels established by your organization. Keep records of these actions and their results.

- If you do not get satisfaction through these channels, consider obtaining a lawyer and filing a complaint with the federal Equal Employment Opportunity Commission (EEOC), your state's Fair Employment Practice Agency, or the federal Department of Education's Office for Civil Rights. Such complaints must be filed within a certain deadline (within 6 months of the most recent incident of harassment, in the case of the EEOC). These agencies may help you settle the case, or they may give you a "right to sue" letter that will facilitate a private lawsuit. If criminal behavior such as sexual assault is involved, you should go directly to the police.

Most large companies provide training programs that cover sexual harassment issues. In fact, such programs may be required by state employment laws. Contracting companies typically provide the training, and it is probably quite effective in increasing awareness of sexual harassment. In the wake of the Weinstein scandal described in Box 16.5, the U.S. Congress mandated such training for its own members.

## 16.9 There Are Three Kinds of Stalkers

**LEARNING OBJECTIVE**

After reading this section you should be able to:

**16.9.1** Explain the differences between intimate partner stalking and delusional stalking.

▲ Actor Mila Kunis was repeatedly stalked by a man, Stuart Dunn, who also tried to break into her home. In 2013 Dunn was convicted of felony stalking and ordered to spend 6 months in a rehab center and to stay away from Kunis for 10 years.

If rape is the dark side of sex, then **stalking** is the dark side of love. A stalker is emotionally obsessed with a particular victim, and that obsession usually has, or once had, a romantic element. Stalkers put their victims in fear by repeatedly following them, harassing them, lying in wait for them, making phone calls or sending messages to them, vandalizing their property, and the like. Sixteen percent of U.S. women, as well as 6% of men, say that they have been the victim of some kind of stalking behavior over their lifetime (CDC, 2018e). **Cyberstalking** (that is, stalking via the internet) is an increasing problem. When workplace romances go sour, it is common for one party to harass or stalk the other online (Mainiero & Jones, 2013).

There are three distinct kinds of stalking. The most common is **intimate partner stalking**, in which the victim is stalked by a current or former spouse, cohabitational partner, boyfriend, girlfriend, or date. It is often assumed that intimate partner stalkers do their stalking after the relationship has broken up, but in actuality stalking can take place while a relationship is still intact (National Institute of Justice, 2012). Intimate partner stalkers often show a controlling or suspicious attitude toward the victims even before the stalking behavior begins. Anger is a major motivational factor in intimate partner stalking. These stalkers often have a prior psychiatric or criminal history (Meloy et al., 2000), and over half are alcohol or drug abusers (Macfarlane et al., 1999).

According to Brian Spitzberg of San Diego State University and William Cupach of Illinois State University, intimate partner stalking is an extreme example of a common behavior pattern that they call **obsessive relational intrusion** (Spitzberg & Cupach, 2014). A rejected lover will frequently make attempts to continue a relationship, perhaps in an attempt to see whether the rejection is wholehearted or not. Most women and men have experienced this kind of unwanted attention at some time or another, as described in Chapter 7. Certain personality traits in the pursuer, such as a tendency toward exploitation, coerciveness, or obsessive thinking, may help turn this behavior into persistent stalking.

In the second kind of stalking, **delusional stalking**, the stalker has the fixed belief that the victim is in love with him or could easily be made to fall in love with him, even though there has never been an intimate relationship between the two of them. This kind of delusional thinking is sometimes called **erotomania**. Anyone may be stalked in this fashion, but celebrities are at particular risk. Halle Berry, Selena Gomez, Miley Cyrus, Usher, Keira Knightley, Justin Bieber, and countless others have been plagued by stalkers, some of whom have broken into the celebrities' homes. Occasionally a stalker insists that he or she is married to the celebrity.

The most notorious delusional stalker was John Hinckley Jr., who stalked actress Jodie Foster. In 1981, after countless rebuffs, Hinckley attempted to assassinate President Reagan as a means to draw Foster's attention. In doing so, he was mimicking the plot of the film *Taxi Driver*, in which Foster played a child prostitute. At trial, Hinckley was found not guilty by reason of insanity and was institutionalized. In a letter to *The New York Times*, Hinckley described his assassination attempt as "the greatest love offering in the history of the world" (Taylor, 1982). Over the ensuing years Hinckley recovered from his mental illness, and he was released in 2016.

**obsessive relational intrusion**
Obsessive pursuit of a person by a rejected lover.

**delusional stalking** Stalking motivated by the delusional belief that the victim is in love with, or could be persuaded to fall in love with, the stalker.

**erotomania** The delusional belief that a sexually desired but unattainable person is actually in love with oneself.

▲ John Hinckley Jr. attempted to assassinate President Reagan in order to impress the object of his delusional passion, actress Jodie Foster (seen here in *Taxi Driver*).

**grudge stalking** Stalking motivated by a non-sexual grudge, often within a work environment.

One example of cyberstalking involved a criminal justice student at Florida International University, Kassandra Cruz, who became fixated on a young woman she saw on a pornographic video (FBI, 2017). Cruz created a fake persona, a U.S. Marine named Giovanni, and "he" sent admiring messages and friend requests to the victim, who in the meantime had quit her porn career. Once friended, "Giovanni" inundated the victim with likes and comments, to the point that the victim unfriended "him." Whereupon Giovanni bombarded her with over 1000 phone calls and text messages, including threats to expose her previous occupation and demands for money. The FBI arranged a sting operation, and Cruz was arrested and sentenced to 22 months in prison for cyberstalking. Cases like this illustrate how easily social networks can become anti-social networks.

The third type of stalking is **grudge stalking**, in which the stalker pursues the victim to seek revenge for some actual or imagined injury. Grudge stalking is not usually sexual.

Being stalked is an extremely traumatic and stressful experience and one that may go on for years. Besides having to deal with the constant harassment, the victim is often in fear that the stalking will escalate to violence—and with good reason. According to a national survey of violence against women, 81% of women who were stalked by a current or former intimate partner were also physically assaulted by the stalker, and 31% were also sexually assaulted (U.S. Department of Justice, 1998). Actress Rebecca Schaeffer was shot dead by a stalker in 1989.

Stalking is illegal in all 50 states, and stalking across state lines is a federal offense. In many states, however, first-offense stalking is only a misdemeanor, in which case the penalties may be minor. Furthermore, it may not be enough just to prove that you were put in fear by the stalker—in some jurisdictions, the stalker must make "credible threats" against you in order to be convicted of a crime.

## Summary

- Sexual assaults are nonconsensual sex acts; rapes are sexual assaults involving penetration accomplished by force or the threat of force. Statutory rapes are those in which the victim cannot give consent on account of age or mental incapacity. Although both men and women of all ages may experience rape, young women face the highest risk. The great majority of perpetrators are male.

- The rape rate has decreased markedly over the past 30 years. Most rapes and sexual assaults are committed by people known to the victims (acquaintances, relatives, or intimate partners). The majority of sexual assaults are not reported to police.

- The prevalence of sexual assaults on college campuses is disputed, but the overall frequency of campus rape has fallen. Most campus rapes are perpetrated by acquaintances or current or former boyfriends. A disproportionate number of campus rapes are committed by college athletes such as football players. There is controversy about how to balance the rights of accusers and accused in the adjudication of campus sexual assaults.

- Drugs such as Ambien may be used in the perpetration of rape, but alcohol (consumed by the perpetrator or the victim) is much more commonly associated with rape, including rapes on college campuses.

- Besides physical injuries, victims of sexual assaults may suffer a variety of ill effects, including post-traumatic stress disorder. These effects may be countered by counseling and by survivors' groups, which help victims regain a sense of control. Male victims of sexual assaults may fear that they will not be taken seriously. LGBT victims are at especially high risk and do not always receive appropriate care.

- The law has become increasingly protective of rape victims, but many victims of rape and sexual assault do not report the crimes. Men who are convicted of rape are typically sentenced to lengthy prison terms, but only a small minority of rapes are reported and prosecuted. A small, but not negligible, proportion of rape accusations turn out to be unfounded.

- Conflicting theories attempt to explain rape. Evolutionary psychologists have raised the possibility that it evolved because it increased the reproductive success of men who committed it.

- Individual men may be predisposed to rape on account of childhood abuse, personality disorders, or a lack of empathy and respect for others. Social forces may encourage a "culture of rape." Conversely, they may discourage rape, as, for example, through the criminal justice system. Rape is often used as an instrument of war or genocide.

- Rape prevention programs teach teenagers rape awareness and avoidance, attempt to overcome gender stereotypes, and promote conflict management skills. Many teens are never exposed to these programs, and their effectiveness is uncertain. It is possible that fostering empathy development in young children would be a more effective long-term strategy.

- Violence between intimate partners causes both physical and psychological injuries. The rate of intimate partner violence has dropped substantially over the past 30 years.

- Intimate partner violence typically follows a three-phase cycle that includes tension building, violence, and reconciliation. As the cycle repeats, the violent phase tends to intensify and may eventually occur without interruption.

- Victims of intimate partner violence often stay with their partners. The reasons for this may include social isolation, economic dependence, low self-esteem, shame, and fear of retribution. Battered women may come to see the violence as inevitable and therefore do little to escape it. Many services are now available to help victims of intimate partner abuse, whether or not they remain in their abusive relationships.

- Unwelcome sexual attention in the workplace (sexual harassment) is a form of illegal sex discrimination. It can take the form of quid pro quo harassment, in which a demand for sex is accompanied by some inducement or threat, or the form of hostile environment harassment, in which one person harasses another on account of her or his sex. Harassment can also occur in other structured environments, such as schools and colleges. Allegations of sexual harassment against Hollywood executive Harvey Weinstein in 2017 triggered an avalanche of similar accusations against "superstars" in diverse fields.

- Sexual harassment causes psychological and practical problems for its victims and reduces workplace productivity. Victims can take steps to end sexual harassment by confronting their harassers or by reporting the harassment.

- Stalking is obsessive following, calling, lying in wait, sending of mail or messages, and the like, all directed at a specific victim. In intimate partner stalking, the stalker is a current or former spouse or romantic partner, and the stalking is motivated by sexual jealousy and anger. In delusional stalking, the stalker is mentally disturbed and believes that the victim (often an acquaintance, teacher, therapist, or celebrity) is in love with him or could be made to fall in love with him. In grudge stalking, the stalker is not motivated by sexual interest. Whatever the type of stalking, it can progress to violence. Stalking is illegal, but legal remedies are of limited effectiveness.

## Discussion Questions

1. "On this campus, men still get away with a lot of sexist talk, sexual harassment, and even date rape." "On this campus, political correctness has got to the point that men are scared to show normal friendly behavior to women." Which of these two statements corresponds more closely to your opinion, and why? Do you think your sex influences your opinion?

2. If you had to establish your college's policy regarding faculty–student sex, what considerations would be most important to you in setting the policy? What would the policy be, and how would it compare with your college's actual policy? (If you don't know what your college's actual faculty–student sex policy is, find out.)

3. How would you advise a female friend who tells you she is being stalked by her former boyfriend? Would your advice be different if it were a male friend being stalked by his former girlfriend?

The **Discovering Human Sexuality** digital resources include activities, animations, flashcards, web links, chapter outlines and summaries, and other study tools.

Learn more with this chapter's digital tools, including the **Oxford Insight Study Guide**, at **oup.com/he/levay5e**.

4. Both men and women may sometimes give unclear signals about whether they are willing to engage in sexual contact when they are in a potentially sexual situation. How can a man or woman best make sure that the other person is really willing to engage in sex? What if you or your companion has had a few drinks?

5. Not uncommonly, victims recant accusations that their partners beat them. Would you support a "no-drop policy" in your community (i.e., a policy to continue a prosecution in these circumstances)? What kind of evidence could be used to get a conviction if the victim recanted?

## Web Resources

Advocates for Human Rights. Sexual harassment   **tinyurl.com/ycntz27c**

Equal Employment Opportunity Commission: Policy guidance on current issues of sexual harassment   **tinyurl.com/y8vzaxnd**

Just Detention International (formerly Stop Prisoner Rape)   **www.justdetention.org**

Men Can Stop Rape   **www.mencanstoprape.org**

National Coalition Against Domestic Violence (hotline: 1-800-799-7233)   **www.ncadv.org**

National Sexual Violence Resource Center   **www.nsvrc.org**

Not Alone (U.S. government site focusing on sexual assault)   **www.notalone.gov**

RAINN—Rape, Abuse & Incest National Network (hotline: 1-800-656-4673)   **www.rainn.org**

Stalking Resource Center   **tinyurl.com/y9t84owt**

## Recommended Reading

Baker, C. N. (2007). *The women's movement against sexual harassment*. Cambridge University Press.

Carpenter, E. (2013). *Life, reinvented: A guide to healing from sexual trauma for survivors and loved ones*. Quantum.

Fisher, B. S., Daigle, L. E. & Cullen, F. T. (2009). *Unsafe in the ivory tower: The sexual victimization of college women*. Sage.

Germain, L. J. (2016). *Campus sexual assault: College women respond*. Johns Hopkins University Press.

Hirsch, J. S. & Khan, S. (2020). *Sexual citizens: A landmark study of sex, power and assault on campus*. W. W. Norton.

Lalumiere, M., Harris, G. T., Quinsey, V. L. & Rice, M. E. (Eds.). (2005). *The causes of rape: Understanding individual differences in male propensity for sexual aggression*. American Psychological Association.

Miller, C. (2019). *Know my name: A memoir*. Viking. (Account of the fallout from Chanel Miller's 2015 sexual assault by Stanford University student Brock Turner.)

Reddington, F. P. & Kriesel, B. W. (Eds.). (2017). *Sexual assault: The victims, the perpetrators, and the criminal justice system* (3rd ed.). Carolina Academic Press.

Spitzberg, B. H. & Cupach, W. R. (2014). *The dark side of relationship pursuit: From attraction to obsession and stalking* (2nd ed.). Routledge.

Walker, L. E. A. (2016). *The battered woman syndrome* (4th ed.). Springer.

Soi Cowboy—Bangkok's red light district.

# 17

# Sex Work

Like anything that people want, sex has a cash value. Indeed, in one way or another, sex fuels a significant part of the U.S. economy. In this chapter, we focus on the selling of sex itself (prostitution) and the commercial production of sexually arousing materials (pornography). The selling of sex raises a variety of practical and ethical concerns, and few aspects of sexuality so sharply divide conservatives and liberals.

## 17.1 Sex Is an Industry

**LEARNING OBJECTIVE**

After reading this section you should be able to:

17.1.1 Explain which activities may be considered sex work.

**sex worker** A person who engages in prostitution, pornography, or another sex-related occupation.

**prostitution** The practice of engaging in sex for pay.

**hustler** A male prostitute.

**sex trafficking** Making money from coerced or juvenile prostitution.

Most people want sex, at least for some portion of their lives. They may get enough of it from noncommercial sources, of course—from spouses, cohabitational partners, dates, or casual sex or from solo sex and sexual fantasies. Even if they don't, they may prefer to go without rather than pay for it. They may believe that to pay for it would be wrong, dangerous, or threatening to their ongoing relationships.

But that leaves everyone else, and so there has to be a sex industry. The size of this industry in the United States is impressive. Just one tiny part of it—male prostitution—is worth over $1 billion annually (Logan, 2017). In just one U.S. county—San Diego—illegal sex trafficking has been valued at $810 million per year—and that amount doesn't include self-employed prostitution or legal facets of the sex industry such as the creation and distribution of pornography, sex toys, and so on (Carpenter & Gates, 2016).

People whose occupations are closely tied to the provision of sexual services are called **sex workers**. Most obviously, this group includes prostitutes, but it also includes those who recruit or control prostitutes, those who make or act in pornographic videos, performers in strip clubs, pornographic webcam actors, and so on. The outer limits of what may be called sex work are fuzzy. Does it include people who make, test, or sell sex toys? Possibly. How about people who write human sexuality textbooks? We think not.

For the most part, sex work—even the legal sector of the industry—is highly stigmatized, and it's worth asking why that should be. After all, plenty of women, and some men, receive their entire financial support from their sex partners without bringing their relationships into disrepute. What is morally offensive to many people about sex work is not simply that money is involved, but that the relationship between prostitute and client is brief and loveless and that the payment is for sex only, not as part of the complex web of commitments, attachments, and dependencies that characterize more lasting relationships. And with pornography the relationship is even more tenuous, as consumers of pornography don't even meet the people whose sexual antics they are watching. In other words, sex work violates a common belief that sex is morally justified only in the context of a loving, committed relationship.

In spite of the stigma attached to sex work, some argue that all sex work should be decriminalized, either because it is a victimless activity, or because criminalization creates more harm than it prevents. We discuss this issue later in the chapter.

## 17.2 Prostitution Is on the Decline

**LEARNING OBJECTIVE**

After reading this section you should be able to:

17.2.1 Explain why prostitution has become less prevalent over time.

A **prostitute** is a person who engages in sex for pay. Obsolete or abusive terms for prostitutes, such as "hooker" and "whore," have to some extent been reclaimed by present-day prostitutes and the organizations that represent them. Male prostitutes are often called **hustlers**. A **sex trafficker** is someone who coerces a person to engage in prostitution or who facilitates prostitution by minors.

### Historically, prostitution was viewed as a necessary evil

Prostitution is often called "the oldest profession," and with good reason. For millennia, prostitution was just about the only way in which unattached women could support themselves. Jewish and Christian scriptures include frequent references to prostitutes (or "harlots"), and Christian tradition holds that one of Jesus's followers, Mary Magdalene, was a reformed prostitute (**FIGURE 17.1**).

Prostitution, like all sex between unmarried people, has been condemned as "fornication" throughout the Christian era. Still, moralists such as St. Augustine and St. Thomas Aquinas condoned the social structure of prostitution because they saw it as providing a necessary "safety valve" for the satisfaction of the male sex drive. Thus, Augustine wrote: "If you do away with harlots, the world will be convulsed with lust" (Dever, 1996). Although most prostitutes were despised and downtrodden, a few mingled with the rich and famous, in which case they were called **courtesans** (**FIGURE 17.2**).

The heyday of prostitution was probably the late 18th and 19th centuries, when large numbers of men migrated to cities, where women were in short supply. In response to the terrible conditions experienced by prostitutes in London, William Booth founded the Salvation Army in 1865; its first shelter for prostitutes and vagrant girls opened 3 years later. Large cities were also rife with male prostitution: In the 1890s at least eight locations in New York's Bowery neighborhood were known as places where men could hire men or male youths for sex (Friedman, 2014).

In the latter part of the 19th century, most U.S. cities saw the development of "red-light districts," in which prostitution was tolerated or, in a few locations, even legal. In the early 20th century, however, a coalition of reformers, early feminists, and health authorities forced most of these districts out of existence. Epidemics of gonorrhea and other diseases during World War I triggered a major campaign against prostitution, and the profession went underground.

▲ **FIGURE 17.1** **St. Mary Magdalene** has often been portrayed with immodestly long red hair—a reference to her supposed earlier life as a prostitute. This painting is by Piero di Cosimo (c. 1490).

### There are moral and practical reasons for the decline

Over the course of the 20th century, prostitution became much less prevalent in the United States and other developed nations. Kinsey estimated that men's usage of female prostitutes had dropped by nearly 50% over the few decades prior to the time of his survey in the 1940s. Still, Kinsey's survey showed that the average unmarried man in his 30s visited a prostitute once every 3 weeks (Kinsey et al., 1948).

A further major decline in prostitution accompanied the sexual revolution of the 1960s and its aftermath. Thanks to oral contraceptives and a sea change in sexual morality, unmarried women became much more willing to have sex with their boyfriends, so the main incentive for men to visit prostitutes lost much of its force. Whereas 7% of men born between 1933 and 1937 lost their virginity to a prostitute, only 1.5% of men born between 1968 and 1974 did so, according to National Health and Social Life Survey (NHSLS) data. During this same period, employment opportunities for many women expanded greatly, so the main incentive for women to work as prostitutes lessened.

Another possible factor in the decline in prostitution has been the increasing availability of other forms of sexual gratification, such as online pornography, webcamming (see below), and the like. The 2020 coronavirus pandemic may have accelerated this shift by making prostitution in the traditional sense more risky for both sex workers and their clients (**BOX 17.1**).

**courtesan** Historical term for a high-class prostitute who moved in aristocratic circles.

▶ **FIGURE 17.2** **A 16th-century Venetian courtesan** painted by Jacopo Tintoretto.

## BOX 17.1
# Sex Work in the Time of Plague

As we approach the end of our work on this edition of the textbook, the COVID-19 pandemic appears to be reaching its peak in the United States, as in many other countries, and it is causing great loss of life as well as economic devastation. While the pandemic has affected millions of people in all walks of life, it has had a particularly severe impact on sex workers.

Prostitution by its very nature requires close bodily contact between strangers—the exact opposite of the social isolation that is the leading strategy for curbing the pandemic. Thus COVID-19 has motivated both prostitutes and their clients to reduce or cease their activities.

Streetwalking prostitutes have largely attempted to continue their activities, however, because they have little economic choice in the matter. Well-known pick-up locations, such as Figueroa Street in South Los Angeles, are still active, but johns can demand lower prices or riskier sex at the same price (e.g., "full service" rather than a "hand job"). "Our circumstances are regularly very dire, and every day we face life-and-death decisions," one crisis counselor told *The Los Angeles Times*. "The coronavirus is just another danger added to the pot" (Newberry, 2020).

Escort (off-street) prostitution has been even more severely affected. Demand has fallen precipitously, because potential clients are more concerned about disease or more anxious about their finances. Travelers, usually a major source of income for escort prostitutes, have almost disappeared. What's more, the social safety net barely exists for sex workers of any kind. In fact, sex workers were specifically excluded from the 2020 federal relief program for small businesses.

Some escort prostitutes have moved into online activities such as "camming." More clients are using these online services, but tips—the main source of income for cammers—have become smaller or even nonexistent. Also, it takes much effort, time, and

Amsterdam's usually bustling red light district was deserted during the 2020 COVID-19 epidemic.

© Dean Mouhtaropoulos/Getty Images

skill to develop a profitable online presence. "From personal experience, I feel like a lot of newer models will flood the cam rooms, but they'll realize it is super hard and not follow through with getting on," one cammer told *Newsweek* (Palmer, 2020).

Visits to pornographic websites have increased dramatically all over the world during the pandemic, according to Pornhub, but most especially in countries that have closed down previously legal brothel industries (López, 2020). That hasn't been much help to the actors, because production has largely ceased. A new genre of coronavirus-themed videos has appeared, however, sometimes with the purported aim of disseminating health-related information.

By the time you read this the COVID-19 pandemic will probably have waned or even reached its end. Yet it is likely that the pandemic will accelerate the ongoing transition to online sex work, as both the sex workers and their clients become used to the experience and more familiar with the technology.

Statistics on the prevalence of prostitution are hard to come by. One of the best studies of prostitution was conducted in Chicago by the Center for Impact Research (O'Leary & Howard, 2001). According to this study, an estimated minimum of 1800 to 4000 women and girls worked as prostitutes in the Chicago metropolitan area at any one time, which is less than 0.1% of the female population. Other sources have estimated (very roughly) that 1 in 100 U.S. women has worked as a prostitute at some point in her life (ProCon.org, 2018).

Although most prostitutes are female, the proportion of prostitutes who are male or transgender is significant in some large cities. Most of the trans women have not undergone genital surgery, but they may have breast implants and/or be taking estrogens.

All forms of prostitution are illegal everywhere in the United States except for 11 nonurban counties of Nevada, in which brothel prostitution is legal. Engaging in prostitution is usually a misdemeanor. Enforcement varies greatly, however. Prostitution that is publicly visible is much more likely to run afoul of the law than are other types of prostitution. Some jurisdictions have instructed their police forces to make the enforcement of prostitution laws a low priority. Other cities have set up "diversion programs" that spare prostitutes jail time and help them move on to other occupations without the stigma of a criminal record. Men who use prostitutes are also breaking the law; if convicted, they may have to attend a "school for johns" (**FIGURE 17.3**). In some jurisdictions they are publicly shamed by having their names and photos posted online.

The United States is something of an exception in criminalizing all forms of prostitution. In Canada, Mexico, and most countries in Western Europe and Central and South America, some forms of prostitution are legal. Usually this is off-street prostitution. Public solicitation for prostitution and living off the earnings of prostitutes (pimping) are often illegal.

© ZUMA Press, Inc/Alamy Stock Photo

▲ **FIGURE 17.3** At a "school for johns," attendees learn about the negative aspects of prostitution.

## 17.3 There Is a Hierarchy of Prostitution

### LEARNING OBJECTIVES

After reading this section you should be able to:

**17.3.1** Describe the different kinds of prostitution.

**17.3.2** Compare the working experiences of female, male, and transgender prostitutes.

**17.3.3** Evaluate the reasons why juveniles may engage in prostitution.

Prostitution is difficult to characterize, because it takes many different forms. In general there is a hierarchy, ranging from forms that are street based, cheap, and dangerous, up to less visible forms involving larger sums of money and greater security for the prostitutes and the prostitutes' clients.

### Street prostitution has many risks

In the Chicago study just described, 30% to 35% of the prostitutes worked on the streets. Street prostitution (or streetwalking) is the most visible and familiar part of the industry. Streetwalkers are usually picked up by clients ("johns") driving automobiles, but they may also be picked up in bars located near recognized streetwalking zones. After agreement between prostitute and client about the kind of sex to be engaged in and the fee, sex takes place in the automobile, in a pay-by-the-hour motel, or at some other location.

Street prostitutes (in the United States and worldwide) occupy the lowest rank of the prostitution hierarchy. Their income from prostitution is low, but higher than they could expect to earn in "straight" work. Some street prostitutes experience a lifetime of social degradation, beginning with a violence-ridden childhood and continuing into homelessness, alcoholism, and drug use (Raphael, 2004). The risk of being beaten or raped exists every time a streetwalker steps into a stranger's car. One study conducted in Colorado concluded that active street prostitutes are nearly 18 times more likely to fall victim to homicide than other women (Potterat et al., 2004).

Street prostitutes are less able or likely to insist on condom use than are other prostitutes, so they face a greater risk of acquiring sexually transmitted infections and becoming pregnant. A British study of street-based prostitutes found that every one of them was drug or alcohol dependent; for most, their days were a nonstop cycle of selling sex, buying and using drugs, and then returning to work (Jeal & Salisbury, 2004; Jeal et al., 2008). In another study, which focused on young men who exchanged sex for money (or drugs) in Harlem, New York, 41% of the men tested HIV-positive (El-Bassel et al., 2000). Some U.S. states have passed "aggravated prostitution" laws, which make it a felony for anyone to engage in prostitution while HIV-positive. In Tennessee, conviction for aggravated prostitution results in lifelong registration as a violent sex offender (Galletly et al., 2014).

The majority of female street prostitutes are mothers (Dalla, 2000). The fathers are not usually the women's customers; however, they are very often unavailable to support the children. The prostitute herself may give up or lose her parental rights. Street prostitutes who retain custody of their children experience considerable shame and anxiety about their own and their children's safety and may be reluctant to avail themselves of social services in case they should be deemed unfit mothers and lose custody of their children (Sloss & Harper, 2004).

### Female, male, and transgender streetwalkers have different experiences

Although female, male, and transgender streetwalkers all service male clients and all receive about the same payment per client, their experiences are otherwise quite different, according to a study led by sociologist Martin Weinberg of Indiana University (Weinberg et al., 1999). Female and transgender prostitutes tend to be in their late 20s, while male prostitutes are younger. Prostitution is more of a full-time occupation for women: They service more clients and earn a larger weekly income from prostitution than do either men or trans women. Men spend about twice as much time with each client as do either natal women or trans women, so their pay per hour is less.

The nonfinancial aspects of prostitution work out better for men, however. Most significantly, male and transgender prostitutes are much less likely to be beaten or raped by a client than are women (but see below). They cannot become pregnant and for the most part do not have children to worry about. Also, men in general have more interest in casual sex and in having multiple sex partners than do women. Accordingly, male prostitutes get more sexual enjoyment and experience orgasm more often in the course of their work than do women, according to the Weinberg study.

Another difference that works to the advantage of male prostitutes is that they tend to be independent agents working only for themselves, whereas women often work for **pimps**. The women give the pimps all or part of their earnings. In return, the pimps set up the women's living and working arrangements, protect their turf, provide drugs, and pay off mobsters and the police (or, if that doesn't work, bail the women out of jail).

A good deal of deception occurs in street prostitution. Prostitutes often con their clients: At least half the prostitutes in the Weinberg study said they had failed to provide promised services or they had demanded more money than initially agreed to. Transgender prostitutes frequently deceive their clients about their anatomical sex. They may tape back their penis and refuse to remove their panties, saying that they are having their period. Alternatively, they may use their anus or even their hands to fake coitus.

Transgender prostitutes do not always need to deceive, however, because plenty of men are specifically attracted to trans women, whom they call "she-males." According to the transgender prostitutes interviewed in the Weinberg study, it happened about 13 times a year that a client initially thought that the transgender prostitute was a natal woman but discovered the truth during the course of the encounter. About 15% of these clients responded violently; of the remainder, about half broke off the encounter, but the others simply carried on, suggesting that the discovery did not affect their enjoyment in a substantial way.

### Some prostitutes work out of massage parlors and strip clubs

Higher up the hierarchy are prostitutes who work at or out of a fixed commercial location such as a **massage parlor** or an exotic dance venue (strip club). Massage

**pimp**  A man who manages prostitutes in exchange for part of their earnings.

**massage parlor**  An establishment for massage that may also offer the services of prostitutes.

parlors are often the most readily available locations for prostitution in suburban areas, but because they have become so associated with prostitution, they have become a frequent target for police raids. In 2011 more than 30 people who were associated with "Goddess Temples" in Phoenix and Sedona, Arizona, were arrested on prostitution-related charges (ABC News, 2011). At the "temples," prosecutors alleged, johns were called "seekers" and coitus was called "sacred union."

Services at these kinds of locations vary, but hand–genital contact is the most common. At strip clubs, exotic dancers may provide sex by rubbing their body against the customer's genitals during a "lap dance." Alternatively, sex may take place in a "VIP room" or off-site after the show. Not all masseuses and exotic dancers are prostitutes, of course, but ads or word of mouth usually make it clear what services are available at a particular establishment.

The one kind of locale for prostitution that is hard to find in the United States today is an old-fashioned **brothel** (also called a bordello or whorehouse), whose traditional red lantern placed in the doorway gave red-light districts their name. Today, legal working brothels can be found only in some rural counties of Nevada (**FIGURE 17.4**). Brothels also function under the radar in some remote mining and logging communities.

A handful of the countless brothels that once flourished in the United States have been preserved for their historical value. The best known of these is the Dumas Brothel in Butte, Montana, which was designated a National Historic Landmark in 1973. After receiving this federal accolade, the brothel continued operating for another 9 years.*

Legal brothels are found in several European countries. The city of Zurich, Switzerland, has built a municipal "drive-in brothel" as part of an effort to reduce street prostitution (Lidz, 2016) (**FIGURE 17.5**). The brothel has a series of carwash-style booths where the action takes place, as well as a café, shower facilities, and a laundry, and security staff are on-site. There is no charge for prostitutes to use the brothel, but pimps are banned from the area.

### Escort services are the main form of prostitution in the United States

The most prevalent form of prostitution in the United States is **escort service** prostitution. This is off-street prostitution that is not tied to a specific service location. **Escorts** (or **call girls**) may promote their services by a variety of means, including ads in newspapers and adult entertainment magazines, but the internet is now their principal advertising medium. Escorts may have their own websites, or they may work for an agency that has a site. Some personal ads that appear to be posted by individuals are actually the product of organized-crime groups (Chan et al., 2019).

In recent years the U.S. government has attempted to clamp down on web-based advertising. The most popular site, Backpage, was seized and closed down in 2018; in the same year President Trump signed legislation making website owners liable for prostitution-related content, with penalties ranging up to 10 years in prison. Nevertheless, websites based overseas still

▲ **FIGURE 17.4  Sex in the sticks** Nevada's Shady Lady Ranch is located far from the bright lights of Las Vegas. This brothel was the first to offer a legal "prostidude"; he served women at $300 per hour but quit for lack of customers.

**brothel**  A house of prostitution.

**escort service**  A service that provides prostitutes, generally contacted by phone or online.

**escort (or call girl)**  Euphemism for a prostitute who advertises by print, word of mouth, or the internet.

▲ **FIGURE 17.5  Zurich street sign** points the way to the city's drive-in brothel.

*The owner of the brothel, Ruby Garrett, was a kindly woman who shot her husband while he was playing cards, killing him instantly. She was acquitted of murder and died in 2012.

operate, and U.S. websites such as Craigslist still carry ads for massage and other services that may be covers for prostitution.

Some websites offer customers "verification membership," which means that the site verifies who the customer is, and the customer can then use his verification to contact escorts. This is a benefit both to the customer, who can avoid giving the escort personal information such as credit card numbers, and to the escort, who can use the verification to be sure of the customer's identity and to avoid police stings. Because prostitution is illegal almost everywhere, code terms are widely used in prostitutes' advertising and communications (**TABLE 17.1**). The sites themselves often state that their advertisers are not selling sex and that any sex that happens has nothing to do with the contracted services.

Another advantage of these sites is that they may allow for customers to review escorts in the same way that they might review restaurants or hotels. Another site, TheEroticReview.com, is wholly dedicated to reviews of escorts by self-described "hobbyists"; it reports receiving about 250,000 unique visitors daily. (Access to this site was blocked in the United States until 2019.) Such sites provide valuable information not only for other customers but also for researchers. In one study of escort service prostitution in the United States and other Westernized countries, researchers matched customers' descriptions of prostitutes with the prices they charged per hour, thus coming up with an estimate of the monetary value of various physical attributes (The Economist, 2014). The woman's build ("very fat" to "athletic") was the most important variable, but hair length, hair color, and bust size all influenced prices (**FIGURE 17.6**). Based on these figures, a woman who spent $3700 on plastic surgery to increase her bust size from flat to D earned about $40 more per hour, so she would recoup her outlay after about 90 hours' work.

None of this is very surprising, given that the objectification of women (and sometimes of men) lies at the very core of prostitution. You might be surprised, however, to learn that having a college degree also increases a prostitute's value, and by a hefty 31%, which is similar to the premium that college graduates enjoy in other fields (Cunningham & Kendall, 2010). This is not because they earn more per hour or have more clients, but because they have much longer sessions with their clients, who tend to be older men wanting a "girlfriend experience." These "talk and cuddle" sessions take more time and require a higher level of education than regular assignments.

Escort service prostitution is much safer for the escorts than street work: Escorts face a lower risk of violence or arrest, and they are better able to require the use of condoms. It is also safer for the client—he is less likely to be robbed or arrested. Compared with "straight" work, however, escort service prostitution is still a risky business. One Oregon man named Neal Falls is suspected of having murdered a series of escorts; his killing spree came to an abrupt end in 2015, when he was shot dead with his own gun by an escort he had planned to torture and kill (NBC News, 2015).

Although much of an escort's work is anonymous and loveless, some escorts see the same clients over and over again, and their relationships with these "regulars" can become quite intimate

**TABLE 17.1** Some coded terms and slang used in prostitution

| | |
|---|---|
| Provider | Escort prostitute |
| Generous (or gen) | Willing to pay for sex |
| Incall | At escort's place |
| Outcall | At customer's place |
| Girlfriend experience | Longer session with romantic flavor |
| Massage rates | Manual stimulation |
| Full companionship (or full service) | Coitus |
| Half-and-half | Fellatio and coitus |
| Interpreter | Condom |
| Bareback | Without a condom |
| Fully functional (in reference to trans prostitute) | Has a penis |
| 420 friendly | Into sex under influence of marijuana |
| Party'n'play (PNP) | Into sex on drugs (usually methamphetamine) |
| Versatile (in male ads) | Into insertive or receptive anal sex |
| Donation | Price |
| Roses | Dollars |

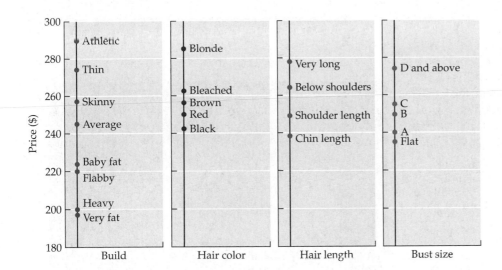

◀ **FIGURE 17.6  Looks matter** This figure shows how physical features influence the price of one hour with a female prostitute, based on data from several countries. (After *The Economist*. 2014. More bang for your buck. *The Economist* 420(1): 18.)

and pleasurable to both parties. Regulars are also desirable because they are predictable and therefore safer for the prostitute.

At the top of the prostitution hierarchy are the premier escorts—beautiful and well-presented young women or men that a client can take to dinner or a show without embarrassment. Such a prostitute might stay with a visiting businessperson or politician for an entire weekend or even travel abroad to spend time with a well-heeled oil sheikh. These top-end escort service prostitutes often work for **madams** who have some access to affluent society. Alternatively, they may work for prostitution rings. One such ring, named the Emperors Club, charged $1000 to $5000 per hour for its escorts' services; it was shut down in a 2008 scandal that cost the job of the then governor of New York, Eliot Spitzer.

A form of sexual moneymaking that attracts many college students is sugaring (**BOX 17.2**). This activity straddles the boundary between prostitution and legitimate sexual relationships.

## Many prostitutes work for pimps

A pimp is a person—usually a man—who facilitates prostitution and lives off prostitutes' earnings. This is the usual meaning of the word, but in legal terms, the crime of pimping refers specifically to receiving a prostitute's earnings; in most states facilitating prostitution is another crime called procuring or pandering.

A pimp may introduce a young woman to the business. He promotes her, arranges her assignations, and provides security in case the client becomes abusive. If the prostitute is a streetwalker, he assigns and protects her turf. In the case of incall prostitution he sets up the incall location. In the case of out-calls, he may come to an arrangement with staff at the client's hotel or motel. A typical pimp manages several prostitutes. The prostitute gives her pimp a part or all of her earnings. In return he may give her clothes and other gifts, and he takes care of her living expenses.

Some pimps have amicable, mutually beneficial relationships with prostitutes, as described here by a pimp in the San Diego study mentioned in Section 17.1 (Carpenter & Gates, 2016):

> *The best pimps are the ones you don't even know exist. Girl feels comfort in that. Most times, the girls don't need the guys, the guy's just her comfort zone, to feel loved, to feel like you're her dad, you're their bodyguard; however they feel, you know you're the protector that knows what's going on. . . . If the money keeps rolling, everything's smooth, nobody gets hurt. People are happy both ways.*

Other pimps may coerce women to engage in prostitution, in which case the pimps are known as sex traffickers (see Section 17.4).

**madam**   A woman who manages a brothel or an escort service.

## BOX 17.2
## Sugaring

A fresh-faced student who's maxed out her loans? And a wealthy businessman who'd like some youthful company? That's a match made in sugar heaven.

She's a sugar baby, and he's a sugar daddy, and they're sugaring. And they're not alone. At least 2.5 million students—mostly women, but also plenty of young men—have registered as sugar babies or sugar boys on sugaring's premier website, SeekingArrangement.com. That doesn't mean that they've all found daddies, but they'd like to. And according to a YouGov poll—not the most reliable of polls, we have to say—8% of women and men age 18 to 34 are involved in sugaring relationships (YouGov, 2017).

What does sugaring actually involve? Socializing, certainly, but most of the daddies want sex too. How many of the sugar babies and sugar boys are willing to give it up is unclear, but you don't get $90,000—the amount a Michigan State University student named Christina said she received over 2 years—for sipping merlot on a few dinner dates (Loudenback, 2017).

Is sugaring prostitution? As far as the law is concerned, probably not, because any sex that happens is—or is said to be—incidental to a social relationship, and any cash donation is made out of the goodness of the sugar daddy's heart, not as part of an explicit pay-to-play deal. On a moral level, sugar babies have to deal with the same social stigma that prostitutes face, but that's just part of the cost of doing business. "At the end of the day, it's benefiting me and it's helping me and my future," said Christina, "and people's opinions aren't going to benefit my future."

Alyssa Ramos, 21, from Madison, Wisconsin, traveled the world for free, courtesy of travel companions like Oliver Wright, a 37-year-old lawyer. Ramos said that no sex took place.

And just as prostitutes are often viewed as socioeconomic victims, the same can be true of sugar babies. Here's what one young woman wrote on Jezebel.com: "What really sucks about sugar baby relationships is that most of the arrangements don't seem like they're entered into freely; they're a desperate response to a shitty set of circumstances—a lack of job opportunities, lack of job abilities, and last, but not least, the insanely high cost of college education" (Ryan, 2013).

### Men who use escorts have liberal attitudes

It has often been claimed, especially in the popular media, that men who use prostitutes are very ordinary men—the "johns next door," as *Newsweek* put it (Bennetts, 2011). This may have been true in the distant past, when prostitution was far more prevalent than it is today and most men had used prostitutes at some time in their lives. Now, however, only 14% of men have ever had sex with a prostitute, and only about 1% have done so during the previous 12 months, according to a study of data from the General Social Survey and other sources by Martin Monto and Christine Milrod of the University of Portland (Monto & Milrod, 2013). This raises the possibility that users of prostitutes have special characteristics that distinguish them from the general male population.

Monto and Milrod found this to be true, at least for the "hobbyists" who are frequent users of internet-based escort-style prostitutes. These men were more highly educated and had higher incomes than the general male population, and they had far more liberal attitudes on sexual matters: Only 6% thought that gay sex was wrong, for example, versus 55% in the control sample. Most of them believed that prostitutes enjoy their work and said that they would be willing to marry a prostitute. Not surprisingly, nearly all of the hobbyists believed that prostitution should be legalized, and they rarely if ever ran into trouble with the law. Thus the users of escort prostitutes are very different from nonusers of prostitutes, but not in pathological ways. Rather, they seem to be free-thinking enthusiasts. Men arrested for seeking to hire street-based prostitutes, on the other hand, tend to be younger, unmarried men who have little experience with prostitution and are therefore more likely to be caught in police sting operations.

**gigolo**  A male prostitute who caters to women.

## Some women use male prostitutes

Male escorts are the only kind of prostitute that women use in any significant numbers. Male escorts who are paid by women are called **gigolos**. Gigolos are usually very presentable young men who are able to interact socially with their clients in addition to providing sexual services. There are some websites, such as cowboys4angels.com, that provide gigolos, but this kind of service forms only a minute portion of the escort industry in the United States. Although gigolos emphasize their social and conversational skills, ripped abs don't hurt (**FIGURE 17.7**).

Rather than hire expensive gigolos, some older white women travel to Africa, the Caribbean (especially Jamaica), or elsewhere for sexual pleasure (Bauer, 2014). In the coastal resort communities of Kenya, for example, female sex tourists can obtain sex and companionship from strapping 20-year-old Maasai tribesmen, sometimes for as little as a pair of sunglasses. It's not just about economics, though: White women who seek out nonwhite men in exotic environments are driven by a particular fantasy—that of violating colonial taboos to find intimacy with a hypermasculine "native" (Jacobs, 2010). No amount of money can fulfill this fantasy in their home countries.

## Juvenile prostitution is of special concern

In spite of the many unfounded guesstimates that you may have heard, the number of juvenile (under 18) prostitutes in the United States is not known. They certainly exist in significant numbers, however, especially in cities where there are large populations of homeless youth (**BOX 17.3**). Most are age 14 to 17, but a few are younger. The older youths often have false IDs that identify them as adults.

These youths have often fled abusive home environments. Some are mentally ill. They have little of marketable value aside from their youthful bodies, so prostitution is often a necessity ("survival sex") rather than the best-paid option out of many. They are vulnerable to further abuse, violence, exploitation, and disease. Some have been brought from out of state (by sex traffickers—see below). When they are caught by the police, they are usually treated as victims, and the criminal focus is on the pimps or the johns. Sometimes they are charged with offenses and detained simply so they can be provided with needed services.

Drug use is very common among juvenile prostitutes, and withdrawal symptoms are often the immediate reason for turning a trick. "When I was on junk [heroin] I'd get so sick without it that I'd have to be working," said a young woman who entered prostitution at age 14. "I'd have to have money for drugs to be OK" (Downe & "Ashley-Mika," 2003).

Not all juvenile prostitutes are homeless. Some still live with their parents, attend school, and have not been abused. They engage in prostitution not to survive but to obtain money for luxuries such as expensive clothes. In 2014 a 17-year-old female high school student in Venice, Florida, was charged with running an underage prostitution ring—according to police, she pimped high school students as young as 15 for $40 to $200 a trick (Womack, 2014). When researchers spoke with staff at 20 San Diego–area high schools, all said that some female students were earning money from prostitution (Carpenter & Gates, 2016).

▲ **FIGURE 17.7**  **Gigolo Nick Hawk** starred in a Showtime reality TV series, *Gigolos*, about the lives of male escorts in Las Vegas.

## BOX 17.3
## Juvenile Prostitutes in Portland, Oregon

As any visitor to Portland knows, this vibrant city has a large population of street-based youths, some of whom survive through prostitution. One of them, "Kendall," told her story to *The Portland Mercury* (Marcus, 2009). At the age of 16, Kendall left home to live with DJ, the homeless, abusive, and alcoholic boyfriend with whom she had fallen in love. Within days he had persuaded her to sell herself on the street—sometimes as often as 25 times in a day. DJ took most of her earnings and also beat her. Although Kendall continued to attend school, she sometimes had to wear sunglasses to conceal a black eye or invent an explanation for visible bruises. As soon as school let out each afternoon, she began turning tricks.

This continued for a year. Eventually she told DJ she was leaving him, and she returned to her parents' home, but DJ came to visit while her parents were out. "In 2 hours your dad is going to come home and find your dead body on the basement floor," he said, and he attacked her and tried to strangle her. Luckily, Kendall was able to dial 911. As the police battered on the door, DJ begged Kendall to say they had just been having sex, but the welt around her neck, and several broken ribs, told the true story. DJ was arrested; he was eventually sentenced to 8 years in prison for assault and for pimping.

Kendall's experience was not unusual. "Most of the teens I meet with have suffered repeated, horrific abuse at the hands of both pimps and johns," said Esther Nelson of Portland's Sexual Assault Resource Center. "Many have been burned, stabbed, shot, strangled, thrown from moving cars, tied up, branded, and starved."

Girls from Seattle and Portland are often trafficked by their pimps down the Interstate 5 corridor to Los Angeles and Las Vegas. In the latter city, over 100 underage girls are picked up by the police for on-street prostitution every year (see

Underage prostitutes are more victims than criminals.

© Chris Matula/Palm Beach Post/Zuma Press

figure). For her master's thesis in criminal justice at the University of Nevada, Las Vegas, Alanna Robinson studied 52 of these girls, along with a comparison group of girls detained for other offenses (Robinson, 2010). Most came from dysfunctional homes where at least one family member had served time in prison. Most had been physically, sexually, or emotionally abused in their home environment. Many had been removed at least once from an abusive family environment by child welfare authorities.

In 2011 actors Ashton Kutcher and Demi Moore began a campaign against juvenile prostitution, in the course of which they claimed that between 100,000 and 300,000 children are lost to prostitution and sex trafficking in the United States every year (McLaughlin, 2011). This figure (which has been cited frequently in the media, including *The New York Times*) is based on a misinterpretation of a 2002 study by social scientists Richard Estes and Neil Weiner of the University of Pennsylvania (Estes & Weiner, 2002). Those researchers actually gave these figures as the number of children who were *at risk* of commercial sexual exploitation, not those who actually fell victim to it. Researchers at the University of New Hampshire have estimated the total yearly arrests for juvenile prostitution in the United States at 1450 (Mitchell et al., 2010), but this does not account for juveniles who engage in prostitution without being arrested.

Kendall's history was actually an unusual one in that she had run away from a stable, loving home environment, and this may have been her ultimate salvation. After recovering from DJ's assault, she completed high school, enrolled in a community college, and now has aspirations for a career in law enforcement.

---

Leaving the United States for a moment, it's worth mentioning that sex work by schoolgirls is rampant in Japan, where it is called "JK" service (*joshi kōsei* is Japanese for "high school girl") (**FIGURE 17.8**). The work may involve sex ("compensated dating") or erotic modeling. The girls wear their school uniforms, which have an almost fetishistic allure for middle-aged Japanese businessmen. "If there are two 16-year old girls, and one's at school and one's not, customers will always choose the one who's at school," according to a man who arranges JK dates (Fifield, 2017). The JK industry is illegal if sex is involved, but there is little public concern about it, and the participants are unlikely to get into trouble.

## 17.4 Sex Trafficking Is a Global Business

### LEARNING OBJECTIVES

After reading this section you should be able to:

17.4.1 Define sex trafficking.

17.4.2 Evaluate the argument that the campaign against transnational sex trafficking infringes on the rights of the women involved.

Sex traffickers coerce people to engage in prostitution or facilitate prostitution by minors. Thus pimps are sex traffickers if they employ some form of coercion, which may include beatings, sexual assault, economic coercion, or imprisonment. Sometimes psychological abuse is all it takes to achieve the pimp's objectives. Here is how one self-identified "gorilla pimp" put it in the San Diego study (Carpenter & Gates, 2016):

> *Girls are very vulnerable and they're very weak minded. You can really crash somebody's dreams down and you can do it to a girl very quick and very fast. You know, in the pimping game, you never compliment your ho. You don't want her to think too fine of herself. You know, you wanna tell her shit like, "go clean your fucking face" when nothing's on her face. You know what I'm saying? You want her to make her feel like she has to prove herself to you. You don't want that to ever stop.*

Sex traffickers commonly move their prostitutes around the country. In Box 17.3 we described how juveniles are trafficked from Portland, Oregon, to Las Vegas. This practice has the main objective of satisfying the high demand in "Sin City," but it has the additional benefit (to the trafficker) of isolating the juveniles from their home environments, thus making them easier to control, and it may make the juveniles harder to trace by law enforcement. If state lines are crossed, however, there will be a violation of federal law.

Transnational trafficking means the transportation of individuals—usually women or girls—from one country to another to supply the demand for prostitutes. The direction of transport is usually from poorer to richer countries (**FIGURE 17.9**). For example, many women are transported from Bangladesh to Pakistan and India, from Myanmar (Burma) to Thailand, from Vietnam to China, and from the Philippines and Thailand to Japan. Women are trafficked to the United States from places all over the world, including Latin America, Southeast Asia, Eastern Europe, and Russia. Western Europe is also a major destination for trafficked prostitutes.

There is a lot of variation in how willingly women participate in transnational sex trafficking. Some women know what they are letting themselves in for and see it as a chance for economic betterment, in which case the practice might not qualify as sex trafficking in legal terms. At the other extreme, some women are deceived, enslaved, held prisoner in the host country, and forced to engage in prostitution against their will. Most cases fall into a gray area: The women travel voluntarily and know that they will be working in the sex industry, but they experience some degree of deception or coercion.

▲ **FIGURE 17.8 When Japanese teenagers offer "JK" services,** their status as schoolchildren is central to their sex appeal.

▲ Juvenile prostitutes are highly visible in some cities around the world, such as here in Bangkok, Thailand.

▶ **FIGURE 17.9** **Traffic in women and girls for prostitution** flows largely from poorer to richer countries. (After National Intelligence Council. 2000. *Global trends 2015: A dialogue about the future with nongovernment experts*. National Intelligence Council: Washington, D.C. https://tinyurl.com/y9ejsrca.)

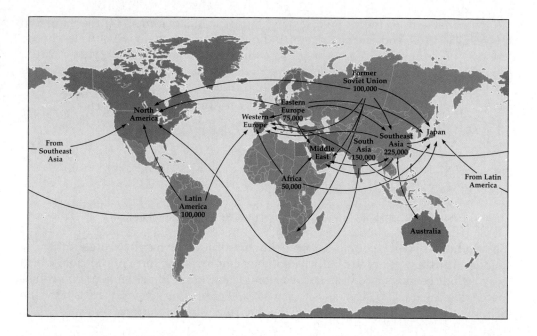

For example, they may have to work longer as prostitutes in the host country to "pay back" their traffickers than they were initially led to believe.

The Coalition Against Trafficking in Women (CATW) takes an unreservedly negative view of this trade. "To say that these women are voluntarily allowing themselves to be trafficked is to ignore the powerful social conditions that push women and girls into that kind of life," says Dorchen Leidholdt, one of CATW's founders. "The valuation of women as commodities in the global marketplace is devastating to the rights of all women."

While CATW opposes all forms of prostitution, another organization, the Global Alliance Against Traffic in Women (GAATW), takes a different stance: Although it also opposes trafficking as exploitation, GAATW affirms the right of women to migrate and to choose their own occupations, including sex work. A similar position has been laid out by Elizabeth Bernstein, a professor of women's studies at Barnard College. She argues that campaigners against sex trafficking are motivated by "feel-good capitalism" and have little real interest in the welfare of women in the source countries or their right to choose their own destiny (Bernstein, 2018).

Although sex trafficking does exist, the magnitude of the problem—especially with regard to juveniles—has sometimes been blown up into a veritable sex panic. In 2013, for example, the *Dallas Morning News* brought ridicule on itself by asserting, "In Houston alone, about 300,000 sex trafficking cases are prosecuted each year" (*Dallas Morning News*, 2013). The actual number in that year was 2 (Bennett, 2013).

The converse of transnational trafficking is **sex tourism**. In this case, instead of the prostitute being brought to the more affluent consumer's country, the consumer travels to the home country of the prostitute. Popular destinations include the Dominican Republic, the Netherlands, Thailand, and Indonesia. The reason for travel may include the legality of prostitution in the countries visited (or the lax enforcement of whatever anti-prostitution laws exist), the low prices sex tourists expect to pay in Third World countries, and the availability of very young prostitutes.

Some men actually relocate to foreign countries on account of the availability and low price of sex. In 1998, for example, Britain's *Sunday Mirror* alleged that the science fiction writer Arthur C. Clarke (1917–2008) was a pedophile who lived in Sri Lanka in order to have sex with underage Sri Lankan boys (Popham, 1998). Clarke denied the allegation but did not sue the newspaper.

**sex tourism** Traveling to a foreign country to find sex partners (usually prostitutes).

# 17.5   There Are Conflicting Views on Prostitution

### LEARNING OBJECTIVES
After reading this section you should be able to:

17.5.1   Evaluate arguments for and against the idea that prostitution is just another part of the gig economy and should therefore be decriminalized.

17.5.2   Explain and evaluate the libertarian perspective on prostitution.

Americans are about equally divided on the question of whether prostitution should be legal, but there are demographic differences: More men than women, and more young people than old people, support legalization (Marist Poll, 2016) (**FIGURE 17.10**). Among those who oppose legalization, the majority do so for moral or religious reasons rather than because of the potential negative effects of prostitution, such as the spread of sexually transmitted infections (STIs). Moral opposition to prostitution is probably rooted in the belief that casual sex itself is morally wrong.

A traditional feminist view is that men's use of prostitutes is misogynistic. A well-known proponent of this view was anti-prostitution and anti-pornography crusader Andrea Dworkin (1946–2005). "When men use women in prostitution, they are expressing a pure hatred for the female body," she wrote. Prostitution, according to Dworkin, is "gang rape punctuated by money exchange" (Dworkin, 1994).

It is certainly true that some men maltreat prostitutes. Yet there are also men who take a great deal of interest in the women they pay and take pains to please them. "I have found that escorts are some of the finest and most interesting women you'll ever meet and it's a real treat to get to know them," writes Marc Perkel, author of an online guide to escort service prostitution. "I recommend that you prepare for your escort's arrival the same way you would for a date. After all, escorts offer more than just sex. Often you can get good conversation and personal companionship as well. And you get these other services by being as nice to them as to any other woman you date" (Perkel, n.d.). Similar ideas are expressed by numerous "hobbyists" on review sites like TheEroticReview.com. "Yes, it's a paid friendship," wrote one reviewer, "but it's still a friendship." Given the existence of these positive attitudes, it's hard to believe that hatred of women is the main driver of female prostitution, any more than hatred of men is the main driver of male prostitution.

In recent years, feminist attitudes toward prostitution have taken two diverging perspectives (Benoit et al., 2019). In one, prostitution is seen as the result of gender inequality in a patriarchal society. Sex work, it's thought, is not like other forms of work that exploit people's bodies, such as laboring, because what is paid for is not simply the work a prostitute does, but also her actual womanhood. In this view, there is no difference between regular prostitution and sex trafficking—both represent the sexual enslavement of women. Feminists who take this perspective tend to believe that prostitution should remain a crime, but that a heavier punitive burden should be placed on the men who hire prostitutes than on the prostitutes themselves.

In the other feminist view, prostitution results from social inequality—that is, from the class structure of society. This is a Marxist perspective: Prostitutes sell their labor in the same way as other unskilled people do in an exploitative capitalist system. The main reason that there are more female than male prostitutes is not gender inequality, in this view; rather, it's because men are more interested in casual sex than women, and most men are heterosexual. Prostitution is part of the gig economy—the system of independent workers who are paid on a per-task basis—and as such offers some pros and cons as compared to unskilled wage-based work: freedom and the possibility of

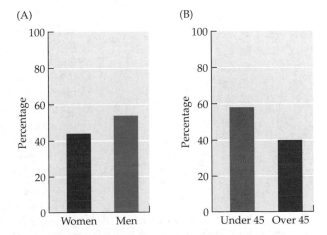

▲ **FIGURE 17.10   Should prostitution be legalized?** (A) The percentage of American women and men who support legalization. (B) The percentage of Americans under and over 45 who support legalization. (After Marist Poll. 2016. *Should prostitution be legalized?* Marist Institute for Public Opinion. Poughkeepsie, NY.)

higher earnings, counterbalanced by greater uncertainties and risks. Feminists who take this perspective tend to support the decriminalization of prostitution.

There is a legitimate question about whether the harms suffered by prostitutes are inherent to prostitution, or whether they result from the way society views and treats the practice (Moen, 2014). The concept of occupational health and safety, for example, which has greatly improved working conditions in many fields, is difficult or impossible to apply to an occupation that is illegal. It has therefore been argued that legalization would greatly reduce the harms associated with prostitution (Ross et al., 2012). In the legal brothels of Nevada, for example, prostitutes seldom experience violence or acquire STIs—and of course they are not arrested in connection with their work (Brents & Hausbeck, 2005). These beneficial effects associated with legalization have been noted in many other countries.

Finally, there is the libertarian point of view. This is the idea that, even if prostitution is intrinsically harmful, governments should allow adults to make choices about their lives, including bad choices, so long as any resulting harm is to the choosers rather than to other people. In the case of prostitution, the prostitute and her client voluntarily make a deal that is unlikely to harm anyone beyond those two people. And to the extent that there is any potential harm to others, such as damaged relationships or the spread of STIs, these harms characterize casual sex in general rather than being specific to sex that is paid for. Thus the Libertarian Party includes prostitution in an extensive list of activities that it believes government has no business concerning itself with (OnTheIssues.org, 2018).

## There are several options for legal reform

If Americans ever come to believe that prostitution—or some forms of prostitution—should no longer be a crime, they will have at least three options. The first is **decriminalization**—that is, the laws banning prostitution would simply be eliminated. This avenue is favored by prostitutes' rights groups (King, 2015). In 2017 one such group brought suit to have California's prostitution laws overthrown, arguing that the laws violate people's rights to have consensual sex. In allowing the suit to proceed, a judge asked, "Why should it be illegal to sell something that it's legal to give away?" (Morris, 2017). A federal appeals court rejected the lawsuit, however, leaving California's prostitution laws intact.

In Rhode Island indoor prostitution was decriminalized in 2003, when a judge spotted a hidden deficiency in existing law. The deficiency was corrected in 2009. Economists working for the National Bureau of Economic Research took advantage of this six-year "holiday" to study the potential effects of decriminalization (Cunningham & Shah, 2014). As might be expected, there was an increase in indoor prostitution. In addition, though, rape offenses decreased by 31% and cases of female gonorrhea decreased by 39%. These findings suggested that, while the decriminalization of indoor prostitution may cause harm (for example, to the women engaged in prostitution), there are likely also to be social benefits.

The second alternative is **legalization with regulation**. This corresponds roughly to the conditions under which Nevada's legal brothels operate. Prostitutes would be allowed to work in prescribed locations and under defined conditions. They might be required to be licensed, to take safe-sex classes, or to have periodic medical examinations for STIs. Proponents argue that this system would reduce the harmful side effects of prostitution, such as disease, unwanted pregnancy, violence, and organized crime.

A third avenue, called the **Nordic model**, is to decriminalize the *selling* of sex but to maintain or strengthen penalties for the *buying* of sex, in line with the gender-inequality feminist perspective described above. It may seem an odd idea for one side of a transaction to be legal and the other side illegal, but this is currently the situation in Norway, Sweden, France, and Iceland. If this model were enacted, prostitutes might be less exposed to extortion and more willing to seek medical care.

**decriminalization** Removal of laws that criminalize activities, such as prostitution.

**legalization with regulation** Conversion of an activity, such as prostitution, from a crime to a governmentally regulated occupation.

**Nordic model** A system in which prostitution is a crime for the client but not for the prostitute.

Prostitution would remain a crime, however, and the stigma associated with it would remain. Thus prostitutes would not be able to function as sex workers with rights and obligations comparable to those of workers in "straight" occupations.

Regardless of the merits of these different perspectives, it's not likely that laws will be changed to make prostitution legal anywhere in the United States, at least in the near future. San Francisco voters had the opportunity to do so in 2008, but the measure was soundly defeated. Given that San Francisco is a liberal city, especially in sexual matters, it's unlikely that a similar measure would fare better anywhere else in the country.

The question of what (if anything) to do about the legal status of prostitution in the United States is a difficult one, and there are merits to diverse views. We hope that you will take advantage of this class to develop your own opinion based on your background, your readings, and discussions inside and outside of the classroom.

## 17.6 There Is More to Sex Work Than Prostitution

**LEARNING OBJECTIVE**

After reading this section you should be able to:

**17.6.1 Describe two forms of sex work that don't involve sexual contact.**

Prostitution—the selling of actual sexual contact—is the most controversial form of commercial sex work, but there are plenty of other forms, such as exotic dancing, or stripping, as well as phone sex and erotic webcamming. These activities straddle the boundary between prostitution and pornography.

### Stripping is going mainstream

Exotic dancers, more commonly known as strippers, may be female or male. They usually perform in strip clubs, but there are also agencies that provide strippers for private parties and other events. Some male strippers ("go-go boys") work in gay bars.

Laws governing what can happen in strip clubs—and whether they can exist at all—vary greatly from place to place. Mostly, strip clubs are legal but are restricted to certain parts of a city. Full nudity may or may not be allowed—most commonly it is. In some places no contact between dancer and customer is permitted, but in others the dancer may grind against the customer's crotch in a lap dance. Many strip clubs have private areas where there is little oversight over what transpires.

The trend, however, is toward greater restraint because strip clubs are becoming more popular with a mainstream audience than previously. Some strip clubs are popular with businesspeople—men and sometimes women too— who visit to have a drink and conduct business or entertain clients. (To some, this practice is just another way in which career advancement is made more difficult for women.) In these establishments the dancers are likely to avoid direct contact with customers and focus mostly on pole dancing and the like. Pole dancing itself has gone mainstream: Middle-aged suburbanites now take pole-dancing classes as a form of fitness workout.

### Phone sex has diversified

In traditional **phone sex** the customer calls an operator who engages him in erotic conversation while he masturbates or fantasizes. The customer is charged about $4 per minute. Billing via premium-rate telephone numbers has

**phone sex** Erotic telephone conversations, usually carried out for pay.

© Guy Corbishley/Alamy Stock Photo

▲ Exotic dancers at a strip club.

largely given way to the use of credit cards. There are also chat lines like Masturline that don't have professional operators; instead, members pay to do some heavy breathing with other members.

Phone sex companies like to create the impression that their operators are motivated by sex, not money, of course. "Missy is a diagnosed nymphomaniac and phone sex is her therapy," announces one website. "Most operators will orgasm with the caller," says another. Anyone who believes this might want to read an amusing account of the "unsexy realities" of the job posted by a retired phone sex operator (Mannen, 2014). Still, she does acknowledge that phone sex serves a purpose for some operators beyond the financial rewards. "They don't like the way they look," she writes, "and pretending to be what the client wants them to be allows them to feel desirable. . . . There are more grandmothers than you'd care to know about in this industry." Phone sex spares the operators most of the risks associated with prostitution, so long as they resist the numerous requests to meet customers in person. In addition, most operators now work from home, so they can fit the work into their daily schedules.

Phone sex operators become more familiar with obscure corners of male sexuality than most professional sexologists. According to the retired operator mentioned above, it's all in a day's work to describe shrinking the client down to an inch in height and flushing him down the toilet, to speak to him in the voice and manner of a 6-year-old, or to converse with him in a wholly made-up "language of the yak people."

## Cam models offer "realness"

A more up-to-date variant on phone sex is **sexual webcamming** (**FIGURE 17.11**). Webcammers, generally known as cam models, perform online, and customers can request specific acts, for which they tip with "tokens" purchased ahead of time. Cam models have to be more presentable than phone sex operators, and they may need to show more authentic signs of sexual engagement, but the potential rewards are greater because the webcammer can service more than one customer simultaneously.

Although most cam models are accessed via websites such as Chaturbate, where they compete for clients' attention with hundreds of other models, once a client has logged onto a particular model he experiences something like authenticity, or "realness," which is only partly feigned. Often the models work in their own bedroom, which gives the experience an amateur flavor, and they interact in lively fashion with their clients. In a survey of cam models by sociologist Angela Jones, one model put it this way:

> Ya know, guys don't spend all that money because they want something fake. I mean, they come because they want to believe that it's a real woman they're talking to and it's a real person. And that they can tell you what to do; they can get exactly what they want . . . For them it's about the interaction . . . Some of them I think could care less about the sex; it's just having someone pay them interest. . . . You're flirting with them and making them feel good about themselves. And I think that means more to them than seeing you bend over and spread your butt cheeks. (Jones, 2020)

Two obvious benefits of camming, for the models, are safety—no physical interactions with clients—and good pay. Another is pleasure: Most cam models get both sexual and social pleasure from their work. In Jones's survey, 87% of respondents said that they were satisfied with their job. Typical comments included:

**sexual webcamming**   Live sexual performances or nudity supplied over the internet for pay.

© Christina Koci Hernandez/San Francisco Chronicle/Corbis

▲ **FIGURE 17.11**   **Melissa Gira Grant,** webcamming pioneer and writer on the sex industry.

"It's a blast," "It's super fun," "I enjoy dressing up and chatting with people online," and "I've had quite a bit of jobs in the past, but not one of them has been as fun and amazing as camming has been." One model, a man, did express a different perspective: "The compliments are nice, but it takes a drag on your sex life. Makes it feel like a chore and the fun goes away . . . Then it just gets boring."

Underage webcamming is a serious problem. The most notorious case involved a Californian boy named Justin Berry, who at the age of 13 began performing in his bedroom at his family home, without his parents' knowledge. He went on to recruit other juveniles. Over the space of a few years Berry received hundreds of thousands of dollars in goods and cash from his male customers. He became well known nationally after *The New York Times* published a story about him (Eichenwald, 2005): He appeared on national talk shows, and he testified before Congress about how he had been victimized online and in the real world. In spite of these traumas, Berry went on to become a successful computer security entrepreneur.

# 17.7 Pornography Has Always Been Part of Human Culture

## LEARNING OBJECTIVES
After reading this section you should be able to:

17.7.1 Cite the legal criteria under which pornography may be banned, according to *Miller v. California*.

17.7.2 Explain what products and activities are illegal under child pornography laws.

The word **pornography** (often abbreviated as "porn") refers to depictions of people or behaviors that are intended to be sexually arousing. The depictions can be in any medium, but the most common ones are photography, video/film, written text, and drawing/painting. Sometimes the term "pornography" is restricted to the more down-market products, or products of which the speaker disapproves. More expensive works, or those that are considered to have literary or artistic merit, may be called **erotica**. This distinction is very subjective, of course. One catchall, nonjudgmental term that is popular with academics and policy makers is **sexually explicit materials,** but on the face of it that phrase encompasses educational materials (such as some of the illustrations in this textbook) that are not intended to be sexually arousing, so we will stick with "pornography."

Pornographic works survive from many ancient cultures. Often, as with the sexually themed ceramics created by pre-Incan and Incan cultures, the intent of the artist remains mysterious. However, some ancient works, such as the sculptures and wall paintings that decorated the brothels of the ancient Roman city of Pompeii, are clearly intended to be sexually arousing.

## Pornography has battled censorship

During the 19th century, almost anything that was potentially arousing was considered **obscene**—that is, sexually offensive or threatening to public morality. In the United States, the federal **Comstock Laws** of 1873, and comparable state laws, criminalized the sale or possession of obscene materials. Some writings were banned as obscene even though they had no content that would be considered pornographic today. These included writings about contraception and homosexuality. The legal suppression of such materials continued well into the 20th century.

At present, the law regarding pornography in the United States is governed by the Supreme Court's decision in the 1973 case **Miller v. California**. According to *Miller*, there is no broad, First Amendment protection for pornography, but states may restrict a pornographic work only under certain conditions:

**pornography** Material (such as art, writing, photographic images, and film) that is intended to be sexually arousing. Also called porn.

**erotica** Sexually themed works, such as books or sculpture, deemed to have literary or artistic merit.

**sexually explicit materials** A nonjudgmental phrase denoting pornography.

**obscene** Related to sexually themed publications, art, films, performances, or behavior that is deemed offensive to public morals or that violates legal standards of acceptability.

**Comstock Laws** Federal and state laws enacted in the late 19th century that criminalized pornography.

***Miller v. California*** A 1973 Supreme Court definition of the characteristics of pornography that can be made illegal.

- The average person, applying contemporary community standards, must find that the work, taken as a whole, appeals to the prurient interest (i.e., is intended to be sexually arousing).

- The work depicts or describes, in a patently offensive way, sexual conduct or excretory functions.

- The work, taken as a whole, lacks serious literary, artistic, political, or scientific merit.

In recent years *Miller* has become difficult to interpret and apply. The reason is the increasing globalization of pornography, facilitated by the internet, which has made it harder to establish which "community standards" should be used to judge any particular work.

In addition, the use of the term "contemporary" has ensured that legal standards must shift with changing public opinion, which has become more tolerant of pornography over the years. In a 2018 poll, 43% of Americans said that pornography was morally acceptable, as compared with 36% in the previous year (Gallup, 2018). Factors associated with tolerant attitudes included young age, male sex, and Democratic party affiliation. The pollsters suggested that the sudden jump in acceptability from 2017 to 2018 might have been the work of a single individual: porn star Stormy Daniels, whose legal battles with President Trump turned her into a celebrity. Whatever the reasons, the practical result of these changing attitudes has been a general lessening or outright abandonment of efforts to restrict print- and internet-based pornography.

## Any involvement with child pornography is a crime

The main exception to this liberalizing trend concerns pornography involving minors. State and federal laws prohibit the manufacture, distribution, and possession of images or videos portraying minors in sexual situations. Simple nude photos of children may also be illegal if they are deemed "sexually suggestive." Moreover, this "child porn" doesn't have to be real, so long as it is believable. Thus materials in which adult actors are made to look like minors, or minors are made to look as if they are engaged in sexual activity, or videos showing believable computer-generated simulations of minors engaged in sexual activity are all illegal under U.S. law. Even unrealistic images such as cartoons may be illegal if they portray minors engaged in acts that are "obscene" by *Miller* criteria.

Legislators love to show that they are tough on child pornography: Between 1987 and 2009 the U.S. Congress increased penalties for the production, distribution, or consumption of child pornography on nine separate occasions. Just possessing child porn carries a first-time minimum penalty of 5 years in prison under federal law, and other sentences can range up to 40 years. Many judges and others have expressed the view that the minimum sentences are excessive (Families Against Mandatory Minimums, n.d.).

Does simply viewing child porn on the internet without intentionally downloading it onto one's computer amount to illegal "possession" of the material? Most courts have ruled that it does, so that the traces of such viewing that remain on a person's computer may be taken as evidence of possession. In 2011 the Oregon Supreme Court ruled that it does not (Green, 2011), but the legislature subsequently criminalized "accessing with intent to view" child pornography. Regardless, in all jurisdictions the viewing must be intentional in order to constitute an offense: Users do not have to deep six their computers or phones simply because they came across images of minors in the course of searching for legal pornography.

Producers of commercial pornographic videos in the United States are legally obliged to document that their actors are over 18. Aggregator sites sometimes include amateur or foreign videos in which this age limit is not respected.

Minors can get into legal trouble for sending sexually explicit photos or videos of themselves to friends—sexting. During the 2016–17 school year, for example, a

16-year-old Maryland girl distributed a cellphone video of herself performing fellatio on an unidentified male. One of the students who saw the video showed it to a police officer. As a result, the girl was charged with filming a minor engaged in a sex act and distributing child pornography—even though the activity itself was legal in Maryland, where the age of consent is 16. She was named as a delinquent and suffered various penalties, including electronic monitoring, drug testing, and restrictions on her movement. The lower court's decision was upheld by Maryland's highest appeals court, which ruled that the child pornography law allowed no exceptions for minors filming their own activities, even when the activity itself is legal (Bekiempis, 2019).

## 17.8 New Technologies Mean New Kinds of Pornography

### LEARNING OBJECTIVES

After reading this section you should be able to:

17.8.1 Give examples of technological advances that have changed pornography.

17.8.2 Explain Pornhub's business model.

Developments in communication technologies have always affected pornography in important ways. The invention of printed books, photography, cinematography, glossy magazines, videocassettes, DVDs, the internet, smartphones, and virtual reality each spurred a new, more explicit, and more accessible genre of pornography. Here are some historical highlights:

- The magazine *Playboy* was founded by Hugh Hefner in 1953; by 1971 it was selling 7 million copies a month. *Playboy* was **softcore** pornography—it included no images of actual penetrative sex. It was followed by magazines that ventured into **hardcore** pornography, such as *Hustler*, founded by Larry Flynt in 1974.

- The pornographic film *Deep Throat* (starring Linda Lovelace) appeared in 1972. Because this film and others that followed it incorporated humor, they helped dissipate the shame and secretiveness that had been associated with the genre (**FIGURE 17.12**), and they won a degree of middle-class acceptance.

- The introduction of videocassettes in the late 1970s, followed by DVDs in the 1990s, made the production and distribution of porn movies much easier, and a great diversity of movies catering to every taste appeared. Because videos could be rented and watched at home, they put most porno theaters out of business.

- Broadband internet connections, which became widespread during the first decade of this century, enabled the streaming of pornographic videos; these now constitute the dominant medium for porn consumption.

There have been considerable stylistic changes in porn videos, driven in part by technological advances. The introduction of lightweight film cameras, for example, has allowed for "gonzo pornography," which is intended to make the viewer feel like a participant in the action rather than a passive onlooker. In gonzo porn the actors themselves often hold the cameras, in which case it may be called point-of-view pornography (**FIGURE 17.13**). In 2013 MiKandi released the first porn video in which both actors

▲ **FIGURE 17.12** *Deep Throat* (1972) is probably the most famous pornographic film of all time. It featured a woman (played by Linda Lovelace) whose sex life was unexciting until a doctor discovered that her clitoris was located in her throat—a finding that triggered a bonanza of oral sex.

**softcore** Related to relatively nonexplicit pornography.

**hardcore** Related to explicit pornography, such as images of penetrative sex and ejaculation.

◄ **FIGURE 17.13** **Point-of-view pornography** shows the action as filmed by one of the participants.

filmed the proceedings with Google Glass—it was viewed over 1 million times within the first 24 hours of its release. Porn actors have to adapt to the rapid changes in the industry, but their experiences on set remain about the same (**BOX 17.4**).

Another way for consumers to immerse themselves in porn is through virtual reality. The online virtual reality game Second Life, for example, has its own red-light district, where the players' avatars take the roles of prostitutes and their customers. More recently, the Oculus Rift virtual reality headset has been used to deliver 3-D erotic games, sometimes in conjunction with a computer-controlled masturbatory device. In 2016 Pornhub began offering free virtual reality porn viewable with Oculus Rift.

Somewhat related to virtual reality is "deepfake porn," in which artificial intelligence is used to substitute the face of some celebrity, such as a well-known actress, for that of the actual porn performer. Current efforts, such as one that turned actress Gal Gadot (of *Wonder Woman* fame) into a porn star, are recognizable as fakes (Clark, 2017). Before long, though, it may become possible for the average porn consumer to insert anyone's face, including their own, into any commercial porn video and

---

### BOX 17.4
## What's It Like to Be a Porn Star?

*I definitely think you need to be a very sexual person, because that's just the nature of the job. . . . I do love sex, but for me, that's not the point of doing porn. Porn, for me, is the ultimate fantasy. I like being on display, I like being on camera, I like turning people on, I like being a sex object. Being a porn star is the ultimate fantasy, to me. —Asa Akira*

*Porn is just an extension of my everyday sex life, but to be honest I tend to become more extreme or aggressive on film. I'm playing a character who knows what he wants and he gets it. Off camera I tend to be more vanilla than extreme. I like my cuddle moments and I like the soft touches and the romantic things that all couples like. —Diesel Washington*

*If it's anal or deep penetration, I generally have two orgasms on set. For me it's all about the intensity. I want hardcore. In real life, you have passion and intimacy, and it's gentler, but overall on camera, I just expect and want a rougher sexual experience. If it's regular sex, I come less often. Maybe once per scene. —Courtney Cummz*

*Deep throating is not always awesome. If a girl's going down on you for a scene, she's going to be at it for a long time. So she gets tired, and eventually you start feeling molars on the head of your dick. Getting paid to receive oral sex is basically like getting your dick chewed on for an hour. —Lance Hart*

*I cannot film more than 1 boy/girl scene in a week, because the sex is so intense and usually with a much-larger-than-average sized penis. My vagina needs a few days to recuperate. —Siri*

*All that bouncing around can really hurt, especially if one of those silicone pumpkins whacks you in the head. —Anonymous*

Sources: E. J. Dickson. 2014. *Porn Star Asa Akira takes us inside her new book, 'Insatiable'*. DailyDot.com; GayDemon. com. 2016. *Interview with Diesel Washington*. GayDemon. com; C. Cummz. 2014. *What it's really like to be a porn star*. Anna Breslaw, byline. Cosmopolitan.com; R. Evans and L. Hart. 2014. *5 reasons being a male porn star is less fun than it looks*. Cracked.com; Siri*. 2013. *What is a day in the life of a porn star like?* Quora.com; S. Harrison. 2008. *The hard life of the male porn star*. YourTango.com

*not the iPhone Siri

have the resulting hybrid be indistinguishable from the real thing. Of course such a development will open the door to all kinds of abuses.

The sexual content of porn has evolved over the years, with larger numbers of videos featuring kinks of various kinds. Sixteen of the top 100 Pornhub searches by men are for incest videos, most commonly for mother–son incest (Stephens-Davidowitz, 2017). Incest videos are often "fauxcest"—that is, the actors are not in fact related—but they may also involve real relatives. Among the latter, the Czech identical twins Elijah and Milo Peters stand out: They don't just have sex on camera but are also live-in lovers in real life—thus defying the "Westermarck effect" that we discussed in Chapter 5 (**FIGURE 17.14**).

It is often stated that pornographic videos are showing ever-increasing amounts of violence, especially portrayals of nonconsensual sexual aggression against women. Yet in a detailed analysis, sociologists at McGill University found no increase in this kind of aggression over the 9 years up to 2016: About 12% of videos included such content throughout that period (Shor & Seida, 2019). The reason for the low proportion of videos portraying nonconsensual sexual violence against women was evidently that they were unpopular with consumers: Out of the 70 most-watched videos, only 1 included this kind of content.

One interesting question is how an increasingly aging population will affect the industry. The answer comes from Japan, where "elder porn" now constitutes nearly 20% of the market. One porn star, Shigeo Tokuda, performed in about 400 videos after retiring from his regular job at the age of 70 (Ryall, 2017) (**FIGURE 17.15**). In elder porn it's only the male actors who are old, however; the female actors remain as young as ever, if not younger. Presumably the older male actors provide characters with whom aging male consumers can identify.

▲ **FIGURE 17.14    Incest porn stars** Elijah and Milo Peters, who are identical twins, are also lovers in real life.

## The porn business model is changing

The U.S. porn industry probably peaked around 2005: In that year 13,588 hardcore titles were released, 957 million adult DVDs and VHS tapes were rented, and the adult entertainment industry as a whole generated $12.6 billion (Lim, 2006). Since then, the increasing availability of free porn on the internet has undercut the industry's profitability. The actors' earnings have stagnated or even fallen, and production values are generally lower than in the past. Until recently porn videos had plots, but current productions are often of the so-called wall-to-wall variety, meaning that you don't even know that it's the cable-repair guy—the video is nothing but sex scenes. In fact, compilation videos are available that simply show the same sex act—for example, a man ejaculating onto a woman's face—repeated over and over by different actors.

Another factor contributing to the decline of commercial pornography is the increasing popularity of amateur porn, which can be uploaded to aggregator websites, generally known as **tube sites**. Pornhub is the dominant tube site: It gets 125 million visits per day. Although the tube sites started with amateur videos, they now also distribute commercial porn for free. This material consists partly of teaser clips from commercial videos—which may not include the "money shot"—but the sites also carry full-length commercial videos. These may or may not violate copyright laws. The tube sites get most of their revenue from advertising.

**tube site**    A website that aggregates amateur and commercial pornographic videos from multiple sources.

© Yoshikazu Tsuno/AFP/Getty Images

▶ **FIGURE 17.15    Elder porn star** Shigeo Tokuda continued making videos into his 80s. In 2020 he was hospitalized with COVID-19 but survived.

Although most consumers access the tube sites for free, a minority of customers do pay—for premium or specialist material. This is an important source of income for the production companies, and so their data analysts study the comments posted by paying customers on the companies' bulletin boards and send very specific requests to the directors. This is how one observer put it:

> To the actors rolling their eyes at yet another prompt to declaim, "But you're my step-dad!" or, "Show me your big black dick," the directors shrug, point at the emailed instructions and say, "That's what they want . . ." (Turner, 2019)

Because the paying customers are older, the preferences that get acted on are for genres that younger consumers may consider outdated or distasteful, such as incest and interracial porn. ("Interracial" always means a black man with a white woman.)

Because of the challenges facing the porn industry, there has been a great deal of consolidation. A single holding company, MindGeek, now owns most of the tube sites, including Pornhub, as well as many production companies. MindGeek consumes more bandwidth than Facebook or Amazon (Hassan, 2018). It mines every scrap of user data: If a viewer stops watching a video when a couple has sex in a swimming pool, that's one more data point out of billions that determine the locations for future productions. Pornhub's data is an invaluable source of information about current trends in porn (**BOX 17.5**).

## There is some pornography for women

Most pornography is produced by men and marketed to men. That doesn't necessarily mean that it's unappealing to women—some women love it, especially those who like to watch porn in male company. Here's how one woman put it:

> It provides stimulation, and inspiration for sexual fantasies. It also provides ideas for trying new things with my partner. It also provides a way to turn us both on when watching it together, and gives us a different kind of sexual experience. (Attwood, 2018)

Among heterosexual porn searches by women,* 25% are for videos featuring violence against women, according to an analysis of Pornhub data (Stephens-Davidowitz, 2017). This finding is certainly surprising, given that only 12% of all videos portray nonconsensual sexual violence, and those are the less popular ones, according to the McGill study mentioned earlier. This suggests that female porn consumers may be more interested in portrayals of sexual violence than male consumers are. That would be consistent with the finding, mentioned in Chapter 5, that many women have fantasies involving sexual coercion. As with those fantasies, though, an interest in violent pornography doesn't mean that women who watch it want to be sexually assaulted in real life.

There are also porn videos made by women with women in mind. Companies such as Sssh.com produce videos that differ from those aimed at men in having romantic storylines in addition to sex scenes. Here's one Sssh.com teaser (Sssh.com, 2009):

> Chloe and Melissa have been hired as domestic staff at a mysterious estate on Rutherford Island. Shortly after arriving, they feel something is "not quite right." Things become even more disturbing as night falls, but a storm has washed out the bridge to the island, making escape impossible.

Porn videos for women feature more attractive men than are typically seen in videos aimed at male consumers. (Some male porn actors, such as longtime star Ron Jeremy, have been average looking at best, but Jeremy had physiological talents that compensated for any shortcomings in appearance**.) Some heterosexual women also

---

*Pornhub doesn't have to ask what sex you are: Google figured that out a long time ago, and it sells the information to Pornhub.

**In 2020 Jeremy was charged with raping three women; he has pleaded not guilty.

## BOX 17.5
## The World According to Pornhub

*In 2019 Pornhub received 42 billion visits and 39 billion searches. Here are some data from the company's 2019 annual report:*

**Sex of visitors (U.S.):** 70% male, 30% female

**Average age of visitors (U.S.):** 39

**Time spent per visit:**
- Overall average worldwide: 10 minutes 28 seconds
- Ages 18–24: 9 minutes 24 seconds
- Age 65+: 12 minutes 13 seconds

**Most popular time:** 11 PM Sunday

**Most viewed categories (worldwide):**
1. Japanese
2. Lesbian
3. Amateur
4. *Hentai* (anime porn)
5. MILF (Mothers I'd Like to Fuck)

**Most searched pornstars (See figures):**
- Female: Lana Rhoades
- Male: Jordi El Niño Polla

**Most viewed category on Pornhub Gay:** Straight guys

**Effect of external events on viewership:**
- New Year's Eve: −45% (worldwide, time-adjusted)
- Superbowl: −27% (U.S.)
- St. Patrick's Day (Ireland): −16%

Top Pornhub porn stars in 2019: Lana Rhoades (left) and Jordi El Niño Polla (right).

- Government shutdown (Jan. 7–11): +6.3% (Washington, D.C.)
- Facebook/Instagram outage (March 13): +19% at 7 PM (U.S.)
- Polar vortex Jan. 30–31 (deep freeze): +22% (Minnesota)

During the 2020 COVID-19 pandemic Pornhub's traffic rose globally. In the United States, usage peaked at 41% above normal on March 25, the day on which Pornhub made its premium content free. The company took this step "to encourage people to stay indoors and distance themselves socially" (Pornhub, 2020).

enjoy gay male porn—in which looks and physique are valued—in the same way that many straight men enjoy "lesbian" sex scenes. In fact, more than one-third of the viewers of gay male porn on Pornhub are women (Pornhub, 2019).

The so-called lesbian videos so popular with men don't usually feature lesbians and are not very likely to appeal to lesbian consumers. Much more to lesbians' taste are videos such as the *Crash Pad* series (produced by Pink and White Productions), which feature women—often tattooed and sporting unconventional hairstyles—who are highly diverse in their skin colors, body shapes, and personalities (Urquhart, 2014) (**FIGURE 17.16**). Their approach to sex is athletic and involves liberal use of sex toys such as strap-on dildos.

A woman-oriented genre that has no close male equivalent is the romance novel. The ubiquitous Harlequin Romance novels belong to this category. Many of these novels would hardly be considered pornographic, because their main emphasis is on relationships rather than on sex acts. There are also romance novels that include steamy sex scenes, but even those typically end with a "happily ever after" emotional union—quite different from the "happy endings" (orgasms) that wrap up most

▶ **FIGURE 17.16** **Lesbian porn** This is an episode of the *Crash Pad* series (Pink and White Productions) being shot.

male-oriented pornography (Ogas & Gaddam, 2011). British author E. L. James has livened up the genre with her *Fifty Shades* series of BDSM-themed romance novels—critical shipwrecks that sailed on to global best-sellerdom.

## 17.9 There Are Conflicting Perspectives on the Value or Harm of Pornography

**LEARNING OBJECTIVE**

After reading this section you should be able to:

**17.9.1** Evaluate the evidence for harmful and beneficial effects of pornography for consumers and actors.

Although pornographers have basically won their battle with the censors, debate continues about pornography's effects. Here we review some of the issues that have been raised and the evidence that bears on them. Because few of these important questions have been definitively answered, we head the following sections with questions rather than statements.

### Does porn promote sexual violence?

Many writers and activists have suggested that pornography teaches men and boys to objectify, degrade, abuse, and sexually assault women (**FIGURE 17.17**). Gail Dines, a retired sociology professor from Wheelock College, put it like this:

*The messages that porn disseminates about women can be boiled down to a few essential characteristics: they are always ready for sex and are enthusiastic to do whatever men want, irrespective of how painful, humiliating, or harmful the act is. The word "no" is glaringly absent from porn women's vocabulary.* (Dines, 2011)

There is some experimental evidence to suggest that watching porn can, in limited circumstances, promote sexual violence. One expert in this field is Neil Malamuth of UCLA, whose "confluence model" of sexual aggression we described in Chapter 16. Consistent with that model, Malamuth's experiments suggest that viewing pornography may indeed increase the risk of sexual violence, but only for men who have certain predisposing factors, such as low empathy, antisocial personality, or a history of childhood abuse (Malamuth, 2018). It is violent or "extreme" pornography, rather than pornography in general, that has this effect, according to Malamuth.

Although violent pornography may trigger sexual violence in some men, there doesn't appear to be any overall effect linking the availability of porn to sex crimes. During the 1990s, when the amount and consumption of video pornography skyrocketed in the United States, the prevalence of rape plunged, falling to previously unheard-of lows (**FIGURE 17.18**). A similar inverse relationship has been noted in other countries, such as Japan (Diamond, 2009). On the basis of these data, it's more believable that the availability of porn actually *lessens* most men's likelihood of committing rape, just as may be the case with the availability of prostitution, to judge by the Rhode Island study mentioned earlier. This would be consistent with the idea that porn and prostitution divert the sex drive of some potentially violent men into less harmful channels. Still, it would take more direct studies to determine whether there really is an effect of this kind, or whether the inverse relationship shown in Figure 17.18 is merely coincidental.

▲ **FIGURE 17.17** **Anti-porn march** through the Times Square area of New York City in 1979. Feminists including Susan Brownmiller, Andrea Dworkin, Gloria Steinem, and Bella Abzug led the march. Dworkin's speech at the closing rally is available online. (Dworkin, 1979.)

## Does porn damage relationships?

It has often been claimed that viewing porn harms established sexual relationships, such as marriages. Intuitively this makes sense, because one's own partner is not likely to be as physically attractive, or as accomplished a sexual athlete, as the actors in pornographic videos, particularly as the couple ages. What's more, it's possible to switch videos as often as desired, thus maintaining novelty, whereas a real-life monogamous relationship features sex with the same partner for years on end, with the resulting likelihood of habituation, as discussed in Chapter 5. Thus the contrast between marital sex and porn sex could diminish a porn user's satisfaction with marital sex over time. This lessening of sexual satisfaction might in turn lead to dissatisfaction with the relationship itself, and hence to a breakup. In a qualitative study of porn use by Taylor Kohut and colleagues at the University of Western Ontario, one interviewee expressed it quite bluntly: "I feel like porn makes my partner look ugly in my eyes. I don't find my partner attractive anymore and my relationship of 20 months is suffering" (Kohut et al., 2017).

Sociologist Samuel Perry of the University of Oklahoma has conducted several studies that appear to document this effect (Perry, 2020). In one study, he and Cyrus Schleifer analyzed data gathered by the General Social Survey, in which a representative panel of Americans were asked about porn use at 2-year intervals (Perry & Schleifer, 2018). The researchers focused on respondents who at a given time were married and not watching porn. Two years later, some of these respondents said they had watched porn since the previous interview, whereas others said

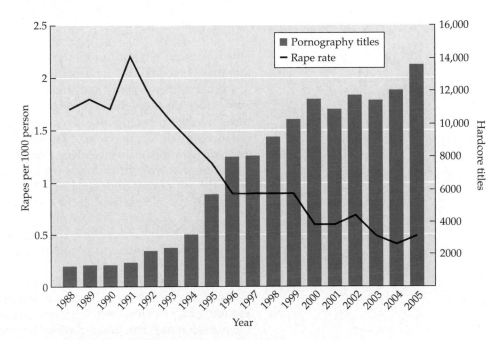

▲ **FIGURE 17.18** **Porn up, rape down** This figure plots the number of hardcore pornographic videos and the rate of forcible rape for the United States between 1988 and 2005. (After C. J. Ferguson and R. D. Hartley. 2009. *Aggress Violent Behav* 14: 323–329.)

they had not. The researchers found that those respondents who had watched porn were twice as likely to have split up during that 2-year period than those who had not done so. The researchers concluded that watching porn was a factor increasing the likelihood of divorce. Unfortunately, it's not really possible to infer the direction of causation in studies of this kind. It's equally plausible that the respondents began using porn *because* they were no longer satisfied with marital sex. Thus convincing evidence for a causal link between porn use and breakups is lacking.

### Does porn use cause performance problems or sex addiction?

Both in the academic literature and in social discourse, this kind of story has become commonplace: A man—it's nearly always a man—masturbates while watching regular porn. He watches it because he likes it, and because it helps him develop an erection and reach orgasm. After a while the porn doesn't work so well, so he watches more of it and shifts to more arousing or more extreme porn. Now he finds that he can't get an erection while having sex with his regular partner, and eventually not even while watching the most extreme porn he can find. Alternatively, he can get an erection but can't reach orgasm, even with the most vigorous and prolonged masturbation. He now believes that he's hooked on porn—addicted—and can't quit watching it, even though doing so is ruining his life and no longer bringing him any pleasure.

The "NoFap" reddit and website are populated by men who say that excessive porn use with masturbation has damaged their capacity for physiological arousal—erection and orgasm—either altogether or during sex with regular partners. ("Fapping" is slang for male masturbation.) Most NoFappers are trying, with variable success, to "reboot"—that is, to abstain from porn and masturbation for a few months in order to recover their sexual responsiveness. Many of these men's comments do suggest that they feel addicted (Reddit.com, 2019):

> For the longest time, I have tried different ways to keep myself from watching porn, like I was some kind of savage beast that needed to be restrained. I tried relying on porn blockers, cold showers, workouts, meditation, everything. But I always ended up masturbating.

> Today (day 22) was a day full of urges. I worked out at home and when I had another urge I took a long walk outside. Glad I made these choices instead of PMO [porn, masturbation, orgasm]. It feels like a personal victory.

NoFappers are not anti-porn or anti-masturbation on principle; rather, they believe that they personally need to abstain for a limited period in order to get their lives back.

Researchers are sharply divided on whether porn does harm sexual function. Some have taken the NoFap perspective, supporting it with detailed case histories that document erectile disorder or anorgasmia in frequent porn users, as well as the recovery of function after a period of abstention (Park et al., 2016). Others have argued that erectile disorder in porn users is rare, and that when it does occur it is associated not with the porn use itself, but with guilt and other negative attitudes or beliefs about porn (Grubbs & Gola, 2019). As to the issue of sex addiction, we have already discussed this issue in the context of hypersexuality (Chapter 14). Regardless of the academic debate, it's clear that a minority of men do devote enough time and energy to porn as to cause difficulties in their daily lives and relationships and make it difficult for them to reduce their porn consumption.

### Does porn harm actors?

One possible negative consequence of acting in pornographic videos is the possibility of acquiring an STI. This possibility is heightened if condoms are not used, which is often the case as many consumers prefer "bareback" sex. STIs among porn actors are not uncommon (King & Evans, 2020), but it is difficult to know whether the transmissions occur in the course of making videos, because many porn actors have multiple sexual relationships, including paid ones, outside of the studio environment (Kendrick et al.,

2016). In Los Angeles County, the center of porn production in the United States, condom use is mandated by law, but some producers have evaded this requirement by moving their operations elsewhere. Most production companies test their actors for STIs frequently—every 2 weeks is typical, and rapid tests may be performed immediately before a shoot. The use of PrEP—pre-exposure prophylaxis against HIV—is common, especially among actors in gay male videos.

Another possibility is that the experience of acting in pornographic videos is traumatizing to the actors, especially to the very young women who are among the most sought-after participants. This possibility is likely heightened by engagement in sexually aggressive pornography. One of the early hardcore porn stars, Linda Lovelace, documented the abuse she suffered in the making of the blockbuster 1972 film *Deep Throat* (Lovelace & McGrady, 1980). Industry practices have become much more professional since that time, however, and the comments cited in Box 17.4 are not suggestive of a psychologically damaging work environment. Still, some abuse no doubt persists. And even if acting in a pornographic video is a wholly agreeable experience, doing so may come back to haunt an actor who later embarks on a "straight" career.

▲ Outdoor porn shoot on a miniature train layout.

© Hugh Mitton/Alamy Stock Photo

## Pornography has beneficial effects

In a qualitative study of men's and women's experiences with the consumption of pornography, the great majority of interviewees denied that they or their partners experienced any negative consequences (Kohut et al., 2017). On the contrary, the interviewees often pointed to positive effects:

- *Pornography provides useful information:* "I feel like pornography helped educate me on how to perform oral sex better;" "When we first met, he didn't know how to use his fingers the way that I liked, and I had trouble explaining and showing him what I liked, so he watched a video, and it helped us improve our sex life."

- *Pornography promotes experimentation:* "She enjoys using toys and positions that we were first exposed to by pornography;" "It has helped me understand my own kinks, and the types of things I dislike, and maybe introduce me to some new things that I hadn't thought of."

- *Pornography improves communication:* "It helps us facilitate a conversation about kinks, fetishes, wants and won'ts in the bedroom, etc.;" "We use it to show each other what we feel like doing with them;" "It's helped me be more frank about what I want."

- *Pornography provides an alternative outlet:* "It can get her an orgasm when I am not available or not in the mood;" "He knows he has carte blanche to jack off to porn if/when he needs to, so hopefully he feels less pressure to look for sex elsewhere."

- *Pornography improves mood:* "Seeing this porn gives me a feeling of life and of joy—a zest for living;" "Helps keep our sex life exciting, which makes both of us happier."

- *Pornography reduces guilty feelings:* "'It's helped me to accept that I enjoy kinky sex;" "I believe it has taught me that the body and sex are meant to be enjoyed."

## Sex is part of the mass media

Sexually themed content on network television and in advertising is rarely as explicit as it is in pornographic videos and the like. However, television and advertising reach a much wider audience, including children and people who may not have chosen to see erotic material. Thus, even mildly provocative sexual material can elicit a great deal of protest.

Images of genitalia, female nipples, anuses, and hardcore sex, as well as the use of sexual slang words such as "fuck," are all off-limits on network TV, and if they do occur, the broadcasters may be penalized by the Federal Communications Commission (FCC). One test case involved the 2002 and 2003 Billboard Music Awards, in which the presenters uttered vulgarities. In the 2003 incident, for example, Nicole Richie said in reference to her city-girls-on-a-farm TV series, "Why do they even call it *The Simple Life*? Have you ever tried to get cow shit out of a Prada purse? It's not so fucking simple." The Fox network, joined by the other networks, argued that the FCC acted arbitrarily in penalizing fleeting obscenities such as these. After a long-running legal battle the Supreme Court sided with Fox on narrow grounds, but it did not reject the FCC's right to penalize even brief obscenities (Liptak, 2012) .

Although explicit sexual vulgarities are uncommon on network TV, television programs in general are rife with sexual content—most of it verbal references to sex. The Parents Television Council (PTC)—a conservative group that works to reduce the amount of sex, violence, and profanity on television—has long complained that the number of sexual references is increasing, and that these references need to be curtailed to spare children and teens from harmful effects. Whether the PTC's campaign against sex on television is having any effect is open to question, because it spreads its condemnation so widely. During one week of ratings that we examined, PTC could not identify a single prime-time show to honor with its green light ("Family-friendly show promoting responsible themes and traditional values"). Sometimes it seems as if a damning critique from the PTC actually helps *increase* a show's viewership (**FIGURE 17.19**). And by linking "sex and violence" in a single mantra of disapproval, the PTC hints at an underlying sex-negativity, as if acts that bring pleasure and acts that bring pain are equally blameworthy.

In 1996 the U.S. television industry was ordered by Congress to introduce a "voluntary" ratings system that indicates the presence and intensity of sexual content (along with violence and foul language) in individual programs. In combination with the V-chip—a device built into all television sets—this system allows parents to filter out entire categories of programs they deem unsuitable for their children. The ACLU opposed the system, saying that it amounted to government censorship.

In any case, as television sets are increasingly used to display streaming content, the filtering of undesirable material becomes more and more difficult. In 2017 videos started appearing on YouTube Kids that were ostensibly designed for children but actually contained quasi-pedophilic content—for example, children using toy-like syringes to make injections into naked buttocks. In response, Google's CEO promised to increase the monitoring of YouTube content (Wojcicki, 2017).

## Sex sells, sometimes

Sex has been used in advertising for as long as advertising has existed, and roughly one-fifth of all contemporary advertising has overt sexual content (Reichert & Lambiase, 2003; Reichert, 2007). People often pay attention to and recall sexy ads better than ads containing nonsexual imagery (G&R Research and Consulting, 2008).

A problem with the use of sexual content in advertising is that it may distract the viewer from attending to or remembering the name of the product or the advertising message. Thus, sexual content is most effective when the product itself is related to sex—as perfume is, for example. Sex doesn't sell lawn mowers so well.

Another problem has to do with the different responses of men and women to sexually themed advertising. An informative study on this topic was performed by an international group led by Darren Dahl of the University of British Columbia (Dahl et al., 2011). They found, first, that men respond favorably to sexually themed advertising that is devoid of any relationship context, whereas women respond negatively to such

▲ **FIGURE 17.19  Backhanded compliment?** The CW channel used a comment from the Parents Television Council to promote the 2008 season of its teen sex drama, *Gossip Girl*.

(A)                                          (B)

▲ **FIGURE 17.20    Sex in advertising**  (A) Women reacted negatively to this ad for Calvin Klein's Obsession perfume. (B) This Dolce & Gabbana ad appears to represent a gay BDSM scene.

material; they only respond favorably when the sexual content is clearly embedded in a committed relationship. So much we might have guessed. For women to react most favorably, however, there must be an indication that the commitment is a resource that is being transferred from the man to the woman. (Think beribboned new car in driveway.) Unfortunately for advertisers, this kind of content is perceived negatively by men—apparently because it reminds them how "high-maintenance" a sexual relationship can be. So advertisers have to figure out which partner is likely to be the decision maker for any particular purchase before they create their ads.

Female nudity in advertisements is something that women say they dislike. When market researchers interviewed women about an ad for Calvin Klein's Obsession perfume, for example (**FIGURE 17.20A**), most women's responses were strongly negative. One woman described it as "obscene—nothing about love—purely physical pornography. Absolutely useless for selling perfume." Obsession was a blockbuster success in the marketplace, however—either because men were doing the buying or because women's unconscious responses didn't correspond with what they told interviewers.

Advertisers are constantly trying to extend the limits of acceptability. For their spring 2007 campaign, Dolce & Gabbana used an ad in which a woman was pinned to the ground by a kneeling, bare-chested man while four other men looked on. It provoked a storm of criticism. NOW, for example, accused Dolce & Gabbana of glorifying gang rape (National Organization for Women, 2014), and in Italy the ad was banned outright. Stefano Gabbana defended the ad by claiming that it was intended to represent an "erotic dream." The company pulled the ad from publications worldwide but has since come out with ads in which men are represented as sexual victims (**FIGURE 17.20B**).

Advertisements have traditionally portrayed women and men in stereotypical gender roles, with women as home-based caregivers and men as outdoorsy go-getters (Furnham, 2016). Recently, however, the pendulum has swung the other way, whether in recognition of changing gender roles or in a proactive attempt to change them. Thus TV spots featuring a man and a woman are now more likely to show the woman as active, smart, and solution-oriented, and the man as none of the above (**FIGURE 17.21**). Ads like the one shown in the figure would have been unthinkable a generation ago, and they would be unthinkable today with the sex roles reversed.

▶ **FIGURE 17.21** Gender role reversal The dialogue in this 2015 spot for Campbell's Soup runs as follows: Woman on way out the door: "Still not feeling well?" Man on couch: "No—you know, when I got sick, my mom used to make me chicken noodle soup." Woman: "Oh, OK . . . You should call your mom . . . Bye!" (Man heats Campbell's soup.) The ad is viewable online. (iSpot.tv, 2017.)

## Summary

- Many relationships involve an exchange of resources for sex. Prostitution—paid sex—is the extreme version of this phenomenon. Prostitutes can be female, male, or transgender, but nearly all users of prostitutes are male. Prostitution is illegal almost everywhere in the United States, but enforcement varies.

- Historically, prostitution has been condemned as wrong but also tolerated as necessary. Concern about STI transmission has been a major factor in anti-prostitution campaigns. Prostitution declined greatly during the 20th century in the United States, probably because unmarried women became more willing to engage in sexual relations with men.

- Streetwalkers are the lowest-paid prostitutes. They face a relatively high risk of violence and STIs, and many use drugs. Street prostitutes who are minors may be runaways or homeless; these prostitutes face a heightened risk of violence and exploitation. Among street prostitutes, women do better economically than men, but men enjoy their work more. Female street prostitutes traditionally worked for pimps, but increasing numbers are independent operators or are controlled by gangs.

- Some prostitutes work at commercial locations such as massage parlors or exotic dance venues. Brothels—establishments that have the sole purpose of prostitution—are rare today and, in the United States, are legal only in some rural counties of Nevada.

- Escorts are off-street prostitutes who obtain clients by advertising or by word of mouth. They may go to the client's location or receive clients at a fixed location. Many work for escort services, which arrange their appointments. Escorts are more numerous than street prostitutes; they charge more, and they work in somewhat safer conditions.

- Women and men prostitute themselves principally because they can earn much more from prostitution than from other occupations available to them, but sexual pleasure plays some role for high-end escorts and for some male prostitutes. Men use prostitutes for a wide variety of reasons, including difficulty in obtaining unpaid partners, the quest for sexual variety, or the excitement of illicit sex. According to some feminists, men use prostitutes to express their hatred of women, but some accounts by men suggest otherwise.

- Feminists have campaigned successfully for increased prosecution and punishment of men who use prostitutes. There is some support for regulated legalization of prostitution, as has happened in some European countries.

- Prostitutes in developing countries work in risky conditions, but the occupation does offer them an above-average income. Some international agencies believe that prostitution should be recognized, governed by fair labor codes, and integrated into regional economies. Some international women's groups believe that activities associated with prostitution, but not prostitutes themselves, should be criminalized.

- Many women are trafficked between countries for purposes of prostitution. Some women participate in this traffic voluntarily in search of economic betterment; others are enslaved and prostituted against their will. In sex tourism, men or women travel to foreign countries where prostitution is legal or cheap. Going overseas to have sex with minors is a crime under U.S. and Canadian laws.

- Pornography consists of depictions of people or behaviors that are intended to be sexually arousing. Censorship of pornography increased greatly in Victorian times but eased after World War II. In 1973, the U.S. Supreme Court ruled that the legality of sexually explicit work must be judged by "contemporary community standards." In practice, very little adult porn is now a cause for prosecution, but any involvement with porn featuring minors risks severe penalties.

- Developments in communication technologies—the printing press, photography, film, and computers—have all affected pornography in important ways. Feature-length pornographic movies became popular in the 1970s. The introduction of the videocassette format made production and consumption easier and allowed for greater diversity of content. Thanks to the internet, consumers can now access a diverse range of pornography—often for free—and they can create their own pornography for sale or exchange. Virtual reality sites allow for the enactment of sexual fantasies with like-minded others.

- Pornography designed for women tends to be less sexually graphic than male-oriented pornography—emphasizing intimacy and romance more than sex alone. Still, there is a trend toward more sexually explicit material for women. Some lesbians have pioneered a more hardcore approach to pornography.

- There is debate about the potential effects of pornography. Research studies suggest that pornography does not incite most men to harm women, but pornography that includes violence may make a few men more likely to do so. Countries with high rates of pornography consumption do not have unusually high rates of violence against women. Whether porn consumption damages relationships or impairs sexual function is uncertain. Users believe that viewing porn offers several benefits, including learning about sex, facilitating sexual communication, improving mood, and reducing guilty feelings about unusual sexual activities.

- Pornography featuring real sexual activity by minors, as well as believable simulations of such activity, is illegal in the United States.

- Sexual content on television has increased greatly. Responding to public and congressional concern, the television industry introduced a rating system that warns of sexual (and violent) content. In combination with the V-chip, it allows parents to filter out material they don't want their children to see, but the system is little used.

- Sexually themed advertising can sell products, but women and men react to such advertising in different ways. Advertisers are constantly pushing the boundaries of what's acceptable in terms of nudity or the kinds of sexual activity shown or suggested by advertisements.

## Discussion Questions

1. Do you think that prostitution should be decriminalized, legalized with regulation, or illegal? Give your reasons.

2. If prostitution remains illegal, should the emphasis be on prosecuting prostitutes or on prosecuting their customers ("johns")? Should law enforcement devote equal resources to reducing street prostitution and escort service prostitution?

3. Should all depictions of sex involving underage people (whether real or simulated) be illegal? Why or why not?

4. Female college students have sometimes been hired as high-priced call girls. What do you think would be the pros and cons of this occupation? If your best friend considered this as a way to pay a tuition bill that was overdue, what would you advise her to do?

5. Parents are often very upset to find their young sons viewing pornographic material. How would you advise parents to respond in that situation?

6. Do you think children should be protected from seeing pornographic material on the internet? If you do, how would you accomplish this?

The **Discovering Human Sexuality** digital resources include activities, animations, flashcards, web links, chapter outlines and summaries, and other study tools.

Learn more with this chapter's digital tools, including the **Oxford Insight Study Guide**, at **oup.com/he/levay5e**.

## Web Resources

Association of Sites Advocating Child Protection (porn industry association) **www.asacp.org**

Coalition Against Trafficking in Women **www.catwinternational.org**

End Child Prostitution (ECPAT) **www.ecpat.net**

International Sex Worker Foundation for Art, Culture and Education **www.iswface.org**

Sex Workers Education Network **www.bayswan.org/penet.html**

## Recommended Reading/Viewing

Bauer, J. & Gradus, R. (Directors). (2015). *Hot Girls Wanted.* (Documentary film exploring the world of amateur porn.)

Boyle, K. (Ed.). (2010). *Everyday pornography.* Routledge.

Brown, C. (2011). *Paying for it: A comic-strip memoir about being a john.* Drawn & Quarterly.

Delacoste, F. & Alexander, P. (Eds.). (1998). *Sex work: Writings by women in the sex industry* (2nd ed.). Cleis.

Dworkin, A. (1981). *Pornography: Men possessing women.* Putnam.

Jones, A. (2020). *Camming: Money, power, and pleasure in the sex work industry.* New York University Press.

Lane, F. S., III. (2000). *Obscene profits: The entrepreneurs of pornography in the cyber age.* Routledge.

McNair, B. (2013). *Porno? Chic!: How pornography changed the world and made it a better place.* Routledge.

Mulholland, M. (2013). *Young people and pornography: Negotiating pornification.* Palgrave Macmillan.

Ogas, O. & Gaddam, S. (2011). *A billion wicked thoughts: What the world's largest experiment reveals about human desire.* Dutton. (Mines internet porn usage and other sources to probe male and female sexuality.)

Reichert, T. & Lambiase, J. (Eds.). (2012). *Sex in advertising: Perspectives on the erotic appeal.* Routledge.

Strossen, N. (2000). *Defending pornography: Free speech, sex, and the fight for women's rights.* NYU Press.

Tarrant, S. (2016). *The pornography industry: What everyone needs to know.* Oxford University Press.

Whisnant, J. & Stark, C. (2005). *Not for sale: Feminists resisting prostitution and pornography.* Spinifex.

# Sex and Evolution

Our sexuality evolved from the sex lives of nonhuman creatures that preceded us in the long history of life on Earth. By studying this evolutionary process, we can hope to find clues to some very basic "why" questions about ourselves: Why are we sexual beings? Why are there two sexes? Why do we find some people more attractive than others? Why don't all sex acts lead to pregnancy? Why are men more interested in casual sex than women are? Why do some of us cheat on our partners? And why do some of us remain faithful? The study of evolution does not provide complete answers to these questions, but it does remind us that answers are needed. Without the evolutionary perspective, it is too easy to view our own sexuality as the natural order of things, requiring no explanation.

Most of the examples and research studies described here feature nonhuman animals. This may seem odd for a textbook on human sexuality. What we are discussing here, however, are general evolutionary principles; in the main text of the book we consider how relevant these principles may be to our own sex lives.

# A.1 Rival Theories Offer Explanations for Sexual Reproduction

**asexual reproduction**
Reproduction in which all the offspring's genes are inherited from a single parent.

**genome** An organism's entire complement of DNA, including all its genes. In some viruses, such as HIV, the genome is composed of RNA.

**sexual reproduction** Reproduction in which the offspring inherit genes from two parents.

**gamete** A germ cell (ovum or sperm) that fuses with another to form a new organism.

**ovum (pl. ova)** A mature female gamete, prior to or immediately after fertilization.

**sperm (or spermatozoon; pl. spermatozoa)** A male gamete, produced in the testis.

**meiosis** A pair of cell divisions that produces haploid gametes.

**zygote** A cell formed by the fusion of gametes; a fertilized ovum.

**adaptive** Helping the propagation of an organism's genes.

**parthenogenesis** Asexual reproduction from an unfertilized ovum; "virgin birth."

**mutation** A change in an organism's genome.

Living organisms produce offspring by two alternative methods: asexual and sexual reproduction. The key feature of **asexual reproduction** is that each individual organism receives its **genome**—the entirety of its genetic endowment—from just one parent. One example that you may be familiar with is the reproduction of hydras and other microscopic animals by a simple budding process; another example is the propagation of plants from cuttings.

In **sexual reproduction**, on the other hand, an organism receives its genome from two parents. Each parent produces specialized reproductive cells known as **gametes**: **ova** in females and **spermatozoa** (or **sperm**) in males (**FIGURE A.1**). What's special about gametes is that they possess half the number of chromosomes that is typical for that species. This halving takes place by means of a two-step process known as **meiosis** (see Animations A.1 Mitosis and A.2 Meiosis, and Activity A.1 Differences and Similarities between Meiosis and Mitosis). Thus, when ovum and sperm unite to form a **zygote**, the full genome is restored, but it's a mixed genome, half coming from the mother and half from the father.

Nearly all multicellular organisms are capable of sexual reproduction, and most vertebrates (including all mammals) rely on it as their only means of reproduction. This tells us that the capacity for sexual reproduction must be **adaptive**; that is, it must help the organism to perpetuate its genes in future generations. How does it do so?

Surprisingly, the answer to this very basic question is a bit of a mystery. On the face of it, asexual reproduction is more adaptive than sexual reproduction. This is because an animal that reproduces asexually devotes all its resources to passing on its own genes, and those genes are perpetuated in all of its descendants (**FIGURE A.2**). An animal that reproduces sexually, however, dilutes its genes with those of another animal, thus reducing the representation of its own genes in future generations. This seems like a pointless self-sacrifice.

The paradox is particularly striking in species in which one sex—usually the female—invests far more in reproduction than the other sex. In such species, it would seem that females would do better to give birth **parthenogenetically** (by asexual "virgin birth") rather than to give some male's genes a free ride into the next generation. If a single parthenogenetically reproducing female arose in a population of a million sexually reproducing individuals, then—other things being equal—it would take less than 50 generations for her clonal descendants to replace the entire population. This advantage to asexual reproduction can be observed experimentally in species consisting of both sexually and asexually reproducing individuals (Gibson et al., 2017). Yet, in nearly all species, females engage in sexual reproduction all or at least some of the time. So other things must not be equal—but in what way, exactly?

## Sexual reproduction removes harmful mutations

One way in which sexual reproduction is adaptive is that it helps organisms cope with the problem of harmful **mutations**. Mutations are random changes in an organism's genome caused by errors in the copying of DNA or by damaging chemicals, sunlight, or radiation. In humans, about 70 new mutations crop up in every generation; this is known from studies that have compared the entire genomes of parents and their children (Kong et al., 2012).

Many mutations are neutral—they have no effect on an organism's ability to survive and reproduce—but of those that are not neutral,

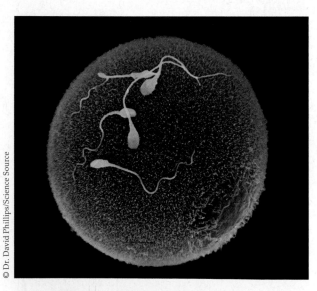

▲ **FIGURE A.1** **Gametes** A human ovum and several sperm. Note the difference in size: The sperm contributes nothing to the zygote except its genes.

far more are harmful than beneficial, just as random changes in computer software are far more likely to degrade its performance than to improve it.

When organisms reproduce asexually, harmful mutations accumulate over the generations. Because all the descendants of a given animal possess copies of that animal's genes, there is no way to get rid of a harmful mutation short of eliminating that entire lineage. When organisms reproduce sexually, however, harmful mutations *can* be eliminated. That's because offspring receive a randomly selected half of their mother's genes and half of their father's genes. If one parent carries a particular damaged gene, about half of that parent's offspring will not inherit it—they will inherit the normal version of the gene from the other parent instead.

In reality, most organisms carry numerous harmful mutations. Thus, each offspring is likely to inherit some harmful mutations from each parent. But because of the lottery-like nature of sexual reproduction, some offspring will receive a greater total load of harmful mutations, and other offspring will receive fewer (**FIGURE A.3**). Natural selection will favor the survival and reproduction of the offspring that have fewer harmful mutations. Thus, sexual reproduction may help maintain an equilibrium state in a population of organisms, in which the appearance of new harmful mutations is balanced by the gradual elimination of old ones. This process has been documented in real life—not in humans, but in humbler, fast-reproducing organisms such as yeast (McDonald et al., 2016) and water fleas (Paland & Lynch, 2006).

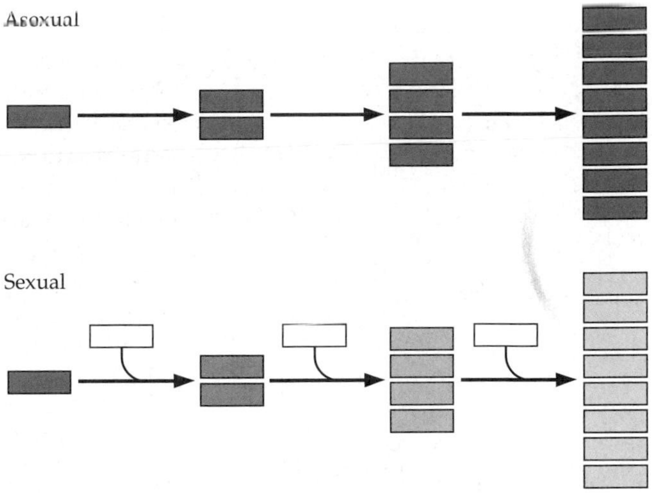

▲ **FIGURE A.2** **The paradox of sexual reproduction** An asexually reproducing female's genes (orange) are propagated without loss into future generations, but a sexually reproducing female's genes are mixed with the genes of unrelated males (white) and thus are reduced by half in each ensuing generation.

## Sexual reproduction may generate beneficial gene combinations

Another possible adaptive function of sexual reproduction is that it can generate advantageous new combinations of genes. This mixing of genes may be useful in dealing with environmental threats, such as attacks by infectious organisms and parasites. These organisms are constantly evolving tricks to elude the host organisms' defense mechanisms, so the host needs to be able to respond. Gene mixing may be an effective way for the host species to do this (Ridley, 2003). In this conception, the

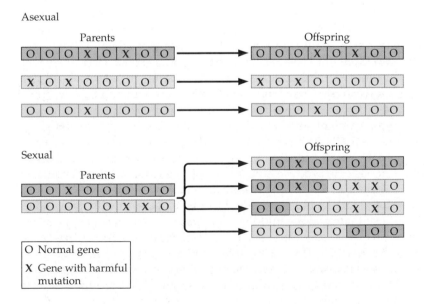

◀ **FIGURE A.3** **Reproduction and harmful mutations** In this diagram, each organism is represented as a genome with eight genes, some of which have harmful mutations (each marked with an X). In asexual reproduction (top), each offspring inherits the entire genome of its parent, along with any harmful mutations. In sexual reproduction (bottom), each offspring inherits random chunks of its father's (purple) and mother's (orange) genomes. Thus, some offspring, such as the lowermost one in the diagram, may inherit few or no harmful mutations. If this lucky offspring enjoys great reproductive success and its unlucky siblings die out, the harmful mutations will be eliminated from the population.

**investment** The commitment or expenditure of resources for a goal, such as reproductive success.

genetic variations among individuals in a sexually reproducing species are like the numbers in combination locks: When a parasite develops the ability to "pick" a common combination of genes, many individuals die, but sexual reproduction quickly reestablishes a population with novel, "unpickable" combinations.

Supporting the idea that sexual reproduction exists to help organisms cope with changes in the environment is the observation that in species that can reproduce either sexually or asexually, the sexual route is often adopted when environmental conditions become stressful. In such conditions the offspring generated by the sexual route are fitter (survive and reproduce better) than those generated asexually (Becks & Agrawal, 2012). In addition, the products of sexual reproduction are often seeds or eggs that are hardier than adult organisms, so species switch to sexual reproduction with the approach of harsh conditions—winter cold or summer drought (Gerber et al., 2018).

## A.2 Why Are There Two Sexes?

The ideas just discussed offer explanations for sexual reproduction, but they don't explain the existence of males and females. Across the biological realm, "male" is the name given to individuals with small gametes (sperm, in the case of humans), and "female" is the name given to individuals with large gametes (ova). But why should these two kinds of individuals exist? Why shouldn't a sexually reproducing species consist of individuals that are all alike, any two of which could pair off and fuse their gametes (sex without sexes, as it were)?

Actually, sex without sexes might well be an ideal arrangement for a species. But because natural selection operates at the individual level and not at the species level, it does not necessarily produce arrangements that are ideal for the species as a whole. Rather, it produces compromises—states in which the conflicting interests of countless individuals are in dynamic equilibrium. Sex without sexes is not generally an equilibrium state, and here's why: Reproduction requires an **investment**—a commitment of resources. For many organisms, that investment is the time and energy required to produce a gamete. That gamete must be endowed with enough nutrient material so that, once it has fused with the other parent's gamete, it can develop into a new organism. How much nutrient material is required? That depends, in part, on how much nutrient material the *other* parent contributes.

Let's consider a hypothetical sex-without-sexes species, in which the gametes of all individuals are isogametes, that is, roughly similar in size and nutrient content (**FIGURE A.4**). Even in this situation, there will be some natural variation, so some individuals will produce slightly larger gametes and some will produce slightly smaller ones. Over time, natural selection will favor individuals that produce larger gametes (containing more nutrients), because those gametes stand a better chance of developing into offspring. But individuals that produce smaller gametes will also be favored because such gametes require a smaller investment and are therefore easier to produce. And as long as there are some larger gametes available to fuse with, those smaller gametes can still develop into offspring. The only individuals that are not especially favored are those that produce middle-sized gametes, because middle-sized gametes are suboptimal in terms of both nutrient content and ease of production. Thus, the individuals producing middle-sized gametes tend to die out, and the population gradually diverges into two groups pursuing different strategies. One group produces large, nutrient-loaded gametes (ova); the other produces small,

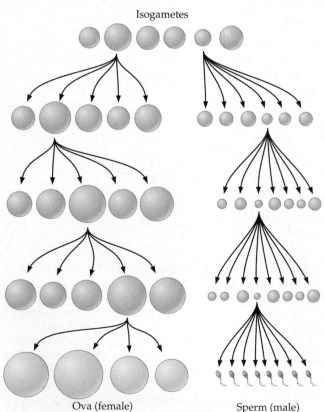

Isogametes

Ova (female)          Sperm (male)

▲ **FIGURE A.4** **Disruptive selection** splits a single population of similar-sized gametes (isogametes) into large (female) and small (male) types.

nutrient-poor gametes (sperm). The two groups that result are females and males, respectively (Bulmer & Parker, 2002; da Silva, 2018).

Several other factors come into play. For one, there is the question of mobility. To fuse, gametes need to come together, which usually means that at least one of the gametes has to be motile. Movement is easier for small gametes than large ones, so gametes produced by males are usually the motile ones. There is also the matter of numbers. Because a small gamete requires so little investment to produce, males can produce many more gametes than females can. In fact, some factors that we'll consider below often make it essential for males to produce large numbers of gametes. Thus, the total investment in gamete production may end up being similar in the two sexes.

### Hermaphrodites combine male and female reproductive functions

Although we usually think of males and females as being two different kinds of individuals within a species, it is not uncommon for individuals to combine male and female reproductive functions within a single body. Such individuals are called **hermaphrodites**. In some species, including most flowering plants and trees as well as some invertebrate animals such as worms and snails, all the individuals are hermaphrodites; there are no pure males or females.

One might imagine that hermaphrodites would fertilize themselves. Such self-fertilization, however, would nullify much of the genetic advantage that sexual reproduction is thought to confer. Thus, in hermaphroditic species there generally exist mechanisms to reduce the likelihood of self-fertilization. Male and female gametes may be generated at different times, or at distant locations on the organism. In the corn plant, for example, the male flower (the tassel) is at the top of the plant and develops early, while the female flower (the ear silk) is lower on the plant and develops somewhat later. As a result, less than 3% of all corn kernels are the result of self-pollination. Nevertheless, the capacity for self-fertilization is useful to plants as a backup means of reproduction; after all, most plants are rooted to the ground and cannot go searching for sex partners, which may not be available in the vicinity.

In hermaphroditic animals, behavioral mechanisms often prevent self-fertilization: The animals simply don't inseminate themselves, even though they are physically capable of doing so. Some hermaphroditic mollusks engage in a bizarre behavior called "penis fencing": Each of the two mating animals acts as if it is trying to inseminate the other while at the same time avoiding being inseminated itself (**FIGURE A.5**). They behave in this way because each animal is advantaged if the other takes on the task of producing their offspring.

▲ **FIGURE A.5  Penis fencing** Each of these nudibranch mollusks is both male and female, but each is trying to play the male role by impaling the other with its penises (the white hornlike structures) without being impaled itself. For a video of this behavior see Web Resources at the end of this appendix.

**hermaphrodite**  An organism that combines male and female reproductive functions.

**sex determination**  The biological mechanism that determines whether an organism will develop as a male or a female.

## A.3  Evolution Has Led to Diverse Methods of Sex Determination

Seeing that so many species throughout the animal kingdom have settled on sexual reproduction, one might expect that the mechanisms of **sex determination**—controlling whether an embryo becomes male or female—would also have become fixed early in evolution and would now be universal. In fact, however, a wide variety of sex-determining mechanisms has evolved (Capel, 2017). For example, in many reptiles the offspring's sex is determined by the temperature at which the fertilized eggs are incubated, but the details vary from species to species: among lizards and alligators, eggs incubated at low temperatures develop into females and those incubated at high temperatures produce males, while among some turtles it's the other way around.

**autosome** Any chromosome other than a sex chromosome.

**sex chromosome** Either of a pair of chromosomes (X or Y in mammals) that differ between the sexes.

**X chromosome** A sex chromosome that is present as two copies in females and one copy in males.

**Y chromosome** A sex chromosome that is present only in males.

**sexual selection** The evolution of traits under the pressure of competition for mates or of choice by mates.

## In mammals, sex is determined by chromosomes

In humans—and in most mammals—an embryo's sex is determined by the chromosomes it possesses. Forty-four of our 46 chromosomes are known as **autosomes**; they come in 22 homologous (corresponding) pairs, regardless of a person's sex. With the remaining two chromosomes, the **sex chromosomes**, the situation is more complicated. Females possess a homologous pair of sex chromosomes, termed **X chromosomes**, but males possess one X chromosome and one much smaller chromosome, called a **Y chromosome**. (The human chromosomes are shown in Figure 4.1.)

As mentioned above, gametes are produced by meiosis, a process of cell division in which the number of chromosomes is halved. Human ova receive 22 autosomes and one X chromosome. Sperm, however, receive 22 autosomes and either one X or one Y. Thus, when the ovum and sperm fuse at fertilization, the resulting zygote receives an X from the ovum and either an X or a Y from the sperm. If an X chromosome is received from the sperm, the zygote will develop as a female (XX); conversely, if a Y chromosome is received from the sperm, the zygote will develop as a male (XY).

Since there are equal numbers of X-bearing and Y-bearing sperm, the chances of a zygote being female or male are also equal. Studies of early human embryos have confirmed the equal numbers of females and males at the start of development (Orzack et al., 2015). At birth, however, males slightly outnumber females: About 105 boys are born for every 100 girls. This male-biased sex ratio is caused by a tendency for more females than males to die during prenatal life.

The technology exists to determine the sex of a fetus long before birth and to abort a fetus if it is not of the sex desired by the parents. Thus countries in which boys are strongly preferred experience sex ratios at birth that are unnaturally high—as much as 115:100 in the case of China (Central Intelligence Agency, n.d.).

The details of human sex determination and sexual development are described in Chapter 4.

## A.4 Sexual Selection Produces Anatomical and Behavioral Differences between Males and Females

In many respects, natural selection acts similarly on females and males. It ensures that women and men are both adapted to life on land, for example, and that female and male fish are both adapted to life in water. Yet marked differences can develop between males and females of a single species. Think of peacocks and peahens, for example: The males strut to and fro and shake their gorgeous tail feathers, while the plainer females watch silently, evaluate their prospective mates, and decide which male to mate with. Such differences in the appearance and behavior of males and females result from competition for mates. Charles Darwin called this process **sexual selection** (Clutton-Brock, 2017).

### Males and females follow different reproductive strategies

Two common, though not universal, features of sexual selection among nonhuman animals are competition among males and choice by females. These features result from the differing strategies adopted by males and females early in the evolution of the two sexes. Females committed themselves to a "nurturing" strategy by virtue of their investment in large, nutrient-rich ova, while males committed themselves to an "exploitative" strategy by virtue of their production of sperm—cells so small and nutrient poor that they contribute little to the zygote beyond a set of genes. In some animals, the evolution of these strategies has led to very marked differences in the roles played by the two sexes in reproduction (Lehtonen et al., 2016).

Female mammals, for example, carry the burden of **internal fertilization** followed by a prolonged period of **gestation** (pregnancy), which may last from 2 or 3 weeks (in rodents) to 22 months (in elephants). After female mammals deliver their young, they continue to nourish them through **lactation** (milk production) and nursing and usually provide most or all of the care and protection that mammalian infants require. This prolonged investment results in offspring that have a far greater chance of surviving to adulthood than the young of other vertebrates, but it also greatly limits the total number of offspring that female mammals can produce in a lifetime. A female frog can produce hundreds or thousands of tadpoles; it's unusual for a woman to produce more than a dozen children.

Males, however, can often get away with a very small investment in reproduction—a few drops of **semen** containing sperm. In theory, a male mammal could father as many offspring as a female frog produces tadpoles, simply by inseminating female after female and walking away from each. But that is reckoning without two practical constraints: competition from other males, and the ability of females to choose which males they mate with, as we'll see below.

## Females and males are exposed to different reproductive risks

Female and male animals typically experience different kinds of risks in their reproductive lives. For a female, the maximum number of potential offspring is relatively low, but her chances of having close to this number are quite good, since there will usually be plenty of males willing to mate with her. The risk for a female is not so much that she will produce few offspring, but that her offspring will fail to survive and reproduce in their turn. To maximize the likelihood that her offspring will survive, she needs not only to invest her own resources in them, but also to ensure that they are fathered by the best available male. (What "best" means, we'll discuss in a moment.)

For males, it's different: Males can father large numbers of offspring, but they can also easily end up fathering none. In some species, for example langur monkeys and elks, dominant males control large harems of females, leaving subordinate males without mates. A dominant male fathers many offspring every year, at least as long as he can maintain his dominant position. Subordinate males will have no offspring unless they can displace a dominant male or evade his surveillance. Although there are wide differences among species, males typically face the real possibility of having few or no offspring. In other words, the variability in reproductive success is greater for males than for females of most species, including humans (Betzig, 2012) (**FIGURE A.6**), and this encourages the evolution of "risky" sexual strategies by males.

## Males often compete for access to females

Because of this difference in reproductive risks experienced by males and females, males often compete with one another for access to females, while females often choose among males. We should emphasize, though, that words such as "compete" and "choose" are really figures of speech. We don't mean to imply that animals consciously try to achieve certain goals—we don't know enough about the basis of animal behavior to make such assertions. All we are saying is that animals behave *as if* they were goal driven.

What traits are influenced by sexual selection? Competition among males naturally leads to selection for traits that confer success in that competition. The most obvious traits are large size and physical strength; males are commonly larger and stronger than females, sometimes markedly so, especially among mammals (**FIGURE A.7**). Along with these physical traits goes the behavioral trait of aggressiveness—the willingness to engage in the interminable bouts of roaring, head butting, biting, and general mayhem that establish a male animal's position in the dominance hierarchy and thus influence his ability to mate with females. The sex differences in size, strength, and aggressiveness are as true for humans as they are for many other species (Puts, 2015).

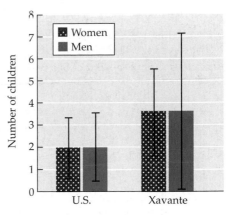

▲ **FIGURE A.6  Reproduction is a riskier game for men.** This bar graph shows the number of children born to women and men in the United States, a monogamous culture (left), and among the Xavante people of Brazil, where men may have multiple wives (right). Each data set is plotted as a mean and a standard deviation (a measure of the dispersion of the data around the mean, shown by the vertical lines). In both cultures, the standard deviation is greater for men than for women, but this difference is more marked for the polygamous Xavante. (Data from G. R. Brown et al. 2009. *Trends Ecol Evol* 24: 297–304.)

**internal fertilization**  Fertilization within the body.

**gestation**  Bearing young in the uterus; pregnancy.

**lactation**  The production of milk in the mammary glands.

**semen**  The fluid, containing sperm and a variety of chemical compounds, that is discharged from the penis (ejaculated) at the male sexual climax.

▶ **FIGURE A.7** **Intermale aggression**
Male elephant seals compete for access to females, so aggressiveness and large size are assets.

**pheromone** A volatile compound that is released by one organism and that triggers a specific behavior in another member of the same species.

**fluctuating asymmetry** A difference between the left and right sides of the body that results from random perturbations of development.

Competition among males also favors traits that assist males in locating receptive females before other males do. Such traits may include well-developed sensory skills that aid them in finding females, such as the ability to detect **pheromones** (sexually attractive volatile compounds) and to home in on their source. Another trait that helps males get to females quickly is early sexual maturation—early in life or early in the breeding season.

## Females often choose among males

What about female choice? One advantageous choice females can make is to mate with healthy, genetically favored males. How can they identify such males? Just the fact that a male has battered other males into submission speaks volumes about his health and fitness, of course. Not all species engage in such male-male contests, however. In these cases, females may choose among males on the basis of their physical appearance or behavior.

CHOICE BASED ON APPEARANCE One aspect of males' appearance to which females often pay attention is their bodily symmetry. Vertebrates are roughly bilaterally symmetrical, at least in outward appearance. The developmental reason for this symmetry is that, aside from obviously asymmetrical structures such as the heart, a single set of genetic instructions directs the development of both sides of the body. Good genes operating in a good environment will therefore produce a highly symmetrical organism. Poor genes, or a poor environment, will disturb this process, leading to asymmetries. This kind of perturbation, in which the direction of asymmetry is random, is called **fluctuating asymmetry** (Graham & Özener, 2016). A high degree of fluctuating asymmetry has been correlated with a number of disadvantageous characteristics or experiences, such as chromosomal defects, infections, exposure to toxins, and environmental stress. Low fluctuating asymmetry, however, has been correlated with a number of advantageous characteristics, such as high sprinting speed in humans (Trivers et al., 2013).

It turns out that animals are very good at assessing the symmetry of other individuals of the same species, and they prefer to mate with highly symmetrical individuals. For example, when researchers manipulated the tail feathers of male barn swallows to make them less symmetrical, those males became less attractive to females (Møller, 1992). Thus, there is sexual selection for symmetry, especially in males. In addition, females are selected for the cognitive skills that are required to evaluate symmetry and the motivation to do so.

Besides symmetry, females often look for other anatomical characteristics in males. Female barn swallows, for example, prefer those males whose outermost tail feathers are not only symmetrical, but also longer than those of other males. Female deer prefer the males with the largest antlers, female fish often prefer the most brightly colored males, and so on. Generally, the rule is "The bigger and brighter, the better"—especially with regard to features that are obviously related to sexual displays (**FIGURE A.8**).

This preference for "bigger and brighter" seems to be open-ended. If one exaggerates the features to which females pay attention—giving a male barn swallow "tail extenders," for example—these artificially enhanced males will be preferred over any "natural" males. Because of this open-ended quality, sexual selection can lead to a runaway process in which the display characteristics of males become highly exaggerated, as has happened with the peacock.

Nevertheless, something holds this process in check. The tails of male barn swallows are not getting longer, for example, even though a male with a superlong tail would attract a lot of females. The most plausible reason why the runaway process comes to a halt is that these displays have a *cost* for males: It takes an investment of food to grow long tail feathers. Large antlers hamper a stag's ability to move through the forest. Bright coloration attracts predators. At some point, the cost of these displays balances their reproductive advantage, and an equilibrium situation is reached.

It is precisely the fact that these attractive features have a cost that makes them attractive (Zahavi & Zahavi, 1997). Only a peacock that is genetically well endowed, is healthy, and has had ample access to food can sustain the cost of a tail ornate enough to attract peahens. What these displays say is "I have been able to take on the incredible burden of this tail (or antlers or coloration) and still survive—so I must be a superior animal." And indeed, there is some evidence that these displays are honest advertisements of reproductive superiority. One study, for example, found that male deer with large, complex antlers also had higher-quality sperm than other males (Malo et al., 2005).

CHOICE BASED ON BEHAVIOR   Besides choosing males on the basis of anatomical features, females also choose on the basis of **courtship behavior**. Sometimes this behavior is of practical use to the female in producing young. Female spiders, for

**courtship behavior**   Behavior that attracts a mate.

◄ **FIGURE A.8   The ornate tail feather display** of a male peacock shows females his general health and the quality of his genes.

example, often demand that their suitors provide some food prior to mating, such as a dead insect (failing which, the male himself may become the snack). Some female birds demand that the male provide a nesting site or actually construct a nest.

Besides the direct value of such gifts to the female, there's another, more subtle benefit. Demanding that a male provide resources tests his genetic fitness in the same way that demanding anatomical features such as ornate tail feathers does. Thus, it may be beneficial to the female to make the male expend resources, even if that expenditure does not benefit her in any direct way.

In fact, in numerous instances courtship by males seems to involve useless make-work. Male bowerbirds, for example, must construct elaborate thatched structures—bowers—and decorate them with hard-to-find items, such as colored shells, berries, and bottle tops, before females will pay attention to their advances (**FIGURE A.9**). The bowers have no direct value to the females—they are not nests—but they do have the indirect value of testing the male's fitness. Courtship song is another example: Singing for hours at a time offers no direct reproductive benefit, but by doing so, a male bird advertises the fact that he is not foraging—and if he can survive so long without foraging, he must be a well-endowed animal. Much courtship behavior has this flavor: Males inflict handicaps on themselves—the behavioral equivalent of peacocks' tails—to prove that they are fit enough to withstand them.

MATE CHOICE COPYING   Another way in which female animals choose mates is by copying the choices of other females, especially attractive females. A male that has been chosen by an attractive female is likely to be a high-quality individual and may therefore be worth pursuing, even without any direct knowledge about that male's qualities. Thus mate choice copying by females has been observed in numerous species (Gibson & Hoglund, 1992). For example, biologists at the University of Texas at Austin observed the behavior of female sailfin mollies (a species of fish) that had the choice of consorting with two similar-looking males (Hill & Ryan, 2006). The test females consistently chose to consort with one of the males, which they apparently judged to be the more desirable mate. The researchers then paired the preferred male with a low-quality female and the nonpreferred male with a high-quality female. After observing these pairs, the test females switched their preference and spent most of their time with the previously nonpreferred male. In other words, the presence of the high-quality female had increased the male's perceived value. Mate choice copying may save the time and risk involved in direct investigation of potential mates. Numerous studies have documented mate choice copying by human females: Women judge men to be more attractive if they have an attractive female partner (Rodeheffer et al., 2016).

© Dave Watts/Alamy Stock Photo

▲ **FIGURE A.9**   **The male satin bowerbird (dark blue)** is not as eye-catching as a peacock, but he makes up for it by building an elaborate bower and decorating its entrances with blue-colored objects, such as shells, berries, bottle tops, or feathers. If a female approves of his work, she will mate with him within the avenue of the bower.

FEMALES MAY INITIATE COURTSHIP   So far, we've given the impression that females choose among males simply by assessing their courtship behavior. In fact, however, females often initiate courtship. If the caterwauling from your neighbor's cat has ever awakened you, for example, you know that female mammals advertise when they are sexually receptive. At around the time when they ovulate, when **copulation** (penile-vaginal sex) can result in fertilization, hormonal changes cause females to undergo **estrus**, or "heat." Besides complex internal processes connected with ovulation, estrus involves the production of auditory, olfactory, or visual signals intended to alert males to the female's receptive state.

Females also may approach individual males and show **proceptive behavior**—behavior designed to elicit reciprocal courtship. Estrous female mice and rats, for example, perform a hopping, darting, and ear-wiggling routine that may induce the male to attempt a mount. During the remainder of their ovarian cycle (when fertilization is not possible), females do not make these displays or approach males, and they forcefully reject male courtship.

## Sometimes males make significant investments in reproduction

Insofar as females induce males to make an investment in reproduction, they may restore some balance between female and male reproductive strategies. The more resources males invest, the more interest they will have in ensuring their investment is not wasted. If a male has to spend days or weeks courting a female, or if he has to provide "expensive" nuptial gifts or accomplish burdensome tasks, he may become as committed as the female to seeing that the offspring of their union survive. Otherwise, he will have to start all over again with another female. His life, or the mating season, may simply not be long enough to allow that.

Thus, while males of many species make little or no contribution to the care of their offspring, in other species, males make contributions as great as those made by females. This kind of cooperative investment can allow for the evolution of lifestyles that would otherwise be impossible. Pairs of seagulls, for example, take alternating shifts at the nest (incubating eggs or protecting hatchlings) and away from the nest (finding food for themselves and the chicks). A single bird cannot accomplish both tasks, so male investment has been essential to the evolution of seagulls, as well as many other species of birds.

In a few species, males take on the entire responsibility of caring for eggs or young. A male stickleback fish, for example, constructs an underwater nest in which females lay eggs; after fertilizing them, the male spends about 2 weeks guarding the eggs and the newly hatched fry. Some male water birds, such as phalaropes and jacanas, also take on the entire responsibility for incubating eggs and feeding the hatchlings.

### If males invest, sexual selection may work differently

If males and females invest about equally in reproduction, sexual selection may not lead to any marked anatomical or behavioral differences between the sexes. Male and female seagulls, for example, are nearly the same size, and neither one has any special display feathers or other sexually distinct characteristics. In fact, the only reliable way to tell the sex of a seagull is to examine its internal anatomy.

If males invest *more* than females in reproduction, and thus are limited in how many offspring they can produce, the effects of sexual selection on the two sexes can actually be reversed. Among the just-mentioned phalaropes, for example, females compete for the sexual favors of males, and males choose among females. Consistent with this pattern, female phalaropes and

**copulation** Sexual intercourse; coitus.

**estrus** The restricted period within the ovarian cycle when females of some species are sexually receptive; "heat."

**proceptive behavior** Behavior by females that may elicit sexual advances by males.

© Roy Mangersnes/Minden Pictures

▲ **FIGURE A.10** **Gender role reversal** Among red phalaropes males invest more in reproduction than females. As a result, females—seen here on the left—are the larger and more brightly colored sex, and they compete aggressively to mate with males.

© 2015 Matthew Silk

▲ **FIGURE A.11 Sexual swellings of female baboons** appear at the time of ovulation and attract a great deal of attention from males.

jacanas are larger, more brightly colored, and more aggressive than males (**FIGURE A.10**).

Sometimes males choose among females because individual females vary in how much they can invest in reproduction. This variation is most obvious in species in which individuals continue to grow after reaching reproductive maturity. Whereas humans stop growing soon after the end of puberty, some animals, such as tortoises, grow throughout their lives. In such species, the oldest and largest females are capable of laying the largest clutches of eggs, so males mate preferentially with the oldest females.

Among some primate species, males invest considerably in reproduction, even if not to the same degree as females. For that reason, there may be competition and choosing by both sexes. Take baboons, for example. Male baboons are larger than females and compete intensely for mates, as is true in so many other species. In addition, however, female baboons compete for the sexual attention of dominant males. They do this by means of "sexual swellings"—patches of pigmented genital and perianal skin that swell around the time of ovulation (**FIGURE A.11**). The females with the largest swellings seem to be genetically favored: They have more offspring than other females, and their offspring are more likely to survive. Thus, males try to copulate with the females with the largest swellings.

It turns out, in fact, that competition among females is much more common than has been thought in the past. Whereas males may compete simply for access to females, females more commonly compete for resources, such as social rank, that enhance their offspring's prospects for survival (Clutton-Brock, 2007).

## Sexual selection protects against extinction

We described earlier how sexual *reproduction* helps remove harmful mutations. Specifically, it creates a range of individuals with both smaller and larger numbers of mutations; selection then winnows out those with the most mutations and preserves those with the fewest. Sexual *selection* plays an important role in the winnowing-out process: When individuals of one sex—usually females—choose among numerous potential mates, they are in effect picking those with fewer harmful mutations and leaving the others to die without progeny.

A research group led by Alyson Lumley of Britain's University of East Anglia carried out a multiyear study that demonstrated this process in action (Lumley et al., 2015) (**FIGURE A.12**). Starting in 2005, the researchers bred two populations of flour beetles. In one population, each female could choose among five males; in the other, she had no choice, as only one male was placed in the enclosure with her ("enforced monogamy").

After 45 generations, the researchers wanted to know whether there was a difference in the number of harmful mutations that had accumulated in the two populations. To find out, they continued mating the beetles over another 20 generations, but now they always mated brother-sister pairs. The progeny of such incestuous matings are highly inbred and are therefore especially likely to show the effects of harmful mutations passed on from their parents (see "Avoiding incest is an evolved behavior," below). As a consequence, the numbers of beetles that survived and reproduced in both populations fell from generation to generation. The important finding, though, was that the beetles that descended from the "enforced monogamy" population fared much worse than the others: As shown in Figure A.12, by nine generations

(A)

(B)

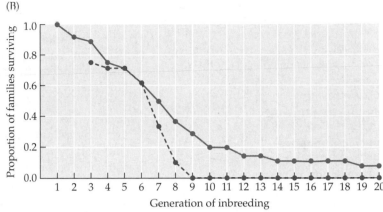

▲ **FIGURE A.12** **Sexual selection prevents extinction.**
(A) Two red flour beetles (*Tribolium castaneum*) in courtship.
(B) The descendants of beetles that reproduced without a
choice of sex partners (dashed curve) died out faster under
conditions of sibling inbreeding than did the descendants
of beetles that had a choice of sex partners (solid curve). The
latter had not completely died out even after 20 generations of
inbreeding. This showed that having a choice of sex partners
helped remove harmful mutations from the population. (After
A. J. Lumley et al. 2015. *Nature* 522: 470–473.)

of incestuous inbreeding they had all died out, whereas some beetles that descended
from the population that had a choice of mates were still alive and reproducing after
20 generations, when the experiment ended.

The results demonstrated that there had indeed been less accumulation of harmful mutations among the beetles that had a choice of sex partners, showing that the
females choose males with fewer mutations. The researchers summed up their findings in the title of their paper: "Sexual selection protects against extinction."

## A.5 Diverse Relationship Styles Have Evolved

Evolution has led to a bewildering variety of sexual relationships, from sexual
free-for-alls to lifelong, sexually exclusive pairings. Understanding the basis for this
diversity can be quite a challenge. Still, we can start with the basic assumption that
evolution is always at work. In other words, animals' genes are likely to promote
sexual behaviors and relationships that offer the best prospects for leaving copies of
those genes in future generations.

### Social and sexual arrangements are not necessarily the same

In looking at animal liaisons, we need to distinguish carefully between two phenomena: *social arrangements* and *sexual reality*. In the past, people (including biologists)
have tended to take animals' social arrangements at face value—as if these arrangements tell us unambiguously who is having sex with whom. Sometimes they do. It
turns out, however, that humans are not the only species in which social and sexual
arrangements are imperfectly aligned.

In many species, individuals are essentially solitary or belong to same-sex groups,
and they reproduce by mating with strangers (either one or many) that they never
see again. This is the pattern seen in the majority of invertebrates, fishes, amphibians,
and reptiles. Among mammals, there is considerable diversity in relationship styles,
even between related species. For example, montane voles (*Microtus montanus*) mate
with strangers and immediately go their separate ways, whereas their prairie cousins
(*Microtus ochrogaster*) form stable pair-bonds (Carter & Getz, 1993).

When reproduction does involve lasting relationships, we see two basic patterns:
monogamy and polygamy. In **monogamous** relationships, two animals (usually of
different sexes) form a **pair-bond** for the duration of the breeding season or even for
their entire lifetimes. Many birds, such as the seagulls described earlier, pair up for

**monogamy** 1. Marriage limited to
two persons. 2. A sexual relationship
in which neither partner has sexual
contact with a third party.

**pair-bond** A durable sexual
relationship between two individuals.

**polygamy** Marriage to or (mostly in animals) mating with more than one partner.

**polygyny** The marriage or mating of one male with more than one female.

**polyandry** The marriage or mating of one female with more than one male.

**sexual monogamy** Pair-bonding that is sexually exclusive.

**social monogamy** Pair-bonding that is not sexually exclusive.

**promiscuity** Engaging in numerous casual or short-lived sexual relationships.

**paternity test** A test to identify an individual's father by DNA analysis.

a season. Swans are famous for forming lifelong pair-bonds. In **polygamous** relationships, one animal forms stable bonds with several individuals of the other sex. In most polygamous species, single males form relationships with multiple females. This "harem" arrangement is technically called **polygyny** ("many females"). The opposite arrangement—a single female with a harem of males—is called **polyandry** ("many males"). It is a rare arrangement, but one animal that does adopt it is the jacana, the waterbird we have already mentioned on account of its unusual "females compete, males choose" behavior. In southern Texas one may come across a pond occupied by a single female jacana and several males in a loose social group.

That polygyny is more common than polyandry is consistent with the greater investment in reproduction by females. It simply would not be possible for females of most species to mate with multiple males and have offspring with all of them. Only when the balance of reproduction investment is reversed, as with jacanas, does polyandry crop up.

The terms "monogamy" and "polygamy," as just described, refer to bonding relationships, not to sexual behavior as such. Some pair-bonding species mate only within the pair-bond and are therefore called **sexually monogamous**. More commonly, pair-bonded individuals will mate not only with their partners but also, on some occasions, with strangers. Species in which this occurs are called **socially monogamous**. Individuals of polygamous species may also mate with strangers. A male lion will readily mate with a female from outside his pride, for example, if he can get to her before the female members of his pride drive her off. We'll call the willingness to engage in sex outside of an animal's established relationship or relationships **promiscuity**—without the negative connotation this word may carry when applied to humans.

## Male promiscuity offers obvious evolutionary benefits

From an evolutionary standpoint, male promiscuity is more or less to be expected: The investment in mating outside the pair-bond ("extra-pair sex") is usually so slight that it is "worth it" for the male, even if the chances that the mating will lead to viable offspring are not very great. Thus, one has to wonder: Why are males of some species less disposed to promiscuity than are males of other species?

In some species, females may impose sexual monogamy on males: Females may simply refuse to engage in extra-pair sex. This is true for some species of birds. Sometimes males mate with only one female simply because they mate only once—period. Deep-sea anglerfishes offer an extreme example (**FIGURE A.13**). In these species, a male homes in on a female and partially fuses with her. His eyes degenerate, and he remains permanently attached to the female, providing her with sperm whenever required. (For a video, see Web Resources.) Once attached to his mate in this manner, he is ill equipped to embark on extramarital affairs!

## Why are females promiscuous?

Male promiscuity makes evolutionary sense, but what about female promiscuity? At first glance, it seems there is no reason for it, since females can usually produce all the offspring they are capable of producing with the aid of a single male. But in fact, female promiscuity is fairly common, even in species that have long been considered sexually monogamous.

The best evidence for female promiscuity comes from DNA analysis. Individuals of the same species have numerous differences in their DNA; these differences can be detected with simple enzymatic tests. Offspring inherit their particular DNA sequences from their parents, so by comparing the sequences from an offspring and the individuals that are candidates to be its parents, the true parents can be identified. Since it is usually the identity of the father that is in doubt, the procedure is generally called **paternity testing**.

© Peter David/Getty Images

▲ **FIGURE A.13  Deep-sea threesome** Two small males have attached themselves permanently to the lower surface of this female anglerfish.

Paternity testing has now been done on a wide variety of species, with a wide variety of results. In some socially monogamous birds, up to three-fourths of a female's offspring are fathered by males other than her social mate (Birkhead, 1998). Among common chimpanzees, as many as half of all offspring are fathered by males from outside the group to which the mother belongs. In the hamadryas baboon, on the other hand, females seem never to cheat on their male partners, even if their partners are sterile, in which case there are no offspring (Birkhead, 2000).

Among western or westernized human populations, only about 1 in 100 children are fathered by someone other the woman's husband or regular partner (Larmuseau et al., 2017). Thus, if women cheat on their partners, they usually take care not to get pregnant. These findings may not apply to nonwestern societies, however. A DNA study of a pastoralist community in Namibia found that 70% of couples raise at least one child whose genetic father is not the husband (Scelza et al., 2000). This very high rate of extra-pair paternity does not necessarily represent "cheating": In most cases both husband and wife are aware that the child was fathered by a different man.

Female promiscuity may be adaptive for a number of reasons, which may differ among species. In species in which males provide resources such as food or protection, obtaining these resources from multiple mates may make promiscuity worthwhile. Another possibility is that socially monogamous females are promiscuous in order to obtain sperm from higher-quality males than their social partners. After all, if males vary in quality, most females will not be partnered with the very best males, so they may seek a higher-quality male to mate with. To test this idea, Susan Smith observed the mating behavior of black-capped chickadees (Smith, 1988). She found that when a female chickadee engages in extra-pair sex, she usually does so with a male that was dominant over her social mate during the previous winter. This finding suggests that promiscuous females are indeed shopping for better genes than their regular mates can provide. In another study of songbirds, the offspring of a female's promiscuous matings were found to be fitter (had more lifetime offspring of their own) than her offspring by her regular mate (Gerlach et al., 2012). This suggests that shopping for better genes really is an adaptive behavior.

## Female promiscuity leads to adaptive responses by males

While female promiscuity benefits females, it harms the reproductive success of the males that are their social mates. As a result, males of many species have developed behavioral strategies to prevent their mates from engaging in sex with other males. A common behavior of this type is **mate guarding**: A male remains close to a female throughout the period when she is fertile and attempts to keep other males away from her. To evaluate the effectiveness of this behavior in a songbird, Dutch researchers observed how closely male birds guarded their mates; later, they determined the paternity of nestlings by DNA analysis (Komdeur et al., 2007). As one might expect, the more closely a female was guarded by her mate, the fewer of her nestlings were fathered by outside males. Thus, mate-guarding behavior really does serve an adaptive function—for males. Do you think that human males ever engage in this kind of behavior?

Another way that males may respond to female promiscuity is by producing large numbers of sperm. By sheer force of numbers these sperm compete with the sperm of other males within the females' reproductive tracts. If we compare our close relatives, the chimpanzees and gorillas, for example, we find that a female chimpanzee mates many times with many different males for every time that she becomes pregnant, whereas female gorillas mate with only one or two males per pregnancy. Correspondingly, the testes of chimpanzees are far larger (in relation to overall body size) than those of gorillas, and this allows chimpanzee males to produce ejaculates that contain far more sperm and to ejaculate more frequently. In humans, testis size is intermediate between that of chimpanzees and gorillas, suggesting that female promiscuity and sperm competition have played a role in human evolution, but not an unusually large one.

**mate guarding**   A behavior in which a male animal prevents sexual contact between his mate and other males.

No primate can compare with pigs, however, in terms of sperm statistics. Pigs mate promiscuously, so sperm competition is probably very strong. Correspondingly, each ejaculate of a male pig (boar) measures a pint (473 mL) or more in volume and contains an average of 750 billion sperm (compared with a mere 350 *million* in men). Furthermore, the boar's penis is long enough to deposit the ejaculate directly into the sow's uterus, rather than into the vagina as in humans—another trait that has been driven by sperm competition.

## Males may copulate with females by force

Forced copulation is seen in a wide variety of animals, from insects to primates. In some of these animals it is clearly an adaptive behavior; that is, it persists because those animals that engage in it have more offspring than they would have otherwise.

Perhaps the most detailed study of forced copulation has been done on scorpionflies by evolutionary psychologist Randy Thornhill of the University of New Mexico (Thornhill & Palmer, 2000). In these insects, a male is able to mate with a female by one of two strategies. In one strategy, he offers the female a nuptial gift, such as a dead insect; the female approaches the gift-bearing male, and they mate. If a male approaches a female without a gift, the female attempts to flee. In this case, however, the male may grasp the female and hold her immobile with a special appendage called a notal organ, which enables him to copulate in the face of the female's resistance. Because the notal organ has no use other than for forced copulation—it is not required for unforced sex—Thornhill concluded that forced copulation is not a random by-product of scorpionfly evolution, but an adaptive behavior resulting from countless generations of sexual selection.

Only a couple of other species (also insects) have anatomical adaptations that facilitate forced copulation. In fact, quite a few species have the opposite—arrangements of the female anatomy that make copulation impossible without her active collaboration. For example, a female rat's **vulva** is situated on the underside of her rump and is inaccessible to males unless she exposes it by arching her rump upward—a behavior called lordosis. It is likely that arrangements of this kind are adaptations to prevent forced copulation.

Most animals do not have anatomical specializations that either facilitate or prevent this behavior, but attempts at forced copulation by males, and resistance by females, have been observed in numerous species, including primates (Muller & Wrangham, 2009) (**FIGURE A.14**). Orangutans are notorious in this respect (Knott et

**vulva** The female external genitalia.

(A)

(B)

Both photos courtesy of John Alcock

▲ **FIGURE A.14** **Unforced sex and coercive sex** in the beetle *Tegrodera aloga*. (A) The male (right) courts the female by drawing her antennae into grooves on his head. The female may or may not respond by copulating with him.

(B) In an alternative strategy, the male (below) runs up to the female, throws her on her side, and inserts his genitalia as she struggles to free herself from his grasp.

al., 2010). Male orangutans exist in two anatomically distinct forms, one larger than the other. During the fertile portion of her menstrual cycle a female orangutan will mate willingly with only the larger type of male. Thus, to impregnate a female, a smaller male must overcome violent resistance on her part. This rape-like behavior may leave one or both parties with significant injuries, but it results in pregnancy often enough to make the behavior adaptive for the smaller type of male. The smaller male can develop into the larger type, but this only happens if larger males are absent.

## A.6  Sometimes, Helping Relatives Reproduce Is a Good Strategy

Genes act within the individual that possesses them. At first thought, therefore, it would seem that genes should cause their owners to focus 100% of their efforts on reproducing themselves. And there is indeed a lot of selfish sexual behavior in this world: The topic we have just discussed—forced copulation—is an extreme example. But selfless, altruistic behavior is also quite common.

One kind of altruistic behavior with an obvious adaptive value is parental care. In evolutionary terms, it's no use having offspring if those offspring don't have offspring in their turn, so it may pay to help one's offspring survive and become sexually mature, even if that limits the number of offspring one can produce. Genes promoting parental care (or at least maternal care) are evidently widespread.

Genes promoting altruistic behavior toward one's offspring survive because the offspring have a good chance of possessing those same genes. (Specifically, any gene in a parent has a 50% chance of being handed down to each offspring.) Therefore, genes for altruism toward one's offspring are helping *themselves* get handed on to the third and future generations. But parents and offspring are not the only kinds of relatives that inherit the same genes. Siblings also co-inherit half of their genes, on average. First cousins co-inherit about one-eighth of their genes, and so on. Thus, if you happen to possess genes that cause you to help a relative reproduce, those same genes may exist in that relative too. If so, your "altruism" helps propagate those genes into the next generation, even if you have no offspring yourself. The mechanism by which genes for altruism toward relatives are maintained in a population is called **kin selection** (Kay et al., 2019).

Kin selection does seem to explain quite a lot of social and sexual behavior in the animal kingdom. For example, subordinate males in lion prides and other groups may have few or no offspring of their own, at least as long as they are subordinate. If the dominant male is their brother or other close relative, however, it may still be worth it for them to remain in the group and help him reproduce, for by doing so, they are propagating copies of some of their own genes. Kin selection also favors the development of "aunting" behavior in primates—the tendency of females to share maternal duties—because the females that share these duties are likely to be sisters or other close relatives.

## A.7  Avoiding Incest Is an Evolved Behavior

Most people believe that incest—sex with a close relative such as a sibling—is morally wrong. And in fact sexual relationships between adult siblings are very uncommon. This is a good thing because any children resulting from sex between siblings stand a higher than usual likelihood of suffering from certain inherited disorders. But it is not just our moral judgments or our knowledge of genetics that cause us to avoid incestuous relationships; rather, evolution has provided us with a psychological mechanism that makes siblings sexually unattractive to each other (Wilson, 2019).

This mechanism, known as the Westermarck effect, depends on the close and prolonged contact that usually exists between siblings, and between children and

**kin selection**  The theory that it can be advantageous, in evolutionary terms, to support the reproductive success of close relatives.

their parents, during childhood. Thus, adopted children are just as unattractive to their siblings as biological siblings, even though there is no rational reason for adoptive siblings to avoid having children together. Conversely, biological siblings or other relatives who *don't* live together during childhood may find each other sexually attractive when they meet in adulthood, and many cases of incest involve that kind of situation. A famous example is recounted in the ancient Greek legend of Oedipus, who unwittingly married his mother and fathered four children; Oedipus had been abandoned at birth and never met his mother during his childhood. More recently, a 19-year-old New Mexico man and his mother were arrested and charged with incest; the man had been adopted out as an infant and, like Oedipus, only met his mother again when he was adult (Associated Press, 2016a).

A similar mechanism operates in nonhuman animals. Infant mice, for example, learn the smell of their littermates (which carries information about a set of variable genes called MHC markers). After puberty, they avoid sex with animals carrying similar MHC markers—animals that might be their close relatives. Whether incest avoidance in humans depends on the sense of smell is not known: Most likely, it depends on a broader array of cues including visual appearance, behavior, and so on. Whatever these cues may be, they operate below the level of consciousness—we're not sexually attracted to our siblings, but we don't know why.

## A.8 Sex Has Acquired Other Functions beyond Reproduction

In evolutionary terms, reproduction was doubtless the original function of sexual behavior. In many species, however, sex has acquired other functions that are not directly connected with establishing pregnancy. We know this because individuals of many species engage in sexual behaviors that cannot produce offspring, such as sex between two males or between two females. Why do they do so?

In part, animals may be motivated to engage in sexual behaviors simply by the physical pleasure that sexual activity brings. Engaging in nonreproductive sex for pleasure alone would not be adaptive in an evolutionary sense. But some species have found functions for nonreproductive sex that are truly adaptive. Notable among these species is our close relative, the bonobo or pygmy chimpanzee (*Pan paniscus*), which lives along the Congo River in Central Africa.

### Female and male bonobos engage in nonreproductive sex

Like most female mammals, female bonobos advertise when they are willing to copulate (estrus). Bonobos, like baboons, do so by means of their genital swellings. In striking contrast to mammals such as mice, however, the estrus of a bonobo extends over almost two-thirds of her entire ovarian cycle, which lasts about 2 months. In fact, the female bonobo is out of estrus for only a few days around the time of menstruation (the periodic shedding of the lining of the uterus). Although the bonobo ovulates at some point during her estrus, the ovum is viable for only a day or two; sperm do not survive in her reproductive tract for more than a day or two, either. In other words, for most of the time when the female bonobo is willing to have sex, there is no chance that sex will result in pregnancy. From your knowledge of human sexuality, this may not strike you as particularly remarkable, but in evolutionary terms it is a real novelty.

Not only are female bonobos sexually receptive for most of the ovarian cycle, but they are also receptive when they are not cycling at all. Bonobo mothers breastfeed their young for several years after they are born, and lactation suppresses ovulation. Thus, bonobos cannot become pregnant while they are still nursing previous offspring. Even so, they are sexually receptive throughout this period.

Further accentuating the nonreproductive nature of much bonobo sex, both female and male bonobos engage in frequent homosexual encounters (**FIGURE A.15**). When two females have sex, they embrace face to face, and each rubs her swollen **clitoris** (the erectile component of the external female genitalia that mediates sexual pleasure) sideways against the other's. This behavior, called genito-genital rubbing, is unique to female-female encounters—it's quite different from the behavior shown by females during sexual encounters with males.

Sexual encounters between males occur in one of two ways. In one kind, the males face away from each other and one male rubs his **scrotum** (the sac containing the testes) against the other male's buttocks. In the other, the two males rub their penises together while hanging from a tree branch.

▲ **FIGURE A.15**   **Two female bonobos** engage in sexual behavior known as genito-genital rubbing.

## Bonobos use sex for conflict resolution and alliance formation

All this nonreproductive sexual activity raises an obvious question—why? Close observation of bonobo colonies in captivity and in the wild indicates that bonobos use sex for the prevention and resolution of conflicts (Gruber & Clay, 2016). Two bonobos that are faced with a conflict in food allocation, for example, will engage in sex and then divide the food peacefully. This happens regardless of the sex or age of the two animals. Alternatively, one animal may take food from another and "pay" with the currency of sex. When an entire troop of bonobos comes upon a food source—a situation that triggers wild fighting in other species, such as common chimpanzees—the bonobos engage in extensive bouts of sex with one another before dividing up the food. The bonobos' motto seems to be "Make love, not war." And bonobos make love amicably—forced copulation is virtually unknown in this species.

A related function of sex in bonobos is the cementing of social relationships and the formation of alliances. This function is particularly important for females. Bonobo females leave their natal (birth) groups and join new ones, whereas males stay in their natal groups. Females joining a group are initially unwelcome, but they solidify their position by forming close alliances with high-ranking females. The activity that bonds females in these alliances is genito-genital rubbing. So effective are these sex-mediated alliances that female bonobos have largely taken the control of bonobo society away from males. In fact, a male's rank depends in large part on the rank of his mother.

Because bonobos, like many humans, see much more to sex than making babies, we might imagine that we have inherited this aspect of our sexuality from bonobos. But such an assumption would be risky, for common chimpanzees—which are about equally closely related to us—are far more restricted in their use of nonreproductive sex. What is remarkable about the Hominoidea—the superfamily that includes gibbons, orangutans, gorillas, common chimpanzees, bonobos, and humans—is the diversity of their sexual and social arrangements. Gibbons are monogamous; orangutans are solitary; gorillas are polygynous; common chimpanzees are polygamous and male dominated; bonobos are polygamous and female dominated. Human culture may cause people to adopt any of these arrangements, but evolutionary forces are still at work in human sexuality, as is discussed in several chapters of this book.

**clitoris**   The erectile organ in females, whose external portion is located at the junction of the labia minora, just in front of the vestibule.

**scrotum**   The sac behind the penis that contains the testicles.

# Summary

- The original function of sex—and its only function in many species—is reproduction. The reasons why many species rely on sexual rather than asexual reproduction are disputed. Two general theories have been presented. First, sexual reproduction may promote the elimination of harmful mutations. Second, by mixing genes from different individuals, sexual reproduction may foster the selection of advantageous traits.

- Natural selection has caused gametes to diverge into female and male forms. Female gametes are large and contain nutrients; male gametes are small and motile.

- Sex may be determined by chromosomal mechanisms, as in mammals, or by the temperature at which eggs are incubated, as in many reptiles.

- Sexual selection, driven by competition for mates, has led to different morphological and behavioral traits in males and females. Because females generally invest more than males in reproduction, males often compete among themselves for access to females. This competition may select for large, aggressive individuals.

- Females often choose among males. Their choices may be based on morphological features, such as symmetry, display feathers, or antler size, or on behavioral traits such as the provision of food. Some female choice seems aimed at forcing males to make a greater investment in reproduction than they otherwise would. In species in which males do make significant investments, males become choosier and females become more competitive. Sexual selection helps remove harmful mutations.

- A wide variety of relationship styles exists. Animals may engage in sex without establishing any social bond, or they may bond in socially monogamous or polygamous relationships. Polygamy usually involves one male and several females (polygyny); the reverse arrangement (polyandry) is uncommon.

- In many socially monogamous or polygynous species, both males and females engage in sex outside these social structures. Promiscuity has obvious benefits for males in terms of increased numbers of offspring. For a female, promiscuity may offer a range of benefits: It may help her gain resources from males, it may give her access to high-quality genes, or it may favorably influence the behavior of males toward her or her offspring.

- Forced copulation has been observed in many species. In a few species, this behavior is clearly adaptive, increasing the male's likelihood of having offspring.

- Because close relatives share many genes, evolution has led to altruistic behavior among relatives, including behavior in the reproductive domain.

- Sexual behavior has developed other functions besides reproduction. Bonobos offer a striking example: In this species, much sex takes place when the female is incapable of becoming pregnant and between individuals of the same sex. Bonobo sex is directed not only toward reproduction, but also toward the avoidance or resolution of conflicts and the establishment of social bonds.

## Web Resources

Colby, C. The TalkOrigins Archive: Introduction to evolutionary biology **tinyurl.com/60qt**

Langin, K. Video of mating deep-sea anglerfish stuns biologists **https://tinyurl.com/tb9u5bn**

Lively, C. M. Evolution of sex and recombination **tinyurl.com/kyzdmbv**

Newman, L. Flatworms penis fencing (video) **tinyurl.com/ybxsvxwy**

PBS: Evolution—Show #5: Why sex? **tinyurl.com/587f2**

UC Museum of Paleontology and the National Center for Science Education: Welcome to evolution 101 **tinyurl.com/yblqkpv9**

## Recommended Reading

Beukeboom, L. & Perrin, N. (2014). *The evolution of sex determination*. Oxford University Press.

Birkhead, T. (2000). *Promiscuity: An evolutionary history of sperm competition*. Harvard University Press.

Buss, D. M. (2003). *The evolution of desire: Strategies of human mating* (4th ed.). Basic Books.

Dawkins, R. (2016). *The selfish gene: 40th anniversary edition*. Oxford University Press.

Geary, D. C. (2009). *Male, female: The evolution of human sex differences*. American Psychological Association.

Ridley, M. (2003). *The red queen: Sex and the evolution of human nature*. Harper Perennial.

Ryan, C. & Jetha, C. (2010). *Sex at dawn: The prehistoric origins of modern sexuality*. Harper.

Sommer, V. & Vasey, P. L. (2006). *Homosexual behaviour in animals: An evolutionary perspective*. Cambridge University Press.

Stevant, I., Papaioannou, M. D. & Nef, S. (2018). A brief history of sex determination. *Molecular and Cellular Endocrinology, 468*, 3–10.

# APPENDIX B

# Sex and the Nervous System

Sexual behavior is under the control of two of the body's three major communication networks: the nervous system and the endocrine system. (The third network—the immune system—plays little role in sex.) Here we consider the role of the nervous system, focusing on very basic functions such as penile and clitoral erection, as well as the brain mechanisms involved in sexual arousal. **BOX B.1** offers a brief refresher course on the organization of the nervous system, emphasizing elements that are referred to in this textbook.

# BOX B.1
## The Nervous System

(A)

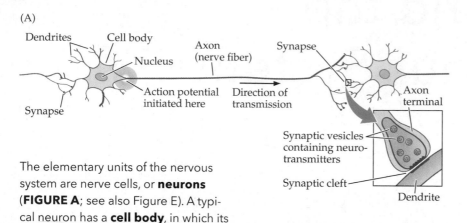

(B)

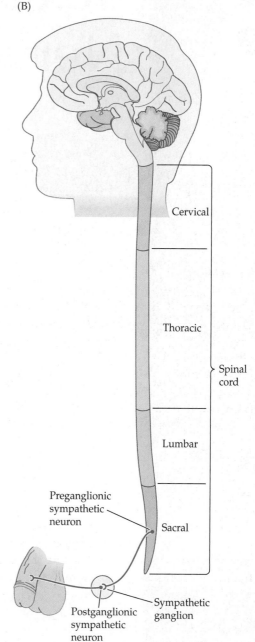

The elementary units of the nervous system are nerve cells, or **neurons** (**FIGURE A**; see also Figure E). A typical neuron has a **cell body**, in which its nucleus and part of its cytoplasm are located, plus two kinds of cytoplasmic extensions: **dendrites**, which receive and integrate numerous input signals from other neurons or from sensory receptors, and an **axon**, or nerve fiber, which transmits the neuron's output signals in the form of electrochemical **action potentials** or nerve impulses. The axon may span many centimeters (e.g., from the spinal cord to the foot), or it may end in the same region as the cell body. (In the latter case, the neuron is called an **interneuron**.) The terminals of the axon form **synapses** with the dendrites of other neurons or with muscle fibers. (In the latter case, the neurons are called **motor neurons** and the synapses are called **neuromuscular junctions**.)

When action potentials reach synapses, they cause the release of chemical **neurotransmitters**, which are small molecules such as amino acids (e.g., glutamate), catecholamines (e.g., norepinephrine), or acetylcholine. Neurotransmitters diffuse rapidly across the narrow **synaptic cleft** and raise or decrease the excitability of the postsynaptic neuron or muscle fiber.

The nervous system is divided into three subsystems: the central nervous system, the peripheral nervous system, and the autonomic nervous system. (There is also an enteric nervous system that controls the gut, which will not concern us here.) The **central nervous system** (**CNS**) comprises the spinal cord and the brain. Most regions of the CNS consist of gray matter and white matter. The **gray matter** is where the CNS carries out its all-important computations; it contains a mix of neuronal cell bodies, dendrites, synapses, and supporting nonneuronal cells, and it is organized into **cortex** (sheets) and **nuclei** (clumps). The **white matter** contains only axons interconnecting various parts of the CNS, along with supporting cells.

The **spinal cord**, although it is a continuous structure, is conventionally divided into segments; these segments are defined by the vertebrae through which the bundles of nerve fibers enter and leave the spinal cord. Counting down from the top, there are eight cervical, twelve thoracic, five lumbar, and five sacral segments (**FIGURE B**). The gray matter of the spinal cord can be divided into two **dorsal horns** and two **ventral horns**, one on either side of the cord (**FIGURE C**). Axons enter and leave these areas through the **dorsal** and **ventral roots**, respectively.

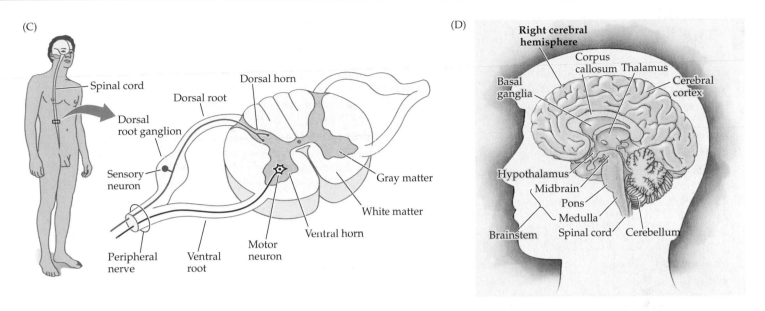

The brain (**FIGURE D**) is divided into two general regions: the forebrain and the brain stem. The main elements of the **forebrain** are the left and right **cerebral hemispheres**, each of which consists of several lobes of **cerebral cortex** and underlying white matter, along with deeper structures known as the **basal ganglia**. The two hemispheres are interconnected via the **corpus callosum**. The **brain stem** includes several subregions: starting from the lower end, these regions are the **medulla**, the **pons** with the attached cerebellum, the **midbrain**, and the **thalamus** with the underlying **hypothalamus**. Several of these regions contain cell groups involved in sexual functions.

The **peripheral nervous system** is the set of motor axons that leave the CNS to innervate striated (voluntary) muscles, plus the sensory axons that bring information into the CNS. These two kinds of axons are also called **efferent** (i.e., carrying signals away from the CNS) and **afferent** (bringing signals into the CNS), respectively. The motor axons belong to motor neurons whose cell bodies are located in the ventral horn of the spinal cord. The sensory axons belong to neurons whose cell bodies are located in **ganglia** within the dorsal roots. Sensory neurons are unusual in that they have no dendrites; rather, a T-shaped axon conveys impulses from the periphery into the dorsal horn of the spinal cord (**FIGURE E**).

The **autonomic nervous system** controls—largely without our volition—the activity of smooth muscles, heart muscle, and glands throughout the body. Within the autonomic nervous system are two subsystems: the parasympathetic and **sympathetic nervous systems**. The parasympathetic nervous system arises from the brain. Some of its branches are distributed to organs in the abdomen, but

they do not reach as far as the pelvis and they therefore play no role in genital function.* For that reason we do not discuss the parasympathetic nervous system in this book, and it is not shown in Figure B. The sympathetic nervous system arises from thoracic, lumbar, and sacral segments of the spinal cord. It consists of two sets of neurons: a set of **preganglionic neurons** that reside in the spinal cord and send their axons to ganglia outside the spinal cord, and a set of **postganglionic neurons** whose cell bodies lie in the ganglia and that send their axons to peripheral targets, such as smooth muscle and glands. Figure B shows only the portion of the sympathetic nervous system that arises from the sacral segments of the spinal cord. The axons

*(Continued)*

---

*Traditional accounts of the autonomic nervous system have described the autonomic outputs from the sacral segments of the spinal cord as being part of the parasympathetic nervous system. More recent work has shown that they are similar in every respect to the sympathetic outputs from higher levels of the cord and are quite different from the parasympathetic outputs that arise in the brain. Espinosa-Medina, I., Saha, O., Boismoreau, F., et al. (2016). The sacral autonomic outflow is sympathetic. *Science, 354,* 893–897; Espinosa-Medina, I., Saha, O., Boismoreau, F. & Brunet, J. F. (2018). The "sacral parasympathetic": ontogeny and anatomy of a myth. *Clinical Autonomic Research, 28,* 13–21. For that reason the sacral outputs should be considered part of the sympathetic nervous system—which means that the entire autonomic innervation of the genitalia is sympathetic.

(E)

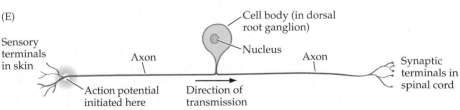

## BOX B.1

## The Nervous System (*continued*)

of these preganglionic neurons run to sympathetic ganglia; from there postganglionic sympathetic neurons innervate the penis, clitoris, and other pelvic structures.

**neuron**    A single nerve cell with all its extensions.

**cell body**    The part of a neuron where the nucleus is located.

**dendrites**    The extensions of a neuron that receive incoming signals from other neurons.

**axon**    The extension of a neuron that conveys impulses, usually in a direction away from the cell body. Also called nerve fiber.

**action potential**    An electrochemical signal that travels rapidly along an axon. Also called *nerve impulse*.

**interneuron**    A neuron whose connections are local.

**synapse**    A junction where signals are transmitted between neurons or from neurons to muscle fibers.

**motor neuron**    A neuron that triggers the contraction of muscle fibers.

**neuromuscular junction**    A synapse between an axon and a muscle fiber.

**neurotransmitter**    A compound released at a synapse that increases or decreases the excitability of an adjacent neuron.

**synaptic cleft**    The narrow space between two neurons at a synapse.

**central nervous system (CNS)**    The brain and spinal cord.

**gray matter**    A region of the CNS containing the cell bodies of neurons.

**cortex**    The outer portion of an anatomical structure, as of the cerebral hemispheres or the adrenal gland.

**nucleus (pl. nuclei)**    In neuroanatomy, a recognizable cluster of neurons in the CNS.

**white matter**    A region of the CNS that contains bundles of axons but no neuronal cell bodies.

**spinal cord**    The portion of the CNS within the vertebral column.

**dorsal horn**    The rear portion of the gray matter of the spinal cord; it has a sensory function.

**ventral horn**    The portion of the gray matter of the spinal cord nearer to the front of the body, where motor neurons are located.

**dorsal root**    A bundle of sensory axons that enters a dorsal horn of the spinal cord.

**ventral root**    A bundle of motor axons that leaves a ventral horn of the spinal cord.

**forebrain**    The cerebral hemispheres and basal ganglia.

**cerebral hemispheres**    The uppermost and largest portion of the brain, divided into left and right halves.

**cerebral cortex**    Convoluted, layered gray matter that covers most of the brain.

**basal ganglia**    Deep noncortical structures of the forebrain.

**corpus callosum**    A band of axons interconnecting the left and right cerebral hemispheres.

**brain stem**    The region of the brain between the forebrain and the spinal cord.

**medulla**    The portion of the brain stem closest to the spinal cord.

**pons**    A region of the brain above the medulla.

**midbrain**    The region of the brain stem between the pons and the thalamus.

**thalamus**    The uppermost region of the brain stem.

**hypothalamus**    A small region at the base of the brain on either side of the third ventricle; it contains cell groups involved in sexual responses and other basic functions.

**peripheral nervous system**    The motor and sensory connections between the CNS and peripheral structures such as muscles and sense organs.

**efferent**    Carrying signals away from the CNS.

**afferent**    Carrying signals toward the CNS.

**ganglia**    Clusters of neurons outside the CNS.

**autonomic nervous system**    The portion of the nervous system that controls smooth muscles and glands without our conscious involvement.

**sympathetic nervous system**    A division of the autonomic nervous system; among other functions, it controls clitoral and penile erection as well as seminal emission and ejaculation.

**preganglionic neuron**    An autonomic motor neuron in the spinal cord.

**postganglionic neuron**    A neuron with its cell body in an autonomic ganglion and an axon that innervates glands or smooth muscles in peripheral organs such as the genitalia.

## B.1 Erection Can Be Mediated by a Spinal Reflex

One simple behavior that illustrates the role of the nervous system in sex is the erection of the penis or clitoris in response to tactile stimulation of the genital area. This behavior requires five elements that collectively form a reflex loop running from the genitals to the spinal cord and back:

1. Sensory nerve endings detect the stimulation.
2. Nerves convey the sensory information to the spinal cord.

3. Information is processed in the spinal cord.

4. Nerves carry an output signal to the penis or clitoris.

5. Vascular elements are responsible for the actual erection.

Although the brain also plays a significant role in promoting or inhibiting erection, this role is not essential. People who have suffered spinal injuries that prevent communication between the brain and the lower portion of the spinal cord are usually still capable of having erections in response to genital stimulation. In women with such injuries, vaginal lubrication may still occur, though it is often reduced in amount (National Institute on Disability and Rehabilitation Research, 2015).

### Sensory innervation of the genitalia

The penis and clitoris possess a unique class of sensory nerve endings termed **genital end-bulbs** or **genital corpuscular receptors**, which we describe and illustrate in Chapter 3 (Figure 3.6). These are thought to sense the kind of tactile stimulation that occurs during sexual behavior. In one study the density of these receptors in the clitoris was found to vary as much as 14-fold among different women (Shih et al., 2013). Such variation might cause one woman's clitoris to be more erotically sensitive than another's, but because studies of this kind are done on tissue from deceased women, it hasn't been possible to make a direct correlation between the variation in innervation density and variations in erotic sensitivity.

### The pudendal and pelvic nerves

If we trace the sensory nerve fibers from the penis or clitoris, we find that they travel toward the spinal cord in the left and right **pudendal nerves** (**FIGURE B.1**). The sensory fibers enter the sacral segments (labeled S2–S4 in the figure) of the spinal cord by passing through the dorsal roots. The cell bodies of the sensory fibers are located within the dorsal roots, but no synaptic connections occur there—signals go directly into the spinal cord.

The central endings of the sensory nerve fibers form synaptic connections with interneurons (local circuit cells) in the gray matter of the sacral segments of the spinal cord. These interneurons in turn form synaptic connections with output neurons, which in this case are preganglionic neurons of the sympathetic* nervous system (see Box B.1, Figure E). The cell bodies of these neurons are located in the sacral segments of the spinal cord, and their efferent axons leave the cord in the ventral roots and travel toward the genitals in the **pelvic nerves**. On reaching ganglia near the bladder, they form synapses with postganglionic sympathetic neurons, whose axons in turn travel to the erectile tissues in the penis and clitoris.

The sympathetic axons that enter the erectile tissue are of two kinds, characterized by the different neurotransmitters that they release within the tissue. One kind releases norepinephrine (also

---

*For the reason why we call these output neurons sympathetic, rather than parasympathetic as earlier accounts have described them, see the footnote to Box B.1.

▶ **FIGURE B.1  Nerve pathways involved in erection**  Erection is controlled by sympathetic inputs to the erectile tissue. Activity in these inputs is influenced by sensory signals carried to the spinal cord by the pudendal nerve, as well as by activity in pathways descending from the brain. Thus erection can be caused either by genital stimulation or by psychological arousal.

**genital end-bulbs (or genital corpuscular receptors)**  Specialized nerve endings, found in the genital area, that probably detect the tactile stimulation associated with sexual activity.

**pudendal nerves**  Peripheral nerves supplying the external genitalia.

**pelvic nerves**  Nerves that convey sympathetic signals from the lower spinal cord to the genitalia and other pelvic organs.

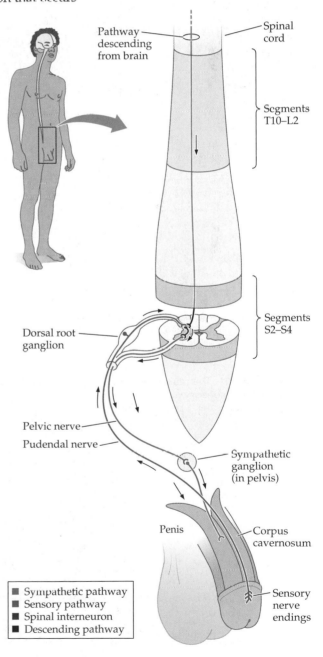

- ■ Sympathetic pathway
- ■ Sensory pathway
- ■ Spinal interneuron
- ■ Descending pathway

**adrenergic**  Using norepinephrine (noradrenaline) as a neurotransmitter.

**cholinergic**  Using acetylcholine (and in some cases nitric oxide) as a neurotransmitter.

**sinusoid**  A vascular space, such as within erectile tissue, capable of being expanded by filling with blood.

called noradrenaline); axons of this kind are called **adrenergic**. The other kind releases two neurotransmitters, acetylcholine and nitric oxide; axons of this type are called **cholinergic**. Activity in these two types of sympathetic axons affects the erectile tissue in different ways.

## B.2  Erectile Tissue Forms a Hydraulic System

The erectile tissue within the corpora cavernosa consists of irregular vascular spaces called **sinusoids**, which are separated by walls of connective tissue called **trabeculae** (**FIGURE B.2A**). Blood enters the sinusoids via arterioles and exits via veins. The trabeculae contain smooth muscle cells, and contraction of these cells shrinks the spaces, thus diminishing the volume of the erectile tissue as a whole. The other major control element consists of smooth muscle cells in the walls of the arterioles. Contraction of these cells constricts the arterioles, diminishing the flow of blood into the sinusoids.

The flaccid state of the penis and clitoris is not simply an inactive condition in which the erectile tissue receives no input from the nervous system. Rather, it is actively maintained by a continuous (tonic) flow of impulses in the adrenergic nerve fibers. The norepinephrine released from

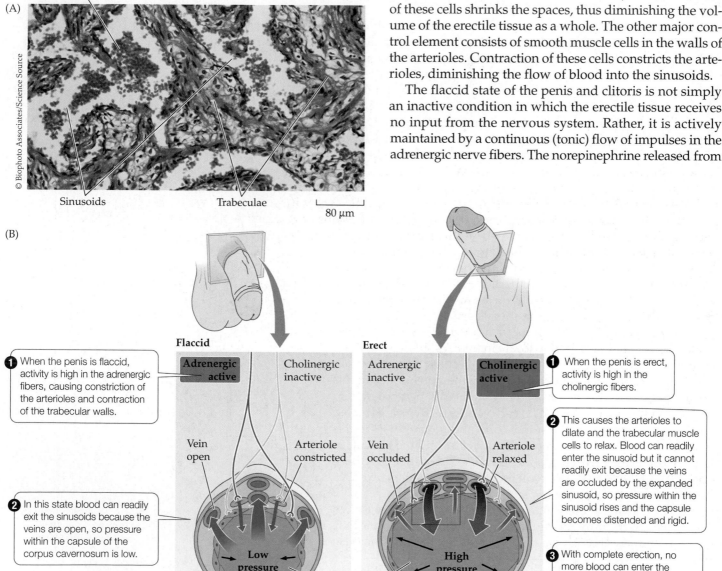

▲ **FIGURE B.2  The mechanism of penile or clitoral erection**  (A) Erectile tissue of a corpus cavernosum, showing sinusoids (some with red blood cells) and trabeculae (the cellular walls between the sinusoids). (B) Diagram of the erectile mechanism. Note that for simplicity, the illustration shows the penis as if it contains a single, large sinusoid. In reality, thousands of microscopic sinusoids make up the erectile tissue of the corpora cavernosa and the corpus spongiosum.

the terminals of these axons causes the smooth muscle cells in the walls of the arterioles to remain in a state of contraction, and the arterioles are constricted and little blood can flow into the sinusoids.

Erection results from an increase in the activity of the cholinergic fibers, such as may happen during activation of the spinal reflex described above. The release of the neurotransmitters acetylcholine and nitric oxide cause the smooth muscle cells of the arterioles and the trabeculae to relax, and the sinusoids fill with blood. Whether the adrenergic input ceases during erection, or whether its influence is simply overridden by the cholinergic inputs, is not clear.

As the erectile tissue expands, it compresses and closes the veins that receive the outflow from the sinusoids, causing the volume of the tissue to increase further and the penis as a whole to become erect (**FIGURE B.2B**).

With complete erection, no more blood can enter the sinusoids, and blood flow ceases. The pooled blood gradually loses its oxygen, taking on the purplish color of venous blood. This color change can be observed in the glans of the penis, which has only a thin, translucent capsule.

## B.3  Muscles Are Also Involved in Erection

Several striated (voluntary) muscles of the pelvic floor are also involved in erection of the penis and clitoris (**FIGURE B.3**). The most important of these are the ischiocavernosus and bulbospongiosus muscles. The action of these muscles is most obvious in the case of the penis. If a man's penis is already erect but hanging down from the body, a light touch on the sensitive areas of the penis, or even on nearby skin, will cause the penis to jump up and project directly forward or upward. At the same time, the glans of the penis will become more enlarged. This involuntary reflex response is caused by contraction of the ischiocavernosus and bulbospongiosus muscles, which pull on and squeeze the corpora cavernosa and corpus spongiosum in the root of the penis. It is also possible to produce the same movement voluntarily, without any stimulation of the genitals. This is the only aspect of erection that is under conscious control.

This reflex has the same afferent pathway we described earlier—the sensory fibers running to the spinal cord through the pudendal nerve—but the efferent pathway is different, and it does not involve the sympathetic nervous system. Instead, the

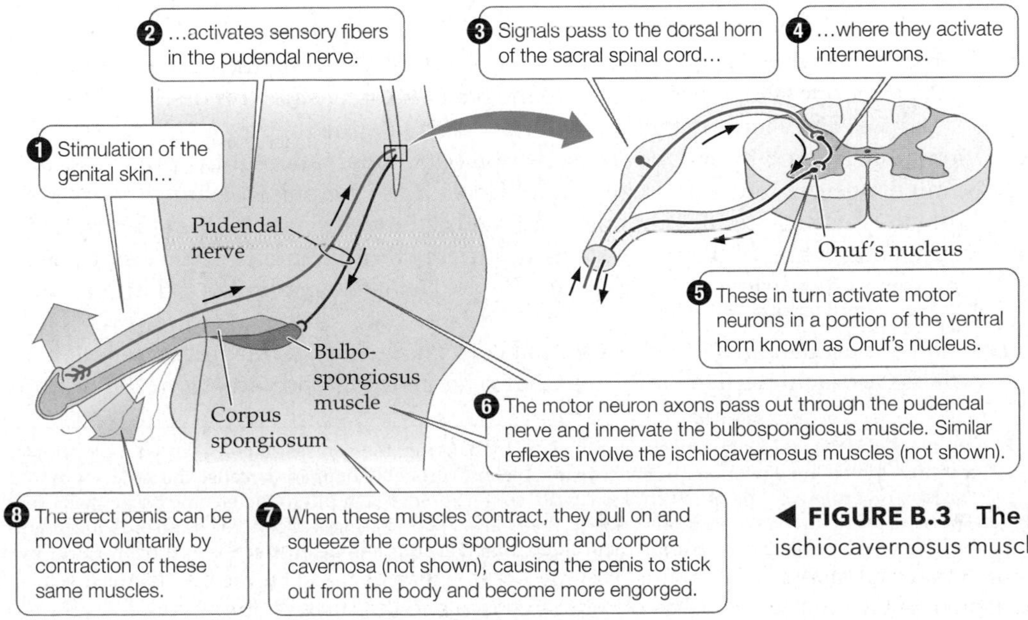

**trabeculae**  Connective tissue partitions separating the sinusoids of erectile tissue.

❷ ...activates sensory fibers in the pudendal nerve.

❸ Signals pass to the dorsal horn of the sacral spinal cord...

❹ ...where they activate interneurons.

❶ Stimulation of the genital skin...

Pudendal nerve

Onuf's nucleus

❺ These in turn activate motor neurons in a portion of the ventral horn known as Onuf's nucleus.

Bulbo-spongiosus muscle

Corpus spongiosum

❻ The motor neuron axons pass out through the pudendal nerve and innervate the bulbospongiosus muscle. Similar reflexes involve the ischiocavernosus muscles (not shown).

❽ The erect penis can be moved voluntarily by contraction of these same muscles.

❼ When these muscles contract, they pull on and squeeze the corpus spongiosum and corpora cavernosa (not shown), causing the penis to stick out from the body and become more engorged.

◀ **FIGURE B.3**  **The bulbospongiosus muscle** and the ischiocavernosus muscle are involved in erectile reflexes.

**Onuf's nucleus** A sexually dimorphic group of motor neurons in the sacral segments of the spinal cord that innervates striated muscles associated with the penis and clitoris.

**sexual dimorphism** An anatomical difference between the sexes.

**locus coeruleus** A nerve center in the pons that helps regulate the state of consciousness.

terminals of the sensory fibers in the sacral segments of the spinal cord activate a set of interneurons, which in turn connect with a set of motor neurons in the ventral horn of the cord. These motor neurons form a cell group known as **Onuf's nucleus**. Onuf's nucleus is significantly larger—and contains more motor neurons—in men than in women. This difference is one of many **sexual dimorphisms**, or anatomical differences between the sexes, in the human central nervous system (CNS); other differences are described elsewhere in this book.

The axons of the motor neurons of Onuf's nucleus run back down the pudendal nerves to the genitalia, where some of them innervate the ischiocavernosus and bulbospongiosus muscles. (Other axons innervate the anal sphincter, the bladder, and other muscles of the pelvic floor.) When impulses reach the endings of the nerves in the muscles (the neuromuscular junctions), they cause the muscles to contract.

## B.4 The Brain Influences Erection and Ejaculation

So far, we have discussed erection as if it were only a spinal reflex triggered by genital stimulation. In fact, however, erection can occur without any tactile stimulation. The stimulus may consist of erotically arousing sights or sounds, or erotic fantasies.

These influences on erection are mediated by higher levels of the CNS (see Box B.1, Figure D). One brain region that is particularly important for the regulation of sexual excitation (and other drives such as hunger and thirst) is the hypothalamus, which is located at the base of the brain. Descending pathways from the hypothalamus activate lower centers in the brain stem, specifically in the pons and medulla, which in turn send control signals to the sympathetic neurons in the spinal cord, increasing or decreasing their activity levels. This higher-level control ensures that the spinal reflexes mediating genital arousal are not fixed and constant, but responsive to circumstances: Tactile stimulation of the penis or clitoris may elicit physiological arousal in some circumstances (in the presence of an attractive partner or during sexual fantasies, for example)—but not in others.

Another example of higher-level control of erection concerns erections during sleep (nocturnal erections). As described in Chapter 3, erections occur during the rapid eye movement (REM) phases of sleep. These erections are controlled from a center in the pons called the **locus coeruleus**. Here's how it works: Most of the time, the locus coeruleus neurons are active; their activity then stimulates activity in the neurons of the lumbar region of the spinal cord, and this activity is relayed to the penis by the adrenergic sympathetic axons, thus keeping the penis flaccid. During REM sleep, however, the activity of the neurons in the locus coeruleus drops; this leads to a corresponding drop in adrenergic activity, shifting the balance in favor of the cholinergic sympathetic inputs to the penis, so an erection occurs.*

Seminal emission—the loading of the semen into the urethra just before ejaculation—is triggered by activity in the sympathetic innervation of the prostate gland, seminal vesicles, and vasa deferentia. Ejaculation—the pulsed expulsion of semen from the urethra—results from the combined activity of sympathetic neurons, which cause contraction of the walls of the urethra, and of the motor neurons of Onuf's nucleus, which trigger contractions of muscles of the pelvic floor that forcefully squeeze the urethra.

Most paraplegic men, whose spinal cords have been damaged or severed, are unable to ejaculate. This indicates that a descending pathway from the brain to

---

*In men who die suddenly, especially if they die by hanging, the penis is often observed to develop an erection immediately after death. This "death erection" probably happens because the connection from the locus coeruleus to the spinal cord is cut off, so the adrenergic input to the erectile tissue falls silent. This causes the arterioles to dilate and—if the heart is still beating—allows the sinusoids to fill with blood and the penis to become erect. Thus nocturnal erections and death erections probably occur by a similar mechanism.

Onuf's nucleus in the spinal cord is important for ejaculation. This pathway originates in the hypothalamus, but a crucial way station is located in the region of the brain stem known as the pons (Facchinetti et al., 2014; Waldinger, 2017) (**FIGURE B.4A**).

In a functional brain-imaging study in men and women, two regions within the pons, named the pelvic organ stimulating center (POSC) and the pelvic floor stimulating center (PFSC), were active during ejaculation (in men) and orgasm (in women) (Huynh et al., 2013) (**FIGURE B.4B**). However, the POSC was only active on the left side of the pons, while the PFSC was only active on the right side. This illustrates the fact that the brain stem, like the cerebral cortex, is not functionally symmetrical but assigns different tasks to the left and right sides. (In the case of the POSC, the right side is concerned with another task in which fluid is ejected from the body—urination.) Both the POSC and PFSC were more active in men than in women, perhaps because Onuf's nucleus is larger in men and innervates a greater mass of muscle.

The PFSC was not active in women during faked orgasms, suggesting that this brain region controls the vaginal and pelvic contractions that women cannot consciously control.

## B.5 Brain Pathways Mediate Attraction and Arousal

Having described the "lower-level" control of genital responses, we now consider how the cerebral cortex and other brain regions create sexual attraction and sexual arousal. We will focus on how a potentially arousing experience, such as seeing a sexually attractive face or watching an erotic video, is processed in such a way as to produce arousal at both the physiological and psychological levels.

The early events have been studied by a German research group using evoked potentials, which are patterns of neural activity recorded on the scalp in response to a visual stimulus such as seeing a face (Carbon et al., 2018). This technique allows for precise timing of brain events. The brain first makes a decision about the face's sex; this decision is made within less than a quarter of a second after the image is presented to the viewer. The analysis of attractiveness doesn't begin until 50 milliseconds later. In other words, the brain knows (or thinks it knows) the sex of the person before deciding how attractive they are. This fits with other studies showing that attractiveness is judged by sex-specific criteria—for example, a broad jaw might be seen as attractive in a man but not in a woman.*

This initial processing takes place in and near the visual areas at the rear of the cerebral cortex, especially in a region dedicated to the analysis of faces (**FIGURE B.5**). Visual stimuli related to the body, including images of the genitals, are probably processed in a similar way to images of faces, but they have not been studied in detail.

(A)
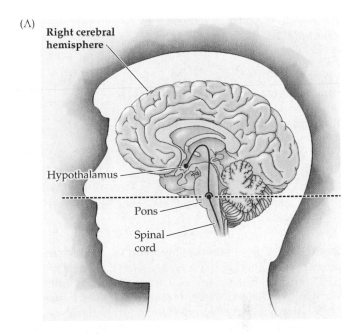

(B)
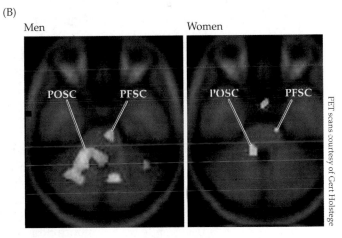

▲ **FIGURE B.4   The pons controls ejaculation and orgasm.** (A) The pons receives inputs from the hypothalamus and sends its output to the spinal cord. The horizontal line indicates the level of the slices shown in B. (B) Activity in the pons of men while ejaculating (left) and women while experiencing orgasm (right), using positron emission tomography (PET). The front of the head is at the top of the scans. Note that the region labeled "POSC" is active only on the left side, whereas the region labeled "PFSC" is active only on the right side. (From H. K. Huynh et al. 2013. *J Sex Med* 10: 3038–3048. Courtesy of Gert Holstege.)

---

*You may have had the experience of looking at a stranger's face and thinking "That's an attractive man (or woman)" but then realizing that the person is of the other sex from what you first thought, whereupon the person's attractiveness changes radically—because you are now using different criteria for attractiveness.

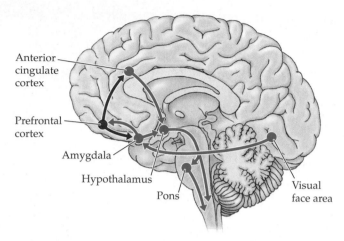

▲ **FIGURE B.5** **Pathways involved in sexual attraction and arousal** This figure shows in a simplified fashion the brain regions involved in sexual arousal such as might follow viewing of an attractive face or erotic video, and their interconnections. Blue pathways are excitatory, red pathways are inhibitory. The front of the brain is to the left.

**amygdala** A group of nuclei in the medial anterior part of the temporal lobe.

**anterior cingulate cortex** A cortical region on the medial surface of the frontal lobe that is involved, among other tasks, in the generation of motivational states.

**prefrontal cortex** The most anterior region of the frontal lobe.

The later stages of arousal have been investigated with imaging technologies such as functional magnetic resonance imaging (fMRI). These methods don't have the temporal resolution of evoked potentials—that is, they cannot tell precisely *when* brain events happen—but they are better at telling *where* they happen, and they can assess the strength of functional connections between active regions. Thus they can identify the brain regions that are active during a sustained period of sexual arousal, such as might accompany the viewing of an erotic video, and they can help define the functional network among those regions.

These imaging methods have revealed the existence of an extensive network of cortical and subcortical regions involved in the generation of sexual arousal. Although this network has not yet been fully explored and understood, it appears that each region within the network makes a specific contribution to promoting or inhibiting sexual excitement (psychological arousal) and genital processes such as penile erection or vaginal lubrication (physiological arousal) (Poeppl et al., 2014; Seok et al., 2016; Ruesink & Georgiadis, 2017).

In the case of arousal to a visual stimulus such as an attractive face or an erotic video, activity in the face area and nearby visual areas is transmitted forward to the **amygdala**, which is a large non-cortical cell group within the temporal lobe. The amygdala is thought to add an emotional quality—a positive emotion in this case—to what was up until then an emotionally neutral sensory signal.

From the amygdala signals are sent to the **anterior cingulate cortex**, the hypothalamus, and the **prefrontal cortex**. The anterior cingulate cortex appears to add a motivational element to the signal—i.e., the drive to do something about it. The hypothalamus—or the parts of it that are involved in sexual functions—convert this drive into specific instructions to lower centers that regulate physiological arousal, including the pons, whose role we discussed in the preceding section, as well as the spinal cord. Electrical stimulation of certain regions of the hypothalamus can elicit organized coital behavior in experimental animals, suggesting that there are pathways leading indirectly from the hypothalamus to regions of the cerebral cortex that control the necessary behaviors.

The prefrontal cortex is involved in conscious control of behavior. It appears that one important role of the prefrontal cortex in sexuality is to suppress sexual behavior in situations where a person knows that it would be inappropriate—which to say most of the time. This suppression is mediated by inhibitory pathways (shown in red in Figure B.5) that run from the prefrontal cortex to the anterior cingulate cortex and the amygdala. By shutting off activity in those two cell groups the prefrontal cortex prevents potentially arousing stimuli from triggering sexual behavior. In men diagnosed with hypersexuality or compulsive sexual behavior these inhibitory pathways are weaker than normal, according to one fMRI study (Schmidt et al., 2017).

Activity patterns in the brain during sexual arousal are similar in everyone, regardless of their sex or sexual orientation, even though the kinds of stimuli that trigger arousal may be very different (Safron et al., 2007; Mitricheva et al., 2019).

Of course, vision is not the only sense through which we can become sexually aroused; the brain structures that we've just described can also be activated by auditory or tactile inputs, either alone or in combination with visual inputs. Olfaction is a particularly interesting sense in connection with sex, because in many animals it plays a key role in the recognition and discrimination of sex partners. Unlike information from other senses, olfactory information can reach the hypothalamus and other subcortical structures directly, without prior analysis by the cerebral cortex. The role of olfaction in human sexual responses is uncertain, but functional imaging studies by a Swedish group indicate that neural activity in the front region of the human hypothalamus is target-selective; that is, this region is activated by male odors in straight women and gay men, and by female odors in straight men and gay women (Savic et al., 2005). Whether these patterns are innate or the product of learning is not known.

The schematic shown in Figure B.5 is certainly an oversimplification, and it may need to be revised as further studies are published. The main point of this section is to make clear that sexual arousal is not something magical or mysterious. Rather, the brain handles sexual arousal just as it handles any other mental process—in a logical sequence of steps involving activation of a functionally specialized pathway.

There is much more to the brain's role in sexuality, of course:

- The hypothalamus, by virtue of its control of the pituitary gland, helps regulate sex hormone levels, the menstrual cycle in women, and spermatogenesis in men.

- Neurotransmitters such as serotonin and dopamine are involved in sexual desire and sexual pleasure.

- Differences in brain structure and function between women and men help create sex differences in cognitive functions and personality.

- Interactions between sex hormones and the brain play a role in the development of a person's sexual orientation.

- Falling in love requires the activation of specific brain regions.

- The brain-derived hormones oxytocin and vasopressin are involved in orgasm, lactation, and possibly falling in love.

In the main text of this book we touch on these and other ways in which the brain plays a central role in human sexuality.

## Summary

- Sexual functions are regulated by the nervous and endocrine systems. In the absence of sexual stimulation, erection of the penis or clitoris is prevented by ongoing activity in the adrenergic sympathetic axons that innervate the genitals. This activity causes constriction of the arterioles supplying the erectile tissue. Erection involves a spinal reflex that begins with stimulation of nerve endings in the genital skin, followed by processing in the spinal cord and outgoing activity in the cholinergic sympathetic axons that innervate the genitals. This activity dilates the arterioles, so more blood enters the sinusoids within the erectile tissue.

- In males, seminal emission (loading of the urethra with semen) involves the coordinated action of sympathetic inputs to the prostate gland, seminal vesicles, and vasa deferentia. Ejaculation is brought about by activity in spinal motor neurons that innervate the muscles of the pelvic floor, causing them to contract in a pulsatile fashion and eject semen from the urethral opening.

- The brain influences these processes in various ways. The hypothalamus influences genital reflexes, so they are modulated by circumstances and erotic images and thoughts. Activity in the locus coeruleus increases the activity of sympathetic neurons in the spinal cord: A decrease in activity in the locus coeruleus during REM sleep leads to a decrease in adrenergic sympathetic input to the genitals and thus to a nocturnal erection. Regions within the pons called the pelvic organ stimulating center (POSC) and the pelvic floor stimulating center (PFSC) trigger the pulsatile muscle contractions associated with male ejaculation and female orgasm.

- When a person views a potentially sexually arousing image such as a face, visual areas at the rear of the cerebral cortex first identify the sex of the face and then assess its attractiveness. Sexual arousal is mediated by a network of brain regions including the amygdala, anterior cingulate area, and hypothalamus. The prefrontal cortex inhibits activity in this network when sexual arousal is not appropriate.

# Glossary

Numbers in brackets refer to the chapter(s) where the term is defined.

**5-alpha-reductase deficiency** A lack of the enzyme that converts testosterone to 5-alpha-dihydrotestosterone. [4]

**5α-dihydrotestosterone (DHT)** An androgen derived from testosterone that plays an important role in the development of the male external genitalia. [3]

## A

**abstinence-only programs** Sex-ed programs that teach abstinence and omit mention of safer-sex practices, homosexuality, etc. [10]

**acquaintance rape** Rape by a person known to the victim. [16]

**acquired immune deficiency syndrome (AIDS)** The disease caused by the human immunodeficiency virus (HIV); its onset is defined by the occurrence of any of a number of opportunistic infections, or on the basis of blood tests. [15]

**acrosome** A structure capping the head of a sperm that contains enzymes necessary for fertilization. [3]

**action potential** An electrochemical signal that travels rapidly along an axon. Also called *nerve impulse*. [App. B]

**adaptive** Helping the propagation of an organism's genes. [App. A]

**adolescence** The period of psychosexual and social maturation that accompanies and follows puberty. [10]

**adrenergic** Using norepinephrine (noradrenaline) as a neurotransmitter. [App. B]

**adult baby** An adult who obtains sexual satisfaction from acting as if he is a baby or toddler. [13]

**afferent** Carrying signals toward the CNS. [App. B]

**afterbirth** The placenta, whose delivery constitutes the final stage of labor. [8]

**afterplay** Sexual behavior engaged in after coitus or orgasm, or at the end of a sexual encounter. [6]

**alveolus (pl. alveoli)** A microscopic cavity, such as one of those in the breast where milk is produced. [2]

**amenorrhea** Absence of menstruation. [2]

**Amethyst** A contraceptive pill designed to completely abolish a woman's periods. [9]

**amniocentesis** The sampling of the amniotic fluid for purposes of prenatal diagnosis. [8]

**amygdala** A group of nuclei in the medial anterior part of the temporal lobe. [App. B]

**anal fold** The posterior portion of the urethral fold, which gives rise to the anus. [4]

**anal sex** Penetration of the anus by the penis, or any sexual behavior involving the anus. [6]

**anatomical sex** An individual's sex based on the appearance of their external genitalia. [4]

**androgen insensitivity syndrome (AIS)** The congenital absence of a functional androgen receptor, making the body unable to respond to androgens. [4]

**androgens** Any of a class of steroids—the most important being testosterone—that promote male sexual development and that have a variety of other functions in both sexes. [2]

**andropause** In men, the gradual decline of fertility with age; a hypothetical male equivalent of menopause. [11]

**androphilic** Sexually attracted to men. [12]

**anilingus** Sexual contact between the tongue or mouth of one person and the anus of another. [6]

**Annovera** A vaginal contraceptive ring that lasts for a year. [9]

**anorgasmia** Difficulty experiencing or inability to experience orgasm. In women, also called *female orgasmic disorder*. [14]

**anterior cingulate cortex** A cortical region on the medial surface of the frontal lobe that is involved, among other tasks, in the generation of motivational states. [App. B]

**anti-Müllerian hormone (AMH)** A hormone secreted by the testes that prevents the development of the female reproductive tract. [4]

**antimiscegenation statutes** State laws that prohibited marriage (and sometimes cohabitation or sex) between persons of different races. [7]

**antiretroviral drugs** Drugs effective against retroviruses. [15]

**anus** The opening from which feces are discharged. [2]

**aphrodisiac** A substance believed to improve sexual performance, enhance sexual pleasure, or stimulate desire or love. [5]

**areola** The circular patch of darker skin that surrounds the nipple. [2]

**artificial insemination by donor (AID)** Artificial insemination using sperm from a man who is not the woman's partner. [8]

**artificial insemination** An assisted reproduction technique that involves the placement of semen in the vagina or uterus with the aid of a syringe or small tube. [8]

**asexual reproduction** The production of offspring genetically related to only one parent. [1, App. A]

**asexual** Describes a person who does not experience sexual attraction. [5]

**assigned sex** An individual's sex as categorized by doctors or others. [4]

**assisted reproductive technology (ART)** In vitro fertilization and related technologies. [8]

**asymptomatic carrier** Someone who is infected with a disease organism but is not experiencing symptoms. [15]

**attachment theory** The idea that relationship styles are influenced by the quality of the early parent–child bond. [7]

**autoerotic** Providing sexual stimulation to oneself or being aroused sexually by oneself. [6]

**autoerotic asphyxia** Self-strangulation for purposes of sexual arousal. [13]

**autogynephilia** A form of male-to-female transsexuality characterized by a man's sexual arousal at the thought of being or becoming a woman. [4, 13]

**autonomic nervous system** The portion of the nervous system that controls smooth muscles and glands without our conscious involvement. [3, App. B]

**autopedophilia** Sexual arousal by the fantasy of being a child. [13]

**autosome** Any chromosome other than a sex chromosome. [App. A]

**aversion therapy** A form of behavior therapy that attempts to eliminate unwanted desires or behaviors by associating them with some unpleasant experience, such as a noxious smell. [13]

**aversive classical conditioning** A form of classical conditioning in which the unconditioned stimulus is painful. [5]

**axon** The extension of a neuron that conveys impulses, usually in a direction away from the cell body. Also called *nerve fiber*. [App. B]

**B**

**bacterial vaginosis** A condition in which the normal microorganisms of the vagina are replaced by other species, causing discomfort and a foul-smelling discharge. [15]

**balanitis** Inflammation of the glans of the penis. [3]

**bar mitzvah** Jewish coming-of-age ceremony for boys. [10]

**barrier method** Any contraceptive technique in which a physical barrier, such as a condom or diaphragm, prevents sperm from reaching the ovum. [9]

**Bartholin's glands** Two mucus-secreting glands that help lubricate the vaginal opening. [2]

**basal ganglia** Deep noncortical structures of the forebrain. [App. B]

**bat mitzvah** Jewish coming-of-age ceremony for girls. [10]

**bathhouse** A facility, usually in the form of a private club, used for casual sex between men. [12]

**BDSM** An all-inclusive term for forms of sexual expression that involve inflicting and receiving physical pain, restraint, or humiliation. [13]

**bear** In gay slang, a burly gay man with plenty of body hair. [12]

**behavior therapy** Treatment of mental disorders by training of behavior. [13]

**behavioral couples therapy (BCT)** Therapy focused on improving styles of communication between partners in relationships. [7]

**benign prostatic hyperplasia** Noncancerous enlargement of the prostate gland. [3]

**bestiality** Sexual contact between a person and an animal. [13]

**bi** Colloquial term meaning "bisexual." [12]

**big data** The search for patterns and trends in very large data sets. [1]

**bigamy** In law, the crime of marrying someone while being already married to another spouse. [11]

**biphobia** Prejudice against bisexuals. [12]

**birth canal** The canal formed by the uterus, cervix, and vagina, through which the fetus passes during the birth process. [2, 8]

**birthing center** A facility specializing in childbirth care. [8]

**bisexual erasure** Ignoring or denying the existence of bisexual people. [12]

**bisexuality** Sexual attraction to persons of both sexes. [12]

**body mass index (BMI)** A person's weight in kilograms divided by the square of their height in meters. [5]

**bondage** The use of physical restraint for purposes of sexual arousal. [13]

**bourgeonal** A floral-scented compound that may be an attractant for spermatozoa. [8]

**Bradley method** A method of childbirth instruction that stresses the partner's role as birth coach and that seeks to avoid medical interventions. [8]

**brain stem** The region of the brain between the forebrain and the spinal cord. [App. B]

**Braxton Hicks contractions** Irregular uterine contractions that occur during the third trimester of pregnancy. Also called *false labor*. [8]

**breast bud** The first stage of breast development at puberty. [10]

**breast implant** A tissue substitute that is inserted to augment or replace a natural breast. [2]

**brothel** A house of prostitution. [17]

**bulbourethral glands (or Cowper's glands)** Two small glands near the root of the penis whose secretions ("pre-cum") may appear at the urethral opening during sexual arousal prior to ejaculation. [3]

**butch** Masculine-acting, often used to describe certain lesbians. [12]

**butt plug** A dildo designed for anal penetration. [6]

**C**

**calendar rhythm method** A fertility awareness method of contraception that takes account of variability in the length of a woman's menstrual cycles. [9]

**Camrese** An extended-use contraceptive pill. [9]

**candidiasis** A fungal infection of the vagina. Also called *thrush* or a *yeast infection*. [2]

**case history** A description of the course of a disorder as it has affected a specific individual. [1]

**castration** Removal of the testicles or testicles and penis. [1]

**casual sex** Sexual encounters that do not take place within a lasting sexual relationship. [7]

**CD4 T lymphocyte** A type of lymphocyte that carries the CD4 receptor; one of the major targets of HIV. [15]

**cell body** The part of a neuron where the nucleus is located. [App. B]

**cell-free fetal DNA analysis** The diagnosis of fetal disorders by sequencing fetal DNA that leaks into the maternal circulation. [8]

**central nervous system (CNS)** The brain and spinal cord. [App. B]

**cerebral cortex** Convoluted, layered gray matter that covers most of the brain. [App. B]

**cerebral hemispheres** The uppermost and largest portion of the brain, divided into left and right halves. [App. B]

**cervical cap** A small rubber or plastic cap that adheres by suction to the cervix, used as a contraceptive. [9]

**cervical mucus method** A fertility awareness method of contraception that depends on observing changes in the cervical mucus. [9]

**cervix** The lowermost, narrow portion of the uterus that connects with the vagina. [2]

**cesarean section (C-section)** The delivery of a baby through an incision in the abdominal wall and the uterus. [8]

**chancre** A primary sore on the skin or a mucous membrane in a person infected with syphilis. (Pronounced SHANK-er.) [15]

**child molester** An adult who has had sexual contact with a prepubescent child. [13]

**chlamydia** A sexually transmitted infection caused by infection with the bacterium *Chlamydia trachomatis.* [15]

**choice blindness** Unawareness of the actual reasons for a preference, along with the unconscious invention of fictive reasons. [5]

**cholinergic** Using acetylcholine (and in some cases nitric oxide) as a neurotransmitter. [App. B]

**chorionic villus sampling (CVS)** The sampling of tissue from the placenta for purposes of prenatal diagnosis. [8]

**chromosomal sex** An individual's sex based on their sex chromosomes. [4]

**chromosome** One of the 46 rod-like structures in human cell nuclei that carry a person's DNA. [4]

**chronic pelvic pain syndrome** An alternative, more inclusive term for "chronic prostatitis." [3]

**cilia** Microscopic, hairlike extensions of cells, often capable of coordinated beating motions. [2]

**Circles of Support and Accountability (COSA)** A program of community support for released sex offenders. [13]

**circumcision** The removal of the male foreskin. In females, a traditional term for "genital cutting." [3]

**cisgender** Having a conventional gender—masculine if anatomically male, feminine if anatomically female. "Cis" is the opposite of "trans." [4]

**civil union** A legal arrangement that confers most or all of the rights and obligations of marriage except the name. [11]

**classical (or Pavlovian) conditioning** A form of behavioral learning in which a novel stimulus is tied to a preexisting reflex. [5]

**climacteric** The transition to infertility at the end of a woman's reproductive life, lasting for several years and culminating in menopause. [11]

**clitoral hood** A loose fold of skin that covers the clitoris. [2]

**clitoridectomy** Removal of the entire external portion of the clitoris (glans, shaft, and hood). [2]

**clitoris** The erectile organ in females, whose external portion is located at the

junction of the inner labia, just in front of the vestibule. [2, App. A]

**cloaca** The common exit of the gastrointestinal and urogenital systems; in humans it is present only in embryonic life. [4]

**cognitive** Related to the aspects of the mind that process knowledge or information. [4]

**cognitive psychology** The study of the information-processing systems of the mind. [1]

**cognitive restructuring** A technique to overcome psychological problems by talking through the negative beliefs that underlie them. [14]

**cognitive therapy** Therapy based on changing a person's beliefs and thought processes. [13]

**cohabitation** A live-in sexual relationship between individuals who are not married to each other. [1, 11]

**coital alignment technique (CAT)** A variation of the man-above position for coitus that increases clitoral stimulation. [14]

**coitus** Penetration of the vagina by the penis. [1, 2, 6]

**colostrum** The milk produced during the first few days after birth; it is relatively low in fat but rich in immunoglobulins. [8]

**colposcopy** The examination of the cervix with the aid of an operating microscope. [2]

**come out of the closet (or come out)** Reveal a previously concealed identity, such as being gay. [12]

**commitment** The cognitive component of love: the decision to maintain a relationship. [7]

**companionate love** Love characterized by intimacy and trust. [7]

**companionate marriage** A form of marriage in which the husband and wife are expected to be emotionally intimate and to engage in social activities together. [11]

**compersion** Pleasure at one's partner's sexual involvement with others. [11]

**comprehensive sex-education programs** Sex-ed programs that discuss abstinence as well as safer-sex practices, sexual and gender diversity, etc. [10]

**Comstock Laws** Federal and state laws enacted in the late 19th century that criminalized pornography. [17]

**concubine** A woman who cohabits with a man but is not his wife, usually in a polygamous culture. [11]

**conditioning** The modification of behavior by learning through association and/or reinforcement. [13]

**congenital adrenal hyperplasia (CAH)** A congenital defect of hormonal metabolism in the adrenal gland, causing

the gland to secrete excessive levels of androgens. [4]

**constant-dose combination pill** An oral contraceptive regimen in which all pills (except any dummy pills) contain the same drug dosage. [9]

**contraception** Prevention of pregnancy. [1]

**contraceptive implant** A device implanted in the body that slowly releases a hormonal contraceptive. [9]

**contraction** In childbirth, a periodic coordinated tightening of the uterine musculature, felt as a cramp. [8]

**control group** A group of participants included in a study for comparison purposes. [1]

**Coolidge effect** The revival of sexual arousal caused by the presence of a novel partner. [5]

**copulation** Sexual intercourse; coitus. [App. A]

**corona** The rim of the glans of the penis. [3]

**corpus callosum** A band of axons interconnecting the left and right cerebral hemispheres. [App. B]

**corpus cavernosum (pl. corpora cavernosa)** Either of two elongated erectile structures within the clitoris or penis that also extend backward into the pelvic floor. [2, 3]

**corpus luteum** A secretory structure in the ovary derived from an ovarian follicle after ovulation. [2]

**corpus spongiosum** A single midline erectile structure that fills the glans; in males it extends backward along the underside of the penis, surrounding the urethra. [2, 3]

**cortex** The outer portion of an anatomical structure, as of the cerebral hemispheres or the adrenal gland. [App. B]

**courtesan** Historical term for a high-class prostitute who moved in aristocratic circles. [17]

**courtship behavior** Behavior that attracts a mate. [App. A]

**courtship disorder** A paraphilia or cluster of paraphilias seen as a disorder of normal courtship behavior. [13]

**covenant marriage** A form of marriage that requires a stronger vow of commitment than a regular marriage and that makes divorce harder to obtain. [11]

**cremaster muscle** A sheet-like muscle that wraps around the spermatic cord and the testicle. [3]

**cross-dressing** Wearing the clothing of the other sex, for any of a variety of reasons. [13]

**crowning**   The appearance of the fetal scalp at the vaginal opening. [8]

**cruising**   Looking for casual sex partners in public spaces. [7]

**crura (sing. crus)**   The two internal extensions of the corpora cavernosa of the clitoris or penis. [2]

**crus (pl. crura)**   Internal extensions of the corpora cavernosa of the clitoris or penis. [3]

**crush**   A short-lived, intense, unreciprocated love, often experienced during adolescence. [7]

**cryptorchidism**   Failure of one or both testicles to descend into the scrotum by 3 months of postnatal age.

**cuckolding**   Being sexually aroused by watching one's partner have sex with another person. [13]

**cultural anthropology**   The study of cultural variations across the human race. [1]

**cunnilingus**   Sexual contact between the tongue or mouth of one person and the vulva of another. [6]

**cyber dating abuse**   Abusive online behavior between dating or other sex partners. [16]

**cyberstalking**   Stalking via the internet. [16]

**cycle of abuse**   The cycle in which some abused children grow up to perform similar forms of abuse on others. Also called *victim–perpetrator cycle*. [13]

## D

**date rape**   Rape by a social acquaintance or someone the individual is dating. [16]

**decriminalization**   Removal of laws that criminalize activities, such as prostitution. [17]

**delayed ejaculation**   Difficulty achieving or inability to achieve orgasm and/or ejaculation. Also called *male orgasmic disorder*. [14]

**delayed labor**   Labor that occurs more than 3 weeks after a woman's due date. [8]

**delayed puberty**   Puberty that begins later than normal. [10]

**delusional jealousy**   Persistent false belief that one's partner is involved with another person. [7]

**delusional stalking**   Stalking motivated by the delusional belief that the victim is in love with, or could be persuaded to fall in love with, the stalker. [16]

**demisexual**   Describes a person who experiences sexual attraction only in the context of a strong emotional bond.

**dendrites**   The extensions of a neuron that receive incoming signals from other neurons. [App. B]

**Depo-Provera**   An injectable form of medroxyprogesterone acetate, used as a contraceptive in women or to decrease the sex drive in male sex offenders. [9]

**Depo-SubQ Provera**   A form of Depo-Provera designed for subcutaneous injection. [9]

**designer steroids**   Synthetic steroids intended to evade detection in drug tests. [3]

**devotee**   Colloquial term for a person whose sexual interests are focused on disabilities. [6]

**diaphragm**   A barrier placed over the cervix as a contraceptive. [9]

**dilation and evacuation (D&E)**
A procedure involving the opening of the cervix and the scraping out of the contents of the uterus with a curette (a metal loop). D&E may be done as an abortion procedure or for other purposes. [9]

**dilation**   In childbirth, the expansion of the cervical canal. Also called *dilatation*. [8]

**dildo**   A sex toy, often shaped like a penis, used to penetrate the vagina or anus. [6]

**discrepant sexual desire**   The situation in which one partner in a relationship has much more interest in sex than the other. [14]

**disorders of sex development**
Medical conditions producing anomalous sexual differentiation or intersexuality. [4]

**dissociation**   The distancing of oneself from the emotions evoked by some traumatic experience or memory. [10]

**domestic partnership**   A legal arrangement that confers some or most of the rights and obligations of marriage. [11]

**dominance**   The use of humiliation or subservience for purposes of sexual arousal. [13]

**dominatrix**   A woman who acts the role of the dominant partner in a BDSM setting. [13]

**dorsal horn**   The rear portion of the gray matter of the spinal cord; it has a sensory function. [App. B]

**dorsal root**   A bundle of sensory axons that enters a dorsal horn of the spinal cord. [App. B]

**double standard**   The idea that acceptable behavior is different for men than for women. [1]

**douche**   To rinse the vagina out with a fluid; the fluid so used. [2]

**Down syndrome**   A collection of birth defects caused by the presence of an extra copy of chromosome 21. [8]

**drag**   The wearing of exaggeratedly feminine clothing by a man, or male clothing by a woman, often for entertainment purposes. [13]

**dysmenorrhea**   Menstrual pain severe enough to interfere with a woman's activities. [2]

**dyspareunia**   Pain during coitus. [14]

## E

**early symptomatic HIV infection**
Health problems caused by HIV, especially those that occur before the criteria for an AIDS diagnosis have been met. [15]

**ectopic pregnancy**   Implantation and resulting pregnancy at any site other than the uterus. [8]

**effacement**   Thinning of the cervix in preparation for childbirth. [8]

**efferent**   Carrying signals away from the CNS. [App. B]

**ejaculatory duct**   Either of the two bilateral ducts formed by the junction of the vas deferens and the duct of the seminal vesicle. The ejaculatory ducts empty into the urethra within the prostate. [3]

**elective abortion**   An abortion performed in circumstances when the woman's health is not at risk. [9]

**ella**   A form of emergency contraception that is effective for 5 days after sex. [9]

**embryo**   In humans, the developing individual up until about 8 weeks of pregnancy. [8]

**emergency contraception**   Use of high-dose contraceptives to prevent pregnancy after unprotected sex.

**emotional jealousy**   Fear that one's partner is becoming emotionally committed to another person. [7]

**empathy**   The ability to share or understand other people's feelings. [16]

**endocrine disruptors**   Substances that interfere with development by mimicking sex hormones. [10]

**endocrinologist**   A physician who specializes in hormonal disorders. [14]

**endometrial cancer**   Cancer of the endometrium of the uterus. [2]

**endometriosis**   The growth of endometrial tissue at abnormal locations such as the oviducts. [2]

**endometrium**   The internal lining of the uterus. [2]

**engagement**   The sinking of a fetus's head into a lower position in the pelvis in preparation for birth. Also called *lightening*. [8]

**epididymis**   A structure, attached to each testicle, where sperm mature and are stored before entering the vas deferens. [3]

**epididymitis** Inflammation of the epididymis. [3, 15]

**epidural anesthesia** Anesthesia administered just outside the membrane that surrounds the spinal cord. [8]

**epiphyseal plates** The growth zones in limb bones, which cease to function after puberty. [10]

**episiotomy** A cut extending the opening of the vagina backward into the perineum, performed by an obstetrician with the intention of facilitating childbirth or reducing the risk of a perineal tear. [8]

**erectile disorder (ED)** A persistent inability to achieve or maintain an erection sufficient to accomplish a desired sexual behavior, such as coitus, to orgasm. Also called *erectile dysfunction*. [14]

**erectile tissue** Tissue that stiffens an organ by filling with blood. [2]

**erogenous zone** A region of the body whose stimulation causes sexual arousal. [2]

**erotic target identity inversion** Sexual arousal by the fantasy of being the kind of person to whom one is sexually attracted. [13]

**erotica** Sexually themed works, such as books or sculpture, deemed to have literary or artistic merit. [17]

**erotomania** The delusional belief that a sexually desired but unattainable person is actually in love with oneself. [16]

**escort (or call girl)** Euphemism for a prostitute who advertises by print, word of mouth, or the internet. [17]

**escort service** A service that provides prostitutes, generally contacted by phone or online. [17]

**Essure** A method of tubal sterilization that blocks the oviducts by use of metal coils. [9]

**estradiol** The principal estrogen, secreted by ovarian follicles. [2]

**estrogens** Any of a class of steroids—the most important being estradiol—that promote the development of female secondary sexual characteristics at puberty and that have many other functions in both sexes. [2]

**estrus** The restricted period within the ovarian cycle when females of some species are sexually receptive; "heat." [App. A]

**ethnography** The study of a cultural group, often by means of extended individual fieldwork. [1]

**eunuch** A man who has been castrated. [1, 11]

**evolutionary psychology** The study of the influence of evolution on mental processes or behavior. [1]

**excitement phase** The beginning phase of the sexual response cycle. [5]

**exhibitionism** Sexual arousal by exposure of the genitals to strangers. [13]

**expedited partner therapy** Giving antibiotics to an infected person to pass on to his or her sexual contacts. [15]

**external genitalia** The sexual structures on the outside of the body. [2]

**extra-pair relationship** A sexual relationship in which at least one of the partners is already married to or partnered with someone else. [7]

**extrafamilial child molester** A person who has had sexual contact with children outside his immediate family. [13]

## F

**fantasy** An imagined experience, sexual or otherwise. [5]

**fellatio** Sexual contact between the mouth of one person and the penis of another. [6]

**female condom** A nitrile rubber pouch inserted into the vagina as a contraceptive and/or to prevent disease transmission. [9]

**female genital cutting** Any of several forms of ritual cutting or excision of parts of the female genitalia. Also called *female genital mutilation* or *female circumcision*. [2]

**female sexual arousal disorder** Lack or insufficiency of physiological sexual arousal in women. [14]

**FemCap** A type of cervical cap that has a raised brim. [9]

**feminism** The movement to secure equality for women; the study of social and psychological issues from women's perspectives. [1]

**femiphobia** Prejudice against femininity, especially of males. [12]

**femme** Feminine-acting, often used to describe certain lesbians or bisexual women. [12]

**fertility awareness methods** Contraceptive techniques that rely on avoiding coitus during the woman's fertile window. Also called *rhythm methods* or *periodic abstinence methods*. [9]

**fertilization** The entry of a spermatozoon into an ovum. [8]

**fetal alcohol syndrome** A collection of physical and behavioral symptoms in a child who was exposed to high levels of alcohol as a fetus. [8]

**fetish** Sexual fixation on an inanimate object, material, or part of the body. [13]

**fibroid** A noncancerous tumor arising from muscle cells of the uterus. [2]

**fimbria** The fringe at the end of the oviduct, composed of fingerlike extensions. [2]

**flagellum** A whiplike cellular structure, such as the tail of a sperm. [3]

**fluctuating asymmetry** A difference between the left and right sides of the body that results from random perturbations of development. [App. A]

**follicle-stimulating hormone (FSH)** One of the two major gonadotropins secreted by the pituitary gland; it promotes maturation of ova (or sperm in males). [2]

**follicle** A fluid-filled sac that contains an egg (ovum), with its supporting cells, within the ovary. [2]

**fondling** Any kind of sexual touching of the partner's body. [6]

**forebrain** The cerebral hemispheres and basal ganglia. [App. B]

**foreplay** Sexual behavior engaged in during the early part of a sexual encounter, with the aim of increasing sexual arousal. [6]

**foreskin (or prepuce)** The loose skin that partially or completely covers the glans in males who have not been circumcised. [3]

**frenulum of the clitoris** An erotically sensitive fold of tissue that connects the labia to the underside of the clitoris. [2]

**frenulum** A strip of loose skin on the underside of the penis, running between the glans and the shaft. [3]

**frotteurism** Sexual arousal from touching or rubbing the genitals against strangers without their consent or without their knowledge, as in a crowded public place. [13]

**fucksaw** A sex toy consisting of a dildo attached to a reciprocating saw. [6]

**furry** A person who socializes in animal costumes. [13]

## G

**gamete** A germ cell (ovum or sperm) that fuses with another to form a new organism. [App. A]

**ganglia** Clusters of neurons outside the CNS. [App. B]

**gay bashing** Hate crimes against gay people. Sometimes includes verbal abuse as well as physical violence. [12]

**gay** Colloquial but now-standard term meaning "homosexual," applicable to men or women. [12]

**gaydar** The ability to recognize gay people on the basis of unconscious behaviors, voice quality, gait, and so on. [12]

**gender dysphoria** The unhappiness caused by discordance between a person's anatomical sex and gender identity.

**gender identity** A person's subjective sense of being male, female, or not exclusively one or the other. [4]

**gender role**   Social behavior thought to be characteristic of one sex or the other, or some blend of the two. [4]

**gender-variant**   Atypical in gender characteristics. [12]

**gender**   The collection of psychological traits that differ between males and females. [1]

**General Social Survey (GSS)**   A long-running periodic survey of the U.S. population run by the National Opinion Research Center. [1]

**genital end-bulbs (or genital corpuscular receptors)**   Specialized nerve endings, found in the genital area, that probably detect the tactile stimulation associated with sexual activity. [3, App. B]

**genital herpes**   An infection of the genital area caused by HSV-1 or HSV-2. [15]

**genital swellings**   Regions of the genitalia in the embryo that give rise to the outer labia (in females) or the scrotum (in males). [4]

**genital tubercle**   A midline swelling in front of the cloaca, which gives rise to the glans of the clitoris (in females) or penis (in males). [4]

**genital warts**   Wartlike growths on or near the genitalia or anus, caused by infection with human papillomavirus. [15]

**genome**   An organism's entire complement of DNA, including all its genes. In some viruses, such as HIV, the genome is composed of RNA. [App. A]

**gestation**   Bearing young in the uterus; pregnancy. [App. A]

**gestational age**   A fetus's age timed from the onset of the mother's last menstrual period. [8]

**gestational surrogacy**   A surrogate pregnancy in which the ovum is provided by some other woman than the surrogate mother. [8]

**gigolo**   A male prostitute who caters to women. [17]

**glans**   The terminal knob of the clitoris or penis. [2, 3]

**glycogen**   A polymer of glucose used for energy storage. [8]

**gonad**   An organ that produces ova or sperm and secretes sex hormones. [2]

**gonadal sex**   An individual's sex based on their possession of testes or ovaries. [4]

**gonadotropin-releasing hormone (GnRH)**   A hormone secreted by the hypothalamus that stimulates the release of gonadotropins from the anterior pituitary gland. [2]

**gonadotropins**   Hormones that regulate the function of the gonads. [2]

**gonorrhea**   A sexually transmitted infection caused by the bacterium *Neisseria gonorrhoeae*. [15]

**Good Lives model**   A form of therapy for sex offenders that focuses on improving the individual's ability to achieve a broad range of life goals. [13]

**Gräfenberg spot (G-spot)**   A possible area of increased erotic sensitivity on or deep within the front wall of the vagina. [2]

**gray matter**   A region of the CNS containing the cell bodies of neurons. [App. B]

**group marriage (or polyfidelity)**   Three or more people living together in a marriage-like relationship. [11]

**grudge stalking**   Stalking motivated by a non-sexual grudge, often within a work environment. [16]

**gynecomastia**   The development of breasts in males. [10]

**gynephilic**   Sexually attracted to women. [12]

## H

**habituation**   A psychological or physiological process that reduces a person's response to a stimulus or drug after repeated or prolonged exposure. [5, 11]

**hardcore**   Related to explicit pornography, such as images of penetrative sex and ejaculation. [17]

**harem**   The quarters for wives and children in a polygamous Muslim household. [11]

**heavy petting**   Sexually touching the partner's genitalia or breasts. [6]

**hebephile**   An adult whose sexual attraction is directed mainly toward pubescent children. [13]

**hepatitis A**   Liver disease caused by the hepatitis A virus. It is sometimes transmitted sexually. [15]

**hepatitis B**   Liver disease caused by the hepatitis B virus, a virus that is often transmitted sexually. [15]

**hepatitis viruses**   Viruses that cause liver disease. [15]

**hermaphrodite**   An organism that combines male and female reproductive functions. [App. A]

**herpes**   An infection caused by herpes simplex virus type 1 or 2 (HSV-1 or HSV-2). [15]

**heteroflexible**   Mostly straight but having some interest in same-sex contacts or relationships. [7]

**heterosexism**   The cultural establishment of heterosexuality as the normal and preferred form of sexual expression. [12]

**heterosexuality**   Sexual attraction to, or behavior with, persons of the opposite sex. [1, 12]

**hijra**   A member of a traditional class of transexual women in northern India and Pakistan. [4]

**homogamy**   The tendency of sexually partnered couples, or married couples, to resemble each other in a variety of respects. [7]

**homologous**   Corresponding— e.g. carrying the same genes. [4]

**homophobia**   Prejudice against homosexuality or gay people. [12]

**homosexuality**   Sexual attraction to, or behavior with, persons of the same sex. [1, 12]

**hooking up**   Uncommitted sex with an acquaintance. [7]

**hostile environment harassment**   Sexual harassment involving a pattern of conduct that creates an intimidating work environment. [16]

**hot flashes (or hot flushes)**   Episodes of reddening and warmth of the skin associated with menopause. [11]

**human chorionic gonadotropin (hCG)**   A hormone secreted by the placenta that maintains the corpus luteum and thus keeps progesterone levels high enough to sustain pregnancy. [8]

**human immunodeficiency virus (HIV)**   The retrovirus that causes AIDS. [15]

**human papillomavirus (HPV)**   Any of a group of viruses that can be sexually transmitted and that cause genital warts or other lesions; some types predispose infected persons to cancer of the cervix or anus. [15]

**human sex pheromones**   Volatile substances released from men's and women's bodies that are thought to influence sexual feelings in others. [5]

**hustler**   A male prostitute. [17]

**hydrocele**   A collection of fluid around a testicle. [3]

**hymen**   A membrane, usually perforated or incomplete, that covers the opening of the vagina. It may be torn by first coitus or by other means. [2]

**hypersexuality**   Excessive sexual desire or behavior. [13, 14]

**hypoactive sexual desire disorder**   Low or absent interest in sex, when this condition causes distress. [14]

**hypogonadal**   Producing insufficient levels of sex hormones. [5]

**hypospadias**   An abnormal location of the male urethral opening on the underside of the penis or elsewhere. [4]

**hypothalamus**   A small region at the base of the brain on either side of the third ventricle; it contains cell groups involved in sexual responses and other basic functions. [2, App. B]

**hysterectomy** Surgical removal of the uterus. [2]

**hysterotomy** An abortion performed via a surgical incision in the abdominal wall and the uterus. [9]

**I**

**illegitimate** When applied to children, an obsolete term meaning born to unmarried parents. [11]

**imperforate hymen** A hymen that completely closes the introitus. [2]

**implantation** The attachment of the embryo to the endometrium. [8]

**implicit association test** A psychological test designed to reveal unconscious or unexpressed feelings. [11]

**in vitro fertilization (IVF)** Any of a variety of assisted reproduction techniques in which fertilization takes place outside the body. [8]

**INAH3** Third interstitial nucleus of the anterior hypothalamus—a neuronal cell group in the hypothalamus that differs in size between men and women and between gay and straight men. [12]

**incapacitated rape** Rape in which the victim was unable to resist on account of intoxication by alcohol or drugs. [16]

**incompetent cervix** A weakening and partial opening of the cervix caused by a previous traumatic delivery, surgery, or other factors. [8]

**indecent exposure** The crime of exposing the genitals or female breasts in public—exact legal definitions vary. [13]

**induced abortion** An abortion performed intentionally by medical or surgical means. [9]

**induced labor** Labor induced artificially by drugs. [8]

**infant formula** Manufactured breast milk substitute. [8]

**infanticide** The intentional killing of a newborn or very young child. [9]

**infantilism** Sexual satisfaction from acting as an infant. [13]

**infertility** Inability (of a man, woman, or couple) to achieve pregnancy. [8]

**infibulation** The most invasive form of female genital cutting, which involves removal of the clitoris, inner labia, and parts of the outer labia, plus the sewing together of the outer labia over the vestibule. [2]

**inguinal canal** A short canal passing through the abdominal wall in the region of the groin in males, through which the spermatic cord passes. [3]

**inner labia (or labia minora)** Thin, hairless folds of skin located between the outer labia and immediately flanking the vestibule. [2]

**internal fertilization** Fertilization within the body. [App. A]

**internalized homophobia** Anti-gay feelings that some gay people absorb from the larger society. [12]

**interneuron** A neuron whose connections are local. [App. B]

**interpersonal scripts** Patterns of behavior that develop between couples. [7]

**intersectionality** Interactions between different aspects of a person's identity, such as race and sexual orientation.

**intersex** Having a biologically ambiguous or intermediate sex. [4]

**interstitial cells** Cells located between the seminiferous tubules in the testicle that secrete hormones. [3]

**intimacy** The sense of connectedness in an established relationship. [7]

**intimate partner stalking** Stalking of a current or former spouse or other intimate partner. [16]

**intimate partner violence** Violence within a sexual or romantic relationship. [16]

**intracytoplasmic sperm injection (ICSI)** Fertilization of an ovum by injection of a single sperm into it. [8]

**intrafamilial child molester** A person who has had sexual contact with his own children or stepchildren. Also called *incest offender*. [13]

**intrauterine device (IUD)** A device placed in the uterus as a contraceptive. Also called *intrauterine contraceptive (IUC)*. [9]

**introitus** The entrance to the vagina, usually covered early in life by the hymen. [2]

**investment** The commitment or expenditure of resources for a goal, such as reproductive success. [App. A]

**isoflavones** Estrogen-like compounds of plant origin. [11]

**J**

**jaundice** Yellowing of the skin and mucous membranes, caused by liver disease. [15]

**jealousy** Fear that one's partner may be sexually or emotionally unfaithful. [7]

**K**

**kathoey** Trans women in Thailand. [4]

**Kegel exercises** Exercises to strengthen pelvic floor muscles, with the aim of improving sexual function or alleviating urinary leakage. [14]

**kin selection** The theory that it can be advantageous, in evolutionary terms, to support the reproductive success of close relatives. [App. A]

**kink** Colloquial term for an unusual sexual desire or behavior; a paraphilia. [13]

**Kinsey scale** A 7-point scale of sexual orientation devised by Alfred Kinsey. [12]

**kisspeptin** A signaling molecule in the hypothalamus that promotes the onset of puberty. [10]

**Klinefelter syndrome** A collection of traits caused by the possession of one or more extra X chromosomes in a male (XXY or XXXY). [4]

**L**

**labia** Two pairs of skin folds that form the sides of the vulva. [2]

**labial adhesion** A condition seen in prepubertal girls in which the left and right inner labia stick together. [2]

**labiaplasty** Surgical modification of the inner labia. [2]

**labor** The process of childbirth. [8]

**lactation** The production of milk in the mammary glands. [8, App. A]

**Lamaze method** A method of childbirth instruction that focuses on techniques of relaxation and other natural means of pain reduction. [8]

**laparoscopy** Abdominal surgery, such as tubal sterilization, performed through a small incision with the aid of a laparoscope (a fiber-optic viewing instrument). [9]

**latent phase** An asymptomatic phase of syphilis or other infectious disease. [15]

**learned helplessness** Depression associated with failure to escape intimate partner violence. [16]

**legalization with regulation** Conversion of an activity, such as prostitution, from a crime to a governmentally regulated occupation. [17]

**leptin** A hormone secreted by fat cells that acts on the hypothalamus. [10]

**lesbian** Homosexual, applicable to women only. [12]

**lobe** A subdivision of a gland or other organ. [2]

**lochia** A bloody vaginal discharge that may continue for a few weeks after childbirth. [8]

**locus coeruleus** A nerve center in the pons that helps regulate the state of consciousness. [App. B]

**lubrication** The natural appearance of slippery secretions in the vagina during sexual arousal, or the use of artificial lubricants to facilitate sexual activity. [2]

**luteinizing hormone (LH)** One of the two major gonadotropins secreted by the pituitary gland; it triggers ovulation and promotes the secretion of sex steroids by the ovaries (or testicles in males). [2]

**lymphogranuloma venereum** Infection of the lymphatic system by certain strains of *Chlamydia trachomatis*. [15]

# M

**madam** A woman who manages a brothel or an escort service. [17]

**mahu** A natal male who took a female gender role in Polynesian society and performed ritual dances. [4]

**male condom** A sheath placed over the penis as a contraceptive and/or to prevent disease transmission. [9]

**mammary glands** The breasts in their functional role as milk-producing glands. [2]

**mammography** Radiographic inspection of the breasts. [2]

**masochism** Sexual arousal from being subjected to pain, bondage, or humiliation. [13]

**massage parlor** An establishment for massage that may also offer the services of prostitutes. [17]

**mastectomy** Surgical removal of a breast. [2]

**mastitis** Inflammation of the breast. [8]

**masturbation** Sexual self-stimulation. Sometimes also used to refer to manual stimulation of another person's genitalia. [6]

**masturbatory reconditioning** The attempt to change a person's sexual attractions by control of fantasy content during masturbation. [13]

**mate guarding** A behavior in which a male animal prevents sexual contact between his mate and other males. [App. A]

**media fetishism** Sexual attraction to materials such as rubber or silk. Also called *material fetishism*. [13]

**medial preoptic area** A region of the hypothalamus involved in the regulation of sexual behaviors typically shown by males. [12]

**medical abortion** An abortion induced with drugs. Also called *medication abortion*. [9]

**medulla** The portion of the brain stem closest to the spinal cord. [App. B]

**meiosis** A pair of cell divisions that produces haploid gametes. [App. A]

**menarche** The onset of menstruation at puberty. (Pronunciations vary; MEN-ar-kee is most common.) [2, 10]

**menopausal hormone therapy** Use of hormones to treat symptoms occurring during or soon after menopause. [11]

**menopause** The final cessation of menstruation at the end of a woman's reproductive years. [11]

**menstrual cramps** Sharp pelvic pains that may accompany or precede menstruation. [2]

**menstrual cup** A cup placed within the vagina that collects the menstrual flow. [2]

**menstrual phase** The days of the menstrual cycle on which menstrual bleeding occurs. [2]

**menstrual toxic shock syndrome** A rare but life-threatening illness caused by a staphylococcal infection and associated with tampon use. [2]

**menstruation** The breakdown of the endometrium at approximately monthly intervals, with consequent loss of tissue and blood through the vagina. [2]

**metoidioplasty** Surgical construction of a small penis from a clitoris. [4]

**midbrain** The region of the brain stem between the pons and the thalamus. [App. B]

**midpiece** The portion of the tail of a sperm closest to the head, containing mitochondria. [3]

**mifepristone** An anti-progesterone drug used to induce abortion. Also known as *RU-486*. [9]

**milk letdown reflex** The letdown of milk in response to nipple stimulation, mediated by oxytocin. [8]

***Miller v. California*** A 1973 Supreme Court definition of the characteristics of pornography that can be made illegal. [17]

**mini-laparotomy** Abdominal surgery, such as tubal sterilization, performed through a short incision. [9]

**minor-attracted person (MAP)** Someone whose predominant sexual attractions are to children or youths under the legal age of consent. [13]

**Mirena** A hormone-releasing IUD that is effective for 5 years. [9]

**misoprostol** A prostaglandin used in medical abortions. [9]

**mittelschmertz (German: middle pain)** Abdominal pain experienced by some women at the time of ovulation. [2]

**molluscum contagiosum** A skin condition marked by small raised growths; it is caused by a pox virus. [15]

**monogamy** 1. Marriage limited to two persons. 2. A sexual relationship in which neither partner has sexual contact with a third party. [App. A]

**mons (or mons veneris)** The frontmost component of the vulva: a mound of fatty tissue covering the pubic bone. [2]

**motor neuron** A neuron that triggers the contraction of muscle fibers. [App. B]

**mucosa** A surface layer of cells that is lubricated by the secretions of mucous glands. [2]

**mucus** A thick or slippery secretion. [2]

**Müllerian duct** Either of two bilateral ducts in the embryo that give rise to the female reproductive tract. [4]

**multiple orgasms** Two or more orgasms, between which the person descends only to the plateau level of arousal. [5]

**mut'a** In Shia Islam, a contract to marry for a fixed period of time. [11]

**mutation** A change in an organism's genome. [App. A]

**mycoplasma genitalium** A group of very small cellular organisms that may cause urethritis. [15]

**myometrium** The muscular layers of the wall of the uterus. [2]

**myotonia** A general increase in muscle tension. [5]

# N

**Naegele's rule** A traditional rule for the calculation of a pregnant woman's due date: 9 calendar months plus 1 week after the onset of the last menstrual period. [8]

**natal sex** A person's anatomical sex at birth. [4]

**National Health and Social Life Survey (NHSLS)** A national survey of sexual behavior, relationships, and attitudes in the United States, conducted in the early 1990s. [1]

**National Survey of Sexual Attitudes and Lifestyles (Natsal)** A periodic British survey of sexual behavior, relationships, and attitudes. [1]

**National Survey of Sexual Health and Behavior (NSSHB)** A national survey of sexual behavior in the United States, based at Indiana University and published in 2010. [1]

**necking** Kissing or caressing of the head and neck. [6]

**necrophilia** A paraphilia involving sexual arousal from viewing or having contact with dead bodies. [13]

**neuromuscular junction** A synapse between an axon and a muscle fiber. [App. B]

**neuron** A single nerve cell with all its extensions. [App. B]

**neuroses** Mental disorders such as depression that, in Freudian theory, are strategies for coping with repressed sexual conflicts. [1]

**neurotransmitter** A compound released at a synapse that increases or decreases the excitability of an adjacent neuron. [App. B]

**Nexplanon** An implanted hormonal contraceptive. [9]

**Next Choice One-Dose** A progestin used for emergency contraception. [9]

**nitric oxide** A dissolved gas that functions as a neurotransmitter in erectile tissue. [3]

**nocturnal orgasm (or nocturnal emission)** Orgasm or ejaculation during sleep. Also called *wet dream*. [3]

**non-binary** Not conforming to either a conventional masculine or feminine gender identity. [4]

**non-cohabiting relationship** An ongoing sexual relationship between two people who do not live together. [7]

**nongonococcal urethritis (NGU)** Urethritis not caused by gonorrhea. [15]

**Nordic model** A system in which prostitution is a crime for the client but not for the prostitute. [17]

**nucleus (pl. nuclei)** In neuroanatomy, a recognizable cluster of neurons in the CNS. [App. B]

**nucleus accumbens** A nucleus within the basal ganglia that is part of the brain's reward system. [5]

**NuvaRing** A contraceptive ring placed in the vagina. [9]

## O

**object fetishism (or objectophilia or objectum sexuality)** Sexual arousal by objects that are not associated with bodies. [13]

**obscene** Related to sexually themed publications, art, films, performances, or behavior that is deemed offensive to public morals or that violates legal standards of acceptability. [17]

**obsessive relational intrusion** Obsessive pursuit of a person by a rejected lover. [7, 16]

**obsessive-compulsive disorder (OCD)** A mental disorder marked by anxiety, repetitive thoughts or urges, and behaviors that temporarily relieve those urges. [13]

**Onuf's nucleus** A sexually dimorphic group of motor neurons in the sacral segments of the spinal cord that innervates striated muscles associated with the penis and clitoris. [App. B]

**oral herpes** Herpes infection of the mouth, caused by HSV-1 or (less commonly) HSV-2. [15]

**orchitis** Inflammation of a testicle. [3]

**orgasm** The intense, pleasurable sensations at sexual climax, along with the physiological processes that accompany them. [5]

**orgasmic platform** The outer portion of the vagina and surrounding tissues, which thickens and tenses during sexual arousal. [5]

**os** The opening in the cervix that connects the vagina with the cervical canal. [2]

**osteoporosis** Reduction in the mineral content of bone, predisposing an individual to fractures. [11]

**outer labia (or labia majora)** Fleshy skin folds, partially covered in pubic hair, that extend from the mons. [2]

**outercourse** Sexual activities other than coitus, promoted as a means for preventing unwanted pregnancy and reducing the risk of STI transmission. [6, 9]

**ovarian cysts** Cysts within the ovary, which can arise from a number of different causes. [2]

**ovary** The female gonad, which produces ova and secretes sex hormones. [2]

**oviduct** Either of two bilateral tubes that lead from the uterus toward the ovaries, the usual site of fertilization. Also called a *fallopian tube*. [2]

**ovotesticular disorder** The possession of both testicular and ovarian tissue in the same individual. [4]

**ovulation** Release of an ovum from an ovary. [2]

**ovum (pl. ova)** A female gamete, or egg. [2, App. A]

## P

**pair-bond** A durable sexual relationship between two individuals. [App. A]

**pansexuality** Sexual attraction to persons of any sex or gender. Also called *omnisexuality*. [12]

**Pap test** The microscopic examination of a sample of cells taken from the cervix or (less commonly) the anus. [2]

**Paragard** A copper-containing IUD. [9]

**paraphilia** A persistent, intense sexual desire or behavior that is uncommon or unusual. [13]

**paraphilic disorder** A paraphilia that causes distress or harms others. [13]

**paraphimosis** Entrapment of the retracted foreskin behind the corona. [3]

**paraplegia** Paralysis affecting the lower half of the body. [6]

**paraurethral glands** Glands situated next to the female urethra, thought to be equivalent to the prostate gland in males. Also known as *Skene's glands*. [2]

**parthenogenesis** Asexual reproduction from an unfertilized ovum; "virgin birth." [App. A]

**partialism** A fetishistic attraction to a specific part of the body. [13]

**parturition** Delivery of offspring; childbirth. [8]

**passionate love** The overwhelming feeling of attraction typical of the early stage of a loving relationship. [7]

**paternity test** A test to identify an individual's father by DNA analysis. [App. A]

**pedophile** A person whose sexual feelings are directed mainly toward prepubescent children. [13]

**pedophilic disorder** Pedophilia that causes distress or that is expressed in sexual contacts with children. [13]

**pelvic examination** A visual and digital examination of the vulva and pelvic organs. [2]

**pelvic floor muscles** A muscular sling that underlies and supports the pelvic organs. [2]

**pelvic inflammatory disease (PID)** An infection of the female reproductive tract, often caused by sexually transmitted organisms. [2, 8, 15]

**pelvic nerves** Nerves that convey sympathetic signals from the lower spinal cord to the genitalia and other pelvic organs. [App. B]

**penile bulb** An expansion of the corpus spongiosum at the root of the penis. [3]

**penile implant** An implanted device for treatment of erectile disorder. [14]

**penis** The erectile, erotically sensitive genital organ in males. [3]

**perfect-use failure rate** The percentage of women using a contraceptive technique correctly who will become pregnant in the course of a year. [9]

**perimenopause** The phase prior to menopause that is marked by irregular menstrual cycles. [11]

**perimetrium** The outer covering of the uterus. [2]

**perineal massage** Manual stretching of the perineum in preparation for childbirth. [8]

**perineum** The region of skin between the anus and the vulva or scrotum. [2]

**peripheral nervous system** The motor and sensory connections between the CNS and peripheral structures such as muscles and sense organs. [App. B]

**persistent genital arousal disorder (PGAD)** Long-lasting physiological arousal in women, unaccompanied by subjective arousal or pleasure. Also called *restless genital syndrome*. [14]

**personality** The collection of mental and behavioral traits, especially those related to emotions and attitudes, that characterizes an individual. [4]

**perversion** An obsolete term for atypical sexual desire or behavior, viewed as a mental disorder. [1]

**petting** Sexually touching the partner's body (often taken to exclude the breasts or genitalia). [6]

**Peyronie's disease** Pathological curvature of the penis. [3]

**pheromone** A volatile compound that is released by one organism and that triggers a specific behavior in another member of the same species. [App. A]

**phimosis** A tightening of the foreskin that prevents its retraction from the glans. [3]

**phone sex** Erotic telephone conversations, usually carried out for pay. [17]

**pimp** A man who manages prostitutes in exchange for part of their earnings. [17]

**pituitary gland** A gland under the control of and situated below the hypothalamus, whose anterior lobe secretes gonadotropins and other hormones. [2]

**placenta previa** An abnormally low position of the placenta, such that it partially or completely covers the internal opening of the cervix. [8]

**placenta** The vascular organ, formed during pregnancy, that allows for the supply of oxygen and nutrients to the fetus and the removal of waste products. [8]

**Plan B One-Step** A progestin used for emergency contraception. [9]

**plateau phase** The phase of the sexual response cycle during which arousal is maintained at a high level. [5]

**pluralistic ignorance** A mistaken belief that one's values, opinions, or behaviors differ from those of one's peers. [10]

**polyamory** The formation of nontransient sexual relationships in groups of three or more. [11]

**polyandry** The marriage or mating of one female with more than one male. [11, App. A]

**polycystic ovary syndrome (PCOS)** A condition marked by excessive secretion of androgens by the ovaries. [2]

**polygamy** Marriage to or (mostly in animals) mating with more than one partner. [1, 11, App. A]

**polygyny** The marriage or mating of one male with more than one female. [11, App. A]

**pons** A region of the brain above the medulla. [App. B]

**pornography** Material (such as art, writing, photographic images, and film) that is intended to be sexually arousing. Also called *porn*. [17]

**post-exposure prophylaxis (PEP)** A drug treatment designed to prevent establishment of an infection after exposure to a disease agent such as HIV. [15]

**post-traumatic stress disorder (PTSD)** A cluster of physical and psychological symptoms that can affect persons who have experienced severe trauma. [10, 16]

**postganglionic neuron** A neuron with its cell body in an autonomic ganglion and an axon that innervates glands or smooth muscles in peripheral organs such as the genitalia. [App. B]

**postnuptial agreement** A financial agreement between spouses. [11]

**postovulatory phase (or luteal phase)** The phase of the menstrual cycle between ovulation and the beginning of menstruation. [2]

**postpartum depression** Depression in a mother during the postpartum phase. [8]

**postpartum depressive psychosis (or postpartum psychosis)** Postpartum depression accompanied by seriously disordered thinking. [8]

**postpartum period** The period after birth. [8]

**pre-exposure prophylaxis (PrEP)** A drug taken before exposure to a disease agent to prevent infection. [15]

**preadolescence** The age range including the beginning of puberty, from approximately age 8 to 12 or 13 years. [10]

**precocious puberty** Puberty that begins earlier than normal. [10]

**preconception care** Medical care and counseling provided to women before they become pregnant. [8]

**prefrontal cortex** The most anterior region of the frontal lobe. [App. B]

**preganglionic neuron** An autonomic motor neuron in the spinal cord. [App. B]

**preimplantation genetic screening (PGS)** Testing of in vitro fertilization embryos for genetic defects prior to implantation. [8]

**premature birth (or preterm birth)** Birth that occurs more than 3 weeks before a woman's due date. [8]

**premature ejaculation** Ejaculation before the man wishes, often immediately on commencement of coitus. Also called *early* or *rapid ejaculation*. [6, 14]

**premenstrual dysphoric disorder** PMS-associated mood changes that are severe enough to interfere with relationships. [2]

**premenstrual syndrome (PMS)** A collection of physical and/or psychological symptoms that may start a few days before the menstrual period begins and continue into the period. [2]

**prenatal care** Medical care and counseling provided to pregnant women. [8]

**prenuptial agreement** A contract signed before marriage, spelling out the disposition of wealth in the event of divorce. [11]

**preovulatory phase (or follicular phase)** The phase of the menstrual cycle during which follicles are developing in the ovaries. [2]

**priapism** A persistent penile erection in the absence of sexual arousal. [3]

**primary amenorrhea** The failure to begin menstruating at puberty. [2, 10]

**primary disorder** A disorder that is not preceded by any period of healthy function. [14]

**primary dysmenorrhea** Painful menstruation that begins at puberty and has no clear cause. [2]

**primary syphilis** The first phase of syphilis, marked by the occurrence of a chancre. [15]

**pro-choice** Believing that abortion should be legal under some or all circumstances. [9]

**pro-life** Opposed to abortion; believing that abortion should be illegal under most or all circumstances. [9]

**proceptive behavior** Behavior by females that may elicit sexual advances by males. [App. A]

**progesterone** The steroid hormone secreted by the ovary and the placenta that is necessary for the establishment and maintenance of pregnancy. [2]

**progestin-only pill** An oral contraceptive that contains progestin but no estrogen. Also called the *mini-pill*. [9]

**progestins** Any of a class of steroids—the most important being progesterone—that cause the endometrium to proliferate and help maintain pregnancy. [2]

**prolactin** A protein hormone, secreted by the anterior lobe of the pituitary gland, that promotes breast development, among other effects. [8]

**prolapse** The slipping out of place of an organ, such as the uterus. [2]

**prolonged exposure (PE) therapy** A form of extended psychotherapy for victims of rape or abuse in which they are encouraged to recall the traumatic event in a safe environment. [16]

**promiscuity** Engaging in numerous casual or short-lived sexual relationships. [App. A]

**prosociality** A positive interest in and concern for others. [7]

**prostaglandin E1** A hormone that can be injected into the penis to produce an erection. [14]

**prostate cancer** Cancer of the prostate gland. [3]

**prostate gland** A single gland located at the base of the bladder and surrounding the urethra; its secretions are a component of semen. [3]

**prostate massager** A butt plug shaped to stimulate the prostate gland. [6]

**prostate-specific antigen (PSA)** An enzyme secreted by the prostate gland; its presence at high levels in the blood is suggestive of, but not diagnostic of, prostate cancer. [3]

**prostatitis** Inflammation of the prostate gland, either acute or chronic. [3]

**prosthesis** An artificial replacement for a body part. [2]

**prostitution** The practice of engaging in sex for pay. [17]

**provoked vestibulodynia** Painful sensitivity of the vestibule to touch or pressure. [14]

**psychology** The study of mental processes and behavior. [1]

**psychosomatic effects** Effects of the mind on the body. [11]

**puberty** The transition to sexual maturity. [4, 10]

**pubic hair** Hair that appears on portions of the external genitalia in both sexes at puberty. [2]

**pubic lice** Insects (*Phthirus pubis*) that preferentially infest the pubic region. [15]

**pubococcygeus muscles** Muscles of the pelvic floor that runs from the pubic bone to the coccyx (tailbone). In women they form a sling around the vagina. [2]

**pudendal nerves** Peripheral nerves supplying the external genitalia. [App. B]

**pulmonary surfactant** A compound produced in the fetal lung that reduces surface tension and thus facilitates inflation of the lungs with air at birth. [8]

## Q

**quadriplegia** Paralysis affecting almost the entire body below the neck. [6]

**qualitative research** In-depth but non-numerical study of social phenomena. [1]

**Quartette** An extended-use contraceptive pill. [9]

**quickening** The onset of movements by the fetus that can be felt by the mother. [8]

**quid pro quo harassment** Unwelcome sexual advances, usually made to a worker in a subordinate position, accompanied by promises or threats. [16]

*quinceañera* Hispanic coming-of-age ceremony for girls. [10]

## R

**radical prostatectomy** Surgical removal of the entire prostate gland and local lymph nodes. [3]

**rape kit** Samples collected from a rape victim's body or clothing for the purpose of identifying the perpetrator. [16]

**rape shield laws** Laws that protect rape victims—for example, by limiting the introduction of evidence about their prior sexual behavior. [16]

**rape** Penetrative sex accomplished by force or the threat of force. [16]

**rapid-onset gender dysphoria** The sudden onset of gender dysphoria in a person who previously had a gender identity congruent with their natal sex.

**recidivism** The tendency of convicted offenders to reoffend. [13]

**rectum** The final, straight portion of the large bowel. It connects to the exterior via the anus. [2, 6]

**refractory period** In males, a period of reduced or absent sexual arousability after orgasm. [5]

**relapse prevention therapy** Therapy aimed at training a person to avoid or cope with situations that trigger the undesirable behavior. [13]

**reportable disease** A disease whose cases must by law be reported to health authorities. [15]

**reproductive tract** The internal anatomical structures in either sex that form the pathway taken by ova, sperm, or the conceptus. [2]

**resolution phase** The phase of the sexual response cycle during which physiological arousal subsides. [5]

**retrovirus** An RNA virus whose genome is transcribed into DNA within the host cell. [15]

**Rh factor** An antigen on the surface of red blood cells that, when present in a fetus but not in its mother, may trigger an immune response by the mother. [8]

**rubella** German measles, a viral infection that can cause developmental defects in fetuses whose mothers contract the disease during pregnancy. [8]

## S

**sadism** Sexual arousal by the infliction of pain, bondage, or humiliation on others, or by witnessing the recipient's suffering. [13]

**sadomasochism (S/M)** The infliction and acceptance of pain or humiliation as a means of sexual arousal. [13]

**saline-induced abortion** An abortion induced by use of a strong salt solution. [9]

**scabies** Infestation with a mite (*Sarcoptes scabiei*) that burrows within the skin. [15]

**script theory** The analysis of sexual and other behaviors as the enactment of socially instilled roles. [1]

**scrotum** The sac behind the penis that contains the testicles. [3, App. A]

**Seasonale** An extended-use contraceptive pill. [9]

**Seasonique** An extended-use contraceptive pill. [9]

**secondary amenorrhea** The cessation of menstruation at some time after menarche. [10]

**secondary disorder** A disorder that follows some period of healthy function. [14]

**secondary dysmenorrhea** Painful menstruation that begins during adult life, usually as a consequence of a pelvic disorder. [2]

**secondary sexual characteristics** Anatomical characteristics, such as breasts and facial hair, that generally differ between the sexes but are not used to define an individual's sex. [2]

**secondary syphilis** The second phase of syphilis, marked by a rash and fever. [15]

**selective serotonin reuptake inhibitors (SSRIs)** A class of drugs, including antidepressants such as Prozac and Lexapro, that may depress sexual function. [13]

**semen** The fluid, containing sperm and a variety of chemical compounds, that is ejaculated from the penis at male sexual climax. [3, App. A]

**seminal emission** The loading of the constituents of semen into the posterior portion of the urethra immediately before ejaculation. [3]

**seminal nurture** The belief that fetuses require repeated infusions of semen to grow. [6]

**seminal vesicles** Two glands situated to either side of the prostate; their secretions are components of semen. [3]

**seminiferous tubules** Convoluted microscopic tubes within the testicle that are the sites of sperm production. [3]

**sensate focus** A form of sex therapy that involves graduated touching exercises. [14]

**serial monogamy** Engagement in a series of monogamous relationships. [7, 10]

**serial orgasms** Two or more orgasms with no more than a few seconds between them. [5]

**seroconversion** The change from negative to positive on an antibody test, such as occurs a few weeks or months after HIV infection. [15]

**sex addiction** The idea that a person may be addicted to sexual behavior by a mechanism similar to that of substance addiction. [14]

**sex chromosome** Either chromosome (X or Y) of a pair that differs between the sexes. [4, App. A]

**sex determination** The biological mechanism that determines whether an organism will develop as a male or a female. [App. A]

**sex play**   A variety of playful activities that add pleasure to sexual interactions. [6]

**sex steroid**   Any of the steroid hormones that are active in sexual and reproductive processes. [2]

**sex surrogate**   A person who engages in sexual relations with a client as part of a sex therapy program. [14]

**sex therapist**   A person who treats sexual disorders, usually by means of psychotherapy and sexual exercises. [14]

**sex tourism**   Traveling to a foreign country to find sex partners (usually prostitutes). [17]

**sex trafficking**   Making money from coerced or juvenile prostitution. [17]

**sex worker**   A person who engages in prostitution, pornography, or another sex-related occupation. [17]

**sex-reassignment surgery (or gender confirmation surgery)**   Surgery to change a person's genitals or other anatomical structures to those of the sex with which the person identifies. [4]

**sex**   The distinction between female and male, or sexual behavior. [1]

**sexology**   The scientific study of sex and sexual disorders. [1]

**sexting**   Sending sexually explicit text or images via cellphone. [3]

**sexual assault**   Coercive or nonconsensual sexual contact; a broader category of behaviors than rape. [16]

**sexual dimorphism**   An anatomical difference between the sexes. [App. B]

**sexual harassment**   Unwanted sexual advances or other intimidating sexual behavior, usually in the workplace. [16]

**sexual intercourse**   Sexual contact, usually understood to involve coitus. [2]

**sexual interest/arousal disorder**   Lack of interest in sex or insufficient sexual arousal, when it causes distress. [14]

**sexual jealousy**   Fear that one's partner is engaging in sexual contacts with another person. [7]

**sexual monogamy**   Pair-bonding that is sexually exclusive. [App. A]

**sexual orientation**   Sexual attraction toward persons of the other sex (heterosexual), the same sex (homosexual), both sexes (bisexual), or neither sex (asexual). [4, 11, 12]

**sexual reproduction**   Reproduction in which the offspring inherit genes from two parents. [1, App. A]

**sexual response cycle**   The sequence of physiological processes that accompany sexual behavior. [5]

**sexual sadism disorder**   Sexual arousal by the suffering of others, viewed as a paraphilic disorder. [13]

**sexual script**   A socially negotiated role that guides sexual behavior. [4]

**sexual selection**   Evolutionary changes driven by competition for mates. [1, App. A]

**sexual webcamming**   Live sexual performances or nudity supplied over the internet for pay. [17]

**sexuality**   The feelings, behaviors, and identities associated with sex. [1]

**sexually explicit materials**   A nonjudgmental phrase denoting pornography. [17]

**sexually transmitted infection (STI)**   Infection with a disease agent during sexual contact. [15]

**shaft of the clitoris**   The portion of the clitoris next to the glans that can be felt under the clitoral hood. [2]

**sinusoid**   A vascular space, such as within erectile tissue, capable of expanding when filled with blood. [3, App. B]

**situational disorder**   A disorder that appears only in certain circumstances. [14]

**Skyla**   A hormone-releasing IUD that is effective for 3 years. [9]

**smegma**   A whitish, greasy secretion that can build up under the hood of the clitoris or the foreskin of the penis. [2, 3]

**social monogamy**   The formation of pair-bonds or marriages that may or may not be sexually exclusive. [7, App. A]

**social psychology**   The study of one's relationships to others. [1]

**sociology**   The scientific study of society. [1]

**sociosexuality**   Interest or engagement in sex without commitment. [7]

**softcore**   Related to relatively nonexplicit pornography. [17]

**softening**   The elimination of connective tissue from the cervix, allowing it to thin out and dilate during labor. Also called *ripening*. [8]

**sperm (or spermatozoon; pl. spermatozoa)**   The male gamete, produced in the testicles. [3, App. A]

**sperm bank**   A facility that collects, stores, and provides semen for artificial insemination. [8]

**spermatic cord**   Either of two bilateral bundles of structures that include the vas deferens, blood vessels, and the cremaster muscle and that pass through the inguinal canal to a testicle. [3]

**spermatogenesis**   The production of sperm. [3]

**spermicide**   A chemical that kills sperm, available as a contraceptive in a variety of forms, such as foams, creams, and suppositories. [9]

**sphincter**   A circular muscle around a tube or orifice whose contraction closes it. [2, 6]

**spina bifida**   A congenital malformation caused by incomplete closure of the neural tube. [8]

**spinal cord**   The portion of the CNS within the vertebral column. [App. B]

**spirochete**   Any of a class of corkscrew-shaped bacteria, including the agent that causes syphilis. [15]

**SRY**   A gene located on the Y chromosome (Sex-determining Region of the Y chromosome) that causes the embryo to develop as a male. [4]

**stalking**   Obsessive pursuit of a previous, current, or desired sex partner in such a way as to put that person in a state of fear. [7, 16]

**standard days method**   A simplified fertility awareness calendar method of contraception usable by women with regular cycles. [9]

**statutory rape**   Penetrative sex when a partner is legally unable to give consent on account of young age, intellectual disability, or unconsciousness. [16]

**stereotypes**   Common opinions about classes of people that are false or overgeneralized. [4]

**sterilization**   A surgical procedure to eliminate fertility in either sex. [9]

**stop-start method**   A sex therapy technique for the treatment of premature ejaculation that involves alternating between stimulating and not stimulating the penis. [14]

**straight**   Colloquial term meaning "heterosexual." [12]

**subfertility**   Difficulty in establishing a pregnancy; arbitrarily defined as the absence of pregnancy after a couple has had frequent unprotected sex for 12 months. [8]

**submission**   Taking the subservient role in BDSM activity. [13]

**suitor**   A person who is seeking to establish a romantic relationship with another. [7]

**sunnah**   Female genital cutting limited to incision or removal of the clitoral hood. [2]

**surgical abortion**   An abortion induced by a surgical procedure. [9]

**surrogate mother**   A woman who carries a pregnancy on behalf of another woman or couple. [8]

**swingers**   Couples who agree to engage in casual sexual contacts with others. [11]

**sympathetic nervous system**   A division of the autonomic nervous system; among other functions, it controls clitoral and penile erection as well as seminal emission and ejaculation. [App. B]

**sympto-thermal method** A fertility awareness method of contraception that depends on the measurement of basal body temperature and the testing of cervical mucus. [9]

**synapse** A junction where signals are transmitted between neurons or from neurons to muscle fibers. [App. B]

**synaptic cleft** The narrow space between two neurons at a synapse. [App. B]

**syphilis** A sexually transmitted infection caused by a spirochete, *Treponema pallidum*. [15]

**T**

**telephone scatalogia** Sexual arousal from making obscene telephone calls. [13]

**tertiary syphilis** The third phase of syphilis, marked by multiple organ damage. [15]

**testicle (or testis; pl. testes)** The male gonad: one of the two glands within the scrotum that produce sperm and secrete sex hormones. [3]

**testicular torsion** Twisting of a testicle that cuts off its blood supply. [3]

**testosterone** The principal androgen, synthesized in the testes and, in lesser amounts, in the ovaries and adrenal glands. [2, 3]

**thalamus** The uppermost region of the brain stem. [App. B]

**therapeutic abortion** An abortion performed to safeguard a woman's life or health. [9]

**third-party sexual harassment** Indirect negative effects of sexual harassment on other employees, or sexual harassment by nonemployees. [16]

**trabeculae** Connective tissue partitions separating the sinusoids of erectile tissue. [App. B]

**trans-attracted** Sexually attracted to transgender persons. [13]

**transexual (or transsexual)** A person who identifies with the other sex and who seeks to transition to the other sex by medical means. [4]

**transgender (or trans)** Having a gender identity that is not fully congruent with one's birth sex. [4]

**transition** The final phase of dilation of the cervix during labor. [8]

**transitioning** Changing one's physical sex and social gender. [4]

**transphobia** Hatred of transgender people. [4]

**transvestism** Wearing clothes of the other sex for purposes of sexual arousal. The term is sometimes applied to cross-dressing for any reason. [4, 13]

**tribadism** Sexual behavior between two women who lie front to front and stimulate each other's vulvas with thrusting motions. [6]

**trichomoniasis (or "trich")** Infection with the protozoan *Trichomonas vaginalis*. [15]

**trimester** One of three 3-month divisions of pregnancy. [8]

**triphasic combination pill** An oral contraceptive regimen that varies the doses of estrogens and progestins around the menstrual cycle. [9]

**triple-X syndrome** A collection of traits caused by the possession, in a female, of three X chromosomes rather than two. [4]

**tubal ligation** A procedure in which the oviducts are blocked by tying them off. [9]

**tubal sterilization** Any procedure that prevents sperm transport in the oviducts. [9]

**tube site** A website that aggregates amateur and commercial pornographic videos from multiple sources. [17]

**Turner syndrome** A collection of traits caused by the possession of one X and no Y chromosome. [4]

**two-spirit person** In Native American cultures, a person with the spirit of both a man and a woman; a transgender person. Also called *berdache*. [4]

**typical-use failure rate** The percentage of women using a contraceptive technique with a typical degree of care who will become pregnant in the course of a year. [9]

**U**

**ultrasound scan** An imaging procedure that depends on the reflection of ultrasonic waves from density boundaries within the body. Also called *ultrasonographic scan*. [8]

**unrequited love** Love that is not reciprocated. [7]

**urethra** The canal that conveys urine from the bladder to the urethral opening. [2]

**urethral folds** Folds of ectodermal tissue in the embryo that give rise to the inner labia (in females) or the shaft of the penis (in males). [4]

**urethritis** Inflammation of the urethra, usually caused by an infection. [15]

**urogenital sinus** The common opening of the urinary and genital systems in the embryo. [4]

**urologist** A physician who specializes in disorders of the urinary and genital systems. [14]

**urophilia** Sexual fixation on urination. [13]

**uterine polyp** A tissue growth from the endometrium that bulges into the uterine cavity. [2]

**uterus** The womb; a pear-shaped region of the female reproductive tract through which sperm pass and where the conceptus implants and develops. [2]

**V**

**vacuum aspiration** An abortion procedure in which the conceptus is destroyed and removed by suction. [9]

**vacuum constriction system** A device for treating erectile disorder that creates a partial vacuum around the penis, thus drawing blood into the erectile tissue. [14]

**vagina** A muscular tube extending 3 to 4 inches (8 to 10 cm) from the vestibule to the uterine cervix. [2]

**vaginal dilator** A plastic cylinder used to enlarge the vagina or to counteract vaginismus. [14]

**vaginismus** Inability to experience coitus due to pain, or fear of pain, and spasm of the muscles surrounding the outer vagina. [14]

**varicocele** Enlargement of the veins that drain the testicle. [3]

**vas deferens (pl. vasa deferentia)** Either of the two bilateral ducts that convey sperm from the epididymis to the ejaculatory ducts. [3]

**vasectomy** A male sterilization technique that involves cutting or tying off the vas deferens from each testicle. [9]

**vasocongestion** Tissue swelling caused by increased filling of local blood vessels. [2, 5]

**vasomotor control** The physiological regulation of peripheral blood flow. [11]

**vasovasostomy** Surgery to reverse a vasectomy. [9]

**venereal disease** Obsolete term for a sexually transmitted infection. [15]

**ventral horn** The portion of the gray matter of the spinal cord nearer to the front of the body, where motor neurons are located. [App. B]

**ventral root** A bundle of motor axons that leaves a ventral horn of the spinal cord. [App. B]

**vestibular bulbs** Erectile structures beneath the inner labia, on either side of the vestibule. [2]

**vestibule** The potential space between the left and right inner labia. [2]

**vibrator** An electrically powered vibrating device used to provide sexual stimulation. [6]

**virginity pledge programs** Programs in which teens take formal pledges not to have sex before marriage. [10]

**virus** An extremely small infectious agent. When not inside a host cell, viruses are metabolically inert but infectious. [15]

**voyeurism** Sexual arousal from watching persons while they are undressing, naked, or engaged in sex. [13]

**vulva** The female external genitalia. [2, App. A]

**vulvodynia** Chronic pain in the vulva with no clear cause. [14]

## W

**Westermarck effect** The lack of sexual attraction between individuals, such as siblings, who lived together during their childhood. [5]

**wet nurse** A woman who breastfeeds someone else's infant. [8]

**white matter** A region of the CNS that contains bundles of axons but no neuronal cell bodies. [App. B]

**withdrawal method** A method of contraception in which the man withdraws his penis from the vagina prior to ejaculation. [9]

**Wolffian duct** Either of two bilateral ducts in the embryo that give rise to the male reproductive tract. [4]

## X

**X chromosome** A sex chromosome that is present as two copies in females and one copy in males. [4, App. A]

**Xulane** A contraceptive patch. [9]

**XYY syndrome** A collection of traits caused by the possession, in a male, of an extra Y chromosome. [4]

## Y

**Y chromosome** A sex chromosome that is present only in males. [4, App. A]

## Z

**zona pellucida** The protective membrane surrounding an ovum and early embryo. [8]

**zoophilia** A persistent preference for sexual contacts with animals. [13]

**zygote** A cell formed by the fusion of gametes; a fertilized ovum. [8, App. A]

# References

Numbers in brackets refer to the chapter(s) where the references are cited.

## A

AASECT. (n.d.). *AASECT position on sex addiction.* (http://tinyurl.com/ya9w8zzx) [14]

Abbey, A. & Ortiz, L. G. (2008). Alcohol and sexual violence perpetration. (http://tinyurl.com/y9psxuoj) [16]

ABC News. (2011). Phoenix Goddess Temple raided as alleged brothel. (http://tinyurl.com/4x3xr36) [17]

Abdelaziz, S. (2017). "It would be good if I too died": Rape as weapon of war against Rohingya. (http://tinyurl.com/ybzgaw88) [16]

Abel, G. G. & Osborn, C. A. (2000). The para-philias. In: M. G. Gelder, J. J. López-Ibor and N. Andreasen (Eds.). *New Oxford textbook of psychiatry.* Oxford University Press. [13]

Abraham, L. (2010). *Can you really predict the success of a marriage in 15 minutes?* (https://tinyurl.com/y27tqu7w) [7]

ACOG. (2016). *Immersion in water during labor and delivery.* (http://tinyurl.com/ybev3lon) [8]

ACOG. (2017a). *Cervical cancer screening.* (https://tinyurl.com/y3bgq7dd) [2]

ACOG. (2017b). *Newborn male circumcision.* (https://tinyurl.com/yyhb8bnz) [3]

ACOG. (2018). *The utility of and indications for routine pelvic examination.* (https://tinyurl.com/y4kchyfk) [2]

ActionAid. (2019). *Chhaupadi and menstruation taboos.* (https://tinyurl.com/y6mb688s) [2]

Adams, H. E., Wright, L. W., Jr. & Lohr, B. A. (1996). Is homophobia associated with homosexual arousal? *Journal of Abnormal Psychology, 105,* 440–445. [12]

Agarwal, A., Mulgund, A., Hamada, A. & Chyatte, M. R. (2015). A unique view on male infertility around the globe. *Reproductive Biology and Endocrinology, 13,* 37. [8]

Agrawal, S. S. & Mishra, G. (2016). Adulteration of synthetic PDE-5 inhibitors viz., sildenafil and tadalafil in marketed herbal aphrodisiacs. *Current Medicine Research and Practice, 6,* 152–156. [5]

AIDSinfo. (2019). The stages of HIV infection. (http://tinyurl.com/yckjvqgb) [15]

Ajlouni, H. K., Daoud, A. S., Ajlouni, S. F. & Ajlouni, K. M. (2010). Infantile and early childhood masturbation: Sex hormones and clinical profile. *Annals of Saudi Medicine, 30,* 471–474. [10]

Akkus, D. E. (2011). Orgasm treatment in migraine: A native and costless choice? A clinical observation. *Archives of Neuropsychiatry, 48,* 268–269. [6]

Akolekar, R., Beta, J., Picciarelli, G., et al. (2015). Procedure-related risk of miscarriage following amniocentesis and chorionic villus sampling: a systematic review and meta-analysis. *Ultrasound in Obstetrics and Gynecology, 45,* 16–26. [8]

Akre, C., Berchtold, A., Gmel, G. & Suris, J. C. (2014). The evolution of sexual dysfunction in young men aged 18–25 years. *Journal of Adolescent Health, 55,* 736–743. [5]

Al Waheidi, M. (2017). Gaza dating site matches widows to men seeking 2nd (or 3rd) wife. *New York Times,* June 4. [11]

Al-Maghafi, N. (2019). In Iraq, religious "pleasure marriages" are a front for child prostitution. *Guardian (London),* October 6. [11]

Al-Sharfi, M., Pfeffer, K. & Miller, K. A. (2016). The effects of polygamy on children and adolescents: A systematic review. *Journal of Family Studies, 22,* 272–286. [11]

Alarie, M. & Gaudet, S. (2013). "I don't know if she is bisexual or if she just wants to get attention": Analyzing the various mechanisms through which emerging adults invisibilize bisexuality. *Journal of Bisexuality, 13,* 191–214. [12]

Alarms.org. (2019). STD statistics 2019: States with the highest rates. (https://tinyurl.com/y4gosegb) [15]

Alexander, B. M., Skinner, D. C. & Roselli, C. E. (2011). Wired on steroids: Sexual differentiation of the brain and its role in the expression of sexual partner preferences. *Frontiers in Endocrinology (Lausanne), 2,* 42. [12]

Alexander, G. M. & Hines, M. (2002). Sex differences in response to children's toys in nonhuman primates (*Cercopithecus aethiops sabaeus*). *Evolution and Human Behavior, 23,* 467–479. [4]

Alexander, M., Bashir, K., Alexander, C., et al. (2018). Randomized trial of clitoral vacuum suction versus vibratory stimulation in neurogenic female orgasmic dysfunction. *Archives of Physical Medicine and Rehabilitation, 99,* 299–305. [14]

Ali, L. & Kelley, R. (2008). The curious lives of surrogates. *Newsweek,* April 7. [8]

Almukhtar, S., Gold, M. & Buchanan, L. (2018). After Weinstein: 71 men accused of sexual misconduct and their fall from power. *New York Times,* February 8. [16]

Altgelt, E. E., Reyes, M. A., French, J. E., et al. (2018). Who is sexually faithful? Own and partner personality traits as predictors of infidelity. *Journal of Social and Personal Relationships, 35,* 600–614. [7]

Althof, S. E. (2007). Treatment of rapid ejaculation: Psychotherapy, pharmacotherapy, and combined therapy. In: S. R. Leiblum (Ed.), *Principles and practice of sex therapy.* Guilford Press. [14]

Althof, S. E. (2016). Psychosexual therapy for premature ejaculation. *Translational Andrology and Urology, 5,* 475–481. [14]

Althof, S. E., McMahon, C. G., Waldinger, M. D., et al. (2014). An update of the International Society of Sexual Medicine's guidelines for the diagnosis and treatment of premature ejaculation (PE). *Journal of Sexual Medicine, 11,* 1392–1422. [14]

Amato, P. R. (2010). Research on divorce: Continuing trends and new developments. *Journal of Marriage and Family, 72,* 650–666. [11]

Amberson, J. I. & Hoon, P. W. (1985). Hemodynamics of sequential orgasm. *Archives of Sexual Behavior, 14,* 351–360. [5]

American Academy of Husband-Coached Childbirth. (2019). *The Bradley method.* (http://tinyurl.com/y9555x3) [8]

American Academy of Pediatrics. (2012). *AAP reaffirms breastfeeding guidelines.* [8]

American Academy of Pediatrics. (2015). *Should the baby be circumcised?* (http://tinyurl.com/pgwkfaj) [3]

American Academy of Pediatrics. (2019). *Sexual behaviors in young children: What's normal, what's not?* (https://tinyurl.com/y2ju39v7) [10]

American Association of Retired Persons. (2010). *Sex, romance, and relationships: AARP Survey of Midlife and Older Adults.* (http://tinyurl.com/yc3uusw8) [11]

American Cancer Society. (2018). *About testicular cancer.* (https://tinyurl.com/y2by9al3) [3]

American Cancer Society. (2019a). *American Cancer Society breast cancer screening guidelines.* (https://tinyurl.com/ycptgeha) [2]

American Cancer Society. (2019b). *Breast reconstruction surgery.* (https://tinyurl.com/y4mx7mp9) [2]

American Cancer Society. (2019c). *Key statistics for anal cancer.* (https://tinyurl.com/ydd4luvn) [15]

American Cancer Society. (2019d). *Survival rates for prostate cancer.* (https://tinyurl.com/ybeswq7l) [3]

American College Health Association. (2016). *Undergraduate student reference group data report, Spring 2016.* (http://tinyurl.com/mql6ntx) [7, 9]

American College Health Association. (2018). *National College Health Assessment II: Fall 2018 reference group executive summary.* (https://tinyurl.com/yxpqx6s4) [6, 9]

American College Health Association. (2019). *National College Health Assessment II: Spring 2019.* (https://tinyurl.com/thg36mp) [16]

American College of Nurse-Midwives. (2005). *Perineal massage in pregnancy.* (http://tinyurl.com/o3ygqos) [8]

American College of Obstetricians and Gynecologists. (2017). *Access to contraception.* (http://tinyurl.com/y9go9nlp) [9]

American College of Obstetricians and Gynecologists. (2019a). *Ectopic pregnancy.* (https://tinyurl.com/y3896wfs) [8]

American College of Obstetricians and Gynecologists. (2019b). *Exercise during pregnancy.* (https://tinyurl.com/y6h25gxn) [8]

American Pregnancy Association. (2017). *Epidural anesthesia.* (http://tinyurl.com/pd95s8p) [8]

American Psychological Association. (2007). *Report of the APA task force on the sexualization of girls.* (https://tinyurl.com/ybmy3v4p) [10]

American Psychological Association. (2011). *Guidelines for psychotherapy with lesbian, gay, and bisexual clients.* (http://tinyurl.com/y88h7ek5) [12]

American Psychological Association. (2017). *APA Division 44.* (http://tinyurl.com/ydz7vlz3) [14]

American Sexual Health Association. (2019). *Statistics: STIs.* (https://tinyurl.com/pdxyd89) [15]

American Society for Reproductive Medicine. (2013). Criteria for number of embryos to transfer: a committee opinion. *Fertility and Sterility, 99,* 44–46. [8]

American Society of Plastic Surgeons. (2019). *2019 national plastic surgery statistics.* (https://tinyurl.com/y5pswzs9) [2]

American Urological Association. (2016). *Penile augmentation surgery.* (http://tinyurl.com/msosoq7) [3]

Amstey, M. S. (1994). The political history of syphilis and its application to the AIDS epidemic. *Women's Health Issues, 4,* 16–19.

Anapol, D. (2010). *Polyamory in the 21st century: Love and intimacy with multiple partners.* Rowman and Littlefield.

Anderson, E., Ripley, M. & McCormack, M. (2019). A mixed-method study of same-sex kissing among college-attending heterosexual men in the U.S. *Sexuality & Culture, 23,* 26–44. [6]

Anderson, N. E., Harenski, K. A., Harenski, C. L., et al. (2019). Machine learning of brain gray matter differentiates sex in a large forensic sample. *Human Brain Mapping, 40,* 1496–1506. [4]

Anderson, T. A., Schick, V., Herbenick, D., et al. (2014). A study of human papillomavirus on vaginally inserted sex toys, before and after cleaning, among women who have sex with women and men. *Sexually Transmitted Infections, 90,* 529–531. [6]

Angulo, J. C., Garcia-Diez, M. & Martinez, M. (2011). Phallic decoration in paleolithic art: Genital scarification, piercing and tattoos. *Journal of Urology, 186,* 2498–2503. [3]

Anonymous (1999). Confessions of a LUG. *Cincinnati CityBeat,* August 26. [7]

Anonymous. (2014a). *Can anyone else orgasm just from nipple stimulation?* (http://tinyurl.com/km6jekq) [5]

Anonymous. (2014b). *I am the guy with two penises.* (http://tinyurl.com/mwpucbm) [3]

Anonymous. (2014c). *The Cosmo sex challenge: 77 positions in 77 days.* (http://tinyurl.com/lbr4wam) [6]

Anonymous. (2019). *My life in sex: I watch my wife sleep with younger men.* (https://tinyurl.com/y3qptsgm) [13]

Antiretroviral Therapy Cohort Collaboration. (2017). Survival of HIV-positive patients starting antiretroviral therapy between 1996 and 2013: A collaborative analysis of cohort studies. (http://tinyurl.com/mychxrg) [15]

Apicella, C. L., Feinberg, D. R. & Marlowe, F. W. (2007). Voice pitch predicts reproductive success in male hunter-gatherers. *Biology Letters, 3,* 682–684. [5]

Arevalo, M., Jennings, V., Nikula, M. & Sinai, I. (2004). Efficacy of the new TwoDay Method of family planning. *Fertility and Sterility, 82,* 885–892. [9]

Ariely, D. & Loewenstein, G. (2006). The heat of the moment: The effect of sexual arousal on sexual decision making. *Journal of Behavioral Decision Making, 19,* 87–98. [16]

Armstrong, K. & Miller, T. C. (2017). When sexual assault victims are charged with lying. *New York Times,* November 24. [16]

Arnold, A. P., Reue, K., Eghbali, M., et al. (2016). The importance of having two X chromosomes. *Philosophical Transactions of the Royal Society of London. Series B: Biological Sciences, 371,* 20150113. [4]

Arroyo, K., Lundahl, B., Butters, R., et al. (2017). Short-term interventions for survivors of intimate partner violence: A systematic review and meta-analysis. *Trauma, Violence & Abuse, 18,* 155–171. [16]

Associated Press. (1996). *Husband seeks divorce over on-line affair.* (http://tinyurl.com/yckhxmk4) [7]

Associated Press. (2008). *Court: Wisconsin law bans sex with the dead, charges against three men reinstated.* (http://tinyurl.com/ychko2y3) [13]

Associated Press. (2011). Texas: Polygamist leader gets life sentence. *New York Times,* August 10. [11]

Associated Press. (2011). *UN group backs gay rights for the first time ever.* (http://tinyurl.com/yav78qky) [12]

Associated Press. (2016a). *Clovis police: Son charged with incest tried to save mom from abuse.* (http://tinyurl.com/yaogaeys) [App. A]

Associated Press. (2016b). *Darren Sharper sentenced to 20 years in L.A. in rape case.* (http://tinyurl.com/yanzaod5) [16]

Associated Press. (2016c). *Purvi Patel to be released after overturned feticide conviction.* (http://tinyurl.com/y9znpk2u) [9]

Associated Press. (2019). *"Free the Nipple" female campaigners lose challenge to US topless conviction.* (https://tinyurl.com/y245cxp9) [3]

Association of LGBTQ Psychiatrists. (2017). *Home page.* (http://www.aglp.org/) [14]

Attwood, F. (2018). Women's pornography. In: K. Harrison & C. A. Ogden (Eds.). *Pornographies: Critical positions.* University of Chester Press. [17]

Averett, P., Yoon, I. & Jenkins, C. L. (2012). Older lesbian sexuality: Identity, sexual behavior, and the impact of aging. *Journal of Sex Research, 49,* 495–507. [14]

AVERT. (2014). *Stories.* (http://tinyurl.com/y93yoxgq) [12]

AVERT. (2019). *Global HIV and AIDS statistics.* (https://tinyurl.com/kusdl78) [15]

Avis, N. E., Colvin, A., Karlamangla, A. S., et al. (2017). Change in sexual functioning over the menopausal transition: Results from the Study of Women's Health Across the Nation. *Menopause, 24,* 379–390. [11]

Avis, N. E., Zhao, X., Johannes, C. B., et al. (2005). Correlates of sexual function among multi-ethnic middle-aged women: Results from the Study of Women's Health Across the Nation (SWAN). *Menopause, 12,* 385–398. [11]

Ayuda, T. (2011). *An Asian American perspective: How to address the stigma surrounding sex* (https://tinyurl.com/y3jzycha) [7]

# B

B4U-ACT. (2017). *Youth, suicidality, and seeking care.* (http://tinyurl.com/y737z3bm) [13]

B4U-ACT. (2019). *Home page.* (www.b4uact.org) [13]

Bach, P. & Brannigan, R. E. (2016). The impact of lifestyle modification on erectile dysfunction. In: L. I. Lipshultz, A. W. Pastuszak, A. T. Goldstein, A. Giraldi & M. A. Perelman (Eds.), *The management of sexual dysfunction in men and women.* Springer. [14]

Bagby, D. (2008). Proud "mama's boys." *Southern Voice*, May 9. [12]

Bailey, J. A., Fleming, C. B., Henson, J. N., et al. (2008). Sexual risk behavior 6 months post–high school: Associations with college attendance, living with a parent, and prior risk behavior. *Journal of Adolescent Health*, 42, 573–579. [7]

Bailey, J. M. (2003). *The man who would be queen: The science of gender-bending and transsexualism.* Joseph Henry Press. [4, 13]

Bailey, M. (2009). *Michael Jackson: Erotic identity disorder?* (https://tinyurl.com/sbnazw4) [13]

Bailey, S. P. (2013). Conservatives say Utah polygamy ruling confirms their worst fears. *Washington Post*, December 16. [11]

BakersfieldNow.com. (2008). Man must pay $12.5M for infecting ex-wife with HIV. (http://tinyurl.com/y7paparv) [15]

Baldwin, J. & Baldwin, J. (2001). *Behavior principles in everyday life (4th ed.).* Prentice Hall. [4]

Bamberg, C., Scheuermann, S., Slowinski, T., et al. (2011). Relationship between fetal head station established using an open magnetic resonance imaging scanner and the angle of progression determined by transperineal ultrasound. *Ultrasound in Obstetrics and Gynecology*, 37, 712–716. [8]

Bancroft, J., Herbenick, D. L. & Reynolds, M. A. (2003). Masturbation as a marker of sexual development. In: J. Bancroft (Ed.), *Sexual development in childhood.* Indiana University Press. [10]

Barnett, M. D., Maciel, I. V., Van Vliet, S. & Marsden, A. D. (2019). Motivations for faking orgasm and orgasm consistency among young adult women. *Personality and Individual Differences*, 149, 83–87. [14]

Barriger, M. & Velez-Blasini, C. J. (2013). Descriptive and injunctive social norm overestimation in hooking up and their role as predictors of hook-up activity in a college student sample. *Journal of Sex Research*, 50, 84–94. [10]

Bartels, A. & Zeki, S. (2000). The neural basis of romantic love. *Neuroreport*, 11, 3829–3834. [7]

Bartels, A. & Zeki, S. (2004). The neural correlates of maternal and romantic love. *Neuroimage*, 21, 1155–1166. [7]

Barth, C., Villringer, A. & Sacher, J. (2015). Sex hormones affect neurotransmitters and shape the adult female brain during hormonal transition periods. *Front Neurosci*, 9, 37. [4]

Barth, J., Bermetz, L., Heim, E., et al. (2013). The current prevalence of child sexual abuse worldwide: A systematic review and meta-analysis. *International Journal of Public Health*, 58, 469–483. [10]

Bartholet, E. (2014). Rethink Harvard's sexual harassment policy. *Boston Globe*, October 15. [16]

Bartz, D. & Greenberg, J. A. (2008). Sterilization in the United States. *Reviews in Obstetrics & Gynecology*, 1, 23–32. [9]

Baseman, J. G. & Koutsky, L. A. (2005). The epidemiology of human papillomavirus infections. *Journal of Clinical Virology*, 32 (Suppl 1), S16–S24. [15]

Basile, K. C., Rostad, W. L., Leemis, R. W., et al. (2018). Protective factors for sexual violence: Understanding how trajectories relate to perpetration in high school. *Prevention Science*, 19, 1123–1132. [16]

Basson, R. (2000). The female sexual response: A different model. *Journal of Sex and Marital Therapy*, 26, 51–65. [5]

Basson, R. (2001). Human sex-response cycles. *Journal of Sex and Marital Therapy*, 27, 33–43. [5, 14]

Basson, R. (2007). Sexual desire/arousal disorders in women. In: S. R. Leiblum (Ed.), *Principles and practice of sex therapy* (4th ed.). Guilford Press. [14]

Basson, R., McInnes, R., Smith, M. D., et al. (2002). Efficacy and safety of sildenafil citrate in women with sexual dysfunction associated with female sexual arousal disorder. *Journal of Women's Health and Gender-Based Medicine*, 11, 367–377. [14]

Bauer, I. L. (2014). Romance tourism or female sex tourism? *Travel Medicine and Infectious Disease*, 12, 20–28. [17]

Baumeister, R. F. & Dhavale, D. (2001). The two sides of romantic rejection. In: M. R. Leary (Ed.), *Interpersonal rejection.* Oxford University Press. [7]

Baumeister, R. F., Wotman, S. R. & Stillwell, A. M. (1993). Unrequited love: On heartbreak, anger, guilt, scriptlessness, and humiliation. *Journal of Personality and Social Psychology*, 64, 377–394. [7]

BBC News. (2018). *Canada province cancels new sex-ed curriculum after protests.* (https://tinyurl.com/y2zspwgc) [6]

Beckerman, S. & Valentine, P. (Eds), (2002). *Cultures of multiple fathers: The theory and practice of partible paternity in lowland South America.* University of Florida Press. [1]

Becks, L. & Agrawal, A. F. (2012). The evolution of sex is favoured during adaptation to new environments. *PLOS Biology*, 10, e1001317. [App. A]

Bedford, J. M. (2015). Human spermatozoa and temperature: The elephant in the room. *Biology of Reproduction*, 93, 97. [3]

Bednarczyk, R. A., Ellingson, M. K. & Omer, S. B. (2019). Human papillomavirus vaccination before 13 and 15 years of age: Analysis of National Immunization Survey teen data. *Journal of Infectious Diseases*, 220, 730–734. [15]

Been, J. V., Nurmatov, U. B., Cox, B., et al. (2014). Effect of smoke-free legislation on perinatal and child health: a systematic review and meta-analysis. *Lancet*, 383, 1549–1960. [8]

Behnia, B., Heinrichs, M., Bergmann, W., et al. (2014). Differential effects of intranasal oxytocin on sexual experiences and partner interactions in couples. *Hormones and Behavior*, 65, 308–318. [5]

Bekiempis, V. (2019). Maryland court: Teen girl who sexted friends violated child pornography laws. *Guardian* (London), August 31. [17]

Belizan, J. M., Althabe, F. & Cafferata, M. L. (2007). Health consequences of the increasing caesarean section rates. *Epidemiology*, 18, 485–486. [8]

Belle, M., Godefroy, D., Couly, G., et al. (2017). Tridimensional visualization and analysis of early human development. *Cell*, 169, 161–173 e112. [4]

Belluck, P. (2018). Federal ban on female genital mutilation ruled unconstitutional by judge. *New York Times*, November 21. [2]

Belva, F., Bonduelle, M., Roelants, M., et al. (2016). Semen quality of young adult ICSI offspring: The first results. *Human Reproduction*, 31, 2811–2820. [3, 8]

Belzer, E., Whipple, B. & Moger, W. (1984). A female ejaculation. *Journal of Sex Research*, 20, 403–406. [5]

Bennett, M. (2013). *Dallas Morning News'* credulity = incredibility (http://tinyurl.com/y9szs5fx) [17]

Bennetts, L. (2011). The john next door. *Newsweek*, July 25. [17]

Benoit, C., Smith, M., Jansson, M., et al. (2019). "The prostitution problem": Claims, evidence, and policy outcomes. *Archives of Sexual Behavior*, 48, 1905–1923. [17]

Bentlage, B. & Eich, T. (2007). *Hymen repair on the Arab Internet.* (http://tinyurl.com/mt8thyl) [2]

Beras, E. (2019). Condom sales lag as millennials have less sex. (https://tinyurl.com/t5bmc7x) [15]

Berdahl, J. L. (2007). The sexual harassment of uppity women. *Journal of Applied Psychology*, 92, 425–437. [16]

Berenbaum, S. A. & Beltz, A. M. (2016). How early hormones shape gender development. *Curr Opin Behav Sci*, 7, 53–60. [4]

Berenbaum, S. A., Bryk, K. K., Nowak, N., et al. (2009). Fingers as a marker of prenatal androgen exposure. *Endocrinology*, 150, 5019–5124. [4]

Bergeron, S., Khalife, S., Dupuis, M. J. & McDuff, P. (2016). A randomized clinical trial comparing group cognitive-behavioral therapy and a topical steroid for women with dyspareunia. *Journal of Consulting and Clinical Psychology*, 84, 259–268. [14]

Bergeron, S., Reed, B. D., Wesselmann, U. & Bohm-Starke, N. (2020). *Vulvodynia.* (https://tinyurl.com/ydadgxvd) [14]

Bergstrand, C. & Blevins Williams, J. (2000). *Today's alternative marriage styles: The case of swingers.* (http://tinyurl.com/na3hx) [11]

Bernstein, E. (2018). *Brokered subjects: Sex, trafficking, and the politics of freedom.* University of Chicago Press. [17]

Bettcher, T. M. (2014). Trapped in the wrong theory: Rethinking trans oppression and resistance. *Signs, 39,* 383–406. [4]

Betzig, L. (2012). Means, variances, and ranges in reproductive success: Comparative evidence. *Evolution and Human Behavior, 33,* 309–317. [App. A]

Biggs, M. A., Rowland, B., McCulloch, C. E. & Foster, D. G. (2016). Does abortion increase women's risk for post-traumatic stress? Findings from a prospective longitudinal cohort study. *BMJ Open, 6,* e009698. [9]

Binik, Y. M., Bergeron, S. & Khalife, S. (2007). Dyspareunia and vaginismus. In: S. R. Leiblum (Ed.), *Principles and practice of sex therapy.* Guilford Press. [14]

Bird, B. S., Schweitzer, R. D. & Strassberg, D. S. (2011). The prevalence and correlates of postcoital dysphoria in women. *International Journal of Sexual Health, 23,* 14–25. [6]

Birkhead, T. R. (1998). *Sperm competition in birds: mechanisms and functions.* In: B. T.R. and A. P. Moller (Eds). Sperm Competition and Sexual Selection. Academic Press. [App. A]

Birkhead, T. R. (2000). *Promiscuity: An evolutionary history of sperm competition.* Cambridge, Mass. Harvard University Press. [7, App. A]

Birnbaum, G. E. (2018). The fragile spell of desire: A functional perspective on changes in sexual desire across relationship development. *Personality & Social Psychology Review, 22,* 101–127. [7]

Birnbaum, G. E. & Reis, H. T. (2019). Evolved to be connected: The dynamics of attachment and sex over the course of romantic relationships. *Current Opinion in Psychology, 25,* 11–15. [7]

Birnbaum, G. E., Kanat-Maymon, Y., Mizrahi, M., et al. (2018). What fantasies can do to your relationship: The effects of sexual fantasies on couple interactions. *Personality & Social Psychology Bulletin,* published online August 18. [5]

Biro, F. M., Galvez, M. P., Greenspan, L. C., et al. (2010). Pubertal assessment method and baseline characteristics in a mixed longitudinal study of girls. *Pediatrics, 126,* e583–e590. [10]

Biro, F. M., Greenspan, L. C., Galvez, M. P., et al. (2013). Onset of breast development in a longitudinal cohort. *Pediatrics, 132,* 1019–1027. [10]

Birth Control Pharmacies. (2019). *Find a birth control pharmacy near you.* (https://tinyurl.com/yyrhlmev) [9]

BishopAccountability. (2019). *Documenting the abuse crisis in the Roman Catholic Church.* (http://tinyurl.com/y7v6utn) [13]

Bivona, J. & Critelli, J. (2009). The nature of women's rape fantasies: An analysis of prevalence, frequency, and contents. *Journal of Sex Research, 46,* 33–45. [5]

Bivona, J. M., Critelli, J. W. & Clark, M. J. (2012). Women's rape fantasies: An empirical

evaluation of the major explanations. *Archives of Sexual Behavior, 41,* 1107–1119. [5]

Blair, E. (2017). Women are speaking up about harassment and abuse, but why now? (http://tinyurl.com/yd48eo53) [16]

Blair, K. L., Cappell, J. & Pukall, C. F. (2018). Not all orgasms were created equal: Differences in frequency and satisfaction of orgasm experiences by sexual activity in same-sex versus mixed-sex relationships. *Journal of Sex Research, 55,* 719–733. [12]

Blake, M. (2014). *Meet the American pastor behind Uganda's anti-gay crackdown.* (http://tinyurl.com/y8bd5y8y) [12]

Blanchard, R. (1993). Varieties of autogynephilia and their relationship to gender dysphoria. *Archives of Sexual Behavior, 22,* 241–251. [13]

Blanchard, R. (2005). Early history of the concept of autogynephilia. *Archives of Sexual Behavior, 34,* 439–446. [4]

Blanchard, R. (2017). Fraternal birth order, family size, and male homosexuality: Meta-analysis of studies spanning 25 years. *Archives of Sexual Behavior, 47*(1), 1–15. [12]

Blanchard, R. & Hucker, S. J. (1991). Age, transvestism, bondage, and concurrent paraphilic activities in 117 fatal cases of autoerotic asphyxia. *British Journal of Psychiatry, 159,* 371–377. [13]

Blanchard, R., Barbaree, H. E., Bogaert, A. F., et al. (2000). Fraternal birth order and sexual orientation in pedophiles. *Archives of Sexual Behavior, 29,* 463–478. [13]

Blanchard, R., Kuban, M. E., Blak, T., et al. (2006). Phallometric comparison of pedophilic interest in nonadmitting sexual offenders against stepdaughters, biological daughters, other biologically related girls, and unrelated girls. *Sexual Abuse, 18,* 1–14. [13]

Bliss, J. (2013). Police, experts: Alcohol most common drug in sexual assaults. (http://tinyurl.com/y9kcxakw) [16]

Boafo, A., Greenham, S., Alenezi, S., et al. (2019). Could long-term administration of melatonin to prepubertal children affect timing of puberty? A clinician's perspective. *Nature and Science of Sleep, 11,* 1–10. [10]

Bockting, W. (1998). Transgender HIV prevention: A qualitative needs assessment. AIDS Care, 10, 505–526.

Bogaert, A. F. (2012). *Understanding asexuality.* Rowman and Littlefield.

Bogaert, A. F., Skorska, M. N., Wang, C., et al. (2018). Male homosexuality and maternal immune responsivity to the Y-linked protein NLGN4Y. *Proceedings of the National Academy of Sciences of the United States of America, 115,* 302–306. [12]

Bongaarts, J. & Sitruk-Ware, R. (2019). Climate change and contraception. *BMJ Sexual & Reproductive Health, 45,* 233–235. [9]

Boone, C. (2017). *Men who sued Eddie Long for sexual misconduct address bishop's death.* (http://tinyurl.com/ya4zqqed) [12]

Boroditsky, L. (2011). How language shapes thought. *Scientific American,* February. [4]

Boroff, D. (2016). *Houston man sentenced to 50 years for producing sick "crush" fetish videos of small animals being tortured, killed.* (http://tinyurl.com/hhw8kf8) [13]

Bos, H. M., Knox, J. R., van Rijn-van Gelderen, L. & Gartrell, N. K. (2016). Same-sex and different-sex parent households and child health outcomes: Findings from the National Survey of Children's Health. *Journal of Developmental and Behavioral Pediatrics, 37,* 179–187. [12]

Bosch, O. J. & Young, L. J. (2018). Oxytocin and social relationships: From attachment to bond disruption. *Currents Topics in Behavioral Neuroscience, 35,* 97–117. [7]

Bossio, J. A., Pukall, C. F. & Steele, S. S. (2016). Examining penile sensitivity in neonatally circumcised and intact men using quantitative sensory testing. *Journal of Urology, 195,* 1848–1853. [3]

Bossip. (2016). *What purity ring, bih? Nick Jonas explains why he broke virginity pledge and started smashing cakes to smithereens.* (http://tinyurl.com/y9e9jagz) [10]

Both, S., Brauer, M., Weijenborg, P. & Laan, E. (2017). Effects of aversive classical conditioning on sexual response in women with dyspareunia and sexually functional controls. *Journal of Sexual Medicine, 14,* 687–701. [5]

Both, S., Spiering, M., Laan, E., et al. (2008). Unconscious classical conditioning of sexual arousal: Evidence for the conditioning of female genital arousal to subliminally presented sexual stimuli. *Journal of Sexual Medicine, 5,* 100–109. [5]

Braithwaite, S. R., Coulson, G., Keddington, K. & Fincham, F. D. (2015). The influence of pornography on sexual scripts and hooking up among emerging adults in college. *Archives of Sexual Behavior, 44,* 111–123. [1]

Brakefield, T. A., Mednick, S. C., Wilson, H. W., et al. (2014). Same-sex sexual attraction does not spread in adolescent social networks. *Archives of Sexual Behavior, 43,* 335–344. [12]

Bramble, M. S., Lipson, A., Vashist, N. & Vilain, E. (2017). Effects of chromosomal sex and hormonal influences on shaping sex differences in brain and behavior: Lessons from cases of disorders of sex development. *Journal of Neuroscience Research, 95,* 65–74. [4]

Brannigan, R. E. & Lipshultz, L. I. (2017). *Sperm transport and capacitation.* (http://tinyurl.com/y92k3brn) [8]

Branstrom, R. & Pachankis, J. E. (2019). Reduction in mental health treatment utilization among transgender individuals after gender-affirming surgeries: A total population study. *American Journal of Psychiatry,* appiajp201919010080. [4]

Bratter, J. L. & King, R. B. (2008). "But will it last?": Marital instability among interracial and same-race couples. *Family Relations, 57,* 160–171. [11]

BreastCancer.org. (2019a). *Breast cancer self-exam.* (https://tinyurl.com/y44gxrk2) [2]

BreastCancer.org. (2019b). *U.S. breast cancer statistics.* (https://tinyurl.com/y7vjo8bn) [2]

Breedlove, S. M. (2010). Organizational hypothesis: instances of the fingerpost. *Endocrinology, 151,* 4116–4122. [4]

Breedlove, S. M. (2019). Replicable data for digit ratio differences. *Science, 365,* 230. [12]

Brennan, R. (2010). *OMG Lady Gaga gives herself mental orgasms!* (http://tinyurl.com/l8yuenu) [6]

Brent, L. J., Franks, D. W., Foster, E. A., et al. (2015). Ecological knowledge, leadership, and the evolution of menopause in killer whales. *Current Biology, 25,* 746–750. [11]

Brents, B. G. & Hausbeck, K. (2005). Violence and legalized brothel prostitution in Nevada. *Journal of Interpersonal Violence, 20,* 270–295. [17]

Bridgeman, B. & Roberts, S. G. (2010). The 4-3-2 method for Kegel exercises. *American Journal of Men's Health, 4,* 75–76. [14]

Bridges, A. J., Sun, C. F., Ezzell, M. B. & Johnson, J. (2016). Sexual scripts and the sexual behavior of men and women who use pornography. *Sexualization, Media, & Society, October-December,* 1–14. [4]

Briggs, N. (2014). Subway rider: I helped take perv down after being sexually assaulted on train. *New York Daily News,* June 23. [13]

Bringle, R. G., Winnick, T. & Rydell, R. J. (2013). *The prevalence and nature of unrequited love.* (http://tinyurl.com/lncsblb) [7]

British Broadcasting Corporation. (2002). *Human instinct: Deepest desires.* (http://tinyurl.com/256jdt) [7]

Brom, M., Both, S., Laan, E., et al. (2014). The role of conditioning, learning and dopamine in sexual behavior: A narrative review of animal and human studies. *Neuroscience and Biobehavioral Reviews, 38,* 38–59. [5]

Brookoff, D., O'Brien, K. K., Cook, C. S., et al. (1997). Characteristics of participants in domestic violence: Assessment at the scene of domestic assault. *JAMA, 277,* 1369–1373. [16]

Brotto, L. A. & Basson, R. (2014). Group mindfulness-based therapy significantly improves sexual desire in women. *Behaviour Research and Therapy, 57,* 43–54. [14]

Brotto, L. A., Bergeron, S., Zdaniuk, B., et al. (2019). A comparison of mindfulness-based cognitive therapy vs cognitive behavioral therapy for the treatment of provoked vestibulodynia in a hospital clinic setting. *Journal of Sexual Medicine, 16,* 909–923. [14]

Brown, A., Barker, E. D. & Rahman, Q. (2019). A systematic scoping review of the prevalence, etiological, psychological, and interpersonal factors associated with BDSM. *Journal of Sex Research,* published online October 16. [13]

Brown, A., Barker, E. D. & Rahman, Q. (2020). Erotic target identity inversions among men and women in an Internet sample. *Journal of Sexual Medicine, 17,* 99–110. [13]

Brown, G. R., Laland, K. N. & Mulder, M. B. (2009). Bateman's principles and human sex roles. *Trends in Ecology & Evolution, 24,* 297–304. [App. A]

Brown, S. L. & Shinohara, S. K. (2013). Dating relationships in older adulthood: A national portrait. *Journal of Marriage & the Family, 75,* 1194–1202. [7]

Brugger, P., Christen, M., Jellestad, L. & Hanggi, J. (2016). Limb amputation and other disability desires as a medical condition. *Lancet Psychiatry, 3,* 1176–1186. [13]

Bryan, E. R., McLachlan, R. I., Rombauts, L., et al. (2019). Detection of chlamydia infection within human testicular biopsies. *Human Reproduction, 34*(10), 1891–1898. [15]

Bryant, D. M., Hoeft, F., Lai, S., et al. (2012). Sex chromosomes and the brain: a study of neuroanatomy in XYY syndrome. *Developmental Medicine and Child Neurology, 54,* 1149–1156. [4]

Buck Louis, G. M., Sundaram, R., Sweeney, A. M., et al. (2014). Urinary bisphenol A, phthalates, and couple fecundity: The Longitudinal Investigation of Fertility and the Environment (LIFE) Study. *Fertility and Sterility, 101*(5), 1359–1366. [3]

Buisson, O. & Jannini, E. A. (2013). Pilot echographic study of the differences in clitoral involvement following clitoral or vaginal sexual stimulation. *Journal of Sexual Medicine, 10,* 2734–2740. [5]

Bulmer, M. G. & Parker, G. A. (2002). The evolution of anisogamy: a game-theoretic approach. *Proceedings of the Royal Society of London. Series B: Biological Sciences, 269,* 2381–2388. [App. A]

Bureau of Justice Statistics. (2011). Intimate partner violence, 1993–2010. (http://tinyurl.com/y9t6nfe7) [16]

Bureau of Justice Statistics. (2013a). Intimate partner violence: Attributes of victimization, 1993–2011. [16]

Bureau of Justice Statistics. (2013b). Sexual victimization in prisons and jails reported by inmates, 2011–12. (http://tinyurl.com/y7kyyc4q) [16]

Bureau of Justice Statistics. (2016). Campus Climate Survey validation study final technical report. (http://tinyurl.com/y9kzxvoy) [16]

Bureau of Justice Statistics. (2017). Rape and sexual assault among college-age females, 1995–2013. (http://tinyurl.com/ycssu99j) [16]

Bureau of Justice Statistics. (2019a). Criminal victimization, 2018. (https://tinyurl.com/yxet3gqd) [16]

Bureau of Justice Statistics. (2019b). Prisoners in 2017. (https://tinyurl.com/yytwbw8o) [16]

Bureau of Justice Statistics. (2019c). Recidivism of sex offenders released from state prison: A 9-year follow-up (2005–14). (https://tinyurl.com/vv5caef) [16]

Burke, A. E. (2011). The state of hormonal contraception today: benefits and risks of hormonal contraceptives: progestin-only contraceptives. *American Journal of Obstetrics and Gynecology, 205,* S14–S17. [9]

Buss, D. M. (2000). *The dangerous passion: Why jealousy is as necessary as love and sex.* Free Press. [7]

Buss, D. M. (2011). *Evolutionary psychology: The new science of the mind* (4th ed.). Pearson. [7]

Buss, D. M. (2013). Sexual jealousy. *Psychological Topics, 22,* 155–182. [4]

Buss, D. M. (2018). Sexual and emotional infidelity: Evolved gender differences in jealousy prove robust and replicable. *Perspectives in Psychological Science, 13,* 155–160. [7]

Buss, D. M. & Schmitt, D. P. (2019). Mate Preferences and Their Behavioral Manifestations. *Annual Review of Psychology, 70,* 77–110. [4]

Bussey, K. & Bandura, A. (1984). Influence of gender constancy and social power on sex-linked modeling. *Journal of Personality and Social Psychology, 47,* 1292–1302. [4]

BuzzFeed News. (2019). *Period tracker apps used by millions of women are sharing incredibly sensitive data with Facebook.* (https://tinyurl.com/y5dexqwb) [9]

Buzzfeed. (2019). *Pornhub just released their 2018 end of year review and it's really something.* (https://tinyurl.com/y6k64jug)

Byne, W., Tobet, S., Mattiace, L. A., et al. (2001). The interstitial nuclei of the human anterior hypothalamus: An investigation of variation with sex, sexual orientation, and HIV status. *Hormones and Behavior, 40,* 86–92. [12]

## C

Cacciatore, R. S., Ingman-Friberg, S. M., Lainiala, L. P. & Apter, D. L. (2020). Verbal and behavioral expressions of child sexuality among 1–6-year-olds as observed by daycare professionals in Finland. *Archives of Sexual Behavior,* Published online, April 15. Burleigh, P. (2019). *A 4-year-old trapped in a teenager's body.* (https://tinyurl.com/y4zq5jjq) [10]

Campanile, C. (2017). *New case of neonatal herpes caused by Jewish circumcision.* (https://tinyurl.com/y62ghblg) [3]

Campbell, D. W. & Eaton, W. O. (1999). Sex differences in the activity level of infants. *Infant and Child Development, 8,* 1–17. [4]

Camperio Ciani, A., Battaglia, U. & Zanzotto, G. (2015). Human homosexuality: A paradigmatic arena for sexually antagonistic selection? *Cold Spring Harbor Perspectives in Biology, 7,* a017657. [12]

Canadian Paediatric Society. (2015). *Newborn male circumcision.* (http://tinyurl.com/l5s7qx8) [3]

Canan, S. N. & Levand, M. A. (2019). A feminist perspective on sexual assault. In: W. T. O'Donohue and P. A. Schewe (Eds.). *Handbook of sexual assault and sexual assault prevention.* Springer. [16]

Cant, M. A. & Croft, D. P. (2019). Life-history evolution: Grandmothering in space and time. *Current Biology, 29,* R215–R218. [11]

Capel, B. (2017). Vertebrate sex determination: evolutionary plasticity of a fundamental owitch. *Nature Reviews Genetics, 10,* 675–689. [App. A]

Capogrosso, P., Colicchia, M., Ventimiglia, E., et al. (2013). One patient out of four with newly diagnosed erectile dysfunction is a young man—worrisome picture from the everyday clinical practice. *Journal of Sexual Medicine, 10,* 1833–1841. [14]

Cappelletti, M. & Wallen, K. (2016). Increasing women's sexual desire: The comparative effectiveness of estrogens and androgens. *Hormones and Behavior, 78,* 178–193. [5, 14]

Cappelletti, S., Aromatario, M., Bottoni, E., et al. (2016). Variability in findings of anogenital injury in consensual and non-consensual fisting intercourse: A systematic review. *Journal of Forensic and Legal Medicine, 44,* 58–62. [6]

Carbon, C. C., Faerber, S. J., Augustin, M. D., et al. (2018). First gender, then attractiveness: Indications of gender-specific attractiveness processing via ERP onsets. *Neuroscience Letters, 686,* 186–192. [App. B]

Carey, B. (2005). Straight, gay or lying? Bisexuality revisited. *New York Times,* July 5. [12]

Carey, K. B., Durney, S. E., Shepardson, R. L. & Carey, M. P. (2015). Incapacitated and forcible rape of college women: Prevalence across the first year. *Journal of Adolescent Health, 56,* 678–680. [16]

Carlsen, E., Giwercman, A., Keiding, N. & Skakkebaek, N. E. (1992). Evidence for decreasing quality of semen during past 50 years. *BMJ, 305,* 609–613. [3]

Carlson, A. & Helling, S. (2017). *Mary Kay Letourneau's former student files for separation from her 21 years after illicit affair.* (http://tinyurl.com/yd75ddwc) [13]

Carnes, P. (2001). *Out of the shadows: Understanding sexual addiction* (3rd ed.). Hazelden. [14]

Carnes, P. J. & Adams, K. M. (2019). *Clinical management of sex addiction.* Routledge. [14]

Caron, S. L. & Ahlgrim, C. J. (2012). Children's understanding and knowledge of conception and birth: Comparing children from England, the Netherlands, Sweden, and the United States. *American Journal of Sexuality Education, 7,* 16–36. [10]

Carpenter, A. & Gates, J. (2016). The nature and extent of gang involvement in sex trafficking in San Diego County. (http://tinyurl.com/yaumuq3e) [17]

Carpenter, L. M. (2005). *Virginity lost: An intimate portrait of first sexual experiences.* New York University Press. [10]

Carter, C. S. & Getz, L. L. (1993). Monogamy and the prairie vole. *Scientific American, 268,* 100–106. [App. A]

Carter, D. (2012). Comprehensive sex education for teens is more effective than abstinence. *American Journal of Nursing, 112,* 15. [10]

Carter, R. B. (1853). *On the pathology and treatment of hysteria.* John Churchill. [2]

Casanova, J. (1789/2015). *The complete memoirs of Casanova.* Benediction Classics. [9]

Cassar, J. (2016). *The woman who married the Eiffel Tower wants to set the record straight about objectum sexuality.* (http://tinyurl.com/jgt8buq) [13]

Catholic Education Resource Center. (2004). *Masturbation: Mortal sin?* (https://tinyurl.com/y5j6vwv9) [6]

*Catholic News-Herald.* (2009). *Birth-control pill is linked to male infertility, says Vatican paper.* (http://tinyurl.com/y9sauvo3) [9]

Caughey, A. B. & Cheyney, M. (2019). Home and birth center birth in the United States: time for greater collaboration across models of care. *Obstetrics and Gynecology, 133,* 1033–1050. [8]

CBC News. (2020). *Sex doll is child porn, but judge finds Kenneth Harrisson not guilty.* (https://tinyurl.com/y4w59fjl) [13]

CDC (Centers for Disease Control and Prevention). (1989). *First 100,000 cases of acquired immunodeficiency syndrome—United States.* (http://tinyurl.com/y7dd8vbs) [12]

CDC (Centers for Disease Control and Prevention). (2007). *Drug use and sexual behaviors reported by adults: United States, 1999–2002.* (http://tinyurl.com/y8rehttj) [10]

CDC (Centers for Disease Control and Prevention). (2011a). *National Intimate Partner and Sexual Violence Survey.* (http://tinyurl.com/y9xo5xcl) [16]

CDC (Centers for Disease Control and Prevention). (2011b). *Sexual behavior, sexual attraction, and sexual identity in the United States: Data from the 2006–2008 National Survey of Family Growth.* (http://tinyurl.com/y9jyzxkc) [11]

CDC (Centers for Disease Control and Prevention). (2012). *First marriages in the United States: Data from the 2006–2010 National Survey of Family Growth.* (http://tinyurl.com/yc4luhg) [11]

CDC (Centers for Disease Control and Prevention). (2013a). *First premarital cohabitation in the United States: 2006–2010 National Survey of Family Growth.* (http://tinyurl.com/y7u796xk) [11]

CDC (Centers for Disease Control and Prevention). (2013b). *The National Intimate Partner and Sexual Violence Survey (NISVS): 2010 findings on victimization by sexual orientation.* (http://tinyurl.com/ybdvmsm8) [16]

CDC (Centers for Disease Control and Prevention). (2013c). *Trends in circumcision for male newborns in U.S. hospitals: 1979–2010.* (http://tinyurl.com/m2w5hju) [3]

CDC (Centers for Disease Control and Prevention). (2014). *Youth Risk Behavior Survey—United States, 2013.* (http://tinyurl.com/j44ph9l) [10]

CDC (Centers for Disease Control and Prevention). (2015a). *Health, United States, 2015.* (http://tinyurl.com/mz88wpe) [2]

CDC (Centers for Disease Control and Prevention). (2015b). *Sexual risk behaviors and academic achievement.* (http://tinyurl.com/y7dhru4t) [10]

CDC (Centers for Disease Control and Prevention). (2016a). *Sexual identity, sex of sexual contacts, and health-related behaviors among students in grades 9–12—United States and selected sites, 2015.* (http://tinyurl.com/ydcvdcnn) [10]

CDC (Centers for Disease Control and Prevention). (2016b). *Youth risk behavior surveillance, United States, 2015.* (http://tinyurl.com/ydahtrfg) [10]

CDC (Centers for Disease Control and Prevention). (2017a). *Effectiveness of family planning methods.* (http://tinyurl.com/ya8t92y4) [9]

CDC (Centers for Disease Control and Prevention). (2017b). *HIV and AIDS in the United States.* (http://tinyurl.com/y7bvnpzs) [15]

CDC (Centers for Disease Control and Prevention). (2017c). *Key statistics from the National Survey of Family Growth* (http://tinyurl.com/y7wxh36u) [10, 11]

CDC (Centers for Disease Control and Prevention). (2017d). *Key statistics from the National Survey of Family Growth—S Listing.* (http://tinyurl.com/y937jswd) [12]

CDC (Centers for Disease Control and Prevention). (2017e). *Key statistics from the National Survey of Family Growth—N listing.* (https://tinyurl.com/y2gluqu8) [11]

CDC (Centers for Disease Control and Prevention). (2017f). *Pre-exposure prophylaxis (PrEP).* (http://tinyurl.com/yddd3xxn) [15]

CDC (Centers for Disease Control and Prevention). (2017g). *State-specific rates of primary and secondary syphilis among men who have sex with men—United States, 2015.* (https://tinyurl.com/t5toldt) [15]

CDC (Centers for Disease Control and Prevention). (2017h). *Two cases of Legionnaires' disease in newborns after water births—Arizona, 2016.* (http://tinyurl.com/yc7szhsh) [8]

CDC (Centers for Disease Control and Prevention). (2017i). *Zika cases in the United States.* (http://tinyurl.com/ybhumxtq) [15]

CDC (Centers for Disease Control and Prevention). (2018a). *Background, methods, and synthesis of scientific information used to inform "Information for providers to share with male patients and parents regarding male circumcision and the prevention of HIV infection, sexually transmitted infections, and other health outcomes."* (https://tinyurl.com/yxaaeakp) [3]

CDC (Centers for Disease Control and Prevention). (2018b). *Before pregnancy.* (http://tinyurl.com/y9xacw8o) [8]

CDC (Centers for Disease Control and Prevention). (2018c). *Breastfeeding report card.* (https://tinyurl.com/yaj7gwl2) [8]

CDC (Centers for Disease Control and Prevention). (2018d). *Provisional number of marriages and marriage rate: United States, 2000–2017.* (https://tinyurl.com/y6b54cjc) [11]

CDC (Centers for Disease Control and Prevention). (2018e). *The National Intimate Partner and Sexual Violence Survey: 2015 data brief—updated release.* (https://tinyurl.com/sm8fdhf) [16]

CDC (Centers for Disease Control and Prevention). (2018f). *Youth Risk Behavior Survey data summary & trends report 2007–2017.* (https://tinyurl.com/y8wojj3a) [10]

CDC (Centers for Disease Control and Prevention). (2019a). *Assisted reproductive technology surveillance—United States, 2016.* (https://tinyurl.com/y6exqqr2) [8]

CDC (Centers for Disease Control and Prevention). (2019b). *Basics about FASDs.* (https://tinyurl.com/y8sjx2u8) [8]

CDC (Centers for Disease Control and Prevention). (2019c). *Births in the United States, 2018.* (https://tinyurl.com/yyld6fkp) [8]

CDC (Centers for Disease Control and Prevention). (2019d). *Expedited partner therapy.* (https://tinyurl.com/yahbochc) [15]

CDC (Centers for Disease Control and Prevention). (2019e). *Gonorrhea.* (https://tinyurl.com/u6ddqsq) [15]

CDC (Centers for Disease Control and Prevention). (2019f). *Increased methamphetamine, injection drug, and heroin use among women and heterosexual men with primary and secondary syphilis—United States, 2013–2017.* (https://tinyurl.com/wdwgshc) [15]

CDC (Centers for Disease Control and Prevention). (2019g). *Pregnancy-related deaths, United States, 2011–2015, and strategies for prevention, 13 states, 2013–2017.* (https://tinyurl.com/yx9uuld2) [8]

CDC (Centers for Disease Control and Prevention). (2019h). *Preventing intimate partner violence.* (https://tinyurl.com/y27fdf5c) [16]

CDC (Centers for Disease Control and Prevention). (2019i). *Sexually transmitted disease surveillance 2018.* (https://tinyurl.com/y6s9furz) [15]

CDC (Centers for Disease Control and Prevention). (2019j). *Smoking, pregnancy, and babies.* (https://tinyurl.com/y68vm8l5) [8]

CDC (Centers for Disease Control and Prevention). (2019k). *Vaginal candidiasis.* (https://tinyurl.com/y4fu3yaq) [2]

CDC (Centers for Disease Control and Prevention). (2020). *Zika virus.* (https://tinyurl.com/h8d3jte) [15]

Central Intelligence Agency. (2019). *World Factbook: Liechtenstein.* (https://tinyurl.com/bsju5zh) [8]

Central Intelligence Agency. (n.d.). *World factbook: Sex ratio.* (https://tinyurl.com/sl2f8qq) [App. A]

Chadwick, S. B., Francisco, M. & van Anders, S. M. (2019). When orgasms do not equal pleasure: Accounts of "bad" orgasm experiences during consensual sexual encounters. *Archives of Sexual Behavior, 48,* 2435–2459. [5]

Chalabi, M. (2015). *How many women don't use tampons?* (http://tinyurl.com/m3ttoyj) [2]

Chalett, J. M. & Nerenberg, L. T. (2000). "Blue balls": A diagnostic consideration in testiculoscrotal pain in young adults: A case report and discussion. *Pediatrics, 106,* 843. [5]

Chan, J., Mojumder, P. & Ghose, A. (2019). The digital sin city: An empirical study of Craigslist's impact on prostitution trends. *Information Systems Research,* published online March 5. [17]

Chang, S., Nazem, T. G., Gounko, D., et al. (2018). Eleven-year longitudinal study of U.S. sperm donors demonstrates declining sperm count and motility. *Fertility and Sterility, 110,* e54–e55. [3]

Changoiwala, P. (2019). *How India fails its rape survivors.* (https://tinyurl.com/v22vlfg) [16]

Chantry, K. & Craig, R. J. (1994). Psychological screening of sexually violent offenders with the MCMI. *Journal of Clinical Psychology, 50,* 430–435. [16]

Chauncey, G. (2019). *Gay New York: Gender, urban culture and the making of the gay male world, 1890–1940* (updated edition). Basic Books. [1]

Chekroud, A. M., Ward, E. J., Rosenberg, M. D. & Holmes, A. J. (2016). Patterns in the human brain mosaic discriminate males from females. *Proceedings of the National Academy of Sciences of the United States of America.* [4]

Chen, L. P., Murad, M. H., Paras, M. L., et al. (2010). Sexual abuse and lifetime diagnosis of psychiatric disorders: systematic review and meta-analysis. *Mayo Clinic Proceedings, 85,* 618–629. [10]

Chen, L. W., Wu, Y., Neelakantan, N., et al. (2016). Maternal caffeine intake during pregnancy and risk of pregnancy loss: a categorical and dose-response meta-analysis of prospective studies. *Public Health Nutrition, 19,* 1233–1244. [8]

Chen, M., Rao, Y., Zheng, Y., et al. (2014). Association between soy isoflavone intake and breast cancer risk for pre- and post-menopausal women: A meta-analysis of epidemiological studies. *PLOS One, 9,* e89288. [11]

Cheval, B., Radel, R., Grob, E., et al. (2016). Homophobia: An impulsive attraction to the same sex? Evidence from eye-tracking data in a picture-viewing task. *Journal of Sexual Medicine, 13,* 825–834. [12]

Chida, Y. & Mao, X. (2009). Does psychosocial stress predict symptomatic herpes simplex virus recurrence? A meta-analytic investigation on prospective studies. *Brain, Behavior, and Immunity, 23,* 917–925. [15]

Children's Bureau. (2018). *The AFCARS report.* (https://tinyurl.com/yxbxcgdh) [8]

Chivers, M. L. (2017). The specificity of women's sexual response and its relationship with sexual orientations: A review and ten hypotheses. *Archives of Sexual Behavior, 46,* 1161–1179. [12]

Choi, Y. D., Park, C. W., Jang, J., et al. (2013). Effects of Korean ginseng berry extract on sexual function in men with erectile dysfunction: A multicenter, placebo-controlled, double-blind clinical study. *International Journal of Impotence Research, 25,* 45–50. [5]

Christensen, K. (2019). The stunning toll of Boy Scout sex abuse: More than 12,200 reported victims. *Los Angeles Times,* May 15. [13]

Chun, A. B., Rose, S., Mitrani, C., et al. (1997). Anal sphincter structure and function in homosexual males engaging in anoreceptive intercourse. *American Journal of Gastroenterology, 92,* 465–468. [6]

Chung, H. S., Hwang, I., Oh, K. J., et al. (2015). The effect of Korean red ginseng on sexual function in premenopausal women: Placebo-controlled, double-blind, crossover clinical trial. *Evidence-Based Complementary & Alternative Medicine, 2015,* 913158. [5]

Cicchese, H. (2014). College class tries to revive the lost art of dating. *Boston Globe,* May 16. [7]

Ciftcioglu, S. & Erci, B. (2009). Coitus interruptus as a contraceptive method: Turkish women's perceptions and experiences. *Journal of Advanced Nursing, 65,* 1686–1694. [9]

City of Philadelphia. (2019). City reports promising reductions in new HIV infections. (https://tinyurl.com/w9y7mkr) [15]

Clark, A. (2015). Burning down the house: Why the debate over *Paris Is Burning* rages on. *Guardian (London),* June 24. [12]

Clark, B. (2017). AI creates fake celebrity porn for Redditors to fap to. (http://tinyurl.com/y9gl2hlh) [17]

Clark, R. D. & Hatfield, E. (1989). Gender differences in receptivity to sexual offers. *Journal of Psychology and Human Sexuality, 2,* 39–55. [7]

Clark, R. D., III & Hatfield, E. (2003). Love in the afternoon. *Psychological Inquiry, 14,* 227–231. [7]

Clark, S. K., Jeglic, E. L., Calkins, C. & Tatar, J. R. (2014). More than a nuisance: The prevalence and consequences of frotteurism and exhibitionism. *Sexual Abuse, 28,* 3–19. [13]

Clarke, D. L., Buccimazza, I., Anderson, F. A. & Thomson, S. R. (2005). Colorectal foreign bodies. *Colorectal Disease, 7,* 98–103. [6]

Clarke, M., Brown, S. & Vollm, B. (2017). Circles of Support and Accountability for sex offenders: A systematic review of outcomes. *Sexual Abuse, 29,* 446–478. [13]

Clarridge, C. (2010). Man who ran animal-sex operation sentenced for probation violation. *Seattle Times,* July 16. [13]

Clement, K., Vaisse, C., Lahlou, N., et al. (1998). A mutation in the human leptin receptor gene causes obesity and pituitary dysfunction. *Nature, 392,* 398–401. [10]

ClinicalTrials.gov. (2020). *Safety and efficacy of 4 investigational HSV 2 vaccines in adults with recurrent genital herpes caused by HSV 2 (HSV15).* (https://tinyurl.com/ya2bmpsu) [15]

Clutton-Brock, T. (2007). Sexual selection in males and females. *Science, 318,* 1882–1885. [App. A]

Clutton-Brock, T. (2017). Reproductive competition and sexual selection. *Philosophical Transactions of the Royal Society of London. Series B: Biological Sciences, 372.* [App. A]

CNN. (2014). *Hopkins to pay $190 million after doctor secretly photographed patients.* (http://tinyurl.com/kzb6wwj) [13]

CNN. (2017a). *California lowers penalty for knowingly exposing partners to HIV.* (http://tinyurl.com/y767n99z) [15]

CNN. (2017b). *Pakistani village elders order retaliatory rape of 17-year-old girl.* (http://tinyurl.com/y6wldxad) [16]

CNN. (2017c). *Sick, dying and raped in America's nursing homes.* (http://tinyurl.com/zz2vwku) [16]

Coalition for Biblical Sexuality. (2017). *Nashville statement.* (http://tinyurl.com/y8f6xrad) [12]

Cochrane Collaboration. (2009). *Antenatal perineal massage for reducing perineal trauma.* (http://tinyurl.com/yac5fdnh) [8]

Cohen, C. R., Lingappa, J. R., Baeten, J. M., et al. (2012). Bacterial vaginosis associated with increased risk of female-to-male HIV-1 transmission: A prospective cohort analysis among African couples. *PLOS Medicine, 9,* e1001251. [15]

Cohen, S. D. & Goldstein, I. (2016). Diagnosis and management of female orgasmic disorder. In: L. I. Lipshultz, A. W. Pastuszak, A. T. Goldstein, A. Giraldi & M. A. Perelman (Eds.), *Management of sexual dysfunction in men and women.* Springer. [14]

Cohen, S. L., Ajao, M. O., Clark, N. V., et al. (2017). Outpatient hysterectomy volume in the United States. *Obstetrics and Gynecology, 130,* 130–137. [2]

Cole, L. A. (2012). The hCG assay or pregnancy test. *Clinical Chemistry and Laboratory Medicine, 50,* 617–630. [8]

Coleman, P. K., Coyle, C. T., Shuping, M. & Rue, V. M. (2009). Induced abortion and anxiety, mood, and substance abuse disorders: isolating the effects of abortion in the National Comorbidity Survey. *Journal of Psychiatric Research, 43,* 770–776. [9]

College Confidential. (2014). *Would you go to prom without a date?* (http://tinyurl.com/yauuf6mu) [10]

Collier, K. L., Horn, S. S., Bos, H. M. & Sandfort, T. G. (2014). Attitudes toward lesbians and gays among American and Dutch adolescents. *Journal of Sex Research, 52,* 140–150. [12]

Collins, G. (2014). This is what 80 looks like. *New York Times,* March 22. [11]

Collins, R. L. (2011). Content analysis of gender roles in media: Where are we now and where should we go? *Sex Roles, 64,* 290–298. [1]

Collins, R. L., Elliott, M. N., Berry, S. H., et al. (2004). Watching sex on television predicts adolescent initiation of sexual behavior. *Pediatrics, 114,* e280–289. [1]

Condomfinder. (2019). *Find free condoms.* (www.condomfinder.org) [9]

Confer, J. C. & Cloud, M. D. (2011). Sex differences in response to imagining a partner's heterosexual or homosexual affair. *Personality and Individual Differences, 50,* 129–134. [7]

Conley, K. (2017). Sex crimes are skyrocketing in NYC subways: State senator. *New York Post,* June 6. [13]

Conley, T. D., Ziegler, A., Moors, A. C., et al. (2013). A critical examination of popular assumptions about the benefits and outcomes of monogamous relationships. *Personality and Social Psychology Review, 17,* 124–141. [11]

Cook, N. R., Lee, I. M., Zhang, S. M., et al. (2013). Alternate-day, low-dose aspirin and cancer risk: Long-term observational follow-up of a randomized trial. *Annals of Internal Medicine, 159,* 77–85. [2]

Cooke, S., Tyler, J. P. & Driscoll, G. L. (1995). Hyperspermia: The forgotten condition? *Human Reproduction, 10,* 367–368. [3]

Cooper, A. (Ed.) (2002). *Sex and the internet: A guidebook for clinicians.* Brunner–Routledge. [7]

Corona, G., Isidori, A. M., Aversa, A., et al. (2016). Endocrinologic control of men's sexual desire and arousal/erection. *Journal of Sexual Medicine, 13,* 317–337. [5]

Cortes, M. E., Carrera, B., Rioseco, H., et al. (2015). The role of kisspeptin in the onset of puberty and in the ovulatory mechanism: A mini-review. *Journal of Pediatric and Adolescent Gynecology, 28,* 286–291. [10]

Cosmopolitan. (2017). *All 25 MTV Movie Awards "Best Kiss" Winners, ranked.* (http://tinyurl.com/lc4r5jn)

Coulter, R. W. S., Mair, C., Miller, E., et al. (2017). Prevalence of past-year sexual assault victimization among undergraduate students: Exploring differences by and intersections of gender identity, sexual identity, and race/ethnicity. *Prevention Science, 18,* 726–736. [16]

Council on Contemporary Families. (2009). *Are babies bad for marriage?* (http://tinyurl.com/y8ar5nuo) [8]

Court of Arbitration for Sport. (2019). *CAS arbitration: Caster Semenya, Athletics South Africa (ASA) and International Association of Athletics Federations (IAAF): Decision.* (https://tinyurl.com/yy4nf7he) [4]

Cowley, A. D. (2014). "Let's get drunk and have sex": The complex relationship of alcohol, gender, and sexual victimization. *Journal of Interpersonal Violence, 29,* 1258–1278. [16]

Coyne, S. M., Linder, J. R., Rasmussen, E. E., et al. (2016). Pretty as a Princess: Longitudinal Effects of Engagement With Disney Princesses on Gender Stereotypes, Body Esteem, and Prosocial Behavior in Children. *Child Development, 87,* 1909–1925. [4]

Coyne, S. M., Stockdale, L., Linder, J. R., et al. (2017). Pow! Boom! Kablam! Effects of Viewing Superhero Programs on Aggressive, Prosocial, and Defending Behaviors in Preschool Children. *Journal of Abnormal Child Psychology.* [4]

Craig, L. K. & Gray, P. B. (2018). Pubic hair removal in cross-cultural perspective. *Cross-Cultural Research, 53,* 215–237. [2]

Cravens, J. D. & Whiting, J. B. (2015). Fooling around on Facebook: The perceptions of infidelity behavior on social networking sites. *Journal of Couple & Relationship Therapy, 15*(3), 213–231. [7]

Crimes Against Children Research Center. (2014). *Trends in unwanted online experiences and sexting.* (http://tinyurl.com/kefavjf) [10]

Crissman, H. P., Berger, M. B., Graham, L. F. & Dalton, V. K. (2017). Transgender

demographics: A household probability sample of US adults, 2014. *American Journal of Public Health, 107,* 213–215. [4]

Crocker, W. H. & Crocker, J. G. (2003). *The Canela: Kinship, ritual and sex in an Amazonian tribe* (2nd. ed.). Wadsworth. [1]

Crompton, L. (2003). *Homosexuality and civilization.* Harvard University Press. [12]

Cui, M. & Donnellan, M. B. (2009). Trajectories of conflict over raising adolescent children and marital satisfaction. *Journal of Marriage and Family, 71,* 479–494. [11]

Cummz, C. (2014). What it's really like to be a porn star. (http://tinyurl.com/y8gt5zxr) [17]

Cunningham, G. R., Stephens-Shields, A. J., Rosen, R. C., et al. (2016). Testosterone treatment and sexual function in older men with low testosterone levels. *Journal of Clinical Endocrinology and Metabolism, 101,* 3096–3104. [14]

Cunningham, S. & Kendall, T. D. (2010). Prostitution labor supply and education. (http://tinyurl.com/y8z8n7at) [17]

Cunningham, S. & Shah, M. (2014). Decriminalizing indoor prostitution: Implications for sexual violence and public health. (https://tinyurl.com/yyme8o5b) [17]

**D**

da Silva, J. (2018). The evolution of sexes: A specific test of the disruptive selection theory. *Ecology & Evolution, 8,* 207–219.

Dadlez, E. M., Andrews, W. L., Lewis, C. & Stroud, M. (2009). Rape, evolution, and pseudoscience: Natural selection in the academy. *Journal of Social Philosophy, 40,* 75–96. [16]

Dahabreh, I. J. & Paulus, J. K. (2011). Association of episodic physical and sexual activity with triggering of acute cardiac events: Systematic review and meta-analysis. *Journal of the American Medical Association, 305,* 1225–1233. [6]

Dahl, D. W., Vohs, K. D. & Sengupta, J. (2011). Sex in advertising: Only on Mars and not on Venus? *GfK Marketing Intelligence Review, 3,* 54–57. [17]

Daily Mirror. (2016). *Incredible moment hungry newborn baby uses natural instinct as he 'breast crawls' to find mum's nipple.* (https://tinyurl.com/y2rt5okq) [8]

Daily Nation. (2016). *Kenya: over 20,000 HIV infections averted by adult make circumcision tool Prepex.* (http://tinyurl.com/kthbs9d) [3]

Daily News. (2019). *Perversion of justice: A proposal to ban subway gropers is a bad idea whose time has not yet come.* (https://tinyurl.com/yxg382rt) [13]

Dalla, R. L. (2000). Exposing the "Pretty Woman" myth: A qualitative examination of the lives of female streetwalking prostitutes. *Journal of Sex Research, 37,* 344–353. [17]

Dallas Morning News. (2013). Editorial: *Cracking down on sex traffickers.* (http://tinyurl.com/yayr59f4) [17]

Darling, C. A., Davidson, J. K., Sr. & Jennings, D. A. (1991). The female sexual response revisited: Understanding the multiorgasmic experience in women. *Archives of Sexual Behavior, 20,* 527–540. [5]

Das, A. (2007). Masturbation in the United States. *Journal of Sex and Marital Therapy, 33,* 301–317. [6]

Davey Smith, G., Frankel, S. & Yarnell, J. (1997). Sex and death: Are they related? Findings from the Caerphilly Cohort Study. *BMJ, 315,* 1641–1644. [11]

Davies, L. (2014). Pope Francis encourages mothers to breastfeed—even in the Sistine Chapel. *The Guardian (London),* January 12. [3]

Davies, S. L., Glaser, D. & Kossoff, R. (2000). Children's sexual play and behavior in pre–school settings: Staff's perceptions, reports, and responses. *Child Abuse and Neglect, 24,* 1329–1343. [10]

Davis, M. K. & Gidycz, C. A. (2000). Child sexual abuse prevention programs: A meta-analysis. *Journal of Clinical Child Psychology, 29,* 257–265. [10]

Davis, S. R. & Davison, S. L. (2012). Current perspectives on testosterone therapy for women. *Menopausal Medicine, 20*(2), S1–S4. [10]

Davis, S. R., Baber, R., Panay, N., et al. (2019). Global consensus position statement on the use of testosterone therapy for women. *Journal of Clinical Endocrinology and Metabolism, 104,* 4660–4666. [14]

Davis, S. R., Worsley, R., Miller, K. K., et al. (2016). Androgens and female sexual function and dysfunction: Findings from the Fourth International Consultation of Sexual Medicine. *Journal of Sexual Medicine, 13,* 168–178. [5]

Dawson, S. J. & Chivers, M. L. (2014). Gender-specificity of solitary and dyadic sexual desire among gynephilic and androphilic women and men. *Journal of Sexual Medicine, 11,* 980–994. [12]

Dawson, S. J., Suschinsky, K. D. & Lalumiere, M. L. (2012). Sexual fantasies and viewing times across the menstrual cycle: A diary study. *Archives of Sexual Behavior, 41,* 173–183. [5]

Days for Girls International. (2019). *Turning periods into pathways.* (https://tinyurl.com/y4qv69lo) [2]

de Graaf, P. M. & Kalmijn, M. (2006). Divorce motives in a period of rising divorce: Evidence from a Dutch life-history survey. *Journal of Family Issues, 27,* 483–505. [11]

de Magalhaes, P. (1576/1922). *The histories of Brazil.* Cortes Society. [4]

De Smet, D., Van Speybroeck, L. & Verplaetse, J. (2014). The Westermarck effect revisited: A psychophysiological study of sibling incest aversion in young female adults. *Evolution and Human Behavior, 35,* 34–42. [5]

de Waal, F. B. M. (2016). Bonobos use sex to cool tempers. Scientific American Mind. [1]

De Zutter, A., Horselenberg, R. & van Koppen, P. J. (2018). Motives for filing a false allegation of rape. *Archives of Sexual Behavior, 47,* 457–464. [16]

Dehlin, J. P., Galliher, R. V., Bradshaw, W. S., et al. (2015). Sexual orientation change efforts among current or former LDS Church members. *Journal of Counseling Psychology, 62,* 95–105. [12]

Del Guidice, M. (2019). Mesuring sex differences and similarities. In: D. P. VanderLaan and W. I. Wong (Eds). *Gender and sexuality development: Contemporary theory and research.* Springer. [4]

Dellis, A. E., Arkoumanis, T., Kyprianou, C. & Papatsoris, A. G. (2018). Paraffinoma, siliconoma and Co: disastrous consequences of failed penile augmentation: A single-centre successful surgical management of a challenging entity. *Andrologia, 50,* e13109. [3]

DeMaris, A. (2013). Burning the candle at both ends: Extramarital sex as a precursor of marital disruption. *Journal of Family Issues, 34,* 1474–1499. [11]

Deng, J. M., Satoh, K., Wang, H., et al. (2011). Generation of viable male and female mice from two fathers. *Biology of Reproduction, 84,* 613–618. [12]

Denizet-Lewis, B. (2004). Friends, friends with benefits and the benefits of the local mall. *New York Times,* May 30. [10]

Depmann, M., Faddy, M. J., van der Schouw, Y. T., et al. (2015). The relationship between variation in size of the primordial follicle pool and age at natural menopause. *Journal of Clinical Endocrinology and Metabolism, 100,* E845–E851. [11]

Depree, B. (2016). *Our new survey: A few stats on vibrator use.* (https://tinyurl.com/y6aauk8h) [6]

Dever, V. M. (1996). Aquinas on the practice of prostitution. (http://tinyurl.com/yaqasxaj) [17]

Devries, K. M., Mak, J. Y., Bacchus, L. J., et al. (2013). Intimate partner violence and incident depressive symptoms and suicide attempts: A systematic review of longitudinal studies. *PLOS Medicine, 10,* e1001439. [16]

Diamond, L. M. (2008). *Sexual fluidity: Understanding women's love and desire.* Harvard University Press. [12]

Diamond, L. M. (2016). Are women more sexually fluid than men? *Archives of Sexual Behavior (in preparation).* [12]

Diamond, L. M., Dickenson, J. A. & Blair, K. L. (2017). Stability of sexual attractions across different timescales: The roles of bisexuality and gender. *Archives of Sexual Behavior, 46,* 193–204. [12]

Diamond, M. (2009). Pornography, public acceptance and sex-related crime: A review. *International Journal of Law and Psychiatry, 32,* 304–314. [17]

Diamond, M. (2013). Transsexuality among twins: Identity concordance, transition, rearing, and orientation. *International Journal of Transgenderism, 14,* 24–38. [4]

Diamond, M. & Sigmundson, H. K. (1997). Sex reassignment at birth. Long-term review and clinical implications. *Archives of Pediatrics and Adolescent Medicine, 151,* 298–304. [4]

Dias, E. & Horowitz, J. (2019). Pope defrocks Theodore McCarrick, ex-cardinal accused of sexual abuse. *New York Times,* February 16. [13]

Diaz, F. (2010). The problem of the undetected rapist: A Texas A&M case study. (http://tinyurl.com/y9vq4qmh) [16]

Dibble, J. L. & Drouin, M. (2014). Using modern technology to keep in touch with back burners: An investment model analysis. *Computers in Human Behavior, 34,* 96–100. [7]

Dickson, E. J. (2014). Porn star Asa Akira takes us inside her new book, *Insatiable.* (http://tinyurl.com/ydgf9fkf) [17]

Dillinger, J. (2019). *Number of sex offenders by state.* (https://tinyurl.com/y37e8yhj) [13]

Dines, G. (2011). *Pornland: How porn has hijacked our sexuality.* Beacon Press. [17]

Dirie, W. (1998). *Desert flower: The extraordinary journey of a desert nomad.* William Morrow. [2]

Disaster Center. (2019). United States crime rates 1960–2018. (http://tinyurl.com/qtj24) [16]

Dixson, A. F. (2009). *Sexual selection and the origins of human mating systems.* Oxford University Press. [6]

Dixson, B. J. & Rantala, M. J. (2016). The role of facial and body hair distribution in women's judgments of men's sexual attractiveness. *Archives of Sexual Behavior, 45,* 877–889. [5]

Djinovic, R. P. (2018). Metoidioplasty. *Clinics in Plastic Surgery, 45,* 381–386. [4]

Domonoske, C. (2017). *Vibrator maker to pay millions over claims it secretly tracked use.* (http://tinyurl.com/zz2f6b9) [6]

Dowbiggin, I. R. (2003). *Keeping America sane: Psychiatry and eugenics in the United States and Canada, 1880–1940.* Cornell University Press. [13]

Downe, P. & "Ashley-Mika" (2003). "The people we think we are": The social identities of girls involved in prostitution. In: K. Gorkoff & J. Runner (Eds.), *Being heard: The experiences of young women in prostitution.* Fernwood Publishing. [17]

Drummond, K. D., Bradley, S. J., Peterson-Badali, M. & Zucker, K. J. (2008). A follow-up study of girls with gender identity disorder. *Developmental Psychology, 44,* 34–45. [4]

Dryden, W. (1999). *Overcoming jealousy.* Sheldon Press. [7]

Dude, A., Neustadt, A., Martins, S. & Gilliam, M. (2013). Use of withdrawal and unintended pregnancy among females 15–24 years of age. *Obstetrics & Gynecology, 122*(3), 595–600. [9]

Duffy, R., Alian, M., Patel, U., et al. (2016). Does bicycling, in otherwise healthy men, increase the risk of erectile dysfunction? *Evidence-Based Practice, 19*(10), 6–7. [14]

Dukers-Muijrers, N. H., Niekamp, A. M., Brouwers, E. E. & Hoebe, C. J. (2010). Older and swinging: Need to identify hidden and emerging risk groups at STI clinics. *Sexually Transmitted Infections, 86,* 315–317. [11]

DW News. (2019). *Japan's problem with subway groping.* (https://tinyurl.com/y4qeyfvq) [13]

Dworkin, A. (1979). *The lie.* (http://tinyurl.com/yadyugcl) [17]

Dworkin, A. (1994). *Prostitution and male supremacy.* (http://tinyurl.com/ycbtr4qq) [17]

## E

Earls, C. M. & Lalumière, M. L. (2002). A case study of preferential bestiality (zoophilia). *Sexual Abuse, 14,* 83–88. [13]

Earls, C. M. & Lalumière, M. L. (2009). A case study of preferential bestiality. *Archives of Sexual Behavior, 38,* 605–609. [13]

Eastwick, P. W. & Finkel, E. J. (2008). Sex differences in mate preferences revisited: Do people know what they initially desire in a romantic partner? *Journal of Personality and Social Psychology, 94,* 245–264. [5]

Eastwick, P. W. & Hunt, L. L. (2014). Relational mate value: Consensus and uniqueness in romantic evaluations. *Journal of Personality and Social Psychology, 106,* 728–751. [5]

Eaton, N. R., Keyes, K. M., Krueger, R. F., et al. (2012). An invariant dimensional liability model of gender differences in mental disorder prevalence: Evidence from a national sample. *Journal of Abnormal Psychology, 121,* 282–288. [10]

Eckert-Lind, C., Busch, A. S., Petersen, J. H., et al. (2020). Worldwide secular trends in age at pubertal onset assessed by breast development among girls: A systematic review and meta-analysis. *JAMA Pediatrics,* published online, February 10. [10]

Eckholm, E. (2007). Boys cast out by polygamists find help. *New York Times,* September 9. [11]

Edmonds, S. E. (2015). Bearing bodies: Physical activity, obesity stigma, and sexuality in the bear community. *Sociology of Sport Journal, 32,* 415–435. [12]

Ehrensaft, D. (2017). Gender nonconforming youth: current perspectives. *Adolesc Health Med Ther, 8,* 57–67. [4]

Eibl-Eibesfeldt, I. (2007). *Human ethology.* Aldine. [7]

Eichel, E. W., Eichel, J. D. & Kule, S. (1988). The technique of coital alignment and its relation to female orgasmic response and simultaneous orgasm. *Journal of Sex and Marital Therapy, 14,* 129–141. [14]

Eichenwald, K. (2005). Through his webcam, a boy joins a sordid online world. *New York Times,* December 19. [17]

Eisinger, R. W., Dieffenbach, C. W. & Fauci, A. S. (2019). HIV viral load and transmissibility of HIV infection: Undetectable equals untransmittable. *JAMA, 321,* 451–452. [15]

Eisner, S. (2013). *Bi: Notes for a bisexual revolution.* Seal Press. [12]

El-Bassel, N., Schilling, R. F., Gilbert, L., et al. (2000). Sex trading and psychological distress in a street-based sample of low-income urban men. *Journal of Psychoactive Drugs, 32,* 259–267. [17]

Elliot, L. M., Booth, M. M., Patterson, G., et al. (2017). Association of state-mandated abstinence-only sexuality education with rates of adolescent HIV infection and teenage pregnancy. *Journal of the Louisiana State Medical Society, 169,* 56. [10]

Elliott, A. J. & Niesta, D. (2008). Romantic red. Red enhances men's attraction to women. *Journal of Personality and Social Psychology, 95,* 1150–1164. [5]

Elliott, S. (2009). Sexuality after spinal cord injury. In: E. C. Field-Fote (Ed.), *Spinal cord injury rehabilitation.* F.A. Davis. [6]

Ellis, B. J. & Malamuth, N. M. (2000). Love and anger in romantic relationships: A discrete systems model. *Journal of Personality, 68,* 525–556. [7]

Ellison, C. R. (2000). *Women's sexualities: Generations of women share intimate secrets of sexual self-acceptance.* New Harbinger. [6]

Ellsworth, R. M., Bailey, D. H., Hill, K. R., et al. (2014). Relatedness, co-residence, and shared fatherhood among Ache foragers of Paraguay. *Current Anthropology, 55,* 647–653. [1]

Elmes, J., Nhongo, K., Ward, H., et al. (2014). The price of sex: Condom use and the determinants of the price of sex among female sex workers in eastern Zimbabwe. *Journal of Infectious Diseases, 210*(Suppl 2), S569–S578. [6]

Eltonsi, T. K., Tawfik, T. M., Rashed, L. A., et al. (2017). Study of the link between dopamine transporter gene polymorphisms and response to paroxetin and escitalopram in patients with lifelong premature ejaculation. *International Journal of Impotence Research, 29*(6), 235–239. [14]

Elwood, C., Money, D., van Schalkwyk, J., et al. (2019). Placentophagy. *Journal of Obstetrics and Gynaecology of Canada, 41,* 679–682. [8]

Emmelot-Vonk, M. H., Verhaar, H. J., Nakhai-Pour, H. R., et al. (2011). Low testosterone concentrations and the symptoms of testosterone deficiency according to the Androgen Deficiency in Ageing Males (ADAM) and Ageing Males' Symptoms rating scale (AMS) questionnaires. *Clinical Endocrinology, 74,* 488–494. [14]

England, P. & Bearak, J. (2014). The sexual double standard and gender differences in attitudes toward casual sex among U.S. university students. *Demographic Research, 30,* 1327–1338. [7]

Epstein, D. & Johnson, R. (1998). *Schooling sexualities.* Open University Press. [10]

Equal Employment Opportunity Commission. (2016). Select Task Force on the Study of Harassment in the Workplace: Report of Co-Chairs Chai R. Feldblum & Victoria A. Lipnic. (http://tinyurl.com/y8xux2gn) [16]

Espelage, D. L., Basile, K. C., Leemis, R. W., et al. (2018). Longitudinal examination of the bullying-sexual violence pathway across early to late adolescence: Implicating homophobic name-calling. *Journal of Youth & Adolescence, 47,* 1880–1893. [16]

Espelage, D. L., Hong, J. S., Rinehart, S. & Doshi, N. (2016). Understanding types, locations, & perpetrators of peer-to-peer sexual harassment in U.S. middle schools: A focus on sex, racial, and grade differences. *Children and Youth Services Review, 71,* 174–183. [16]

Espinosa-Medina, I., Saha, O., Boismoreau, F. & Brunet, J. F. (2018). The "sacral parasympathetic": ontogeny and anatomy of a myth. *Clinical Autonomic Research, 28,* 13–21. [App. B]

Espinosa-Medina, I., Saha, O., Boismoreau, F., et al. (2016). The sacral autonomic outflow is sympathetic. *Science, 354,* 893–897. [App. B]

Estes, R. J. & Weiner, N. A. (2002). *The commercial sexual exploitation of children in the U.S., Canada and Mexico* (revised ed.). University of Pennsylvania Press. [17]

Esteves, S. C., Roque, M., Bedoschi, G., et al. (2018). Intracytoplasmic sperm injection for male infertility and consequences for offspring. *Nature Reviews Urology, 15,* 535–562. [8]

Estill, A., Mock, S. E., Schryer, E. & Eibach, R. P. (2018). The effects of subjective age and aging attitudes on mid- to late-life sexuality. *Journal of Sex Research, 55*(2), 146–151. [11]

Evans, R. (2014). 5 reasons being a male porn star is less fun than it looks. (http://tinyurl.com/p5635pp) [17]

Evans, R. W. & Couch, R. (2001). Orgasm and migraine. *Headache, 41,* 512–514. [6]

Evers, Y. J., Dukers-Muijrers, N. H. T. M., Kampman, C. J. G., et al. (2020). Prevalence of drug use during sex among swingers and perceived benefits and risks: A cross-sectional internet survey in the Netherlands. *Sexually Transmitted Infections, 96*(1), 40–46. [11]

Experience Project. (2014). *I have been raped.* (http://tinyurl.com/yadg4y6l) [16]

## F

Facchinetti, P., Giuliano, F., Laurin, M., et al. (2014). Direct brain projections onto the spinal generator of ejaculation in the rat. *Neuroscience, 272,* 207–216. [App. B]

Faderman, L. (1981). *Surpassing the love of men: Romantic friendship and love between women from the Renaissance to the present.* William Morrow. [7]

Faderman, L. (2016). *The gay revolution: The story of the struggle.* Simon & Schuster. [12]

Fagot, B. I., Leinbach, M. D. & O'Boyle, C. (1992). Gender labeling, gender stereotyping, and parenting behaviors. *Developmental Psychology, 28,* 440–443. [4]

Fales, M. R., Frederick, D. A., Garcia, J. R., et al. (2016). Mating markets and bargaining hands: Mate preferences for attractiveness and resources in two national U.S. studies. *Personality and Individual Differences, 88,* 78–87. [5]

Families Against Mandatory Minimums. (n.d.). *An introduction to child pornography sentencing.* (https://tinyurl.com/yx39bh58) [17]

Family Research Council. (2019). *Ten arguments from social science against same-sex marriage.* (http://tinyurl.com/2a2c6te) [11]

Faria, N. R., Rambaut, A., Suchard, M. A., et al. (2014). The early spread and epidemic ignition of HIV-1 in human populations. *Science, 346,* 56–61. [15]

Farr, R. H. (2016). Does parental sexual orientation matter? A longitudinal follow-up of adoptive families with school-age children. *Developmental Psychology, 53*, 252–264. [12]

FBI. (2017). *Woman sentenced for harassing victim on social media* (http://tinyurl.com/ybc38zqp) [16]

FBI. (2019). *Crime in the United States 2018.* (https://tinyurl.com/yytj7yjp) [16]

Fecteau, J. (2017). *Katy Perry on 'I Kissed a Girl': 'Truth be told, I did more than that!'.* (http://tinyurl.com/sk8fd84) [7]

Feinberg, D. R., DeBruine, L. M., Jones, B. C. & Perrett, D. I. (2008). The role of femininity and averageness of voice pitch in aesthetic judgments of women's voices. *Perception, 37*, 615–623. [5]

Ferdenzi, C., Delplanque, S., Atanassova, R. & Sander, D. (2016). Androstadienone's influence on the perception of facial and vocal attractiveness is not sex specific. *Psychoneuroendocrinology, 66*, 166–175. [5]

Ferguson, C. E. & Malouff, J. M. (2016). Assessing police classifications of sexual assault reports: A meta-analysis of false reporting rates. *Archives of Sexual Behavior, 45*, 1185–1193. [16]

Ferguson, C. J. & Hartley, R. D. (2009). The pleasure is momentary . . . the expense damnable?: The influence of pornography on rape and sexual assault. *Aggression and Violent Behavior, 14*, 323–329. [17]

Fergussen, A. & Fergussen, L. (2019). *The worst (& safest) countries for LGBTQ+ travel in 2019.* (https://tinyurl.com/wec6anl) [12]

Ferraris, P., Yssel, H. & Misse, D. (2019). Zika virus infection: An update. *Microbes and Infection, 21*(8–9), 353–360. [15]

Ferreira, C. H., Dwyer, P. L., Davidson, M., et al. (2015). Does pelvic floor muscle training improve female sexual function? A systematic review. *International Urogynecology Journal, 26*, 1735–1750. [14]

Ferris, D. G., Samakoses, R., Block, S. L., et al. (2017). 4-valent human papillomavirus (4vHPV) vaccine in preadolescents and adolescents after 10 years. *Pediatrics, 140*(6), e20163947. [15]

Ferron, A., Lussier, Y., Sabourin, S. & Brassard, A. (2017). The role of Internet pornography use and cyber infidelity in the associations between personality, attachment, and couple and sexual satisfaction. *Social Networking, 6*, 1–18. [7]

Field, C. J., Kimuna, S. R. & Straus, M. A. (2013). Atitudes toward interracial relationships among college students: Race, class, gender, and perceptions of parental views. *Journal of Black Studies, 44*, 741–776. [7]

Fifield, A. (2017). For vulnerable high school girls in Japan, a culture of "dates" with older men. *Washington Post*, May 16. [17]

FindLaw. (2019a). *State rape laws.* (http://tinyurl.com/oldmw4w) [16]

FindLaw. (2019b). *State sexual assault laws.* (http://tinyurl.com/ybwh2gm3) [16]

Fine, C. (2010). *Delusions of gender.* W.W. Norton. [4]

Finer, L. B. & Philbin, J. M. (2013). Sexual initiation, contraceptive use, and pregnancy among young adolescents. *Pediatrics, 131*, 886–891. [10]

Finer, L. B., Frohwirth, L. F., Dauphinee, L. A., et al. (2005). Reasons U.S. women have abortions: quantitative and qualitative perspectives. *Perspectives on Sexual & Reproductive Health, 37*, 110–118. [9]

Fink, B., Neave, N., Manning, J. T. & Grammer, K. (2006). Facial symmetry and judgements of attractiveness, health and personality. *Personality and Individual Differences, 41*, 491–499. [5]

Finkelhor, D., Hotaling, G., Lewis, I. A. & Smith, C. (1990). Sexual abuse in a national survey of adult men and women: prevalence, characteristics, and risk factors. *Child Abuse and Neglect, 14*, 19–28. [10]

Finkelhor, D., Vanderminden, J., Turner, H., et al. (2014). Youth exposure to violence prevention programs in a national sample. *Child Abuse and Neglect, 38*, 677–686. [10]

Finkelstein, J. W., Susman, E. J., Chinchilli, V. M., et al. (1998). Effects of estrogen or testosterone on self-reported sexual responses and behaviors in hypogonadal adolescents. *Journal of Clinical Endocrinology and Metabolism, 83*, 2281–2285. [5]

Finkelstein, K. E. (2001). Man is sentenced to 5 years in attacks in Central Park. *New York Times*, May 19. [16]

First, M. B. (2014). DSM-5 and paraphilic disorders. *Journal of the American Academy of Psychiatry and the Law, 42*, 191–201. [13]

Fish, E. W., Murdaugh, L. B., Zhang, C., et al. (2019). Cannabinoids exacerbate alcohol teratogenesis by a CB1-Hedgehog interaction. *Scientific Reports, 9*, 16057. [8]

Fisher, H. E. (1989). Evolution of human sexual pair-bonding. *American Journal of Physical Anthropology, 78*, 331–354.

Fisher, H. E. (2006). Broken hearts: The nature and risks of romantic rejection. In: A. C. Crouter & A. Booth (Eds.), *Romance and sex in adolescence and emerging adulthood: Risks and opportunities*. Lawrence Erlbaum. [7]

Fisher, H. E., Aron, A. & Brown, L. L. (2006). Romantic love: A mammalian brain system for mate choice. *Philosophical Transactions of the Royal Society of London. Series B: Biological Sciences, 361*, 2173–2186. [7]

Fisher, M. M. & Eugster, E. A. (2014). What is in our environment that effects puberty? *Reproductive Toxicology, 44*, 7–14. [10]

Fleischman, A. R., Oinuma, M. & Clark, S. L. (2010). Rethinking the definition of "term pregnancy". *Obstetrics and Gynecology, 116*, 136–139. [8]

Flore, P. C., Mulder, J. & Wicherts, J. M. (2019). The influence of gender stereotype on mathematics test scores of Dutch high school students: A registered report. *Comprehensive Results in Social Psychology*, Published online at https://tinyurl.com/y5otn233. [4]

Flores, A. R., Herman, J. L., Brown, T. N. T., et al. (2017). *Age of individuals who identify as transgender in the United States.* (http://tinyurl.com/msmsvk8) [4]

Flynn, A. B., Johnson, R. M., Bolton, S. L. & Mojtabai, R. (2016). Victimization of lesbian, gay, and bisexual people in childhood: Associations with attempted suicide. *Suicide and Life-Threatening Behavior, 46*, 457–470. [12]

Fogg, A. (2013). The startling facts on female sexual aggression. (http://tinyurl.com/yckkjjkp) [16]

Fonteille, V., Redoute, J., Lamothe, P., et al. (2019). Brain processing of pictures of children in men with pedophilic disorder: A positron emission tomography study. *NeuroImage: Clinical, 21*, 101647. [13]

Foo, Y. Z., Simmons, L. W. & Rhodes, G. (2017). Predictors of facial attractiveness and health in humans. *Scientific Reports, 7*, 39731. [5]

Forcey, D. S., Vodstrcil, L. A., Hocking, J. S., et al. (2015). Factors associated with bacterial vaginosis among women who have sex with women: A systematic review. *PLOS One, 10*, e0141905. [15]

Ford, C. S. & Beach, F. A. (1951). *Patterns of sexual behavior*. Harper. [3, 6]

Ford, K. S. (2019). Marrying within the alma mater: Understanding the role of same-university marriages in educational homogamy. *Sociological Research Online* (published online July 11). [7]

Foshee, V. A., Bauman, K. E., Ennett, S. T., et al. (2004). Assessing the long-term effects of the Safe Dates program and a booster in preventing and reducing adolescent dating violence victimization and perpetration. *American Journal of Public Health, 94*, 619–624. [16]

Foshee, V. A., Benefield, T., Chen, M. S., et al. (2016). The effects of the Moms and Teens for Safe Dates Program on dating abuse: A conditional process analysis. *Prevention Science, 17*, 357–366. [16]

Fossos, N., Neighbors, C., Kaysen, D. & Hove, M. C. (2007). Intimate partner violence perpetration and problem drinking among college students: The roles of expectancies and subjective evaluations of alcohol aggression. *Journal of Studies on Alcohol and Drugs, 68*, 706–713. [16]

Foubert, J. D., Clark-Taylor, A. & Wall, A. F. (2020). Is campus rape primarily a serial or one-time problem? Evidence from a multicampus study. *Violence Against Women, 26*(3–4), 296–311. [16]

Foubert, J. D., Newberry, J. T. & Tatum, J. L. (2007). Behavior differences seven months later: Effects of a rape prevention program on first-year men who join fraternities. *Journal of Student Affairs Research and Practice, 44*, 728–749. [16]

Fournier, A., Dos Santos, G., Guillas, G., et al. (2014). Recent recreational physical activity and breast cancer risk in postmenopausal women in the E3N cohort. *Cancer Epidemiology, Biomarkers and Prevention, 23*, 1893–1902. [2]

Fowler, G. A. (2012). When the most personal secrets get outed on Facebook. *Wall Street Journal*, October 15. [10]

Fraley, C. (2010). *A brief overview of adult attachment theory and research.* (http://tinyurl.com/7ttlkgo) [7]

Fraley, M. (2016). Gwen Araujo murder 14 years later: Transgender teen's killers face parole. *Mercury News*, Octrober 14. [4]

Frayser, S. G. (1994). Defining normal childhood sexuality: An anthropological approach. *Annual Review of Sex Research, 4*, 173–217. [10]

Frazer, J. G. (1922). *The golden bough: A study of magic and religion* (abridged ed.). Macmillan.

Frederick, D. A. & Jenkins, B. N. (2015). Height and body mass on the mating market: Associations with number of sex partners and extra-pair sex among heterosexual men and women aged 18–65. *Evolutionary Psychology, 13*(3), 1–14. [5]

Frederick, D. A., Lever, J., Gillespie, B. J. & Garcia, J. R. (2017). What keeps passion alive? Sexual satisfaction is associated with sexual communication, mood setting, sexual variety, oral sex, orgasm, and sex frequency in a national U.S. study. *Journal of Sex Research, 54*, 186–201. [7]

Freud, S. (1905/1975). *Three essays on the theory of sexuality.* Basic Books. [12]

Freund, K. & Blanchard, R. (1986). The concept of courtship disorder. *Journal of Sex and Marital Therapy, 12*, 79–92. [13]

Freund, K. & Blanchard, R. (1993). Erotic target location errors in male gender dysphorics, paedophiles, and fetishists. *British Journal of Psychiatry, 162*, 558–563. [13]

Freund, K. W. (1974). Male homosexuality: An analysis of the pattern. In: J. A. Lorraine (Ed.), *Understanding homosexuality: Its biological and psychological bases.* Elsevier. [12]

Freund, K., Watson, R. & Rienzo, D. (1989). Heterosexuality, homosexuality, and erotic age preference. *Journal of Sex Research, 26*, 107–117. [13]

Freunscht, I. & Feldmann, R. (2011). Young adults with fetal alcohol syndrome (FAS): social, emotional and occupational development. *Klinische Padiatrie, 223*, 33–37. [8]

Frias-Navarro, D., Monterde, I. B. H., Pascual-Soler, M. & Badenes-Ribera, L. (2015). Etiology of homosexuality and attitudes toward same-sex parenting: A randomized study. *Journal of Sex Research, 52*, 151–161. [12]

Fricker, J. & Moore, S. (2008). Internet infidelity and its correlates. *Australian Journal of Counselling Psychology, 9*, 15–22. [7]

Friedman, M. (2014). Male sex work from ancient times to the near present. In: V. Minichiello & J. Scott (Eds.). *Male sex work and society.* Harrington Park Press. [17]

Friedrich, W. N., Fisher, J., Broughton, D., et al. (1998). Normative sexual behavior in children: A contemporary sample. *Pediatrics, 101*, E9. [10]

Friedrich, W. N., Sandfort, T. G. M., Oostveen, J. & Cohen-Kettenis, P. T. (2000). Cultural differences in sexual behavior: 2–6-year-old Dutch and American children. *Journal of Psychology and Human Sexuality, 12*, 117–129. [10]

Furnham, A. (2016). Are men and women portrayed differently in TV ads? (http://tinyurl.com/yb5gnub7) [17]

## G

G&R Research and Consulting. (2008). Sex in advertising. (http://tinyurl.com/y7qod2gf) [17]

Gaither, T. W., Awad, M. A., Osterberg, E. C., et al. (2017). Prevalence and motivation: Pubic hair grooming among men in the United States. *American Journal of Men's Health, 11*, 620–640. [2]

Gaitskell, K., Green, J., Pirie, K., et al. (2016). Tubal ligation and ovarian cancer risk in a large cohort: substantial variation by histological type. *International Journal of Cancer, 138*, 1076–1084. [9]

Galenson, E. (1990). Observation of early infantile sexual and erotic development. In: M. E. Perry (Ed.), *Handbook of sexology, vol. 7. Childhood and adolescent sexology.* Elsevier. [10]

Galletly, C., Lazzarini, Z., Sanders, C. & Pinkerton, S. D. (2014). Criminal HIV exposure laws: Moving forward. *AIDS and Behavior, 18*, 1011–1013. [17]

Gallup Organization. (2001). *Over half of Americans believe in love at first sight.* (http://tinyurl.com/y8rkdae3) [7]

Gallup, A. M. & Newport, F. (2008). *The Gallup Poll: Public opinion 2007.* Rowman and Littlefield. [11]

Gallup. (2006). *Americans at odds over gay rights.* (http://tinyurl.com/yca5t3lv) [12]

Gallup. (2013). *In U.S., 87% approve of black-white marriage, vs. 4% in 1958.* (https://tinyurl.com/yboqa4sc) [1]

Gallup. (2018). *More Americans say pornography is morally acceptable.* (https://tinyurl.com/vbk4qus) [17]

Gallup. (2019a). *Abortion.* (https://tinyurl.com/y5zx4nfo) [9, 11]

Gallup. (2019b). *Americans still greatly overestimate U.S. gay population.* (https://tinyurl.com/y5qlcxn2) [12]

Gangestad, S. W. & Thornhill, R. (1997). The evolutionary psychology of extrapair sex: The role of fluctuating asymmetry. *Evolution and Human Behavior, 18*, 69–88. [7]

Ganna, A., Verweij, K. J. H., Nivard, M. G., et al. (2019). Large-scale GWAS reveals insights into the genetic architecture of same-sex sexual behavior. *Science, 365*(6456). doi:10.1126/science.aat7693 [12]

Gannon, T. A., Collie, R. M., Ward, T. & Thakker, K. (2008). Rape: Psychopathology, theory, and treatment. *Clinical Psychology Review, 28*, 982–1008. [16]

Ganong, L. & Coleman, M. (2016). *Stepfamily relationships: Development, dynamics, and interventions* (2nd ed.). Springer. [11]

Garcia-Falgueras, A. & Swaab, D. F. (2008). A sex difference in the hypothalamic uncinate nucleus: Relationship to gender identity. *Brain, 131*, 3132–3146. [4, 12]

Gartoulla, P., Worsley, R., Bell, R. J. & Davis, S. R. (2018). Moderate to severe vasomotor and sexual symptoms remain problematic for women aged 60 to 65 years. *Menopause, 25*, 1331–1338. [11]

Gaskins, A. J., Mendiola, J., Afeiche, M., et al. (2014). Physical activity and television watching in relation to semen quality in young men. *British Journal of Sports Medicine, 49*, 265–270. [3]

Gates, G. J. (2013). *LGBT parenting in the United States.* (http://tinyurl.com/yda3aq3e) [12]

Gates, K. (2017). *Deviant desires: A tour of the erotic edge.* powerHouse Books. [13]

GayDemon.com. (2016). *Interview with Diesel Washington.* (http://tinyurl.com/yacntpjh) [17]

Geddes, R. & Lueck, D. (2000). *The gains from self-ownership and the expansion of women's rights.* (http://tinyurl.com/y75e72t7) [16]

Gender Dysphoria Affirmative Working Group. (2020). *The gender affirmative model.* (https://tinyurl.com/w4nfs2m) [4]

Georgiadis, J. R., Kortekaas, R., Kuipers, R., et al. (2006). Regional cerebral blood flow changes associated with clitorally induced orgasm in healthy women. *European Journal of Neuroscience, 24*, 3305–3316. [5]

Gerber, N., Booksmythe, I. & Kokko, H. (2018). Sex allocation theory for facultatively sexual organisms inhabiting seasonal environments: The importance of bet hedging. *The American Naturalist, 192*, 155–170. [App A]

Gerlach, N. M., McGlothlin, J. W., Parker, P. G. & Ketterson, E. D. (2012). Promiscuous mating produces offspring with higher lifetime fitness. *Proceedings of the Royal Society of London. Series B: Biological Sciences, 279*, 860–866. [App A]

Gerressu, M., Mercer, C. H., Graham, C. A., et al. (2008). Prevalence of masturbation and associated factors in a British national probability survey. *Archives of Sexual Behavior, 37*, 266–278. [6]

Gesselman, A. N., Webster, G. D. & Garcia, J. R. (2017). Has virginity lost its virtue? Relationship stigma associated with being a sexually inexperienced adult. *Journal of Sex Research, 54*, 202–213. [11]

Gibson, A. K., Delph, L. F. & Lively, C. M. (2017). The two-fold cost of sex: Experimental evidence from a natural system. *Evolution Letters, 1*, 6–15. [App A]

Gibson, L. E. & Leitenberg, H. (2000). Child sexual abuse prevention programs: Do they decrease the occurrence of child sexual abuse? *Child Abuse and Neglect, 24*, 1115–1125. [10]

Gibson, R. M. & Hoglund, J. (1992). Copying and sexual selection. *Trends in Ecology & Evolution, 7*, 229–232. [App A]

Gilfoyle, N. F. P. (2010). *Brief of the American Psychological Association, the California Psychological Association, the American Psychiatric Association, and the American*

*Association for Marriage and Family Therapy as amici curiae in support of plaintiff-appellees.* (http://tinyurl.com/b94oa58) [12]

Gilmore, A. K., Granato, H. F., Simpson, T., et al. (2018). After the assault: Effective treatments for survivors. In: L. M. Orchowski and C. A. Gidycz (Eds.). *Sexual assault risk reduction and resistance: Theory, research, and practice.* Elsevier. [16]

Giorgi, G. & Siccardi, M. (1996). Ultrasonographic observation of a female fetus' sexual behavior in utero. *American Journal of Obstetrics and Gynecology, 175,* 753. [10]

Giovanardi, G. (2017). Buying time or arresting development? The dilemma of administering hormone blockers in trans children and adolescents. *Porto Biomedical Journal, (in press).* [4]

Glina, S., Sharlip, I. D. & Hellstrom, W. J. (2013). Modifying risk factors to prevent and treat erectile dysfunction. *Journal of Sexual Medicine, 10,* 115–119. [14]

Goedel, W. C. & Duncan, D. T. (2016). Contextual factors in geosocial-networking smartphone application use and engagement in condomless anal intercourse among gay, bisexual, and other men who have sex with men who use Grindr. *Sex Health, 13,* 549–544. [7]

Goldberg, H., Stupp, P., Okoroh, E., et al. (2016). Female genital mutilation/cutting in the United States: Updated estimates of women and girls at risk, 2012. *Public Health Reports, 131,* 340–347. [2]

Goldman, R. & Goldman, J. (1982). *Children's sexual thinking: A comparative study of children aged 5 to 15 years in Australia, North America, Britain and Sweden.* Routledge and Kegan Paul. [10]

Goldmeier, D., Sadeghi-Nejad, H. & Facelle, T. M. (2014). Persistent genital arousal disorder. In: Y. M. Binik & K. S. K. Hall (Eds.), *Principles and practice of sex therapy.* Guildford Press. [14]

Goldstein, I. (2000). The mutually reinforcing triad of depressive symptoms, cardiovascular disease, and erectile dysfunction. *American Journal of Cardiology, 86,* 41F–45F. [14]

Goldstein, I. & Berman, J. R. (1998). Vasculogenic female sexual dysfunction: Vaginal engorgement and clitoral erectile insufficiency syndromes. *International Journal of Impotence Research, 10*(Suppl 2), S84–S90; discussion S98–S101. [14]

Goldstein, I., Kim, N. N., Clayton, A. H., et al. (2017). Hypoactive sexual desire disorder: International Society for the Study of Women's Sexual Health (ISSWSH) expert consensus panel review. *Mayo Clinic Proceedings, 92,* 114–128. [14]

Goldstein, L. & Otterman, S. (2018). Catholic priests abused 1,000 children in Pennsylvania, report says. *New York Times,* August 14. [13]

Gomez Caballero, N., Almenara, S., Tevar Terol, A. & Horga de la Parte, J. F. (2019). Anaphylaxis probably induced by transfer of amoxicillin via oral sex. *BMJ Case Reports, 12.* doi:10.1136/bcr-2018-227398 [6]

Gomez Jimenez, F. R., Court, L. & Vasey, P. L. (2020). A retrospective study of childhood sex-typed behavior in Istmo Zapotec men, women, and muxes. *Archives of Sexual Behavior, 49*(2), 467–477. [12]

Gondim, R., Teles, F. & Barroso, U., Jr. (2018). Sexual orientation of 46, XX patients with congenital adrenal hyperplasia: A descriptive review. *Journal of Pediatric Urology, 14,* 486–493. [12]

Good Lives Model. (2014). *The Good Lives Model of offender rehabilitation.* (http://tinyurl.com/y7w532ff) [13]

Goode, E. (2012). Researchers see decline in child sex abuse rate. *New York Times,* June 28. [10]

Gottlieb, L. (2014). Does a more equal marriage mean less sex? *New York Times,* February 6. [11]

Gottman, J. M. (2011). *The science of trust: Emotional attunement for couples.* W.W. Norton. [7]

Gottman, J. M. & Gottman, J. (2011). *How to keep love going strong.* (http://tinyurl.com/2ewjv2n) [7]

Gottman, J. M. & Levenson, R. W. (1999). What predicts change in marital interaction over time? A study of alternative models. *Family Process, 38,* 143–158. [7]

Gottman, J. M. & Levenson, R. W. (2000). The timing of divorce: Predicting when a couple will divorce over a 14-year period. *Journal of Marriage and the Family, 62,* 737–745. [7]

Gottman, J. M. & Notarius, C. I. (2000). Decade review: Observing marital interaction. *Journal of Marriage and the Family, 62,* 927–947. [7, 8]

Gottman, J. M. & Schwartz Gottman, J. (2017). *The science of couples and family therapy: Behind the scenes at the "love lab."* W.W. Norton. [7]

Gottman, J. M., Coan, J., Carrere, S. & Swanson, C. (1998). Predicting marital happiness and stability from newlywed interactions. *Journal of Marriage and the Family, 60,* 5–22. [7]

Grace, D. M., David, B. J. & Ryan, M. K. (2008). Investigating preschoolers' categorical thinking about gender through imitation, attention, and the use of self-categories. *Child Development, 79,* 1928–1941. [4]

Grady, D. (2016). Cancer survivor receives first penis transplant in the United States. *New York Times,* May 16. [3]

Graham, C. A., Crosby, R., Yarber, W. L., et al. (2006). Erection loss in association with condom use among young men attending a public STI clinic: potential correlates and implications for risk behaviour. *Sexual Health, 3,* 255–260. [9]

Graham, J. H. & Özener, B. (2016). Fluctuating asymmetry of human populations: A review. *Symmetry, 8,* 12: 11°36. [App. A]

Graham, L. M., Jensen, T. M., Givens, A. D., et al. (2019). Intimate partner violence among same-sex couples in college: A propensity score analysis. *Journal of Interpersonal Violence, 34*(8), 1583–1610. [16]

Grebe, N. M., Sarafin, R. E., Strenth, C. R. & Zilioli, S. (2019). Pair-bonding, fatherhood, and the role of testosterone: A meta-analytic review. *Neuroscience and Biobehavioral Reviews, 98,* 221–233. [3]

Green, A. (2011). Oregon Supreme Court rules that simply viewing child pornography on the Internet isn't illegal. *The Oregonian,* January 6. [17]

Green, R. (1987). *The "sissy-boy syndrome" and the development of homosexuality.* New Haven. Yale University Press. [4]

Green, R. (1987). *The "sissy-boy syndrome" and the development of homosexuality.* Yale University Press. [12]

Griffin, L., Clyde, K., Byng, R. & Bewley, S. (2020). Sex, gender and gender identity: A re-evaluation of the evidence. *BJPsych Bulletin,* published online July 21. [4]

Griffin, R. (2018). Almost half of U.S. births happen outside marriage, signaling cultural shift. (https://tinyurl.com/yb7gzxgn) [1]

Grimes, D. A. & Schulz, K. F. (2011). Nonspecific side effects of oral contraceptives: nocebo or noise? *Contraception, 83,* 5–9. [9]

Groth, A. N. (1979). *Men who rape: The psychology of the offender.* Plenum. [16]

Grubbs, J. B. & Gola, M. (2019). Is pornography use related to erectile functioning? Results from cross-sectional and latent growth curve analyses. *Journal of Sexual Medicine, 16,* 111–125. [17]

Gruber, T. & Clay, Z. (2016). A comparison between bonobos and chimpanzees: A review and update. *Evolutionary Anthropology, 25,* 239–252. [App. A]

Grunbaum, J. A., Lowry, R., Kann, L. & Pateman, B. (2000). Prevalence of health risk behaviors among Asian American/Pacific Islander high school students. *Journal of Adolescent Health, 27,* 322–330. [10]

Guiora, A. Z., Beit-Hallahmi, B., Fried, R. & Yoder, C. (1982). Language environment and gender identity attainment. *Language Learning, 32,* 289–304. [4]

Guo, M., Heran, B., Flannigan, R., et al. (2016). Persistent sexual dysfunction with finasteride 1 mg taken for hair loss. *Pharmacotherapy, 36,* 1180–1184. [5, 14]

Guth, M. A. S. (n.d.). *Prostate self-examination.* (https://tinyurl.com/y44xvs3j) [3]

Guttmacher Institute. (2006). *Asian American adolescents' first sexual intercourse: Gender and acculturation differences.* (http://tinyurl.com/ya3rpvxv) [10]

Guttmacher Institute. (2014). Moving forward: Family planning in the era of health reform. (http://tinyurl.com/yd3mxfsu) [1]

Guttmacher Institute. (2017a). *American teens' sexual and reproductive health.* (http://tinyurl.com/zp3ugng) [10]

Guttmacher Institute. (2017b). *Sex and HIV education.* (http://tinyurl.com/gwq4dvy) [10]

Guttmacher Institute. (2019). *Sex and HIV education.* (https://tinyurl.com/gwq4dvy) [10]

Guttmacher Institute. (2019a). *Induced abortion in the United States.* (http://tinyurl.com/l789emu) [9]

Guttmacher Institute. (2019b). *State abortion policy landscape: from hostile to supportive.* (https://tinyurl.com/yxbyqhom) [9]

Guttmacher Institute. (2019c). *Unintended pregnancy in the United States.* (http://tinyurl.com/zoqe5ue) [9]

Guttmacher Institute. (2020). *An overview of abortion laws.* (https://tinyurl.com/hs29h3b) [9]

# H

Haake, P., Exton, M. S., Haverkamp, J., et al. (2002). Absence of orgasm-induced prolactin secretion in a healthy multi-orgasmic male subject. *International Journal of Impotence Research, 14,* 133–135. [5]

Haase, C. M., Holley, S. R., Bloch, L., et al. (2016). Interpersonal emotional behaviors and physical health: A 20-year longitudinal study of long-term married couples. *Emotion, 16,* 965–977. [11]

Hackney, A. C., Lane, A. R., Register-Mihalik, J. & O'Leary, C. B. (2017). Endurance exercise training and male sexual libido. *Medicine and Science in Sports and Exercise, 49,* 1383–1388. [14]

Hadj-Moussa, M., Agarwal, S., Ohl, D. A. & Kuzon, W. M., Jr. (2019). Masculinizing genital gender confirmation surgery. *Sex Med Rev, 7,* 141–155. [4]

Hadwan, M. H., Almashhedy, L. A. & Alsalman, A. R. (2012). Oral zinc supplementation restores high-molecular-weight seminal zinc binding protein to normal value in Iraqi infertile men. *BMC Urology, 12,* 32. [3]

Hagerty, B. B. (2008). *Some Muslims in U.S. quietly engage in polygamy.* (http://tinyurl.com/2vbrcpe) [11]

Haider-Markel, D. P. & Joslyn, M. R. (2008). Beliefs about the origins of homosexuality and support for gay rights. *Public Opinion Quarterly, 72,* 291–310. [12]

Haider, K. S., Haider, A., Doros, G. & Traish, A. (2018). Long-term testosterone therapy improves urinary and sexual function and quality of life in men with hypogonadism: Results from a propensity-matched subgroup of a controlled registry study. *Journal of Urology, 199*(1), 257–265. [11]

Haines, M. (2008). Fertility and mortality in the United States. (http://tinyurl.com/yd6bbgwe) [1]

Halata, Z. & Munger, B. L. (1986). The neuroanatomical basis for the protopathic sensibility of the human glans penis. *Brain Research, 371,* 205–230. [1]

Hales, A. (2019). *Chatting with a Virtuous Pedophile.* (https://tinyurl.com/yyt26hvv) [13]

Halpern–Meekin, S., Manning, W. D., Giordano, P. C. & Longmore, M. A. (2013). Relationship churning in emerging adulthood: On/off relationships and sex with an ex. *Journal of Adolescent Research, 28,* 166–188. [7]

Halpern, C. J. T., Udry, J. R., Suchindran, C. & Campbell, B. (2000a). Adolescent males' willingness to report masturbation. *Journal of Sex Research, 37,* 327–232. [10]

Halpern, C. T., Joyner, K., Udry, J. R. & Suchindran, C. (2000b). Smart teens don't have sex (or kiss much either). *Journal of Adolescent Health, 26,* 213–225. [10]

Halpern, C. T., Kaestle, C. E. & Halltors, D. D. (2007). Perceived physical maturity, age of romantic partner, and adolescent risk behavior. *Prev Sci, 8,* 1–10. [10]

Hamer, D. H. (2002). Genetics of sexual behavior. In: J. Benjamin, R. P. Ebstein and R. H. Belmaker (Eds). *Molecular genetics and human personality.* American Psychiatric Publishing. [12]

Hamermesh, D. S. (2011). *Beauty pays: Why attractive people are more successful.* Princeton University Press.

Hanson, R. K., Harris, A. J., Helmus, L. & Thornton, D. (2014). High-risk sex offenders may not be high risk forever. *Journal of Interpersonal Violence, 29,* 2792–2813. [13]

Harder, H., Starkings, R. M. L., Fallowfield, L. J., et al. (2019). Sexual functioning in 4,418 postmenopausal women participating in UKCTOCS: A qualitative free-text analysis. *Menopause, 26,* 1100–1009. [11]

Hare, L., Bernard, P., Sanchez, F. J., et al. (2009). Androgen receptor repeat length polymorphism associated with male-to-female transsexualism. *Biological Psychiatry, 65,* 93–96. [4]

Hare, R. M., Schlatter, S., Rhodes, G. & Simmons, L. W. (2017). Putative sex-specific human pheromones do not affect gender perception, attractiveness ratings or unfaithfulness judgements of opposite sex faces. *Royal Society Open Science, 4,* 160831. [5]

Harker, L. & Keltner, D. (2001). Expressions of positive emotion in women's college yearbook pictures and their relationship to personality and life outcomes across adulthood. *Journal of Personality and Social Psychology, 80,* 112–124. [7]

Härkönen, J. (2015). Divorce. In: R. Scott and S. Kosslyn (Eds.), *Emerging trends in the social and behavioral sciences.* Wiley. [11]

Harms, W. (2019). *There's a queer purge happening in Chechnya. Is the US going to do anything about it?* (https://tinyurl.com/yyfejfba) [12]

Harper, J. C. & Sengupta, S. B. (2012). Preimplantation genetic diagnosis: state of the art 2011. *Human Genetics, 131,* 175–186. [8]

Harper, K. N., Zuckerman, M. K., Harper, M. L., et al. (2011). The origin and antiquity of syphilis revisited: An appraisal of Old World pre-Columbian evidence for treponemal infection. *American Journal of Physical Anthropology, 146* (Suppl 53), 99–133. [15]

Harrison, S. (2014). The hard life of the male porn star. (http://tinyurl.com/ych9p8bl) [17]

Harte, C. B. & Meston, C. M. (2012). Recreational use of erectile dysfunction medications and its adverse effects on erectile function in young healthy men: the mediating role of confidence in erectile ability. *Journal of Sexual Medicine, 9,* 1852–1859. [14]

Hartmann, U. & Waldinger, M. D. (2007). Treatment of delayed ejaculation. In: S. R. Leiblum (Ed.), *Principles and practice of sex therapy* (4th ed.). Guilford Press. [14]

Harvard Mental Health Letter. (2010). *Pessimism about pedophilia.* (https://tinyurl.com/yb3wm6mj)

Harvard Women's Health Watch. (2013). *Testosterone therapy: Is it for women?* (http://tinyurl.com/y84emac9) [14]

Haselton, M. G. & Gildersleeve, K. (2016). Human ovulation cues. *Current Opinion in Psychology, 7,* 120–125. [5]

Haselton, M. G., Mortezaie, M., Pillsworth, E. G., et al. (2007). Ovulatory shifts in human female ornamentation: Near ovulation, women dress to impress. *Hormones and Behavior, 51,* 40–45. [5]

Hassan, A. (2018). Porn sites collect more user data than Netflix or Hulu. This is what they do with it. (https://tinyurl.com/y9c6aqq2) [17]

Hassett, J. M., Siebert, E. R. & Wallen, K. (2008). Sex differences in rhesus monkey toy preferences parallel those of children. *Hormones and Behavior, 54,* 359–364. [4]

Hatfield, E. & Rapson, R. L. (2005). *Love and sex: Cross-cultural perspectives.* University Press of America. [7]

Hatfield, E. & Rapson, R. L. (2011). Equity theory in close relationships. In: P. A. M. Van Lange, A. W. Kruglanski & E. T. Higgins (Eds.), *Handbook of theories of social psychology* (Volume 2). Sage. [7]

Hatfield, E., Forbes, M. & Rapson, R. L. (2012). Marketing love and sex. *Society, 49,* 506–511. [5]

Hatfield, E., Pillemer, J. T., O'Brien, M. U. & Le, Y.-C. L. (2008). The endurance of love: Passionate and companionate love in newlywed and long-term marriages. *Interpersona, 2,* 35–64. [7]

Hatzenbuchler, M. L. & Pachankis, J. E. (2016). Stigma and minority stress as social determinants of health among lesbian, gay, bisexual, and transgender youth: Research evidence and clinical implications. *Pediatric Clinics of North America, 63,* 985–997. [14]

Hayden, R. P., Flannigan, R. & Schlegel, P. N. (2018). The role of lifestyle in male infertility: diet, physical activity, and body habitus. *Current Urology Reports, 19,* 56. [8]

Haydon, A. A., Cheng, M. M., Herring, A. H., et al. (2014). Prevalence and predictors of sexual inexperience in adulthood. *Archives of Sexual Behavior, 43,* 221–230. [11]

Hayes, R. D., Dennerstein, L., Bennett, C. M., et al. (2008). Risk factors for female sexual dysfunction in the general population: Exploring factors associated with low sexual function and sexual distress. *Journal of Sexual Medicine, 5,* 1681–1693. [11]

Hayes, R. M. & Dragiewicz, M. (2018). Unsolicited dick pics: Erotica, exhibitionism or entitlement? *Women's Studies International Forum, 71,* 114–120. [13]

Hayes, S. L. & Carpenter, B. J. (2010). *Absence of malice: Constructing the female sex offender.* (http://tinyurl.com/ycjrs66d) [13]

Hayes, T. B., Khoury, V., Narayan, A., et al. (2010). Atrazine induces complete feminization and chemical castration in male African clawed frogs (*Xenopus laevis*). *Proceedings of the National Academy of Sciences of the United States of America, 107,* 4612–4617. [9]

Hazan, C. & Shaver, P. (1987). Romantic love conceptualized as an attachment process. *Journal of Personality and Social Psychology, 52*, 511–524. [7]

Healthline. (2019). *Everything you need to know about butt implants.* (https://tinyurl.com/y27evfez)

Heiman, J. R. (2007). Orgasmic disorders in women. In: S. R. Leiblum (Ed.), *Principles and practice of sex therapy* (4th ed.). Guilford Press. [14]

Helms, J. L. & Waters, A. M. (2016). Attitudes toward bisexual men and women. *Journal of Bisexuality, 16*, 454–467. [12]

Helmus, L., Hanson, R. K., Thornton, D., et al. (2012). Absolute recidivism rates predicted by Static-99R and Static-2002R sex offender risk assessment tools vary across samples: A meta-analysis. *Criminal Justice and Behavior, 39*, 1148–1171. [13]

Hembree, W. C., Cohen-Kettenis, P. T., Gooren, L., et al. (2017). Endocrine treatment of gender-dysphoric/gender-incongruent persons: An endocrine society clinical practice guideline. *Journal of Clinical Endocrinology and Metabolism, 102*, 3869–3903. [4]

Hens, K., Dondorp, W., Handyside, A. H., et al. (2013). Dynamics and ethics of comprehensive preimplantation genetic testing: a review of the challenges. *Human Reproduction Update, 19*, 366–375. [8]

Henton, C. L. (1976). Nocturnal orgasm in college women: Its relation to dreams and anxiety associated with sexual factors. *Journal of Genetic Psychology, 129*, 245–251. [3]

Herbenick, D., Eastman-Mueller, H., Fu, T. C., et al. (2019). Women's sexual satisfaction, communication, and reasons for (no longer) faking orgasm: Findings from a U.S. probability sample. *Archives of Sexual Behavior, 48*, 2461–2472. [14]

Herbenick, D., Fu, T. J., Arter, J., et al. (2018). Women's experiences with genital touching, sexual pleasure, and orgasm: Results from a U.S. probability sample of women ages 18 to 94. *Journal of Sex and Marital Therapy, 44*, 201–212. [14]

Herbenick, D., Fu, T.-C. & Dodge, B. (2019). The alcohol contexts of consent, wanted sex, sexual pleasure, and sexual assault: Results from a probability survey of undergraduate students. *Journal of American College Health, 67*, 144–162. [16]

Herbenick, D., Reece, M., Sanders, S. A., et al. (2009). Prevalence and characteristics of vibrator use by women in the United States: Results from a nationally representative study. *Journal of Sexual Medicine, 6*, 1857–1866. [6]

Herbenick, D., Reece, M., Sanders, S. A., et al. (2010a). Women's vibrator use in sexual partnerships: Results from a nationally representative survey in the United States. *Journal of Sex and Marital Therapy, 36*, 49–65. [6]

Herbenick, D., Reece, M., Schick, V. & Sanders, S. A. (2014). Erect penile length and circumference dimensions of 1,661 sexually active men in the United States. *Journal of Sexual Medicine, 11*, 93–101. [3]

Herbenick, D., Reece, M., Schick, V., et al. (2010b). Sexual behavior in the United States: Results from a national probability sample of men and women ages 14–94. *Journal of Sexual Medicine, 7*(Suppl 5), 255–265. [6, 10]

Herdt, G. (2005). *The Sambia: Ritual, sexuality, and change in Papua New Guinea*. Wadsworth. [6, 10]

Herdt, G. (2019). Intimate consumption and new sexual subjects among the Sambia of Papua New Guinea. *Oceania, 89*, 36–67. [6]

Herek, G. M., Norton, A. T., Allen, T. J. & Sims, C. L. (2010). Demographic, psychological, and social characteristics of self-identified lesbian, gay, and bisexual adults in a US probability sample. *Sexuality Research & Social Policy, 7*, 176–200. [12]

Herman-Giddens, M. E., Steffes, J., Harris, D., et al. (2012). Secondary sexual characteristics in boys: Data from the Pediatric Research in Office Settings Network. *Pediatrics, 130*, e1058–1068. [10]

Hermanson, M. (2019). *Relatório registra 420 vítimas fatais de discriminação contra LGBTs no Brasil em 2018.* (https://tinyurl.com/y9mp79bd) [12]

Hertlein, K. M. & Weeks, G. R. (2007). Two roads diverging in a wood. *Journal of Couple and Relationship Therapy, 6*, 95–107. [7]

Herzog, H. (2017). *What's the deal with "furries"?* (http://tinyurl.com/y9bue5wa) [13]

Hewlett, B. S. & Hewlett, B. L. (2010). Sex and searching for children among Aka foragers and Ngandu farmers of Central Africa. *African Study Monographs, 31*, 107–125. [6]

Heyman, R. E. & Smith Slep, A. M. (2001). The hazards of predicting divorce without cross-validation. *Journal of Marriage and the Family, 63*, 473–479. [7]

HHS Office of Adolescent Health. (2016). *Teen births.* (http://tinyurl.com/kbmplbh) [10]

HHS.gov. (2019). *Hepatitis B basic information.* (https://tinyurl.com/yb7kbesc) [15]

Hickey, E., Aggrawal, A. & Mellor, L. (2016). *Understanding necrophilia: A global multidisciplinary approach* Cognella Academic Publishing. [13]

Hill, S. E. & Ryan, M. J. (2006). The role of model female quality in the mate choice copying behaviour of sailfin mollies. *Biology Letters, 2*, 203–205. [App. A]

Hines, M. (2006). Prenatal testosterone and gender-related behaviour. *European Journal of Endocrinology, 155*, S115–S121. [4]

Hines, M., Constantinescu, M. & Spencer, D. (2015). Early androgen exposure and human gender development. *Biol Sex Differ, 6*, Published online at https://tinyurl.com/y5ldkwuc. [4]

Hite, S. (2003). *The Hite report: A nationwide study of female sexuality*. Seven Stories Press. [6]

HIV.gov. (2019a). *Long-acting HIV prevention tools.* (https://tinyurl.com/rssebvb) [15]

HIV.gov. (2019b). *U.S. statistics.* (https://tinyurl.com/y77feftg) [15]

HIV.gov. (2019c). *U.S. statistics: Fast facts.* (https://tinyurl.com/y77feftg) [15]

HIVandHepatitis.com. (2016). *ASM Microbe 2016: PrEP use is rising fast in U.S., but large racial disparities remain.* (http://tinyurl.com/y8zs7szs) [15]

Hoag, N., Keast, J. R. & O'Connell, H. E. (2017). The "G-spot" is not a structure evident on macroscopic anatomic dissection of the vaginal wall. *Journal of Sexual Medicine, 14*, 1524–1532. [2]

Hoekzema, E., Barba-Muller, E., Pozzobon, C., et al. (2017). Pregnancy leads to long-lasting changes in human brain structure. *Nature Neuroscience, 20*, 287–296. [8]

Hoffman, J. (2017). Hunting a killer: Sex, drugs and the return of syphilis. *New York Times*, August 24. [15]

Hoffmann, H. (2017). Situating human sexual conditioning. *Archives of Sexual Behavior, 46*, 2213–2229. [5]

Holman, A. & Sillars, A. (2012). Talk about "hooking up": The influence of college student social networks on nonrelationship sex. *Health Communication, 27*, 205–216. [10]

Holmes, R. M. (2012). The outdoor recess activities of children at an urban school: Longitudinal and intraperiod patterns. *American Journal of Play, 4*, 327–351. [4]

Holstege, G., Georgiadis, J. R., Paans, A. M., et al. (2003). Brain activation during human male ejaculation. *Journal of Neuroscience, 23*, 9185–9193. [5]

Honan, W. H. (1994). Professor ousted for lecture gets job back. *New York Times*, September 17. [16]

Hong, D. S. & Reiss, A. L. (2014). Cognitive and neurological aspects of sex chromosome aneuploidies. *Lancet Neurol, 13*, 306–318. [4]

Hook, E. B. & Warburton, D. (2014). Turner syndrome revisited: review of new data supports the hypothesis that all viable 45,X cases are cryptic mosaics with a rescue cell line, implying an origin by mitotic loss. *Human Genetics*. [4]

Hoskins, A. W. & Ellis, L. (2014). Fetal testosterone and criminality: Test of evolutionary neuroandrogenic theory. *Criminality, 53*. [4]

Howard, S. R., de Roux, N., Leger, J., et al. (2019). Puberty and its disorders. In: M. T. Dattani & C. G. D. Brook (Eds.), *Brook's clinical pediatric endocrinology* (7th ed.). Wiley. [10]

Hsu, K. J. & Bailey, J. M. (2017). Autopedophilia: Erotic-target identity inversions in men sexually attracted to children. *Psychological Science, 28*, 115–123. [13]

Hsu, K. J. & Bailey, J. M. (2019). The "furry" phenomenon: Characterizing sexual orientation, sexual motivation, and erotic target identity inversions in male furries. *Archives of Sexual Behavior, 48*, 1349–1369. [13]

Hu, S., Pattatucci, A. M., Patterson, C., et al. (1995). Linkage between sexual orientation and chromosome Xq28 in males but not in females. *Nature Genetics, 11,* 248–256. [12]

Huang, C., Li, B., Xu, K., et al. (2017). Decline in semen quality among 30,636 young Chinese men from 2001 to 2015. *Fertility and Sterility, 107,* 83–88.[3]

Hucker, S. J. (2011). Hypoxyphilia. *Archives of Sexual Behavior, 40,* 1323–1326. [13]

Hughes, S. M., Harrison, M. A. & Gallup, G. G. J. (2007). Sex differences in romantic kissing among college students: An evolutionary perspective. *Evolutionary Psychology, 5,* 612–631. [6]

Huh, W. K., Joura, E. A., Giuliano, A. R., et al. (2017). Final efficacy, immunogenicity, and safety analyses of a nine-valent human papillomavirus vaccine in women aged 16–26 years: A randomised, double-blind trial. *Lancet, 390*(10108), 2143–2159. [15]

Human Rights Campaign. (2017). *State maps of laws and policies: Hate crimes.* (http://tinyurl.com/y7qmyyvn) [12]

Human Rights Campaign. (2019). *State maps of laws & policies.* (https://tinyurl.com/y5hlmzld) [12]

Human Rights Campaign. (2020). *A national epidemic: Fatal anti-transgender violence in America in 2019.* (https://tinyurl.com/y4db2v62) [4]

Human Rights Watch. (2013). *Raised on the registry: The irreparable harm of placing children on sex offender registries in the US.* (https://tinyurl.com/qc66ykz) [13]

Huo, S., Scialli, A. R., McGarvey, S., et al. (2016). Treatment of men for "low testosterone": A systematic review. *PLOS One, 11,* e0162480. [14]

Huppin, M., Malamuth, N. M. & Linz, D. (2019). An evolutionary perspective on sexual assault and implications for interventions. In: W. T. O'Donohue and P. A. Schewe (Eds.). *Handbook of sexual assault and sexual assault prevention.* Springer. [16]

Huynh, H. K., Willemsen, A. T., Lovick, T. A. & Holstege, G. (2013). Pontine control of ejaculation and female orgasm. *J Sex Med, 10,* 3038–3048. [App. B]

Hyde, J. S. (2016). Sex and cognition: Gender and cognitive functions. *Current Opinion in Neurobiology, 38,* 53–56. [4]

**I**

ILGA. (2019). *Sexual orientation laws in the world—2019.* (https://tinyurl.com/y68n29ru) [12]

Inhorn, M. C. (1996). *Infertility and patriarchy: The cultural politics of gender and family life in Egypt.* University of Pennsylvania Press. [11]

International Professional Surrogates Association. (n.d.). *Home page.* (http://tinyurl.com/kpmweg) [14]

iSpot.tv. (2017). Campbell's Soup TV commercial, "Real real life: Mom." (http://tinyurl.com/y7z2rwa7) [17]

**J**

Jabbour, J., Holmes, L., Sylva, D., et al. (2020). Robust evidence for bisexual orientation among men. *PNAS,* published online, July 20. [12]

Jackson, J. B., Miller, R. B., Oka, M. & Henry, R. G. (2014). Gender differences in marital satisfaction: A meta-analysis. *Journal of Marriage and Family, 76,* 105–129. [11]

Jackson, S. E., Yang, L., Koyanagi, A., et al. (2020). Declines in sexual activity and function predict incident health problems in older adults: Prospective findings from the English Longitudinal Study of Ageing. *Archives of Sexual Behavior, 49*(3), 929–940. [11]

Jacobs, J. (2010). *Sex, tourism, and the postcolonial encounter.* Ashgate. [17]

Jain, T., Schwarz, E. B. & Mehrotra, A. (2019). A study of telecontraception. *New England Journal of Medicine, 381,* 1287–1288. [9]

James-Kangal, N., Weitbrecht, E. M., Francis, T. E. & Whitton, S. W. (2018). Hooking up and emerging adults' relationship attitudes and expectations. *Sexuality and Culture, 22,* 706–723. [7]

Janecka, M., Rijsdijk, F., Rai, D., et al. (2017). Advantageous developmental outcomes of advancing paternal age. *Translational Psychiatry, 7,* e1156. [8]

Jankowiak, W. R. & Fischer, E. F. (1992). A cross-cultural perspective on romantic love. *Ethnology, 31,* 149 155. [7]

Jankowiak, W. R., Volsche, S. L. & Garcia, J. R. (2015). Is the romantic–sexual kiss a near human universal? *American Anthropologist, 117,* 535–539. [6]

Jannic, A., Mammeri, H., Larcher, L., et al. (2019). Orogenital transmission of *Neisseria meningitidis* causing acute urethritis in men who have sex with men. *Emerging Infectious Diseases, 25,* 175–176. [15]

Jaspers, L., Feys, F., Bramer, W. M., et al. (2016). Efficacy and safety of flibanserin for the treatment of hypoactive sexual desire disorder in women: A systematic review and meta-analysis. *JAMA Internal Medicine, 176,* 453–462. [14]

Jeal, N. & Salisbury, C. (2004). A health needs assessment of street-based prostitutes: Cross-sectional survey. *Journal of Public Health (Oxford), 26,* 147–151. [17]

Jeal, N., Salisbury, C. & Turner, K. (2008). The multiplicity and interdependency of factors influencing the health of street-based sex workers: A qualitative study. *Sexually Transmitted Infections, 84,* 381–385. [17]

Jeffery, A. J., Shackelford, T. K., Zeigler-Hill, V., et al. (2019). The evolution of human female sexual orientation. *Evolutionary Psychological Science, 5,* 71–86. [12]

Jennings, V. H. & Arevalo, M. (2011). Fertility awareness methods. In: R. A. Hatcher, J. Trussell, A. L. Nelson, et al. (Eds.), *Contraceptive technology* (20th ed.). Ardent Media. [9]

Jiang, H., Qian, X., Carroli, G. & Garner, P. (2017). Selective versus routine use of episiotomy for vaginal birth. *Cochrane Database of Systematic Reviews, 2,* CD000081. [8]

Jiang, L. C. & Hancock, J. T. (2013). Absence makes the communication grow fonder: Geographic separation, interpersonal media, and intimac in dating relationships. *Journal of Communication, 63,* 556–577. [7]

Johansson, P., Hall, L., Tärning, B., et al. (2014). Choice blindness and preference change: You will like this paper better if you (believe you) chose to read it! *Journal of Behavioral Decision Making, 27,* 281–289. [5]

Johnson, A. A., Hatcher, B. J., El-Khorazaty, M. N., et al. (2007). Determinants of inadequate prenatal care utilization by African American women. *Journal of Health Care for the Poor and Underserved, 18,* 620–636. [8]

Johnson, M. A. (2007). *Essential Reproduction* (6th edition). Blackwell. [8]

Johnson, M. H. (2018). *Essential reproduction* (8th ed.). Wiley-Blackwell. [3]

Johnson, S. D., Phelps, D. L. & Cottler, L. B. (2004). The association of sexual dysfunction and substance use among a community epidemiological sample. *Archives of Sexual Behavior, 33,* 55–63. [5]

Johnson, S., Cushion, M., Bond, S., et al. (2015). Comparison of analytical sensitivity and women's interpretation of home pregnancy tests. *Clinical Chemistry and Laboratory Medicine, 53,* 391–402. [8]

Jones, B. C., Debruine, L. M., Little, A. C., et al. (2006). Integrating gaze direction and expression in preferences for attractive faces. *Psychological Science, 17,* 588–591. [5]

Jones, B. C., Hahn, A. C., Fisher, C. I., et al. (2018). General sexual desire, but not desire for uncommitted sexual relationships, tracks changes in women's hormonal status. *Psychoneuroendocrinology, 88,* 153–157. [2]

Jones, C., Chan, C. & Farine, D. (2011). Sex in pregnancy. *Canadian Medical Association Journal, 183,* 815–818. [8]

Jonsson, H., Sulem, P., Kehr, B., et al. (2017). Parental influence on human germline de novo mutations in 1,548 trios from Iceland. *Nature, 549,* 519–522. [8]

Josephs, L. (2015). How children learn about sex: A cross-species and cross-cultural analysis. *Archives of Sexual Behavior, 44,* 1059–1069. [10]

Joyal, C. C. & Carpentier, J. (2017). The prevalence of paraphilic interests and behaviors in the general population: A provincial survey. *Journal of Sex Research, 54,* 161–171. [13]

Joyal, C. C., Cossette, A. & Lapierre, V. (2014). What exactly is an unusual sexual fantasy? *Journal of Sexual Medicine, 12,* 328–340. [5]

Ju, H., Jones, M. & Mishra, G. (2014). The prevalence and risk factors of dysmenorrhea. *Epidemiologic Reviews, 36,* 104–113. [2]

Jud, A., Fegert, J. M. & Finkelhor, D. (2016). On the incidence and prevalence of child maltreatment: A research agenda. *Child & Adolescent Psychiatry & Mental Health, 10,* 17. [10]

Just Detention International. (2014). *Survivor stories*. (http://spr.igc.org/en/survivorstories/taz-ca.html (Accessed September 23, 2014) [16]

Juzwiak, R. (2015). *What it's like to be a gay little person*. (http://tinyurl.com/gou69gw) [12]

## K

Kafka, M. P. (2008). Neurobiological processes and comorbidity. In: D. R. Laws and W. T. O'Donohue (Eds.). *Sexual deviance: Theory, assessment, and treatment* (2nd ed.). Guilford. [13]

Kafka, M. P. (2013). The development and evolution of the criteria for a newly proposed diagnosis for DSM-5: Hypersexual disorder. *Sexual Addiction & Compulsivity, 20*, 19–29. [14]

Kahlenberg, S. M. & Wrangham, R. W. (2010). Sex differences in chimpanzees' use of sticks as play objects resemble those of children. *Current Biology, 20*, R1067–1068. [4]

Kaiser Family Foundation. (2019). *The HPV vaccine: Access and use in the U.S.* (https://tinyurl.com/y7h4czju) [15]

Kaiser Health News. (2019). *Despite federal protections, rape victims still get billed for forensic exams*. (https://tinyurl.com/y6nkjjao) [16]

Kaiser, T., Del Giudice, M. & Booth, T. (2019). Global sex differences in personality: Replication with an open online dataset. *Journal of Personality*, Published online, July 15. [4]

Kane, P. (2014). *Queer flight: Does the success of gay rights mean the end of gay culture?* (http://tinyurl.com/y7tgb2we) [12]

Kantor, J. & Twohey, M. (2017). Harvey Weinstein paid off sexual harassment accusers for decades. *New York Times*, October 5. [16]

Kaplan, H. S. (1979). *Disorders of sexual desire*. Simon and Schuster. [

Kaplan, S. (2015). Former Iowa legislator Henry Rayhons, 78, found not guilty of sexually abusing wife with Alzheimer's. *Washington Post*, April 23. [6]

Kaplowitz, P. & Bloch, C. (2016). *Evaluation and referral of children with signs of early puberty*. (http://tinyurl.com/y9uuqnva) [10]

Kärgel, C., Massau, C., Weiss, S., et al. (2017). Evidence for superior neurobiological and behavioral inhibitory control abilities in non-offending as compared to offending pedophiles. *Human Brain Mapping, 38*, 1092–1104. [13]

Kashdan, T. B., Goodman, F. R., Stiksma, M., et al. (2018). Sexuality leads to boosts in mood and meaning in life with no evidence for the reverse direction: A daily diary investigation. *Emotion, 18*, 563–576. [6]

Katz, G. (2006). Not standing still for subway gropers. *New York Times*, July 5. [13]

Katz, J. & Jhally, S. (2000). Put the blame where it belongs: On men. *Los Angeles Times*, June 25. [16]

Kaunitz, A. M., Pinkerton, J. V. & Manson, J. E. (2018). Hormonal contraception and risk of breast cancer: a closer look. *Menopause, 25*, 477–479. [9]

Kavanaugh, M. L. & Jerman, J. (2018). Contraceptive method use in the United States: trends and characteristics between 2008, 2012 and 2014. *Contraception, 97*, 14–21. [9]

Kay, T., Lehmann, L. & Keller, L. (2019). Kin selection and altruism. *Current Biology, 29*, R438–R442. [App. A]

Kazmi, D., Bailey, J., Yau, M., et al. (2017). New developments in prenatal diagnosis of congenital adrenal hyperplasia. *Journal of Steroid Biochemistry and Molecular Biology, 165*, 121–123. [4]

Keane, K. (2020). *I'm self-isolating with someone I've only been dating for 2 months*. (https://tinyurl.com/yx6xw5zw) [11]

Kearney, M. S. & Levine, P. B. (2017). *The economics of non-marital childbearing and the "marriage premium for children."* (https://tinyurl.com/y6hjjpkr) [11]

Keesling, B. (2006). *Sexual healing: The completest guide to overcoming common sexual problems* (3rd ed.). Hunter House. [14]

Kenagy, G. P. (2005). Transgender health: Findings from two needs assessment studies in Philadelphia. *Health and Social Work, 30*, 19–26. [16]

Kendrick, K., Brown, V., Lords, C., et al. (2016). Full house: A retrospective analysis of high sexually transmitted infection prevalence among adult film actors at a singular residence. *Sexually Transmitted Diseases, 43*, 556–559. [17]

Kennedy, E. L. & Davis, M. D. (1983). *Boots of leather, slippers of gold: The history of a lesbian community*. Routledge. [12]

Kerckhof, M. E., Kreukels, B. P. C., Nieder, T. O., et al. (2019). Prevalence of sexual dysfunctions in transgender persons: Results from the ENIGI follow-up study. *Journal of Sexual Medicine, 16*(12), 2018–2029. [14]

Kerpelman, J. L., Pittman, J. F., Adler-Baeder, F., et al. (2009). Evaluation of a statewide youth-focused relationships education curriculum. *Journal of Adolescence, 32*, 1359–1370. [11]

Kessler, A., Sollie, S., Challacombe, B., et al. (2019). The global prevalence of erectile dysfunction: A review. *BJU International* (E-pub before print, July 2). [14]

Killingsworth, M. A. & Gilbert, D. T. (2010). A wandering mind is an unhappy mind. *Science, 330*, 932. [6]

Kilpatrick, D. G. & Resnick, H. S. (2013). Drug-facilitated, incapacitated, and forcible rape: A national study. BiblioGov. [16]

Kim, B., Benekos, P. J. & Merlo, A. V. (2016). Sex offender recidivism revisited: Review of recent meta-analyses on the effects of sex offender treatment. *Trauma Violence Abuse, 17*, 105–117. [13]

King, E. (2015). 3 sex workers' rights organizations that fight every day to end the stigma. (http://tinyurl.com/y9ef4vl9) [17]

King, G. P. & Evans, D. T. (2020). Behind the camera: Sexual health testing patterns and outcomes amongst UK adult film performers. *International Journal of STD and AIDS, 31*, 62–65. [17]

King, R. & Belsky, J. (2012). A typological approach to testing the evolutionary functions of human female orgasm. *Archives of Sexual Behavior, 41*, 1145–1160. [5]

King, R., Belsky, J., Mah, K. & Binik, Y. (2011). Are there different types of female orgasm? *Archives of Sexual Behavior, 40*, 865–875. [5]

Kingston, D. A. (2018). Hypersexuality: Fact or fiction? *Journal of Sexual Medicine, 15*, 613–615. [14]

Kingston, D. A., Graham, F. J. & Knight, R. A. (2017). Relations between self-reported adverse events in childhood and hypersexuality in adult male sexual offenders. *Archives of Sexual Behavior, 46*, 707–720. [14]

Kinsey, A. C., Pomeroy, W. B. & Martin, C. E. (1948). *Sexual behavior in the human male*. Saunders. [3, 6, 10, 17]

Kinsey, A. C., Pomeroy, W. B., Martin, C. E. & Gebhard, P. H. (1953). *Sexual behavior in the human female*. Saunders. [6, 10]

Kippen, R., Chapman, B. & Yu, P. (2013). What's love got to do with it? Homogamy and dyadic approaches to understanding marital instability. *Journal of Population Research, 30*, 213–247. [7]

Kirschbaum, A. L. & Peterson, Z. D. (2018). Would you say you "had masturbated" if . . . ?: The influence of situational and individual factors on labeling a behavior as masturbation. *Journal of Sex Research, 55*, 263–272. [6]

Kjaer, T., Albieri, V., Jensen, A., et al. (2014). Divorce or end of cohabitation among Danish women evaluated for fertility problems. *Acta Obstetricia et Gynecologica Scandinavica, 93*, 269–276. [11]

Klein, A. (2018). *Cause of polycystic ovary syndrome discovered at last*. (https://tinyurl.com/y3u92keb) [2]

Klein, R. (1999). *Penile augmentation surgery*. (http://tinyurl.com/lp5bgxh) [3]

Kleinplatz, P. J., Menard, A. D., Paquet, M. P., et al. (2009). The components of optimal sexuality: A portrait of "great sex." *Canadian Journal of Human Sexuality, 18*, 1–13. [6]

Kleinplatz, P. J., Menard, A. D., Paquet, M. P., et al. (2009). The components of optimal sexuality: A portrait of "great sex." *Canadian Journal of Human Sexuality, 18*, 1–13. [11]

Klifto, K. M. & Dellon, A. L. (2020). Persistent genital arousal disorder: Review of pertinent peripheral nerves. *Sexual Medicine Reviews, 8*(2), 265–273. [14]

Kluger, J. (2014). A preemie revolution. *Time*, June 2. [8]

Knickmeyer, R. & Baron-Cohen, S. (2006). Fetal testosterone and sex differences. *Early Human Development, 82*, 755–760. [4]

Knott, C. D., Emery Thompson, M., Stumpf, R. M. & McIntyre, M. H. (2010). Female reproductive strategies in orangutans, evidence for female choice and counterstrategies to infanticide in a species with frequent sexual coercion. *Proceedings of the Royal Society of London. Series B: Biological Sciences, 277,* 105–113. [App. A]

Knox, D., Zusman, M. & McNeely, A. (2008). University students' beliefs about sex: Men vs. women. *College Student Journal, 42,* 181–185. [14]

Kohut, T., Fisher, W. A. & Campbell, L. (2017). Perceived effects of pornography on the couple relationship: Initial findings of open-ended, participant-informed, "bottom-up" research. *Archives of Sexual Behavior, 46,* 585–602. [17]

Kolata, G. (2007). Training through pregnancy to be marathon's fastest mom. *New York Times,* November 3.

Komdeur, J., Burke, T. & Richardson, D. S. (2007). Explicit experimental evidence for the effectiveness of proximity as mate-guarding behaviour in reducing extra-pair fertilization in the Seychelles warbler. *Molecular Ecology, 16,* 3679–3688. [App. A]

Komisaruk, B. R., Beyer-Flores, C. & Whipple, B. (2006). *The science of orgasm.* Johns Hopkins University Press.

Komisaruk, B. R., Whipple, B., Crawford, A., et al. (2004). Brain activation during vaginocervical self-stimulation and orgasm in women with complete spinal cord injury: fMRI evidence of mediation by the vagus nerves. *Brain Research, 1024,* 77–88. [6]

Kong, A., Frigge, M. L., Masson, G., et al. (2012). Rate of de novo mutations and the importance of father's age to disease risk. *Nature, 488,* 471–475. [App. A]

Korn, S. Y. L. (2010). When no means yes. (https://tinyurl.com/tptelze) [16]

Kornrich, S., Brines, J. & Leupp, K. (2012). Egalitarianism, housework, and sexual frequency in marriage. *American Sociological Review, 78,* 26–50. [11]

Kort, R., Caspers, M., van de Graaf, A., et al. (2014). Shaping the oral microbiota through intimate kissing. *Microbiome, 2,* 41. [6]

Korzeniewski, K. (2012). Sexually transmitted infections among Army personnel in the military environment. In: N. Malla (Ed.), *Sexually Transmitted Infections.* IntechOpen. [15]

Kosters, J. P. & Goetzsche, P. C. (2008). *Regular self-examination or clinical examination for early detection of breast cancer.* (http://tinyurl.com/kqhrs8y) [2]

Kowal, D. (2011). Coitus interruptus (withdrawal). In: R. A. Hatcher, J. Trussell, A. L. Nelson et al. (Eds.), *Contraceptive technology* (20th ed.). Ardent Media. [9]

Kozhimannil, K. B., Macheras, M.,5869999999 & Lorch, S. A. (2014). Trends in childbirth before 39 weeks' gestation without medical indication. *Medical Care, 52,* 649–657. [8]

Krahe, B., Bieneck, S. & Scheinberger-Olwig, R. (2007). The role of sexual scripts in sexual aggression and victimization. *Archives of Sexual Behavior, 36,* 687–701. [4]

Krakowsky, Y. & Grober, E. D. (2016). Hypoactive sexual desire in men. In: L. I. Lipshultz, A. W. Pastuszak, A. T. Goldstein, A. Giraldi & M. A. Perelman (Eds.), *Management of sexual dysfunction in men and women.* Springer. [14]

Kroeger, R. A. & Smock, P. J. (2014). Cohabitation: Recent research and implications. In: J. Treas, J. Scott and M. Richards (Eds.), *The Wiley-Blackwell companion to the sociology of families.* Wiley. [11]

Kross, E., Berman, M. G., Mischel, W., et al. (2011). Social rejection shares somatosensory representations with physical pain. *Proceedings of the National Academy of Sciences of the United States of America, 108,* 6270–6275. [7]

Kruger, T. H., Haake, P., Haverkamp, J., et al. (2003). Effects of acute prolactin manipulation on sexual drive and function in males. *Journal of Endocrinology, 179,* 357–365. [5]

Kruger, T. H., Hartmann, U. & Schedlowski, M. (2005). Prolactinergic and dopaminergic mechanisms underlying sexual arousal and orgasm in humans. *World Journal of Urology, 23,* 130–138. [5]

Kuperberg, A. (2014). Age at coresidence, premarital cohabitation, and marriage dissolution: 1985–2009. *Journal of Marriage and Family, 76,* 352–369. [11]

Kuperberg, A. (2019). Premarital cohabitation and direct marriage in the United States: 1956–2015. *Marriage and Family Review, 55,* 447–475. [11]

Kwek, K. (2016). Fundamentalist Mormon polygamy and the traffic in women. *Women's Studies International Forum, 58,* 25–33. [11]

**L**

Laan, E., Rellini, A. H., Barnes, T. & International Society for Sexual Medicine. (2013). Standard operating procedures for female orgasmic disorder: Consensus of the International Society for Sexual Medicine. *Journal of Sexual Medicine, 10,* 74–82. [14]

Labelle, A., Bourget, D., Bradford, J. M., et al. (2012). Familial paraphilia: A pilot study with the construction of genograms. *ISRN Psychiatry,* published online January 1, 692813. [13]

Ladas, A. K., Whipple, B. & Perry, J. D. (2004). *The G spot and other recent discoveries about human sexuality.* Holt. [2]

Lakehomer, H., Kaplan, P. F., Wozniak, D. G. & Minson, C. T. (2013). Characteristics of scheduled bleeding manipulation with combined hormonal contraception in university students. *Contraception, 88,* 426–430. [2]

Lamaze International. (2019). *Trusted leader from pregnancy to parenthood.* (www.lamaze.org) [8]

Langdridge, D. & Lawson, J. (2019). The psychology of puppy play: A phenomenological investigation. *Archives of Sexual Behavior,* published online August 8. [13]

Långstrom, N. & Zucker, K. J. (2005). Transvestic festishism in the general population: Prevalence and correlates. *Journal of Sex and Marital Therapy, 31,* 87–95. [13]

Langstrom, N., Babchishin, K. M., Fazel, S., et al. (2015). Sexual offending runs in families: A 37-year nationwide study. *International Journal of Epidemiology, 44,* 713–720. [13, 16]

Långström, N., Rahman, Q., Carlström, E. & Lichtenstein, P. (2010). Genetic and environmental effects on same-sex sexual behavior: A population study of twins in Sweden. *Archives of Sexual Behavior, 39,* 75–80. [12]

Larivee, N., Suissa, S., Coulombe, J., et al. (2017). Drospirenone-containing oral contraceptive pills and the risk of venous thromboembolism: an assessment of risk in first-time users and restarters. *Drug Safety, 40,* 583–596. [9]

Larmuseau, M. H. D., Claerhout, S., Gruyters, L., et al. (2017). Genetic-genealogy approach reveals low rate of extrapair paternity in historical Dutch populations. *American Journal of Human Biology,* published online, July 25. [7]

Larmuseau, M. H. D., Claerhout, S., Gruyters, L., et al. (2017). Genetic-genealogy approach reveals low rate of extrapair paternity in historical Dutch populations. *American Journal of Human Biology,* Published online, July 25. [App. A]

Larsson, I. & Svedin, C. G. (2002a). Sexual experiences in childhood: Young adults' recollections. *Archives of Sexual Behavior, 31,* 263–273. [10]

Larsson, I. & Svedin, C. G. (2002b). Teachers' and parents' reports on 3- to 6-year-old children's sexual behavior: A comparison. *Child Abuse and Neglect, 26,* 247–266. [10]

Larsson, I., Svedin, C. G. & Friedrich, W. N. (2000). Differences and similarities in sexual behavior among preschoolers in Sweden and USA. *Nordic Journal of Psychiatry, 54,* 151–157. [10]

Laumann, E. O. & Michael, R. T. (Eds.). (2000). *Sex, love, and health in America: Private choices and public policies.* University of Chicago Press. [10]

Laumann, E. O., Gagnon, J. H., Michael, R. T. & Michaels, S. (1994). *The social organization of sexuality: Sexual practices in the United States.* Chicago. University of Chicago Press. [1, 10]

Laumann, E. O., Masi, C. M. & Zuckerman, E. W. (1997). Circumcision in the United States: Prevalence, prophylactic effects, and sexual practice. *Journal of the American Medical Association, 277,* 1052–1057. [3]

Laurenson, J. P., Bloom, R. A., Page, S. & Sadrieh, N. (2014). Ethinyl estradiol and other human pharmaceutical estrogens in the aquatic environment: a review of recent risk assessment data. *AAPS Journal, 16,* 299–310. [9]

Lavin, M. (2008). Voyeurism: Psychopathology and theory. In: D. R. Laws and W. T. O'Donohue (Eds.). *Sexual deviance: Theory, assessment, and treatment* (2nd ed.). Guilford. [13]

Lavner, J. A., Karney, B. R. & Bradbury, T. N. (2013). Newlyweds' optimistic forecasts of their marriage: For better or for worse? *Journal of Family Psychology, 27,* 531–540. [11]

Lavner, J. A., Karney, B. R. & Bradbury, T. N. (2016). Does couples' communication predict marital satisfaction, or does marital satisfaction predict communication? *Journal of Marriage and the Family, 78,* 680–694. [7]

Lavner, J. A., Weiss, B., Miller, J. D. & Karney, B. R. (2018). Personality change among newlyweds: Patterns, predictors, and associations with marital satisfaction over time. *Developmental Psychology, 54,* 1172–1185. [11]

Lawrence, A. A. (2017). Autogynephilia and the typology of male-to-female transsexualism: Concepts and controversies. *European Psychologist, 22,* 39–54. [4]

Lawrence, E., Rothman, A. D., Cobb, R. J. & Bradbury, M. T. (2008). Marital satisfaction across the transition to parenthood. *Journal of Family Psychology, 22,* 41–50. [11]

Laws, D. R. & O'Donohue, W. T. (2008). *Sexual deviance: Theory, assessment, and treatment* (2nd ed.). Guilford. [13]

Leahy, R. L. & Tirch, D. D. (2008). Cognitive behavioral therapy for jealousy. *International Journal of Cognitive Therapy, 1,* 18–32. [7]

Lee, J. M., Wasserman, R., Kaciroti, N., et al. (2016). Timing of puberty in overweight versus obese boys. *Pediatrics, 137,* e20150164. [10]

Lee, P. A. & Houk, C. P. (2016). Constitutional delayed puberty. In: P. Kumanov & A. Agarwal (Eds.), *Puberty: Physiology and abnormalities.* Springer. [10]

Lee, P. A., Nordenstrom, A., Houk, C. P., et al. (2016). Global disorders of sex development update since 2006: Perceptions, approach and care. *Horm Res Paediatr, 85,* 158–180. [4]

Leger, J. & Carel, J. C. (2016). Precocious puberty. In: P. Kumanov & A. Agarwal (Eds.), *Puberty: Physiology and abnormalities.* Springer. [10]

Lehmiller, J. J., Ley, D. & Savage, D. (2018). The psychology of gay men's cuckolding fantasies. *Archives of Sexual Behavior, 47,* 999–1013. [13]

Lehtonen, J., Parker, G. A. & Scharer, L. (2016). Why anisogamy drives ancestral sex roles. *Evolution, 70,* 1129–1135. [App. A]

Leiblum, S. R. (2007). Sex therapy today: Current issues and future perspectives. In: S. R. Leiblum (Ed.), *Principles and practice of sex therapy* (4th ed.). Guilford Press. [14]

Lenschow, C., Copley, S., Gardiner, J. M., et al. (2016). Sexually monomorphic maps and dimorphic responses in rat genital cortex. *Current Biology, 26,* 106–113. [10]

Lepage, J. F., Hong, D. S., Raman, M., et al. (2014). Brain morphology in children with 47,XYY syndrome: a voxel- and surface-based morphometric study. *Genes Brain Behav, 13,* 127–134. [4]

Leppink, E. W. & Grant, J. E. (2016). Behavioral and pharmacological treatment of compulsive sexual behavior/problematic hypersexuality. *Current Addiction Reports, 3,* 406–413. [14]

LeTendre, G. K. (2020). Cultural beliefs about adolescence. In: S. Hupp and J. D. Jewell (Eds.) *Encyclopedia of child and adolescent development.* Wiley. [10]

LeVay, S. (1991). A difference in hypothalamic structure between heterosexual and homosexual men. *Science, 253,* 1034–1037. [12]

LeVay, S. (2006). *Same sex—different rules.* (http://tinyurl.com/m47u42q) [6]

LeVay, S. (2017). *Gay, straight, and the reason why: The science of sexual orientation* (2nd ed.). Oxford University Press. [12]

Levenson, J. S. (2018). Sex offender management policies and evidence-based recommendations for registry reform. *Current Psychiatry Reports, 20,* 21. [13]

Levenson, J. S. & Macgowan, M. J. (2004). Engagement, denial, and treatment progress among sex offenders in group therapy. *Sexual Abuse, 16,* 49–63. [13]

Lever, J. (1994). Sexual revelations: The 1994 *Advocate* survey of sexuality and relationships: The men. *The Advocate,* August 23. [12]

Lever, J. (1995). Lesbian sex survey. *The Advocate,* August 22. [6]

Lever, J., Frederick, D. A. & Peplau, L. A. (2006). Does size matter? Men's and women's views on penis size across the lifespan. *Psychology of Men and Masculinity, 7,* 129–143. [3]

Levesque, R. J. R. (2011). Puberty rites. In: R. J. R. Levesque (Ed.), *Encyclopedia of adolescence.* Springer.

Levin, R. J. (2015). Sexuality of the ageing female: The underlying physiology. *Sexual and Relationship Therapy, 30,* 25–36. [11]

Levin, R. J. (2019). The clitoris: An appraisal of its reproductive function during the fertile years: Why was it, and still is, overlooked in accounts of female sexual arousal. *Clinical Anatomy,* published online. [2]

Levin, R. J. & Wagner, G. (1985). Orgasm in women in the laboratory—quantitative studies on duration, intensity, latency, and vaginal blood flow. *Archives of Sexual Behavior, 14,* 439–449. [5]

Levine, E. C., Herbenick, D., Martinez, O., et al. (2018). Open relationships, nonconsensual nonmonogamy, and monogamy among U.S. adults: Findings from the 2012 National Survey of Sexual Health and Behavior. *Archives of Sexual Behavior, 47,* 1439–1450. [11]

Levis, S., Strickman-Stein, N., Ganjei-Azar, P., et al. (2011). Soy isoflavones in the prevention of menopausal bone loss and menopausal symptoms: A randomized, double-blind trial. *Archives of Internal Medicine, 171,* 1363–1369. [11]

Lewis, R. J. & Janda, L. H. (1988). The relationship between adult sexual adjustment and childhood experiences regarding exposure to nudity, sleeping in the parental bed, and parental attitudes toward sexuality. *Archives of Sexual Behavior, 17,* 349–362. [10]

Lewis, T., McElroy, E., Harlaar, N. & Runyan, D. (2016). Does the impact of child sexual abuse differ from maltreated but non-sexually abused children? A prospective examination of the impact of child sexual abuse on internalizing and externalizing behavior problems. *Child Abuse and Neglect, 51,* 31–40. [10]

Ley, D. (2009). *Women who stray and the men who love them.* Rowman and Littlefield. [13]

Ley, D., Prause, N. & Finn, P. (2014). The emperor has no clothes: A review of the "pornography addiction" model. *Current Sexual Health Reports,* February. [14]

Li, C. Y., Kayes, O., Kell, P. D., et al. (2006). Penile suspensory ligament division for penile augmentation: Indications and results. *European Urology, 49,* 729–733. [3]

Li, D. H., Newcomb, M., Macapagal, K., et al. (2020). Condom-associated erectile function, but not other domains of sexual functioning, predicts condomless insertive anal sex among young men who have sex with men. *Archives of Sexual Behavior.* [9]

Li, D. K. (2019). *Massachusetts high court upholds Michelle Carter's conviction for texts encouraging boyfriend's suicide.* (https://tinyurl.com/y7vfuvon) [16]

Li, S. H. & Graham, B. M. (2017). Why are women so vulnerable to anxiety, trauma-related and stress-related disorders? The potential role of sex hormones. *Lancet Psychiatry, 4,* 73–82. [4]

Li, Z., Wan, H., Feng, G., et al. (2016). Birth of fertile bimaternal offspring following intracytoplasmic injection of parthenogenetic haploid embryonic stem cells. *Cell Research, 26,* 135–138. [12]

Liao, L. M., Lunn, S. & Baker, M. (2015). Midlife menopause: Male partners talking. *Sexual and Relationship Therapy, 30,* 167–180. [11]

Lidz, G. (2016). *Why Zurich is turning its red-light district into a drive-through.* (http://tinyurl.com/h7wrpc3) [17]

Lieberman, D. & Billingsley, J. (2016). Current research in sibling detection. *Current Opinion in Psychology, 7,* 57–60. [5]

Liew, Z., Ritz, B., Rebordosa, C., et al. (2014). Acetaminophen use during pregnancy, behavioral problems, and hyperkinetic disorders. *JAMA Pediatrics, 168,* 313–320. [8]

Lifelong Adoptions. (2019). *LGBT adoption laws.* (http://tinyurl.com/hjl2xxc) [12]

Lim, G. (2006). *In lust we trust: Adventures in adult cinema.* Monsoon. [17]

Limoncin, E., Carta, R., Gravina, G. L., et al. (2014). The sexual attraction toward disabilities: A preliminary internet-based study. *International Journal of Impotence Research, 26,* 51–54. [6]

Lindberg, L. D., Maddow-Zimet, I. & Marcell, A. V. (2019). Prevalence of sexual initiation before age 13 years among male adolescents and young adults in the United States. *JAMA Pediatrics, 173,* 553–560. [10]

Lindberg, L. D., Santelli, J. S. & Desai, S. (2018). Changing patterns of contraceptive use and the decline in rates of pregnancy and birth among U.S. adolescents, 2007–2014. *Journal of Adolescent Health, 63*, 253–256. [9]

Lindberg, L., Santelli, J. & Desai, S. (2016). Understanding the decline in adolescent fertility in the United States, 2007–2012. *Journal of Adolescent Health, 59*, 577–583. [10]

Lindh, I., Ellstrom, A. A. & Milsom, I. (2011). The long-term influence of combined oral contraceptives on body weight. *Human Reproduction, 26*, 1917–1924. [9]

Linz, D., Blumenthal, E., Donnerstein, E., et al. (2000). Testing legal assumptions regarding the effects of dancer nudity and proximity to patron on erotic expression. *Law and Human Behavior, 24*, 507–533. [3]

Lippa, R. A. (2008). Sex differences and sexual orientation differences in personality: Findings from the BBC Internet survey. *Archives of Sexual Behavior, 37*, 173–187. [12]

Lippa, R. A. (2020). Interest, personality, and sexual traits that distinguish heterosexual, bisexual, and homosexual individuals: Are there two dimensions that underlie variations in sexual orientation? *Archives of Sexual Behavior, 49*, 607–622. [12]

Lipshultz, L. I., Pastuszak, A. W., Goldstein, A. T., et al. (Eds.). (2016). *Management of sexual dysfunction in men and women: An interdisciplinary approach.* Springer. [14]

Liptak, A. (2012). Supreme Court rejects F.C.C. fines for indecency. *New York Times*, June 21. [17]

Liptak, A. (2016). Supreme Court strikes down Texas abortion restrictions. *New York Times*, June 27. [9]

Lisak, D. & Miller, P. M. (2002). Repeat rape and multiple offending among undetected rapists. *Violence and Victims, 17*, 75–83. [16]

Little, A. C., Apicella, C. L. & Marlowe, F. W. (2007). Preferences for symmetry in human faces in two cultures: Data from the UK and the Hadza, an isolated group of hunter-gatherers. *Proceedings: Biological Sciences, 274*, 3113–3117. [5]

Little, A. C., Debruine, L. M. & Jones, B. C. (2014). Sex differences in attraction to familiar and unfamiliar opposite-sex faces: Men prefer novelty and women prefer familiarity. *Archives of Sexual Behavior, 43*, 973–981. [5]

Little, A. C., Jones, B. C. & DeBruine, L. M. (2011). Facial attractiveness: Evolutionary based research. *Philosophical Transactions of the Royal Society of London. Series B: Biological Sciences, 366*, 1638–1659. [5]

Littman, L. (2018). Parent reports of adolescents and young adults perceived to show signs of a rapid onset of gender dysphoria. *PLOS One, 13*, e0202330. [4]

Littman, L. (2020). The use of methodologies in Littman (2018) is consistent with the use of methodologies in other studies contributing to the field of gender dysphoria research: Response to Restar (2019). *Archives of Sexual Behavior, 49*, 67–77. [4]

Lobmaier, J. S., Fischbacher, U., Wirthmuller, U. & Knoch, D. (2018). The scent of attractiveness: Levels of reproductive hormones explain individual differences in women's body odour. *Proceedings: Biological Sciences, 285*(1886).

Loftus, E. F. & Davis, D. (2006). Recovered memories. *Annual Review of Clinical Psychology, 2*, 469–498. [10]

Logan, T. D. (2017). *Economics, sexuality, and male sex work.* Cambridge University Press. [17]

Loh, C., Gidycz, C. A., Lobo, T. R. & Luthra, R. (2005). A prospective analysis of sexual assault perpetration: Risk factors related to perpetrator characteristics. *Journal of Interpersonal Violence, 20*, 1325–1348. [16]

Lokeshwar, S. D., Patel, P., Shah, S. M. & Ramasamy, R. (2020). A systematic review of human trials using stem cell therapy for erectile dysfunction. *Sexual Medicine Reviews, 8*, 122–130. [14]

Lönnerdal, B. (2003). Nutritional and physiological significance of human milk proteins. *American Society for Clinical Nutrition, 77*, 1537S–1543S. [8]

López Bernal, A. & TambyRaja, R. L. (2000). Preterm labour. *Baillieres Best Practice and Research in Clinical and Obstretrics and Gynecology, 14*, 133–153. [8]

Lopez, B. (2013). Sliver of sky: Confronting the trauma of sexual abuse. *Harper's Magazine*, January, 41–48. [10]

López, C. (2020). Porn views have sharply increased in some countries since coronavirus quarantines started worldwide. (https://tinyurl.com/yc2saw27) [17]

Lorenz, T., Rullo, J. & Faubion, S. (2016). Antidepressant-induced female sexual dysfunction. *Mayo Clinic Proceedings, 91*, 1280–1286. [14]

Los Angeles LGBT Center. (2019). Domestic violence services. (http://tinyurl.com/yd3dz6lt) [16]

Lösel, F. & Schmucker, M. (2005). The effectiveness of treatment for sexual offenders: A comprehensive meta-analysis. *Journal of Experimental Criminology, 1*, 117–146. [16]

Loudenback, T. (2017). Millions of college students are so terrified of loans they're turning to "sugar daddies" for help paying for school. (http://tinyurl.com/ya4f3yu8) [17]

Lovelace, L. & McGrady, M. (1980). *Ordeal: An autobiography.* Carol Publishing Group. [17]

Lumley, A. J., Michalczyk, L., Kitson, J. J., et al. (2015). Sexual selection protects against extinction. *Nature, 522*, 470–473. [App. A]

Lumley, V. A. & Scotti, J. R. (2001). Supporting the sexuality of adults with mental retardation. *Journal of Positive Behavior Interventions, 3*, 109–119. [6]

Lussier, P. & Piché, L. (2008). Frotteurism: Psychopathology and theory. In: D. R. Laws and W. T. O'Donohue (Eds.). *Sexual deviance: Theory, assessment, and treatment* (2nd ed.). Guilford. [13]

Lyden, M. (2007). Assessment of sexual consent capacity. *Sexuality and Disability, 25*, 3–20. [6]

Lynch, D. (2015). *Colin Farrell on addiction, self-control and confronting his inner sex beast.* (http://tinyurl.com/yd753xh2) [14]

**M**

Maccoby, E. E. (1998). *The two sexes: Growing up apart, coming together.* Harvard University Press. [4]

Macedo, G. S., Alemar, B. & Ashton-Prolla, P. (2019). Reviewing the characteristics of BRCA and PALB2-related cancers in the precision medicine era. *Genetics and Molecular Biology, 42*, 215–231. [2]

Macfarlane, J. M., Campbell, J. C., Wiot, S., et al. (1999). Stalking and intimate partner femicide. *Homicide Studies, 3/4*, 300–317. [16]

Magga, G. (2010). *Female circumcision and Ugandan politics.* (http://tinyurl.com/lj85jmk) [2]

Maharaj, S. & Trevino, K. (2015). A comprehensive review of treatment options for premenstrual syndrome and premenstrual dysphoric disorder. *Journal of Psychiatric Practice, 21*, 334–350. [2]

Mahic, M., Mjaaland, S., Bovelstad, H. M., et al. (2017). Maternal immunoreactivity to herpes simplex virus 2 and risk of autism spectrum disorder in male offspring. *mSphere, 2*. [8]

Mahmoudzadeh, M., Wallois, F., Kongolo, G., et al. (2017). Functional maps at the onset of auditory inputs in very early preterm human neonates. *Cerebral Cortex, 27*, 2500–2512. [8]

Mainiero, L. A. & Jones, K. J. (2013). Workplace romance 2.0: Developing a communication ethics model to address potential sexual harassment from inappropriate social media contacts between coworkers. *Journal of Business Ethics, 114*, 367–379. [16]

Malamuth, N. (2018). "Adding fuel to the fire"? Does exposure to non-consenting adult or to child pornography increase risk of sexual aggression? *Aggression and Violent Behavior, 41*, 74–89. [1, 17]

Malamuth, N. M. & Hald, G. M. (2017). The Confluence Mediational Model of sexual aggression. In: D. P. Boer (Ed.). *The Wiley handbook on the theories, assessment, and treatment of sexual offending.* Wiley. [16]

Malamuth, N. M., Huppin, M. & Linz, D. (2018). Sexual assault interventions may be doing more harm than good with high-risk males. *Aggression and Violent Behavior, 41*, 20–24. [16]

Male Contraceptive Initiative. (2019). *Home page.* (http://tinyurl.com/zkse2d4) [9]

Malo, A. F., Roldan, E. R., Garde, J., et al. (2005). Antlers honestly advertise sperm production and quality. *Proceedings of the Royal Society of London. Series B: Biological Sciences, 272*, 149–157. [App. A]

Mamo, L. (2007). *Queering reproduction: Achieving pregnancy in the age of technoscience.* Duke University Press. [12]

Maniglio, R. (2013). Child sexual abuse in the etiology of anxiety disorders. *Trauma, Violence, & Abuse, 14*, 96–112. [10]

Manktelow, B. N., Seaton, S. E., Field, D. J. & Draper, E. S. (2013). Population-based estimates of in-unit survival for very preterm infants. *Pediatrics, 131*, e425–e432. [8]

Mannen, A. (2014). 6 unsexy realities of being a phone sex operator. (http://tinyurl.com/ydcnlze2) [17]

Manning, J. (2015). Paradoxes of (im)purity: Affirming heteronormativity and queering heterosexuality in family discourses of purity pledges. *Women's Studies in Communication, 38*, 99–117. [10]

Manning, J., Kilduff, L., Cook, C., et al. (2014). Digit ratio (2D:4D): A biomarker for prenatal sex steroids and adult sex steroids in challenge situations. *Front Endocrinol (Lausanne), 5*, 9. [4]

Manning, W. D. & Cohen, J. A. (2012). Premarital cohabitation and marital dissolution: An examination of recent marriages. *Journal of Marriage and the Family, 74*, 377–387. [11]

Manson, J. E., Aragaki, A. K., Rossouw, J. E., et al. (2017). Menopausal hormone therapy and long-term all-cause and cause-specific mortality: The Women's Health Initiative Randomized Trials. *Journal of the American Medical Association, 318*, 927–938. [11]

Marazziti, D., Di Nasso, E., Masala, I., et al. (2003). Normal and obsessional jealousy: A study of a population of young adults. *European Psychiatry, 18*, 106–111. [7]

Marcus, R. (2009). Confessions of a teenage prostitute. *Portland Mercury*, September 3. [17]

Marist Poll. (2016). Should prostitution be legalized? (http://tinyurl.com/yankhu8r) [17]

Markman, H. J., Renick, M. J., Floyd, F. J., et al. (1993). Preventing marital distress through communication and conflict management training: A 4- and 5-year follow-up. *Journal of Consulting and Clinical Psychology, 61*, 70–77. [7]

Marques, J. K., Wiederanders, M., Day, D. M., et al. (2005). Effects of a relapse prevention program on sexual recidivism: Final results from California's Sex Offender Treatment and Evaluation Project (SOTEP). *Sexual Abuse, 17*, 79–107. [13]

Marshal, M. P., Dietz, L. J., Friedman, M. S., et al. (2011). Suicidality and depression disparities between sexual minority and heterosexual youth: A meta-analytic review. *Journal of Adolescent Health, 49*, 115–123. [12]

Marshall, D. S. (1971). Sexual behavior on Mangaia. In: D. S. Marshall & D. N. Suggs (Eds.), *Human sexual behavior*. Basic Books. [10]

Marshall, T. C., Bejanyan, K., Di Castro, G. & Lee, R. A. (2013). Attachment styles as predictors of Facebook-related jealousy and surveillance in romantic relationships. *Personal Relationships, 20*, 1–22. [7]

Marshall, W. L. & Fernandez, Y. M. (2003). *Phallometric testing with sexual offenders*. Safer Society Press. [13]

Marshall, W. L. & Marshall, L. E. (2016). The treatment of adult male sex offenders. In: D. P. Boer (Ed.). *Wiley handbook on the theories, assessment and treatment of sexual offending: Volume III, Treatment*. Wiley. [16]

Martijn, F. M., Babchishin, K. M., Pullman, L. E. & Seto, M. C. (2020). Sexual attraction and falling in love in persons with pedohebephilia. *Archives of Sexual Behavior*, published online February 21. [13]

Martin-Tuite, P. & Shindel, A. W. (2019). Management options for premature ejaculation and delayed ejaculation in men. *Sexual Medicine Review* (E-pub before print, October 23). [14]

Martin, D. (2008). Mildred Loving, who fought marriage ban, dies. *New York Times*, May 6. [7]

Martinson, F. M. (1976). Eroticism in infancy and childhood. *Journal of Sex Research, 2*, 251–262. [10]

Martyn-St. James, M., Cooper, K., Ren, S., et al. (2017). Phosphodiesterase-5 inhibitors for premature ejaculation: A systematic review and meta-analysis. *European Urology Focus, 3*, 119–129. [14]

Maruthupandian, J. & Marimuthu, G. (2013). Cunnilingus apparently increases duration of copulation in the Indian flying fox, *Pteropus giganteus. PLOS One, 8*, e59743. [6]

Maseroli, E., Scavello, I., Rastrelli, G., et al. (2018). Outcome of medical and psychosexual interventions for vaginismus: A systematic review and meta-analysis. *Journal of Sexual Medicine, 15*, 1752–1764. [14]

Masters, W. H. & Johnson, V. (1970). *Human sexual inadequacy*. Boston. Little, Brown. [14]

Masters, W. H. & Johnson, V. (1979). *Homosexuality in perspective*. Little, Brown. [12]

Masters, W. H. & Johnson, V. E. (1966). *Human sexual response*. Little, Brown. [6]

Masters, W. H., Johnson, V. E. & Kolodny, R. C. (1982). *Human sexuality*. Little, Brown. [10]

Mather, V. & Longman, J. (2019). Ruling leaves Caster Semenya with few good options. *New York Times*, July 31.

Matthews, M. (1994). *Horseman: Obsessions of a zoophile*. Prometheus Books. [13]

Maurer, T. W. & Robinson, D. W. (2008). Effects of attire, alcohol, and gender on perceptions of date rape. *Sex Roles, 58*, 423–434. [16]

Maxim. (2013). *Maxim's 2013 sex survey results*. (http://tinyurl.com/lzxf2cr)

Maxwell, J. A., Muise, A., MacDonald, G., et al. (2017). How implicit theories of sexuality shape sexual and relationship well-being. *Journal of Personality and Social Psychology, 112*, 238–279. [7]

Mayo Clinic. (2014). *Kegel exercises: A how-to-guide for women*. (http://tinyurl.com/y94uh6dx) [14]

Mayo Clinic. (2017a). *Hypospadias*. (http://tinyurl.com/kn4sv2j) [4]

Mayo Clinic. (2017b). *Undescended testicle*. (http://tinyurl.com/h344jth) [4]

Mayo Clinic. (2017c). *Vaginal dryness*. (http://tinyurl.com/y8w6eggj) [11]

Mayo Clinic. (2019a). *Could an abortion increase the risk of problems in a subsequent pregnancy?* (https://tinyurl.com/y2nuzjfq) [9]

Mayo Clinic. (2019b). *Genital herpes*. (https://tinyurl.com/y326y4sd) [15]

Mayo Clinic. (2019c). *Home pregnancy tests: can you trust the results?* (http://tinyurl.com/y7nm9ycl) [8]

Mayo Clinic. (2019d). *Kegel exercises: A how-to guide for women*. (https://tinyurl.com/ydczohq9) [14]

Mayo Clinic. (2019e). *Molluscum contagiosum*. (https://tinyurl.com/qnvotgy) [15]

Mayo Clinic. (2019f). *Painful intercourse (dyspareunia)*. (https://tinyurl.com/tb3gcb4) [14]

Mayo Clinic. (2019g). *Performance-enhancing drugs: Know the risk*. (http://tinyurl.com/n6dbegr) [3]

Mayo Clinic. (2019h). *Premature ejaculation*. (http://tinyurl.com/yads3kv6) [14]

Mayo Clinic. (2019i). *Prenatal cell-free DNA screening*. (https://tinyurl.com/yxgc5bbe) [8]

Mayo Clinic. (2019j). *Toxic shock syndrome*. (https://tinyurl.com/y675skqt) [2]

Mazur, D. J. & Lipshultz, L. I. (2018). Infertility in the aging male. *Current Urology Reports, 19*, 54. [8]

McCabe, M. P. & Goldhammer, D. L. (2013). Prevalence of women's sexual desire problems: What criteria do we use? *Archives of Sexual Behavior, 42*, 1073–1078. [14]

McCabe, M. P., Sharlip, I. D., Lewis, R., et al. (2016). Incidence and prevalence of sexual dysfunction in women and men: A consensus statement from the Fourth International Consultation on Sexual Medicine 2015. *Journal of Sexual Medicine, 13*, 144–152. [14]

McCarty, E. J., Quah, S., Maw, R., et al. (2011). Post-exposure prophylaxis following sexual exposure to HIV: A seven-year retrospective analysis in a regional centre. *International Journal of STD and AIDS, 22*, 407–408. [15]

McConaghy, N. (2005). Sexual dysfunction and disorders. In: J. E. Maddux and B. A. Winstead (Eds.). *Psychopathology: Foundations for a contemporary understanding*. Erlbaum. [13]

McCormack, M. & Anderson, R. E. (2014). The influence of declining homophobia on men's gender in the United States: An argument for the study of homohysteria. *Sex Roles, 71*, 109–120. [12]

McDonald, E. A. & Brown, S. J. (2013). Does method of birth make a difference to when women resume sex after childbirth? *British Journal of Obstetrics and Gynaecology, 120*, 823–830. [8]

McDonald, M. J., Rice, D. P. & Desai, M. M. (2016). Sex speeds adaptation by altering the dynamics of molecular evolution. *Nature, 531*, 233–236. [App. A]

McElrath, M. J., Smythe, K., Randolph-Habecker, J., et al. (2013). Comprehensive assessment of HIV target cells in the distal human gut suggests increasing HIV susceptibility toward the anus. *Journal of Acquired Immune Deficiency Syndromes, 63*, 263–271. [15]

McEntyre, G. (2017). *"I'm twisted": Infamous Columbus serial groper speaks about decades of sexual assaults*. (http://tinyurl.com/yat2swhp) [13]

McLaughlin, K. (2011). Moore, Kutcher: Join our crusade to end child sex trafficking. (http://tinyurl.com/y8h4d8rq) [17]

McMillan, J. (2014). The kindest cut? Surgical castration, sex offenders and coercive offers. *Journal of Medical Ethics, 40*, 583–590. [13]

McNulty, J. K., Maxwell, J. A., Meltzer, A. L. & Baumeister, R. F. (2019). Sex-differentiated changes in sexual desire predict marital dissatisfaction. *Archives of Sexual Behavior, 48*(8), 2473–2489. [11]

McNulty, J. K., Olson, M. A., Meltzer, A. L. & Shaffer, M. J. (2013). Though they may be unaware, newlyweds implicitly know whether their marriage will be satisfying. *Science, 342*, 1119–1120. [11]

McShane, L. (2009). David Carradine a fan of "potentially deadly" deviant sex acts, ex-wife said in court papers. *New York Daily News*, June 5. [13]

Meixel, A., Yanchar, A. & Fugh-Berman, A. (2015). Hypoactive sexual desire disorder: Inventing a disease to sell low libido. *Journal of Medical Ethics, 41*, 859–862. [14]

Meizner, I. (1987). Sonographic observation of in utero fetal "masturbation." *Journal of Ultrasound in Medicine, 6*, 111. [10]

Mejak, S. L., Bayliss, J. & Hanks, S. D. (2013). Long-distance bicycle riding causes prostate-specific antigen to increase in men aged 50 years and over. *PLOS One, 8*, e56030. [3]

Meloy, J. R., Rivers, L., Siegel, L., et al. (2000). A replication study of obsessional followers and offenders with mental disorders. *Journal of Forensic Sciences, 45*, 147–152. [16]

Meltzer, A. L., McNulty, J. K., Jackson, G. L. & Karney, B. R. (2014). Sex differences in the implications of partner physical attractiveness for the trajectory of marital satisfaction. *Journal of Personality and Social Psychology, 106*, 418–428. [11]

Mendonca, B. B., Batista, R. L., Domenice, S., et al. (2016). Steroid 5alpha-reductase 2 deficiency. *Journal of Steroid Biochemistry and Molecular Biology, 163*, 206–211. [4]

Meneses, L. M., Orrell-Valente, J. K., Guendelman, S. R., et al. (2006). Racial/ethnic differences in mother–daughter communication about sex. *Journal of Adolescent Health, 39*, 128–131. [10]

Meston, C. & Stanton, A. M. (n.d.). *Female sexual interest/arousal disorder*. (https://tinyurl.com/rmsf7ns) [14]

Meston, C. M. & Buss, D. M. (2007). Why humans have sex. *Archives of Sexual Behavior, 36*, 477–507. [5]

Meston, C. M. & Buss, D. M. (2009). *Why women have sex: The psychology of sex in women's own voices*. Times Books. [14]

Meyer-Bahlburg, H. F., Dolezal, C., Baker, S. W. & New, M. I. (2008). Sexual orientation in women with classical or non-classical congenital adrenal hyperplasia as a function of degree of prenatal androgen excess. *Archives of Sexual Behavior, 37*, 85–99. [12]

Miletski, H. (2017). Zoophilia: Another sexual orientation? *Archives of Sexual Behavior, 46*, 39–42. [13]

Miller, G., Tybur, J. M. & Jordan, B. D. (2007). Ovulatory cycle effects on tip earnings by lap dancers: Economic evidence for human estrus? *Evolution and Human Behavior, 28*, 375–381. [5]

Miller, L. (2014). Rape: Sex crime, act of violence, or naturalistic adaptation? *Aggression and Violent Behavior, 19*, 67–81. [16]

Miller, S. A. & Byers, E. S. (2004). Actual and desired duration of foreplay and intercourse: Discordance and misperceptions within heterosexual couples. *Journal of Sex Research, 41*, 301–309. [6]

Min, K. J., Lee, C. K. & Park, H. N. (2012). The lifespan of Korean eunuchs. *Current Biology, 22*, R792–R793. [14]

Mitchell, K. J., Finkelhor, D. & Wolak, J. (2010). Conceptualizing juvenile prostitution as child maltreatment: Findings from the National Juvenile Prostitution Study. *Child Maltreatment, 15*, 18–36. [17]

Mitchell, K. J., Jones, L. M., Finkelhor, D. & Wolak, J. (2013). Understanding the decline in unwanted online sexual solicitations for U.S. youth 2000–2010: Findings from three Youth Internet Safety Surveys. *Child Abuse and Neglect, 37*, 1225–1236. [10]

Mitchell, K. R., Geary, R., Graham, C. A., et al. (2017). Painful sex (dyspareunia) in women: Prevalence and associated factors in a British population probability survey. *British Journal of Obstetrics and Gynaecology, 124*, 1689–1697. [14]

Mitricheva, E., Kimura, R., Logothetis, N. K. & Noori, H. R. (2019). Neural substrates of sexual arousal are not sex dependent. *Proceedings of the National Academy of Sciences of the United States of America, 116*, 15671–15676. [App. B]

Moen, O. M. (2014). Is prostitution harmful? *Journal of Medical Ethics, 40*, 73–81. [17]

Mogilski, J. K., Reeve, S. D., Nicolas, S. C. A., et al. (2019). Jealousy, consent, and compersion within monogamous and consensually non-monogamous romantic relationships. *Archives of Sexual Behavior, 48*, 1811–1828. [11]

Molina, J. M., Charreau, I., Spire, B., et al. (2017). Efficacy, safety, and effect on sexual behaviour of on-demand pre-exposure prophylaxis for HIV in men who have sex with men: An observational cohort study. *Lancet HIV, 4*, e402–e410. [15]

Møller, A. P. (1992). Female swallow preference for symmetrical male sexual ornaments. *Nature, 357*, 238–240. [App. A]

Molnar, B. E., Buka, S. L. & Kessler, R. C. (2001). Child sexual abuse and subsequent psychopathology: Results from the National Comorbidity Survey. *American Journal of Public Health, 91*, 753–760. [10]

Mondaini, N., Ponchietti, R., Muir, G. H., et al. (2003). Sildenafil does not improve sexual function in men without erectile dysfunction but does reduce the postorgasmic refractory time. *International Journal of Impotence Research, 15*, 225–228. [14]

Montgomery, M. J. & Sorell, G. T. (1998). Love and dating experience in early and middle adolescence: Grade and gender comparisons. *Journal of Adolescence, 21*, 677–689. [7]

Monto, M. A. & Carey, A. G. (2014). A new standard of sexual behavior? Are claims associated with the "hookup culture" supported by general social survey data? *Journal of Sex Research, 51*, 605–615. [7]

Monto, M. A. & Milrod, C. (2013). Ordinary or peculiar men? Comparing the customers of prostitutes with a nationally representative sample of men. *International Journal of Offender Therapy and Comparative Criminology, 20*, 1–19. [17]

Moore, A. & Reynolds, P. (2018). *Childhood and sexuality: Contemporary issues*. Palgrave Macmillan. [10]

Moore, T. J., Glenmullen, J. & Mattison, D. R. (2014). Reports of pathological gambling, hypersexuality, and compulsive shopping associated with dopamine receptor agonist drugs. *JAMA Internal Medicine, 174*, 1930–1933. [14]

Morch, L. S., Skovlund, C. W., Hannaford, P. C., et al. (2017). Contemporary hormonal contraception and the risk of breast cancer. *New England Journal of Medicine, 377*, 2228–2239. [9]

Morin, R. (2016). *Can child dolls keep pedophiles from offending?* (https://tinyurl.com/y5fnw8t5) [13]

Morley, K. (2017). Tampon sales fall as working women choose contraceptives to stop their monthly cycles. *The Telegraph (London)*, January 16. [9]

Morris, C. (2017). California courts may consider legalizing prostitution. (http://tinyurl.com/ycxs5eko) [17]

Morris, D. H., Jones, M. E., Schoemaker, M. J., et al. (2012). Body mass index, exercise, and other lifestyle factors in relation to age at natural menopause: Analyses from the Breakthrough Generations Study. *American Journal of Epidemiology, 175*, 998–1005. [11]

Morris, P. H., White, J., Morrison, E. R. & Fisher, K. (2013). High heels as supernormal stimuli: How wearing high heels affects judgements of female attractiveness. *Evolution and Human Behavior, 34*, 176–181. [5]

Moskowitz, D. A. & Hart, T. A. (2011). The influence of physical body traits and masculinity on anal sex roles in gay and bisexual men. *Archives of Sexual Behavior, 40*, 835–841. [12]

Moskowitz, D. A., Rieger, G. & Roloff, M. E. (2008). Tops, bottoms and versatiles. *Sexual and Relationship Therapy, 23*, 191–202. [12]

Moskowitz, D. A., Turrubiates, J., Lozano, H. & Hajek, C. (2013). Physical, behavioral, and psychological traits of gay men identifying as bears. *Archives of Sexual Behavior, 42*, 775–784. [12]

Mother and Child Health and Education Trust. (2016). *Initiation of breastfeeding by breast crawl.* (https://tinyurl.com/8v9j4dp) [8]

Mott, M. (2018). The new Title IX guidelines benefit survivors. (https://tinyurl.com/qv5msgm) [16]

Movement Advancement Project. (2019). *Conversion therapy laws.* (https://tinyurl.com/y6dpzsj8) [12]

Moye, D. (2018). *Denver 9-year-old dies by suicide after reported bullying for being gay.* (https://tinyurl.com/y3bk8r4c) [12]

Mroz, J. (2011). From one sperm donor, 150 children. *New York Times*, September 5. [8]

Mroz, J. (2019). Their mothers chose donor sperm. The doctors used their own. *New York Times*, August 21. [8]

Mrug, S., Elliott, M. N., Davies, S., et al. (2014). Early puberty, negative peer influence, and problem behaviors in adolescent girls. *Pediatrics, 133*, 7–14. [10]

Muehlenhard, C. L. & Shippee, S. K. (2010). Men's and women's reports of pretending orgasm. *Journal of Sex Research, 47*, 552–567. [14]

Muise, A., Christofides, E. & Desmarais, S. (2009). More information than you ever wanted: Does Facebook bring out the green-eyed monster of jealousy? *CyberPsychology & Behavior, 12*, 441–444. [7]

Muller, M. N. & Wrangham, R. W. (Eds), (2009). *Sexual coercion in primates and humans: An evolutionary perspective on male aggression against females.* Harvard University Press. [App. A]

Mundell, E. J. (2019). *Study: Many poor women can't afford tampons, pads.* (https://tinyurl.com/y58uukfd) [2]

Muneer, A., Arya, M., Jordan, G. H., et al. (2014). Augmentation procedures for the penis. In: A. Muneer, M. Arya & G. H. Jordan (Eds.), *Atlas of male genitourethral surgery.* John Wiley & Sons. [3]

Munson, M. & Stelbourn, J. P. (Eds), (2013). *The lesbian polyamory reader: Open relationships, non-monogamy, and casual sex.* Harrington Park Press. [7]

Murphy, M. R., Checkley, S. A., Seckl, J. R. & Lightman, S. L. (1990). Naloxone inhibits oxytocin release at orgasm in man. *Journal of Clinical Endocrinology and Metabolism, 71*, 1056–1058. [5]

Murphy, M., Demers, J. M., Ostroff, M. L. & Ostroff, J. L. (2018). Oral PDE5 inhibitors for erectile dysfunction. *U.S. Pharmacist, 43*, 29–33. [14]

Murphy, W. D. & Page, I. J. (2008). Exhibitionism: Psychopathology and theory. In: D. R. Laws and W. T. O'Donohue (Eds.). *Sexual deviance: Theory, assessment, and treatment* (2nd ed.). Guilford. [13]

Musick, K. & Bumpass, L. (2006). *Cohabitation, marriage, and trajectories in well-being and relationships.* [11]

Muslims for Progressive Values. (2017). *LGBTQI resources.* (http://tinyurl.com/ycwfskv5) [12]

## N

Nagrath, A. & Singh, M. (2012). Sex during pregnancy. In: A. Nagrath, N. Malhotra & S. Seth (Eds.), *Progress in Obstetrics & Gynecology—3.* Jaypee Brothers (Available at http://tinyurl.com/sexduringpregnancy). [8]

Najman, J. M., Dunne, M. P. & Boyle, F. M. (2007). Childhood sexual abuse and adult sexual dysfunction: Response to commentary by Rind and Tromovitch (2007). *Archives of Sexual Behavior, 36*, 107–109. [10]

Najman, J. M., Dunne, M. P., Purdie, D. M., et al. (2005). Sexual abuse in childhood and sexual dysfunction in adulthood: An Australian population-based study. *Archives of Sexual Behavior, 34*, 517–526. [10]

Nath, J. K. & Nayar, V. R. (1997). India. In: R. T. Francoeur (Ed.), The international encyclopedia of sexuality. Continuum. [1]

Nath, J. K. & Nayar, V. R. (1997). India. In: R. T. Francoeur (Ed.), *The international encyclopedia of sexuality.* Continuum. [6]

National Center for Health Research. (2019). *The cycle of domestic violence.* (https://tinyurl.com/udas9fd) [16]

National Domestic Violence Hotline. (2017). *LGBTQ relationship violence.* (http://tinyurl.com/y6wqewp8) [16]

National Down Syndrome Society. (2019). *What is Down syndrome?* (http://tinyurl.com/y9wacrhk) [8]

National Institute of Justice. (2012). *Intimate partner stalking: Duration and trajectory.* (http://tinyurl.com/y74h8mb2) [16]

National Institute on Disability and Rehabilitation Research. (2015). *Sexuality & sexual functioning after spinal cord injury.* (http://tinyurl.com/ycyumy6v) [App. B]

National Institutes of Health. (n.d.). *Rh incompatibility.* (https://tinyurl.com/y3e9e3rv) [8]

National Marriage Project. (2010). *The state of our unions: Marriage in America 2012.* (http://tinyurl.com/y8y3ye4g) [11]

National Opinion Research Center. (2016). *Abortion if woman wants for any reason.* (http://tinyurl.com/y8b9d7ey) [9]

National Organization for Women. (2014). *Dolce & Gabbana.* (http://tinyurl.com/yc3ee57g) [17]

National Poll on Healthy Aging. (2019). *Let's talk about sex.* (https://tinyurl.com/y445hrcw) [11]

National Public Radio. (2017). *In majority Catholic Philippines, Duterte orders better access to birth control.* (http://tinyurl.com/zjv5jvc) [9]

National Survey of Sexual Health and Behavior. (2019). *About the National Survey of Sexual Health and Behavior.* (https://tinyurl.com/y5y6tv76) [1]

National Vital Statistics Reports. (2017). *Births: Final data for 2015.* (http://tinyurl.com/ha6gx6o) [8]

National Vital Statistics Reports. (2018). *Timing and adequacy of prenatal care in the United States, 2016.* (https://tinyurl.com/y3lvou3l) [8]

National Vital Statistics Reports. (2019a). *Births: Provisional data for 2018.* (https://tinyurl.com/y4r2tor8) [1]

National Vital Statistics Reports. (2019b). *Total fertility rates by state and race and Hispanic origin: United States, 2017.* (https://tinyurl.com/y4y4u9sp) [1]

Natsal. (2019). *The National Survey of Sexual Attitudes and Lifestyles.* (https://tinyurl.com/v2yg6o6) [1]

Nattrass, S., Croft, D. P., Ellis, S., et al. (2019). Postreproductive killer whale grandmothers improve the survival of their grandoffspring. *Proceedings of the National Academy of Sciences of the United States of America,* Published online December 9. [11]

Naturist Education Foundation. (2009). *NEF California poll 2009.* (http://tinyurl.com/l59cfje) [3]

NBC News. (2015). "Textbook case": W.Va. sex worker stopped a serial killer, authorities say. (http://tinyurl.com/ybuse2yh) [17]

Nelson, L. D. & Morrison, E. L. (2005). The symptoms of resource scarcity: Judgments of food and finances influence preferences for potential partners. *Psychological Science, 16*, 167–173. [5]

Netting, N. S. & Reynolds, M. K. (2018). Thirty years of sexual behavior at a Canadian university: Romantic relationships, hooking up, and sexual choices. *Canadian Journal of Human Sexuality, 27*, 55–68. [7]

Newberry, L. (2020). Coronavirus fears haven't stopped the sex trade on Los Angeles streets. *Los Angeles Times*, April 15. [17]

Newcomb, M. E., Hill, R., Buehler, K., et al. (2019). High burden of mental health problems, substance use, violence, and related psychosocial factors in transgender, non-binary, and gender diverse youth and young adults. *Archives of Sexual Behavior.* [4]

Newcomb, M. E., Ryan, D. T., Garofalo, R. & Mustanski, B. (2014). The effects of sexual partnership and relationship characteristics on three sexual risk variables in young men who have sex with men. *Archives of Sexual Behavior, 43*, 61–72. [15]

Newmahr, S. (2011). *Playing on the edge: Sadomasochism, risk, and intimacy.* Indiana University Press. [1, 13]

Neyt, B., Vandenbulcke, S. & Baert, S. (2019). Are men intimidated by highly educated women? Undercover on Tinder. *Economics of Education Review, 73*, 101914. [5]

Ngun, T. C., Ghahramani, N., Sanchez, F. J., et al. (2011). The genetics of sex differences in brain and behavior. *Frontiers in Neuroendocrinology, 32*, 227–246. [4]

Nhlekisana, R. O. B. (2017). From childhood to womanhood: Puberty rites of !Xoo girls of Zutshwa. *Marang: Journal of Language and Literature, 29*, 31–41. [2]

Nobre, P. J. (2017). Treating men's erectile problems. In: Z. D. Petersen (Ed.), *The Wiley handbook of sex therapy.* Wiley. [14]

Nottinger, O. (2014). *Teen mom — minus the MTV*. (http://tinyurl.com/yc2gubog) [10]

Noonan, A. & Taylor Gomez, A. (2010). Who's missing: Awareness of gay, lesbian, bisexual and transgender people with intellectual disability. *Sexuality and Disability, 29*, 175–180. [6]

Nordling, L. (2016). South Africa ushers in a new era for HIV. *Nature, 535*, 214–217. [15]

North American Menopause Society. (2017). Hormone therapy position statement. *Menopause, 24*, 728–753. [11]

Nosek, M. A., Howland, C. A., Rintala, D. H., et al. (2001). National study of women with physical disabilities: Final report. *Sexuality and Disability, 19*, 5–40. [6]

Nossiter, A. (1996). 6-year-old's sex crime: Innocent peck on cheek. *New York Times*, September 27. [16]

Nowak, N. T., Murali, A. & Driscoll, I. (2015). Factors related to sex differences in navigation a computerized maze. *Journal of Environmental Psychology, 43*, 136–144. [4]

Nummenmaa, L., Suvilehto, J. T., Glerean, E., et al. (2016). Topography of human erogenous zones. *Archives of Sexual Behavior, 45*, 1207–1216. [2]

Nunes, K. L., Hermann, C. A., Renee Malcom, J. & Lavoie, K. (2013). Childhood sexual victimization, pedophilic interest, and sexual recidivism. *Child Abuse and Neglect, 37*, 703–711. [13]

Nurnberg, H. G., Hensley, P. L., Heiman, J. R., et al. (2008). Sildenafil treatment of women with antidepressant-associated sexual dysfunction: A randomized controlled trial. *JAMA, 300*, 395–404. [14]

## O

O'Hara, M. E. (2017). *Judge grants Oregon resident the right to be genderless*. (http://tinyurl.com/lcqf2sn) [4]

O'Crowley, P. (2004). Student orientation: More teenage girls are testing gender boundaries. *Star-Ledger*, May 26. [7]

O'Kane, C. (2019). *Woman with two wombs gives birth twice, less than a month apart*. (https://tinyurl.com/yxr932pf) [2]

Oakley, S. H., Vaccaro, C. M., Crisp, C. C., et al. (2014). Clitoral size and location in relation to sexual function using pelvic MRI. *Journal of Sexual Medicine, 11*(4), 1013–1022. [14]

Objectum-Sexuality Internationale. (2013). *Welcome to Objectum-Sexuality Internationale*. (http://tinyurl.com/djnks2) [13]

Ocean, F. (2012). *Whoever you are, wherever you are . . . I'm starting to think we're a lot alike*. (http://tinyurl.com/y768axrl) [12]

Odukogbe, A. A., Afolabi, B. B., Bello, O. O. & Adeyanju, A. S. (2017). Female genital mutilation/cutting in Africa. *Translational Andrology and Urology, 6*, 138–148. [2]

Office of Population Research. (2014). *Are emergency contraceptive pills effective for overweight or obese women?* (http://tinyurl.com/ojn2n9t) [9]

Office on Women's Health. (2013). *Date rape drugs fact sheet*. (http://tinyurl.com/y9ywtpbs) [16]

Office on Women's Health. (2018a). *Premenstrual dysphoric disorder (PMDD)*. (https://tinyurl.com/y9nhn4lx) [2]

Office on Women's Health. (2018b). *Premenstrual syndrome (PMS)*. (https://tinyurl.com/y4vdzsrw) [2]

Office on Women's Health. (2018c). *Your guide to breastfeeding*. (https://tinyurl.com/ya34cnyz) [8]

Ogas, O. & Gaddam, S. (2011). *A billion wicked thoughts: What the world's largest experiment reveals about human desire*. Dutton. [17]

Okami, P., Olmstead, R. & Abramson, P. R. (1997). Sexual experiences in early childhood: 18-year longitudinal data from the UCLA Family Lifestyles Project. *Journal of Sex Research, 34*, 339–347. [10]

Okami, P., Olmstead, R., Abramson, P. R. & Pendleton, L. (1998). Early childhood exposure to parental nudity and scenes of parental sexuality ("primal scenes"): an 18-year longitudinal study of outcome. *Archives of Sexual Behavior, 27*, 361–384. [10]

OKtrends. (2010). *The big lies people tell in online dating*. (http://tinyurl.com/y8g8h9e7) [12]

OnTheIssues.org. (2018). Libertarian Party on crime. (http://tinyurl.com/ycnpanbv) [17]

Opperman, E., Braun, V., Clarke, V. & Rogers, C. (2014). "It feels so good it almost hurts": Young adults' experiences of orgasm and sexual pleasure. *Journal of Sex Research, 51*, 503–515. [14]

Orzack, S. H., Stubblefield, J. W., Akmaev, V. R., et al. (2015). The human sex ratio from conception to birth. *Proceedings of the National Academy of Sciences of the United States of America, 112*, E2102–2111. [App. A]

Osterberg, E. C., Gaither, T. W., Awad, M. A., et al. (2017). Correlation between pubic hair grooming and STIs: Results from a nationally representative probability sample. *Sexually Transmitted Infections, 93*, 162–166. [2]

Ostroff, J. (2016). *Baby Storm now: Dad David Stocker on the uproar and Storm's gender identity*. (http://tinyurl.com/lramlm4) [4]

Ostrzenski, A., Krajewski, P., Ganjei-Azar, P., et al. (2014). Verification of the anatomy and newly discovered histology of the G-spot complex. *BJOG, 121*, 1333–1339. [2]

Oswalt, S. B. & Wyatt, T. J. (2013). Sexual health behaviors and sexual orientation in a U.S. national sample of college students. *Archives of Sexual Behavior, 42*, 1561–1572. [7]

Ottaviano, G., Zuccarello, D., Menegazzo, M., et al. (2013). Human olfactory sensitivity for bourgeonal and male infertility: a preliminary investigation. *European Archives of Oto-Rhino-Laryngology, 270*, 3079–3086. [8]

Otterson, J. (2017). *Steroid abuse in high school and college athletes*. (https://tinyurl.com/y689rgov) [3]

Overby, L. M. (2014). Etiology and attitudes: Beliefs about the origins of homosexuality and their implications for public policy. *Journal of Homosexuality, 61*, 568–587. [12]

O'Connor, D. B., Lee, D. M., Corona, G., et al. (2011). The relationships between sex hormones and sexual function in middle-aged and older European men. *Journal of Clinical Endocrinology and Metabolism, 96*, E1577–E1587. [11]

O'Leary, C. & Howard, O. (2001). The prostitution of women and girls in metropolitan Chicago: A preliminary prevalence report. (http://tinyurl.com/y8rqa5vs) [17]

O'Neal, E. N., Spohn, C., Tellis, K. & White, C. (2014). The truth behind the lies: The complex motivations for false allegations of sexual assault. *Women & Criminal Justice, 24*, 324–340. [16]

## P

Paechter, C. & Clark, S. (2007). Learning gender in primary school playgrounds: Findings from the Tomboy Identities Study. *Pedagogy, Culture and Society, 15*, 317–331. [4]

Pai, D. (2018). *10 celebrities who are all about their bush*. [2]

Paik, A. (2010). "Hookups," dating, and relationship quality: Does the type of sexual involvement matter? *Social Science Research, 39*, 739–753. [7]

Pal, N., Broaddus, R. R., Urbauer, D. L., et al. (2018). Treatment of low-risk endometrial cancer and complex atypical hyperplasia with the levonorgestrel-releasing intrauterine device. *Obstetrics and Gynecology, 131*, 109–116. [9]

Palacios, S., Henderson, V. W., Siseles, N., et al. (2010). Age of menopause and impact of climacteric symptoms by geographical region. *Climacteric, 13*, 419–428. [11]

Paland, S. & Lynch, M. (2006). Transitions to asexuality result in excess amino acid substitutions. *Science, 311*, 990–992. [App. A]

Palmer, E. (2020). Sex workers say online market is saturated with performers, fans are canceling subscriptions during coronavirus pandemic. (https://tinyurl.com/y72y6tuz) [17]

Panja, T. (2019). Russia banned from Olympics and global sports for 4 years over doping. *New York Times*, December 10.

Pappas, K. B., Wisniewski, A. B. & Migeon, C. J. (2008). Gender role across development in adults with 46,XY disorders of sex development including perineoscrotal hypospadias and small phallus raised male or female. *Journal of Pediatric Endocrinology and Metabolism, 21*, 625–630. [4]

Parent, A. S., Franssen, D., Fudvoye, J., et al. (2016). Current changes in pubertal timing: Revised vision in relation with environmental factors including endocrine disruptors. In: J. P. Bourguignon & A. S. Parent (Eds.), *Puberty from bench to clinic: Lessons for clinical management of pubertal disorders*. Karger. [10]

Parfrey, A. (2000). *Apocalypse culture*. Feral House. [13]

Park, A. (2019). Yale opts out of DKE punishment. (https://tinyurl.com/ru6q32o) [16]

Park, B. Y., Wilson, G., Berger, J., et al. (2016). Is internet pornography causing sexual dysfunctions? A review with clinical reports. *Behavioral Sciences, 6*(3), 17. [17]

Parsemus Foundation. (2019). *Vasalgel, a multi-year contraceptive.* (http://tinyurl.com/y8heakag) [9]

Patchin, J. W. & Hinduja, S. (2019). The nature and extent of sexting among a national sample of middle and high school students in the U.S. *Archives of Sexual Behavior, 48*(8), 2333–2343. [3]

Patel, P., Borkowf, C. B., Brooks, J. T., et al. (2014). Estimating per-act HIV transmission risk: A systematic review. *AIDS, 28,* 1509–1519. [15]

Paul, E. L. & Hayes, K. A. (2002). The casualties of 'casual' sex: A qualitative exploration of the phenomenology of college students' hookups. *Journal of Social and Personal Relationships, 19,* 639–661. [7]

Pawlowski, M., Atwal, R. & Dunbar, R. I. M. (2008). Sex differences in everyday risk-taking behavior in humans. *Evolutionary Psychology, 6,* 29–42. [1]

Payscale.com. (2019). *The state of the gender pay gap 2019.* (https://tinyurl.com/yd6zpznk) [11]

PBS. (2019). Years-old rape kits are being tested around U.S. with help from Manhattan DA, DOJ. (https://tinyurl.com/y3j2pfop) [16]

Pell, E. (2013). The race grows sweeter near its final lap. *New York Times,* January 24. [11]

Peloquin, K., Brassard, A., Lafontaine, M. F. & Shaver, P. R. (2014). Sexuality examined through the lens of attachment theory: Attachment, caregiving, and sexual satisfaction. *Journal of Sex Research, 51,* 561–576. [7]

Peltason, R. (2008). *I am not my breast cancer: Women talk openly about love and sex, hair loss and weight gain, mothers and daughters, and being a woman with breast cancer.* William Morrow. [2]

Penner, D. (2013). *Woman freed after plea agreement in baby's death.* (http://tinyurl.com/y98ot7uk) [9]

Peplau, L. A., Spalding, L. R., Conley, T. D. & Veniegas, R. C. (1999). The development of sexual orientation in women. *Annual Review of Sex Research, 10,* 70–99. [7]

Perelli-Harris, B. & Styrc, M. (2018). Mental well-being differences in cohabitation and marriage: The role of childhood selection. *Journal of Marriage and Family, 80,* 239–255. [11]

Perelman, M. A. (2013). Delayed ejaculation. *Journal of Sexual Medicine, 10,* 1189–1190. [14]

Perelman, M. A. (2016a). Introduction: Advocating for a transdisciplinary approach to the management of sexual disorders. In: L. I. Lipshultz, A. W. Pastuszak, A. T. Goldstein, A. Giraldi & M. A. Perelman (Eds.), *Management of sexual dysfunction in men and women.* Springer. [14]

Perelman, M. A. (2016b). Psychosexual therapy for delayed ejaculation based on the Sexual Tipping Point model. *Translational Andrology and Urology, 5,* 563–575. [14]

Perez-Fuentes, G., Olfson, M., Villegas, L., et al. (2013). Prevalence and correlates of child sexual abuse: A national study. *Comprehensive Psychiatry, 54,* 16–27. [10]

Perez, S., Brown, C. & Binik, Y. (2016). Vaginismus: When genito-pelvic pain/penetration disorder makes intercourse seem impossible. In: L. I. Lipshultz, A. W. Pastuszak, A. T. Goldstein, A. Giraldi & M. A. Perelman (Eds.), *Management of sexual dysfunction in men and women.* Springer. [14]

Perkel, M. (n.d.). *How to use escort services: A men's guide.* (http://tinyurl.com/5s7y7) [17]

Perrett, D. (2010). *In your face: The new science of human attraction.* Palgrave Macmillan.

Perrett, D. I., Lee, K. J., Penton-Voak, I., et al. (1998). Effects of sexual dimorphism on facial attractiveness. *Nature, 394,* 884–887. [5]

Perry, D., Walder, K., Hendler, T. & Shamay-Tsoory, S. G. (2013). The gender you are and the gender you like: sexual preference and empathic neural responses. *Brain Research, 1534,* 66–75. [1]

Perry, S. L. (2020). Pornography and relationship quality: Establishing the dominant pattern by examining pornography use and 31 measures of relationship quality in 30 national surveys. *Archives of Sexual Behavior, 49*(4), 1199–1213. [17]

Perry, S. L. & Schleifer, C. (2018). Till porn do us part? A longitudinal examination of pornography use and divorce. *Journal of Sex Research, 55,* 284–296. [17]

Pettijohn, T. F., Sacco, D. F. & Yerkes, M. J. (2009). Hungry people prefer mature mates: A field test of the environmental security hypothesis. *Journal of Social, Evolutionary, and Cultural Psychology, 3,* 216–132. [5]

Pew Research Center. (2014). *Four-in-ten couples are saying "I do," again.* (http://tinyurl.com/kk3hunl) [11]

Pew Research Center. (2015). *Americans are still divided on why people are gay.* (http://tinyurl.com/kbsmeym) [12]

Pew Research Center. (2016). *Vast majority of Americans know someone who is gay, fewer know someone who is transgender.* (http://tinyurl.com/y9ll3b77) [12]

Pew Research Center. (2017a). *6 facts about American fathers.* (http://tinyurl.com/y7hxvw8w) [11]

Pew Research Center. (2017b). *As U.S. marriage rate hovers at 50%, education gap in marital status widens.* (https://tinyurl.com/yy9w7t3k) [11]

Pew Research Center. (2017c). *Key facts about race and marriage, 50 years after Loving v. Virginia.* (https://tinyurl.com/y5gnnbut) [1, 7]

Pew Research Center. (2017d). *Number of U.S. adults cohabiting with a partner continues to rise, especially among those 50 and older.* (http://tinyurl.com/ydhlggdv) [11]

Pew Research Center. (2017e). *Public opinion on abortion.* (http://tinyurl.com/yc2vnavz) [9]

Pew Research Center. (2019a). *Generation Z looks a lot like Millennials on key social and political issues.* (https://tinyurl.com/y6qo38u4) [11]

Pew Research Center. (2019b). *Public opinion on abortion.* (https://tinyurl.com/y6xg3jar) [9]

Pew Research Center. (2019c). *Why is the teen birth rate falling?* (https://tinyurl.com/y6h2h97b) [10]

Phillips, D. M., Sudol, K. M., Taylor, C. L., et al. (2004). Lubricants containing N-9 may enhance rectal transmission of HIV and other STIs. *Contraception, 70,* 107–110. [6]

Pierce, A. P. (2000). The coital alignment technique (CAT): An overview of studies. *Journal of Sex and Marital Therapy, 26,* 257–268. [14]

Pincus, J. H. (2001). *Base instincts: What makes killers kill?* W.W. Norton. [13]

Pines, A. M. (2005). *Falling in love: Why we choose the lovers we choose* (2nd ed.). Routledge. [7]

Pique Resilience Project. (2019). *Detransition Q&A.* (https://tinyurl.com/y3ur6vpb) [4]

Planned Parenthood. (2019). *What's the cervical mucus method of FAMs?* (https://tinyurl.com/y54j4caf) [9]

Plaud, J. J. & Martini, J. R. (1999). The respondent conditioning of male sexual arousal. *Behavior Modification, 23,* 254–268. [13]

Plaud, J., Gaither, G. A., Amato Henderson, S. & Devitt, M. K. (1997). The long-term habituation of sexual arousal in human males: A crossover design. *Psychological Record, 47,* 385–398. [13]

Poeppl, T. B., Langguth, B., Laird, A. R. & Eickhoff, S. B. (2014). The functional neuroanatomy of male psychosexual and physiosexual arousal: a quantitative meta-analysis. *Human Brain Mapping, 35,* 1404–1421. [13, App. B]

Polackwich, A. S. & Shoskes, D. A. (2016). Chronic prostatitis/chronic pelvic pain syndrome: A review of evaluation and therapy. *Prostate Cancer and Prostatic Diseases, 19,* 132–138. [3]

Pollard, M. & Mullan Harris, K. (2013). *Cohabitation and marriage intensity: Consolidation, intimacy, and commitment.* (https://tinyurl.com/y2arpkxh) [11]

PollingReport.com. (2014). *Abortion and birth control.* (http://tinyurl.com/76bag) [9]

Popham, P. (1998). The mysterious Sri Lankan world of Arthur C. Clarke. *The Independent* (London), February 3. [17]

Population Council. (2019). *MENT: subdermal implants for men.* (https://tinyurl.com/y3gp96mk) [9]

Pornhub. (2019). The 2019 year in review. (https://tinyurl.com/qmfe8yx) [17]

Pornhub. (2020). Coronavirus update: April 14. (https://tinyurl.com/r9ucmpy) [17]

Portman, D. J., Edelson, J., Jordan, R., et al. (2014). Bremelanotide for hypoactive sexual desire disorder: Analyses from a Phase 2B dose-ranging study. *Obstetrics and Gynecology, 123*(Suppl 1), 31S. [14]

Postma, R., Bicanic, I., van der Vaart, H. & Laan, E. (2013). Pelvic floor muscle problems mediate sexual problems in young adult rape victims. *Journal of Sexual Medicine, 10,* 1978–1987. [16]

Poston, D. L. & Baumle, A. K. (2010). Patterns of asexuality in the United States. *Demographic Research, 23,* 509–530. [5]

Potterat, J. J., Brewer, D. D., Muth, S. Q., et al. (2004). Mortality in a long-term open cohort of prostitute women. *American Journal of Epidemiology, 159,* 778–785. [17]

Pound, N., Lawson, D. W., Toma, A. M., et al. (2014). Facial fluctuating asymmetry is not associated with childhood ill-health in a large British cohort study. *Proceedings: Biological Sciences*, 281(1792).

Pound, P., Langford, R. & Campbell, R. (2016). What do young people think about their school-based sex and relationship education? A qualitative synthesis of young people's views and experiences. *BMJ Open*, 6, e011329. [10]

Power to Decide. (2019). *Teen pregnancy.* (https://tinyurl.com/y4yfludh) [10]

PR Newswire. (2016). *Non-surgical male circumcision device approved for use in adolescents by the World Health Organization.* (https://tinyurl.com/yyq77gyv) [3]

Prause, N. & Graham, C. A. (2007). Asexuality: Classification and characterization. *Archives of Sexual Behavior*, 36, 341–356. [5]

Prause, N., Steele, V. R., Staley, C., et al. (2015). Modulation of late positive potentials by sexual images in problem users and controls inconsistent with "porn addiction." *Biological Psychology*, 109, 192–199. [14]

Priest, R. J. (2001). Missionary positions: Christian, modernist, postmodernist. *Current Anthropology*, 42, 29–68. [6]

Pringle, J., Mills, K. L., McAteer, J., et al. (2017). The physiology of adolescent sexual behaviour: A systematic review. *Cogent Social Sciences*, 3, 1368858. [10]

ProCon.org. (2018). *How many prostitutes are in the United States and the rest of the world?* (http://tinyurl.com/y9fpkmpj) [17]

*Psychology Today*. (2019). *Find a transgender therapist.* (https://tinyurl.com/rsqg29a) [14]

Public Health England. (2020). Surveillance of type-specific HPV in sexually active young females in England, to end 2018. (https://tinyurl.com/udqfavh) [15]

Puts, D. (2015). Human sexual selection. *Current Opinion in Psychology*, 7, 28–32. [App. A]

Puts, D. A., Bailey, D. H., Cardenas, R. A., et al. (2013). Women's attractiveness changes with estradiol and progesterone across the ovulatory cycle. *Hormones and Behavior*, 63, 13–19. [5]

## Q

Quart, A. (2008). When girls will be boys. *New York Times*, March 16. [4]

Quartz. (2017). *Trump's budget would devote $277 million to the least effective contraceptive method known to humankind.* (http://tinyurl.com/y84c94vr) [10]

Queen, C. (1998). Bend over boyfriend: A couple's guide to male anal pleasure. Fatale Video. [6]

Quora. (2014). *What is a day in the life of a porn star like?* (http://tinyurl.com/y9bre6oc) [17]

## R

Rahman, Q., Xu, Y., Lippa, R. A. & Vasey, P. L. (2020). Prevalence of sexual orientation across 28 nations and its association with gender equality, economic development, and individualism. *Archives of Sexual Behavior*, 49, 595–606. [12]

Rahnema, C. D., Crosnoe, L. E. & Kim, E. D. (2015). Designer steroids: Over-the-counter supplements and their androgenic component: Review of an increasing problem. *Andrology*, 3, 150–155. [3]

Raley, R. K., Sweeney, M. M. & Wondra, D. (2015). The growing racial and ethnic divide in U.S. marriage patterns. *Future of Children*, 25, 89–109. [11]

Ramachandran, V. S. & Blakeslee, S. (1999). *Phantoms in the brain: Probing the mysteries of the human mind.* William Morrow.

Rametti, G., Carrillo, B., Gomez Gil, E., et al. (2011a). White matter microstructure in female to male transsexuals before cross-sex hormonal treatment. A diffusion tensor imaging study. *Journal of Psychiatric Research*, 45, 199–204. [4]

Rametti, G., Carrillo, B., Gomez-Gil, E., et al. (2011b). The microstructure of white matter in male to female transsexuals before cross-sex hormonal treatment. A DTI study. *Journal of Psychiatric Research*, 45, 949–954. [4]

Raphael, J. (2004). *Listening to Olivia: Violence, poverty, and prostitution.* Routledge. [17]

Reddit.com. (2019). r/NoFap. (https://tinyurl.com/pvlsvhd) [17]

Reece, A. S. & Hulse, G. K. (2019). Cannabis teratology explains current patterns of Coloradan congenital defects: The contribution of increased cannabinoid exposure to rising teratological trends. *Clinical Pediatrics*, 58, 1085–1123. [8]

Reece, M., Herbenick, D., Dodge, B., et al. (2010a). Vibrator use among heterosexual men varies by partnership status: Results from a nationally representative study in the United States. *Journal of Sex and Marital Therapy*, 36, 389–407. [6]

Reece, M., Herbenick, D., Fortenberry, J. D., et al. (2010b). *National Survey of Sexual Health and Behavior.* (http://tinyurl.com/okc9829) [4]

Regan, P. C., Levin, L., Sprecher, S., et al. (2000). Partner preferences: What characteristics do men and women desire in their short-term sexual and long-term romantic partners? *Journal of Psychology and Human Sexuality*, 12, 1–21. [5]

Regnerus, M. (2019). *New data show "gender-affirming" surgery doesn't really improve mental health. So why are the study's authors saying it does?* (https://tinyurl.com/w3xfntg) [4]

Regnerus, M. & Uecker, J. (2011). *Premarital sex in America: How young Americans meet, mate, and think about marrying.* Oxford University Press. [7, 11]

Regnerus, M., Price, J. & Gordon, D. (2017). Masturbation and partnered sex: Substitutes or complements? *Archives of Sexual Behavior*, 46(7), 2111–2121. [6]

Reichert, T. (Ed.) (2007). *Investigating the use of sex in media promotion and advertising.* Haworth Press. [17]

Reichert, T. & Lambiase, J. (Eds.) (2003). *Sex in advertising: Perspectives on the erotic appeal.* Lawrence Erlbaum Associates. [17]

Reilly, D., Neumann, D. L. & Andrews, G. (2015). Sex differences in mathematics and science achievement: A meta-analysis of National Assessment of Educational Progress assessments. *Journal of Educational Psychology*, 107, 645–662. [4]

Reilly, D., Neumann, D. L. & Andrews, G. (2019). Gender differences in reading and writing achievement: Evidence from the National Assessment of Educational Progress (NAEP). *American Psychologist*, 74, 445–458. [4]

Reiner, W. G. (2004). Psychosexual development in genetic males assigned female: the cloacal exstrophy experience. *Child and Adolescent Psychiatric Clinics of North America*, 13, 657–674. [4]

Reinert, A. E. & Simon, J. A. (2017). "Did you climax or are you just laughing at me?" Rare phenomena associated with orgasm. *Sexual Medicine Reviews*, 5(3), 275–281.

Reischel, J. (2006). *Crush me, kill me.* (http://tinyurl.com/y9km9zu3) [13]

Religious Tolerance. (2011). *Diversity of Roman Catholic beliefs about masturbation: Part 2: Church catechism. Is masturbation a venial or a mortal sin?* (https://tinyurl.com/y3dsmz98)

Religious Tolerance.org. (2012). *Bisexuality: Part 1: Quotations.* (http://tinyurl.com/y9kctvy9) [12]

Restar, A. J. (2020). Methodological critique of Littman's (2018) parental-respondents' accounts of "rapid-onset gender dysphoria". *Archives of Sexual Behavior*, 49, 61–66. [4]

Reverby, S. M. (2011). "Normal exposure" and inoculation syphilis: A PHS "Tuskegee" doctor in Guatemala, 1946–48. *Journal of Policy History*, 23, 6–28. [15]

Revesz, R. (2017). *Paedophiles "could be prescribed child sex dolls" to prevent real attacks, says therapist.* (https://tinyurl.com/y3uy596v) [13]

Reynolds, M. A., Herbenick, D. L. & Bancroft, J. (2003). The nature of childhood sexual experiences. In: J. Bancroft (Ed.), *Sexual development in childhood.* Indiana University Press. [10]

Rhodes, S. D., Mann, L., Siman, F. M., et al. (2015). The impact of local immigration enforcement policies on the health of immigrant Hispanics/Latinos in the United States. *American Journal of Public Health*, 105, 329–337. [8]

Rice, K. (2015). Pansexuality. In: P. Whelehan and A. Bolin (eds.), *The international encyclopedia of human sexuality.* Wiley. [12]

Rice, M. E. & Harris, G. T. (2002). Men who molest their sexually immature daughters: Is a special explanation required? *Journal of Abnormal Psychology*, 111, 329–339. [13]

Rider, J. R., Wilson, K. M., Sinnott, J. A., et al. (2016). Ejaculation frequency and risk of prostate cancer: Updated results with an additional decade of follow-up. *European Urology*, 70, 974–982. [6]

Ridley, M. (2003). *The red queen: Sex and the evolution of human nature.* Harper Perennial. [App. A]

Rieger, G., Chivers, M. L. & Bailey, J. M. (2005). Sexual arousal patterns of bisexual men. *Psychological Science*, 16, 579–584. [12]

Rieger, G., Linsenmeier, J. A., Gygax, L. & Bailey, J. M. (2008). Sexual orientation and childhood gender nonconformity: Evidence from home videos. *Developmental Psychology, 44,* 46–58. [12]

Rieger, G., Rosenthal, A. M., Cash, B. M., et al. (2013). Male bisexual arousal: A matter of curiosity? *Biological Psychology, 94,* 479–489. [12]

Rind, B. (2001). Gay and bisexual adolescent boys' sexual experiences with men: An empirical examination of psychological correlates in a nonclinical sample. *Archives of Sexual Behavior, 30,* 345–368. [10]

Rind, B. (2018). First postpubertal male same-sex sexual experience in the National Health and Social Life Survey: Current functioning in relation to age at time of experience and partner age. *Archives of Sexual Behavior, 47,* 1755–1768. [10]

Rind, B., Tromovitch, P. & Bauserman, R. (1998). A meta-analytic examination of assumed properties of child sexual abuse using college samples. *Psychological Bulletin, 124,* 22–53. [10]

Ritchie, S. J., Cox, S. R., Shen, X., et al. (2018). Sex differences in the adult human brain: Evidence from 5,216 UK Biobank participants. *Cerebral Cortex, 28,* 2959–2975. [4]

Robinson, A. (2010). *Characteristics of adolescent females sexually exploited through prostitution.* (http://tinyurl.com/yc29o42z) [17]

Robinson, L. (2016). *Adele, queen of hearts.* (http://tinyurl.com/gn5ddun) [8]

Rodeheffer, C. D., Leyva, R. P. L. & Hill, S. E. (2016). Attractive female romantic partners provide a proxy for unobservable male qualities: The when and why behind human female mate choice copying. *Evolutionary Psychology,* Online ahead of print, May 31. [App. A]

Rodrigue, C., Blais, M., Lavoie, F., et al. (2018). Passion, intimacy, and commitment in casual sexual relationships in a Canadian sample of emerging adults. *Journal of Sex Research, 55,* 1192–1205. [7]

Rodriguez-Martinez, H. (2007). Role of the oviduct in sperm capacitation. *Theriogenology, 68*(Suppl 1), S138–S146. [8]

Rogers, S. M., Turner, C. F., Hobbs, M., et al. (2014). Epidemiology of undiagnosed trichomoniasis in a probability sample of urban young adults. *PLOS One, 9,* e90548. [15]

Rolland, M., Le Moal, J., Wagner, V., et al. (2013). Decline in semen concentration and morphology in a sample of 26,609 men close to general population between 1989 and 2005 in France. *Human Reproduction, 28,* 462–470. [3]

Rosario, I. J., Kasabwala, K. & Sadeghi-Nejad, H. (2013). Circumcision as a strategy to minimize HIV transmission. *Current Urology Reports, 14,* 285–290. [3]

Rosario, M., Schrimshaw, E. W. & Hunter, J. (2011). Different patterns of sexual identity development over time: Implications for the psychological adjustment of lesbian, gay, and bisexual youths. *Journal of Sex Research, 48,* 3–15. [12]

Rosario, M., Schrimshaw, E. W., Hunter, J. & Braun, L. (2006). Sexual identity development among gay, lesbian, and bisexual youths: Consistency and change over time. *Journal of Sex Research, 43,* 46–58. [12]

Rosario, M., Schrimshaw, E. W., Hunter, J. & Levy-Warren, A. (2009). The coming-out process of young lesbian and bisexual women: Are there butch/femme differences in sexual identity development? *Archives of Sexual Behavior, 38,* 34–49. [12]

Roselli, C. E. & Stormshak, F. (2009). The neurobiology of sexual partner preferences in rams. *Hormones and Behavior, 55,* 611–620. [12]

Rosen, R. C. (2007). Erectile dysfunction: Integration of medical and psychological approaches. In: S. L. Leiblum (Ed.), *Principles and practice of sex therapy* (4th ed.). Guilford Press. [14]

Rosenbaum, J. E. (2009). Patient teenagers? A comparison of the sexual behavior of virginity pledgers and matched nonpledgers. *Pediatrics, 123,* e110–e120. [10]

Rosenthal, A. M., Hsu, K. J. & Bailey, J. M. (2017). Who are gynandromorphophilic men? An internet survey of men with sexual interest in transgender women. *Archives of Sexual Behavior, 46,* 255–264. [13]

Rosenthal, A. M., Sylva, D., Safron, A. & Bailey, J. M. (2011). Sexual arousal patterns of bisexual men revisited. *Biological Psychology, 88,* 112–115. [12]

Rosman, J. P. & Resnick, P. J. (1989). Sexual attraction to corpses: A psychiatric review of necrophilia. *Bulletin of the American Academy of Psychiatry and the Law, 17,* 153–163. [13]

Ross, J. A., Davison, A. Z., Sana, Y., et al. (2013). Ovum transmigration after salpingectomy for ectopic pregnancy. *Human Reproduction, 28,* 937–941. [2]

Ross, M. W., Crisp, B. R., Mansson, S. A. & Hawkes, S. (2012). Occupational health and safety among commercial sex workers. *Scandinavian Journal of Work and Environmental Health, 38,* 105–119. [17]

Rothman, L. (2016). *Exclusive: New "happiness index" number reveals how Americans feel right now.* (https://tinyurl.com/y2hzuaea) [11]

Rothschild, B. M., Calderon, F. L., Coppa, A. & Rothschild, C. (2000). First European exposure to syphilis: the Dominican Republic at the time of Columbian contact. *Clinical Infectious Diseases, 31,* 936–941. [1]

Rowland, D., McMahon, C. G., Abdo, C., et al. (2010). Disorders of orgasm and ejaculation in men. *Journal of Sexual Medicine, 7,* 1668–1686. [14]

Rubin, A. J. (2000). Public more accepting of gays, poll finds. *Los Angeles Times,* June 18. [12]

Rudder, C. (2010). *The case for an older woman.* (http://tinyurl.com/kzpkuom)

Rue, V. M. (1997). *The psychological safety of abortion: the need for reconsideration.* (http://tinyurl.com/y86525ar) [9]

Ruesink, G. B. & Georgiadis, J. R. (2017). Brain imaging of human sexual response: Recent developments and future directions. *Current Sexual Health Reports, 9,* 183–191. [App. B]

Ruigrok, A. N., Salimi-Khorshidi, G., Lai, M. C., et al. (2013). A meta-analysis of sex differences in human brain structure. *Neuroscience and Biobehavioral Reviews.* [4]

Ruiz, R. R. (2016). Russia's track and field team barred from Rio Olympics. *New York Times,* June 17. [3]

Rule, N. O. (2017). Perceptions of sexual orientation from minimal cues. *Archives of Sexual Behavior, 46,* 129–139. [12]

Russell, D. E. H. (1984). *Sexual exploitation: Rape, child sexual abuse, and workplace harassment.* Sage. [16]

Ryall, J. (2017). In conversation with Japan's 82-year-old porn star. (http://tinyurl.com/ybmev629) [17]

Ryan, B. (2020). *Long-acting injectable PrEP proves as effective as Truvada.* (https://tinyurl.com/ycwu978u) [15]

Ryan, C. & Jethá, C. (2010). *Sex at dawn: The prehistoric origins of modern sexuality.* Harper. [1]

Ryan, E. G. (2013). Exposé on Miami's "sugar baby" culture is most depressing thing ever. (http://tinyurl.com/yay9qs9k) [17]

Ryan, W. S., Legate, N. & N., W. (2015). Coming out as lesbian, gay, or bisexual: The lasting impact of initial disclosure experiences. *Self and Identity, 14,* 549–569. [12]

**S**

Sabo, E. (2010). Understanding genital herpes. (http://tinyurl.com/ocbdqr7) [15]

Sacher-Masoch, L. v. (1870/2000). *Venus in furs.* Viking Penguin. [13]

Sadowski, D. J., Butcher, M. J. & Kohler, T. S. (2016). A review of pathophysiology and management options for delayed ejaculation. *Sexual Medicine Reviews, 4,* 167–176. [14]

Sadr, J. & Krowicki, L. (2019). Face perception loves a challenge: Less information sparks more attraction. *Vision Research, 157,* 61–83. [5]

Safarinejad, M. R., Azma, K. & Kolahi, A. A. (2009). The effects of intensive, long-term treadmill running on reproductive hormones, hypothalamus-pituitary-testis axis, and semen quality: A randomized controlled study. *Journal of Endocrinology, 200,* 259–271. [14]

Safron, A., Barch, B., Bailey, J. M., et al. (2007). Neural correlates of sexual arousal in homosexual and heterosexual men. *Behavioral Neuroscience, 121,* 237–248. [App. B]

Saigal, S., Day, K. L., Van Lieshout, R. J., et al. (2016). Health, wealth, social integration, and sexuality of extremely low-birth-weight prematurely born adults in the fourth decade of life. *JAMA Pediatrics, 170,* 678–686. [8]

Saincome, M. (2013). *Meet the man who had sex with a dolphin (and wrote a book about it).* (http://tinyurl.com/yc828czj) [13]

Saint Louis, C. (2017). *Learning to talk like a woman (or a man).* (http://tinyurl.com/lq9wxta) [4]

Salama, S., Boitrelle, F., Gauquelin, A., et al. (2015). Nature and origin of "squirting" in female sexuality. *Journal of Sexual Medicine, 12,* 661–666. [5]

Salazar, L. F., DiClemente, R. J., Wingood, G. M., et al. (2004). Self-concept and adolescents' refusal of unprotected sex: A test of mediating mechanisms among African American girls. *Prevention Science, 5,* 137–149. [10]

Samal, P. K., Farber, C., Farooque, N. A. & Rawat, D. S. (1997). Polyandry in a central Himalayan community: An eco-cultural analysis. *Man in India, 76,* 51–56. [11]

Sami, N. & Ali, T. S. (2006). Psycho-social consequences of secondary infertility in Karachi. *Journal of the Pakistan Medical Association, 56,* 19–22. [11]

San Francisco AIDS Foundation. (2017). *Anal douching safety tips.* (https://tinyurl.com/s4y3vud) [6]

San Lazaro Campillo, I. S., Meaney, S., O'Donoghue, K. & Corcoran, P. (2018). Ectopic pregnancy hospitalisations: a national population-based study of rates, management and outcomes. *European Journal of Obstetrics, Gynecology, and Reproductive Biology, 231,* 174–179. [8]

Sanchez-Garrido, M. A. & Tena-Sempere, M. (2013). Metabolic control of puberty: Roles of leptin and kisspeptins. *Hormones and Behavior, 64,* 187–194. [10]

Sanchez, F. J. & Vilain, E. (2012). "Straight-acting gays": the relationship between masculine consciousness, anti-effeminacy, and negative gay identity. *Archives of Sexual Behavior, 41,* 111–119. [12]

Sand, M. & Fisher, W. A. (2007). Women's endorsement of models of female sexual response: The Nurses' Sexuality Study. *Journal of Sexual Medicine, 4,* 708–719. [14]

Sanders, A. R., Martin, E. R., Beecham, G. W., et al. (2015). Genome-wide scan demonstrates significant linkage for male sexual orientation. *Psychological Medicine, 45,* 1379–1388. [12]

Santelli, J. S., Kaiser, J., Hirsch, L., et al. (2004). Initiation of sexual intercourse among middle school adolescents: The influence of psychosocial factors. *Journal of Adolescent Health, 34,* 200–208. [10]

Santelli, J. S., Kantor, L. M., Grilo, S. A., et al. (2017). Abstinence-only-until-marriage: An updated review of U.S. policies and programs and their impact. *Journal of Adolescent Health, 61,* 273–280. [10]

Santos-Iglesias, P., Sierra, J. C. & Vallejo-Medina, P. (2013). Predictors of sexual assertiveness: the role of sexual desire, arousal, attitudes, and partner abuse. *Archives of Sexual Behavior, 42,* 1043–1052. [5]

Santtila, P., Jern, P., Westberg, L., et al. (2010). The dopamine transporter gene (DAT1) polymorphism is associated with premature ejaculation. *Journal of Sexual Medicine, 7,* 1538–1546. [14]

Sassler, S., Michelmore, K. & Holland, J. A. (2016). The progression of sexual relationships. *Journal of Marriage and Family, 78,* 587–597. [11]

Sauvageau, A. & Geberth, V. J. (2009). Elderly victim: An unusual autoerotic fatality involving an 87-year-old male. *Forensic Science, Medicine, and Pathology, 5,* 233–235. [13]

Sauvageau, A. & Racette, S. (2006). Autoerotic deaths in the literature from 1954 to 2004: A review. *Journal of Forensic Sciences, 51,* 140–146. [13]

Savic, I., Berglund, H. & Lindstrom, P. (2005). Brain response to putative pheromones in homosexual men. *Proceedings of the National Academy of Sciences of the United States of America, 102,* 7356–7361. [App. B]

Savin-Williams, R. (2016). *Becoming who I am: Young men on being gay.* Harvard University Press. [12]

Savin-Williams, R. (2018). An exploratory study of exclusively heterosexual, primarily heterosexual, and mostly heterosexual young men. *Sexualities, 21*(1 2), 16 29. [12]

Savin-Williams, R. C. & Vrangalova, Z. (2013). Mostly heterosexual as a distinct sexual orientation group: A systematic review of the empirical evidence. *Developmental Review, 33,* 58–88. [12]

Sayle, A. E., Savitz, D. A., Thorp, J. M., Jr., et al. (2001). Sexual activity during late pregnancy and risk of preterm delivery. *Obstetrics and Gynecology, 97,* 283–289. [8]

Scelza, B. A., Prall, S. P., Swinford, N., et al. (2000). High rate of extrapair paternity in a human population demonstrates diversity in human reproductive strategies. *Science Advances, 6,* Published online February 19. [App. A]

Schaal, B., Doucet, S., Soussignan, R., et al. (2019). The human mammary odour factor: variability and regularities in sources and functions. In: C. D. Buesching (Ed.), *Chemical signals in vertebrates 14.* Springer. [8]

Schmidt, C., Morris, L. S., Kvamme, T. L., et al. (2017). Compulsive sexual behavior: Prefrontal and limbic volume and interactions. *Human Brain Mapping, 38,* 1182–1190. [14, App. B]

Schmidt, G. (Ed.) (2000). *Kinder der sexuellen Revolution.* Psychosozial-Verlag. [6]

Schmitt, D. P. (2004). Patterns and universals of mate poaching across 53 nations: The effects of sex, culture, and personality on romantically attracting another person's partner. *Journal of Personality and Social Psychology, 86,* 560–584. [7]

Schneider, H. J., Pickel, J. & Stalla, G. K. (2006). Typical female 2nd-4th finger length (2D:4D) ratios in male-to-female transsexuals-possible implications for prenatal androgen exposure. *Psychoneuroendocrinology, 31,* 265–269. [4]

Schneuer, F. J., Milne, E., Jamieson, S. E., et al. (2018). Association between male genital anomalies and adult male reproductive disorders: a population-based data linkage study spanning more than 40 years. *Lancet Child Adolesc Health, 2,* 736–743. [4]

Schubach, G. (2001). *Urethral expulsions during sensual arousal and bladder catheterization in seven human females.* (http://tinyurl.com/28wa8g)

Schuler, M., Mohnke, S., Amelung, T., et al. (2019). Empathy in pedophilia and sexual offending against children: A multifaceted approach. *Journal of Abnormal Psychology, 128,* 453–464. [13]

Schultz, W. W., van Andel, P., Sabelis, I. & Mooyaart, E. (1999). Magnetic resonance imaging of male and female genitals during coitus and female sexual arousal. *BMJ, 319,* 1596–1600. [6]

Schulz, K. M. & Sisk, C. L. (2016). The organizing actions of adolescent gonadal steroid hormones on brain and behavioral development. *Neuroscience and Biobehavioral Reviews, 70,* 148–158. [10]

Schwartz, C. R. & Graf, N. L. (2009). Assortative matching among same-sex and different-sex couples in the United States, 1990–2000. *Demographic Research, 21,* 843–878. [12]

Scorolli, C., Ghirlanda, S., Enquist, M., et al. (2007). Relative prevalence of different fetishes. *International Journal of Impotence Research, 19,* 432–437. [13]

Scott-Sheldon, L. A. J. & Chan, P. A. (2020). Increasing sexually transmitted infections in the U.S.: A call for action for research, clinical, and public health practice. *Archives of Sexual Behavior, 49*(1), 13–17. [15]

Scott-Sheldon, L. A., Carey, K. B., Kaiser, T. S., et al. (2016). Alcohol interventions for Greek letter organizations: A systematic review and meta-analysis, 1987 to 2014. *Health Psychology, 35,* 670–684. [7]

Seehuus, M., Stanton, A. M. & Handy, A. B. (2019). On the content of "real-world" sexual fantasy: Results from an analysis of 250,000+ anonymous text-based erotic fantasies. *Archives of Sexual Behavior, 48,* 725–737. [5]

Seelman, K. L. (2015). Unequal treatment of transgender individuals in domestic violence and rape crisis programs. *Journal of Social Service Research, 41,* 307–325. [16]

Segal, N. (2000). *Entwined lives: Twins and what they tell us about human behavior.* Plume. [4]

Sell, A., Lukazsweski, A. W. & Townsley, M. (2017). Cues of upper body strength account for most of the variance in men's bodily attractiveness. *Proceedings: Biological Sciences, 284*(1869).

Semenyna, S. W. & Vasey, P. L. (2016). The relationship between adult occupational preferences and childhood gender nonconformity among Samoan women, men, and fa'afafine. *Human Nature, 27,* 283–295. [12]

Semon, T. L., Hsu, K. J., Rosenthal, A. M. & Bailey, J. M. (2017). Bisexual phenomena among gay-identified men. *Archives of Sexual Behavior, 46,* 237–245. [12]

Seok, J. W., Park, M. S. & Sohn, J. H. (2016). Neural pathways in processing of sexual arousal: a dynamic causal modeling study. *International Journal of Impotence Research, 28,* 184–188. [App. B]

Servin, A., Bohlin, G. & Berlin, L. (1999). Sex differences in 1-, 3-, and 5-year-olds' toy-choice in a structured play-session. *Scandinavian Journal of Psychology, 40,* 43–48. [4]

Seto, M. C. (2008). Pedophilia: Psychopathology and theory. In: D. R. Laws and W. T. O'Donohue (Eds.). *Sexual deviance: Theory, assessment, and treatment* (2nd ed.). Guilford. [13]

Shacham, E., Godlonton, S. & Thornton, R. L. (2014). Perceptions of male circumcision among married couples in rural Malawi. *Journal of the International Association of Providers of AIDS Care, 13*(4), 443–449. [3]

Shackelford, T. K. & Mouzos, J. (2005). Partner killing by men in cohabiting and marital relationships: A comparative, cross-national analysis of data from Australia and the United States. *Journal of Interpersonal Violence, 20,* 1310–1324. [11]

Shah, J. & Christopher, N. (2002). Can shoe size predict penile length? *British Journal of Urology International, 90,* 586–587. [3]

Shamloul, R. & Ghanem, H. (2013). Erectile dysfunction. *Lancet, 381,* 153–165. [11]

Shamonki, M. I., Jin, H., Haimowitz, Z. & Liu, L. (2016). Proof of concept: preimplantation genetic screening without embryo biopsy through analysis of cell-free DNA in spent embryo culture media. *Fertility and Sterility, 106,* 1312–1318. [8]

Sharpe, R. M. (1997). Do males rely on female hormones? *Nature, 390,* 447–448. [10]

Sharpe, R. M. (2012). Sperm counts and fertility in men: A rocky road ahead. *EMBO Reports, 13,* 398–403. [3]

Shatz, N. (2016). *Doe v. Brandeis*: In a unique decision, federal judge found lack of "basic fairness" in college sexual misconduct proceedings. (http://tinyurl.com/ybcfz3sg) [16]

Shell-Duncan, B. & Hernlund, Y. (Eds), (2000). *Female "circumcision"" in Africa: Culture, controversy, and change.* Lynne Rienner. [2]

Shepardson, R. L., Walsh, J. L., Carey, K. B. & Carey, M. P. (2016). Benefits of hooking up: Self-reports from first-year college women. *International Journal of Sexual Health, 28,* 216–220. [7]

Sheppard, L. D. & Johnson, S. K. (2019). The femme fatale effect: Attractiveness is a liability for businesswomen's perceived truthfulness, trust, and deservingness of termination. *Sex Roles, 81*(11–12), 779–796. [5]

Sheppard, M. & Mayo, J. B. (2013). The social construction of gender and sexuality: Learning from two-spirit traditions. *The Social Studies, 104,* 259–270. [1]

Sheridan, M. (2010). California elects nation's first openly transgender judge, Victoria Kolakowski. *New York Daily News,* November 17. [4]

Shih, C., Cold, C. J. & Yang, C. C. (2013). Cutaneous corpuscular receptors of the human glans clitoris: descriptive characteristics and comparison with the glans penis. *Journal of Sexual Medicine, 10,* 1783–1789. [App. B]

Shilts, R. (1982). *The mayor of Castro Street: The life and times of Harvey Milk.* St. Martin's Press. [12]

Shilts, R. (1987). *And the band played on: Politics, people, and the AIDS epidemic.* St. Martin's Press. [12]

Shor, E. & Seida, K. (2019). "Harder and harder"? Is mainstream pornography becoming increasingly violent and do viewers prefer violent content? *Journal of Sex Research, 56,* 16–28. [17]

Shostak, M. (2000). *Nisa: The life and words of a !Kung woman.* Harvard University Press. [7]

Shupe, J. (2019). *I was America's first 'nonbinary' person. It was all a sham.* (https://tinyurl.com/y2tn8fx4) [4]

Sifakis, S., Androutsopoulos, V. P., Tsatsakis, A. M. & Spandidos, D. A. (2017). Human exposure to endocrine-disrupting chemicals: Effects on the male and female reproductive systems. *Environmental Toxicology & Pharmacology, 51,* 56–70. [3]

Sigl-Glöckner, J., Maier, E., Takahashi, N., et al. (2019). Effects of sexual experience and puberty on mouse genital cortex revealed by chronic imaging. *Current Biology, 29,* 3588–3599. [10]

Silverberg, C. (2008). *How to achieve male multiple orgasms.* (http://tinyurl.com/35gkan)

Silverthorne, Z. A. & Quinsey, V. L. (2000). Sexual partner age preferences of homosexual and heterosexual men and women. *Archives of Sexual Behavior, 29,* 67–76. [5]

Simon, S. (2002). AIDS scare at tiny college shakes town. *Los Angeles Times,* April 30. [15]

Simpson, E. A., Nicolini, Y., Shetler, M., et al. (2016). Experience-independent sex differences in newborn macaques: Females are more social than males. *Sci Rep, 6,* 19669. [4]

Simpson, J. A., Collins, W. A., Tran, S. & Haydon, K. C. (2007). Attachment and the experience and expression of emotions in romantic relationships: A developmental perspective. *Journal of Personality and Social Psychology, 92,* 355–367. [7]

Sinclair, H. C. & Frieze, I. H. (2001). Initial courtship behavior and stalking: How should we draw the line? In: K. E. Davis, I. H. Frieze & R. D. Maiuro (Eds.), *Stalking: Perspectives on victims and perpetrators.* Springer. [7]

Sinding, C., Kemper, E., Spornraft-Ragaller, P. & Hummel, T. (2013). Decreased perception of bourgeonal may be linked to male idiopathic infertility. *Chemical Senses, 38,* 439–445. [8]

Singer, P. (2001). *Heavy petting.* (https://tinyurl.com/y8qzj2vf) [13]

Sionean, C., DiClemente, R. J., Wingood, G. M., et al. (2002). Psychosocial and behavioral correlates of refusing unwanted sex among African-American adolescent females. *Journal of Adolescent Health, 30,* 55–63. [10]

Sipski, M. L., Alexander, C. J. & Rosen, R. (2001). Sexual arousal and orgasm in women: Effects of spinal cord injury. *Annals of Neurology, 49,* 35–44. [6]

Sisk, C. L. (2017). Development: Pubertal hormones meet the adolescent brain. *Current Biology, 27,* R706–R708. [10]

Sivalingam, V. N., Duncan, W. C., Kirk, E., et al. (2011). Diagnosis and management of ectopic pregnancy. *Journal of Family Planning and Reproductive Health Care, 37,* 231–240. [9]

Skakkebaek, A., Moore, P. J., Chang, S., et al. (2018). Quality of life in men with Klinefelter syndrome: the impact of genotype, health, socioeconomics, and sexual function. *Genet Med, 20,* 214–222. [4]

Skakoon-Sparling, S., Cramer, K. M. & Shuper, P. A. (2016). The impact of sexual arousal on sexual risk-taking and decision-making in men and women. *Archives of Sexual Behavior, 45,* 33–42. [15]

Skenazy, L. (2017). *Teen girl sent teen boy 5 inappropriate pictures. He faced lifetime registry as a "violent sex offender" or 350 years in jail.* (http://tinyurl.com/zopx5gv) [10]

Skjaerven, R., Wilcox, A. J. & Lie, R. T. (1999). A population-based study of survival and childbearing among female subjects with birth defects and the risk of recurrence in their children. *New England Journal of Medicine, 340,* 1057–1062. [8]

Skorupskaite, K., George, J. T. & Anderson, R. A. (2014). The kisspeptin–GnRH pathway in human reproductive health and disease. *Human Reproduction Update, 20*(4), 485–500. [10]

Skovlund, C. W., Morch, L. S., Kessing, L. V. & Lidegaard, O. (2016). Association of hormonal contraception with depression. *JAMA Psychiatry, 73,* 1154–1162. [9]

Skuse, D., Printzlau, F. & Wolstencroft, J. (2018). Sex chromosome aneuploidies. In: D. H. Geschwind, H. L. Paulson and C. Klein (Eds.) *Handbook of Clinical Neurology, Vol. 147.* Elsevier. [4]

Sloss, C. M. & Harper, G. W. (2004). When street sex workers are mothers. *Archives of Sexual Behavior, 33,* 329–341. [17]

Smith, D. K., Herbst, J. H. & Rose, C. E. (2015). Estimating HIV protective effects of method adherence with combinations of preexposure prophylaxis and condom use among African American men who have sex with men. *Sexually Transmitted Diseases, 42,* 88–92. [9, 15]

Smith, M. (2019). Ex-Michigan State president to get $2.4 million in retirement deal. *New York Times,* July 30. [16]

Smith, S. M. (1988). Extra-pair copulation in black-capped chickadees: the role of the female. *Behaviour, 107,* 15–23. [App. A]

SmithBattle, L. (2007). "I wanna have a good future": Teen mothers' rise in educational aspirations, competing demands, and limited school support. *Youth and Society, 38,* 348–371. [10]

Snowden, J. M., Tilden, E. L., Snyder, J., et al. (2015). Planned out-of-hospital birth and birth outcomes. *New England Journal of Medicine, 373,* 2642–2653. [8]

Society for Adolescent Health and Medicine (2017). Abstinence-only-until-marriage policies and programs: An updated position paper of the Society for Adolescent Health and Medicine. *Journal of Adolescent Health, 61,* 400–403. [10]

Society for Assisted Reproductive Technology. (2019). *Latest data from SART show increasing use of cryopreservation for fertility preservation.* (https://tinyurl.com/w7wkfv5) [8]

Soh, D. W. & Cantor, J. M. (2015). A peek inside a furry convention. *Archives of Sexual Behavior, 44,* 1–2. [13]

Solomon, T. M., Halkilis, P. N., Moeller, R. M., et al. (2011). Sex parties among young gay, bisexual, and other men who have sex with men in New York City: Attendance and behavior. *Journal of Urban Health, 88,* 1063–1075. [7]

Sommers, C. H. (2017). A panic is not an answer: We're at imminent risk of turning this #metoo moment into a frenzied rush to blame all men. *New York Daily News,* November 26. [16]

Sonderland, A. L., O'Brien, K., Kremer, P., et al. (2014). The association between sports participation, alcohol use and aggression and violence: A systematic review. *Journal of Science and Medicine in Sport, 17,* 2–7. [16]

Soper, T. (2014). Yahoo exec countersues for defamation in sexual harassment case. (http://tinyurl.com/ycazfhvx) [16]

Sorokowski, P., Sorokowska, A., Butovskaya, M., et al. (2017). Love influences reproductive success in humans. *Frontiers in Psychology, 8,* 1922. [7]

Southern Poverty Law Center. (2007). *Bishop Eddie Long.* (http://tinyurl.com/yclauhba) [12]

Spencer, R. (2014). Libidos, vibrators and men, oh my! This is what your ageing sex drive looks like. *Guardian (London),* March 25. [11]

Spielmann, S. S., Joel, S. & Impett, E. A. (2019). Pursuing sex with an ex: Does it hinder breakup recovery? *Archives of Sexual Behavior, 48,* 691–702. [7]

Spitzberg, B. H. & Cupach, W. R. (2014). *The dark side of relationship pursuit: From attraction to obsession and stalking* (2nd ed.). Routledge. [16]

Sprecher, S. (1999). "I love you more than yesterday": Romantic partners' perceptions of changes in love and related affect over time. *Journal of Personality and Social Psychology, 76,* 46–53. [7]

Sprecher, S. (2014). Evidence of change in men's versus women's emotional reactions to first sexual intercourse: A 23-year study in a human sexuality course at a midwestern university. *Journal of Sex Research, 51,* 466–472. [10]

Sprecher, S. & Hendrick, S. (2004). Self-disclosure in intimate relationships: Associations with individual and relationship characteristics over time. *Journal of Social and Clinical Psychology, 23,* 836–856. [7]

Sprecher, S. & Regan, P. C. (2002). Liking some things (in some people) more than others: Partner preferences in romantic relationships and friendships. *Journal of Social and Personal Relationships, 19,* 463–481. [5]

Sreenivasan, S. & Weinberger, L. E. (2016). Surgical castration and sexual recidivism risk. In: A. Phenix and H. Hoberman (Eds.). *Sexual offending.* Springer. [13]

Sssh.com. (2009). Sssh.com is everything you desire and more. (http://tinyurl.com/y9en3a39) [17]

Stack, L. (2017). Killer of transgender woman is sentenced under U.S. hate crime law. *New York Times,* May 17. [4]

Stafford, L. (2011). *Maintaining long-distance and cross-residential relationships.* Routledge. [7]

Stander, V. A., Thomsen, C. J. & McWhorter, S. K. (2016). Impact of childhood sexual abuse severity on the adjustment of Navy recruits: An evaluation of the importance of the nature of the abusive relationship. In: S. M. Wadsworth & D. S. Riggs (Eds.), *War and family life.* Springer. [10]

Starkweather, K. E. & Hames, R. (2012). A survey of non-classical polyandry. *Human Nature, 23,* 149–172. [11]

Statistics Canada. (2017). *Families, households and marital status: Key results from the 2016 Census.* (http://tinyurl.com/ycto54wl) [11]

Steensma, T. D., McGuire, J. K., Kreukels, B. P. C., et al. (2013). Factors associated with desistence and persistence of childhood gender dysphoria: A quantitative follow-up study. *Journal of the American Academy of Child and Adolescent Psychiatry, 52,* 582–590. [4]

Stein, N. (1999). Incidence and implications of sexual harassment in K–12 schools. (http://tinyurl.com/y9v79y77) [16]

Steinberg, J. R. & Finer, L. B. (2011). Examining the association of abortion history and current mental health: a reanalysis of the National Comorbidity Survey using a common-risk-factors model. *Social Science and Medicine, 72,* 72–82. [9]

Stephens-Davidowitz, S. (2017). *Everybody lies: Big data, new data, and what the Internet can tell us about who we really are.* Dey St. [1, 9, 10, 12, 17]

Stern, S. R. & Willis, T. J. (2007). What are teenagers up to online? In: S. R. Mazarella (Ed.), *20 questions about youth and the media.* Peter Lang Publishing. [7]

Sternberg, R. J. (1986). A triangular theory of love. *Psychological Review, 93,* 119–135. [7]

Sternberg, R. J. (1997). Construct validation of a triangular love scale. *European Journal of Social Psychology, 27,* 313–335. [7]

Stewart, D. E. & Vigod, S. N. (2019). Postpartum depression: pathophysiology, treatment, and emerging therapeutics. *Annual Review of Medicine, 70,* 183–196. [8]

Stief, M. C., Rieger, G. & Savin-Williams, R. C. (2014). Bisexuality is associated with elevated sexual sensation seeking, sexual curiosity, and sexual excitability. *Personality and Individual Differences, 66,* 193–198. [12]

Stolk, L., Perry, J. R., Chasman, D. I., et al. (2012). Meta-analyses identify 13 loci associated with age at menopause and highlight DNA repair and immune pathways. *Nature Genetics, 44,* 260–268. [11]

Stoneage, D. (2012). *Donkey love.* Different Drummer Films. [13]

Stop Street Harassment. (2014). *Harassed in public spaces: A national street harassment report.* (http://tinyurl.com/lqsmchk) [13]

Strikwerda, L. (2017). Legal and moral implications of child sex robots. In: J. Danaher and N. McArthur (Eds.). *Robot sex: Social and ethical implications.* MIT Press. [13]

Stuart, H. (2013). *Not all pedophiles have mental disorder, American Psychiatric Association says in new DSM.* (http://tinyurl.com/y86wlsjt) [13]

Sturdivant, N. (2019). *"I would say that this the beginning for me": Once convicted as a teen, now Genarlow Wilson is dedicated to mentoring youth.* (https://tinyurl.com/yxsrw6sc) [10]

Su, R. & Rounds, J. (2015). All STEM fields are not created equal: People and things interests explain gender disparities across STEM fields. *Front Psychol, 6,* 189. [4]

Su, R., Rounds, J. & Armstrong, P. I. (2009). Men and things, women and people: A meta-analysis of sex differences in interests. *Psychological Bulletin, 135,* 859–884. [4]

Sumner, R. N., Tomlinson, M., Craigon, J., et al. (2019). Independent and combined effects of diethylhexyl phthalate and polychlorinated biphenyl 153 on sperm quality in the human and dog. *Scientific Reports, 9,* 3409. [3]

Sumter, S. R., Vandenbosch, L. & Ligtenberg, L. (2017). Love me Tinder: Untangling emerging adults' motivations for using the dating application Tinder. *Telematics and Informatics, 34,* 67–78. [7]

Sundaram, A., Vaughan, B., Kost, K., et al. (2017). Contraceptive failure in the United States: estimates from the 2006–2010 National Survey of Family Growth. *Perspectives on Sexual & Reproductive Health, 49,* 7–16. [9]

Sunil, T. S., Spears, W. D., Hook, L., et al. (2010). Initiation of and barriers to prenatal care use among low-income women in San Antonio, Texas. *Maternal & Child Health Journal, 14,* 133–140. [8]

Survive-UK. (2001). *It happened to me.* (http://survive.org.uk/stories.html (Accessed September 3, 2005) [16]

Suschinsky, K. D., Lalumiere, M. L. & Chivers, M. L. (2009). Sex differences in patterns of genital sexual arousal: Measurement artifacts or true phenomena? *Archives of Sexual Behavior, 38,* 559–573. [5]

Sussman, L. & Bordwell, S. (1981). *The rapist file: Interviews with convicted rapists.* Chelsea House. [16]

Swami, V. & Tovee, M. J. (2006). Does hunger influence judgments of female physical attractiveness? *British Journal of Psychology, 97,* 353–363. [5]

Swamy, G. K., Ostbye, T. & Skjaerven, R. (2008). Association of preterm birth with long-term survival, reproduction, and next-generation preterm birth. *Journal of the American Medical Association, 299,* 1429–1436. [8]

Swartout, K. M., Koss, M. P., White, J. W., et al. (2015). Trajectory analysis of the campus serial rapist assumption. *JAMA Pediatrics*, *169*, 1148–1154. [16]

Swerdloff, R. S. & Ng, C. M. (2019). *Gynecomastia: Etiology, diagnosis, and treatment.* (https://tinyurl.com/y5w9nwhf) [10]

## T

Tan, M., Jones, G., Zhu, G., et al. (2009). Fellatio by fruit bats prolongs copulation time. *PLOS One*, *4*, e7595. [6]

Tanner, C. (2019). Brigham Young University announces more Honor Code updates—promising to tell students what they're accused of. *Salt Lake Tribune*, August 21. [16]

Tanner, J. L. & Arnett, J. J. (2016). The emergence of emerging adulthood: The new life stage between adolescence and young adulthood. In: A. Furlong (Ed.), *Routledge handbook of youth and young adulthood* (2nd ed.). Routledge. [10]

Tattoli, L., Solarino, B., Tsokos, M., et al. (2017). Two extraordinary autoerotic fatalities. *Forensic Science, Medicine, and Pathology*, *13*, 102–106. [13]

Taylor, J. (1992). *Born that way?* (documentary film). Windfall Films, London. [12]

Taylor, R. D. (2010). Risk and resilience in low-income African American families: Moderating effects of kinship social support. *Cultural Diversity and Ethnic Minority Psychology*, *16*, 344–351. [11]

Taylor, S. (1982). Hinckley hails "historical" shooting to win love. *New York Times*, July 9. [16]

Taylor, S. N., Marrazzo, J., Batteiger, B. E., et al. (2018). Single-dose zoliflodacin (ETX0914) for treatment of urogenital gonorrhea. *New England Journal of Medicine*, *379*, 1835–1845. [15]

TelAbortion, (2020). *About the project.* www.telabortion.org. [9]

Tenga. (2019). *2019 self-pleasure report: How Americans masturbate and its role in self-care.* (https://tinyurl.com/y2mjjkh2) [6]

Ter Kuile, M. M., Melles, R. J., Tuijnman-Raasveld, C. C., et al. (2015). Therapist-aided exposure for women with lifelong vaginismus: Mediators of treatment outcome: A randomized waiting list control trial. *Journal of Sexual Medicine*, *12*, 1807–1819. [14]

Terrorism Research Center. (1998). *Trafficking in women and children.* (http://www.terrorism.com/documents/pub45270/pub45270chap2.html#5 (Accessed October 1, 2002) [17]

The Economist. (2014). *More bang for your buck.* (http://tinyurl.com/yan34zsh) [17]

The Knot. (2019). *The national average cost of a wedding is $33,931.* (http://tinyurl.com/zabfk58) [11]

Thirumalai, A. & Page, S. T. (2019). Recent developments in male contraception. *Drugs*, *79*, 11–20. [9]

Thomas, J. N., Crosby, L. & Milford, J. (2015). Gender differences among self-reported genital piercing stories. *Deviant Behavior*, *36*, 441–462. [2]

Thompson, J. A. (2019). Disentangling the roles of maternal and paternal age on birth prevalence of Down syndrome and other chromosomal disorders using a Bayesian modeling approach. *BMC Medical Research Methodology*, *19*, 82. [8]

Thornborrow, T., Jucker, J. L., Boothroyd, L. G. & Tovée, M. J. (2018). Investigating the link between television viewing and men's preferences for female body size and shape in rural Nicaragua. *Evolution and Human Behavior*, *39*, 538–546. [5]

Thornhill, R. & Palmer, C. T. (2000). *A natural history of rape: Biological bases of sexual coercion.* Cambridge, Mass. MIT Press. [16, App. A]

Thrasher, S. W. (2019). H.I.V. is coming to rural America. *New York Times*, December 1. [15]

Tiefer, L. (2002). Sexual behaviour and its medicalisation. Many (especially economic) forces promote medicalisation. *BMJ*, *325*, 45. [14]

Tilcsik, A., Anteby, M. & Knight, C. R. (2015). Concealable stigma and occupational segregation: Toward a theory of gay and lesbian occupations. *Administrative Science Quarterly*, *60*, 446–481. [12]

Tirtayasa, P. M., Prasetyo, R. B. & Rodjani, A. (2013). Diphallia with associated anomalies: A case report and literature review. *Case Reports in Urology*, *2013*, 192960. [3]

Todd, B. K., Fischer, R. A., Di Costa, S., et al. (2018). Sex differences in children's toy preferences: A systematic review, meta-regression, and meta-analysis. *Infant and Child Development*, *27*, Online at https://tinyurl.com/y4mqtbq3. [4]

Tong, Y. (2013). Acculturation, gender disparity, and the sexual behavior of Asian American youth. *Journal of Sex Research*, *50*, 560–573. [10]

Toomey, R. B., Syvertsen, A. K. & Shramko, M. (2018). Transgender adolescent suicide behavior. *Pediatrics*, *142*(4). [10]

Tovee, M. J., Swami, V., Furnham, A. & Mangalparsad, R. (2006). Changing perceptions of attractiveness as observers are exposed to a different culture. *Evolution and Human Behavior*, *27*, 443–456. [5]

Townsend, L. (2007). *Leatherman's handbook II.* Booksurge Publishing. [7]

Trenholm, C., Devaney, B., Fortson, K., et al. (2007). *Impacts of four Title V, Section 510 abstinence education programs* (https://aspe.hhs.gov/report/impacts-four-title-v-section-510-abstinence-education-programs) [10]

Trivers, R., Palestis, B. G. & Manning, J. T. (2013). The symmetry of children's knees is linked to their adult sprinting speed and their willingness to sprint in a long-term Jamaican study. *PLOS One*, *8*, e72244. [App. A]

Tronstein, E., Johnston, C., Huang, M. L., et al. (2011). Genital shedding of herpes simplex virus among symptomatic and asymptomatic persons with HSV-2 infection. *JAMA*, *305*, 1441–1449. [15]

Truesdale, M. D., Osterberg, E. C., Gaither, T. W., et al. (2017). Prevalence of pubic hair grooming-related injuries and identification of high-risk individuals in the United States. *JAMA Dermatology*, *153*, 1114–1121. [2]

Trussell, J., Schwartz, E. B. & Guthrie, K. (2009). Obesity and oral contraceptive pill failure. *Contraception*, *79*, 334–338. [9]

Tulviste, T. & Koor, M. (2005). "Hands off the car, it's mine!" and "The teacher will be angry if we don't play nicely": Gender-related preferences in the use of moral rules and social conventions in preschoolers' dyadic play. *Sex Roles*, *53*, 57–66. [4]

Tunell, A. (2018). *Inside Skirt Club, the secret, worldwide sex party for bisexual women.* (https://tinyurl.com/yyn2d7up) [7]

Turanovic, J. J., Pratt, T. C. & Piquero, A. R. (2017). Exposure to fetal testosterone, aggression, and violent behavior: A meta-analysis of the 2D:4D ratio. *Aggression and Violent Behavior*, *(In press)*. [4]

Turner, G. (2019). My stepdad's huge dataset. (https://tinyurl.com/w2u7xpm) [17]

Twenge, J. M., Sherman, R. A. & Wells, B. E. (2016). Changes in American adults' reported same-sex sexual experiences and attitudes, 1973–2014. *Archives of Sexual Behavior*, *45*, 1713–1730. [7]

Twenge, J. M., Sherman, R. A. & Wells, B. E. (2017). Declines in sexual frequency among American adults, 1989–2014. *Archives of Sexual Behavior*, *46*, 2389–2401. [11]

## U

U.S. Census Bureau. (2010). *America's families and living arrangements.* (http://tinyurl.com/y7jeke9s) [11]

U.S. Census Bureau. (2013). *America's families and living arrangements: 2012.* (http://tinyurl.com/yb6kbm45) [12]

U.S. Census Bureau. (2017). *America's families and living arrangements: 2016.* (http://tinyurl.com/yc8gjcq2) [11]

U.S. Census Bureau. (2019). *Historical marriage status tables.* (https://tinyurl.com/y7uty5lz) [11]

U.S. Census Bureau. (2020). *U.S. marriage and divorce rates by state.* (https://tinyurl.com/vnzeq4q) [11]

U.S. Department of Education. (2011). "Dear colleague" letter. (http://tinyurl.com/ydg4659z) [16]

U.S. Department of Education. (2020). *Secretary DeVos takes historic action to strengthen Title IX protections for all students.* (https://tinyurl.com/yd2q6uxj) [16]

U.S. Department of Justice. (1998). *Stalking in America: Findings from the National Violence Against Women Survey.* (http://tinyurl.com/hpuc2wt) [16]

U.S. Department of State. (2019). *Annual report on intercountry adoption.* (https://tinyurl.com/y2u2jolf) [8]

U.S. Food and Drug Administration (2016). *Depo-Provera: full prescribing information.* http://tinyurl.com/yclmj3zw. [9]

U.S. Food and Drug Administration. (2017). *Mercury levels in commercial fish and shellfish.* (http://tinyurl.com/yayg6ur5) [8]

U.S. Preventive Services Taskforce. (2016). Primary care screening for and treatment of depression in pregnant and postpartum women. *Journal of the American Medical Association, 315*, 388–406. [8]

UCSF Health. (2019). *Ashkenazi Jewish carrier testing.* (https://tinyurl.com/y496fuv6) [11]

Ueno, K., Roach, T. & Peña-Talamantes, A. E. (2013). Sexual orientation and gender typicality of the occupation in young adulthood. *Social Forces, 92*, 81–108. [12]

Ullman, M. T. (2016). The declarative/procedural model: A neurobiological model of language learning, knowledge and use. In: G. Hickok and S. A. Small (Eds). *The neurobiology of language.* Elsevier. [4]

Ulrich, H., Randolph, M. & Acheson, S. (2005/6). Child sexual abuse. *Scientific Review of Mental Health Practice, 4* (Fall/Winter), 37–51. [10]

UN News. (2018). *Women's rights face global pushback from conservativism, fundamentalism—UN experts warn.* (https://tinyurl.com/y5q5fned) [11]

United Educators. (2019). Large loss report, 2019. (https://tinyurl.com/yx6os9nr) [16]

United Nations. (1994). Security Council Resolution 955, 8 November 1994. (http://tinyurl.com/y8ycbbl7) [16]

United Nations. (2008). *Convention on the Rights of Persons with Disabilities.* (https://tinyurl.com/yyselnc2) [9]

United Nations. (2017). *End abuse and detention of gay men in Chechnya, UN human rights experts tell Russia.* (https://tinyurl.com/y4bhruaz) [12]

United Nations. (2019). *Progress in family planning: did the Millennium Development Goals make a difference?* (https://tinyurl.com/y6yacar3) [9]

Upadhya, K. K., Santelli, J. S., Raine-Bennett, T. R., et al. (2017). Over-the-counter access to oral contraceptives for adolescents. *Journal of Adolescent Health, 60*(6), 634–640. [9]

Urban Thesaurus. (2019). *Slang for choking your chicken.* (https://tinyurl.com/y4xopfhg) [6]

Urquhart, V. V. (2014). Straight porn is full of "lesbians." So why is lesbian porn so boring? (http://tinyurl.com/lnwu3uh) [17]

Utian, W. H. & Woods, N. F. (2013). Impact of hormone therapy on quality of life after menopause. *Menopause, 20*, 1098–1105. [11]

## V

Van Dongen, S. (2014). Associations among facial masculinity, physical strength, fluctuating asymmetry and attractiveness in young men and women. *Annals of Human Biology, 41*, 205–213. [5]

van Wieringen, J. C., Wafelbakker, F., Verbrugge, H. P. & de Haas, J. H. (1971). *Growth diagrams 1965 Netherlands: Second National Survey on 0–24-year-olds.* Netherlands Institute for Preventative Medicine TNO, Leiden and Wolters Noordhoff. [10]

Vance, E. B. & Wagner, N. N. (1976). Written descriptions of orgasms: A study of sex differences. *Archives of Sexual Behavior, 5*, 87–98. [5]

VanderLaan, D. P., Petterson, L. J. & Vasey, P. L. (2017). Elevated kin-directed altruism emerges in childhood and is linked to feminine gender expression in Samoan fa'afafine: A retrospective study. *Archives of Sexual Behavior, 46*, 95–108. [12]

Vanita, R. (2001). *Same-sex love in India: Readings from literature and history.* Palgrave Macmillan. [6]

Vannier, S. A. & O'Sullivan, L. F. (2017). Passion, connection, and destiny: How romantic expectations help predict satisfaction and commitment in young adults' dating relationships. *Journal of Social and Personal Relationships, 34*, 235–257. [11]

Vardi, Y., Har-Shai, Y., Gil, T. & Gruenwald, I. (2008). A critical analysis of penile enhancement procedures for patients with normal penile size: Surgical techniques, success, and complications. *European Urology, 54*, 1042–1050. [3]

Vatsyayana (1991). *The Kama Sutra of Vatsyayana* (R.F. Burton, trans.). Arkana. [1]

Vejar, A. (2020). Here are 5 high-profile bills Utah's governor just signed into law. *Salt Lake Tribune*, March 29. [11]

Vennemann, B. & Pollak, S. (2006). Death by hanging while watching violent pornographic videos on the Internet: Suicide or accidental autoerotic death? *International Journal of Legal Medicine, 120*, 110–114. [13]

Ventus, D., Gunst, A., Arver, S., et al. (2019). Vibrator-assisted start-stop exercises improve premature ejaculation symptoms: A randomized controlled trial. *Archives of Sexual Behavior* (E-pub before print, November 18). [14]

Verbakel, E. & Kalmijn, M. (2014). Assortative mating among Dutch married and cohabiting same-sex and different-sex couples. *Journal of Marriage and Family, 76* (February), 1–12. [12]

Vicinus, M. (1989). Distance and desire: English boarding school friendships, 1870–1920. In: L. Duberman, M. Vicinus & G. Chauncey (Eds.), *Hidden from history: Reclaiming the gay and lesbian past.* NAL Books. [7]

Villarosa, L. (2013). *Chirlane McCrae: From gay trailblazer to politician's wife.* (http://tinyurl.com/mpruxzu) [12]

Vingilis-Jaremko, L. & Maurer, D. (2013). The influence of symmetry on children's judgments of facial attractiveness. *Perception, 42*, 302–320. [5]

Virtuous Pedophiles. (2017). *Welcome to Virtuous Pedophiles.* (www.virped.org) [13]

Voracek, M., Hofhansl, A. & Fisher, M. L. (2005). Clark and Hatfield's evidence of women's low receptivity to male strangers' sexual offers revisited. *Psychological Reports, 97*, 11–20. [7]

Vossler, A. (2016). Internet infidelity 10 years on: A critical review of the literature. *Family*

*Journal. Counseling and Therapy for Couples and Families, 24*, 359–366. [7]

Vrangalova, Z. & Savin-Williams, R. C. (2011). Adolescent sexuality and positive well-being: A group-norms approach. *Journal of Youth and Adolescence, 40*, 931–944. [10]

## W

Wade, L. (2017). *American hookup: The new culture of sex on campus.* W.W. Norton. [7]

Wade, T. J. & Feldman, A. (2016). Sex and the perceived effectiveness of flirtation techniques. *Human Ethology Bulletin, 31*(2), 30–44. [7]

Wadman, M. (2019). 'Rapid onset' of transgender identity ignites storm *Science, 361*, 958–959. [4]

Wadman, M. (2019). 'Rapid onset' of transgender identity ignites storm *Science, 361*, 958–959. [4]

Waite, L. J. & Joyner, K. (2001). Emotional and physical satisfaction with sex in married, cohabiting, and dating sexual unions: Do men and women differ? In: E. O. Laumann and R. T. Michael (Eds.), *Sex, love, and health in America: Private choices and public policies.* University of Chicago Press. [11]

Waldinger, M. D. (2017). Physiology of ejaculation. In: S. Minhas and J. Mulhall (Eds). *Male sexual dysfunction: A clinical guide.* Wiley Blackwell. [App. B]

Waldinger, M. D., de Lint, G. J., van Gils, A. P., et al. (2013). Foot orgasm syndrome: A case report in a woman. *Journal of Sexual Medicine, 10*, 1926–1934. [5]

Waldinger, M. D., Quinn, P., Dilleen, M., et al. (2005). A multinational population survey of intravaginal ejaculation latency time. *Journal of Sexual Medicine, 2*, 492–497. [14]

Waldinger, M. D., Zwinderman, A. H. & Olivier, B. (2001). Antidepressants and ejaculation: A double-blind, randomized, placebo-controlled, fixed-dose study with paroxetine, sertraline, and nefazodone. *Journal of Clinical Psychopharmacology, 21*, 293–297. [14]

Walker, L. E. A. (2009). *The battered woman syndrome* (3rd ed). Springer. [16]

Walker, R. S., Flinn, M. V. & Hill, K. R. (2010). Evolutionary history of partible paternity in lowland South America. *Proceedings of the National Academy of Sciences of the United States of America.* [1]

Wallen, K. & Lloyd, E. A. (2011). Female sexual arousal: Genital anatomy and orgasm in intercourse. *Hormones and Behavior, 59*, 780–792. [14]

Waller, K. L. & MacDonald, T. K. (2010). Trait self-esteem moderates the effect of initiator status on emotional and cognitive responses to romantic relationship dissolution. *Journal of Personality, 78*, 1271–1299. [7]

Wallien, M. S. & Cohen-Kettenis, P. T. (2008). Psychosexual outcome of gender-dysphoric children. *Journal of the American Academy of Child and Adolescent Psychiatry, 47*, 1413–1423. [4]

Walton, M. T., Cantor, J. M., Bhullar, N. & Lykins, A. D. (2017). Hypersexuality: A critical review and introduction to the "sexhavior cycle." *Archives of Sexual Behavior, 46*(8), 2231–2251. [14]

Wang, A. B. (2017). A supermodel reveals she is intersex, was subjected to 'traumatizing' and 'unnecessary' surgeries. *Washington Post*, January 25. [4]

Wang, H., Yuan, J., Hu, X., et al. (2014). The effectiveness and safety of avanafil for erectile dysfunction: A systematic review and meta-analysis. *Current Medical Research and Opinion, 30*, 1565–1571. [14]

Wang, K., Rendina, H. J. & Pachankis, J. E. (2016). Looking on the bright side of stigma: How stress-related growth facilitates adaptive coping among gay and bisexual men. *Journal of Gay and Lesbian Mental Health, 20*, 363–375. [14]

Wang, Y. & Kosinski, M. (2018). Deep neural networks are more accurate than humans at detecting sexual orientation from facial images. *Journal of Personality and Social Psychology, 114*(2), 246–257. [12]

Wang, Y. E., Kakigi, C., Barbosa, D., et al. (2016). Oral contraceptive use and prevalence of self-reported glaucoma or ocular hypertension in the United States. *Ophthalmology, 123*, 729–736. [9]

Wanshel, E. (2017). *Pastor warns hurricanes will hit cities that don't repent "sexual perversion."* (http://tinyurl.com/yaaawpvp) [12]

Ward, T. & Beech, A. R. (2008). An integrated theory of sexual offending. In: D. R. Laws and W. T. O'Donohue (Eds.). *Sexual deviance: Theory, assessment, and treatment* (2nd ed.). Guilford. [13]

Warner, L. & Steiner, M. J. (2011). Male condoms. In: R. A. Hatcher, J. Trussell, A. L. Nelson, et al. (Eds.), *Contraceptive technology* (20th ed.). Ardent Media. [9]

Warner, P. & Bancroft, J. (1987). A regional clinical service for sexual problems: A three-year survey. *Sexual and Marital Therapy, 2*, 115–126. [14]

Warren, J. T., Harvey, S. M. & Henderson, J. T. (2010). Do depression and low self-esteem follow abortion among adolescents? Evidence from a national study. *Perspectives on Sexual & Reproductive Health, 42*, 230–235. [9]

Waterman, J. M. (2010). The adaptive function of masturbation in a promiscuous African ground squirrel. *PLOS One, 5*(9), e13060. [6]

Wawer, M. J., Gray, R. H., Sewankambo, N. K., et al. (2005). Rates of HIV-1 transmission per coital act, by stage of HIV-1 infection, in Rakai, Uganda. *Journal of Infectious Diseases, 191*, 1403–1409. [15]

WebMD. (2019). *Genital piercings.* (https://tinyurl.com/y6h8n3ma) [3]

Weeks, G. R., Gambescia, N. & Hertlein, K. M. (2015). *A clinician's guide to systemic sex therapy* (2nd ed.). Routledge. [14]

Weinberg, M. S., Shaver, F. M. & Williams, C. J. (1999). Gendered sex work in the San Francisco Tenderloin. *Archives of Sexual Behavior, 28*, 503–521. [17]

Weiner, L. & Avery-Clark, C. (2017). *Sensate focus in sex therapy.* Routledge. [14]

Weinrott, M. R. & Saylor, M. (1991). Self-report of crimes committed by sex offenders. *Journal of Interpersonal Violence, 6*, 286–300. [16]

Weiss, E. (2004). *Surviving domestic violence: Voices of women who broke free.* Volcano Press. [16]

Wellings, K., Field, J., Johnson, A. M. & Wadsworth, J. (1994). *Sexual behavior in Britain: The National Survey of Sexual Attitudes and Lifestyles.* Penguin Books. [12]

Wellings, K., Palmer, M. J., Machiyama, K. & Slaymaker, E. (2019). *Changes in, and factors associated with, frequency of sex in Britain: Evidence from three National Surveys of Sexual Attitudes and Lifestyles (Natsal).* (https://tinyurl.com/yythxvcn) [11]

Wellman, J. D. & McCoy, S. K. (2014). Walking the straight and narrow: Examining the role of traditional gender norms in sexual prejudice. *Psychology of Men and Masculinity, 15*, 181–190. [12]

Wentland, J. J. & Reissing, E. (2014). Casual sexual relationships: Identifying definitions for one-night stands, booty calls, fuck buddies, and friends with benefits. *Canadian Journal of Human Sexuality, 23*, 167–177. [7]

Werner, M. A., Ford, T., Pacik, P. T., et al. (2014). Botox for the treatment of vaginismus: A case report. *Journal of Women's Health Care, 3*(2). [14]

Wessells, H., Lue, T. F. & McAninch, J. W. (1996). Complications of penile lengthening and augmentation seen at one referral center. *Journal of Urology, 155*, 1617–1620. [3]

Whipple, B. & Brash-McGreer, K. (1997). Management of female sexual dysfunction. In: M. L. Sipski, M. L. & Alexander, C. J. (Eds.), *Sexual function in people with disability and chronic illness: A health professional's guide.* Aspen Publishers.

Whipple, B., Myers, B. & Komisaruk, B. R. (1998). Male multiple ejaculatory orgasms: A case study. *Journal of Sex Education and Therapy, 23*, 157–162. [5]

Whipple, B., Ogden, G. & Komisaruk, B. R. (1992). Physiological correlates of imagery-induced orgasm in women. *Archives of Sexual Behavior, 21*, 121–133. [6]

Whisman, M. A. & Snyder, D. K. (2007). Sexual infidelity in a national sample of American women: Differences in prevalence and correlates as a function of method of assessment. *Journal of Family Psychology, 21*, 147–154. [7]

Whisman, M. A., Gilmour, A. L. & Salinger, J. M. (2018). Marital satisfaction and mortality in the United States adult population. *Health Psychology, 37*, 1041–1044. [11]

White House. (2011). *Statement by the President on the killing of David Kato.* (http://tinyurl.com/ychlgwuf) [12]

White, N. D., Hill, D. M. & Bodemeier, S. (2008). Male condoms that break in use do so mostly by a "blunt puncture" mechanism. *Contraception, 77*, 360–365. [9]

Wibowo, E. & Wassersug, R. J. (2016). Multiple orgasms in men: What we know so far. *Sexual Medicine Reviews, 4*, 136–148. [5]

Wiederman, M. W. (2015). Sexual script theory: Past, present, and future. In: J. DeLamater and R. F. Plante (Eds).

Wilcox, A. J., Dunson, D. & Baird, D. D. (2000). The timing of the "fertile window" in the menstrual cycle: day specific estimates from a prospective study. *BMJ, 321*, 1259–1262. [9]

Wile, D. (1992). *The art of the bedchamber: The Chinese sexual yoga practices including women's solo meditation texts.* SUNY Press. [6]

Wilkinson, J., Malpas, P., Hammarberg, K., et al. (2019). Do a la carte menus serve infertility patients? The ethics and regulation of in vitro fertility add-ons. *Fertility and Sterility, 112*, 973–977. [8]

Williams Institute. (2012). *Serving our youth: Findings from a national survey of services providers working with lesbian, gay, bisexual and transgender youth who are homeless or at risk of becoming homeless.* (http://tinyurl.com/bmr7ztf) [12]

Williams, C. J. & Weinberg, M. S. (2003). Zoophilia in men: A study of sexual interest in animals. *Archives of Sexual Behavior, 32*, 523–535. [13]

Williams, D. H. & Johnson, B. A. (2016). Clinical evaluation and treatment of disorders of ejaculation. In: L. I. Lipshultz, A. W. Pastuszak, A. T. Goldstein, A. Giraldi & M. A. Perelman (Eds). *Management of sexual dysfunction in men and women.* Springer. [14]

Williams, P. T. (2013). Breast cancer mortality vs. exercise and breast size in runners and walkers. *PLOS One, 8*, e80616. [2]

Williams, T. J., Pepitone, M. E., Christensen, S. E., et al. (2000). Finger-length ratios and sexual orientation. *Nature, 404*, 455–456.

Williams, T. M. (1986). *The impact of television: A natural experiment in three communities.* Academic Press. [1]

Williams, W. L. (1986). *The spirit and the flesh: Sexual diversity in American Indian culture.* Beacon Press. [4]

Willness, C. R., Steel, P. & Lee, K. (2007). A meta-analysis of the antecedents and consequences of workplace sexual harassment. *Personnel Psychology, 60*, 127–162. [16]

Willoughby, B. J. & Belt, D. (2016). Marital orientation and relationship well-being among cohabiting couples. *Journal of Family Psychology, 30*, 181–192. [11]

Wilson, I. M., Graham, K. & Taft, A. (2017). Living the cycle of drinking and violence: A qualitative study of women's experience of alcohol-related intimate partner violence. *Drug & Alcohol Review, 36*, 115–124. [16]

Wilson, J. D. & Roehrborn, C. (1999). Long-term consequences of castration in men: lessons from the Skoptzy and the eunuchs of the Chinese and Ottoman courts. *Journal of Clinical Endocrinology and Metabolism, 84*, 4324–4331. [1]

Wilson, R. A. (2019). Incest, incest avoidance, and attachment: Revisiting the Westermarck effect. *Philosophy of Science, 86*, 391–411. [App. A]

Wilson, S. J., Jaremka, L. M., Fagundes, C. P., et al. (2017). Shortened sleep fuels inflammatory responses to marital conflict: Emotion regulation matters. *Psychoneuroendocrinology, 79*, 74–83. [11]

Wimpissinger, F., Tscherney, R. & Stackl, W. (2009). Magnetic resonance imaging of female prostate pathology. *Journal of Sexual Medicine, 6*, 1704–1711. [5]

Wincze, J. P. (2009). *Enhancing sexuality: A problem-solving approach to treating dysfunction* (2nd ed.). Oxford University Press. [14]

Wisch, F. W. (2017). *Table of state animal sexual assault laws.* (http://tinyurl.com/oht542d) [13]

Wise, N. J., Frangos, E. & Komisaruk, B. R. (2017). Brain activity unique to orgasm in women: An fMRI analysis. *J Sex Med, 14*, 1380–1391. [1]

Witchel, S. M. (2018). Disorders of sex development. *Obstetrics and Gynaecology, 48*, 90–102. [4]

Wlodarski, R. & Dunbar, R. I. M. (2014). What's in a kiss? The effect of romantic kissing on mate desirability. *Evolutionary Psychology, 12*, 178–199. [6]

Wofford, W. (2016). Finding love again, this time with a man. *New York Times*, April 23. [12]

Wojcicki, S. (2017). Expanding our work against abuse of our platform. (http://tinyurl.com/y9anamtw) [17]

Wolfram, S. (2013). *Data science of the Facebook world.* (http://tinyurl.com/arougs8) [7]

Wollan, M. (2012). San Francisco officials approve a ban on public nudity. *New York Times*, November 20. [3]

Womack, C. (2014). Police: Sarasota High School student led prostitution ring. *Sarasota Herald-Tribune*, November 24. [17]

Wong, J. S. & Gravel, J. (2018). Do sex offenders have higher levels of testosterone? Results from a meta-analysis. *Sexual Abuse, 30*(2), 147–168. [16]

Wong, W. I., Pasterski, V., Hindmarsh, P. C., et al. (2013). Are there parental socialization effects on the sex-typed behavior of individuals with congenital adrenal hyperplasia? *Archives of Sexual Behavior, 42*, 381–391. [4]

Wood, B. M. & Marlowe, F. W. (2013). Household and kin provisioning by Hadza men. *Human Nature, 24*, 280–317. [7]

Wood, J. M., Koch, P. B. & Mansfield, P. K. (2006). Women's sexual desire: A feminist critique. *Journal of Sex Research, 43*, 236–244. [14]

Wood, P. L. (2018). Cosmetic genital surgery in children and adolescents. *Best Practice and Research: Clinical Obstetrics & Gynaecology, 48*, 137–146. [2]

Woodstock, M. (2017). *Male? Female? Jamie Shupe battles for a third option.* (https://tinyurl.com/y22a2znc) [4]

Working Group for a New View of Women's Sexual Problems. (2001). A new view of women's sexual problems. In: E. Kaschak & L. Tiefer (Eds.), *A new view of women's sexual problems*. Haworth Press. [14]

World Association for Sexual Health. (2014). *Declaration of sexual rights.* (https://tinyurl.com/unm383t) [1]

World Association for Sexual Health. (2019). *Declaration on sexual pleasure.* (https://tinyurl.com/r8t4khd) [1]

World Bank. (2019). *Fertility rate, total (births per woman)—Japan.* (https://tinyurl.com/yxv3haaa) [11]

World Health Organization. (2014). Male circumcision for HIV prevention. (http://tinyurl.com/2zjakx) [15]

World Health Organization. (2017). *Voluntary medical male circumcision for HIV prevention in 14 priority countries in eastern and southern Africa.* (https://tinyurl.com/yynhubcr) [3]

World Health Organization. (2018a). *Family planning/contraception.* (http://tinyurl.com/d2kr9bt) [9]

World Health Organization. (2018b). *Female genital mutilation.* (https://tinyurl.com/ybshlrqv) [2]

World Health Organization. (2019). *Herpes simplex virus.* (https://tinyurl.com/y4wggmp6) [15]

World Professional Association for Transgender Health. (2017). *Standards of care for the health of transsexual, transgender, and gender-nonconforming people, Version 7.* (http://tinyurl.com/okc9829) [4]

Wright, P. J. (2011). Mass media effects on youth sexual behavior: Assessing the claim for causality. *Annals of the International Communication Association, 35*, 343–385. [4]

Wu, J. P., McKee, K. S., McKee, M. M., et al. (2017). Use of reversible contraceptive methods among U.S. women with physical or sensory disabilities. *Perspectives on Sexual & Reproductive Health, 49*(3), 141–147. [9]

Wu, J., Braunschweig, Y., Harris, L. H., et al. (2019). Looking back while moving forward: a justice-based, intersectional approach to research on contraception and disability. *Contraception, 99*, 267–271. [9]

Wurtele, S. K., Simons, D. & Moreno, T. (2014). Sexual interest in children among an online sample of men and women: Prevalence and correlates. *Sexual Abuse, 26*(6), 546–568. [13]

Wylie, K. R. & Eardley, I. (2007). Penile size and the "small penis syndrome." *BJU International, 99*, 1449–1455. [3]

**X**

Xiao, S. X., Cook, R. E., Martin, C. L., et al. (2019). Will they listen to me? An examination of in-group gender bias in children's communication beliefs. *Sex Roles, 80*, 172–185. [4]

Xie, R. H., He, G., Liu, A., et al. (2007). Fetal gender and postpartum depression in a cohort of Chinese women. *Social Science and Medicine, 65*, 680–684. [8]

Xu, Y. & Zheng, Y. (2017). Does sexual orientation precede childhood sexual abuse? Childhood gender nonconformity as a risk factor and instrumental variable. *Sexual Abuse, 29*(8), 786–802. [12]

Xu, Y., Norton, S. & Rahman, Q. (2017). Sexual orientation and neurocognitive ability: A meta-analysis in men and women. *Neuroscience and Biobehavioral Reviews, 83*, 691–696. [12]

Xu, Y., Norton, S. & Rahman, Q. (2019). Early life conditions and adolescent sexual orientation: A prospective birth cohort study. *Developmental Psychology, 55*, 1226–1243. [12]

**Y**

Yafi, F. A., Jenkins, L., Albersen, M., et al. (2016). Erectile dysfunction. *Nature Reviews Disease Primers, 2*, 16003. [14]

Yang, M. L., Fullwood, E., Goldstein, J. & Mink, J. W. (2005). Masturbation in infancy and early childhood presenting as a movement disorder: 12 cases and a review of the literature. *Pediatrics, 116*, 1427–1432. [10]

Yang, Y. (2016). *China made 85 billion sanitary pads last year, and not one tampon. Here's why.* (https://tinyurl.com/y4b42sbt) [2]

Yarab, P. E., Sensibaugh, C. C. & Allgeier, E. R. (1998). More than just sex: Gender differences in the incidence of self-defined unfaithful behavior in heterosexual dating relationships. *Journal of Psychology and Human Sexuality, 10*, 45–57. [7]

Yeung, J. & Pauls, R. N. (2016). Anatomy of the vulva and the female sexual response. *Obstetrics and Gynecology Clinics of North America, 43*, 27–44. [5]

Yoffe, E. (2019). "I'm radioactive." (https://tinyurl.com/yyb6se27) [16]

Yonkers, K. A. & Simoni, M. (2018). Evidence-based treatments for premenstrual disorders. *American Journal of Obstetrics and Gynecology, 219*, 215–216. [2]

YouGov. (2017). *Do you know what a sugar baby is? 61% of Americans do.* (http://tinyurl.com/y7uqroab) [17]

Young-Bruehl, E. (1996). *The anatomy of prejudices.* Harvard University Press. [12]

Young, B. R., Desmarais, S. L., Baldwin, J. A. & Chandler, R. (2017). Sexual coercion practices among undergraduate male recreational athletes, intercollegiate athletes, and non-athletes. *Violence Against Women, 23*, 795–812. [16]

Young, L. J. & Wang, Z. (2004). The neurobiology of pair bonding. *Nature Neuroscience, 7*, 1048–1054. [7]

YouTube. (2019). *Alessandro Moreschi sings Ave Maria.* (https://tinyurl.com/knb2uwk) [10]

Yule, M. A., Brotto, L. A. & Gorzalka, B. B. (2014). Biological markers of asexuality: Handedness, birth order, and finger length ratios in self-identified asexual men and women. *Archives of Sexual Behavior, 43*, 299–310. [5]

Yule, M. A., Brotto, L. A. & Gorzalka, B. B. (2017a). Human asexuality: What do we know about a lack of sexual attraction? *Current Sexual Health Reports, 9,* 50–56. [5]

Yule, M. A., Brotto, L. A. & Gorzalka, B. B. (2017b). Sexual fantasy and masturbation among asexual individuals: An in-depth exploration. *Archives of Sexual Behavior, 46,* 311–328. [5]

**Z**

Zahavi, A. & Zahavi, A. (1997). *The handicap principle: A missing piece of Darwin's puzzle.* Oxford University Press. [App. A]

Zaleski, A. (2019). *Meet the wounded veteran who got a penis transplant.* (https://tinyurl.com/vd8xz97) [3]

Zamboni, B. D. (2019). A qualitative exploration of adult baby/diaper lover behavior from an online community sample. *Journal of Sex Research, 56,* 191–202. [13]

Zandbergen, D. L. & Brown, S. G. (2015). Culture and gender differences in romantic jealousy. *Personality and Individual Differences, 72,* 122–127. [7]

Zava. (2019). *Preferred positions.* (https://tinyurl.com/y6bm7raz) [6]

Zeifman, D. M. (2019). Attachment theory grows up: a developmental approach to pair bonds. *Current Opinion in Psychology, 25,* 139–143. [7]

Zeigler, C. (2017). *Former Patriots and Chiefs tackle Ryan O'Callaghan comes out as gay.* (http://tinyurl.com/y8gmuzp8) [12]

Zeki, S. & Romaya, J. P. (2010). The brain reaction to viewing faces of opposite- and same-sex romantic partners. *PLOS One, 5,* e15802. [7]

Zeleke, B. M., Bell, R. J., Billah, B. & Davis, S. R. (2017). Hypoactive sexual desire dysfunction in community-dwelling older women. *Menopause, 24,* 391–399. [14]

Zerjal, T., Xue, Y., Bertorelle, G., et al. (2003). The genetic legacy of the Mongols. *American Journal of Human Genetics, 72,* 717–721. [16]

Zhang, J. & Gong, M. (2018). Review of the role of leptin in the regulation of male reproductive function. *Andrologia, 50,* e12965. [10]

Zhang, J. W., Piff, P. K., Iyer, R., et al. (2014). An occasion for unselfing: Beautiful nature leads to prosociality. *Journal of Environmental Psychology, 37,* 61–72. [7]

Zhang, J., Troendle, J., Reddy, U. M., et al. (2010). Contemporary cesarean delivery practice in the United States. *American Journal of Obstetrics and Gynecology, 203,* e321–e326. [8]

Zhang, L., Lee, A. J., Debruine, L. M. & B.C., J. (2019). Are sex differences in preferences for physical attractiveness and good earning capacity in potential mates smaller in countries with greater gender equality? *PsyArXiv Preprints,* Posted online at https://psyarxiv.com/mtsx8. [4]

Zhao, J., Lau, M., Vermette, D., et al. (2016). Communication between Asian American adolescents and health care providers about sexual activity, sexually transmitted infections, and pregnancy prevention. *Journal of Adolescent Research, 32,* 127–154. [7]

Zhou, V. (2016). *China has world's most skewed sex ratio at birth—again.* (http://tinyurl.com/yaxbgum6) [8]

Zhou, W., Yang, X., Chen, K., et al. (2014). Chemosensory communication of gender through two human steroids in a sexually dimorphic manner. *Current Biology, 24,* 1091–1095. [5]

Zhu, B., Kong, A., Sun, Z. & Zhu, R. (2011). Transition from paroxysmal disorder in infancy to the masturbatory orgasm in childhood. *International Journal of Sexual Health, 23,* 278–281. [10]

Zhu, W., Chen, C. J., Thomas, C. E., et al. (2011). Vaccines for gonorrhea: Can we rise to the challenge? *Frontiers in Microbiology, 2,* 124. [15]

Ziegler, A. & Conley, T. D. (2016). The importance and meaning of sexual fantasies in intimate relationships. In: Aumer, K. (Ed.), *The psychology of love and hate in intimate relationships.* Springer. [5]

Zietsch, B. P., Westberg, L., Santtila, P. & Jern, P. (2015). Genetic analysis of human extrapair mating: Heritability, between-sex correlation, and receptor genes for vasopressin and oxytocin. *Evolution and Human Behavior, 36,* 130–136. [7]

Zivony, A. & Lobel, T. (2014). The invisible stereotypes of bisexual men. *Archives of Sexual Behavior, 43,* 1167–1176. [12]

Zopotosky, M. (2017). Detroit-area doctor charged with performing genital mutilation on girls. *Washington Post,* April 13. [2]

Zverina, J., Hampl, R., Sulocava, J. & Starka, L. (1990). Hormonal status and sexual behaviour of 16 men after surgical castration. *Archivio Italiano di Urologia, Nefrologia, Andrologia, 62,* 55–58. [13]

Zweig, J. M., Dank, M., Yahner, J. & Lachman, P. (2013). The rate of cyber dating abuse among teens and how it relates to other forms of teen dating violence. *Journal of Youth & Adolescence, 42,* 1063–1077. [16]

# Index

Page numbers in *italic* type indicate the information will be found in an illustration.